FAMILY LAW

SEVENTH EDITION

William P. **Statsky**

Cengage

Australia • Brazil • Canada • Mexico • Singapore • United Kingdom • United States

Family Law, **Seventh Edition**
William P. Statsky

SVP, Higher Education & Skills Product: Erin Joyner

Product Director: Matt Seeley

Associate Product Manager: Abbie M. Schultheis

Product Assistant: Anne E. Van Vorst

Director, Learning Design: Rebecca von Gillern

Senior Manager, Learning Design: Leigh Hefferon

Learning Designer: Mara C. Vuillaume

Marketing Director: Sean H. Chamberland

Marketing Manager: Andrew Ouimet

Director, Content Creation: Juliet Steiner

Content Creation Manager: Alexis Ferraro

Senior Content Manager: Betty L. Dickson

Digital Delivery Lead: Steven McMillan

Designer: Erin Griffin

Interior Credit: iStock.com/krblokhin

Cover image: Rena Schild/ShutterStock.com

For product information and technology assistance, contact us at
Cengage Customer & Sales Support, 1-800-354-9706
or support.cengage.com.

For permission to use material from this text or product, submit all requests online at **www.copyright.com.**

Library of Congress Control Number: 2020901572

Book Only ISBN: 978-1-337-91753-7
Looseleaf Edition: ISBN: 978-1-337-91760-5

Cengage
200 Pier 4 Boulevard
Boston, MA 02210
USA

Cengage is a leading provider of customized learning solutions with employees residing in nearly 40 different countries and sales in more than 125 countries around the world. Find your local representative at: **www.cengage.com.**

To learn more about Cengage platforms and services, register or access your online learning solution, or purchase materials for your course, visit **www.cengage.com.**

Notice to the Reader

Publisher does not warrant or guarantee any of the products described herein or perform any independent analysis in connection with any of the product information contained herein. Publisher does not assume, and expressly disclaims, any obligation to obtain and include information other than that provided to it by the manufacturer. The reader is expressly warned to consider and adopt all safety precautions that might be indicated by the activities described herein and to avoid all potential hazards. By following the instructions contained herein, the reader willingly assumes all risks in connection with such instructions. The reader is notified that this text is an educational tool, not a practice book. Since the law is in constant change, no rule or statement of law in this book should be relied upon for any service to the client. The reader should always refer to standard legal sources for the current rule or law. If legal advice or other expert assistance is required, the services of the appropriate professional should be sought. The publisher makes no representations or warranties of any kind, including but not limited to, the warranties of fitness for particular purpose or merchantability, nor are any such representations implied with respect to the material set forth herein, and the publisher takes no responsibility with respect to such material. The publisher shall not be liable for any special, consequential, or exemplary damages resulting, in whole or part, from the readers' use of, or reliance upon, this material.

Printed in the United States of America
Print Number: 02   Print Year: 2022

FAMILY LAW

SEVENTH EDITION

Options.

We understand that affordable options are important. Visit us at cengage.com to take advantage of our new textbook rental program, which can be bundled with our MindTap products!

Over 300 products in every area of the law: MindTap, textbooks, online courses, reference books, companion websites, and more – Cengage helps you succeed in the classroom and on the job.

Support.

We offer unparalleled course support and customer service: robust instructor and student supplements to ensure the best learning experience, custom publishing to meet your unique needs, and our sales representatives are always ready to provide you with dependable service.

Feedback.

As always, we want to hear from you! Your feedback is our best resource for improving the quality of our products. Contact your sales representative or write us at the address below if you have any comments about our materials or if you have a product proposal.

Accounting and Financials for the Law Office • Administrative Law • Alternative Dispute Resolution • Bankruptcy Business Organizations/Corporations • Careers and Employment • Civil Litigation and Procedure • CP Exam Preparation • Computer Applications in the Law Office • Constitutional Law • Contract Law • Criminal Law and Procedure • Document Preparation • Elder Law • Employment Law • Environmental Law • Ethics • Evidence Law • Family Law • Health Care Law • Immigration Law • Intellectual Property • Internships • Interviewing and Investigation • Introduction to Law • Introduction to Paralegalism • Juvenile Law • Law Office Management • Law Office Procedures • Legal Research, Writing, and Analysis • Legal Terminology • Legal Transcription • Media and Entertainment Law • Medical Malpractice Law • Product Liability • Real Estate Law • Reference Materials • Social Security • Torts and Personal Injury Law • Wills, Trusts, and Estate Administration • Workers' Compensation Law

---

5 Maxwell Drive
Clifton Park, New York 12065-2919

For additional information, find us online at: cengage.com

In memory of Patricia Farrell Statsky
whose life was a gift and a blessing to me (in a marriage of 50 years),
to her family, to her students, and to the many friends she enriched
by her presence and love.

William P. Statsky

BY THE SAME AUTHOR

For all publications by William Statsky, see: www.statsky.blogspot.com

The California Paralegal: Essential Rules, Documents, and Resources. Cengage, 2008 (with S. Sandberg)

Case Analysis and Fundamentals of Legal Writing, 4th ed. West Group, 1995 (with J. Wernet)

Essentials of Paralegalism, 5th ed. Cengage, 2010

Essentials of Torts, 3rd ed. Cengage, 2012

Family Law: The Essentials, 3rd ed. Cengage, 2015

Family Law, 7th ed. Cengage, 2021

The Florida Paralegal: Essential Rules, Documents, and Resources. Cengage, 2009 (with B. Diotalevi & P. Linquist)

Inmate Involvement in Prison Legal Services: Roles and Training Options for the Inmate as Paralegal. American Bar Association, Commission on Correctional Facilities and Services, 1974

Introduction to Paralegalism: Perspectives, Problems, and Skills, 8th ed. Cengage, 2016

Legal Desk Reference. West Group, 1990 (with B. Hussey, M. Diamond, & R. Nakamura)

The Legal Paraprofessional as Advocate and Assistant: Training Concepts and Materials. Center on Social Welfare Policy and Law, 1971 (with P. Lang)

Legal Research and Writing: Some Starting Points, 5th ed. Cengage, 1999

Legal Thesaurus/Dictionary: A Resource for the Writer and Computer Researcher. West Group, 1985

Legislative Analysis and Drafting, 2nd ed. West Group, 1984

The New York Paralegal: Essential Rules, Documents, and Resources. Cengage, 2009 (with R. Sarachan)

The Ohio Paralegal: Essential Rules, Documents, and Resources. Cengage, 2008 (with K. Reed & B. Moore)

Paralegal Employment: Facts and Strategies for the 1990s, 2nd ed. West Group, 1993

Paralegal Ethics and Regulation, 2nd ed. West Group, 1993

The Pennsylvania Paralegal: Essential Rules, Documents, and Resources. Cengage, 2009 (with J. DeLeo & J. Geis)

Rights of the Imprisoned: Cases, Materials, and Directions. Bobbs-Merrill Company, 1974 (with R. Singer)

The Texas Paralegal: Essential Rules, Documents, and Resources. Cengage, 2009 (with L. Crossett)

Torts: Personal Injury Litigation, 6th ed. Carolina Academic Press, 2019

What Have Paralegals Done? A Dictionary of Functions. National Paralegal Institute, 1973

BRIEF CONTENTS

CONTENTS

7 CHAPTER   237

DIVORCE GROUNDS AND PROCEDURE

8 CHAPTER   291

SPOUSAL SUPPORT, PROPERTY DIVISION, AND THE SEPARATION AGREEMENT

9 CHAPTER   370
CHILD CUSTODY

16 CHAPTER 606
THE NEW SCIENCE OF MOTHERHOOD

17 CHAPTER 632
TORTS AND FAMILY LAW

APPENDIX A 650
GENERAL INSTRUCTIONS FOR THE ASSIGNMENTS AND PROJECTS IN THE BOOK

APPENDIX B 677
COMPUTER-GENERATED REPORTS: THE DIVORCE OF MARGARET AND NELSON PARIS

APPENDIX C 690

INTERROGATORIES ON FINANCIAL ASSETS

APPENDIX D 701

FAMILY LAW IN YOUR STATE

PREFACE

Say it isn't true. A recent *New York Times* story reported that a well-known divorce attorney was giving out pens to prospective clients that said, "Sue Someone You Love." This is not the image the legal profession wishes to project to the public. Yet newspapers, magazines, talk shows, and social media do seem to give the impression that our society is in a litigation frenzy: "Son Sues to Divorce His Mother," "Wife Demands Half of Husband's Medical Practice in Divorce Settlement," "Surrogate Mother Refuses to Turn Over Baby," "Live-in Lover Seeks Palimony," "Facebook Divorces on the Rise."

Our goal in this book is to sort through the headlines to find an accurate picture of the state of family law today and the role of the attorney-paralegal team within it. We are living in an era of great change in the practice of family law. The primary focus of the family law practitioner is no longer limited to adultery and who gets the children.

No-fault divorce has made marriage relatively easy to dissolve. The women's movement has helped bring about major shifts in determining what property can be split after a divorce and how to split it. The country has declared war on the "deadbeat" parent who fails to pay child support. Major new enforcement mechanisms have been designed to find these parents and make them pay. To the surprise of many, courts have come to the aid of some unmarried fathers seeking to undo the adoption of their children. Science and technology have unleashed new concepts of motherhood and parentage. The law has not been able to keep pace with the scientific revolution taking place in the test tube and in the womb.

In short, there is a lot to talk about! It's a fascinating time to study family law.

CHAPTER FORMAT

Each chapter includes features designed to assist students in understanding the material:

- A Chapter Outline at the beginning of each chapter provides a preview of the major topics discussed in the chapter.
- Chapter Objectives, also at the beginning of each chapter, present a more detailed listing of the themes and skills covered in the chapter.
- Exhibits and tables are used extensively to clarify concepts and present detailed information in an organized chart form.
- Assignments that ask students to apply concepts to particular fact situations are included in the chapters. The assignments cover critical skills such as analysis, investigation, interviewing, and drafting.

- Key Terms are printed in boldface type throughout the chapters. A list of Key Terms also appears at the end of each chapter to help students review important terminology introduced in that chapter.
- Each Key Term is also defined in the margin next to the text to which the terms are relevant.
- Paralegal roles are highlighted toward the end of each chapter.
- At the end of most chapters, there is a Check the Cite exercise in which the student is sent to a specific case found on the Internet that is relevant to the material covered in the chapter.
- At the end of every chapter, there is a Project assignment in which the student is asked to use Internet sources to develop a particular theme related to the chapter.
- Following each Project assignment, there is an exercise called Ethics in a Family Law Practice, which asks the student to read a fact situation and identify ethical problems that may exist. These exercises build on the principles of ethics covered in Chapter 2.
- At the end of most chapters, there is a Writing Sample assignment in which the student is asked to draft a family-law document that could be developed into a writing sample when searching for employment.
- A Summary at the end of each chapter provides a concise review of the main concepts discussed.
- Each chapter has Review Questions covering the major themes in the chapter.
- Helpful Websites are added at the end of each chapter to provide additional materials on the topics of the chapter.

CHANGES IN THE SEVENTH EDITION

- The material in all of the chapters has been updated.
- Additional material has been added on the relationship between the practice of family law and the Internet and social media.
- New sections have been added to many of the chapters, such as the unique characteristics of family-law cases, the questions left open by the recognition of same-sex marriage, and the recognition of three-parent relationships.
- Greater emphasis has been placed on family laws that are available on the Internet.

SUPPORT MATERIALS

This seventh edition is accompanied by a support package that will assist students in learning and aid instructors in teaching:

INSTRUCTOR COMPANION WEBSITE

Spend less time planning and more time teaching. This instructor companion website to accompany *Introduction to Law* allows you "anywhere, anytime" access to all of your resources.

- The Instructor's Manual contains various resources for each chapter of the book.
- The **Testbank** In Cognero, Word, and several LMS-friendly formats makes generating tests and quizzes fast and easy. With many questions and different styles to choose from, you can create customized assessments for your students with the click of a button. Add your own unique questions and print rationales for easy class preparation.
- Customizable **PowerPoint® Presentations** focus on key points for each chapter. (PowerPoint® Is a registered trademark of the Microsoft Corporation.)

To access additional course materials (including MindTap), go to login.cengage.com, then use your SSO (single sign on) login to access the materials.

MINDTAP:

MINDTAP: EMPOWER YOUR STUDENTS

CENGAGE
_____
MINDTAP

MindTap is a platform that propels students from memorization to mastery. It gives you complete control of your course, so you can provide engaging content, challenge every learner, and build student confidence. Customize interactive syllabi to emphasize priority topics, then add your own material or notes to the eBook as desired. This outcomes-driven application gives you the tools needed to empower students and boost both understanding and performance.

ACCESS EVERYTHING YOU NEED IN ONE PLACE

Cut down on preparation with the preloaded and organized MindTap course materials. Teach more efficiently with interactive multimedia, assignments, quizzes, and more. Give your students the power to read, listen, and study on their phones, so they can learn on their terms.

EMPOWER STUDENTS TO REACH THEIR POTENTIAL

Twelve distinct metrics give you actionable insights into student engagement. Identify topics troubling your entire class and instantly communicate with those struggling. Students can track their scores to stay motivated toward their goals. Together, you can be unstoppable.

CONTROL YOUR COURSE—AND YOUR CONTENT

Get the flexibility to reorder textbook chapters, add your own notes, and embed a variety of content including Open Educational Resources (OER). Personalize course content to your students' needs. They can even read your notes, add their own, and highlight key text to aid their learning.

Supplements At-A-Glance

SUPPLEMENT:	WHAT IT IS:	WHAT'S IN IT:
Instructor Companion Website	Resources for the Instructor, via Cengage SSO	• Instructor's Manual with sample syllabi, lecture keys, answers to text questions, and test bank and answer key • PowerPoint® presentations • Testbank In Cognero, Word, and LMS-friendly formats, with many questions to choose from to create customized assessments for your students
MindTap: 	To learn more go to www.cengage.com/Mindtap or ask your instructor to try it out	• eBook with ReadSpeaker, highlighting, note-taking and more • Chapter quizzes • Case Studies • Customizable flashcards • Assignments • Additional resources

CENGAGE UNLIMITED The first-of-its-kind digital subscription designed specially to lower costs. Students get total access to everything Cengage has to offer on demand—in one place. That's 20,000 eBooks, 2,300 digital learning products, and dozens of study tools across 70 disciplines and over 675 courses. Currently available in select markets. Details at **www.cengage.com/unlimited**

ACKNOWLEDGMENTS

A word of thanks to the reviewers who made valuable suggestions for improving the text:

Bob White
IBMC College
Greeley, CO

John C. Daniel, JD, CPCU, CIC
IBMC College
Greeley, CO

Christy James Musgrove, J.D.
Professor of Paralegal Studies and Criminal Justice
Georgia Military College
Valdosta, GA

Felicia Williams-Winston
Paralegal Professor
Hinds Community College
Raymond, MS

Kim D. Phifer
Mississippi Gulf Coast Community College
Gulfport, MS

Please note that the Internet resources are of a time-sensitive nature and URL addresses may often change or be deleted.

CHAPTER 1

Introduction to Family Law and Practice

CHAPTER OUTLINE

CHAPTER OBJECTIVES

After completing this chapter, you should be able to:

- Identify the major themes of family law in the twenty-first century.
- List major terminology changes in family law.
- List other areas of law with which family-law practitioners should be familiar.
- State the tests used by a court when a family law is challenged as a violation of due process of law or of equal protection of law.
- State the impact of social media on the practice of family law.
- List the variety of paralegal roles in various family-law offices and settings.
- Identify the dangers of bias in the practice of family law.
- Be aware of the danger of violence in high-conflict family-law cases.
- Know the main legal-research sources of family law.

FAMILY LAW IN THE TWENTY-FIRST CENTURY

family law
The body of law that defines relationships, rights, and duties in the formation, ongoing existence, and dissolution of marriage and other family units.

marriage
The legal union of two persons as spouses with designated rights and obligations to each other.

Family law consists of legal principles that govern marital and nonmarital families. The principles cover rights and duties as families are created, maintained, and dissolved. More specifically, family law is the body of law that defines relationships, rights, and duties in the formation, ongoing existence, and dissolution of marriage and other family units.

For centuries, marriage has remained relatively unchanged. Not so, however, in recent decades. The world of our grandparents was dramatically different from today's world:

> [U]ntil a generation ago there was a social consensus as to what marriage meant. Marriage was permanent and monogamous; children were automatic, essential, and central; husbands earned money and made decisions; wives stayed home taking care of house, children, and husband. The legal system reinforced the social norms for marriage. Now the clarity and unity of the domestic picture is gone. Only a small percentage of American families still have all the characteristics associated with the traditional nuclear family ideal. In place of a single socially approved ideal we have compelling demands for autonomy and privacy, and multiple models of intimacy: single parents [more than 40 percent of new mothers are unmarried], working wives, house husbands, living-together arrangements without marriage, [same-sex marriage], serial marriage, stepchildren, [surrogate parents and children with more than two parents at the same time, etc.]. The changes are legion, and their message is clear: the destruction of traditional marriage as the sole model for adult intimacy is irreversible.[1]

See Exhibit 1.1 on the percentage of babies born to unwed mothers and the percentage of children who live with both parents.

Indeed, we live in a society that sometimes appears to be in a state of perpetual change. One scholar maintains that "marriage has changed more in the past 30 years than in the previous 3,000."[2] A recent survey came to the provocative conclusion that 39 percent of respondents feel that marriage is obsolete.[3] Another survey found that just under half of young Americans do not believe that government should be in the business of issuing marriage licenses.[4] According to Justice Scalia of the United States Supreme Court, a "culture war" is underway in this area of the law as society debates whether change has gone too far or not far enough.[5]

EXHIBIT 1.1   Changing Family Structure: A Seventy-Five-Year Overview

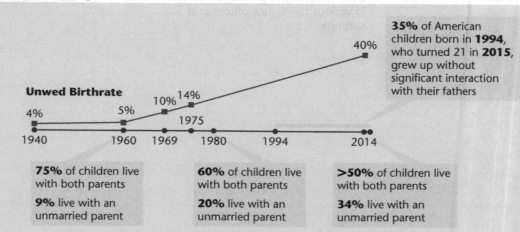

35% of American children born in **1994**, who turned 21 in **2015**, grew up without significant interaction with their fathers

Unwed Birthrate

4% (1940)   5% (1960)   10% 14% (1969)   40%   1975

1940   1960   1969   1980   1994   2014

75% of children live with both parents
9% live with an unmarried parent

60% of children live with both parents
20% live with an unmarried parent

>50% of children live with both parents
34% live with an unmarried parent

Source: "Child Support Report." Office of Child Support Enforcement. U.S. Dept. of Health & Human Services, Feb/Mar 2016 (www.acf.hhs.gov/sites/default/files/programs/css/february_march_2016_child_support_report.pdf).

Courts and legislatures have not always been able to fit traditional family-law principles into this environment of debate and change. New principles have been—and still are—needed. One of the central themes in this book will be how family law has evolved in response to the shifting boundary lines of how people choose to live together.

Five important developments in family law are a product of this turmoil. They have shaped our recent history and will continue to play major roles in the twenty-first century. Here is an overview of these developments.

EQUALITY OF THE SEXES: THE STRUGGLE CONTINUES

There was a time in our history when a wife could not make her own will or bring a lawsuit in her own name. Without her husband's consent, there was relatively little that she could do. Two centuries ago, the greatest scholar of the day, Blackstone, declared that "the very being or legal existence of a woman was suspended during the marriage, or at least was incorporated and consolidated into that of her husband."[6] Indeed, in the eyes of the law, the husband and wife were one person, and that person was the husband. "Under the centuries-old doctrine of **coverture**, a married man and woman were treated by the State as a single, male-dominated legal entity."[7] Carried to its logical extreme, the rule meant that a wife could not sue her husband (the suit would be the equivalent of the husband suing himself), and a husband could not be convicted of raping his wife.

Much progress has been made in abandoning this theory of the law based on male dominance. To a large extent, the law has equalized the legal status of husbands and wives. Some changes, however, have had unintended consequences that have served to perpetuate the inequality. For example, the emergence of no-fault divorce (which we will study in Chapter 7) gave both spouses an equal right to end a marriage without having to prove adultery, cruelty, or other marital misconduct. Yet some have argued that this reform removed a substantial bargaining chip of wives on the issues of money and custody, particularly for long-term marriages. With a no-fault divorce, a husband did not have to bargain so hard to get out of the marriage if the divorce was relatively easy to obtain. Also, for many couples, the standard of living of an ex-husband usually increases after divorce, while that of an ex-wife decreases.[8] Some feminists say that "equality" has led to a diminution of women's rights. A Columbia law professor, author of *The Illusion of Equality*, has argued that "Equality is being applied with a vengeance against women."[9]

Furthermore, it is important to keep in mind that reforms in the law do not always translate into changes in human behavior. Not that long ago, for example, a court was asked to interpret a written marital agreement between Mr. and Mrs. Spires that contained the following provisions:

Mrs. Spires:

- may not withdraw any money from the bank without Mr. Spires's express permission

- may not "attempt to influence the status/intensity" of any relationship that Mr. Spires may have "with other individuals outside of the marriage unless the husband verbally requests input from the wife"

- may not "dispute" Mr. Spires in public "on any matter"

- must "conduct herself in accordance with all scriptures in the Holy Bible applicable to marital relationships germane to wives and in accordance with the husband's specific requests"

- must "carry out requests of the husband in strict accordance, i.e., timeliness, sequence, scheduling, etc."

coverture
The legal status of a married woman whereby her civil existence for many purposes was merged with (was covered up by) her husband's legal status. Also called *unity of person, doctrine of oneness, spousal-unity rule, unity of identity.*

- may not receive any loan or gift without first obtaining Mr. Spires's permission
- must maintain a sexual relationship that "remains spontaneous and solely with the husband"[10]

The parties entered into this agreement in 1991, not 1791 or 1891. Although the court eventually declared the agreement to be unenforceable, the fact that such a case had to be litigated close to the beginning of the twenty-first century suggests that not everyone in society accepts the legal principle of equality between the sexes. Fortunately, many do accept it. Nevertheless, anyone engaged in the practice of family law must be prepared to find serious discrepancies between the laws on the books and how people, in fact, conduct their lives. These discrepancies will continue to generate considerable business for family-law practices.

INCREASED FEDERALIZATION OF FAMILY LAW

The U.S. Constitution has specific enumerated powers that are the responsibility of the United States (federal) government, e.g., to raise armies and regulate patents. Family-law matters are *not* among these enumerated powers. Under the Tenth Amendment, the "powers not delegated to the United States by the Constitution, nor prohibited by it to the States, are reserved to the States respectively, or to the people." Hence, family law is substantially within the responsibility of state law. As Chief Justice William Rehnquist of the United States Supreme Court once said, domestic relations "has been left to the states from time immemorial."[11] Congress, federal courts, and federal administrative agencies have historically played relatively minor roles in family law. When parties want a divorce, for example, they go to a state court, not to a federal court.

Although state law continues to dominate the field, federal law is becoming increasingly important. The following are some examples:

- Competent legal representation in a divorce settlement must include advice on how federal tax laws affect alimony and property division (particularly prior to 2019 when the tax law changed).
- The same is true for the impact of our federal bankruptcy laws.
- The legalization of abortion occurred through an interpretation by a federal court (the U.S. Supreme Court) of the federal constitution.
- Major changes in the state law of paternity have been due to interpretations of the federal (U.S.) Constitution.
- Interstate child-custody disputes are substantially regulated by federal statutes, such as the Parental Kidnaping Prevention Act (PKPA).
- Perhaps the most dramatic inroad of federal law has been in the area of child support. Congress passed laws that have led to substantial changes in the enforcement of child-support obligations. Child support is still governed by state law, but Congress has told states that if they want to receive specified federal funds (e.g., grants for public assistance), they must pass specified state laws designed to increase collection of child support from delinquent parents. All states have made such changes.

federalization
Changes in state law that result mainly from (a) laws written by the federal legislature (Congress) and (b) interpretations of the U.S. Constitution by federal courts.

constitutionalization
Changes in state law that result from interpretations of the U.S. Constitution by the U.S. Supreme Court and other federal courts. (See the glossary for another meaning.)

When federal law leads to changes in an area of law once controlled mainly by state law, we refer to the change as the **federalization** of that area of the law. If the federal law consists of interpretations of the U.S. Constitution by the U.S. Supreme Court and other federal courts, we refer to the change as the **constitutionalization** of that area of the law. Of course, state family law has not been swallowed up by federalization or constitutionalization. The bulk of family law today is still written by state legislatures and state courts. Yet federal law's role in family law is significant and continues to increase. As we will see, not everyone is happy with this trend.

CONTRACT DIMENSION OF FAMILY LAW

A great deal of family law is governed by the **status** of the participants. By status, we mean the bundle of legal rights and obligations that are imposed by law, often without regard to the consent or contract desires of the persons involved. For example, once parties are married, they cannot agree (contract) on their own to dissolve their marriage in order to marry someone else. In other words, spouses cannot divorce themselves. They need a court order of divorce. Nor can they agree (contract) that either or both will have additional spouses. A basic requirement of the law is one spouse at a time. The *status* of marriage would trump such contractual desires. Phrased another way, such contracts are unenforceable because of the duties and obligations imposed by the status of marriage.

Yet there is still considerable room for the parties to enter into agreements (contracts) about their marriage so long as they do not tamper with basic rights and obligations that are central to the status of marriage. In fact, a relatively recent major development in family law has been a substantial increase in the capacity of parties to enter into enforceable contracts that help define their rights and obligations. When we study **premarital agreements**, for example, we will see that parties can enter into contracts that define important components of the impending marriage they are about to enter, particularly in the area of finances. To an increasing degree, marriage is viewed as an economic partnership that is subject to some mutual modification, rather than as an eternal union of love benevolently presided over by the husband. Again, however, there are limits on what parties can do by contract. Courts will not approve (enforce) everything the parties agree to do.

It is sometimes said that in every marriage there is a third party—the state—that imposes rights and obligations on the spouses. The state's right to do so is based on its **police power**, which is the inherent power of a government to impose laws deemed necessary and proper for public security, health, morality, and general welfare. Despite this role of the state, we have begun to see more flexibility in what the parties are allowed to do by contract.

SCIENCE AND FAMILY LAW

Scientific breakthroughs have created substantial challenges for family law. Nowhere is this more evident than in the evolving science of motherhood. New ways to create babies have given us the reality of multiple parents—more than two. "Reproductive technology has made it possible for one person to supply an egg, another to fertilize it, a third to gestate it and a fourth and fifth to be deemed the parents."[12] This reality has forced legislatures and courts to redefine traditional areas of the law and to confront new categories of disputes. For example, who is the legal parent when a surrogate mother changes her mind about turning the baby over to the couple that provided the embryo for the child? (We will find out in Chapter 16.)

DEREGULATION OF SEXUALITY

At one time, society imposed severe restrictions on intimate conduct. The law contained numerous examples of crimes related to sexuality, such as the sale of contraceptives, homosexual conduct, and abortion. All restrictions on sexuality have not been eliminated, but they have been substantially reduced for adults. In the dramatic case of *Lawrence v. Texas*, which decriminalized private homosexual conduct between consenting adults, the U.S. Supreme Court said that the liberty guarantee in the U.S. Constitution "presumes an autonomy of self that includes. . . certain intimate conduct" and that such conduct between consenting adults had "transcendent dimensions" protected by the Constitution."[13] Although there is a segment of

status
A person's legal condition by which rights and obligations are imposed by law, often without regard to the consent or contract desires of the person involved.

premarital agreement
A contract by persons about to be married that can cover (1) financial and related matters once the marriage occurs and (2) spousal support, property division, and related matters in the event of separation, divorce, annulment, or death. Also called *prenuptial agreement* ("*prenup*"), *antenuptial agreement*.

police power
The inherent power of a government to impose laws deemed necessary and proper for public security, health, morality, and general welfare.

society that wants to maintain—and indeed, increase—government regulation of "intimate conduct," the law, is moving in the other direction.

———————————

As family-law continues into the twenty-first century, these are some of the major themes that will continue to demand the attention of courts and legislatures and, therefore, will be part of family-law practices where attorneys and paralegals serve the needs of clients.

FAMILY LAW CASES ARE UNIQUE

There is an important difference between family-law cases and most other civil cases in our court system. In a garden-variety negligence, defamation, or breach-of-contract case, the events usually involve one isolated set of prior facts. In many family-law cases, however, the facts are often shifting as the case is underway in court:

> Unlike [other] civil cases, which frequently involve a snapshot in time of past events, the issues in many domestic relations cases evolve throughout the course of a case and well into the future. Resolution of family disputes requires an assessment of past events to shape future behaviors and relationships. The dispute resolution process itself must be fluid and flexible in this evolving environment. . . . Where children are involved, the relationship between the parties continues well beyond the resolution of the case. [Parties] frequently come back to the court to adjust for new circumstances, resolve new disputes, or resolve pre-existing disputes that were not effectively addressed the first time.[14]

The issue in many civil cases is who should pay for the damages caused by an accident or by the failure to deliver promised goods. In family-law cases, the facts are often in flux and the issue before the court is how the parties are going to be able to live together (or apart) in the future. As we will see, a remedy that satisfies this goal requires greater sensitivity and flexibility from our legal system than a single award of monetary damages for a past accident or injury.

THE NEW TERMINOLOGY OF FAMILY LAW

One of the consequences of changes in family law over recent decades has been the development of new terminology to describe some of the participants and procedures that make up family law. Below are some examples of new family-law terminology (with older terms in the parentheses):

- Dissolution (divorce)
- Spousal support (alimony)
- Maintenance (alimony)
- Nonmarital child (illegitimate child, out-of-wedlock child, bastard)
- Caregiver (custodian)
- Parenting (mothering, fathering)
- Parenting plan, parenting schedule, parenting functions, parental responsibility, residential schedule, co-parenting plan (custody)
- Parenting time (visitation)
- Unmarried couple (persons living in a meretricious relationship)

Some of the changes in terminology are cosmetic. Others have a more substantial purpose, such as emphasizing responsibilities rather than rights, downplaying an emphasis on morality, and toning down the rhetoric that can contribute to the hostility that some family-law disputes can engender. A major goal is to move away from terminology that encourages parties to view themselves as "winners" or "losers" so that there can be a greater focus on an amicable resolution of conflict, particularly when children are involved.

Not all states use the new terminology. Indeed, you are likely to find that most states use both the old and the new terminology at the same time. This is inevitable as courts apply prior decisions (precedents) to current fact situations. The prior decisions, of course, use the old terminology. In this book, we will be examining both the old and the new terminology.

precedent
A decision made in a prior case that can be used as a standard or guide in a later case, which raises a similar issue.

SCOPE OF FAMILY LAW

To work in an office where family law is practiced, you need compassion, flexibility, skill, and above all, an ability to handle a wide diversity of problems. Although many cases are straightforward and "simple," some are not. A veteran attorney observed that a family-law practice requires everyone "to become an expert in many fields of law, not just one."[15] In this sense, the specialty of family law requires one to be a generalist.

Let's examine this diversity through an example. It will provide you with an overview of many of the topics we will examine in this book. Assume that you are a paralegal working for Karen Smith, an attorney in your state. One of the clients of the office is Susan Miller, who lives out of state. Karen receives the following email message from Susan:

2/7/19
Karen Smith:
I am leaving the state in a week to live with my mother in your state. She will help me move everything so that we can start a new life. I need to see you as soon as I arrive. Yesterday, Joel, my husband, called from his business. He threatened me and our three children. I will bring the twins with me, but I don't know where my oldest boy is. He is probably with Joel and getting into more trouble.
Susan Miller

The checklist below lists many of the questions that are potentially relevant to the case of Susan Miller. Most of the technical terms in this list will be defined in subsequent chapters and in the glossary. Our goal here is to demonstrate that the scope of the law covered in a family-law practice can be quite broad.

One final word before we begin the overview. Some state bar associations have **specialty certification** programs for attorneys who practice family law. At least one state (Texas) also has a specialty certification for paralegals in family law.[16] Certification requires meeting designated qualifications such as experience in the specialty and passing an exam in the law of the specialty. Most attorneys and paralegals, however, do not have specialty certification because the state does not offer it or there is a perception that one is not needed.

specialty certification
A recognition of competency (often by a bar association) in a particular area of law.

EXHIBIT 1.2   Checklist: Areas of Law Often Covered in a Family-Law Practice: The Example of *Miller v. Miller*

Criminal Law

- Has Joel Miller committed a crime? What kind of threats did he make? Did he assault his wife, Susan Miller, and children? Has domestic violence been committed or threatened?
- If Joel has been violent, should Susan report him to the police?
- Has Joel failed to support his family? If so, is the nonsupport serious enough to warrant state or federal criminal action against him?

(continued)

Exhibit 1.2 *(continued)*

- Is there a danger of further criminal acts by Joel? If so, what can be done, if anything, to prevent them? Can Susan obtain a restraining or protective order to keep him away?
- Is Susan subject to criminal penalties for taking the children out of state?

Divorce/Separation/Annulment Law

- What does Susan want? An end of the marriage?
- Does she know what Joel wants to do?
- Does she have grounds for a divorce?
- Does she have grounds for an annulment? (Were the Millers validly married?)
- Does she have grounds for a legal separation?
- Does Joel have grounds for a divorce, annulment, or legal separation against his wife?

Custody Law

- Does Susan want sole physical and sole legal custody of all three children? Is she the biological mother of all three? Is Joel their biological father? Are there any paternity problems? Will Joel want custody? What is the lifestyle of the parent or parents seeking custody? Is joint physical custody or joint legal custody an option?
- If Susan does not want a divorce, annulment, or legal separation, how can she obtain legal custody of the children?
- Does Susan want anyone else to be given custody of any of the children (e.g., a relative)? Could such a person make a claim for custody *against* her?
- If Susan wants custody, has she jeopardized her chances of being awarded custody by taking the children out of state?

Support Law

- Is Joel supporting his wife? Is she supporting him?
- Is Joel supporting the three children? Is she supporting them? Do they have any special medical or educational needs? If so, are these needs being met?
- Are the children now covered under Joel's health insurance policy? Is Susan covered? Is there a danger that the policy will be changed? Who has the authority under the policy to change the beneficiaries?
- Does either spouse have a pension plan from prior or present employment? Can one spouse (or ex-spouse) obtain rights in the pension plan of the other spouse (or ex-spouse)? (This is an issue of employee-benefits law.)
- Can Susan obtain a court order forcing Joel to provide support while she is deciding whether she wants to terminate the marital relationship?
- If Susan files for divorce, annulment, or legal separation, can she obtain a temporary support order while the case is in progress?
- If Susan files for divorce, annulment, or legal separation and loses for substantive or procedural reasons, can she still obtain a support order for separate maintenance against Joel?
- While Susan is living apart from her husband, can she enter into contracts with merchants for the purchase of food, clothing, furniture, medical care, prescriptions, transportation, and other necessities (called "necessaries") and make *him* pay for them? Can she use his credit?
- Does Joel have assets (personal property or real property) against which a support order can be enforced? Is there a danger he might try to hide these assets? Is there a danger he might try to give the assets to persons he controls such as by transferring title into the names of these other persons? If so, can this be prevented?

(continued)

Exhibit 1.2 *(continued)*

- If Joel cannot be relied upon for support and Susan cannot work, does she qualify for public assistance such as Temporary Assistance to Needy Families (TANF)? (This is an issue of public-benefits law.)

- Is Joel supporting any other children, such as from a previous marriage? If so, how would this affect his duty to support the three children he had with Susan?

Contract Law and Agency Law

- Has Joel entered into any contacts for which Susan could be found liable if he fails to perform the contracts?

- Can Joel obligate Susan on any of his current or future debts?

- Has she ever worked for him or otherwise acted as his agent?

- Has he ever worked for her or otherwise acted as her agent?

- Have the children (particularly the oldest child) entered into any contracts under their own names? If so, who is liable for such contracts? Can they be canceled (disaffirmed)?

Real Property Law and Personal Property Law

- Do either or both spouses own real property (e.g., land)? If so, how is the real property owned? How is title held? Individually? As tenants by the entirety? As community property?

- Who provided the funds for the purchase of this property? Were the funds earned during the marriage or did any of the funds come from money either of them brought into the marriage?

- What rights, if any, does Susan have in Joel's separate property?

- What rights, if any, does Joel have in Susan's separate property?

- What is Joel's income? Can his wages be garnished?

- What other personal property exists—cars, bank accounts, stocks, bonds, or furniture? Who owns this property? With what funds were they purchased?

Corporate Law and Business Law

- Does Joel own or have an interest in a business? If so, is it a corporation? A partnership? A sole proprietorship? If the parties separate and obtain a divorce, will Susan be entitled to a share of the business as part of the division of marital property?

- What are the assets and liabilities of the business?

- The same questions need to be asked about any business(es) of Susan.

Bankruptcy Law

- Is there a danger that Joel or his business might go into bankruptcy? If so, how would this affect Susan's rights to support and to her share of the marital property? How would it affect his duty of spousal or child support?

- The same bankruptcy questions need to be asked regarding Joel's personal and business assets.

Tort Law

- Has Joel committed any torts against Susan (e.g., assault, fraud, conversion, intentional infliction of emotional distress)?

- Has she committed any torts against him?

- Can one spouse sue another in tort?

- Have the children (particularly the oldest) damaged any property or committed any torts for which the parents might be liable?

Civil Procedure Law

- If a court action is brought (e.g., for divorce, custody, separate maintenance), what court would have jurisdiction? A court in this state? A court in the state where Joel resides?

(continued)

Exhibit 1.2 *(continued)*

- How can service of process be made?

- Whose depositions should be taken as part of discovery?

- If Susan sues and obtains a judgment in this state, can it be enforced in another state? Would she have to travel to the other state to enforce her rights and that of the children?

- What divorce law applies: the law of the state where Joel lives or the state to which Susan has now moved? (This is a *conflict-of-law* issue.)

Evidence Law

- What factual claims will Susan be making, e.g., that Joel has hidden money or other assets that should be part of a property settlement or used to support the family? Is there evidence of dissipation (squandering marital assets)?

- What testimonial evidence (oral statements of witnesses) exists to support Susan's claims?

- How much of this evidence is admissible in court?

- What documentary evidence should be obtained (e.g., marriage license, birth certificates, records of purchases, financial statements, loan applications)?

- What claims will Joel make against Susan? What evidence is he likely to use to support these claims? What objections can be made to this evidence?

Juvenile Law

- Can a dependency or child-neglect petition be brought against Joel or Susan?

- Why is Susan upset about her eldest son? Has he committed an act of delinquency or other status offense?

- Is Susan's son a Person in Need of Supervision (PINS), a Child in Need of Supervision (CHINS), or a Child in Need of Protection and Services (CHIPS)?

Tax Law

- Have Joel and Susan filed joint tax returns in the past?

- Is any money due or are any refunds expected on past returns?

- In a property settlement following a divorce or separation, what would be the most advantageous settlement for Susan from a tax perspective?

- What arrangement might Joel seek in order to obtain the best tax posture for him? What is negotiable? What will he be willing to give up to obtain his tax objectives? Will he, for example, cooperate in allowing Susan to have sole physical custody and sole legal custody of the children in exchange for her cooperation in obtaining the most advantageous tax position for him?

Estate Law

- Do the Millers each have their own wills? If so, who are the beneficiaries? Do they have a joint will? If there is no divorce, can Joel leave Susan out of his will entirely?

- Who receives their property if they die without a valid will (i.e., intestate) while they are separated or after a divorce?

- Does Joel have a life insurance policy on which Susan or the children are beneficiaries? If so, is he allowed to change these beneficiaries?

Social Security Law

- When will Joel be eligible for social security? Can Susan be eligible for Social Security through his earnings if she is not eligible independently?

- How do Social Security benefits affect support obligations?

(continued)

Exhibit 1.2 *(continued)*

Professional Responsibility & Ethics

- Is Joel represented by counsel? If so, can we contact Joel directly, or must all communications to him be made through his attorney? If he is not yet represented, are there limitations on what we can and cannot say to him?

- If Susan can find her eldest son, can she simply take him away from her husband when the latter is not around? Would this be illegal? What is the ethical obligation of an attorney whose client is about to do something illegal?

Attorney Fees and Court Costs

- Can Joel be forced to pay attorney fees and court costs that Susan will incur in her legal disputes with him?

- Can Susan be forced to pay Joel's attorney fees and court costs?

The purpose of this book is to examine questions such as those in the checklist regarding Joel and Susan Miller. More specifically, our purpose is to equip you to raise and answer such questions that could arise in your state.

OVERVIEW OF MAJOR CONSTITUTIONAL PRINCIPLES

INTRODUCTION

As indicated, a good deal of family law has been changed because of constitutional-law rulings of the courts, particularly interpretations of the U.S. Constitution by the U.S. Supreme Court. We will be covering such changes in later chapters. Here, our goal is to provide basic constitutional principles that will provide a background for understanding these changes.

Family law consists of a vast array of rules found in the statutes of the legislature and in the **common law** opinions of the courts. The rules cover (a) what can and cannot be done in family relationships and (b) the steps that must be followed to do what is allowed. The rules can range from eligibility to enter into the state of marriage to residency requirements for when a court can hear a divorce case. Eventually, almost every rule is challenged by persons who believe that the rule wrongly restricts what they want to do because, they assert, the restriction is unconstitutional. The argument is that the restriction violates the state constitution, the federal (United States) constitution, or both constitutions.

common law
Law created by courts in the absence of controlling statutory law or other higher law. (See glossary for additional meanings.)

When a court agrees to hear such a challenge, it will use its power of **judicial review** to determine the constitutionality of the rule, including its power to invalidate the rule if the court concludes that it violates the constitution.

Constitutional challenges fall into three main groups: (1) those that violate the U.S. Constitution, (2) those that violate the state constitution, and (3) those that violate both constitutions.

judicial review
(1) The power of a court to determine the constitutionality of a statute or other law, including the power to refuse to enforce it if the court concludes that it violates the constitution.
(2) The power of a court to determine the correctness of what a lower tribunal has done.

- Assume that a state writes a statute that grants a benefit to legitimate children that is denied to illegitimate children. This state law could be challenged as a violation of the 14th Amendment of the U.S. Constitution. The 14th Amendment covers actions taken by a state government.

- The same statute denying the benefit to illegitimate children might also be challenged as a violation of the state constitution.

- Assume that Congress writes a federal statute on the enforcement of child support against out-of-state parents. This federal law could be challenged as a violation of the 5th Amendment of the U.S. Constitution. The 5th Amendment covers actions taken by the federal (United States) government.

Let's examine each of these three kinds of constitutional challenges, the first of which will be our primary concern in this book.

CHALLENGING STATE GOVERNMENT ACTION AS A VIOLATION OF THE 14TH AMENDMENT OF THE U.S. CONSTITUTION

There are two major challenges to state action based on the 14th Amendment of the U.S. Constitution. First, the challenge alleges that the state action violates due process of law (DPL) in the 14th Amendment. Second, the challenge alleges that the state action violates equal protection of law (EPL) in the 14th Amendment. Some challenges allege that the state action violates both DPL and EPL.

Due Process of Law (DPL)

The 14th Amendment to the U.S. Constitution provides that no state shall "deprive any person of life, liberty or property, without due process of law."[17] The phrase **due process of law** means both procedural due process and substantive due process:

- **Procedural due process (PDP).** The constitutional requirement that the government provide fair procedures such as adequate notice and an opportunity to be heard whenever the government seeks to deprive someone of life, liberty, or property.
- **Substantive due process (SDP).** The constitutional requirement that the government avoid arbitrary and capricious actions that deprive someone of life, liberty, or property, regardless of how fair the government might be in the procedures that lead to the deprivation.

The focus of SDP is the *content* of what the government is doing (e.g., terminate parental rights). The focus of PDP is the *method* or steps used by the government to implement that content (e.g., provide a hearing).

PROCEDURAL DUE PROCESS (PDP) To comply with PDP, the government must provide fair procedures when it deprives someone of life, liberty, or property. Which procedures? The answer depends on the seriousness of what is being deprived by the government. If, for example, the government is taking away a poor person's welfare benefits, terminating the parental rights of a parent, or expelling a student from public school (all very serious deprivations), then the procedures must include rights such as a notice of the reasons for the government action and an opportunity to contest the deprivations at a hearing, including the right to bring an attorney to represent you at the hearing. The failure to provide these procedures is a violation of PDP. Less serious deprivations may not require all of these procedural rights.

SUBSTANTIVE DUE PROCESS (SDP) Many of the due-process challenges against state family-law restrictions have alleged SDP. When a court must decide if a family-law restriction violates SDP, it often goes through the following steps:

- The court must determine whether the restriction is of a **fundamental right** (e.g., the right to marry) or is a restriction of a nonfundamental right (e.g., the right to adopt a child). A fundamental right falls into one of the following three categories: The right (a) is specifically guaranteed in the U.S. Constitution, (b) is implicit in the concept of ordered liberty, or (c) is deeply rooted in the nation's history and tradition. If a right does not fall into one of these three categories, it is a nonfundamental right.

---

due process of law (DPL)
Both procedural due process and substantive due process.

procedural due process (PDP)
The constitutional requirement that the government provide fair procedures—such as adequate notice and an opportunity to be heard—whenever it seeks to deprive someone of life, liberty, or property.

substantive due process (SDP)
The constitutional requirement that the government avoid arbitrary and capricious actions that deprive someone of life, liberty, or property, regardless of how fair the government might be in the procedures that lead to the deprivation.

fundamental right
A right that falls into one of the following three categories: The right (a) is specifically guaranteed in the U.S. Constitution, (b) is implicit in the concept of ordered liberty, or (c) is deeply rooted in the nation's history and tradition.

- The court must determine the constitutionality of a restriction of a fundamental right or of a nonfundamental right. To make this determination, the court applies a test or standard. The test is called a *level of scrutiny* and is different for fundamental rights and nonfundamental rights. As we will see, the test for the constitutionality of a restriction of a fundamental right is much higher (and more difficult for a state to meet) than if the restriction is of a nonfundamental right.

- Because there are two levels or tiers of rights (fundamental rights and nonfundamental rights), the analysis of whether a restriction violates SDP is called a *two-tier analysis:*

  1. If the restriction is of a fundamental right, then it must pass the **strict-scrutiny test** to be valid. This test is met if the restriction is **narrowly tailored** to serve a **compelling state interest**.

  2. If the restriction is of a nonfundamental right, then it must pass the broader (and easier-to-meet) **rational-basis test** to be valid (also called a *rational-relation test*). This test is met if the restriction is **reasonably related** to a **legitimate state interest** or purpose.

If a government restriction does not meet these tests, the restriction violates SDP. Exhibit 1.3 summarizes these principles of SDP.

strict-scrutiny test
The government's action must be narrowly tailored to serve a compelling state interest. Also phrased as *necessary to serve a compelling state interest.*

narrowly tailored
No more than needed to maintain the effectiveness of a goal; no broader than absolutely necessary.

compelling state interest
An interest that is of the highest order; an interest that has a clear justification in the necessities of national or community life.

rational-basis test
The government's action must be reasonably related to a legitimate state interest or purpose. Also called *minimal-scrutiny test* and *rational-relation test.*

reasonably related
Logically connected (pertaining to any means used to achieve a goal that is reasonably likely to be successful).

legitimate state interest
Any government objective that the state has the authority to pursue, such as to provide for public safety.

EXHIBIT 1.3   Constitutional Challenges to State Family-Law Restrictions Based on Substantive Due Process (SDP) of the 14th Amendment

Substantive Due Process (SDP): The constitutional requirement that the government avoid arbitrary and capricious actions that deprive someone of life, liberty, or property, regardless of how fair the government might be in the procedures that lead to the deprivation.

Guideline: Whether a state family-law restriction violates SDP depends on whether the restriction is (1) of a fundamental right or (2) of a nonfundamental right. The highest test or level of scrutiny is used to determine whether a restriction on a fundamental right violates SPD (the strict-scrutiny test). A broader and easier-to-meet test is used to determine whether a restriction on a nonfundamental right violates SDP (the rational-basis test).

Kind of Right the Restriction Interferes With	Definition	Examples	Test, Standard, or Level of Scrutiny Used by a Court to Decide If the Restriction Violates SDP	Definitions
Fundamental Right	*Fundamental right:* A right that falls into one of the following three categories: The right (a) is specifically guaranteed in the U.S. Constitution, (b) is implicit in the concept of ordered liberty or (c) is deeply rooted in the nation's history and tradition.	*Family-Law Examples:* • Right to marry. • Right of a couple to use contraceptives. • Right to direct the education and upbringing of one's children • Right to have an abortion without undue burden. *Other Examples:* • Right to vote • Right to interstate travel.	*Strict Scrutiny:* The restriction on the fundamental right must be *narrowly tailored* to serve a *compelling state interest.* Also phrased as *necessary to serve a compelling state interest.*	*Narrowly Tailored:* No more than needed to maintain the effectiveness of a goal; no broader than absolutely necessary. *Compelling State Interest:* An interest that is of the highest order and that has a clear justification in the necessities of national or community life.

(continued)

Exhibit 1.3 (continued)

Kind of Right the Restriction Interferes With	Definition	Examples	Test, Standard, or Level of Scrutiny Used by a Court to Decide If the Restriction Violates SDP	Definitions
Nonfundamental Right	A nonfundamental right is any right that does not fall into one of the three categories listed above.	*Family Law Examples:* • Right of adults to engage in private same-sex intimate conduct. • Right of grandparents to have a relationship with their grandchildren. *Other Examples:* • Right to use a public park. • Right to buy a boat.	*Rational Basis:* The restriction on the nonfundamental right must be reasonably related to a *legitimate state interest* or purpose.	*Reasonably Related:* Logically connected (pertaining to any means used to achieve a goal that is reasonably likely successful). *Legitimate State Interest or Purpose:* Any government objective that the state has the authority to pursue, such as to provide for public safety.

Equal Protection of Law (EPL)

equal protection of law (EPL)
The constitutional requirement that the government treats one group or class the same as it treats another group or class *in like circumstances*; often shortened to *equal protection*.

classification
(1) A group or class that the government treats differently from another group or class in that the government discriminates for or against that group or class. (2) The government's different treatment of one group or class over another. (3) The identification of property as either separate property or marital property.

Equal protection of law (EPL), often shortened to *equal protection*, is the constitutional requirement that the government treats one group or class the same as it treats another group or class *in like circumstances*. The focus of EPL is the unequal treatment of groups or classes that result from a law. To classify something means to divide it into groups or classes. **Classification** (or class) has different meanings in the law. In divorce proceedings, for example, the word refers to the identification of property as either separate property or marital property. In constitutional law, the word often refers to a group or class that the government treats differently from another group—meaning the government has discriminated for or against a certain group or class. The constitutional question we are addressing here is whether a classification violates EPL.

Under the EPL constitutional requirement, if two groups or classes are similarly situated, the government must treat them the same. The origin of this rule is the Equal Protection Clause of the 14th Amendment to the U.S. Constitution, which provides that no state shall "deny to any person within its jurisdiction the equal protection of the laws."[18] An example of discrimination that violates EPL would be a rule that allows ex-wives, but not ex-husbands, to obtain alimony in a divorce.

Not all classifications, however, violate EPL. "Equal protection does not require that all persons be dealt with identically."[19] It is not a violation of EPL, for example, for the government to mandate treatment for mentally ill persons but not for persons who are mentally healthy. The two groups or classes of people (mentally ill and healthy) are not *in like circumstances*.

To determine whether a particular discrimination violates EPL, we must examine (a) the kind of discrimination involved, and (b) the *reason* the government believes the discrimination is needed. Here are the steps that a court would take in an EPL case:

Step 1: Determine which of the following four categories the discrimination fits into:
- Discrimination involving a fundamental right,
- Discrimination involving a suspect class,
- Discrimination involving a quasi-suspect class, or
- Discrimination involving any other class.

Step 2: If the discrimination involves a fundamental right or if it involves a *suspect class* (a class based on race, national origin, or alienage), then it must pass the *strict-scrutiny test*. As we have seen, this test is met if the discrimination is *narrowly tailored* to meet a *compelling state interest*.

Step 3: If the discrimination involves a **quasi-suspect class** (a class based on gender or on a child's legitimacy), then it must pass the **intermediate-scrutiny test**. This test is met if the classification is *substantially* related to serve an *important* state interest. Intermediate scrutiny is also called *heightened scrutiny* and *elevated scrutiny*.

Step 4: If the discrimination does not fit into any of these three categories—fundamental right, suspect class, or quasi-suspect class—then it must pass the broader (and easier-to-meet) *rational-basis test* to be valid (also called rational-relation test). As we have seen, this test is met if the restriction is *reasonably related* to a *legitimate state interest* or purpose.

Step 5: Because there are three tiers of rights, the analysis of whether a restriction violates EPL is called a *three-tier analysis*. The first tier is a classification that impacts fundamental rights or a suspect class (the same test applies to both). The second tier is a classification that impacts quasi-suspect classes. The third tier is every other kind of classification, i.e., one that does not involve a fundamental right, suspect class, or quasi-suspect class.

Exhibit 1.4 summarizes these principles.

suspect class
A group based on race, national origin, or alienage. *Alienage* is the condition of being an alien—that is, a person who was born outside the United States, is still a subject of a foreign nation, and has not been naturalized in the United States.

quasi-suspect class
A group based on gender or on a child's legitimacy.

intermediate-scrutiny test
The classification must be substantially related to serve an important state interest. Also called *heightened scrutiny* or *elevated scrutiny*.

EXHIBIT 1.4 Constitutional Challenges to Family-Law Restrictions Based on Equal Protection of Law (EPL) of the 14th Amendment

Equal Protection of Law (EPL): The constitutional requirement that the government treats one group or class the same as it treats another group or class *in like circumstances*.

Guideline: Whether a family-law classification violates EPL depends on whether the discrimination involves (1) a fundamental right, (2) a suspect class, (3) a quasi-suspect class, or (4) any other class. The highest test (the *strict-scrutiny test)* is used to determine the constitutionality of a classification involving a fundamental right or a suspect class. Broader (and easier to meet) tests are used when the classification involves a quasi-suspect class (*intermediate-scrutiny test*) and when the classification involves any other group (*rational-basis test*).

Type of Classification	Definitions	Examples	Test Used by a Court to Decide If the Classification Violates EPL	Definitions
Classification Involving a *Fundamental Right* **or** **Classification Involving a** *Suspect Class*	*Fundamental Right*: A right that falls into one of the following three categories: The right (a) is specifically guaranteed in the U.S. Constitution, (b) is implicit in the concept of ordered liberty or (c) or is deeply rooted in the nation's history and tradition. *Suspect Class*: A class based on race, national origin, or alienage.	*Family-Law Example That Violates EPL*: • A statute allowing same-race couples to marry but not mixed-race couples	*Strict-Scrutiny Test*: The classification must be *narrowly tailored* to serve a *compelling state interest*. Also phrased as *necessary to serve a compelling state interest*.	*Compelling State Interest*: An interest that is of the highest order and that has a clear justification in the necessities of national or community life.

(continued)

Exhibit 1.4 *(continued)*

Type of Classification	Definitions	Examples	Test Used by a Court to Decide If the Classification Violates EPL	Definitions
Classification Involving a *Quasi-Suspect Class*	*Quasi-Suspect Class*: A class based on gender or on a child's legitimacy	*Family-Law Examples That Violate EPL:* • A statute that allows ex-wives to receive alimony but not ex-husbands. • A statute that allows children of married couples to inherit from their parents but not the illegitimate children of their parents.	*Intermediate-Scrutiny Test*: The classification must be *substantially related* to serve an *important state interest* or purpose.	*Important State Interest*: An interest that is significant.
Classification That Does *NOT* Involve a Fundamental Fight, a Suspect Class, or a Quasi-Suspect Class		*Family-Law Example That Violates EPL:* • An ordinance that restricts use of a city-owned pool to adults with children.	*Rational-Basis Test*: The classification must be *reasonably related* to a *legitimate state interest* or purpose.	*Legitimate State Interest or Purpose*: Any government objective that the state has the authority to pursue, such as to provide for public safety.

CHALLENGING FEDERAL GOVERNMENT ACTION AS A VIOLATION OF THE 5TH AMENDMENT OF THE U.S. CONSTITUTION

The constitutional rules outlined in Exhibits 1.3 and 1.4 cover *state* government laws that are challenged as a violation of the 14th Amendment of the U.S. Constitution. Suppose, however, that the challenge is against an action of the *federal* government, such as a statute of Congress. Federal government action is covered by the 5th Amendment. The challenge to a federal statute is that it violates the 5th Amendment.

Both the 14th Amendment (governing state action) and the 5th Amendment (governing federal action) have Due Process Clauses. Although the 5th Amendment does not have an Equal Protection Clause, the liberty protected under its Due Process Clause has been interpreted as including equal protection rights. Hence, there are cases in which the federal government has been found to have violated equal protection under the 5th Amendment. A major recent example is the landmark case of *United States v. Windsor* (2013). In this case, the U.S. Supreme Court held that it was unconstitutional for the federal government to define marriage as a union of a man and woman for purposes of federal benefits and duties, even in a state that allowed same-sex marriage under state law. The Court was interpreting the Due Process Clause of the 5th Amendment, which, as indicated, includes equal protection rights. (We will examine the *Windsor* case in Chapter 5.)

CHALLENGING STATE GOVERNMENT ACTION AS A VIOLATION OF THE STATE CONSTITUTION

The overview thus far has focused on *federal* constitutional challenges—those based on the U.S. Constitution; however, each state has its own constitution. Some of the states have provisions similar to those in the U.S. Constitution. It is quite possible for a state court to conclude that its state constitution requires a family-law restriction to meet a higher standard of scrutiny than what would be allowed under the U.S. Constitution. For example, gender-based discrimination will be upheld under the U.S. Constitution if it meets the standard of intermediate scrutiny. A state, however, can set the bar higher than the federal constitution and rule that its own state constitution requires gender-based discrimination to meet the standard of strict scrutiny for it to be allowed within its state. A state cannot go below a standard set by the U.S. Constitution, but it can exceed that standard for its own state.

SAME-SEX RELATIONSHIPS AND THE U.S. CONSTITUTION

The constitutional law outlined in Exhibits 1.3 and 1.4 has undergone changes in recent decisions of the U.S. Supreme Court when the issue before the Court involves matters of same-sex intimacy and marriage. Instead of the tiered analysis and levels of scrutiny, the Court (lead by Justice Kennedy) based its decisions on constitutional rights to personal dignity and autonomy. We will examine these controversial variations in Chapter 5 when we cover same-sex relationships.

FAMILY LAW IN THE AGE OF ELECTRONIC EXHIBITIONISM

Computers have affected the practice of family law in a number of important ways beyond the fact that computers sit on the desks of every attorney, paralegal, and secretary in the office. As we will see later in this chapter (and in Appendix D), a great deal of legal research in family law can be done online on fee-based sites and on free sites.

In addition, computers have had other important roles in family law. In Chapter 9, for example, we will discuss virtual visitation (e-visitation) in which the custodial parent allows the other parent to visit the children through programs such as Skype that allow real-time communication over the Internet. We will also look at equally helpful online programs for scheduling virtual and physical visitation. Such technology can lessen the chances of continued bitterness following a divorce. In Chapter 15, we will discuss how the Internet has been successfully used by persons seeking to adopt a child and by adoptees seeking to reconnect with their biological parents.

There is also a darker side of the Internet. On search engines such as Google or Bing, run the search, "Facebook ruined my marriage." The results will give you examples of the damage that popular sites can do. Spouses in shaky marriages have been using social media as a source of evidence of marital wrongs such as a spouse communicating flirtatiously with a nonspouse. As one blogger recently commented, "Facebook may not be good for your marriage, but it might be good for your divorce."[20]

Family-law attorneys are also making use of social media. According to the president of the American Academy of Matrimonial Lawyers, an organization of family-law attorneys, "In just about every case now, to some extent, there is some electronic evidence. . . . It has completely changed our field."[21] By one estimate, 81 percent of the members of the Academy "have used or faced evidence plucked from Facebook, Twitter, and other social networking sites over the past five years."[22] A Denver attorney commented, "You're finding information that you just never get in the normal discovery process—ever. . . . People are just blabbing things all over Facebook. People don't yet quite connect what they're saying in their divorce cases is completely different from what they're saying on Facebook.

It doesn't even occur to them that they'd be found out."[23] Another attorney says that battles over infidelity often become ugly when the parties are confronted with damaging text messages. "It's much different than rumors running around about a husband. . .with a babe," he said. "It's in the spouse's face. They read it over and over again. It's harsh and hurtful."[24]

It is now becoming part of standard procedure for family-law attorneys to advise clients "about the location and preservation of evidence in the family's 'digital vault.' The location and preservation of this digital evidence to support a client's case requires a new skill set. Family-law attorneys must know how to economically and effectively locate, preserve, collect, review, and utilize electronically stored information (ESI)."[25] Bar associations offer seminars for attorneys on how to locate and make tactical use of Word documents, PDF files, spreadsheets, email posts, text messages, browsing history, and activity on social media. When parties are in litigation, the discovery of this material (**e-discovery**) can be critical. Attorneys often make formal demands to each other that they instruct their clients to preserve all social media accounts. Parties cannot simply erase or delete their online data. They could be sanctioned by a court and be subject to a tort suit for **spoliation**.

The country's fascination with the Internet—particularly the urge to tell the world about yourself on a social network—has been described by some family-law attorneys as electronic exhibitionism.[26] Here are some examples and consequences of this trend:

- A New York attorney says she routinely asks for a court order to seize and copy the hard drives of the spouses of her clients in order to collect evidence of financial resources for property division and for information relevant to child custody.

- An attorney for the wife in a divorce case hires a **forensic** investigator to retrieve bank records and other files that her spouse tried to delete from their computer.

- A husband suspected his wife of having an affair. He secretly installed a program that took snapshots of every Internet site she visited and every email she sent. He discovered that she was romantically involved with the parent of a classmate of their son.

- A wife introduced evidence that her husband went on an online dating site (match.com) and declared that he was single and childless, even though he was seeking sole custody of the child he had with his soon-to-be ex-wife.

- A father seeking legal custody introduced records he subpoenaed from a gaming site (WorldofWarcraft.com), which indicated that the mother of their child was online playing the game at the time she testified that she was unable to attend their child's school event. The records showed that on some days the mother played for ten hours.

- A teenager's mother accused her ex-husband of not adequately supervising their daughter. He disputed this—until his ex-wife introduced screen captures of photos the daughter had posted on her Facebook page showing her and friends playing drinking games at her father's apartment.

- A mother denies in court that she smoked marijuana, but on her Facebook page she has pictures of herself partying and smoking pot.

- A mother testified in court that her husband forced their son to defriend her on Facebook.

- A woman sought an annulment on the grounds of bigamy, suspecting that her husband was married in Europe at an earlier time. He denied this. On his computer, however, she found a wedding photo of him and another woman (in a bridal gown) exchanging vows in front of a minister.

e-discovery
Electronic data discovery (EDD). The discovery of data found in emails, spreadsheets, databases, videos, text messages, and other digital formats.

spoliation
Intentionally destroying, altering, or concealing evidence.

forensic
Pertaining to the use of scientific techniques to discover and examine evidence. (See glossary for additional definitions.)

- As a result of Facebook's practice of recommending friends, a woman received a routine request to be the friend of another woman, both of whom, Facebook said, were probably connected to a certain man. Unknown to Facebook and to the two women, the connection the women had was that they were both currently married to the man! At the time, he married wife #2, he had not divorced wife #1. He is now facing a charge of bigamy.

Social networks are not the only source of electronic evidence. Cell phones, smartphones, Global Position System (GPS) receivers, and E-ZPass records are also sources. "We had one woman," reports a New York attorney, "who said her husband was beating her, and we found the E-ZPass records showing her crossing the George Washington Bridge at the precise time she said she was being beaten."[27]

Furthermore, the Internet allows parties to continue their bitterness after the divorce has been concluded. For example, a father who is upset about a child custody decision might create a blog in order to air his hostility toward his ex-wife. Enraged spouses have uploaded videos on YouTube describing the alleged unfairness of the other side's divorce tactics. (Example: type "*Tricia Walsh Smith*" *divorce* in YouTube.) In a recent case, a judge ordered an ex-husband to stop attacking his ex-wife on his Facebook page and to post an apology on the page for his past attacks.

To confront these online realities, many family-law attorneys have standard advice for their clients:

- One divorce attorney says that she includes a confidentiality clause in every separation agreement that prohibits both spouses from publishing factual or fictional accounts of their marriage.

- A family-law attorney regularly advises his clients to change all their passwords and privacy settings to prevent their spouses from being able to gain access to their sites during (and after) the divorce. This approach, however, does not always work. In a recent custody dispute, a judge ordered the parties to exchange each other's passwords for their Facebook and dating websites to allow mutual opportunity for discovery of evidence relevant to their disputes.

Some paralegals in family-law practices are frequently assigned the task of surfing the Internet for evidence (or leads to evidence) on their clients and opponents.

- A father tells the court that his child-support payments are too high? Find out if there are photos of him online driving his new Audi.

- A parent seeking sole custody denies that she drinks? Find out if there are photos of her in her apartment partying with a drink in her hand next to a liquor bottle.

The search can sometimes be fruitful:

- In one case, the firm won shared custody for the father after finding out that his wife had posted sexually explicit comments on her boyfriend's online page.

- In another case, the credibility of a husband's claim of marital fidelity was questioned when the office found an online profile stating that he was single and looking.

Such evidence is not always verifiable or admissible in court. But attorneys have found that they can sometimes gain bargaining leverage by simply suggesting that the evidence exists.

PARALEGALS IN FAMILY-LAW CASES

The media (particularly television dramas) often give a distorted view of a family-law practice, and indeed, of attorneys in general. The practice of law is not an endless series of confessions and concessions that are pried loose from

contested
Challenged; opposed or disputed.

opponents. Every attorney does not spend all day engaged in the kind of case that makes front-page news. It is rare for the legal system to become the spectacle—some would say the circus—exhibited by some high-profile **contested** cases. While excitement and drama can be part of the legal system, they are not everyday occurrences. What is common is painstaking, time-consuming, and meticulous hard work. This reality is rarely portrayed in the media.

Nevertheless, it is true that the day-to-day work of paralegals in a family-law practice can expose them to intense emotions and occasional drama. In many ways, paralegals who work in family law are unique as indicated by the following comments from an experienced paralegal:

> *Perhaps in no other area of the law can paralegals have such substantive impact than in family law matters. From the moment the client seeks an attorney's services to the conclusion of the attorney's representation, paralegals can and do have real impact. Not only can they prepare most, if not all, pleadings under the direction of their supervising attorney, but they often become the client's most frequent contact during an extremely traumatic time in their life. Whether the matter involves a divorce, child custody, or paternity action, post-judgment support modification, or adoption, the paralegal develops a close bond with the client.*[28]

We will now take a more specific look at the possible range of paralegal responsibilities in a family-law practice. Keep in mind, however, that no two paralegals will have identical job descriptions. According to veteran paralegal, Yasmin Spiegel, "Your skills and interests, as well as the degree of trust and communication between you and your boss, will determine the tasks that you will be assigned."[29] Nevertheless, it is possible to list some of the commonly performed tasks of many paralegals.[30] (See Exhibit 1.5.) Following this list of tasks, we will read more from Yasmin Spiegel as she provides a flesh-and-bones perspective of life in the trenches. (See Exhibit 1.6.) Paralegal tasks will also be presented at the end of many of the remaining chapters in the book.

Although some definitions will be provided in the following descriptions, definitions of the major family-law terms are found in the glossary and in later chapters.

EXHIBIT 1.5   Examples of Paralegal Roles in Family Law

The following tasks pertain mainly to paralegals working on divorce cases:

New Clients

- Screen prospective family-law clients who telephone the office seeking information about the law firm.
- Schedule appointments of prospective clients with attorney.
- Help identify problems that can be referred to others, e.g., to government agencies that provide public assistance.
- Conduct a **conflicts check** on a prospective client to make sure that the law firm would not have a **conflict of interest** that would disqualify the law firm from representing the client (e.g., because the firm once represented the spouse of the prospective client).
- After the attorney has accepted the person as a client (a) attend (and take notes at) the initial interview of the client conducted by the attorney, or (b) conduct the initial interview of the client.
- Open a case file for the new client.
- Draft letters for the new client to sign authorizing the release of his or her confidential information, e.g., medical records, tax returns, and employment records.

conflicts check
Finding out whether a conflict of interest exists that might disqualify a law office from representing a prospective client or from continuing the representation of a current client.

conflict of interest
Divided loyalties that actually or potentially harm (or disadvantage) someone who is owed undivided loyalty.

(continued)

Exhibit 1.5 *(continued)*

- Maintain contact with the client (a) by keeping the client apprised of the status of the case, (b) by answering client questions that do not involve giving **legal advice**, and (c) by referring legal questions to the attorney.
- Set up the calendar or **tickler** system of important dates that must be monitored throughout the case.
- Help the client assemble relevant documents, e.g., marriage certificate, divorce decree on prior marriage (if any), proof of residences, birth certificates of children, pay stubs, prior year tax returns, copies of deeds, and medical records on the health of the client and children. (For more details on what documents are needed, see Chapter 3 on compiling a family history.)
- Prepare a chronology (**timeline**) of relevant events, e.g., tasks and time spent raising the children.

Commencement of Action

- Conduct follow-up interviews with the client to obtain information needed for drafting the petition, summons, and accompanying affidavits.
- Prepare the first draft of these documents.
- Prepare special orders as needed (e.g., ordering the parties not to take the children out of the state, ordering the parties not to sell or otherwise transfer marital assets).
- Arrange for service of process and service of discovery documents. Ensure that **proof of service** has been filed for each document.
- Maintain and update the tickler systems to monitor due dates, such as the date when the defendant must respond to the petition and when interrogatories must be answered.
- Prepare **stipulations** covering agreements between the parties on facts, procedures, or plans.

Financial Data

- Assist the client in compiling an inventory of financial data on the personal and business assets and liabilities of (a) the client and (b) the client's spouse. (See also Chapter 3 on compiling a family history.)
- Prepare financial **affidavits** on this data.
- Assist the client in preparing (or obtaining) a **financial statement** of assets and liabilities (debts).
- Prepare a report that compares the inventory of assets and liabilities identified by the client and the inventory of assets and liabilities according to his or her spouse.
- Classify real property and personal property as (a) separate property or (b) as marital/community property.
- Help the client trace the source of funds used to purchase specific property.
- Research the background and availability of experts needed to assemble financial data, e.g., an accountant or a financial adviser.
- Hire experts (e.g., an accountant) selected by the attorney to assemble financial data.
- Hire an appraiser to assess the value of personal property (e.g., jewelry) and real property (e.g., a home) in which either spouse has an interest. (Specialized assessors are often needed to assess company or business assets.)
- Hire and monitor a private investigator used on the case.

Support Needs

- Assist the client in compiling financial data on the day-to-day living needs and expenses of (a) the client, (b) the children, and (c) other dependents.
- Prepare affidavits of these support needs pending the outcome of the case.

legal advice
A statement or conclusion that applies the law or legal principles to the facts of a specific person's legal problem in an attempt to help resolve that problem.

tickler
A paper or computer system designed to provide reminders of important dates.

timeline
A chronological presentation of significant events, often using text and diagrams.

proof of service
A sworn statement (or other evidence) that a summons or other process has been served on (delivered to) a person. Also called *certificate of service* or *return of service*.

stipulation
An agreement between opposing parties about a particular matter. The verb is *stipulate*. (See glossary for an additional meaning.)

affidavit
A written or printed statement containing facts given under oath by a person (called the *affiant*) before someone with authority to administer the oath.

financial statement
A report covering assets (e.g., income, investments) and debts of a person or business as of a particular date or over a designated period. A financial accounting or balance sheet.

(continued)

arrearages
Payments that are due but have not yet been made. Also called *arrears*.

discovery
Methods used by parties to force information from each other before trial to aid in trial preparation. Examples of such methods include interrogatories and depositions. The methods can also be used to aid in the enforcement of a judgment.

interrogatories ("rogs")
A method of discovery by which one party sends written questions to another party.

protective order
A court order directing a person to refrain from inappropriate conduct such as harming or harassing another. Also called *order of protection*.

deposition
A method of discovery by which one party questions another (or questions the other party's witness), usually outside the courtroom. The person questioned is called the *deponent*.

subpoena
1. A command to appear at a certain time and place. 2. To command that someone appear at a certain time and place.

subpoena duces tecum
A command to appear at a certain time and place and bring specified things such as documents or jewelry for inspection.

Exhibit 1.5 *(continued)*

- Obtain child support worksheets and assist the client in filling them out.
- Calculate **arrearages** of child support, if any.

Temporary Orders

- Interview the client and others for information relevant to requests for temporary orders from the court on (a) child custody, (b) child support, (c) spousal support, (d) payment of attorney fees (including paralegal fees), and (e) maintaining the status quo on marital/community property.
- Determine the amount of child support to be requested based on the state's guidelines for calculating child support.
- Document special needs of children that will be the basis of child support beyond what the state's guidelines require.
- Prepare a draft of the pleadings needed for the temporary orders.
- Arrange for the service of the pleadings for the temporary orders.

Settlement

- Assemble and organize the package of documents and other materials the attorney will need for negotiation sessions with the opposing counsel.
- Be available to obtain additional facts and materials the attorney may need during negotiation sessions.
- Draft proposed settlement offers.
- Draft agreements (stipulations) that the attorneys have reached during settlement negotiations.
- Draft other settlement documents, e.g., releases.
- Prepare a draft of the proposed parenting plan.
- Prepare a draft of the separation agreement.
- Draft proposed temporary and final orders based on the settlement agreements.

Discovery

- Prepare and distribute the **discovery** documents that are subject to automatic disclosure to the opposing party. (*Automatic* means the documents must be sent without a request for them.)
- Prepare a checklist of the automatic-disclosure documents that the other side must provide and monitor their receipt.
- Draft proposed stipulations on discovery.
- Draft **interrogatories** to be sent to the opponent. Arrange for their delivery (service).
- Enter due dates for discovery responses in the office tickler system.
- Digest (summarize) and index the responses to the interrogatories when received.
- Identify interrogatories (or other discovery requests) sent by the opponent that could be the basis of an objection or a **protective order**.
- Draft responses to interrogatories sent by opponent.
- Draft **deposition** notices and **subpoenas**.
- Draft the **subpoena duces tecum** identifying documents or other things the deponent (the person being deposed) should bring to the deposition.
- Coordinate the hiring of court reporters or providers of other recording systems (e.g., video) for the deposition.
- Help draft deposition questions for the attorney conducting the deposition.
- Assemble a notebook or package of documents the attorney will use at the deposition.

(continued)

Exhibit 1.5 *(continued)*

- Help prepare the client for his or her deposition by the opponent, e.g., by role playing a question-and-answer session with the client.
- Attend the deposition and take notes.
- Order the deposition transcripts.
- Digest and index deposition transcripts.
- Maintain a database of all discovery data.
- Draft other discovery demands to be submitted to the opponent, e.g., **requests for production (RFPs)** and **requests for admissions (RFAs)**.
- Enter due dates for responses to RFPs and RFAs in the office tickler system.
- Help prepare the client's responses to other discovery demands sent to the client.
- Digest and index responses to other discovery materials.
- Accompany the client to an **independent medical examination (IME)**.

Alternative Dispute Resolution (ADR)

- Provide the client with information on **alternative dispute resolution (ADR)** options or requirements.
- Help schedule **mediation** or other ADR sessions.
- When the client must attend ADR (mandatory mediation), help prepare the client for the ADR sessions.
- Monitor documentation of the client's attendance at the ADR sessions.

Interstate Practice

- Draft documents needed to obtain and/or enforce custody orders when a child and the parent(s) reside in different states in compliance with the Uniform Child Custody Jurisdiction and Enforcement Act (UCCJEA).
- Draft documents needed to obtain and/or enforce support orders when a child and the parent(s) reside in different states in compliance with the Uniform Interstate Family Support Act (UIFSA).

Trial Preparation

- Using the Internet and other resources, research the credentials, fees, and availability of expert witnesses.
- Coordinate meetings between the attorney and proposed expert witnesses.
- Perform legal research, particularly on procedural issues.
- Organize documents the attorney will use to **impeach** opposing witnesses.
- Organize the **trial notebook**.
- Prepare or order exhibits, e.g., blow-ups of receipts and pie charts of expenses.
- Draft a list of exhibits.
- Assemble and organize trial exhibits.
- Prepare needed trial subpoenas for witnesses and arrange for their service.
- Prepare affidavits of **court costs** and attorney fees (detailing specific tasks performed by the attorneys and paralegals on the case) that must be submitted to the court.
- Draft and file requests to set court hearing dates.
- Help prepare the client for trial.
- Ensure that client, witnesses, and office personnel have the court's address and are aware of dress requirements and other etiquette norms that must be observed in the courtroom.

request for production (RFP)
A method of discovery by which one party requests that another party provide access to electronically stored data, paper documents, or other tangible things for copying or inspection. The method can also include a request to enter the party's land for inspection.

request for admissions (RFA)
A method of discovery by which one party sends a request to another party that the latter agree that a certain fact or legal conclusion is true or valid so that there will be no need to present proof or arguments about such matters during the trial.

independent medical examination (IME)
A method of discovery by which a party obtains a court order for a professional examination of a person whose physical or medical condition is in controversy.

alternative dispute resolution (ADR)
A method or procedure for resolving a legal dispute without litigating it in a court or administrative agency. ADR methods include mediation, arbitration, and Med-Arb.

mediation
A method of alternate dispute resolution (ADR) in which the parties avoid litigation by submitting their dispute to a neutral third person (the mediator) who helps the parties resolve their dispute but does not render a decision that resolves it for them.

impeach
To challenge; to attack the credibility of.

trial notebook
A collection of documents, arguments, and strategies that an attorney plans to use during a trial.

court costs
Charges or fees (imposed by and paid to the court) that are related to litigation in that court. An example is a court-filing fee.

(continued)

pretrial conference
A meeting of the attorneys and the judge (or magistrate) before the trial to attempt to narrow the issues, secure stipulations, make a final effort to settle the case without a trial, and cover other preliminary matters. Also called a *trial management conference.*

appellate brief
A document that a party files with an appellate court (and serves on an opponent) in which the party presents arguments on why the appellate court should affirm (approve), reverse, vacate (cancel), or otherwise modify what a lower court has done.

execution
1. The process of carrying out or satisfying the judgment of a court. 2. A command or writ to a court officer (e.g., sheriff) to seize and sell the property of the losing litigant (now called the *judgment debtor*) in order to satisfy the judgment debt to the winning litigant (now called the *judgment creditor*). Execution is also called *general execution* and *writ of execution.*

garnishment
A court proceeding by a creditor to force a third party in possession of the debtor's property (e.g., wages) to turn the property over to the creditor to satisfy the debt owed to the creditor.

instrument
A formal written document that gives expression to or embodies a legal act or agreement (e.g., a contract or a will). (See glossary for an additional meaning.)

Exhibit 1.5 *(continued)*

- Prepare documents for the **pretrial conference**, such as the case status statement.
- Draft the case management report.

Trial

- Drive the client to the court, if needed.
- Attend the trial to provide general assistance to the trial attorney.
- Compile a list of exhibits submitted into evidence.
- Take notes on the testimony of witnesses.
- Draft a proposed decree of dissolution, an order, and other documents to be submitted to the court.

Post-Trial

- Draft a motion for a new trial.
- Order a transcript of the trial.
- Draft a notice of appeal.
- Read the transcript to identify testimony and rulings the attorney wishes to highlight when the attorney drafts the **appellate brief**.
- File the appeal documents in court and serve them (or arrange for them to be served) on opposing counsel.
- Assemble documents the attorney will need for the settlement conference with the appellate judge.
- Assemble documents the attorney will need for oral arguments.
- Draft the letter to the client providing instructions on what he or she needs to do as a result of the final judgment.
- Draft documents needed for the enforcement or **execution** of the judgment, e.g., **garnishment** of wages.
- Coordinate the drafting of **instruments** needed for the transfer of assets pursuant to the final judgment.
- Coordinate the filing and recording of transfer instruments.

EXHIBIT 1.6   Family Law for Paralegals: An Insider's View

by Yasmin Cogswell Spiegel

The role of a paralegal in a family-law practice is exciting and varied. Whereas all areas of law can be interesting, the opportunities for client contact, full involvement, and case responsibility in family law make it a truly satisfying area of specialty. Family law affords tremendous scope for helping people going through basic changes in their lives. With the divorce rate at roughly 50 percent, there are few families who haven't been touched in some way by the problems and trauma of a court action. Our job as paralegals can be to help smooth the way through this difficult time for the client, making the experience kinder, easier to understand, more efficient, and hopefully, less expensive.

Divorce is not the only area covered in family law. Adoption, grandparent visitation issues, and emancipation of minors are just a few of the other areas in our files. In addition, we sometimes need to know about and apply bankruptcy law, business law, and criminal law.

The teamwork between attorney and paralegal is crucial to the success of a paralegal working in family law. Your skills and interests, as well as the degree of trust and

Exhibit 1.6 *(continued)*

communication between you and your boss, will determine the tasks that you will be assigned. If there is good communication and rapport between you as team members, the clients will come to rely on both of you in handling the case, and your participation will be invaluable.

In my office the attorney conducts the initial interview with the client. This is done to establish the attorney/client bond, which is crucial to the successful processing of the case. Any general questions the client has about the dissolution process, as well as strategy, fees, and expectations are all covered at this stage. If there is an immediate need for temporary orders, such as restraining orders, temporary custody, or support, the attorney will begin the information-gathering process by taking detailed notes of the client's situation.

The initial interview is usually concluded by inviting me into the office to be introduced as the "paralegal who will be assisting me with your case." This gives me the authority to contact the client on behalf of the attorney in order to gather more detailed information and to answer the client's questions on general procedure. I find that clients are, for the most part, pleased to know that a paralegal will be working on their case. I am usually more accessible than the attorney to answer their questions, or to convey information, and they are billed at a lower rate for my time.

It is often my responsibility to draft the opening documents. These include the summons, petition, and related pleadings. With the recent adoption by the courts of income-and-expense forms, this job has become critical. The forms are complicated, and in some instances intimidating; clients often need a lot of assistance in filling them out. Some of our female clients don't understand that the forms are meant to demonstrate "need" for support. They spend all their time trying to make their income on the form come out even with their expenses, but that is often impossible. It is my job to tell them that if they don't show the court evidence of the need for support, the judge won't order any.

I am also responsible for drafting stipulations on mediation, counseling, property declarations, orders to show cause, and motions for *pendente lite* relief to be granted during the litigation, pending the final outcome of the case. I rely on notes from the attorney as well as my own interviews with the client to obtain the facts needed to create these documents. The attorney reviews them for accuracy. We then obtain the signature of the client. When the documents are filed, I see that the papers are served on the client's spouse and keep the client informed of subsequent developments.

Discovery plays an important role in family law. Over the years my office has developed a set of family law interrogatories on our computer, which can be modified and used to flush out the details of marital property and separate property. For the property division between the spouses, all real property and pension plans must be appraised to determine their value. This is also the responsibility of the paralegal. Building a strong working relationship with various legal support personnel (such as appraisers, actuaries, deposition reporters, mediation and rehabilitation counselors, process servers, and photocopy services) is essential. These people trust and respect my role as a professional and as a representative of my office; they often go out of their way to assist us in emergencies because of the relationship we have built over the years.

Preparing and arranging the service of the deposition notices is another important part of a family-law practice, which falls within the scope of the paralegal's responsibility. Once the attorney conducts the deposition and the transcript of the deposition comes back from the reporter, it is my job to index and summarize it for the attorney's use in trial preparation. Comparing the bank account dates, numbers, balances, and other descriptions of property with the opposing party's previous descriptions helps to establish the full extent of a marital interests and separate property interests, thereby achieving an appropriate division.

Child custody and visitation can be the most traumatic aspect of a family-law case. Parents who are separating are often terrified of the effect the separation will have on

(continued)

Exhibit 1.6 *(continued)*

their children, and are frequently afraid that dividing their households will result in loss of closeness and opportunities for quality parenting time. Fortunately, courts lean heavily in favor of joint custody whenever feasible.

Mediation counseling programs have been set up to assist parents in working out arrangements for custody and visitation with the assistance of trained facilitators. The agreements they work out are then presented as stipulations to the court. Wherever possible, a judge will not hear a motion for custody or visitation until the parties have been to mediation. It is my job as paralegal to coordinate contact between the mediator and the parties, to prepare the mediation counseling stipulations, to see that they are signed by all parties and attorneys, and to make sure that they are filed with the court.

Mediation sessions are practical and beneficial because they are often the first time the parties have been able to sit down and actually *listen* to each other since their problems began. The sessions can also be a major step in achieving the level of cooperation they will need as separated parents with children in common.

If the parties are unable to settle their disputes (and we try very hard to settle every family-law case without the necessity of a trial), then I draft a *trial brief* setting out the facts, the history of the case, the contested and uncontested issues, our proposal for division of property, and a memorandum setting forth the applicable law. Updated income-and-expense statements and property declarations must be filed along with the trial brief, and any appraisals or actuarial analyses of pension funds as of the time of trial.

Before the day of the trial, I contact the client to make sure that he or she is psychologically prepared to attend, and I make arrangements with the client for last-minute prepping by the attorney. I organize the file so that all exhibits and necessary documents are finger-tip-accessible to the attorney trying the case. I subpoena any witnesses who may be needed. It can be difficult to get a firm court date because of case congestion. The client must be assisted in dealing with the resulting anxiety and inconvenience. If the case goes to trial, I sometimes go along to help my boss keep organized with respect to the documents, to take notes on the areas of inquiry to be explored, to run emergency errands, and to keep the witnesses organized and at-the-ready.

When the judgment is prepared (either by stipulation in the form of a marital settlement agreement or by reducing a decision by the trial court to judgment form), I often draft the first document for review by the attorney and client. Keeping track of dates, such as deadlines for appeal and eligibility for final judgment is also my responsibility. Some of my wrap-up details include preparing transfer deeds and notifying the administrator of the ex-spouse's pension plan of the rights of our client in the plan as ordered by the court.

Although I have had to skip over many areas of a paralegal's responsibilities in the area of family law, I have tried to give you a sense of some of the duties that a paralegal may have. Your particular tasks will be assigned by the attorney. Short of giving the client legal advice and appearing as his or her representative in court, there is tremendous scope for the utilization of paralegals in a family-law practice.

As a family-law case progresses, a paralegal becomes intimately familiar with the client's life and affairs. You are in a unique position to offer comfort and guidance to people in deep transition. While a legal professional's role should never be confused with that of a therapist or psychiatrist, your positive attitude and sensitivity to the client's situation can make a big difference in how he or she experiences the adjustment to what often amounts to an entirely new life. Over the past six years in a practice predominantly devoted to family law, I have watched hundreds of clients pass through this difficult change in their lives, heal their wounds, and create more successful and satisfying lifestyles. Being part of these transitions is a very rewarding part of my job.

Source: The Journal (Sacramento Valley Paralegal Association, June 1986). Reprinted with permission of Yasmin Cogswell Spiegel.

FREELANCERS, GOVERNMENT PARALEGALS, AND CASAs

FREELANCERS IN FAMILY LAW

Family law is a popular area of law for freelance paralegals. These are persons who have their own business; they operate as independent contractors rather than as employees of law offices. There are two main categories of individuals that a freelancer might serve: attorneys or the general public.

- *Attorneys.*

Freelancers who serve attorneys receive specific assignments from one or more attorneys around town, e.g., to digest (summarize) the transcript of a divorce deposition or to file an adoption petition in court. Attorney supervision of freelancers is required even though they may work out of a home office rather than in the office of the attorney who hired them. Success as a freelancer in family law depends to a very large extent on the experience of the paralegal. It is relatively rare for someone to go into business as a freelancer without years of prior experience as a traditional employee of a law office.

- *General Public.*

Most freelancers who serve the general public do not work under attorney supervision. They sell what are called self-help services directly to the public. State laws restrict the services freelancers can provide and what they can call themselves. In some states, for example, they cannot call themselves paralegals if they do not work under attorney supervision. Also, they run the risk of being charged with the unauthorized practice of law (UPL) *if they perform services that only attorneys can perform. In Chapter 2, we will cover UPL rules that apply to all freelancers as well as to traditional paralegals employed by attorneys.*

GOVERNMENT PARALEGALS

Family-law paralegals are also in demand in government. For example, every state has child-support enforcement agencies (called IV-D agencies), and most of them use paralegals that help parents collect child support. Here is an example of the duties of a child-support paralegal in one state:

Duties of Child-Support Government Paralegal

- Interview custodial and noncustodial parents who have appointments at the agency, who are walk-ins, and who telephone the agency. The paralegal must ensure that those who seek child-support services are assisted in a manner consistent with office policies, as well as local, state, and federal laws and regulations.
- Complete all follow-up case processing within the assigned time frame.
- Work all file requests and transfer files weekly. Cite cases into court in a timely manner.
- Prepare cases for court two weeks prior to the court date.
- See that all case numbers and notes for the court are on the docket.
- See that the bench warrant stamp has been completed on the inside of the file.
- Review files and complete court preparation sheets to prepare cases for hearing.
- Transport the court files to the appropriate person in the time frame given.
- After the court proceedings, complete all dispositions on cases within twenty-four hours. Complete follow up on all cases in court.
- Review and send out income withholding orders to employers.

unauthorized practice of law (UPL)
(1) A nonattorney's performance of tasks in a law office without adequate attorney supervision when those tasks are part of the practice of law. (2) Delegating tasks to a nonattorney that only an attorney is authorized to perform. (3) Using or attempting to use legal skills to help resolve a specific person's legal problem when the assistance is provided by someone who does not have a license to practice law and when the kind of assistance provided requires such a license or other authorization.

- Answer and process calls using a multi-line phone system.
- Attend court to assist individual court participants and deputy prosecuting attorneys.
- Participate in the planning, review, and evaluation of the intake procedures, goals, and objectives.
- Thoroughly learn the policies and procedures of the Child Support Division so that accurate information is given to custodial and noncustodial parents, as well as staff of other agencies.[31]

We will cover the work of these child-support agencies in greater detail in Chapter 10.

COURT APPOINTED SPECIAL ADVOCATES (CASAs)

court appointed special advocate (CASA)
A volunteer (who can be an attorney, a paralegal, or other nonattorney) appointed by the court to perform special assignments pertaining to children in the court system.

In most states, paralegals and other nonattorneys can provide volunteer advocacy services on behalf of children in the court system. The volunteers are called **court appointed special advocates (CASAs).** Paralegals who are CASAs devote several hours a week of their volunteer time to the CASA program where the focus is on children in abuse and neglect cases, particularly children in the foster care system. Typically, a CASA volunteer will be assigned one case with duties such as the following:

- Interview the child, parents, foster parents and any other concerned parties or relatives.
- Review appropriate records and reports.
- Work with the attorney **guardian ad litem** in pursuit of the best interests of the child.

guardian ad litem (GAL)
A special guardian (often, but not always, an attorney) appointed by the court to appear in court proceedings on behalf of a person who is a minor, mentally incompetent, or otherwise incapacitated.

- Confer with counselors, teachers, social workers, etc. involved in the case.
- Submit thorough, independent written reports to the court and guardian ad litem prior to court hearings.
- Appear in court as needed to answer questions or to testify on findings or recommendations.
- Maintain records of all findings (documenting all contacts).
- Visit institutions, foster homes, or group homes where the child is placed or may be placed.
- Monitor court orders to ensure services to the child are being furnished in a timely manner and that the placement is appropriate.
- Remain involved in the case until the court's jurisdiction is terminated.[32]

practice of law
Using or attempting to use legal skills to help resolve a specific person's legal problem when the assistance requires a license to practice law or other authorization.

CASAs are not substitutes for attorneys, social workers, or other child welfare personnel. A CASA cannot give legal advice or engage in the **practice of law.** The CASA's role is to be an independent voice for the child, assisting the judge to better understand the needs of the child.

CASAs undergo training conducted by the local CASA program. Training requirements vary from program to program, but an average course is approximately thirty hours. Volunteers learn about courtroom procedure from judges, lawyers, social workers, and court personnel. They also learn effective advocacy techniques for children and cover topics on child sexual abuse, early childhood development, and adolescent behavior.[33]

ASSESSING YOUR OWN BIASES

The paralegal in Exhibit 1.6 talked about the "traumatic" aspects of some family-law cases. Working in this area of the law is not for the faint of heart. "One of the worst kept secrets in legal practice is the toll that domestic relations work can take on a lawyer's staff, resources, and psyche."[34] The unfolding of some client cases can be emotionally draining. The client's world may be falling apart in a volcano of pain, anger, and confusion. Someone once said that in a criminal-law practice, you deal with bad people at their best, and in a family-law practice, you deal with good people at their worst.[35]

Inevitably, you will have personal feelings about a particular case. A client's objective or personality might give you a sense of discomfort or unease. Will these personal feelings become the basis of a **bias**, which is an inclination, tendency, or predisposition to think or act in a certain way? How would you answer the following question about yourself?

> *"Am I objective enough that I can assist a person even though I have a personal distaste for what that person wants to do or what that person has done?"*

Many of us would quickly answer "yes" to this question. We all like to feel that we are levelheaded and not susceptible to letting our prejudices interfere with the job we are asked to accomplish. Many of us, however, are unaware of how our personal likes and dislikes affect us.

bias
(1) An inclination, tendency, or predisposition to think or act in a certain way. (2) Prejudice for or against something or someone. (3) A danger of prejudgment.

ASSIGNMENT 1.1

In the following cases, to what extent might an individual be hampered in delivering legal services because of personal reactions toward the client? Identify *potential* bias.

a. Craig Smith, the client of your office, is being sued by his estranged wife, Nancy Smith, for custody of their two small children. The Smiths live separately, but Craig has had custody of the children during most of their lives while Nancy has been in the hospital. Nancy has charged that Craig often yells at the children, leaves them with neighbors and day-care centers for most of the day, and is an alcoholic. Your investigation reveals that Nancy will probably be able to prove all these allegations in court.

b. Rebecca Jones is being sued by Harold Jones for divorce on the ground of adultery. Rebecca is the client of your office. Thus far, your investigation has revealed that there is considerable doubt over whether Rebecca did, in fact, commit adultery. During a recent conversation with Rebecca, however, she tells you that she is a prostitute.

c. Jane Anderson is seeking an abortion. She is not married. The father of the child wants to prevent her from having the abortion. Jane comes to your office for legal help. She wants to know her rights. You belong to a church that believes abortion is murder. You are assigned to work on the case.

d. Paul Gibson and Victor Ortega are a gay couple who want to adopt Sammy, a six-month-old baby whose parents recently died in an automobile accident. (Paul is a second cousin of one of the deceased parents.) Sammy's maternal grandmother is not able to adopt him because of her age and health. She opposes the adoption by Paul and Victor because of their lifestyle. Paul and Victor are clients of your office in their petition for adoption. You have been assigned to work on their case. You agree with the grandmother's position.

e. Tom Donaldson is a client of your office. His former wife, Greta, claims that he has failed to pay court-ordered alimony and that the payments should be increased because of her needs and his recently improved financial status. Your job is to help Tom collect a large volume of records concerning his past alimony payments and his present financial worth. You are the only person in the office who is available to do this record gathering. It is clear, however, that Tom does not like you. On a number of occasions, he has indirectly questioned your ability.

objectivity
The state of being dispassionate; the absence of a bias.

Having analyzed the hypothetical situations in Assignment 1.1, do you still feel the same about your assessment of your own **objectivity**? Would you have a bias in any of them? Clearly, we cannot simply wish our personal feelings away or pretend that they do not exist. Nor are there any absolute rules or techniques that apply to every situation you will be asked to handle. Nor are the following admonitions very helpful: "Be objective," "Be dispassionate," "Don't get personally involved," "Control your feelings." Such admonitions are too general, and when viewed in the abstract, they may appear to be unnecessary because most of us believe that we can be objective, dispassionate, detached, and in control.

We must recognize that there are facts and circumstances that arouse our emotions and tempt us to impose our own value judgments. Perhaps if we know where we are vulnerable, we will be in a better position to prevent our reactions from interfering with our work. It is not desirable to be totally dispassionate and removed. A paralegal who is cold, unfeeling, and incapable of empathy is not much better than a paralegal who self-righteously scolds a client. It is not improper for a paralegal to express sympathy, surprise, and perhaps even shock at what unfolds from the client's life story. If these feelings are genuine and if they would be normal reactions to the situation at a given moment, then they should be expressed. The problem is *how to draw the line* between expressing such feelings and reacting so judgmentally that you interfere with your ability to communicate with the client now and in the future. Again, there are no absolute guidelines. As you gain experience in the art of dealing with people, you will develop styles and techniques that will enable you to avoid going over that line. The starting point in this development is to recognize how easy it is to go over the line.

Some paralegals apply what is called the "stomach test." If your gut tells you that your personal feelings about the case are so intense that you may not be able to do a quality job for the client, you need to take action.[36] Talk with your supervisor. You may have some misunderstandings about the case that your supervisor can clear up. You may be able to limit your role in the case or be reassigned to other cases. Without breaching client confidentiality (see Chapter 2), contact your local paralegal association to try to talk with other paralegals who have handled similar situations. They may be able to give you some guidance.

Attorneys often take unpopular cases involving clients who have said or done things that run the gamut from being politically incorrect to being socially reprehensible. As professionals, attorneys are committed to the principle that *everyone* is entitled to representation. Paralegals should have this same commitment. But attorneys and paralegals are human. No one can treat every case identically. In the final analysis, you need to ask yourself whether your bias is so strong that it might interfere with your ability to give the needs of the client 100 percent of your energy and skill. If so, you have an obligation not to work on the case.

Ethical concerns dictate this result. As we will see in Chapter 2, attorneys have an ethical obligation to avoid a conflict of interest. Such a conflict exists when an attorney has divided loyalties. An obvious example is an attorney who represents both parties in a legal dispute they have with each other. A less obvious example is an attorney whose personal feelings could interfere with his or her obligation to give a client vigorous representation. The attorney's personal feelings should not be in conflict with a client's legitimate need for undiluted advocacy. Is the attorney going to be loyal to his or her personal feelings and values, or to the client's cause? Clients should not be subjected to such conflicts of loyalties. When a conflict of this kind exists, the attorney has an ethical obligation not to take the case. The same obligation applies to paralegals who might be asked to work on the case. There should be no interference with a client's entitlement to your total commitment.

ASSIGNMENT 1.2

In the relationship among a husband, wife, and child, many things can be done that would be wrong (i.e., illegal, immoral, or improper) according to your personal system of values. Make a list of the five things that could be done by a husband, wife, or child to another family member (e.g., husband to wife, child to parent) that would be most offensive to your sense of values. Assume that a client in the office where you work has done one of these five things and is being challenged in court by someone because of it. Your office is defending the client against this challenge. What difficulties do you see for yourself in being able to assist this client?

VIOLENCE IN A FAMILY LAW PRACTICE

Unfortunately, violence must be one of the concerns of a family-law practice. In Chapter 10, for example, we will see that special measures must be taken to protect a mother from violence once she asserts a claim for child support against an estranged father. In Chapter 12, we will examine other dimensions of domestic violence.

Unfortunately, violence can also be directed at family-law offices. At a conference of attorneys, the speaker asked a group of about 120 experienced family-law attorneys if anyone in the room had experienced violent actions or threats in their practice. Almost all the attorneys in the room raised their hand. One woman told the group, "Just yesterday, I [learned that] my client and I were in grave danger."[37] Many attorneys are upgrading their office security systems; some acknowledge that when interviewing a new client, they consciously assess whether taking the case might pose personal risks to anyone in the office. Famed divorce attorney Raoul Felder reportedly keeps a pistol in his desk drawer. "Everyone hates divorce lawyers," he said, "sometimes even their clients."[38]

Family-court personnel are also concerned. Violence has erupted in the corridors of some courthouses and occasionally in the courtroom itself. In a recent case, a San Jose man fighting for custody of his three children shot and wounded three deputies. Abe Gorenfeld is a family-law court commissioner. At his retirement party, he pointed to the "bullet hole still visible in the ceiling outside his fifth-floor courtroom where a woman fired her pistol at her soon-to-be ex-husband and missed."[39] Many courthouses now have elaborate security systems at the entrances. Some courts, however, have been slow to add such security. One court did not do so until a bailiff discovered a gun in the lunch box of a distraught husband sitting in a courtroom.

Of course, violence is not an everyday occurrence in family-law offices and courthouses. Many paralegals rarely or never witness extreme behavior of this kind. Yet out-of-control, angry, frustrated citizens exist throughout our society. We all should be aware of the reality that volatile emotions often exist within families undergoing disintegration. Individuals who perceive themselves as victims are sometimes capable of lashing out against anyone involved in what they may irrationally feel is an unresponsive legal system. Thus, caution is the order of the day.

FAMILY LAW SOURCES

The many different sources of family law are outlined in Exhibit 1.7.

EXHIBIT 1.7   Sources of Family Law

PRIMARY AUTHORITY

primary authority
Any law written by one of the three branches of government (legislative, judicial, and executive).

Primary authority is the main source of family law. Primary authority is any law written by one of the three branches of government—legislative, judicial, and executive. The main primary authorities are constitutions, statutes, court opinions, court rules (rules of court), and administrative regulations. Primary authorities exist at the federal, state, and local levels of government. Here is an overview of these primary authorities at the state, local, and federal levels of government:

State and Local Law Sources

- *State constitution:* The state constitution is the highest state law to which all other state laws must conform.

- *Statutes of the state legislature:* All states have family-law statutes that cover a broad range of family-law topics such as divorce and adoption. The statutes on family law may be scattered throughout the statutory code of your state legislature, although in most states, a large number of these statutes are collected together in several volumes or titles, often called "domestic relations," "family law," or "families." (See Appendix D for family-law statutes in your state and Appendix A for more about using statutory codes.)

    Many states have enacted *uniform laws*, e.g., the Uniform Parentage Act and the Uniform Marriage and Divorce Act. Uniform acts are proposed statutes initially written by a private organization in areas where uniformity among the states is deemed appropriate. The acts are then offered to state legislatures. Each state can adopt, modify, or reject the proposals. Once a uniform law is accepted by a state (often with modifications), it becomes a statute of that state.

- *State court opinions interpreting the state constitution, state statutes, and state administrative regulations.*

- *State court opinions creating and interpreting common law. Common law* is judge-made law in the absence of controlling statutory law or other higher law. If a problem exists for which there is no governing statute, a court may have the authority to create common law to solve that problem.

- *State court rules (also called rules of court) governing the mechanics of litigation before a particular court.* They cover many of the procedural aspects of divorces, annulments, adoptions, etc. The rules often contain standard court forms that are either required or recommended.

- *State administrative regulations of agencies that carry out statutes:* An example is the agency that administers child-support enforcement laws.

- *Local law:* A major example is a zoning ordinance on single-family residences.

Federal Law Sources

- *United States Constitution:* The federal constitution is the highest law to which all other federal *and* state laws must conform in areas covered by the U.S. Constitution.

- *Federal statutes:* An example is a statute of Congress that requires states to enact child-support enforcement laws as a condition for receiving federal grants.

- *Federal court opinions interpreting federal laws.*

- *Federal regulations:* An example is a regulation of the Internal Revenue Service on the tax consequences of a divorce.

- *International law:* An example is the Hague Convention on the Civil Aspects of International Child Abduction.

(continued)

Exhibit 1.7 *(continued)*

SECONDARY AUTHORITY

Secondary authority is any nonlaw that summarizes, describes, or explains the law but is not a law itself. The major examples of secondary authorities are legal treatises, legal encyclopedias, and legal periodicals. Secondary sources are sometimes used by the courts to help them interpret primary authority. In this sense, secondary authorities influence family law and can be included as a source of family law.

secondary authority
Any nonlaw that summarizes, describes, or explains the law but is not a law itself.

Wikipedia

Perhaps the largest secondary authority is the online legal encyclopedia, *Wikipedia*. You need to be cautious about the content of legal materials on *Wikipedia*, not simply because the site allows users to make corrections and additions to its millions of entries, but mainly because the site does not contain the full text of reliable and current primary authority. Attorneys or paralegals would look foolish if, for example, they cited *Wikipedia* as their only source for the law on a divorce topic. Yet free private sites such as *Wikipedia* can be valuable because they will often provide references and links to a primary authority. (The same is also often true of sites of law firms, organizations, or associations.) Furthermore, when you need to do background research on a family-law topic, the sites can be useful so long as you do not rely on them as substitutes for the only 100 percent reliable sources of family law—primary authorities.

FAMILY LAW ONLINE

It is possible to obtain a great deal of online information that is relevant to a family-law practice. In addition to research into court opinions, statutes, and other primary authorities, a law firm often must do factual research. An example of factual research is to try to uncover personal and business assets that an estranged spouse may be trying to hide.

Three major fee-based online databases, for which the firm pays a subscription fee, are Westlaw (www.westlaw.com), LexisNexis (www.lexis.com), and Bloomberglaw (www.bna.com/bloomberglaw). In addition, you can obtain a great deal of free material online. (See Exhibit 1.8 for a list of mostly free sites.) Greater

EXHIBIT 1.8   Finding Family Law on Mostly Free Online Sites

FINDING PRIMARY AUTHORITY ON THE FAMILY LAW OF YOUR STATE

Statutes

- **Google, Bing, and Yahoo**
- Go to the general search engines of Google, Bing, or Yahoo.
- In the search box, type a broad or narrow topic and the name of your state. Examples:

  family law Florida

  child custody Pennsylvania

  divorce Delaware

- **Your State Legislature**
- Go to the site of your state legislature.
- Use the search features on the site to locate current or pending statutes on family law.
- See the sites for your state in Appendix D of this book.

(continued)

Exhibit 1.8 *(continued)*

Court Opinions

- **Google Scholar**
- Go to scholar.google.com.
- Click "Case law."
- Click "Select courts" and check the courts you want.
- Click "Done" and type the search term you want covered in opinions.
- If you already know the citation of an opinion that you want to read, enter it into the search box (e.g., "487 N.W.2d 484").

- **Findlaw**
- caselaw.findlaw.com
- caselaw.findlaw.com/summary.html

- **Additional Links to Court Opinions (and Other Laws)**
- www.justia.com (click *Laws: Cases & Codes*)
- www.plol.org

Note: If you are led to a site of a law firm, find out if the site provides an overview of laws and links to the family law of your state.

Finding Secondary Authority on the Family Law of Your State

- **Google, Bing, and Yahoo**
- Go to the general search engines of Google, Bing, or Yahoo.
- In the search box, type a broad or narrow topic and the name of your state. Examples:
  family law Florida

  child custody Pennsylvania

  divorce Delaware

- **Google Scholar**
- Go to scholar.google.com.
- Select "Articles."
- Run the same searches as mentioned above.

- **Other Sites**
- See the sites for your state in Appendix D of this book.

Note: If you are led to a site of a law firm, find out if the site provides an overview of laws and links to the family law of your state.

Other Sites that Are Portals to Family Law of Your State

- guides.ll.georgetown.edu/familylaw
- www.law.cornell.edu/wex/table_family
- www.justia.com/family
- statesidelegal.org/family-law-overview
- www.law.cornell.edu/wex/table_divorce
- openjurist.org/law/family-law
- www.expertlaw.com/library/family_law
- en.wikipedia.org/wiki/Category:Family_law
- en.wikipedia.org/wiki/Family_law
- www.youtube.com (enter a legal topic in the search box, e.g., child custody)

caution is needed when using free sites than when using the fee-based ones. In general, the fee-based sites are more comprehensive, current, and user-friendly than the free sites. The latter, however, are becoming increasingly reliable, particularly those run by the government itself. (For links to federal, state, local, and tribal governments and laws, see www.loc.gov/law/help/guide/states.php.)

SKILLS ASSIGNMENTS IN THE BOOK

To help you develop the ability to perform paralegal tasks, several categories of skills assignments are presented in the chapters of this book. Your instructor will decide which of these assignments you will be doing. Some of the instructions for these assignments are found in Appendix A. The categories of assignments are as follows:

1. *Legal analysis assignment*

There are two main kinds of legal analysis assignments in the book. First, you are given a set of facts and asked to apply one or more of the legal principles discussed in the text to those facts. Second, you are asked to apply the holding of a court opinion to a new set of facts. A holding is the court's answer to one of the legal issues the court has resolved in the opinion.

2. *State code assignment*

A great deal of family law is found in the statutes of your state statutory code. In the state code assignment, you will be asked to determine what your state code says about a particular topic.

3. *Court opinion assignment*

Two of the major categories of court opinions are those that interpret statutes and those that create and interpret *common law,* which is judge-made law in the absence of controlling statutory law or other higher law (see glossary for additional meanings.) In the court opinion assignment, you may be asked to find both kinds of court opinions written by state courts in your state on a family-law issue.

4. *Complaint drafting assignment*

In this assignment, you will be asked to draft a complaint (called a *petition* in some states) acceptable in your state on a specific family-law matter.

5. *Agreement drafting assignment*

Agreements are often used in a family-law practice by parties who wish to define an aspect of their relationship. In this assignment, you will be asked to draft such an agreement.

6. *Checklist formulation assignment*

Here, you will examine a statute or common-law principle and design a checklist of questions that an interviewer would ask (or that an investigator would pursue) to help determine whether that statute or common-law principle applies.

7. *Investigation strategy assignment*

This assignment asks you to formulate a plan for gathering new facts or for substantiating facts that you already have on a family-law problem.

8. *Interview assignment*

In this assignment, you will role-play as an interviewer who will conduct a legal interview on a hypothetical (i.e., assumed) set of facts in a family-law case.

legal analysis
The application of one or more rules to the facts of a client's case in order to answer a legal question that will help (a) avoid a legal dispute, (b) resolve a legal dispute that has arisen, or (c) prevent a legal dispute from becoming worse.

holding
A court's answer to one of the legal issues in a case.

hypothetical
Assumed to exist solely for purposes of discussion.

9. *Interrogatory assignment*

In this assignment, you will draft a set of interrogatories, which are questions sent to an opposing party in litigation to help your side prepare for trial.

10. *Flowchart assignment*

This assignment requires the presentation of a step-by-step outline of a particular legal procedure in your state.

11. *Systems assignment*

In the systems assignment, you will contact someone who now works in a family-law office to determine what system the office uses to accomplish some aspect of client service.

12. *Writing Sample*

At the end of each chapter, an idea is presented on a topic that you could write about and turn into a writing sample when looking for employment upon graduation.

———————————

Within each assignment, you will find specific instructions. Again, you will also be referred to Appendix A, where you will find General Instructions for that category of assignment.

SUMMARY

Family law is the body of law that defines relationships, rights, and duties in the formation, ongoing existence, and dissolution of marriage and other family units. Some of the major themes in the development of family law are equality of the sexes, increased federalization of family law, contract dimension of family law, science and law, and deregulation of sexuality. To accommodate changes in family law, many states are using newer terminology that downplays conflict in family-law cases.

Someone working in a family-law practice may encounter legal problems in a wide variety of areas in addition to basic family law. These other areas include criminal law, contract law, agency law, real property law, personal property law, corporate and business law, bankruptcy law, tort law, civil procedure law, evidence law, juvenile law, tax law, estate law, Social Security law, and ethics law.

Courts are often asked to review the constitutionality of family laws. At the federal level, the major challenges are those that allege a violation of due process of law and equal protection of law. The two categories of due process are procedural due process (PDP) and substantive due process (SDP). PDP requires fair procedures before the government can restrict life, liberty, or property. SDP requires the government to avoid arbitrary or capricious actions that deprive someone of life, liberty, or property. Interferences with fundamental rights must meet the test of strict scrutiny. Interferences with nonfundamental rights must meet the rational-basis test. Challenges that allege a violation of equal protection must meet the test of strict

scrutiny (for fundamental rights and for a suspect class), intermediate scrutiny (for a quasi-suspect class), or rational basis (for all other categories). Social media have provided family-law attorneys with new avenues to evidence that can be used in negotiation and litigation.

Paralegals in family law perform many functions, such as interviewing clients, drafting temporary orders and other court pleadings, collecting financial data, coordinating client and witness appearances for hearings and trials, maintaining case files, and assisting in discovery and at trial. Paralegals also use family-law skills in government employment and freelance work. Volunteer options are possible as Court Appointed Special Advocates (CASAs).

Because the cases handled in a family-law practice can be emotionally charged, the need for professionalism and objectivity (avoiding bias) is paramount, particularly if the office is representing a client who has done something that clashes with a worker's personal values. Violence is an ongoing concern in family law.

The primary sources (authorities) of family law are constitutions, statutes, court opinions (opinions interpreting statutes and common-law opinions), court rules (rules of court) and administrative regulations. Secondary authorities, such as legal periodicals and legal treatises, can also be important for a family-law practitioner. Many family-law attorneys are able to use the Internet to find material that is relevant to the legal disputes of their clients.

KEY TERMS

family law	suspect class	request for admissions (RFA)
marriage	quasi-suspect class	independent medical examination (IME)
coverture	intermediate-scrutiny test	alternative dispute resolution (ADR)
federalization	e-discovery	mediation
constitutionalization	spoilation	impeach
status	forensic	trial notebook
premarital agreement	contested	court costs
police power	conflicts check	pretrial conference
precedent	conflict of interest	appellate brief
specialty certification	legal advice	execution
common law	tickler	garnishment
judicial review	timeline	instruments
due process of law (DPL)	proof of service	unauthorized practice of law (UPL)
procedural due process (PDP)	stipulation	court appointed special advocate (CASA)
substantive due process (SDP)	affidavit	guardian ad litem (GAL)
fundamental right	financial statement	practice of law
strict-scrutiny test	arrearages	bias
narrowly tailored	discovery	objectivity
compelling state interest	interrogatories	primary authority
rational-basis test	protective order	secondary authority
reasonably related	deposition	legal analysis
legitimate state interest	subpoena	holding
equal protection of law (EPL)	subpoena duces tecum	hypothetical
classification	request for production (RPA)	indigent

PROJECT

This project will require you to use the Internet to compile a list of some of the major family-law publications and resources for your state. To begin compiling this list, answer the questions in (a) to (f) below. Also look for leads in Exhibit 1.8 and Appendix D on the family law of your state.

Family Law of Your State

a. What is the name of the statutory code containing the statutes of your legislature? If more than one code exists, list each one. (See Appendix D.)

b. In this code, find any statute on divorce. Quote and cite the first line from this statute that mentions the word *divorce*.

c. Go to the website of the state courts in your state. (See Exhibit 1.8 and Appendix D.) Find the court rules of any civil court in your state that hears divorce cases. Quote from any court rule that uses the word *divorce*.

d. In this question, you will use Google Scholar to find court opinions on divorce written by your state courts. Follow these steps:

- Go to scholar.google.com.
- Click "Case law."
- Click "Select courts" and check the state courts for your state.
- Click "Done" and type *divorce* in the search box.

Give the citation of any two opinions written by different state courts in your state that cover any aspect of divorce. For each opinion, include the name of the opinion, the reporter in which it is found, the court that wrote the opinion, and the date of the opinion. Briefly describe the facts of each opinion.

e. In this question, you will use Google Scholar to find a periodical article that covers divorce in your state (e.g., New York divorce, Alaska divorce). Follow these steps:

- Go to scholar.google.com.
- Select "Articles."
- In the search box, type your search terms.
- Look for articles (not books) in the list generated by the search.

Give the citation of two periodical articles that have the word *divorce* and the name of your state in the title of the articles. Some of the results from this search may give you only the first page of the article, which is all you need for this assignment. (Reading the full article may require payment of a fee.)

f. Run this search in Google, Bing, or Yahoo: blog aa "family law" (substitute the name of your state for aa). List any blogs that cover the family law of your state. For each blog, give the site's address and a brief description of what it covers.

ETHICS IN A FAMILY-LAW PRACTICE

An ethical obligation of every legal professional is to help extend legal services to persons in society who cannot afford to pay private attorneys. Every state has *pro bono* programs that provide free (or reduced-cost) legal services to **indigent** or low-income persons with family-law problems. While in school, you may not be able to devote time to pro bono work, but you should know how to find out what pro bono opportunities are available in the area of family law so that you can consider donating time at a later date. To find out, conduct the following search in Google, Bing, or Yahoo: aa "pro bono" "family law" (substitute the name of your city and state for aa in the search, e.g., Cleveland Ohio "pro bono" "family law").

Many of the links will direct you to organizations seeking pro bono help from attorneys. Determine if the website of such organizations tells you if it also seeks pro bono help from paralegals. Locate two different organizations in the state that accept pro bono help from paralegals in the area of family law. Give the name of the organization, its street and website address, and the kind of assistance that paralegals can provide to the clients of the organization.

indigent
Poor; without means to afford something such as a private attorney or filing fees.

REVIEW QUESTIONS

1. What is family law?
2. What are five major developments that affect the practice of family law in the twenty-first century?
3. What are some of the changes in family-law terminology, and why have such changes been made?
4. When working on family-law cases, what are some of major areas of law that could be involved?
5. What are the two categories of due-process challenges to a family-law rule under the U.S. Constitution?
6. How will a court resolve a substantive due process (SDP) challenge to a state family-law rule?
7. What are the main categories of discrimination that have been challenged as a violation of equal protection and how have the courts resolved such challenges?
8. How have social media affected the practice of family law?
9. What are some of the major roles of paralegals in the practice of family law?
10. What is the role of a CASA?
11. What is a bias and in what way can it interfere with job performance by workers in a law office?
12. To what extent is violence a concern in the practice of family law?
13. What are the main categories of primary authority in family law?
14. What is the distinction between primary and secondary authority?

HELPFUL WEBSITES

Your State

See Appendix D for links to the family law of your state on the topics covered in this chapter.

Roles of Paralegals in Family Law and Other Areas of Practice

- The 'Lectric Law Library—www.lectlaw.com/files/pap01.htm (scroll down to *Family Law*)
- www.paralegals.org/files/Paralegal_Responsibilities.pdf (click *Domestic Relations/Family Law*)
- www.cobar.org (enter *"Family Law Paralegal"* in the search box)
- www.paralegalalliance.com/?s=family+law
- legaltalknetwork.com/podcasts/paralegal-voice/2014/10/paralegals-role-family-law-practice

Societal Changes and Family Law

- aaml.org
- ncfmr.bgsu.edu
- www.pewsocialtrends.org (type *marriage* in the search box)
- www.census.gov (type *family profiles* in the search box)
- quod.lib.umich.edu/m/mfr/4919087.0005.105?rgn=main;view=fulltext

Research Guide to Family Law

- See Exhibits 1.7 and 1.8

Google, Bing, or Yahoo

(on these search engines, run the following searches, substituting your state for "aa")

- "family law" aa
- divorce aa
- "family law" bias aa
- "paralegal roles" aa
- "family law" violence aa
- "family law" research aa

- constitution "family law" aa
- paralegal jobs "family law" aa
- "family law" "social media" aa
- freelance paralegal "family law" aa
- Facebook divorce aa

YouTube

On YouTube run the same searches listed above for Google, Bing, Yahoo. The caution mentioned in the chapter about using *Wikipedia* also applies to videos about the law on YouTube. The videos are rarely subjected to serious editorial scrutiny. Yet even when the video clips are trying to entice you to retain an attorney, buy a book, or enroll in a course, they can provide useful overviews and references to primary authority.

Twitter, Reddit, and Facebook

On Twitter, Reddit, and Facebook, conduct the following searches (substitute your state for *aa* in your searches; run the searches with and without the name of your state). Look for links to family-law developments in your state.

- family law aa
- divorce aa

ENDNOTES

Note: All or most of the court opinions in these Endnotes can be read online. To do so, go to Google Scholar (scholar.google.com), select "Case law," and in the search box, enter the cite (e.g., "539 U.S. 558") or the name of the case (e.g., "Lawrence v. Texas") that is given in the endnote.

[1] Marjorie Maguire Shultz, *Contractual Ordering of Marriage: A New Model for State Policy*, 70 Cal. L. Rev. 204, 207 (March 1982).

[2] Claudia Dreifus, *Where Have You Gone, Norman Rockwell? A Fresh Look at the Family* (interview of Dr. Stephanie Coontz), N.Y. Times, June 14, 2005, at D3 (www.nytimes.com/2005/06/14/science/14conv.html).

[3] *The Decline of Marriage and the Rise of New Families* (Pew Research Center Publications November 18, 2010) (www.pewresearch.org) (enter *declining marriage* in the search box).

[4] Harry D. Krause & David D. Meyer, *Family Law in a Nutshell* 16 (5th ed. 2007) (6th ed. 2017).

[5] *Lawrence v. Texas*, 539 U.S. 558, 602 (dissent) (2003).

[6] Quoted in *Warren v. State*, 336 S.E.2d 221, 223 (Ga. 1985).

[7] *Obergefell v. Hodges*, 135 S. Ct. 2584, 2595 (2015).

[8] Lenore Weitzman, *The Divorce Revolution* 382 (1985).

[9] Elizabeth Gleick, *Hell Hath No Fury*, Time Magazine (October 7, 1996).

[10] *Spires v. Spires*, 743 A.2d 186, 193 (D.C. 1999).

[11] *Santosky v. Kramer*, 455 U.S. 745, 770 (1982) (dissent).

[12] Ruth Padawer, *Who Knew I was Not the Father?* N.Y. Times, November 17, 2009 at MM38.

[13] *Lawrence v. Texas*, supra note 5 at 562.

[14] National Center for State Courts et al, *Family Justice Initiative*, 2 (2019).

[15] John Greenya, *Family Affairs: Seven Experts in Family Law Discuss Their Experiences*, 9 Washington Lawyer 23, 31 (Nov./Dec. 1994).

[16] Board Certified Paralegal (www.tbls-bcp.org).

[17] U.S. Const. amend. XIV, § 1 (usconstitution.net/const.html).

[18] U.S. Const. amend. XIV, § 1 (usconstitution.net/const.html).

[19] *Baxtrom v. Herold*, 383 U.S. 107, 111 (1966).

[20] Stephanie Rabiner, *Facebook Divorce: Evidence from Wall Posts* (February 9, 2011) (blogs.findlaw.com).

[21] Brad Stone, *Tell-All PCs and Phones Transforming Divorce*, N.Y. Times, September 15, 2007, at A1.

[22] Leanne Italie, *Divorce Lawyers: Facebook Tops in Online Evidence in Court*, June 29, 2010 (www.usatoday.com /tech/news/2010-06-29-facebook-divorce_N.htm).

[23] Ibid.

[24] Laura Holson, *Text Messages: Digital Lipstick on the Collar*, N.Y. Times, December 9, 2009, at A1.

[25] William Hamilton & Wendy Akbar, *E-Discovery in the Age of Facebook, Twitter, & the Digital Family*, 33 Family Advocate 16 (Fall 2010).

[26] Carolyn Davis, *Divorce Facebook Style*, The Philadelphia Enquirer (July 12, 2010).

[27] Nadine Brozan, *Divorce Lawyers' New Friend: Social Networks*, N.Y. Times, May 15, 2011 at ST17.

[28] Beverly Ann Miller and Sherryll Babboni-Stripp, *The Role of the Legal Assistant in Family Matters*, 74 Michigan Bar Journal 54 (January 1995). (The phrase legal assistant was changed to paralegal in the quote).

[29] Yasmin Spiegel, *Family Law for Paralegals*, 6 The Journal 7 (Sacramento Valley Paralegal Association, June 1986).

[30] See Shelley Riseden, *10 Most Common Tasks of a Family Law Paralegal*, Paralegal Alliance (May 2013) (www.paralegalalliance.com); State Bar of Texas, *Attorney's Guide to Practicing with Legal Assistants* (1986); and Colorado Bar Association Paralegal Committee, *Guidelines for the Utilization of Paralegals*, "Family Law Paralegal" (2008).

[31] Child Support Paralegal, Office of Marion County Prosecutor, Indiana (www.indy.gov/eGov/County/Pros /ChildSupport/Pages/ChildSupport.aspx).

[32] CASA *Volunteer Job Description* (heartlandcasa.org /page12115233.aspx).

[33] William Statsky and Lynn Crossett, *The Texas Paralegal: Essential Rules, Documents, and Resources*, 49 (Cengage 2010).

[34] Jennifer J. Rose, *The Ten Commandments of Family Law. . .*, 39 Practical Lawyer 85 (Jan. 1993).

[35] *The Volokh Conspiracy* (March 11, 2011) (reason.com /volokh).

[36] Shari Caudron, *Crisis of Conscience*, 12 Legal Assistant Today 73, 75 (Sept./Oct. 1994).

[37] A.P. Roth, *Dangerous Divorces*, California Lawyer 23, 24 (Feb. 1994).

[38] www.raoulfelder.com.

[39] Deborah Belgum, *82-Year-Old Jurist Bows Out. . .*, Los Angeles Times, Jan. 6, 1997, at B1.

CHAPTER 2

Ethics in a Family Law Practice

CHAPTER OUTLINE

CHAPTER OBJECTIVES

After completing this chapter, you should be able to:

- Recognize the major ethical violations that can be committed in a family-law office.
- Know when an attorney-client relationship is formed.
- State the ethical dangers of attorney websites.
- Explain the ethical obligation of competence.
- List examples of digital competence.
- Distinguish unethical incompetence and legal malpractice.
- Know the ethical rules governing limited-scope representation.

- Define collaborative law.
- State when attorney fees and paralegal fees are ethical.
- Know whether an attorney can pay someone for a client referral.
- Explain the ethical duty of diligence.
- Identify when an attorney is allowed to reveal client confidences.
- List major conflicts of interest in a family-law practice.
- State the attorney's ethical duty on safeguarding client property.
- Define the anticontact rule.

- State the ethics rules on attorney withdrawals from a case.
- State the duty to be truthful and to disclose adverse authority.
- Describe when Internet "friending" is unethical.
- Explain the ethical rules governing solicitation and advertising.
- Describe when attorneys and paralegals violate rules on the unauthorized practice of law (UPL).

INTRODUCTION

ethics
Rules or standards of behavior to which members of an occupation, profession, or other organization are expected to conform. Ethics governing attorneys are called *legal ethics*, *codes of professional responsibility*.

Ethics are rules or standards of behavior to which members of an occupation, profession, or other organization are expected to conform. An ethics survey in one state revealed that 25 percent of all grievances filed against attorneys involved family-law cases.[1] This was almost double the percentage for every other area of practice. An uncomfortably large number of family-law clients eventually turn on their own attorney with a charge of unethical conduct. "The intensely personal and very emotional tone of many family law proceedings undoubtedly contributes to the fact that family law practitioners are on the receiving end of a disproportionately high percentage of professional grievances filed against lawyers."[2]

Many ethics rules are based on the *Model Rules of Professional Conduct*, which we will briefly examine in the context of a family-law practice. The *Model Rules* were written by the American Bar Association (ABA). Although the ABA publishes ethical rules, it does not discipline attorneys for unethical conduct. The ABA rules are not binding on any attorney. If a state court adopts an ABA rule, then attorneys in that state are governed by the rule. Attorney conduct is regulated by the state court, often in collaboration with the state bar association. The role of the ABA is to *propose* ethical rules for consideration by the various states. A state is free to adopt, modify, or reject the ethical rules recommended by the ABA. In view of the prestige of the ABA, however, many states have adopted its proposals with little change. The rule references in this chapter (e.g., Rule 1.1) will be to the *Model Rules*. For the full text of the *Model Rules*, see the Helpful Websites at the end of the chapter.

Exhibit 2.1 summarizes the major ethical standards (based on the *Model Rules*) that should guide all paralegals working in a family-law office.

EXHIBIT 2.1   Checklist of Ethical Guidelines for Paralegals in a Family Law Practice

1. *Disclosure of status.* Be sure that everyone with whom you come in contact knows that you are not an attorney. Do not allow people to assume that you are an attorney, which is likely when they see that you work in a law office.

2. *Accepting cases.* Do not "accept" a case on behalf of the office. You can tell someone what kinds of family-law cases the office handles, but you cannot say or imply that the office will take someone's case. Only an attorney can accept a case and thereby establish an attorney-client relationship.

3. *Setting fees.* Do not "set" a fee. You can tell someone the amount of an attorney's initial consultation fee, if any, but when questioned further about fees, you must say that fees need to be discussed with the attorney.

4. *Sharing fees.* Do not accept all or part of the fee of a particular client even if the attorney offers it to you. Attorneys cannot share (split) fees of particular clients with nonattorneys. Your salary will come out of the fees generated by the office from *all* clients, but it is unethical for an attorney to agree in advance to give you a bonus or other compensation on the fee that will be generated by a particular client's case. This is so even if you referred the client to the office, even if you did great work on the case, and even if the client agrees to let you have all or part of the fee.

5. *Compensation for referring clients.* Do not accept anything of value for recommending an attorney or for referring a case to an attorney. Something of value can include increased salary, a bonus, time off, a promotion, etc. You can recommend an attorney, but you cannot be given extra compensation or anything of value for the recommendation.

(continued)

Exhibit 2.1 *(continued)*

6. *Confidentiality.* Do not discuss the facts of a case with anyone outside the office (including your spouse or parent) without permission from your supervisor. If you have information related to the case, you must keep the information confidential. This rule is not limited to secrets or personal information about the case. It includes *all* information related to the case, including the fact that a particular person is a family-law client of the office. Although some information about a client may already be public knowledge, abide by the rule that you will not discuss any aspect of the case without permission from your supervisor. KEC: Keep Everything Confidential.

7. *Confidentiality.* Before sending documents prepared on a computer (or before filing them in court), remove the **metadata**. Metadata can consist of confidential information.

8. *Confidentiality.* When sending messages or documents over the Internet (e.g., as email attachments), be sure that the client understands that the communication may not be secure and agrees to let you send it. Know how to **encrypt** the communication if your supervisor deems this precaution to be necessary. Extra caution is needed when placing client data on smartphones, tablets, and other small media devices, which are easy to lose and often relatively easy to hack.

9. *Conflict of interest.* Let your supervisor know immediately if in your prior employment (or volunteer activities) you worked for other law offices with clients who have any connection or relationship with clients of the law office where you now work (or volunteer) even if that prior work or activity did not involve a family-law matter. Your supervisor must determine if such connections create a **conflict of interest**.

10. *Conflict of interest.* Avoid romantic or financial relationships with current clients, with opposing parties, with relatives of opposing parties, or with attorneys, paralegals, or secretaries of opposing parties.

11. *Conflict of interest.* Understand how the office performs its **conflicts check** on every prospective family-law client so that the office can avoid taking cases that would create a conflict of interest.

12. *Conflict of interest.* Let your supervisor know if a client has offered you a gift. If the gift requires the preparation of a document, the document may have to be prepared by an attorney who does not work in your office.

13. *Competence.* If you do not know how to perform an assigned task, let your supervisor know that you need additional training or a different assignment.

14. *Competence.* Never stop learning the substantive and procedural law that pertains to the family-law tasks you are assigned. Clients are entitled to **competent** assistance. Once employed, competence is maintained primarily through self-study and through **continuing legal education (CLE)**.

15. *Communication with other side.* Do not contact an opponent (or anyone connected with an opponent) unless you have the permission of your supervisor and the opponent's attorney. Without such permission, do not try to become a Facebook friend (or try to establish other kinds of online communication) with an opponent and anyone connected with the opponent.

16. *Communication with other side.* If the other side is proceeding **pro se** and your supervisor allows you to communicate with him or her, you must not give the impression that you are **disinterested** or unconnected with the case. He or she must know that you work for the other side.

17. *Solicitation.* Do not initiate contacts with anyone in person, by phone, or online (such as by email, on a social media site, in a chat room, etc.) in order to encourage him or her to hire (and pay fees to) your law office unless the person already has a relationship with the law office. (You can, however, recommend your office if someone asks you for a recommendation.)

(continued)

metadata
Data about data. Data about an electronic document that are hidden within the document itself, e.g., earlier versions of the document.

encrypt
Convert text into a code that renders it incomprehensible until it is reconverted into a readable format by an authorized recipient with the right software. The noun is *encryption*.

conflict of interest
Divided loyalties that actually or potentially harm (or disadvantage) someone who is owed undivided loyalty.

conflicts check
Finding out whether a conflict of interest exists that might disqualify a law office from representing a prospective client or from continuing the representation of a current client.

competent
Taking the time needed to prepare so that you are using the knowledge and skill that are reasonably necessary to represent a particular client. The noun is *competency*. (See glossary for additional definitions.)

continuing legal education (CLE)
Training in the law (usually short term) that a person receives after completing his or her formal legal training or after becoming employed.

pro se (on one's own behalf)
Representing oneself; not represented by an attorney. Also called *in propria persona* (abbreviated *in pro per*).

disinterested
(1) Not working for one side or the other in a dispute. (2) Not deriving benefit if one side of a dispute wins or loses; objective.

Exhibit 2.1 *(continued)*

18. *Advertising.* Do not make misrepresentations or false claims in advertising.

19. *Unauthorized practice of law.* Do not give **legal advice**.

20. *Unauthorized practice of law.* Avoid performing any task in the office without attorney supervision, even if you have performed the task before and know how to perform it.

21. *Unauthorized practice of law.* Do not sign a pleading or any document that is filed in court even if the attorney asks you to sign it.

22. *Commingling.* Do not deposit client funds (e.g., proceeds of the sale of a home that is part of a property division in a divorce) into the same account that the law office uses for rent, salaries, or other office expenses. Avoid **commingling**.

23. *Misconduct.* Do not lie or otherwise misrepresent facts. Examples: pretending to be a stranger in order to obtain information from someone in an office or online; notarizing a signature on a document even though you were not present to see the signer place his or her signature on the document.

24. *Misconduct.* Do not pad your timesheets by stating that you performed a task you did not perform or by falsely stating the amount of time you spent on a task.

25. *Misconduct.* Do not use (or pass on to others) any nonpublic information you learn while in the office that could be used in the purchase or sale of stock (**insider trading**).

26. *Misconduct.* Do not tell anyone how to hide assets so that the assets will not be available to an opponent in litigation, and do not tell anyone how to avoid a **subpoena** or other legal **process**.

_____

27. *Finally:* Know the common rationalizations for unethical conduct:
    - It's always done.
    - The other side does it.
    - The cause of our client is just.
    - If I don't do it, I will jeopardize my job.

Promise yourself that you will not allow any of these rationalizations to entice you to participate in unethical conduct even if there are attorneys, paralegals, and others around you who use the rationalizations.

FORMATION OF THE ATTORNEY-CLIENT RELATIONSHIP

When an attorney first meets with a prospective client, one of the first concerns is whether to accept the case. The attorney may reject a case for a number of reasons, such as (a) the belief that the prospective client does not have a **meritorious** case, (b) the presence of a conflict of interest (see discussion below), (c) the office does not have the expertise needed to take the case, and (d) the likelihood that the office would not be able to collect its fees and costs of representation.

Once the office decides not to take the case, it should send out a **letter of nonengagement** to avoid or refute a later claim by prospective clients who say they thought the office was going to provide representation. Initial contacts with the office may have involved a meeting and some phone calls without a clear indication of whether the attorney was going to take the case. As time passes, the matter can become ugly if the **statute of limitations** has run (expired) so that a claim can no longer be asserted. The attorney does not want to be blamed for the fact that the claim is now **time-barred**. Sending a letter of nonengagement helps

---

legal advice
A statement or conclusion that applies the law or legal principles to the facts of a specific person's legal problem in an attempt to help resolve that problem.

commingling
(1) Mixing what should be kept separate. (Example: depositing client funds in an account that also contains general operating funds of the office.) (2) Any mixing of items of different categories. The verb is *commingle*.

insider trading
Improperly using (or passing on to others) any nonpublic information that could provide a financial advantage when used to buy or sell shares in a company.

subpoena
(1) A command to appear at a certain time and place. (2) To command that someone appear at a certain time and place.

process
The means (e.g., a summons, writ, or other court order) used by a court to acquire or exercise its power or jurisdiction over a person.

meritorious
Having merit; having a reasonable basis to believe that a person's claim or defense will succeed.

letter of nonengagement
A letter sent to prospective clients that explicitly states the law office will not be representing them.

statute of limitations
A law stating that civil or criminal actions are barred if not brought within a specified period of time. The action is time-barred if not brought within that period.

time-barred
Prevented (barred) from bringing a civil or criminal action because of the passage of a designated period of time without commencing the action. Being unable to sue because of the *statute of limitations*.

prove that the attorney never had an ethical or professional duty to act on the case before the claim was barred by the statute of limitations because the attorney never agreed to provide representation.

The test of whether an attorney-client relationship has been formed is whether a reasonable person would interpret the attorney's conduct as an agreement to provide legal services to a specific person. It does not depend on whether a **retainer** agreement or letter of engagement was signed, although this is the most common way in which to enter the relationship. The test is not whether the attorney wanted or intended to become someone's attorney. The test is how a reasonable person would interpret what the attorney said or did. In the absence of clear evidence of nonengagement, attorneys can find themselves in an unwanted and unintended attorney-client relationship, as seen in the following example:

> *Harry Davis is an attorney. He meets Mary Patterson at a party. They have never met before. When Mary finds out that Davis is an attorney, she tells him that she recently separated from her husband, Kevin Patterson, and that she suspects he is starting to hide the assets they have accumulated during their marriage. Davis tells her that she could get copies of bank statements and close any joint accounts with her husband. He also answers her questions about her custody rights. During the conversation, Davis is called away, but before he leaves the party, he gives Mary his card. Nothing else is said.*

Is Davis Mary's attorney? Has an attorney-client relationship been formed? The question is critical because if such a relationship exists, Davis has ethical duties pertaining to confidentiality and conflict of interest. He must treat what Mary told him as confidential and he would not be allowed to represent Mary's husband in the divorce, even if Mary later hires someone else to represent her in the divorce.

Did Davis become Mary's attorney at the party? On the one hand, he gave her legal advice along with his business card after she gave him details about her legal problem. On the other hand, they never signed an agreement or discussed fees. He never said that he would represent her. As indicated, however, a formal agreement and fees are not essential. As of the time of the party, if a reasonable person in Mary's position could believe that Davis agreed to provide legal services, then an attorney-client relationship was formed. It can always be ended (see the discussion of withdrawal below), but once it is formed, serious consequences can result if the attorney does not act properly before it is ended.

Some prospective clients shop around for an attorney on the phone, in person, by email, or through attorney websites. While doing so, they may give information about their case to the attorneys they contact. Until a formal attorney-client relationship is created, preferably in writing, attorneys must use great care to make clear that they are not providing representation. Websites are a particular cause for concern. When you go to the website of an attorney, you will often see statements that caution visitors that no attorney-client relationship is created simply by reason of the fact that the site is visited or that an email query is sent to the attorney through a link on the site. Before allowing a visitor to send an email question, cautious attorneys make visitors click "yes" to the question, "Do you understand that the receipt of your email does not in and of itself create an attorney-client relationship between us?"

Here is what the American Bar Association says about websites and the attorney-client relationship:

> *Websites have become a common means by which lawyers communicate with the public. Lawyers must not include misleading information on websites, must be mindful of the expectations created by the website, and must carefully manage inquiries invited through the website. Websites that invite inquiries may create a prospective client-lawyer relationship.*[3] *(Rule 1.18)*

retainer
(1) The act of hiring or engaging the services of someone, usually a professional. (The verb is *retain*.) (2) An amount of money (or other property) paid by a client as a deposit or advance against future fees, costs, and related expenses of providing services.

COMPETENCE

Attorneys have an ethical obligation to represent their clients competently (Rule 1.1). A classic example of an incompetent family-law attorney is one who accepts more cases than his or her office can handle. As a consequence, the law is not adequately researched, filing deadlines are missed, etc. Such an attorney is practicing law unethically.

The standard of competence required of attorneys is that they must use the knowledge and skill commonly applied under similar circumstances by attorneys in good standing in the same area of practice. The level of knowledge and skill needed depends on the complexity of the case. A great deal may be needed when representing a wife in a divorce case where the issue is the disputed valuation of a husband's partially vested pension or his partnership interest in a foreign business. Relatively less is required for a garden-variety, uncontested divorce in which the parties have no children and no assets. This does not mean that every attorney handling uncomplicated cases is competent. In fact, a number of attorneys have been charged with incompetence, in part, because of their failure to hire additional attorney or paralegal help for a high-volume practice consisting of relatively uncomplicated cases. The skill of managing a caseload is a component of competence.

How do ethical attorneys become competent? They draw on the general principles of analysis learned in law school. They take the time needed to prepare themselves. They spend time in traditional and online law libraries. They talk with their colleagues. When needed, they also formally associate themselves with more experienced attorneys in the area. They do not accept cases that are beyond their capacity. Attorneys who fail to take such steps are acting unethically if they are not using the knowledge and skill that is commonly applied under similar circumstances by attorneys in good standing in the same area of practice.

Attorneys in a family-law practice must also make sure that their paralegals are competent. Steps to insure this include:

- Supervising every task performed by paralegals.
- Encouraging paralegals to attend *continuing legal education (CLE)* programs relevant to their assigned tasks on family-law cases.
- Encouraging paralegals to engage in self-study, e.g., by reading material online on the family law of the state (see Appendix D for links to such material).

Victory is not the measure of competence. Competent attorneys can lose cases. There is nothing unethical about losing a case if the attorney used the knowledge and skill required by the standard of competence.

Clients, particularly family-law clients, often seek reassurances about their case. Responding to this anxiety can sometimes be delicate, especially for clients who have unreasonable expectations about their case's outcome. Consequently, everyone in the law firm, paralegals included, must avoid saying anything that could be interpreted as guaranteeing a particular result. For example, compare the following statements:

- "The court will grant you full custody."
- "Although we can never predict what a court will do, we have good arguments that we will use to try to persuade the court to grant you full custody."

The first statement can be interpreted as a guarantee or warranty that the client will be given full custody. If this result does not occur, the attorney might lose a breach-of-contract suit brought by the client. In such a suit, attorneys cannot raise the defense that they competently represented the client in the custody

uncontested
Unchallenged; without opposition or dispute.

dispute. A guarantee, once provided, is measured by the result promised, not by whether reasonably necessary knowledge and skill were used. The second statement properly avoids promising a result.

DIGITAL COMPETENCE

Computer knowledge and skill are also components of ethical competence. In the past, a law office looked with amusement at the older attorneys who refused to join the computer bandwagon in the practice of law. No more. Indeed, all attorneys (young or old) can be disciplined for failing to "keep abreast" of the "benefits and risks associated with relevant technology." (Rule 1.1, Comment 8).

Today, attorneys must know how to do basic computer tasks, including the following:

- Back up files
- Perform computerized legal research
- Install and update virus and malware protection
- Avoid violating confidentiality when using computer devices in public
- Safeguard confidentiality in the cloud
- Create secure passwords
- Remove ("scrub") metadata
- Conduct e-discovery
- Avoid spoliation of digital evidence

Paralegal competence includes an ability to assist attorneys in these areas of computer use.

ETHICAL INCOMPETENCE AND LEGAL MALPRACTICE

Two major consequences can result when an attorney is found to be incompetent. First, the attorney might be disciplined for unethical conduct pursuant to the rules of ethics. The discipline can lead to sanctions such as a reprimand or disbarment. Second, the attorney might be sued for **legal malpractice**, which is the failure of an attorney to use the knowledge and skill commonly applied under similar circumstances by attorneys in good standing in the same area of practice. An attorney is reasonable (and thereby avoids liability for legal malpractice) when he or she uses such knowledge and skill. The ethics case and the malpractice case are separate proceedings, although the same conduct might be the basis of both.

The three major errors most commonly committed by family-law attorneys are:

- *Failure to know the law or to apply it properly.* According to the claims statistics of one legal-malpractice insurance company, "A failure to know or apply the law is almost three times more likely to occur in family law than in other areas of practice."[4]
- *Failure to follow client instructions.* Attorneys sometimes fail to document everything they tell the client and everything clients tell their attorneys. In the absence of such documentation, courts tend to side with clients when they allege that the attorney went against the client's instructions.
- *Failure to obtain client consent or to provide the client with needed information about the case.*

e-discovery
The discovery of data found in emails, spreadsheets, databases, videos, and other digital formats. Also called *electronic data discovery (EDD)*.

spoliation
Intentionally destroying, altering, or concealing evidence.

legal malpractice
The failure of an attorney to use the knowledge and skill commonly applied under similar circumstances by attorneys in good standing in the same area of practice.

To the extent that errors are based on communication problems, paralegals have an important role to play. Once a case commences, the paralegal might be the person the client speaks to most often. The paralegal provides information on the status of the case and relays messages between the attorney and client. Every such contact with the client should be noted in the client's file, indicating the date of the contact and the specifics of what was said. These notes can become important evidence in a legal-malpractice action in which the client and the attorney disagree about what instructions were given, when they were given, and what the client did in response.

Legal malpractice requires proof of actual harm.

Attorney John Hamilton represents Mary Smith in her divorce action against her husband, Ed Smith. Hamilton tells Mary that she is not entitled to a share of a business that Ed started during the marriage. A year after the divorce, Mary suspects that Hamilton was incorrect in this advice and sues him for legal malpractice.

To win this case, Mary has the burden of proving that the divorce advice Hamilton gave her about the business fell below the standard of skill that is commonly applied by attorneys in the same area of practice. She must *also* prove that this incompetence caused her actual harm. To prove harm, Mary must prove that Ed's business had value (it was not insolvent, meaning it had more assets than liabilities) so that there was something to divide other than business debts. If she cannot prove causation, then she lost nothing by Hamilton's incompetent advice, and the legal-malpractice claim fails.

In this regard, the legal-malpractice case differs from an *ethics* case brought against the attorney. In an ethics case against Hamilton, there is no requirement that he cause actual harm, although such harm is often asserted. Attorneys can be disciplined for unethical conduct if they are incompetent even if this failure does not lead to an actual loss by a client.

Can a paralegal in a family-law practice be sued for negligence? Yes. Every person is personally liable for negligence that causes harm. The paralegal's supervisor can *also* be liable for the paralegal's negligence. Under the doctrine of **respondeat superior**, an employer is responsible for the conduct of employees while they are acting within the **scope of employment**.

LIMITED SCOPE REPRESENTATION

Most attorney services consist of a mix, or bundle, of tasks such as legal advice on the grounds for divorce, investigation of marital assets, document preparation, document review, document filing, legal research, negotiation, and court representation. Collectively, these tasks are called **bundled legal services**.

Suppose, however, that a client does not want the full range of attorney services. The client might be representing him or herself (pro se) but would like the attorney to perform specific tasks, such as reviewing a separation agreement that the client has prepared or drafting a letter that the client wants to send to the employer of his or her spouse. Attorneys who agree to provide discrete task representation of this kind are providing limited-scope representation known as **unbundled legal services.** (Charging for discrete tasks is called *task-based billing, unit billing,* or *project billing.*) Increasingly, clients are turning to the Internet for self-help assistance in preparing some of their own legal documents. They then might look for attorneys willing to provide unbundled services on aspects of their case where they need attorney assistance.

The main ethical danger in providing unbundled legal services is that the client does not have a clear understanding of the limited nature of the representation. (Rule 1.2) A nightmare example is the attorney who agrees to review a document

respondeat superior
"Let the master [boss] answer." An employer is responsible (liable) for the wrongs committed by an employee committed within the scope of employment.

scope of employment
Conduct of an employee (1) that is foreseeable by the employer and (2) that is performed for the employer's business under the employer's specific or general control.

bundled legal services
All tasks needed to represent a client on a legal matter; all-inclusive legal services.

unbundled legal services
Discrete task representation for which the client is charged per task. When performing such tasks, the attorney is providing limited-scope legal services rather than the full range (the full bundle) of legal services that may be needed on a legal matter.

prepared by a pro se client who is under the misimpression that the attorney will also file a claim based on that document. The client then loses the claim when it is not filed before the statute of limitations expires. Attorneys have an ethical obligation to avoid such misunderstandings on the limited scope of representation in unbundled cases.

In some states, documents filed in court that were prepared by an attorney must state the attorney's name on the document. In such states, for example, a client who hires an attorney for the limited purpose of drafting a divorce complaint cannot allow the court to believe that the client drafted it.

COLLABORATIVE LAW

Collaborative law is an example of limited-scope representation in family-law cases. Collaborative law is a method of practicing law in which the attorneys refuse to continue representing the parties if the parties cannot settle their dispute through mediation or another form of alternative dispute resolution (ADR). Collaborative law is limited because the collaborative-law attorneys do not litigate.

Each party hires his or her own attorney who practices collaborative law. A four-way agreement is then reached in which the parties consent to the limited role of their attorneys. To encourage settlement, the agreement provides that the attorneys will refuse to continue representing the parties if litigation becomes necessary because ADR fails to resolve the disputes. The parties must find other attorneys if the case goes to trial. The collaborative-law attorneys, therefore, do not have a financial incentive to drag the dispute into litigation in order to increase the number of their hourly fees. When collaborative law is successful, the role of the court is to review the agreements reached by the parties and decide whether to approve the agreements.

Most states say that practicing collaborative law is ethical so long as clients give informed consent to the restriction on litigation in a collaborative-law arrangement. There is a danger that a client who hires a collaborative-law attorney will not understand the litigation restriction and may not realize that they can hire other attorneys who are not subject to the restriction.

> Obtaining the client's informed consent requires that the lawyer communicate adequate information and explanation about the material risks of [and reasonably available alternatives to] the limited representation. The lawyer must provide adequate information about the rules or contractual terms governing the collaborative process, its advantages and disadvantages, and the alternatives. The lawyer also must assure that the client understands that, if the collaborative law procedure does not result in settlement of the dispute and litigation is the only recourse, the collaborative lawyer must withdraw and the parties must retain new lawyers to prepare the matter for trial.[5]

Another troublesome ethical question is whether the four-way agreement on the limited scope of the representation places an attorney under a contractual commitment to an opposing party. This was the concern of one of the few bar associations to take the position that practicing collaborative law is unethical.[6] Most state bars (and the American Bar Association) disagree. It is true that it is unethical for an attorney to represent a party if the representation will be "materially limited" by the attorney's responsibilities to a "third person." (Rule 1.7(b)) In this instance, the third person is the opposing party to whom the attorney has made a contractual commitment to cease providing services to the attorney's own client if ADR collapses and litigation becomes necessary. If, however, a client gives informed consent to the arrangement, the ethical objection is eliminated. The contractual agreement to withdraw from the case places no limits on the attorney's duty to provide competent and vigorous representation prior to the

collaborative law
A method of practicing law in which the attorneys refuse to continue representing the parties if the parties cannot settle their dispute through mediation or another form of alternative dispute resolution (ADR).

mediation
A method of alternate dispute resolution (ADR) in which the parties avoid litigation by submitting their dispute to a neutral third person (the mediator), who helps the parties resolve their dispute but does not render a decision that resolves it for them.

alternative dispute resolution (ADR)
A method or procedure for resolving a legal dispute without litigating it in a court or an administrative agency. ADR methods include mediation, arbitration, and Med-Arb.

informed consent
Agreement to let something happen based on having a reasonable understanding of its benefits, risks, and available alternatives.

time litigation becomes necessary. This is the view of most bar associations. They also do not believe that the agreement to withdraw interferes with the attorney's independent judgment of whether litigation is needed.

Collaborative law will not work in every family-law case. The parties must be willing and able, through their attorneys, to engage in robust negotiation in order to reach a settlement of all the issues involved. Some spouses might be pressured into agreeing to try collaborative law without fully understanding what it entails. If there is a serious power imbalance between the spouses—or if one of the spouses has committed domestic violence in the past and the other spouse feels that the threat of violence still exists—collaborative law may not work. At a minimum, the parties must be strong enough to engage in the give-and-take that is needed. Although the client's attorney will take the lead in the negotiations, the client must believe in the process and not be threatened by it.

FEES

REASONABLE FEE

Attorney fees must be reasonable (Rule 1.5). There is no absolute rule on when a family-law fee is excessive and therefore unreasonable. A number of factors must be considered, such as the amount of time and labor involved, the complexity of the matter, the experience and reputation of the attorney, the customary fee in the locality for the same kind of case, etc. The amount of the fee should be communicated to the client before or soon after the attorney starts to work on the case. Almost all states require contingent-fee agreements (discussed next) to be in writing. Most states recommend (but do not require) that other fee agreements (e.g., an hourly fee) be in writing as well.

CONTINGENT FEE

contingent fee
A fee that is paid only if the case is successfully resolved by litigation or settlement regardless of the number of hours spent on the case. (The fee is also referred to as a *contingency*.)

Most family-law attorneys charge an hourly fee for tasks that they perform and a lower hourly fee for the tasks performed by their paralegals. Hourly fees are paid regardless of whether the attorney achieves the objectives sought by the client. A **contingent fee** is different because it is paid only if the case is successfully resolved by litigation or settlement.

Serious ethical problems can arise if contingent fees are charged in family-law cases.

Tom hires Malinda, an attorney, to obtain a divorce from his wife, JoAnne. The fee will be $25,000 if the divorce is granted. No fee is due if it is not granted.

public policy
The principles inherent in the customs, morals, and notions of justice that prevail in a state; the foundation of public laws; the principles that are naturally and inherently right and just.

This $25,000 contingent fee is unethical and is against **public policy**. In this example, assume that a glimmer of hope arises that Tom and JoAnne might reconcile. Note the potential pressure on Malinda. She has an interest in obtaining the $25,000 fee for a completed divorce. This interest could conflict with the interest of Tom, her client, to keep the possibility of reconciliation alive. This conflict of interests might lead Malinda to discourage reconciliation or to set up roadblocks to it. Reconciliation obviously removes the possibility of the divorce from occurring.

In family-law cases, therefore, the following three contingent fees are unethical:

- Receiving a designated fee *if* the divorce is granted,
- Receiving a designated fee *if* the court issues an alimony or support order of a specified amount, or
- Receiving a designated fee *if* the court issues or approves a property division that functions as or takes the place of (is in lieu of) an alimony or support order (Rule 1.5(d)).

These fees are unethical even if the amount of the contingent fee is reasonable and is agreed to by the client.

Some states have limited exceptions to this prohibition on contingent fees in family-law cases. For example, a state might forbid a contingent fee when a client is seeking *future* support but allow it if the client is seeking to collect **arrearages** on a support judgment that has already been rendered. If a judgment already exists and the attorney is seeking recovery of a post-judgment balance, the attorney's desire to collect the contingent fee is less likely to interfere with the continuation or reconciliation of family relationships. Rule 1.5 of the *Model Rules* of the American Bar Association does not prohibit "a contract for a contingent fee for legal representation in connection with the recovery of post-judgment balances due under support, alimony or other financial orders."[7]

arrearages
Payments that are due but have not yet been made. Also called *arrears*.

ASSIGNMENT 2.1

(1) Pauline Adams hires an attorney to help her establish the paternity of a child she says she had with Tom Canter. They are not married. The attorney will charge her $5,000 if he wins a court judgment establishing Tom as the father. If such a judgment is not obtained, no fee will be paid. Is the fee ethical? (See General Instructions for the Legal Analysis Assignment in Appendix A.)

(2) Dan and Elaine Bolton were divorced in 2018. The divorce decree ordered Dan to pay $350 a month in child support for their daughter, which he has faithfully paid. A year later, Elaine goes to an attorney to seek help in obtaining an increase in child support to $500 a month. Is there any policy reason against the attorney taking this case for a fee of 20 percent of everything a court orders Dan to pay above $350 a month? (See General Instructions for the Legal Analysis Assignment in Appendix A.)

FEE-SPLITTING

Next, we examine the problem of **fee-splitting**. There are two main categories of fee-splitting. The first category is the splitting of a fee between two or more attorneys who are not in the same law firm. Such splitting is allowed if certain conditions are met such as (1) an agreement by the client to allow the split and (2) the amount of the total fee is reasonable. The second category is the splitting of a fee between an attorney and a nonattorney even if they work in the same firm.

It is unethical for an attorney to share the fee of a particular client with a nonattorney. For example, if a paralegal does particularly outstanding work on the divorce case of a client, the attorney cannot reward the paralegal by paying him or her a portion of the fee that the attorney charged the client. Of course, a law firm uses client fees to pay paralegal salaries and benefits such as an annual bonus and contributions to a retirement plan. Such payments, however, are ethical because they are not paid out of particular client fees.

fee-splitting
(1) The splitting (division) of a single client's fee between two or more attorneys who are not in the same law firm. (2) The splitting (division) of a single client's fee between an attorney and a nonattorney. Also called *fee-sharing* or *division of fees*.

PARALEGAL FEES IN FAMILY LAW CASES

Most attorneys charge a client **paralegal fees** for the work done on the client's case by the attorney's paralegal. The fees go to the attorney, not to the paralegal. The following case reviews the standards a court uses when awarding paralegal fees. It also acknowledges the important role that paralegals play in the practice of family law.

paralegal fees
Fees that attorneys can collect for the nonclerical work of their paralegals on client cases.

CASE | McMackin v. McMackin
651 A.2d 778 (1993)
Family Court of Delaware

Background: *The attorney fees of the husband and wife in this divorce case include work performed by the paralegals of the attorneys. Under Delaware law, a court "after considering the financial resources of both parties may order a party to pay all or part of" the other party's attorney fees (Delaware Code Annotated, title 13, § 1515; see delcode.delaware.gov/title13/c015/index.shtml). An award of attorney fees can include paralegal fees if the standards for awarding paralegal fees are met. After reviewing the standards, the court must then decide how the fees are to be paid in view of the income of the husband and wife.*

OPINION OF THE COURT:

Crompton, Judge

The following is my decision regarding attorney's fees in the above-captioned matter. I have reviewed Affidavits for Fees submitted by counsel for both James H. McMackin (hereinafter "Husband") and Marianne C. McMackin (hereinafter "Wife"). Wife's total attorney's fees, paralegal fees and costs amount to $12,785.50. Husband's total attorney fees, paralegal fees and costs are $9,768.35. . . .

The United States Supreme Court has found that the term "attorney's fee" refers not only to the work performed by members of the Bar but also to reasonable fees for the work product of an attorney, which includes the work of paralegals, law clerks and recent law graduates at market rates for their services. *Missouri v. Jenkins,* 491 U.S. 274 (1989).

The definition of a legal assistant or paralegal was defined in *ABA By-Laws,* § 21-12 (1986) as follows:

Persons who, although not members of the legal profession, are qualified through education, training, or work experience, are employed or retained by a lawyer, law office, governmental agency, or other entity in a capacity or function which involves the performance, under the direction and supervision of an attorney, of specifically delegated substantive legal work, which work, for the most part, requires a sufficient knowledge of legal concepts such that, absent that legal assistant, the attorney would perform the task.

Paralegal fees are not a part of the overall overhead of a law firm. Paralegal services are billed separately by attorneys, and these legal assistants have the potential for greatly decreasing litigation expenses and, for that matter, greatly increasing the efficiency of many attorneys. By permitting paralegal fees, the danger of charging these fees off as the attorney's work is hopefully extinguished. By the same token, the danger of charging off a secretary's services as those of a paralegal is very real and present, thereby mandating

that certain information be provided by the supervising attorney before paralegal fees can be awarded by this Court in the future. Those criteria are as follows:

1. The time spent by the person in question on the task;

2. The hourly rate as charged to clients (will vary based on expertise and years of experience);

3. The education, training or work experience of the person which enabled him or her to acquire sufficient knowledge of legal concepts. The Court recognizes that not all those who work in a paralegal capacity have a paralegal degree or license, but many of these people do possess expertise, which should be recognized in family law matters;

4. The type of work involved in detail. The work must *not* be purely clerical or secretarial in nature. Such work would fall under costs and may not be charged as paralegal fees at the market rate. The task must contain substantive legal work under the direction or supervision of an attorney such that if the assistant were not present, the work would be performed by the attorney and not a secretary. However, the assistant may not do work that only an attorney is allowed to do under the rules of practice and ethics. Substantive legal work which may be performed by legal assistants and billed at the market rate includes, but is not limited to, such activities as:

(a) Factual investigation, including locating and interviewing witnesses;

(b) Assistance with depositions, interrogations and document production;

(c) Compilation of statistical and financial data;

(d) Checking legal citations;

(e) Correspondence with clients/opposing counsel/courts; and

(f) Preparing/reviewing/answering petitions and other pleadings.

Applying the above standards to the two affidavits received in the matters sub judice, it is evident that both of them contain the required information. Both affidavits clearly comply with all four criteria previously discussed. For example, they describe the time spent by the paralegal, the hourly rate, and the education training or work experience of the paralegal. The type of affidavit submitted by Husband's counsel is exactly what this Court expects when reviewing fees. The affidavit of Wife's counsel leaves a bit to be desired in that it merely attaches invoices sent to the client. These invoices are very difficult to read and should be consolidated into one document with a separate affidavit attached by the paralegal. Husband's affidavit complies in

(continued)

every respect, but Wife's affidavit is certainly within the guidelines. Both attorneys have described in detail the type of work performed by the paralegal. This work includes such activities as reviewing depositions, preparing subpoenas, reviewing discovery, assisting in preparing Rule 52(d) Submissions, conferences with clients and correspondence. Clearly the type of work involved is that which would normally have been prepared or accomplished by the attorney and not a secretary. . . .

Husband has stated in his answer to Wife's Motion for Counsel Fees that he has no cash available to pay her fees. It is my opinion that his substantial income of approximately $82,000 per year versus Wife's income of approximately $35,600 per year mandates that he pay 60% of her fees. . . . This amount is to be added to the lump sum which Husband owes to Wife and is to be paid at the same time.

IT IS SO ORDERED.

PAYMENT FOR REFERRALS

An attorney cannot give someone any form of compensation or payment for referring clients to the attorney. With few exceptions, a "lawyer shall not give anything of value to a person for recommending the lawyer's services." "Lawyers are not permitted to pay others for channeling professional work" (Rule 7.2(b)).

Alice Davis, a paralegal, works for the law firm of Sullivan and Sullivan. For every divorce client that Alice refers to the firm, she receives one extra day a year in vacation time.

Alice is receiving something of value—added vacation time—for referring business to an attorney. This is unethical even if the client consents to this payment to the paralegal.

DILIGENCE AND UNWARRANTED DELAY

Attorneys have an ethical duty to be diligent in the representation of their clients. It is unethical for an attorney to use **dilatory** tactics that cause unwarranted delay in representing a client. An attorney must act with reasonable diligence and promptness (Rule 3.2).

Angry clients sometimes complain that attorneys keep clients in the dark about what is happening and take too long to complete a case. "He never answers my calls." "It took months to file the case in court." "She keeps telling me that everything is fine, but nothing ever gets done." Such complaints, however, do not necessarily indicate dilatory tactics or other unethical behavior by the attorney. Events may be beyond the attorney's control: for example, the court calendar is crowded or the other side is not responding. Yet this does not excuse a lack of regular communication with clients to keep them reasonably informed about the status of their case. In contrast, other explanations for a lack of diligence and promptness are more serious and probably indicate unethical conduct. Here are some examples of serious unethical conduct:

dilatory
Causing delay, often without merit or justification.

- The attorney is disorganized. The law office has not developed adequate systems to process its family-law cases. The delays are due to careless mistakes and a lack of skill.

- The attorney is taking more cases than the office can handle. Cases are taking much longer to process than they should. Additional personnel should be hired to do the needed work, or new cases should not be accepted.

- The office fails to designate backup attorneys to handle ongoing cases of attorneys who are away on vacation or who are otherwise unavailable because of pressing work on other cases. As a result, casework stagnates for unacceptably long periods of time.
- The attorney is trying to "wear the opponent down" with unnecessary motions and stalling tactics that are not required for competent representation on the merits of the case.

CONFIDENTIALITY

confidential
(1) Pertaining to information that others do not have a right to receive. (2) Pertaining to all information related to the representation of a client whatever its source, including the fact that someone is a client.

Information is confidential if it relates to the representation of a client and others do not have a right to receive it. In a law office, the ethical rule of confidentiality is summarized in Exhibit 2.2.

EXHIBIT 2.2   Rule on Confidentiality in a Law Office

GENERAL RULE: An attorney must not disclose information relating to the representation of a client.

EXCEPTIONS TO THE GENERAL RULE

- *Consent*: A client can always expressly agree to allow the disclosure of confidential information. Also, an attorney has implied consent from the client to disclose confidential information when disclosure is needed to carry out the representation for which the attorney was hired.
- *Preventing Death or Substantial Bodily Harm*: Confidential information can be disclosed if the attorney reasonably believes disclosure is necessary to prevent reasonably certain death or substantial bodily harm.
- *Preventing Substantial Injury to Financial Interests or Property*: Confidential information can be disclosed if the following two conditions are met:
  - the attorney reasonably believes disclosure is necessary to prevent the client from committing a crime or fraud that is reasonably certain to cause substantial injury to the financial interests or property of another, and
  - the client is using the services of the attorney in committing the crime or fraud that the attorney now seeks to prevent by the disclosure.
- *Suits between Attorney and Client*: If the client sues the attorney or vice versa, the attorney can reveal whatever confidential information is necessary for the attorney to defend against the client's suit or to assert the attorney's claims against the client (Model Rule 1.6).

The confidentiality rule applies to *all* information relating to the representation of a client, whatever its source. The prohibition is not limited to so-called secrets or matters explicitly communicated in confidence. Here are some examples of unethical breaches of confidentiality:

- At home, a paralegal tells her husband that J.K. Thompson is one of the new divorce clients in the office where the paralegal works. (The client's identity should not be disclosed to anyone outside the office.)
- In an elevator crowded with strangers, a paralegal tells her supervisor that the adoption notice in the Smith case came in today's mail. (Confidential information should not be discussed in public places where strangers can hear what is being said.)
- In an attorney's office, a client file is left open on the desk, where child custody documents are visible to (and are glanced at by) an electrician who is in the office repairing a light fixture. (Extra care should be used to prevent strangers from seeing anything in documents that contain confidential information.)

The confidentiality rule is designed to encourage clients to discuss their cases fully and frankly with the law office they have hired, including embarrassing or legally damaging information. Arguably, clients would be reluctant to be forthcoming with the office if they had to worry whether an attorney, paralegal, or other staff member might reveal confidential information to others.

Many law offices communicate with clients by email. Some offices store documents on smartphones and on digital record-keeping services that are in the cloud. Of course, client information should never be mentioned on any open social networks such as Facebook or Twitter. Even "private" or restricted online communications are vulnerable to hacking and other unauthorized access. Cautious attorneys warn clients about the dangers of online communication and obtain written client permission to use any of them. Precautions such as *encryption* are also highly recommended, and in some instances, required.

Confidentiality can also be breached by sending inappropriate metadata. When you send someone a document online (e.g., a memo created in Microsoft Word that you send as an attachment to an email message), you are sending more than the data that will be read on the screen when the document is opened. Digital documents also contain metadata, which are data about data. They could consist of hidden information about the document such as the language used in earlier drafts of the document or it could include "margin" comments from the writer of the memo on the strengths and weaknesses of the client's position. It may be helpful for you to be able to read these earlier drafts and comments, but recipients of the document should not be able to read them, particularly opposing attorneys to whom you send the documents! Yet they can read them if they know how to locate the metadata in what you send. Hence, before you send a document online, you need to find out how to erase the document's metadata. (For guidance, run the search "removing metadata" in Google, Bing, or Yahoo.)

Careless online disclosure of confidential information can also occur when the wrong email address is typed into the email message. Most email programs allow you to accept a suggested addressee after you type the first few letters of a person's email address. When in a hurry, you may hit the *send* button before realizing that the addressee the program suggested was not the person you wanted.

A great fear of law office personnel is that the wrong person will obtain material that should be protected by ethics, by the **attorney-client privilege** or by the **work-product rule**. This mistake can have devastating consequences. For example, if a stranger overhears a confidential communication by a client to the attorney or to the attorney's paralegal, a court might rule that the attorney-client privilege has been waived on the theory that it is inconsistent to let a stranger or any third party hear what you claim was confidential. Media celebrity Martha Stewart was confronted with this reality when a court ruled in her trial that she waived the attorney-client privilege covering the contents of an email with her attorney when Stewart mailed a copy of the email to her daughter.

In some situations, however, it is proper for a law office to breach confidentiality, as illustrated in the following situation:

> An attorney represents a husband in a bitter divorce case against his wife. During a meeting at the law firm, the husband shows the attorney a gun and says he is going to use it to kill his wife later the same day.

In this example, can the attorney tell the police what the husband said? Yes. It is not unethical for an attorney to reveal information about a client if the attorney reasonably believes the disclosure is necessary to prevent the client from committing a criminal act that could lead to someone's reasonably certain death or substantial bodily harm.

attorney-client privilege
A client or a client's attorney can refuse to disclose any confidential (private) communication between them if the purpose of the communication was to facilitate the provision of legal services to the client.

work-product rule
Notes, working papers, memoranda, or similar things prepared by or for an attorney in anticipation of litigation are not discoverable by an opponent, absent a showing of substantial need. They are protected by privilege. Also called *attorney work product*.

CONFLICT OF INTEREST

A *conflict of interest* is divided loyalty that actually or potentially harms (or disadvantages) someone who is owed undivided loyalty (Rule 1.7). Assume, for example, that a salesman does part-time work selling the same kind of products of two competing companies. The salesman has a conflict of interest. How can he serve two masters with the same loyalty? How does he divide his customers between the two companies? There is an obvious danger that he will favor one over the other. The fact that he may try to be fair in his treatment of both companies does not eliminate the conflict of interest. The *potential* exists for one of the companies to be disadvantaged. It may be that the two companies are aware of the problem and are not worried; they consent to his working for both of them with full knowledge of the risks. This does not mean that there is no conflict of interest; it simply means that the affected parties are willing to take the risks involved in the conflict. As we shall see, consent can be a valid defense to some (but not all) conflict-of-interest charges. Consent, however, does not mean that there was no conflict of interest.

In a family-law practice, a number of conflict-of-interest issues can arise, such as the following:

- Multiple representation
- Former client/present adversary
- Law firm disqualification
- Identity of the client
- Business transactions with a client
- Gifts from a client
- Loaning money to a client
- Sex with a client
- Bias

MULTIPLE REPRESENTATION

Bob and Patricia Farmer are separated, and they both want a divorce. They are contesting who should have sole custody of the children and how the marital property should be divided. Mary Franklin, Esq., is an attorney that Bob and Patricia know and trust. They decide to ask Franklin to represent both of them in the divorce.

multiple representation
Representation by the same attorney of more than one side in a controversy or other legal matter. Also called *joint representation* or *common representation*.

adverse interests
A goal or claim of one person that is different from (or opposed to) the goal or claim of another person.

contested
Challenged; opposed or disputed.

In this case, Franklin has a conflict of interest due to **multiple representation**. How can she give her undivided loyalty to both sides? They have **adverse interests**, which means different goals or claims. On the custody question, for example, how can Franklin vigorously argue that Bob should have sole custody, and at the same time vigorously argue that Patricia should have sole custody? A client is entitled to the *independent professional judgment* of an attorney, particularly in a **contested** case where the parties are disputing a factual or legal issue. How can Franklin act independently for two different people who are at odds with each other? Franklin's commitment to be fair and objective in giving her advice to the parties will not solve the difficulty. Her role as an attorney is to be a *partisan advocate* for the client. It is impossible for Franklin to play this role for two clients engaged in such a dispute. A clear conflict of interest exists. In every state, it would be unethical for Franklin to represent both Bob and Patricia in this case, even though both parties consent to the multiple representation. Consent would not be a defense to a conflict-of-interest charge when the parties have the kind of adverse interests that Bob and Patricia have.

Suppose, however, that the divorce case involved different facts:

Jim and Mary Smith are separated, and they both want a divorce. They have been married only a few months. There are no children and no marital assets to divide. George Davidson, Esq., is an attorney that Jim and Mary know and trust. They decide to ask Davidson to represent both of them in the divorce.

Can Davidson ethically represent both sides here? Some states *will* allow him to do so on the theory that there are no adverse interests between the parties—meaning the spouses have no disputes regarding support, custody, or property division. Hence, in such cases the potential for harm in multiple representation is almost nonexistent. Other states, however, disagree. They frown on multiple representation even in so-called **friendly divorces**. The divorce may have been "friendly" when granted, but years later one of the ex-spouses may attack the attorney for having had a conflict of interest. When reminded that both parties consented to the multiple representation, the ex-spouse will inevitably respond by saying, "I didn't understand what I was being asked to consent to."

Ethical problems involving multiple representation are not limited to divorces. When we study adoption in Chapter 15, we will see that attorneys are sometimes hired to facilitate the adoption among the various parties. An attorney-facilitator performs tasks such as bringing together a birth mother and the parties who want to adopt the child (the prospective adoptive parents). Such facilitation is not unethical in most cases. If, however, disputes arise between birth mothers and prospective parents and they have adverse interests, it is unethical for an attorney to represent the birth mother and the prospective parents.

friendly divorce
A divorce proceeding in which the spouses are not contesting the dissolution of the marriage, or anything related thereto. An uncontested divorce.

FORMER CLIENT/PRESENT ADVERSARY

Jessica Winters, Esq., represented Gregory Noonan in his divorce action against his former wife, Eileen Noonan. In this action, Eileen received custody of their children and alimony. Five years later, Eileen wants to reopen the case in order to obtain more alimony. Winters no longer represents Gregory, who now has a different attorney. Eileen hires Winters in her action for increased alimony.

In this situation, a former client (Gregory) is now an **adversary**. Winters once represented Gregory; she now represents a party who is suing Gregory. Without Gregory's *informed consent*, it is unethical for Winters to "switch sides" and represent Eileen against him. Consent is needed (1) when the second case is the same as the first one or when the two cases are substantially related and (b) when the former client and the present client have **materially** adverse interests in the current case (Rule 1.9(a)).

The necessity of consent is not limited to cases in which the same sets of parties are involved. Without Gregory's consent, it would be equally unethical for Winters to represent one of his children who later sues Gregory for support to force him to pay college expenses. Such an action would be substantially related to Gregory's original divorce action against Eileen.

Why is this so? If the cases are the same or are substantially related, the likelihood is strong that the attorney will use information learned in the first case to the detriment of the former client in the second case. Winters undoubtedly found out a good deal about Gregory when she represented him in the divorce case. Winters might now be able to use this information *against* Gregory in Eileen's attempt to increase her alimony or in a child's attempt to force him to pay college expenses.

adversary
An opponent. (See glossary for an additional meaning.)

materially
Serious and substantial. (See glossary for an additional meaning.)

ASSIGNMENT   2.2

Is there a conflict problem in any of the following cases? (See General Instructions for the Legal Analysis Assignment in Appendix A.)

a. Irene Farrell is an attorney who represented Bill and Gail Davis, a married couple, when they set up a business. Two months later, Bill and Gail separate. Gail asks Irene to represent her in the divorce.

b. Ted Harris is an attorney who represents Jim O'Toole in a negligence case in which Jim is seeking damages he suffered in an automobile collision. A year after the negligence case is over, Jim's wife asks Ted to represent her in her divorce against Jim.

c. Bob Richards makes an appointment with Alex Jacobson, an attorney, to discuss the possibility of Alex representing him in his divorce against his wife, Lena Richards. They discuss fees, the grounds for divorce, and Bob's prospects of obtaining sole custody of their child. Bob decides not to hire Alex. Instead, he hires Dan Henderson, Esq., to represent him. Lena Richards hires Alex Jacobson to represent her in the divorce.

LAW FIRM DISQUALIFICATION

> *John Farrell, Esq., is an attorney at Williamson, Harris & Richards. Two years ago, John represented the father in a custody dispute with the child's grandmother (the mother of the father's deceased ex-wife). The father won the case, but the grandmother was awarded limited visitation rights. The grandmother now wants to sue the father for failure to abide by the visitation order. She asks John to represent her. (The father is now using a different law firm.) John declines because of a conflict of interest, but he sends her to his law partner at Williamson, Harris & Richards down the corridor.*

imputed disqualification
The disqualification of every attorney in a law office from representing a client solely because of an actual conflict of interest caused by one of the attorneys in the office. Also called *vicarious disqualification*.

Under Rule 1.10, if an attorney is disqualified from representing a client because of a conflict of interest, every attorney in the *same law firm* is also disqualified unless the client being protected by this rule consents to the representation. In the John Farrell example, the *father* would have to consent to the representation of the grandmother by John's law partner. The disqualification of the partner and the entire law firm is called an **imputed disqualification**. This type of disqualification occurs when an attorney causes another attorney or law firm to be disqualified. In effect, John's knowledge about the father is imputed (i.e., attributed) to the partner and everyone else in the law firm of Williamson, Harris & Richards.

In addition, a paralegal can cause the imputed disqualification of a law firm. This situation most commonly arises when the paralegal switches jobs.

> *Claire Anderson is a paralegal at the firm of Lawrence Burton, Esq. Her sole assignment is to work on the Vickers divorce case. The firm represents Sam Vickers. One of Claire's tasks is to make an inventory of all the assets of Sam Vickers. His wife, Karen Vickers, is represented by Edward Walsh, Esq. Before this case goes to trial, Claire quits her paralegal job with Burton and becomes a paralegal with Walsh, who immediately assigns her to the Vickers case. When Burton finds out that Claire has performed substantial work on the Vickers case while working for Walsh, he makes a motion in court to disqualify Walsh from continuing to represent Karen Vickers.*

tainted
Having or causing a conflict of interest.

Claire Anderson is **tainted**. (Any attorney, paralegal, or other employee who creates a conflict of interest is deemed to be tainted.) Will Burton's motion to disqualify Walsh be granted? Yes, if the paralegal (Claire) reveals any information about the Vickers case to Walsh, her new employer.

Suppose, however, there is no evidence that the paralegal revealed anything about the case. How does the court decide the disqualification motion? In most states, the court will handle the motion by asking two questions: (1) Did the paralegal obtain confidences and secrets about the case while at the first firm? (2) Did the paralegal reveal any of these confidences and secrets about the case at the second firm? To help answer these questions, the court will use two **presumptions**:

- *Irrebuttable (conclusive) presumption.* An **irrebuttable presumption** is an assumption or inference of fact that a party will not be allowed to disprove by showing that the assumption or inference is false. (An irrebuttable presumption is also called a *conclusive presumption.*) If the paralegal did *any* work on the case in the first firm, a conclusive presumption is raised that the paralegal obtained confidences and secrets about the case. In short, evidence cannot be introduced to show that the paralegal did not obtain confidences and secrets. For example, the paralegal will not be allowed to testify that he or she did no more than carry the case file back and forth between attorneys in the office. Such evidence is inadmissible because the presumption is irrebuttable (conclusive) that confidences and secrets about the case were obtained at the first firm if it is established that the paralegal did *any* work on the case.

- *Rebuttable presumption.* Once it is established that confidences and secrets were indeed obtained at the first firm, the next question is whether any of these confidences or secrets were revealed at the second firm. Another presumption helps answer this question, but this time the presumption is rebuttable. A **rebuttable presumption** is an assumption or inference of fact that a party will be allowed to try to dispute (rebut). The rebuttable presumption is that the confidences and secrets were revealed by the paralegal at the second firm. (See Exhibit 2.3.) An assumption or inference of fact in a rebuttable presumption will be treated as true if it is not disproved.

presumption
An assumption or inference that a certain fact is true once another fact is established. The presumption is *irrebuttable* (conclusive) if a party is not allowed to introduce evidence to try to show that the assumption is false. The presumption is *rebuttable* if a party is allowed to introduce evidence to try to show that the assumption is false.

irrebuttable presumption
An assumption or inference of fact that a party will not be allowed to try to disprove (rebut). Also called *conclusive presumption.*

rebuttable presumption
An assumption or inference of fact that a party will be allowed to try to disprove (rebut), but that will be treated as true if it is not disproved.

EXHIBIT 2.3   Presumptions When a Paralegal Switches Jobs

Paralegal does some work on a case at the first firm.	=	This creates an irrebuttable presumption that the paralegal obtained confidences and secrets about the case at the first firm.	+	It also creates a rebuttable presumption that the paralegal shared (revealed) those confidences and secrets about the case at the second firm.

The attorney at the second firm can disprove the rebuttable presumption that the confidences and secrets were shared by proving that he or she set up a **Chinese Wall** around the paralegal at the second firm. A Chinese Wall is a series of screening steps taken to prevent a tainted worker (e.g., attorney, paralegal, secretary, or clerk) from having any contact with the case of a particular client because of the conflict of interest the tainted worker has created in that case. A tainted worker who is shielded or screened by a Chinese Wall becomes a *quarantined worker.* The screening steps can include making sure that the worker never works on the case at the new firm, ordering the worker not to say anything about the case to any employee of the office, instructing all others in the firm to refrain from discussing the case with the worker, and physically storing the file on the case in an area of the office away from the worker.

If a tainted paralegal with a conflict of interest is effectively screened from the case in this manner, most states will not impose an imputed disqualification on the paralegal's employer. Tainted attorneys, however, are often treated differently. Most states will order a disqualification even if an effective Chinese Wall was set up around the tainted attorney.

Chinese Wall
A screening that prevents a tainted worker (such as an attorney or a paralegal) from having any contact with the case of a particular client in the office, because the tainted worker has created a conflict of interest between that client and someone else. Also called an *ethical wall* or *cone of silence.* A tainted worker is also called a *contaminated worker.* Once a Chinese Wall is set up around the tainted worker, he or she is referred to as a *quarantined worker.*

IDENTITY OF THE CLIENT

In most family-law cases, it is clear who the client is. There is no doubt who is entitled to the attorney's zealous advocacy and undivided loyalty. In some cases, however, this is not clear. The attorney may interact with multiple family members who do not always have the same interests. Each may need independent legal advice. Consider the following cases:

- Family members contact an attorney about an aging parent, seeking advice on ways to protect the parent's health and assets. In some instances, the elderly person may be the one who comes to the attorney accompanied by relatives, such as the person's children, all of whom are potential heirs.

- A client asks an attorney to draft a will in which he makes provisions for his wife and children. After the client dies, some of the deceased's relatives contact the attorney with questions about the will. The surviving spouse has heard that she has a right to reject what the deceased provided for her in the will and instead select (elect) a percentage of the deceased's estate. She asks the attorney about this option. The attorney also suspects that some of the deceased's children have disagreements about the estate.

- For years, a man has physically abused his wife and children. In a recent incident, the police arrest the man and a prosecution begins. The wife and one of the children call an attorney and ask the attorney to represent the husband/father in the criminal case (which the prosecution is refusing to drop). The wife and children, anxious to have the scandal disappear, tell the attorney that they will pay all attorney fees.

- A pregnant woman agrees to allow Mr. and Mrs. Smith to adopt her child upon birth. The Smiths are the proposed adoptive parents. The parties have been brought together by an attorney hired by the Smiths. A week after the child is born (but before the adoption is final), the Smiths separate and file for divorce. The birth mother calls the attorney and asks if she can stop the adoption. The soon-to-be ex-wife tells the attorney that she wants to adopt the child as a single person. The soon-to-be ex-husband tells the attorney that he wants to adopt the child with a woman he met online who has agreed to marry him.

Each of these situations involves persons who have actual or possible conflicting interests. In later chapters, we will discuss the substantive law that governs such situations (e.g., the right of a surviving spouse to elect against the will). Here, our concern is the ethical landmine that can exist when the same attorney interacts with different family members. The temptation of the attorney is to try to satisfy everyone so that the case does not fall apart. Yet to avoid a conflict of interest, the ethical obligation of the attorney is to avoid giving legal advice to persons who do not have the same interests. Once the attorney has identified who the client is, everyone else should be told in writing that the attorney does not represent them and that they should obtain their own attorney. In reality, however, this is seldom done unless there is open hostility among the people involved.

BUSINESS TRANSACTIONS WITH A CLIENT

Paul Kelly, Esq., is Ed Johnson's attorney in a divorce case. Johnson owns a cleaning business for which Paul does some legal work. Ed offers to allow Paul to buy a 30 percent interest in the business. Paul does so and continues as Ed's attorney.

Assume that the business runs into difficulties and that Ed considers bankruptcy. He goes to Paul for advice on bankruptcy law. Paul has dual concerns: to give Ed competent legal advice and to protect his own 30 percent interest in the business.

Bankruptcy may be good for Ed, but disastrous for Paul's investment, or vice versa. How can Paul give Ed independent professional advice when the advice may go against Paul's own interest?

This is not to say, however, that it is always unethical for an attorney to enter into a business transaction with a client. If certain strict conditions are met, it can be proper. The conditions are as follows: (1) the terms of the transaction are "fair and reasonable" and are clearly explained to the client in writing, (2) the client has an opportunity to consult with another attorney on the advisability of entering into the transaction, and (3) the client gives his or her written consent to entering into the transaction (Rule 1.8). In the Paul Kelly example, Ed must be given the chance to consult with an attorney other than Paul on the advisability of letting Paul buy a 30 percent interest in the business; Paul must give Ed a clear, written explanation of their business relationship; Ed must consent in writing; and the relationship must be fair and reasonable.

GIFTS FROM A CLIENT

William Stanton, Esq., has been the family attorney of the Tarkington family for years. At Christmas, Patricia Tarkington gave William an expensive computer and told him to change her will so that William's daughter would receive funds to cover her college education.

Generally, attorneys are allowed to accept a gift from a client. If, however, a document must be prepared to carry out the gift, it is unethical for the attorney to prepare that document. Note the conflict in the William Stanton example. It would be in Patricia's interest to have the will written so that a set or maximum sum is identified for this gift to William's daughter, as well as a cutoff date for its use. In contrast, William would probably want the will drafted so that there is no maximum amount stated and no cutoff date. Suppose his daughter obtains a bachelor's degree and then wants to go to graduate school. If the language of the will is vague (and no time limits are inserted), an argument could be made that the gift covers both undergraduate and graduate tuition. Other questions could arise as well, e.g., does the gift cover room and board at college, and what if the daughter does not go to college until after she marries and raises her own children? It is in William's interest to draft the will to benefit his daughter under all these contingencies; however, this may not be in Patricia's interest.

Because of this conflict of interest, an attorney cannot prepare a document such as a will, trust, or contract that results in any substantial gift from a client to the attorney or to the attorney's children, spouse, parents, or siblings. If a client wants to make such a gift, another attorney who is not part of the same law firm must prepare the document. There is, however, one exception. If the client-donor is related to the person receiving the gift, the attorney can prepare the document (Rule 1.8(c)).

Lastly, there does not appear to be any ethical problem in taking the gift of the expensive computer from Mrs. Tarkington. No documents are involved.

LOANING MONEY TO A CLIENT

Henry Harris, Esq., is Barbara Atkinson's attorney in a divorce action against her husband in which the main dispute is over the property division. While the case is pending, Henry agrees to lend Barbara living expenses and court filing fees.

It can be a conflict of interest for an attorney to give financial assistance to a client in connection with current or planned litigation. A *loan* covering litigation expenses, however, is an exception to this rule. Such a loan is ethical. In the Henry Harris example, the main difficulty is the loan to cover the client's living expenses.

Suppose that the husband makes an offer to settle the case with Barbara. There is a danger that Henry's advice will be colored by the fact that he has a financial interest in Barbara—he wants to have his loan for living expenses repaid. The offer to settle from the husband may not be enough to cover the loan. Should Henry advise Barbara to accept the offer? It may be in Barbara's interest to accept the offer, but not in Henry's own interest. Such divided loyalty is the essence of a conflict of interest. Hence, the loan of living expenses is unethical. As indicated, however, an exception exists for a loan to cover the expenses of litigation, such as filing fees and other court costs. It is not unethical for an attorney to lend the client money to cover such expenses (Rule 1.8(e)).

SEX WITH A CLIENT

One of the more dramatic examples of a conflict of interest is the attorney who develops a romantic relationship with a current client, particularly a sexual relationship. Family-law clients often seek an attorney when they are most vulnerable. Under such circumstances, it is unconscionable for the attorney to take advantage of this vulnerability. An attorney with a physical or emotional interest in a client will be looking for ways to increase that interest and to inspire a reciprocal interest from the client. This pressure is not what the client needs. The attorney's own need could cloud the duty to put the client's welfare first. The only way to maintain professional independence is for attorneys—and their paralegals and other employees as well—to avoid these kinds of relationships with current clients. When the case is over and they cease being clients, such relationships are less likely to constitute a conflict of interest.

The American Bar Association prohibits sexual relations between attorney and client, even if it is consensual, *unless* the sexual relationship began before the attorney-client relationship began (Rule 1.8(j)). Surprisingly, however, not all states specifically mention this subject in their codes of ethics, and those that do are hesitant to impose prohibitions. In the Florida ethics code, for example, sexual conduct is prohibited only if it can be shown that the conduct "exploits or adversely affects" the client.[8]

BIAS

adversary system
A method of resolving a legal dispute whereby the parties (alone or through their advocates) argue their conflicting claims before a neutral (impartial) decision maker.

bias
(1) An inclination, tendency, or predisposition to think or act in a certain way. (2) Prejudice for or against something or someone. (3) A danger of prejudgment.

In our **adversary system** (where disputes are resolved by advocates arguing before a neutral decision maker), clients are entitled to vigorous representation within the bounds of law and ethics. If attorneys or paralegals have strong personal feelings that go against what a client is trying to accomplish, they have a **bias**. In such cases, there is a likelihood—not a guarantee—that their feelings will interfere with their ability to provide vigorous representation. If there is interference, it is unethical to continue. The American Bar Association says that such interference can exist when the objectives of the client are "repugnant" to the attorney (Rule 6.2).

In New York State, attorneys are cautioned that they "should decline employment if the intensity of personal feelings . . . may impair effective representation of a prospective client."[9] For more on how bias in an attorney or paralegal can be a conflict of interest, see "Assessing Your Own Biases" in Chapter 1.

SAFEKEEPING OF CLIENT PROPERTY

An attorney shall hold client property separate from the attorney's own property (Rule 1.15). Every family-law law office has an account that is used to pay items such as salaries, rent, and other office expenses. Client funds must not be placed in this account; client funds *must* be kept in separate accounts (Rule 1.15).

CHAPTER 2 ETHICS IN A FAMILY LAW PRACTICE

The *commingling* of funds is unethical no matter how accurate the records are on whom owns the amounts in the account. In a commingled account, the danger is too great that client funds will be used for nonclient purposes. This is extremely important for paralegals to know, as they are sometimes placed in charge of bookkeeping records in a law firm. Their supervising attorney may tell them "it's OK to put everything in a single account." Doing something unethical, however, is never OK.

ANTICONTACT RULE

If Attorney A knows that an opposing party is represented by Attorney B, then A cannot communicate with that party about the case unless B consents to the communication (Rule 4.2). This is called the **anticontact rule**. If an attorney knows that an opposing party is not represented, that attorney must not give this party the impression that the attorney is *disinterested* (uninvolved) in the case (Rule 4.3). Someone is disinterested if he or she is not working for one side or the other in a dispute and will not derive any benefit if either side wins or loses.

> *Dan and Theresa Kline have just separated and are thinking about a divorce. Each claims the marital home. Theresa hires Thomas Kirby, Esq., to represent her. Kirby calls Dan to ask if Dan is willing to settle the case.*

It is unethical for Kirby to contact Dan about the case if Kirby knows that Dan has his own attorney. The same would be true of efforts to contact Dan made by paralegals or other employees of Kirby. The communication must be with Dan's attorney. Only the latter can give Kirby permission to communicate with Dan. If Dan does not have an attorney, Kirby can talk with Dan, but he must not allow Dan to be misled about Kirby's role. Dan must be made to understand that Kirby works for the other side. It would be unethical for Kirby to say anything that would suggest that he is disinterested. The only advice Kirby can ethically give Dan in such a situation is to obtain his own attorney.

The anticontact rule also covers electronic communication. The rule is violated if a represented party is contacted (without permission) by email or through social network sites such as Facebook.

anticontact rule
An advocate must not contact an opposing party without permission of the latter's attorney. Also called *no-contact rule*.

WITHDRAWAL

Attorneys are not required to take every case. Furthermore, once attorneys begin a case, they are not obligated to stay with a client until the case is over. If, however, the attorney has been appointed or assigned to the case by a judge, or if the case has already begun in court, the permission of the court must usually be obtained before withdrawal is ethical.

The following are circumstances in which an attorney must not accept a case or must withdraw from a case:

- The representation of the client would violate the law, e.g., the attorney is asked for advice on how to defraud the Internal Revenue Service on a property division in a divorce case.

- The representation of the client would violate ethical rules, e.g., the attorney discovers he or she has a conflict of interest with the client that cannot be overcome (cured) by consent.

- The client dismisses (fires) the attorney.

- The attorney's physical or mental condition has deteriorated, e.g., due to alcoholism or depression, to the point where the attorney's ability to represent the client has been materially impaired (Rule 1.16).

An attorney has the option of withdrawing for reasons such as failing to pay attorney fees and having a fundamental disagreement with the client about the case.

Withdrawal, if allowed, must be done reasonably. An attorney should not abruptly withdraw on the eve of an important hearing or on the day before the client's cause of action dies because of the expiration of the statute of limitations. The client will need time to find other representation.

FALSE EVIDENCE AND STATEMENTS; FAILURE TO DISCLOSE

Attorneys must not knowingly offer false evidence or make false statements. They have an ethical obligation to be truthful to a court. If they later discover that they made a *material* statement in court that they now realize was false, they must correct the statement in court (Rule 3.3).

Suppose that a divorce client asks his or her attorney to offer into evidence a document that falsely states the earnings of the client's company. If the attorney knows that the document contains false statements, it would be unethical for the attorney to offer it into evidence unless the attorney informs the court of the falsity.

The obligation of truthfulness applies to statements made to opponents as well as to courts. For example, it would be unethical for an attorney representing a husband to tell an opposing attorney that the maximum coverage on the husband's liability policy is $100,000 when the attorney knows that the maximum is $300,000. Of course, making such a false statement to a judge would also be unethical.

Attorneys must not make false or misleading statements on Facebook, LinkedIn, or other social media. Attorneys have been disciplined for exaggerating their experience in their online profiles such as by falsely stating that they have handled cases in federal court or by listing specialty experience that they did not have.

Chances are high that attorneys who offer false evidence or who lie to a court will pressure their employees to participate in the deception. A paralegal or other employee might be asked to give a false statement to a court clerk, help a client lie (commit perjury), backdate a document, or improperly notarize a deed. Do not compromise your integrity no matter how much you believe in the cause of the client, no matter how much you detest the tactics of the opposing side, no matter how much you like the attorney for whom you work, and or no matter how important the job is to you.

Finally, failure to disclose legal authority can be unethical. An attorney must tell a tribunal about a case, statute, or other authority that the attorney knows will hurt the cause of the attorney's own client if the opposing attorney has failed to tell the tribunal about this authority (Rule 3.3(a)(2)).

MISCONDUCT

Attorneys shall not commit a criminal act that reflects adversely on their fitness. Nor shall they engage in any conduct involving dishonesty, fraud, or misrepresentation (Rule 8.4). Conduct of an attorney that constitutes a crime (e.g., stealing a client's property) can lead to criminal prosecution by the government and to ethical discipline by the state court that regulates attorneys. If the government decides not to prosecute, discipline for ethical misconduct is still possible if a state court determines that the attorney engaged in dishonesty, fraud, or misrepresentation.

ETHICS ONLINE: FRAUDULENT "FRIENDING"

Assume that a family-law attorney wants to conduct a **deposition** of a witness in preparation for a divorce trial. The witness is not a party in the litigation but could give testimony that is **adverse** to the attorney's client in the divorce case. While deposing this witness, the attorney learns that the witness has a Facebook page that is private. The attorney would like to find out what is on the page. Its content might be useable to **impeach** the witness if he or she later testifies in the trial itself. The attorney wants to ask his paralegal to "friend" the witness without revealing that the paralegal works for the attorney. If accepted as a friend, the content of the Facebook pages could then be read.

Is this online "friending" ethical? Assume that the attorney is not sure. He is also not sure if communicating with the witness would violate the anticontact rule since the witness is unrepresented. To help resolve these ethical questions, the attorney asks the ethics committee of the local bar association for an opinion on whether the Facebook contact would be ethical. (Most bar associations provide this service for its members.) The following opinion is the response of the ethics committee. Note that, in the opinion, the attorney is referred to as the "inquirer" who is asking the committee for ethics advice. The "third person" or "third party" mentioned in the opinion is the person the attorney asks to do the online friending. Additionally, the opinion uses the word **implicate** or *implicated* several times. In this context, the word means *may apply* or *may be relevant to.* If someone says an activity implicates a rule, the comment simply means that the rule might apply and therefore should be considered or examined.

deposition
A method of discovery by which one party questions another party (or questions the other party's witness) usually outside the courtroom. The person questioned (deposed) is called the *deponent.*

adverse
(1) Opposed to. (2) Hostile. (See glossary for additional meanings.)

impeach
To challenge; to attack the credibility of.

implicate
(1) May apply or be relevant to. (2) May involve or affect.

ETHICS OPINION **The Philadelphia Bar Association Professional Guidance Committee Opinion 2009-02**

The inquirer deposed an 18 year old woman (the "witness"). The witness is not a party to the litigation, nor is she represented. Her testimony is helpful to the party [who is] adverse to the inquirer's client.

During the course of the deposition, the witness revealed that she has "Facebook" and "MySpace" accounts. Having such accounts permits a user like the witness to create personal "pages" on which he or she posts information on any topic, sometimes including highly personal information. Access to the pages of the user is limited to persons who obtain the user's permission, which permission is obtained after the user is approached online by the person seeking access. The user can grant access to his or her page with almost no information about the person seeking access, or can ask for detailed information about the person seeking access before deciding whether to allow access.

The inquirer believes that the pages maintained by the witness may contain information relevant to the matter in which the witness was deposed, and that could be used to impeach the witness's testimony should she testify at trial. [At the deposition, the] inquirer did not ask the witness to reveal the contents of her pages, either by permitting access to them online or otherwise. He has, however, either himself or through agents, visited Facebook and MySpace and attempted to access both accounts. When that was done, it was found that access to the pages can be obtained only by the witness's permission, as discussed in detail above.

The inquirer states that based on what he saw in trying to access the pages, he has determined that the witness tends to allow access to anyone who asks (although it is not clear how he could know that), and states that he does not know if the witness would allow access to him if he asked her directly to do so.

The inquirer proposes to ask a third person, someone whose name the witness will not recognize, to go to the Facebook and MySpace websites, contact the witness and seek to "friend" her, to obtain access to the information on the pages. The third person would state only truthful information, for example, his or her true name, but would not reveal that he or she is affiliated with the lawyer or the true purpose for which he or she is seeking access, namely, to provide the information posted on the pages to a lawyer for possible use antagonistic to the witness. If the witness allows access, the third person would then provide the information posted on the pages to the inquirer who would evaluate it for possible use in the litigation.

(continued)

The inquirer asks the Committee's view as to whether the proposed course of conduct is permissible under the Rules of Professional Conduct, and whether he may use the information obtained from the pages if access is allowed. Several Pennsylvania Rules of Professional Conduct (the "Rules") are implicated in this inquiry.

Rule 5.3. Responsibilities Regarding Nonlawyer Assistants provides in part that,

With respect to a nonlawyer employed or retained by or associated with a lawyer: . . .

(c) a lawyer shall be responsible for conduct of such a person that would be a violation of the Rules of Professional Conduct if engaged in by a lawyer if:

(1) the lawyer orders or, with the knowledge of the specific conduct, ratifies the conduct involved; . . .

Since the proposed course of conduct involves a third person, the first issue that must be addressed is the degree to which the lawyer is responsible under the Rules for the conduct of that third person. The fact that the actual interaction with the witness would be undertaken by a third party who, the Committee assumes, is not a lawyer does not insulate the inquirer from ethical responsibility for the conduct.

The Committee cannot say that the lawyer is literally "ordering" the conduct that would be done by the third person. That might depend on whether the inquirer's relationship with the third person is such that he might require such conduct. But the inquirer plainly is procuring the conduct, and, if it were undertaken, would be ratifying it with full knowledge of its propriety or lack thereof, as evidenced by the fact that he wisely is seeking guidance from this Committee. Therefore, he is responsible for the conduct under the Rules even if he is not himself engaging in the actual conduct that may violate a rule. . . .

Rule 8.4 [on] misconduct provides in part that, "It is professional misconduct for a lawyer to (a) violate or attempt to violate the Rules of Professional Conduct, knowingly assist or induce another to do so, or do so through the acts of another; . . . (c) engage in conduct involving dishonesty, fraud, deceit or misrepresentation. . . ."

Turning to the ethical substance of the inquiry, the Committee believes that the proposed course of conduct contemplated by the inquirer would violate Rule 8.4(c) because the planned communication by the third party with the witness is deceptive. It omits a highly material fact, namely, that the third party who asks to be allowed access to the witness's pages is doing so only because he or she is intent on obtaining information and sharing it with a lawyer for use in a lawsuit to impeach the testimony of the witness. The omission would purposefully conceal that fact from the witness for the purpose of inducing the witness to allow access, when she may not do so if she knew the third person was associated with the inquirer and the true purpose of the access was to obtain information for the purpose of impeaching her testimony.

The fact that the inquirer asserts he does not know if the witness would permit access to him if he simply asked in forthright

fashion does not remove the deception. The inquirer could test that by simply asking the witness forthrightly for access. That would not be deceptive and would of course be permissible. Plainly, the reason for not doing so is that the inquirer is not sure that she will allow access and wants to adopt an approach that will deal with her possible refusal by deceiving her from the outset. In short, in the Committee's view, the possibility that the deception might not be necessary to obtain access does not excuse it.

The possibility or even the certainty that the witness would permit access to her pages to a person not associated with the inquirer who provided no more identifying information than would be provided by the third person associated with the lawyer does not change the Committee's conclusion. Even if, by allowing virtually all would-be "friends" onto her Facebook and MySpace pages, the witness is exposing herself to risks like that in this case, excusing the deceit on that basis would be improper. Deception is deception, regardless of the victim's wariness in her interactions on the Internet and susceptibility to being deceived. The fact that access to the pages may readily be obtained by others who either are or are not deceiving the witness, and that the witness is perhaps insufficiently wary of deceit by unknown Internet users, does not mean that deception at the direction of the inquirer is ethical.

The inquirer has suggested that his proposed conduct is similar to the common—and ethical—practice of videotaping the public conduct of a plaintiff in a personal injury case to show that he or she is capable of performing physical acts he claims his injury prevents. The Committee disagrees. In the video situation, the videographer simply follows the subject and films him as he presents himself to the public. The videographer does not have to ask to enter a private area to make the video. If he did, then similar issues would be confronted, as for example, if the videographer took a hidden camera and gained access to the inside of a house to make a video by presenting himself as a utility worker.

Rule 4.1 (Truthfulness in Statements to Others) provides in part that, "In the course of representing a client a lawyer shall not knowingly (a) make a false statement of material fact or law to a third person; . . ." The Committee believes that in addition to violating Rule 8.4c, the proposed conduct constitutes the making of a false statement of material fact to the witness and therefore violates Rule 4.1 as well. Furthermore, since the violative conduct would be done through the acts of another third party, this would also be a violation of Rule 8.4a.

The Committee is aware that there is controversy regarding the ethical propriety of a lawyer engaging in certain kinds of investigative conduct that might be thought to be deceitful. For example, the New York Lawyers' Association Committee on Professional Ethics, in its Formal Opinion No. 737 (May, 2007), approved the use of deception, but limited such use to investigation of civil right or intellectual property right violations where the lawyer believes a violation is taking place or is imminent, other means are not available to obtain evidence, and rights of third parties are not violated.

(continued)

ETHICS OPINION (continued)

Elsewhere, some states have seemingly endorsed the absolute reach of Rule 8.4. In *People v. Pautler*, 47 P. 3d 1175 (Colo. 2002), for example, the Colorado Supreme Court held that no deception whatever is allowed, saying,

> "Even noble motive does not warrant departure from the Rules of Professional Conduct. . . . We reaffirm that members of our profession must adhere to the highest moral and ethical standards. Those standards apply regardless of motive. Purposeful deception by an attorney licensed in our state is intolerable, even when undertaken as a part of attempting to secure the surrender of a murder suspect. . . . Until a sufficiently compelling scenario presents itself and convinces us our interpretation of Colo. RPC 8.4(c) is too rigid, we stand resolute against any suggestion that licensed attorneys in our state may deceive or lie or misrepresent, regardless of their reasons for doing so."

The Oregon Supreme Court in *In Re Gatti*, 8 P3d 966 (Ore 2000), ruled that no deception at all is permissible, by a private or a government lawyer, even rejecting proposed carve-outs for government or civil rights investigations, stating,

> As members of the Bar ourselves—some of whom have prior experience as government lawyers and some of whom have prior experience in private practice—this court is aware that there are circumstances in which misrepresentations, often in the form of false statements of fact by those who investigate violations of the law, are useful means for uncovering unlawful and unfair practices, and that lawyers in both the public and private sectors have relied on such tactics. However, . . . [f]aithful adherence to the wording of [the analog of Pennsylvania's Rule 8.4], and this court's case law does not permit recognition of an exception for any lawyer to engage in dishonesty, fraud, deceit, misrepresentation, or false statements. In our view, this court should not create an exception to the rules by judicial decree."

Following the *Gatti* ruling, Oregon's Rule 8.4 was changed. It now provides:

> [It] shall not be professional misconduct for a lawyer to [engage in] lawful covert activity in the investigation of violations of civil or criminal law or constitutional rights, provided the lawyer's conduct is otherwise in compliance with these Rules of Professional Conduct. "Covert activity," as used in this rule, means an effort to obtain information on unlawful activity through the use of misrepresentations or other subterfuge. 'Covert activity' may be commenced by a lawyer or involve a lawyer as an advisor or supervisor only when the lawyer in good faith believes there is a reasonable possibility that unlawful activity has taken place, is taking place or will take place in the foreseeable future."

Iowa has retained the old Rule 8.4, but adopted a comment interpreting the Rule to permit the kind of exception allowed by Oregon. . . .

The Committee also considered the possibility that the proposed conduct would violate Rule 4.3 (Dealing with Unrepresented person), which provides in part that

(a) In dealing on behalf of a client with a person who is not represented by counsel, a lawyer shall not state or imply that the lawyer is disinterested. . .

(c) When the lawyer knows or reasonably should know that the unrepresented person misunderstands the lawyer's role in the matter the lawyer should make reasonable efforts to correct the misunderstanding.

Since the witness here is unrepresented, this rule addresses the interactions between her and the inquirer. However, the Committee does not believe that this rule is implicated by this proposed course of conduct. Rule 4.3 was intended to deal with situations where the unrepresented person with whom a lawyer is dealing knows he or she is dealing with a lawyer, but is under a misapprehension as to the lawyer's role or lack of disinterestedness. In such settings, the rule obligates the lawyer to insure that unrepresented parties are not misled on those matters. One might argue that the proposed course here would violate this rule because it is designed to induce the unrepresented person to think that the third person with whom she was dealing is not a lawyer at all (or lawyer's representative), let alone the lawyer's role or his lack of disinterestedness. However, the Committee believes that the predominating issue here is the deception discussed above, and that that issue is properly addressed under Rule 8.4.

ASSIGNMENT 2.3

Tom and Gail Owen have been married for twenty years. Gail contacts an attorney to seek advice about a divorce. Gail suspects that Tom is having an affair with Rachel Adams and that there are pictures of Tom and Rachel on Rachel's Facebook page. Gail says that she has tried to access Rachel's Facebook page, but it is restricted to friends and Gail did not want to ask Rachel to allow Gail to friend her. At the conclusion of the attorney's interview with Gail, the attorney asks a paralegal in the office to find out what is on Rachel's Facebook page. Discuss the paralegal's options in completing this assignment. What can the paralegal do ethically and what would be unethical?

FALSE NOTARIZATION

affidavit
A written or printed statement containing facts given under oath by a person (called the *affiant*) before someone with the authority to administer the oath.

Documents must sometimes be notarized in family-law cases. An example is an **affidavit** to be filed in court. Unfortunately, paralegals who are also notaries are sometimes asked by their supervisors to notarize documents that should not be notarized. In fact, when paralegals are sued, the most common reason is false notarization of a signature. A signature should never be notarized unless the notary personally watches the person sign the document. A supervisor who is pressed by deadlines might ask the notary to notarize a document that the client signed earlier without the notary watching the signing. The attorney might say that the attorney saw the signing or that the document is simply one of many minor documents that still require a notary's seal. "The client is out of town and we must file the document by the end of the day today," says the frantic attorney to the paralegal. This pressure should be resisted. False notarization is illegal.

attestation clause
A formal statement stating that a person witnessed another person signing a document or performing other tasks related to the validity of the document.

Closely related to affidavits are **attestation clauses** in documents stating that you saw (witnessed) someone sign the document or perform other tasks related to the validity of the document. Do not sign a clause saying you witnessed something being performed or executed unless you actually did witness it.

SOLICITATION

solicitation
An appeal or request for clients or business. (See glossary for an additional meaning.)

Compare the following two categories of **solicitation**:

1. *In-person, live telephone, or real-time electronic contact.* Solicitation of clients through such contact is unethical if the attorney's goal is to seek fees or other financial benefit ("**pecuniary** gain") unless the contact is (a) with another attorney or (b) with someone with whom the attorney has a family, close personal, or prior professional relationship.

real-time
Occurring now; happening as you are watching; able to respond immediately or within seconds.

2. *Written, recorded, or standard (not **real-time**) electronic contact.* Solicitation of clients through such contact is ethical unless (a) the attorney knows that the prospective client does not want to be solicited, (b) the solicitation involves coercion, duress, or harassment, or (c) the solicitation is untruthful or misleading. (Rule 7.3)

pecuniary
Relating to money. (A pecuniary interest is a financial interest.)

People in family distress are sometimes so distraught that they are not in a position to evaluate their need for legal services. They should not be subjected to pressures from an attorney who shows up wanting to be hired, particularly if the attorney is not a relative, close friend, or has never represented them in the past. Such in-person solicitation of clients is unethical if the attorney has a monetary or other financial goal such as generating fees.

Frank Ellis, Esq., stands outside the office of a marriage counselor and gives a business card to any depressed, angry, or otherwise distraught spouse coming out of the office after a therapy session. The card says that Ellis is an attorney specializing in divorce cases.

ambulance chasing
Approaching accident victims (or others who might have a legal problem or claim of any kind) to encourage them to hire a particular attorney. If the attorney uses someone else to do the soliciting, the latter is called a *runner*. If this other person uses deception or fraud in the solicitation, he or she is sometimes called a *capper* or a *steerer*.

Ellis's method of looking for prospective divorce clients is pejoratively (disparagingly) referred to as **ambulance chasing**. There is no indication that Ellis is related to any of the people coming out of the therapy sessions, nor that he has any prior professional relationship with them, e.g., as former clients. Ellis's goal appears to be strictly monetary (**pecuniary**): finding a source of fees. His conduct is therefore unethical.

Likewise, it would be improper for Ellis to ask his paralegal or other employee to try to "drum up business" by such solicitation.

DOCKET MINING

When a divorce action is filed, the filing becomes a part of the court's docket, which is accessible to the public. In what is called "docket mining," attorneys looking for clients might read the docket for recently filed divorce cases, obtain the names of defendants, and send them letters offering their legal services. (Or, the attorneys will have their paralegals go to court to get these names from the docket.)

Such solicitation is allowed in most states. In a few states, however, it is unethical to send solicitation letters to defendants unless it is clear in the record that the defendant has been served with the divorce papers. A proof-of-service document or notation in the file would demonstrate that this has occurred.

ADVERTISING

An attorney must not engage in false or misleading advertising in the newspaper, on television, on the Internet, or in other media (Rule 7.2). One of the ways in which the public can be misled is by advertising that creates unjustified expectations of the results the attorney will be able to obtain in the case. The following advertisement, for example, would be unethical:

"If you are owed more than $5,000 in child support, we will collect it for you."

UNAUTHORIZED PRACTICE OF LAW (UPL)

There are three major categories of the **unauthorized practice of law (UPL)** that we need to cover:

1. A nonattorney's performance of tasks in a law office without adequate attorney supervision when those tasks are part of the practice of law.

2. Delegating tasks to a nonattorney that only an attorney is authorized to perform.

3. Using or attempting to use legal skills to help resolve a specific person's legal problem when the assistance is provided by someone who does not have a license to practice law and when the kind of assistance provided requires such a license or other authorization.

unauthorized practice of law (UPL)
(1) A nonattorney's performance of tasks in a law office without adequate attorney supervision when those tasks are part of the practice of law. (2) Delegating tasks to a nonattorney that only an attorney is authorized to perform. (3) Using or attempting to use legal skills to help resolve a specific person's legal problem when the assistance is provided by someone who does not have a license to practice law and when the kind of assistance provided requires such a license or other authorization.

INADEQUATE SUPERVISION IN A LAW OFFICE

Attorneys act unethically if they do not properly supervise paralegals. This includes paralegals who are salaried employees of individual attorneys and freelance paralegals who have their own business and perform tasks (often out of their home office) for one or more attorneys around town. The supervision attorneys must give these paralegals (employees or freelance) should include "appropriate instruction" on the ethical rules governing an attorney's conduct (Rule 5.3). Paralegals who function without proper supervision are engaged in the UPL, as the following example illustrates:

Thomas Monroe, Esq., has a busy family-law practice consisting of himself and a part-time secretary who recently quit. He decides to hire Alex Ogden, a paralegal who recently graduated from a paralegal program. Ogden did not take a family-law course in school and has never worked in this area of the law. Monroe gives him the files of all current divorce cases and asks him to read through them to get an idea of the kind of cases the office handles. Since Ogden arrived, Monroe has spent a great deal of time in court. Ogden is often alone in the office. During these times, divorce clients call with questions about their cases.

Ogden takes these calls and answers the questions as best he can, based on whatever information he finds in the files and on his general understanding of family law. Here are examples of questions he has answered:

- *"When is the date of my next hearing?"*
- *"Have you received the appraisal from my husband's lawyer?"*
- *"Can I sue my ex-husband for the slanderous things he has been saying about me to our daughter?"*

Monroe is unethically failing to supervise his paralegal. Indeed, there seems to be almost no supervision at all. An attorney cannot hire a paralegal and then disappear. Employees must be given needed on-the-job training and supervision. According to one expert in a high-volume office, excessive delegation of tasks without supervision can be a serious problem, "[e]specially in the domestic relations area, where paralegals are extensively utilized. . . . I have seen attorneys allow their paralegals to do all of the client's work except for court appearances. There are situations where the client never once met or talked to an attorney."[10] The potential for ethical violations and legal-malpractice claims in such offices is high.

One of the dangers of having unsupervised employees is that they might give clients *legal advice*, which is a statement or conclusion that applies the law or legal principles to the facts of a particular person's legal problem in an attempt to help resolve that problem. This is unethical even if the advice is correct. The first two examples of questions Ogden answered (on the date of a hearing and the receipt of an appraisal) do not call for legal advice. They are factual questions that do not require the application of law or legal principles to the facts of a particular client's legal problem. The opposite is true of the last example. Ogden would be providing legal advice if he tells a client whether her husband can be sued for slander.

It is appropriate to give someone **legal information**, which is general information about the law or about a client's case that does not constitute legal advice. Although the line between legal advice and legal information is blurry, the core of the distinction must be understood. This following statement is legal information:

- "Our state has specific guidelines on how much child support a parent must pay."

It is a general statement that does not apply the law to the facts of a particular client's case. The following statement, however, is legal advice:

- "Our state guidelines on how much child support a parent must pay entitles you to receive extra support because of your child's disability."

The line is crossed when you cover the specific facts of a specific person's legal problem in an attempt to help resolve the problem.

IMPROPER DELEGATION OF TASKS

There are some tasks that only an attorney can perform. They include representing clients in court, conducting depositions, and giving legal advice. It is the unauthorized practice of law for any nonattorney in the office to engage in such tasks.

SELF-HELP AND THE UPL

We turn now to a different component of the UPL: freelancers who sell self-help services directly to the general public. These freelancers do not work for, and are not supervised by, attorneys. The buyers of self-help services are representing themselves, but they go to freelancers for some assistance in their self-representation effort. The number of self-represented litigants is huge. A recent study concluded that 72 percent of divorce and separation cases involve at least one self-represented party.[11] Some of them seek the assistance of a freelancer who might sell them a do-it-yourself divorce kit containing legal forms that the

legal information
A general statement about the law or about a client's case that does not apply the law or legal principles and hence does not attempt to help resolve a legal problem in the specific facts of a specific person.

freelancer might complete. Freelancers providing such services have different titles, such as paralegal, independent paralegal, or legal document preparer. (In a few states, however, the paralegal title cannot be used if the nonattorney does not have attorney supervision.)

Nonattorneys can sell self-help services so long as they do not mislead anyone into thinking they are attorneys and do not provide legal advice by selecting the forms for a buyer or by helping the buyer fill them out. Providing legal information or generalized legal instructions to the public at large is not legal advice or the practice of law. Do-it-yourself kits for getting a divorce, suing your landlord, and incorporating a business, etc., are illegal only when legal advice is provided along with the kits. Buyers must make their own decisions on which forms to use and how to use them. When the nonattorney fills out the forms, the language used on them must come exclusively from the client.

Some traditional attorneys are worried by the large number of nonattorneys who are providing these services. A management seminar of the American Bar Association on "nonlegal vendors" commented on the "shrinking legal monopolies" once enjoyed by the legal profession. "There's been a permanent shift to self-representation in the majority of divorce proceedings in states such as California" where "increased competition from nonlawyer entities" have "blurred distinctions between legal and nonlegal work."[12]

practice of law
Using or attempting to use legal skills to help resolve a specific person's legal problem when the assistance requires a license to practice law or other authorization.

Interactive Computer Programs

Courts have struggled with interactive Internet programs (e.g., www.complete-case.com) that are designed to help individuals engage in many legal activities such as drafting pleadings for their uncontested divorce. The question-and-answer format of these programs allows documents to be selected and prepared in response to the specific facts typed in by the users. Some courts have said that these online programs are the equivalent of providing personal assistance on a person's specific legal problem and hence is the practice of law.

Most courts, however, disagree by concluding that the website is nothing more than the equivalent of a more detailed, user-friendly how-to-do-it book or kit. Do-it-yourself-divorce sites are careful to point out that they cannot give legal advice. They make referrals to attorneys whenever a standard question cannot be answered by standardized answers. If, however, the site has human interaction with the user by making corrections and suggestions based on the answers provided by the user, there is a danger that a court will rule that the program is more than a mere self-help service and that the human interaction turns the transaction into the UPL.

As expected, many traditional attorneys are hostile toward computer-driven self-help services. A well-known family-law attorney argues that they delude and exploit people. "It's like the sick person who calls the doctor and the doctor says 'cough on the phone, I'll tell you what's wrong with you.'"[13]

Assisting in the UPL

Sometimes a nonattorney who sells law-related kits or other legal material will hire an attorney to help them prepare or implement the kits or materials without having the attorneys provide day-to-day supervision.

> Sam Grondon is a nonattorney who sells Do-It-Yourself Divorce Kits. A kit contains all the forms for a divorce in the state, plus written instructions on how to use the forms. Paula Unger, a local attorney, wrote the kit and obtains a royalty from Sam on every sale. She never talks to any buyers of the kits. Most customers make their purchase on the Internet without talking to Sam. A few customers go to Sam's house to buy the kits. Occasionally, Sam will answer questions to help these buyers decide which forms they need to file and how to fill them out. If he does not know the answer, he calls Paula for help.

It is unethical for an attorney to aid a nonattorney in the UPL (Rule 5.5). Has Paula done this? Yes, but only with respect to the customers who come to Sam's home and receive in-person instruction on selecting and filling out the forms. Such activity is the UPL. By being available on the phone to answer Sam's questions, Paula is assisting Sam's UPL. It is proper for a nonattorney to sell how-to-do-it material and to give written instructions on using the material so long as the instructions are not directed at a particular person. Sam does the latter when he advises some of the buyers on which forms to purchase and helps fill them out. An attorney acts unethically to the extent that he or she is associated with and assists a nonattorney engaged in providing such assistance to particular persons.

ASSIGNMENT   2.4

You are a paralegal working at the law office of David Smith, Esq. Your first assignment is to draft a divorce petition for the case of *Harris v. Harris*, which is to be heard the next day. Your office represents Elaine Harris in her divorce action against her husband, Paul Harris. You never took family law in school. After Smith gives you this assignment, he leaves for the day and asks you to bring the petition to him in court tomorrow. You do the best you can. On your way to court, you see a woman crying on the steps of the court. As you pass by, you give her one of Smith's business cards and tell her that she may want to contact Smith if she has any family legal problems. Inside the building, you see a man standing alone next to a phone booth. He looks like the photo of Paul Harris that is in the file. You ask him if he is Paul Harris, and he says that he is. You tell him that you represent his wife and you ask him if he is going to contest the divorce. After he tells you that his wife is lying about his assets, you walk away. What ethical problems do you see? (See the General Instructions for the Legal Analysis Assignment in Appendix A.)

MY SISTER'S DIVORCE

Most people are fascinated by family law and almost always have a question or two that they would like to ask someone. Once your relatives, friends, neighbors, and acquaintances find out that you work in a family-law office or that you are a freelancer, you will probably become a target of inquiries. Inevitably, while talking to someone in a social gathering, you will find yourself being asked about child support rights or about "my sister's divorce." Be careful. If you answer a legal question about the facts of a particular person's case, you are giving legal advice and may be engaging in the UPL. It makes no difference whether you answer the question correctly or incorrectly. Nor is it relevant that your advice is free. Nonattorneys cannot give legal advice on matters that ultimately require resolution by a court. There are some areas, such as Social Security, where you do not have to be an attorney to answer legal questions. This is rarely true in family law.

It may be awkward for you to decline to answer legal questions, especially when they cover topics on which you may be more knowledgeable than some attorneys. People you know may not appreciate being told that they should consult an attorney for legal questions they ask you. Yet this is the proper response. Do not risk misleading someone and being charged with the UPL. There are many self-help books and Internet sites that provide information about the law. If you are aware of some good ones (see Appendix D for legal sites covering your state), refer people to them. This is quite different from telling someone what laws apply to particular facts. Of course, if you work for an attorney, you can also suggest that the person contact your law office for legal assistance from an attorney.

PARALEGAL ROLES

- For an overview of paralegal roles in family-law cases, see Exhibit 1.5 and Exhibit 1.6 in Chapter 1.
- For financial issues covered in Chapter 2 (e.g., entering into a business transaction with a client), a paralegal may be asked to help collect the documents and facts outlined in:
  - the checklist in Exhibit 3.1 of Chapter 3
  - the interrogatories in Appendix C
- Conflicts Specialists. In larger firms, some paralegals (often called *conflicts specialists*) have specific ethics duties designed to help the office identify possible conflicts of interest. They may carry out these duties full time or in combination with traditional paralegal duties on cases in the office.

EXAMPLES OF DUTIES OF A CONFLICTS SPECIALIST:

- Maintain a database that contains the names of (a) all clients that the office represents or has represented in the past, and (b) all persons who have had significant relationships with such clients, e.g., spouses or ex-spouses of clients (including maiden names, for women), parent and subsidiary corporations of clients, and major business partners and associates of clients.
- For each prospective client, search the conflicts database to determine whether personal, business, or other connections exist between the prospective client and current or past clients.
- If such connections exist, bring them to the attention of the supervising attorney who will determine whether a conflict of interest exists.
- When a new attorney or paralegal is about to be hired, examine a list of cases the attorney or paralegal worked on in prior jobs and identify possible conflicts between (a) parties on this case list and (b) current and former clients of the new office where the attorney or paralegal is being considered for employment. Bring all possible conflicts to the attention of the supervising attorney.

SUMMARY

Ethics are rules or standards of behavior to which members of an occupation, profession, or other organization are expected to conform. Ethical duties arise when an attorney-client relationship is formed, which sometimes can occur without the attorney intending to form such a relationship, particularly on the Internet. The standard of conduct required of attorneys is that they must use the knowledge and skill commonly applied under similar circumstances by attorneys in good standing in the same area of practice. Some unethical incompetence can be the basis of a legal-malpractice action if the client can prove actual harm. It is ethical to provide limited-scope representation (including collaborative law) if the client understands and consents to the limited scope of the services. It is unethical for an attorney to charge an unreasonable fee or to charge a contingent fee if the fee is dependent on securing a divorce, the amount of alimony or support obtained, or the amount of property settlement in lieu of alimony or support. It is unethical to share part of a particular client fee with a nonattorney. Paralegal fees are collected for the nonclerical work of a paralegal. An attorney cannot give something of value to someone for a client referral. Attorneys must avoid dilatory tactics that cause unwarranted delay. All information pertaining to a case must be kept confidential. There are exceptions, however, such as when the attorney reasonably believes the disclosure is necessary to prevent reasonably certain death or substantial bodily harm.

Conflicts of interest must be avoided in situations involving multiple representation, representing someone in opposition to a person who was once a client, job switches, multiple family members contacting the attorney, business transactions with a client, gifts from a client, loans to a client, romantic relationships with a client, and bias because of personal preferences and belief systems. Attorneys have an ethical duty to safeguard client property such as by not commingling client and office funds. Under the anticontact rule, an office cannot contact an opposing party without permission of the latter's attorney. Unrepresented parties must not be led to believe that the office is disinterested. In some cases, an attorney must withdraw from a case; in others, attorneys have the option to withdraw. The attorney must not knowingly make false statements to a tribunal; offer false evidence; or engage in any conduct involving dishonesty, fraud, or misrepresentation (including the use of deception to obtain information on social media). Some forms of solicitation are improper such as through in-person contact with strangers in order to generate fees. Advertising must be truthful. An attorney has an ethical obligation to give proper supervision to paralegals. Nonattorneys offering self-help engage in the unauthorized practice of law if they give legal advice to their clients in cases that require a license to practice law or other authorization. Attorneys must not aid nonattorneys in the unauthorized practice of law.

KEY TERMS

ethics	respondeat superior	imputed disqualification
metadata	scope of employment	tainted
encrypt	bundled legal services	presumption
conflict of interest	unbundled legal services	irrebuttable presumption
conflicts check	collaborative law	rebuttable presumption
competent	mediation	Chinese Wall
continuing legal education (CLE)	alternative dispute resolution (ADR)	adversary system
pro se	informed consent	bias
disinterested	contingent fee	anticontact rule
legal advice	public policy	deposition
commingling	arrearages	adverse
insider trading	fee-splitting	impeach
subpoena	paralegal fees	implicate
process	dilatory	affidavit
meritorious	confidential	attestation clause
letter of nonengagement	attorney-client privilege	solicitation
statute of limitations	work-product rule	real-time
time-barred	multiple representation	pecuniary
retainer	adverse interests	ambulance chasing
uncontested	contested	unauthorized practice of law (UPL)
e-discovery	friendly divorce	legal information
spoliation	adversary	practice of law
legal malpractice	materially (material)	

CHECK THE CITE

In the divorce case of Norman Mailer ("a writer of substantial acclaim"), his wife made a motion to disqualify Norman's attorney. What was the reason for the motion? How did the appellate court rule on the motion? *Mailer v. Mailer*, 390 Mass. 371, 455 N.E.2d 1211 (1983). To read the opinion online: (1) Run a citation search ("455 N.E.2d 1211") in the *Case law* database of Google Scholar (scholar.google .com). (2) Run a citation search ("455 N.E.2d 1211") or a case name and state search ("Mailer v. Mailer" Massachusetts) in the general search engines of Google, Bing, or Yahoo.

PROJECTS

Project 2.1

In Google, Bing, or Yahoo, run the following search: aa "collaborative law" (substitute the name of your state for aa in the search). Write a short essay in which you compare at least two collaborative law offices in your state. Describe how these offices operate. In what ways are they similar and different in how they pursue the goals of collaborative law?

Project 2.2

Ted is a paralegal who works for Edward Davis, Esq. Davis has a caseload of more than one hundred divorces. Ted feels overwhelmed because he constantly receives calls from clients asking him legal questions and wanting to know the status of their cases. Davis is almost always in court and hence is not available to supervise Ted. Examine the three ethical codes of the major national associations of paralegals and legal assistants. Quote rules and guidelines from these codes that might be relevant to potential ethical problems in the Davis office. The three codes are:

- National Association of Legal Assistants, *NALA Code of Ethics And Professional Responsibility* (www.nala .org) (enter "code of ethics" in the search box)

- National Federation of Paralegal Associations, *Model Code of Ethics and Professional Responsibility and Guidelines for Enforcement* (www.paralegals.org) (Under "Positions & Issues" click "Ethics")

- NALS The Association for Legal Professionals, *NALS Code of Ethics & Professional Responsibility* (www.nals .org/page/history)

WRITING SAMPLE

Write a memo to your supervisor on the ethical obligations in your state of an attorney whose client is charged with domestic violence against his spouse and children. The client confides to the attorney that the charge of domestic violence is true but that he wants to deny it in court. The client said to the attorney, "I'm telling you the truth because I know you'd never tell anyone." In Google, Bing, or Yahoo, run this search: aa "domestic violence" (for aa substitute the name of your state). Also run searches such as: "ethical responsibilities of an attorney who represents a spouse suspected of domestic violence" (without the quotation marks). For more leads, run this search in the *Articles* database of Google Scholar (scholar.google.com): aa ethics attorney "domestic violence" (for aa, substitute the name of your state). Try to find relevant sources such as your state code of ethics, opinions of state courts and bar associations in your state, the American Bar Association's *Model Rules,* and ethics opinions from other states. (See General Instructions for the Writing Sample in Appendix A.)

REVIEW QUESTIONS

1. What are ethics?
2. Why are many family-law attorneys charged with unethical conduct?
3. What is the *Model Rules of Professional Conduct* and is it binding?
4. What are the main ethical guidelines for paralegals in a family-law practice?
5. How are most attorney-client relationships created?
6. How can an attorney-client relationship be entered into without the attorney intending to form such a relationship?
7. How is it possible to create an attorney-client relationship through website interaction?
8. What is the standard of attorney competence? What is digital competence?
9. What steps can attorneys take to increase the competence of their paralegals?
10. How can an attorney avoid giving a guarantee to a client?
11. What is the relationship between ethical incompetence and legal malpractice?
12. What are the three major errors committed by family-law attorneys that have led to legal-malpractice suits?
13. What role can paralegals play in avoiding errors based on communication problems?
14. What is the distinction between bundled and unbundled legal services?
15. What is limited-scope representation and when is it ethical for an attorney to provide it?
16. What is collaborative law and when is it ethical to practice it?
17. How is a reasonable fee determined?
18. Are contingent fees allowed in family-law cases?
19. What is fee-splitting?
20. When will a court grant paralegal fees in a family-law case?
21. Can an attorney pay for client referrals?
22. What is the attorney's ethical duty regarding diligence and delay?
23. What is confidential information?
24. When is it ethical for an attorney to divulge confidential information?
25. What is a conflict of interest?
26. When is multiple representation ethical?
27. When is consent needed to represent a client against a former client?
28. What is imputed disqualification?
29. How does a court determine if an office should be disqualified because of a paralegal's prior employment?
30. When is it ethical for attorneys to enter into a business transaction with their clients?
31. When is taking a gift from a client a conflict of interest?
32. When is a loan to a client ethical?
33. Is it unethical for an attorney to have a sexual relationship with a client?
34. What is unethical commingling of funds?
35. What is the anticontact rule?
36. When must an attorney withdraw from a case and when is withdrawal at the option of the attorney?
37. What is the attorney's duty on truthfulness and disclosure of adverse authority?

38. In what ways can it be unethical to obtain information from online social networks?

39. Give an example of false notarization.

40. When is solicitation ethical and unethical?

41. In what ways can advertising be unethical?

42. What is a consequence of failing to provide proper supervision of paralegals?

43. When do nonattorneys offering self-help services to the public without attorney supervision engage in the unauthorized practice of law (UPL)?

HELPFUL WEBSITES

Ethical Rules in Your State

- www.sunethics.com/state-and-national-ethics-resources-home.html
- www.law.cornell.edu/ethics/listing.html

Guides to Legal Ethics on the Internet

- guides.ll.georgetown.edu/legal_ethics
- www.hg.org/practic.html
- www.washlaw.edu/subject/ethics.html
- web.law.duke.edu/lib/researchguides/legale
- paralegal-ethics.blogspot.com
- www.freivogelonconflicts.com

ABA *Model Rules of Professional Conduct*

- www.americanbar.org (enter *model rules* in the search box)

Ethics Opinions

- guides.ll.georgetown.edu/legal_ethics
- www.paralegalethics.net/site/index.htm

Bounds of Advocacy of the American Academy of Matrimonial Lawyers

- familylawfla.org/wp-content/uploads/2015/12/Family-Law-Bounds-of-advocacy.pdf

International Academy of Collaborative Professionals

- www.collaborativepractice.com

A Basic Guide for Paralegals: Ethics, Confidentiality, and Privilege

- www.cfpainc.com/images/Paralegal_Guide-Ethics.pdf
- www.cfpainc.com/legalethics.html

Google Scholar

(scholar.google.com)

- Choose "Articles" and enter in the search box any of the key terms discussed in the chapter. Add the name of your state to the search term.
- Choose "Case law" and "Select courts". Select your state, click "Done", and enter in the search box any of the key terms discussed in the chapter. Add the name of your state to the search term.

Google, Bing, or Yahoo

(on these search engines, run the following searches, substituting your state for "aa")

- attorney ethics aa
- paralegal ethics aa
- family law ethics aa
- solicitation attorney aa
- confidentiality attorney aa
- Chinese Wall attorney aa
- collaborative law aa
- attorney fees aa
- conflict of interest attorney aa
- unauthorized practice of law aa
- legal malpractice aa

YouTube

Run the same searches on YouTube listed above for Google, Bing, Yahoo searches. Although the video clips may be trying to entice you to retain an attorney, buy a book, or enroll in a course, they can provide useful overviews and references to primary authority.

Twitter, Reddit, and Facebook

On Twitter, Reddit, and Facebook, run the following searches (substitute your state for *aa*; run the searches with and without the name of your state). Look for links to family-law developments in your state.

- attorney ethics aa
- unauthorized practice of law aa

ENDNOTES

1 *Report: Lawyer Discipline, Washington State Bar News* 37 (Aug. 1993).

2 Kathleen Hogan, *Not-So-Innocent Bystanders*, 33 Family Advocate 4 (Fall 2010).

3 American Bar Association Standing Committee on Ethics and Professional Responsibility, *Formal Opinion 10-457* (August 5, 2010) (www.americanbar.org) (enter *model rules* in the search box).

4 Dan Pinnington, *Family Law: Increasingly a Risky Business* (American Bar Association, Law Practice Today, July 2005).

5 American Bar Association Standing Committee on Ethics and Professional Responsibility, *Formal Opinion 07-447* (August 9, 2007).

6 Ethics Committee of the Colorado Bar Association, *Ethics Opinion 115* (February 24, 2007).

7 American Bar Association, *Model Rules of Professional Conduct*, Rule 1.5, Comment 6.

8 Rule 4-8.4(i), *Florida Rules of Professional Conduct* (2002).

9 *New York Lawyer's Code of Professional Responsibility*, Ethical Consideration 2–39 (formerly 2-30) (2005).

10 Stacey Hunt, *Attorney Supervision of Paralegals*, Recap 10 (California Alliance of Paralegal Associations, Fall 1998).

11 National Center for State Courts, *Family Justice Initiative: The Landscape of Domestic Relations Cases in State Courts* ii (2018).

12 Rachael Zahorsky, *As Nonlawyer Vendors, Would-Be Clients Take on More Legal Tasks, How Can Practitioners Get Ahead?* (www.ABAJournal.com) (August 5, 2011).

13 Dee McAree, *Online Divorce Services Spark Debate*, National Law Journal (July 22, 2003).

CHAPTER 3

Compiling a Family History

CHAPTER OUTLINE

CHAPTER OBJECTIVES

After completing this chapter, you should be able to:

- Recognize when a family history is needed in a family-law case.

- Understand the reasons a client is not always sure what he or she wants.

- Know the major guidelines for interviewing clients in a family-law case.

- List the major documents that the family-law office often needs to collect.

- Know the kinds of information that should be obtained to identify a possible conflict of interest.

- Identify the emergency concerns that may need to be addressed immediately.

- Know the facts that need to be obtained about the marriage, the children, prior marriages, contracts about the marriage, expenses, insurance, family assets and debts, and business assets and debts.

- Identify some of the major roles of paralegals in the compilation of a family history.

INTRODUCTION

Many family-law clients go through life-changing events. Competent representation of such clients can require an enormous amount of fact gathering, particularly when there are **contested** legal issues, complex factual disputes, relatively large sums of property, and suspected hiding of assets.

contested
Challenged; opposed or disputed.

Often, the family-law office must compile the equivalent of a life history of the client and the client's family. This history can have social, psychological, spiritual, and financial dimensions—each of which can involve numerous detailed facts. In this chapter, we introduce some of the essential factual building blocks for compiling this history through interviewing and investigation.

Attorneys frequently ask new clients to fill out a lengthy questionnaire on their married life, including relevant events before the marriage and after the separation. Some clients might be asked to write a detailed narrative that describes major events of the marriage, including the following:

- Wrongs or improprieties committed by both spouses.
- Strengths and weaknesses of each as a marital partner and as a parent.
- Changes in each spouse's standard of living before and during the marriage.
- Major purchases before and during the marriage.
- Contributions each spouse made to the raising of the children.
- Circumstances of separations.

In addition, of course, there is an extended interview early in the case and a series of follow-up interviews on different aspects of the case as it unfolds.

Before we begin our introduction to comprehensive fact gathering, we will explore some sensitive dimensions of legal interviewing in a family-law practice.

WHAT DOES THE CLIENT WANT?

Recently, a veteran family-law paralegal was asked what her greatest challenges were in this specialty. She responded as follows:

We see the best in people, the worst, and everything in between. Different clients need different levels and types of support from their legal team. Sometimes it takes several interactions with a client and some wrong turns to figure out their needs and expectations.[1]

Another family-law paralegal cautions that many clients come into an office with "unrealistic perceptions." Often, a client's "ideas of separation, divorce, and child custody may be shaped by television, tabloids, and well-meaning acquaintances," which results, unfortunately, in "common misunderstandings" about our legal system.[2]

Sometimes, prospective clients will tell the attorney that they are struggling in their marriage and thinking about divorce. One divorce attorney noted that such clients are known as "tire kickers":

They come in and say, "Look, I'm not ready to get divorced, but things aren't as good as I thought they'd be and I'm thinking about it." The first thing I try to do is educate people about their rights and obligations when it comes to marriage.[3]

A number of assumptions can be made about many clients with family-law problems, particularly clients who have never encountered lawyers and the legal system in any significant way:

- They are not sure what they want.
- They change their minds about what they want.
- Their understanding of legal and nonlegal options is incomplete and often incorrect.

- The legal problem they convey to the office staff involves other legal problems they are not aware of—even the office may be unaware of all of them at the outset.

Suppose that a client, Jane Dodson, walks into the office and tells the attorney, "I want a divorce." The following are observations that *might* be possible about Jane:

- Jane has an incomplete understanding of what a divorce entails.

- Jane says she wants a divorce because she thinks this is the only legal remedy available to solve her problem. If the client knew that other remedies existed (e.g., annulment, judicial separation, a support order, or a restraining order), she would consider these options.

- What really troubles Jane is that her husband beats the children. A divorce is the only way she thinks she can stop it.

- Jane does not want a divorce. She is being pressured by her husband to institute divorce proceedings. He has threatened her with violence if she refuses.

- If Jane knew that marriage or family counseling was available, she would consider using it before taking the drastic step of going to a law office for a divorce.

If any of these observations is correct, think of how damaging it would be for someone in the law office to take out the standard divorce forms and start filling them out immediately after Jane says that she wants a divorce.

This response would not be appropriate until an attorney first probes beneath the statement to determine what, in fact, the client seeks to accomplish. The danger exists that Jane might be steered in the direction of a divorce because no other options are presented to her. No one takes the time to help Jane express the ideas, intentions, and desires that are lurking beneath the seemingly clear statement, "I want a divorce."

This is not to say that the office must psychoanalyze every client or that it must always distrust what the client initially says. It is rather an acknowledgement of the fact that *most people are confused about the law and make requests based upon misinformation as to what courses of action are available to solve problems.* Furthermore, a client's ability to communicate may be substantially limited because of the emotional crisis that prompted the office visit. Common sense tells us to avoid taking all statements at face value. An important part of an attorney's obligation, therefore, is to present options for the client to consider. Clients may not know what they want until all of the options are carefully explained.

Here is how a family-law attorney handles initial contacts with potential clients contemplating a divorce:

> *The first thing I try to do is educate people about their rights and obligations when it comes to marriage. Marriage is the most legally significant thing you will do, other than dying. It changes your property ownership rights. It changes your obligations when it comes to support. It changes all kinds of legal rights. You don't even get a pamphlet when you get married that explains it all to you. You don't get a one-page document that says, "By the way,"*
>
> ○ *your inheritance rates have automatically changed,*
> ○ *your ability to select a beneficiary for your life insurance policy has just changed,*
> ○ *your ability to hold property in your sole name just changed.*
>
> *The first thing I do anytime anyone comes to my office, wherever they're at in their marriage, is I just try to get them up to speed on what they're already involved in. Then, as a divorce lawyer who sincerely tries to be ethical, I talk to people about steps they might take to avoid the worst-case scenario. I suggest counseling or therapy and I'll offer referrals. I try to make sure that they've exhausted all their options before making this final decision.[4]*

ASSIGNMENT 3.1

For each of the following statements made by a client, what areas do you think would be reasonable to probe to determine if the statement is an accurate reflection of what the client wants? What misunderstandings do you think the client might have? What further questions would you ask to be sure that you have identified what the client wants?

a. "I want to commit my husband to a mental institution."

b. "I want to put my baby daughter up for adoption."

(See General Instructions for the Interview Assignment in Appendix A. You can ignore Instruction 5.)

INTERVIEWING GUIDELINES

This section outlines additional sensitivity guidelines for conducting a client interview in a family-law case. Often, a paralegal will conduct a follow-up client interview, which occurs after the attorney has discussed fees, accepted the case, explained major options, provided preliminary legal advice, and obtained the basic facts. Here are guidelines for conducting a follow-up client interview in which the paralegal's assignment is to compile s family history:

1. The interview's primary objective is to establish a relationship of confidence and trust with the client. Initial contacts can be crucial. All aspects of highly sensitive information must be explored as the office compiles a family history. The client needs to feel that he or she is working with a competent professional who treats the case as extremely important and who is keenly sensitive to the myriad possible predicaments, embarrassments, defeats, angers, and frustrations that can be part of the client's narrative.

2. Set aside an adequate amount of time to conduct the interview. You do not want to be rushed. Try to avoid taking phone calls during the interview. Do not hold or look at any electronic devices during the interview, even if the client decides to use such devices he or she has brought.

3. Dress conservatively and professionally.

4. Clear away open files and papers of other clients from your desk and the general interview area. You do not want to violate client confidentiality by allowing a stranger to see anything in their files. Confidentiality is another reason to avoid taking calls during the interview. A client in the office should not be able to hear you discuss the cases of other clients on the phone. For the same reason, you should never tell the client about other named cases in the office (past or present).

5. Make sure the client is comfortable. Offer the client a cup of coffee or a bottle of water. Have a supply of tissues available.

6. At the beginning of the interview, give the client your business card that states your name, title, business address, email address, and phone number. Repeat your name even if you provided it at an earlier date when you first met the client. You should assume that clients will not remember the names of everyone they meet in the law office.

7. Make sure the client knows you are not an attorney. It is usually not enough to tell the client that you are a "paralegal" or a "legal assistant." In addition to stating your title, use the word "nonattorney" or the phrase "I am not an attorney," so that there will be no misunderstanding. Also point out that you will be working closely with the attorney handling the case.

8. Prepare the client for what will happen during the interview. Explain that you may need to meet with the client more than once. Let the client know you will be taking detailed notes because you consider everything the client says about the case to be important and you want to obtain an accurate account of the case.

9. Maintain eye contact as much as possible even though you are taking notes.

10. Use great sensitivity in obtaining facts from the client. You will be hearing highly personal facts about the client's life. Think of how you would feel if you were revealing such facts about yourself to a stranger. Think of how you would want this other person to react to what you are revealing. At such a vulnerable time, clients need understanding and compassion. (For a discussion of the sensitivity required when interviewing a woman who has been a victim of domestic violence, see Exhibit 12.3 in Chapter 12.)

11. Listen attentively. The best way to build rapport with a client is to demonstrate that you are listening to everything the client is saying. A useful technique of attentive listening is to repeat back a portion of what the client has just told you. Not only does this technique tend to assure the client that you have been listening, it can often trigger the client's memory into providing more detail or further explanation. Another active-listening technique is to refer back to something the client said earlier and to use this reference as the basis of a new or follow-up question (e.g., "Earlier, you said that you rarely used the vacation home. Could you tell me more about the vacation home?").

12. Encourage the client to do most of the talking. If you receive a one-or two-word answer, ask the client to explain the answer in greater detail.

13. Encourage the client to express his or her feelings whenever this might be helpful in obtaining underlying facts (e.g., "How did you feel when your husband told you that your son wanted to live with him?").

14. Interpret the client's body language. Sitting posture, eye contact (or its absence), and facial expressions are nonverbal communications that can indicate levels of trust, interest, and confusion. Be ready to make adjustments in the way you are phrasing or sequencing questions so that you and the client are working together on the same level of clarity and trust. Also, be aware of your own body language. You do not want your gestures or mannerisms to indicate anything other than the highest level of professionalism, attention, and respect.

15. Take your notes in the language of the client. Use quotation marks for important language (e.g., the client said she is "certain the father is unable to raise the children on his own"). Avoid extensive paraphrasing in which you restate what the client said in your own words.

16. Never talk down to or criticize a client.

17. Avoid disparaging comments about the opposing attorney or about the client's spouse.

18. Do not give **legal advice**, which is a statement or conclusion that applies the law or legal principles to the facts of a specific person's legal problem in an attempt to help resolve that problem. If the client asks you a legal question, say that you are not permitted to give legal advice but that you would be glad to bring the question to the attorney's attention. This response is necessary even when you know the answer and even when your good relationship with the client makes it awkward to pull back. The reality, however, is that when you answer a legal question by giving legal advice, you are probably engaging in the **unauthorized practice of law (UPL)**.

legal advice
A statement or conclusion that applies the law or legal principles to the facts of a specific person's legal problem in an attempt to help resolve that problem.

unauthorized practice of law (UPL)
Using or attempting to use legal skills to help resolve a specific person's legal problem when the assistance is provided by someone who does not have a license to practice law and when the kind of assistance provided requires such a license or other authorization. (See the glossary for additional meanings.)

19. Clients may ask you what their chances of success are. The only appropriate answer you can give is that every case is different and that the office will be using its skills and experience to put the best case forward on the client's behalf. Never give a client any reason to believe you think the client will win, even if you do have this belief. An expression of confidence in the outcome of a case might be interpreted as a guarantee. A client may have a breach-of-contract action against the office for failure to deliver what a court later interprets was a promised or guaranteed result.

20. Let the client know how to reach you if he or she thinks of other relevant information after the interview is concluded.

21. Make mental notes on the client's personality. When attorneys decide to take a case, their preliminary assessment is that the office can help the client. Yet there still may be some doubts about whether the relationship between the office and the client will work. When such doubts exist, the attorneys may ask their paralegals to be on the lookout for signs of difficulty. For example, one attorney told his paralegals who would be doing follow-up interviews to "assess the client's personality" and decide whether the office "could work with this person." In addition, beware of potential red flags or danger signals, including the client who demonstrates any of the following characteristics:

- Appears emotionally distraught or vengeful,
- Provides an inconsistent story or avoids answering questions,
- Has unrealistic objectives,
- Suggests use of improper influence or other unethical or illegal conduct,
- Rambles, wanders off the subject, or constantly interrupts you,
- Tells the office "how to run" the case,
- Has already discharged or filed disciplinary complaints against other lawyers,
- Has a personality disorder, or
- Is flirtatious.[5]

In your report or memorandum to your supervisor on the interview, be sure to include your observations and assessments relevant to concerns such as these. They, of course, would never be mentioned to the client.

FAMILY HISTORY CHECKLIST

The inclination of a cautious office is to be thorough about facts. A comprehensive checklist, such as the one presented in Exhibit 3.1, can assist in this objective. The checklist can be used as a guide in conducting client interviews and in investigations that often continue up until the time when the case has been resolved through settlement or litigation.

E-RECORDS

Many of the categories on the checklist refer to records that will be relevant to various issues that can arise in family-law cases. Before the age of computers and the Internet, most of these records were printed on paper. Obviously, this has changed significantly. Although we have by no means seen the end of paper, a great deal of information today consists of electronic records (e-records). Examples include emails, spreadsheets, social media posts, and other digital formats in a variety of databases.

Today's American family is a digital family living in a digital ecosphere that can tell family stories and reveal family secrets better than any after-the-fact human recollection. The volume of a family's household data now rivals that of a small business. Simply put, family members do not just use some digital tools, they live digitally: email, Facebook, Twitter, instant messaging, texting. Young people today were "born digital." . . . The family's financial records will be stored electronically. Banking, investments, retirement accounts, and profit-sharing plans will likely be managed electronically from home computers. Emails abound from the school organizations, college networks, neighborhood associations, and sports teams. Employer-owned laptops brought home for doing work in the evenings also may contain these personal records.[6]

It is important, therefore, during initial client interviews to find out (1) what computers all family members have access to, (2) what cell phones and other digital devices they have, (3) what email programs they use, and (4) what interactive websites and social networks they regularly use by uploading photos and posting other data about themselves and their special interests.

electronic data discovery (EDD)
The discovery of data found in emails, spreadsheets, databases, texts, social-media posts, and other digital formats. Also called *e-discovery.*

Yet even comprehensive client interviews may not reveal all of this digital information. **Electronic data discovery (EDD)** (sometimes called *e-discovery*) during the pretrial discovery stage of litigation will often be crucial in uncovering relevant facts and records. E-discovery experts may be needed to locate the assets of spouses who use elaborate stratagems to conceal what they own or control.

When a wealthy businessman sets out to divorce his wife, his fortune may appear to vanish. The quest to find it might reveal an offshore financial system bigger than the U.S. economy. [Some spouses have] become astonishingly effective at "offshoring" wealth—detaching assets, through complex layers of ownership and legal planning, from their actual owners, often by hiding them in another country. Created by lawyers, accountants and private bankers and operating out of a global archipelago of European principalities, former British colonies and Asian city-states, the [strategies have] one main purpose: to make the richest people in the world appear to own as little as possible.[7]

The starting point in complex cases, and in relatively simple cases, is what the client knows and what he or she is able to find in the categories listed in the checklist outlined in Exhibit 3.1.[8] Once the attorney gathers the most critical information at the time the case is accepted, paralegals might be asked to help assemble the myriad of details outlined in the checklist.

A checklist, of course, is no more than a point of departure. Effective interviewers are willing to add questions to a checklist, even if they do not appear to be directly on point. Relevant facts have a way of materializing from seemingly irrelevant lines of inquiry. Sometimes, you do not know what you are looking for until you find it.

EXHIBIT 3.1   Checklist for Compiling a Family History

Table of Contents

 1. Basic Information
 2. Documents the Client Should Bring to a Law Office
 3. Conflict-of-Interest Facts
 4. Emergency Concerns
 5. Background
 6. Marital Facts
 7. Prior Contracts
 8. Itemized Expenses
 9. Health Information
10. Wills and Trusts

(continued)

Exhibit 3.1 *(continued)*

11. Rearing and Custody of Children
12. Business Interests
13. Employment History
14. Education
15. Contributions to Career Enhancement
16. Real Property
17. Stocks, Bonds, and Related Accounts
18. Other Personal Property
19. Insurance
20. Miscellaneous Income
21. Claims
22. Frequently Overlooked Assets
23. Liabilities
24. Tax Returns
25. Assets of the Children
26. Professionals Hired or Consulted
27. Next Steps

1. BASIC INFORMATION

- Client's name.
- Street address of residence.
- Email address(es).
- Social Security number.
- Facebook, Instagram, and other social media address(es).
- Phone number at residence.
- Phone number and Web address(es) of business.
- Cell phone number(s).
- Same information for the client's spouse.
- DOM (date of marriage).
- DOS (date of separation).
- How did the client select the law office? Referral?
- Is the spouse represented by an attorney? If so, when was the attorney retained? Who is paying for his or her services? What is the attorney's name, address, phone number, email address, Web address, and fax number?

  - *If the other spouse is represented by an attorney, all contacts with the spouse must be through that attorney. (See the anticontact rule in Chapter 2.)*

2. DOCUMENTS THE CLIENT SHOULD BRING TO A LAW OFFICE

If some of the documents are digital, download them and bring in what you were able to download. Here are the types of documents the client should bring to the office:

- Marriage license.
- Prior divorce or annulment decree with current or other spouse(s).
- Powers of attorney the client and spouse have given each other.
- Premarital agreement.
- Document(s) the client was given prior to signing the premarital agreement.
- Other written agreements between client and spouse entered into before and during the marriage, e.g., child-custody agreements.

(continued)

Exhibit 3.1 *(continued)*

- Federal, state, and local tax returns for the past five years.
- Net worth statements (financial statements) of client, spouse, or business (e.g., financial statement filed when applying for a mortgage or other loan).
- Tax assessments or bills.
- Deeds to property the client or spouse obtained as a gift or that was purchased prior to the marriage.
- Deeds to property the client or spouse obtained as a gift or that was purchased during the marriage.
- Recent pay stubs of the client and spouse.
- Business formation records (e.g., articles of incorporation, partnership agreement, board of director minutes).
- Recent bank statements for all personal and business accounts of the client and spouse.
- Recent securities statements (e.g., mutual fund report).
- Recent statements from pension fund.
- Loan or refinancing applications made by the client or spouse.
- Recent major bills (e.g., mortgage, tuition, rent).
- Credit reports on the client, spouse, or business from TransUnion, Experian, Equifax, or another consumer credit reporting company).
- Wills and codicils (additions) to wills.
- Trusts.
- Medical records of the client on major current ailments.
- Police records, if relevant, to domestic violence committed during the marriage or since the separation.
- Separation agreement the parties have signed or drafts of such an agreement the parties considered.
- Birth certificates of the children.
- Court documents on litigation in which the client, the spouse, or both, were parties.
- Client's résumé.
- Spouse's résumé.

> - If the client does not have any of these documents, ask the client if he or she thinks they exist and, if so, where they might be obtained. For some documents, the client may be asked to sign a form giving the office authorization to obtain a copy of the document.

3. CONFLICT-OF-INTEREST FACTS

- Client's maiden name (if a woman).
- Other names used by the client.
- Has this office ever represented the client before?
- Has this office ever represented any relatives of the client?
- Has this office ever represented any business associates of the client?
- Names of other attorneys the client has contacted about this case.
- Names of attorneys who have represented the client on any other matter in the past.
- Spouse's full name.
- Other names used by the spouse.
- Has this office ever represented the spouse before?
- Has this office ever had any contact with the spouse before?
- Has this office ever represented any relatives of the spouse?
- Has this office ever represented any business associates of the spouse?

> - Before accepting a case, a law office must do a conflicts check to determine whether a conflict of interest would prevent it from representing the prospective client (e.g., because the office once represented an opponent of the prospective client). (See Chapter 2.)
>
> - If a person once contacted the office about the marriage, the office might be prevented from representing that person's spouse even if the person eventually hires another attorney. Some communications with an attorney can create attorney-client obligations regardless of whether the attorney is hired. (See Chapter 2.)

(continued)

Exhibit 3.1 *(continued)*

- Details of any contact the spouse has had with this office in the past (e.g., a general inquiry about a legal matter during the marriage).
- Names of other attorneys who have represented the spouse on any matter in the past.

4. EMERGENCY CONCERNS

- If court proceedings have already been initiated by the client or spouse, what are the next court dates on which the client is required to make an appearance or to file pleadings?
- Does the client think there is a danger the spouse will remove the children out of state?
- Is the spouse abusing the client or the children?
- Does the client think there is a danger the spouse will give away marital assets?
- Does the client think there is a danger the spouse will conceal (hide) marital assets?
- Does the client's spouse know that the client is seeking legal services? If not, is there a danger of a hostile reaction when this becomes known (e.g., domestic violence)?
- While waiting for a court date on the divorce case, do the client and children have immediate support needs?
- Is the client suffering emotional trauma? (If so, the office will provide the client with a referral list of psychologists, other counselors, or support agencies.)
- Do the parties have joint credit cards?
- If such cards are cancelled (to prevent further charges by the spouse), will the client have access to other credit cards?
- Do the parties have other joint accounts at other financial institutions?
- Did the client cosign or guarantee a loan secured by the spouse?
- Is the client or spouse currently pregnant? Due date? What prenatal care is underway?
- If the client, spouse, or children are not citizens, inquire about their immigration status.

5. BACKGROUND

Client

- How long has the client lived at the current address?
- How many consecutive months has the client been a resident of this county?
- Addresses of the most recent three prior residences of the client and the dates at each residence.
- Client's date of birth.
- Client's place of birth.
- Client's race.
- Client's religious affiliation and extent of involvement.
- Client's present occupation and length of time in this field.
- Business address, phone/cell number(s), email address(es), and Web address(es).
- Prior occupations of the client.
- Highest year of school or college completed. Date(s) completed.

Spouse

- Length of time the spouse has lived at current residence.
- Number of consecutive months the spouse has been a resident of this county.
- Addresses of the most recent three prior residences of the spouse and the dates at each residence.
- Spouse's date of birth.

Side notes:

- *Protective orders may be needed if there is a danger of violence or of a change in the status of marital property such as by a spouse selling it or moving it out of the state. (See Chapter 8.)*

- *A motion for temporary support and attorney fees may be needed pending the outcome of the case — pendente lite — while the litigation is going on. (See Chapter 8.)*

- *The client might be advised by the attorney to cancel all joint accounts, apply for an account in his or her own name, and notify lenders to cancel future loans for which the client provided earlier authorization. (See Chapter 8.)*

- *Length of residence may be important to establish the court's in rem jurisdiction (through domicile) and to establish venue. (See Chapter 7.)*

- *Race and religious practices may become relevant in child-custody issues, although custody decisions cannot be based solely on race. (See Chapter 9.)*

(continued)

Exhibit 3.1 *(continued)*

- Spouse's place of birth.
- Spouse's race.
- Spouse's religious affiliation and extent of involvement.
- Spouse's present occupation and length of time in this field.
- Business address of the spouse, phone/cell number(s), email address(es), and Web address(es).
- Prior occupations of the spouse.
- Highest year of school or college completed. Date(s) completed.

6. MARITAL FACTS

Marriage

- Date of current marriage.
- Place where marriage ceremony occurred.
- Date on marriage license.
- Compliance with blood tests (in some states) or other formalities required to obtain the license.
- Name and address of person who performed marriage ceremony.
- Names and addresses of witnesses to the marriage ceremony.
- If doubt exists on whether the parties are married, did they use the same last name while together and did they introduce each other to others as "my husband" and "my wife"?
- At the time of the marriage, did either spouse have a prior marriage that was not ended by divorce or death?
- How old were the client and spouse when they married?
- Are they related to each other by blood (e.g., cousins) or by marriage (e.g., in-laws)?
- Were both able to perform all marital functions (financial, sexual, social, etc.) upon marriage?
- Did both go through the marriage ceremony with the full and free intention to become spouses?
- When the parties went through the marriage ceremony, did either lie about or misrepresent important facts that would have led to a cancellation of the ceremony if the facts were known (e.g., a willingness to have children)?

- *The belief of others on whether the parties are married could be relevant to whether a common law marriage was formed (in states that allow such marriages). (See Chapter 5.)*
- *These questions are relevant to whether grounds for an annulment might exist (e.g., nonage, fraud). (See Chapter 6.)*

Children

- For each child born to the marriage, state his or her full name, date of birth, place of birth, current address, prior address(es), length of time the child has spent at current address and at each prior address, Internet addresses (e.g., Facebook, Instagram, and email), adults with whom the child has lived since birth, past sources of support, current sources of support, and the child's desire and ability to attend college.
- For each child to whom the client or the spouse was an adoptive parent, guardian, or stepparent, state the child's full name, date of birth, place of birth, current address, prior address(es), Internet addresses (e.g., Facebook, Instagram, and email), length of time the child has spent at current address and at each prior address, adults with whom the child has lived since birth, past sources of support, current sources of support, and the child's desire and ability to attend college. Also state the names and addresses of the birth parents and the circumstances of the child's coming into the family.
- Have any of the children been emancipated?

- *A child who is emancipated is legally independent of his or her parent or legal guardian. (See Chapter 14.)*

Prior Marriages

- If the client was married before the current marriage, state the name of each former spouse; his or her current or last known address; the date, place, and circumstances of each marriage; how each marriage was terminated; the names of all children who were born, adopted, or otherwise lived with the family during this marriage; and how these children are (and were) supported.

Exhibit 3.1 *(continued)*

- Same questions if the spouse of the client had a prior marriage or marriages.
- Known sources of support (employment, family business) of former spouses.
- Outstanding debts or obligations owed to or by former spouses, e.g., alimony, child support, property division. Was a court order used to enforce these debts?

Deterioration of Marriage

- Does the client want a divorce? Why or why not?
- Does the client's spouse want a divorce? Why or why not?
- Has the client considered the alternative of a legal separation or annulment?
- When did the marriage start to deteriorate? State the circumstances.
- Length of time the parties have had marital difficulties.
- Date of the most recent sexual intimacy with spouse.
- Has there been domestic violence or the threat of such violence? State the circumstances.
- Are the parties now separated?
- If so, what was the DOS (date of separation), who initiated it, the reason the client thinks the separation occurred, and the reason the spouse thinks the separation occurred.
- Where has each party and the children lived since the DOS? Include the dates.
- How has each party and the children been supported since the DOS?
- Have the parties had other separations in the past?
  - If so, for each separation, state the dates involved, who initiated the separation, the reason the client thinks the separation occurred, the reason the spouse thinks the separation occurred, where each party and the children lived during the separation, how each party and the children were supported during the separation, and the circumstances of the end of the separation leading to a resumption of the marital relationship.
- Does the client think there is a realistic chance of reconciliation? Why or why not?
- Does the spouse think there is a realistic chance of reconciliation? Why or why not?
- Have the parties attempted marital counseling? If so, who initiated each effort and to what extent was the effort successful?
- Who was the marital counselor? Who selected the counselor and how was he or she paid?
- Does either party now want to try marital counseling? Why or why not?

• Because of no-fault divorce, facts on who caused the breakdown of the marriage (marital fault) are generally not relevant to whether a divorce will be granted, but it may be relevant to other issues such as child custody. (See Chapters 7 to 9.)

7. PRIOR CONTRACTS

Premarital Agreement

- Do the parties have a premarital agreement?
- Date that the premarital agreement was signed.
- Names and addresses of the attorneys, if any, who represented either party during the negotiation and drafting of the premarital agreement.
- Other individuals consulted, e.g., accountant, financial planner, business associate, clergy, friend, or relative.
- Describe the nature of the disclosure the spouse gave the client concerning the spouse's financial assets and worth before the client signed the agreement.
- Describe the nature of the disclosure the client gave the spouse concerning the client's financial assets and worth before the spouse signed the agreement.
- What rights did each side waive in the agreement, e.g., right of support?
- Summarize the major provisions in the agreement for the client and for the spouse in the event of a divorce.

• The validity of a premarital agreement may depend, in part, on whether there was adequate disclosure of each other's assets and liabilities prior to signing the premarital agreement. (See Exhibit 4.3 in Chapter 4.)

(continued)

Exhibit 3.1 *(continued)*

- Summarize the major provisions in the agreement for the client and for the spouse upon the death of either during or after the marriage.
- Location of the original agreement.

Separation Agreement

- Have the parties discussed or entered into a separation agreement?
- Date the separation agreement was signed.
- Were the parties already separated when the agreement was signed?
- Names and addresses of the attorneys, if any, who represented either party during the negotiation and drafting of the separation agreement.
- Summarize the major provisions in the agreement on support, child custody, and property division.
- Location of the original agreement.

Other Agreements

- Have the client and spouse entered into employment agreements with each other at a place of business?
- Summarize the major provisions in the agreement.
- Has either spouse lent the other money?
- If so, describe the major terms of the agreement, e.g., interest charged. What is the present status of the loan? What amounts have been repaid?
- Location of the agreements.
- Names and addresses of the attorneys, if any, who represented either party during the negotiation and drafting of the agreement(s).
- Has the spouse ever borrowed money from a relative of the client or entered into any other kind of agreement with a relative? Describe the circumstances and present status of the agreement(s).
- Has the client ever borrowed money from a relative of the spouse or entered into any other kind of agreement with a relative? Describe the circumstances and present status of the agreement(s).

8. ITEMIZED EXPENSES

Where relevant, state whether the expense is for the client only or for the children only. Use monthly figures where appropriate. To obtain a monthly figure for a recurring expense incurred less frequently than monthly, add the total spent for that item for the year and divide by twelve.

- Mortgage (state if payments include taxes and insurance).
- Rent.
- Real property taxes.
- Homeowner association fees.
- Utilities: gas/oil.
- Utilities: electric.
- Utilities: water and sewer.
- Utilities: recycle service.
- Water softener.
- Phones (landline, cell, other).
- Internet service provider.
- Maintenance of house.
- Maintenance of swimming pool.
- Gardener.

(continued)

Exhibit 3.1 *(continued)*

- Groceries.
- Restaurants.
- Clothes: purchase.
- Clothes: maintenance (tailor, laundry, etc.).
- Shoes.
- Maid.
- Cleaning service.
- Baby-sitter.
- Day care center.
- School expenses: tuition.
- School expenses: books and supplies.
- School expenses: tutoring.
- School expenses: transportation.
- School expenses: after-school programs.
- School expenses: miscellaneous.
- Extracurricular lessons: music, dance, sports, theater, etc.
- Equipment maintenance: music, sports, etc.
- Summer camp.
- Visitation expenses when a child visits the noncustodial parent (transportation, phone calls, meals, etc.).
- Car: payments.
- Car: gas.
- Car: maintenance.
- Car: registration.
- Car: tolls.
- Car: automobile club dues.
- Insurance premium: house.
- Insurance premium: car.
- Insurance premium: life.
- Insurance premium: dental.
- Insurance premium: health.
- Insurance premium: disability.
- Insurance premium: umbrella.
- Health costs (not covered by insurance) for medical doctors, dentists, orthodontists, homeopathic/holistic practitioners, prescription and nonprescription drugs, glasses and eye care, and other medical-related costs.
- Hairdresser.
- Haircuts.
- Toiletries and cosmetics.
- Pets: veterinarian.
- Pets: food and supplies.
- Entertainment.
- Cable TV access.
- Vacation.

(continued)

Exhibit 3.1 *(continued)*

- Computer supplies.
- Camera supplies.
- Contributions: church/synagogue.
- Contributions: charities.
- Newspaper/magazine subscriptions.
- Allowance for children.
- Membership: country club.
- Other membership, e.g., YMCA gym.
- Cost of gifts (birthdays, holidays, etc.).
- Payments to IRA or other retirement fund.
- Accountant/tax preparer fees.
- Court-ordered payments of child support or alimony from a prior marriage.
- Miscellaneous expenses.

9. HEALTH INFORMATION

- Current health of client.
- Current health of spouse.
- Current health of children.
- Physical and mental health history of the client (covering periods before marriage, during marriage, and since separation): major problems, names and addresses of treating physicians or counselors, dates of hospitalizations or other major treatments, diagnosis for future, etc.).
- Same questions on the physical and mental health history of spouse.
- Same questions on the physical and mental health history of each child.

- *The health of a party can be relevant to many issues (e.g., future medical expenses, need for alimony, ability to care for a child, capacity to understand agreements signed before and during the marriage). (See Chapters 4, 8, and 9.)*

10. WILLS AND TRUSTS

Wills

- What wills exist? (Client's separate will, spouse's separate will, joint will, etc.). Address the following topics for each will:
  - Date signed/executed.
  - Name and address of attorney who prepared the will.
  - Names and addresses of witnesses.
  - Name and addresses of initial executor and alternate/successor executors.
  - Guardian for minor children, if needed.
  - Primary beneficiaries (who receives what).
  - Remainder beneficiaries.
  - Codicils or amendments (reasons for changes, dates executed, summary of changes).
  - Names and addresses of witnesses.
  - Location of original will and codicils.

Trusts

- Kinds of trusts in existence (testamentary trust, family trust, inter vivos trust, etc.). Address the following topics for each trust:
  - Date signed/executed.
  - Name and address of attorney who prepared the trust.
  - Names and addresses of witnesses.

Exhibit 3.1 *(continued)*

- Names and addresses of initial trustee and alternate/successor trustees.
- Description of assets (principal) in the trust.
- Lifetime beneficiaries.
- Remainder beneficiaries.
- Amendments (reasons for changes, dates executed, summary of changes).
- Location of the original and amendments.

11. REARING AND CUSTODY OF CHILDREN

- Names of natural (birth) children, adopted children, stepchildren, and other children living with client or spouse. Address the following topics for each child:
  - Age.
  - Location of birth certificate.
  - Names and addresses of biological parents.
  - Who should have custody according to the client? (What are the client's views on the options of sole physical custody, joint physical custody, sole legal custody, and joint legal custody?)
  - Who should have custody according to the client's spouse? (What are the spouse's views on the options of sole physical custody, joint physical custody, sole legal custody, and joint legal custody?)
  - Strengths and weaknesses of the client as a parent.
  - Strengths and weaknesses of the spouse as a parent.

  - *All of these topics will be relevant to a court's decision on child custody. (See Chapter 9.)*

- Career responsibilities and goals of the client and how they affect the availability of the client to care for the child.
- Career responsibilities and goals of the spouse and how they affect availability of the spouse to care for the child.
- What relatives of the client in the area are available (and willing) to help the client with child care?
- What relatives of the spouse in the area are available (and willing) to help the spouse with child care?
- What is each child's relationship with other children in the home?
- Does either the client or the spouse expect to move to another area in the future? If so, why, and how will the move affect visitation opportunities of the other parent—the noncustodial parent?
- Court actions or orders to date, e.g., paternity, child support, guardianship, adoption, and juvenile delinquency (include dates, courts and agencies involved, attorneys for parties, reasons court or agency action was initiated, outcomes/decisions of the courts or agencies, major events since).
- Police involvement, e.g., misconduct by child, abuse of child by others (include dates, enforcement agencies involved, reasons police became involved, action taken by police, major events since).
- Same questions for child protective services.
- Religious activities of child: describe the role of each parent in fostering these activities.
- Major school events (teacher conferences, assembly performances, etc.): describe role of each parent in these events.
- Homework (assistance provided, checking for completion, etc.): describe the role of each parent.
- After-school activities at home, at friend's house, at playground (amount of supervision, transportation provided, etc.): describe the role of each parent.
- Sports (transportation provided, attendance at games, etc.): describe the role of each parent.
- Medical and dental appointments: describe the role of each parent.
- Birthdays: describe role of each parent.

  - *All of these factors are relevant to a court's custody decision based on the best interests of the child. (See Chapter 9.)*

(continued)

Exhibit 3.1 *(continued)*

- Vacations: describe role of each parent.
- Discipline at home: describe role of each parent.
- Other major events in child's life: describe the role of each parent.
- Attitude of child toward each parent. Where would child like to live?
- Client's efforts to encourage the child to have a positive or a negative attitude about the spouse.
- Spouse's efforts to encourage the child to have a positive or a negative attitude about the client.
- Child's awareness of the client's romantic relationships with others before and since the separation from the spouse. Impact on the child.
- Child's awareness of the spouse's romantic relationships with others before and since the separation from the client. Impact on the child.
- Third parties who might be witnesses to the home environment, e.g., neighbors, relatives, teachers, day care providers, clergy, counselors, friends.

- *Depending upon the age and maturity of the child, a court will consider his or her wishes on where to live. (See Chapter 9.)*

- *When a child is hostile to one of the parents, some courts consider evidence of parental alienation syndrome. (See Chapter 9.)*

12. BUSINESS INTERESTS

- Business in which the client or spouse had an ownership interest (solely owned by client, solely owned by spouse, jointly owned). Address the following topics for each business:
  - Name of business. Description of its products or services.
  - Address, phone, email, website.
  - Legal status of business (partnership, corporation, limited liability company, business trust, sole proprietorship, other).
  - Addresses and other contact information of all major branches or sub-entities of the business.
  - Names and addresses of accountants or others responsible for compiling and storing financial records of the business.
  - Date the business was created or entered into.
  - Source of funds used to start the business.
  - Source of funds used to develop the business.
  - Distribution of profits in the past.
  - Location of bank accounts in which profits are or were deposited. Ownership of these accounts.
  - Most recent financial statement for the business. Who prepared it? Where is the statement located?
  - Nature and extent of business debts, losses, or liabilities.
  - Location of business tax returns for prior years and names of persons who prepared them.
- Partnership: kind (family, limited, general, etc.).
- Partnership: profit and loss history.
- Partnership: percentage interest of the client and of the spouse.
- Partnership: names of other partners.
- Partnership: provisions for sale of a partner's interest.
- Partnership: provisions for termination.
- Corporation: kind (public, closely held, etc.).
- Corporation: state of incorporation.
- Corporation: names and addresses of incorporators.
- Corporation: total issued shares. Kinds of shares.
- Corporation: profit and loss history.
- Corporation: number and kind of shares owned by the client or the spouse.

(continued)

Exhibit 3.1 *(continued)*

- Corporation: names of officers of corporation.
- Corporation: names of members of the board of directors.
- Corporation: provisions for the sale of stock.
- Corporation: provisions for dissolution.
- Limited liability company: percentage owned by the client and the spouse.
- Limited liability company: other owners or principals and their roles.
- Limited liability company: profit and loss history.
- Sole proprietorship: profit and loss history.
- Other business entities: description, method of operation, profit-and-loss history.

13. EMPLOYMENT HISTORY

Answer separately for the client and for the spouse.

- Name, address, email, website of employers. Cover the following topics for the current employer and for each prior employer for the last ten years:
  - Occupation or profession.
  - Dates employed.
  - Title and responsibilities.
  - Name of supervisor.
  - Compensation history. Methods of payment (periodic salary, commission, deferred compensation, royalties, dividends, etc.).
  - Salary: gross.
  - Salary: net.
  - Deferred salary or other compensation.
  - Bonus availability. Other incentive plans.
  - Cost-of-living adjustments.
  - Benefits: pension (defined-benefit plan, defined-contribution plan, other).
  - Benefits: deferred-savings plan, profit-sharing plan, stock options.
  - Benefits: life insurance (names of beneficiaries, amount of cash surrender value, who has power to change beneficiaries).
  - Benefits: health insurance (persons covered).
  - Benefits: dental insurance (persons covered).
  - Benefits: disability insurance.
  - Benefits: vacation.
  - Benefits: sick leave.
  - Benefits: severance pay.
  - Benefits: union.
  - Benefits: perks (payment of membership fees at clubs or professional associations, company car, company yacht, recreational facilities, entertainment allowance, sports tickets, other).
  - Expense account: details.

14. EDUCATION

In the following list, answer separately for the client, the spouse, and each child:

- Education: highest grade or degree achieved, dates, institutions attended, special training received (e.g., certificates), etc.

(continued)

Exhibit 3.1 *(continued)*

- How was the education financed?
- What are future education/training plans?
- Is there an interest and ability to pursue further education/training?
- Assess potential interferences (e.g., health, transportation, cost, need to care for others, etc.).

15. CONTRIBUTIONS TO CAREER ENHANCEMENT

- Before the parties were married, to what extent did either contribute to the career enhancement of the other? Explain (e.g., took a job to support the family, used personal funds to help pay for the other's education, agreed to assume all child-raising and household chores while the other pursued education).
- During the marriage, did the client or spouse enhance his or her own career, such as by obtaining education or training?
- Did one spouse postpone his or her own career enhancement during the marriage so that the other's career could be enhanced?

In a property division, most courts will try to find ways to "compensate" the spouse who sacrificed his or her own education or career so that the other spouse could obtain an education or career. (See Chapter 8.)

16. REAL PROPERTY

- Ownership (e.g., solely owned by client, solely owned by spouse, jointly owned, ownership with others). Cover the following topics for each real property:
- Legal status (e.g., joint tenancy, tenancy by the entirety, tenancy in common, landlord-tenant interest, other).
- How is legal title held?
- Nature of the real property (e.g., residence, vacation, time-share, business, rental property, vacant land, other).
- Location/address.
- Persons currently using/benefiting from the real property.
- Original cost and date of purchase.
- Name and address of the seller.
- Source of funds used for the purchase.
- Amount owed on the property. Name and address of the creditor/mortgagee.
- Source of funds used to pay ongoing debt.
- Current fair market value of property. Amount of the most recent written appraisal.
- If acquired by gift, name and address of the donor, and the circumstances of the gift. To whom was the gift made, and when? Relationship between donor and donee. Relative? Friend? Business associate?
- If acquired by inheritance, name and address of the decedent transferor. Circumstances of the inheritance: to whom was the inheritance given? on what date? Relationship between the transferor and the recipient. Relative? Friend? Business associate?
- Improvements made to the property. Dates and sources of funds used.
- Sources of funds used to pay insurance covering the property.
- Sources of funds used to pay taxes on the property.
- Sources of funds used to pay maintenance costs on the property.

Although the law office should determine who has legal title to all property, the distribution of property upon divorce is usually not dependent on the identity of the title holder. It is more important knowing when the property interest was acquired and whether the property is marital/community property (as opposed to separate property), regardless of who holds title. (See Chapter 8.)

In most states, property (real or personal) acquired by gift or inheritance to one spouse only is the separate property of that spouse and not subject to property division upon divorce. (See Chapter 8.)

17. STOCKS, BONDS, AND RELATED ACCOUNTS

Address the following topics for each separately owned item:

- Stocks: names of corporations.
- Stocks: name of owner(s) as shown on stock certificate.

(continued)

Exhibit 3.1 *(continued)*

- Stocks: number of shares.
- Stocks: actual or approximate current value.
- Stocks: certificate numbers.
- Stocks: dates acquired.
- Stocks: cost of shares.
- Stocks: source of funds used to purchase.
- Bonds: name of corporation or obligor.
- Bonds: name of owner(s) as shown on bond certificate.
- Bonds: dates acquired.
- Bonds: bond numbers.
- Bonds: face amounts at maturity; maturity dates.
- Bonds: actual or approximate present value.
- Bonds: interest rate.
- Bonds: coupons attached.
- Bonds: cost of bond.
- Bonds: source of funds used to purchase.
- Other. For each of the following, state the owner(s), beneficiaries, issuing banks or other institutions, dates opened and renewed, amount used to purchase, source of funds used to purchase, maturity dates, interest earned, penalties, and current balance:
  - Certificates of deposit.
  - Money market accounts.
  - Mutual funds.
  - IRA accounts.
  - 401 (k) account.
  - Keogh plan.
  - Checking accounts.
  - Savings accounts.
  - Christmas club accounts.
  - Other financial accounts or instruments.
  - Safe deposit box (banks or institutions where located, dates opened, number of box, persons authorized to enter, contents).

18. OTHER PERSONAL PROPERTY

Address the following topics for each item of personal property with a fair market value of more than $500:

- Ownership (solely owned by client, solely owned by spouse, jointly owned, owned with others).
- Nature of the property (e.g., furniture, jewelry, precious metal, antique, art, china, fur, car, boat, sporting equipment, coin collection, stamp collection, airplane, pet, other).
- Location/address.
- Persons currently using/benefiting from the property.
- Original cost and dates of purchase.
- Name and address of sellers.
- Source of funds used to purchase.

(continued)

Exhibit 3.1 (continued)

- Amount owed on the property. Names and addresses of creditors.
- Source of funds used to pay ongoing debt.
- Current fair market value of property (method of valuation, e.g., written appraisal).
- If acquired by gift, name and address of the donor. Circumstances of the gift. To whom was the gift made? On what date? Relationship between the donor and donee. Relative? Friend? Business associate?
- If acquired by inheritance, name and address of the deceased transferor. Circumstances of the gift. To whom was the inheritance made? On what date? Relationship between the transferor and recipient. Relative? Friend? Business associate?
- Improvements made to property. Dates and sources of funds used.
- Sources of funds to pay insurance covering the property.

19. INSURANCE

For each category of insurance listed below, provide as much of the following information as is relevant to the kind of insurance involved: (1) the name of the insurance company, (2) the policy number, (3) the date policy was issued, (4) beneficiaries, (5) whether the beneficiaries are irrevocable (i.e., can they be changed?), (6) the face amount and the amount of premium, (7) the source of funds used to pay premiums, (8) the date premiums are due, (9) assignability of policy, (10) any loans against the policy, and (11) other features of the insurance.

- Life insurance.
- Health insurance.
- Fire/homeowner insurance on residence or vacation home.
- Title insurance.
- Vehicle insurance.
- Boat insurance.
- Disability insurance.
- General liability insurance.
- Commercial property insurance.
- Product liability insurance.
- Business interruption insurance.
- Other insurance.

20. MISCELLANEOUS INCOME

If not covered elsewhere in this checklist, state whether any of the following sources of income apply, including the names of the recipient(s) and the amounts received (monthly, annually, one-time, etc.):

- Social Security income of the client and spouse.
- Other Social Security income (e.g., survivor benefits, disability) and the name of recipients.
- Unemployment compensation income of the client and spouse.
- Workers' compensation income of the client and spouse.
- Income from veterans' benefits of the client and spouse.
- Public assistance, e.g., TANF—Temporary Assistance for Needy Families.
- Anticipated tax refund of the client and spouse.
- Income from annuity of the client and spouse.
- Income from trusts of the client and spouse.
- Income from alimony/maintenance obligation of the client and spouse.

(continued)

Exhibit 3.1 *(continued)*

- Income from book or patent royalties of the client and spouse.
- Income from rental property of the client and spouse.
- Interest income from personal loans of the client and spouse.
- Gifts from friends or relatives of the client and spouse.
- Other income of the client and spouse.

21. CLAIMS

- Is the client or spouse currently a plaintiff in a civil action? If so, state the circumstances.
- Does the client or spouse anticipate filing a civil court action in the future? If so, state the circumstances, e.g., what damages might be sought?
- Has the client or spouse filed (or does either expect to file) a claim against an insurance company, e.g., a claim arising out of a recent automobile accident? State the circumstances.
- Is the client or spouse awaiting recovery from an insurance claim or court judgment? If so, state the circumstances.
- For each insurance or court claim, explain whether the recovery will cover a loss of income or other property that was lost or interfered with during the marriage.

- *Anticipated court damage awards may be marital property that can be divided upon divorce, depending on whether the amount received is personal to the victim (e.g., pain and suffering) or is designed to replace income that would have been earned during the marriage. If the latter, the award can be marital property. (See Chapter 8.)*

22. FREQUENTLY OVERLOOKED ASSETS

For each of the following assets listed below, state (1) who owns the asset, (2) the date(s) it was acquired, (3) the resources used to acquire it, (4) the current method of valuing it, and (5) any expiration restrictions:

- Cryptocurrencies such as bitcoin.
- Frequent flier points.
- Hotel discount program based on accumulated points.
- Credit-card or cash discount program based on accumulated points.
- Department store discount program based on accumulated points.
- Unused sports season tickets; the right to purchase season tickets at a discount.
- Accumulated equity in a car lease.
- Expected medical reimbursement.
- Unused sick leave.
- Lottery tickets purchased during the marriage that may produce winnings in the future.

23. LIABILITIES

For each of the following liabilities (debts) listed below, address (1) the nature of the debt, (2) the reason it was incurred, (3) who benefited from taking on the debt, (4) the creditors' names, (5) the debtors' names, (6) the loan numbers, (7) the date the debt was incurred, (8) the source of funds used in the past (and currently) to pay the debt, (9) the original amount of the debt, (10) the amount outstanding, (11) the date and amount of next payment, and (12) whether the client or spouse can increase the amount of the debt on his or her own.

- Mortgage on primary residence.
- Mortgage on second home or vacation home.
- Mortgage on business property.
- Other mortgages.
- Mechanic's liens.
- Credit cards.

(continued)

Exhibit 3.1 *(continued)*

- Charge cards.
- Car loans.
- Boat loans.
- Student loans.
- Loans against cash value of life insurance policy.
- Loans from a friend.
- Other notes or loans.
- Court judgments for money in which the client or spouse is or will be a defendant or may otherwise be responsible for the judgment and thereby become a judgment debtor. State the circumstances.
- Bankruptcy payments (e.g., under a Chapter 13 bankruptcy).

24. TAX RETURNS

Provide the following information on each of the returns listed below for the last three years: (1) adjusted gross income; (2) taxable income; (3) taxes due; (4) source of funds used to pay the taxes; (5) accountant, attorney, or tax service used to prepare the return; (6) extent to which the client or spouse was involved in the preparation of the return, and (7) location of a copy of the return.

(Provide the same information if an amended return was filed for any of the returns.)

- Federal income tax return.
- Federal corporate (or other business) tax return.
- State income tax return.
- State corporate (or other business) tax return.
- City or other local tax return.
- City or other local corporate (or other business) tax return.
- Gift tax return.
- Estate tax return.
- Returns filed abroad.
- Other returns.

- *Under the innocent-spouse doctrine, a spouse may be able to avoid liability for delinquent taxes that result from a tax return prepared by the other spouse. (See Chapter 11.)*

25. ASSETS OF THE CHILDREN

- List any real or personal property the children own (more than $100 in value) in their own name or jointly with another, e.g., cash, securities, land.
- How was this property acquired? On what date? A gift by whom? An inheritance from whom? Purchased with the child's own funds?
- Who controls this property? The child? A parent? A guardian or custodian? A trustee?
- Has the client, the spouse, or anyone else used or consumed any of this property?
- When will the child have unrestricted access to this property?

26. PROFESSIONALS HIRED OR CONSULTED

For each of the following persons listed below, state (1) their name and address, (2) the dates hired or consulted, (3) whether they were hired or consulted by the client or by the spouse, (4) the fees paid, (5) the source of funds to pay the fees, (6) the nature of the services they provided, and (7) the kinds of financial or other records they have (or had) in their possession:

- Attorneys.
- Accountants.
- Real estate agents or brokers.

Exhibit 3.1 *(continued)*

- Insurance agents.
- Bankers.
- Stockbrokers.
- Clergy.
- Others.

27. NEXT STEPS

The client needs clear instructions on what further steps he or she should take. The following are some examples:

- Locate documents identified during the interview as important (e.g., copies of tax returns).
- Cancel joint accounts with spouse.
- Take photos of the contents of the house.
- Start keeping a journal on the behavior of the spouse, interactions with the children, expenses, etc.

The checklist in Exhibit 3.1 is not the only place in the book where there are guidelines on fact gathering. In some of the remaining chapters, you will find Interviewing and Investigation Checklists that pertain to specific issues under discussion in a chapter. (See also the technique of fact particularization discussed in Appendix A under the heading "Fact-Gathering Assignments.")

ASSIGNMENT   3.2

Your instructor will play the role of a new client in the office where you work as a paralegal. Assume that you have been asked to conduct a comprehensive interview of this client in order to compile a family history. The client is a spouse in a marriage where there are substantial personal and business assets over which the spouses are expected to have bitter disputes. They are also expected to contest the custody of their two minor children. The marriage was the second marriage for both parties. To date, the client has not been asked to bring anything to the interview. You must let the client know what you want him or her to bring to the office in subsequent meetings.

Everyone in the class will play the role of interviewer. Raise your hand when you have questions. Everyone should ask numerous questions in this potentially complex case. (You do not have to follow the outline of questions in Exhibit 3.1, but you should be as comprehensive in the topics covered.) Take detailed notes on the questions and answers, regardless of who asks the questions. Do not limit your notes to the answers to the questions you ask.

If you feel that another student failed to elicit sufficient detail on a question, re-ask the question in your own way to try to obtain greater detail.

After the interview, prepare a detailed report (sometimes called an *intake memorandum*) on what you learned from the interview. Use headings for different categories of data. Choose an overall organization for the report that you feel would best facilitate reading. The format of the beginning of the report should be as follows:

> OFFICE MEMORANDUM
> TO: [name of your instructor]
> FROM: [your name]
> DATE: [date of the interview]
> RE: Comprehensive Interview of [name of client]

(See General Instructions for the Interview Assignment in Appendix A.)

EXHIBIT 3.2   Example of Software used for the Intake of New Family-Law Clients

Intake Form: Abacus Family Law Divorce Case Intake Form   [?][X]

Please enter information about the case.

Client v. Spouse   Mitchell v. Mitchell   [Check for duplicates]

Court   SD FAMILY LAW   [^]

Court Case Number   900000012

Opened   05/30/18   [^]

Attorney   BRF   [^]

Date Married   02/11/02   [^]   State Married   CA   [^]

Date Separated   03/16/18   [^]   State Separated   CA   [^]

State Residency Reqs Met?   [ ]   County Reqs Satisfied?   [ ]

Minor Children?   [✓]

Child 1 Full Name   George Mitchell   Child 1 Date of Birth   11/25/11   [^]   Child 1 Gender   M   [^]

Child 1 Legal Custody   Petitioner   [^]   Child 1 Physical Custody   Petitioner   [^]   Child 1 Visitation   Respondent   [^]

Child 2 Full Name   Sarah Mitchell   Child 2 Date of Birth   05/21/13   [^]   Child 2 Gender   F   [^]

Child 2 Legal Custdy   Petitioner   [^]   Child 2 Physical Custody   Petitioner   [^]   Child 2 Visitation   Respondent   [^]

Please enter contact information for the client below

Last name   Mitchell   [Check for duplicates]

First name   Donald

Dear

Addressee   Donald Mitchell

Address 1   2000 South Street apt#3

Source: © AbacusLaw (www.abacuslaw.com). Reprinted with permission.

SOFTWARE

Many family-law offices use special software to record the basic facts obtained during client interviews. See Exhibit 3.2 for an example. For more examples of the use of computers in a family-law practice, see Exhibits B.1 to B.11 in Appendix B.

PARALEGAL ROLES

Paralegals and other staff of law firms can have a large role in helping identify and locate the large variety of facts that can be involved in a family-law case. Rose Reitz, a veteran paralegal, states, "I love digging for information and finding relevant facts on a case. Documents will always tell the story, and I enjoy going through those documents and finding out what that story is."[9]

- For an overview of paralegal roles in family-law cases, see Exhibits 1.5 and 1.6 in Chapter 1.
- In addition to the large number of documents and facts outlined in Chapter 3 that paralegals help an office to collect for a case, see:
    - The comprehensive checklists on separation agreements found at the beginning of Chapter 8, and
    - The list of documents and facts sought in the **interrogatories** on financial assets in Appendix C.

interrogatories
A method of discovery by which one party sends written questions to another party. Also called *rogs*.

- *Interviewing*. Depending on the kind of office where the client is seeking legal services, paralegal interviewing and data collection duties can vary considerably. In private law offices, for instance, the attorney conducts the initial interview (sometimes with the paralegal taking notes) that establishes the attorney-client relationship, sets fees, and collects basic facts. The paralegal may then conduct follow-up interviews as needed. In some publicly funded law offices (e.g., a **legal aid office**), paralegals can have a much larger role. They may be asked to make a preliminary determination of the client's eligibility for free legal services (based on income guidelines of the office), interview the client, and start preparing the pleadings. In busy offices, clients with relatively simple cases may not see an attorney until the date of the first court hearing.

- *Conflicts Check*. The paralegal may also have the duty of checking the list of all current and prior clients and of all the opponents of these clients in order to identify possible conflicts of interest. In a large office, **conflicts checks** are initially assigned to one staff member (a conflicts specialist), who might be a paralegal. (On conflicts of law and conflicts checks, see Chapter 2.)

- *Client Assistance on Data Collection*. Paralegals often have a role helping clients assemble the large volume of financial and related records (outlined in Exhibit 3.1) that must be collected and reviewed. Clients need to sign authorization forms that allow the office to obtain confidential records from schools, hospitals, and employers. Paralegals often prepare such forms and coordinate their signing and distribution.

- *Liaison to Experts*. Where appraisers, accountants, and other experts need to be hired, paralegals search for candidates that the attorneys will consider. Once hired, the paralegal might be the main liaison between the office and the experts.

legal aid office
An office of attorneys (and paralegals) that provides free legal services to persons who cannot afford standard legal fees.

conflicts check
Finding out whether a conflict of interest exists that might disqualify a law office from representing a prospective client or from continuing the representation of a current client.

SUMMARY

In light of the potential complexity of a family-law case, a law office may need to compile a comprehensive family history, particularly when there are contested legal issues, complex factual disputes, relatively large sums of property, or suspected hiding of assets. The family history is collected primarily by legal interviews and investigation. Because clients are not always sure what they want, thoughtful attorneys provide clear explanations and options. Often, clients are confused about the law. Guidelines for paralegals conducting follow-up client interviews include having uninterrupted time to conduct the interviews, preserving confidentiality, listening attentively, avoiding legal advice, and not stating outcome guarantees. Any emergency concerns (e.g., physical safety) should be dealt with soon after the client arrives.

To compile a family history, facts are collected on the marriage, its deterioration, emergency concerns, prior contracts between the spouses, expenses, health history, wills and trusts, children, businesses, employment history, education and training, contributions each made to the education and career of the other, real and personal property, insurance, debts and liabilities, tax returns, assets of the children, and professionals either has consulted.

KEY TERMS

contested	electronic data discovery (EDD)	conflicts check
legal advice	interrogatories	
unauthorized practice of law (UPL)	legal aid office	

PROJECT

Some family-law attorneys post online interview checklists that they ask prospective clients to fill out or to be ready to discuss. Find three such forms or checklists online. To find them, run the following searches in Google, Bing, or Yahoo:

> divorce law interview
>
> family law checklist
>
> divorce interview

Also run the same searches in Pinterest (pinterest.com) and in the Images link in Google, Bing, or Yahoo. (You can also add the name of your state to the search terms, but you are not limited to interview forms used in your state.)

How do the three checklists compare with each other? Discuss relative strengths and weaknesses. How do the three checklists compare with the checklist in Exhibit 3.1? What items would you add to Exhibit 3.1 based on what you learned online?

ETHICS IN A FAMILY-LAW PRACTICE

You are a paralegal working at the law office of Smith & Smith. You have referred a divorce client to the firm. The client is a close friend of yours. During an interview, the client asks you whether a wife is ever obligated to pay alimony to a husband. The client was concerned that she might be ordered to pay alimony to the husband she is divorcing. Last week, you happened to be discussing the same topic with your attorney supervisor. You tell the client what the attorney told you; namely, that either spouse can be liable for alimony. Any ethical problems?

WRITING SAMPLE

Assume that you have completed an interview with a client (Nancy Franklin) and are now preparing a memo to your supervisor (Helen Foley, Esq.) on the interview. For purposes of the memo, you can make up the facts that the client told you during the interview so long as the facts are consistent with the following scenario:

Nancy and her husband, James Franklin, have been married three years. They have one child. They have agreed to split all their assets and debts equally and to have joint legal custody of their child (meaning they would make all major decisions together on matters such as education, religion, and medical care) with

Nancy having sole physical custody (meaning that the child would live with Nancy).

The main points to cover in the memo are the factual details of what the spouses own and owe and the client's wishes on visitation. Organize the memo under headings that you think will make it easy for a busy attorney to read. Again, you will make up all of the facts for your memo (e.g., what the assets and debts are and how much visitation Nancy wants the father to have) consistent with the scenario outlined above. You do not need to know any law to conduct this interview. The heading and first line of your memo will be as follows:

Interview Memo

TO: Helen Foley, Esq.   RE: Interview of Nancy Franklin
FR: Your name   2020-Div-Franklin
Date: Today's date

    You have asked me to interview Nancy Franklin to determine the assets and debts of the parties and the client's wishes on visitation.

(See General Instructions for the Writing Sample in Appendix A.)

REVIEW QUESTIONS

1. In what ways do attorneys obtain facts that will be needed to represent a client in a family-law case?

2. When is a family-law attorney most likely to want a detailed family history of a client?

3. What concerns must an attorney have when determining what a client wants?

4. What are some of the major guidelines for conducting an interview of a family-law client?

5. What steps should be taken to preserve client confidentiality during an interview?

6. What misunderstanding about the paralegal's role should a paralegal avoid when interviewing a client?

7. What is legal advice, and why should a paralegal avoid giving it?

8. How can an interviewer avoid giving guarantees during an interview?

9. What observations for a supervisor should the interviewer be making of the client's personality during the interview?

10. What are the main categories of facts that make up a family history?

11. What documents should a client be asked to bring to interviews?

12. What information does an office need to avoid a conflict of interest?

13. What emergency concerns should be inquired into at the outset of a client interview?

HELPFUL WEBSITES

Interviewing a Family Law Client

- www.busby-lee.com/pdf/Client-Info-Sheet(Divorce).pdf
- www.tinamhall.com/resources.html

The Anxious Family-Law Client

- winattrial.com/Calming Down the Anxious Family Law Client.htm

Interviewing: Selected Articles

- www.rongolini.com/Interviewing.html

Attentive Listening

- www.businesslistening.com/listening_skills-3.php
- peterstark.com/attentive-listening-skills/#

Google, Bing, Yahoo

(on these search engines, run the following searches)

- intake memo
- attentive listening
- "kinds of questions"
- "legal interviewing"
- interviewing clients
- "difficult clients"

YouTube

Run the following search on YouTube:

- client interviewing

ENDNOTES

[1] *My Specialty: Divorce Law*, 27 Paralegal Today 27 (April/June 2010).

[2] Amy H. Johnson, *What I Wish You Knew*, Facts & Findings 35 (NALA, May/June 2016).

[3] Sean Illing, *A Divorce Lawyer's Guide to Staying Together*. Vox (February 13, 2019) (www.vox.com/2018/12/3/18075794/marriage-divorce-happiness-relationships-james-sexton).

[4] Ibid.

[5] James Feldman, *The Initial Interview: That First Contact is Crucial*, 12 Family Advocate 6 (Summer 1990).

[6] William Hamilton and Wendy Akbar, *E-Discovery in the Age of Facebook, Twitter, & the Digital Family*, 33 Family Advocate 16 (Fall 2010).

[7] Nicholas Confesorre, *How to Hide $400 Million*, N.Y. Times Magazine (November 30, 2016) (www.nytimes.com/2016/11/30/magazine/how-to-hide-400-million.html).

[8] Some of the checklist questions are based on or adapted from Form 4, *Affidavit* [on financial resources] (Supreme Court of the United States, 2003); *What Your Lawyer Needs to Know*, 15 Family Advocate 28 (Summer 1992); Louis Brown, *A Family Legal Information Check List*, 3 Practical Lawyer 60 (no. 6, Oct. 1957); Leo Barrett, *The Initial Interview with a Divorce Client*, 23 Practical Lawyer 75 (no. 4, June 1977); Louis Brown, *Manual for Periodic Checkup* (1983); and Allan Chay & Judith Smith, *Legal Interviewing in Practice* (1996).

[9] Reitz Sets It Right at Quarles & Brady (search.proquest.com/openview/e1539d6d00754e55bd2507faae75cd97/1?pq-origsite=gscholar&cbl=2026554) (December 5, 2018).

CHAPTER 4

Premarital, Postnuptial, and Cohabitation Agreements

CHAPTER OUTLINE

CHAPTER OBJECTIVES

After completing this chapter, you should be able to:

- Define the four major kinds of agreements that can be entered into by persons in intimate relationships:
  (1) cohabitation agreement,
  (2) premarital agreement,
  (3) postnuptial agreement, and
  (4) separation agreement.
- Identify some of the major reasons couples enter into premarital agreements.
- Know what can and cannot be included in a premarital agreement.

- State the requirements for a valid premarital agreement.
- Distinguish between procedural and substantive fairness, and explain when an agreement is unconscionable.
- Know the malpractice dilemma faced by an attorney who represents the financially weaker party in a premarital agreement.
- Know what can be included in a postnuptial agreement.

- Know what can be included in a cohabitation agreement.
- State the holding and impact of *Marvin v. Marvin* on the law of cohabitation.
- List the remedies that are possible in cohabitation cases that agree with *Marvin v. Marvin*.
- Know why many courts are reluctant to provide remedies for cohabitants other than an action for breach of contract.

KINDS OF AGREEMENTS

Persons in an intimate relationship can create four major kinds of agreements: (1) cohabitation, (2) premarital, (3) postnuptial, and (4) separation. (See Exhibit 4.1.) The parties using these agreements may be about to enter into an intimate relationship, may already be in it, or may want to end it. Our main focus in Chapter 4 will be premarital, postnuptial, and cohabitation agreements. Separation agreements will be covered in Chapter 8.

EXHIBIT 4.1 Kinds of Agreements Made by Persons in an Intimate Relationship

Kind of Agreement	Definition	Examples
Cohabitation Agreement	A contract by persons in an intimate relationship who are not married to each other (and who intend to stay unmarried indefinitely) that covers financial and related matters while living together and upon the end of the cohabitation by separation or death.	Ed and Claire meet at a bank where they work. After dating several years, they decide to live together. Although they give birth to a child, they do not want to be married (at least for now). They enter into an agreement that specifies what property is separately owned and how they will divide property purchased with joint funds if the relationship ends.
Premarital Agreement (Also called a *prenuptial agreement*, or *prenup*, and an *antenuptial agreement*)	• A contract by persons about to be married that can cover (1) financial and related matters once the marriage occurs and (2) spousal support, property division, and related matters in the event of separation, divorce, annulment, or death. • The Uniform Premarital Agreement Act (§ 1) defines it as "an agreement between prospective spouses made in contemplation of marriage and to be effective upon marriage."	Jim and Mary want to marry. Before the wedding, they enter into an agreement that makes clear what property each brings to the marriage and what will remain separate property. The agreement states that neither will have any rights in the separate property of the other; upon death, it will go to whomever each designates in his or her individual will. In addition, the agreement provides that all income earned by either party during the marriage shall be marital (community) property to which each shall be entitled to half in the event of a divorce.
Postnuptial Agreement (Also called a *postnup* or *midnup*)	A contract between married persons that covers specific matters, usually financial in nature. The spouses may have no intention of separating. If they have this intention, the contract is commonly called a *separation agreement*.	• While happily married, George and Helen enter into an agreement whereby George lends Helen $5,000 at 5% interest. She is to make monthly payments of $300. (For this loan, George uses money he recently inherited from his mother.) • While still happily married, George and Helen decide to amend the premarital agreement they entered into before marrying. They will now change some of its financial terms. • Jim and Mary were married in 2012. They separate in 2016. They do not obtain a divorce. In 2019, they reconcile and move back together. When they do so, they enter into a reconciliation agreement that covers financial and custody issues that they want clarified.
Separation Agreement (Also called a *marital settlement agreement (MSA)*—Because the separation agreement is entered into during the marriage, it is sometimes referred to as a *postnuptial agreement*, although when separation is contemplated, the more common term is *separation agreement*.	A contract between married persons who have separated (or who are about to separate) that can cover support, child custody, property division, and other terms of their separation and likely divorce.	Sam and Joe, a married couple, have separated. In anticipation of their divorce, they enter into an agreement that specifies how their marital property will be divided, who will have custody of their adopted child, and what their support obligations to each other will be. Later, they will ask the divorce court to approve this agreement.

PREMARITAL AGREEMENTS

INTRODUCTION

premarital agreement
A contract by persons about to be married that can cover (1) financial and related matters once the marriage occurs and (2) spousal support, property division, and related matters in the event of separation, divorce, annulment, or death. Also called a *prenuptial agreement*, a *prenup*, or an *antenuptial agreement*.

Not all states define a premarital agreement in the same way. In general, a premarital agreement is a contract by persons about to be married that can cover (1) financial and related matters once the marriage occurs and (2) spousal support, property division, and related matters in the event of separation, divorce, annulment, or death. The agreement is also called a *prenuptial agreement* (*prenup*) and an *antenuptial agreement*. Premarital agreements allow the parties to define many of the major terms of a marriage.

Why, you might ask, would two individuals about to enter into the blissful state of marriage discuss such matters as "who gets what" if they divorce? According to one family-law attorney, "The typical young couple starting out does not need" a premarital agreement. "For the middle-aged couple or older couple who has accumulated significant assets, it can be appropriate."[1] Other attorneys are more emphatic about who needs a prenup: *every* couple contemplating marriage. "If you're going to get married and you don't want a prenuptial," exclaims a New York attorney, "you need to see a psychiatrist, not a lawyer."[2]

Needs and emotions, however, are not always in accord. Raising the "P" word (prenuptial) during an engagement can sometimes be unsettling. When famous Beatle band member, Paul McCartney, separated from his second wife, Heather Mills, "Legal experts estimated that he could lose up to a quarter of his $1 billion fortune because he reportedly felt that asking her to sign a prenup was unromantic."[3]

Here are some of the categories of persons most likely to enter into premarital agreements:

- They are older.
- They have substantial property that was acquired independently of each other.
- They have an independent interest in a business, particularly a family-run business.
- They have had prior marriages.
- They have children and perhaps grandchildren from prior relationships.

The numbers in these categories are large. For example, at least one spouse in 22 percent of currently married couples is in his or her second marriage; another 6 percent have a spouse in a third marriage.[4] Such individuals may want to make clear that the new spouse is not to have any claim on designated property or that the children of the former marriage will have first claim to property acquired before the new marriage.

Another large category of couples favoring premarital agreements is young professionals, particularly those in their early thirties with separate careers. (See Exhibit 4.2.) Although the women's movement of the 1980s and 1990s did not crusade in favor of premarital agreements, the "protect yourself" message of the movement helped increase the popularity of premarital agreements among brides-to-be. Finally, the high divorce rate (almost 50 percent of all marriages) has made more young couples aware of the need to preplan for the possible crisis of separation and dissolution. One preplanning tool that might decrease the likelihood of divorces becoming protracted and emotionally brutal is the premarital agreement.

WHAT CAN AND CANNOT BE INCLUDED

In most states, parties have considerable flexibility on what they can include in a premarital agreement. Valid agreements allow the parties to waive or limit some of the marital rights they would otherwise have upon divorce or death. To understand this flexibility, here are two examples (using salaries and wills) of what happens *without* a premarital agreement and the changes such agreements can make:

EXHIBIT 4.2   Popping the Question

"It's a prenuptial agreement silly! I'm asking you to *marry* me!"

Source: Mark Hannabury, 90 Case and Comment 34 (Mar.–Apr. 1985). Reprinted with permission.

- *Salary.* In most states, the salary earned by either spouse during the marriage is marital property, which can be divided in the event of a divorce. A husband, for example, could not say that his soon-to-be ex-wife is not entitled to any of the wages he earned during the marriage. A valid premarital agreement, however, can change this result. The parties can decide to treat salaries and other income as the separate property of the spouse who earned it so that it would not become **divisible** marital property upon divorce.

- *Wills.* In most states, a surviving spouse has a right to elect to receive a designated portion (called an **elective share**) of the estate of a deceased spouse even if the latter's will gives the survivor considerably less or nothing at all. A valid premarital agreement can change this result. The parties can waive this right of election so that the will of a deceased spouse could not be overridden by the surviving spouse (i.e., the latter would not be allowed to "elect against the will").

For states that have adopted the **Uniform Premarital Agreement Act (UPAA)**, the scope of what parties can control in a premarital agreement is quite broad:

Uniform Premarital Agreement Act § 3

   (a) Parties to a premarital agreement may contract with respect to:

      (1) the rights and obligations of each of the parties in any of the property of either or both of them whenever and wherever acquired or located;

      (2) the right to buy, sell, use. . ., dispose of, or otherwise manage and control property;

      (3) the disposition of property upon separation, marital dissolution, death, or the occurrence or nonoccurrence of any other event;

      (4) the modification or elimination of spousal support;

      (5) the making of a will, trust, or other arrangement to carry out the provisions of the agreement;

divisible
Capable of being divided.

elective share
The percentage of a deceased spouse's estate that the surviving spouse can choose (elect) to receive despite what the will of the deceased spouse provided for the surviving spouse. Also called *right of election, statutory share*, or *forced share.*

Uniform Premarital Agreement Act (UPAA)
A model statute adopted by many states that governs the legality of premarital agreements.

(6) the ownership rights in and disposition of the death benefit from a life insurance policy;

(7) the choice of law governing the construction of the agreement; and

(8) any other matter, including their personal rights and obligations, not in violation of public policy or a statute imposing a criminal penalty.

(b) The right of a child to support may not be adversely affected by a premarital agreement.[5]

ASSIGNMENT   4.1

What restrictions exist in your state on what a premarital agreement can and cannot do? (See the General Instructions for the State Code and the Court Opinion Assignments in Appendix A.)

---

public policy
The principles inherent in the customs, morals, and notions of justice that prevail in a state; the foundation of public laws; the principles that are naturally and inherently right and just.

Note the admonition in Section 3(a)(8) of the UPAA that the premarital agreement must not violate public policy or criminal statutes. **Public policy** consists of the principles inherent in the customs, morals, and notions of justice that prevail in a state. For example, the parties cannot agree that neither will ever bring a divorce action or any other suit against the other. It is against public policy to discourage the use of the courts in this way, as legitimate grievances might go unheard. Let's take a closer look at specific clauses that may or may not violate public policy.

Facilitating Divorce

At one time, many courts considered financial clauses in premarital agreements to be against public policy because they *facilitated* (or encouraged) *divorce*. The thinking was that divorce planning before marriage might incline a party to seek a divorce if he or she knows what funds or other property will be available upon divorce, particularly, of course, if the financial terms upon divorce are favorable.

no-fault divorce
A divorce that is granted without having to prove marital wrongs that caused the break-up.

Today, courts do not place such limitations on premarital agreements. In the era of **no-fault divorce**, terminating the marriage is no longer difficult. There is no pressure from society to keep marriages together at all costs. A spouse who wants a divorce can obtain one with relative ease and probably does not need the inducement of a favorable premarital agreement to end the marriage.

Alimony Clause

waive
To relinquish or to give up a right or privilege because of an explicit rejection of it or because of a failure to take appropriate steps to claim it at the proper time.

Most courts allow clauses in premarital agreements that provide a designated amount of spousal support (alimony) or, indeed, that provide for no spousal support in the event of a divorce. These courts will allow parties to **waive** (relinquish or give up) spousal support.

public charge
An individual who is primarily dependent on the government for subsistence or support, as demonstrated by either the receipt of cash assistance for income maintenance or by institutionalization for short- or long-term care at government expense.

Suppose, however, that a divorce occurs and, because of changed circumstances between the time that the agreement was signed and the time of the divorce, one of the ex-spouses is about to become a **public charge**—meaning, a person in need of public (government) assistance. As events unfolded, the ex-spouse made a bad bargain if he or she agreed in the premarital agreement to waive (or to take almost no) spousal support if the parties were to divorce. To prevent an ex-spouse from becoming destitute or a public charge, a court can force the other ex-spouse to provide spousal support despite the no-support clause in the premarital agreement. Here is how the UPAA states this rule:

If a provision of a premarital agreement . . . eliminates spousal support and such . . . elimination causes one party to the agreement to be eligible for support under a program of public assistance at the time of separation or marital dissolution, a court, notwithstanding the terms of the agreement, may require the other party to provide support to the extent necessary to avoid such eligibility.[6]

Suppose that an ex-spouse is not about to become a public charge but is dissatisfied with the financial terms of the premarital agreement that he or she signed before the marriage. We will examine this issue later in the chapter.

Death Clause

As indicated earlier, most states give a surviving spouse the right to an *elective share* of his or her deceased spouse's estate. The elective share is a percentage of a deceased spouse's estate that the surviving spouse can choose (elect) to receive despite what the will of the deceased spouse provided for the surviving spouse. The right to an elective share is designed to prevent a deceased spouse from disinheriting the surviving spouse by a will (see Chapters 8 and 12).

In premarital agreements, parties often give up (waive) their right to an elective share in each other's estates. (This waiver is sometimes called the *death clause*.) The agreement, for example, might say that a surviving spouse will receive a specified amount (e.g., $100,000) upon the death of the other spouse in lieu of the elective share.

Life-Insurance Clause

A clause found in premarital agreements might commit a spouse to purchase and fund a life insurance policy of a designated amount with the other spouse as the beneficiary.

Property-Division Clause

Premarital agreements can spell out what property belongs to each spouse during the marriage and upon its termination. The enforceability of clauses on property division in premarital agreements (and in separation agreements) depends, in part, on whether there was adequate disclosure to each other of the property that each owned at the time they signed the agreement.

property division
The distribution of community or marital property between spouses (or ex-spouses) after a legal separation or divorce. Also called *property settlement* or *property distribution*.

Retirement-Benefits Clause

Premarital agreements sometimes provide that each party waives any rights that either has in the pension retirement benefits of the other, e.g., a 401(k) plan. (See Chapter 8 for a discussion of such plans.) There is some doubt, however, as to the legality of such clauses under federal law. A *married* person (a spouse) may be able to waive such rights, but it is not clear that someone contemplating marriage (a fiancée or fiancé) can do so. In light of this uncertainty, the premarital agreement should have a clause requiring both parties within a short time *after* they are married to sign waiver forms approved by the administrator of the pension or retirement plan. The form would confirm the agreement of the parties that one of the spouses will not receive any benefit from the funds in the plan.

Child-Support Clause

Parents have an equal duty to support their children pursuant to child-support guidelines that mandate the minimum amount of support each must provide (see Chapter 10). A premarital agreement can specify child-support amounts that are higher than the minimum, but it cannot have a child-support clause that goes below the minimum unless approved by the court. Furthermore, a clause that purports to absolve one of the parents from contributing to child support is unenforceable.

Child-Custody Clause

The main child-custody standard used by courts is the best interests of the child (see Chapter 9). The desires of both parents are taken into consideration, but what they want is never controlling. Hence, a clause in a premarital agreement on child custody is never binding on a court.

Debts Clause

Debts that a spouse brings into the marriage are the debts of that spouse alone. Individual debts do not become joint debts simply because of the marriage. Individual debts can be considerable, particularly for recent graduates of undergraduate and professional schools. It is not uncommon for such individuals to enter into the marriage with more than $100,000 in school debts. To prevent later misunderstandings (e.g., "You said you would help me pay my school loans"), the premarital agreement might include a clause that specifies what debts are being brought into the marriage and who is responsible for them. To protect the nondebtor, the clause could say that "any assistance on the other's debt does not constitute an agreement to assume joint responsibility for the debt."

Lifestyle-Clause

Some premarital agreements try to regulate very specific and sensitive aspects of the marriage relationship by including lifestyle clauses. Examples of such life-style clauses include the following:

- Who performs what household chores.
- How often sexual relations will occur.
- Requiring children to be vegetarian.
- How much time the couple will spend with the in-laws.
- Whose career takes priority in the event one of the spouses is laid off from work.
- What night the husband can watch football with his friends.
- How long a spouse will work until retirement.
- How much weight a wife can gain (with a fine of $500 per excess pound!).[7]

Some lifestyle clauses try to regulate post-divorce conduct such as inserting a clause in the premarital agreement that would prohibit a party from dating another person in public for a designated period of time in the event of a divorce.

The practical and legal effect of such lifestyle clauses is questionable, as it is unlikely that a court would become involved in enforcing terms of this nature. (Most "jurisdictions will not enforce agreements with respect to personal services rendered during marriage."[8]) Yet some family-law attorneys still recommend that these lifestyle clauses be included in the premarital agreement in order to clarify expectations and help prevent (or minimize) future marital bickering or tension.

Remaining-Childless Clause

Occasionally, a clause in a premarital agreement will assert that the parties will always use birth control so that they will remain childless. Such a clause is often insisted upon by an older man—who already has children from a prior marriage—and who is about to marry a younger woman. There is some doubt about the legality of such a clause in states that consider having children as one of the purposes of marriage.[9] More importantly, if the clause is violated and a child is born, the violation would have no effect on the obligation of both parents to support the child. Yet an attorney might want to include the clause, again to clarify expectations while candidly acknowledging to the client that the clause would probably be unenforceable.

Confidentiality Clause

A feature of some confessional television and social media is the ex-spouse telling the world about the horrors of a former marriage. (See the examples of "electronic exhibitionism" in Chapter 1.) To try to head off such exposés, the premarital agreement may require the parties to maintain confidentiality about what occurs in their impending marriage. Although difficult to enforce in the age of the Internet, the confidentiality clause is often sought by well-to-do and powerful clients. The confidentiality clause could also cover the contents of the premarital agreement itself. A client may be reluctant to place financial data in the agreement without such a clause.

Automatic-Termination Clause

The parties can agree that all or some of the terms of the premarital agreement will automatically terminate or expire after a designated number of years (e.g., five) if the parties are still married at that time. This will force the now-married couple to renegotiate the terms of their relationship. (See the discussion below on postnuptial agreements.) Wealthy clients rarely agree to such automatic-termination (or sunset) clauses. Attorneys for a less-wealthy client may try to negotiate it into the agreement on the theory that the client would probably do better in a new agreement.

Severability Clause

A severability clause states that if any single portion of the agreement is found to be invalid, the remaining valid provisions of the agreement should still be enforced. This type of clause is designed to prevent a party from arguing that the entire premarital agreement should be discarded if a court rules that any part of it is invalid. Something is severable if it can be removed without destroying what remains. (The opposite of severable is *essential* or *indispensable*.)

VALID CONTRACT

A premarital agreement is an example of a contract, which is a legally enforceable agreement. Premarital agreements are also executory contracts because performing the terms of such contracts will take place in the future (after the marriage). The traditional requirements or elements of most contracts are offer, acceptance, and consideration. Consideration is something of value that is exchanged between parties. The consideration for the premarital agreement is the mutual promise of the parties to enter into the marriage. In most states, however, the premarital agreement (contract) is enforceable without proof of consideration.

Like all contracts, the parties to a premarital contract must have the capacity to enter into a contract. Someone who is underage or mentally incompetent, for example, cannot form a valid contract. Contracts must be entered into voluntarily. Fraud and duress can invalidate the contract, as we will see. The statute of frauds requires some categories of contract to be in writing, although not all states have this requirement for premarital agreements.

Premarital contracts are different from commercial contracts in important respects. A singular characteristic of most commercial contracts is that the parties are allowed to treat each other at arm's length—that is, as if they are strangers both looking out solely for their own self-interests. This is not entirely true of couples engaged to be married. Both parties must make a financial disclosure to each other before signing the premarital agreement and both must be given the opportunity to consult with his or her own attorney and other advisers on whether to sign it. *Married* couples are in a fiduciary relationship with each other, requiring loyalty and fair treatment. States differ, however, on whether an *engaged* couple is in such a relationship with each other when they enter into a premarital agreement. Yet they have a duty of financial disclosure and cannot treat each other as strangers. Overreaching is forbidden.

We need to examine some of these themes more closely.

---

sunset
Automatic termination or expiration upon a designated time or event.

severability clause
A clause in an agreement stating that if any part of the agreement is declared invalid, the remaining valid portions of the agreement should be be carried out (enforced).

severable
Removable without destroying what remains. Something is severable when what remains after it is taken away has legal force and can survive without it. The opposite of severable is *essential* or *indispensable*.

contract
A legally enforceable agreement. The elements of most contracts are an offer, acceptance, and consideration. Some contracts must be in writing.

executory contracts
A contract in which the parties bind themselves to future activity; a contract that is not yet fully completed or performed.

consideration
Something of value that is exchanged between parties. It can be an act, a forbearance (not performing an act), a promise to perform an act, or a promise to refrain from performing an act.

capacity
The legal power to do something, such as enter into a contract or a relationship. Also called *legal capacity*. (See glossary for an additional meaning.)

statute of frauds
A law requiring some contracts (example: one that cannot be performed within a year of its making) to be in writing and signed by the parties to be bound by the contract.

arm's length
Pertaining to how parties would treat each other if they were strangers looking out for their own self-interests with no confidential or other special relationship between them that would cause one to expect the other to provide a special advantage or to act with fairness.

fiduciary relationship
The relationship that exists when one party (called the fiduciary) owes loyalty, candor, and fair treatment to another party. The fiduciary is required to act in the interest of and for the benefit of the other. Also called a *confidential relationship*.

overreaching
Taking unfair advantage of another's naiveté or other vulnerability, especially by deceptive means.

Voluntary

voluntary
By choice; proceeding from a free and unrestrained will.

duress
The unlawful use of force or threats to pressure or compel someone to do something he or she does not want to do. Illegal coercion.

The agreement must be **voluntary**, meaning that it must proceed from a free and unrestrained will. A court will not enforce an agreement that a party was forced to sign or that is the product of **duress**, which is the unlawful use of force or threats to pressure or compel someone to do something he or she does not want to do. Note that, in most cases, it is not duress for a party to threaten to call off the engagement if the other party does not sign the premarital agreement. This is not an unlawful threat.

Leo and Helen are engaged to be married. Leo's attorney drafts a premarital agreement and Leo tells Helen he will cancel the engagement if she does not sign it. She signs it and they marry. Five years later, they separate. In the divorce proceeding, Leo asks the court to enforce the terms of the premarital agreement. Helen argues that the agreement is invalid because it was the product of duress.

Helen will lose her argument if at the time she signed the agreement, she was an intelligent woman, had an adequate command of the English language, was given full disclosure of Leo's finances, and had adequate time to consult her own attorney or other advisers. She may have felt pressure to sign, but the pressure was not unlawful if she had the information she needed (or the opportunity to obtain it) and proceeded to sign the agreement of her own free will. The result might be different if Helen was still learning English, had limited life experience, was pregnant, in poor health, or was presented with the agreement for the first time on the day of the wedding with hundreds of guests (many from out of town) about to file into church.

rebut
To attack, dispute, or refute.

To help **rebut** the charge of duress, some attorneys recommend that the premarital agreement be presented to the other party at least three months before the marriage.

Fraud

fraud
An intentionally false statement of fact that (a) is material, (b) is made to induce reliance by the plaintiff, and (c) results in harm because of the reliance. Also called *deceit* or *misrepresentation*.

Fraud is an intentionally false statement of fact that is *material*, made to induce reliance, and results in harm because of the reliance. If, for example, a party lies about what he or she owns in order to obtain the consent of the other party to the premarital agreement, the agreement will not be enforced. The false statement must be **material**, meaning that the fact was serious and substantial, and important enough to influence the decision to sign.

material
(1) Serious and substantial. (2) Important enough to influence the decision that was made.

FINANCIAL DISCLOSURE

Parties must make a sufficient disclosure of their finances to each other before signing the premarital agreement. States differ on how much disclosure is required. Some insist on a full and detailed disclosure of assets and liabilities. In other states, it is enough to provide a general picture of one's financial worth. Once the general picture is provided, the other party has a duty to make inquiries or to consult with experts in order to obtain more financial details. Cautious attorneys, however, will always try to provide maximum financial disclosure to rebut a later claim by a spouse that he or she did not know the scope of the other spouse's wealth when signing the premarital agreement. Such attorneys will not only list all assets but will also state the estimated or actual value of each asset, being careful to avoid undervaluation.

Often, the agreement includes a clause that says full disclosure has been made. This clause, however, is not always controlling, particularly if it can be shown that the party was tricked or unduly coerced into signing the agreement.

Finally, although the right to receive financial disclosure is critical to the validity of a premarital agreement, the right can be waived in most states. Parties can agree to a clause saying that the offer of a full financial disclosure was waived or that whatever the other party has disclosed is sufficient and that no further disclosure is needed.

FAIRNESS AND UNCONSCIONABILITY

Courts differ on how they treat the issue of the fairness of a premarital agreement. In some courts, the enforceability of the agreement is based on the distinction between procedural and substantive fairness. In other courts, enforceability depends on whether the agreement was unconscionable. These concepts, however, are not mutually exclusive; there is overlap in the meanings of procedural unfairness, substantive unfairness, and unconscionability.

Fairness

There are two kinds of fairness:

- **Procedural fairness.** Sufficient financial disclosure, sufficient opportunity to consult with others, voluntariness, and the absence of duress and fraud. Informed consent.

- **Substantive fairness.** Equitable in the sense that the terms are reasonable and mutually favorable, the hallmarks of a good deal for both spouses.

The focus of procedural fairness is the *process* the parties went through when they entered into the premarital agreement. Was it open, voluntary, and informed? The focus of substantive fairness is the *content* of the agreement itself. Was it mutually favorable? If a state does not use the language of procedural or substantive fairness, it might instead use the standard of unconscionability along with the requirement of sufficient disclosure and voluntariness.

Let's take a closer look at these terms.

PROCEDURAL FAIRNESS A procedurally fair agreement in one in which the parties were given sufficient financial disclosure, entered into the agreement voluntarily, had sufficient time to seek advice from others on whether to sign, and were not subjected to duress or fraud. Competent attorneys advise their clients to give their prospective spouses time to study and think about the terms of the premarital agreement before signing. Waiting until the morning of the wedding to bring up the subject of a premarital agreement is not wise, particularly if the parties have substantially different education and business backgrounds. The more immature a person is in age and in worldly matters, the more time he or she should be given to consider the agreement and to consult with independent experts or friends who are able to explain (1) the present and future financial worth of the prospective spouse and (2) the waivers asked for in the premarital agreement.

SUBSTANTIVE FAIRNESS At one time, society viewed women as vulnerable and in need of special protection. There was almost a presumption that a woman's prospective husband would try to take advantage of her through the premarital agreement. Courts that took this view tended to scrutinize such agreements to make sure they were procedurally *and* substantively fair to the prospective bride. The agreement had to be free of coercion and deception, and also had to be equitable in the sense of being a reasonably good deal under the circumstances.

The women's movement has helped change this perspective. Today, there is a greater degree of equality between the sexes. Consequently, if a woman makes a bad bargain in a premarital agreement, many courts are inclined to force her to live with it so long as the following occurred:

- It was entered into voluntarily,

- There was no duress or fraud.

- There was adequate disclosure of the identity and value of the other's assets and debts.

- There was an opportunity to seek advice from independent counsel, financial advisers, and others.

procedural fairness
Sufficient financial disclosure, sufficient opportunity to consult with others, voluntariness, and the absence of duress and fraud. Informed consent.

substantive fairness
Equitable in the sense that the terms are reasonable and mutually favorable.

In short, procedural fairness is all that is required. An agreement will not be struck down simply because there is an inequality in what each party receives. A wife cannot undo the agreement because of "buyer's remorse" or a wish that a better deal had been negotiated. Of course, the same is true of males of modest means who later regret signing premarital agreements with relatively wealthy women.

In a few states, if the terms of the agreement are not substantively fair, the court will presume that the other party concealed assets and failed to make a complete financial disclosure (procedural fairness), requiring this party to overcome the presumption by proving that the disclosure was sufficient. This gives the weaker party an advantage. He or she does not have to prove that the disclosure was inadequate; the other party has the burden of proving that it was adequate.

The rule that procedural fairness is enough to enforce a premarital agreement is subject to a major exception. As we have seen, if the terms of the agreement leave a spouse in such poverty that he or she is likely to become a public charge when the other spouse seeks to enforce it, most courts will step in and require enough spousal support to avoid this result.

Unconscionability

Some states do not use the terms procedural and substantive fairness but simply conclude that the agreement will be enforced so long as (1) there was sufficient disclosure and voluntariness and (2) the agreement was not unconscionable. An agreement is **unconscionable** when it is shockingly unfair or unjust; it shocks the conscience by heavily favoring one side, together with an absence of meaningful choice and a highly unequal bargaining posture of the parties. One court defined *unconscionability* as "the absence of meaningful choice on the part of one party due to one-sided contract provisions, together with terms which are so oppressive that no reasonable person would make them and no fair and honest person would accept them."[10] In effect, when an agreement is unconscionable, a party is unduly cornered into accepting very little and giving up a great deal in a highly pressurized take-it-or-leave-it environment.

See the Interviewing and Investigation Checklist on factors relevant to the validity of a premarital agreement.

unconscionable

(1) Shockingly unfair or unjust. (2) Shocking the conscience by heavily favoring one side together with an absence of meaningful choice and a highly unequal bargaining posture of the parties.

ASSIGNMENT   4.2

a. Jim and Mary are about to be married. Mary is a wealthy actress. Jim is a struggling artist. Both agree that it would be a good idea to have a premarital agreement. Mary suggests that Jim make an appointment to visit her tax preparer whom Mary will instruct to give Jim a complete understanding of her assets. Laughing, Jim replies, "Not necessary. I'm insulted at the suggestion, my love." A year after the marriage, they divorce. Mary seeks to enforce the premarital agreement, which provides that Jim waives spousal support and is not entitled to any of Mary's property in the event of a divorce. Jim argues that the agreement is unenforceable. Discuss whether he is correct. (See General Instructions for the Legal Analysis Assignment in Appendix A.)

b. Do women have enough equality in today's society that they should be forced to live with agreements that, in hindsight, they should not have entered into? Is it more demeaning to a woman to rescue her from a poorly bargained agreement or to force her to live in drastically poorer economic circumstances because of the premarital agreement she signed?

☑ INTERVIEWING AND INVESTIGATION CHECKLIST

Factors Relevant to the Validity of a Premarital Agreement

LEGAL INTERVIEWING QUESTIONS TO ASK THE CLIENT

(D = Defendant-Spouse)

1. On what date did you begin discussing the premarital agreement?

2. Whose idea was it to have an agreement?

3. On what date did you first see the agreement?

4. Who wrote the agreement?

5. Did you read the agreement? If so, how carefully?

6. Did you understand everything in the agreement?

7. Describe in detail what you thought was in the agreement.

8. Did you sign the agreement? If so, why?

9. Were any changes made in the agreement? If so, describe the circumstances, such as the nature of each change, who proposed it, etc.

10. Do you recall anything said during the discussions on the agreement that was different from what was eventually written down?

11. Who was present at the time you discussed and signed the agreement?

12. Where is the agreement kept? Were you given a copy at the time you signed?

13. Before you signed the agreement, did you consult with anyone, e.g., attorney, accountant, or relative? Were you encouraged to have such consultations? Explain.

14. If you did consult with anyone, describe that person's relationship, if any, with D. Friend of D? Business associate of D? Paid by D?

15. What were you told by the individuals with whom you consulted? Did they think it was wise for you to sign the agreement? Why or why not?

16. How old were you when you signed the agreement? How old was D?

17. What is your educational background and business or work experience. Same question for D.

18. How much did you know about D's background before you agreed to marry D? What knowledge or impressions did you have of D's wealth and standard of living?

19. How did you reach these conclusions on D's wealth and standard of living? What were you told, what did you observe, etc.?

20. While you were considering the premarital agreement, describe what you specifically knew about the following: D's bank accounts (e.g., savings, checking, trust), insurance policies, home ownership, business property, salary, investments (e.g., stocks, bonds), rental income, royalty income, inheritances (recent or expected), cars, planes, boats, etc. How did you obtain this knowledge?

21. What did you know about D's debts and other liabilities? How did you obtain this knowledge?

22. When you signed the agreement, did you know that D owned (_____)? (Insert items in parentheses that the client learned about only after the agreement was signed.)

23. Do you think you were given an honest accounting of all D's assets at the time you signed? Why or why not?

24. Do you think the agreement you signed was fair to you and to the children you and D had? Why or why not?

POSSIBLE INVESTIGATION TASKS

- Obtain copies of the premarital agreement that was signed.

- If possible, obtain copies of earlier drafts of the agreement, if any. Compare them to the agreement that was signed.

- Contact and interview anyone who has knowledge of and/or who was present during the discussions and/or signing of the agreement.

- Try to obtain bank records, tax records, etc., that would help identify the wealth and standard of living of D and of the client at the time they signed the premarital agreement. Focus on records that reflect the extent of their assets and liabilities (debts).

- Prepare an inventory of every asset that the client thought D owned at the time the agreement was signed, and an inventory of every asset the investigation has revealed D in fact owned at the time of the signing.

INDEPENDENT COUNSEL

The preferred practice is for each party to a premarital agreement to have independent counsel. If one of them cannot afford to pay an attorney, the other should offer funds to hire one. If funds are provided for this purpose, the attorney hired should have no obligations, allegiance, or prior professional or business dealings with the party providing the funds.

What happens if a party signs a premarital agreement without the benefit of independent counsel? Is it evidence that the agreement could not have been voluntarily entered into? The celebrated case of *In re Marriage of Bonds* answers this question. In the *Bonds* case, a multimillionaire baseball player, Barry Bonds, entered into a premarital agreement with his prospective wife, Sun Bonds. Paragraph 10 of their premarital agreement provided as follows:

> 10. CONTROL AND EARNINGS OF BOTH HUSBAND AND WIFE DURING MARRIAGE. We agree that all the earnings and accumulations resulting from the other's personal services, skill, efforts and work, together with all property acquired with funds and income derived therefrom, shall be the separate property of that spouse.

This clause meant that Sun Bonds would have no marital rights in the baseball salary of Barry Bonds, clearly the largest asset in the coming marriage. She did not have independent counsel when she signed the agreement.

The case arose in California, a **community property** state in which each spouse has a 50 percent interest in marital property such as a spouse's salary, regardless of which spouse earned the salary. A valid premarital agreement can change this rule. If the *Bonds* case had arisen in a **common-law property** state, the same issue would have had to be decided. The question before the court would still be whether the absence of independent counsel rendered the premarital agreement involuntary and therefore unenforceable.

community property
Property in which each spouse has a 50 percent interest if the property was acquired during the marriage other than by gift, will, or intestate succession (inheritance) to only one of the spouses. (See Chapter 8.)

common-law property
Property acquired during the marriage in a state other than a community-property state. (Older definition: Property acquired during the marriage that is the separate property of the spouse who earned it or who has title to it.) (See Chapter 8.)

CASE | In re Marriage of Bonds
24 Cal. 4th 1, 5 P.3d 815 (2000)
Supreme Court of California

Background: *When Barry Bonds married Susann (Sun) Bonds in 1988, he was earning $106,000 a year with the Pittsburgh Pirates. When he divorced her in 1994, he was earning millions a year with the San Francisco Giants. Before they married, they signed a premarital agreement prepared by Barry's counsel in which Sun waived any interest in Barry's earnings during the marriage. Sun Bonds did not have independent counsel. She argued that the agreement was invalid because she did not sign it voluntarily. The trial court found that Sun entered into the agreement voluntarily with a full understanding of its terms. Sun appealed to the Court of Appeal, which reversed and directed a retrial on the issue of voluntariness. Barry then appealed to the California Supreme Court. In the following court opinion, Barry is the petitioner; Sun is the respondent.*

Decision on Appeal: *The California Supreme Court reversed the decision of the Court of Appeal. There was substantial evidence that Sun Bonds signed voluntarily despite the lack of independent counsel.*

OPINION OF THE COURT

Chief Justice GEORGE delivered the opinion of the court: . . .

Sun and Barry met in Montreal in the summer of 1987 and maintained a relationship during ensuing months through telephone contacts. In October 1987, at Barry's invitation, Sun visited him for 10 days at his home in Phoenix, Arizona. In November 1987, Sun moved to Phoenix to take up residence with Barry and, one week later, the two became engaged to be married. In January 1988, they decided to marry before the commencement of professional baseball's spring training. On February 5, 1988, in Phoenix, the parties entered into a written premarital agreement in which each party waived any interest in the earnings and acquisitions of the other party during marriage. [The agreement was signed in the office of Barry's attorney, Leonard Brown. Sun did not have an attorney when she signed. After the signing, Barry and Sun flew to Las Vegas, and were married the following day.]

Each of the parties then was 23 years of age. Barry, who had attended college for three years and who had begun his career in professional baseball in 1985, had a contract to play for the Pittsburgh Pirates. His annual salary at the time of the marriage ceremony was approximately $106,000. Sun had emigrated to Canada from Sweden in 1985, had worked as a waitress and bartender, and had undertaken some training as a cosmetologist, having expressed an interest in embarking upon a career as a makeup artist for celebrity clients. Although her native language was Swedish, she had used both French and English in her employment, education, and personal relationships when she lived in Canada. She was unemployed at the time she entered into the premarital agreement. . . .

[The trial court concluded that Barry had demonstrated by clear and convincing evidence that the agreement and its execution were free from the taint of fraud, coercion, or undue influence and that Sun entered the agreement with full knowledge of the property involved and her rights therein. The

(continued)

court of appeal reversed, concluding that the trial court erred in failing to give proper weight to the circumstance that Sun was not represented by independent counsel. Barry has now appealed to the Supreme Court.]

Pursuant to Family Code section 1615, a premarital agreement will be enforced unless the party resisting enforcement of the agreement can demonstrate . . . that he or she did not enter into the contract voluntarily. . . . *Black's Law Dictionary* defines "voluntarily" as "Done by design. . . . Intentionally and without coercion." (Black's Law Dict. (6th ed. 1990) p. 1575.) The same source defines "voluntary" as "Proceeding from the free and unrestrained will of the person. Produced in or by an act of choice. Resulting from free choice, without compulsion or solicitation. The word, especially in statutes, often implies knowledge of essential facts." (Ibid.) The *Oxford English Dictionary* defines "voluntarily" as "[o]f one's own free will or accord; without compulsion, constraint, or undue influence by others; freely, willingly." (19 *Oxford English Dict.* (2d ed. 1989) p. 753.). . . .

[The circumstance that one of the parties was not represented by independent counsel is only one of several factors that must be considered in determining whether a premarital agreement was entered into voluntarily. In addition, a court should consider the impact upon the parties of such factors as

- coercion that may arise from the proximity of execution of the agreement to the wedding, or from surprise in the presentation of the agreement;
- inequality of bargaining power in some cases indicated by the relative age and sophistication of the parties;
- whether there was full disclosure of assets; and
- the parties' understanding of the rights being waived under the agreement or at least their awareness of the intent of the agreement.]

The trial court determined that there had been no coercion. . . . Several witnesses, including Sun herself, stated that she was not threatened. The witnesses were unanimous in observing that Sun expressed no reluctance to sign the agreement, and they observed in addition that she appeared calm, happy, and confident as she participated in discussions of the agreement. [Barry's attorney, Leonard Brown] testified that Sun had indicated a desire at their first meeting to enter into the agreement, and that during the discussion preceding execution of the document, she stated that she understood the agreement. As the trial court determined, although the wedding between Sun and Barry was planned for the day following the signing of the agreement, the wedding was impromptu—the parties had not secured a license or a place to be married, and the few family members and close friends who were invited could have changed their plans without difficulty. (For example, guests were not arriving from Sweden.)

In view of these circumstances, the evidence supported the inference, drawn by the trial court, that the coercive force of the normal desire to avoid social embarrassment or humiliation was diminished or absent. Finally, Barry's testimony that the parties early in their relationship had discussed their desire to keep separate their property and earnings, in addition to the testimony of Barry and [his attorney] that they had met with Sun at least one week before the document was signed to discuss the need for an agreement, and the evidence establishing that Sun understood and concurred in the agreement, constituted substantial evidence to support the trial court's conclusion that Sun was not subjected to the type of coercion that may arise from the surprise and confusion caused by a last-minute presentation of a new plan to keep earnings and property separate during marriage. . . .

Brown testified that [he] informed Sun that he represented Barry and that therefore it might be in her best interest to have her own attorney. She declined. Brown testified that at the February 5, 1988, session he explained the basics of community property law, telling Sun that she would be disavowing the protection of community property law by agreeing that income and acquisitions during marriage would be separate property. He informed her of her right to separate counsel, and told both parties that the agreement did not have to be signed that day. He again informed Sun that he represented Barry. He testified that Sun stated that it was not necessary for her to have counsel, and that she said she understood how the contract affected her interests under the community property law. . . . Sun did not forgo separate legal advice out of ignorance. Instead, she declined to invoke her interests under the community property law because she agreed, for her own reasons, that Barry's and her earnings and acquisitions after marriage should be separate property. . . .

[The] basic purport of the agreement—that the parties would hold their earnings and accumulations during marriage as separate property, thereby giving up the protection of marital property law—was a relatively simple concept that did not require great legal sophistication to comprehend and that was, as the trial court found, understood by Sun. Finally, we observe that the evidence supports the inference that Sun was intrepid rather than a person whose will is easily overborne. She emigrated from her homeland at a young age, found employment and friends in a new country using two languages other than her native tongue, and in two years moved to yet another country, expressing the desire to take up a career and declaring to Barry that she "didn't want his money." These circumstances support the inference that any inequality in bargaining power—arising primarily from the absence of independent counsel who could have advised Sun not to sign the agreement or urged Barry to abandon the idea of keeping his earnings separate—was not coercive. . . .

Family Code Section 1615 places on the party seeking to avoid a premarital agreement the burden of demonstrating that the agreement was involuntary. The trial court determined that Sun did not carry her burden, and we believe that its factual findings in support of this conclusion are supported by substantial evidence.

The judgment of the Court of Appeal is reversed. . . .

ASSIGNMENT 4.3

a. Assess the voluntariness of the premarital agreement in the fact situations in (i)–(iv) below. Assume in each instance that the parties did not have independent counsel. How would the *Bonds* case apply to each?

   (i) Harry presented Linda with the premarital agreement for the first time at the jewelry store where they were buying a ring the day before the wedding. Immediately after the wedding, they were scheduled to begin an expensive honeymoon cruise.

   (ii) Sam presented Mary with the premarital agreement for the first time two weeks before the wedding, just after Mary's elderly and frail parents arrived for the wedding from abroad.

   (iii) When Diane signed the premarital agreement, she was a pregnant teenager, anxious about the legitimacy of her child. Her husband-to-be and the father of the child, Bill, was an older man.

   (iv) The spouse preparing the premarital agreement was an attorney. The spouse of this attorney was a paralegal.

b. Should the law *require* each party to have his or her own independent counsel in order for the premarital agreement to be valid?

c. Do you think that there should be a difference between determining the voluntariness of a confession in a criminal case and the voluntariness of a premarital agreement in a civil case? Why or why not?

DO NOT SIGN THIS AGREEMENT!

Under some circumstances, attorneys run the risk of being sued for legal malpractice when their clients are presented with lopsided premarital agreements by their future spouse.

Assume the following facts:
(1) There is a substantial disparity between the wealth of the parties to a premarital agreement, and
(2) The financially weaker party is being asked to waive all or substantially all of the property rights normally accorded spouses.

An attorney representing the weaker party is in a potentially vulnerable position. It is easy to say that the attorney should fight hard and bargain for better terms for the client. If, however, the wealthy party insists on no changes and if the attorney's client is prepared to go along and sign the agreement, there is not much that the attorney can do.

To be sure, the attorney needs to provide clear explanations of what the client is giving up. This, however, may not be enough to prevent the client from suing the attorney for legal malpractice years later when the premarital agreement is being enforced and the full brunt of the agreement is felt. Inevitably, the client says that she (it's usually a woman) did not understand the terms of the agreement and was not given proper advice by her attorney.

To protect themselves in such situations, some attorneys feel that they need to advise their clients in writing *not* to sign the agreement. Another strategy is to withdraw from the representation. If the attorney feels that the client is relatively immature and not capable of handling the intense emotional pressure she is under, the ultimate step of self-protection that the attorney can take is to formally withdraw from representing the client.

It is not much consolation to say that the premarital agreement might eventually be attacked on grounds such as unconscionability. It can take years to bring such litigation. Furthermore, if the litigation is brought, the chances of winning are compromised when it is made known that the agreement was signed against the advice of the party's own attorney! She understood that it was a bad deal because her attorney told her not to sign it or because her attorney withdrew from representing her. Yet she went ahead and signed anyway.

DRAFTING GUIDELINES

The Premarital Agreements Checklist contains guidelines for drafting a premarital agreement. After the guidelines, you will find a sample premarital agreement.

☑ PREMARITAL AGREEMENTS: A CHECKLIST OF DRAFTING GUIDELINES

Ensuring the Enforceability of a Premarital Agreement
(FH = Future Husband; FW = Future Wife)

Although all the steps listed in this checklist may not be required in your state, they will help ensure the enforceability of the agreement. This checklist assumes that the attorney drafting the agreement represents the future husband (FH), who is going to enter into the marriage with considerably more wealth than the future wife (FW). If a same-sex marriage is involved, the same guidelines apply. For such marriages, substitute S1 (Spouse 1) for FH, and S2 (Spouse 2) for FW in the following guidelines:

PREPARATION

- Verify the accuracy of the names, addresses, and relationships of every individual to be mentioned in the premarital agreement.

- Research the requirements for premarital agreements in the state, e.g., whether they must be subscribed (signed), acknowledged (affirmed as a genuine document), notarized (affirming the authenticity of signatures), or recorded (deposited with an official office or body such as a county clerk's office).

- Determine if the FH and the FW plan to move to another state during the marriage. If so, research the requirements for premarital agreements in such state in order to ensure that the premarital agreement would be valid there in the event that they do move. (Even if there is a move, however, the parties can designate the state whose law will govern the agreement. See below.)

- Weeks (and, if possible, months) before the marriage, notify the FW when the agreement will be ready to examine and that she should obtain independent counsel.

- The greater the disparity in the age, wealth, education, and business experience of the FH and the FW, the more time the FW should be given to study the agreement.

- Have the FW sign a statement acknowledging that she has been advised to hire independent counsel and that the FH will, if needed, provide funds for such hiring.

- Have the FW sign a statement acknowledging that she has been told that the persons hired by the FH represent the FH and do not represent the FW even though such persons may discuss the law and FW's options.

- Make sure the FW is old enough to have the legal capacity to enter into a valid contract in the state.

- Determine whether the FW has ever been treated for mental illness or if any question could be raised about the FW's current mental health for purposes of understanding the agreement. If needed, assist the FW in selecting a mental health professional who is qualified to issue a certificate or affidavit of competency following an evaluation.

- Prepare a list of all current personal and business assets of of the FH with the exact or approximate value of each asset. Use market value (what it could be sold for in an open market), not book value (the amount stated on the books). (Include real property, vehicles, jewelry, household furnishings, stocks, bonds, other securities, cash, and other personal property.) This list should be referred to in the agreement, shown to the FW, to her independent counsel, and to her other advisers, and attached to the agreement.

- Have the FW (and her independent counsel and other advisers) sign a statement acknowledging receipt of this list.

- Prepare a list of all known future assets that the FH expects to acquire during the marriage, with the exact or approximate market value of each asset. (Include future employment contracts, options, and anticipated purchases.) This list should be referred to in the agreement, shown to the FW, to her independent counsel, and to her other advisers, and attached to the agreement.

- Have the FW (and her independent counsel and other advisers) sign a statement acknowledging receipt of this list.

- Prepare a list of all current debts and other liabilities of the FH. This list should be referred to in the agreement, shown to the FW, to her independent counsel, and to her other advisers, and attached to the agreement.

- Have the FW (and her independent counsel and other advisers) sign a statement acknowledging receipt of this list.

- Alternatively, hire an accountant to prepare a financial statement of the FH detailing his assets and liabilities. This statement should be referred to in the agreement, shown to the FW, to her independent counsel, and to her other advisers, and attached to the agreement.

- Have the FW (and her independent counsel and other advisers) sign a statement acknowledging receipt of this financial statement.

(continued)

PREMARITAL AGREEMENTS: A CHECKLIST OF DRAFTING GUIDELINES (*continued*)

- Obtain copies of recent personal tax returns, business tax returns, existing contracts of employment, deeds, purchase agreements, credit-card bills, pension statements, and brokerage reports. Make a list of these documents. The documents and the list should be referred to in the agreement, shown to the FW, to her independent counsel, and to her other advisers. The list should be attached to the agreement.

- Have the FW (and her independent counsel and other advisers) sign a statement acknowledging the receipt of the list and their examination of these documents.

- To preserve confidentiality of sensitive financial data, the participants might acknowledge having access to and reading the lists, statements, and documents referred to above but not have them attached to the premarital agreement.

PARTICIPANTS AND THEIR ROLES

- The FH's attorney, financial advisers, and other experts who have any communication with the FW should make clear to the FW (a) that they represent the FH only, (b) that the FW should not rely on them to protect her interests, and (c) that the FW should seek independent counsel or other advice.

- If needed, suggestions should be made to the FW about where she can find independent counsel and other experts who have never had any business or social dealings with the FH.

- If needed and if possible, funds should be made available to the FW to hire independent counsel or other experts.

- If no independent counsel of the FW is used, representatives of the FH will explain the terms of the agreement to the FW. When doing so, they should again remind the FW that their sole role is to protect the best interests of the FH, not the FW.

- If English is the second language of the FW, arrange for a translator to be present. Encourage the FW to select this translator.

- There should be at least two witnesses present who will observe the execution of the agreement. (Paralegals are sometimes asked to act as witnesses to such documents.)

- The agreement should contain a clause stating that when the agreement was negotiated, discussed, and signed neither party was under the influence of alcohol, prescribed medication, or any drug that would affect their ability to understand the rights granted and waived in the agreement.

CONTENT OF THE AGREEMENT

- State the reasons the parties are entering into the agreement.
- Include a separate list of the names, addresses, and titles of every individual who helped the FW prepare and/or understand the agreement.

- State whether the assets of the FH and of the FW listed as separate property will remain separate property during the marriage.

- State whether the appreciation (i.e., increase in value) of separate property during the marriage will constitute separate property.

- List the FH's existing children, other relatives, or friends and specify what assets, if any, they will be given (to the exclusion of the FW) during the marriage or upon the termination of the marriage.

- List the FW's existing children, other relatives, or friends and specify what assets, if any, they will be given (to the exclusion of the FH) during the marriage or upon the termination of the marriage.

- List the documents that were shown to, read by, and understood by the FW (e.g., lists of the assets, lists of debts, copies of tax returns, and financial statements). State which of these documents are attached to the agreement.

- Include a statement that the FW acknowledges receipt of details on the FH's assets and liabilities, that this disclosure is comprehensive, that the FW has had _____ [specify a number of days, weeks or months] to examine these details, which is a sufficient amount of time, and that the FW is fully satisfied that this disclosure adequately apprises her of the FH's financial condition.

- Briefly summarize the major property and support rights that the FW and the FH would have upon dissolution of a marriage or upon the death of either in the absence of a premarital agreement (e.g., the right to an equitable share in all marital property, the right to alimony, and the right to elect against the will of a deceased spouse). Then include a statement that the parties understand that by signing the premarital agreement, they are waiving some or all of these rights.

- State whether there is specific business or nonbusiness property that the FH will have the right to manage and dispose of without the consent or participation of the FW.

- If the parties are waiving rights to each other's pension benefits, include a clause that the parties will acknowledge this waiver in writing immediately after they are married.

- State whether the FW will own and be entitled to the death benefits of specific life insurance policies.

- Indicate which state's law will govern the interpretation and enforcement of the agreement.

- State whether arbitration will be used if the FW and the FH have disagreements over the agreement and whether the arbitrator's findings can be appealed. If used, state how the arbitrator will be chosen and compensated.

- State the method the FH and the FW will use to modify or terminate the agreement during the marriage.

- Do not ask for a waiver of disclosure of assets. (It is legal to ask for such a waiver, but the request should be avoided if possible.)

- Do not ask for a waiver of mutual support during the marriage. (Such a request may raise a red flag of unconscionability.)

- Do not ask for a waiver of child support. (Such a waiver cannot be enforced. See Chapter 10.)

- Do not ask for a waiver of the right to seek custody or visitation. (Such a waiver cannot override the court's role in deciding custody based on the best interests of the child. See Chapter 9.)

- Do not specify a date on which the prospective marriage will be dissolved. (Including such a date may be evidence of a sham marriage and grounds for an annulment. See Chapter 6.)

- State that if either party provides financial or other help to the other to pursue his or her education during the marriage that the help shall be considered gifts without expectation of repayment in any form.

- If the parties are of child-bearing age, do not state that either or both will not have children. (See earlier discussion on the enforceability of such clauses.)

- State that each party will keep the contents of the agreement confidential and will not disclose such contents in traditional or social media.

- State what documents, if any, the parties will be obligated to sign or obtain within a specified time after they are married (e.g., a waiver of rights in each other's retirement benefits, a life insurance policy, or an amendment to an existing will or trust).

- Include a severability clause stating that if any specific clause in the agreement is found to be invalid, the intent of the parties is to have the remaining valid parts of the agreement enforced.

SIGNING THE AGREEMENT

- Videotape the signing session, particularly while the FW is explaining (a) why she is signing, (b) whom she relied upon for advice in accepting the terms of the agreement, (c) her understanding of the FH's present and future assets, (d) her understanding of what she is waiving in the agreement, (e) that she has been advised to obtain independent counsel, and (e) if she does not have independent counsel, why she chose not to have such counsel.

- The FH and the FW should sign every page of the agreement.

- The signatures should be notarized.

- Minor changes or corrections to the agreement should be dated and signed by the parties in the margin next to the change. Major changes should prompt a new version of the document.

RECORDKEEPING

- Keep copies of the agreement and all of the attachments (the latter are often called schedules attached to the agreement).

- Keep copies of all documents that were changed before the final agreement was signed. They may be needed to help prove the state of mind of the participants.

- Store these documents indefinitely. They may not be needed until decades later when the parties separate or when one of them dies and the agreement is enforced or challenged.

ASSIGNMENT 4.4

a. Assume you are about to be married and that you are substantially more well-to-do than your spouse-to-be. Draft a premarital agreement for you and your future spouse. You can make up facts about the financial affairs and interests of each of you. Number each clause of the agreement separately and consecutively. Try to anticipate as many difficulties as possible that could arise during the marriage and state in the agreement how you want them resolved. Before you draft the agreement, prepare a checklist of topics to cover in the agreement. Review all the material in this chapter on premarital agreements and check online for additional ideas for topics that a couple should discuss and cover in such an agreement. (See General Instructions for the Agreement-Drafting Assignment in Appendix A.)

b. After your instructor makes note of the fact that you have drafted an agreement, you will be asked to exchange agreements with another student and analyze that student's agreement. Go through each numbered clause in the agreement and determine all possible legal problems that might be raised according to the standards identified in this chapter. When you cannot apply a standard, in whole or in part, because you need more facts, simply list the factual questions to which you would like answers and state how they might be relevant to the validity of the clause in question. (See General Instructions for the Legal-Analysis Assignment in Appendix A.)

EXAMPLE OF A PREMARITAL AGREEMENT

Exhibit 4.3 contains an example of a premarital agreement. Margin comments are provided to highlight important themes in the clauses. For terms you do not understand in the clauses, consult the glossary at the end of the book.

EXHIBIT 4.3   Example of a Premarital Agreement

PREMARITAL AGREEMENT

This premarital agreement is made on [date], between [name of future husband] of [address] and [name of future wife] of [address].

RECITALS

A. The parties have represented to each other that each is single and legally free to marry.

B. The parties presently contemplate marriage to each other, such marriage to be solemnized in the near future.

C. The parties have fully and completely disclosed the nature and approximate value of all of their presently existing assets, liabilities, and income to each party's satisfaction on the respective Schedules annexed to this agreement.

D. Each party recognizes that certain rights and claims may accrue to each of them in the property and interests of the other as a result of their marriage. These rights include, but are not limited to, the right to spousal support upon separation or divorce and the right to an elective share of the estate of a deceased spouse. The parties understand that such rights are being modified by this agreement.

E. The parties desire to define certain obligations arising out of their marriage to each other and to fix, limit, and determine the rights and claims that may accrue in the property of the other by reason of their marriage and to accept the provisions of this agreement in lieu of and in full satisfaction of any and all rights and claims that otherwise each might have in the property of the other, in the event of the parties' separation or dissolution of their marriage.

F. To each party's satisfaction, they enter into this premarital agreement with full knowledge of the extent and approximate present value of each other's property, and with full knowledge that this agreement alters rights to such property that may be conferred by law by virtue of their marriage.

G. The future husband has had the benefit of independent legal advice, prior to the execution of this agreement, from _____ [name], Esq., of _____ [address].

H. The future wife has had the benefit of independent legal advice, prior to the execution of this agreement, from _____ [name], Esq., of _____ [address].

In consideration of the matters described above, and of the mutual benefits and obligations set forth in this agreement, the parties agree as follows:

SECTION 1—FINANCIAL DISCLOSURE

The parties acknowledge that, to their mutual satisfaction, each has had the opportunity to ascertain, has been informed by a full and frank disclosure by the other, and is fully acquainted with and aware of the approximate assets, liabilities, income, and general financial circumstances of the other; that each has ascertained and weighed all of the facts, conditions and circumstances likely to influence his or her judgment in all matters embodied here; that each has given due consideration to all such matters and questions, and clearly understands

Margin comments:

- *A recital is a preliminary statement in a document covering its background or purpose.*

- *Clauses D, E, and F point out that the parties know that valuable legal rights accrue to married couples. The clauses also state that the parties realize that a valid premarital agreement can eliminate or otherwise modify these rights. The clauses help rebut a later claim that either of the parties did not realize what the agreement changed or waived.*

- *One of the strongest arguments for the validity of a premarital agreement is the fact that both sides had independent counsel advising them.*

(continued)

Exhibit 4.3 *(continued)*

and consents to all the provisions contained here; and that each has had the opportunity to have or has in fact had the benefit and advice of independent counsel of his or her own choice and is willing to accept the provisions of this agreement in lieu of all other rights each may have.

SECTION 2—SEPARATE PROPERTY: PROPERTY BROUGHT INTO THE MARRIAGE

After the solemnization of the marriage between the parties, each of them will separately retain all rights in his or her own property now owned and more fully set forth in the Schedules that are annexed to this agreement. Each party will have the absolute and unrestricted right to dispose of their separate property free from any claim that may be made by the other by reason of their marriage and with the same effect as if no marriage has been entered between them.

SECTION 3—APPRECIATION OF SEPARATE PROPERTY

The attached Schedules list the property of [future husband] and [future wife], respectively, as that property is now constituted. Each party will separately retain all rights to the property in its present form and in any form that is traceable to it, including any appreciation in the value of the property as a direct or indirect result of the contribution or efforts of either party or due to market factors, except as may be provided to the contrary in this agreement.

SECTION 4—PROPERTY ACQUIRED AFTER MARRIAGE

Any property either party acquires after the marriage—except for such property that has been specifically excepted in this agreement and that has not been commingled with joint or otherwise marital property—will be divided between the parties upon separation or divorce as provided in this agreement.

SECTION 5—PARTIES' UNDERSTANDING OF RIGHTS WAIVED

The parties intend that the disposition of the property referred to in this agreement be deemed a disposition of this property that would fully satisfy any claims either party may have against the other including each party's rights to equitable distribution under [cite statute] upon a divorce.

SECTION 6—GENERAL STATEMENT OF INTENTION

While the parties fully intend to commit themselves to achieving a successful long-term marriage, each is personally aware of the practicalities and realities of married life. Each therefore intends by entering into this agreement to minimize the time, financial cost, and emotional strain involved in the event of a future separation or dissolution of marriage between them.

SECTION 7—CHILD SUPPORT OF CHILDREN FROM A PRIOR MARRIAGE

[Future husband] has children from his prior marriage. [Future wife] has children from her prior marriage. Each party will continue to be responsible for all legal obligations (including the duty of support) concerning his or her own children and in no event will either be responsible, now or in the future, for any legal obligations concerning the other party's children.

SECTION 8—RETIREMENT BENEFITS

The parties each have retirement plans either through their employer or self-procured. The parties intend by entering into this agreement that neither party will acquire any rights at any time, in any form or nature, to the other's retirement benefits. If further agreements are needed to effectuate Section 8 after the marriage, the parties agree to execute such agreements.

- *Financial disclosure of assets and liabilities is critical for a valid agreement. Throughout the agreement there are references to attachments that are included ("annexed") to the agreement. The attachments - called "Schedules" - provide this financial disclosure.*

- *Property that a person brings into the marriage is separate property, not marital or community property. (See Chapter 8.) The attached Schedules will list this property to prevent later misunderstandings.*

- *Chapter 8 will discuss the issue of whether the appreciation of separate property is marital or separate property, which may depend on whether the appreciation is active or passive. In either event, a premarital agreement can state how the parties wish to treat the appreciation.*

- *This agreement in Exhibit 4.3 is written for a couple in a common-law property state that divides property upon divorce on the basis of an equitable distribution. The same clause could be written if the parties were in a community property state. (See Chapter 8.)*

- *Once the marriage occurs, the parties want to make clear that they do not intend to obligate themselves for the child support of their respective stepchildren. (See Chapter 10.)*

- *A waiver of retirement rights may have to occur after the marriage takes place. Section 22 covers this concern by providing that the parties will cooperate in creating (executing) any documents or instruments needed to carry out the intentions of the parties in this agreement.*

(continued)

Exhibit 4.3 *(continued)*

SECTION 9—MARITAL PROPERTY ACQUIRED DURING MARRIAGE

Nothing contained in this agreement will be construed to preclude any rights either party may have in the event of the dissolution of their marriage in those assets that are acquired during the marriage except to the extent that agreement (or any subsequent agreement entered by the parties) specifically alters any of those rights.

SECTION 10—WAIVER OF SPOUSAL SUPPORT (ALIMONY) UPON SEPARATION OR DIVORCE

Both parties are presently employed. [Future husband] is employed by _____, and [future wife] is employed by _____. Both [future husband] and [future wife] are entering into the marriage financially independent and self-sufficient. If the parties separate or the marriage is dissolved, each party understands and agrees to waive, relinquish, and release the other from any duty or obligation to support the other in any fashion or manner. No claim or demand for such support may be made. If a separation or dissolution of marriage is sought by either party, and it appears that the financial circumstances of either party has changed to such a degree that such party can sufficiently demonstrate that he or she would be left without a means of support, destitute or a public charge, or at a standard of living far below that which the party enjoyed before the marriage, as a result of this agreement, then in that event, the party who is not left in any of the foregoing circumstances agrees to provide support for the other in an amount not to exceed $_____ per month, for a period not to exceed _____ years.

SECTION 11—INSURANCE

If the parties separate or the marriage is dissolved, the parties mutually agree that neither will be responsible for maintaining any policy of insurance for the benefit of the other, including, but not limited to, health, life, and automobile insurance.

SECTION 12—PROPERTY RIGHTS UPON DEATH

The parties waive any right to an elective share of each other's estate upon death and make no commitment to transfer any of their separate property to each other upon the death of either party.

SECTION 13—DEDICATION OF INCOME

The parties specifically make no delineation as to the precise use of their income, except to state that it is their general intention to pool their income for their mutual benefit, for the purpose of maintaining their agreed-upon lifestyle and for the accumulation of marital assets. For purposes of this provision, retirement income will not be deemed income but will instead be deemed separate property, as provided in Section 8.

SECTION 14—DEBT BROUGHT INTO THE MARRIAGE

The parties represent that prior to the marriage neither has incurred any debt, charge, obligation or liability for which the other is or may become liable. Any assistance of one party on the other's debt does not constitute an agreement to assume joint responsibility for the debt. Each party agrees to indemnify and hold the other harmless of loss, expenses (including reasonable attorney fees), and damages in the event that a claim is made on the other arising out of or in connection with a breach by either party of Section 14.

SECTION 15—DEBT INCURRED AFTER THE MARRIAGE

Neither party will incur any debts, charges, obligations, or liability over the amount of $_____ for which the other may become liable without first providing the other with reasonable notice and obtaining the other's written consent. Each party agrees to

- *Section 9 says that the parties do not intend to make any changes in how the state divides marital or community property if there is a divorce unless this agreement or a subsequent agreement specifies any such changes.*

- *If there is a separation or divorce, Section 10 waives spousal support (alimony) unless one of the parties faces a drastically lower standard of living or needs public assistance. In such circumstances the agreement lists a specific (liquidated) amount of money for a specific number of years. Note, however, that a court is not bound by this limitation if it determines that more support for a longer period is needed. (See Chapter 8.)*

- *Section 14 clarifies that the debts the parties bring into the marriage are separate debts. Without written consent, one party will not be responsible for the other's separate debts. Furthermore, helping someone on his or her debts does not in and of itself constitute an agreement to be jointly responsible for them.*

(continued)

Exhibit 4.3 *(continued)*

indemnify and hold the other harmless of loss, expenses (including reasonable attorney fees), and damages in the event that a claim is made on the other arising out of or in connection with a breach of Section 15.

SECTION 16—DISTRIBUTION OF MARITAL PROPERTY

The parties acknowledge and understand that each enters this marriage with the same approximate total value of assets. The parties further acknowledge and understand that they intend to pool their financial resources in a joint effort to acquire various undetermined assets such as real estate, financial investment accounts, and other marital property. In the event of separation or marriage dissolution, the parties will agree on how such acquired marital property will be distributed between them. If the parties cannot agree, the property will be liquidated with the net proceeds derived from the liquidation to be evenly distributed between them. "Net proceeds" are the sales price or total liquidated value of any asset less any liens, taxes, and other necessary costs of the liquidation.

- *Section 16 states that in the event of a separation or divorce, if the parties cannot agree on how their marital property should be divided, the division should be equal.*

SECTION 17—FULL DISCLOSURE

The parties acknowledge and represent to each other that they have made a full, fair, and complete disclosure to the other of the nature and approximate value of their assets, liabilities, and income as presently constituted in accordance with their attached Schedules, and that each accepts those disclosures as accurate. The parties represent and acknowledge that based upon the foregoing representations, each knowingly, voluntarily, and without undue pressure, waives further discovery relative to the nature and value of the other's current and future assets, and liabilities.

- *Section 17 says that the financial disclosures are adequate and that further disclosure (discovery) is waived.*

SECTION 18—GIFT OR INHERITANCE TO ONE PARTY

Property acquired during the marriage to one party by way of gift or inheritance from a relative or other third party will be deemed the separate property of that party including any income or profits, increments, accretions, or increases in value of such property at any time, whether due to market conditions or the services, skills, or efforts of either party, and that all such property will be kept separate and not commingled with joint or otherwise marital property. To the extent that any such property is commingled or not kept separate from marital property, it will be deemed joint property.

SECTION 19—GIFT OR INHERITANCE TO BOTH PARTIES

Property acquired by the parties jointly during the marriage by way of gift or inheritance from a relative or other third party shall be deemed joint property acquired during the marriage, the distribution of which, in the event of the parties' separation or dissolution of marriage, is governed by this agreement and by any subsequent agreement the parties decide to enter.

- *Sections 18 and 19 state that property from a gift or an inheritance to one spouse is the separate property of that spouse unless that property is mixed (commingled) with their joint assets. If the gift or inheritance is to both parties, it is marital or joint property (See Chapter 8.)*

SECTION 20—INTERSPOUSAL TRANSFERS, DEVISES, AND BEQUESTS

Notwithstanding any provision of this agreement to the contrary, any other right acquired by either party by virtue of any transfer or conveyance of property between the parties during their lifetime, or by devises or bequests made by either party for the benefit of the other pursuant to a last will and testament, will not be limited or restricted.

SECTION 21—BUSINESS PROPERTY MANAGEMENT

In the event that one of the parties establishes an independent business, the other party shall have no participation in the management of that business.

SECTION 22—ADDITIONAL DOCUMENTS

Both parties agree to execute all documents or instruments necessary to give full force and effect to this agreement, including, but not limited to, documents necessary to waive all rights in each other's retirement benefits pursuant to Section 8.

(continued)

Exhibit 4.3 *(continued)*

SECTION 23—ATTORNEY FEES

In the event of a court proceeding concerning their marital relationship or the dissolution of their marriage, each party will pay and be responsible for payment of his or her own attorney fees and all ancillary costs incurred in connection with any such proceeding.

- *A court would not be bound by Section 23 if it concluded that one of the spouses could not finance private counsel on his or her own. It could order the other spouse to provide funds for this purpose despite what Section 23 says.*

SECTION 24—TIMING OF EXECUTION

This agreement is being executed in sufficient time prior to the scheduled wedding date of _____. The parties acknowledge that each had sufficient opportunity prior to executing this agreement to consult with counsel, to reschedule the wedding date if necessary, and to not proceed with the marriage, but each agrees that the timing of the execution of this agreement relative to their wedding date has no effect on his or her decision to execute this agreement. Each party further waives his or her right to argue that he or she had insufficient time to make an informed and calculated decision to execute it. The parties further represent that this agreement has been discussed between them for a period of _____ [days or weeks or months] prior to the date of executing this agreement, and it is only as a result of their deliberations and thoughtful consideration of the provisions contained in this agreement that it is being executed at this time.

- *Section 24 addresses the problem of a party claiming that the pressures of wedding arrangements prevented him or her from calmly and thoroughly studying the agreement before deciding to sign it.*

SECTION 25—VOLUNTARY EXECUTION

This agreement has been executed by each of the parties free from persuasion, fraud, undue influence, or economic, physical or emotional duress of any kind imposed by the other party or by other persons. During the discussions, negotiations, and signing of this agreement, neither party was under the influence of alcohol, prescribed medication, or any drug that would affect their ability to understand the rights granted and waived in the agreement.

- *Undue influence is improper persuasion, coercion, force, or deception.*

SECTION 26—INDEPENDENT COUNSEL

The parties acknowledge that each has procured and has been advised as to all aspects of this agreement by independent counsel of his or her own choice and understand he or she has the right to seek additional advice of counsel and of others but has expressly waived that right. Each party is satisfied that he or she has freely negotiated the contents of this agreement free from the persuasion of the other or any third party.

- *By including Section 26, the parties are being extra cautious. The section makes explicit the fact that the parties have consulted with their own independent counsel and waive any right they have to seek additional advice.*

SECTION 27—AGREEMENT AS EVIDENCE

This agreement may be offered in evidence in any proceeding instituted by either of the parties in any court of competent jurisdiction in which a determination of the status of the parties' relationship is sought and may, subject to the approval of the court, be incorporated and merged into any order or judgment rendered in that action.

SECTION 28—VALIDITY AND ENFORCEABILITY OF AGREEMENT

The parties further agree that this agreement is valid and enforceable in any action that may subsequently be commenced by either party that may require the use of this agreement as evidence to demonstrate the parties' intent and understanding on any issues addressed in this agreement.

SECTION 29—SEVERABILITY

Should any provision of this agreement be held invalid or unenforceable by any court of competent jurisdiction, all other valid provisions will nonetheless continue in full force and effect.

SECTION 30—MODIFICATION OR WAIVER

No modification or waiver of any terms of this agreement will be valid unless in writing and executed by the parties.

(continued)

Exhibit 4.3 *(continued)*

SECTION 31—GOVERNING LAW

The laws of the state of _____ [name of state] will govern the execution and enforcement of this agreement.

SECTION 32—CONSIDERATION

The consideration for this agreement is the mutual promises contained in this agreement and the marriage about to be solemnized. If the marriage does not take place, this agreement shall be void.

SECTION 33—ENTIRE AGREEMENT

This agreement contains the entire agreement and understanding of the parties, and no representations or promises have been made except those set forth in this agreement.

SECTION 34—BINDING EFFECT

This agreement is binding on and inures to the benefit of the parties and their respective heirs, executors, and administrators.

SECTION 35—EFFECTIVE DATE OF AGREEMENT

This agreement shall become effective upon the date the parties are married.

SECTION 36—ARBITRATION

In the event of any disagreement over the meaning or application of this agreement, the parties will resolve the matter by arbitration. The parties shall mutually agree on who the arbitrator shall be and they will pay for such arbitrator equally.

SECTION 37—CONFIDENTIALTY

Each party agrees that the following matters will be kept confidential: the terms of this premarital agreement and the terms of any other agreement made between the parties during and after the marriage including, but not limited to, the terms of any separation agreement in the event that a separation or divorce occurs.

Dated: _____

_____

[*Name and Signature of Party*]

_____

[*Name and Signature of Party*]

Witnesses:

_____

_____

Notary Public:

_____(Seal)

My commission expires on _____ [expiration date].

This instrument was prepared by _____ [name] of

_____ [address].

[Attach schedules]

Source: Adapted from 98 *American Jurisprudence Legal Forms 2d*, § 139:19 (May 2011) with permission of Thomson Reuters.

POSTNUPTIAL AGREEMENTS

postnuptial agreement
A contract between married persons that covers specific matters, usually financial in nature. Also called *postnup* and *midnup*.

separation agreement
A contract between married persons who have separated (or who are about to separate) that can cover support, custody, property division, and other terms of their separation and likely divorce. Also called *marital settlement agreement (MSA)*.

coverture
The legal status of a married woman whereby her civil existence for many purposes merged with (was covered up by) that of her husband. Also called *unity of person, doctrine of oneness, spousal-unity rule, unity of identity*.

As mentioned in Exhibit 4.1, a **postnuptial agreement** (also called a *postnup* or a *midnup*) is a contract between married persons that covers specific matters, usually financial in nature. They may have no intention of separating or divorcing. If they have this intention, the contract is commonly called a **separation agreement**. (Note, however, that in some states the separation agreement is also referred to as a postnuptial agreement because it is created after (post) the parties entered the marriage.)

At one time in our early history, a wife could not enter into a valid contract with her husband. Under the common-law rule of the **coverture**, the legal identity of a wife was subsumed into the legal identity of the husband. The husband and wife was one person and that person was the husband. Hence, for a wife to enter into a contract with her husband was the equivalent of the husband contracting with himself. This rule no longer exists. Today, of course, a wife has her own independent legal identity and can enter into contracts with anyone, including her husband. Furthermore, spouses can sue each other for breach of these contracts.

Postnuptial contracts, like premarital agreements, can designate what each spouse would receive upon the death of one of them or in the event of a divorce. In addition, here are some specific purposes that such agreements can have:

- Update or change the premarital agreement;
- Revoke the premarital agreement entirely;
- Ratify (formally acknowledge and approve) the premarital agreement after a child is born to help rebut a potential claim that a pregnant spouse-to-be acted under undue pressure or duress because of the pregnancy when she signed the premarital agreement;
- Change (or purchase) a life insurance policy with a commitment to keep it funded and to designate one of the spouses as the beneficiary;
- Clarify what will be done with a large inheritance given to one of the spouses during the marriage;
- Specify the terms of a reconciliation after the parties resumed living together after a separation;
- Set the terms of a financial transaction between the spouses such as a plan to form a business partnership together or a loan to one spouse from the personal (separate) funds of the other spouse;
- Specify how funds will be distributed from the sale of a business that one spouse began before the marriage and that both spouses ran during the marriage.

Of course, not all married couples enter into postnuptial agreements in such circumstances. One family-law attorney comments that "Postnups, like prenups, aren't everybody's idea of problem solving. Skeptics say even mentioning a marital contract is asking for trouble. 'How do you sit down with your spouse and say, I just got a bonus and I'd like to keep it all. Can we sign an agreement [to confirm this]?' Who's going to feel good about that? It's kind of tacky."[11]

Despite this concern, however, postnuptial agreements are becoming increasingly popular, particularly in times of economic uncertainty when both spouses have separate financial lives. A fair number of spouses have their own individual businesses and manage their own finances. "It is impossible to know how many couples are signing postnuptial agreements, since they are drafted by private lawyers and usually not reviewed by the courts unless they are challenged. But lawyers who specialize in family and matrimonial law say the demand has been growing."[12]

The requirement of procedural fairness discussed earlier for premarital agreements also applies to postnuptial agreements. They must be entered into voluntarily by both spouses without duress or undue influence. Sufficient financial disclosure is essential.

Some postnuptial agreements, however, are not valid even if they are entered into voluntarily and with informed consent. For example, one spouse cannot enter into a contract to support the other spouse. Spouses already have a duty of mutual support. A promise of support would not meet the contract requirement of consideration, which is something of value (e.g., a promise) that is exchanged. You are not receiving something of value if you already have what is being promised. For the same reason, an agreement to provide standard household services is not backed by consideration. Spouses already have a duty to provide such services to each other. Furthermore, clauses on child custody and child support are treated the same in premarital and postnuptial agreements. Such clauses do not restrict the court's right to make an independent decision of what support and custody needs will best serve the interests of a child.

Although most states will enforce postnuptial agreements for valid purposes, there remains a lingering concern that a spouse is being taken advantage of. According to one family-law attorney, "If you look at the agreements, they're almost always to increase the rights of the wealthier partner and decrease the rights of the less wealthy one."[13] The tendency of many courts, therefore, is to scrutinize the agreements carefully to make sure that procedural fairness existed when they were entered into and that they are not unconscionable.

Some states go even further and will not enforce postnuptial agreements in the absence of substantive fairness. In these states, married couples have a *fiduciary relationship* with each other, unlike unmarried couples and unlike most strangers. Persons in a fiduciary relationship owe each other loyalty, candor, and fair treatment. By definition, therefore, a court in these states will scrutinize the terms of a postnuptial agreement to ensure that they are substantively fair to both parties.

ASSIGNMENT 4.5

In a famous postnup case, a married couple (Jamie and Frank McCourt) had a dispute over the terms of their postnuptial agreement and the ownership of the Los Angeles Dodgers. The couple were married and living in Massachusetts when they entered into the postnuptial agreement. After purchasing the Dodgers, they decided to move to California (a community-property state). One of the objectives of the postnuptial agreement was to try to shield some of their assets from creditors. Do a search (McCourt Dodgers postnup) in Google, Bing, or Yahoo on the controversy.

a. What dispute did Jamie and Frank have about the postnup and the ownership of the Dodgers?

b. How was the dispute resolved? What decisions were made by the courts?

c. What could the attorneys have done to prevent the dispute?

COHABITATION AGREEMENTS

By **cohabitation** we mean living together in an intimate (usually sexual) relationship. Married couples, of course, also cohabit. Hence, you will sometimes see the term *nonmarital cohabitation,* which refers to unmarried couples living together. (Texas refers to the relationship as "nonmarital conjugal cohabitation."[14]) Most often, however, the word *cohabitation* refers only to unmarried couples and we will use the word in this sense. Parties who are cohabiting are called **cohabitants.**

cohabitation
Living together in an intimate (usually sexual) relationship in the manner of spouses. A de facto husband and wife relationship. The verb is *cohabit.*

cohabitants
Two persons living together in an intimate (usually sexual) relationship.

Once relatively rare, cohabitation is today the norm among a vast segment of the population. At one time, the inclination of society was to punish couples who lived together without being married. (They were "living in sin" or what the church calls "public concubinage.") **Adultery** and **fornication** were crimes in most states. Until 2018, for example, it was a second-degree misdemeanor for an unmarried couple in Florida to "lewdly and lasciviously associate and cohabit together." Criminal prosecution, however, was rare even in states that still had such a law on its books. Today, the prevailing value in the land is privacy in how couples chose to live their lives together. This is not to say that anything goes, but the shift is substantially toward the elimination of restrictions.

Parties have different reasons for living in a marriage-like relationship without actually getting married:

- They may want to live together to find out if they are sufficiently compatible for marriage.
- They may not believe in marriage. (As we saw in Chapter 1, a recent national survey reported that 39 percent of respondents said that marriage was obsolete.[15])
- The parties may not be eligible to marry (e.g., they are underage).
- One of the parties might be receiving alimony from a divorce decree and does not want to jeopardize its continuation; the terms of the divorce might provide that the alimony would end or be reduced if the recipient remarried.
- One of the parties might be receiving public assistance of some kind that would end or be reduced if the recipient marries.

Whatever the reason, the numbers of couples living together continues to grow.

In this section, we will examine the **cohabitation agreement**, which is a contract by persons in an intimate relationship who are not married to each other (and who intend to stay unmarried indefinitely). The contract covers financial and related matters while living together and upon the end of the cohabitation by separation or death.

CONSIDERATION

First, let's look at the contract dimension of cohabitation agreements. As mentioned earlier, a contract is a legally enforceable agreement and most contracts consist of the three elements: offer, acceptance, and consideration. Not all consideration, however, will qualify for a cohabitation agreement. Compare the following two situations:

Case I. Jim hires Mary as a maid for his house. She receives weekly compensation plus room and board. For a three-month period, Jim fails to pay Mary's wages, even though she faithfully performs all of her duties. During this period, Jim seduces Mary and they have a brief affair. After the affair ends, Mary sues Jim for breach of contract due to nonpayment of wages for cleaning services.

Case II. Barbara is a prostitute. Sam hires Barbara for an evening but refuses to pay her fee the next morning. Barbara sues Sam for breach of contract due to nonpayment of the fee.

In Case II, Barbara cannot sue Sam for breach of contract because sex for hire is illegal in most states. Thus, a contract for sex is not enforceable in court because it is against public policy. While there was consideration because Sam promised to pay money for sex and Barbara promised and provided sexual services, the contract for sex is void. Most states refer to payment for sexual services as **meretricious**, which means pertaining to prostitution or unlawful sexual relations.[16]

---

adultery
Voluntary sexual intercourse between a married person and someone other than his or her spouse. (See glossary for an expanded meaning.)

fornication
Voluntary sexual intercourse between unmarried persons.

cohabitation agreement
A contract by persons in an intimate relationship who are not married to each other (and who intend to stay unmarried indefinitely) that covers financial and related matters while living together and upon the end of the cohabitation by separation or death.

meretricious
1. Pertaining to prostitution or unlawful sexual relations. 2. Vulgar or tawdry. (See the glossary for the special meaning of *meretricious* in Washington State.)

In Case I, Mary has a valid claim for breach of contract. Her agreement to have a sexual relationship with Jim is incidental and, therefore, irrelevant to her right to collect compensation that is due her as a maid. She did not sell sexual services to Jim. There is no indication in the facts that the parties bargained for sexual services or that she engaged in sex in exchange for anything from Jim (e.g., continued employment, a raise in pay, lighter work duties). The sex they had with each other is a *severable* part of their relationship and should not affect her main claim. As we have seen, something is severable when what remains after it is removed has legal force and can survive without it.

There are two ways to determine whether something is severable. First, the parties might explicitly state that it is severable such as by inserting a severability clause in their agreement. (For an example of such a clause, see Section 29 in Exhibit 4.3.) Second, if no such explicit agreement exists, we ask whether the parties would probably have carried out the rest of what happened if the questionable part did not exist. In Case I, we can say that the cleaning services would have been legitimately provided and paid for even if a sexual relationship had not developed between Jim and Mary. Hence, the sexual relationship was severable. In Case II, we can say that the payment would not have been made if sexual services had not been provided. Hence, sex was not a severable part of the arrangement; it was an essential part.

Now we come to a more difficult case:

Dan and Helen meet in college. They soon start living together. They move into an apartment, pool their resources, and have children. They never marry. Twenty years after they entered into this relationship, they decide to separate. Helen now sues Dan for a share of the property acquired during the time they lived together.

The fact that Dan and Helen never married does not affect their obligation to support their children, as we shall see in Chapter 10. What about Dan and Helen themselves? They cohabited and never married. They built a relationship, acquired property together, and helped each other over a long period of time. Do they have any support or property rights in each other now that they have separated?

For years, the law denied any rights to an unmarried person who made financial claims based upon a period of cohabitation. The traditional reasons for this denial were as follows:

- To grant financial or property rights to unmarried persons would treat them as if they were married. Our laws favor the institution of marriage. To recognize unmarried relationships would denigrate marriage and discourage people from entering into it. (Why marry if you can obtain all or most of the benefits of marriage without marrying?)

- Most states have abolished **common-law marriage**, as we will see in Chapter 5. The preference of the law is for **ceremonial marriages**. To allow substantial financial rights to be awarded upon the termination of an unmarried relationship would be the equivalent of giving the relationship the status of a common-law marriage.

- Sexual relations are legal and morally acceptable within marriage. If the law recognizes unmarried cohabitation, then illicit and illegal sex is being condoned.

The last point on illegal sex is controversial. We will see in Chapter 5 that the U.S. Supreme Court has recently established a measure of constitutional protection for unmarried adults who engage in consensual sexual conduct. To date, this protection has not been extended to such conduct occurring in prostitution. Nevertheless, it should be noted that there is some uncertainty as to whether the government can continue to criminalize sexual behavior between consenting unmarried adults. As of now, however, prostitution remains illegal in all states (with

common-law marriage
A marriage entered into without complying with statutory formalities (e.g., obtaining a marriage license, having the marriage performed by an authorized person before witnesses) when the parties (a) agree to marry, (b) live together as spouses, and (c) hold themselves out as married. A marriage of persons who have not gone through a ceremonial marriage. Called an *informal marriage* in Texas.

ceremonial marriages
A marriage entered in compliance with statutory formalities (e.g., obtaining a marriage license, having the marriage performed by an authorized person before witnesses). A marriage other than a common-law marriage. Also called *conventional marriage, formal marriage, statutory marriage.*

the narrow exception of several counties of Nevada). Hence, the following discussion will continue to examine cohabitation in light of the current law that payment for sexual services is meretricious and illegal.

MARVIN v. MARVIN

In 1979, the important case of *Marvin v. Marvin* was decided in California.[17] This case held that parties living together would not be denied a financial remedy in court upon their separation solely because they never married. Although widely discussed in the media, most states have *not* followed all of the holdings in the *Marvin* case,

The parties in *Marvin v. Marvin* lived together for seven years without marrying. The plaintiff was Michelle Marvin (formerly Michelle Triola) and the defendant was Lee Marvin, a famous actor. Although they never married, Michelle changed her last name to Marvin. She alleged that she and Lee Marvin had an oral agreement (1) that he would support her, and (2) that while "the parties lived together they would combine their efforts and earnings and would share equally any and all property accumulated as a result of their efforts whether individual or combined." She further alleged that she agreed to give up her career as a singer in order to devote full time to the defendant (Lee) as a companion, homemaker, housekeeper, and cook. During the seven years that they were together, the defendant accumulated in his name more than $1 million in property. When they separated, she sued for her share of this property.

The media viewed Michelle's support claim as an alimony action between two unmarried "ex-pals" and dubbed it a palimony suit. **Palimony** has come to mean support payments ordered after the end of a nonmarital relationship if the party seeking support was induced to enter or stay in the relationship by a promise of support or if ordering support is otherwise equitable. In addition to support, the *Marvin* case covered the broader topics of earnings, expenses, and other property agreements between unmarried parties.

The *Marvin* case addressed two main issues: the presence of an illicit relationship and the design of an appropriate remedy.

Illicit Relationship

One of the first hurdles for the plaintiff in the *Marvin* case was the "meretricious sexual services." Lee, the defendant, argued that even if a contract did exist (which he denied), it was unenforceable because it involved an illicit relationship. The parties were not married but were engaging in sexual relations. The court, however, ruled that

> [A] contract between nonmarital partners is unenforceable only to the extent that it explicitly rests upon the immoral and illicit consideration of meretricious sexual services. . . . The fact that a man and woman live together without marriage, and engage in a sexual relationship, does not in itself invalidate agreements between them relating to their earnings, property, or expenses. . . . [Adults] who voluntarily live together and engage in sexual relations are . . . as competent as any other persons to [enter into contracts] respecting their earnings and property rights.[18]

The agreement will be invalidated only if sex is an express or explicit condition of the relationship. If the sexual aspect of their relationship is *severable* from their agreements on finances, the agreements will be enforced. An example of an *unenforceable* agreement would be a promise by a man to provide for a woman in his will in exchange for her agreeing to live with him in order to become the natural mother of his children. This agreement is *explicitly* based on a sexual relationship. Thus, sex in such a case cannot be separated from the agreement and is *not* severable.

palimony
Support payments ordered after the end of a nonmarital relationship (a) if the party seeking support was induced to enter or stay in the relationship by a promise of support or (b) if ordering support is otherwise equitable.

Appropriate Remedy

The next concern of the court in *Marvin* was the theory of *recovery*. Married parties have financial rights in each other because of their *marital status,* which gives rise to duties imposed by law. What about unmarried parties? The *Marvin* court suggested more than one **remedy** (theory of recovery) for such individuals:

- Express contract
- Implied-in-fact contract
- Implied-in-law contract (quasi contract)
- Constructive trust
- Partnership
- Joint venture

Before we examine these remedies, two points must be emphasized. First, most states do not agree with *Marvin* that all of these remedies can apply to unmarried couples when they separate. States are reluctant to grant rights to unmarried couples in a way that would undermine the strong preference for *ceremonial marriage.* Many states are favorable to the express-contract remedy, but not the implied-contract remedies. The fear is that opening the door to implied-contract theories can present huge problems of proof, encourage litigation, and create substantial uncertainty that could have been avoided if the parties had entered into an express contract, or, indeed, a marriage. It is too easy for a cohabitant to fabricate or exaggerate a claim after the cohabitation has ended, particularly after one of the cohabitants dies and the claim is made against his or her estate. Second, all of the remedies will be of no avail if it can be shown that meretricious sexual services were at the heart of the relationship and cannot be separated (are not severable) from the other aspects of the relationship.

EXPRESS CONTRACT

An **express contract** is an agreement or contract whose terms are explicitly stated by the parties. Unfortunately, cohabitation agreements are rarely express contracts. The cohabitants do not often spell out the terms of their relationship (e.g., a written agreement that says, "If you agree to support me, I'll agree to stay home, take care of the house, entertain guests, etc.") Without a written express contract or strong evidence of an express oral contract, it can be extremely difficult (although not impossible) to prove what agreements the parties reached on financial matters just prior to and during their cohabitation.

Next, we examine some of the even-more-difficult-to-establish theories of recovery (remedies) endorsed by the court in the *Marvin* case.

IMPLIED CONTRACT

There are two kinds of implied contracts: implied-in-fact contracts and implied-in-law contracts.

Implied-in-Fact Contract

An **implied-in-fact contract** is a contract that is not created by an express agreement between the parties but is inferred as a matter of reason and justice from their conduct and the surrounding circumstances. The contract exists when it is reasonable to conclude that the parties had a **tacit** understanding that they were bound by a contract even though the terms of the contract were never expressly discussed. Consider the following example:

While on vacation, you make an appointment with a hairstylist. When you arrive at the salon, you ask for a haircut and describe the style you want. At no time is

remedy
The means by which a right is enforced or the violation of a right is prevented, compensated for, or otherwise redressed. The plural is *remedies.* (See the glossary for an additional meaning.)

express contract
An agreement or contract whose terms are explicitly stated by the parties.

implied-in-fact contract
A contract that is manifested by conduct and circumstances rather than by words of agreement. A contract whose existence could be inferred by a reasonable person, even in the absence of an express agreement to create it. Also called a *contract implied-in-fact.*

tacit
Understood without being openly stated; implied by silence or conduct other than words.

there any mention of payment. On the way out when you are asked to pay, you will not be able to avoid payment by proving that you never expressly agreed to pay for the haircut and that there were no signs in the facility or flyers mentioning costs. Under traditional contract principles, you have entered into an implied-in-fact contract to pay for the hairstyling service, which is as binding as an express contract. Unless the state has enacted special laws to change this result, you must pay for the haircut.

In the case of unmarried individuals living together, we must similarly determine whether an implied-in-fact contract existed.

Sally and Frank are unmarried. After twenty years together, they separate. Sally now sues Frank for an equal share of the income from the rental properties purchased while they lived together. All the properties were placed in Frank's name only. They never discussed sharing rental income. Sally performed all bookkeeping services, collected the rents, and paid bills for all of the properties. She never took a salary. Both Sally and Frank always told everyone that they were "a team" who worked together "like a pair of gloves."

There was no express contract to share rental income. Was there an implied-in-fact contract to do so? Looking at all the evidence, a court would have to determine if it is reasonable to conclude from their conduct that they were entering into an agreement to share the profits from the rental business. Is it reasonable to conclude that the intent of Sally and Frank was that she would be exchanging her financial and support services for her share of the business? Did both sides expect "compensation" in some form to be provided for what each did? If so, an implied-in-fact contract existed, which can be as enforceable as an express contract.

Nonbusiness services between unmarried couples are often seen in a different light. Most courts are reluctant to imply a contract of compensation for persons in a romantic relationship who perform personal services such as doing household chores, cooking, and entertaining guests. When parties in an intimate relationship provide such personal services for each other, their usual intent is to do so without expecting compensation. The presumption is that such mutual services are **gratuitous**, rendered without expectation of payment. If asked why certain services were provided, the probable response is that it was convenient or gratifying to do so. Courts are unlikely to "order compensation for services performed by one partner that can be characterized as part of the ordinary give-and-take of a shared life."[19]

gratuitous
Performed without expectation of payment.

IMPLIED-IN-LAW CONTRACT (QUASI CONTRACT)

Another *Marvin* remedy is **implied-in-law contract** (also called *quasi contract*), which is an obligation created by law to avoid **unjust enrichment**. Although an implied-in-law contract is referred to as a contract, it is a legal fiction to use the word contract because it does not involve an express or implied agreement. The doctrine of implied-in-law contract is simply a device designed by the courts to prevent unjust enrichment. The latter occurs when someone receives a benefit in the form of goods or services that in fairness should be returned or paid for even though there was no express or implied promise to do so. When the benefit provided is a service, the amount the recipient should pay is called **quantum meruit**, which is the reasonable value of the service provided.

Suppose, for example, that a doctor provides medical care to an unconscious motorist on the road. The doctor can recover the reasonable cost of medical services under the theory of an implied-in-law contract, even though the motorist never expressly or impliedly asked for such services. Another example might be a

implied-in-law contract
An obligation created by the law to avoid unjust enrichment in the absence of an express or implied contract creating this obligation. Also called a *quasi contract*.

unjust enrichment
The receipt of a benefit in the form of goods or services that in fairness should be returned or paid for even though there was no express or implied promise to do so.

quantum meruit
"As much as he deserves." An award of the reasonable value of services provided despite the absence of an express or implied agreement to pay for the services.

man who arranges for a foreign woman to come to this country to live in his home and provide household services. Assume that they never married and that there was no express or implied understanding between them that she would be paid. If what she provided was not meretricious, the law might obligate him to pay the reasonable value of her services (quantum meruit), less the value of any support she received from him during the time they were together.

CONSTRUCTIVE TRUST

The next remedy discussed by the *Marvin* court – constructive trusts – can be a valuable option for plaintiffs, but the remedy is narrow and limited.

A **trust** is a property arrangement or device involving three parties:

- The creator of the trust (called the *settlor* or *trustor*).
- The person who holds legal title to the property (called the *trustee*).
- The person who is to benefit from the property (called the *beneficiary* or *cestui que trust*); the beneficiary has a **beneficial interest** in the property.

The property itself is called the *corpus*. A trust comes into existence when the creator transfers legal title of the corpus to the trustee who holds it for the benefit of the beneficiary.

Most trusts are created by express agreement. At times, however, the law will imply the existence of a trust even if the parties did not intend to create one. Such a trust is called a **constructive trust**. It comes into existence by **operation of law** rather than (or even despite) what the parties intended. A constructive trust is imposed as an **equitable remedy** to prevent unjust enrichment by someone who has improperly obtained property through fraud, duress, abuse of confidence, or other wrongful conduct.

> *Tim and Sandra, an unmarried cohabiting couple, decide to buy a house. The funds for the house come from an inheritance from Sandra's father; hence, the house is her separate property. Without telling Sandra, Tim places the title to the house in his name only, although he told her that he would put it in their joint names. After the couple separates, Tim refuses to acknowledge Sandra's interest in the house. He sells the house and keeps the proceeds for himself.*

On such facts, Tim obtained title to the house wrongfully. A court will impose a constructive trust on the funds for Sandra's benefit. She will be entitled to all or most of the proceeds from the sale.

One final note before we examine two court opinions that reach opposite conclusions on the rights of unmarried cohabitants. In some states, unjust enrichment is a separate remedy and not solely one of the components of the remedies of implied-in-law contracts and constructive trusts.

The following two cases, *Hewitt v. Hewitt* and *Watts v. Watts*, are examples of the contrasting points of view among courts of different states on whether unmarried cohabitants should be given support or other financial rights upon the termination of the cohabitation. The *Watts* case says no. The *Hewitt* case is more inclined to adopt the approach of *Marvin v. Marvin*. Note the interaction among the three cases:

- The *Hewitt* case cites and refuses to follow the *Marvin* case.
- The *Watts* case cites the *Marvin* case with approval.
- The *Watts* case cites and distinguishes the *Hewitt* case.

---

trust
A property arrangement by which its creator (the settlor or trustor) transfers property (the corpus) to a person (the trustee) who holds legal title for the benefit of another (the beneficiary or *cestui que trust*).

beneficial interest
A right to a benefit from something (e.g., property) whose legal ownership is in another.

constructive trust
A trust created by operation of law to prevent unjust enrichment by someone who has improperly obtained property through fraud, duress, abuse of confidence, or other wrongful conduct.

operation of law
The means by which legal consequences are imposed by law, regardless of (or even despite) the intent or wishes of the parties involved.

equitable remedy
A form of relief (e.g., injunction, specific performance, or constructive trust) that may be available when remedies at law (e.g., damages) are not adequate.

CASE

Hewitt v. Hewitt
77 Ill. 2d 49, 394 N.E.2d 1204, 3 A.L.R. 4th 1 (1979)
Supreme Court of Illinois

Background: *Victoria Hewitt met Robert Hewitt in college. When she became pregnant, he told her they were husband and wife and that no formal ceremony was necessary. He said he would "share his life, his future, his earnings and his property" with her. They announced to their parents that they were married and held themselves out as husband and wife while residing in Illinois. She helped him in his education and business. During fifteen years together, they had three children. They never entered into a ceremonial marriage. (Since 1905, Illinois has not allowed parties to enter a common-law marriages, which is a marriage entered into without going through a ceremonial marriage.) Upon their separation, she sued him for "an equal share of the profits and properties accumulated" while together. Her theories of recovery included express contract, implied contract, constructive trust, and unjust enrichment. The circuit court dismissed her complaint. She appealed. The lower appellate court reversed and ruled that she could sue him for violating an express oral contract. Robert then appealed. The case is now on appeal before the Supreme Court of Illinois.*

Decision on Appeal: *Judgment for Robert. It is against public policy in Illinois to enforce property rights of unmarried cohabitants.*

OPINION OF THE COURT:

Justice UNDERWOOD delivered the opinion of the court. . . .

In finding that plaintiff's complaint stated a cause of action on an express oral contract, the appellate court adopted the reasoning of the California Supreme Court in the widely publicized case of *Marvin v. Marvin* (1976), 557 P.2d 106,. . . We are aware, of course, of the increasing judicial attention given the individual claims of unmarried cohabitants to jointly accumulated property, and the fact that the majority of courts considering the question have recognized an equitable or contractual basis for implementing the reasonable expectations of the parties unless sexual services were the explicit consideration. . . .

The issue of unmarried cohabitants' mutual property rights, however,. . . cannot appropriately be characterized solely in terms of contract law, nor is it limited to considerations of equity or fairness as between the parties to such relationships. There are major public policy questions involved in determining whether, under what circumstances, and to what extent it is desirable to accord some type of legal status to claims arising from such relationships. Of substantially greater importance than the rights of the immediate parties is the impact of such recognition upon our society and the institution of marriage. Will the fact that legal rights closely resembling those arising from conventional marriages can be acquired by those who deliberately choose to enter into what have heretofore been commonly referred to as "illicit" or "meretricious" relationships encourage formation of such relationships and weaken marriage as the foundation of our family-based society? In the event of death shall the survivor have the status of a surviving spouse for purposes of inheritance, wrongful death actions, workmen's compensation, etc.?

And still more importantly: what of the children born of such relationships? What are their support and inheritance rights and by what standards are custody questions resolved? What of the sociological and psychological effects upon them of that type of environment? Does not the recognition of legally enforceable property and custody rights emanating from nonmarital cohabitation in practical effect equate with the legalization of common law marriage at least in the circumstances of this case? And, in summary, have the increasing numbers of unmarried cohabitants and changing mores of our society. . . reached the point at which the general welfare of the citizens of this State is best served by a return to something resembling the judicially created common law marriage our legislature outlawed in 1905?

Illinois' public policy regarding agreements such as the one alleged here was implemented long ago in *Wallace v. Rappleye* (1882), 103 Ill. 229, 249, where this court said: "An agreement in consideration of future illicit cohabitation between the plaintiffs is void." This is the traditional rule,. . . It is true, of course, that cohabitation by the parties may not prevent them from forming valid contracts about independent matters, for which it is said the sexual relations do not form part of the consideration. *Restatement of Contracts* secs. 589, 597 (1932). . . .

The real thrust of plaintiff's argument here is that we should abandon the rule of illegality because of certain changes in societal norms and attitudes. It is urged that social mores have changed radically in recent years, rendering this principle of law archaic. It is said that because there are so many unmarried cohabitants today the courts must confer a legal status on such relationships. . . . If this is to be the result, however, it would seem more candid to acknowledge the return of varying forms of common law marriage than to continue displaying the naiveté we believe involved in the assertion that there are involved in these relationships contracts separate and independent from the sexual activity, and the assumption that those contracts would have been entered into or would continue without that activity. . . .

[J]udicial recognition of mutual property rights between unmarried cohabitants would, in our opinion, clearly violate the policy of our recently enacted Illinois Marriage and Dissolution of Marriage Act. . ."[to] strengthen and preserve the integrity of marriage and safeguard family relationships." (Ill. Rev. Stat. 1977, ch. 40, par. 102.) We cannot confidently say that judicial recognition of property rights between unmarried cohabitants will not make that alternative to marriage more attractive by allowing the parties to engage in such relationships with greater security. . . . The policy of the Act gives the State a strong continuing interest in the institution

(continued)

of marriage and prevents the marriage relation from becoming in effect a private contract terminable at will. This seems to us another indication that public policy disfavors private contractual alternatives to marriage. . . .

[W]e believe that these questions are appropriately within the province of the legislature, and that, if there is to be a change in the law of this State on this matter, it is for the legislature and not the courts to bring about that change. We accordingly hold that plaintiff's claims are unenforceable for the reason that they contravene the public policy, implicit in the statutory scheme of the Illinois Marriage and Dissolution of Marriage Act, disfavoring the grant of mutually enforceable property rights to knowingly unmarried cohabitants.

Appellate court reversed; circuit court affirmed.

CASE

Watts v. Watts
137 Wis. 2d 506, 405 N.W.2d 303 (1987)
Supreme Court of Wisconsin

Background: *Sue Watts alleges that she quit her job and abandoned her career in exchange for James Watts's promise to take care of her. For more than twelve years, they raised a family and worked in a family business together in Wisconsin. They never married. (Common-law marriages are not allowed in Wisconsin.) When the relationship deteriorated, she sued him in circuit court for her share of the property they had accumulated. Among her legal theories were breach of an express or implied contract and unjust enrichment. The circuit court dismissed the case, arguing that the legislature, not the court, should provide relief to parties who have accumulated property in nonmarital cohabitation relationships. The case is now on appeal before the Supreme Court of Wisconsin.*

Decision on Appeal: *Reversed. The court does not have to wait until the legislature acts. Sue Watts should be allowed to bring her claims against James Watts.*

OPINION OF THE COURT:

Justice ABRAHAMSON delivered the opinion of the court. . . .

Nonmarital cohabitation does not render every agreement between the cohabiting parties illegal. . . . The plaintiff alleges that during the parties' relationship, and because of her domestic and business contributions, the business and personal wealth of the couple increased. Furthermore, the plaintiff alleges that she never received any compensation for these contributions to the relationship and that the defendant indicated to the plaintiff both orally and through his conduct that he considered her to be his wife and that she would share equally in the increased wealth.

The plaintiff asserts that since the breakdown of the relationship the defendant has refused to share equally with her the wealth accumulated through their joint efforts or to compensate her in any way for her contributions to the relationship. . . . [H]er claim. . .is that she and the defendant had a contract to share equally the property accumulated during their relationship. The essence of the complaint is that the parties had a contract, either an express or implied in fact contract, which the defendant breached. . . .

The defendant appears to attack the plaintiff's contract theory on three grounds. First, the defendant apparently asserts that the court's recognition of plaintiff's contract claim for a share of the parties' property contravenes the Wisconsin Family Code. Second, the defendant asserts that the legislature, not the courts, should determine the property and contract rights of unmarried cohabiting parties. Third, the defendant intimates that the parties' relationship was immoral and illegal and that any recognition of a contract between the parties or plaintiff's claim for a share of the property accumulated during the cohabitation contravenes public policy.

The defendant rests his argument that judicial recognition of a contract between unmarried cohabitants for property division violates the Wisconsin Family Code on *Hewitt v. Hewitt*, 77 Ill. 2d 49, 394 N.E.2d 1204, 3 A.L.R. 4th 1 (1979). In *Hewitt* the Illinois Supreme Court concluded that judicial recognition of mutual property rights between unmarried cohabitants would violate the policy of the Illinois Marriage and Dissolution Act because enhancing the attractiveness of a private arrangement contravenes the Act's policy of strengthening and preserving the integrity of marriage. The Illinois court concluded that allowing such a contract claim would weaken the sanctity of marriage, put in doubt the rights of inheritance, and open the door to false pretenses of marriage. . . .

The defendant has failed to persuade this court that enforcing an express or implied in fact contract between these parties would in fact violate the Wisconsin Family Code. The Family Code, chs. 765–68, Stats. 1985–86, is intended to promote the institution of marriage and the family. We find no indication, however, that the Wisconsin legislature intended the Family Code to restrict in any way a court's resolution of property or contract disputes between unmarried cohabitants.

(continued)

CASE • Watts v. Watts (continued)

The defendant also urges that if the court is not willing to say that the Family Code proscribes contracts between unmarried cohabiting parties, then the court should refuse to resolve the contract and property rights of unmarried cohabitants without legislative guidance. The defendant asserts that this court should conclude, as the *Hewitt* court did, that the task of determining the rights of cohabiting parties is too complex and difficult for the court and should be left to the legislature. We are not persuaded by the defendant's argument. Courts have traditionally developed principles of contract and property law through the case-by-case method of the common law. While ultimately the legislature may resolve the problems raised by unmarried cohabiting parties, we are not persuaded that the court should refrain from resolving such disputes until the legislature gives us direction. . . .

We turn to the defendant's third point, namely, that any contract between the parties regarding property division contravenes public policy because the contract is based on immoral or illegal sexual activity. . . . Courts have generally refused to enforce contracts for which the sole consideration is sexual relations, sometimes referred to as "meretricious" relationships. See *In Matter of Estate of Steffes*, 95 Wis. 2d 490, 514, 290 N.W.2d 697 (1980), citing *Restatement of Contracts*, Section 589 (1932). Courts distinguish, however, between contracts that are explicitly and inseparably founded on sexual services and those that are not. This court, and numerous other courts, have concluded that "a bargain between two people is not illegal merely because there is an illicit relationship between the two so long as the bargain is independent of the illicit relationship and the illicit relationship does not constitute any part of the consideration bargained for and is not a condition of the bargain." *Steffes*, supra, 95 Wis. 2d at 514, 290 N.W.2d 697.

While not condoning the illicit sexual relationship of the parties, many courts have recognized that the result of a court's refusal to enforce contract and property rights between unmarried cohabitants is that one party keeps all or most of the assets accumulated during the relationship, while the other party, no more or less "guilty," is deprived of property which he or she has helped to accumulate. See e.g., *Marvin v. Marvin*, 557 P.2d 106, 121 (1976).

The *Hewitt* decision, which leaves one party to the relationship enriched at the expense of the other party who had contributed to the acquisition of the property, has often been criticized by courts and commentators as being unduly harsh. Moreover, courts recognize that their refusal to enforce what are in other contexts clearly lawful promises will not undo the parties' relationship and may not discourage others from entering into such relationships. *Tyranski v. Piggins*, 44 Mich. App. 570, 577, 205 N.W.2d 595 (1973). A harsh, per se rule that the contract and property rights of unmarried cohabiting parties will not be recognized might actually encourage a partner with greater income potential to avoid marriage in order to retain all accumulated assets, leaving the other party with nothing.

In this case, the plaintiff has alleged many facts independent from the parties' physical relationship which, if proven, would establish an express contract or an implied in fact contract that the parties agreed to share the property accumulated during the relationship. The plaintiff has alleged that she quit her job and abandoned her career training upon the defendant's promise to take care of her. A change in one party's circumstances in performance of the agreement may imply an agreement between the parties. *Steffes*, supra, 95 Wis. 2d at 504, 290 N.W.2d 697; *Tyranski*, supra, 44 Mich. App. at 574, 205 N.W.2d at 597. In addition, the plaintiff alleges that she performed housekeeping, childbearing, childrearing, and other services related to the maintenance of the parties' home, in addition to various services for the defendant's business and her own business, for which she received no compensation. Courts have recognized that money, property, or services (including housekeeping or childrearing) may constitute adequate consideration independent of the parties' sexual relationship to support an agreement to share or transfer property. See *Tyranski*, supra, 44 Mich. App. at 574, 205 N.W.2d at 597; *Steffes*, supra 95 Wis. 2d at 501, 290 N.W.2d 697.

[Until recently, the prevailing view was that services performed in the context of a "family or marriage relationship" were presumed gratuitous. However, that presumption was rebuttable. In *Steffes*, we held the presumption to be irrelevant where the plaintiff can show either an express or implied agreement to pay for those services, even where the plaintiff has rendered them "with a sense of affection, devotion and duty." Id. 95 Wis. 2d at 503, 290 N.W.2d at 703–704.]

According to the plaintiff's complaint, the parties cohabited for more than twelve years, held joint bank accounts, made joint purchases, filed joint income tax returns, and were listed as husband and wife on other legal documents. Courts have held that such a relationship and "joint acts of a financial nature can give rise to an inference that the parties intended to share equally." *Beal v. Beal*, 282 Or. 115, 122, 577 P.2d 507, 510 (1978). The joint ownership of property and the filing of joint income tax returns strongly implies that the parties intended their relationship to be in the nature of a joint enterprise, financially as well as personally.

Having reviewed the complaint and surveyed the law in this and other jurisdictions, we hold that the Family Code does not preclude an unmarried cohabitant from asserting contract and property claims against the other party to the cohabitation. We further conclude that public policy does not necessarily preclude an unmarried cohabitant from asserting a contract claim against the other party to the cohabitation so long as the claim exists independently of the sexual relationship and is supported by separate consideration. Accordingly, we conclude that the plaintiff in this case has pleaded the facts necessary to state a claim for damages resulting from the defendant's breach of an express or an implied in fact contract to share with the plaintiff the property accumulated through the efforts

(continued)

of both parties during their relationship. . . . [W]e do not judge the merits of the plaintiff's claim; we merely hold that she be given her day in court to prove her claim. . . .

The plaintiff's [next] theory of recovery involves unjust enrichment. Essentially, she alleges that the defendant accepted and retained the benefit of services she provided knowing that she expected to share equally in the wealth accumulated during their relationship. She argues that it is unfair for the defendant to retain all the assets they accumulated under these circumstances and that a constructive trust should be imposed on the property as a result of the defendant's unjust enrichment. . . .

As we have discussed previously, allowing no relief at all to one party in a so-called "illicit" relationship effectively provides total relief to the other, by leaving that party owner of all the assets acquired through the efforts of both. Yet it cannot seriously be argued that the party retaining all the assets is less "guilty" than the other. Such a result is contrary to the principles of equity. Many courts have held, and we now so hold, that unmarried cohabitants may raise claims based upon unjust enrichment following the termination of their relationships where one of the parties attempts to retain an unreasonable amount of the property acquired through the efforts of both. . . .

In summary, we hold that the plaintiff's complaint has stated a claim upon which relief may be granted. . . . Accordingly, we reverse the judgment of the circuit court, and remand the cause to the circuit court for further proceedings consistent with this opinion.

ASSIGNMENT 4.6

a. Why did the *Hewitt* court rule that it should not provide a remedy for unmarried cohabitating couples? Why did the *Watts* court rule that a remedy should be provided for them?

b. The *Watts* court referred to criticism of the *Hewitt* court as "unduly harsh." Do you agree? Which opinion was correctly decided, *Hewitt* or *Watts*?

c. Assume that James Watts died without leaving a will while he still had a good relationship with Sue Watts. Would she be able to claim a share of his estate as one of his heirs?

Thus far, we have examined four of the possible remedies discussed in the *Marvin* case for unmarried cohabitants: express contract, implied-in-fact contract, implied-in-law contract, and constructive trust, focusing mainly on express contracts. *Marvin* also suggested partnership and joint venture as remedies.

PARTNERSHIP

A **partnership** is a voluntary association of two or more persons to place their resources in a jointly owned business or enterprise, with a proportional sharing of profits and losses. A court might find that an unmarried couple entered the equivalent of a partnership and thereby acquired rights and obligations in the property involved in the partnership.

partnership
A voluntary association of two (or more) persons to place their resources in a jointly owned business or enterprise with a proportional sharing of profits and losses.

JOINT VENTURE

A **joint venture** is a business or profit-seeking activity of two or more persons who each participate and control the activity (or who have the right of participation and control). A court might use the joint-venture theory to cover enterprises entered into by two unmarried individuals while living together (e.g., the purchase of a farm). Once a joint venture is established, the parties have legally enforceable rights in the fruits of their endeavors.

joint venture
A business or profit-seeking activity of two or more persons who each participate and control the activity (or who have the right of participation and control).

ASSIGNMENT   4.7

a. Tom and George, a gay couple, live together. George agrees to support Tom while the latter completes engineering school, at which time Tom will support George while the latter completes law school. After Tom obtains his engineering degree, he leaves George. George now sues Tom for the amount of money that would have been provided as support while George attended law school. What result? (See General Instructions for the Legal-Analysis Assignment in Appendix A.)

b. Richard and Lena have lived together for ten years without being married. This month, they separated. They never entered a formal contract, but Lena says that they had an informal understanding that they would equally divide everything acquired during their relationship together. Lena sues Richard for one-half of all property so acquired. You work for the law firm that represents Lena. Draft a set of interrogatories for Lena that will be sent to Richard in which you seek information that would be relevant to Lena's action. (See General Instructions for the Interrogatories Assignment in Appendix A.)

See the Interviewing and Investigation Checklist on factors relevant to the property rights of unmarried couples, and Exhibit 4.4 for an example of a cohabitation agreement.

✔ INTERVIEWING AND INVESTIGATION CHECKLIST

Property Rights of Unmarried Couples

LEGAL INTERVIEWING QUESTIONS

1. When and how did the two of you meet?

2. When did you begin living together?

3. On what dates did you live together?

4. What changes, if any, had to be made in your personal, social, or business lives in order to start living together?

5. Why did the two of you decide to start living together? What exactly did you say to each other about your relationship at the time?

6. Did you discuss the living arrangement together? If so, what was said?

7. Do the two of you have a sexual relationship together? If so, when did it begin?

8. What was said or implied about the continuing sexual relationship between you? Was there an express or implied understanding that either of you would provide sex in exchange for other services, for money, or for other property?

9. If sexual relations had not been a part of your relationship, would you have still lived together?

10. Were the two of you faithful to each other? Did either of you ever date others? Explain.

11. What was your understanding about how the following items would be paid for: rent, house purchase, mortgage, furniture, food, clothing, medical bills, health insurance, etc.?

12. Describe the extent to which you both maintained separate financial lives. Describe the extent to which you had a joint or communal financial life. For example, did you agree to keep separate or joint bank accounts? Why?

13. What other commitments were made, if any? For example, was there an agreement on providing support, making a will, giving each other property or shares in property?

14. What discussions occurred, if any, about having children together?

15. Did you ever discuss marriage? If so, what was said by both of you on the topic?

(continued)

16. What did you give up in order to live with him or her? Was this understood by both of you? How do you know?

17. What did he or she give up in order to live with you? Was this understood by both of you? How do you know?

18. What other promises were made or implied between you? Why were they made?

19. Is there a way for you to substantiate the existence of any of these promises, agreements, or understandings? Were any commitments put in writing?

20. How did you introduce each other to others?

21. What understanding did others have of the nature of your relationship together? How did they come to this understanding?

22. What were your roles in the house? How were these roles decided upon? Through agreement? Explain.

23. Did either of you have a separate business before or during the cohabitation? If so, explain how the business was financed and run.

24. Did you both have a jointly run business together before or during the cohabitation? If so, how it was financed and run?

25. Have either of you received compensation or any form of payment from the other or from a business that was solely or jointly run? If so, explain.

26. Did he or she ever pay you for anything you did? Did you ever pay him or her? If not why not? If so, explain the circumstances.

27. If no payment was ever made, was payment expected in the future? Explain.

28. Did you use each other's money for any purpose? If so, explain the circumstances. If not, why not?

29. Did you ever feel pressured or coerced by any aspect of your relationship together? If so, explain.

30. Did you ever feel you were cheated or taken advantage of by any aspect of your relationship together? If so, explain.

POSSIBLE INVESTIGATION TASKS

- Obtain copies of bank statements, deeds for property acquired while the parties were together, loan applications, tax returns, etc.

- Interview persons who knew the parties.

- Contact professional housekeeping companies to determine the going rate for housekeeping services.

EXAMPLE OF A COHABITATION AGREEMENT

EXHIBIT 4.4   Cohabitation Agreement

COHABITATION AGREEMENT

Intention of the Parties

[1] _____ and _____ declare that they are not married to each other, but they are living together under the same roof, and by this agreement intend to protect and define each other's rights pertaining to future services rendered, earnings, accumulated property and furnishings and other matters that may be contained herein.

[2] It is expressly set forth herein that the consent of either party to cohabit sexually with the other is not a consideration, either in whole or in part, for the making of this agreement.

[3] It is further expressly set forth herein that the general purpose of this agreement is that the earnings, accumulations and property of each party herein shall be the separate property of the person who earns or acquires said property, and shall not be deemed community property, joint property, common law property or otherwise giving the non-earning or non-acquiring party an interest in same.

- *In this general statement of intention, the parties want to make clear that their sexual relationship is not the essence of their relationship and of their agreement. If it was, a court might declare the agreement to be invalid.*

(continued)

Exhibit 4.4 *(continued)*

Representations to the Public

[4] It is agreed that should either or both of the parties to this agreement represent to the public, in whatever manner, that they are husband and wife, that said representation shall be for social convenience only, and shall in no way imply that sexual services are a consideration for any part of this agreement, nor shall it imply that sexual cohabitation is taking place.

Property, Earnings, and Accumulations

[5] It is agreed that all property of any nature or in any place, including but not limited to the earnings and income resulting from the personal services, skill, effort, and work of either party to this agreement, whether acquired before or during the term of this agreement, or acquired by either one of them by purchase, gift or inheritance during the said term, shall be the separate property of the respective party, and that neither party shall have any interest in, and both parties hereby waive any right or interest he or she may have in, the property of the other. This waiver includes any appreciation of the property covered in this clause, regardless of how the appreciation occurs or who contributes to the appreciation.

Services Rendered

[6] It is agreed that whatever household, homemaking, or other domestic work and services that either party may contribute to the other or to their common domicile shall be voluntary, free, and without compensation, and each party agrees that work of this nature is done without expectation of monetary or other reward from the other party.

Debts and Obligations

[7] It is agreed that all debts and obligations incurred by either party which is to the benefit of that party shall be the debt or obligation of that party only, and that the other shall not be liable for same. Should one party be forced to pay a debt rightfully belonging to and benefiting the other, the other promises to reimburse, indemnify, and hold harmless the one who has paid said debt or obligation. Those debts and obligations, which are to the benefit of both parties, such as utilities, garbage, local telephone service, rent, and renter's insurance shall be paid in such sums and in such proportion by each party as shall be mutually agreeable.

Money Loaned

[8] All money, with the exception of mortgage or rent payments, transferred by one party to the other, either directly or to an account, obligation, or purchase of the other, shall be deemed a loan to the other, unless otherwise stated in writing. This shall include such things as down payments on a home or vehicle, and deposits in either party's separate bank account.

Rented Premises

[9] It is agreed that should the parties share rented premises, said rented premises shall "belong" to the person who first rented the same, and should the parties separate, the second one shall leave (even if his or her name is on the lease at the time) taking only such belongings as he or she owned prior to moving in or purchased while living together. If the parties both rent the premises from the beginning, then it is agreed that they will have a third person flip a coin to see who "owns" the premises, and the winner will have the option to remain while the loser leaves.

- *If parties hold themselves out to be spouses, a court might conclude that they have entered a common-law marriage if such marriages are allowed in the state where they live or where they spend significant time. See, however, Clause 17 in which they explicitly disclaim an intent to enter a common-law marriage.*

- *Note that Clause 6 does not cover business or professional services they render to each other. Such services are covered in clauses [11] to [13].*

(continued)

Exhibit 4.4 *(continued)*

Rent or Mortgage

[10] It is agreed that the parties may split the rent or mortgage payments in whatever proportion they choose, each contributing such sum as is mutually agreeable. It is also agreed that if one party contributes to the mortgage payment of a premises belonging to or being purchased in the name of the other party, that such contribution shall be deemed rent only, and shall be non-refundable and shall not create in the person who is living in the premises owned or being purchased by the other, any interest in said property or in the equity therein.

Business Arrangements

[11] It is agreed that should one party contribute services, labor, or effort to a business enterprise belonging to the other, that the party contributing said services, labor, or effort shall not acquire by reason thereof any interest in, ownership of, or claim to said business enterprise, nor shall said person be compensated in any way for said services, labor, or effort, unless the terms of said compensation are expressly agreed to in writing by both parties.

[12] Should the parties share services, labor, or effort in a jointly owned business enterprise the relative interests of each party shall be apportioned according to a separate partnership agreement, or, if there is no express agreement, then in proportion that each contributed thereto.

[13] It is agreed that the business known as _____ is the individual and separate business of _____, and is not to be deemed a jointly owned business of both parties.

Separate Accounts

[14] In conformity with the intentions of the parties set forth herein, both parties agree to maintain separate bank accounts, insurance accounts (except for insurance to insure the contents of an apartment, house, etc., which the parties may jointly hold), tax returns, credit accounts, credit union accounts, medical accounts, automobile registration and ownership, and deeds to property, and to make all purchases of personal property, including furniture, appliances, records, books, works of art, stereo equipment, etc., separate, in order to avoid confusion as to the ownership of same, and also in order to avoid nullifying the general intent of this agreement.

Duration of This Agreement

[15] This agreement shall remain in effect from the date the parties start cohabiting until either party leaves or removes himself or herself from the common domicile with the intention not to return, or until they marry, or until they make a new written agreement that is contrary to the terms of this agreement.

Attorney Fees and Costs

[16] Each party agrees to act in good faith with the provisions of this agreement, and should one party breach the agreement or fail to act in good faith therewith, such party agrees to pay to the other such attorney fees and costs as may be reasonable in order to properly enforce the provisions herein.

No Common-Law Marriage Intended

[17] Even though the parties hereto are cohabiting under the same roof and may give the appearance of being married, or from time to time represent to the public that they are husband

(continued)

Exhibit 4.4 (continued)

and wife, they do not intend by such acts to acquire the status of common-law marriage, and expressly state herein that this is not an agreement to marry, that they are not now married, and that they understand they are not married to each other during the term of this agreement.

Waiver of Support

[18] Both parties waive and relinquish any and all rights to alimony, spousal support, palimony, or other separate maintenance from the other in the event of a termination of their living together arrangement.

Estates at Death

[19] Upon death, neither party shall have any claim upon the estate of the other.

Dated: _____

_____
[Name and Signature of Party]

_____
[Name and Signature of Party]

Names of Witnesses:

_____

_____

Notary Public:

_____(Seal)

My commission expires on _____ [Expiration Date]

Source: Reprinted from William Mulloy, *West's Legal Forms* § 3.54, pp. 225–29 (2d ed., West Group, 1983) with permission of Thomson Reuters.

ASSIGNMENT 4.8

Draft a cohabitation agreement for Helen Smith and Sam Jones who have just decided to move in together. Assume the following facts:

- They are not married and do not intend to become married.
- They would like to enter into a contract that spells out their rights and responsibilities.
- They want to make clear that the house in which they will live belongs to Helen even though Sam will be doing extensive remodeling work on it.
- They each have separate bank accounts and one joint account.
- They want to clarify that only the funds in the joint account belong to both of them equally.
- In the following year, they hope to have or adopt a child. In either event, they want the contract to specify that the child will be given the surname, Smith-Jones, a combination of their own last names.

You will need additional facts to prepare the agreement. You can make these facts up so long as they are reasonably consistent with the facts given above. Before you draft the agreement, prepare a checklist of topics to cover in the agreement such as how they will pay for everyday expenses and what separate property they will each initially bring with them to the relationship. Review all the material in this chapter on cohabitation agreements and check online for additional ideas for topics that a couple should discuss and cover in such an agreement. (See General Instructions for the Agreement-Drafting in Appendix A.)

PARALEGAL ROLES

- For an overview of paralegal roles in family-law cases, see Exhibits 1.5 and 1.6 in Chapter 1.
- For all financial issues covered in Chapter 4, a paralegal may be asked to help collect documents and facts outlined in:
  - The checklist in Exhibit 3.1 of Chapter 3,
  - The checklists on separation agreements at the beginning of Chapter 8, and
  - The interrogatories in Appendix C.
- The interviewing and investigation checklists in Chapter 4 also cover fact-finding roles of paralegals.
- Give the client a list of all documents that he or she should bring to the office pertaining to the premarital, postnuptial, or cohabitation agreement.
- Conduct extensive follow-up interviews of the client to identify all facts on the circumstances of the agreements.
- Schedule follow-up meetings of the client with the attorney to discuss client objectives for the negotiation and drafting of the agreements.
- Research the background of potential accountants, appraisers, or other experts who may be hired to prepare a financial statement of current assets and liabilities for disclosure to the other party to the premarital agreement.
- Compile exhibits or documents the attorney will need for the negotiation of the agreements with opposing counsel.
- Prepare a memorandum that states the terms that the attorney has negotiated with opposing counsel.
- Label, date, and file each draft of the agreement as it is changed during client discussions and the attorney's negotiations with opposing counsel.
- Compile and label financial statements and other disclosure documents that will become attachments (schedules) to the agreement.
- Prepare a first draft of the agreement, using digital copies of prior agreements of the same kind as a template and starting point.
- Read the draft of the agreement proposed by opposing counsel, noting discrepancies from the negotiated terms.
- Schedule the execution of the agreements.
- On the office calendar, note the dates on which further forms, affidavits, or agreements must be executed, e.g., filing the form needed to waive pension rights. Monitor compliance of these events.

SUMMARY

The four main kinds of agreements that parties in intimate relationships enter into before and after marriage are as follows:

1. Premarital agreements
2. Postnuptial agreements
3. Cohabitation agreements
4. Separation agreements

A *premarital agreement* is a contract by persons about to be married that can cover (a) financial and related matters once the marriage occurs and (b) spousal support, property division, and related matters in the event of separation, divorce, annulment, or death. In most states, the agreement can waive spousal support so long as one of the spouses is not left destitute at the time it is enforced. Some clauses may necessitate further action after the marriage, e.g., waiver of retirement benefits. In general, courts are not receptive to enforcing lifestyle clauses that cover personal services during the marriage.

For a premarital agreement to be valid, all states require sufficient financial disclosure, an opportunity to consult with others, voluntariness, and the absence of duress and fraud. Most states do not require substantive fairness but will not enforce the agreement if it is *unconscionable*—which means shocking the conscience by heavily favoring one side in the absence of meaningful choice and highly unequal bargaining positions of the parties. Independent counsel for each party is not required, although each must be given the opportunity to consult such counsel.

A *postnuptial agreement* is a contract between married persons that covers financial and related matters between them, usually financial in nature. The parties may have no intention of separating. If they have this intention, the agreement is commonly called a *separation agreement*. The requirement of procedural fairness applies to postnuptial agreements. Some states also require substantive fairness because of the fiduciary relationship that exists between spouses.

A *cohabitation agreement* is a contract by persons in an intimate relationship who are not married to each other (and who intend to stay unmarried indefinitely) that covers financial and related matters while living together and upon the end of the relationship by separation or death. Valid consideration is required; the consideration cannot be *meretricious* (pertaining to prostitution or unlawful sexual relations). The sexual aspect of the relationship, if any, must be severable from the rest of the agreement.

Most states are reluctant to enforce a cohabitation agreement unless the parties have an express agreement. If the aggrieved party cannot establish the existence of an express cohabitation contract, other remedies that some courts will entertain (to avoid the unfairness of one of the parties walking away from the relationship with nothing) include implied-in-fact contract, implied-in-law contract (quasi contract), constructive trust, partnership, and joint venture.

KEY TERMS

premarital agreement	overreaching	meretricious
divisible	voluntary	common-law marriage
elective share	duress	ceremonial marriage
Uniform Premarital Agreement Act (UPAA)	rebut	palimony
public policy	fraud	remedy
no-fault divorce	material	express contract
waive	procedural fairness	implied-in-fact contract
public charge	substantive fairness	tacit
property division	unconscionable	gratuitous
sunset	community property	implied-in-law contract
severability clause	common-law property	unjust enrichment
severable	postnuptial agreement	quantum meruit
contract	separation agreement	trust
executory contract	coverture	beneficial interest
consideration	cohabitation	constructive trust
capacity	cohabitants	operation of law
statute of frauds	adultery	equitable remedy
arm's length	fornication	partnership
fiduciary relationship	cohabitation agreement	joint venture

CHECK THE CITE

Mary Allesandro Hardee is a legal assistant who developed a romantic relationship with and eventually married Jay Hardee, a client of the office where Mary worked. The office was representing Jay on his second divorce. At the time Mary and Jay signed a premarital agreement, her assets totaled $48,200; Jay's totaled $1,536,642. Some years later, they divorced. During the divorce, what position did each party take on the effect of the premarital agreement? How did the court rule on their positions? Read *Hardee v. Hardee*, 348 S.C. 84, 558 S.E.2d 264 (2001). To read the opinion online: (1) Run a citation search ("558 S.E.2d 264") in the *Case law* database of Google Scholar (scholar.google.com). (2) Run a citation search ("558 S.E.2d 264") or a case name and state search ("Hardee v. Hardee" South Carolina) in the general search engines of Google, Bing, or Yahoo.

PROJECT

In Google, Bing, or Yahoo, run the following search: aa "cohabitation agreement" (substitute the name of your state for aa in the search, e.g., California "cohabitation agreement"). Write an essay on the requirements for cohabitation agreements in your state. You must cite and quote from a minimum of four different online sources. At least two of these sources should be the actual language of statutes, court opinions, or other laws.

ETHICS IN A FAMILY LAW PRACTICE

You are a paralegal working at the law office of Paul Silverman, Esq. Alice Henderson has asked the office to write a cohabitation agreement for her and her boyfriend, Fred Lincoln. Both Alice and Fred come to the firm's office.

Paul Silverman describes the agreement that he has drafted for them, telling them that it is a standard agreement considered fair to both parties. Alice and Fred are happy with the agreement and sign it. Any ethical problems?

WRITING SAMPLE

The following assignments in this chapter could be used as the basis of a writing sample: Assignment 4.4(a) and Assignment 4.8. The same is true of the Project on researching cohabitation agreements in your state just mentioned. (See General Instructions for the Writing Sample in Appendix A.)

REVIEW QUESTIONS

1. What are the four main categories of agreements that persons in an intimate relationship can enter into?
2. What is a premarital agreement?
3. Why do couples enter into premarital agreements?
4. What does the Uniform Premarital Agreement Act say about what can be included in a premarital agreement?
5. What is meant by public policy?
6. What is meant by contracts that facilitate divorce?
7. When will a court not enforce a spousal-support clause?
8. What is an elective share and can it be waived?
9. What difficulty might exist when parties waive retirement benefits in a premarital agreement and how can this difficulty be resolved?
10. Can child support be waived?
11. Can the parties decide who will have custody of the children?
12. How are debts sometimes handled?
13. What are lifestyle clauses and do courts enforce them?
14. What is covered by a confidentiality clause?
15. What is the effect of a sunset clause?
16. What is the function of a severability clause?
17. What is a contract? When is it executory?
18. What are the requirements for a valid contract?
19. In what ways are commercial contracts and premarital agreements treated differently in the law?
20. When is an agreement voluntary?
21. What is duress and fraud?
22. What is the obligation of financial disclosure?
23. What is the distinction between procedural fairness and substantive fairness?
24. Do courts require substantive fairness in premarital agreements?
25. When is an agreement unconscionable?
26. Is each party required to have independent counsel?
27. Why did the *Bonds* case hold that the premarital agreement was voluntary even though both sides did not have independent counsel?
28. What dilemma does an attorney face when he or she represent the less well-to-do party who is being asked to sign (and is willing to sign) a premarital agreement that substantially favors the better-off party?
29. What is a postnuptial agreement?
30. What are some of the reasons couples enter them?
31. What is cohabitation?
32. What is a cohabitation agreement?
33. What consideration for the agreement would be invalid?
34. What did the *Marvin* case hold?
35. What is palimony?
36. What remedies did the *Marvin* court say were possible?
37. Why do most courts disfavor remedies other than an action for breach of an express contract?
38. What is an implied-in-fact contract?
39. What is an implied-in-law contract?
40. What is quantum meruit?
41. What is a trust?
42. What is the operation of law?
43. What is an equitable remedy?
44. When could a partnership be a remedy for a cohabitant?
45. What is a joint venture?

HELPFUL WEBSITES

Your State

See Appendix D for links to the family law of your state on the topics covered in this chapter.

Premarital Agreements

- www.expertlaw.com/library/family_law/prenuptial_agreements.html
- www.bankrate.com/brm/prenup.asp
- www.prenuptialagreements.org
- family.findlaw.com/marriage/sample-premarital-prenuptial-agreement.html

Uniform Premarital Agreement Act (UPAA)

- en.wikipedia.org/wiki/Uniform_Premarital_Agreement_Act
- www.uniformlaws.org (enter *premarital* in the search box)

Thirteen Famous Prenups

- www.abajournal.com/gallery/famous_prenups_gallery/1893

Postnuptial Agreements

- www.thespruce.com/postnuptial-agreements-2302012
- en.wikipedia.org/wiki/Postnuptial_agreement

Cohabitation Agreements

- family.findlaw.com/living-together/sample-cohabitation-agreement.html
- en.wikipedia.org/wiki/Cohabitation_agreement
- www.palimony.com

Jewish Law

- www.jlaw.com/Articles/antenuptial_agreement4.html

Google Scholar (scholar.google.com)

- Choose "Articles" and enter in the search box any of the key terms discussed in the chapter. Add the name of your state to the search term.
- Choose "Case law" and "Select courts". Select your state, click "Done," and enter in the search box any of the key terms discussed in the chapter. Add the name of your state to the search term.

Google, Bing, Yahoo

(on these search engines, run the following searches, substituting your state for "aa")

- "premarital agreement" aa
- "antenuptial agreement" aa
- "separation agreement" aa
- meretricious aa
- "Marvin v. Marvin" aa
- "postnuptial agreement" aa
- "cohabitation agreement" aa
- palimony aa
- "unjust enrichment" aa

YouTube

Run the same searches on YouTube listed above for Google, Bing, Yahoo searches. Even when the video clips are trying to entice you to retain an attorney, buy a book, or enroll in a course, they can provide useful overviews and references to primary authority.

Twitter, Reddit, and Facebook

On Twitter, Reddit, and Facebook, run the following searches (substitute your state for *aa*; run the searches with and without the name of your state). Look for links to family-law developments in your state.

- prenuptial agreement aa
- cohabitation agreement aa

ENDNOTES

Note: The court opinions in these endnotes can be read online. To do so, go to Google Scholar (scholar.google.com), select "Case law," and in the search box, enter the cite (e.g., "5 P.3d 815") or name of the case (e.g., "In re Marriage of Bonds") that is given in the endnote.

[1] Pamila Yip, *To Have and to Hold*, San Jose Mercury News, January 26, 2003, at 3F.

[2] David Rovella, *Pre-Nups No Longer Just for the Wealthy*, National Law Journal 9/6/99, at A1.

[3] Kerry Hannon, *Planning for Love and Money*, U.S. News & World Report, 56 (July 16, 2006).

[4] Rose Kreider, *How Many Trips Do We Take Down the Aisle?* U.S. Census Bureau (May 18, 2011).

[5] See, for example, the Texas Premarital Agreement Act (www.statutes.legis.state.tx.us/Docs/FA/htm/FA.4.htm). See also the Uniform Premarital and Marital Agreements Act (uniformlaws.org) (type *premarital* in the search box).

[6] See for example, Connecticut General Statutes, § 46b-36g(b).

[7] Geoffrey Gray, *With This Ring (and This Contract), I Thee Wed*, New York, 51 (March 26, 2006); Jan Hoffman, *The Rich; How They Keep It*, The New York Times Magazine, 102 (November 19, 1995).

[8] *In re Marriage of Bonds*, 24 Cal. 4th 1, 25, 5 P.3d 815, 830 (2000), quoting Katharine Silbaugh, *Marriage Contracts and the Family Economy* 93 N.W.U.L.Rev. 65, 123 (1998).

[9] Jill Brooke, *A Promise to Love, Honor and Bear No Children*, N.Y. Times, October 13, 2002, at ST1.

[10] *Holler v. Holler*, 612 S.E.2d 469, 476 (S.C. Ct. App., 2005).

[11] Susan Berfield, *Does Your Marriage Need a Postnup?* Business Week, 80 (April 16, 2007).

[12] Tamar Lewin, "Among Nuptial Agreements, Post- Has Now Joined Pre-," N.Y. Times, July 7, 2001.

[13] Ibid.

[14] Vernon's Texas Statutes and Codes Annotated, Family Code, § 1.108 (1997).

[15] *The Decline of Marriage and the Rise of New Families* (Pew Research Center Publications November 18, 2010) (www.pewresearch.org) (enter *declining marriage* in the search box).

[16] Washington State has its own meaning for meretricious. It defines a meretricious relationship as a stable, marital-like relationship where both parties cohabit with knowledge that a lawful marriage between them does not exist. *Connell v. Francisco*, 898 P.2d 831, 834 (Wash. 1995).

[17] 557 P.2d 106 (Cal. 1976).

[18] 557 P.2d at 112, 113, 116 (emphasis in original).

[19] Ann Estin, *Unmarried Partners and the Legacy of Marvin v. Marvin*, 76 Notre Dame Law Review 1381, 1400 (2001).

CHAPTER 5

Marriage

CHAPTER OUTLINE

CHAPTER OBJECTIVES

After completing this chapter, you should be able to:

- Explain whether causes of action can be brought for breach of promise to marry (or for inducing a breach).
- Know when gifts must be returned upon breaking off an engagement.
- Know when restraints on marriage are enforceable.
- Understand what is meant by marriage as a fundamental right.
- List the times when a person will likely want to know if he or she is married.

- Distinguish between ceremonial and common-law marriages.
- State the technical or procedural requirements for a ceremonial marriage.
- Know when a proxy marriage is allowed.
- State what is meant by the ABM (Anything But Marriage) movement.
- On what legal theory did the U.S. Supreme Court end the ban on same-sex marriage?

- Explain how a covenant marriage is entered into and terminated.
- List the requirements for a common-law marriage.
- State why common-law marriages are disfavored.
- Know how a conflict-of-laws issue is resolved in a state where common-law marriage is not allowed.
- Identify the elements of a putative marriage.
- Explain *marriage by estoppel* and *de facto marriage*.

LEGAL ISSUES PRIOR TO MARRIAGE

Before we examine the law of marriage formation, we will explore three important issues that can arise when a planned marriage does not occur.

1. Can someone be sued for failing to fulfill a promise to marry? If so, what is the theory of the suit? What is the **cause of action**?

2. When a marriage is called off, what happens to the engagement ring and wedding gifts that have already been exchanged?

3. Is a promise *not* to marry enforceable?

BREACH OF PROMISE TO MARRY

More than 100,000 wedding engagements are broken each year. This can be a costly experience. In some cities, traditional weddings can cost between $50,000 and $100,000, and "as the wedding day approaches, less and less of the expense of the event can be recovered if the event is canceled." In New York City, for example, many caterers and hotels charge for services and rooms that cannot be rebooked when canceled with less than six months' notice.[1] Faced with such costs, some victims of broken engagements consider suing for breach of contract or, more specifically, for breach of promise to marry.

In a *minority* of states, one person can sue another for breach of promise to marry. Such suits are called **heart-balm actions** because they are based on the loss of love and relationship—a broken heart. (In Chapter 17, we will examine more of these actions such as alienation of affections and seduction.) The main relief available in such actions is **compensatory damages**. This is an amount of money that will restore an injured party to his or her position prior to the injury or other loss. Examples of such losses are payments to buy a wedding dress, rent a hall, and purchase rings. Damages for humiliation and mental anguish may also be allowed.

The remedy of **specific performance** (which orders a party to perform a contract as promised) is not available. No court would force parties to enter into a marriage that one of the parties no longer wants. At one time, **expectation damages**—money to compensate for the loss of what was reasonably anticipated from a contract—were allowed. Today, however, this is no longer so. For example, the **aggrieved** party cannot be compensated for a loss of the lifestyle he or she would have enjoyed if the marriage had occurred. **Punitive damages** can be awarded if the party breaching the promise to marry acted out of **malice** (e.g., intentionally humiliating the other party or recklessly disregarding the upheaval and pain that the breach would cause).

As indicated, however, not all states allow heart-balm actions such as breach of promise to marry. The states that have abolished such actions have done so mainly by what is called a **heart-balm statute**. Such statutes were enacted for a number of reasons. The emotions involving a refusal to marry are usually so personal, intense, and possibly bitter that a court is not a proper setting to handle them. Furthermore, persons should be allowed to correct their mistakes of the heart without fear of a lawsuit. As one judge said, the courtroom should not become a "grotesque" setting for the exposure of heart-rending episodes of wounded pride, which should be best kept private rather than public."[2] Courts were also afraid of being flooded with breach-of-promise lawsuits, particularly by unscrupulous "gold diggers and blackmailers" who become engaged in order to use the threat of publicity to force a lucrative settlement.[3]

cause of action
1. A legally acceptable reason for bringing a suit. 2. A rule that constitutes a legal theory for bringing a suit. 3. The facts that give a person a right to judicial relief. When you *state a cause of action,* you list the facts that give you a right to judicial relief against the alleged wrongdoer.

heart-balm actions
An action based on the loss of love and relationships - on a broken heart (e.g., breach of promise to marry, alienation of affections, and seduction).

compensatory damages
Money paid to restore an injured party to his or her position prior to the injury or other loss.

specific performance
A remedy for breach of contract that forces the wrongdoing party to complete the contract as promised. It is an equitable remedy.

expectation damages
Money to compensate for the loss of what was reasonably anticipated from a contract that was not performed.

aggrieved
Injured or wronged and thereby entitled to a remedy.

punitive damages
Damages that are added to actual or compensatory damages in order to punish malicious, outrageous, or reckless conduct and to deter similar conduct in the future. Also called *exemplary damages, smart money,* or *vindictive damages.*

malice
1. The intent to inflict injury or other wrongful harm. 2. Reckless disregard of what is right. 3. Animosity or ill will.

heart-balm statute
A statute that abolishes heart-balm actions.

CASE | Stanard v. Bolin
88 Wash. 2d 614, 565 P.2d 94 (1977)
Supreme Court of Washington

Background: *During their courtship, the male defendant assured the female plaintiff that he was worth in excess of $2 million, that he was planning to retire in two years, and that the two of them would then travel. He promised the plaintiff that she would never have to work again and that he would see to the support of her two teenaged sons. He also promised that the plaintiff's mother would never be in need. After he proposed, the parties found a suitable home for their residence and they signed a purchase agreement. At the insistence of the defendant, the plaintiff placed her home on the market for sale and sold most of her furniture at a public auction. The parties set the wedding date, reserved a church, and hired a minister to perform the service. Dresses for the plaintiff, her mother, and the matron of honor were ordered, and a reception was arranged at a local establishment. The parties began informally announcing their plans to a wide circle of friends.*

After the wedding date was set, the plaintiff's employer hired another person to take over her job and asked the plaintiff to assist in teaching the new employee the duties of her job. A month before the wedding, the defendant informed the plaintiff that he would not marry her. This came as a great shock to the plaintiff and caused her to become ill and to lose sleep and weight. She sought medical advice and was treated by her physician. The plaintiff also had to take her home off the market and repurchase furniture at a cost in excess of what she received for her old furniture. In addition, she had to cancel all wedding plans and reservations, return wedding gifts, and explain to her friends, family, and neighbors what had happened. The plaintiff sued the defendant for breach of promise to marry. The trial court ruled for the defendant. The plaintiff appealed to the Supreme Court of Washington.

Decision on Appeal: The trial court is reversed. The plaintiff should be allowed to sue for breach of promise, although there are limitations on the kind of damages that can be awarded. The court addressed two main issues on damages: (1) expectation damages and (2) emotional damages.

OPINION OF THE COURT:

Justice HAMILTON delivered the opinion of the court.

This appeal presents the question of whether the . . . action for breach of promise to marry should be abolished. . . . The breach-of-promise-to-marry action is one not easy to classify. Although the action is treated as arising from the breach of a contract (the contract being the mutual promises to marry), the damages allowable more closely resemble a tort action. . . .

When two persons agree to marry, they should realize that certain actions will be taken during the engagement period in reliance on the mutual promises to marry. Rings will be purchased, wedding dresses and other formal attire will be ordered or reserved, and honeymoon plans with their attendant expenses will be made. . . . When the plans to marry are abruptly ended, it is certainly foreseeable that the party who was unaware that the future marriage would not take place will have expended some sums of money and will suffer some forms of mental anguish, loss to reputation, and injury to health. We do not feel these injuries should go unanswered merely because the breach-of-promise-to marry action may be subject to abuses; rather, an attempt should be made to eradicate the abuses from the action.

One major abuse of the action is allowing the plaintiff to bring in evidence of the defendant's wealth and social position . . . under the theory that the plaintiff should be compensated for what she or he has lost by not marrying the defendant. [We do not believe such damages are justified in light of modern society's concept of marriage, which is a coming together out of love, not in order to secure property. Hence, damages] for loss of expected financial and social position should no longer be recoverable under the breach-of-promise-to-marry actions. This means that evidence of the defendant's wealth and social position becomes immaterial in assessing the plaintiff's damages.

Other damages subject to criticism are those damages given for mental anguish, loss to reputation, and injury to health. It is argued that these injuries are "so vague and so little capable of measurement in dollars that they give free rein to the jury's passions, prejudices and sympathies." See Homer Clark, *The Law of Domestic Relations in the United States* 12 (1968). This argument has little merit, for it places no faith in the jury's ability to evaluate objectively the evidence regarding plaintiff's injuries and render a just verdict. If a jury's verdict is tainted by passion or prejudice, or is otherwise excessive, the trial court and the appellate court have the power to reduce the award or order a new trial. See *Hogenson v. Service Armament Co.*, 77 Wash. 2d 209, 461 P.2d 311 (1969). Lack of ability to quantify damages in exact dollar amounts does not justify abolishing the breach-of-promise-to-marry action. In her complaint plaintiff alleged that she had suffered pain, impairment to health, humiliation, and embarrassment as a result of the defendant's breach of his promise to marry. If this is true. . . , she is entitled to compensation for these injuries. . . .

In conclusion, we have decided that the breach-of-promise-to-marry action should be retained . . . for the recovery of the foreseeable special and general damages which are caused by a defendant's breach of promise to marry. However, the action is modified to the extent that a plaintiff cannot recover for loss of expected financial and social position,. . .

The judgment of the trial court is reversed. . . .

ASSIGNMENT 5.1

a. Give (i) specific examples of evidence of damages you think the plaintiff will try to introduce at the new trial and (ii) specific examples of evidence of damages she will be forbidden to introduce.

b. Do you agree with the result reached by the court in the *Stanard* case? Why or why not? Is marriage a property transaction today? Should expectation damages be awarded in such cases?

ASSIGNMENT 5.2

Assume that you live in a state where heart-balm actions can be brought. Dan asks Carol to marry him. Carol says yes. The date is set for the wedding. Two weeks before the wedding, Carol learns that Dan has just married Linda. At the time Dan was engaged to Carol, Carol was already married to Bill, but Dan did not know this. Carol was in the process of divorcing Bill and hoped the divorce would be finalized before her marriage to Dan. Carol wanted to wait until the divorce was final before telling Dan about the prior marriage and divorce. Dan did not learn about any of this until after his marriage to Linda. When Carol's divorce to Bill became final, she sues Dan for breach of promise to marry. Should Carol be allowed to bring this action? (See General Instructions for the Legal-Analysis Assignment in Appendix A.)

INDUCING A BREACH OF PROMISE TO MARRY

In the commercial world, it is a *tort* to induce a person to break a contract with someone else. It is called **interference with contract relations**. For example, Jones Company persuades Smith Company to break Smith's contract with Miller Company so that Smith can enter into a contract with Jones. Miller has a tort action against Jones for interfering with its contract relations with Smith.

Suppose that Jim and Mary are engaged to be married. Mary's mother is opposed to the marriage and persuades Mary to break her promise to marry Jim. Can Jim sue Mary's mother for interference with contract relations by inducing a breach of Mary's promise to marry him? Most states would say no, even in states that allow actions for breach of promise to marry. Courts do not want to discourage relatives from advising against what they consider to be a bad match. Indeed, relatives have a **privilege** to provide such advice in order to protect those close to them.

FRAUD

If a heart balm-statute exists, some plaintiffs have tried to get around it by bringing an action for *fraud* rather than for breach of promise to marry. The action would be for fraudulently inducing someone to enter into a marriage. **Fraud** is an intentionally false statement of fact that is material, made to induce reliance by the plaintiff, and results in harm because of the reliance.

Elements of the Tort of Fraud

(Sometimes called deceit and misrepresentation)

- There must be a false statement of present fact by the defendant.
- The defendant must know that the statement is false. (This element is called **scienter**).

interference with contract relations
Intentionally encouraging or provoking a breach of contract that exists between or among other persons. Also called *tortious interference with contractual relations*.

privilege
A right to act contrary to the right of another without being subject to tort or other liability. It is a defense that authorizes conduct that would otherwise be wrong. (See glossary for an additional meaning.)

fraud
An intentionally false statement of fact that (a) is material, (b) is made to induce reliance by the plaintiff, and (c) results in harm because of the reliance. Also called *deceit* or *misrepresentation*.

scienter
Knowledge of the falsity of a statement, a lack of honest belief in its truth, or a reckless disregard of its truth or falsity. (See glossary for an additional meaning.)

- The defendant must intend that the plaintiff rely upon the statement.
- The plaintiff must rely on the defendant's statement and be reasonable in so relying.
- The plaintiff must suffer harm due to the reliance.

Here is an example of how an aggrieved party might try a fraud cause of action based on a broken engagement.

> *Don tells Phyllis that he wants to marry her. At the time he makes this statement of fact, it is false because Don never wants to marry her. His goal—his intention—is to obtain a loan of $25,000 from her. He knows that without a marriage proposal, she will refuse. Phyllis believes he wants to marry her and lends him the money in reliance on his promise of marriage. Soon thereafter, she learns that he never wanted to marry her and that he has spent the money she lent him. Her reliance on his promise resulted in her loss of $25,000.*

Or, suppose that Don falsely promises to marry Phyllis in order to persuade her to give up her virginity to him. Assume that Phyllis and Don live in a state with a heart-balm statute that has abolished the breach-of-promise-to-marry cause of action. Can Phyllis overcome this obstacle by suing Don for fraud in the loan case or in the virginity case? The answer depends on whether the legislature intended the heart-balm statute to eliminate both causes of action even though the act may specifically mention only the breach-of-promise action. Some states allow the fraud action. Others have said that the heart-balm statute eliminates both the breach-of-promise and the fraud action.

INTENTIONAL INFLICTION OF EMOTIONAL DISTRESS (IIED)

intentional infliction of emotional distress (IIED)
Intentionally causing severe emotional distress by extreme or outrageous conduct.

Another tort action some plaintiffs have tried to bring is **intentional infliction of emotional distress (IIED)**. The plaintiff must convince a court that the heart-balm statute does not bar this action as well. If this can be done, the next step is to prove that he or she was the victim of particularly shocking conduct by the defendant. For example, a man knows his fiancée is emotionally unstable because she is a former mental patient. He proposes marriage for the sole purpose of humiliating her by changing his mind just after she makes elaborate, public, and expensive wedding plans. A state might conclude that this is sufficiently outrageous and shocking conduct. A more common change-of-mind case, on the other hand, would probably not be enough for this tort, no matter how upset the jilted party becomes. The behavior of the culprit must shock the conscience.

GIFTS

gift
The voluntary delivery of property with the present intent to transfer title and control, for which no payment or consideration is made.

consideration
Something of value that is exchanged between parties. It can be an act, a forbearance (not performing an act), a promise to perform an act, or a promise to refrain from performing an act.

donor
The person who gives a gift.

donee
The person who receives a gift.

testamentary gift
A gift made in a will.

revocable
Capable of being altered, revoked, cancelled, or recalled.

inter vivos gift
A gift that takes effect (becomes irrevocable) while the donor is living.

irrevocable
Not capable of being altered, revoked, cancelled, or recalled.

A **gift** is a voluntary delivery of property with the present intent to transfer title and control, for which no payment or consideration is made. (**Consideration** is something of value that is exchanged.) The two parties in a gift are the **donor** (the giver) and the **donee** (the recipient).

There are two main categories of gifts: testamentary and inter vivos. A **testamentary gift** is a gift made in a will. Donors of testamentary gifts can always change their mind before they die by changing their will. Hence, testamentary gifts are **revocable**. Our primary concern in this chapter is the **inter vivos gift**, which is a gift that takes effect while the donor is living. It is not commonly known that once an inter vivos gift is made, it is **irrevocable**; the donor cannot revoke the gift and reclaim it from the donee. The one exception in some states is an inter vivos gift made while the donor knows that death is near ("impending death"). In these states, an inter vivos gift made in view of impending death is revocable while the donor is still alive.

Irrevocable Gifts

For a gift to be irrevocable, all of the elements of a gift must be present:

Elements of an Irrevocable Gift

- There must be a delivery of the property. (For some kinds of property, delivery is accomplished by a symbolic act such as giving the donee a key to the house or a key to a safe deposit box.)
- The transfer must be voluntary.
- The donor must intend to relinquish title and dominion over what is given.
- There must be no consideration such as a cash payment for the gift.
- The donor must intend that the gift take effect immediately; there must be a present intention to give an unconditional gift.
- The donee must accept the gift.

If Pat says to Bill, "I'll definitely give you my car next year," no gift has taken place. There was no intent that an immediate transfer would occur. Also, there was no delivery. Similarly, no gift has been made if Pat says to Bill, "Maybe I'll let you keep the pen you borrowed." There was no intent by Pat to relinquish her title and dominion over the pen now. This is so even though Bill already had possession of the pen.

Conditional Gifts

Suppose that Pat says to Bill, "I'll give you this car if you make the honor roll." No gift has occurred because a condition exists that must be fulfilled before the gift becomes effective (i.e., Bill must make the honor roll). There is no present intention to relinquish title and dominion.

Now let's apply these rules to a wedding engagement. The general rule is that gifts given in contemplation of marriage are conditional gifts, meaning that they are subject to a condition—the occurrence of the marriage. The gifts are not irrevocable if the condition is not met due to a cancellation of the engagement. With some exceptions, most states allow the donor to force the return of such conditional gifts. Examine the following sequence of events:

January 1, 2018: Mary and Bob meet.

January 2, 2018: On a date at a restaurant, Bob gives Mary a bracelet.

February 13, 2018: Mary and Bob become engaged; he gives her an engagement ring. The marriage date will be in eight months.

March 26, 2018: This is Mary's birthday; Bob gives Mary a new car.

June 5, 2018: Bob and Mary change their minds about getting married.

Assume that Bob now wants the bracelet, ring, and car back. When Mary refuses, Bob sues her, contending in court that the elements of a gift were not met when he gave Mary the items because he intended that she keep them only if they married. Will a court infer this condition of marriage? The answer depends on Bob's intention at the time he gave each of the items to Mary. The court must turn the clock back to the time when the gifts were given and determine what the intention was at those times.

When the bracelet was given, the parties were not engaged. A jury might conclude that Bob's intent was to please Mary, but not necessarily to win her hand in marriage. The bracelet was given the day after they met, when marriage was probably not on his mind. If so, the bracelet was a courting gift (called a gift of pursuit). It is unlikely, therefore, that a court would rule that the gift of the bracelet was conditional and force Mary to return it. In contrast, the facts show that about six weeks after the bracelet was given, the parties became engaged. This short time period does raise the possibility, however slight, that marriage *was* on Bob's mind when he gave Mary the bracelet (i.e., that the gift was conditional).

The birthday gift of the car is troublesome. Again, the central issue is Bob's intent at the time he gave her the car. Mary would argue that no condition of marriage was attached to the gift. She would say that a birthday gift would have been given whether or not they were engaged. Bob would argue that the extraordinary cost of a new car is persuasive evidence that it would not have been given as a birthday gift unconnected with the impending marriage. This is a strong argument.

ASSIGNMENT 5.3

What further facts would you seek in order to assess whether the car was a gift in the case of Bob and Mary? (See General Instructions for the Investigation-Strategy Assignment in Appendix A.)

Engagement Rings

What about the engagement ring? When the decision to break the engagement is mutual, most courts say that a condition of marriage was implied and, therefore, the ring must be returned. Suppose, however, that one of the parties unilaterally breaks the engagement without any plausible reason or justification. This person is considered to be at fault. Must the ring be returned in such a case? Some courts will order the return of the ring if the person receiving it (the donee) is the one who broke the engagement without justification, but not if he or she is the "innocent" party. Most courts, however, will order the return of the ring regardless of who was at fault.

Of course, Internet sites have been created to try to cash in on the predicament faced by no-longer-engaged couples. For example, one site (www.idonow-idont.com) is designed to be a clearinghouse for the sale of engagement rings that are no longer suitable for their original purpose because of the breakup.

ASSIGNMENT 5.4

Roy and Brooke have been dating for months. Roy is a football player who is often on the road. While away at a game just before Valentine's Day, Roy calls Brooke and asks her if she received the gift he sent her. She says the package just came. He tells her to open it, which she does. It's a ring valued at $76,000. She thanks him and says she loves the ring. Roy then says, "You're going to look good with that ring wherever you go. How about wearing it to our wedding?" Brooke tells Roy that she is going to marry someone else that she has recently met. Roy asks for the ring back. She refuses. Does she have to return it? (See the General Instructions for the Legal-Analysis Assignment in Appendix A.)

Third-Party Gifts

Third parties (e.g., relatives and friends) often give wedding gifts. When the marriage does not take place, these parties can force a return of the gifts in most states because courts will conclude that such gifts were conditional. In a few states, however, they may have trouble getting the gifts back. Earlier, we saw that heart-balm statutes abolished the cause of action for breach of promise to marry. Some of these statutes are worded so broadly that courts might interpret them to mean that *any* cause of action growing out of a broken engagement will not be allowed, including a cause of action to obtain the return of conditional gifts.

ASSIGNMENT 5.5

Examine the following sequence of events:

February 13, 2018: Jim says to Bob, "Please introduce me to Joan. I want to meet her because I know that she is the girl I want to spend the rest of my life with." Bob does so. Jim is so happy that he gives Bob a gold wristwatch and says to him, "I want you to have this. Thanks for being my friend. I want you to wear this watch to my wedding someday."

March 1, 2018: Joan brings Jim home to meet her mother. When the evening is over, Jim gives Joan's mother an expensive family Bible.

September 5, 2018: They agree to marry. The wedding date is to be February 18, 2019. On the day that they agree to marry, Jim gives Joan a diamond bracelet, saying, "I want you to have this no matter what happens."

December 14, 2018: They both agree to break the engagement.

Jim asks Bob for the wristwatch back. Bob refuses. Jim asks Joan's mother for the Bible back. The mother refuses. Jim asks Joan for the bracelet back. Joan refuses.

a. Can Jim obtain the wristwatch from Bob, the Bible from the mother, and the bracelet from Joan? (See General Instructions for the Legal-Analysis Assignment in Appendix A.)

b. Draft a complaint against Joan in which Jim seeks the return of the bracelet. (See General Instructions for the Complaint-Drafting Assignment in Appendix A.)

Unjust Enrichment

The theory of recovery we have been discussing thus far is the existence of a conditional gift. An alternative theory of recovery that is available in some states is **unjust enrichment**. When allowed, this remedy is used when someone has received a benefit that was not intended as a gift and that should be returned or for which compensation should be paid.

See this chapter's Interviewing and Investigation Checklist on the status of gifts.

unjust enrichment
The receipt of a benefit in the form of goods or services that in fairness should be returned or paid for even though there was no express or implied promise to do so.

☑ INTERVIEWING AND INVESTIGATION CHECKLIST

The Status of Gifts

LEGAL INTERVIEWING QUESTIONS

(C = client; D = defendant)

1. On what date did you and D first agree to be married?

2. Where were you at the time of this agreement? Were you in this state? If not, in what state?

3. How old were you at the time? How old was D?

4. What specific language did D use when D promised to marry you? What specific language did you use when you accepted or promised to marry D? (Try to obtain exact quotations.)

5. When did you first learn that D no longer wished to marry you? What specifically was said and done?

6. What reason did D give?

7. Did D give you any gifts?

8. For each gift received, describe the gift, the date you were told about it, and what was said when it was given. Specify whether the gift was received before or after the engagement.

9. Has D ever given you gifts on special occasions such as birthdays; holidays such as Easter, Christmas, or Hanukkah; or on recognition days such as the day you won a race or other prize? Describe the circumstances of all such gifts.

10. When did each gift come into your possession?

11. Answer Questions 7 through 10 for any gifts you gave to D.

12. Before or after the engagement, did D give gifts to any of your relatives or close friends? If so, describe the circumstances.

13. Before or after the engagement, did you give gifts to any of D's relatives or close friends? If so, describe the circumstances.

(continued)

14. Did you or D receive any shower gifts or wedding gifts from others before the engagement was broken? If so, describe the circumstances.

15. Did you have a shower or wedding registry in which you indicated what gifts you would welcome? To what extent was the registry used?

POSSIBLE INVESTIGATION TASKS

- Locate all letters or other written communications D sent to C about their relationship.
- Draft an inventory of every gift connected with D's relationship with C. For each gift, identify the donor (the giver), donee (the recipient), date of the gift, kind and value of the gift, circumstances surrounding the gift, present location of the gift, etc.

RESTRAINT OF MARRIAGE

restraint of marriage
A condition in a contract or gift that a benefit will be lost upon marriage or remarriage.

What happens if a contract or gift contains a condition that a benefit will be lost if a marriage or remarriage occurs? Such a condition is called a **restraint of marriage**. The law looks with disfavor on attempts to limit the right to marry, even with the consent of the person subject to the limitation. Not all restrictions, however, are invalid. A distinction must be made between a general restraint on marriage and a reasonable limitation on marriage.

General Restraint

A general restraint on marriage is a total or near-total prohibition against marriage and is unenforceable. For example:

- In exchange for a large sum of money to be given to her by her father, Mary agrees never to marry.

- As John leaves for a military tour of duty, Jane says, "It is you that I want to marry. Even if you don't want to marry me, even if you marry someone else, even if you die, I promise you that I will never marry anyone else as long as I live." John leaves without promising to marry Jane.

Mary's father cannot sue her to hold her to her agreement never to marry, nor can Jane be sued by John for breach of her promise should she marry someone other than him. People may decide never to marry, but no court will force them to abide by that decision.

The John/Jane agreement is unenforceable for another reason. For a contract to exist, there must be consideration (something of value that is exchanged between the parties). Jane's consideration was her promise never to marry anyone, but John gave no consideration in exchange. Hence, Jane's promise is unenforceable because she received no consideration; there was no valid contract to breach.

Reasonable Limitation

A reasonable limitation on marriage is one that (1) is a partial rather than a general prohibition, (2) serves what the court feels is a useful purpose, and (3) is not otherwise illegal. Consider the following situations:

- Jim enters into a contract in which he promises that he will never marry a woman who is not of his religious faith.

- Mary enters into a contract in which she promises never to marry anyone who has a criminal record.

- Jill enters into a contract in which she promises that she will not marry before she turns eighteen years old, and that she will obtain the permission of her parents if she decides to marry between the ages of eighteen and twenty-one.

- Linda enters into a contract in which she promises that she will not marry until she completes her college education.

Assume that Jim, Mary, Jill, and Linda received consideration (e.g., cash) from a relative in exchange for their promises. Are the promises enforceable? If Jim, Mary, Jill, and Linda later decide to marry contrary to their promises, can they be forced through litigation to return whatever consideration they received as a remedy for their breach of promise? Not all states answer this question in the same way, but generally the answer is yes. The restraints on marriage to which they agreed are enforceable.

All of the restraints in the examples are partial: they do not totally prohibit marriage or come near such a total prohibition. All of the restraints arguably serve a useful purpose: to protect a person or to preserve a valuable tradition or culture. There is no illegality evident in any of the restraints, e.g., no one is being asked to refrain from marriage in order to engage in adultery or fornication. Hence, all of the restraints could be considered reasonable limitations on one's right to marry and are enforceable in most states.

Thus far, we have been examining *contracts* that restrain marriage. Suppose, however, that the attempted restriction on marriage came as a condition attached to a *gift* (inter vivos or testamentary) rather than through a contract. For example:

- In Bob's will, he promises to give $100,000 to Fran "so long as she remains unmarried." When Bob dies, Fran is not married. She is given the **bequest** of $100,000. One year later, Fran marries. Bob's estate brings a suit against Fran to have the money returned.

- John has a deed drafted that states, "I convey all my property to my widowed sister, Joan, to be owned and used by her until she remarries, at which time said property shall go to the Red Cross."

bequest
A gift of personal property in a will. (In some states, a bequest can be a gift of personal property or real property in a will.)

In theory, the same rules on marriage restrictions apply to such gifts as apply to contracts. Some courts, however, are more inclined to find the restrictions to be reasonable (and hence enforceable) when the restriction is attached to a gift than when it is embodied in a contract.

In the Bob/Fran example, Fran might have an additional argument in her favor. The condition in the will is that the $100,000 bequest will be made to Fran "so long as she remains unmarried." The condition does not say she must remain unmarried forever. A reasonable interpretation of the will is that she must remain unmarried up until the time the will takes effect—when he dies. Under this interpretation, Fran met the condition because her marriage occurred after Bob died.

ASSIGNMENT 5.6

Closely examine each of the following situations. Determine which restraints on marriage, if any, are enforceable. Give specific reasons you think the restraint is or is not enforceable. (See General Instructions for the Legal-Analysis Assignment in Appendix A.)

a. John is married to Brenda. John enters into a contract with Brenda's father stating that if children are born from the marriage and if Brenda dies before John, John will never remarry. In exchange, John is given the father's large farm to live on rent-free for life. Children are born, and Brenda does die first. John marries Patricia. Brenda's father then sues to evict John from the farm. Does John have a defense to this suit?

(continued)

ASSIGNMENT (*continued*)	5.6

b. Joan enters into a contract with her aunt stating that she will not have children before she turns twenty-one. In exchange, Joan is given a sum of money when she signs the contract. Before she turns twenty-one, Joan has a baby (out of wedlock). The aunt sues Joan for breach of contract. Does Joan have a defense?

c. Fred enters into a contract with his father in which the father agrees to pay for Fred's entire medical education if Fred agrees to marry a doctor or a medical student if he decides to marry. When Fred becomes a doctor, he marries Sue, an electrician. The father sues Fred for the cost of the medical education. Does Fred have a defense?

d. Bill and Jean live together, but they do not wish to marry. They enter into a contract by which Jean promises to continue to live with Bill, to care for him, and to help raise their child in the event that they have a child. Bill agrees to place $500 per month in a bank account for Jean so long as she carries out her promise. Jean cannot receive the money until Bill dies. Also, if she marries anyone before Bill dies, she forfeits the right to all the money in the account. After living with Bill for twenty years (and remaining childless), Jean leaves him to marry Tom. Can Jean sue Bill to obtain $120,000 (plus interest), the amount in the account at the time she married Tom?

Antinepotism

In Chapter 12, we will learn that discrimination on the basis of marital status is often illegal as a violation of civil rights. For example, it is illegal for a bank to deny credit to someone solely because the applicant is not married.

nepotism
Favoritism shown to relatives. A rule against nepotism is called an *antinepotism rule*.

Nepotism is favoritism shown to relatives. Suppose that an employer has an *antinepotism* policy that forbids its employees to be married to each other. Under this policy, if one employee marries another employee, one or both must be terminated. Is this policy an unenforceable restriction on marriage?

Most courts have said that the antinepotism policy is reasonable because it (1) avoids spousal quarrels in the workplace, (2) avoids the appearance of management favoritism if a spouse has supervisory authority over his or her spouse, and (3) cuts down on scheduling problems when, for example, the spouses seek the same vacation dates.

Antinepotism policies do not discriminate on the basis of marital status. They do not say that only single persons can be employed. The restriction is against marrying a particular person—someone who works for the same employer. Although not all states agree with the conclusion that antinepotism policies are enforceable, most states do.

INTRODUCTION TO MARRIAGE

Marriage is a coming together for better or for worse, hopefully enduring and intimate to the degree of being sacred. It is an association that promotes a way of life, not causes; a harmony in living, not political faiths; a bilateral loyalty, not commercial or social projects. Yet it is an association for as noble a purpose as any involved in our prior decisions. Griswold v. Connecticut, 381 U.S. 479, 486 (1965) (Douglas, J.).

marriage
The legal union of two persons as spouses with designated rights and obligations to each other.

We now begin our examination of the law governing the formation of **marriage**. The definition of marriage in America changed dramatically in 2004 when Massachusetts became the first state to allow same-sex marriage, and in 2015, when the U.S. Supreme Court required all states to do so in the landmark decision of *Obergefell v. Hodges*.

- Prior definition of *marriage*: The legal union of a man and woman as husband and wife with designated rights and obligations to each other.
- Current definition: The legal union of two persons as spouses with designated rights and obligations to each other.

FUNDAMENTAL RIGHT

As individuals, we have different categories of rights as we saw in Chapter 1. The highest category is a **fundamental right**. The right to marry is such a right. A fundamental right is a right that (a) is specifically guaranteed in the U.S. Constitution, (b) is implicit in the concept of ordered liberty, or (c) is deeply rooted in the nation's history and tradition. Marriage falls into the third category—a right that is deeply rooted in the nation's history and tradition. According to the U.S. Supreme Court, "The freedom to marry has long been recognized as one of the vital personal rights essential to the orderly pursuit of happiness by free men."[4]

Over the years there have been major shifts in the exercise of this essential (fundamental) right. Forty-eight percent of Americans aged fifteen and older are married; fifty years ago, the number was 72 percent.[5] The marriage rate has declined, in part, because of the large number of couples living together (cohabiting) without marrying. (See Chapter 4.) Considerable diversity exists among those that do marry. Although most couples are men and women in their first marriage, an increasing number are in their second and third marriages. (In a recent cartoon, the confused minister accidently asked the bride, "Do you take this man to be your first husband?"[6]) Gender diversity also exists among the population of married couples; there are more than 550,000 same-sex marriages in the country.[7]

AM I MARRIED?

A client is not likely to walk into a law office and ask, "Am I married?" The existence of a marriage becomes an issue when the client is trying to obtain some other objective, such as asserting or seeking the following:

- A divorce (you can't divorce someone to whom you are not married).
- Pension benefits as the surviving spouse of a deceased employee.
- Social Security benefits as the surviving spouse of a deceased worker.
- Workers' compensation death benefits as the surviving spouse of an employee fatally injured on the job.
- Damages due to the **wrongful death** of a spouse.
- Assets of a deceased spouse who died **intestate** (i.e., without leaving a valid will).
- Assets under a clause in the will of a spouse (who died **testate**) that gives property "to my wife" or "to my husband."
- An **elective share** of the estate of a deceased spouse (who died testate). (This share can be selected—elected—in place of what is provided for the surviving spouse in the will of the deceased spouse.)

fundamental right
A right that falls into one of the following three categories: The right (a) is specifically guaranteed in the U.S. Constitution, (b) is implicit in the concept of ordered liberty, or (c) is deeply rooted in the nation's history and tradition.

wrongful death
A death caused by a tort or other wrong.

intestate
(1) Pertaining to someone who dies without a valid will. (2) A person who dies without a valid will.

testate
(1) Pertaining to someone who dies with a valid will. (2) A person who dies with a valid will.

elective share
The percentage of a deceased spouse's estate that the surviving spouse can choose (elect) to receive despite what the will of the deceased spouse provided for the surviving spouse. Also called *right of election, statutory share*, and *forced share*.

- Entrance into the United States (or avoidance of deportation) as a result of being married to a U.S. citizen.

- The **marital-communications privilege**, the right of spouses not to testify and to prevent each other from testifying about confidential communications between them during the marriage).

In all of these examples, the seeking party must establish that he or she is a spouse, i.e., that a marriage existed.

CEREMONIAL AND COMMON-LAW MARRIAGES

There are two main kinds of marriage:

- **Ceremonial marriage.** A marriage entered in compliance with statutory formalities (e.g., obtaining a marriage license, having the marriage performed by an authorized person before witnesses). A marriage other than a common-law marriage. Also called a *conventional marriage, traditional marriage, formal marriage,* or *statutory marriage.*

- **Common-law marriage.** A marriage entered without complying with statutory formalities by persons who (a) agree to marry, (b) live together as spouses, and (c) hold themselves out as married. A marriage by persons who have not gone through a ceremonial marriage. Called an *informal marriage* in Texas.

Although most states have abolished common-law marriage, the law governing such marriages must still be understood, as we will see later in the chapter.

Both ceremonial marriages and common-law marriages are the result of contracts that the parties have entered into. It is often said, however, that there are three parties in every marriage: the two spouses and the state. The state is always present because of its regulatory power over the formation of marriages, the custody and support of children, and the termination of marriages. As we saw in Chapter 4 on premarital agreements, parties are allowed to enter into contracts that alter many aspects of a marriage, but the state remains a powerful definer and enforcer of marriage basics.

CEREMONIAL MARRIAGE

The hallmark of a valid ceremonial marriage is compliance with statutory requirements such as obtaining a license. These requirements have not always existed. For most of Western history, marriage was a private contract between two families that did not require the permission or involvement of the state or of the church. For centuries, society's main ecclesiastical authority (the Roman Catholic Church) required church marriages but accepted the validity of marriages that were based solely on the couple's exchange of marital vows.

> In 1215, the church decreed that a "licit" marriage must take place in church. But people who married illicitly had the same rights and obligations as a couple married in church: their children were legitimate; the wife had the same inheritance rights; the couple was subject to the same prohibitions against divorce. Not until the 16th century did European states begin to require that marriages be performed under legal auspices. In part, this was an attempt to prevent unions between young adults whose parents opposed their match.[8]

Although some American colonies required marriages to be registered, common-law marriages were widely accepted as valid until the latter part of the 19th century when many (but by no means all) states decreed that only ceremonial marriages would be recognized as valid.

---

marital-communications privilege
A person can refuse to testify and can prevent his or her spouse or ex-spouse from testifying about any confidential communications made between them during their marriage. Also called *marital privilege, husband-wife privilege.*

ceremonial marriage
A marriage entered into in compliance with statutory formalities.

common-law marriage
A marriage entered into without complying with statutory formalities by persons who (a) agree to marry, (b) live together as spouses, and (c) hold themselves out as married.

TECHNICAL/PROCEDURAL REQUIREMENTS

We need to distinguish between (a) technical or procedural requirements for marriage (e.g., obtaining a marriage license, having witnesses to the ceremony) and (b) the essential requirements for marriage that pertain to the intent to marry and the capacity to marry (e.g., being of minimum age, having no serious mental disability). Most of the essential requirements will be discussed in Chapter 6 when we cover annulments. For now, our focus is on the technical/procedural requirements for a ceremonial marriage.

Not all states have the same technical/procedural requirements. (See Appendix D for links to the requirements for your state.) Here are the requirements most often found in statutory codes:

- Marriage license (in some states, both parties must apply for the license in person).
- Waiting period between the time the marriage license is obtained and the wedding.
- Solemnization. The formal steps taken in a public ceremony performed by an authorized person, the officiant (e.g., a member of the clergy, a judge, or other designated person).
- Witnesses to the ceremony.
- Marriage declaration (during the ceremony, before the officiant and witnesses, the parties must indicate that they take each other as husband and wife (or as spouses, for same-sex marriages).
- Recording of the marriage by the officiant in a designated government office (e.g., the county clerk) following the ceremony (the process is called recordation).

Some states require a blood test or other medical procedure to determine the presence of venereal disease, sickle cell disease, or rubella, although such requirements are becoming less common.

In a few states, parties who wish their marriage to be private can choose what is called a confidential marriage. Such marriages have fewer technical/procedural requirements (e.g., no witnesses are needed) and information about the marriage that is recorded in a government office is not available to the general public.[9]

The requirement of solemnization varies among the states. In most states, all that is required to solemnize a marriage is for the parties to declare in the presence of the clergy member, judge, or other officiant that they take each other as husband and wife (or as spouses). Some states do not require a ceremony. New York, for example, allows a couple to become married by a written contract (called a *marriage by contract*) signed before two witnesses and acknowledged by a judge.[10] In Colorado, no officiant is needed; the couple can solemnize their own marriage (sometimes referred to as a *self-solemnization*).[11]

States impose different time periods for the marriage license. For example, a state may say that the license expires if the parties are not married within ninety days after the license is issued. There might be an additional waiting period for persons who wish to marry after having obtained a divorce decree. In one state, a license can be used in any county of the state, whereas in another state the parties may have to be married in the county where they obtained the license.

VIOLATING TECHNICAL/PROCEDURAL REQUIREMENTS

In Chapter 6, we will examine whether a marriage can be annulled if it is entered into in violation of one of the technical/procedural requirements (e.g., the officiant did not have proper authorization to marry the parties). In general, such violations are *not* grounds for an annulment.

solemnization
Formal steps taken in a public ceremony to enter into a status or contract. The verb is *solemnize*.

officiant
One who leads or performs a ceremony, often a religious service.

recordation
Filing a document with a government body so that it becomes part of an official record.

confidential marriage
A ceremonial marriage entered into with fewer technical/procedural requirements and greater privacy than a traditional ceremonial marriage.

SURNAMES

There is no requirement that one party take the other's surname. In some states, parties are given specific notice that marriage does not automatically change anyone's name. Although it is traditional for women to take their husband's last name, there is nothing to prevent her from keeping her own name or using a hyphenated name consisting of the surnames of both spouses. The husband-to-be also has the option of keeping his own name, taking his wife's name, or using a hyphenated name. We will have more to say about change-of-name laws in later chapters.

PROXY MARRIAGE

proxy marriage
A ceremonial marriage in which agents (or stand-ins) take the place of one or both of the prospective spouses who are not present at the ceremony.

Is the physical presence of the bride and groom at the ceremony a requirement for a ceremonial marriage? You might think so, but most states allow a proxy marriage, in which the ceremony takes place with one or both parties being absent (e.g., the groom is overseas in the military). A third-party agent must be given the authority (usually in writing) to act on behalf of the missing party or parties during the ceremony.

Immigration officials are often suspicious of proxy marriages. The concern is that an American citizen is entering into a proxy marriage with someone who lives abroad solely to qualify that person for an entry status as the spouse of a U.S. citizen. It may not succeed. Immigration law provides as follows:

> *The term "spouse," "wife," or "husband" does not include a spouse, wife, or husband by reason of any marriage ceremony where the contracting parties thereto are not physically present in the presence of each other, unless the marriage shall have been consummated.*[12]

Note, however, that a proxy marriage with a foreign bride or groom might be valid under *state* law even if the immigration authorities do not recognize it for purposes of entry into the country.

POSTHUMOUS MARRIAGE

posthumous
Existing or occurring after death.

Proxy marriages occur in the absence of one or both spouses. Suppose that one of the would-be spouses is no longer alive. Can you marry a dead person? Are posthumous marriages allowed? Not in America, with the possible exception of Utah. Some European countries, however, allow posthumous marriages. In France, for example, anyone "wishing to marry a dead person must send a request to the president, who then forwards it to the justice minister, who sends it to the prosecutor in whose jurisdiction the surviving person lives. If the prosecutor determines that the couple planned to marry before the death and if the parents of the deceased approve, the prosecutor sends a recommendation back up the line. The president, if so moved, eventually signs a decree allowing the marriage."[13] A ceremony is held in which the bride or groom stands beside a photo of the deceased. "The phrase 'till death do us part' is eliminated from the vows and 'I do' is replaced by saying 'I did.'"[14]

Although posthumous marriage is not practiced in America, there have been several rare cases under the unique laws and culture of Utah in which local courts have allowed the celebration or recognition of a marriage to a deceased person.[15]

ASSIGNMENT 5.7

Go to your state statutory code and identify all of the technical or procedural requirements for entering into a ceremonial marriage (e.g., obtaining a license, paying a fee). (See General Instructions for the State-Code Assignment in Appendix A.)

SAME-SEX MARRIAGE

The most controversial issue in family law—other than abortion—is whether same-sex couples should be allowed to marry. In 2015, the U.S. Supreme Court resolved this issue in the case of *Obergefell v. Hodges* when it held that

> [The] right to marry is a fundamental right inherent in the liberty of the person, and under the Due Process and Equal Protection Clauses of the Fourteenth Amendment couples of the same-sex may not be deprived of that right and that liberty.

Before examining this case in detail, we need to understand the turbulent background that led to it.

MARRIAGE ALTERNATIVES IN THE UNITED STATES

For centuries, in most of the world, marriage was limited to opposite-sex couples. In some cultures, a person was allowed to be part of a multiple marriage at the same time (**polygamy**, **polygyny**, or **polyandry**), but such practices applied only to persons of the opposite sex.

Throughout the 1990s, no state in the United States was ready to legalize same-sex marriage despite intense pressure to do so. Some states created marriage alternatives for same-sex couples in the hope that this would satisfy the demand for formal recognition by the state. In these alternatives, the couples would enjoy many of the benefits of marriage but would not be married. The strategy was ABM: anything but marriage (sometimes called EBM: everything but marriage).

The newly created ABM status had different names, and in some states, was made available to both opposite-sex and same-sex couples. The most common terms were **civil union** and **domestic partnership**. Because each was a legal status, formal steps were required to enter into them and to terminate them. The following are some of the requirements that were often imposed by law to enter the ABM status (the references to domestic partnership can also apply to most civil unions):

- Both parties are at least eighteen years old.
- Both parties are mentally competent to consent to entering into a contract and neither is acting under force or duress.
- Neither party is married to or legally separated from any other person and neither is in another domestic partnership.
- Neither party is related to each other by blood or marriage in a degree of closeness that would constitute grounds for annulment of a marriage.
- Each party acknowledges being in a committed relationship of mutual caring and support for each other and are jointly responsible for each other's common welfare.

Another requirement might be that the parties have shared a residence or be financially interdependent for a designated period of time, e.g., three months. If the status is restricted to same-sex couples, the parties must declare that they are in such a relationship. If the status is available to opposite-sex couples, special restrictions might apply. For example, in California, domestic partnerships were not open to opposite-sex couples unless one partner was at least sixty-two years old.

In most states, couples could enter into the new status by filing a document (such as a Declaration of Domestic Partnership) with a government official (e.g., the county clerk). No solemnization ceremony was required. In relatively uncomplicated cases, the ABM status could be terminated by simply filing a corresponding

polygamy
The condition or practice of having more than one spouse at the same time.

polygyny
The condition or practice of having more than one wife at the same time.

polyandry
The condition or practice of having more than one husband at the same time.

civil union
A same-sex legal relationship of unmarried individuals who have many of the same state benefits and responsibilities as individuals in a marriage.

domestic partnership
A same-sex or opposite-sex legal relationship of unmarried individuals who are emotionally and financially interdependent and who have many of the same state benefits and responsibilities as individuals in a marriage.

document—(e.g., Notice of Termination of Domestic Partnership) with the same official. A court filing to terminate the status might be needed if the parties had children (natural or adopted) or acquired a designated amount of assets or debts during the relationship.

The marriage-like benefits bestowed on couples in the new ABM status varied. The most common benefits included the following:

- Allowing your partner to be a covered person on your health insurance policy.
- Receiving workers' compensation benefits when a partner dies from a work-related injury or disease.
- Being able to bring a lawsuit for the wrongful death of your partner.
- Being allowed to visit a partner in a hospital and to make medical decisions for an incapacitated partner.
- Filing joint state tax returns.
- Receiving a portion of the estate of a partner who dies intestate (without a valid will).

HAWAII, CONFLICT OF LAWS, AND FULL FAITH AND CREDIT

Not all states joined the movement to create new ABM relationships for same-sex couples. Opponents of the ABM status felt it legitimated immoral conduct and took an uncomfortable step in the direction of full recognition of same-sex marriage.

In 1993, the Hawaii Supreme Court reached the surprising conclusion that the denial of same-sex marriage is presumed to be unconstitutional under its *state* constitution and sent the case back to the lower court for further proceedings.[16] This decision made international news. Many gay activists were ecstatic. Could this state decision be the breakthrough they had been hoping for? In essence, the ongoing Hawaii litigation could have led to a lifting of the ban on same-sex marriage. To say that conservatives in Hawaii and in the nation were alarmed would be an understatement.

The fear of same-sex marriage opponents in other states was that if Hawaii eventually authorized same-sex marriage, they might be forced to recognize such marriages within their own states. For example, assume that State X allowed same-sex marriage but State Y did not and the following events occurred:

- *Ted and Bob marry in State X.*
- *They then move to State Y, where they continue to live together. Bob dies in State Y.*
- *Ted now goes to a court in State Y and asks for a share of Bob's estate as his surviving spouse.*

    Or:

- *After Ted and Bob move to State Y, they decide to separate.*
- *They go to a State Y court and ask for a divorce and an order dividing their marital property.*

In either event, the State Y court must decide whether to recognize the marriage entered into in State X. Does the State Y court apply its own law (where same-sex marriage is illegal) or the law of State X (where same-sex marriage is allowed)? This is a **conflict-of-laws** question. As we will see later in this chapter (and in Chapter 6), the traditional conflict-of-law rule is as follows:

conflict-of-laws
An inconsistency between the laws of different legal systems such as the laws of two states or the laws of two countries.

Conflict of Laws and the Validity of a Marriage

The validity of a marriage is determined by the law of the state in which the marriage was entered into or contracted (the state of celebration). Another state will recognize that marriage unless to do so would violate a strong public policy of the state asked to recognize it.

Under this conflict-of-law rule, State Y would be required to recognize the same-sex marriage entered into in State X *unless* State Y determined that to do so would violate a strong public policy of State Y.

In our example, we said that same-sex marriages are not allowed in State Y. There are undoubtedly hundreds (perhaps thousands) of activities that are not allowed in State Y (e.g., driving over the speed limit, underage drinking). All of these prohibitions do not necessarily violate the strong public policy of the state. State Y would have to categorize its position on same-sex marriage. Would recognizing such a marriage in a conflict-of-law case violate the strong public policy of State Y? If the answer is yes, State Y would not give Ted a share of Bob's estate or allow Ted and Bob to divorce in State Y, because to do so would require it to acknowledge (recognize) the marriage as valid.

Would this settle the question in State Y? Not necessarily. *State* conflict-of-interest law would allow State Y to avoid recognizing same-sex marriage, but *federal* full-faith-and-credit constitutional law might do the opposite.

The Full Faith and Credit Clause

Under the **full faith and credit clause** of the U.S. Constitution, states must recognize (give full faith and credit to) each other's official decisions. The U.S. Constitution is superior in authority to state laws. Assume that Ted and Bob have a judgment from a court in State X that declares their marriage to be legal under the law of State X. Would other states be constitutionally required to give full faith and credit to the judgment of this State X court, even if State Y declared that doing so would be against its strong public policy to recognize a same-sex marriage?

This was a complex question that had no clear answer at the time. The courts would have had to answer it if Hawaii had indeed recognized same-sex marriage, and other states were asked to recognize a gay marriage entered into in Hawaii. To the great relief of conservatives, this recognition did not happen because the Hawaiian legislature took the issue out of the courts by passing a law banning same-sex marriage. Hence at least for now, other states (1) did not have to decide if same-sex marriage was against their strong public policy and (2) would not have to give full faith and credit to a state law that allowed such marriages.

DEFENSE OF MARRIAGE ACT (DOMA)

The drama was over in Hawaii, but what about in other states? What if another state actually authorized same-sex marriages? (As of the early 1990s when the Hawaii issue was unresolved, no state had done so.) Rather than wait for this to happen, more than thirty-five state legislatures quickly enacted statutes that (1) banned same-sex marriages and (2) declared that it would be against their strong public policy to recognize such marriages entered into in another state. In fact, a story in the *New York Times* on this development was titled, "Fearing a Toehold for Gay Marriages, Conservatives Rush to Bar the Door."[17]

These legislative actions took care of the conflict-of-law question in these states, but what about full faith and credit? Does the U.S. Constitution require recognition (full faith and credit) to same-sex marriages validly entered into in *other* states? Although the federal courts had not answered this question, Congress decided to answer it. In 1996, Congress passed, and President Bill Clinton signed,

full faith and credit clause (FFC) The obligation of one state to recognize and enforce the laws and court decisions of another state. The obligation is based on the U.S. Constitution, which provides that "Full Faith and Credit shall be given in each State to the public Acts, Records, and judicial Proceedings of every other State." Article IV, § 1.

Defense of Marriage Act (DOMA)
A federal statute that says (1) one state is not required to give full faith and credit to a same-sex marriage entered in another state (28 U.S.C. § 1738C), and (2) for federal purposes, only opposite-sex marriage is recognized (1 U.S.C. § 7).

the Defense of Marriage Act (DOMA), which said that a state is not required to give full faith and credit to a same-sex marriage entered into in another state:

> No State . . . shall be required to give effect to any public act, record, or judicial proceeding of any other State . . . respecting a relationship between persons of the same sex that is treated as a marriage under the laws of such other State. . . .[18]

If a state wanted to recognize another state's same-sex marriage, it could, but DOMA said that this recognition was not required. DOMA did not make same-sex marriages illegal. It simply provided that one state could not be forced to recognize such a marriage if another state ever allowed one.

FEDERAL DEFINITION OF MARRIAGE: § 3 OF DOMA

DOMA did more than declare that states did not have to recognize the same-sex marriages of other states. Section 3 of DOMA also said that for *federal* purposes, marriage "means only a legal union between one man and one woman as husband and wife."[19] Section 3 of DOMA did not ban same-sex marriages and had no effect on states that might want to allow same-sex marriage. It simply said that for purposes of administering *federal* laws, such as Social Security, immigration, and federal income tax, same-sex marriages were not recognized. There are more than one thousand federal benefits and rights that are granted to married couples. Under § 3 of DOMA, same-sex couples were not eligible for them even in a state that decided to authorize same-sex marriage. For example, married same-sex couples would not be eligible for surviving-spouse benefits under Social Security and could not file a joint federal income tax return. In a state that allowed same-sex marriages, such couples could file a joint *state* tax return as spouses, but they had to file two individual *federal* tax returns (one for each partner) because DOMA stated that only opposite-sex marriage was recognized for federal purposes.

STATE RECOGNITION OF SAME-SEX MARRIAGE

The hostility to same-sex marriage at the federal level under DOMA, however, did not dampen efforts to change state laws to allow such marriages. Quite the contrary. In 2003, Massachusetts made headlines when its Supreme Judicial Court became the first state in the country to allow same-sex marriage.[20] The decision was based on the court's interpretation of the Massachusetts constitution. Relatively soon thereafter, other states came to the same conclusion. They did so by various routes. Some, like Massachusetts, interpreted their own state constitution to allow same-sex marriage. Other states passed statutes authorizing them. Still others reached the same conclusion through the ballot box in which voters used the initiative and referendum process to force the state to change its marriage laws so that same-sex couples could marry.

U.S. SUPREME COURT DECISIONS: *LAWRENCE, WINDSOR,* AND *OBERGEFELL*

While all of this activity was taking place, everyone waited to see what the U.S. Supreme Court would do. The answer unfolded over time with three landmark cases written by Justice Anthony Kennedy: *Lawrence, Windsor,* and *Obergefell*.

Lawrence v. Texas

In the 2003 case of *Lawrence v. Texas*, the U.S. Supreme Court ruled that it was unconstitutional for Texas to make it a crime for consenting adults to engage in intimate same-sex conduct in private.[21] Writing for the majority, Justice Kennedy held that such laws violated **substantive due process (SDP)**. The focus of the opinion

substantive due process (SDP)
The constitutional requirement that the government avoid arbitrary and capricious actions that deprive someone of life, liberty, or property regardless of how fair the government might be in the procedures that lead to the deprivation.

was the liberty interest protected by the Due Process Clause of the Fourteenth Amendment (states cannot deprive persons of "live, liberty, or property without due process of law.") Although many in society condemn homosexual conduct as immoral, the Court said that the liberty interest enjoyed by every individual cannot be dictated by the moral code of others. (The "fact that the governing majority in a State has traditionally viewed a particular practice as immoral is not a sufficient reason for upholding a law prohibiting the practice.")

Justice Kennedy used broad language in concluding that "liberty presumes an autonomy of self that includes freedom of thought, belief, expression, and certain intimate conduct. The instant case involves liberty of the person both in its spatial and more transcendent dimensions." The Court held that the state of Texas had no justification for criminalizing conduct that occurs within these dimensions. "The Texas statute furthers no **legitimate state interest** which can justify its intrusion into the personal and private life of the individual."[22]

United States v. Windsor

Recall that § 3 of DOMA said that for all *federal* purposes, marriage "means only a legal union between one man and one woman as husband and wife." In the 2013 case of *United States v. Windsor*, the U.S. Supreme Court ruled that § 3 was unconstitutional.[23]

In this case, two New York women—Edith Windsor and Thea Spyer—entered into a valid marriage in Canada. (At the time, same-sex marriage was not allowed in New York but New York recognized same-sex marriages that were validly entered into outside the state.) After they returned to New York, Spyer died, leaving her estate to Windsor. Windsor sought to claim the marital exemption from the federal estate tax for surviving spouses. The marital exemption excludes from estate taxation "any interest in property which passes or has passed from the decedent to his surviving spouse."[24] Because of § 3 of DOMA, however, Windsor did not qualify as a surviving spouse and the exemption was denied. For federal purposes, the women were not married, and therefore, Windsor did not qualify as a surviving spouse. The result was that Windsor had to pay $363,053 in estate taxes that a spouse in an opposite-sex marriage would not have had to pay.

The Court said that § 3 of DOMA created "two contradictory marriage regimes within the same State." New York State law recognized the validity of a marriage that federal law refused to recognize. Hence, § 3 forced "same-sex couples to live as married for the purpose of state law but unmarried for the purpose of federal law, thus diminishing the stability and predictability of basic personal relations the state has found it proper to acknowledge and protect." The "purpose and effect" of § 3 was to "injure" the same class that New York sought to protect. Hence, § 3 "demeaned" the married same-sex couple whose relationship New York has sought to "dignify." The statute impermissibly disparaged same-sex couples "who wanted to affirm their commitment to one another before their children, their family, their friends, and their community."

Consequently, § 3 violated due process and the equal protection principles applicable to the federal government in the 5th Amendment.[25] Section 3 sought to harm a politically unpopular group, thereby denying them the equality guaranteed by the U.S. Constitution. There was no legitimate government purpose such as efficiency that could justify this discrimination.

Note that the *Windsor* case did not hold that the ban on same-sex marriage was unconstitutional. It simply ended the discrepancy between how the federal government and the states treated same-sex marriage. After the *Windsor* decision:

- *If* a state allowed couples to enter into a same-sex marriage, then the federal government must recognize that marriage for federal purposes. The 1,000+ federal benefits and rights that depend on marriage would be granted to validly married opposite-sex couples *and* to validly married same-sex couples.

legitimate state interest
Any government objective that the state has the authority to pursue, such as providing for public safety.

- If a state did not allow same-sex marriage, then nothing changed for same-sex couples in those states. They are not entitled to the 1,000+ federal benefits and rights that depend on the existence of a valid marriage. This, of course, was also true for unmarried opposite-sex couples. They are not entitled to the 1,000+ federal benefits and rights that depend on the existence of a valid marriage. If you were not married, you could not claim a marriage-based federal benefit.

Obergefell v. Hodges

This legal backdrop set the stage for the dramatic opinion in 2015 of Justice Kennedy in *Obergefell v. Hodges,* which struck down state laws that prevented same-sex couples from marrying. Supreme Court justices have a reputation for being dispassionate and reserved in expressing their disagreements with each other. The *Obergefell* case, however, did not live up to this reputation. Indeed, justices were surprisingly candid and blunt in their dissent. For example, in his dissent in *Obergefell*, Justice Scalia scoffed at the "soaring rhetoric" of the majority opinion. He said that he would hide his head in a bag if he ever voted for an opinion that began with the following sentence:

> *The Constitution promises liberty to all within its reach, a liberty that includes certain specific rights that allow persons, within a lawful realm, to define and express their identity.*

In Justice Scalia's view, such concepts misunderstand the mandate of liberty in the Constitution, are broad enough to justify whatever social policy the majority of the Court wants to impose on the country, and interfere with the role of the legislature, whose political and constitutional responsibility is to debate and resolve issues as profound as the definition of marriage.

CASE | Obergefell v. Hodges
135 S. Ct. 2584 (2015)
Supreme Court of the United States

Background: *Several same-sex couples sued state officials in federal court for failing to allow same-sex marriages or for failing to give full recognition to the same-sex marriage they entered into elsewhere. Federal trial courts ruled in favor of the same-sex couples. On appeal, the U.S. Court of Appeals for the 6th Circuit reversed. The couples then appealed to the U.S. Supreme Court where the cases of the couples were consolidated.*

Decision on Appeal: The U.S. Supreme Court held that the right to marry is a fundamental right inherent in the liberty of the person. Under the Due Process and Equal Protection Clauses of the Fourteenth Amendment, same-sex couples may not be deprived of the right to marry.

OPINION OF THE COURT

Justice Kennedy delivered the opinion of the Court. . .

The Constitution promises liberty to all within its reach, a liberty that includes certain specific rights that allow persons, within a lawful realm, to define and express their identity. The petitioners in [the cases before us] seek to find that liberty by marrying someone of the same sex and having their marriages deemed lawful on the same terms and conditions as marriages between persons of the opposite sex.

I

[Two questions are before the Court]: The first . . . is whether the Fourteenth Amendment requires a State to license a marriage between two people of the same sex. The second . . . is whether the Fourteenth Amendment requires a State to recognize a same-sex marriage licensed and performed in a State which does grant that right.

II

Before addressing the principles and precedents that govern these cases, it is appropriate to note the history of the subject now before the Court.

A

From their beginning to their most recent page, the annals of human history reveal the transcendent importance of marriage. The lifelong union of a man and a woman always has promised nobility and dignity to all persons, without regard to their station in life.

(continued)

Marriage is sacred to those who live by their religions and offers unique fulfillment to those who find meaning in the secular realm. Its dynamic allows two people to find a life that could not be found alone, for a marriage becomes greater than just the two persons. Rising from the most basic human needs, marriage is essential to our most profound hopes and aspirations.

The centrality of marriage to the human condition makes it unsurprising that the institution has existed for millennia and across civilizations. Since the dawn of history, marriage has transformed strangers into relatives, binding families and societies together. Confucius taught that marriage lies at the foundation of government . . . . There are untold references to the beauty of marriage in religious and philosophical texts spanning time, cultures, and faiths, as well as in art and literature in all their forms. It is fair and necessary to say these references were based on the understanding that marriage is a union between two persons of the opposite sex.

That history is the beginning of these cases. The respondents say it should be the end as well. To them, it would demean a timeless institution if the concept and lawful status of marriage were extended to two persons of the same sex. Marriage, in their view, is by its nature a gender-differentiated union of man and woman. This view long has been held—and continues to be held—in good faith by reasonable and sincere people here and throughout the world.

The petitioners acknowledge this history but contend that these cases cannot end there. Were their intent to demean the revered idea and reality of marriage, the petitioners' claims would be of a different order. But that is neither their purpose nor their submission. To the contrary, it is the enduring importance of marriage that underlies the petitioners' contentions. This, they say, is their whole point. Far from seeking to devalue marriage, the petitioners seek it for themselves because of their respect—and need—for its privileges and responsibilities. And their immutable nature dictates that same-sex marriage is their only real path to this profound commitment.

Recounting the circumstances of three of these cases illustrates the urgency of the petitioners' cause from their perspective. Petitioner James Obergefell, a plaintiff in the Ohio case, met John Arthur over two decades ago. They fell in love and started a life together, establishing a lasting, committed relation. In 2011, however, Arthur was diagnosed with amyotrophic lateral sclerosis, or ALS. This debilitating disease is progressive, with no known cure. Two years ago, Obergefell and Arthur decided to commit to one another, resolving to marry before Arthur died. To fulfill their mutual promise, they traveled from Ohio to Maryland, where same-sex marriage was legal. It was difficult for Arthur to move, and so the couple were wed inside a medical transport plane as it remained on the tarmac in Baltimore. Three months later, Arthur died. Ohio law does not permit Obergefell to be listed as the surviving spouse on Arthur's death certificate. By statute, they must remain strangers even in death, a state-imposed separation Obergefell deems "hurtful for the rest of time.". . . He brought suit to be shown as the surviving spouse on Arthur's death certificate.

April DeBoer and Jayne Rowse are co-plaintiffs in the case from Michigan. They celebrated a commitment ceremony to honor their permanent relation in 2007. They both work as nurses, DeBoer in a neonatal unit and Rowse in an emergency unit. In 2009, DeBoer and Rowse fostered and then adopted a baby boy. Later that same year, they welcomed another son into their family. The new baby, born prematurely and abandoned by his biological mother, required around-the-clock care. The next year, a baby girl with special needs joined their family. Michigan, however, permits only opposite-sex married couples or single individuals to adopt, so each child can have only one woman as his or her legal parent. If an emergency were to arise, schools and hospitals may treat the three children as if they had only one parent. And, were tragedy to befall either DeBoer or Rowse, the other would have no legal rights over the children she had not been permitted to adopt. This couple seeks relief from the continuing uncertainty their unmarried status creates in their lives.

Army Reserve Sergeant First Class Ijpe DeKoe and his partner Thomas Kostura, co-plaintiffs in the Tennessee case, fell in love. In 2011, DeKoe received orders to deploy to Afghanistan. Before leaving, he and Kostura married in New York. A week later, DeKoe began his deployment, which lasted for almost a year. When he returned, the two settled in Tennessee, where DeKoe works full-time for the Army Reserve. Their lawful marriage is stripped from them whenever they reside in Tennessee, returning and disappearing as they travel across state lines. DeKoe, who served this Nation to preserve the freedom the Constitution protects, must endure a substantial burden.

The cases now before the Court involve other petitioners as well, each with their own experiences. Their stories reveal that they seek not to denigrate marriage but rather to live their lives, or honor their spouses' memory, joined by its bond.

B

The ancient origins of marriage confirm its centrality, but it has not stood in isolation from developments in law and society. The history of marriage is one of both continuity and change. That institution—even as confined to opposite-sex relations—has evolved over time.

For example, marriage was once viewed as an arrangement by the couple's parents based on political, religious, and financial concerns; but by the time of the Nation's founding it was understood to be a voluntary contract between a man and a woman. See N. Cott, Public Vows: A History of Marriage and the Nation 9–17 (2000); S. Coontz, Marriage, A History 15–16 (2005). As the role and status of women changed, the institution further evolved. Under the centuries-old doctrine of coverture, a married man and woman were treated by the State as a single, male-dominated legal entity. See 1 W. Blackstone, Commentaries on the Laws of England 430 (1765). As women gained legal, political, and property rights, and as society began to understand that women have their own equal dignity, the law of coverture was abandoned. . . . These and other developments in the institution of marriage over the past

(continued)

centuries were not mere superficial changes. Rather, they worked deep transformations in its structure, affecting aspects of marriage long viewed by many as essential. . . .

These new insights have strengthened, not weakened, the institution of marriage. Indeed, changed understandings of marriage are characteristic of a Nation where new dimensions of freedom become apparent to new generations, often through perspectives that begin in pleas or protests and then are considered in the political sphere and the judicial process.

This dynamic can be seen in the Nation's experiences with the rights of gays and lesbians. Until the mid–20th century, same-sex intimacy long had been condemned as immoral by the state itself in most Western nations, a belief often embodied in the criminal law. For this reason, among others, many persons did not deem homosexuals to have dignity in their own distinct identity. A truthful declaration by same-sex couples of what was in their hearts had to remain unspoken. Even when a greater awareness of the humanity and integrity of homosexual persons came in the period after World War II, the argument that gays and lesbians had a just claim to dignity was in conflict with both law and widespread social conventions. Same-sex intimacy remained a crime in many States. Gays and lesbians were prohibited from most government employment, barred from military service, excluded under immigration laws, targeted by police, and burdened in their rights to associate. . . .

For much of the 20th century, moreover, homosexuality was treated as an illness. When the American Psychiatric Association published the first Diagnostic and Statistical Manual of Mental Disorders in 1952, homosexuality was classified as a mental disorder, a position adhered to until 1973. . . . Only in more recent years have psychiatrists and others recognized that sexual orientation is both a normal expression of human sexuality and immutable. . . .

In the late 20th century, following substantial cultural and political developments, same-sex couples began to lead more open and public lives and to establish families. This development was followed by a quite extensive discussion of the issue in both governmental and private sectors and by a shift in public attitudes toward greater tolerance. As a result, questions about the rights of gays and lesbians soon reached the courts, where the issue could be discussed in the formal discourse of the law.

This Court first gave detailed consideration to the legal status of homosexuals in *Bowers v. Hardwick*, 478 U.S. 186 (1986). There it upheld the constitutionality of a Georgia law deemed to criminalize certain homosexual acts. Ten years later, in *Romer v. Evans*, 517 U.S. 620 (1996), the Court invalidated an amendment to Colorado's Constitution that sought to foreclose any branch or political subdivision of the State from protecting persons against discrimination based on sexual orientation. Then, in 2003, the Court overruled *Bowers*, holding that laws making same-sex intimacy a crime "demea[n] the lives of homosexual persons." *Lawrence v. Texas*, 539 U.S. 558, 575.

Against this background, the legal question of same-sex marriage arose. In 1993, the Hawaii Supreme Court held Hawaii's law restricting marriage to opposite-sex couples constituted a classification on the basis of sex and was therefore subject to strict scrutiny under the Hawaii Constitution. *Baehr v. Lewin*, 74 Haw. 530, 852 P.2d 44. Although this decision did not mandate that same-sex marriage be allowed, some States were concerned by its implications and reaffirmed in their laws that marriage is defined as a union between opposite-sex partners. So too in 1996, Congress passed the Defense of Marriage Act (DOMA), defining marriage for all federal-law purposes as "only a legal union between one man and one woman as husband and wife." 1 U.S.C. § 7.

The new and widespread discussion of the subject led other States to a different conclusion. In 2003, the Supreme Judicial Court of Massachusetts held the State's Constitution guaranteed same-sex couples the right to marry. See *Goodridge v. Department of Public Health*, 440 Mass. 309, 798 N.E.2d 941 (2003). After that ruling, some additional States granted marriage rights to same-sex couples, either through judicial or legislative processes. . . . Two Terms ago, in *United States v. Windsor*, 570 U.S. 744, 133 S. Ct. 2675 (2013), this Court invalidated DOMA to the extent it barred the Federal Government from treating same-sex marriages as valid even when they were lawful in the State where they were licensed. DOMA, the Court held, impermissibly disparaged those same-sex couples "who wanted to affirm their commitment to one another before their children, their family, their friends, and their community." 133 S. Ct., at 2689. . . .

III

Under the Due Process Clause of the Fourteenth Amendment, no State shall "deprive any person of life, liberty, or property, without due process of law." The fundamental liberties protected by this Clause include most of the rights enumerated in the Bill of Rights. . . . In addition, these liberties extend to certain personal choices central to individual dignity and autonomy, including intimate choices that define personal identity and beliefs. . . .

The identification and protection of fundamental rights is an enduring part of the judicial duty to interpret the Constitution. That responsibility, however, "has not been reduced to any formula." *Poe v. Ullman*, 367 U.S. 497, 542 (1961) (Harlan, J., dissenting). Rather, it requires courts to exercise reasoned judgment in identifying interests of the person so fundamental that the State must accord them its respect. See ibid. That process is guided by many of the same considerations relevant to analysis of other constitutional provisions that set forth broad principles rather than specific requirements. History and tradition guide and discipline this inquiry but do not set its outer boundaries. See *Lawrence*, supra, at 572. That method respects our history and learns from it without allowing the past alone to rule the present.

The nature of injustice is that we may not always see it in our own times. The generations that wrote and ratified the Bill of Rights and the Fourteenth Amendment did not presume to know the extent of freedom in all of its dimensions, and so they entrusted to future generations a charter protecting the right of all persons to enjoy

(continued)

liberty as we learn its meaning. When new insight reveals discord between the Constitution's central protections and a received legal stricture, a claim to liberty must be addressed.

Applying these established tenets, the Court has long held the right to marry is protected by the Constitution. In *Loving v. Virginia*, 388 U.S. 1, 12 (1967), which invalidated bans on interracial unions, a unanimous Court held marriage is "one of the vital personal rights essential to the orderly pursuit of happiness by free men." The Court reaffirmed that holding in *Zablocki v. Redhail*, 434 U.S. 374, 384 (1978), which held the right to marry was burdened by a law prohibiting fathers who were behind on child support from marrying. The Court again applied this principle in *Turner v. Safley*, 482 U.S. 78, 95 (1987), which held the right to marry was abridged by regulations limiting the privilege of prison inmates to marry. Over time and in other contexts, the Court has reiterated that the right to marry is fundamental under the Due Process Clause. . . .

It cannot be denied that this Court's cases describing the right to marry presumed a relationship involving opposite-sex partners. The Court, like many institutions, has made assumptions defined by the world and time of which it is a part. This was evident in *Baker v. Nelson*, 409 U.S. 810, a one-line summary decision issued in 1972, holding the exclusion of same-sex couples from marriage did not present a substantial federal question.

Still, there are other, more instructive precedents. This Court's cases have expressed constitutional principles of broader reach. In defining the right to marry these cases have identified essential attributes of that right based in history, tradition, and other constitutional liberties inherent in this intimate bond. . . . And in assessing whether the force and rationale of its cases apply to same-sex couples, the Court must respect the basic reasons why the right to marry has been long protected. . . .

This analysis compels the conclusion that same-sex couples may exercise the right to marry. The four principles and traditions to be discussed demonstrate that the reasons marriage is fundamental under the Constitution apply with equal force to same-sex couples.

A first premise of the Court's relevant precedents is that the right to personal choice regarding marriage is inherent in the concept of individual autonomy. This abiding connection between marriage and liberty is why *Loving* invalidated interracial marriage bans under the Due Process Clause. . . . Like choices concerning contraception, family relationships, procreation, and childrearing, all of which are protected by the Constitution, decisions concerning marriage are among the most intimate that an individual can make. See *Lawrence*, supra, at 574, 123 S. Ct. 2472. Indeed, the Court has noted it would be contradictory "to recognize a right of privacy with respect to other matters of family life and not with respect to the decision to enter the relationship that is the foundation of the family in our society." *Zablocki*, supra, at 386, 98 S. Ct. 673.

Choices about marriage shape an individual's destiny. As the Supreme Judicial Court of Massachusetts has explained, because "it fulfils yearnings for security, safe haven, and connection that express our common humanity, civil marriage is an esteemed institution, and the decision whether and whom to marry is among life's momentous acts of self-definition." *Goodridge*, 798 N.E.2d, at 955.

The nature of marriage is that, through its enduring bond, two persons together can find other freedoms, such as expression, intimacy, and spirituality. This is true for all persons, whatever their sexual orientation. . . . There is dignity in the bond between two men or two women who seek to marry and in their autonomy to make such profound choices. . . .

A second principle in this Court's jurisprudence is that the right to marry is fundamental because it supports a two-person union unlike any other in its importance to the committed individuals. This point was central to *Griswold v. Connecticut*, which held the Constitution protects the right of married couples to use contraception. 381 U.S. 479, 485 (1965). Suggesting that marriage is a right "older than the Bill of Rights," *Griswold* described marriage this way: "Marriage is a coming together for better or for worse, hopefully enduring, and intimate to the degree of being sacred. It is an association that promotes a way of life, not causes; a harmony in living, not political faiths; a bilateral loyalty, not commercial or social projects. Yet it is an association for as noble a purpose as any involved in our prior decisions." Id., at 486.

And in *Turner*, the Court again acknowledged the intimate association protected by this right, holding prisoners could not be denied the right to marry because their committed relationships satisfied the basic reasons why marriage is a fundamental right . . . The right to marry thus dignifies couples who "wish to define themselves by their commitment to each other." *Windsor*, supra, 133 S. Ct., at 2689. Marriage responds to the universal fear that a lonely person might call out only to find no one there. It offers the hope of companionship and understanding and assurance that while both still live there will be someone to care for the other.

As this Court held in *Lawrence*, same-sex couples have the same right as opposite-sex couples to enjoy intimate association. *Lawrence* invalidated laws that made same-sex intimacy a criminal act. And it acknowledged that "[w]hen sexuality finds overt expression in intimate conduct with another person, the conduct can be but one element in a personal bond that is more enduring." 539 U.S., at 567. But while *Lawrence* confirmed a dimension of freedom that allows individuals to engage in intimate association without criminal liability, it does not follow that freedom stops there. Outlaw to outcast may be a step forward, but it does not achieve the full promise of liberty.

A third basis for protecting the right to marry is that it safeguards children and families and thus draws meaning from related rights of childrearing, procreation, and education. . . . The Court has recognized these connections by describing the varied rights as a unified whole: "[T]he right to 'marry, establish a home and bring up children' is a central part of the liberty protected by the Due Process Clause." *Zablocki*, 434 U.S., at 384. . . . Under the laws of the several States, some of marriage's protections for children and families are material. But marriage also confers more profound

(continued)

benefits. By giving recognition and legal structure to their parents' relationship, marriage allows children "to understand the integrity and closeness of their own family and its concord with other families in their community and in their daily lives." *Windsor*, supra, 133 S. Ct., at 2694–2695. Marriage also affords the permanency and stability important to children's best interests. . . .

As all parties agree, many same-sex couples provide loving and nurturing homes to their children, whether biological or adopted. And hundreds of thousands of children are presently being raised by such couples. . . . Most States have allowed gays and lesbians to adopt, either as individuals or as couples, and many adopted and foster children have same-sex parents. This provides powerful confirmation from the law itself that gays and lesbians can create loving, supportive families.

Excluding same-sex couples from marriage thus conflicts with a central premise of the right to marry. Without the recognition, stability, and predictability marriage offers, their children suffer the stigma of knowing their families are somehow lesser. They also suffer the significant material costs of being raised by unmarried parents, relegated through no fault of their own to a more difficult and uncertain family life. The marriage laws at issue here thus harm and humiliate the children of same-sex couples. . . .

That is not to say the right to marry is less meaningful for those who do not or cannot have children. An ability, desire, or promise to procreate is not and has not been a prerequisite for a valid marriage in any State. In light of precedent protecting the right of a married couple not to procreate, it cannot be said the Court or the States have conditioned the right to marry on the capacity or commitment to procreate. The constitutional marriage right has many aspects, of which childbearing is only one.

Fourth and finally, this Court's cases and the Nation's traditions make clear that marriage is a keystone of our social order. Alexis de Tocqueville recognized this truth on his travels through the United States almost two centuries ago: "There is certainly no country in the world where the tie of marriage is so much respected as in America . . . [W]hen the American retires from the turmoil of public life to the bosom of his family, he finds in it the image of order and of peace. . . . [H]e afterwards carries [that image] with him into public affairs." 1 *Democracy in America* 309 (1990).

In *Maynard v. Hill*, 125 U.S. 190 (1888), the Court echoed de Tocqueville, explaining that marriage is "the foundation of the family and of society, without which there would be neither civilization nor progress." . . . This idea has been reiterated even as the institution has evolved in substantial ways over time, superseding rules related to parental consent, gender, and race once thought by many to be essential. . . . Marriage remains a building block of our national community.

For that reason, just as a couple vows to support each other, so does society pledge to support the couple, offering symbolic recognition and material benefits to protect and nourish the union. Indeed, while the States are in general free to vary the benefits they confer on all married couples, they have throughout our history made marriage the basis for an expanding list of governmental benefits, rights, and responsibilities. These aspects of marital status include: taxation; inheritance and property rights; rules of intestate succession; spousal privilege in the law of evidence; hospital access; medical decision-making authority; adoption rights; the rights and benefits of survivors; birth and death certificates; professional ethics rules; campaign finance restrictions; workers' compensation benefits; health insurance; and child custody, support, and visitation rules. . . . Valid marriage under state law is also a significant status for over a thousand provisions of federal law. . . . The States have contributed to the fundamental character of the marriage right by placing that institution at the center of so many facets of the legal and social order.

There is no difference between same- and opposite-sex couples with respect to this principle. Yet by virtue of their exclusion from that institution, same-sex couples are denied the constellation of benefits that the States have linked to marriage. This harm results in more than just material burdens. Same-sex couples are consigned to an instability many opposite-sex couples would deem intolerable in their own lives. As the State itself makes marriage all the more precious by the significance it attaches to it, exclusion from that status has the effect of teaching that gays and lesbians are unequal in important respects. It demeans gays and lesbians for the State to lock them out of a central institution of the Nation's society. Same-sex couples, too, may aspire to the transcendent purposes of marriage and seek fulfillment in its highest meaning.

The limitation of marriage to opposite-sex couples may long have seemed natural and just, but its inconsistency with the central meaning of the fundamental right to marry is now manifest. With that knowledge must come the recognition that laws excluding same-sex couples from the marriage right impose stigma and injury of the kind prohibited by our basic charter.

[Opponents incorrectly argue that the petitioners seek] a new and nonexistent "right to same-sex marriage." . . . *Loving* did not ask about a "right to interracial marriage"; *Turner* did not ask about a "right of inmates to marry"; and *Zablocki* did not ask about a "right of fathers with unpaid child support duties to marry." Rather, each case inquired about the right to marry in its comprehensive sense, asking if there was a sufficient justification for excluding the relevant class from the right. . . .

The right to marry is fundamental as a matter of history and tradition, but rights come not from ancient sources alone. They rise, too, from a better informed understanding of how constitutional imperatives define a liberty that remains urgent in our own era. Many who deem same-sex marriage to be wrong reach that conclusion based on decent and honorable religious or philosophical premises, and neither they nor their beliefs are disparaged here. But when that sincere, personal opposition becomes enacted law and public policy, the necessary consequence is to put the imprimatur of the State itself on an exclusion that soon demeans or stigmatizes those whose own liberty is then denied. Under the Constitution, same-sex couples seek in marriage the same legal treatment as opposite-sex couples, and it would disparage their choices and diminish their personhood to deny them this right.

(continued)

The right of same-sex couples to marry that is part of the liberty promised by the Fourteenth Amendment is derived, too, from that Amendment's guarantee of the equal protection of the laws. The Due Process Clause and the Equal Protection Clause are connected in a profound way, though they set forth independent principles. Rights implicit in liberty and rights secured by equal protection may rest on different precepts and are not always co-extensive, yet in some instances each may be instructive as to the meaning and reach of the other. In any particular case one Clause may be thought to capture the essence of the right in a more accurate and comprehensive way, even as the two Clauses may converge in the identification and definition of the right. . . . This interrelation of the two principles furthers our understanding of what freedom is and must become.

The Court's cases touching upon the right to marry reflect this dynamic. In *Loving* the Court invalidated a prohibition on interracial marriage under both the Equal Protection Clause and the Due Process Clause. The Court first declared the prohibition invalid because of its unequal treatment of interracial couples. It stated: "There can be no doubt that restricting the freedom to marry solely because of racial classifications violates the central meaning of the Equal Protection Clause." 388 U.S., at 12. With this link to equal protection the Court proceeded to hold the prohibition offended central precepts of liberty: "To deny this fundamental freedom on so unsupportable a basis as the racial classifications embodied in these statutes, classifications so directly subversive of the principle of equality at the heart of the Fourteenth Amendment, is surely to deprive all the State's citizens of liberty without due process of law." Ibid. The reasons why marriage is a fundamental right became more clear and compelling from a full awareness and understanding of the hurt that resulted from laws barring interracial unions.

The synergy between the two protections is illustrated further in *Zablocki*. There the Court invoked the Equal Protection Clause as its basis for invalidating the challenged law, which, as already noted, barred fathers who were behind on child-support payments from marrying without judicial approval. The equal protection analysis depended in central part on the Court's holding that the law burdened a right "of fundamental importance." 434 U.S., at 383. It was the essential nature of the marriage right, discussed at length in *Zablocki* that made apparent the law's incompatibility with requirements of equality. Each concept—liberty and equal protection—leads to a stronger understanding of the other.

Indeed, in interpreting the Equal Protection Clause, the Court has recognized that new insights and societal understandings can reveal unjustified inequality within our most fundamental institutions that once passed unnoticed and unchallenged. To take but one period, this occurred with respect to marriage in the 1970's and 1980's. Notwithstanding the gradual erosion of the doctrine of coverture, . . . invidious sex-based classifications in marriage remained common through the mid–20th century. . . . These classifications denied the equal dignity of men and women. One State's law, for example, provided in 1971 that "the husband is the head of the family and the wife is subject to him; her legal civil existence is merged in the husband, except so far as the law recognizes her separately, either for her own protection, or for her benefit." Ga. Code Ann. § 53–501 (1935). Responding to a new awareness, the Court invoked equal protection principles to invalidate laws imposing sex-based inequality on marriage. . . . Like *Loving* and *Zablocki*, these precedents show the Equal Protection Clause can help to identify and correct inequalities in the institution of marriage, vindicating precepts of liberty and equality under the Constitution.

Other cases confirm this relation between liberty and equality. In *M.L.B. v. S.L.J.*, the Court invalidated under due process and equal protection principles a statute requiring indigent mothers to pay a fee in order to appeal the termination of their parental rights. See 519 U.S. 102, 119–124 (1996). In *Eisenstadt* v. Baird, the Court invoked both principles to invalidate a prohibition on the distribution of contraceptives to unmarried persons but not married persons. See 405 U.S. 438, 446–454 (1972). And in *Skinner v. Oklahoma ex rel. Williamson*, the Court invalidated under both principles a law that allowed sterilization of habitual criminals. See 316 U.S. 535, 538–543 (1942).

In *Lawrence* the Court acknowledged the interlocking nature of these constitutional safeguards in the context of the legal treatment of gays and lesbians. . . . Although *Lawrence* elaborated its holding under the Due Process Clause, it acknowledged, and sought to remedy, the continuing inequality that resulted from laws making intimacy in the lives of gays and lesbians a crime against the State. *Lawrence* therefore drew upon principles of liberty and equality to define and protect the rights of gays and lesbians, holding the State "cannot demean their existence or control their destiny by making their private sexual conduct a crime." Id., at 578.

This dynamic also applies to same-sex marriage. It is now clear that the challenged laws burden the liberty of same-sex couples, and it must be further acknowledged that they abridge central precepts of equality. Here the marriage laws enforced by the respondents are in essence unequal: same-sex couples are denied all the benefits afforded to opposite-sex couples and are barred from exercising a fundamental right. Especially against a long history of disapproval of their relationships, this denial to same-sex couples of the right to marry works a grave and continuing harm. The imposition of this disability on gays and lesbians serves to disrespect and subordinate them. And the Equal Protection Clause, like the Due Process Clause, prohibits this unjustified infringement of the fundamental right to marry. . . .

These considerations lead to the conclusion that the right to marry is a fundamental right inherent in the liberty of the person, and under the Due Process and Equal Protection Clauses of the Fourteenth Amendment couples of the same-sex may not be deprived of that right and that liberty. The Court now holds that same-sex couples may exercise the fundamental right to marry. No longer may this liberty be denied to them. *Baker v. Nelson* must be and now is overruled, and the State laws challenged by Petitioners in these cases are now held invalid to the extent they exclude same-sex couples from civil marriage on the same terms and conditions as opposite-sex couples.

(continued)

IV

There may be an initial inclination in these cases to proceed with caution—to await further legislation, litigation, and debate. The dynamic of our constitutional system [however] is that individuals need not await legislative action before asserting a fundamental right. The Nation's courts are open to injured individuals who come to them to vindicate their own direct, personal stake in our basic charter. An individual can invoke a right to constitutional protection when he or she is harmed, even if the broader public disagrees and even if the legislature refuses to act. The idea of the Constitution "was to withdraw certain subjects from the vicissitudes of political controversy, to place them beyond the reach of majorities and officials and to establish them as legal principles to be applied by the courts." *West Virginia Bd. of Ed. v. Barnette*, 319 U.S. 624 (1943). This is why "fundamental rights may not be submitted to a vote; they depend on the outcome of no elections.". . .

A ruling against same-sex couples would . . . be unjustified under the Fourteenth Amendment. The petitioners' stories make clear the urgency of the issue they present to the Court. James Obergefell now asks whether Ohio can erase his marriage to John Arthur for all time. April DeBoer and Jayne Rowse now ask whether Michigan may continue to deny them the certainty and stability all mothers desire to protect their children, and for them and their children, the childhood years will pass all too soon. Ijpe DeKoe and Thomas Kostura now ask whether Tennessee can deny to one who has served this Nation the basic dignity of recognizing his New York marriage. Properly presented with the petitioners' cases, the Court has a duty to address these claims and answer these questions. . . .

The respondents also argue that allowing same-sex couples to wed will harm marriage as an institution by leading to fewer opposite-sex marriages. This may occur, the respondents contend, because licensing same-sex marriage severs the connection between natural procreation and marriage. That argument, however, rests on a counterintuitive view of opposite-sex couple's decision-making processes regarding marriage and parenthood. Decisions about whether to marry and raise children are based on many personal, romantic, and practical considerations; and it is unrealistic to conclude that an opposite-sex couple would choose not to marry simply because same-sex couples may do so. . . .

Finally, it must be emphasized that religions, and those who adhere to religious doctrines, may continue to advocate with utmost, sincere conviction that, by divine precepts, same-sex marriage should not be condoned. The First Amendment ensures that religious organizations and persons are given proper protection as they seek to teach the principles that are so fulfilling and so central to their lives and faiths, and to their own deep aspirations to continue the family structure they have long revered. The same is true of those who oppose same-sex marriage for other reasons. In turn, those who believe allowing same-sex marriage is proper or indeed essential, whether as a matter of religious conviction or secular belief, may engage those who disagree with their view in an open and searching debate. The Constitution, however, does not permit the State to bar same-sex couples from marriage on the same terms as accorded to couples of the opposite sex.

V

These cases also present the question whether the Constitution requires States to recognize same-sex marriages validly performed out of State . . . . The Court, in this decision, holds same-sex couples may exercise the fundamental right to marry in all States. It follows that the Court also must hold—and it now does hold—that there is no lawful basis for a State to refuse to recognize a lawful same-sex marriage performed in another State on the ground of its same-sex character.

No union is more profound than marriage, for it embodies the highest ideals of love, fidelity, devotion, sacrifice, and family. In forming a marital union, two people become something greater than once they were. As some of the petitioners in these cases demonstrate, marriage embodies a love that may endure even past death. It would misunderstand these men and women to say they disrespect the idea of marriage. Their plea is that they do respect it, respect it so deeply that they seek to find its fulfillment for themselves. Their hope is not to be condemned to live in loneliness, excluded from one of the civilization's oldest institutions. They ask for equal dignity in the eyes of the law. The Constitution grants them that right.

The judgment of the Court of Appeals for the Sixth Circuit is reversed.

It is so ordered.

Chief Justice ROBERTS, dissenting.

Petitioners make strong arguments rooted in social policy and considerations of fairness. They contend that same-sex couples should be allowed to affirm their love and commitment through marriage, just like opposite-sex couples. That position has undeniable appeal; over the past six years, voters and legislators in eleven States and the District of Columbia have revised their laws to allow marriage between two people of the same sex.

But this Court is not a legislature. Whether same-sex marriage is a good idea should be of no concern to us. Under the Constitution, judges have power to say what the law is, not what it should be. . . . The fundamental right to marry does not include a right to make a State change its definition of marriage. . . . Stripped of its shiny rhetorical gloss, the majority's argument is that the Due Process Clause gives same-sex couples a fundamental right to marry because it will be good for them and for society. If I were a legislator, I would certainly consider that view as a matter of social policy. But as a judge, I find the majority's position indefensible as a matter of constitutional law. . . . [We do not sit as a super-legislature to weigh the wisdom of legislation simply because we find it unwise, improvident, or out of harmony with a particular school of thought.] . . .

Hard questions arise when people of faith exercise religion in ways that may be seen to conflict with the new right to same-sex marriage—when, for example, a religious college provides married

(continued)

student housing only to opposite-sex married couples, or a religious adoption agency declines to place children with same-sex married couples. Indeed, the Solicitor General candidly acknowledged that the tax exemptions of some religious institutions would be in question if they opposed same-sex marriage. . . .

If you are among the many Americans—of whatever sexual orientation—who favor expanding same-sex marriage, by all means celebrate today's decision. Celebrate the achievement of a desired goal. Celebrate the opportunity for a new expression of commitment to a partner. Celebrate the availability of new benefits. But do not celebrate the Constitution. It had nothing to do with it.

Justice SCALIA, dissenting. . . .

Today's decree says that my Ruler, and the Ruler of 320 million Americans coast-to-coast, is a majority of the nine lawyers on the Supreme Court. The opinion in these cases is the furthest extension in fact—and the furthest extension one can even imagine—of the Court's claimed power to create "liberties" that the Constitution and its Amendments neglect to mention. This practice of constitutional revision by an unelected committee of nine, always accompanied (as it is today) by extravagant praise of liberty, robs the People of the most important liberty they asserted in the Declaration of Independence and won in the Revolution of 1776: the freedom to govern themselves. . . .

When the Fourteenth Amendment was ratified in 1868, every State limited marriage to one man and one woman, and no one doubted the constitutionality of doing so. That resolves these cases. When it comes to determining the meaning of a vague constitutional provision—such as "due process of law" or "equal protection of the laws"—it is unquestionable that the People who ratified that provision did not understand it to prohibit a practice that remained both universal and uncontroversial in the years after ratification. We have no basis for striking down a practice that is not expressly prohibited by the Fourteenth Amendment's text, and that bears the endorsement of a long tradition of open, widespread, and unchallenged use dating back to the Amendment's ratification. Since there is no doubt whatever that the People never decided to prohibit the limitation of marriage to opposite-sex couples, the public debate over same-sex marriage must be allowed to continue.

But the Court ends this debate, in an opinion lacking even a thin veneer of law. . . .

The opinion is couched in a style that is as pretentious as its content is egotistic. . . . [The] opinion's showy profundities are often profoundly incoherent. "The nature of marriage is that, through its enduring bond, two persons together can find other freedoms, such as expression, intimacy, and spirituality." (Really? Who ever thought that intimacy and spirituality [whatever that means] were freedoms? And if intimacy is, one would think Freedom of Intimacy is abridged rather than expanded by marriage. Ask the nearest hippie. Expression, sure enough, is a freedom, but anyone in a long-lasting marriage will attest that that happy state constricts, rather than expands, what one can prudently say.) Rights, we are told, can "rise . . . from a better informed understanding of how constitutional imperatives define a liberty that remains urgent in our own era." (Huh? How can a better informed understanding of how constitutional imperatives [whatever that means] define [whatever that means] an urgent liberty [never mind], give birth to a right?). . . . The world does not expect logic and precision in poetry or inspirational pop-philosophy; it demands them in the law. The stuff contained in today's opinion has to diminish this Court's reputation for clear thinking and sober analysis.

Justice THOMAS, dissenting.

The Court's decision today is at odds not only with the Constitution, but with the principles upon which our Nation was built. Since well before 1787, liberty has been understood as freedom from government action, not entitlement to government benefits. The Framers created our Constitution to preserve that understanding of liberty. Yet the majority invokes our Constitution in the name of a "liberty" that the Framers would not have recognized, to the detriment of the liberty they sought to protect. . . .

[The] majority goes to great lengths to assert that its decision will advance the "dignity" of same-sex couples. The flaw in that reasoning, of course, is that the Constitution contains no "dignity" Clause, and even if it did, the government would be incapable of bestowing dignity. . . .

Our Constitution—like the Declaration of Independence before it—was predicated on a simple truth: One's liberty, not to mention one's dignity, was something to be shielded from—not provided by—the State. Today's decision casts that truth aside. In its haste to reach a desired result, the majority misapplies a clause focused on "due process" to afford substantive rights, disregards the most plausible understanding of the "liberty" protected by that clause, and distorts the principles on which this Nation was founded. Its decision will have inestimable consequences for our Constitution and our society. I respectfully dissent.

Justice ALITO, dissenting. . . .

While, for many, the attributes of marriage in 21st-century America have changed, those States that do not want to recognize same-sex marriage have not yet given up on the traditional understanding. They worry that by officially abandoning the older understanding, they may contribute to marriage's further decay. It is far beyond the outer reaches of this Court's authority to say that a State may not adhere to the understanding of marriage that has long prevailed, not just in this country and others with similar cultural roots, but also in a great variety of countries and cultures all around the globe. . . .

Perhaps recognizing how its reasoning may be used, the majority attempts, toward the end of its opinion, to reassure those who oppose same-sex marriage that their rights of conscience will be protected. We will soon see whether this proves to be true. I assume that those who cling to old beliefs will be able to whisper their thoughts in the recesses of their homes, but if they repeat those views in public, they will risk being labeled as bigots and treated as such by governments, employers, and schools. . . .

ASSIGNMENT 5.8

a. The majority opinion said four "principles and traditions" support the view that marriage is a fundamental right and that they apply to both same-sex couples and opposite-sex couples. What are the four principles and traditions?

b. The majority opinion said that a marriage license cannot be denied to couples of mixed race, to someone who has failed to pay child support from a prior relationship, and to someone who is incarcerated. Can a church refuse to marry a same-sex couple? Should it be allowed to do so?

THE LEGACY OF *OBERGEFELL V. HODGES*

The *Obergefell* decision has been controversial. Its impact has been the subject of considerable debate. One critic complained that the opinion was not "analytically rigorous" in its treatment of liberty:

> As a roadmap to future courts in discerning the content and limits of substantive liberty, [the opinion] leaves much to be desired. . . . Even readers who are enthusiastic about the result in Obergefell and believe it fully justified as a matter of doctrine and principle could react with dismay at the lack of clear guidance that the Court gives for the future administration of these important principles.[26]

strict-scrutiny test
The government's action must be narrowly tailored to serve a compelling state interest. Also phrased as *necessary to serve a compelling state interest.*

rational-basis test
The government's action must be reasonably related to a legitimate state interest or purpose. Also called *minimal-scrutiny test, rational-relation test.*

In Chapter 1, we said that the traditional analysis of due process and equal protection was based on tiered analysis and levels of scrutiny (see Exhibits 1.2 and 1.3 in Chapter 1). For example, if a state imposed a restriction on a fundamental right, the courts would determine the constitutionality of the restriction by applying the **strict-scrutiny test**. Under this test, the state's action would have to be narrowly tailored to serve a compelling state interest. Restrictions on other rights were judged under the **rational-basis test**. Under this test, the state's action would have to be reasonably related to a legitimate state interest or purpose.

Obergefell and Levels of Scrutiny

Justice Kennedy did not use tiered analysis and levels of scrutiny in the opinions we have been examining, particularly in *Obergefell v. Hodges*. Instead, he based his analysis on personal dignity and autonomy. Some legal scholars have said that Justice Kennedy's broad language in support of gay rights have made it "surprisingly easy" for later Court decisions to cut back on the rights he articulated for the Court. Two law professors, for example, wrote an article called "Kennedy's Shaky Gay Rights Legacy," in which they argued that he should have relied on the more traditional levels-of-scrutiny analysis that applied the strict-scrutiny test, the rational-basis test, or some other level of scrutiny:

> He [Justice Kennedy] never adequately explained why if "dignity rights" are protected by the Constitution they could not be claimed by those who want to marry more than one person or to marry a cousin. . . . In the marriage cases, a fair analysis should have depended less on "the universal fear" of loneliness and more on whether the bans were subject to rational basis review or something stricter.[27]

Chief Justice Roberts would agree. "It is striking," he said, "how much of the majority's reasoning would apply with equal force to the claim of a fundamental right to plural marriage. If '[t]here is dignity in the bond between two men or two women who seek to marry and in their autonomy to make such profound choices,' why would there be any less dignity in the bond between three people who, in exercising their autonomy, seek to make the profound choice to marry?"[28]

Obergefell and the Business Community

Questions also arose among some members of the business community. "Since same-sex marriage became the law of the land, the battle over LGBT rights has shifted from the altar to the cash register. As wedding vendors have turned away same-sex couples for moral reasons, lawsuits have pitted the right to be served against the right to refuse."[29]

In a recent case, a Colorado baker refused to make a wedding cake for a gay wedding because of the baker's religious convictions against same-sex marriage. The couple sued the baker under the anti-discrimination laws of Colorado. The baker asserted his First Amendment rights to freedom of speech and to the free exercise of religion. The baker lost and was fined for refusing to bake the cake. He then appealed in federal court. The U.S. Supreme Court ruled in favor of the baker, but the ruling of the Court was narrow. The Court did not rule that businesses could refuse to serve same-sex couples simply by asserting that to do so would violate their religion. Rather, the Court said that Colorado failed to give due consideration to the baker's religious beliefs. During the hearings in Colorado on the case, state officials expressed hostility to religion. This "hostility was inconsistent with the First Amendment's guarantee that our laws be applied in a manner that is neutral toward religion."[30] Hence, the Court did not provide clear guidelines on whether businesses could refuse to provide goods and services to same-sex couples.

Some states are considering changing the law that requires county officials to issue marriage licenses so that officials opposed to same-sex marriage would not have to sign licenses that are issued, whether for opposite-sex or same-sex couples. The proposal would eliminate the requirement of obtaining a license. Parties who wish to marry would simply file an affidavit with the county that they meet the requirements to marry (e.g., are of age and are not married to anyone else).

Finally, the broader issue of discrimination against gays and lesbians continues to be debated in the legislatures and courts of the country. "There is no federal law that bans discrimination based on sexual orientation in employment, housing, or education. Some states have laws that impose such bans, but many do not. As one scholar commented, 'You can get married, put a picture on your desk from the wedding and then be fired because the boss sees the picture'."[31]

COVENANT MARRIAGE

As indicated earlier in this chapter, to enter into a ceremonial marriage all that is required are the following:

- Compliance with the technical/procedural requirements (e.g., witnesses and a waiting period), and
- The intent and capacity requirements (e.g., being old enough) that we will discuss in the next chapter.

To dissolve a ceremonial marriage in the era of **no-fault divorce** (discussed in Chapter 7), all that is required in most states is for one spouse to declare that the parties are no longer compatible or that their differences are irreconcilable; there is no need to prove who was at fault in the collapse of the marriage.

Many people are alarmed at the high incidence of divorce in America. In a few states, reformers have argued that one way to reduce the divorce rate is to increase the requirements for entering into and for dissolving a marriage. As a result, they created the *covenant marriage*, which is based on the principle of "harder to enter and harder to get out of." A **covenant marriage** is a form of ceremonial marriage (a) that is entered into with proof of premarital counseling and a promise to seek marital counseling when needed during the marriage, and (b) that is dissolved upon

no-fault divorce
A divorce that is granted without having to prove marital wrongs that caused the break-up.

covenant marriage
A ceremonial marriage is (a) entered into with proof of premarital counseling and a promise to seek marital counseling when needed during the marriage, and (b) that is dissolved upon separation for a designated period or upon proof of marital fault. Also called a *high-test marriage*.

separation for a designated period or upon proof of marital fault, such as adultery. These are substantial departures from standard marriage and divorce practice in the United States where counseling is not required before or during marriage and where no-fault divorce is the norm, as we will see in Chapter 7.

Three states allow covenant marriages: Louisiana, Arkansas, and Arizona. These states do *not* require every couple contemplating marriage to go through a covenant marriage. A two-tiered marriage system exists in these states. Couples are given a choice between a covenant marriage and a conventional marriage. If they choose the latter, they do not need to comply with the additional requirements for entering into and dissolving their marriage. These requirements apply only if they choose the covenant-marriage option.

Proponents of covenant marriage argue that premarital counseling will better prepare the parties for handling the difficulties that marriage can entail. Furthermore, when such difficulties do, in fact, arise in the marriage, marital counseling may be able to help resolve the difficulties. The result could be a reduction in the divorce rate.

Proponents also hope that if a man wants to choose a conventional marriage, his fiancée might ask him why he wants a marriage that is so easy to dissolve. This frank discussion may lead to a decision to cancel the marriage or at least to postpone it until they have more serious discussions about marriage. Through such discussions, potentially weak marriages might be avoided.

Although some differences exist, the essence of covenant marriage is the same in Louisiana, Arkansas, and Arizona (mandatory premarital counseling, agreement to seek marital counseling if needed, and restrictive grounds for divorce). In Louisiana, the first state to create this option, a couple that selects a covenant marriage must submit an affidavit from a therapist, minister, or other member of the clergy that the couple has been given premarital counseling on the "nature and purpose" of marriage. The couple must also sign a statement that says:

> We do solemnly declare that marriage is a covenant between a man and a woman who agree to live together as husband and wife for so long as they both may live. We have chosen each other carefully and disclosed to one another everything which could adversely affect the decision to enter into this marriage. We have received premarital counseling on the nature, purposes, and responsibilities of marriage. We have read the Covenant Marriage Act, and we understand that a Covenant Marriage is for life. If we experience marital difficulties, we commit ourselves to take all reasonable efforts to preserve our marriage, including marital counseling. With full knowledge of what this commitment means, we do hereby declare that our marriage will be bound by Louisiana law on Covenant Marriages and we promise to love, honor, and care for one another as husband and wife.[32]

The acknowledgement that the marriage will last "as long as they both may live," does not mean that divorce has been abolished. Divorce is possible, but only on specified grounds, most of which are fault-based. In Louisiana, the grounds are adultery, a sentence of death or imprisonment for a felony, abandonment of the matrimonial domicile for a year, physical or sexual abuse, and living separate and apart continuously without reconciliation for a period of two years. Fault or a two-year separation is *not* required to dissolve a conventional Louisiana marriage. Such a marriage can be dissolved simply by a showing that the parties have lived separate and apart for a designated period of time.

Will covenant marriages reduce the rate of divorce? It is too early to tell. One study of Louisiana marriages over an eight-year period concluded that "covenant couples have only a little over half the odds (.55) of divorce or separation that standard couples have."[33] Yet the study concluded that this result was due more to the religious views of the couple (particularly the wife) than to the covenant marriage itself. Furthermore, only a very small number of couples chose covenant marriages in the state (about 2 percent). Nevertheless, other states have explored the possibility of creating their own covenant-marriage option. States are uneasy about reintroducing fault in the law of divorce, but they want to remain open to policy changes that might reduce the divorce rate.

ASSIGNMENT 5.9

a. Explain why you think it is a good or bad idea for every state to force couples to choose between conventional and covenant marriages.

b. Explain why you think it is a good or bad idea for every state to abolish conventional marriages and to require every marriage to be a covenant marriage.

COMMON-LAW MARRIAGE

INTRODUCTION

A *common-law marriage* is a marriage entered into without complying with statutory formalities—e.g., obtaining a marriage license and having the marriage performed by an authorized person before witnesses—when the parties (a) agree to marry, (b) live together as spouses, and (c) hold themselves out as married.

The marriages of couples that enter into a common-law marriage are as valid as the marriages of couples that enter into a ceremonial marriage. To end a common-law marriage, for example, one of the parties must die, or they must go through a divorce proceeding in the same manner as any other married couple seeking to dissolve a marriage.[34] There is no such thing as a common-law divorce in which the spouses end their marriage by simply declaring themselves to be divorced.

Common-law marriages are not allowed in every state. In fact, most states have abolished them as of certain dates. For several of the following reasons you need to know about common-law marriage even in states that have abolished them:

- Parties may enter into a common-law marriage in a state where such marriages are valid and then move to another state that has abolished such marriages. Under conflict-of-laws principles, as we will see, the second state may have to recognize the marriage as valid.

- In our highly mobile society, parties who live together should be aware that if they travel through states that recognize common-law marriages for vacations or for other temporary purposes, one of the parties might later try to claim that they entered into a common-law marriage in such a state.

- It may be that your state once recognized common-law marriages as valid, but then, as of a certain date, abolished all such marriages for the future. The law abolishing them is not **retroactive**. A number of people may still live in your state who entered into valid common-law marriages before the law was changed, and hence, their marriages are still valid.

retroactive
Applying to facts that arose before a particular event or date.

Requirements for Common-law Marriage

In states that recognize common-law marriages, it is not enough that the parties lived together, even for an extended period of time. The following elements must be established:

- *Capacity*. The parties must have **capacity** to marry. (For example, they must be of age and not be already married to someone else. Some states impose a minimum age (e.g., eighteen) to enter a common-law marriage that is higher than the age required to enter a ceremonial marriage.) Capacity is the legal power to do something.

capacity
The legal power to do something such as enter into a contract or a relationship. Also called *legal capacity*. (See glossary for an additional meaning.)

- *Present intent and agreement.* There must be a present intent to marry and a present agreement to enter a marital relationship. It is not enough for the couple to discuss marriage in the future. The intent and agreement to become spouses to each other must be **in praesenti**—meaning, undertaken at present. (Some states require an **express** agreement; others allow the agreement to be inferred from the manner in which the parties relate to each other.)

- *Cohabitation.* The parties must actually live together as spouses (i.e., there must be **cohabitation**). In some states, cohabitation must include sexual relations. In other states, however, living openly together as spouses is sufficient even if the relationship was never consummated, particularly if illness prevented **consummation**. (Note that consummation is never a requirement for a valid ceremonial marriage.)

- *Holding out.* There must be an openness about the relationship; the parties must make representations to the world that they are spouses. This is referred to as **holding out**. The holding-out requirement functions as a major deterrent of fraudulent claims that a common-law marriage was entered.

A popular misconception about common-law marriages is that the parties must live together for seven years before the marriage becomes legal. There is no such time requirement.

Courts generally are reluctant to find that a common-law marriage exists. During America's pioneer days, there may have been a need for common-law marriage because of the scarcity of officials to perform ceremonial marriages. This, of course, is no longer true today. More importantly, common-law marriages are disfavored (even in states where they are legal) because it is relatively easy to fabricate a claim that the parties married by common law, particularly after one of them has died. As one court said of a common-law marriage, "It tends to weaken the public estimate of the sanctity of the marriage relation. It puts in doubt the certainty of the rights of inheritance. It opens the door to false pretenses of marriage and the imposition on estates of questionable heirs. . . . It places honest, God-ordained matrimony and mere meretricious cohabitation too nearly on a level with each other."[35]

Although millions of adults live together in an intimate relationship, their intent or goals are not always clear. In many relationships, neither party may want a marriage, although in some, one of the adults may have this intention or hope. Most states require strong evidence (**clear and convincing evidence** rather than just a **preponderance of the evidence**) that both parties had the intent to marry before concluding that a common-law marriage was entered. According to one court, the "mutual understanding or consent must be conveyed with such a demonstration of intent and with such clarity on the part of the parties that marriage does not creep up on either of them and catch them unawares. One cannot be married unwittingly or accidentally."[36]

Another reason common-law marriages are disfavored is because there is no public record of the marriage. It is important for society to have accurate records on its various populations in order to identify needs, allocate resources, and provide protection. This goal is hampered if a large segment of the population is married without the state knowing about it. (Some states allow couples to register their common-law marriage with the county, but few couples do so.) Also, bypassing the technical requirements for a ceremonial marriage defeats other government objectives. Blood tests, for example, help prevent the spread of certain diseases and waiting periods discourage hasty marriages. None of these goals can be achieved with a common-law marriage.

See the Interviewing and Investigation Checklist on the factors relevant to the formation of a common-law marriage.

ASSIGNMENT   5.10

Paul and Fran live in a state that recognizes common-law marriage. They become engaged. The wedding will take place in eight months. Three months after the engagement, Paul dies in an automobile accident. Is Fran the widow of Paul for purposes of inheritance and state government benefits such as Social Security? (See the General Instructions for the Legal-Analysis Assignment in Appendix A.)

power of attorney
(1) A document that authorizes another to act as one's agent or attorney in fact. (An attorney in fact is someone who is authorized to act in place of or for another, often in a business transaction. An attorney in fact may or may not be an attorney at law.) (2) The authority itself.

✔ INTERVIEWING AND INVESTIGATION CHECKLIST

Factors Relevant to the Formation of a Common-Law Marriage between the Client (C) and the Defendant (D).

LEGAL INTERVIEWING QUESTIONS

1. On what date did you first meet D?

2. When did the two of you first begin talking about living together? Describe the circumstances. Where were you? Who said what, etc.?

3. Did you or D ever discuss with anyone else your plans to live together? If so, with whom and what was said?

4. On what date did you actually move in together? How long have you been living together? (Obtain precise dates.)

5. Have you and D had sexual relations? If so, when was the first time?

6. In whose name was the lease to the apartment or the deed to the house in which you lived?

7. Do you have separate or joint bank accounts? If joint, what names appear on the account?

8. Who pays the rent or the mortgage?

9. Who pays the utility bills?

10. Who pays the food bills?

11. Since you have been living together, have you filed separate or joint tax returns?

12. Other than everyday purchases, what did the two of you purchase with joint funds?

13. What attitudes have you both expressed to each other about marriage in general? For example, did either of you feel that there was a difference between commitment and marriage?

14. Did you and D have a written or oral agreement that you and D were going to be married? What precise language did you use when the two of you discussed marriage?

15. Why didn't you and D have a marriage ceremony?

16. Did you ever introduce each other as "my husband," "my wife," or "my spouse"? If so, to whom? Name the specific individuals.

17. Name any relatives, neighbors, business associates, friends, etc., who think of you and D as married. State why each thinks so.

18. Did you and D ever discuss making individual or joint wills? Do you have them? What attorneys, if any, did you use?

19. Did either of you give each other a **power of attorney** for business or healthcare? If so, what are the details?

20. Did you and D ever separate for any period of time? If so, describe the circumstances.

21. Did you and D have children? If so, what last name did the children have? Same questions as to adopted children.

22. On insurance policies, is either of you the beneficiary? How is the premium paid?

23. During your life with D, what other indications exist that the two of you treated each other as married?

24. Have the two of you ever spent significant time on vacation or for any other reason in the District of Columbia or in any of the following states: Alabama, Colorado, Georgia, Idaho, Iowa, Kansas, Montana, New Hampshire, Ohio, Oklahoma, Pennsylvania, Rhode Island, South Carolina, Texas, or Utah? (These states recognize or once recognized common-law marriage. See Exhibit 5.1.) If so, describe the circumstances. How long were you there? Did you discuss your relationship while there?

POSSIBLE INVESTIGATION TASKS

- Obtain copies of leases or deeds.

- Obtain copies of bills, receipts, tax returns, etc., to determine how the names of C and D appear on them.

- Obtain copies of any written agreements between C and D.

- Interview anyone C indicates would think of C and D as married.

- Obtain birth certificates of children, if any.

EXHIBIT 5.1   States That Allow Common-Law Marriage

State	Requirements for Common-Law Marriage Established by Case or Statute
Alabama (allowed only before 2017)	■ After 2017: No common-law marriage may be entered into in this state on or after January 1, 2017. Ala. Code § 30-1-20. ■ Before 2017: Common-law marriages entered into before 2017 are valid. Requirements: (1) capacity; (2) present, mutual agreement to permanently enter the marriage relationship to the exclusion of all other relationships; and (3) public recognition of the relationship as a marriage and public assumption of marital duties and cohabitation.
Colorado	■ Case: Requirements: A common-law marriage is established by the mutual consent or agreement of the parties to be husband and wife, followed by a mutual and open assumption of a marital relationship. *People v. Lucero*, 747 P.2d 660, 663 (Colo., 1987). Statute: ■ (1) A common-law marriage entered into on or after September 1, 2006, shall not be recognized as a valid marriage in this state unless, at the time the common-law marriage is entered into: (a) Each party is eighteen years of age or older; and (b) The marriage is not prohibited.
District of Columbia	■ Case: Requirements: In the District of Columbia, when a man and woman who are legally capable of entering into the marriage relation, mutually agree, in words of the present tense, to be husband and wife, and consummate their agreement by cohabiting as husband and wife, a "common-law marriage" results. *U.S. Fidelity & Guaranty Co. v. Britton*, 269 F.2d 249, 251 (D.C. Cir. 1959).
Georgia (allowed only for marriages entered before 1997)	■ After 1997 No common-law marriage shall be entered into in this state on or after January 1, 1997. Ga. Code Ann., § 19-3-1.1. ■ Before 1997 Common-law marriages entered into before 1997 are valid. Requirements: In order for there to be a "common law marriage," the three essential elements of marriage . . . must be met all at one time: (1) the parties must be able to contract, (2) there must be an actual contract, and (3) there must be consummation according to law. *Brown v. Brown*, 215 S.E.2d 671, 672 (Ga. 1975).
Idaho (allowed only for marriages entered before 1996)	■ After 1996 No common-law marriage shall be entered into in this state after 1996. Statute. I.C. § 32-201. ■ Before 1996 Common-law marriages entered into before 1996 are valid. Requirements: The parties were both capable of giving consent (and did in fact consent) to the common-law marriage at its inception. The parties must assume the rights, duties and obligations of marriage. The parties' consent may be either expressed or implied by their conduct. If consent is implied, the best and most common, although not exclusive, method of proving consent is to show cohabitation, general reputation in the community as husband and wife, and holding oneself out as married. From such evidence, the court may infer that, at the outset, mutual consent was present. *Wilkins v. Wilkins*, 48 P.3d 644, 649 (Idaho, 2002).
Iowa	■ Case Requirements: The elements and conditions necessary to establish the existence of a common-law marriage [are] . . . intent and agreement *in praesenti* as to marriage on the part of both parties together with continuous cohabitation and public declaration that they are husband and wife; [there must be] a general and substantial "holding-out" or open declaration thereof to the public by both parties thereto. *In re Dallman's Estate*, 228 N.W.2d 187, 189, 190 (Iowa 1975).

(continued)

Exhibit 5.1 *(continued)*

State	Requirements for Common-Law Marriage Established by Case or Statute
Kansas	■ Statute (b) The state of Kansas shall not recognize a common-law marriage contract if either party to the marriage contract is under 18 years of age. Kan. Stat. §23-2502. ■ Case Requirements: The basic elements essential in the creation of a common-law marriage are the capacity of the parties to marry, a present marriage agreement, and a holding out of each other as husband and wife to the public. *In re Mazlo's Estate*, 505 P.2d 762, 763 (Kan. 1973).
Montana	■ Statute The statutes on ceremonial marriage do not invalidate common-law marriages. Mont. Code Ann. § 40-1-403 ■ Case Requirements: Under our common law, such a marriage is established when a couple: (1) is competent to enter into a marriage, (2) mutually consents and agrees to a common law marriage, and (3) cohabits and is reputed in the community to be husband and wife. Snetsinger v. Montana University System, 104 P.3d 445, 451 (Mont. 2004).
New Hampshire (effective only at death for purposes of inheritance and death benefits)	■ Statute Requirements: Persons cohabiting and acknowledging each other as husband and wife, and generally reputed to be such, for the period of 3 years, and until the decease of one of them, shall thereafter be deemed to have been legally married. N.H. Rev. Stat. § 457:39 ■ Case Requirements: [T]he status of "common law" spouse obtains only as to the survivor of two people who had cohabited and acknowledged each other as husband and wife, and who had been generally reputed as such, for a period of three years and until the decease of one of them. *Joan S. v. John S.*, 427 A.2d 498, 499 (N.H., 1981).
Ohio (allowed only for marriages entered before October 1991)	■ After 1991: Statute: No common-law marriage may be entered into in this state on or after 1991. On and after October 10, 1991, . . . common law marriages are prohibited in this state. Ohio Rev. Code Ann. § 3105.12. ■ Before 1991: Case Common-law marriages entered into before 1991 are valid. Requirements: An agreement of marriage *in praesenti* when made by parties competent to contract, accompanied and followed by cohabitation as husband and wife, they being so treated and reputed in the community and circle in which they move, establishes a valid marriage at common law . . . Although cohabitation and reputation are necessary elements of a common law marriage, this court has previously held that standing alone they do not constitute a common law marriage. *Fitzgerald v. Mayfield*, 584 N.E.2d 13, 17 (Ohio Ct. App. 1990).
Oklahoma	■ Case The law is unclear as to whether they are allowed only for marriages entered before November 1999. As of November 1, 1999, the State of Oklahoma does not recognize common law marriages. *Roed v. Jerry Scott*, 2001 WL 35972774 (Dist.. Ct. of OK, Cleveland County). Requirement: A common-law marriage occurs upon the happening of three events: a declaration by the parties of an intent to marry, cohabitation, and a holding out of themselves to the community of being husband and wife. *Brooks v. Sanders* 190 P.3d 357, 362 (Okla. Civ. App. 2008). ■ If you entered into a common law marriage in Oklahoma after 1998, your marital status is complicated. Courts today may go either way when it comes to these marriages, and in order to gain the benefits of marriage, you may have to have a traditional legal ceremony. (marriage.laws.com/common-law-marriage-oklahoma)

(continued)

Exhibit 5.1 *(continued)*

State	Requirements for Common-Law Marriage Established by Case or Statute
Pennsylvania (allowed only for marriages entered before 2005)	▪ After 2005: Statute No common-law marriage contracted after January 1, 2005, shall be valid. Nothing in this part shall be deemed or taken to render any common-law marriage otherwise lawful and contracted on or before January 1, 2005, invalid. 23 Pa.C.S.A. § 1103. ▪ Before 2005: Common-law marriages entered into before 2005 are valid. Requirements: In Pennsylvania, a common law marriage is a marriage by express agreement of the parties without ceremony, and usually without a witness, and *verba de praesenti* [words of present intention], uttered with the purpose of establishing a relation of husband and wife. However, common law marriage will still be recognized without use of *verba de praesenti*, where the intention of the parties as expressed by their words, is that they were married. While cohabitation and reputation alone will not suffice to establish a common law marriage, they are relevant factors which a court may consider in determining whether the parties have entered into a common law marriage. *Cann v. Cann*, 632 A.2d 322, 325 (Pa. Super. Ct. 1993).
Rhode Island	▪ Case Requirements: The existence of such a marriage "must be established by clear and convincing evidence that the parties seriously intended to enter into the husband-wife relationship." The conduct of the parties must have been "of such a character as to lead to a belief in the community that they were married." The just-mentioned requirements must be proven through "inference from cohabitation, declarations, reputation among kindred and friends, and other competent circumstantial evidence. *Zharkova v. Gaudreau*, 45 A.3d 1282, 1290–91 (R.I. 2012).
South Carolina (allowed only for marriages entered before 2019)	▪ After 2019: From "this date forward—that is, purely prospectively—parties may no longer enter into a valid marriage in South Carolina without a license." *Stone v. Thompson*, 833 S.E.2d 266 (S.C. 2019). ▪ Before 2019: Common law marriages entered before 2019 are valid. S.C. Code Ann. § 20-1-360. See also § 20-1-100. Requirement: The key element in discerning whether parties are common-law married is mutual assent: each party must intend to be married to the other and understand the other's intent. Some factors to which courts have looked to discern the parties' intent include tax returns, documents filed under penalty of perjury, introductions in public, contracts, and checking accounts.
Texas (common law marriage is called informal marriage in Texas)	▪ Statute Requirements: (a) [T]he marriage of a man and woman may be proved by evidence that . . . the man and woman agreed to be married and after the agreement they lived together in this state as husband and wife and they represented to others that they were married. . . . (c) A person under 18 years of age may not . . . be a party to an informal marriage. V.T.C.A., Family Code § 2.401. *Note* A couple in an informal marriage has the option of filing (registering) a Declaration of Informal Marriage in the county clerk's office. V.T.C.A., Family Code § 2.402. ▪ Case Requirements: A valid common-law marriage consists of three elements: (1) an agreement presently to be husband and wife; (2) living together as husband and wife; and (3) holding each other out to the public as such. *Claveria's Estate v. Claveria*, 615 S.W.2d 164, 166 (Tex. 1981).
Utah	▪ Statute Requirements: (1) A marriage which is not solemnized according to this chapter shall be legal and valid if a court or administrative order establishes that it arises out of a contract between a man and a woman who: (a) are of legal age and capable of giving consent; (b) are legally capable of entering a solemnized marriage under the provisions of this chapter; (c) have cohabited; (d) mutually assume marital rights, duties, and obligations; and (e) who hold themselves out as and have acquired a uniform and general reputation as husband and wife. U.C.A. 1953 § 30-1-4.5.

Two situations remain to be considered on the topic of common-law marriage: conflict of laws and impediment removal.

CONFLICT OF LAWS

A conflict of laws exists when a court is asked to apply inconsistent laws of two different legal systems such as two different states or countries. In such cases, the court must make a **choice of law**. Let's look at two examples:

- Case #1. Bill and Pam live in State X, where common-law marriages are legal. They enter into such a marriage. Then they move to State Y, where common-law marriages have been abolished. They could have entered into a ceremonial marriage in State Y, but they chose not do so because they did not want a ceremonial marriage and they knew that their marriage was valid in State X. Bill is injured on the job and dies in State Y. Pam claims workers' compensation benefits as the "wife" of Bill. Will State Y recognize Pam as married to Bill?

- Case #2. Ed and Mary are both fourteen years of age living in State A. Fourteen is the minimum age to marry in State A. They enter into a valid marriage in State A. They then move to State B where the minimum age to marry is sixteen. (If they had tried to marry in State B, their marriage would not have been valid because of **nonage**—being below the required minimum age.) Ed is injured on the job and dies in State B. He is fifteen at the time of death. Mary claims workers' compensation benefits as the "wife" of Ed. Will State B recognize Mary as married to Ed?

In Case #1, the conflict of law is over the validity of common-law marriages: State X recognizes them; State Y does not. In Case #2, the conflict of law is over the minimum age to marry: States A and B have different minimum ages to marry. The couples are now domiciled in a state that would not recognize their marriage if entered into there.

Domicile is the place where a person has been physically present (a) with the intent to make that place a permanent home or (b) with no intent to make any other place a permanent home. A **domiciliary** is a person domiciled in a particular place. The state where someone is domiciled is called the **domiciliary state**. The current domiciliary state in Case #1 is State Y; the current domiciliary state in Case #2 is State B. The issue in both cases is whether the domiciliary state will recognize the marriage entered into in another state.

Earlier in the chapter when we covered same-sex marriage, we discussed the general conflict-of-law rule on the validity of marriage.

Conflict of Laws and the Validity of a Marriage

The validity of a marriage is determined by the law of the state in which the marriage was entered into or contracted (the state of celebration). Another state will recognize that marriage *unless* to do so would violate a strong public policy of the state asked to recognize it.

Under this general rule:

- Case #1. State Y will recognize as valid the marriage of Bill and Pam that was entered into in State X *unless* State Y determines that recognizing common-law marriages violates the strong public policy of State Y.

- Case #2. State B will recognize as valid the marriage of Ed and Mary that was entered into in State A *unless* State B determines that recognizing underage marriages violates the strong public policy of State B.

choice of law
A selection of which law to apply when a court is being asked to apply the law of different legal systems such as two states or two countries.

nonage
Below the required minimum age to enter into a relationship or perform a task. Minority.

domicile
The place where a person has been physically present (a) with the intent to make that place a permanent home or (b) with no intent to make any other place a permanent home. The place to which one intends to return when away.

domiciliary
One who is domiciled in a particular place.

domiciliary state
The state where one has a domicile.

We will study this general rule (and the meaning of strong public policy) in Chapter 6 on annulment. For now, here is how the general conflict-of-law rule would apply to our two cases:

- Case #1. Most domiciliary states would recognize as valid common-law marriages that were entered into in other states. It is not against the strong public policy of most domiciliary states to recognize out-of-state common-law marriages even if such marriages cannot be entered into in the domiciliary state.

- Case #2. Not all states agree on whether to recognize a marriage in which the parties were of age in the state where they entered into the marriage but would not be of age if they had entered it in the domiciliary state. Some states would consider it against their strong public policy to recognize such marriages. Other states disagree and would recognize it.

IMPEDIMENT REMOVAL

An impediment is a legal obstacle that prevents the formation of a valid marriage or other contract. The following is an example to help illustrate the concept of impediment removal:

In 1999, Ernestine enters into a valid ceremonial marriage with John. After several years, they begin having marital troubles and separate, but they do not divorce. In 2005, Ernestine and Henry begin living together. They cohabitate and hold each other out as husband and wife in a state where common-law marriages are valid (They do not enter into a ceremonial marriage.) Except for the existence of the 1999 marriage to John, it is clear that Ernestine and Henry would have a valid common-law marriage. In 2011, John obtains a divorce from Ernestine. Henry and Ernestine continue to live together in the same manner as they have since 2005. In 2019, Henry dies on the job. Ernestine claims death benefits under the state's workers' compensation laws as his surviving "wife." Was she ever married to Henry?

impediment
A legal obstacle that prevents the formation of a valid marriage or other contract.

Until 2011, a serious **impediment** existed to their being able to marry: Ernestine was already married to someone else (John). When Ernestine's marriage to John was dissolved by the divorce in 2011, the impediment was removed. The issue is (1) whether Ernestine and Henry would be considered to have entered into a valid common-law marriage at the time the impediment was removed, or (2) whether at that time they would have had to enter into a *new* common-law marriage agreement, express or implied.

In most states, a new agreement would not be necessary. An earlier agreement to marry (by common law) will carry forward to the time the impediment is removed so long as the parties continued to live together openly as husband and wife. Accordingly, Ernestine automatically became the wife of Henry when the impediment of the prior marriage was removed, because she and Henry continued to live together openly as husband and wife after that time. As one court explained:

It is not to be expected that parties once having agreed to be married will deem it necessary to agree to do so again when an earlier marriage is terminated or some other bar to union is eliminated.[37]

In the states that reach this conclusion, it makes no difference that either or both of the parties knew of the impediment at the time they initially agreed to live as husband and wife.

ASSIGNMENT 5.11

Examine the following sequence of events:

- Ann and Rich meet in State Y where they agree to live together as husband and wife forever. They do not want to go through a marriage ceremony, but they agree to be married and openly hold themselves out as such. State Y, however, does not recognize common-law marriages.

- Rich accepts a job offer in State X, where common-law marriages are legal, and they both move there.

- After three years in State X, Rich and Ann move back to State Y. One year later, Rich dies. In his will, he leaves all of his property to his "wife." Ann is not mentioned by name in his will.

- From the time they met until the time of Rich's death, they lived together as husband and wife, and everyone who knew them thought of them as such.

Can Ann claim anything under the will? State Y provides tax benefits to "widows." Can Ann claim these benefits? (See the General Instructions for the Legal-Analysis Assignment in Appendix A.)

ASSIGNMENT 5.12

State Y does not recognize common-law marriages. Vivian and Tom begin living together in State Y in 2005 and continuously do so until Tom's death in 2014. During this time, pursuant to mutual agreement, they cohabited and held themselves out as husband and wife, but never went through a marriage ceremony. They purchased real property in their joint names as husband and wife. On four different occasions, they went on vacation fishing trips to a resort in State X, where they registered as husband and wife, held themselves out as such, and lived together during their stay. Two trips in 2007 were of three days' duration each. Two other trips were of seven days' duration each, one in 2008 and one in 2009. State X recognizes common-law marriages. Were the parties married in 2014? (See General Instructions for the Legal-Analysis Assignment in Appendix A.)

ASSIGNMENT 5.13

What is the feminist argument in favor of allowing common-law marriages? (In Google, Bing, or Yahoo, run this search: feminist common law marriage.)

PUTATIVE MARRIAGE

In some states, courts will treat unmarried parties as putative spouses for purposes of providing limited rights such as the right to receive support and the right to inherit from the other putative spouse. A **putative spouse** is a person who believes he or she entered into a valid marriage even though there

putative spouses
A person who believes in good faith that he or she entered into a valid marriage even though an impediment made the marriage invalid.

was an impediment that made the marriage unlawful. The marriage is referred to as a *putative marriage*. Here is how one court described a putative marriage:

> A putative marriage is one that has been contracted in good faith and in ignorance of some existing impediment on the part of at least one of the contracting parties. Three circumstances must occur to constitute this species of marriage:
>
> 1. There must be bona fides. At least one of the parties must have been ignorant of the impediment, not only at the time of the marriage, but must also have continued ignorant of it during his or her life.
> 2. The marriage must be duly solemnized.
> 3. The marriage must have been considered lawful in the estimation of the parties or of that party who alleges the bona fides.[38]

Here is an example of a putative marriage:

> *Brenda goes through a marriage ceremony in good faith and does not find out until after her "husband" Jim dies that he was still married to another woman who was still alive. In the few states that recognize putative marriages, Brenda would be given some protection (e.g., she would be awarded the reasonable value of the services she rendered or a share of the property the parties accumulated during the relationship).*

Note, however, that only the innocent party can benefit from the putative marriage. If Brenda had died first in our example, Jim, her bigamist "husband," could not claim benefits as her putative spouse. A putative spouse can collect Social Security as the widow or widower of his or her deceased putative spouse if the applicant for benefits "in good faith went through a marriage ceremony" that resulted "in a purported marriage," which "but for a legal impediment not known to the applicant at the time of such ceremony, would have been a valid marriage."[39]

Uniform Marriage and Divorce Act

States differ on whether putative marriages require cohabitation. Most states do not. States that have adopted the Uniform Marriage and Divorce Act do require it as you can see from the definition of putative spouse in § 209 of the act:

> Any person who has cohabited with another to whom he is not legally married in the good faith belief that he was married to that person is a putative spouse until knowledge of the fact that he is not legally married terminates his status and prevents acquisition of further rights. A putative spouse acquires the rights conferred upon a legal spouse, including the right to maintenance following termination of his status.

Good faith is measured by a subjective standard. The test is whether the innocent party actually believed that the marriage was valid. The test is not whether a reasonable person would have believed it was valid. Reasonableness is an objective standard. The test is not objective; it is subjective.

MARRIAGE BY ESTOPPEL

In Chapter 7, we will discuss invalid marriages that are treated as valid because one of the parties is estopped (prevented) from asserting the invalidity of the marriage. In the absence of someone who can challenge the validity of the marriage, the marriage is treated as valid—it is a marriage by estoppel. This is a relationship that is recognized as a marriage because a party is prevented from

---

bona fides
Good faith. The absence of wrongful intent or desire to take inappropriate advantage of someone.

Uniform Marriage and Divorce Act (UMDA)
A model statute on marriage and divorce proposed to the states for adoption.

subjective standard
A standard that measures something by what a particular person actually knew, felt, or did.

objective standard
A standard that measures something by comparing (1) what a particular person actually knew, felt, or did with (2) what a reasonable person would have known, felt, or done under the same or similar circumstances.

estopped
Prevented from asserting a right or a defense because it would be unfair or inequitable to allow the assertion. The noun is *estoppel*.

marriage by estoppel
A relationship that is recognized as a marriage because a party is prevented from asserting the invalidity of the marriage even though grounds for its invalidity may exist.

asserting the invalidity of the marriage even though grounds for its invalidity may exist. Here is an example:

> Ted is married to Alice. Ted goes to another state and obtains an invalid divorce from Alice. Ted then marries Helen. Some years later, Helen files a divorce action against Ted seeking alimony and attorney fees. Ted's defense is that he was never legally married to Helen because his marriage to Alice was not terminated by a valid divorce.

On these facts, Ted will be prevented from raising this defense because he is the one who procured the "divorce" that he now acknowledges was invalid. He will not be allowed to take inconsistent positions. He took advantage of the "divorce" to Alice by marrying Helen. It is inconsistent and unfair to allow him to try to undo the marriage to Helen. Hence, the marriage to Helen is treated as valid because there is no one who can challenge its validity. If he could challenge it, a court would rule that the marriage to Helen is invalid because it was entered into at a time when Ted was still married to Alice. But because Ted cannot raise this challenge, the marriage to Helen becomes a marriage by estoppel. Consequently, Helen has the right to go to court and seek a divorce (including alimony, attorney fees, and other spousal rights) from the man whom the court will treat as her legal husband.

DE FACTO MARRIAGE

Assume that a couple lives together for an extended period but never had a ceremonial marriage, never held themselves out as husband and wife, and never had a good-faith belief they were married. After years of being together, one of them dies. Does the survivor have any rights? There was no common-law marriage because the couple did not meet the holding-out requirement for such marriages. There was no putative marriage because neither had a good-faith belief that they were married.

The couple had what a few states call a **de facto marriage**, a marriage in fact as opposed to a legal marriage. A de facto marriage is a relationship recognized as a marriage for limited purposes even though the relationship does not meet the requirements of a ceremonial, common-law, or putative marriage, although the couple has acted in a marriage-like manner. Only a minority of states recognize de facto marriages. In such states, if one of the cohabitants dies on the job, the surviving cohabitant might be given workers' compensation benefits as the "spouse" of the deceased. Most states, however, do not recognize de facto marriages and will not grant marital benefits to cohabitants in such relationships. Of course, if the parties had entered into a cohabitation agreement (expressed or implied), they might be able to obtain the kind of contract and related benefits discussed in Chapter 4.

There is another less-common meaning of de facto marriage in some states. The phrase is sometimes applied to cases in which a man is paying alimony to his ex-wife and asks a court to end his alimony obligation because his ex-wife is cohabiting with another man and living in a marriage-like relationship with that man. Her relationship with this other man is referred to as a de facto marriage. In several states, this is sufficient to end the ex-husband's alimony obligation. In West Virginia, for example, a statute provides as follows:

> In the discretion of the court, an award of spousal support may be reduced or terminated upon specific written findings by the court that since the granting of a divorce and the award of spousal support a de facto marriage has existed between the spousal support payee and another person.[40]

We will examine this issue again in Chapter 8.

de facto marriage
A marriage in fact. A relationship of a cohabiting couple that is recognized as a marriage for limited purposes when the couple has acted in a marriage-like manner even though the relationship does not meet the requirements of a ceremonial, common-law, or putative marriage.

THE STRUGGLE TO FIND A REMEDY

Sometimes, a court will stretch a legal definition in order to cover facts that call out for a remedy even though traditional legal concepts do not seem to fit. It is not true that courts will bend every legal definition in order to find a way to reach a decision that is appropriate. Many people come away from the legal system without a remedy because their case does not fit within the elements of a traditional remedy. Yet it is clear from our discussions in this text that family law is still evolving. Legislatures and courts are often receptive to the creation of new legal relationships and of retooling some of the old legal relationships to accommodate the rich diversity of how people in our society form families. This trend is aptly demonstrated by the expanding contractual rights of unmarried cohabitants discussed in Chapter 4. It is also demonstrated in this chapter by the discussions of civil unions, domestic partnerships, same-sex marriages, putative spouses, and de facto marriages.

PARALEGAL ROLES

- For an overview of paralegal roles in family-law cases, see Exhibits 1.5 and 1.6 in Chapter 1.
- For all financial issues covered in Chapter 5, a paralegal may be asked to help collect documents and facts outlined in:
  - The checklist in Exhibit 3.1 of Chapter 3.
  - The checklists on separation agreements at the beginning of Chapter 8.
  - The interrogatories in Appendix C.

SUMMARY

Most states do not allow the heart-balm action of breach of promise to marry. Nor do they allow suits for inducing someone to breach this promise. States differ on whether they also prohibit a tort action for fraud based on the breach. For states that do allow an action for breach of promise to marry, recovery is limited to compensatory damages. Expectation damages are not allowed. If the breach is particularly shocking, the tort of intentional infliction of emotional distress (IIED) might have been committed.

When a planned marriage does not occur, conditional gifts (those dependent on the marriage occurring) must be returned. This is also true of engagement rings except in the few states where the ring does not have to be returned to the person who broke the engagement without justification. This person is not entitled to have the ring returned to him or her. A contract that imposes a total or a near total prohibition on marriage is an unenforceable, general restraint on marriage. In contrast, contracts that impose reasonable limitations on one's right to marry can be enforceable. Most states enforce anti-nepotism job rules that forbid married employees from working together for the same employer.

Marriage is a fundamental right. The two major categories of marriage are ceremonial and common-law marriages. Ceremonial marriages must comply with technical or procedural requirements such as obtaining a marriage license and observing a waiting period. There is no requirement that either party take the surname of the other party when the marriage occurs. In most states, the failure to comply with technical or procedural requirements does not invalidate the marriage. Most states allow proxy marriages when the bride, groom, or both is not present for the marriage ceremony.

Civil unions and domestic partnerships give same-sex couples (and some opposite-sex couples) all or most of the state rights and responsibilities that apply to married couples. After the U.S. Supreme Court ruled that same-sex intimate contact in private between consenting adults could not be criminalized (*Lawrence*) and that federal benefits could not be denied to same-sex married couples in states that authorized same-sex marriage (*Windsor*), the Court ruled that states could no longer ban same-sex marriage (*Obergefell*).

A covenant marriage is a ceremonial marriage (a) that is entered upon proof of premarital counseling and a promise to seek marital counseling when needed during the marriage, and (b) that is dissolved upon separation for a designated period or upon proof of marital fault. It is more difficult to dissolve a covenant marriage than a conventional one.

In states where common-law marriages are allowed, the requirements are the legal capacity to marry, a present intent and agreement to enter into a marital relationship, living together as spouses (cohabitation), and an openness about living together as spouses (holding out). Under conflict-of-laws rules, the validity of a marriage is governed by the state in which it was entered or contracted. Hence, if a couple enters a valid common-law marriage in a state where it is valid but moves to a state where such marriages have been abolished, the latter state will recognize the marriage as valid unless recognition would violate its strong public policy.

Occasionally, an impediment exists to an otherwise valid common-law marriage. If the impediment is removed while the parties are still openly living together, a valid common-law marriage will be established as of the date of the removal. In most states, a new agreement to enter a common-law marriage is not needed when the impediment is removed.

A putative spouse is a person who believes in good faith that he or she entered (and cohabitated in) a valid marriage even though an impediment made the marriage invalid. The putative spouse can obtain some of the benefits of the resulting putative marriage despite the impediment. A marriage by estoppel is a relationship that is recognized as a marriage because a party is prevented from asserting the invalidity of the marriage even though grounds for its invalidity may exist. A de facto marriage is a relationship of a cohabiting couple that is recognized as a marriage for limited purposes when the couple has acted in a marriage-like manner even though the relationship does not meet the requirements of a ceremonial, common law, or putative marriage.

KEY TERMS

cause of action
heart-balm action
compensatory damages
specific performance
expectation damages
aggrieved
punitive damages
malice
heart-balm statute
interference with contract relations
privilege
fraud
scienter
intentional infliction of emotional
    distress (IIED)
gift
consideration
donor
donee
testamentary gift
revocable
inter vivos gift
irrevocable
unjust enrichment
restraint of marriage
bequest
nepotism

marriage
fundamental right
wrongful death
intestate
testate
elective share
marital-communications privilege
ceremonial marriage
common-law marriage
solemnization
officiant
recordation
confidential marriage
proxy marriage
posthumous
polygamy
polygyny
polyandry
civil union
domestic partnership
conflict of laws
full faith and credit (FFC)
Defense of Marriage Act (DOMA)
substantive due process (SDP)
legitimate state interest
strict-scrutiny test
rational-basis test

no-fault divorce
covenant marriage
retroactive
capacity
in praesenti
express
cohabitation
consummation
holding out
clear and convincing evidence
preponderance of the evidence
power of attorney
choice of law
nonage
domicile
domiciliary
domiciliary state
impediment
putative spouse
bona fides
Uniform Marriage and Divorce Act
subjective standard
objective standard
estopped
marriage by estoppel
de facto marriage

CHECK THE CITE

The United States Supreme Court held in *Turner v. Safley* that the restriction on marriage imposed on inmates was unconstitutional. What was the restriction and why was it held unconstitutional? See *Turner v. Safley*, 482 U.S. 78, 107 S. Ct. 2254 (1987). To read the opinion online:

(1) Run a citation search ("482 U.S. 78") in the *Case law* database of Google Scholar (scholar.google.com). (2) Run a citation search ("482 U.S. 78") or a case name search ("Turner v. Safley") in the general search engines of Google, Bing, or Yahoo.

PROJECT

Find out what courts in your state have said about the *Obergefell* case on same-sex marriage. Go to Google Scholar (scholar.google.com), click *Case law*, click *Select courts*, and check the box for the courts of your state. After you click *done*, run the following search (substituting your state for "aa" in the search):

"Obergefell v. Hodges" aa

Try to find three cases in your state that have cited *Obergefell*. Briefly state what these cases said about *Obergefell*.

Run the same search in the *Articles* database of Google Scholar. What are some of the views expressed in the literature about the impact of *Obergefell* in your state?

ETHICS IN A FAMILY LAW PRACTICE

Mary and Ted live in Louisiana. They want to enter into a covenant marriage. They visit Reverend Sharon Fox for the required premarital counseling. Reverend Fox is also a part-time paralegal. The couple spends two hours with Reverend Fox. She spends over half this time answering questions from Ted and Mary about the grounds for the divorce of a covenant marriage, the kind

of testimony that will be admissible in court to prove marital fault, the court that can grant such a divorce, and whether Ted's earlier divorce in another state is valid in Louisiana. Reverend Fox did the best she could in answering these questions. Any ethical problems? Do not focus on Louisiana family law. Examine ethics issue(s) only.

WRITING SAMPLE

Polygamy is the practice of having more than one spouse at the same time. Write a memorandum in which you apply *Obergefell v. Hodges* to whether the ban on polygamous marriage violates the U.S. Constitution. In

addition to reading the majority and dissenting opinions of the case, run this search in Google, Bing, or Yahoo: *Obergefell polygamy*. (See General Instructions for the Writing Sample in Appendix A.)

REVIEW QUESTIONS

1. What is a cause of action?
2. What is a heart-balm action?
3. What is the distinction between compensatory and expectation damages? How do they differ from punitive damages?
4. What is specific performance?
5. What is an action for breach of promise to marry and why have many states abolished the action?
6. What is a heart-balm statute?
7. What is the holding in *Stanard v. Bolin*?
8. What are the elements of fraud?
9. When can a fraud action be brought in a state that has a heart-balm statute?
10. What is scienter?
11. Under what circumstances can a breach of promise to marry be the basis of an action for intentional infliction of emotional distress (IIED)?
12. When is a gift irrevocable?
13. What is the distinction between an inter vivos and a testamentary gift?
14. When is a gift conditional?
15. When do engagement rings have to be returned?
16. Why do wedding gifts have to be returned after an engagement is broken?
17. What is unjust enrichment?
18. What is a restraint of marriage?

19. What is the difference between a general restraint and a reasonable limitation on marriage?
20. What is a bequest?
21. Do antinepotism policies at work constitute an unenforceable restraint on marriage?
22. What is a fundamental right?
23. Under what circumstances is a client likely to face the question of whether he or she is married?
24. What does intestate mean?
25. What is a wrongful death?
26. What is an elective share?
27. What is the marital-communications privilege?
28. What is the distinction between a ceremonial and a common-law marriage?
29. What technical/procedural requirements often apply to ceremonial marriages?
30. What is a confidential marriage?
31. How are marriages solemnized?
32. Is there an obligation for one person to take the other's surname?
33. What is a proxy marriage?
34. What is the ABM movement?
35. What is a civil union and a domestic partnership?
36. What is the conflict-of-law rule on the validity of marriages?
37. What was the full-faith-and-credit controversy?
38. What is the Defense of Marriage Act (DOMA)?
39. What did *Lawrence v. Texas* decide?
40. What did *U.S. v. Windsor* decide?
41. What did *Obergefell v. Hodges* decide?
42. What is a covenant marriage?
43. What are the requirements for a common-law marriage?
44. What is meant by capacity?
45. When is something done *in praesenti*?
46. How is holding out accomplished?
47. Why are common-law marriages disfavored?
48. What is the distinction between clear and convincing evidence and preponderance of the evidence?
49. What is a conflict of laws?
50. What is meant by domicile?
51. What is a domiciliary and a domiciliary state?
52. What is an impediment?
53. What happens when an impediment to a valid common-law marriage is removed?
54. What is a putative spouse?
55. What is the distinction between a subjective and an objective standard?
56. What is marriage by estoppel?
57. What is a de facto marriage?

HELPFUL WEBSITES

Your State

See Appendix D for links to the family law of your state on the topics covered in this chapter.

Heart Balm Actions

- heartbalmlaws.uslegal.com
- www.johnsonturner.com/heart-balm-actions
- en.wikipedia.org/wiki/Breach_of_promise

Conditional Gifts

- www.jud.ct.gov/lawlib/Notebooks/Pathfinders/Marry.PDF
- en.wikipedia.org/wiki/Engagement_ring
- gifts.uslegal.com/revocation-of-conditional-gift

Marriage Requirements in All States

- topics.law.cornell.edu/wex/table_marriage
- www.usmarriagelaws.com
- www.1800bride2b.com/articles/marriagelaws_chart.htm

Same-Sex Marriage

- www.pewresearch.org/search/same-sex%20marriage
- www.history.com/topics/gay-rights/gay-marriage
- en.wikipedia.org/wiki/Same-sex_marriage

Common-Law Marriage

- www.buddybuddy.com/common.html
- www.unmarried.org
- www.ncsl.org/GoogleResults.aspx?q=common%20law%20marriage
- en.wikipedia.org/wiki/Common-law_marriage_in_the_United_States

Marriage by Proxy

- marriagebyproxy.com
- en.wikipedia.org/wiki/Proxy_marriage

Covenant Marriage

- en.wikipedia.org/wiki/Covenant_marriage

Gay & Lesbian Advocates & Defenders

- www.glad.org

National Organization for Marriage

- www.nationformarriage.org

Google Scholar (scholar.google.com)

- Choose "Articles" and enter in the search box any of the key terms discussed in the chapter. Add the name of your state to the search term.
- Choose "Case law" and "Select courts". Select your state, click "Done," and enter in the search box any of the key terms discussed in the chapter. Add the name of your state to the search term.

Google, Bing, and Yahoo

(on these search engines, run the following searches, substituting your state for "aa")

- "heart balm" aa
- "breach of promise to marry" aa
- "conditional gift" aa
- "restraint of marriage" aa

- marriage law bias aa
- DOMA aa
- "covenant marriage" aa
- "putative marriage" aa
- "de facto marriage" aa
- "domestic partnership" aa
- "same-sex marriage" aa
- "common law marriage" aa
- "marriage by estoppel" aa

YouTube

Run the same searches on YouTube listed above for Google, Bing, Yahoo searches. Even when the video clips are trying to entice you to retain an attorney, buy a book, or enroll in a course, they can provide useful overviews and references to primary authority.

Twitter, Reddit, and Facebook

On Twitter, Reddit, and Facebook, run the following searches (substitute your state for aa in your searches; run the searches with and without the name of your state). Look for links to family-law developments in your state.

- same sex marriage aa
- common law marriage aa

ENDNOTES

Note: All or most of the court opinions in these Endnotes can be read online. To do so, go to Google Scholar (scholar. google.com), select "Case law," and in the search box, enter the cite (e.g., "368 N.Y.S.2d 980") or name of the case (e.g., "Friedman v. Geller") that is given in the Endnote.

[1] Keith Bradsher, *Modern Tale of Woe: Being Left at the Altar*, N.Y. Times, March 7, 1990, at B8.

[2] *Friedman v. Geller*, 368 N.Y.S.2d 980, 983 (Civil Court, City of New York 1975).

[3] W. Page Keeton et al., *Prosser and Keeton on the Law of Torts* 929 (5th ed. 1984); *Askew v. Askew*, 22 Cal. App. 4th 942 (note 22) (Cal. Ct. App. 1994).

[4] *Loving v. Virginia*, 388 U.S. 1, 12 (1967).

[5] Gretchen Livingston, *Family Life is Changing . . .* (Fact Tank, www.pewresearch.org) (June 2018); Vera Cohn, et al., *Barely Half of U.S. Adults are Married - A Record Low* (Pew Research Center 2011).

[6] Laura Peterson, *Divorce*, N.Y. Times, May 5, 1996, at 8.

[7] Adam P. Romero, *Estimates of Marriages of Same-Sex Couples . . .* (williamsinstitute.law.ucla.edu/experts/ adam-romero/obergefell-effect) (June 2017).

[8] Stephanie Coontz, *Taking Marriage Private*, N.Y. Times, November 26, 2007, at A27.

[9] For an example of an application for a confidential marriage in California, see losangelesmarriagelicense.com/ confidential-marriage-license.html.

[10] New York Domestic Relations, § 11(4)(2015).

[11] Colorado Revised Statutes, § 14-2-109(1)(1993).

[12] 8 U.S.C. § 1101(a)(35) (uscode.house.gov).

[13] Craig Smith, *A Love that Transcends Death is Blessed by the State*, N.Y. Times, February 19, 2004 (www.nytimes. com/2004/02/19/international/europe/19WIDO.html).

[14] Mark Mancini, *Can You Legally Marry a Dead Person?* Mental Floss, (mentalfloss.com/article/53829/can-you-legally-marry-dead-person) (12/2/13).

[15] Holly Honderich, *Judge Rules Utah Woman Legally Married to Deceased Partner* (2018) (www.bbc.com/ news/world-us-canada-45335851); Dennis Romboy, *Relatives Cannot Intervene in Woman's Marriage to Deceased Spouse, Court Rules* (2014) (www.ksl. com/?nid=148&sid=32689976). See also *Gardiner v. Taufer*, 342 P.3d 269 (Utah 2014).

[16] *Baehr v. Lewin*, 852 P.2d 44 (Haw. 1993).

[17] David Dunlap, *Fearing a Toehold for Gay Marriages, Conservatives Rush to Bar the Door*, N.Y. Times, March 6, 1996, at A13.

[18] 28 U.S.C. § 1738C (uscode.house.gov).

[19] 1 U.S.C. § 7 (uscode.house.gov).

[20] *Goodridge v. Department of Public Health*, 798 N.E.2d 941 (Mass. 2003).

[21] 539 U.S. 558 (2003).

[22] 539 U.S. at 577.

[23] 570 U.S. 744 (2013).

[24] 570 U.S. at 753; 26 U.S.C. § 2056(a).

[25] The *Lawrence* case applied the 14th Amendment, whereas the *Windsor* case applied the 5th Amendment. DOMA is a *federal* statute. Challenges to federal laws are based on the clause in the 5th Amendment that prohibits the deprivation of life, liberty, or property without due process of law. *Windsor*, therefore, is a 5th Amendment case. Challenges to *state* laws (such as the state sodomy law of Texas) are based on the clauses in the 14th Amendment that prohibit the deprivation of life, liberty, or property without due process of law and that prohibit the denial of the equal protection of the laws. A case that challenges the constitutionality of a state ban on same-sex marriage will, therefore, be a 14th Amendment case. Both the 5th Amendment and the 14th Amendment have a Due Process Clause, but only the 14th Amendment has an Equal Protection Clause. Such differences, however, are not significant. The U.S. Supreme Court has said that the liberty protected by the 5th Amendment's Due Process Clause includes an equal-protection requirement. In short, there is substantial similarity in how the Court interprets challenges under both the 5th and 14th Amendments.

[26] Tobias Barrington Wolff, *The Three Voices of Obergefell*, L.A. Law., December 2015, at 28, 34.

[27] Kent Greenfield & Adam Winkler, *Kennedy's Shaky Gay Rights Legacy*, N.Y. Times, June 29, 2018, at A25.

[28] *Obergefell v. Hodges*, 135 S. Ct. 2584, 2621-2622 (2015) (Roberts, Dissent).

[29] Katy Steinmetz, *The Supreme Court is No Cakewalk*, Time, June 18, 2018, at 25.

[30] *Masterpiece Cakeshop,Ltd. v. Colorado Civil Rights Com'n*, 138 S. Ct. 1719 (2018).

[31] Adam Liptak, *Groups Counting on the Court's Defender of Gay Rights*, N.Y. Times, July 18, 2017, at A9.

[32] Louisiana Department of Justice, Office of the Attorney General, *Louisiana Laws on Community Property and Covenant Marriage*; Louisiana Revised Statutes Annotated tit. 9, § 273.1.

[33] Laura A. Sanchez & James D. Wright, *Covenant Marriage: The Movement to Reclaim Tradition in America* 117 (2008).

[34] Texas is an exception. A couple in an informal marriage (which is what Texas calls common-law marriages) in Texas does not need to go through a divorce procedure if they have been separated for two years and meet other requirements. Tex. Fam. Code Ann. § 2.401(b).

[35] *Sorensen v. Sorensen*, 100 N.W. 930, 932 (Neb. 1904).

[36] *Collier v. City of Milford*, 537 A.2d 474, 479-480 (Conn. 1998).

[37] *John Crane, Inc. v. Puller*, 899 A.2d 879, 917 (Md. Ct. Spec. App. 2006).

[38] *United States Fidelity & Guarantee Co. v. Henderson*, 53 S.W.2d 811, 816 (Tex. Civ. App. 1932).

[39] 42 U.S.C § 416 (www.ssa.gov/OP_Home/ssact/title02/0216.htm).

[40] Annotated Code of West Virginia, § 48-5-707(a)(1).

CHAPTER 6

Annulment

CHAPTER OUTLINE

ANNULMENT, DIVORCE, AND LEGAL SEPARATION

EFFECTIVE DATE OF THE ANNULMENT

THE DISTINCTION BETWEEN VOID AND VOIDABLE
Grounds That Determine Void versus Voidable
The Necessity of a Court Decision
Annulment Action after Death
Ratification
Conflict of Laws

WHO CAN SUE?

OVERVIEW OF GROUNDS FOR ANNULMENT

GROUNDS THAT RELATE TO THE CAPACITY TO MARRY
Gender
Prior Existing Marriage
Consanguinity and Affinity
Nonage
Physical Disability

GROUNDS THAT RELATE TO THE INTENT TO MARRY
Sham Marriages
Mental Disability
Duress
Fraud

VIOLATION OF TECHNICAL/ PROCEDURAL REQUIREMENTS

CHURCH ANNULMENT

CONFLICT OF LAWS
Conflict-of-Laws Rule in Annulment Actions
Marriage Evasion Statutes

CONSEQUENCES OF AN ANNULMENT DECREE
Legitimacy of Children from an Annulled Marriage
Custody and Child Support
Alimony and Property Division
Revival
Inheritance
Bigamy
Interspousal Immunity in Some Tort Actions
Marital Communications Privilege
Income Tax Status

CHAPTER OBJECTIVES

After completing this chapter, you should be able to:

- Define and distinguish annulment, divorce, and legal separation.
- Identify the kinds of annulment cases brought in the era of no-fault divorce.
- Know why the phrase "annulled marriage" is technically incorrect.
- State the effective date of an annulment.
- Identify the two categories of annulment grounds.
- Distinguish between a voidable marriage and a void marriage.

- Identify who has standing to bring an annulment action.
- List and explain the capacity and the intent/state-of-mind grounds for annulment.
- Know the effect of the last-in-time and the Enoch Arden marriage presumptions.
- Explain how immigration officials treat green-card marriages.
- Distinguish between a civil annulment and a church annulment.

- Explain the conflict-of-laws rule in annulment cases.
- Describe the effect of marriage-evasion statutes.
- Explain the consequences of an annulment on the legitimacy of children, alimony and property division, child custody and child support, inheritance, bigamy, interspousal immunity, marital-communication privilege, and income-tax status.

ANNULMENT, DIVORCE, AND LEGAL SEPARATION

In this chapter, we cover annulment, the first of the three major relationship changes we will examine in the text—see Exhibit 6.1. An **annulment** is a declaration by a court that a valid marriage never existed, even though the parties may have obtained a marriage license, gone through a ceremony, lived together, and perhaps had children together over a period of many years. In contrast, a **divorce** is a declaration by a court that a validly entered marriage is terminated so that the parties are no longer married to each other. In a divorce, there is something to dissolve. In an annulment, there is simply a judicial statement or declaration that the parties never entered into a marital relationship. A divorce is granted because of facts that occurred after the marriage was entered. With few exceptions, an annulment is granted because of facts in existence at the time the parties attempted to enter into the marriage. Lastly, a **legal separation** is a declaration by a court that the spouses can live separate and apart even though they remain married. The legal separation ends the "bed and board" relationship but not the marriage relationship. If the parties want to marry someone else, they must obtain an annulment or a divorce.

Not many annulments are granted in American courts today, but this was not always the case. Years ago, when a divorce was more difficult to obtain, an annulment was a major way to end an unhappy marriage. In the current era of **no-fault divorce**, however, the option of divorce is readily available. Parties, therefore, are less likely to seek an annulment. Nevertheless, the following are reasons why a party might want an annulment:

- *Religion*. A spouse may want to end the marital relationship but is opposed to divorce because divorce is not allowed by his or her religion.

- *Restoring a benefit*. A pension or a government benefit may have ended when a party married. To have the benefit restored, the party may try to annul the marriage.

These are among the themes we will explore in this chapter.

The law of annulment originated in **canon law** of the **ecclesiastical courts**. For centuries in Europe, and later in the American colonies, divorce as we know it today, was unavailable. The main way to end a dysfunctional marriage was to ask an ecclesiastical court to declare that the marriage was defective. If successful, the parties could remarry, not because the court divorced them, but because the court decreed that there never was a valid marriage. By the late nineteenth century, the exclusive jurisdiction of the ecclesiastical courts in this area ended. Laws were enacted allowing parties to obtain an annulment, a divorce, or a legal separation in the secular or civil courts of the country.

annulment
A declaration by a court that a valid marriage never existed. Also called a *declaration of invalidity of marriage* or a *marital annulment*.

divorce
A declaration by a court that a validly entered marriage is terminated so that the parties are no longer married to each other. Also called a *dissolution, marital dissolution,* or *divorce a vinculo matrimonii* (divorce from the chains of marriage).

legal separation
A declaration by a court that the parties can live apart, even though they are still married to each other. Also called a *judicial separation, limited divorce, divorce a mensa et thoro,* or *separation from bed and board*.

no-fault divorce
A divorce that is granted without having to prove marital wrongs that caused the break-up.

canon law
Church law or ecclesiastical law.

ecclesiastical court
A court that resolves disputes on church matters; a court that applies canon law.

EXHIBIT 6.1   Annulment, Divorce, and Legal Separation

Decree of Court	Definition	Also Called	Can Parties Now Marry?
Annulment	A declaration by a court that a valid marriage never existed.	• Declaration of invalidity of marriage • Marital annulment	Yes
Divorce	A declaration by a court that a validly entered marriage is terminated so that the parties are no longer married to each other.	• Dissolution • Marital dissolution • Divorce a vinculo matrimonii	Yes
Legal Separation	A declaration by a court that the spouses can live apart even though they are still married to each other.	• Judicial separation • Limited divorce • Divorce a mensa et thoro • Separation from bed and board	No

Not all states use the same terminology to describe court proceedings for an annulment. The following list contains the most common terms:

- Action for a declaration of invalidity.
- Action for a *declaratory judgment* that the marriage is invalid.
- Action for a judgment of *nullity*.
- Action for annulment.
- Action to declare a marriage void
- Action to declare the nullity of a void marriage.
- Libel for annulment.
- Petition for annulment.
- Petition to issue a judgment of nullity.
- Suit to annul.

nullity
Legally void.

declaratory judgment
A court judgment that establishes (declares) rights or duties but does not order their enforcement.

marriage
The legal union of two persons as spouses with designated rights and obligations to each other.

purported
Claimed, reputed. (See glossary for an additional definition.)

Nullity means legally void. A **declaratory judgment** is a binding judgment that establishes (declares) rights or duties but does not order their enforcement.

It is technically incorrect to refer to an annulment as an "annulled marriage." The word **marriage** means the legal union of two persons as spouses. To bring an action to "annul a marriage" means that you are seeking to invalidate something that never existed. It would be more logical to say that you are seeking to "annul an attempted marriage." (Some states use the phrases *supposed marriage* and *alleged marriage*.) Because of habit and convenience, however, phrases such as *annulled marriage* are widely used throughout family law in spite of the slight lapse in logic this language entails.

The same problem exists with the terms *spouse, husband,* and *wife*. These terms refer to persons in a legal marriage. In the context of annulment actions, some courts prefer the phrases *purported spouse, purported husband, purported wife,* and *purported marriage*. **Purported** means claimed or reputed. Convenience, however, trumps logic, and most courts do not use the qualifiers such as *purported, alleged,* and *supposed* before the words *marriage* and *spouse*. (We will adopt this convenience in the chapter.)

EFFECTIVE DATE OF THE ANNULMENT

Dates are important in annulment actions. In most states, the effective date of an annulment is the date the parties entered into the marriage and not the date a court invalidates the marriage.

> *Paul and Karen are married on March 13, 2015. In 2018, Paul is killed while on the job. Karen claims work benefits from Paul's employer as his surviving widow. Paul's parents, however, assert that the 2015 marriage was invalid and bring an annulment action to have it declared annulled. The marriage is annulled in 2019 and the parents now claim the work benefits as the only surviving relatives of Paul.*

relation-back rule
An act done (or a decision made) at a later time is treated as if it had occurred at an earlier time. Here, a court's invalidation of a marriage after the parties have entered into the marriage is treated as if the invalidity existed at the time the parties entered the marriage.

In this example, a 2015 marriage was declared invalid in 2019. In most states, the effective date of the invalidity would be 2015, not 2019. The invalidity "relates back" to the time when the parties tried to enter the marriage. The invalidity does not begin on the date the court declares the marriage to be invalid. Hence, Karen was not Paul's widow when he died in 2018. The logic of an annulment decree is that Paul never had a widow. Paul's parents, not Karen, are eligible for whatever work benefits that are available.

This is dramatically different from divorce cases. If parties are married in 2015 and divorced in 2019, the effective date of the divorce is 2019, not 2015. When, however, we examine the consequences of annulments later in the chapter, we will see that the courts do not always follow the logic of the **relation-back rule**.

THE DISTINCTION BETWEEN VOID AND VOIDABLE

GROUNDS THAT DETERMINE VOID VERSUS VOIDABLE

To obtain an annulment, grounds (legally sufficient reasons) must be established. There are two categories of grounds for annulment: (1) those that render the marriage void and (2) those that render it voidable. Although both grounds are serious, those that render a marriage void are the most serious because they offend a strong public policy of the state. Before we examine each of these grounds in detail, we need to cover some important points about the void-voidable distinction. Even though some modern courts blur the distinction, it is still a factor in many court decisions. (See Exhibit 6.2.)

THE NECESSITY OF A COURT DECISION

A voidable marriage requires a court decision to establish its invalidity. Voidable marriages are valid unless a court declares them to be invalid. A void marriage is invalid whether or not a court declares it invalid. (A void marriage is void ab initio, meaning that it is invalid from the beginning.) Something is void if it has no legal effect. If, however, something is voidable, it is treated as valid unless it is cancelled or invalidated. Hence, a voidable marriage is valid for all intents and purposes unless someone is successful in convincing a court to declare its invalidity. (This distinction can be critical, as you will see in the *Miller* case opinion later in this chapter.)

Assume that two individuals in a voidable marriage die without anyone bringing an annulment action. The effect of this inaction is that the law treats the marriage as if it is valid. In effect, there is no practical difference between a marriage that complies with all legal requirements and a voidable marriage that no one challenges. Of course, if a voidable marriage is successfully challenged in court, the marriage is declared invalid.

Although there is no need for a court to declare void marriages to be invalid, courts are often asked do so. The reason for this request is that a party may want to use the courts to remove any uncertainty (cloud) about the status of the marriage and to have a public record of the invalidity.

grounds
Reasons that are legally sufficient to obtain a particular remedy or result.

void
Of no legal effect; invalid whether or not a court declares it so.

voidable
Of no legal effect but valid unless cancelled or invalidated.

voidable marriage
A marriage that is invalid but that is treated as valid unless a court declares its invalidity.

void marriage
A marriage that is invalid even if no court ever declares its invalidity.

void ab initio
Invalid from the beginning or from the time something started.

EXHIBIT 6.2   Grounds for Void or Voidable Marriages

GROUNDS THAT RENDER A MARRIAGE VOID:

- Prior existing marriage.
- Consanguinity and affinity—that is, too closely related by blood (*consanguinity*) or by marriage (*affinity*).
- Sham marriage.

GROUNDS THAT RENDER A MARRIAGE VOIDABLE:

- Nonage (underage).
- Physical disability.
- Mental disability.
- Duress.
- Fraud.

ANNULMENT ACTION AFTER DEATH

Can a voidable marriage be declared invalid after the death of one of the spouses? No. A void marriage, however, is treated differently. It can be challenged in court and annulled after the death of one of the parties.

RATIFICATION

ratification
The approval of something after it has occurred. Approval retroactively by agreement, conduct, or any inaction that can reasonably be interpreted as an approval. The verb is *ratify.*

There can be a *ratification* of voidable marriages, but not all void marriages can be ratified. **Ratification** is the approval of something after it has occurred. The approval is manifested by agreement, by conduct, or by any inaction that can be reasonably interpreted as approval.

> *Bill and Gail are married in 2017. In 2018, Bill finds out that Gail lied to him about her age when she agreed to marry him. She was underage at the time but she led him to believe otherwise. They continue living together until 2020 when Bill brings an annulment against Gail on the ground of her being underage when they married.*

cohabit
To live together in an intimate (usually sexual) relationship in the manner of spouses. The noun is *cohabitation.* Although a married couple cohabits, the word is more often used in reference to unmarried couples.

The annulment action will be dismissed. Paul continued to **cohabit** with Gail after he discovered in 2018 that she was underage (nonage) in 2017. This conduct will constitute a ratification of the voidable marriage and will prevent Bill from obtaining the annulment. His conduct—his continued cohabitation—will be interpreted as an approval of the marriage despite the defect of age. This result will apply to all of the grounds discussed in this chapter that render a marriage voidable.

Suppose that Bill discovered in 2018 that Gail was married to Fred when Bill married her in 2017 and that the marriage to Fred had never been dissolved. Does Bill's continued cohabitation after discovering the ground for the annulment constitute a ratification of the marriage, thereby preventing Bill from winning the annulment action in 2020? No. Bill can still bring the annulment action. The ground for the annulment (a prior existing marriage to Fred) renders the marriage void. In most states, you cannot ratify a void marriage.

CONFLICT OF LAWS

Later in this chapter, we will examine what happens when State #1 is asked to recognize a marriage entered into in State #2 under the following circumstances:

> *Ted and Grace marry in State #2, where the marriage is valid. They then move to State #1, where they want to file a joint tax return as a married couple. The marriage, however, would have been invalid if it had been entered into in State #1.*

Will State #1 recognize the State #2 marriage so that Ted and Grace can file a joint return in State #1? The answer to this conflict-of-law question will depend on whether State #1 considers the marriage void or voidable. In general, if it is voidable, State #1 will recognize the marriage, but not if it is void.

WHO CAN SUE?

standing
The right to state a claim or to bring a case and seek relief from a court.

The right to state a claim or to bring an action is called **standing**. Who has standing to bring an annulment action? A number of persons might want the opportunity to annul a particular marriage. Possibilities include:

- *The wrongdoer spouse.* This is the spouse who knowingly did the act that constituted the ground for the annulment. Example: The spouse who commits fraud in order to convince the innocent spouse to enter into the marriage.

- *The innocent spouse.* This spouse did nothing that would give the other spouse grounds to annul the marriage.

- *Parent or guardian ad litem (GAL) of the innocent spouse.*

As we discuss each ground for annulment in this chapter, we will indicate who does and does not have standing to bring the annulment action on that ground. For some grounds, there are no restrictions on who can sue. For others, standing may be denied to the wrongdoer spouse who knowingly did the act that constituted the ground for annulment. This spouse has **dirty hands** and should not be allowed to "profit" from what he or she did by giving him or her standing to bring the annulment. In such cases, the wrongdoing party is prevented (**estopped**) from using an annulment action to get out of what might clearly be an invalid marriage. Suppose that the innocent spouse (who has standing) does not want an annulment. The marriage, therefore, is never invalidated. As we saw in Chapter 5, such a marriage is called a **marriage by estoppel**. Of course, if a spouse cannot obtain an annulment, he or she can terminate the relationship through divorce (if the other spouse is still alive).

For some grounds, a parent or guardian ad litem may have independent standing to bring the annulment action even if the spouses are either unwilling to sue or are prevented from doing so.

Again, we will point out who has standing and who does not have standing when we cover the individual grounds for annulment.

OVERVIEW OF GROUNDS FOR ANNULMENT

There are two main categories of grounds for annulment: (1) capacity grounds and (2) intent grounds. The grounds in both categories constitute **impediments**, which prevent the formation of a valid marriage. First, we will examine those that relate to a party's capacity to marry. **Capacity** is the legal power to do something, such as enter into a contract or a relationship. Then, we will turn to the grounds that focus on whether a party who has the capacity to marry formed the requisite *intent* to marry. See Exhibit 6.3.

guardian ad litem (GAL)
A special guardian (often, but not always, an attorney) appointed by the court to appear in court proceedings on behalf of a person who is a minor, insane, or otherwise incapacitated or under a disability.

dirty hands
Wrongdoing or other inappropriate behavior that would make it unfair or inequitable to allow persons to assert a right or a defense they would normally have. Also called *unclean hands.* A person without dirty hands is said to have *clean hands.*

estopped
Prevented from asserting a right or a defense because it would be unfair or inequitable to allow the assertion. The noun is *estoppel.*

marriage by estoppel
A relationship that is recognized as a marriage because a party is prevented from asserting the invalidity of the marriage even though grounds for its invalidity may exist.

impediment
A legal obstacle that prevents the formation of a valid marriage or other contract.

capacity
The legal power to do something, such as enter into a contract or a relationship. Also called *legal capacity.* (See glossary for an additional meaning.)

EXHIBIT 6.3 Grounds for Annulment

CAPACITY GROUNDS

- Prior existing marriage.
- Consanguinity and affinity: too closely related by blood (consanguinity) or by marriage (affinity).
- Nonage (underage).
- Physical disability.

INTENT OR STATE-OF-MIND GROUNDS

- Sham marriage.
- Mental disability.
- Duress.
- Fraud.

ASSIGNMENT 6.1

List the grounds for annulment in your state. (See General Instructions for the State-Code Assignment in Appendix A.)

GROUNDS THAT RELATE TO THE CAPACITY TO MARRY

GENDER

Until recently, no state recognized same sex-marriage. During this period, a marriage between two men or two women would be void and hence could be annulled. Today, of course, gender cannot be a ground for annulment because same-sex marriage is allowed in all fifty states. The other grounds for annulment, however, still apply. For example, a same-sex marriage can be annulled if one of the same-sex spouses was underage or had a prior existing marriage that was not dissolved.

PRIOR EXISTING MARRIAGE

Prior existing marriage is a capacity ground of annulment. A person lacks the capacity to marry when he or she marries while still in a valid, undissolved marriage with someone else. If a person tries to live with more than one spouse at the same time, it is called **polygamy**. In most states, the existence of a prior undissolved marriage renders the second marriage void. In only a few states is the second marriage voidable.

Entering into a marriage when a prior one exists is called **bigamy**. Bigamy is a crime in most states. Hence, someone facing a civil action of annulment may also have to face a possible criminal **prosecution** for bigamy. One famous historical example of bigamy involved the seventh president of the United States:

In 1791, when U.S. President Andrew Jackson married his wife, Rachel Jackson, he mistakenly thought her first husband had already divorced her. When it was discovered that Rachel was not divorced from her first husband, the president's marriage was considered bigamous. To rectify this situation, the president and Rachel remarried after the divorce was finalized.

Several important *presumptions* need to be considered in annulment cases on the ground of prior existing marriage. A **presumption** is an assumption or inference that a certain fact is true once another fact is established. Most presumptions are rebuttable, meaning that the other side can introduce evidence to try to **rebut** (attack or refute) the presumption. The two major **rebuttable presumptions** in this area of the law are the last-in-time-marriage presumption and the Enoch Arden presumption.

Last-in-Time-Marriage Presumption

When an action is brought to annul a second marriage, defendants—those who oppose the annulment—sometimes will claim that the first marriage ended because of the death of a spouse or because the earlier marriage ended by divorce or annulment. Sometimes, however, marriage records, particularly old ones, are difficult to obtain; and for common-law marriages, there are no records. Consequently, proving the status of a prior marriage can be a monumental task. Was that marriage properly entered? Was it dissolved? To assist parties in this difficult situation, the law has created the **last-in-time-marriage presumption**, which provides that if more than one marriage is alleged to exist, the most recent marriage is presumed to be valid.

In Chapter 7, we will learn that a marriage is presumed to be valid unless someone comes forward and proves its invalidity. Of course, this presumption does not help us in a case involving two marriages. It makes no sense to presume that both marriages are valid. Hence, in such cases, we apply the last-in-time-marriage presumption. The effect of this presumption is that the court will treat the first marriage as having been dissolved by death, divorce, or annulment. Because the presumption is rebuttable, the party seeking to annul the second marriage can attempt to rebut

polygamy
The condition or practice of having more than one spouse at the same time. (*Polygyny* is having more than one wife at the same time; *polyandry* is having more than one husband at the same time.)

bigamy
Marrying while still in a valid undissolved marriage with someone else.

prosecution
(1) Bringing and processing criminal proceedings against someone. The words *prosecution* and *prosecute* can also refer to bringing and processing *civil* proceedings against someone, although the words are more commonly used in criminal proceedings. (2) The attorney representing the government in a criminal case. Also called the *prosecutor*.

presumption
An assumption or inference that a certain fact is true once another fact is established. The presumption is *rebuttable* if a party is allowed to introduce evidence to try to show that the assumption is false. The presumption is *irrebuttable* (conclusive) if a party is not allowed to introduce evidence to try to show that the assumption is false.

rebut
To attack, dispute, or refute.

rebuttable presumption
An assumption or inference of fact that a party will be allowed to try to disprove (rebut) but that will be treated as true if it is not disproved.

last-in-time-marriage presumption
If more than one marriage is alleged to exist, the most recent marriage is presumed to be valid.

the presumption by introducing evidence that the first marriage was not dissolved. Yet proving a negative is not always easy. For example, it can be difficult to find evidence that a divorce has *not* occurred. You would have to go to every county where the spouse lived, check the records, and show that no record of divorce exists.

> *Frank seeks to annul his marriage to Diane because he believes that Diane was married to Ted at the time Frank married her and that the marriage to Ted was never dissolved. Diane does not want her marriage to Frank annulled and she asserts the last-in-time-marriage presumption. Under this presumption, the court will treat her marriage to Ted as having been dissolved and, therefore, her marriage to Frank (the most recent marriage) as valid. Frank, therefore, will lose his annulment action against Diane unless he can prove that the marriage to Ted was not dissolved.*

The value to Diane of the last-in-time-marriage presumption is that she does not have to prove that her marriage to Ted was dissolved; Frank has the burden of proving that it was not dissolved.

Enoch Arden Presumption

Consider the following sequence of events:

- Spouse #1 disappears.
- The left-behind spouse marries spouse #2.
- Spouse #1 reappears after the marriage to spouse #2.

> *Paul marries Cynthia. A few months later, Cynthia disappears. Paul has not heard from her for fifteen years in spite of all his efforts to locate her. Paul then marries Mary in the honest belief that his first wife (Cynthia) is dead. Mary does not know anything about Cynthia. Suddenly Cynthia reappears, and Mary learns about the first marriage. Mary immediately brings an action against Paul to annul her marriage to him on the ground of a prior existing marriage.*

These facts leads us to the second presumption: the **Enoch Arden presumption**. In states that allow this presumption, a spouse is presumed to be dead after being missing without explanation for a designated number of years (often five to seven) despite **due diligence** in attempting to locate him or her. (The name of the presumption comes from the narrative poem Enoch Arden, by Alfred Lord Tennyson, about a sailor who returned to his home years after being shipwrecked to discover that his wife had married again.)

Parties might try to raise the Enoch Arden presumption in the following two different proceedings:

1. In an annulment case such as Mary's action in which the prior existing marriage is raised as a ground for an annulment against Paul.

2. In a criminal case in which the presumption is raised as a defense to the crime of bigamy. In the criminal case, defendants argue that their second marriage was not illegal (bigamous) because the law should presume that the first wife died.

States, however, do not agree on when the Enoch Arden presumption can be used in annulment and criminal cases:

- In most states, Enoch Arden applies only as a defense to a *criminal* prosecution for bigamy. The presumption of death does not apply to annulment proceedings. In these states, the second marriage would be annulled because the first spouse is not presumed to be dead even if he or she never reappears.

- In some states, Enoch Arden applies to annulment proceedings as well as to criminal prosecutions. In the annulment case, however, these states treat the reappearance of the missing spouse in one of two ways: (1) the second marriage is valid and cannot be annulled even if the missing spouse reappears, or (2) the second marriage can be annulled if the missing spouse reappears, so

Enoch Arden presumption
A spouse is presumed to be dead after being missing without explanation for a designated number of years, despite due diligence in attempting to locate him or her.

due diligence
Reasonable efforts to find and verify factual information that is needed to carry out an obligation, to avoid harming someone, or to make an important decision.

that the Enoch Arden presumption is effective in the annulment action only if the missing spouse stays missing.

Exhibit 6.4 summarizes the prior-existing-marriage ground for an annulment.

EXHIBIT 6.4   Summary: Prior Existing Marriage

Definition: A marriage in which one or both parties lacked the capacity to marry because one or both already had a prior valid marriage that had not been dissolved.

Void or Voidable: In most states, the establishment of this ground renders the second marriage void.

Who Can Sue: In most states, either party to the second marriage can bring the annulment action on this ground; both have standing.

Major Defenses:

1. The first spouse is presumed dead (Enoch Arden presumption).
2. The first marriage ended by divorce or annulment.
3. The plaintiff has "dirty hands" (available in a few states).

Is this ground for annulment also a ground for divorce? Yes, in some states, but it is rarely used. It is called an *Enoch Arden divorce*.

Intent

As indicated, bigamy is a crime. In most states, *intent* is an element of the crime so that when entering a second marriage, the spouse must know that the prior marriage had not been dissolved. Intent is not required in an annulment action on the ground of prior existing marriage. The annulment ground can exist even if a spouse innocently (but mistakenly) thought that his or her first spouse died or that the earlier marriage ended by a proper proceeding such as divorce.

The media is always interested in bigamy-related cases. Recently, a woman was prosecuted for applying for twenty-seven marriage licenses over several years as part of an immigration scam to help foreign men obtain green cards. According to a city clerk, "these career brides earn $3,000 to $10,000 per fake marriage."[1] In another widely reported case, a wife initiated a bigamy prosecution after discovering on Facebook that her husband was still married to another woman.[2]

CONSANGUINITY AND AFFINITY

Next, we examine the relationship ground for annulment. People may lack the capacity to marry because they are too closely related to each other. There are two ways that you can be related to someone: by **consanguinity** (blood) and by **affinity** (marriage). Here are examples of an attempted marriage of individuals related by consanguinity and affinity:

consanguinity
Relationship by blood.

affinity
Relationship by marriage rather than by blood.

- A father marries his daughter (consanguinity).
- A sister marries her brother (consanguinity).
- A man marries his son's former wife (affinity).
- A woman marries her stepson (affinity).

Most of the relationship prohibitions on who can marry are based on consanguinity. The state has an interest in preventing genetic disorders that might occur in children of parents related by blood. An additional concern is the possibility of sexual exploitation of vulnerable family members when blood relatives marry, particularly when there is a significant disparity of age between the spouses. Only a few states prohibit marriages of persons related by affinity. Where affinity prohibitions still exist, they mainly cover marriage between stepparents and stepchildren because of the danger of sexual exploitation of children in such relationships.

Not all consanguinity relationships are prohibited. Most states have statutes that indicate which relationships can be the basis of annulments. All states prohibit marriage within the immediate family, such as brother and sister, father and daughter, and grandmother and grandson. Most states prohibit uncle-niece and aunt-nephew marriages. About half the states prohibit first-cousin marriages, but only a few prohibit second-cousin marriages. (In the media, the husband in a cousin-cousin marriage is sometimes referred to as a *cusband*.) States differ on whether persons can marry their adopted sibling. Most states say that they can.

Notes on Consanguinity and Affinity

1. The Uniform Marriage and Divorce Act (§ 207) would prohibit all marriages between ancestors and descendants (e.g., father and daughter, grandmother and grandson); brother-sister marriages; and adopted brother-sister marriages. The act would permit first-cousin marriages and all affinity marriages.

2. The crime of **incest** consists of sexual relations between two people who are too closely related to each other as defined by law. In many states, the relationships that are incestuous under the criminal law are the same relationships that could lead to annulment if the parties married.

incest
Sexual relations between two people who are too closely related to each other as defined by law.

Exhibit 6.5 summarizes the consanguinity and affinity grounds for an annulment.

ASSIGNMENT 6.2

In the following list, you will find pairs of individuals. For each pair, check your state code and answer three questions: Can the individuals marry? If the marriage is prohibited, is it void or voidable? What code section gives you the answer? (See General Instructions for the State-Code Assignment in Appendix A.)

	Can They Marry?	Void or Voidable?	Code Section
Mother/son			
Father/daughter			
Brother/sister			
Grandparent/grandchild			
Uncle/niece or aunt/nephew			
First cousin/first cousin			
Second cousin/second cousin			
Half-brother/half-sister			
Father-in-law/daughter-in-law			
Mother-in-law/son-in-law			
Brother-in-law/sister-in-law			
Stepparent/stepchild			
Adoptive parent/adoptive child			

(If your state code does not provide a direct answer to any of the above questions, you may have to check court opinions. See General Instructions for the Court-Opinion Assignment in Appendix A.)

EXHIBIT 6.5   Summary: Consanguinity or Affinity

Definition: A marriage by parties who lack the capacity to marry because their relationship by consanguinity (blood) or by affinity (marriage) is prohibited by law.

Void or Voidable: In most states, the prohibited marriage is void.

Who Can Sue: Either party can be the plaintiff in the annulment action; both have standing.

Is this annulment ground also a ground for divorce? Yes, in most states.

NONAGE

nonage
Below the required minimum age to enter into a relationship or to perform a task. Minority.

In order to marry, a party must be a certain minimum age, e.g., sixteen with parental or court consent and eighteen without needing consent. A person marrying below the minimum age lacks the capacity to marry. The ground to annul a marriage in which one or both spouses are underage is called **nonage**. At one time, states imposed different age requirements for males and females. At common law, the minimum age to marry was fourteen for males and twelve for females. In most states, this has been changed either by a statute or by a court ruling that this kind of sex discrimination is unconstitutional.

Within a state, the minimum age may differ depending upon whether:

• Parental or court consent exists.

• The female is pregnant.

• A child has already been born out of wedlock.

Where parental consent is required, the consent of one parent is usually sufficient. In some states, a court may have the power to authorize a marriage of parties who are underage even if a parent has refused to consent to the marriage. In these states, the court will consider factors such as the maturity of the parties, their financial resources, and whether children (to be born or already born) would be "illegitimate" if the marriage were not authorized. Still another variation found in some states is that the courts have the authority to require that underage individuals go through premarital counseling as a condition of being allowed to marry.

If an underage child marries, most states allow him or her to sue for annulment, as can the person he or she attempted to marry. States differ, however, on whether the spouse who lied about his or her age can obtain an annulment on the ground of nonage. Because of this spouse's *dirty hands*, some states refuse to allow him or her to bring the annulment action. Other states allow it despite the lie.

A parent or guardian ad litem also has standing to seek the annulment in most states even if the minor does not want the annulment. There are, however, time limits. The annulment cannot be brought if the parties cohabit after the child reaches the statutory minimum age. Such conduct constitutes a *ratification* of the marriage.

Exhibit 6.6 summarizes the nonage ground for an annulment.

EXHIBIT 6.6   Summary: Nonage

Definition: A marriage in which one or both parties lacked the capacity to marry because at the time of the marriage one or both were under the minimum age to marry and did not have special permission to marry.

Void or Voidable: In most states, the marriage is voidable. In some states, however, a marriage of someone below the age of seven is void.

(continued)

Exhibit 6.6 *(continued)*

Who Can Sue: Either party in most states. In some states, the spouse who lied about his or her age cannot sue for annulment on the ground of nonage. In many states, a parent or guardian ad litem also has standing.

Major Defenses:

1. The party who lied about his or her age lacks standing in some states.

2. The under-aged party affirmed or ratified the marriage by cohabitation after that party reached the statutory minimum age.

Is this ground for annulment also a ground for divorce? Yes, in some states.

PHYSICAL DISABILITY

A person with certain physical disabilities lacks the capacity to marry. States differ on which disabilities constitute incapacity. Examples include impotence (the most commonly cited in annulment statutes), epilepsy, pulmonary tuberculosis in advanced stages, and venereal disease.

Impotence

Impotence is the inability to have sexual intercourse. In some states, it is called an incapacity to consummate the marriage. An allegation of impotence can raise several issues:

- Inability to copulate that is incurable.
- Inability to copulate that is curable.
- Sterility (infertility).
- Refusal to have sexual intercourse.

In most states, only the first situation, an incurable inability to copulate, is a ground for annulment. The standard for incurability is not the impossibility of a cure; rather, it is the present unlikelihood of a cure. The standard for copulation is the ability to perform the physical sex act naturally, without pain or harm to the other spouse. The "mere" fact that a spouse does not derive pleasure from the act is not what is meant by an inability to copulate. The *refusal* to copulate is not an inability to copulate, although the refusal is sometimes an indication of (is evidence of) the inability to copulate.

In most states, it makes no difference whether the inability is due to physical (organic) causes or to psychogenic or emotional causes, nor does it matter whether the person is impotent only with his or her spouse. If normal coitus is not possible with one's spouse, whatever the cause, the ground exists. There once was a rule called the doctrine of triennial cohabitation under which a man was presumed to be impotent if his wife remained a virgin after three years of cohabitating together. The doctrine no longer applies today.

It is a defense to an annulment action that the party seeking the annulment knew of the party's impotence (or other physical disability) at the time of the marriage and yet still went through with the marriage. Finally, time limits may exist for bringing the action on this ground. For example, a state may bar the action if it is not brought within a designated number of years (e.g., four or five years) after the marriage was entered.

Venereal Disease (Sexually Transmitted Disease, STD)

In a few states, marrying while suffering from a communicable sexually transmitted disease (STD) is a ground for annulment, although in most states it is not. In some states, it is a crime to knowingly marry or have sexual

impotence
The inability to engage in sexual intercourse. For males, it is often the inability to achieve or maintain an erection.

copulate
To engage in sexual intercourse.

sterility
Inability to have children; infertility.

triennial cohabitation
A rule by which a man was presumed to be impotent if his wife remained a virgin after three years of cohabitating together.

intercourse with someone who has an infectious STD. A state might have a statutory requirement that parties contemplating marriage go through a medical examination as a condition of obtaining a marriage license. An important objective of this exam is to determine whether either party has a communicable STD. For a number of reasons, however, a spouse might marry despite having an STD:

• The medical exam may have failed to detect the STD that was present.
• The parties were able to falsify the results of the medical exam.
• The parties did not take the medical exam because they entered a common-law marriage in a state where such marriages are allowed.

Note on Testing for HIV

In some states, applicants for marriage must be given information about the human immunodeficiency virus (HIV) and acquired immunodeficiency syndrome (AIDS).[3] The applicants must sign a statement that they have been offered a list of sites in the state that offer HIV tests. At one time, Illinois went even further by requiring that every applicant be tested "to determine whether either of the parties to the proposed marriage has been exposed to HIV or any other identified causative agent of AIDS." During the first six months of the program, the number of marriage licenses issued in Illinois dropped by 22.5 percent, and the number of licenses issued to Illinois residents in surrounding states increased significantly.[4] Rather than bother with the test, many couples simply crossed state lines to obtain their marriage license. Consequently, Illinois abolished its program of mandatory testing. Today Illinois law simply provides that county clerks must give marriage applicants a brochure on "sexually transmitted diseases and inherited metabolic diseases."[5]

Exhibit 6.7 summarizes the physical disability ground for an annulment.

ASSIGNMENT	6.3

Should Congress pass a federal law requiring every state to impose mandatory HIV testing? What problems would such a law solve and cause?

EXHIBIT 6.7 Summary: Physical Disability

Definition: A marriage in which one or both parties lacked the capacity to marry because one or both suffered from impotence or other designated physical disability.

Void or Voidable: Voidable.

Who Can Sue: In most states, either spouse; both have standing. In some states, the nondisabled spouse who knew of the other's disability at the time of the marriage cannot sue.

Major Defense:

The plaintiff waited too long to bring the annulment action on this ground.

Is this ground for annulment also a ground for divorce? Yes, in some states.

GROUNDS THAT RELATE TO THE INTENT TO MARRY

SHAM MARRIAGES

An essential element of a marriage contract is the intent to enter into a marriage. Examine the following four cases in which couples went through all the marriage formalities (obtaining a license, having the blood test, etc.) and completed the marriage ceremony:

- Dennis and Janet enter into a marriage solely to obtain permanent resident alien status for Dennis, who is not a U.S. citizen. Janet is a citizen. Dennis wants to use his marriage status to avoid deportation by immigration officials. They do not want to live together.

- After a great deal of laughing and boasting at a college graduation party, Edna dares Stanley to marry her. He accepts the dare and they marry. They live in different countries to which they return after the marriage, never wanting to live together.

- Frank and Helen have an affair. Helen becomes pregnant. Neither wants the child to be born illegitimate. They never want to live together, but decide to be married solely for the purpose of having the child born legitimate. They agree that the child will live with Helen.

- Rachel and Ken have been dating for a number of months. They decide to get married "just to try it out." They feel this is a modern and rational way of determining whether they will want to stay together forever. Both fully understand that there will be "no hard feelings" if either of them wants to dissolve the marriage after six months.

All four of these couples go through the steps required to become married. To any reasonable outside observer of their outward actions, nothing unusual happened. They all intended to go through a marriage ceremony; they all intended to go through the outward appearances of entering into a marriage contract. Subjectively, however, each couple had a hidden agenda.

According to traditional contract principles, if individuals give clear outward manifestations of mutual assent to enter into a contract, the law will bind them to their contract, even though their unspoken motive was *not* to enter into a binding contract. Many courts, however, apply a different principle to marriage contracts. The first three couples above engaged in sham marriages—that is, the parties never intended to live together as husband and wife. They had a limited purpose of avoiding deportation, displaying braggadocio, or avoiding illegitimacy of a child. Many courts would declare such marriages to be void and would grant an annulment to either party. There is a minority of courts, however, that would conclude that a valid marriage exists once the formalities of marriage are followed regardless of the unspoken objectives or motives of the parties.

Assume that the first three couples cohabit for a period of time *after* they go through the marriage ceremony. Such cohabitation is strong evidence that they *did* intend to be married at the time of the ceremony and that they are now inventing reasons to get out of the marriage through an annulment.

What about the fourth case in which Rachel and Ken entered into a *trial marriage*? The fact that they cohabited is evidence that they intended to be married at the time they entered into the marriage contract. Most courts would find this marriage valid and deny an annulment to anyone who later claims that the parties never intended to assume the marital status. It cannot be said that they married in jest or that they married for a limited purpose. The fact that they did not promise to live together forever as husband and wife does not mean that they lacked the intent to be married at the time they entered into the marriage.

Exhibit 6.8 summarizes the sham ground for an annulment.

sham marriage
A pretend or counterfeit marriage in which parties never intended to live together as husband and wife.

EXHIBIT 6.8　Summary : Sham Marriage

Definition: A marriage in which one or both parties lacked the intent to marry in spite of the fact that they voluntarily went through all the formalities of a marriage. The parties never intended to live together as husband and wife.

Void or Voidable: Void.

Who Can Sue: Either party; both have standing.

Major Defense: The parties did have the intention to marry at the time they entered into the marriage ceremony. A major item of evidence that this intention existed is that they cohabited after the ceremony. (*Note:* In some states, the annulment will be denied if the parties went through all the outward formalities of the marriage no matter what their unspoken objective was.)

Is this ground for annulment also a ground for divorce? Usually not.

Sham Marriages and Immigration Law

alien
A person who was born outside the United States, is still a subject of a foreign nation, and has not been naturalized in the United States.

green-card marriage
A marriage of a foreigner (alien) with an American citizen that entitles the foreigner to permanent resident status in the United States.

A green card entitles an immigrant or **alien** to permanent resident status in the United States. One way to obtain a green card is to enter into a marriage in good faith with a U.S. citizen. Such a marriage is sometimes referred to as a **green-card marriage**. The marriage, however, is a sham marriage if the parties never intended to be married and were simply seeking the alien's legal entry into the country. In a green-card marriage, the alien can be deported and the marriage annulled.

To deter immigration-related marriage fraud, aliens deriving their immigrant status based on a marriage of less than two years are classified as *conditional* immigrants. To remove their conditional status, the immigrants must file an application with the U.S. Citizenship and Immigration Services during the 90-day period before their second-year anniversary of receiving conditional status. If the aliens cannot show that the marriage is a valid one, their conditional immigrant status may be terminated and they become deportable. There must be proof that the couple has maintained a valid marriage during the two-year period. As part of this proof, immigration officials interview the parties separately and together. In these official interviews, the spouses are asked questions that a truly married couple would be expected to know about each other. For example, each spouse might be asked the following questions in separate interviews:

- How did you meet?
- When did you meet each other's families?
- What was the wedding like and who attended?
- What's the color of your spouse's toothbrush?
- Where do you keep the laundry hamper?
- Who cooks the meals? What did you eat the last time you had a meal together?
- What is your spouse's favorite music?
- What did the two of you do last New Year's Eve?
- What did your spouse wear on your wedding day? Where did you go to celebrate?
- What is your spouse's birthday?

- How much do you pay for rent?
- What piece of jewelry means the most to you and to your spouse?

If the interviewer finds significant discrepancies in the answers given during the separate interviews, the application to remove their conditional status (and hence the green card itself) can be denied and the alien can face deportation.[6]

Sham Marriages and College Tuition

In most states, public universities have different tuition rates for in-state students and out-of-state students. In California, it can take up to two years for out-of-state students to establish residency so that they qualify for the substantially lower in-state tuition fees. One of the requirements is that students be financially independent of their parents. Simply saying you are independent is not sufficient. Being married, however, does qualify as independence.

Recently, a student from the Midwest attending a state university in California posted on Facebook that she was looking for a husband from California. "An out-of-state student whom she did not know responded to her [Facebook] post, and they married in 2007, the summer before her junior year. She graduated in 2009 and estimated that the marriage had saved her $50,000. The couple has divorced."[7] Websites exist that help students enter into such "marriages of convenience." Because the parties to such marriages never intended to marry (and rarely live together as husband and wife), the marriages could be annulled as shams.

ASSIGNMENT 6.4

a. Elaine is twenty years old, and Philip, a bachelor, is seventy-five. Philip asks Elaine to marry him. Philip has terminal cancer and wants to die a married man. He and Elaine know that he probably has less than six months to live and that he will spend the rest of his life in a hospital bed. Under their arrangement, she does not have to continue as his wife after six months if he is still alive. They go through all the formal requirements to be married. On the day after the marriage ceremony, Elaine changes her mind and wants to end the marriage. Can she obtain an annulment? Philip does not want the marriage annulled. (See General Instructions for the Legal-Analysis Assignment in Appendix A.)

b. Draft a set of interrogatories from Philip to Elaine. Draft a separate set of interrogatories from Elaine to Philip. (See General Instructions for the Interrogatory Assignment in Appendix A.)

Multiple Purposes to Marry

In the *Miller* case, which follows, Edward Christoph was alleged to have entered into a common-law marriage to avoid prosecution for a crime. Even if your state does not recognize common-law marriages (see Exhibit 5.1 in Chapter 5), the case is important because the issue would be the same if he had entered a ceremonial marriage in order to avoid criminal prosecution. The case raised the question of what to do when someone has multiple purposes or intentions when entering into a marriage and cautions us to distinguish motive to marry and intention to marry.

CASE | In the Interest of Melissa Miller
301 Pa. Super. 511, 448 A.2d 25 (1982)
Superior Court of Pennsylvania.

Background: *Edward Christoph was a thirty-six-year-old English teacher who began a romantic relationship with one of his eighth-grade students, Melissa Miller (also called Missy). She was fourteen years old at the time. Her mother had been having difficulty with her at home. Melissa would sneak out of the house through her bedroom window in the early morning hours and stay away for three or four hours. Her mother found letters to Melissa from Christoph that said, "You gave yourself fully," and "I love you." When the police began investigating Christoph for sexual involvement with a minor, he consulted an attorney who advised him how to enter a common-law marriage. He then entered into a common-law marriage with Melissa. (At the time, common-law marriages were allowed in Pennsylvania. Though the minimum age to enter into a ceremonial marriage was sixteen, the age of consent to enter into a common-law marriage in the state was seven.) The mother asked the state to declare Melissa to be a dependent child because of her incorrigibility. The juvenile division of the lower court did so and ordered her placed in a foster home. Since Christoph's motive in marrying Melissa was to avoid criminal prosecution, the court also invalidated the common-law marriage. Melissa, as appellant, appealed this decision in the Superior Court of Pennsylvania. She did not want the marriage invalidated.*

Decision on Appeal: *The Superior Court of Pennsylvania reversed the lower court's order. The common-law marriage was valid. Melissa should not have been declared a dependent child.*

OPINION OF THE COURT

Judge SPAETH delivered the opinion of the court. . . .

Mr. Christoph testified that his motive [in entering the common-law marriage] was that appellant should "be my wife" and that his understanding, when he told her this, was that no criminal charges were going to be brought against him:

Q. What did you say to Melissa . . . on that occasion?
A. I said, "I marry you, Melissa." . . .
Q. And what did you intend when you said you married her?
A. I intended that she be my wife.
Q. And as your wife, what was your intention towards her?
A. To take her home to live with me as my wife.
Q. Did you recognize any responsibility when you said these words?
A. Yes.
Q. What were the responsibilities that you recognized?
A. To take her, provide a home and all the necessities that you would normally provide for your wife.
Q. Mr. Christoph, at the time this alleged marriage is to have taken place between you and Missy, do you know—were

you aware of the fact that the police were investigating you?
A. I had talked to the police at the time, yes.
Q. Were you afraid that charges would be filed against you by the police as a result of your involvement with Missy.
A. No.
Q. You were not afraid of that?
A. No.
Q. The crime, corrupting the moral[s] of minors, have you ever heard of that at the time you got married to Missy?
A. Yes, I did.
Q. Did you have any concerns at the time this alleged marriage is to have taken place with you being charged by the police.
A. No.
Q. Why not?
A. Because when I talked to Detective Slupski he said . . . he was going to recommend to the D.A. that no charges be brought....

Mr. Christoph's sister, Virginia Byers, who was a witness to the marriage ceremony, testified that "one of Mr. Christoph's express motives in marrying Melissa Miller was to avoid criminal prosecution." . . . However, the sister also testified that another of Mr. Christoph's motives was that he loved appellant. . . . It seems to us that the fairest inference to be drawn from the evidence is that Mr. Christoph may have had at least two motives for marrying appellant—his love for her, and his desire to avoid criminal prosecution for his relationship with her. We find no support in the record for the lower court's assignment of priority to the second of these motives. . . .

Accepting the lower court's finding that Mr. Christoph married appellant to avoid criminal prosecution, still, we are unable to uphold its order. For contrary to the court's opinion, such a motive does not invalidate a common law marriage.

The controlling decision is *Estate of Gower,* 445 Pa. 554, 284 A.2d 742 (1971). In *Gower,* as here, the parties had by words in the present tense expressed their intent to marry one another. The lower court nevertheless held the marriage invalid because the appellant's motive in entering into the marriage was to avoid conscription for military service. Reversing, the Supreme Court held that "[t]he reason or motive underlying a decision to marry is not relevant to a finding of the *intention* to marry." Id. at 557, 284 A.2d at 744. (emphasis in original). Therefore, the appellant's motive to avoid conscription could not render invalid their otherwise valid common law marriage.

The record here establishes—and the lower court did not question—appellant's and Mr. Christoph's *intention* to marry. The fact—as the lower court found it to be—that Mr. Christoph's *motive*

(continued)

was to avoid prosecution could not render invalid their otherwise valid common law marriage. . . .

We have not overlooked the arguments of counsel for appellant's mother, urging that we re-examine the doctrine of common law marriage, and either abolish it or align the age of consent [for a common law marriage, 7] to that required for statutory marriage [16]. However, we have declined previous opportunities to abolish or modify the doctrine of common law marriage. . . . Past efforts in the Legislature to abolish common law marriage have failed. . . .

In conclusion, we wish to note that neither have we overlooked the anguish that this marriage has caused appellant's mother. We may hope that her fears are unfounded, as they may be, for the most devoted mother is sometimes mistaken about what is good for her child. But if we knew that the marriage would prove unhappy and short, that would not deflect us from our decision. Our responsibility is to interpret and apply the law. If a marriage is lawful, that is the end of our inquiry. For as judges, we are agents of the State, and whether a lawful marriage is happy or unhappy is none of the State's affair.

Reversed.

ASSIGNMENT 6.5

a. Why couldn't the *Miller* marriage be annulled?

b. Assume that Edward Christoph filed for divorce the day after the statute of limitations for corrupting the morals of a minor expired. If Melissa Miller then filed for an annulment, do you think Judge Spaeth would have reached a different result?

Sham Marriages and Statutory Rape

Matthew was twenty years old when he started dating twelve-year-old Chrystal in Nebraska. Their sexual relationship began when she was thirteen years old. When she became pregnant, they traveled to neighboring Kansas where the minimum age for a girl to marry is twelve if her parents consent. Chrystal's parents gave their consent. The minimum age to marry in their own state of Nebraska is 17. Annulment was not an issue because Matthew, Chrystal, and her parents did not want the marriage to end.

In addition to the fact that Chrystal was under age for a valid marriage in Nebraska, there was the separate issue of statutory rape. Matthew had sexual relations with a thirteen-year-old girl *before* and after the marriage. In Nebraska, it is **statutory rape** for a person over eighteen to have sexual relations with someone under age fifteen. Consequently, when the couple returned to Nebraska, Matthew was convicted of a sex crime (called sexual assault in the first degree) and received a sentence of eighteen to thirty months in prison. It was not a defense to the criminal charge of statutory rape that Chrystal had given her consent to the sexual relations nor that the couple was validly married.

One editorial commented, "Prosecuting this case should send a warning to other adults who imagine they can turn sex crimes into romance by marrying their victims."[8]

statutory rape
Sexual intercourse with a person under a designated age even if the latter consents.

MENTAL DISABILITY

A primary reason *mental disability* is a ground for annulment is to prevent people from marrying who are incapable of understanding the nature and responsibilities of the marriage relationship. Unfortunately, however, mental disability is very difficult to define. Various state statutes use different terms to describe this condition, such as insane, want of understanding, unsound mind, idiot, weak-minded, feeble-minded, mentally retarded, lack of mental capacity, imbecile, lunatic, incapable of consenting to a marriage, mentally ill, legally incompetent, mental defective, etc. One court provided the following definition:

> While there has been a hesitancy on the part of the courts to judicially define the phrase "unsound mind," it is established that such term has reference to the mental capacity of the parties at the very moment of inception of the marriage contract. Ordinarily, lack of mental capacity, which renders a party incapable of entering into a valid marriage contract, must be such that it deprives him of the ability to understand the objects of marriage, its ensuing duties and undertakings, its responsibilities and relationship. There is a general agreement of the authorities that the terms "unsound mind" and "lack of mental capacity" carry greater import than eccentricity or mere weakness of mind or dullness of intellect.[9]

Not all states would agree with every aspect of this definition of mental disability, although, in general, it is consistent with the definitions used by many courts.

Presumption of Mental Competence

All individuals are presumed to be sane (mentally competent) unless the contrary is proven. Suppose that someone was once committed to a mental institution and, upon release, seeks to be married. Surely, the fact of prior institutionalization does not prove that the person is *presently* incapable of understanding the marriage contract at the time he or she attempts to marry. Hence, prior institutionalization is not, in and of itself, sufficient to establish the mental-disability ground for annulment.

Assume that a person is mentally disabled but marries during a brief period of mental health before relapsing again to his or her prior state of mental disability. The marriage took place during what is called a **lucid interval**, and many states will validate such a marriage if there was cohabitation. Furthermore, some states will deny the annulment if the parties freely cohabited during a lucid interval at *any* time after the marriage was entered even if one or both parties were not lucid at the time the marriage was entered.

Mental Disability and the Influence of Drugs and Alcohol

Suppose that a person is intoxicated or under the influence of drugs at the time the marriage contract is entered. In most states, this, too, would be a ground for annulment if the alcohol or drugs rendered the person incapable of understanding the marriage contract. Nevada law allows annulments for "want of understanding" that renders a party incapable of assenting to marriage.[10] Most of the cases interpreting this provision have involved persons who were intoxicated at the time of the marriage.

Exhibit 6.9 summarizes the mental-disability ground for an annulment.

lucid interval
A period of time during which a mentally ill or insane person had the mental capacity to understand what he or she was doing before the mental illness or insanity returned.

EXHIBIT 6.9   Summary: Mental Disability

Definition: A marriage in which one or both parties lacked the intent to marry because one or both were unable to understand the marriage contract and the duties of marriage at the time they attempted to enter into the marriage due to mental illness or to the influence of alcohol or drugs.

Void or Voidable: Voidable in most states.

Who Can Sue: In some states, only the mentally ill person (or his or her parent or guardian ad litem) can bring the annulment action. In other states, only the mentally healthy person can sue. In many states, either can sue; both have standing.

(continued)

Exhibit 6.9 *(continued)*

Major Defenses:

1. The marriage occurred during a lucid interval.
2. After the marriage began, there was a lucid interval during which the parties freely cohabited.

Is this ground for annulment also a ground for divorce? Yes, in most states.

Mental Illness in Civil and Criminal Cases

Mental illness can be an issue in different kinds of civil and criminal cases. The definition of *mental illness* may not be the same in all of these cases. The differences can be slight or substantial. A state may have one standard of mental illness that will disable a person from being able to marry, another standard that will disable a person from being able to enter an ordinary business contract and handle his or her business affairs, another standard that will disable a person from being able to write a will, and still another standard to determine whether a person has the mental capacity to commit a crime.

DURESS

Duress is the unlawful use of force or threats to pressure or compel someone to do something he or she does not want to do. Anyone forced to consent to marry does not have the requisite intent to be married. There are four main ways to commit duress:

- Physical violence.
- Threats of physical violence.
- Malicious or groundless threats of criminal prosecution.
- Malicious or groundless threats of civil litigation.

Applying physical force or threatening its use is clearly sufficient for this ground. If an individual is faced with a choice between a wedding and a funeral and chooses the wedding, the resulting marriage will be annulled as one induced by duress. The same is true if the choice is between bodily harm and marriage.

Suppose, however, that the choice does not involve physical violence or the threat of physical violence. Consider the following example of duress:

George is courting Linda. They have sexual relations several times. Linda announces that she is pregnant. Linda's father is furious at George and threatens to "turn him in" to the county district attorney to prosecute him for the crime of statutory rape (Linda is underage). Furthermore, Linda and her father will sue George in the county civil court for support of the child. On the other hand, no criminal prosecution will be brought and no civil action will be initiated if George agrees to marry Linda. George agrees, and the wedding promptly takes place. After the wedding, it becomes clear that Linda was not pregnant; everyone made an honest mistake. George then brings an action to annul the marriage on the ground of duress.

Most courts would rule against George and deny him the annulment if he had a choice in deciding whether to enter into the marriage despite the threat of criminal and civil litigation. The court, however, might rule differently if Linda's father had held a gun to George's head and threatened to shoot him if he did not marry Linda. Faced with a literal "shotgun wedding," George has a good annulment case.

duress
The unlawful use of force or threats to pressure or compel someone to do something he or she does not want to do. Illegal coercion.

malicious
1. Pertaining to a wrongful act that is done intentionally and without just cause or excuse.
2. Pertaining to conduct that is certain or almost certain to cause harm.

In most states, marriages induced by duress are voidable rather than void, but only the innocent party will have standing to bring the annulment action on that ground. If, however, this innocent party voluntarily cohabited with the "guilty" party (i.e., the one who did the coercing) after the effects of the duress have worn off, then the annulment action will be denied on the theory that there has been a ratification of the marriage.

Exhibit 6.10 summarizes the duress ground for an annulment.

EXHIBIT 6.10   Summary: Duress

Definition: A marriage in which a party lacked the intent to marry because he or she was induced to enter into the marriage by unlawful force or threats.

Void or Voidable: Voidable in most states.

Who Can Sue: The party who was coerced. In some states, his or her parent or guardian ad litem also has standing.

Major Defenses:

1. The plaintiff did not believe the threat of violence and therefore was not coerced by it.
2. The plaintiff has "dirty hands" and lacks standing because this is the party who used duress.
3. The plaintiff voluntarily cohabited with the defendant after the effects of the duress had worn off (ratification).

Is this ground for annulment also a ground for divorce? Yes, in some states.

FRAUD

fraud
An intentionally false statement of fact that (a) is material, (b) is made to induce reliance by the plaintiff, and (c) results in harm because of the reliance. Also called *deceit*, intentional *misrepresentation*.

Fraud is an intentionally false statement of fact that is material, made to induce reliance by the plaintiff, and results in harm because of the reliance. A valid marriage requires an intent to marry, but the intent is compromised if the decision to marry has a foundation in fraud. In short, a spouse-to-be intends one thing and gets another!

Generally, for fraud to be a ground of annulment, the defendant must intentionally misrepresent or conceal a critically important fact and the person deceived must rely upon this fact in the decision to enter into the marriage. Not every false representation, however, will be sufficient to grant an annulment. As one court put it:

> [T]he fact that a brunette turned to a blond overnight, or that the beautiful teeth were discovered to be false, or the ruddy pink complexion gave way suddenly to pallor, or that a woman misstated her age or was not in perfect health, would lead no court to annul the marriage for fraud.[11]

The Fraud Must Be Material

material
(1) Serious and substantial. (2) Important enough to influence the decision that was made.

What kind of false representation *is* ground for an annulment? Many courts require the representation to be **material** and essential. A representation is material if it pertains to something that was important enough to influence the decision to enter into the marriage. Even a blatant and serious lie would *not* be material if a person knew about the lie and decided to enter the marriage anyway.

The Essentials Test

essentials test
Did the matter go to the heart or essence of the marriage or relationship?

A representation is essential if it pertains to the heart or core of the marital relationship. (This is the **essentials test**.) Most courts say that the essentials are those marital duties that relate to sexual relations and having children. An example would be a man who misrepresents his intention to have children or who conceals a sexually transmitted disease from his partner. In general, misrepresentations about one's wealth ("I'm very well off"), health ("I am cancer-free"), character ("I never drink"), or affection ("I love you very much") would *not* be about the essentials.

It should be noted, however, that some states take a broader view of what is essential. Such states say that something is essential if it is *vital* to the marriage relationship, which can encompass matters other than sexual relations and having children. An example is a misrepresentation about one's religion. In these states, lying about whether one is a practicing Catholic or an observant Jew might be considered vital to the marriage and serious enough to warrant the annulment on the ground of fraud.

Can a man obtain an annulment on the ground of fraud if his wife lied about whether she became pregnant by him before the marriage? If she is pregnant by another man and falsely tells her husband that he is the father, many states would grant the annulment on the ground of fraud.

Intentional Misrepresentation

The state of mind of the deceiving party is critical. In most states, there must be an *intentional misrepresentation* of fact or an *intentional concealment* of fact. See the first two forms of communication in Exhibit 6.11 on the methods by which false facts are communicated. The third and fourth forms (*innocent nondisclosure* and *innocent misrepresentation*) will not be sufficient in most states.

Sometimes it is difficult to categorize a misrepresentation. For example:

> One hour after Joe marries Mary, he gets on a bus and disappears forever. They never had sexual relations before or after marriage and never discussed the subject.

From Joe's conduct, we may be able to draw an *inference* that at the time he married Mary, he never intended to consummate the marriage. More evidence of

EXHIBIT 6.11 Forms of Communication in Fraud Cases

1. Just before their marriage, Joe tells Mary that he is anxious to have children with her. In fact, he intends to remain celibate after their marriage.	1. Joe's statement about children is an *intentional misrepresentation* of fact.
2. Joe says nothing about his planned celibacy because he knows that if he tells Mary, she will not marry him. He says nothing about children or celibacy, and the subject never comes up before their marriage.	2. Joe's silence is an *intentional concealment* of fact.
3. Joe does not tell Mary that he intends to remain celibate after the wedding because he incorrectly assumed that Mary already knew this fact.	3. Joe's silence is an *innocent* (or *good faith*) *nondisclosure* of fact. It was not intentional. At worst, it was a careless nondisclosure of fact.
4. Before their marriage, Joe tells Mary that he is a virgin (which is true) but that he definitely is able to have children and wants to have them with her after they marry. To his surprise, Joe finds out that he is impotent.	4. Joe's statement about his ability to have children is an *innocent* (or *good faith*) *misrepresentation* of fact. It was not intentional. At worst, it was a careless misrepresentation of fact.

misrepresentation, however, would be needed to determine whether the annulment could be granted on the ground of fraud.

In most states, marriages induced by fraud are voidable rather than void, but only the innocent party will have standing to bring the annulment action on that ground. If, however, this innocent party voluntarily cohabited with the "guilty" party (i.e., the one who committed the fraud) after learning of the fraud, then the annulment action will be denied on the theory that there has been a ratification of the marriage.

Exhibit 6.12 summarizes the fraud ground for an annulment.

EXHIBIT 6.12 Summary: Fraud

Definition: A marriage in which one of the parties lacked the intent to marry because of an intentional misrepresentation or intentional concealment of a fact that was material and essential (or in some states, was vital) to the marriage.

Void or Voidable: Voidable in most states.

Who Can Sue: The innocent party. In some states, his or her parent or guardian ad litem also has standing.

Major Defenses:

1. The fraud was not about an essential fact or was not about a vital fact.
2. The fraud was not material; the plaintiff did not rely on the fraud in his or her decision to marry.
3. The fraud occurred after the marriage was entered into (again, no reliance).
4. After the plaintiff discovered the fraud, he or she consummated the marriage or otherwise freely cohabited with the fraudulent party (ratification).
5. The misrepresentation or nondisclosure was innocent; it was made in good faith with no intention to deceive.
6. The plaintiff has no standing to bring the annulment action, because the plaintiff was the deceiver.

Is this ground for annulment also a ground for divorce? Yes, in some states.

I Take This Man for Richer Only: Who Wants to Marry a Multimillionaire?

At one time, Fox TV aired a program called *Who Wants to Marry a Multimillionaire?* in which a bachelor selected a bride from among fifty contestants he had never met before the show. Immediately after his selection, marriage vows were exchanged before 23 million viewers. Apparently, however, the honeymoon of the instant bride and groom did not go well. Soon after the newlyweds returned, the bride asked a Nevada court for an annulment based on fraud. They had not consummated their relationship. The bride became disenchanted when she learned that a prior girlfriend had obtained a restraining order against him for **domestic violence (DV)**. His failure to disclose his "history of problems with prior girlfriends," she told the court, constituted fraud. This was not a particularly strong argument, however, because she knew that one of the show's main attractions was that she was willing to take her chances. If she did not have all the facts needed to make the marriage decision, she arguably was willfully ignorant.

domestic violence (DV)
Actual or threatened injury or abuse of one member of a family or household by another member.

Nevertheless, the court granted the annulment. As a condition of appearing on the show, the bachelor and all the contestants signed individual premarital agreements in which they agreed not to challenge any annulment action that might be filed in the future. In granting the annulment, however, the court did not base its decision on this agreement. Indeed, it is doubtful that such agreements are enforceable. As a matter of public policy, courts do not want to encourage the dissolution of marriages by such agreements. (See Chapter 4 on premarital agreements.)

Why then was the annulment granted, particularly when the factual basis for fraud was relatively weak? The answer is not clear. First of all, the Nevada hearing was **uncontested**. The husband neither appeared nor was represented by counsel. Hence, there was no opposition to the petition to annul on the ground of fraud. Nor did anyone appeal. There was no written opinion in which the trial judge stated a rationale for granting the annulment. Some have speculated that the judge may have been influenced by the negative public outcry over what had taken place. Of course, if the annulment had been denied, the parties would not have been forced to stay married. The option of divorce would have been readily available.

uncontested
Unchallenged; without opposition or dispute.

ASSIGNMENT 6.6

a. Do you think the annulment in the multimillionaire case could have been granted on the ground that the marriage was a sham? (See the General Instructions for the Legal-Analysis Assignment in Appendix A.)

b. Later, we will study no-fault divorce in which marital fault is no longer relevant to the granting of divorce. Is there any reason why we should not have a system of no-fault annulment?

The Tort of Fraud

Occasionally, spouses try to sue each other for the **tort** of fraud. In one case, a husband's fraud suit against his wife alleged that she falsely told him that she loved him and was sexually attracted to him. He said he would not have married her if he had known this. The court, however, dismissed the action. In Chapter 17, we will see that some tort actions are allowed between spouses (e.g., a civil battery action). Torts based on the loss of love, however, are generally not allowed. They are called **heart-balm actions**.

In the fraud suit, the court said, "[w]ords of love, passion and sexual desire are simply unsuited to the cumbersome strictures of common law fraud and deceit. The idea that a judge, or jury of 12 solid citizens, can arbitrate whether an individual's romantic declarations at a certain time are true or false, or made with intent to deceive, seems almost ridiculously wooden."[12]

tort
A civil wrong (other than a breach of contract) that causes injury or other harm for which our legal system deems it just to provide a remedy such as damages. Injury or harm can be to a person (a personal tort); to land and anything attached to the land (a real-property tort); to property other than land, called personal property and movable property (a personal-property tort); or to economic interests (an economic tort).

heart-balm actions
An action based on the loss of love and relationships—on a broken heart (e.g., breach of promise to marry, alienation of affections, and seduction).

VIOLATION OF TECHNICAL/PROCEDURAL REQUIREMENTS

In Chapter 5, we examined technical or procedural requirements for entering into a ceremonial marriage. Examples include obtaining a marriage license from the correct county and observing a waiting period. Suppose that such requirements for a ceremonial marriage have been violated. What consequences would follow?

- Len and Helen want their good friend, Fred (a dentist), to marry them. Fred signs up with an online ministry, which ordains 10,000 ministers a month. He becomes "ordained" simply by typing his name and address on the ministry's online form and by sending in a fee. He then marries Len and Helen. Later, they learn that Fred's ordination did not meet the state's criteria to be an **officiant** authorized to perform marriage ceremonies.

- Joe and Mary live in a state that requires a three-day waiting period between the date a marriage license is issued and the date of the ceremony. Because they wish to be married right away, they find a minister who marries them on the same day they obtained the license.

Are these couples validly married? In most cases, a marriage is valid even when there has been a failure to comply with one of the technical/procedural requirements discussed in Chapter 5 for a ceremonial marriage. In general, noncompliance with the requirements for a ceremonial marriage cannot later be used as a ground for annulment. The policy of the law is to recognize the validity of a marriage whenever possible.

Violating these requirements is simply not serious enough for a court to declare that a marriage is invalid, particularly when the parties have lived together as husband and wife for a long time, raised a family, and amassed considerable property in the process. Courts conclude that the legislature did not intend to impose the penalty of invalidity for violating these requirements.

officiant
One who leads or performs a ceremony, often a religious service.

CHURCH ANNULMENT

The Roman Catholic Church has its own separate system of annulment, which it calls a *declaration of nullity*. The church does not recognize divorce. Nor does it recognize the annulments discussed in this chapter that are granted by the civil courts. Having a civil annulment does not automatically lead to a church annulment (and vice versa). In the eyes of the church, the only way to terminate a marriage (other than by the death of one of the parties) is by seeking a petition of nullity in a church court applying canon law. This court can declare the marriage "null." Technically, the church does not dissolve the marriage. Rather, it makes a finding that a valid sacramental marriage was not created or entered into on the wedding day. This will allow a Catholic to remarry in the church, to receive communion, and to participate in all the other sacraments. Full participation is denied to a Catholic who remarries without obtaining a church annulment—even if he or she obtains a civil annulment.

The main ground for a church annulment is *defective consent*. "The reasons (or grounds) for defective consent can vary greatly. Some would include a grave lack of discretion of judgment; consent resulting from force and fear; an intention against permanence of marriage; an intention against having children; an inability to consent to the obligations of marriage because of a serious psychological anomaly, and a consent made subject to a condition about the future."[13]

To initiate a church annulment, the petitioner pays a processing fee (approximately $500) in order to have a formal hearing presided over by a tribunal judge. An advocate presents the case of the petitioner seeking the annulment. Also present is a *defender of the bond,* who monitors the proceeding to ensure that rights are protected and church law properly observed. The hierarchy in Rome has criticized American bishops for allowing too many church annulments. More than 30,000 annulments are granted each year in the 119 dioceses of the United States. This constitutes 70 percent of the annulments granted by the church worldwide.

CONFLICT OF LAWS

A **conflict of laws** exists when there is an inconsistency between the laws of different legal systems, such as two states or two countries. For example, two states could have different minimum ages to marry or different consanguinity requirements. (See also Chapter 5 where we examined conflict of laws on the issue of common-law marriage.)

In annulment cases, the most common conflicts question arises when the parties are married in one state and then moved to another state where one of the parties seeks an annulment. If these two states do not have the same annulment law, a **choice of law** must be made between:

- The law of the state where the parties were married (called the *state of celebration* and also *lex loci celebrationis, state of contract,* and *lex loci contractus*), and

- The law of the state where the parties have a permanent home (called the state of **domicile** or the **domiciliary state**). A **domiciliary** is a person domiciled in a particular place.

> For example:
>
> *Jim and Jane are first cousins. They marry in State X, where their marriage is valid. They then move to State Y. If they had married in State Y, their marriage would not have been valid because first cousins cannot marry in State Y. Jim sues Jane in State Y for an annulment, alleging the invalidity of first-cousin marriages. What annulment law does the court in State Y apply—the law of State X or the law of State Y?*

State X is the state of celebration or the state of contract (i.e., the state where the parties entered into the marriage contract). State Y is the domiciliary state (i.e., the state where the parties are now domiciled). The state where the parties file the suit is called the **forum** state. (A forum is a court, or more specifically, the court or tribunal hearing the case.) In our example, State Y is both the domiciliary state and the forum state.

Assume that Jim dies **intestate** (i.e., without a valid will). Assume further that he has children from a prior marriage that ended in divorce but no children with his second spouse, Jane. Under the intestacy laws of most states, his spouse and children receive designated portions of his estate. If there is no spouse, the children have more of an estate to share. Therefore, it is in the interest of the children to claim that Jane cannot be the surviving spouse of Jim because they were never validly married. The success of this claim may depend on which law applies—that of State X or State Y.

CONFLICT-OF-LAWS RULE IN ANNULMENT ACTIONS

In Chapter 5, we discussed the general conflict-of-laws rule on the validity of marriage:

Conflict of Laws and the Validity of a Marriage

> The validity of a marriage is determined by the law of the state in which the marriage was entered or contracted (the state of celebration). Another state will recognize that marriage unless to do so would violate a strong **public policy** of the state asked to recognize it.

Exhibit 6.13 states this same rule, using the language of the domiciliary state.

conflict of laws
An inconsistency between the laws of different legal systems such as the laws of two states or the laws of two countries.

choice of law
A selection of which law to apply when a court is being asked to apply the law of different legal systems such as two states or two countries.

domicile
The place where a person has been physically present (a) with the intent to make that place a permanent home or (b) with no intent to make any other place a permanent home. The place to which one intends to return when away. A *residence*, on the other hand, is simply the place where you are living at a particular time. A person can have more than one residence but generally can have only one domicile.

domiciliary state
The state where one has a domicile.

domiciliary
One who is domiciled in a particular place.

forum
(1) A court. (2) The place where the parties are presently litigating their dispute. (3) A court or tribunal hearing a case.

intestate
(1) Pertaining to someone who dies without a valid will. (2) A person who dies without a valid will.

public policy
The principles inherent in the customs, morals, and notions of justice that prevail in a state; the foundation of public laws; the principles that are naturally and inherently right and just.

EXHIBIT 6.13 Conflict of Laws and the Validity of a Marriage

A domiciliary state will recognize as valid a marriage that was entered into in another state if:

• The marriage was valid in the state where it was entered, and

• Recognizing the marriage would not violate a strong public policy of the domiciliary state.

If both of these conditions are met, the domiciliary marriage will treat the marriage as valid *even if* the marriage would not have been valid if it had been entered into in the domiciliary state.

In most states, a violation of public policy depends on whether the state would consider the marriage to be void or voidable.

• *Void marriages.* The domiciliary state would *refuse* to recognize a marriage that is valid in the state of celebration if that marriage would have been void if the parties had tried to enter it in the domiciliary state. It is against the strong public policy of the domiciliary state to be asked to recognize what it considers to be a void marriage even though it is valid in the state of celebration.

• *Voidable marriages.* The domiciliary state *would* recognize a marriage that is valid in the state of celebration even if that marriage would have been voidable if the parties had tried to enter it in the domiciliary state. It is not against the strong public policy of the domiciliary state to be asked to recognize what it considers to be a voidable marriage if it was valid in the state of celebration.

consanguinity
Relationship by blood.

Let's apply these rules to the Jim and Jane example. The state of celebration is State X where their marriage is valid because first-cousin marriages do not violate the **consanguinity** laws of State X. Now we must ask whether State Y (the domiciliary state) considers marriages between first cousins to be void or voidable:

• *Void.* If State Y considers marriages between first cousins to be void, then it will refuse to recognize it. In the annulment action of Jim against Jane, the annulment would be granted because State Y would apply its own annulment law, not that of State X. It is against the strong public policy of State Y to recognize a marriage that it considers void even if it is valid in the state of celebration.

• *Voidable.* If State Y considers marriages between first cousins to be voidable, then it will recognize it. In the annulment action of Jim against Jane, the annulment would be denied because State Y would apply the law of State X where the marriage is valid. It is not against the strong public policy of State Y to recognize a marriage that it considers voidable if it is valid in the state of celebration.

MARRIAGE EVASION STATUTES

Next, we consider the conflicts problem that occurs when the parties travel to another state solely to evade the marriage law of their own state.

Bob and Mary are domiciled in State A. They cannot marry in State A because they are underage (nonage). After checking the law of neighboring states, they discover that they would not be underage in State B. They go to State B and are married. (State B is the state of celebration.) After the marriage, they return to State A (the domiciliary state). Later, Mary sues Bob in State A for an annulment. What annulment law does the court in State A apply—the law of the domiciliary state (A) or the law of the state of celebration (B)?

In this example, Bob and Mary went to the state of celebration solely to evade the marriage law of the domiciliary state. Several states have enacted *marriage-evasion* statutes to cover this situation. In such states, the choice of law depends upon the presence or absence of an intent to evade. The statute might provide that the domiciliary state will refuse to recognize the marriage if the parties went to the state of celebration for the purpose of evading the marriage laws of the domiciliary state to which they later returned. This is what arguably occurred in the case of Bob and Mary. Hence, if the domiciliary state (State A) has a marriage-evasion statute, it would refuse to recognize the marriage and would grant the annulment to Mary. If, however, Bob can prove that they did not go to State B to evade the marriage law of State A, then State A would apply the law of the state of celebration (State B) and deny the annulment.

It is sometimes difficult to prove whether the parties went to the other state with the intent to evade the marriage laws of their domiciliary state. It may depend on circumstantial evidence, such as how long they remained in the state of celebration and whether they returned to their initial domiciliary state or established a domicile in another state altogether. The Interviewing and Investigation Checklist is designed to assist you in collecting evidence on intent.

✔ INTERVIEWING AND INVESTIGATION CHECKLIST

Factors Relevant to the Intent to Evade Marriage Laws

Assume that the parties live in State A but were married in State B. (See also the Interviewing and Investigation Checklist on determining domicile in Chapter 7.)

LEGAL INTERVIEWING QUESTIONS

1. How long have the two of you lived in State A?
2. Why didn't you marry in State A?
3. When did you decide to go to State B?
4. Have either of you ever lived in State B?
5. Do either of you have relatives in State B? In State A?
6. Was either of you born in State B? In State A?
7. On what date did you both go to State B?
8. Did you sell your home or move out of your apartment in State A?
9. When you left State A, did you intend to come back?
10. After you arrived in State B, when did you apply for a marriage license?
11. On what date were you married?
12. While you were in State B, where did you stay? Did you have all your clothes and furniture with you?
13. Who attended the wedding ceremony in State B?
14. Did you have sexual relations in State B?
15. Did either of you work or apply for work in State B?
16. How long did you both stay in State B?
17. Did you both vote or pay taxes in State B?
18. Did you both open a checking account in a bank in State B?
19. Did you both obtain a library card in State B?
20. What utility bills did each of you pay while in State B?
21. Where did you both go after you left State B?

POSSIBLE INVESTIGATION TASKS

- Obtain copies of all records that tend to establish the kind of contact the parties had with State B (e.g., motel receipts, bank statements, rent and utility receipts, employment records).
- Interview friends, relatives, and associates of the parties to determine what light they can shed on the intent of the parties in going to State B.

Thus far, our main focus has been on marriages that are valid in the state of celebration but invalid and annullable in the domiciliary state if the marriages had been contracted in the domiciliary state (see Exhibit 6.14).

Suppose, however, that the marriage was invalid in the state of celebration. The parties then move to a new state where they establish a domicile. If they had been married in their new domicile state, their marriage would have been valid. An annulment action is brought in their new domiciliary state (see Exhibit 6.15).

If a marriage is invalid where it was entered (in the state of celebration), can it be recognized (considered valid) in any other state? Will a domiciliary state validate a marriage that is invalid according to the law of the state of celebration? Contrary to the general conflict-of-laws rule on the validity of marriages, the answer in some states is *yes*. In such states, the domiciliary state will deny an annulment of a marriage that would have been valid if entered into in the domiciliary state but that is clearly invalid in the state where it was actually entered. Such states take this position, in part, because of the public policy (and indeed the presumption) favoring the validity of marriages.

EXHIBIT 6.14 Marriages Valid in State of Celebration

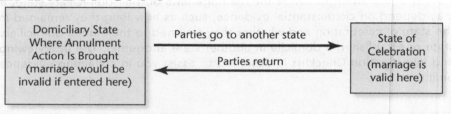

EXHIBIT 6.15 Marriages Invalid in State of Celebration

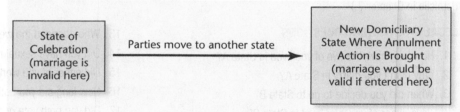

CONSEQUENCES OF AN ANNULMENT DECREE

Many events usually occur between the time the parties enter into an invalid marriage and the date of its annulment. What are the legal consequences of these events? In theory, an annulled marriage never existed. The old rule was that once a void or a voidable marriage was declared invalid, the declaration was **retroactive**; it related back to the time the parties attempted to enter the marriage. This rule, when strictly applied, resulted in some harsh consequences. A child born to parents before their marriage was annulled was, in effect, born out of wedlock and thus an **illegitimate child**. (Such children were referred to as "retroactive bastards.") Rigid application of the relation-back rule could also harshly impact support rights. Suppose that a woman lives with a man for forty years before their marriage is

retroactive
Applying to facts that arise before a particular event or date.

illegitimate child
A child born to parents who are not married to each other, who never married thereafter, and who never took steps to legitimate the child. Also called *nonmarital child, child of an informal relationship, child out of wedlock, child with no presumed father, bastard.*

annulled. She would not be entitled to support payments. A man has no duty to support someone who was never his wife! Clearly, these were unfair consequences, and all states have taken steps, often using the **equity** power of a court, to offset them. What follows is an overview of the present law in this area.

LEGITIMACY OF CHILDREN FROM AN ANNULLED MARRIAGE

Most states have passed statutes that declare the **legitimation** of children from an annulled marriage. In later chapters, we will see that, in most instances, the rights of (and duties to) children are *not* dependent on whether they are legitimate.

CUSTODY AND CHILD SUPPORT

There is no difference in how courts handle child custody and child support in annulment and divorce cases. It makes no difference whether the parents have a valid marriage, an invalid marriage, or no marriage at all. Child-custody decisions are based on the best interests of the child, and child-support decisions are based on the support needs of the child within the framework of child-support guidelines. We will discuss child custody in Chapter 9 and child support in Chapter 10.

ALIMONY AND PROPERTY DIVISION

In some states, **alimony** cannot be awarded in annulment proceedings. In most states, however, statutes exist that allow alimony in such actions. This includes temporary alimony pending the final outcome of the action and permanent alimony following the annulment decree. It may be, however, that alimony will be denied to the "guilty" party (e.g., the party who committed the fraud, who used duress to pressure the other party to enter the marriage, or who committed other wrongful acts that created the ground for the annulment).

Another limitation on alimony in some states is that only defendants can receive it. By definition, the plaintiff seeking the annulment is saying that no marriage ever existed. A few courts say that it is inconsistent for the plaintiff to take this position and yet ask for alimony.

What about property that was accumulated during the marriage? Logically, if there was no marriage, there is no *marital* property to divide. Courts, however, have devised various theories to provide a measure of fairness to parties in annulment cases. Examples:

- A court might refuse to apply the annulment retroactively so that property acquired during the marriage would be divided in a manner similar to property division upon divorce.
- A court might allow a party to bring a suit on a theory of **implied-in-law contract** (also called *quasi contract*) to prevent **unjust enrichment**. Under this theory, the party may be able to obtain a return of goods acquired or the reasonable value of services provided during the relationship.
- A court might apply the putative-spouse doctrine. A **putative spouse** is a person who believes in good faith that he or she entered into a valid marriage even though an impediment existed that rendered the marriage invalid. An example of an impediment would be the existence of a prior existing marriage. For more on putative spouses, see Chapter 5.

In Chapter 4, we discussed similar theories to obtain relief for parties who cohabited but never entered into a valid marriage or never tried to enter one.

equity
(1) Justice administered according to fairness in a particular case, as contrasted with the strictly formalized rules followed by common-law courts. (2) The system of justice administered in courts of equity. (3) Fairness.

legitimation
(1) The declaration that a child is legitimate. The verb is *legitimate*. (2) The steps taken to declare that a child is legitimate.

alimony
Money or other property paid in fulfillment of a duty to support one's spouse (or ex-spouse) after a legal separation, a divorce, and, in most states, an annulment. Also called *maintenance, spousal support*.

implied-in-law contract
An obligation created by the law to avoid unjust enrichment in the absence of an express or implied contract creating this obligation. Also called *quasi contract*.

unjust enrichment
The receipt of a benefit in the form of goods or services that in fairness should be returned or paid for even though there was no express or implied promise to do so.

putative spouse
A person who believes in good faith that he or she entered into a valid marriage, even though an impediment made the marriage invalid. The marriage with such a spouse is called a *putative marriage*.

REVIVAL

Bob is validly married to Elaine. In 2016, they go through a valid divorce proceeding, which provides that Bob will pay Elaine alimony until she remarries. In 2018, Elaine marries Dan, and Bob stops his alimony payments. In 2020, Elaine's marriage to Dan is annulled.

What effect does this annulment have on Bob's earlier obligation to pay alimony to Elaine? Several possibilities exist:

- *Option 1.* Bob does not have to resume paying alimony. His obligation ceased forever when Elaine married Dan. The fact that the second marriage was annulled is irrelevant.

- *Option 2.* Bob does not have to resume paying alimony. Dan must start paying alimony in 2020 if the state authorizes alimony in annulment actions.

- *Option 3.* There is a **revival** of Bob's alimony obligation. Bob must resume paying alimony starting in 2020, the date of the annulment decree.

- *Option 4.* There is a revival of Bob's alimony obligation. Bob must resume paying alimony retroactive to when he stopped paying in 2018.

Option 4 is the most logical. Because the technical effect of an annulment decree is to say that the marriage never existed, the decree should be retroactive to the date when Elaine and Dan entered into the marriage that was later annulled. Although Option 4 is the most logical of the four presented, it is arguably as unfair to Bob as Option 1 is unfair to Elaine. Most states adopt Options 2 or 3.

INHERITANCE

There are two main categories of **decedents**: those who die **testate** (leaving a valid will) and those who die *intestate* (without leaving a valid will). If a person dies testate, his or her estate is distributed according to the terms of the will. If a person dies intestate, his or her estate is distributed according to the state's laws of **intestacy**, which generally provide that a certain percentage of the estate goes to the surviving spouse, another percentage to children, etc. The transfer of property under these laws is called **intestate succession**.

Assume that the marriage of a decedent has been annulled and that the decedent never remarried. What are the consequences if the decedent died intestate or if he or she died testate with a provision in the will to a surviving "spouse"?

- *Intestate.* A person who dies intestate does not have a surviving spouse if the marriage was annulled. An annulment (as well as a divorce) terminates mutual intestate rights of former spouses. Under the intestacy laws, all of the decedent's estate would go to other relatives such as children.

- *Testate.* The will of a person who dies testate does not have a surviving spouse if the marriage was annulled even if the will had a provision in it for a surviving "spouse." Under statutes such as the **Uniform Probate Code**, an annulment (or a divorce) automatically terminates or revokes provisions in a will for a surviving spouse unless the will specifically says otherwise. Furthermore, if before death the decedent had appointed his or her spouse as **executor**, **trustee**, or **conservator**, the annulment also automatically revokes these appointments.

---

revival
Restoration of what was once inoperative or terminated.

decedent
The person who has died; the deceased.

testate
(1) Pertaining to someone who dies with a valid will. (2) A person who dies with a valid will. (In older cases, if the testate was a man, he was also called *testator* and, if a woman, *testatrix*.)

intestacy
The condition of dying without a valid will.

intestate succession
The transfer of a decedent's property to state-designated relatives of the decedent who dies without leaving a valid will. Also called *descent and distribution, hereditary succession.*

Uniform Probate Code
A law adopted by some states that covers (1) the probating of wills and (2) the distribution of the estate of persons who die without wills (*intestate succession*).

executor
A person designated in a will to carry out the terms of the will and to handle related matters. (If a woman, this person is sometimes called an *executrix*.)

trustee
The person or company holding legal title to property for the benefit of another.

conservator
A person appointed by the court to manage the affairs of persons who are not competent to do so on their own.

BIGAMY

Ed marries Diane. He leaves her without obtaining a divorce. He now marries Claire. This marriage to Claire is later annulled. He is charged with the crime of bigamy.

Can Ed use the defense that his marriage with Claire was annulled, and therefore, he was never married to Claire? Most of the cases that have answered this question have said that the subsequent annulment is *not* a defense to the bigamy charge.

INTERSPOUSAL IMMUNITY IN SOME TORT ACTIONS

An immunity is a defense that prevents someone from being sued for what would otherwise be wrongful conduct. As we shall see in Chapter 17, spouses may have the benefit of an interspousal immunity that prevents certain kinds of tort litigation between spouses. The immunity does not cover *property* torts such as conversion and trespass. Spouses can still sue each other for property torts in most states. States differ on whether the immunity covers *personal* torts such as the tort of assault.

Assume, for example, that George assaults his wife, Pauline, in a state where the interspousal immunity bars personal torts between spouses. She would not be able to sue him for the tort of assault in such states. She might be able to initiate a *criminal* action against him for the crime of assault or battery, but she could not bring a civil assault action against him.

Now assume that the marriage of George and Pauline is annulled. After the annulment, can Pauline sue George for an assault that occurred during the marriage? Because the annulment means that they were never married, the tort action for assault should, in theory, be allowed. Yet most courts would hold that the annulment does not wipe out the impact of the interspousal immunity for personal torts. Therefore, in such states, the assault action could not be brought; the immunity would bar the action despite the annulment.

There is no immunity, however, for torts committed *after* the parties go through an annulment or a divorce.

immunity
A defense that is granted because of a special relationship or status that operates to block litigation and liability whether or not wrongful conduct was committed. The defense prevents someone from being sued for what might be wrongful conduct.

interspousal immunity
Spouses cannot sue each other for designated categories of torts. Also called *husband-wife immunity.*

civil
Noncriminal.

MARITAL COMMUNICATIONS PRIVILEGE

A privilege is a special legal benefit, right, exemption, or protection. Under the marital-communications privilege, a husband and a wife can refuse to disclose confidential communications between them during the marriage. The policy behind the privilege is to encourage open communication between spouses without fear that they might one day have to give court testimony about the communications. The privilege, however, does not apply to suits between the spouses themselves such as for divorce. The main value of the privilege is in third-party litigation. For example:

Sam is married to Helen. Their marriage is annulled. A year later, Sam is sued by a neighbor who claims that Sam negligently damaged the neighbor's property. The alleged damage was inflicted while Sam was still married to Helen. At the trial, the neighbor calls (subpoenas) Helen as a witness and asks her to testify about what Sam told her concerning the incident while they were still living together.

privilege
A special legal benefit, right, exemption, or protection. (See glossary for an additional definition.)

marital-communications privilege
A person can refuse to testify and can prevent his or her spouse or ex-spouse from testifying about any confidential communications made between them during their marriage. Also called *marital privilege* or *husband-wife privilege.*

subpoena
(1) To command that someone appear at a certain time and place. (2) A command to appear at a certain time and place.

According to the marital-communications privilege, Helen can refuse to testify about what she and her husband told each other during the marriage. Their marriage, however, was annulled, so that in the eyes of the law they were never married. Does this change the rule on the privilege? Can Helen give this testimony? The answer is not clear; few cases have considered the issue. Of those that have, some have concluded that the annulment does not destroy the privilege, while others have reached the opposite conclusion.

INCOME TAX STATUS

A husband and wife can file a joint income tax return so long as they were married during the taxable year. Suppose, however, that after ten years of marriage and ten years of filing joint returns, the marriage is annulled. Must the parties now file *amended* returns for each of those ten years? Should the returns now be filed as separate returns rather than joint ones, again on the theory that the annulment meant the parties were never validly married? According to the Internal Revenue Service, you are considered unmarried for the whole year if you obtained a decree of annulment: "You must file amended returns [e.g., as a single taxpayer] for all tax years affected by the annulment not closed by the [three-year] period of limitations."[14]

ASSIGNMENT   6.7

Fred and Jill are married. Fred is killed in an automobile accident with a truck of the ABC Tire Company. Jill brings a wrongful death action against the ABC Tire Company. Such actions give spouses the right to sue for the wrongful death of their deceased spouse. The attorney of ABC learns that Jill was married to someone else at the time she married Fred. The attorney claims that Jill cannot bring the wrongful death action, since she was never validly married to Fred. How would your state resolve this claim? You may have to check both statutory law and case law. (See General Instructions for the State-Code Assignment and General Instructions for the Court-Opinion Assignment in Appendix A.)

ASSIGNMENT   6.8

Prepare a flowchart of annulment litigation in your state. (See General Instructions for the Flowchart Assignment in Appendix A.)

PARALEGAL ROLES

- Investigate facts that are relevant to the grounds for annulment.
- Draft pleadings for the annulment action.
- Provide referrals to religious annulments.
- The Interviewing and Investigation Checklist can also cover fact-finding roles of paralegals.
- For an overview of paralegal roles in family-law cases, see Exhibits 1.5 and 1.6 in Chapter 1.
- For all financial issues covered in Chapter 6, a paralegal may be asked to help collect documents and facts outlined in:
  - The checklist in Exhibit 3.1 of Chapter 3.
  - The interrogatories in Appendix C.

SUMMARY

An annulment is a declaration by a court that a valid marriage never existed. For convenience, we refer to an annulment as an "annulled marriage"—although it would be more accurate to call it an *alleged* or *purported marriage*. The effective date of an annulment is the date the parties attempted to enter into the marriage, not the date of the annulment decree. To obtain an annulment, a party must establish grounds and must have standing.

A divorce is a declaration by a court that a validly entered marriage is terminated so that the parties are no longer married to each other. A legal separation is a declaration by a court that parties can live apart even though they are still married to each other. Some grounds render a marriage void; others will render it voidable. A voidable marriage is valid unless a court annuls it. A void marriage is invalid whether or not a court declares it so. Voidable marriages cannot be annulled after death; void marriages can. Voidable marriages can be ratified; void marriages cannot. If a party lacks standing, a marriage by estoppel may occur, which is a relationship that is recognized as a marriage because a party is prevented from asserting the invalidity of the marriage even though grounds for its invalidity may exist.

There are four grounds relating to the legal capacity to marry:

1. *Prior existing marriage.* At the time of the marriage, a prior marriage had not been terminated.

2. *Consanguinity and affinity.* The parties married in violation of a prohibition against the marriage of certain categories of individuals who are too closely related to each other.

3. *Nonage.* A party was underage at the time of the marriage.

4. *Physical disability.* A party was impotent at the time of the marriage or had another physical disability.

There are four grounds relating to the intent to marry:

1. *Sham marriage.* The parties never intended to marry, i.e., they never intended to live together as husband and wife.

2. *Mental disability.* At the time of the marriage, a party was incapable of understanding the nature and duties of the marriage relationship.

3. *Duress.* A party was induced to enter into the marriage by the unlawful use of force or threats.

4. *Fraud.* A party intentionally misrepresented or concealed a fact that was essential (or vital) to the marriage.

Under the last-in-time-marriage presumption, if more than one marriage is alleged to exist, the most recent marriage is presumed to be valid. Under the Enoch Arden presumption, a spouse is considered dead after being missing without explanation for a designated number of years despite due diligence in attempting to locate him or her. In most states, a violation of a technical/procedural requirement for a ceremonial marriage is not a ground for an annulment.

Under conflict-of-law principles, a marriage will be considered valid in a domiciliary state if (a) the marriage is valid according to the state where it was contracted and (b) recognizing the validity of the marriage would not violate a strong public policy of the domiciliary state. If both conditions are met, the domiciliary state will deny the annulment, even though the marriage could have been annulled if it had been entered into in the domiciliary state. Generally, if a marriage would have been void had it been contracted in the domiciliary state, the latter state will not apply the law of the state of celebration, where the marriage is valid.

A state may have a statute that invalidates marriages contracted in other states solely to evade the domiciliary state's marriage laws. Some states will validate a marriage entered into in another state (even though the marriage is invalid in the state where it was entered) so long as the marriage would have been valid if it had been entered into in the state where the parties are now domiciled. In effect, this state will deny the annulment even though the state of celebration would have granted it.

In most states, children born from an annulled marriage are considered legitimate. In an annulment proceeding, the court must award custody of the children and provide for their support. If the state does not allow alimony or property division in annulment cases, the court might use the theory of implied-in-law contract (quasi contract) to prevent unjust enrichment. Another possible theory is putative spouse.

If a divorced person's second marriage is annulled, states disagree on whether benefits and duties arising from the divorce in the first marriage are revived. Revival issues might also arise in cases that involve inheritance, bigamy, tort liability, marital-communications privilege, and income-tax status.

KEY TERMS

annulment	canon law	marriage
divorce	ecclesiastical court	purported
legal separation	declaratory judgment	relation-back rule
no-fault divorce	nullity	grounds

void	nonage	intestate
voidable	impotence	public policy
voidable marriage	copulate	consanguinity
void marriage	sterility	retroactive
void ab initio	triennial cohabitation	illegitimate child
ratification	sham marriage	equity
cohabit	alien	legitimation
standing	green-card marriage	alimony
guardian ad litem (GAL)	statutory rape	implied-in-law contract
dirty hands	lucid interval	unjust enrichment
estopped	duress	putative spouse
marriage by estoppel	malicious	revival
impediment	fraud	decedent
capacity	material	testate
polygamy	essentials test	intestacy
bigamy	domestic violence (DV)	intestate succession
prosecution	uncontested	Uniform Probate Code
presumption	tort	executor
rebut	heart-balm action	trustee
rebuttable presumption	officiant	conservator
last-in-time-marriage presumption	conflict of laws	immunity
Enoch Arden presumption	choice of law	interspousal immunity
due diligence	domicile	civil
consanguinity	domiciliary state	privilege
affinity	domiciliary	marital-communications privilege
incest	forum	subpoena

CHECK THE CITE

What was the basis of the fraud alleged by the husband in his annulment action in the case of *Husband v. Wife*, 262 A.2d 656 (Del. Super. Ct. 1970)? How did the court rule on the fraud issue? To read the opinion online:

(1) Run a citation search ("262 A.2d 656") in the *Case law* database of Google Scholar (scholar.google.com). (2) Run this search in the general search engines of Google or Bing.

PROJECT

In the Articles database of Google Scholar (scholar.google.com), enter the search: aa annulment (substitute the name of your state for "aa"). Give the citation of two articles that discuss the law of annulment in your state. Provide a short summary of what each article says about

annulment in the state. For some articles, you may be given only the first page of the article. If so, base your summaries on what is provided. Avoid articles that do not clearly indicate on the first page of the article that it covers annulment in your state.

ETHICS IN A FAMILY-LAW PRACTICE

You are a paralegal working at a law office that is representing Mary Smith in her annulment action against Paul Smith. The case is uncontested. Both parties want the annulment. After a trial court grants the annulment, Paul Smith asks you to represent him as an independent

paralegal in the petition he now wants to file for an annulment from the Catholic Church. Assume that the Church allows nonattorney representation in Church annulment cases. Are there any ethical problems in your doing so?

WRITING SAMPLE

Draft a complaint for Elaine for her annulment action against Philip based on the facts in Assignment 6.4. Assume that Elaine files an action for annulment, which Philip opposes. (See General Instructions for the

Writing Sample in Appendix A. Also check the General Instructions for the Complaint-Drafting Assignment in Appendix A.)

REVIEW QUESTIONS

1. How do annulment, divorce, and legal separation differ?
2. Why are few annulments granted today?
3. Why is it important to understand annulment law despite the fact that few annulments are currently granted?
4. What is the historical origin of annulments?
5. What are some of the common terms for an annulment action?
6. Why is it technically incorrect to refer to an "annulled marriage"?
7. What is the effective date of an annulment?
8. What are the main grounds that render a marriage void?
9. What are the main grounds that render a marriage voidable?
10. What is the distinction between a voidable and a void marriage?
11. Can a marriage be annulled after the death of a spouse?
12. What is ratification and can an annullable marriage be ratified?
13. What is standing?
14. What is a guardian ad litem?
15. What is a marriage by estoppel?
16. What are the capacity grounds for annulment?
17. What are the intent/state-of-mind grounds for annulment?
18. When can a prior existing marriage (bigamy) be the basis of an annulment?
19. What is the last-in-time-marriage presumption?
20. How does the Enoch Arden presumption affect annulments?
21. When can consanguinity and affinity be the basis of an annulment?
22. When can nonage be the basis of an annulment?
23. When can physical disabilities be the basis of an annulment?
24. When can sham marriage be the basis of an annulment?
25. How do immigration officials attempt to identify marriages that are not entered into in good faith?
26. When can mental disability be the basis of an annulment?
27. What is a lucid interval?
28. When can duress be the basis of an annulment?
29. When can fraud be the basis of an annulment?
30. Can an annulment be granted because the parties failed to comply with the technical or procedural requirements for a ceremonial marriage?
31. What is the main ground for an annulment in the Catholic Church?
32. What is meant by conflict of laws?
33. What is the general conflict-of-laws rule in marriage validity cases?
34. What is a marriage-evasion statute?
35. When will a domiciliary state recognize an out-of-state marriage if the marriage is valid in the state of celebration but would have been invalid if entered into in the domiciliary state?
36. What effect does an annulment have on the legitimacy of children?
37. What effect does an annulment have on child custody and child support?
38. In an annulment action, can a court award alimony and rule on property division?
39. What is the problem of revival and how do different states handle it?
40. In what way can an annulment affect intestate succession, bigamy, interspousal tort immunity, the marital-communications privilege, and income-tax status?

HELPFUL WEBSITES

Your State
See Appendix D for links to the family law of your state on the topics covered in this chapter.

Annulment Overview
- www.expertlaw.com/library/family_law/annulment.html
- www.womansdivorce.com/marriage-annulment.html
- www.thespruce.com/how-to-obtain-a-civil-annulment-2300462
- en.wikipedia.org/wiki/Annulment

Green-Card Marriage
- en.wikipedia.org/wiki/Green_card_marriage
- www.immihelp.com/greencard/familybasedimmigration/persons-in-us.html

Church Annulment

- www.newadvent.org/cathen/07695a.htm
- www.ewtn.com/catholicism/library/explaining-an-annulment-1010

Google Scholar (scholar.google.com)

- Choose "Articles" and enter in the search box any of the key terms discussed in the chapter. Add the name of your state to the search term.
- Choose "Case law" and "Select courts". Select your state, click "Done," and enter in the search box any of the key terms discussed in the chapter. Add the name of your state to the search term.

Google, Bing, or Yahoo

(on these search engines, run the following searches, substituting your state for "aa")

- annulment aa
- void marriage aa
- bigamy aa
- revival annulment aa

- Catholic annulment aa
- fraud annulment aa
- Enoch Arden annulment aa
- green card marriage aa

YouTube

Run the same searches on YouTube listed above for Google, Bing, Yahoo searches. Even when the video clips are trying to entice you to retain an attorney, buy a book, or enroll in a course, they can provide useful overviews and references to primary authority.

Twitter, Reddit, and Facebook

On Twitter, Reddit, and Facebook, run the following search (substitute your state for aa in your searches; run the searches with and without the name of your state). Look for links to family-law developments in your state.

- annulment aa

ENDNOTES

Note: All or most of the court opinions in these endnotes can be read online. To do so, go to Google Scholar (scholar.google.com), select "Case law," and in the search box, enter the cite (e.g., "104 N.W.2d 8") or name of the case (e.g., "Johnson v. Johnson") that is given in the endnote.

[1] Jennifer Leavitt-Wipf, *Marriage for a Green Card* (2008) (www.knowitallmall.com/od/familybased/a/marriage-fraud.htm).

[2] John Wetenhall, *Alleged Bigamist's Defense: Never Married to First Wife* (Aug. 4, 2010) (abcnews.go.com/US/alleged-facebook-bigamists-defense-marriage-legal/story?id=11306824).

[3] Mandatory Premarital HIV Testing (www.cga.ct.gov/PS98/rpt/olr/htm/98-R-0995.htm).

[4] Bernard Turnock and Chester Kelly, *Mandatory Premarital Testing*, 261 Journal of the American Medical Association 3415 (Jun. 15, 1989) (www.ncbi.nlm.nih.gov/pubmed/2635877).

[5] Illinois Compiled Statutes, 750 ILCS 5/204 (from Ch. 40, par. 204) (www.ilga.gov/legislation/ilcs/ilcs.asp).

[6] Nina Bernstein, *Do You Take This Immigrant?* N.Y. Times, June 13, 2010 at 31; James A. Jones, *The Immigration Marriage Fraud Amendments: Sham Marriages or Sham Legislation?* 24 Florida State University Law Review 679 (1997) (8 U.S.C. §§ 1154, 1184, 1186a (1994)).

[7] Tess Townsend, *Get Married, Save Thousands on Tuition*, N.Y. Times, Feb. 6, 2011, at A27.

[8] *What's the Matter With Kansas?*, Editorial, N.Y. Times, Aug. 31, 2005, at A18.

[9] *Johnson v. Johnson*, 104 N.W.2d 8, 14 (N.D. 1960).

[10] Nevada Revised Statutes, § 125.330.

[11] *Cervone v. Cervone*, 155 Misc. 543, 547, 280 N.Y.S. 159, 164 (N.Y. Sup. Ct. 1935).

[12] *Askew v. Askew*, 22 Cal. App. 4th 942, 959 (Cal. Ct. App. 1994).

[13] *Archdiocese of Baltimore, Type of Annulments* (www.archbalt.org/marriage-tribunal/types-of-annulments-formal-case-defect-of-consent).

[14] *Divorce or Separated Individuals*, 3, Publication 504 (017) Internal Revenue Service, 2018) (www.irs.gov/pub/irs-pdf/p504.pdf).

CHAPTER 7

Divorce Grounds and Procedure

CHAPTER OUTLINE

INTRODUCTION
Overview
Historical Background
The Shift from Fault to No-Fault
Divorce
Cautionary Notes
A Return to Fault?
Marital Misconduct in No-Fault
Divorce
Tort Claims Brought within a
Divorce Action

**NO-FAULT GROUNDS FOR
DIVORCE**
Living Apart
Incompatibility
Irreconcilable Differences

FAULT GROUNDS FOR DIVORCE
Adultery
Cruelty
Desertion
Other Grounds
Defenses to the Fault Grounds

LEGAL SEPARATION

SEPARATE MAINTENANCE

**INTRODUCTION TO DIVORCE
PROCEDURE**

DOMICILE
Intent

**DURATIONAL RESIDENCY
REQUIREMENT**

FULL FAITH AND CREDIT

DIVISIBLE DIVORCE

JURISDICTION
Types of Jurisdiction
Person Attacking the Divorce
Judgment
Jurisdictional Analysis: More
Examples
Child Custody Jurisdiction

VENUE

SUMMARY DISSOLUTION

**ALTERNATIVE DISPUTE
RESOLUTION (ADR)**
Arbitration
Mediation
Med-Arb
Private Judging
Neutral Evaluation
Collaborative Law

PRETRIAL MATTERS
Notice and Opportunity to be Heard

Representation
Guardian Ad Litem (GAL)
Pleadings
Default Judgment; Default
Divorce
Pretrial Conferences
Waiting Period
Discovery
Inventory of Assets and Liabilities
Preliminary Orders

TRIAL

DIVORCE JUDGMENT

**ENFORCEMENT OF DIVORCE
JUDGMENT**
Civil Contempt
Execution
Garnishment
Attachment
Receivership
Constructive Trust

**RELIGION AND DIVORCE
PROCEDURE**
Religious Divorces
Religious Traditions in Civil Court

CHAPTER OBJECTIVES

After completing this chapter, you should be able to:

- Know the three eras of divorce in our legal history.
- Distinguish between limited and absolute divorce.
- Explain why states added no-fault grounds for divorce.
- Describe the role of marital misconduct in a no-fault divorce.
- Describe the main no-fault grounds for divorce.
- Describe the main fault grounds for divorce and their defenses.

- Distinguish legal separation, separate maintenance, and divorce.
- Explain how domicile is determined.
- Know the meaning of full faith and credit.
- Explain what is meant by divisible divorce.
- Identify the three main kinds of jurisdiction.
- Know the kind of jurisdiction a court needs to dissolve a

marriage and how it obtains this kind of jurisdiction.

- Know the kind of jurisdiction a court needs to order spousal support, child support, and property division and how it obtains this kind of jurisdiction.
- Explain when a party will be prevented from attacking the jurisdiction of a court that issued a divorce judgment.

- Know when a state is a *home state* for purposes of child-custody jurisdiction.
- Know how venue is determined.
- Explain what a summary dissolution is.
- State the requirement of procedural due process in divorce cases.
- Describe the role of a guardian ad litem (GAL).

- Identify the components of a divorce complaint/petition.
- Know when a court will issue a default divorce.
- Explain what happens at a pretrial conference.
- Describe the main methods of discovery in divorce cases.
- List the major preliminary orders.
- Summarize what occurs in a divorce trial.

- Explain the main methods of alternative dispute resolution (ADR).
- Identify the major remedies available to enforce a divorce judgment.
- Describe divorce in the Jewish and Islamic traditions and know whether such traditions can be enforced in secular civil courts.

INTRODUCTION

Marriage can be dissolved in three ways: the death of one of the spouses, annulment, or divorce. A **divorce** is a declaration by a court that a validly entered marriage (opposite-sex or same-sex) is terminated so that the parties are no longer married to each other. In this chapter, we cover the termination of a marriage by divorce. In separate chapters, we will examine in detail the topics of spousal support and property division (Chapter 8), child custody (Chapter 9), and child support (Chapter 10).

OVERVIEW

The history of divorce in the United States has gone through three main eras:

- The era of *restrictive divorce*, when it was very difficult to obtain a divorce because of the need to prove marital wrongdoing (fault). A dominant theme of divorce law was morality. Divorces were granted for specific wrongdoing (immorality), such as adultery, cruelty, and desertion.

- The era of *collusive divorce*, when a very large number of spouses lied to the court in order to make it appear that the fault **grounds** for divorce existed. Lying was one way to get around the often onerous, expensive, and debilitating task of presenting evidence to prove whose fault caused the break-up. Lying was also common when parties wanted to bypass a procedural requirement for obtaining a divorce in their state.

- Currently we are in the era of *unilateral divorce* when most divorces can be granted even if only one spouse wants to terminate the marriage. Under the system of **no-fault divorce**, either party could precipitate the divorce without having to prove the marital wrongs that caused the break-up. Hence there was no longer a need to lie about such wrongs. Economics has always been a major theme of divorce, but in the era of the unilateral divorce, the dominant theme shifted from fault (who was in the wrong) to economics (how will the parties be supported and, most importantly, how should marital property be divided). It takes two people to create a marriage, but in the era of unilateral divorce, it can take only one of them to initiate and conclude the process of dissolving the marriage by divorce.[1]

These are some of the themes we will be examining in this chapter.

HISTORICAL BACKGROUND

Under early English law, marriage law was within the province of the **ecclesiastical** courts of the Roman Catholic Church, which applied its own **canon law**. To understand church law in this area, we need to distinguish two kinds of divorce:

divorce
A declaration by a court that a validly entered marriage is terminated so that the parties are no longer married to each other. Also called *dissolution*, *marital dissolution*, or *divorce a vinculo matrimonii* (divorce from the chains of marriage).

collusive divorce
A divorce obtained in a proceeding in which the spouses agreed to lie to the court in order to facilitate the granting of the divorce.

grounds
Reasons that are legally sufficient to obtain a particular remedy or result.

no-fault divorce
A divorce that is granted without having to prove marital wrongs that caused the break-up.

ecclesiastical
Pertaining to the church.

canon law
Church law; ecclesiastical law.

- **Limited divorce.** A declaration by a court that the spouses can live apart although they are still married to each other. Also called *legal separation, judicial separation, separation from bed and board*, and *divorce a mensa et thoro* (divorce from board and hearth).

- **Absolute divorce.** A declaration by a court that the marriage is terminated so that the parties are no longer married to each other. Also called *complete divorce* and *divorce a vinculo martimonii* (divorce from the chains of marriage).

Canon law considered marriage to be a sacrament and an indissoluble bond. Hence, ecclesiastical courts were restricted to granting limited divorces; they could not grant an absolute divorce. They could, however, grant an annulment on the basis that a valid marriage never existed. Only an annulment would allow the parties to remarry.

One consequence of the Protestant Reformation in the sixteenth century was that the ecclesiastical courts began to lose their exclusive jurisdiction over divorce. As the secular courts took over, absolute divorce became possible so long as marital fault (e.g., adultery, cruelty, and desertion) could be established. In early American history, the New England colonies gave the legislature the power to grant an absolute divorce (called a *legislative divorce*), although such divorces were rare. Eventually, this power was given to the courts, often the courts of equity.[2]

THE SHIFT FROM FAULT TO NO-FAULT DIVORCE

For many years, the main grounds for divorce were those based on fault, the premise being that a marriage should not be terminated unless there was evidence of serious wrongdoing by one of the spouses. In short, blame had to be established. Many believed that stringent divorce laws would help prevent the failure of marriages. The fact that a couple could no longer get along was not enough of a reason to grant a divorce unless substantial wrongdoing existed. As one court commented in the mid-1950s:

> Testimony which proves merely an unhappy union, the parties being high strung temperamentally and unsuited to each other and neither being wholly innocent of the causes which resulted in the failure of their marriage, is insufficient to sustain a [divorce] judgment.[3]

Even when serious misconduct was alleged, states often required **corroboration** (additional evidence) of the misconduct. In our early history, only the innocent party—the spouse who was not at fault in the breakdown of the marriage—could obtain a divorce. The innocent party could receive alimony, a favorable division of the marital property, and custody of the children. The guilty or at-fault party was punished on the issues of support, property division, and child custody. If a divorce was granted, it was common to deny the guilty spouse the right to remarry. In short, guilt, wrongdoing, and punishment were predominant themes of our divorce laws.

Fault-based divorce, however, encouraged widespread dishonesty. More than 90 percent of the divorces were **uncontested**, meaning that there was no dispute between the parties. The percentage of uncontested divorces was so high, in large part, because parties often flagrantly committed **perjury** (lied to the courts) about the facts of their case in order to establish that fault existed or that they met all the procedural requirements for a divorce. While such conduct was obviously illegal, the parties were seldom caught. Both sides wanted the divorce, so there was little incentive to reveal the truth. Judges were not unaware of what was going on; many simply looked the other way.

The fault system also encouraged **migratory divorces**, where one of the parties would "migrate" or travel to another state solely to take advantage of its more

limited divorce
A declaration by a court that parties can live apart although they are still married to each other.

absolute divorce
A declaration by a court that the marriage is terminated so that the parties can remarry.

corroboration
Additional evidence of a fact in dispute.

uncontested
Unchallenged; without opposition or dispute.

perjury
Making a false statement under oath concerning a material matter with the intent to provide false testimony. Also called *false swearing*.

migratory divorces
A divorce obtained in a state to which one of the spouses traveled before returning to his or her home state.

contested
Challenged; opposed or disputed.

lenient divorce laws before returning to his or her own state. Some of these states gained the reputation of being divorce mills. At one time, a favorite destination for a "quickie" divorce was Reno, Nevada, where someone could "take the cure" (as a Reno divorce was known) by meeting Nevada's minimal procedural requirements.[4]

On those occasions when a divorce action was **contested**, court proceedings sometimes resembled a soap opera. A famous attorney, looking back over his long career, recalled the time when an indignant woman accused of infidelity broke down on the witness stand and screamed, "What you say isn't true. I've been faithful to my husband dozens of times."[5] In a similar vein, another attorney commented that for decades New York's divorce system was:

> built on a foundation of winks and falsehoods. If you wanted to split quickly, you and your spouse had to give one of the limited number of allowable reasons—including adultery, cruelty, imprisonment or abandonment—so there was a tendency to pick one out of a hat. Pregnant women have insisted they have not had sex in a year, one of the existing grounds; spouses claimed psychological cruelty for getting called fat; and [prominent parties denied adultory even though their affairs were mentioned in society columns]. One legendary ploy involved listing the filing lawyer's secretary as the partner in adultery (which may even have been true in a few cases).[6]

In this environment, Elizabeth Gilbert, author of the best-seller *Eat, Pray, Love* offered this caution in her book, "Here I pause to offer a prayer for my gentle reader: may you never, ever, have to get a divorce in New York."[7] Unfortunately, the trauma and chaos experienced by parties within the fault system of divorce were not unique to New York.

Reform was obviously needed. In 1969, California enacted the first no-fault divorce law in the country. Soon, other states followed. Today no-fault grounds exist in every state. Some states have eliminated the word "divorce" and replaced it with the word **dissolution** as a symbolic gesture that a new day has arrived. The change from fault to no-fault dramatically increased the rate of divorce in the country. In the years between 1970 and 1996, the number of divorced people living in the country more than quadrupled from 4.3 million to 18.3 million.[8] Estimates vary on the number of all current marriages that will eventually end in divorce. The range of estimates is between 40 and 50 percent. Some researchers believe that the more accurate estimate is 41 percent.[9]

dissolution
A divorce. A court's termination of a marriage for specified grounds. (See the glossary for another meaning of dissolution.)

CAUTIONARY NOTES

Not everyone has been happy with the shift to no-fault divorce. There are social conservatives who regret that marriage is now too easy to dissolve. No-fault divorce has also removed an emotional outlet. Some clients want and need the opportunity to tell the world about the abuse they have received from their spouse. They become frustrated when they learn that they cannot do so in divorce court. In this sense, no-fault divorce prevents some spouses from attaining "emotional closure" through the divorce.[10]

Finally, it has been argued that the end of fault grounds has placed some wives at a disadvantage. With divorce now so easy to obtain, a husband who wants to get out of the marriage does not have to bargain so hard on the issues of spousal support, child custody, and property division.

Suppose, however, that the husband wants to stay in the marriage. If he is the more powerful of the spouses, it may be that no-fault divorce can give the bargaining edge to the wife:

> In the United States, the availability of divorce has increased with unilateral divorce, which allows either member of the couple to dissolve the union. The change has been associated with lower rates of female suicide and domestic

violence, and fewer wives murdered by their husbands. Unilateral divorce shifts the bargaining power to the person who is getting less out of the marriage and thus is most likely to leave. The partner getting more from the marriage has to work harder to keep the other person around, which can be good for the marriage and good for the couple. In other words, unilateral divorce benefits victims and potential victims.[11]

A RETURN TO FAULT?

In a few states (e.g., Louisiana), conservatives were able to reintroduce fault grounds into the law of divorce. In these states, parties wishing to marry can choose a conventional/standard marriage (which can be dissolved with no-fault grounds) and a **covenant marriage** (which requires a separation or fault grounds to dissolve). Not many states, however, allow covenant marriages, and few couples choose them in states that do allow them. See Chapter 5 for a discussion of covenant marriages.

MARITAL MISCONDUCT IN NO-FAULT DIVORCE

No-fault divorce does not always mean that marital fault has no role in divorce litigation:

- For some of the no-fault grounds (e.g., incompatibility and irreconcilable differences), it will be very difficult to describe the facts that support the grounds without alleging who was at fault in creating those facts.

- As we will see in Chapter 8, a court's decision on property division is generally unrelated to fault, but there are some "economic faults" that can be considered, such as **dissipation**, which occurs when a spouse squanders marital assets just before or during the divorce litigation.

- As we will see in Chapter 9, evidence of parental fault can be important in child-custody disputes.

According to the president of the American Academy of Matrimonial Lawyers, "No-fault does not mean that fault is irrelevant." On child-custody issues, it can be very important to introduce evidence that the opposing spouse has shown bad behavior in front of the children or that the spouse has an untreated substance abuse problem. Lying about money can also be key. "Once you catch them in one lie, nothing else they say is credible to the judge."[12]

Also, most states have retained the fault grounds for divorce along with the no-fault grounds. (See Exhibit 7.1.) A party filing for divorce can choose which grounds to use. Most choose no-fault grounds. Some no-fault grounds, however, require that the parties have lived apart for designated periods of time, a requirement that most fault grounds do not have. A party might choose a fault ground to avoid this waiting period.

A spouse might **plead** a no-fault ground and, in the alternative, plead a fault ground. This is done in the hope that the evidence of fault will lead to a more favorable ruling on other issues, such as child custody.

covenant marriage
A form of ceremonial marriage (a) that is entered upon proof of premarital counseling and a promise to seek marital counseling when needed during the marriage, and (b) that is dissolved upon separation for a designated period or upon proof of marital fault. Also called *high-test marriage*.

dissipation
The improper reduction or waste of marital assets that should have been available for property division or for support upon divorce.

plead
To file a pleading, a formal document that asserts or responds to court claims or defenses. (See the glossary for additional definitions.)

EXHIBIT 7.1   Grounds for Divorce

Major No-Fault Grounds for Divorce	Major Fault Grounds for Divorce
• Living apart	• Adultery
• Incompatibility	• Cruelty
• Irreconcilable differences	• Desertion

TORT CLAIMS BROUGHT WITHIN A DIVORCE ACTION

tort
A civil wrong (other than a breach of contract) that causes injury or other loss for which our legal system deems it just to provide a remedy, such as damages. Injury or loss can be to a person (a personal tort); to land and anything attached to the land (a real-property tort); to property other than land, called personal property and movable property (a personal-property tort); or to economic interests (an economic tort).

interspousal immunity
Spouses cannot sue each other for designated categories of torts. Also called *husband-wife immunity*.

Before we take a close look at these grounds for divorce, we need to examine the relationship between no-fault divorce and fault-based **tort** claims. In Chapter 17, we will learn that there are some marital torts that cannot be brought between spouses. The **interspousal immunity** bars suits for such torts. But the immunity does not cover all torts. Assume that a spouse seeks a no-fault divorce and in the same proceeding wants damages from the other spouse for a tort that is not barred by the immunity. For example, when former governor of New Jersey Jim McGreevey and his wife divorced, one of his wife's claims was that he had committed the tort of fraud by tricking her into marrying a gay man who needed a wife to advance his political career.

States differ on whether such torts can be brought in a divorce action or must be brought in a separate proceeding. Some states are against allowing torts to be asserted in the divorce action because most marital torts are based on marital fault and introducing evidence of such fault is inconsistent with the reason no-fault divorce was created. Other states, however, take the view that it would be a waste of time and a needless expense to require two separate suits, one for the divorce and another for the tort.

ASSIGNMENT 7.1

a. In your state code, find the statute that lists the grounds for divorce. Give the citation to this statute and list all the grounds for divorce provided therein. (See General Instructions for the State-Code Assignment in Appendix A.)

b. Select two of the grounds of divorce in your state, a fault ground and a no-fault ground. For each ground, draft a checklist of questions to help determine whether the ground exists. If fault grounds are not allowed in your state, select two no-fault grounds. (See General Instructions for the Checklist-Formulation Assignment in Appendix A.)

NO-FAULT GROUNDS FOR DIVORCE

As indicated in Exhibit 7.1, the three major no-fault grounds for divorce are living apart, incompatibility, and irreconcilable differences.

LIVING APART

living apart
A no-fault ground for divorce that is established when spouses live separately for a designated period of consecutive time during which their intent was to end the marriage.

Living apart (sometimes called *living separate and apart*) is a no-fault ground for divorce in many states. The statute authorizing this ground (or any other ground) must be carefully read; slight differences in wording in the statutes of different states may account for major differences in meaning.

The living-apart ground is established when spouses live separately for a designated period of consecutive time during which their intent was to end the marriage. (They do not have to prove that one of them was at fault in causing the separation.) Most living-apart statutes require that the parties intend to end their marriage when they live separately for the designated period of consecutive time, as outlined below. Some states impose additional and more restrictive requirements. For example, the statute might specify that the living apart must be required by a court order or by a separation agreement of the parties.

APART The parties must be living apart, usually in different buildings. In some states, if they are living in separate parts of the same place ("under the same roof"), they are *not* living apart even if their sexual relationship has ended.

TIME In all states, the statute requires that the parties live apart for a designated period of time, ranging from six months to three years. A major purpose of the time limitation is to force the parties to think seriously about whether reconciliation is possible.

CONSECUTIVENESS The separated time must be consecutive. Off-and-on separations do not qualify if one of the separations does not last the requisite length of time. This is true even if the total time spent apart from intermittent separations exceeds the required minimum. Furthermore, the qualifying period of separation must continue right up to the time one of the spouses brings the divorce action on the ground of living apart.

CONSENT Several states require that the period of separation be consensual or voluntary on the part of *both* spouses. Thus, if one spouse is drafted into the service or is hospitalized for an extended period of time, the separation is not considered voluntary.

CAUSE Sometimes the *cause* of the separation may be relevant to its voluntariness. Suppose, for example, that Bob deserts his wife, Linda, and they live apart for a period in excess of the time required by statute. Arguably, the parties did not separate voluntarily; they separated as a result of the *fault* of Bob. Most states, however, will grant the divorce to either party on the basis that voluntariness and marital fault are irrelevant so long as there was a living apart for the requisite period of time.

The following Checklist covers some of the interviewing and investigation tasks when living apart is an issue in a divorce case.

✔ INTERVIEWING AND INVESTIGATION CHECKLIST

Living Apart

LEGAL INTERVIEWING QUESTIONS

1. How long have you lived apart? Are you now living separate from D (the defendant)?

2. On what date did you separate?

3. Since that date, what contact have you had with D?

4. Have you had sexual relations with D since you separated?

5. Describe the circumstances of your separation with D.

6. When you separated, did you intend a permanent separation? If so, what indications of this did you give?

7. Did D intend a permanent separation? If so, what indications did D give?

8. What was the condition of your marriage at the time of separation?

9. Did you leave D? Did D leave you? Did you both leave at the same time by mutual agreement?

10. When the separation occurred, did either of you protest? Were you or D dissatisfied with the separation?

11. Since you separated, has either of you asked or suggested that the two of you get back together again? If so, when, what was said, and what was the response of the other?

12. Has either of you obtained a legal separation or a judgment of separate maintenance? If so, when? Have you been living separate since that time? Have both of you abided by the terms of the legal separation or maintenance judgment?

13. Since you separated, at what address(es) have you lived? (Same question about D.)

14. Do you and D have a separation agreement? If so, when was it signed?

15. If you separated and resumed living together, answer the above questions for each subsequent separation.

POSSIBLE INVESTIGATION TASKS

- Collect evidence that the parties have lived separate and apart (e.g., rent receipts from the apartments of the parties, copies of separate utility bills).

- Obtain witness statements from people aware of the separation.

ASSIGNMENT   **7.2**

Assume that a statute provides that one of the grounds for divorce is voluntary separation for a period of two consecutive years. This living-apart ground is the only ground authorized in the state. Fred and Gail are married. On June 10, 2015, Fred moves out when they agree to separate. On May 15, 2017, when he learns that she is thinking about filing for divorce, he calls Gail and pleads with her to let him come back. She refuses. On July 25, 2017, she files for divorce on the ground of living apart. Could a divorce be granted on the ground of living apart? (See General Instructions for the Legal-Analysis Assignment in Appendix A.)

As we shall see, most states allow parties to seek a *legal separation*, which is a court authorization that the parties can live separate lives under specified terms (e.g., court orders on alimony and child custody) while still being married to each other. In some states, this legal separation can be *converted* into a divorce after a designated period of time. Similarly, a judgment of *separate maintenance* (spousal support), discussed later in the chapter, can often be converted into a divorce after this period of time.

Exhibit 7.2 summarizes the living-apart ground for divorce.

INCOMPATIBILITY

incompatibility
A no-fault ground for divorce that is established when there is such discord between spouses that it is impossible for them to live together in a normal marital relationship.

Some states list *incompatibility* as a ground for divorce. Incompatibility consists of such rift or discord between spouses that it is impossible to live together in a normal marital relationship. "Petty quarrels" and "minor bickering" are usually not enough. For most of the states that have this ground, fault is not an issue; the plaintiff does not have to show that the defendant was at fault in causing the incompatibility, and the defendant cannot defend the action by introducing

EXHIBIT 7.2   Summary of Ground for Divorce: Living Apart

Definition: Living separately for a designated period of consecutive time during which their intent was to end the marriage.

Who Can Sue: In most states, either party, including the party who wrongfully caused the separation.

Major Defenses:

1. The parties never separated.
2. The parties did not separate for the period designated in the statute.
3. The parties reconciled and cohabitated before the statutory period was over (i.e., the separation was not consecutive).
4. Living apart was a trial separation only; they did not intend to end the marriage.
5. The separation was not voluntary (this defense is available in some states).
6. The agreement to separate was obtained by fraud or duress.
7. The court lacks jurisdiction (discussed later in this chapter).

Is living apart also a ground for annulment? No.

Is living apart also a ground for legal separation? Yes, in many states.

Is living apart also a ground for separate maintenance? Yes, in many states.

evidence that the plaintiff committed marital wrongs. There are a few states, however, that do require a showing of fault. In such states, incompatibility is not a no-fault ground.

When the plaintiff alleges that the parties are incompatible, what happens if the defendant responds by disagreeing? Do *both* husband and wife have to feel that it is impossible to live together? Assuming that the plaintiff is able to establish that more than "petty quarrels" are involved, most courts will grant the divorce to the plaintiff even though the defendant insists that they can still work it out. If, however, the court feels that the marriage is salvageable, some states will allow the judge to order the spouses into counseling or mediation. In many states, this problem is avoided by the additional requirement that the parties be separated (live apart) for a designated period of time (e.g., one year). When a separation of this duration has existed, courts are likely to accept the view of one party that the no-fault ground has been established despite what the other spouse thinks.

If the court is convinced that the spouses are seeking a **sham divorce**, it can refuse to divorce them. Suppose, for example, that the parties try to divorce at the end of the year in order to take advantage of a tax benefit and then remarry at the beginning of the next year. The complaint or petition stating that the parties are incompatible (or that there is an irretrievable breakdown in the marriage) would be fraudulent. (See the discussion below on collusion.)

When a no-fault ground asserted by one spouse is sufficient for a court to grant the divorce, it is referred to as a *unilateral no-fault ground.*

sham divorce
A divorce sought by parties who do not intend to stay divorced from each other once the divorce is granted. When they obtained the divorce, their intent was to remarry at the earliest opportune time.

ASSIGNMENT 7.3

One married partner says to the other, "I no longer love you." By definition, are they incompatible for purposes of this ground for divorce? (See General Instructions for the Legal-Analysis Assignment in Appendix A.)

Exhibit 7.3 summarizes the incompatibility ground for divorce.

IRRECONCILABLE DIFFERENCES

The newest and most commonly used no-fault ground in many states is **irreconcilable differences**, which consist of such discord between spouses that there has been an irremediable breakdown of the marriage. (Something is irremediable if it can't be repaired or corrected.) The goal of the legislatures that have enacted this ground has been to focus on the central question of whether it makes

irreconcilable differences
A no-fault ground for divorce that is established when there is such discord between the spouses that there has been an irremediable breakdown of the marriage.

EXHIBIT 7.3 Summary of Ground for Divorce: Incompatibility

Definition: Such discord between the spouses that it is impossible for them to live together in a normal marital relationship.

Who Can Sue: Either party in most states.

Is incompatibility also a ground for annulment? No.

Is incompatibility also a ground for legal separation? Yes, in many states.

Is incompatibility also a ground for separate maintenance? Yes, in many states.

any sense to continue the marriage. The statutes of various states have similar language and content in describing this ground. For example:

- Irretrievable breakdown of the marriage.
- Discord or conflict of personalities that destroys the legitimate ends of marriage and prevents any reasonable expectation of reconciliation.
- Breakdown of the marriage to such an extent that the legitimate objects of marriage have been destroyed and there remains no reasonable likelihood that the marriage can be preserved.
- Irreconcilable differences are those grounds that a court determines to be substantial reasons for not continuing the marriage and which make it appear that the marriage should be dissolved.
- Insupportability, where discord or conflict of personalities destroys the legitimate ends of the marital relationship and prevents any reasonable expectation of reconciliation.

In some states, an additional requirement is that the parties be separated (live apart) for a designated period of time (e.g., a year).

What happens if the defendant denies that the breakdown of the marriage is irremediable and feels that marriage counseling would help? In most states, this is simply one item of evidence that the court must consider in deciding whether remediation is possible. It is likely, however, that if one party adamantly refuses to participate in any reconciliation efforts, the court will conclude that the breakdown of the marriage is total even if the other party expresses a conciliatory attitude.

If the court concludes that there is a reasonable possibility of reconciliation, its options may be limited to delaying the divorce proceedings—granting a **stay**—for a limited number of days (e.g., thirty) to give the parties additional time to try to work out their difficulties.

stay
The suspension or postponement of a judgment or proceeding.

ASSIGNMENT   7.4

Dan and Helen were married in your state. Helen does not want to be married anymore. She loves Dan and enjoys being his wife, but simply wants to live alone indefinitely. Dan does not want a divorce. Can she obtain a divorce in your state? (See General Instructions for the State-Code Assignment and the Court-Opinion Assignment in Appendix A.)

Exhibit 7.4 summarizes the irreconcilable-differences ground for divorce.

EXHIBIT 7.4   Summary of Ground for Divorce: Irreconcilable Differences

Definition: Such discord between the spouses that there has been an irremediable breakdown of the marriage.

Who Can Aue: Either party.

Is irreconcilable differences also a ground for annulment? No.

Is irreconcilable differences also a ground for legal separation? Yes, in many states.

Is irreconcilable differences also a ground for separate maintenance? Yes, in many states.

The following Checklist covers some of the interviewing and investigation tasks in cases asserting the no-fault grounds of irreconcilable differences or incompatibility.

✔ INTERVIEWING AND INVESTIGATION CHECKLIST

Irreconcilable Differences or Incompatibility

LEGAL INTERVIEWING QUESTIONS

1. Are you and D (the defendant) now living together? If not, how long have you been separated, and what were the circumstances of the separation?

2. How long have you been married to D?

3. Describe your relationship with D at its worst.

4. How often do you and D communicate meaningfully? When was the last time this occurred?

5. How often did you and D argue? Were the arguments intense or bitter? Explain.

6. Does D insult you, ridicule your religion, your political views, or your family?

7. Does D do this in front of anyone? Who else knows that D does this? How do they know?

8. How does D get along with the children? What is your relationship with them?

9. Do you think that D has tried to turn the children against you? If so, how do you know? What specifically have the children or others said or done to make you think so?

10. Have your friends, relatives, or associates told you that D has ridiculed or criticized you behind your back?

11. Does D drink or use drugs? Do you? If so, how much, how often, and how has it affected your marriage?

12. Have the two of you ever hit each other or threatened domestic violence? If so, describe the circumstances. How often has it happened? Did the children see such behavior? Has anyone else seen it?

13. Were there any other major events or scenes that were unpleasant for you? If so, describe them.

14. Did you or D ever call the police?

15. Did you or D receive medical attention as a result of your arguments or fights?

16. How would you describe your sexual relationship with D?

17. Have either of you ever accused the other of infidelity?

18. Have either of you stayed away from home overnight due to marital difficulties. If so, how often?

19. Have you seen or have you considered seeing a psychiatrist or some other mental-health professional?

20. How was your physical and mental health before D started behaving this way?

21. Do you have any difficulty sleeping?

22. Do you have any difficulty doing your regular work because of D?

23. What is D's opinion of you as a spouse?

24. Do you think that you will ever be able to live in harmony with D? Explain why or why not.

25. Does D think the two of you will ever be able to get back together again? Explain why or why not.

26. Have you or D sought marital counseling or therapy of any kind? If so, describe the circumstances.

27. Are you now interested in any such help in order to try to save the marriage? Do you feel it would work? How do you think D feels about this?

28. Have you asked a court for spousal support (separate maintenance) or for a legal separation? If so, what was the result?

POSSIBLE INVESTIGATION TASKS

• Obtain all of the client's medical records, if any, from medical providers that have treated the client as a result of marital difficulties.

• If the children are old and mature enough, find out how they viewed D's relationship with the client, and also how D treated them.

• Obtain police records, if any, resulting from fights or disturbances in which the police became involved.

• Obtain copies of documents such as a legal-separation judgment or separate-maintenance judgment, if any.

FAULT GROUNDS FOR DIVORCE

The three major fault grounds for divorce are adultery, cruelty, and desertion. Although they are less often used today, they remain in force in many states. As indicated, a party will sometimes plead a no-fault ground and also one of the fault grounds, particularly cruelty.

ADULTERY

adultery
(1) Voluntary sexual intercourse between a married person and someone other than his or her spouse. (2) Voluntary intimate sexual relations between a spouse and someone other than his or her spouse, irrespective of the specific sexual acts performed, the marital status of the nonspouse, or the gender of the nonspouse.

corespondent
The person who had sexual relations with a defendant charged with adultery.

circumstantial evidence
Evidence of one fact from which another fact (not personally observed or known) can be inferred. Also called *indirect evidence*.

Adultery is voluntary sexual intercourse between a married person and someone to whom he or she is not married. There are some states that use a broader definition, such as voluntary intimate sexual relations between a spouse and someone other than his or her spouse, irrespective of the specific sexual acts performed, the marital status of the nonspouse, or the gender of the nonspouse. The person who has sexual relations with the defendant is called the **corespondent**.

Intercourse is not voluntary, of course, if the defendant is raped or if the defendant is insane at the time. Because direct evidence of adultery is seldom available, **circumstantial evidence** must be relied upon. Specifically, the plaintiff must prove that the defendant had the *opportunity* (e.g., overnight trips taken with the corespondent) and the *inclination* (e.g., romantic texts sent to the corespondent) to commit adultery.

Although rarely enforced, adultery is a crime in several states. In Michigan, for example, adultery is a felony, which is committed by "sexual intercourse of 2 persons, either of whom is married to a third person."[13] Such criminal laws, however, are of questionable constitutionality after the U.S. Supreme Court held in *Lawrence v. Texas* that a state could not criminalize private, consensual, intimate same-sex conduct by adults.[14] Arguably, the same conclusion could apply to criminal prosecutions for private, consensual, adulterous conduct by adults. (See Chapter 5 on the *Lawrence* case.) *Lawrence*, however, would not affect the right of a state to allow divorce as a ground for adultery.

CRUELTY

In most marriage ceremonies, the parties take each other "for better or worse." This concept was viewed quite literally early in our history, particularly when the woman was the one claiming to have received too much of the "worse." It was expected that a good deal of fighting, nagging, and mutual abuse would occur within a marriage. The concept of permitting marriage to be dissolved because of "mere" meanness or indignities was alien to our legal system for a long time.

cruelty
The infliction of serious physical or mental suffering on another.

Eventually, **cruelty**—the infliction of serious physical or mental suffering on another—became a ground for divorce. Not all states, however, have the same standard for determining when cruelty exists. A state might require that it be "extreme" or "inhumane" before the divorce can be granted. Furthermore, some states limit the ground to actual or threatened *physical* violence. (A 1956 Virginia court held that an attack by a husband in which he "grabbed her, threw her against the wall, and threatened her with a butcher knife" was not enough to amount to physical cruelty.[15]) Later, *mental anguish* came to be recognized as a form of cruelty, but there was often a requirement that the psychological cruelty result in an impairment of the plaintiff's health. Some states will accept a minimal-health impairment (e.g., a loss of sleep).

domestic violence (DV)
Actual or threatened physical injury or abuse of one member of a family or household by another member. (See the glossary for the definition of the *Model Code*.)

stalking
A pattern of repeated and unwanted attention, harassment, contact, or any other course of conduct directed at a specific person that would cause a reasonable person to feel fear.

Cruelty can lead to criminal prosecution for violating laws against **domestic violence (DV)** and stalking. DV is actual or threatened physical injury or abuse of one member of a family or household by another member. **Stalking** is a pattern of repeated and unwanted attention, harassment, contact, or any other course of conduct directed at a specific person that would cause a reasonable person to feel fear. (We will examine DV and stalking in Chapter 12.)

DESERTION

Desertion (also called *abandonment*) is the voluntary and unjustified departure of one spouse from another. The specific components of this ground are as follows:

(1) one spouse voluntarily leaves another,
(2) for an uninterrupted period of time (e.g., two years),
(3) with the intent not to return to resume cohabitation,
(4) the separation occurred without the consent of the other spouse, and
(5) there was no justification or reasonable cause for the separation.

An example of desertion would be a husband who leaves his wife to live with his mistress for several years after telling his wife that he no longer wants to live with her.

It is also possible to commit desertion without leaving the home. **Constructive desertion** consists of either:

(1) Engaging in conduct that justifies the other spouse's departure from the home (e.g., refusing all future sexual relations), or
(2) Rejecting a sincere offer of reconciliation from the other spouse who initially left the home without justification.

In effect, the spouse who stayed home becomes the deserter! When constructive desertion has occurred, the spouse who left would be allowed to sue the other spouse for divorce on the ground of desertion.

OTHER GROUNDS

A number of other closely related and sometimes overlapping grounds exist in many states. Here is a partial list (some of which are also grounds for annulment):

- Bigamy
- Impotence
- Nonage
- Fraud
- Duress
- Incest
- Imprisonment for three consecutive years
- Conviction of a serious crime
- Insanity; mental incapacity for three years
- Habitual drunkenness
- Drug addiction
- Nonsupport
- Unexplained absence
- Neglect of duty
- Obtaining an out-of-state divorce that is invalid
- Sexually transmitted diseases (e.g., venereal disease) or AIDS
- Unchastity
- Pregnancy by someone else
- Treatment injurious to health
- Deviant sexual conduct
- Any other cause deemed by the court to be sufficient, if the court is satisfied that the parties can no longer live together

In some states, a spouse's unexplained absence for a designated number of years (e.g., five) is a ground for divorce if there has been **due diligence** in the search for the missing spouse and a belief that he or she is dead. It is called an **Enoch Arden divorce**. As we explained in Chapter 6, the *Enoch Arden marriage presumption* allowed a spouse to presume that the absent spouse was dead.

desertion
The voluntary and unjustified departure of one spouse from another. Also called *abandonment*.

constructive desertion
(1) A spouse's conduct that justifies the other spouse's departure from the home. (2) A spouse's rejection of a sincere offer of reconciliation from the spouse who initially left the home without justification.

due diligence
Reasonable efforts to find and verify factual information needed to carry out an obligation, to avoid harming someone, or to make an important decision.

Enoch Arden divorce
A divorce granted on the ground that a spouse has disappeared for a designated number of years with no explanation.

DEFENSES TO THE FAULT GROUNDS

The basic defenses to the fault grounds for divorce are defined as follows:

collusion
(1) An agreement to commit fraud. (2) An agreement by spouses that one or both will lie to the court in order to help secure their divorce.

- **Collusion.** An agreement by spouses that one or both will lie to the court in order to help secure their divorce. The lie pertains to grounds for the divorce (e.g., the spouses lie about violence in the marriage); or about procedural requirements for obtaining the divorce (e.g., the spouses lie about whether one or both are domiciled in the state).

connivance
A willingness or a consent by one spouse that a marital wrong be committed by the other spouse.

- **Connivance.** A willingness or a consent by one spouse that a marital wrong be committed by the other spouse (e.g., encouraging someone to seduce one's spouse).[16] A main difference between connivance and collusion is that connivance covers conduct that was actually committed, whereas collusion is an agreement to assert false facts.

condonation
An express or implied forgiveness by the innocent spouse of the marital fault committed by the other spouse.

- **Condonation.** An express or implied forgiveness by the innocent spouse of the marital fault committed by the other spouse (e.g., a spouse continues to live with the other spouse for over a year after finding out that the latter had a weekend affair with an office worker on a business trip).

recrimination
A serious marital wrong committed by the spouse seeking a divorce even though this spouse is charging the other spouse with committing a serious marital wrong.

- **Recrimination.** A serious marital wrong committed by the spouse seeking the divorce even though this spouse is charging the other spouse with committing a serious marital wrong (e.g., petitioning a court for a divorce on the ground of adultery even though the petitioner has also committed adultery). If both spouses are "guilty," the court might apply the doctrine of **comparative rectitude** and award the divorce to the spouse least at fault.

comparative rectitude
A comparison of the wrongdoing of two spouses in causing the breakdown of the marriage so that the divorce can be given to the spouse least at fault.

- **Provocation.** Inciting the conduct that constitutes the marital wrong by the other spouse.

Of course, because of the extensive use of no-fault grounds for divorce, these defenses to the fault grounds are seldom used or needed.

provocation
Inciting the conduct that constitutes the marital wrong by the other spouse.

LEGAL SEPARATION

Two kinds of separation can exist when parties are having serious marital difficulties: an informal separation and a legal separation. Living apart from each other is an *informal separation* if it is not officially granted or approved by the courts. A **legal separation**, on the other hand, is a declaration or judgment by a court that two people can live apart—from bed and board—while still remaining husband and wife. A legal separation is also known as a:

legal separation
A declaration by a court that parties can live apart even though they are still married to each other.

- Judicial separation
- Limited divorce
- *Divorce a mensa et thoro* (divorce from board and hearth)
- Separation from bed and board

Parties subject to a legal separation are not free to remarry. The marriage relationship remains until it is dissolved by the death of one of the parties, by an annulment, or by a divorce.

Parties seek legal separations for several reasons. One's religion may be opposed to divorce. A divorce might result in the termination of medical care that is available through the other spouse's healthcare policy at work. Some spouses might not be emotionally ready to accept the finality of a divorce. Yet they may need a court decree that covers financial support and child custody. In such cases, a legal separation is an option in most states. Spouses who separate without seeking a divorce are sometimes referred to as the *un-divorced*.

To obtain a legal separation, *grounds* must be established in the same manner as grounds must be established to obtain a divorce. In fact, the grounds for legal separation are often similar, if not identical, to the grounds for a divorce (e.g., no-fault grounds such as incompatibility or irreconcilable differences and fault grounds such as adultery or cruelty).

When a court grants a legal separation, it often also makes rulings on spousal support, property division, child support, and child custody while the spouses are living apart. All of these decisions require special categories of jurisdiction. They are the same categories that a court must have when it grants a divorce. Hence, we will discuss them later in this chapter when we cover divorce jurisdiction and procedure. To preview this discussion, a court needs *in rem jurisdiction* to order a legal separation or divorce and *personal jurisdiction* to order property division and spousal support. The details of jurisdiction needed for child custody and child support will be covered in Chapters 9 and 10.

We should distinguish a legal separation from a separation agreement. A **separation agreement** is a contract between spouses who have separated (or who are about to separate) that can cover support, custody, property division, and other terms of their separation and likely divorce. The agreement may or may not become part of (i.e., be incorporated and merged in) the divorce judgment if one is later sought. Also, it is important to use the words "separated" and "separation" carefully. Alone, these words mean a *physical* separation between the spouses. If, however, a court-sanctioned or court-ordered separation is involved, the reference should be to a *legal separation* or comparable term used in the state.

Dates are important in separation cases, whether or not the parties obtain a formal judgment of legal separation. In most cases, the date of separation helps determine whether property is classified as *marital property* or as *separate property*, as we will see in Chapter 8. The date of separation (**DOS**) refers to the date the spouses stopped living together on a permanent basis—the date on which continuing to live together was no longer an option.

In most states, once the parties are permanently living apart, the property that each individually accumulates is considered *separate property*, even though they are still legally married to each other. Also in most states, separate property is not divided upon divorce. As we will discuss later, only marital (or community) property is subject to property division.

separation agreement
A contract by married persons who have separated (or who are about to separate) that can cover support, custody, property division, and other terms of their separation and likely divorce. Also called *marital settlement agreement (MSA)*.

DOS
Date of separation—date the spouses stopped living together on a permanent basis.

ASSIGNMENT 7.5

Does your state have an action for a legal separation?

a. If so, what is the action called?

b. What is the citation of the statute authorizing this action?

c. What are the grounds in your state for a legal separation?

d. Are there any grounds for legal separation that are *not* grounds for divorce? (See General Instructions for the State-Code Assignment in Appendix A.)

e. Prepare a flowchart of the procedural steps that are necessary for a legal separation in your state. (See General Instructions for the Flowchart Assignment in Appendix A.)

After a court issues a legal-separation judgment, the fact that the parties reconcile and resume cohabitation does not mean that the judgment becomes inoperative. It remains effective until a court declares otherwise. Hence, a spouse who is under an order to pay spousal support pursuant to a legal-separation judgment must continue to pay alimony even though the parties have subsequently reconciled and are living together again. To be relieved of this obligation, a petition must be made to the court to change the judgment.

An important consequence of a legal separation in many states is its **conversion** feature. A legal separation can be converted into a divorce. In effect, the existence of the legal separation for a designated period of time can become a ground for a divorce. The Uniform Marriage and Divorce Act provides that "[n]o earlier than 6 months after entry of a judgment of legal separation, the court on motion of either party shall convert the judgment to a judgment of dissolution of marriage."[17] The resulting dissolution or divorce is called a *conversion divorce* or a *convertible divorce*.

conversion
Changing a legal separation into a divorce after the parties have lived apart for a designated period of time. (See the glossary for an additional meaning.)

SEPARATE MAINTENANCE

separate maintenance
Court-ordered spousal support while the parties are separated but still married. Also called *separate support* or *alimony without divorce*.

An action for **separate maintenance** is a proceeding brought by a spouse to secure support. The action is usually filed by wives, but an increasing number of husbands are seeking spousal support by this route. Like the legal-separation judgment, a separate-maintenance judgment does not alter the marital status of the parties; they remain married to each other while living separately.

Some states use an action for spousal maintenance as their version of an action for a legal separation.

The major ground for a separate-maintenance judgment is the refusal of one spouse to support the other without just cause. In addition, most states provide that all of the grounds for divorce will also be grounds for separate maintenance. Furthermore, in a divorce action, if the court refuses to grant either party a divorce, it usually can still enter an order for separate maintenance.

If the plaintiff refuses a good-faith offer by the defendant to reconcile, the plaintiff becomes a wrongdoer, which in some states may justify the defendant in refusing to provide support. If the separate-maintenance action is still pending, the plaintiff will lose the action. If a separate-maintenance judgment has already been awarded, the defendant may be able to discontinue making payments under it.

The court determines the amount and form of a separate-maintenance award in the same way that it makes the alimony determination in a divorce case (see Chapter 8). If needed, the court can also make child-support and child-custody decisions in the separate-maintenance action. In general, *property division* is not resolved by the court in a judgment of separate maintenance. If the parties cannot agree on how their marital property should be divided, they need to seek other avenues of relief, such as a divorce or legal separation.

When we discuss divorce procedure, we will cover the personal jurisdiction needed by a court to make an alimony order. The same kind of jurisdiction is needed when a court orders separate maintenance.

ASSIGNMENT   7.6

a. Does your state have an action for separate maintenance or its equivalent? If so, on what grounds will the action be granted? (See General Instructions for the State-Code Assignment in Appendix A.)

b. Prepare a flowchart of all the procedural steps required in a proceeding for separate maintenance or its equivalent. (See General Instructions for the Flowchart Assignment in Appendix A).

INTRODUCTION TO DIVORCE PROCEDURE

The overwhelming number of divorce cases are uncontested because (1) the other side does not show up in court or (2) the other side shows up but does not dispute what the person filing for divorce is seeking. In many cases, the spouses have negotiated an agreement (on their own or through counsel) on the termination of the marital relationship, as well as on alimony, property division, child custody, and child support. In such cases, divorce procedure can be relatively simple.

There are two main kinds of divorces depending on who is before the court when the judgment was rendered. In a **bilateral divorce**, both spouses are before the court when the divorce case is heard. In an **ex parte divorce** only one of the spouses (the petitioner or plaintiff) is before the court when the divorce case is heard, usually because the other spouse does not appear. (**Ex parte** means only one side is present in court.)

In some states, short-term marriages with no children and no significant marital property can be dissolved (ex parte or bilaterally) under an accelerated or **expedited procedure**, often involving few or no trips to the court other than to file court documents such as a divorce petition and a statement of assets and debts. (See the section on Summary Dissolution later in this chapter.) If, however, the bitterness of the past has not subsided and agreements have not been reached, resolving substantive and procedural disputes can be complicated. Major characteristics of most contested bilateral divorces are tension, cost, and time.

A recent trend among a relatively small number of couples who have amicably uncoupled is to post divorce selfies on Facebook or Instagram (pictures of themselves together smiling soon after the divorce). Holding the hand of his former mate, one man commented, "I couldn't have picked a better ex-wife." These are not the kinds of divorces we will be discussing in the remainder of this chapter.

bilateral divorce
A divorce granted by a court when both spouses are present before the court.

ex parte divorce
A divorce granted by a court when only one of the spouses participates or appears in court. Also called a *unilateral divorce*.

ex parte
With only one side present (usually the plaintiff or petitioner) when a court is asked to do something.

expedited procedure
An accelerated procedure achieved by bypassing some of the procedural steps that are normally required.

DOMICILE

To obtain a divorce, one or both parties must have a domicile in the state. Unfortunately, the terms *domicile* and *residence* are sometimes confused. There are distinct differences between the two terms, although they are often used interchangeably.

- **Residence.** The place where someone is living. A person can have many residences (e.g., a home in the city, plus a beach house, plus an apartment in another state or country).

- **Domicile.** The place where a person has been physically present (a) with the intent to make that place a permanent home, or (b) with no intent to make any other place a permanent home. It is the place to which one intends to return when away. With rare exceptions, a person can have only one domicile.

Here are some related terms:

- *Resident*: a person who has a residence in the state.
- *Nonresident*: a person who does not have a residence in the state.
- *Domiciliary*: a person who has a domicile (is domiciled) in the state.
- *Nondomiciliary*: a person who does not have a domicile (is not domiciled) in the state.

For example, if we say that George is a nondomiciliary of New York, we are saying that he does not have a domicile in New York. Again keep in mind, however, that

residence
The place where someone is living.

domicile
The place where a person has been physically present (a) with the intent to make that place a permanent home or (b) with no intent to make any other place a permanent home.

residence and domicile are sometimes used synonymously. A case or a statute might refer to a nonresident but mean a nondomiciliary.

For several reasons, it is important to identify a person's domicile. For example:

- A court does not have divorce jurisdiction to dissolve a marriage unless at least one of the spouses is domiciled in the state where that court sits. (Later, we will see that the jurisdiction to dissolve a marriage is called *in rem jurisdiction.*)
- Liability for the **estate tax** may depend upon the domicile of the decedent at the time of death.

Children cannot acquire a domicile of their own until they reach the **age of majority** (e.g., eighteen years of age) or otherwise become emancipated. (They are **emancipated** or **unemancipated** depending on whether they are legally independent or dependent on their parent).

- Unemancipated children acquire a domicile by **operation of law** rather than by choice. The law operates to impose a domicile on the child regardless of what the child may want. The domicile of the parents automatically (by operation of law) becomes the domicile of their unemancipated children. If the parents are separated, the child's domicile is that of the parent who has **legal custody**, even if the child happens to be living with the other parent in a different state.
- Emancipated children (like all adults) can pick any domicile they want (**domicile by choice**).

There was a time in the law when the wife's domicile was also determined by operation of law. Her domicile was that of her husband no matter what state she lived in—even if she lived in a state different from her husband. Only the husband was entitled to a domicile of choice. This, of course, is no longer the law. If the rule still existed, it would certainly be struck down as a violation of the **equal protection of law.**

Special rules may apply to the military. A state, for example, may say that a member of the military is presumed to be domiciled in the state where he or she is stationed for a designated period of time (e.g., three months).[18]

INTENT

Domicile requires proof of someone's intent to have a permanent home. Intent is a state of mind; the main way to determine a state of mind is by interpreting external acts. External acts include verbal statements, although such statements are not always the best evidence of a person's state of mind. Suppose, for example, that Bill is domiciled in Connecticut and becomes violently ill during a visit to Maine. He knows that if he dies domiciled in Maine, his beneficiaries will pay a lower state estate tax than if he died domiciled in Connecticut. While lying in a Maine sick bed just before he dies, Bill openly says, "I hereby declare that I intend Maine to be my permanent home." This statement in itself fails to prove that Bill was domiciled in Maine at the time of his death. Other evidence may show that he made the statement simply to give the appearance of changing his domicile and that, if he had regained his health, he would have returned to Connecticut. If so, his domicile at death is Connecticut in spite of his declared intent; a court will conclude that Bill never actually intended to make Maine his permanent home, at least as of the time of his death.

The following Checklist covers interviewing and investigation tasks when domicile is an issue in a divorce case.

estate tax
A tax on money or other property that is transferred by someone who dies leaving a valid will (testate) or without such a will (intestate). There is a federal estate tax and some states impose a state estate tax.

age of majority
The age at which children reach legal adulthood, usually eighteen, entitling them to many civil rights, such as the right to manage their own affairs.

emancipated
Legally independent of one's parent or legal guardian. The noun is *emancipation*.

unemancipated
Legally dependent of one's parent or legal guardian.

operation of law
The means by which legal consequences are imposed by law, regardless of (or even despite) the intent or wishes of the parties involved.

legal custody
The right to make the major child-rearing decisions on health, education, religion, discipline, and general welfare. Also called *decision-making responsibility.*

domicile by choice
A domicile selected by a person with the legal capacity to choose.

equal protection of law
The constitutional requirement that the government treat one group or class the same as it treats another group or class in like circumstances. Shortened to *equal protection.*

☑ INTERVIEWING AND INVESTIGATION CHECKLIST

Domicile

Tasks to Help Determine When a Person Has Established a Domicile

LEGAL INTERVIEWING QUESTIONS

1. When did you come to the state?
2. How often have you been in the state in the past? (Describe the details of your contacts with the state.)
3. Why did you come to the state?
4. Was your intention to stay there for a short period of time? A long period? Indefinitely? Forever?
5. While you were in the state, did you also have a home or apartment elsewhere in the state, and/or in another state, and/or in another country? If so, give details (addresses, how long you spent at each home or apartment, etc.).
6. In what state(s) do you own real property (land)? In what state(s) do you rent real property? For every place owned or rented, specify the location, dates of purchase/lease, length of time owned/leased, details on time spent there, etc.
7. Where do you consider your permanent home to be?
8. Have you ever changed your permanent home in the past? If so, give details.
9. Where are you registered to vote? Where did you vote in the last election? In the election before that?
10. Where is your job or business?
11. In what state is your car registered?
12. What state issued your driver's license?
13. In what states do you have a library card?
14. In what states do you have bank accounts?
15. In what states do you have club memberships?
16. In what state is your pet licensed?
17. In what state do you attend church or other house of worship?
18. If you have a will or trust, what address is listed for you in the will or trust?
19. Did you change your will or trust to mention your new state? If not, why not?
20. What is your address according to the credit-card companies you use? Where are your statements sent?
21. Where were you born?
22. Where do your relatives live?
23. Where did you go to school (elementary, middle, high school, and college)?

POSSIBLE INVESTIGATION TASKS

- Obtain copies of records that would indicate the extent of contact with the state (e.g., state tax returns, bank statements, land ownership papers, leases, hotel receipts, voting records, library cards, and utility bills).
- Interview persons with whom the client may have discussed the move to the state (e.g., relatives, neighbors, business associates).

(For a related checklist, see Chapter 6 on factors relevant to determining the intent of parties who may have traveled to another state in order to evade the marriage law of their domiciliary state.)

ASSIGNMENT 7.7

In the following situations, determine in what state the person was domiciled at the time of death. (See General Instructions for the Legal-Analysis Assignment in Appendix A.)

a. While living in Illinois, Fred hears about a high-paying job in Alaska. He decides to move to Alaska. He no longer wants to live in Illinois. He sells everything he owns in Illinois and rents an apartment in Alaska. There, he discovers that jobs are not easy to find. He decides to leave if he cannot find a job in three months. If this happens, he arranges to move in with his sister in New Mexico. Before the three months are over, Fred dies jobless in Alaska.

b. Gloria moves to New York from Montana to attend New York University. Her husband lives in Montana. Gloria plans to rejoin her husband in Montana when she finishes school in six months. Two months before graduation, her husband decides to move to Oregon. Gloria is opposed to the move and tells him that she will not leave New York if he does not return to Montana. Her husband refuses to move back to Montana. One month before graduation, Gloria dies in New York.

DURATIONAL RESIDENCY REQUIREMENT

durational residency requirement
The requirement that a party be a resident of the state for a specified period of time before being allowed to exercise a right, such as the right to petition a court for a divorce.

Many states have a requirement that a party be a resident of the state for a specified period of time before being allowed to seek a divorce. A time requirement of this kind is called a **durational residency requirement**. States differ on the amount of time the residency must exist. The range is six weeks to a year. States also differ on the nature of the requirement. In a few states, the requirement is a substitute for the requirement of domicile. In most states, however, the residency requirement must be met in addition to domicile. To add further confusion, some states mean domicile when they impose the residency requirement.

We said earlier that a court lacks jurisdiction to issue a divorce decree if at least one of the spouses is not domiciled in the state. Assume that a state imposes a thirty-day residency requirement in addition to the domicile requirement. What happens if a party establishes a domicile immediately upon arriving in the state (there is no minimum amount of time you must spend in a state to make it your domicile), but files for a divorce (ex parte) before meeting the thirty-day durational residency requirement? Does the state lose its jurisdiction to hear the divorce case? In most states, the answer is no. Unlike domicile, residency is not a prerequisite for the court's jurisdiction.

FULL FAITH AND CREDIT

We live in a mobile society; individuals and families change their domiciles relatively often. This is particularly true of persons in families facing domestic difficulties.

> *Ted and Helen are married in Texas. After five years of marriage, Helen moves to California and files for divorce in a California court. Ted remains in Texas, but often travels abroad. The California court grants the divorce and awards her $2,000 a month in alimony. A year later, Helen moves back to Texas and asks a Texas court to enforce the alimony order against Ted.*

forum state
The state in which the case is now being litigated.

foreign divorce
A divorce obtained in another state or country. A divorce that was not obtained in the forum state where the parties are now in litigation. If, for example, you live in Florida and obtain a divorce in Ohio, you have a foreign divorce.

full faith and credit (FFC)
The obligation of one state to recognize and enforce the laws and court decisions of another state. The obligation is based on the U.S. Constitution. Article IV, § 1.

Texas is being asked to recognize and enforce a California judgment. Texas is the **forum state**, which is the state where the case is now being litigated. In the Texas litigation, the California divorce is considered a **foreign divorce**. *Foreign* means any state or country other than the forum state or country.

Is Texas required to recognize and enforce the California divorce judgment? This is a constitutional question. Under the U.S. Constitution, one state must give **full faith and credit (FFC)** to the legal decisions of another state. FFC is the obligation of one state to recognize and enforce the laws and court decisions of another state. The obligation is based on the U.S. Constitution, which provides that "Full Faith and Credit shall be given in each State to the public Acts, Records, and judicial Proceedings of every other State."[19]

Is Texas required to give FFC to the California judgment of divorce? The answer will depend on whether California had proper jurisdiction to render the divorce judgment. Furthermore, it is possible that the FFC obligation may apply to only part of the California judgment. To understand this reality, we need to cover what is called a *divisible divorce*.

Before we examine divisible divorce, it must be stressed that we are talking about divorces issued and enforced in the United States. Our courts are not required to give FFC to a divorce judgment granted in a foreign country such as Mexico or France. A court in the United States may decide to recognize a judgment from another country as a matter of deference and mutual respect (comity), but there is no FFC obligation to do so.

DIVISIBLE DIVORCE

The enforceability of an order in a divorce judgment depends on two factors:

(1) Whether the court had proper jurisdiction to issue that order, and
(2) Whether the defendant had proper due-process notice of (and an opportunity to participate in) the proceeding that resulted in the order.

We will be spending most of our time in this chapter on the first factor.

A divorce judgment can consist of five major orders. The judgment can:

- Dissolve the marriage.
- Award spousal support (alimony).
- Divide marital property (called a property division).
- Award child support.
- Award child custody.

In our Texas/California example involving Ted and Helen, the California court issued two orders: It dissolved the marriage and awarded spousal support (alimony). Which of these two California orders must be given FFC by a Texas court? Both orders? Only one of them? The answer depends on the jurisdiction that California had when it issued its divorce judgment. If, for example, California had jurisdiction to dissolve the marriage (thus divorcing the spouses), but did not have jurisdiction to resolve other issues such as property division, support, and custody, then Texas must give FFC to the order of dissolution (divorce) but is not obligated to give FFC to the order on property division, support, and custody. When a divorce judgment dissolves a marriage but does not properly resolve other marriage issues, it is a **divisible divorce** and therefore, is only partially enforceable.

Because different orders require different kinds of jurisdiction, we must ask the following questions:

1. What kind of jurisdiction does a court need to dissolve a marriage?
2. What kind of jurisdiction does a court need to award spousal support (alimony)?
3. What kind of jurisdiction does a court need to divide marital property (property division)?
4. What kind of jurisdiction does a court need to award child support?
5. What kind of jurisdiction does a court need to award child custody?

We will be focusing on the first three questions. The latter two questions will be covered in Chapter 9 on child custody and Chapter 10 on child support.

We begin with a general introduction to jurisdiction.

JURISDICTION

There are two broad definitions of **jurisdiction**:

- *Power definition.* The power of a court to act in a particular case to resolve a legal matter. There are three major kinds or categories of power jurisdiction: subject-matter jurisdiction, in rem jurisdiction, and personal jurisdiction.

comity
A court's decision to give effect to the laws and court decisions of another state as a matter of deference and mutual respect even if no obligation exists to do so. (Most often applied to the laws and court decisions of another nation.)

divisible divorce
(1) A divorce judgment that dissolves the marriage but does not resolve other divorce issues such as property division, support, and child custody. Also called a *bifurcated divorce.* (2) A divorce that is enforceable only in part. An example is a divorce judgment issued in one court that dissolves the marriage and makes an award of alimony, but only the dissolution is enforceable in another court, not the alimony order.

jurisdiction
(1) The power of a court to act in a particular case to resolve a legal matter. There are three major types of power jurisdiction: subject-matter jurisdiction, in rem jurisdiction, and personal jurisdiction. (2) The geographic area over which a particular court has authority or power.

- *Geographic definition.* The geographic area over which a particular court has authority or power. This definition of jurisdiction refers to a place on the map. A Nevada state court, for example, will often refer to its entire state as "this jurisdiction." Similarly, the U.S. Court of Appeals for the Tenth Circuit covers six states in the Midwestern part of the country. When the Tenth Circuit refers to "this jurisdiction," it is referring to any one of these six states or to all six states collectively.

When we use the word *jurisdiction* in the remainder of the chapter, we will be referring to the power definition. Our examination will focus on the three kinds of power jurisdiction a court can have in a divorce case: subject-matter jurisdiction, in rem jurisdiction, and personal jurisdiction. Specifically, our concern will be challenges to a divorce decree because the court lacks one of these three kinds of jurisdiction.

Such challenges rarely arise in *bilateral divorces* when both spouses are before the court. The main arena in which challenges arise is when only one party is before the court asking for the divorce—the petitioner spouse seeks a divorce judgment against an absent spouse. If the divorce is granted, it is an ex parte divorce. When the petitioner seeks to enforce the judgment, the absent spouse appears and tries to challenge the validity of the ex parte divorce on the ground that the court lacked jurisdiction to grant it. To understand how such a jurisdictional attack will be resolved, let's take a closer look at the three main types of power jurisdiction.

TYPES OF JURISDICTION

As indicated, the three main types of jurisdiction that relate to the power of a court are subject-matter jurisdiction, in rem jurisdiction, and personal jurisdiction.

Subject-Matter Jurisdiction

subject-matter jurisdiction
The court's power to resolve a particular type of legal dispute and to grant a particular type of relief.

void
Of no legal effect.

Subject-matter jurisdiction is the court's power to resolve a particular type of legal dispute and to grant a particular type of relief. Subject-matter jurisdiction is required for all five orders that can be part of a divorce judgment. A criminal law court, for example, would not have subject-matter jurisdiction to hear a divorce case. A divorce judgment rendered by a court without subject-matter jurisdiction over divorces is void. The divorce judgment is void in the state that granted it and in every other state. Such a judgment is not entitled to FFC. Therefore, another state is not required to enforce the divorce judgment.

How does a court acquire subject-matter jurisdiction? The state constitution and/or a state statute determine the subject-matter jurisdiction of state courts.

States differ on which courts are given subject-matter jurisdiction in family-law cases. In some states, divorce and other family-law cases are heard in a special division or section of the trial courts. Other states have established separate family-law or domestic-relations courts that have subject-matter jurisdiction in this area of the law. In some states, even more specialized courts have been created, such as a *Fathering Court* to provide special attention and services to fathers who fall substantially behind in their child-support obligations.[20] Finally, some states give subject-matter jurisdiction to more than one kind of court, each of which has concurrent jurisdiction to hear some or all family-law cases.

concurrent jurisdiction
Subject-matter jurisdiction that resides in more than one kind of court in the same judicial system.

stipulate
To enter into an agreement with an opposing party on a particular matter. The noun is *stipulation*.

Parties have no control over whether a particular court has subject-matter jurisdiction. They cannot stipulate, for example, that a court has this jurisdiction if, in fact, the laws indicated above do not specify that the court has it. This is different from *personal jurisdiction*, which is discussed below. Consent between the parties can confer personal jurisdiction on a court.

In the *federal* court system, there are no family courts or family-law divisions. The vast majority of family-law cases are heard in state courts. Federal courts almost never have subject-matter jurisdiction over such cases even if there is **diversity of citizenship** among the parties. When parties are citizens of different states, the federal courts have diversity jurisdiction, but under the **domestic-relations exception**, federal courts will not hear cases involving the granting of divorce, alimony, or child custody even if the parties are from different states. Suppose, however, that a spouse wants to litigate an issue other than divorce, alimony, or child custody in a federal court, and there is diversity of citizenship among the parties. An example might be a tort action that a mother wants to bring against the father of their child.[21] In such cases, the domestic-relations exception does not apply and a federal court could hear the tort action. Such cases, however, are relatively rare.

diversity of citizenship
The disputing parties are citizens of different states and the amount in controversy exceeds $75,000. This diversity gives subject-matter jurisdiction to a federal trial court—a U.S. District Court. It is called *diversity jurisdiction*.

domestic-relations exception
Federal courts do not have subject-matter jurisdiction over the granting of divorce, alimony, or child custody even if there is diversity of citizenship among the parties.

In Rem Jurisdiction

In rem jurisdiction is required for a court to dissolve a marriage, the first of the five major orders that a court can issue in a divorce case. **In rem jurisdiction** is a court's power over a particular **res**, which is a thing or status that is located within the territory over which the court has authority. An example of a thing is land; an example of a status is a marriage.

How does a court acquire in rem jurisdiction in divorce cases? It is acquired by the domicile of at least one of the spouses in the state. In divorce actions, the *res* is the marriage, which is "located" in any state where one or both spouses are domiciled. In rem jurisdiction gives a court the power to terminate the marriage. A court lacks in rem jurisdiction if it renders a divorce judgment when neither party is domiciled in that state. Such a judgment is not entitled to FFC. Therefore, another state is not required to enforce the divorce judgment. In rem jurisdiction, however, is *not* sufficient to give the court power to issue rulings on financial matters such as alimony and most property-division issues. Such issues require personal jurisdiction.[22]

in rem jurisdiction
The court's power over a particular *res*, which is a thing (e.g., land) or a status (e.g., a marriage) that is located within the territory over which the court has authority.

res
A thing (e.g., land) or a status (e.g., marriage). (See the glossary for an additional meaning.)

Personal jurisdiction

Personal jurisdiction is required for a court to order spousal support (alimony), property division, and child support. **Personal jurisdiction** is a court's power over a person to determine his or her personal rights and duties. Personal jurisdiction is not required to dissolve the marriage; in rem jurisdiction is sufficient. If, however, a court makes an alimony, property-division, or child-support order in an ex parte divorce proceeding without having personal jurisdiction over the defendant, the order can be attacked on jurisdictional grounds; it is not entitled to FFC.

With this background, let's return to the example we looked at earlier:

personal jurisdiction
A court's power over a person to determine (adjudicate) his or her personal rights and duties. Also called *in personam jurisdiction*.

Ted and Helen are married in Texas. After five years of marriage, Helen moves to California and files for divorce in a California court. Ted remains in Texas, but often travels abroad. The California court grants the divorce and awards her $2,000 a month in alimony. A year later, Helen moves back to Texas and asks a Texas court to enforce the alimony order against Ted.

- Helen obtained a California divorce. If she was domiciled in California at the time, the California court had proper in rem jurisdiction to dissolve the marriage. The domicile of only one of the parties is needed for this jurisdiction. It is not necessary for Ted to have been domiciled in California. Hence, the part of the divorce judgment that dissolved the marriage must be enforced—and be given FFC—by a Texas court.

- The California court also ordered Ted to start paying Helen $2,000 a month in alimony. This is a property order that requires personal jurisdiction over the party who is ordered to make this payment—Ted. There is no indication in the facts that California had personal jurisdiction over Ted. If this is so, the part of the divorce judgment that ordered alimony cannot be enforced—and is not entitled to FFC—by a Texas court. If Helen wants alimony, she must take steps that will allow a California court or a Texas court to acquire personal jurisdiction over Ted.

How does a court acquire personal jurisdiction in divorce cases? Here are the main ways:

- **Service of process** on the defendant when he or she is physically present in the forum state (the state where the action is being brought). The **process** documents that must be served (e.g., the complaint or petition and summons) are delivered (handed) to the defendant (or to the defendant's authorized representative) in the forum state. (Such hand delivery is called *personal service* or *actual service*.) Proper service of process gives the court personal jurisdiction over the defendant even if the defendant is a nonresident or a nondomiciliary who happens to be in the state temporarily.

- *Consent.* A defendant can consent (agree) to be subject to the personal jurisdiction of the forum state's court. This is usually done simply by appearing in court and defending the case.[23]

- *Long-arm statute.* A **long-arm statute** allows a state to obtain personal jurisdiction over a nonresident defendant because of the latter's minimum contacts with the state. (The statute would not be needed in Helen's suit against Ted in Texas because Ted is a resident of Texas.) Personal jurisdiction over a nonresident using a long-arm statute is acquired by **substituted service** (also called *constructive service*), which consists of mailing the process documents to the defendant, publishing them in a newspaper, or using other approved alternatives to hand delivery. The personal jurisdiction acquired through a long-arm statute is called **long-arm jurisdiction. Minimum contacts** are those activities in or connected with a state by a nonresident that are substantial and sufficiently purposeful so that it can be said that the nonresident has invoked the benefits and protections of the state, thereby making it fair for the state to assert personal jurisdiction over the nonresident. Here are some of the factors that a court will consider in determining whether such minimum contacts exist, no one of which is necessarily conclusive:

  ○ The defendant was domiciled in the state at one time before he or she left the state.

  ○ The defendant cohabited with his or her spouse in the state before the defendant left the state.

  ○ The defendant visits the state.

  ○ The defendant arranges schooling for his or her children in the state, etc.

We will be returning to the topic of long-arm jurisdiction in Chapters 8 and 10 when we examine the Uniform Interstate Family Support Act (UIFSA).

Exhibit 7.5 summarizes our discussion thus far on subject-matter jurisdiction, in rem jurisdiction, and personal jurisdiction.

service of process
A formal delivery of notice to a defendant that a suit has been initiated to which he or she must respond.

process
The means (e.g., a summons, writ, or other court order) used by the court to acquire or exercise its power or jurisdiction over a person.

long-arm statute
A statute that allows a state to obtain personal jurisdiction over a nonresident defendant because of the latter's minimum contacts with the state.

substituted service
Service of process by mail, by publication in a newspaper, or by other approved methods that are alternatives to the personal service of hand delivering the process documents to the defendant (or to the defendant's authorized representative). Also called *constructive service*.

long-arm jurisdiction
The personal jurisdiction that a state acquires over a nonresident defendant under a long-arm statute.

minimum contacts
Activities in or connected with a state by a nonresident that are substantial and sufficiently purposeful so that it can be said that the nonresident has invoked the benefits and protections of the state, thereby making it fair for the state to assert personal jurisdiction over the nonresident.

EXHIBIT 7.5   Types of Divorce Jurisdiction

Types of Jurisdiction a Court Can Have	Definition	How This Type of Jurisdiction is Acquired in Divorce Cases	What the Court Can Do with this Type of Jurisdiction	What Else is Required?	Full Faith and Credit (FFC) Consequences
Subject-Matter Jurisdiction	The court's power to resolve a particular type of legal dispute and to grant a particular type of relief.	The state constitution or a state statute that gives the court the power to hear cases involving the subject matter of divorce.	The court can hear divorce cases, but it cannot issue any orders unless it *also* has the proper jurisdiction for the order. (See in rem jurisdiction and personal jurisdiction below. See also child-custody jurisdiction in Chapter 9.)	The defendant must be given proper due-process notice of the proceeding and an opportunity to be heard.	If a state court issues a divorce judgment but the court did not have subject-matter jurisdiction to grant divorces, other states do not have to enforce (i.e., do not have to give FFC to) the divorce judgment.
In Rem Jurisdiction	The court's power over a particular *res*. The res may be a thing (e.g., land) or a status (e.g., marriage) located within the territory over which the court has authority.	One or both of the spouses are domiciled in the state.	The court can dissolve the marriage.	The defendant must be given proper due-process notice of the proceeding and an opportunity to be heard.	Other states must give FFC to the judgment that dissolves the marriage. If, however, a court issues a divorce judgment but neither spouse was domiciled in the state at the time, the judgment is not entitled to FFC.
Personal Jurisdiction	A court's power over a person to determine (adjudicate) his or her personal rights and duties.	• Service of process on the defendant in the state. • Consent to be subject to personal jurisdiction. • Long-arm statute if there are minimum contacts with the state.	The court can issue financial orders for spousal support (alimony), child support, and property division.	The defendant must be given proper due-process notice of the proceeding and an opportunity to be heard.	Other states must give FFC to the judgment on spousal support (alimony), child support, and property division. Without personal jurisdiction, however, a judgment on spousal support, property division, or child support is not enforceable and is not entitled to FFC.

PERSON ATTACKING THE DIVORCE JUDGMENT

Assume that a defendant has a good argument that the divorce judgment rendered against him or her is invalid because the court did not have jurisdiction to render it. Can the defendant raise this argument when the plaintiff attempts to enforce it? In most cases, yes. There are times, however, when a party may be barred from asserting a jurisdictional challenge. To understand when this occurs, we need to identify the role that the party had in the original divorce proceeding. Here are the major possibilities:

1. *The person who now wants to raise the jurisdictional challenge is the person who obtained that judgment.*

   Example: In 2014, Jim files for and obtains a divorce judgment against his wife. In 2018, Jim goes to court to argue that the 2015 divorce judgment is invalid because the court did not have jurisdiction to render it. In most states, Jim would not be allowed to raise the jurisdictional challenge. He will be **estopped** (prevented) from denying the validity of the divorce judgment that he sought and successfully obtained. This rule prevents a person from attacking a divorce judgment even though the judgment may be clearly invalid. Note, however, that a few courts do not follow this rule and will allow persons to attack a divorce judgment they participated in obtaining or from which they obtained benefits.

2. *The person who now wants to raise the jurisdictional challenge to the divorce judgment was the person against whom the judgment was obtained.* Whether the person against whom the divorce judgment was obtained can attack the judgment on jurisdictional grounds will depend on several factors, including the following:

   • *The divorce was a bilateral divorce; both sides appeared.* Assume that the divorce judgment was granted after both sides appeared before the court and argued their positions. Can either side now attack the divorce judgment on jurisdictional grounds? Answer: No. If the person now attacking the divorce judgment on jurisdictional grounds appeared as the defendant in that action, he or she will not be allowed to attack the judgment in a later proceeding. He or she should have raised the jurisdictional attack in the original divorce action.

   • *The divorce was an ex parte divorce; only one party appeared—the petitioner.* Assume that the divorce was granted after only one side appeared before the court to argue for the divorce. Can the *absent* party against whom the divorce was obtained attack the divorce judgment on jurisdictional grounds? Answer: Yes.

   • *Accepted the benefits. Can a party against whom the divorce was obtained attack the divorce judgment on jurisdictional grounds if that party has accepted benefits from the divorce (e.g., alimony payments)?* Answer in many states: *No.*

   • *Remarriage. Can a party against whom the divorce was obtained attack the divorce judgment on jurisdictional grounds if that party has remarried and now wants to invalidate the second marriage?* This person's argument is that the second marriage is invalid because the first marriage is still valid due to a jurisdictional flaw (e.g., no domicile) when the divorce judgment was rendered on the first marriage. In most states, this person will not be allowed to make this argument. If the person against whom the divorce was obtained has remarried, he or she will not be allowed to claim that the second marriage is invalid due to jurisdictional defects in the divorce judgment on the first marriage. There are, however, some states that will allow the jurisdictional attack on the divorce judgment if the person making the attack did not know about the jurisdictional defect (e.g., no domicile) at the time.

3. *The person who now wants to raise the jurisdictional challenge to the divorce judgment was not a party to the divorce action.* Finally, we consider jurisdictional attacks against a divorce judgment brought by persons who were not parties to the proceeding that granted the divorce judgment. Assume that after John divorces Mary, he marries Diane. Diane, of course, was not a party

---

estopped
Prevented from asserting a right or a defense because it would be unfair or inequitable to allow the assertion. The noun is *estoppel*.

in the divorce action between John and Mary. Assume that Diane now wants to have her marriage to John annulled. In her annulment action, she argues that when she married John, he was still married to Mary because the court that divorced John and Mary had no jurisdiction to award the divorce. Can a second spouse who was not a party to the prior divorce action challenge the validity of that divorce on jurisdictional grounds? Answer: No. The second spouse relied on the validity of the divorce when he or she entered the marriage and should not now be allowed to upset the validity of that marriage by challenging the validity of the divorce judgment. (Diane's attack against John's divorce is an example of a collateral attack against a judgment because the attack was not raised in the same proceeding that led to the judgment. Diane raised it in her annulment action.)

collateral attack
A challenge or attack against the validity of a judgment raised in a different proceeding from the one that rendered the judgment. A *direct attack* would be a challenge or an attack against the validity of a judgment raised in the *same* proceeding that rendered the judgment such as during the trial or during a direct appeal of that judgment.

JURISDICTIONAL ANALYSIS: MORE EXAMPLES

Let's look at some additional examples of the rules we have been examining.

1. *Bill and Pat are married in Idaho, where both are domiciled. Pat sues Bill for divorce in Idaho. The trial begins after Pat arranges service of process on Bill. In the suit, Pat asked for alimony. The judge granted it ($1,200 a month) over Bill's objections. Bill then moved to Oregon where he established domicile. When he stops paying alimony, Pat sues him in Oregon to enforce the Idaho judgment on alimony. In the Oregon action, Bill argues that the Idaho divorce judgment was invalid because the Idaho court did not have jurisdiction to make the alimony award.*

Jurisdictional Analysis

- Bill's argument will fail. The Idaho divorce was a bilateral divorce. Both spouses were before the court. Idaho had in rem jurisdiction to divorce the parties because of their domicile in Idaho. (The domicile of Pat would have been sufficient, but in this case, both parties were domiciliaries of Idaho.) Idaho needed personal jurisdiction over Bill to be able to order him to pay alimony. It had personal jurisdiction once service of process was made on him and he fully participated in the divorce proceeding. Even if he is correct that Idaho's personal jurisdiction over him was defective, he should have raised this objection when he was before the Idaho case. Oregon, therefore, must give full faith and credit (FFC) to the Idaho judgment of divorce and enforce the alimony award against Bill.

2. *Tom and Mary are married in Massachusetts, where both are domiciled. Mary moves to Ohio, which is now her state of domicile. Tom remains in Massachusetts. Mary obtains a divorce judgment from an Ohio state court. The judgment dissolves the marriage and awards Mary $5,500 a month in alimony. Tom was notified of the action by mail but did not appear. He was not served with process in Ohio. He has never been in Ohio. Mary travels to Massachusetts and brings an action against Tom to enforce the alimony award of the Ohio court.*

Jurisdictional Analysis

- The Ohio divorce was an ex parte divorce. Only one party (Mary) was before the Ohio Court. Ohio had in rem jurisdiction to dissolve the marriage because of Mary's domicile in Ohio. This part of the divorce judgment is entitled to full faith and credit (FFC) in Massachusetts (i.e., Massachusetts *must* recognize this aspect of the Ohio divorce judgment if the Massachusetts court determines that Mary was, in fact, domiciled in Ohio at the time of the divorce judgment).

- The Ohio court did not have personal jurisdiction over Tom to render an alimony award. Recall the methods of acquiring personal jurisdiction over a nonresident defendant: (1) service of process in the forum state, (2) consent through appearance in the action in the forum state, or (3) the long-arm statute. Tom was not served with process in Ohio, he did not consent to Ohio's assertion of personal jurisdiction over him by appearing in the Ohio action, and the long-arm statute did not give Ohio personal jurisdiction of him because he had no minimum contacts with Ohio. In fact, he had no contact with Ohio other than receiving notice by mail of Mary's action. This is not enough to confer personal jurisdiction over him. Therefore, the part of the Ohio divorce judgment that awarded alimony is not entitled to FFC in Massachusetts (i.e., the Massachusetts court does not have to enforce the Ohio alimony award).

3. *Ed and Sam are married in New York, where both are domiciled. Ed moves to Delaware, which is now his state of domicile. Sam remains in New York. Ed obtains a divorce judgment from a Delaware court. The judgment dissolves the marriage and rules that Ed is not obligated to pay alimony to Sam. Sam was notified of the action by mail but did not appear. He was not served with process in Delaware. He has had no contacts with Delaware. In a New York court, Sam brings an action seeking alimony from Ed. Ed argues that the Delaware ruling on alimony should be recognized and enforced in New York.*

Jurisdictional Analysis

- The Delaware divorce was an ex parte divorce. Only one party (Ed) was before the Delaware court. Delaware had in rem jurisdiction to dissolve the marriage because of Ed's domicile in Delaware. This part of the divorce judgment is entitled to FFC in New York (i.e., New York *must* recognize this aspect of the Delaware divorce judgment if the New York court determines that Ed was, in fact, domiciled in Delaware at the time of the divorce judgment).

- The Delaware court did not have personal jurisdiction to decide whether Sam is entitled to alimony because it did not have personal jurisdiction over Sam. He was not served with process in Delaware, he did not consent to Delaware's assertion of personal jurisdiction over him by appearing in the Delaware action, and the long-arm statute did not give Delaware personal jurisdiction of him because he had no minimum contacts with Delaware. Therefore, the part of the Delaware divorce judgment that declared no alimony for Sam is not entitled to FFC in New York (i.e., the New York court does not have to enforce the Delaware alimony decision). A New York court can decide whether Ed must pay Sam alimony.

4. *Ben and Paulene are married in New Jersey, where both are domiciled. Ben travels to Michigan and files for divorce in a Michigan court. Once the divorce is granted, he returns to New Jersey. Neither he nor Paulene were ever domiciled in Michigan. Ben then marries Leona in New Jersey. Ben and Leona separate after having marital difficulties. Leona brings a support action (a separate-maintenance action) against Ben in New Jersey. Ben's defense is that he is not married to Leona because the Michigan divorce is invalid due to the fact that neither he nor Paulene was domiciled in Michigan when he obtained the Michigan divorce, and hence, the Michigan court did not have in rem jurisdiction to dissolve the marriage. Thus, Ben is still married to Paulene and has no duty to support Leona.*

Jurisdictional Analysis

- The Michigan divorce was an ex parte divorce. Only one party (Ben) was before the Michigan court. Ben is the person who obtained the Michigan divorce judgment. In most states, he will be estopped from attacking the judgment on jurisdictional grounds. Even if he can prove that neither he nor Paulene was domiciled in Michigan, he will not be allowed to do so. He relied on the divorce judgment and took the benefits of the divorce when he married Leona. He should not be allowed to attack the very thing he helped accomplish.

5. *Joe and Helen are married in Arizona, where both are domiciled. Helen goes to New Mexico and obtains a divorce judgment against Joe. Joe knows about the action but does not appear. Neither Joe nor Helen was ever domiciled in New Mexico. Joe marries Priscilla. When Helen dies, Joe claims part of her estate. His position is that he is her surviving husband because the New Mexico court had no jurisdiction to divorce them, because neither he nor Helen was ever domiciled there.*

Jurisdictional Analysis

- The New Mexico divorce was an ex parte divorce. Only one party (Helen) was before the New Mexico court. Joe was not the party who sought and obtained the New Mexico divorce. Normally, he would be allowed to attack the divorce judgment on the ground that no one was domiciled in New Mexico at the time of the divorce. But Joe relied upon the divorce and accepted its benefits by marrying Priscilla. It would be inconsistent to allow him to change his mind now, and it could be unfair to Priscilla. Hence, Joe will be estopped from attacking the New Mexico divorce from Helen on jurisdictional grounds.

6. *Wayne and Olivia are married in Oregon, where both are domiciled. They have two children. Olivia decides she can no longer live with Wayne. She takes the children to Pennsylvania where she establishes domicile. Wayne stays in Oregon, although he visits the children about twice a year. During one of the visits, he cohabits with Olivia but leaves after a week due to renewed marital difficulties. Olivia files for and is granted a divorce judgment in Pennsylvania. The judgment dissolves the marriage and awards Mary the car that she and Wayne owned in Oregon, which Wayne still uses in Oregon. Wayne was never served with process in Pennsylvania. He was notified of the divorce action by mail but did not appear. Olivia also published a notice of the pending divorce action in a general circulation newspaper.*

Jurisdictional Analysis

- The Pennsylvania divorce was an ex parte divorce. Only one party (Olivia) was before the Pennsylvania court. Pennsylvania had in rem jurisdiction because of Olivia's domicile in Pennsylvania. This part of the divorce judgment is entitled to FFC in every other state.

- The Pennsylvania court also awarded the Oregon car to Olivia. The vehicle is marital property; it was owned by both parties during the marriage. An award of marital property (a property division) requires personal jurisdiction. Did the Pennsylvania court have personal jurisdiction over Wayne, a nonresident of Pennsylvania? If Pennsylvania has a long-arm statute, it could acquire personal jurisdiction over a nonresident by substituted service if the nonresident has had minimum contacts with Pennsylvania so that it is reasonable and fair to require the nonresident to appear and be subjected to full personal jurisdiction in the state. Wayne had such minimum contacts through his visits with the children in Pennsylvania and his cohabitation with Olivia in the state during a visit. Hence, Pennsylvania had personal jurisdiction (called long-arm jurisdiction) so that it could order the property division; this order is entitled to FFC in every other state.

ASSIGNMENT 7.8

John and Sandra were married in Alabama. After marital difficulties, John takes a job in Georgia and Sandra moves to Florida with their two children. John has never been to Florida. He sometimes calls his children on the phone, and they come to visit him pursuant to arrangements he makes with Sandra. Once he asked his mother to go to Florida to look after the children while Sandra was sick. Sandra files for a divorce in Florida. John does not appear, although he is given notice of the action. (Florida has a long-arm statute.) Sandra is granted the divorce and John is ordered to give her a one-time payment of $25,000 to cover her share of all their marital property. She later travels to Georgia and asks a Georgia court to enforce the $25,000 property-division order, which John has been ignoring. What result? (See General Instructions for the Legal-Analysis Assignment in Appendix A.)

CHILD CUSTODY JURISDICTION

The domicile of a child in a state is usually sufficient to give the state jurisdiction to render a custody decree. In our mobile society where parents and children can easily move among the states, a major basis of custody jurisdiction is the home state of the child. A **home state** is the state where the child has lived with a parent (or anyone acting as a parent) for at least six consecutive months immediately before the commencement of a child-custody proceeding or since birth if the child is less than six months old. We will examine custody jurisdiction in detail in Chapter 9.

VENUE

Venue means the place of the trial. Venue is different from subject-matter jurisdiction. The latter concerns the power of a court to hear a particular type of legal dispute and grant a particular type of relief. Venue concerns the choice among several courts that have the power (subject-matter jurisdiction) to hear the case.

Every county in the state, for example, may contain a superior or county court with subject-matter jurisdiction to grant divorces. The choice of which superior or county court a party selects to file for divorce is called *choice of venue*. The state's statutory code will specify the requirements for the selection of venue. The requirements often relate to the residence (which may mean domicile) of the plaintiff or defendant. For example, the statute might specify that a divorce action can be filed in the county where the defendant spouse resides or in the county where either the plaintiff or the defendant has been a resident for three months preceding the commencement of the action. This venue residency requirement may be in addition to the durational residency requirement discussed earlier that a party be a resident of the state for a designated period of time (e.g., six months) immediately before filing the action.

home state
The state where the child has lived with a parent (or anyone acting as a parent) for at least six consecutive months immediately before the commencement of a child-custody proceeding or since birth if the child is less than six months old.

venue
(1) The place of the trial. (2) The proper county or geographical area in which a court with subject-matter jurisdiction may hear a case. When more than one court has subject-matter jurisdiction to hear a particular kind of case, the selection of the court is called *choice of venue*.

ASSIGNMENT 7.9

Tara, a member of the armed services, is temporarily stationed in your state. She and her husband, George, are domiciled in another state. Under what circumstances, if any, can Tara obtain a divorce in your state? Assume that George has never been in your state. (See General Instructions for the State-Code Assignment in Appendix A.)

SUMMARY DISSOLUTION

In some states, it is possible to obtain a divorce primarily through the mail without going through elaborate court procedures. Such a divorce is often referred to as a **summary dissolution** or a *simplified dissolution.* The requirements for taking advantage of this option are quite strict. In Illinois, for example, the couple must be childless, be married for five years or less, have no real property (other than a lease on a residence), waive any rights to spousal support, etc. In short, there must be very little need for courts, attorneys, and the protection of the legal system. The less conflict between parties over children, property, and support, the easier it is to obtain a divorce.

Unfortunately, however, even simple divorce cases can sometimes drag on for substantial periods of time because of crowded court calendars.

summary dissolution
A divorce obtained in an expedited manner because of the brevity of the marriage, the minimal amount of marital property, and the lack of controversy between the spouses.

ALTERNATIVE DISPUTE RESOLUTION (ADR)

The parties can use informal and formal methods to try to resolve differences in a divorce case without expensive discovery and a full trial. They often use a combination of both methods. First, they engage in informal negotiation (on their own or through counsel) on property division, child custody, spousal support, child support, and other issues pertaining to the marriage. Second, they engage in the more formal process called alternative dispute resolution. **Alternative dispute resolution (ADR)** is a method or procedure for resolving a legal dispute without litigating it in a court or an administrative agency. All states encourage the use of ADR. In Texas, for example, a party seeking a divorce is asked to sign a statement that he or she has been informed of the availability of ADR and will attempt in good faith to resolve the case through ADR. The issues resolved through informal negotiation and ADR are often formalized in a *separation agreement* that the parties then ask the court to approve. (We will cover separation agreements in Chapter 8.)

The major ADR programs are arbitration, mediation, med-arb, private judging, neutral evaluation, and collaborative law.

alternative dispute resolution (ADR)
A method or procedure for resolving a legal dispute without litigating it in a court or an administrative agency.

ARBITRATION

Arbitration is a method of ADR in which the parties avoid litigation by submitting their dispute to a neutral third person (the arbitrator) who renders a decision resolving the dispute. The arbitrator is usually a professional arbitrator hired through organizations such as the American Arbitration Association (www.adr.org).

In some states, the court can order the parties to arbitrate property-division issues involving relatively small property totals (e.g., under $50,000). A premarital agreement (see Chapter 4) may have a clause requiring arbitration of disputes. If the parties have already negotiated a separation agreement, it also might have an arbitration clause.

Spouses in arbitration appear before the arbitrator on their own or through their attorneys. Arbitrators do not have to be attorneys, but many are. The arbitration process is subject to agreement by the parties:

arbitration
A method of alternative dispute resolution (ADR) in which the parties avoid litigation by submitting their dispute to a neutral third person (the arbitrator) who renders a decision resolving the dispute.

> Each party has a right to be represented by an attorney, and the attorneys and the parties [can] agree on the ground rules for the hearing, including, for example, the presentation of evidence, the scope of testimony, the scheduling of hearings, and the allocation of arbitration expenses. The benefits of arbitration are many. The process is confidential and private, and unless the parties agree otherwise, no record is kept of the proceedings. . . . Finally, the arbitrator's decision, unless explicitly made subject to appellate review by the parties, is final and binding on the parties.[24]

MEDIATION

mediation
A method of alternative dispute resolution (ADR) in which the parties avoid litigation by submitting their dispute to a neutral third person (the mediator) who helps the parties resolve their dispute; he or she does not render a decision resolving it for them.

Mediation is a method of ADR in which the parties avoid litigation by submitting their dispute to a neutral third person (the mediator) who helps the parties resolve their dispute; he or she does not render a decision resolving it for them. The *Model Standards of Practice for Family and Divorce Mediation* defines *mediation* as "a process in which a mediator, an impartial third party, facilitates the resolution of family disputes by promoting the participants' voluntary agreement. The family mediator assists communication, encourages understanding and focuses the participants on their individual and common interests. The family mediator works with the participants to explore options, make decisions and reach their own agreements."[25] At the end of mediation, the mediator will draft a memorandum covering the agreements reached by the spouses. An attorney for one of the parties might then draft a formal agreement based on this memorandum, which is then submitted to the opposing attorney for approval or modification.

Although mediators do not render a decision resolving disputes for the parties, they may make suggestions or recommendations for a resolution. If the spouses are unrepresented, mediation is not recommended for cases in which there is a substantial power imbalance between the spouses or where there has been a history of domestic violence between them. For mediation to be effective, there must be considerable give-and-take between the spouses as the mediator guides them toward mutual agreements. This is unlikely to work if one of the spouses cowers before the other or if one of them fears a continuation of prior violence.

Mediation is the most commonly used ADR method in divorce cases. In some states, mediation is mandatory; the parties are required to try to work out their differences before they ask a court for its final rulings, particularly when the judge learns that the parties do not agree on custody and visitation issues. In many courts, the parties can attend mediation within the family-court services unit of the court itself.

For an example of a mediation conducted by an attorney, see Exhibit 7.6. Mediators, however, do not have to be attorneys. In fact, some paralegals have received special training and certification to be mediators in family-law cases. Allan Weltman, a former paralegal in Florida, believes that paralegals "who want rewarding work with a great deal of responsibility and self-direction should look into this area of endeavor."[26]

EXHIBIT 7.6   An Example of Mediation in Family Law

REVELATIONS OF A FAMILY LAW MEDIATOR:
WHAT GOES ON BEHIND CLOSED DOORS TO HELP DIVORCING COUPLES REACH AGREEMENT?

by Joshua Kadish

Over the past seven or eight years, I have mediated a substantial number of family-law cases. My office mates often inquire, "Just what happens behind those closed doors, anyway?" "What was the loud screaming about, followed by hysterical laughter and silence?" "How do you get these embattled couples to agree on anything if they hate each other so much?" I usually parry these questions with a crafty smile and a muttered, "I have my ways . . . " as I scuttle down the hallway.

Bowing to pressure from various fronts, I have decided that the time has come to tell all. What follows is fiction, which I hope reveals the truth.

Fred and Wilma were a young couple in the process of divorcing. They had significant disagreement about custody of their two children, ages 11 and 6. Both had consulted with attorneys and, after receiving estimates of the cost of a custody battle, had followed their attorneys' recommendation to at least try mediation. Wilma had called me to set up an appointment, and at the appointed hour I ushered them into my office.

(continued)

Exhibit 7.6 *(continued)*

My office is somewhat different from many lawyers' offices. I do have a desk in one corner. Most of the office is given over to a sitting area consisting of a large, comfortable couch and two chairs grouped around a coffee table. I always let the couple enter my office first and seat themselves as they wish. Depending upon how they arrange themselves, I can get a preliminary idea of how hotly the battle is raging. Some couples will sit together on the couch. Most position themselves as far away from each other as possible. Fred and Wilma put a good deal of distance between themselves.

After we were settled, I spent a few minutes describing mediation to them. First, my job was to remain neutral and to help them reach agreements for themselves. My job was not to reach decisions for them. Second, what transpired in the mediation sessions was confidential and would not later be disclosed in a courtroom. Third, the process was voluntary and anyone was free to terminate the mediation at any time. Fourth, we would consider the interests of their children to be of paramount importance.

Without looking at either one of them, I then asked them to tell me about their current situation while I studiously looked down at my legal pad. I like to see who will start talking first. This gives me a clue about where the balance of power may lie in the relationship. I am always concerned about one party overpowering the other in mediation.

Fred started talking. Speaking angrily, he told me about their ten-year marriage, the two children and Wilma's affair and withdrawal from the marriage. He stated that although he worked hard, he spent more than an average amount of time caring for the children. He felt that in having an affair, Wilma had proved herself to be an unstable person and that he would be a preferable custodial parent. He pointed out that Wilma had worked during the course of the marriage and that parenting duties had been shared between them more or less equally.

During the course of his statement, Wilma had interrupted Fred to point out that although she had had an affair, it occurred after they had separated and that Fred had been emotionally distant and withdrawn from the marriage for a number of years. Her statement ignited a loud argument between them. I let them argue for a minute or two to get a sense of their style of arguing. This argument was a well-rehearsed one, which they must have been through a hundred times. As each one spoke, I could see that neither party was listening but was marshaling arguments with which to respond, making sure that his or her position was well defended.

I interrupted the argument by stating that I suspected they had had this argument before. This brought a slightly sheepish smile to both faces. Humor is often useful in easing tension and getting people on another track. I then borrowed an idea from an excellent mediator, John Haynes, and asked each of them to take a few minutes to think about what was the absolute worst outcome they could imagine in mediation. By asking this question, I wanted to get them further off the track they had been racing down and to give them a few minutes to calm down. After a few minutes, I asked each to answer. Fred said he was afraid of losing everything, including his children. Wilma stated that she was afraid of the same thing.

I remarked that it was interesting that they were both afraid of exactly the same thing, specifically a loss of their children to the other party. I then asked whether it would be possible for them to agree that whatever the outcome of mediation was it would not result in a complete loss of the children to the other person. They both indicated that they would agree to this.

From that point, the atmosphere eased considerably. Both Fred and Wilma had dramatically realized that each was concerned about exactly the same thing. When people realize that they have the same concerns, it makes them feel closer or at least less adversarial. Moreover, they had been able to reach their first agreement. They realized they had a common interest in not becoming estranged from their children and that they could agree this would not be a result of the mediation.

I then asked what the current situation was regarding the children. Fred stated that he had moved out and was living in a small apartment. He was seeing the children every other weekend. However, he emphasized that he was a very involved father and he wanted the children to spend at least half of their time with him on an alternating weekly basis. Wilma thought this would be bad for the children. She wanted them to be at home with her and see Fred every other weekend. She clearly wished to be the primary parent and felt that the children needed a mother's love. She was quite concerned about the children being in Fred's care for more than one overnight at a time. Fred interrupted her to state that he felt he was just as good a parent as she was. Wilma responded by telling an anecdote about Fred forgetting to feed the children lunch about three weeks ago.

Again, I interrupted. Taking a bit of a risk, I asked whether each parent thought the children loved and needed the other parent. Again, each parent responded affirmatively. My asking this question had the effect of derailing the disagreement and again bringing Fred and Wilma back to some common ground of understanding. Most parents will at least admit the children love and need the other parent.

The next task was to help Fred and Wilma learn to listen to each other and to start separating their positions from their interests. I asked them each if they thought they could state what the other person's position was regarding custody and visitation and the reasons for it. Fred thought he could, but when he tried, Wilma felt he was inaccurate. I then asked Wilma to tell him again what she was

(continued)

Exhibit 7.6 *(continued)*

concerned about, which she did. Fred was then able to repeat Wilma's position back to her. We then reversed the process, and after a couple of tries, Wilma was able to state Fred's concerns back to him.

This is a simple technique known as "active listening" which I borrowed from the field of psychology. It is not too difficult to learn the rudiments, particularly when you are married to a clinical psychologist, as I am. The goal in active listening is to make each person feel understood. There is great power in helping each party feel his or her position is genuinely understood by the other person. In most marital disputes, as one party talks, the other party is not listening, but is preparing arguments to respond to the other. This results in long, well worked out and pointless disputes. Active listening slows the pace down and helps couples improve their communication; if you are assured that you will be listened to, you will be much more likely to be able to listen to another.

At this point Fred and Wilma understood not only each other's positions but the interests and reasons behind the positions. Wilma was concerned about being separated from the children for too many overnight periods in a row. Fred was concerned about long periods of time going by without seeing the children. I pointed out that although their positions (alternating weekly versus every other weekend visitation) conflicted, their interests did not necessarily conflict. Perhaps it would be possible to work out a schedule where Fred saw the children frequently, but not for a long string of overnights. Perhaps every other weekend visitation with some shorter but frequent midweek visitations, plus frequent telephone contact would be acceptable.

I then hauled out a blank calendar. Using the calendar as the focus of discussion, we worked out a visitation schedule that seemed acceptable to both of them. During this discussion, I emphasized to them that they were fortunate to have the opportunity to experiment with different patterns of visitation because it is very difficult to sit in a room and decide what will and will not work in the long run. I suggested that they should commit to trying a certain pattern of visitation for perhaps two months and also commit to reviewing it and altering it as indicated by their needs and the children's.

By finally working out a schedule, I was trying to do several things. First, I was trying to show them that in some ways their interests could be meshed. Second, big problems can be broken down into small, manageable pieces. Rather than creating a visitation schedule, which was engraved in stone and would last for the next twenty years, they could try something for two months. Finally, I had introduced the idea of experimentation and flexibility. They could adjust the situation based upon how they and the children actually reacted to the plan.

I ended the session by telling them I would write their agreement in memo form, which they could review with their attorneys. I then asked each of them to comment on the process of the session. Did either of them have any concerns about what had happened? What did they like about the session? What could we do differently next time when we moved to a discussion of financial issues? I try to make people feel that they are in control of the process. Fred and Wilma both stated that they were pleased with the session and surprised that they had been able to reach agreement. Fred asked how I had done it. "I have my ways . . . " I muttered as I ushered them to the door.

Source: Joshua Kadish. 52 *Oregon State Bar Bulletin* 27 (February/March 1992) (www.mediate.com/kadish).

MED-ARB

med-arb
A method of alternative dispute resolution (ADR) in which the parties first try mediation, and if it does not work, they try arbitration.

Med-arb is a method of ADR in which the parties first try mediation, and if it does not work, they try arbitration. Once it is clear that mediation will not be successful, the mediator switches roles and makes a decision as an arbitrator.

PRIVATE JUDGING

private judging
A method of alternative dispute resolution (ADR) consisting of arbitration or mediation in which the arbitrator or mediator is a retired judge.

Private judging is a method of ADR consisting of arbitration or mediation in which the arbitrator or mediator is a retired judge. It is sometimes misleadingly referred to as *rent-a-judge*. The name is misleading because the retired judge has no more authority or power than any other arbitrator or mediator. Private judging is not a government proceeding.

NEUTRAL EVALUATION

neutral evaluation
A method of alternative dispute resolution (ADR) in which both sides hire an experienced attorney or an expert in the area involved in the dispute who will listen to an abbreviated version of the evidence and arguments of each side and offer an evaluation in the hope that this will stimulate more serious settlement discussions. Sometimes called *case evaluation*.

Neutral evaluation is a method of ADR in which both sides hire an experienced attorney or an expert in the area involved in the dispute who will examine an abbreviated version of the evidence, listen to the arguments of each side, and offer an evaluation in the hope that this will stimulate more serious settlement discussions.

COLLABORATIVE LAW

Collaborative law is a method of practicing law in which the attorneys and parties seek to resolve their family-law differences without litigation. It is a form of *limited-scope representation* (discussed in Chapter 2) because collaborative-law attorneys do not litigate. It is a form of alternative dispute resolution (ADR) because of its emphasis on mediation and other alternatives to litigation. Each party hires his or her own attorney who practices collaborative law. A four-way agreement is then reached in which the parties consent to the limited role of their attorneys. (The parties might agree to share a financial expert who will provide a neutral assessment of the assets and liabilities involved in the marriage.)

To encourage settlement, the four-way agreement provides that the attorneys will refuse to continue representing the parties if litigation becomes necessary because ADR has failed to resolve the disputes. The parties must find other attorneys if the case goes to trial. The collaborative-law attorneys, therefore, do not have a financial incentive to drag the dispute into litigation in order to increase their hourly fees. When collaborative law is successful, the role of the court is limited to reviewing the agreements reached by the parties. Courts often approve such agreements.

collaborative law
A method of practicing law in which the attorneys refuse to continue representing the parties if the parties cannot settle their dispute through mediation or other form of alternative dispute resolution (ADR).

PRETRIAL MATTERS

NOTICE AND OPPORTUNITY TO BE HEARD

It is not enough that a court has proper jurisdiction to issue any of the five orders that often comprise a divorce judgment. Under the Due Process Clause of the U.S. Constitution, defendants have a right to procedural due process consisting of fair procedures, such as receiving notice of the divorce proceedings filed against them and an opportunity to be heard at the proceedings. The U.S. Supreme Court has said that the notice must be "reasonably calculated, under all the circumstances, to apprise interested parties of the pendency of the action and afford them an opportunity" to be heard in it.[27] Notice is achieved by proper service of process, usually by hand delivering the process documents to the defendant or to his or her authorized representative.

A concern of the courts is that some plaintiffs hope that the defendant will not show up in court so that the plaintiff can obtain a default judgment (discussed below). The plaintiff might make little or no effort to locate the defendant for in-person service of process and then fraudulently swear to the court that the defendant could not be found despite extensive (due diligence) location efforts. The plaintiff then asks the court to allow substituted (constructive) service, statistically a weak method of notifying defendants of pending divorce litigation. Aware of the danger of fraudulent service, here is how one court conditions its permission to allow substituted (constructive) service:

procedural due process
The constitutional requirement that the government provide fair procedures (such as adequate notice and an opportunity to be heard) whenever the government seeks to deprive someone of life, liberty, or property.

default judgment
A judgment against a party for failure to appear, plead, or otherwise respond to an opponent's claim.

> [It is] incumbent upon a plaintiff in a divorce action to furnish the court with the following information before an order authorizing constructive notice is entered:
>
> (1) the time and place at which the parties last resided together as spouses;
> (2) the last time the parties were in contact with each other;
> (3) the name and address of the last employer of the defendant either during the time the parties resided together or at a later time if known to the plaintiff;
> (4) the names and addresses of those relatives known to be close to the defendant; and
> (5) any other information which could furnish a fruitful basis for further inquiry by one truly bent on learning the present whereabouts of the defendant.
>
> From such basic information, the plaintiff should then detail for the court the particular efforts which have been made in the effort to ascertain the defendant's present address.[28]

proof of service
A sworn statement (or other evidence) that the requirements of in-person or substituted (constructive) service of process on a party have been followed. Also called *certificate of service* or *return of service*.

indigent
Poor or without means to afford something, such as a private attorney or filing fees.

pro se
(1) On one's own behalf. (2) Representing oneself; not being represented by an attorney. Also called *in propria persona* (abbreviated *in prop per*).

unbundled legal services
Discrete task representation for which the client is charged per task. When performing such tasks, the attorney is providing limited-scope legal services rather than the full range (the full bundle) of legal services that may be needed on a legal matter.

guardian ad litem (GAL)
A special guardian (often, but not always, an attorney) appointed by the court to appear in court proceedings on behalf of a person who is a minor, is insane, or is otherwise incapacitated.

court appointed special advocate (CASA)
A volunteer (who can be an attorney, a paralegal, or other nonattorney) appointed by the court to perform special assignments pertaining to children in the court system.

Once the plaintiff has completed service of process (in-person or, if authorized, substituted), the plaintiff must file a proof of service, which is a sworn statement (or other evidence) that the requirements of in-person or substituted service of process on a party have been followed.

REPRESENTATION

Parties to a divorce can be represented by counsel. If there is an imbalance of wealth at the outset of the divorce litigation, the court can order the wealthier spouse to pay the attorney fees and court costs of the other spouse. In many divorce cases, however, this option is not available because there is no significant disparity of wealth between the spouses.

One method used by some spouses is to seek funds from a company that specializes in funding divorce cases. The funding can cover fees charged by attorneys, investigators, and expert witnesses, as well as court costs. "Divorce funding companies don't all operate in the same way, and they aren't all paid in the same way. Some take a percentage of the final proceeds, some charge a flat fee and others charge only the interest on the money spent to finance the case."[29]

With few exceptions, indigent parties do not have a right to attorney representation at government expense. We will examine the limited exceptions in Chapter 10 when we cover child-support enforcement proceedings and in Chapter 13 when we cover paternity actions. As we will see, however, even in these limited areas of the law, a free government-paid attorney is not required in every child-support or paternity case. Free attorney representation is often available in legal aid offices, although the waiting list at such offices is often long because of their large caseload.

It has been estimated that in 70 to 80 percent of divorce and separation cases, at least one of the parties is a self-represented litigant (SRL).[30] More and more courts are providing different kinds of assistance to parties representing themselves (pro se) in uncomplicated divorce and other family-law cases. The assistance might consist of online self-help centers, standard forms and instructions on court procedures, and volunteer facilitators who are available in the courthouse to assist pro se parties. In addition, numerous websites sell various forms of do-it-yourself assistance.

Occasionally, pro se parties seek the assistance of an attorney for discrete tasks rather than for full legal representation. See Chapter 2 for a discussion of the ethical issues involved in such limited-scope representation (called unbundled legal services) provided by attorneys. Chapter 2 also covers the legality of assistance provided by independent paralegals to pro se parties.

GUARDIAN AD LITEM (GAL)

If an individual in the litigation is a minor, is insane, or is otherwise incapacitated at the time of the divorce action, the court can appoint a guardian—called a guardian ad litem (GAL)—to protect his or her interests during the proceeding. Many GALs are attorneys who provide full representation of the individual being protected. Some GALs, however, have a narrower role of ensuring that the best interests of the child are brought to the court's attention. They might, for example, prepare a home-study report on the living conditions of the child of a divorcing couple. In this role, courts can allow a nonattorney to be a GAL.

Courts often use court appointed special advocates (CASAs). They are volunteers who act as fact-finders, interviewers, and investigators in cases involving child welfare. (Many paralegals have been appointed as CASA volunteers.) They do not represent the child, but they gather pertinent information on the child's welfare and report on these findings to the court. You can find CASA programs in your area by checking the main CASA website (casaforchildren.org). For more on CASAs, see the end of Chapter 1.

PLEADINGS

Pleadings are the formal documents that contain claims or defenses of parties in litigation. Most states have what is called a *forms-driven practice*, which means that official standard forms have been prepared by the courts and must be used in divorce and other family-law cases. In such states, attorneys do not write (draft) many pleadings from scratch. Rather, the attorneys and their paralegals fill out and adapt the required standard forms.

To see a random sample of divorce forms in your state, go to Google or Bing, select the "Images" option, and run this search (substituting the name of your state for "aa":

> aa divorce forms

See also the links to your state in Appendix D.

The first pleading in a divorce case is called the **complaint** (or in some states, the **petition**). It states the claim or cause of action a party is seeking. The claim we are discussing here is a divorce. The party filing the complaint/petition is the plaintiff or **petitioner**; the opposing party is the defendant or **respondent**. See Exhibit 7.7 for an example of a divorce complaint/petition. (If both spouses have no significant disagreements between them, some states allow them to file a *joint petition* for the divorce.)

Pleadings
Formal litigation documents (e.g., a complaint or petition, an answer) filed by parties that state or respond to the claims and defenses the parties have against each other.

complaint
A plaintiff's first pleading that states a claim against the defendant. Also called a *petition*. (See the glossary for an additional definition.)

petition
A complaint. (See the glossary for an additional definition.)

petitioner
A party who files a petition or complaint. Also called a *plaintiff*. (See the glossary for an additional meaning.)

respondent
The party responding to a position or claim of another party. Also called the *defendant*. (See the glossary for an additional meaning.)

EXHIBIT 7.7   Basic Structure of a Divorce Complaint/Petition

STATE OF _____
COUNTY OF _____
FAMILY COURT BRANCH

Mary Smith, Plaintiff | *Caption* |
v.   Civil Action No. _____
Fred Smith, Defendant

COMPLAINT FOR DIVORCE

The plaintiff, through her attorney, alleges:

(1) The jurisdiction of this court is based upon section _____ , title _____ of the State Code (2013). | *Jurisdiction and Venue* |
(2) The plaintiff is fifty years old.
(3) The plaintiff is a resident of the State of _____ , County of _____ . She has resided here for five years immediately preceding the filing of this complaint.
(4) The parties were married on March 13, 1983, in the State of _____ , County of _____ .
(5) There are no children born of this marriage.
(6) The plaintiff and defendant lived and cohabitated together from the date of their marriage until February 2, 2016, at which time they both agreed to separate because of mutual incompatibility. This separation has continued voluntarily and without cohabitation for more than two years until the present time. | *Body* |
(7) Since the separation, the plaintiff has resided at _____ , and the defendant has resided at _____ .
(8) There is no reasonable likelihood of reconciliation.
WHEREFORE, the plaintiff PRAYS:
(1) For an absolute divorce.
(2) For alimony and a division of property. | *Prayer for Relief* |
(3) For restoration of her maiden name.
(4) For reasonable attorney's fees and costs.
(5) For such other relief as this Court may deem just and proper.

_____   _____ | *Subscription* |
Linda Stout   Mary Smith, Plaintiff
Attorney for Plaintiff
234 Main St.
_____ , _____ 07237

STATE of _____ | *Verification* |
COUNTY of _____
    Mary Smith, being first duly sworn on oath according to law, deposes and says that she has read the foregoing complaint by her subscribed and that the matters stated therein are true to the best of her knowledge, information, and belief.

_____

Mary Smith

Subscribed and sworn to before me on this _____ day of _____ , 2018 _____ | *Notarization* |

My commission expires _____

Notary Public, Ted Doyle _____

The main parts of the complaint/petition are as follows:

- *Caption.* The **caption** consists of the heading or introductory part of a pleading or other document that identifies what it is (e.g., Complaint for Divorce, Petition for Dissolution or In the Matter of the Marriage of David Foley and Helen Foley), the names of the parties, the court involved, the docket number if one has been assigned by the court, etc.

- *Jurisdiction and venue.* The beginning of the complaint/petition contains a citation to the statute or constitutional provision giving the court subject-matter jurisdiction over divorces. It also states facts on why the venue of this court is appropriate including how long the party has been a resident of the state and county. Basic facts about the parties and the marriage are stated here or in the body of the pleading.

- *Body.* The body is the part of the pleading that contains the main allegations of the party.

- *Prayer for relief.* A **prayer** is a formal request. The prayer for relief asks the court for specific results, e.g., to dissolve the marriage and divide the marital property.

- *Subscription.* A **subscription** is a signature. Local law specifies who must subscribe (sign) the pleading, often the party and his or her attorney.

- *Verification.* The **verification** is a formal declaration stating that a party has read the pleading and swears that it is true to the best of his or her knowledge. The party thereby *verifies* the pleading.

- *Notarization.* To **notarize** means to certify or attest to something (e.g., the authenticity of a signature).

There are a number of assignments in this book that ask you to draft a complaint/petition. The general instructions for this assignment are found in Appendix A. Review these instructions now. They provide a good overview of the law governing this pleading.

As indicated earlier, many courts have standard forms on pleadings such as complaints/petitions that parties can (or must) use. In addition, high-volume offices that handle many of the same kinds of cases have their own forms for a complaint/petition and for other pleadings that they adapt for particular client cases. Many commercial companies also sell document-assembly software with **templates** that provide the basic structure of the document that can be adapted. For example, see www.ProDoc.com and www.HotDocs.com.

The lawsuit begins when the plaintiff files the complaint/petition with the court (along with the appropriate filing fee). The court then issues a **summons**, which is a formal notice informing the defendant that a lawsuit has been filed and ordering the defendant to appear and answer the allegations of the plaintiff or face a *default judgment*. A copy of the complaint and the summons are served on the defendant (see earlier discussion on notice). If the plaintiff is poor (indigent), he or she can apply to the court for a waiver of filing fees and related court costs in order to proceed **in forma pauperis** (as a poor person). The waiver must be granted. It would be a denial of due process of law to deny parties access to the courts because of their inability to pay filing fees and court costs.[31] (On paying for an attorney, see the earlier discussion on Representation.)

The response of the defendant is the **answer**, which is the pleading filed by the party who responds to the pleading of an opposing party. For our purposes, the defendant's answer is a response to the plaintiff's complaint/petition, which asserts a claim for a divorce. For some claims, the defendant may want to file an

caption
The heading or introductory part of a pleading or other document that identifies what it is, the names of the parties, the court involved, if any, etc.

prayer
A formal request.

subscription
(1) A signature. (2) The act of signing one's name.

verification
A formal declaration that a party has read a document (e.g., a pleading) and swears that it is true to the best of his or her knowledge.

notarize
To certify or attest to something, e.g., the authenticity of a signature.

template
(1) A file containing text and a format that can be used as the starting point for creating frequently used documents. (2) A set of formulas used to perform a designated task.

summons
A court notice served on the defendant ordering him or her to appear and answer the allegations of the plaintiff or face a default judgment.

in forma pauperis
As a poor person who is allowed to proceed without paying certain filing fees and other court costs.

answer
(1) A party's pleading that responds to the pleading of an opposing party. (2) The first pleading of the defendant that responds to the plaintiff's claims.

affirmative defense, which raises facts or arguments that will defeat the opponent's claim even if the opponent's allegations are true. In most states, the defendant can raise his or her own claim (called a counterclaim) against the plaintiff in the answer. Hence, when the complaint asks that the plaintiff be granted a divorce, the counterclaim in the answer can ask that the defendant be granted a divorce. Although both parties may want the divorce, strategic advantage may be sought based on who is granted the divorce.

DEFAULT JUDGMENT; DEFAULT DIVORCE

The summons issued by the court and served on the defendant warns the defendant that if he or she does not respond within a designated number of days, a *default judgment* can be entered against him or her. (Such a judgment can be granted against a party for failure to respond to an opponent's claim.) Unlike other civil proceedings, the default judgment is not automatic in many family-law cases. In divorce cases, a plaintiff who moves for (requests) a default judgment is still required to introduce sufficient evidence to establish his or her case. (This is done in what is often called a prove-up hearing.) When a divorce is granted in a default judgment, the divorce is sometimes called a default divorce.

PRETRIAL CONFERENCES

Before the trial begins, the judge holds one or more pretrial conferences in order to narrow the issues, secure stipulations, establish parameters for discovery, make a final effort to settle the case without a trial, and cover other preliminary matters. (See the discussion of preliminary orders below for a list of the kinds of orders that might be made in a preliminary conference.) The decisions made at the conference become the blueprint for the case and are sometimes referred to as the *case management plan* or, collectively, as the *case management order.*

WAITING PERIOD

Some states have a compulsory *waiting period* or "cooling-off" period (e.g., sixty days) that usually begins to run from the time the divorce complaint/petition is filed. During this period of time, no further proceedings are held in the hope that tempers might calm down, producing an atmosphere of reconciliation.

DISCOVERY

Divorce cases can involve many facts, particularly when finances are in dispute: "Usually the parties have numerous assets and liabilities that need to be documented, discovered, and produced for review in order to settle or try cases."[32] (See the large list of relevant facts and documents outlined in the family history covered in Exhibit 3.1 in Chapter 3.)

Discovery consists of methods or devices used by parties to force information from each other before trial to aid in trial preparation. For cases that involve substantial assets, discovery is "the most time-intensive and expensive phase of a family-law case."[33] One of the reasons for this is the broad scope of what is discoverable.

Much of what is sought in discovery is digital data. As pointed out in Chapter 3, "Today's American family is a digital family living in a digital ecosphere that can tell family stories and reveal family secrets better than any after-the-fact human recollection."[34] Hence, attorneys and paralegals in family-law practices must be adept at e-discovery.

affirmative defense
A defense raising facts or arguments that will defeat the opponent's claim, even if the opponent's allegations in the claim are true.

counterclaim
A claim by one side in a case (usually the defendant) that is filed in response to a claim asserted by an opponent (usually the plaintiff).

prove-up
The presentation of sufficient evidence to support one's claims, even if they are unopposed.

default divorce
A divorce that is granted because of the failure of a spouse to appear, plead, or otherwise defend the divorce action of the other spouse.

pretrial conference
A meeting of the attorneys and the judge (or magistrate) before the trial to attempt to narrow the issues, secure stipulations, make a final effort to settle the case without a trial, and cover other preliminary matters. Also called a *trial management conference.*

discovery
Methods used by parties to force information from each other before trial to aid in trial preparation. The methods can also be used to aid in the enforcement of a judgment.

discoverable
Pertaining to information or materials an opponent can obtain through deposition, interrogatories, or other discovery methods.

e-discovery
Electronic data discovery (EDD). The discovery of data found in emails, spreadsheets, databases, videos, text messages, and other digital formats.

privilege
A special legal benefit, right, exemption, or protection. (See the glossary for an additional meaning.)

attorney-client privilege
A client or a client's attorney can refuse to disclose any confidential (private) communication between them if the purpose of the communication was to facilitate the provision of legal services to the client.

doctor-patient privilege
A patient or a patient's doctor can refuse to disclose any confidential (private) communications between them if the purpose of the communication was to facilitate the provision of medical services to the patient.

interrogatories ("rogs")
A method of discovery by which one party sends written questions to another party.

deposition
A method of discovery by which one party questions another party (or questions the other party's witness) usually outside the courtroom.

deponent
A person questioned in a deposition.

transcribed
Taken down in a word-for-word account. (The account is called a *transcript*.)

subpoena
(1) To command that someone appear at a certain time and place. (2) A command to appear at a certain time and place.

subpoena duces tecum
A command to appear at a certain time and place and bring specified things such as documents or jewelry for inspection.

request for admissions (RFA)
A method of discovery by which one party sends a request to another party that the latter agree that a certain fact or legal conclusion is true or valid so that there will be no need to present proof or arguments about such matters during the trial.

request for production (RFP)
A method of discovery by which one party requests that another party provide access to electronically stored data, paper documents, or other tangible things for copying or inspection. The method can also include a request to enter the party's land for inspection.

independent Medical Examination (IME)
A method of discovery by which a party obtains a court order for a professional examination of a person whose physical or mental condition is in controversy.

privileged
Protected from disclosure; not discoverable.

protective order
A court order directing a person to refrain from inappropriate conduct such as harming or harassing another. Also called an *order of protection*.

Parties can use the discovery methods to obtain any facts that are relevant to their case so long as the facts are not protected by **privilege** such as the **attorney-client privilege** and the **doctor-patient privilege**. The major formal discovery methods are as follows:

- **Interrogatories ("rogs")**. A method of discovery by which one party sends written questions to another party. "Rogs," as they are called, cannot be sent to nonparties. For an example of a set of interrogatories, see Appendix C.

- **Deposition**. A method of discovery by which one party questions another party (or questions the other party's witness), usually in the office of one of the attorneys. The person questioned is called the **deponent**. When someone is questioned, we say that he or she is being *deposed*. Most depositions are **transcribed** so that a word-for-word account of what took place is available to the parties. Some depositions are videotaped, particularly when the deponent is a child in a custody case. If a nonparty is being deposed, that person usually must be served with a **subpoena** to appear at the deposition. Parties and non-parties must be served with a **subpoena duces tecum** when you want them to bring to the deposition specific things such as documents.

- **Request for admissions (RFA)**. A method of discovery by which one party sends a request to another party that the latter agree that a certain fact or legal conclusion is true or valid so there will be no need to present proof or arguments about such matters during the trial.

- **Request for production (RFP)**. A method of discovery by which one party requests that another party provide access to electronically stored data, paper documents, or other tangible things for copying or inspection. The method can also include a request to enter the party's land for inspection.

- **Independent Medical Examination (IME)**. A method of discovery by which a party obtains a court order for a professional examination of a person whose physical or mental condition is in controversy. If paternity is at issue, for example, the court might order a man to undergo a blood-grouping or DNA test.

Limitations on Discovery

There are some limitations on the use of discovery methods. For example, most states have restrictions on who can be deposed and on the number of questions one divorce party can ask of another in interrogatories. These restrictions may vary depending on the complexity of the case. The parties can always make requests to the court to have these restrictions lifted or waived based on the specific needs of a party.

Duty to Supplement Responses

Parties responding to discovery requests have a duty to supplement answers already given in depositions, interrogatories, and other discovery methods if the facts change or if further facts become known and the changed or new facts affect the accuracy or completeness of the facts given earlier to the other party. For example, if a spouse answered an interrogatory on the value of specific property and this value changes substantially after the interrogatory was answered, the responding spouse has a duty to provide the new value to the requesting spouse.

Discovery Abuse

If a party abuses the discovery process by harassing the other side or by demanding information that is **privileged** or otherwise protected from disclosure, the responding party may bring a motion for a **protective order**. Upon motion by any party or by the person from whom discovery is sought, and for **good cause** shown, the court in which the action is pending may make any order that justice requires to protect a party or person from annoyance, embarrassment, oppression, or undue burden or expense.

good cause
A legally sufficient ground or reason. Also called *just cause* or *sufficient cause*.

Some feel that discovery abuse in divorce cases is all-too-common. According to one seasoned family-law attorney:

> In many cases, thousands of pages of documents exchange hands, and parties submit to a variety of mental health, financial, and other discovery examinations. Even nonparties whose lives somehow touch the litigants often are subject to deposition under compulsion of a subpoena and court orders. The universe of what is discoverable, the power to compel compliance with discovery demands, and the penalties for noncompliance all have been greatly enlarged. Practitioners and parties have benefited from the meaningful exchange of information necessary to resolve a case fairly. Yet, there is a trend toward excessive discovery, pushed in many cases by the defensive practice of law by attorneys who are far less concerned about what the discovery will reveal than they are about potential criticism from clients if they fail to obtain the information.[35]

INVENTORY OF ASSETS AND LIABILITIES

Discovery also includes information that the parties must exchange without being asked to do so (sometimes called *mandatory self-disclosure*). For example, at the beginning of the case, they must exchange and file with the court an *inventory of assets and liabilities* (also called *declaration of disclosure*, and *statement of net worth*). The inventory lists all the assets and debts that each spouse says are relevant to the support and property-division issues in the case, including assets a spouse claims is his or her separate property. In some states, they must also file a final inventory at the end of the case to reflect changes and updates since the last inventory.

net worth
The total assets of a person or business less the total liabilities.

If the data provided by a spouse in an inventory is unclear, incomplete, and deceptive, the other side can use the discovery methods outlined above to try to obtain a more accurate account of assets and liabilities. Suppose, for example, that the inventory says certain jewelry is separate (rather than marital) property because it was a gift from the spouse's parent. The interrogatories of the other spouse can seek details on the value of the jewelry, the date the spouse obtained it, the reason it was allegedly given as a gift, etc. A *request for production* could ask that the jewelry be turned over for purposes of inspection and independent evaluation by an independent appraiser.

A spouse's failure to be truthful in the inventory and during discovery can have severe consequences. In a widely publicized California case, a wife failed to tell her husband that her social group had won the lottery. The wife's share of the winnings was $1.3 million. Because of this fraudulent concealment, the court ruled that the entire $1.3 million had to be given to her ex-husband.[36]

ASSIGNMENT 7.10

Pick any well-known married couple in the media. Assume that they are getting a divorce and that you work for the law firm that is representing the wife. You are asked to draft interrogatories meant to elicit as much relevant information as possible about the husband's personal and business finances. The information will be used in the firm's representation of the wife on alimony, child-support, and property-division issues. Draft the interrogatories. You do not need to know actual information about the finances of the person questioned through the interrogatories. A major purpose of the interrogatories is to find out what you do not know. You can obtain ideas for topics to cover in your "rogs" by examining Exhibit 3.1 in Chapter 3 and in Appendix C. (See General Instructions for the Interrogatories Assignment in Appendix A.)

PRELIMINARY ORDERS

Sometimes, obtaining a divorce can be time-consuming, even when the matter is uncontested. The court's calendar may be so crowded that it could take months to have the case heard. If the case is contested and bitterness exists between the parties, the litigation can last a long time.

Pending the outcome of the litigation (**pendente lite**), parties may ask the court (as part of what is called *motion practice*) to issue a number of *preliminary* orders (also called temporary orders), which remain in effect only until final determinations are made later. A motion is made for the order, often accompanied by an **affidavit** that states what is being requested and why. (A **movant** is a person making a motion; an **affiant** is a person making an affidavit.) Unless the request is routine, the movant will also include citations to legal authority that supports the granting of the request. The preliminary orders can include the following:

- Granting temporary physical custody of the children to one of the parents, who will become the *custodial parent,* the parent with whom the child is living. (Often, temporary custody orders become permanent because of the reluctance of courts to disrupt the living environment of children.) A court can also grant temporary *legal* custody to one of the parents, which gives the parent the right to make the major child-rearing decisions on health, education, religion, discipline, and general welfare. (Child custody will be covered in Chapter 9.)

- Granting temporary child visitation to the *noncustodial parent*—the parent who is not living with the child.

- Granting temporary exclusive occupancy of the marital home to one of the spouses (often the custodial parent).

- Granting temporary child support.

- Granting temporary spousal support (alimony).

- Granting temporary attorney fees and related court costs. In divorce cases, spouses are responsible for paying their own fees and costs. If, however, one spouse does not have the resources to pay private counsel and the other spouse has substantial resources, the court will often order the latter to pay the former's fees and costs.

- Enjoining one spouse from bothering or molesting the other spouse and children. (To **enjoin** something is to prohibit it through an **injunction**; an injunction is a court order requiring a person or organization to do or to refrain from doing a particular thing. The injunction may take the form of a **restraining order** designed to prevent family violence.)

- Enjoining a spouse from transferring any property if the transfer might make it unavailable for property division or for the support of the other spouse and children. We will discuss the consequences of **dissipation** (the improper reduction or waste of marital assets that should have been available for property division or support upon divorce) in the next chapter.

- Appointing a **receiver** to manage a spouse's property in order to prevent him or her from squandering the property or otherwise making it unavailable to meet the spouse's obligations.

- Issuing a **ne exeat**, which is a **writ** that forbids a person from leaving the state, country, or jurisdiction of the court; or from removing a child or property therefrom.

- Enjoining the parties from changing insurance policies.

- Ordering an inventory and appraisal of all family assets and debts.

- Granting one spouse control of a business operated by one or both spouses.

- Enjoining the defendant from obtaining a foreign divorce.

---

pendente lite
Pending the [outcome of the] litigation.

affidavit
A written or printed statement containing facts given under oath by a person (called the *affiant*) before someone with authority to administer the oath.

movant
A person who is making a motion.

affiant
A person who is making an affidavit.

enjoin
To prohibit something through an injunction.

injunction
A court order that requires a person or organization to perform, or refrain from doing, a particular thing.

restraining order
A form of injunction, usually issued ex parte (with only one side present), to restrain the defendant from doing a threatened act or from contacting designated individuals. Also called an *order of protection, a personal protection order (PPO),* or a *protection from abuse (PFA).*

dissipation
The improper reduction or waste of marital/community assets that should have been available for property division or support upon divorce.

receiver
A person appointed by the court to protect and manage property in litigation or property in the process of bankruptcy.

ne exeat
A writ that forbids a person from leaving the state, country, or jurisdiction of the court; or from removing a child or property therefrom.

writ
A court order to do or refrain from doing something.

In some states, orders such as these are not necessary because some of them are automatically imposed. For example, a state might provide that once the divorce action begins and service of process is made, the parties are automatically restrained from transferring marital property, canceling insurance that now benefits family members, and removing minor children from the state.

When a court issues a preliminary order, it usually does so after a full **adversary proceeding** where both parties are present to argue their respective positions on the proposed order. Some orders, however, are made in *ex parte* proceedings where only one party appears before the judge. Ex parte preliminary orders are often limited to emergency matters in which there is no time to have a full adversary proceeding or where a danger of domestic violence requires the court to act quickly. At a later date, the party against whom the ex parte order is issued will have the opportunity to contest the order before a judge in an adversarial proceeding.

Preliminary orders can also pertain to discovery that is underway or about to begin. The judge might issue an order that limits discovery to certain areas of inquiry in order to prevent harassment or undue burden on the responding party. Alternatively, if a party has been reluctant to respond to legitimate discovery requests, the judge can grant motions to compel discovery.

TRIAL

Only a few states permit jury trials in divorce cases. If there is no jury, the judge conducts a **bench trial** in which he or she resolves disputes on questions of fact (normally the responsibility of the jury), as well resolving any questions of law. If a jury trial is allowed, the jurors are selected through a procedure known as **voir dire**. During this procedure, the lawyers and/or judge ask questions of prospective jurors to assess their eligibility (e.g., the absence of **bias**) to sit on the jury.

A goal of the trial is to resolve all divorce issues in one proceeding. This would include the issues of dissolving the marriage, spousal support, property division, child support, and child custody. Sometimes, however, these issues must be resolved in separate proceedings. As we saw earlier, if a court has in rem jurisdiction but not personal jurisdiction over the defendant, it can dissolve the marriage but cannot issue property division or support orders. A separate proceeding would be needed to resolve the property and support matters. When separate proceedings are required, the divorce is a *divisible divorce*. (We will examine the special rules governing child custody later.)

The attorneys begin the trial by making *opening statements* outlining the evidence they intend to try to prove during the trial. The plaintiff's side will usually present its case first. The attorney will call the plaintiff's witnesses and directly examine them. The other side can cross-examine these witnesses. Physical evidence (e.g., documents) is introduced as exhibits. Some evidence may have to be *corroborated*, meaning that additional evidence must be introduced to support the position taken by the party. The plaintiff's side will "rest" its case after presenting all of its witnesses and evidence. The defendant's attorney then begins his or her case through direct examination of witnesses, introduction of exhibits, etc.

When a party has the burden of proving a fact, the standard of proof is usually a **preponderance of the evidence**: the fact finder must be able to say from the evidence introduced and found admissible that the existence of a disputed fact is more likely than its nonexistence. Occasionally, however, the law requires a fact to meet a higher standard of proof (e.g., **clear and convincing evidence**).

Who has the **burden of proof**? In general, the party asserting or alleging a fact has the burden of proof on that fact. For example, a spouse who claims that the other spouse has a hidden bank account and physically assaulted the children has the burden of proof on these facts.

---

adversary proceeding
A proceeding in which both sides appear and argue their positions when a court is asked to do something.

bench trial
A nonjury trial.

voir dire
Jury selection.

bias
(1) An inclination, tendency, or predisposition to think or act in a certain way. (2) Prejudice for or against something of someone. (3) A danger of prejudgment.

preponderance of the evidence
A standard of proof that is met when the evidence establishes that the existence of a disputed fact is more likely than its nonexistence. Also called *fair preponderance of evidence*.

clear and convincing evidence
A standard of proof that is met when the evidence demonstrates that the existence of a disputed fact is much more probable than its nonexistence. This standard is stronger than *preponderance of the evidence* but not as strong as *beyond a reasonable doubt*.

burden of proof
The responsibility of proving a fact at trial.

The **marital-communications privilege** does not apply to the divorce action. The privilege allows a spouse to refuse to testify about any confidential communications made between them during their marriage, and one spouse can prevent the other spouse (or ex-spouse) from giving such testimony. But they are allowed to testify about what each said to the other when the testimony is relevant to issues such as support, property division, and child custody. Nor does the privilege apply to criminal proceedings in which one spouse is alleged to have committed a crime against the other or against the children. The privilege allowing spouses to refuse to disclose their confidential marital communications is mainly limited to cases in which a third party is suing one or both of the spouses and attempts to introduce into evidence what one spouse said to the other. When objected to, such evidence is inadmissible.

DIVORCE JUDGMENT

In many states, after the court has reached its decision to grant a divorce, an **interlocutory** judgment (or a *judgment nisi*) of divorce is issued. This means that the judgment will not become final until the passage of a specified period of time (e.g., sixty days). During the time that the interim judgment is in force, the parties are still married. The divorce judgment can be set aside if the parties reconcile before the judgment becomes final.

Final divorce judgments can resolve the questions of alimony, child custody, child support, and property division (assuming, of course, that the court had proper jurisdiction to make these determinations as outlined earlier). In addition, the judgment will often restore the woman's maiden name, if that is her wish, and determine what the surname of the children will be as part of the custody decision. We will have more to say about surnames in Chapters 9 and 12.

Appeals of trial court judgments are possible, but unless the case involves substantial property or bitterness over child custody, it is relatively rare for parties to appeal.

ENFORCEMENT OF DIVORCE JUDGMENT

Most of the controversy involving the enforcement of a divorce judgment has centered on enforcing support and custody orders, particularly across state lines. These topics will be examined at length in Chapters 8, 9, and 10. Here, we begin our examination of enforcement options, which we will continue to examine in these later chapters.

CIVIL CONTEMPT

A party who is ordered to pay a money judgment (e.g., an alimony order) is called the **judgment debtor**. The person in whose favor a money judgment is ordered is the **judgment creditor**. Judgment debtors who disobey such orders can be held in **civil contempt**, which can lead to jail time until they comply with the order. The remedy of jail through civil contempt is not used, however, if the judgment debtor does not have the present financial ability to pay. Inability to pay does not mean burdensome or inconvenient to pay. All resources currently available (or that could become available with reasonable effort) must be used. If the judgment debtor still is unable to pay, incarceration for civil contempt is not imposed.

States differ on whether civil contempt can be used to enforce property-division orders. The latter are more often enforced by execution, attachment, receivership, and constructive trust, which are discussed below.

EXECUTION

The **execution** of the judgment is a command or writ to a court officer (e.g., sheriff) to seize and sell the property of the losing litigant (the judgment debtor) in order to satisfy the judgment debt owed to the judgment creditor. For support orders payable in installments, execution is usually possible only if the orders are *final* and *nonmodifiable* by the court:

- In some states, each unpaid installment automatically becomes a final and non-modifiable judgment of nonpayment to which execution will be available.

- In other states, each unpaid installment does not become a final and nonmodifiable judgment until the judgment creditor makes a specific application to the court for such a judgment and one is entered. Execution is available only after the judgment is so entered or docketed.

execution
(1) The process of carrying out or satisfying the judgment of a court. (2) A command or writ to a court officer (e.g., sheriff) to seize and sell the property of the losing litigant (the judgment debtor) in order to satisfy the judgment debt to the winning litigant (the judgment creditor). Execution is also called *general execution* and *writ of execution.*

GARNISHMENT

When **garnishment** is used, the court authorizes the judgment creditor to reach money or other property of the judgment debtor that is in the hands of a third party such as the employer (who holds wages of the judgment debtor) or a bank (which holds deposits of the judgment debtor).

garnishment
A court proceeding by a creditor to force a third party in possession of the debtor's property (e.g., wages) to turn the property over to the creditor to satisfy the debt owed to the creditor.

ATTACHMENT

Property of the judgment debtor is *attached* when the court authorizes its seizure to bring it under the control of the court so that it can be used to satisfy a judgment or be held as security for such satisfaction. The process is called **attachment**.

attachment
(1) A court authorization of the seizure of a person's property so that it can be used to satisfy a judgment against him or her. (2) The seizure of property as security for such a judgment.

RECEIVERSHIP

The court can appoint a receiver over some or all the judgment debtor's property to prevent him or her from squandering it or otherwise making it unavailable to satisfy the judgment.

CONSTRUCTIVE TRUST

Assume that a judgment debtor conveys property to a "friendly" third party (e.g., the judgment debtor's mother) in an effort to make it appear that he or she no longer owns the property. To reach such property in order to make it available to satisfy the judgment debtor's debts, the court can impose a **constructive trust** on the property. This is a trust created by operation of law to prevent **unjust enrichment** by someone who has improperly obtained property (the mother is this example) through fraud, duress, abuse of confidence, or other wrongful conduct.

constructive trust
A trust created by operation of law to prevent unjust enrichment by someone who has improperly obtained property through fraud, duress, abuse of confidence, or other wrongful conduct.

unjust enrichment
The receipt of a benefit in the form of goods or services that in fairness should be returned or paid for, even though there was no express or implied promise to do so.

ASSIGNMENT   7.11

Prepare a flowchart of the procedural steps that are necessary for a divorce in your state. Assume that the divorce you will be flowcharting is contested. (See General Instructions for the Flowchart Assignment in Appendix A.)

ASSIGNMENT	7.12

Interview a paralegal, attorney, or legal secretary who has been involved in divorce actions in your state. (See General Instructions for the Systems Assignment in Appendix A.) Questions to ask in the interview:

a. Approximately how many divorce cases have you worked on?

b. How many of them have been uncontested?

c. Approximately how long does it take to process an uncomplicated, uncontested divorce?

d. Is there a difference between working on a divorce case and working on another kind of case in the law office? If so, what is the difference?

e. What are the major steps for processing a divorce action in this state?

f. What formbook, manual, or other legal treatise do you use, if any, that is helpful? Who is the publisher?

g. What websites are the most helpful? In what ways are they helpful?

h. Does your office have its own internal manual that covers any aspect of divorce practice?

i. In a divorce action, what is the division of labor among the attorney, the paralegal, and the legal secretary?

j. What computer software is used in divorce cases? What is its function and how useful is it? What would the office have to do if such software did not exist?

RELIGION AND DIVORCE PROCEDURE

Finally, we address two themes involving religion and divorce procedure. First, what divorce laws exist within the Jewish and Islamic traditions? Second, can religious laws be enforceable in our civil courts?

RELIGIOUS DIVORCES

Jewish Divorce

> *When a man hath taken a wife, and married her, and it come to pass that she find no favor in his eyes, because he hath found some uncleanliness in her: then let him write her a bill of divorcement, and give it in her hand, and send her out of his house.* Deuteronomy 24:1 (King James)

get
A document that grants a Jewish divorce.

A Jewish couple seeking a religious divorce can go to a special court called a *Beth Din,* presided over by a rabbi. There, the husband obtains a document called a **get** or bill of divorcement, which the husband hands to his wife. Fault does not have to be shown. In some Jewish traditions, the wife must consent to the divorce. In some Jewish communities in New York, a religious divorce is allowed only if a secular (i.e., civil) divorce or annulment is in process or has already been granted. If a Jewish man has a civil divorce but not a religious divorce, he can still be remarried by a rabbi. But a Jewish woman who does not have a *get*—even if divorced in a civil court—is called an *agunah,* or abandoned wife, and cannot be remarried by a rabbi.[37]

Agunah, Inc., is an organization of Orthodox Jewish women "chained to dead marriages" because their husbands refuse to grant them a Jewish divorce or get.[38] Some rabbis allege that increasing numbers of husbands try to withhold the get as a bargaining chip to obtain reduced support payments or more favorable custody rights. If the husband disappears, the wife's plight is even more desperate. Rabbi Shlomo Klein, based in Israel, travels the world in search of such husbands in order to pressure them into signing the divorce.[39]

A strategy used by some Jewish women is to ask their groom-to-be to sign a premarital agreement in which he agrees that in the event of a civil divorce, he will pay her $150 a day after they separate for every day that they have not obtained a religious divorce, which, of course, requires him to give her a get.[40]

Islamic Divorce

Under **Shariah** (Islamic law), a divorce is traditionally performed by a husband pronouncing the word *talak* (I divorce you) three times. The wife need not be present. One Islamic court recently ruled that sending her an email announcing the talak is not sufficient, although the senior religious adviser in Malaysia has ruled that Muslim men can legally divorce their wives through text messages sent from their mobile phones ("I D4C U").[41]

In some countries, the process is public. In Pakistan, for example, the husband must notify the chairman of an arbitration council that he has pronounced the talak. The council will then attempt to reconcile the parties. If this fails, the divorce becomes absolute ninety days after the husband pronounced the talak. In Egypt, the husband must pronounce the talak in the presence of two witnesses, who are usually officers of a special court.[42] If a wife wants a divorce, she must go to court and prove that her husband has mistreated her. Wives are not often successful. According to one person familiar with Islamic justice, if a husband slaps his wife "only once . . . , [she] has to forgive."[43] A recent change in Egyptian law allows a woman to obtain a divorce without proving mistreatment. She must, however, return her dowry and agree that there will be no alimony.

RELIGIOUS TRADITIONS IN CIVIL COURT

What happens when parties ask a secular (civil) court to enforce a religious marriage or divorce? Our courts cannot settle religious disputes, nor can they favor one religion over another. This would violate the First Amendment. There must be no impermissible entanglement in religious doctrine. Courts can, however, enforce contractual promises based on religious traditions if doing so involves applying neutral principles of law.

In a recent New Jersey divorce case involving an Islamic couple of Bangladeshi descent, the court ordered an ex-wife to return $12,500 to her ex-husband because of a dowry-like commitment that she made under Islamic marriage law. When the parties entered into an arranged marriage in Maryland, they both agreed to be united "under the law of Islam." Pursuant to Islamic custom, a sum of $12,500 was paid to the wife as an initial payment of "sadaq" or "mahr" by the husband or his family. The payment and retention of the sadaq is contingent upon neither party being at fault in precipitating a divorce. The husband alleged that the wife was at fault in the breakdown of the marriage, e.g., she refused to engage in marital relations and left the state on her own and relocated to another state. The court agreed that she was at fault and held that her commitment to return the sadaq was enforceable under basic contract law principles.[44]

Similarly, a New York court enforced an agreement entered into by a Jewish couple that they would appear before a designated Jewish tribunal. When the couple married, they signed a Ketubah, which said the following:

> "[W]e, the bride and bridegroom . . . hereby agree to recognize the Beth Din of the Rabbinical Assembly and the Jewish Theological Seminary of America . . . as having authority to counsel us in the light of Jewish tradition . . . and to summon either party at the request of the other, in order to enable the party so requesting to live in accordance with the standards of the Jewish law of marriage throughout his or her lifetime. We authorize the Beth Din to impose such terms of compensation as it may see fit for failure to respond to its summons or to carry out its decision."

Shariah
Islamic law.

talak
An Arabic word meaning "I divorce you." For a Muslim divorce, the word is spoken three times by a husband to his wife.

After the defendant (the ex-husband) obtained a divorce in a New York civil (secular) court, the plaintiff (the ex-wife) sought to have him summoned before the Beth Din. Her hope was that the Jewish court would order him to give her a *get* so that she could remarry in the Jewish tradition. He refused to appear before the Beth Din. She then sued him in a New York civil (secular) court on the theory that he had violated his contractual commitment to appear before the Beth Din. The lower court dismissed her complaint on the basis that the Ketubah was a liturgical agreement that was entered into as part of a religious ceremony and as such was unenforceable in a civil New York court. This decision was reversed by the New York Court of Appeals. The ex-husband's contractual agreement to appear before a Jewish body can be enforced. Doing so does not require the court to become involved in religious beliefs or disputes. The court said that "the relief sought by plaintiff in this action is simply to compel defendant to perform a secular obligation to which he contractually bound himself. In this regard, no doctrinal issue need be passed upon, no implementation of a religious duty is contemplated, and no interference with religious authority will result. Certainly nothing the Beth Din can do would in any way affect the civil divorce. To the extent that an enforceable promise can be found by the application of neutral principles of contract law, plaintiff will have demonstrated entitlement to the relief sought. Consideration of other substantive issues bearing upon plaintiff's entitlement to a religious divorce, however, is appropriately left to the forum the parties chose for resolving the matter."[45]

The dissenting justices on the Court of Appeals were adamant that the majority had made a serious mistake. "We are of the opinion," said the dissenters, "that to grant the relief plaintiff seeks in this action, even to the limited extent contemplated by the majority, would necessarily violate the constitutional prohibition against entanglement of our secular courts in matters of religious and ecclesiastical content."[46]

Some states are fearful that religious law, particularly Sharia law, will be applied in civil courts. In 2010, for example, Oklahoma amended its constitution to provide that its courts "shall not consider . . . Sharia Law." The Oklahoma amendment discriminated against religions and was successfully challenged as a violation of the First Amendment of the U.S. Constitution. The ruling was controversial. One constitutional scholar commented that he was "no fan of the amendment" but questioned whether it was unconstitutional given that judges already may not impose religious law or take sides on religious questions.[47]

PARALEGAL ROLES

- There are a great variety of roles that a paralegal can have in divorce litigation depending on the kind of practice where the paralegal works. For an overview of paralegal roles in family-law litigation (particularly during pretrial proceedings, discovery, alternative dispute resolution, trial, and post-trial enforcement of divorce judgments), see Exhibits 1.5 and 1.6 in Chapter 1.
- For all financial issues covered in Chapter 7, a paralegal may be asked to help collect documents and facts outlined in:
  - The checklist in Exhibit 3.1 of Chapter 3.
  - The checklists on separation agreements at the beginning of Chapter 8.
  - The interrogatories in Appendix C.

SUMMARY

A divorce is a declaration by a court that a validly entered marriage (opposite-sex or same-sex) is terminated so that the parties are no longer married to each other. There have been three eras in the history of divorce: the eras of restrictive, collusive, and unilateral divorce. American divorce law is derived from the canon law of the Roman Catholic Church in early English history. Until the late 1960s, the main grounds for divorce were those based on fault. No-fault grounds were created, in part, because of the dishonesty fostered by the fault system. Some individuals, however, say that no-fault places some women at a bargaining disadvantage. No-fault divorce does not mean that marital misconduct no longer has a role in divorce litigation. For example, marital fault that affects the children is relevant to child custody.

The major no-fault grounds are living apart, incompatibility, and irreconcilable differences. Living apart is established when spouses live separately for a designated period of consecutive time during which they intend to end the marriage. Incompatibility is established when there is such discord between the spouses that it is impossible for them to live together in a normal marital relationship. Irreconcilable differences are established when there is such discord between the spouses that there has been an irremediable breakdown of the marriage. The major fault grounds are adultery, cruelty, and desertion. The major defenses to the fault grounds of divorce are collusion, connivance, condonation, recrimination, and provocation.

A legal separation is a declaration by a court that parties can live apart even though they are still married to each other. Separate maintenance is court-ordered spousal support while the parties are separated but still married.

Domicile is the place where a person has been physically present (a) with the intent to make that place a permanent home, or (b) with no intent to make any other place a permanent home. Residence is the place where someone is living. Many states have a durational residency requirement that a party be a resident of the state for a specified period of time before being allowed to seek a divorce.

Full faith and credit (FFC) is the obligation of one state to recognize and enforce the legal decisions of another state. The enforceability of a divorce order depends on whether the court had proper jurisdiction to issue that order, and whether the defendant had proper due-process notice of (and an opportunity to participate in) the proceeding that resulted in the order. A divorce judgment can dissolve a marriage, award spousal support, divide marital property, award child support, and award child custody. A divisible divorce is a divorce judgment that dissolves the marriage but does not resolve other divorce issues such as property division, support, and child custody.

Subject-matter jurisdiction is the court's power to resolve a particular type of dispute and to grant a particular type of relief. In rem jurisdiction is the court's power over a particular res, which is a thing or status that is located within the territory over which the court has authority. In rem jurisdiction is needed to dissolve a marriage and is acquired when at least one of the spouses is domiciled in the state. Personal jurisdiction is a court's power over a person to determine (adjudicate) his or her personal rights and duties. Personal jurisdiction is needed for a court to order spousal support, child support, and property division. It is acquired by service of process, consent, or substituted service through a long-arm statute. There are times when a party with a valid jurisdictional challenge to a divorce decree will be estopped from bringing the challenge. An example is the spouse who obtained the divorce judgment

is now challenging its jurisdiction. States differ on when a court has jurisdiction to award child custody. A critical factor is the home state of the child. Venue is the proper county or geographical area in which a court with subject-matter jurisdiction may hear a case.

Summary dissolution is a divorce obtained in an expedited manner because of the brevity of the marriage, the minimal amount of marital property, and the lack of controversy between the spouses. Alternative dispute resolution (ADR) is a method or procedure for resolving a legal dispute without litigating it in a court or an administrative agency. The major vehicles for ADR are arbitration, mediation, med-arb, private judging, neutral evaluation, and collaborative law.

Procedural due process requires that defendants be given notice of divorce proceedings brought against them and an opportunity to be heard in those proceedings. Parties are responsible for the payment of their own attorney fees and court costs in divorce cases, although the court has the power to order the wealthier spouse to pay for the fees and costs of a needy spouse. Many divorce parties represent themselves, sometimes with the assistance of unbundled services from attorneys. A guardian ad litem (GAL) is a special guardian (often an attorney) appointed by the court to appear in court proceedings on behalf of a minor or an incompetent person.

The major pleading of the party seeking a divorce is the complaint/petition. Its main parts are the caption, statement of jurisdiction and venue, body, prayer for relief, subscription, and verification. A default divorce is granted because of the failure of a party to appear, plead, or otherwise defend the divorce action of the other party. A pretrial conference is a meeting of the attorneys and the judge (or magistrate) before the trial to attempt to narrow the issues, secure stipulations, make a final effort to settle the case without a trial, and cover other preliminary matters. The major formal discovery devices are interrogatories, deposition, request for admissions, requests for production, and independent medical examination. Another form of discovery is mandatory self-disclosure such as the inventory of assets and liabilities. Examples of preliminary orders a court can issue are temporary physical and legal child custody, temporary child support, and enjoining a party from transferring marital property. If a state does not allow juries in divorce cases, the judge decides all issues in a bench trial.

An interlocutory judgment of divorce is a judgment that will not become final until the passage of a specified period of time (e.g., sixty days). The main options for enforcing a divorce judgment include civil contempt, execution, garnishment, attachment, receivership, and constructive trust. The Jewish and Islamic religions have their own systems (including special courts) to grant a divorce within their traditions. Some secular civil courts will enforce agreements made within these religions so long as the court does not favor one religion over another, does not settle religious disputes, and applies neutral principles of law.

KEY TERMS

divorce
collusive divorce
grounds
no-fault divorce
ecclesiastical
canon law
limited divorce
absolute divorce
corroboration
uncontested
perjury
migratory divorce
contested
dissolution
covenant marriage
dissipation
plead
tort
interspousal immunity
living apart
incompatibility
sham divorce
irreconcilable differences
stay
adultery
corespondent
circumstantial evidence
cruelty
domestic violence (DV)
stalking
desertion
constructive desertion
due diligence
Enoch Arden divorce
collusion
connivance
condonation
recrimination
comparative rectitude
provocation
legal separation
separation agreement
DOS
conversion
separate maintenance
bilateral divorce
ex parte divorce
ex parte
expedited procedure
residence
domicile
estate tax
age of majority
emancipated
unemancipated
operation of law
legal custody

domicile by choice
equal protection of law
durational residency requirement
forum state
foreign divorce
full faith and credit (FFC)
comity
divisible divorce
jurisdiction
subject-matter jurisdiction
void
concurrent jurisdiction
stipulate
diversity of citizenship
domestic-relations exception
in rem jurisdiction
res
personal jurisdiction
service of process
process
long-arm statute
substituted service
long-arm jurisdiction
minimum contacts
estopped
collateral attack
home state
venue
summary dissolution
alternative dispute resolution (ADR)
arbitration
mediation
med-arb
private judging
neutral evaluation
collaborative law
procedural due process
default judgment
proof of service
indigent
pro se
unbundled legal services
guardian ad litem (GAL)
court appointed special advocate
  (CASA)
pleadings
complaint
petition
petitioner
respondent
caption
prayer
subscription
verification
notarize
template
summons

in forma pauperis
answer
affirmative defense
counterclaim
prove-up
default divorce
pretrial conference
discovery
discoverable
e-discovery
privilege
attorney-client privilege
doctor-patient privilege
interrogatories ("rogs")
deposition
deponent
transcribed
subpoena
subpoena duces tecum
request for admissions (RFA)
request for production (RFP)
independent medical examination (IME)
privileged
protective order
good cause
net worth
pendente lite
affidavit
movant
affiant
enjoin
injunction
restraining order
dissipation
receiver
ne exeat
writ
adversary proceeding
bench trial
voir dire
bias
preponderance of the evidence
clear and convincing evidence
burden of proof
marital-communications privilege
interlocutory
judgment debtor
judgment creditor
civil contempt
execution
garnishment
attachment
constructive trust
unjust enrichment
get
Shariah
talak

CHECK THE CITE

Welfare recipients seeking a divorce in Connecticut could not afford to pay court fees and the costs for service of process. What constitutional challenge did they raise to the requirement to pay these fees and costs? How did the U.S. Supreme Court rule on this challenge? Read *Boddie* *v. Connecticut*, 401 U.S. 371 (1971). To read this opinion online: (1) Run a citation search ("401 U.S. 371") in the *Case law* database of Google Scholar (scholar.google. com). (2) Run a citation search ("401 U.S. 371") in Google, Bing, or Yahoo.

PROJECTS

(1) In Google, Bing, or Yahoo, run the following search: aa wiretapping evidence divorce (substitute the name of your state for aa in the search). Write an essay in which you explain whether one spouse can wiretap another spouse and use the evidence obtained in wiretapping in a divorce case against the spouse in your state. You must cite and quote from a minimum of three different sources that you find on the Internet. At least two of these sources should be the actual language of statutes, court opinions, or other laws.

(2) List any five documents that could be filed in a divorce case in your state (e.g., petition, summons, return of service). On the Internet, try to find two examples of each of the five documents you selected and give a brief summary of the function of each document. The examples can be blank or filled out. Begin your search by determining if your state courts have recommended or required standard forms.

(3) a. What are the names of the court(s) in your state that have the power (subject-matter jurisdiction)

to grant a divorce? Give the citation to (and a brief quote from) the state constitution or state code that supports your answer.

b. Attend a divorce hearing in one of these courts and answer the following questions concerning what you observe:

1. What court heard the case?
2. What was the name of the case?
3. Were both sides represented by counsel? What were the names of the attorneys?
4. Were both parties present?
5. What kind of evidence, if any, was introduced?
6. Use Google, Bing, or Yahoo to find information about the opposing attorneys (e.g., the name of the law firms where they work, their Web addresses, and the kind of practices they have). Summarize what you find.

ETHICS IN A FAMILY LAW PRACTICE

You are a paralegal working at the law office of Smith & Smith. The office represents David Gerry in a divorce action against his wife, Lena Gerry. One of the disputes is how to divide business assets acquired during the marriage. In an effort to pressure Lena to divide the assets in his favor, David tells his attorney to request sole physical and legal custody of their two children even though David has no desire to raise the children. He knows, however, that Lena is terrified at the thought of losing sole custody herself. David wants his attorney to engage in extensive discovery (depositions, interrogatories, etc.) on the custody issue for the sole purpose of wearing Lena down in the hope that she will reduce her claims on the business assets. Any ethical problems?

WRITING SAMPLE

Draft a divorce complaint/petition on behalf of either the husband or the wife who is seeking a divorce in your state. Make up the names and addresses of the parties. You can also make up other facts you need so long as they are consistent with the following facts: the parties have two minor children, a house that is jointly owned, and other substantial property; your client wants sole legal and physical custody, spousal support from the other spouse, and attorney fees paid by the other spouse. (See General Instructions for the Writing Sample in Appendix A.)

REVIEW QUESTIONS

1. What is a divorce?
2. What are the main features of the three historical eras of divorce (restrictive, collusive, and unilateral)?
3. What are the historical origins of American divorce law?
4. What prompted the creation of no-fault grounds for divorce?
5. What are some of the criticisms of the no-fault divorce reforms?
6. What roles can marital misconduct play in no-fault divorce cases?
7. What are the main no-fault and fault grounds for divorce?
8. How is living apart established?
9. How is incompatibility established?
10. How are irreconcilable differences established?
11. How is adultery established?
12. How is cruelty established?
13. How is desertion established?
14. What are the major defenses to the fault grounds of divorce?
15. What is a legal separation, and how does it differ from a divorce?
16. What is separate maintenance, and how does it differ from legal separation and divorce?
17. What is the distinction between a bilateral and an ex parte divorce?
18. How does residence differ from domicile?
19. How do children acquire a domicile?
20. What is a durational residency requirement?
21. What is full faith and credit?
22. What two factors determine the enforceability of a divorce judgment?
23. What is a divisible divorce?
24. What are the five major orders that can be part of a divorce judgment?
25. What is the distinction between the power and the geographic definition of jurisdiction?
26. What is subject-matter jurisdiction and how is it established?
27. What is the domestic-relations exception?
28. What is in rem jurisdiction and how is it acquired?
29. What is personal jurisdiction, and how is it acquired?
30. What is long-arm jurisdiction?
31. What kind of jurisdiction is needed to dissolve a marriage?
32. What kind of jurisdiction is needed to order spousal support, child support, and property division?
33. When will a spouse with a valid jurisdictional challenge to a divorce judgment be estopped from bringing the challenge?
34. How does a court acquire jurisdiction to decide child custody?
35. How is venue determined?
36. What is a summary dissolution?
37. What is the procedural-due-process right of notice?
38. How are attorney fees and court costs paid in divorce cases?
39. When will a court appoint a guardian ad litem?
40. What is a complaint/petition?
41. What are the components of a complaint/petition for divorce?
42. What is a default divorce?
43. What happens at a pretrial conference?
44. What is a waiting period?
45. What are the main formal discovery devices?
46. What is e-discovery?
47. How can a party respond to discovery abuse?
48. What is an inventory of assets and liabilities?
49. What are some of the main preliminary orders a court can issue?
50. What is a bench trial?
51. How do the following ADR methods work: arbitration, mediation, med-arb, private judging, neutral evaluation, and collaborative law?
52. What is an interlocutory judgment?
53. How can the following options be used to enforce a divorce judgment: civil contempt, execution, garnishment, attachment, receivership, and constructive trust?
54. When will a civil court enforce an agreement within a religious tradition?

HELPFUL WEBSITES

Your State

See Appendix D for links to the family law of your state on the topics covered in this chapter.

Divorce Grounds

- www.divorcesource.com
- en.wikipedia.org/wiki/Grounds_for_divorce

- www.hg.org/divorce-law-center.html
- www.americanbar.org/groups/family_law/resources/family_law_in_the_50_states.html

Divorce Procedure

- www.divorcelawinfo.com
- www.law.cornell.edu/wex/table_divorce
- en.wikipedia.org/wiki/Divorce

Divorce Forms

- family.findlaw.com/divorce/divorce-forms.html

Divorce Mediation

- divorceinfo.com/mediation.htm
- apfmnet.org

Family Courts

- www.afccnet.org

Jewish Divorce; Muslim Divorce

- en.wikipedia.org/wiki/Get_(divorce_document)
- www.jewishvirtuallibrary.org/divorce-in-judaism
- en.wikipedia.org/wiki/Divorce_in_Islam

Google Scholar (scholar.google.com)

- Choose "Articles" and enter in the search box any of the key terms discussed in the chapter. Add the name of your state to the search term.

- Choose "Case law" and "Select courts." Select your state, click "Done," and enter in the search box any of the key terms discussed in the chapter. Add the name of your state to the search term.

Google, Bing, or Yahoo

(on these search engines, run the following searches, substituting your state for "aa")

- divorce aa
- divorce grounds aa
- divorce fraud aa
- "separate maintenance" aa
- divorce jurisdiction aa
- divorce pleadings aa
- divorce "e-discovery" aa
- divorce mediation aa
- divorce enforcement aa
- no-fault divorce aa
- divorce adultery aa
- "legal separation" aa
- divorce domicile aa
- divorce "long-arm" aa
- divorce discovery aa
- divorce subpoena aa
- divorce arbitration aa
- divorce "pro se" aa

YouTube

Run the same searches on YouTube listed above for Google, Bing, Yahoo searches. Even when the video clips are trying to entice you to retain an attorney, buy a book, or enroll in a course, they can provide useful overviews and references to primary authority.

Twitter, Reddit, and Facebook

On Twitter, Reddit, and Facebook, run the following search (substitute your state for *aa* in your searches; run the searches with and without the name of your state). Look for links to family-law developments in your state.

- divorce aa

ENDNOTES

Note: All or most of the court opinions in these endnotes can be read online. To do so, go to Google Scholar (scholar.google.com), select "Case law," and in the search box, enter the cite (e.g., "124 A.2d 639") or name of the case (e.g., "Rankin v. Rankin") that is given in the endnote.

[1] Harry D. Krause & David D. Meyer, *Family Law in a Nutshell* 249 (5th ed. 2007).

[2] John DeWitt Gregory et al., *Understanding Family Law* 236 (3d ed. 2005).

[3] *Rankin v. Rankin*, 124 A.2d 639, 644 (PA Super. Ct. 1956).

[4] Patricia Leigh Brown, *A Push to Preserve Reno's Landmarks As Divorce Capital*, N.Y. Times, Apr. 22, 2002, at A1.

[5] Erie Pace, *Louis Nizer, Lawyer to the Famous, Dies at 92*, N.Y. Times, Nov. 11, 1994, at A15.

[6] William Glaberson, *Change to Divorce Law Could Recall a TV Quiz Show: "To Tell the Truth,"* N.Y. Times, Jun. 16, 2010 at A25.

[7] Elizabeth Gilbert, *Eat, Pray, Love*, 30 (Viking 2006).

[8] Arlene F. Saluter and Terry A. Lugaila, *Marital Status and Living Arrangements*, Current Population Reports (Mar. 1998) (www.census.gov/prod/3/98pubs/p20-496.pdf).

[9] Dan Hurley, *Divorce Rate: It's Not as High as You Think*, N.Y. Times, Apr. 19, 2005; National Center for Health Statistics (2017) (www.cdc.gov/nchs/nvss/marriage-divorce.htm).

[10] Brae Canlen, *No More Mrs. Nice Guy*, California Lawyer 51, 95 (Apr. 1994).

[11] Tyler Cowen, *Matrimony Has Its Benefits, and Divorce Has a Lot to Do with That*, N.Y. Times, Apr. 19, 2007, at C3.

[12] Nadine Brozan, *Divorce Lawyers' New Friend: Social Networks*, N.Y. Times, May 15, 2011 at ST17.

[13] Mich. Comp. Laws Ann. § 750.29 & § 750.30.

[14] *Lawrence v. Texas*, 539 U.S. 558 (2003).

[15] *DeMott v. DeMott*, 92 S.E.2d 342, 345 (Va. 1956).

[16] John DeWitt Gregory et al., *Understanding Family Law* 269 (2005).

[17] Uniform Marriage and Divorce Act, § 314(b).

[18] See the Uniform Marriage and Divorce Act, § 302(a)(1). The...court shall enter a decree of dissolution of marriage if...one of the parties...was stationed in this State while a member of the armed services [and] military presence has been maintained for 90 days."

[19] U.S. Const. art. IV, § 1.

[20] National Center for Fathering, www.fathers.com (enter *fathering court* in the search box). Wash. DC has such a court (cssd.dc.gov/page/fathering-court).

[21] *Ankenbrandt v. Richards*, 504 U.S. 689 (1992).

[22] An exception exists for land located in the state. A state has in rem jurisdiction over such land and does not need personal jurisdiction over the defendant to issue a ruling affecting that land.

[23] Note, however, that if the defendant is not domiciled in the state (is a nondomiciliary), he or she can appear solely to contest the court's jurisdiction without submitting to full personal jurisdiction. *Any* appearance by a domiciliary, however, constitutes consent to full personal jurisdiction over the defendant by the court.

[24] Nancy Gordon, *This Judge Does Care About ADR*, 31 Family Advocate 12 (Fall 2008).

[25] Association of Family and Conciliation Courts, *Model Standards of Practice for Family and Divorce Mediation*, 1 (2000) (www.afccnet.org).

[26] Allan J. Weltman, *Family Mediation*, 28 Facts & Findings 27 (National Association of Legal Assistants, Nov. 2001).

[27] *Mullane v. Central Hanover Bank & Trust Co.*, 339 U.S. 306, 314 (1950).

[28] *Bearstop v. Bearstop*, 377 A.2d 405, 408 (D.C. 1977).

[29] Daniel Bukszpan, *These Three People will Fund Your Divorce*, Fortune (April 23, 2016) (fortune.com/2016/04/23/divorce-money-funding-assets).

[30] National Center for State Courts, *The Landscape of Domestic Relations Cases in State Court*, 2 (2018).

[31] *Boddie v. Connecticut*, 401 U.S. 371 (1971).

[32] Lindi Massey, *Discovery: Just What Are You Looking For?*, 9 Legal Assistant Today 128 (Jul./Aug. 1992).

[33] Donald Glenn, *Discovery*, 31 Family Advocate 8 (Spring 2009).

[34] William Hamilton and Wendy Akbar, *E-Discovery in the Age of Facebook, Twitter, & the Digital Family*, 33 Family Advocate 16 (Fall 2010).

[35] Samuel Schoonmaker, *Two Generations of Practitioners Assess the Evolution of Family Law*, 42 Family Law Quarterly 687, 690 (2008).

[36] *In re Marriage of Rossi*, 90 Cal. App. 4th 34, 108 Cal. Rptr. 2d 270 (Cal. Ct. App. 2001).

[37] Lisa Green Markoff, *How Couples "Get" a Religious Divorce*, National Law Journal, Aug. 15, 1988, at 8.

[38] Rivka Haut, *Letter to the Editor*, N.Y. Times, Oct. 12, 1994, at A18. See also Agunah International (www.agunahinternational.com).

[39] John Donnelly, *Rabbi Is an Unorthodox Manhunter*, San Diego Union Tribune, Oct. 28, 1995, at A-22.

[40] Mark Oppenheimer, *Where Divorce Can Be Denied, Orthodox Jews Look to Prenuptial Contracts*, N.Y. Times, March 17, 2012, at A16.

[41] Leela Jacinto, *"I D4C U" Declaring "I Divorce You" by Mail or Mobile Phone Is Easy for Muslim Men—Too Easy, Say Women*, ABCNEWS.com (Aug. 31, 2004).

[42] *The Religious Effect of Religious Divorces*, 37 Modern Law Review 611-13 (1974). *Divorce (Islamic)* (en.wikipedia.org/wiki/Divorce_in_Islam).

[43] Elaine Sciolino, *Britain Grapples with Role for Islamic Justice*, N.Y. Times, Nov. 19, 2008, at A1.

[44] *Rahman v. Hossain*, 2010 WL 4075316 (N.J. Super. Ct. 2010).

[45] *Avitzur v. Avitzur*, 446 N.E.2d 136, 137, 139 (N.Y. 1983).

[46] *Avitzur*, 446 N.E.2d at 139.

[47] *Awad v. Ziriax*, 670 F.3d 1111 (10th Cir. 2012).

CHAPTER 8

Spousal Support, Property Division, and the Separation Agreement

CHAPTER OUTLINE

CHAPTER OBJECTIVES

After completing this chapter, you should be able to:

- Define separation agreement.
- State when courts become involved in separation agreements.
- List the characteristics of an effective separation agreement.
- Identify the main checklists used in the preparation of a separation agreement.

- Give examples of when a court will refuse to approve/enforce a separation agreement.
- State a spouse's duty of disclosure.
- List the main differences between alimony and property division.
- Explain the factors a court will use when deciding whether a clause

in a separation agreement is alimony or property division.
- Distinguish the different kinds of alimony.
- Explain the criteria for awarding alimony.
- State when a court will modify an alimony award.

- Identify the main ways a payee can enforce an alimony obligation.
- State whether alimony and property-division debts are dischargeable in bankruptcy.
- Describe necessaries.
- Explain the tactic of spousal refusal.
- List the main steps in property division.
- Describe the different categories of property.

- List the main kinds of separate property.
- Explain the differences between common-law and community-property states.
- Explain transmutation.
- Explain the criteria for equitable distribution.
- Distinguish between marital and economic fault.
- Explain when appreciation is divisible.
- Know the effect of commingling.

- Explain how property division occurs for pensions, degrees/licenses, businesses, and goodwill.
- Describe how a court will treat debts, taxes, wills, insurance, and legal expenses.
- Know the effect of mutual mistake in a separation agreement.
- Explain the role of alternative dispute resolution (ADR).
- Understand the consequences of reconciliation on a separation agreement.

INTRODUCTION

It is sometimes said that marriage is about love, and divorce is about money.[1] Chapter 8 is largely based on this reality as we begin a comprehensive study of two of the major financial dimensions of divorce: spousal support (alimony) and property division. We will examine attempts by the parties to reach agreement on these matters in a separation agreement, as well as how a court will force a resolution on the parties in the event that they cannot agree. In addition to alimony and property division, we will also cover other separation-agreement issues except for child custody (see Chapter 9) and child support (see Chapter 10).

SEPARATION AGREEMENTS AND LITIGATION

A **separation agreement** is a contract by married persons who have separated (or who are about to separate) that can cover support, custody, property division, and other terms of their separation and likely divorce. If the parties want a **divorce** based on the terms of the separation agreement, they must ask the divorce court to approve the terms. Between 80 and 90 percent of divorces include some form of contractual agreement such as a separation agreement.[2] If the separating parties do not want to divorce, at least at the present time, they might seek a **legal separation** from the court based on the separation agreement that they negotiate.

The separation agreement is an example of a **postnuptial agreement**, one made after the parties have been married. (See Exhibit 4.1 in Chapter 4 for a chart comparing the definitions and functions of separation agreements, premarital agreements, postnuptial agreements, and cohabitation agreements.)

Separation agreements find their way into court in the following situations:

- The parties file for a divorce after negotiating the separation agreement; they ask the court to approve the terms of the agreement and perhaps to incorporate those terms in the divorce decree.
- One party sues the other for breach of contract (i.e., for violating the separation agreement); in this contract suit, one of the parties asks the court to enforce the separation agreement.
- After the divorce, one of the parties brings a suit to ask the court to modify the separation agreement (e.g., to reduce the amount of alimony).
- After the divorce, one of the parties brings a suit to set aside the separation agreement (e.g., because it was induced by fraud or because of mutual mistake).

separation agreement
A contract by married persons who have separated (or who are about to separate) that can cover support, custody, property division, and other terms of their separation and likely divorce. Also called *marital settlement agreement (MSA).*

divorce
A declaration by a court that a validly entered marriage is terminated so that the parties are no longer married to each other. Also called *dissolution, marital dissolution,* and *divorce a vinculo matrimonii* (divorce from the chains of marriage).

legal separation
A declaration by a court that parties can live apart even though they are still married to each other. Also called *judicial separation, limited divorce, divorce a mensa et thoro,* and *separation from bed and board.*

postnuptial agreement
A contract between married persons that covers specific matters, usually financial in nature. (Also called *postnup* and *midnup.*) The spouses may have no intention of separating. If they have this intention, the contract is commonly called a *separation agreement.*

The law encourages parties to enter into separation agreements. So long as certain basic public policies (to be discussed below) are not violated, the law gives a great deal of leeway to the parties to resolve their difficulties and, in effect, to decide what their relationship will be upon the dissolution of their marriage. The role of the attorney and paralegal is to assist the client in this goal.

A high priority of the family-law practitioner must always be to avoid litigation, which is often time-consuming, expensive, and emotionally draining for everyone involved. The marital breakdown of the parties was probably a most painful experience for the entire family. Litigation tends to remind the parties of old wounds and to keep the bitterness alive. Although an effective separation agreement will not guarantee harmony between the spouses, it can help keep their disputes on a constructive level.

EFFECTIVE SEPARATION AGREEMENTS

Bargaining or negotiation begins the process of achieving an effective separation agreement. Initially, the spouses may attempt some bargaining on their own before they find attorneys and turn the task over to them.

What is an effective separation agreement? Obviously, this will vary according to individual circumstances. Nevertheless, some general observations can be made about the characteristics of an effective separation agreement: It is comprehensive, fair, accurate, legal, and readable. (See Exhibit 8.1.)

EXHIBIT 8.1   Characteristics of an Effective Separation Agreement

1. *Comprehensive.* It covers all major matters. If a problem arises months or years later, the parties will not have to say, "We never thought of that when we drafted the agreement."

2. *Fair.* If the agreement is not fair to both sides, it may be unworkable, which will force the parties into expensive and potentially bitter litigation to interpret and enforce the agreement. Hence, the worst kind of legal assistance a law office can provide is to "outsmart" the other side into "giving up" close to everything. Little is accomplished by winning the war but losing the peace. "You gain no advantage in depriving your ex-spouse of what he/she is entitled to. Remember, your ex-spouse has the ability to make your life miserable."[3]

3. *Accurate.* The agreement should accurately reflect the intentions of the parties. What they orally agreed to do in formal or informal bargaining sessions should be stated in the written agreement. No clause in the agreement should ever prompt one of the parties to exclaim, "That's not what we agreed to do when we talked about it!"

4. *Legal.* Certain things can and cannot be done in a separation agreement; the agreement must not attempt to do anything that is illegal.

5. *Readable.* The agreement should be written in language that the parties can understand without having to hire or rehire an attorney every time a question arises.

CHECKLISTS FOR THE PREPARATION OF A SEPARATION AGREEMENT

Before an effective separation agreement can be drafted, a great deal of information is needed. The following checklists identify what is needed. (Also relevant are the data on family history in Chapter 3 and the interrogatories in Appendix C.) The checklists identify topics that the spouses need to negotiate on their own and/or through their attorneys.

For same-sex marriages, the references in the checklists to husband and wife should be referred to as Spouse1 and Spouse2.

DATA NEEDED ON INDIVIDUALS

- Names and addresses of spouses and children (include phone numbers, email addresses, all Internet addresses, e.g., Facebook, Instagram, and LinkedIn pages).
- Name and address of present attorney of the other spouse.
- Names and addresses of prior attorneys, if any, retained by either spouse at any time during the marriage.
- Name and addresses of business associates (e.g., partners, senior employees) of each spouse.
- Name and addresses of major service providers (e.g., accountant, investment advisor, stockbroker, real estate agent) of each spouse.
- Names and addresses of individuals who might serve as character references (if needed on custody or credibility issues).

EXHIBIT 8.2   Financial Checklists

- All prior agreements between spouses (e.g., premarital agreement, postnuptial agreements, such as a loan between the spouses or drafts of separation agreements).
- All property held by the husband in his separate name.
- All property held by the wife in her separate name.
- All property held jointly (in both names).
- All property the husband brought into the marriage and kept as his separate property.
- All property the wife brought into the marriage and kept as her separate property.
- All property the husband brought into the marriage that was jointly used during the marriage and/or whose upkeep/maintenance was jointly paid for during the marriage.
- All property the wife brought into the marriage that was jointly used during the marriage and/or whose upkeep/maintenance was jointly paid for during the marriage.
- All property received by one spouse alone (before or during the marriage) as a gift from a relative or from someone other than the other spouse.
- All property received by one spouse alone (before or during the marriage) from the will (or trust) of a relative or of anyone else.
- All property received by one spouse alone (before or during the marriage) from a relative or from anyone else who died without leaving a valid will and whose property, therefore, passed by **intestate succession**.
- All income earned or other property acquired by the husband after the **DOS** (date of the separation) but before the date of the final divorce.
- All income earned or other property acquired by the wife after the DOS but before the date of the final divorce.
- All pending contracts for the purchase or sale of real property.
- All insurance policies currently in force.
- All insurance policies canceled in the last five years.
- All debts currently **outstanding**, with an indication of who incurred each debt.

intestate succession
The transfer of a decedent's property to state-designated relatives of the decedent who dies without leaving a valid will. Also called *descent and distribution* and *hereditary succession*.

DOS
Date of separation; the date the spouses stopped living together on a permanent basis.

outstanding
(1) Unpaid. (2) To be collected.

(continued)

Exhibit 8.2 *(continued)*

- Copies of all tax returns filed during the marriage and since the DOS.
- All wills, trusts, or other family **instruments**.
- All **financial statements** prepared before the marriage, during the marriage, and after the DOS (e.g., statements filed with the government, a bank, or other institution).
- All income from any source earned by the husband.
- All income from any source earned by the wife.
- Projected future income of both parties (e.g., salary, dividends, interest, Social Security, workers' compensation, pension rights, royalties, loans that will be repaid, future trust income, expected inheritance).
- All present and projected living expenses of the husband.
- All present and projected living expenses of the wife.
- All present and projected living expenses of the children.

instruments
A formal written document that gives expression to, or embodies, a legal act or agreement (e.g., a contract or will). (See the glossary for an additional meaning.)

financial statement
A report covering the assets (e.g., income, investments) and debts of a person or business as of a particular date or over a designated period. A financial accounting or balance sheet.

EXHIBIT 8.3
Checklists for Individual Clauses in the Separation Agreement

1. Spousal support (alimony):
   - Waived by both spouses?
   - If included, who pays? (Who is the **payor**, the **obligor**?)
   - How much?
   - What is the method of payment?
   - What is the frequency of payment?
   - Does payment fluctuate with the income of the payor? Does it fluctuate with the income of the **payee** (the **obligee**)?
   - What security will the payee have in the event of nonpayment by the payor?
   - Does payment terminate on the remarriage or the death of either party?
   - Does payment terminate if the payee **cohabits** with another?
   - Should the agreement include a no-modification clause stating that neither party will ask a court to modify the agreement once it is approved by the court?
   - What are the methods of enforcement?
   - What are the tax consequences of spousal-support payments?
   - Are there any prior agreements about spousal support in the premarital agreement?
2. Child support (see Chapter 10):
   - Who pays?
   - How much? (Will there be a request to modify (increase or reduce) the amount specified by the state's child-support guidelines?)
   - Is the amount modifiable?
   - What is the method of payment?
   - What is the frequency of payment?
   - What is the security for payment?
   - Does it terminate when a child reaches a certain age?
   - Does it terminate if the child is **emancipated** other than by reaching the age of majority?

payor
One who makes a payment of money or who is obligated to do so.

obligor
One who has a legal obligation to do something, usually to make a payment.

payee
One to whom money is paid or is to be paid.

obligee
One to whom a legal obligation is owed.

cohabit
To live together in an intimate (usually sexual) relationship in the manner of spouses. Although a married couple cohabits, the word is more often used in reference to persons not married to each other. The noun is *cohabitation*.

emancipated
Legally independent of one's parent or legal guardian. The noun is *emancipation*.

(continued)

Exhibit 8.3 *(continued)*

- Who will pay daycare expenses?
- Who will pay education expenses covering private schools, college, graduate school, etc.?
- What are the tax consequences of child-support payments?
- Are there any prior agreements about child support in the premarital agreement?

3. Child custody (see Chapter 9):
   - Custody options: Who has **physical custody** (sole or joint) and who has **legal custody** (sole or joint)?
   - What is the method of communicating/consulting on major child-rearing decisions, such as health and education (if parties have joint legal custody)?
   - What are the visitation rights of the **noncustodial parent (NCP)**?
   - Do others have visitation rights (e.g., grandparents)?
   - Where will the child stay during summer vacations and on birthdays and special holidays?
   - Who will pay the child's transportation expenses?
   - Can the child be moved to another city or state on a temporary or permanent basis?
   - Can the last name of the child be changed?
   - What will be the child's participation in religious activity?
   - Are there any prior agreements about child custody in the premarital agreement?

4. Health expenses of **custodial parent (CP)** and children:
   - Who pays?
   - What is the method of payment?
   - What is the security for payment?
   - What medical expenses will be covered?
   - What dental expenses will be covered?
   - How will the cost of drugs be paid?
   - How will any special medical needs of the CP and child be met?
   - Who will pay for expenses not covered by insurance?
   - Are there any prior agreements about healthcare expenses in the premarital agreement?

5. Insurance:
   - Who pays the premiums?
   - What is the method of payment?
   - Who are the beneficiaries?
   - Life insurance?
   - Health insurance?
   - Comprehensive vehicle insurance?
   - Disability insurance?
   - Homeowner's insurance?
   - Umbrella insurance?
   - What is the security for payment?
   - Can the names of beneficiaries be changed?
   - Are there any prior agreements about insurance in the premarital agreement, particularly life and medical insurance?

physical custody
(1) The right of an adult to have a child reside with the adult. Also called *residential custody.* (2) Where the child is actually living.

legal custody
The right to make the major child-rearing decisions on healthcare, education, religion, discipline, and general welfare. Also called *decision-making responsibility.*

noncustodial parent (NCP)
The parent who is not living with the child; the parent who does not have physical custody of the child. Also called *nonresidential parent.*

custodial parent (CP)
The parent with whom the child is living and who has physical custody of the child. Also called *residential parent.*

(continued)

Exhibit 8.3 *(continued)*

6. Estate documents:
   - Are any changes needed in wills that are already in existence (individual or mutual)?
   - Family trust: changes needed?
   - Trust accounts for children: changes needed?
   - Are there any prior agreements about the estate in the premarital agreement?

7. Debts still to be paid:
   - Incurred by whom?
   - When incurred?
   - Why incurred?
   - Who pays?
   - What is the security for payment?
   - Will there be a **hold-harmless** clause for the party who did not incur a debt but is asked by a creditor to pay it?
   - Are there any prior agreements about debts in the premarital agreement?

8. Personal property:
   - List of all personal property in which either spouse has an ownership or other interest (over a value of $50).
   - Who gets what?
   - Cash?
   - Joint and separate bank accounts (savings, checking, certificates of deposit, IRAs, etc.)?
   - Stocks, bonds, mutual funds, other kinds of securities?
   - Motor vehicles?
   - Works of art, jewelry, etc.?
   - Household furniture?
   - Rights to receive money in the future (e.g., retirement pay, stock options, royalties, rents, anticipated court judgment awards)?
   - Are there any prior agreements about personal property in the premarital agreement?

9. Pension
   - Does either spouse have a pension?
   - What kind of a pension is it?
   - When does it vest?
   - What is its current value?
   - Are there any prior agreements about pensions in the premarital agreement?

10. Real property:
   - List of all real property in which either spouse has an ownership or other interest.
   - Residences?
   - Vacation home?
   - Tax shelters?
   - Leases?
   - Are there any prior agreements about real property in the premarital agreement?

hold harmless
To assume any liability in a transaction and thereby relieving another from responsibility or loss arising out of the transaction. Also called *save harmless*.

(continued)

Exhibit 8.3 *(continued)*

11. Business assets:
    - What business interests does each spouse have?
    - Business real estate?
    - Business personal property?
    - How will the business interests be valued? By use of a professional appraiser? If so, how will this person be selected?
    - Who will make management decisions during the separation and after the divorce?
    - Are there any prior agreements about business interests in the premarital agreement?

12. Income tax returns:
    - What returns will be filed after the separation but before the divorce?
    - Will each spouse cooperate in the filing of all returns still to be filed?
    - Who will be responsible to pay deficiencies and penalties if the tax authorities audit the current year's tax return and the returns of prior years when the parties filed joint returns?
    - Will one spouse agree to give the other spouse a hold-harmless clause on tax deficiencies and penalties?
    - Are there any prior agreements about tax returns in the premarital agreement?

13. Attorney fees and court costs:
    - Will each spouse pay his or her own fees and costs?
    - Will one spouse pay the other's fees and costs (part or whole)?

14. Separation agreement:
    - Will the agreement be incorporated and merged into the divorce judgment?
    - Will it be incorporated but not merged into the divorce judgment?

15. Conflict resolution for disagreements after the separation agreement is signed and approved by the court:
    - Will the parties use arbitration to settle the conflict?
    - Mediation?
    - Another method of alternative dispute resolution (ADR)?
    - How will a neutral third party be selected as the arbitrator or mediator?
    - Who will pay the expenses involved?

16. Reconciliation (What happens to the terms of the separation agreement if parties reconcile after the agreement is executed?):
    - What to do about the parts of the separation agreement that were already carried out before the **reconciliation**?
    - What to do about the parts of the separation agreement that were not carried out before the reconciliation?

reconciliation
The full resumption of the marital relationship.

PRELIMINARY CONSIDERATIONS

Before we begin our examination of alimony and property division, we need to consider some preliminary matters that pertain to the legality of separation agreements. To highlight some of the major issues that we will consider, read the sample introductory clauses in Exhibit 8.4 that are sometimes found in separation agreements.

EXHIBIT 8.4   Sample Introductory Clauses in a Separation Agreement

SEPARATION AGREEMENT

[1] THIS AGREEMENT is entered on this 21st day of September, 2019, by Fred Jones (referred to in this agreement as Husband), residing at 465 East 8th Street, Braintree, MA, and by Linda Jones (referred to in this agreement as Wife), residing at 8 Florida Street, Dorchester, MA.

WITNESSETH:

[2] WHEREAS, the parties were married on June 22, 2003 in the state of Ohio, city of Blue Creek, and

[3] WHEREAS, two children were born of this marriage: Ava Jones (October 19, 2005) and Myles Jones (July 5, 2007), and

[4] WHEREAS, as a result of irreconcilable marital disputes, the parties have been voluntarily living apart since June 1, 2018, which both parties feel is in their own best interests and that of their children, and

[5] WHEREAS, both parties wish to enter this agreement for the purpose of settling all custody, support, and property rights between them, and any other matter pertaining to their marriage relationship, and

[6] WHEREAS, both parties acknowledge that they have received a full and accurate disclosure from each other of all assets (separate and marital) and debts (separate and marital) that are relevant to spousal support, child support, child custody, property division, and all other matters pertinent to their separation and divorce (see Attachment "A" containing a summary of these financial disclosures), and

[7] WHEREAS, both parties acknowledge that they have had separate and independent legal advice from counsel of their own choosing on the advisability of entering this agreement, that they have not been coerced or pressured into entering the agreement, and that they voluntarily decide to enter it.

[8] NOW THEREFORE, in consideration of the promises and the mutual commitments contained in this agreement, the parties agree as follows:

[The full text of the agreement goes here.]

ILLEGAL CLAUSES

- The agreement in Exhibit 8.4 between Fred and Linda Jones is careful to point out that a separation has already occurred. Clause [4] says they have been living apart since June 1, 2018. When parties are still living together despite their decision to separate, the law operates on the assumption that there is still hope. Yet a separation agreement provides *benefits* to the parties in the form of money, freedom, etc. The very existence of such an agreement is viewed as an *inducement* to obtain a divorce unless the parties have already separated or are about to do so shortly. A separation agreement between two parties who are still living together and who intend to remain together indefinitely might be declared unenforceable. It would be the equivalent of one spouse saying to another, "If you leave me now, I'll give you $25,000." The agreement is invalid because it is **conducive to divorce**. This is against **public policy**. Although the reform of no-fault divorce has lessened a court's inclination to invalidate separation agreements that are conducive to divorce, the prohibition still exists in many states. The problem is resolved, however, if the agreement says the parties have already separated or are about to do so shortly and that the agreement is simply a statement of the terms of their separation.

conducive to divorce
Tending to encourage divorce.

public policy
The principles inherent in the customs, morals, and notions of justice that prevail in a state; the foundation of public laws; the principles that are naturally and inherently right and just.

- It would also be against public policy for the parties to agree to have a "private divorce." Suppose a husband and wife enter into the following brief separation agreement:

  "We hereby declare that our marriage is over and that we will have nothing to do with each other henceforth. As we part, we ask nothing of each other, including support or property."

Assume further that this agreement is not shown to anyone. To permit parties to make such a contract would be to enable them to "divorce" themselves without the involvement of a court. At the time the parties attempted to enter into this contract, it may have seemed fair and sensible. Suppose, however, that months or years later, one of them becomes destitute and sues the other for support or for part of the property they accumulated while together. The defendant could not defend the action by relying on the promise the parties made in the agreement not to ask for support or property from each other. Furthermore, if either party later tries to marry someone else, he or she can be charged with the crime of **bigamy**.

- Another category of illegal agreement between a husband and wife is **collusion**, which is an agreement to commit fraud. An example of a fraudulent agreement would be a plaintiff who falsely asserts that the defendant deserted her on a certain date, and the defendant falsely admits to this or remains silent even though he knows that the assertion is false. Their *collusive* objective is usually to *facilitate* the granting of the divorce. Before no-fault divorce became part of our legal system (see Chapter 7), this kind of falsehood was common, although rarely uncovered and punished.

- Examine the following two clauses:

  "The wife agrees that she will file for a divorce against the husband within three months."

  _____

  "None of the terms of this separation agreement shall be effective unless and until either of the parties is granted a divorce."

The first clause is invalid as conducive to divorce; a party cannot promise to file for a divorce. The clause doesn't merely encourage divorce; it makes it close to inevitable. The second clause appears to be as bad as the first. Neither of the parties will obtain any of the benefits in the separation agreement unless one of them obtains a divorce. Arguably, this clause encourages one of the parties to file for divorce and the other party to refrain from contesting the divorce. Oddly, however, the courts have not interpreted the second clause in this way. It *is* legal to condition the entire separation agreement on the granting of a divorce.

  "In the event that the wife travels to another state to file for divorce, the husband agrees to go to that state, appear in the action, and participate therein."

Courts differ on the legality of this clause. The parties are clearly contemplating an out-of-state divorce, perhaps because they both realize that obtaining the divorce in their own state would be procedurally more difficult than obtaining it out of state. Such **migratory divorces** were once quite common. Is a clause conducive to divorce if it obligates the defendant to appear in the **foreign divorce** action? Some states think that it is and invalidate the agreement. Other states, however, uphold the clause.

---

bigamy
Marrying another while still in a valid, undissolved marriage with someone else.

collusion
(1) An agreement to commit fraud. (2) An agreement by spouses that one or both will lie to the court in order to help secure their divorce.

migratory divorce
A divorce obtained in a state to which one or both of the spouses traveled before returning to their state of domicile.

foreign divorce
A divorce obtained in another state or country. A divorce that was not obtained in the forum state where the parties are now in litigation. If, for example, you are domiciled in Florida and obtain a divorce in Ohio, you have a foreign divorce.

ASSIGNMENT   8.1

Do the following clauses improperly facilitate divorce? Are they collusive? (See General Instructions for the Legal-Analysis Assignment in Appendix A.)

a. "In the event that the wife files for a divorce, legal separation, or annulment, the husband agrees to cooperate fully in the wife's action."

b. "In the event that the wife files a divorce action, the husband will pay in advance all expenses incurred by the wife in bringing said action."

CAPACITY TO CONTRACT

There was a time in our history when the very thought of a wife entering into a contract with her husband was anathema. A married woman lacked the **capacity** to contract with her husband, because **at common law**, the husband and wife were one, and "the one" was the husband. You could not make a contract with yourself. This rule, of course, has been changed. A wife can enter into a contract, such as a separation agreement, with her husband. (See also Chapter 4 on post-nuptial agreements and Chapter 12 on women's rights generally.)

Today, the major question of capacity involves mental health. A separation agreement is invalid if either party lacked the capacity to understand the agreement and the consequences of signing it. The traditional test is that a person must understand the nature and consequences of his or her act at the time of entering into the separation agreement. This understanding may not exist due to insanity, mental retardation, senility, temporary delirium due to an accident, intoxication, drug addition, etc.

MUTUAL DISCLOSURE, FRAUD, AND DURESS

Clause [6] of the agreement in Exhibit 8.4 states that the parties have received a full and accurate disclosure of all assets and debts. Attachment "A" of the agreement contains a summary of this disclosure.

Spouses negotiating a separation agreement have a duty to make a full and accurate disclosure to each other of all the assets and debts that pertain to the marriage. They cannot treat each other at **arm's length** as two strangers in a business transaction can. This duty is based on the status of the parties as a married couple. Many states say that a husband and wife have a **fiduciary relationship** with each other, which requires mutual loyalty, candor (openness), and fair treatment. Their fiduciary duty does not end until the divorce. The failure to make a full and accurate disclosure during negotiations for the separation agreement can be a violation of the fiduciary duty the parties owe each other.

Serious nondisclosure or lying about assets can lead to the invalidation of part or all of the agreement on the ground of *fraud*. **Fraud** is an intentionally false statement of fact that is **material**, made to induce reliance by the plaintiff, and results in harm because of the reliance. (Something is material if it is important enough to influence a decision.) An example of fraud is a spouse who intentionally fails to disclose or undervalues marital assets that should be part of the property division in the separation agreement.

Unfortunately, many spouses start hiding assets as soon as separation becomes a possibility. ("In a divorce, valuable items often mysteriously turn up 'missing.'"[4]) Unscrupulous spouses would probably agree with the advice a financial adviser gave to a husband who was about to start divorce proceedings: "You know what's the object in a divorce? . . . Pre-emptive retaliation. Here's what I want you to do. Clean out your bank account before she does it for you. Hide your assets."[5]

---

capacity
The legal power to do something, such as enter into a contract or a relationship. Also called *legal capacity*. (See the glossary for an additional meaning.)

at common law
During a time in early U.S. history when law was created by court opinions and legislatures, often before it was changed by later legislatures.

arm's length
Pertaining to how parties would treat each other if they were strangers looking out for their own self-interests with no confidential or other special relationship between them that would cause one to expect the other to provide a special advantage or to act with fairness.

fiduciary relationship
The relationship that exists when one party (called the *fiduciary*) owes loyalty, candor, and fair treatment to another party. The fiduciary is required to act in the interest (and for the benefit) of the other party. Also called a *confidential relationship*.

fraud
An intentionally false statement of fact that (a) is material, (b) is made to induce reliance by the plaintiff, and (c) results in harm because of the reliance. Also called *deceit* and *intentional misrepresentation*.

material
(1) Serious and substantial. (2) Important enough to influence the decision that was made.

Indeed, some spouses have kept assets and debts secret throughout the marriage. The task of uncovering this financial data can be daunting. One divorce attorney advises her clients to start making copies of financial records as soon as possible:

> If you are the spouse in the marriage who is clueless about family finances, use this time to get dialed in while you still have access to all of the accounts. Try to download at least six months of statements from all financial accounts, including assets, debts, and credit cards. You may only have access to this prior to signing the legal separation agreement, so time is of the essence.[6]

The discovery devices discussed in Chapter 7 are important tools for uncovering marital assets. (See also Appendix C for a set of interrogatories designed to uncover assets and debts.)

Several times at the beginning of the agreement in Exhibit 8.4 the parties mention that they are acting "voluntarily." (See clauses [4] and [7].) According to traditional contract principles, if a party enters into a contract because of duress, it will not be enforced. Duress the unlawful use of force or threats to pressure or compel someone to do something he or she does not want to do. (It is sometimes said that the pressure must be severe enough to overcome the will.) Suppose that a wife is physically threatened if she does not sign the separation agreement. Clearly, the agreement would not be valid. The husband could not sue her for breaching it or attempt to enforce it in any other way.

Of course, simply because the separation agreement says that the parties enter it "voluntarily" does not necessarily mean that no duress existed. Either spouse could have been forced to say the agreement was signed "voluntarily." But to have the agreement say that it was "voluntarily" signed is at least *some* indication (however slight) that no duress existed. An aggrieved party, however, can still introduce evidence to the contrary. The same is true of clause [6] that says there has been full and accurate financial disclosure.

At one time, many courts presumed that a husband took unfair advantage of his wife unless he demonstrated otherwise. The women's movement has helped change this attitude. Courts no longer so blatantly protect women. Both sides will be forced to live with the agreement they signed if (1) there was sufficient mutual disclosure of assets and debts, (2) there was no fraud, duress, or overreaching, (3) the agreement is not unconscionable, (4) neither party is about to become a public charge, and (5) both parties had the opportunity to seek independent advice before they signed. If these conditions are met, most courts will presume that the agreement is valid and enforceable, even if one of the parties later regrets signing it.

Ex-spouses who are stuck with a bad bargain sometimes turn against the attorney who represented them on the separation agreement. In one case, for example, an ex-wife won a $1.5 million judgment against her attorney for legal malpractice in failing to do enough investigation of the value of her ex-husband's business before advising her to sign the separation agreement with him.[7]

SEPARATE COUNSEL

There is no requirement that both spouses be represented by counsel; an agreement is not necessarily unconscionable or infected by duress if only one spouse is represented. The last WHEREAS clause [7] in the Jones separation agreement in Exhibit 8.4 states that both Fred and Linda had the benefit of "separate and independent legal advice" on the advantages and disadvantages of signing the agreement. This fact can be significant in a court's deliberation on whether to set the agreement aside on a ground such as duress. It is relatively difficult to challenge the validity of a separation agreement that was signed after both sides consulted with their own attorney—even if the spouse with most of the resources paid for both attorneys.

---

duress
The unlawful use of force or threats to pressure or compel someone to do something he or she does not want to do. Illegal coercion.

aggrieved
Injured or wronged and thereby entitled to a remedy.

overreaching
Taking unfair advantage of another's naiveté or other vulnerability, especially by deceptive means.

unconscionable
(1) Shockingly unfair or unjust. (2) Shocking the conscience by heavily favoring one side together with an absence of meaningful choice and a highly unequal bargaining posture of the parties.

public charge
An individual who is primarily dependent on the government for subsistence or support, as demonstrated by either the receipt of cash assistance for income maintenance or by institutionalization for short- or long-term care at government expense.

legal malpractice
The failure of an attorney to use the knowledge and skill commonly applied under similar circumstances by attorneys in good standing in the same area of practice.

CONSIDERATION

Most contracts must be supported by *consideration* to be valid. (Consideration is something of value that is exchanged between the parties.) The separation agreement is a set of promises by the parties of what they will do. The exchange of these promises is the consideration for the separation agreement. A wife's promise to relinquish all claims she may have against her husband's estate when he dies is an example of her consideration to him. A husband's comparable release of claims in her estate or his promise to transfer to his wife full title to land he solely owns are examples of his consideration to her.

The main consideration in the separation agreement is the separation itself. A husband and wife have the right to live with each other as husband and wife (i.e., the right of cohabitation). By reason of the separation agreement, the parties promise each other that they will never again claim this cohabitation right.

consideration
Something of value that is exchanged between parties. It can be an act, a forbearance (not performing an act), a promise to perform an act, or a promise to refrain from performing an act.

cohabitation
Living together in an intimate (usually sexual) relationship in the manner of spouses.

ALIMONY PAYMENTS AND PROPERTY DIVISION: A SUMMARY OF CONSEQUENCES

We now begin our coverage of alimony and property division. Alimony is money or other property paid in fulfillment of a duty to support one's spouse (or ex-spouse) after a legal separation, a divorce, and, in most states, an annulment. Other terms for alimony include *maintenance* and *spousal support*. Property division is the distribution of community or marital property between spouses after a legal separation or divorce. Although alimony is awarded in most states, its availability is in decline; the main way in which our legal system rearranges the financial lives of spouses upon divorce is through property division.

Exhibit 8.5 presents a summary of the major legal consequences of alimony and property division that we will be examining.

alimony
Money or other property paid in fulfillment of a duty to support one's spouse (or ex-spouse) after a legal separation, a divorce, and, in most states, an annulment. Also called *maintenance* and *spousal support*.

property division
The distribution of community or marital property between spouses after a legal separation or divorce. In a few states, *separate property* can be included in the property division and some states allow property division in an annulment. Also called *property settlement* and *property distribution*.

EXHIBIT 8.5   Alimony and Property Division Terms of a Separation Agreement: A Summary

Definitions

Payor: One who makes a payment of money or who is obligated to do so.

Example: An ex-spouse who must pay alimony or child support is a payor.

Obligor: One who has a legal obligation to do something, usually to make a payment.

Example: An ex-spouse who must pay alimony or child support is an obligor.

Payee: One to whom money is paid or is to be paid.

Creditor: Someone to whom a debt is owed. A payee is a creditor of the payor.

Examples: An ex-spouse who is awarded alimony is a payee; a child who is awarded child support is a payee. The ex-spouse and child are creditors of the payor.

Obligee: One to whom a legal obligation is owed. An obligee is a creditor of the obligor.

Examples: An ex-spouse who is awarded alimony is an obligee. A child who is awarded child support is an obligee.

Debtor: One who owes a debt.

Examples: An ex-spouse who must pay alimony is a debtor. An ex-spouse who must transfer property to the other ex-spouse as part of a property division is a debtor.

Transferor: The person who transfers an interest in property.

Example: The ex-spouse who gives his or her share of the marital home to the other ex-spouse as part of the property division is a transferor.

Transferee: The person to whom an interest in property is transferred.

Example: The ex-spouse who will receive the other ex-spouse's share in the marital home as part of the property division is a transferee.

Interest: A legal share or right in something, which can often be sold or transferred.

Examples: An IRA account that one owns or co-owns is an interest; a tenant's right to leased property is an interest.

(continued)

Exhibit 8.5 *(continued)*

Effect of Bankruptcy on Alimony and Property-Division Obligations

Alimony

- Domestic-support obligations (DSO), such as alimony debts of the payor are *not* extinguished (discharged) by bankruptcy. After bankruptcy, the debtor (payor) who has an alimony obligation to the other spouse (the payee) continues to owe all arrears (unpaid or delinquent alimony debts) and must continue to pay all future alimony debts. The same is true of child-support debts.

- Domestic-support obligations (DSOs) are not dischargeable regardless of whether the debtor files for bankruptcy under Chapter 7 or under Chapter 13 of the Bankruptcy Code.

Property Division

- If the debtor files for bankruptcy under Chapter 7 of the Bankruptcy Code, his or her property-division obligations cannot be discharged.

- If the debtor files for bankruptcy under Chapter 13 of the Bankruptcy Code, his or her property-division obligations (which are not domestic-support debts) *can* be discharged upon certifying that all outstanding alimony and child-support obligations have been met.

Effect of Remarriage on Alimony and Property-Division Obligations

Alimony

- If the person receiving alimony (the payee) remarries, the alimony payments cease (the payor no longer owes them) *unless* the separation agreement or a court specifically provides that the payments continue after the payee's remarriage.

- If the person paying alimony (the payor) remarries, the alimony payments to the first spouse must continue *unless* the separation agreement or a court provides that the payments cease or are reduced.

Property Division

- The remarriage of either the payor or the payee does not affect the terms of the property division. All remaining obligations under the property division must be fulfilled despite the remarriage of the payor or the payee.

Effect of Death on Alimony and Property-Division Obligations

Alimony

- If the payee dies, alimony payments cease.

- If the payor dies, alimony payments cease unless the separation agreement or a court provides that the payments continue.

Property Division

- The death of either the payor or the payee does not affect the terms of the property division. All remaining obligations under the property division must be fulfilled despite the death of the payor or the payee. The obligations would be carried out by or through the estates of the deceased.

Effect of Cohabitation on Alimony and Property-Division Obligations

Alimony

- In some states, cohabitation by the payee either terminates the alimony or is some evidence that alimony is no longer needed.

- Cohabitation by the payor does not affect the payor's alimony obligation to the payee.

Property Division

- The cohabitation of either the payor or the payee does not affect the terms of the property division. All remaining obligations under the property division must be fulfilled despite the cohabitation of the payor or the payee.

Availability of Civil Contempt for Enforcement of Alimony and Property-Division Obligations

Alimony

- If an ex-spouse fails to pay alimony according to the terms of a separation agreement and falls into arrears, a court can use civil contempt to enforce payment if the separation agreement has been incorporated and merged into the divorce decree.

- To use the enforcement remedy of civil contempt, the debtor must have the ability to pay the support.

Property Division

- If an ex-spouse fails to transfer property according to the property-division terms of a separation agreement, states differ on whether a court can use civil contempt to enforce the transfer obligation. In many states, civil contempt can be used if the debtor has violated a court order to transfer the property, but not if the debtor's duty to transfer the property is based on the separation agreement alone.

(continued)

Exhibit 8.5 *(continued)*

The Court's Power to Modify Alimony or Property-Division Terms of the Separation Agreement

Alimony

- Courts differ on when (or if) they have the power to modify alimony awards.
- When they have this power, they will exercise it if there has been a substantial change of circumstances of a continuing nature affecting the payor's ability to pay or the likelihood that the needy spouse will become a public charge unless a modification is ordered.

Property Division

- If either party later becomes dissatisfied with the terms of an otherwise valid property division, the court will rarely, if ever, modify those terms.

Federal Income Tax Treatment of Alimony and Property Division

Alimony

- After 2018, the recipient (payee) of alimony does not pay taxes on what is received. (The same has always been true of child-support payments.) Alimony (and child-support) payments are not taxable income of the payee.
- After 2018, alimony payments are not deductible by the payor. (The same has always been true of child-support payments.)
- Before 2019, alimony was deductible by the payor and taxable to the payee.

Property Division

- Transfers of property incident to a divorce are not reportable as income by the transferee or deductible by the transferor.
- The tax basis of the property in the hands of the transferee is the same as the transferor's tax basis. (See Chapter 11.)

DISTINGUISHING BETWEEN ALIMONY AND PROPERTY DIVISION

The separation agreement will transfer many different kinds of assets: cash, stock, cars, houses, etc. All of these assets fall into the category of property. Unfortunately, it is not always easy to determine whether property mentioned in a separation agreement is alimony or is a part of a property division, particularly when the term transfers **liquid** property such as cash or an asset that can be easily converted into cash. The classification hinges on the intent of the parties at the time they entered into the separation agreement.

Assume, for example, that the agreement provides that one party will make a five-year annual payment of $50,000 to the other party. Is this alimony or property division? The parties may either be confused about the distinction or pay little attention to it. At a later date, however, when the parties realize the importance of the distinction, they may make conflicting claims about what their intentions were. Here are two examples of when the distinction can make a difference:

- *Bankruptcy.* If one party files for bankruptcy, alimony is not dischargeable (it must still be paid), but property-division obligations might be dischargeable.
- *Tax.* If the parties were divorced before 2019, alimony is deductible by the payor, and the payee must pay taxes on the alimony received. Although this is no longer true after 2018, family-law offices will have clients who were divorced before 2019 and hence are still subject to pre-2019 tax laws.

In such situations, the distinction between alimony and property division can be critical.

liquid
Pertaining to cash or property that can be readily converted into cash.

When a court must make this distinction, it will turn the clock back to when the parties were negotiating the separation agreement and determine what their intent was at that time. The test is *not* what the payee actually uses the money or other property for. Proof that a payment was used for rent and groceries, for example, does not show that the payment was alimony. The test is the intent of the parties at the time of the agreement, *before the money or other property is spent or used*.

To determine intent, the court will consider a number of factors:

- Labels used in the agreement.
- Contingencies.
- Method of payment.
- The kind of property transferred.

Usually, none of these factors is conclusive by itself. All of them must be considered. Unfortunately, the factors do not always point in the same direction. One of the factors may clearly indicate an intent that a term is alimony. If, however, the other factors clearly suggest that the term is part of a property division, the court may conclude that it is the latter.

LABELS USED IN THE AGREEMENT Often, the separation agreement will explicitly label a provision as "alimony" or as a "property settlement" or "property division." These labels, however, do not always control. An annual payment of $10,000 given to the wife might be labeled "Property Division," but if it is otherwise clear to the court that the parties intended this payment to be in the nature of support, the court will classify it as alimony in spite of the label. If, for example, the wife clearly needed support but the agreement failed to mention or provide support for her, the parties probably intended the "Property Division" to be her support, or the parties had this intent but wanted to disguise the alimony as property division.

CONTINGENCIES Terms that are **contingent** on the occurrences of certain events are often interpreted as alimony rather than as a property division (e.g., $10,000 a year to the wife until she finishes school or turns sixty years old). The presence of such contingencies suggests an intent to provide support while needed rather than an intent to divide property.

METHOD OF PAYMENT A term in the agreement may provide for:

- A single **lump-sum payment** (e.g., $10,000),
- **Periodic payments** (e.g., $10,000 a year), or
- Fluctuating payments (e.g., $10,000 a year to be increased or decreased depending upon earnings in a particular year).

Periodic and fluctuating payments usually suggest alimony. Lump-sum payments usually suggest a property division. The evidence, however, may show that the parties intended periodic or fluctuating payments to be property division and a lump-sum payment to be alimony. (A lump-sum payment that is intended to be alimony is called **alimony in gross**.)

THE KIND OF PROPERTY TRANSFERRED A conveyance of property other than cash (e.g., a house, a one-half interest in a business) often suggests a property division. Cash alone, however, usually suggests alimony.

Again, these factors are only guides. All of the circumstances must be examined in order to determine the intent of the parties. It may be that a court will conclude that a transfer of a house was intended as alimony or support. The court might also conclude that a one-time lump-sum payment of $75,000 was intended as alimony. Although a court will be inclined to rule otherwise in these examples, proof of intent will control.

contingent
Conditional; dependent on something that may or may not happen.

lump-sum payment
A single payment of an amount of money rather than ongoing payments.

periodic payments
Payments to be made over a period of time as opposed to a single (lump-sum) payment.

alimony in gross
Alimony in the form of a single (lump-sum) payment. Also called *lump-sum alimony*.

ALIMONY

Next, we turn to a close examination of alimony. First, we will look at how courts resolve alimony disputes when the parties cannot resolve the issue between themselves and then we will cover options the parties consider when they try to negotiate alimony terms in their separation agreement. Knowing how courts have ruled on alimony in the past can guide spouses and their attorneys in negotiating realistic terms. They need to know what a court is likely to do if they fail to reach agreement.

INTRODUCTION

At common law, the husband, as head of the household, had a legal duty to support his wife for life. This duty existed even after a divorce so long as the wife's misconduct did not cause the break-up of the marriage. A wife did not have a duty to support her husband during or after marriage. After giving him her **dowry**, her duty was to provide her husband with services, not financial support.

dowry
The cash or other property given to the husband by the wife upon marriage.

Today, however, the financial support duty is mutual. To impose the duty only on a man (the ex-husband) would amount to unconstitutional sex discrimination in violation of the Equal Protection Clause of the U.S. Constitution[8] and in violation of comparable clauses in state constitutions. In most divorces, however, it is the woman who is the recipient of support through a separation agreement and/or through a court order.[9] As more women become successful in their careers, however, the number of ex-wives paying alimony to their ex-husbands has increased. (Occasionally, the media will use the nonlegal word "manimony" for support payments paid to an ex-husband by his more affluent ex-wife.)

The mutual duty of spouses to support each other is based on the common law and on statutes such as the **family expense act**, which requires both spouses to provide for the basic support needs of each other and the rest of the family. (We'll return to this obligation later in the chapter when we cover the rules on *necessaries*.)

family expense act
A state statute that makes spouses jointly liable for the basic support needs of the family.

Once divorce occurs, there are a number of different kinds of alimony that are possible in most states. See Exhibit 8.6 for the types of alimony we will be discussing.

EXHIBIT 8.6   Types of Alimony

GENERAL DEFINITION: Alimony is money or other property paid in fulfillment of a duty to support one's spouse (or ex-spouse) after a legal separation, a divorce, and, in most states, an annulment. Also called *maintenance* and *spousal support*.

Category	Definition
Alimony in Gross	Alimony in the form of a single (lump-sum) payment. Also called *lump-sum alimony*.
Alimony Pendente Lite	Alimony pending the outcome of the litigation or court case. See *temporary alimony* below.
Bridge-the-Gap Alimony	See *rehabilitative alimony* below.
Caregiver Alimony	Alimony for an ex-spouse who cannot be self-supporting because of his or her need to care for a disabled child.
Durational Alimony	See *rehabilitative alimony* below.
Incapacity Alimony	Alimony, usually long-term, for an ex-spouse unable to be self-supporting because of a physical or mental incapacity.
Lump-Sum Alimony	See *alimony in gross* above.
Permanent Alimony	Alimony that is awarded periodically (e.g., monthly) until a designated date or indefinitely without a termination date. Also called *traditional alimony*.
Rehabilitative Alimony	Support payments to an ex-spouse for a limited time to allow him or her to return to financial self-sufficiency through employment or job training. (Also called *durational alimony, transitional alimony*, and *bridge-the-gap alimony*.)

(continued)

Exhibit 8.6 *(continued)*

Category	Definition
Reimbursement Alimony	Alimony that repays an ex-spouse who worked or made other financial contributions during the marriage so that the other spouse could obtain training or otherwise enhance his or her future earning capacity. Also called *restitutional alimony*.
Restitutional Alimony	See *reimbursement alimony*.
Temporary Alimony	Alimony awarded on an interim basis before the court makes its final decision on alimony. Also called *alimony pendente lite*.
Traditional Alimony	See *permanent alimony*.
Transitional Alimony	See *rehabilitative alimony*.

Related Support Categories

- **Separate maintenance.** Court-ordered spousal support while the parties are separated but still married. (See Chapter 7.)

- **Palimony.** Support payments ordered after the end of a nonmarital relationship (a) if the party seeking support was induced to enter or stay in the relationship by a promise of support or (b) if ordering support is otherwise equitable. (See Chapter 4.)

CRITERIA FOR AWARDING ALIMONY

permanent alimony
Alimony that is awarded periodically (e.g., monthly) until a designated date or indefinitely without a termination date. Also called *traditional alimony*.

In recent years, alimony has become disfavored, particularly **permanent alimony**, which is alimony awarded periodically (e.g., monthly) until a designated date or indefinitely (without a termination date). In some states, alimony cannot be granted for more than a specific number of years (e.g., three years) except in extreme cases. Hostility toward long-term alimony can be found in the observation sometimes heard from judges that a failed marriage should not be a ticket to a lifetime pension.

Statistics vary, but according to some estimates only between 9 and 16 percent of divorce cases include alimony as part of a divorce settlement or court award. Before 2019, about 600,000 federal taxpayers claimed the alimony deduction on their returns, with an average claim of $12,500 per return.[10] These numbers are expected to be substantially different now that payors no longer can deduct alimony they pay and payees no longer must pay taxes on alimony they receive.

On financial matters other than child support, there is a "clean-break" mentality among many parties, attorneys, and judges. Alimony, particularly long-term alimony, prolongs the interaction and probable bitterness between ex-spouses. As much as possible, a clean-break philosophy seeks to end the financial interdependency of the parties.

This was not always so. There was a time in our history when courts gave substantial alimony awards to wives, particularly when the husband tended to control the family finances and to place all property in his name alone. Today, large alimony awards are less common because reforms in the law of property division (considered later in the chapter) have placed women in a less vulnerable position. Indeed, many courts will not address the alimony question until after they have divided the marital property. This division will be critical to obtaining a realistic assessment of a spouse's need for support. An ex-spouse who has received millions in the property division is unlikely to need (or be granted) alimony. Hence, the trend is to have short-term or no alimony in separation agreements and court awards unless (a) there is little or no marital property to divide or (b) the more needy spouse's ability to earn a living after the separation is hampered by a lack of job skills, age, and/or by a need to care for children.

Temporary alimony can be awarded while the parties are waiting for a final court decision on property division.

The modern view on court-ordered alimony is expressed in the **Uniform Marriage and Divorce Act (UMDA)**, which refers to alimony as *maintenance*:

> *The maintenance order shall be in amounts and for periods of time the court deems just, without regard to marital misconduct, and after considering all relevant factors, including:*
>
> *(1) the financial resources of the party seeking maintenance, including marital property apportioned to him, his ability to meet his needs independently, and the extent to which a provision for support of a child living with the party includes a sum for that party as custodian;*
>
> *(2) the time necessary to acquire sufficient education or training to enable the party seeking maintenance to find appropriate employment;*
>
> *(3) the standard of living established during the marriage;*
>
> *(4) the duration of the marriage;*
>
> *(5) the age and the physical and emotional condition of the spouse seeking maintenance; and*
>
> *(6) the ability of the spouse from whom maintenance is sought to meet his needs while meeting those of the spouse seeking maintenance.*[11]

Not all states agree with the position of the UMDA that alimony should be awarded "without regard to marital misconduct," as we will see. Yet most states will consider the same kinds of factors listed in (1) to (6) of the UMDA. A common catch-all factor used in many states allows a court to consider anything else that the court deems "necessary to do equity and justice between the parties."

These standards for the award of alimony give judges considerable discretion on when to award alimony and on how much. Some complain that the standards are too broad. Judges "are on their own in deciding how to prioritize the various factors and how to translate them into dollar amounts, resulting in wildly inconsistent alimony awards. When asked how much alimony a lifelong homemaker married to a doctor deserved, judges in an Ohio survey estimated as little as $5,000 a year and as much as $175,000."[12] Some states have addressed this problem by establishing formulas, particularly as to the length of time that alimony payments must be made. For example, for a marriage that lasted one to five years, the formula might say that alimony can be awarded for no more than half of the number of months of the marriage.

REHABILITATIVE ALIMONY

The most popular form of short-term alimony is called **rehabilitative alimony**. It consists of support payments to an ex-spouse for a limited time to allow him or her to return to financial self-sufficiency through employment or job training. How long should this take? The answer, of course, depends on the payee's skills and health, and on the state of the economy. To assess a payee's employability, the court might order a vocational evaluation by an expert who will administer skills tests and research realistic employment opportunities that are available in the area. A minority of states take a broader view of rehabilitative alimony by pegging the standard for its award not to minimal self-sufficiency but to what would be needed to restore the ex-spouse to some measure of the standard of living enjoyed during the marriage.

Rehabilitative alimony may be impractical if the ex-spouse has special needs or must care for a younger child. If the ex-spouse cannot return to self-sufficiency because of a physical or mental incapacity, the alimony provided is sometimes called **incapacity alimony**. Similarly, an ex-spouse raising school-age children will usually have considerably less time to transition back into the outside work world (or to obtain job training) than an ex-spouse without

temporary alimony
Alimony awarded on an interim basis before the court makes its final decision on alimony. Also called *alimony pendente lite* (pending the outcome of the litigation or court case).

Uniform Marriage and Divorce Act (UMDA)
A model statute on marriage and divorce proposed to the states for adoption.

rehabilitative alimony
Support payments to an ex-spouse for a limited time to allow him or her to return to financial self-sufficiency through employment or job training. Also called *durational alimony, transitional alimony,* and *bridge-the-gap alimony.*

incapacity alimony
Alimony, usually long-term, for an ex-spouse unable to be self-supporting because of a physical or mental incapacity.

caregiver alimony
Alimony for an ex-spouse who cannot be self-supporting because of his or her need to care for a disabled child.

reimbursement alimony
Alimony that repays an ex-spouse who worked or made other financial contributions during the marriage so that the other spouse could obtain training or otherwise enhance his or her future earning capacity. Also called *restitutional alimony.*

child-rearing duties. Caregiver alimony covers ex-spouses who cannot be self-supporting because of his or her need to care for a disabled child. Of course, all of these categories of alimony are separate from (and in addition to) the child support that must be paid for a child's needs.

REIMBURSEMENT ALIMONY

Reimbursement alimony seeks to repay a spouse who worked (or made other financial contributions) during the marriage so that the other spouse could obtain training or otherwise enhance his or her future earning capacity. An example would be a wife who held a full-time job in order to help pay her husband's tuition in dental school. When the couple divorces, there may be no property to divide because of the short length of the marriage and the sacrifices that both made to meet the expenses of dental school. The amount she contributed to his education could be returned to her upon divorce as reimbursement alimony payable in a lump sum or periodically over a designated period of time. Although called alimony, the funds or other property given to the payee are primarily designed to serve the cause of fairness and justice rather than to meet a need for support.

Later, we will discuss the separate issue of whether a degree or occupational license is marital property that can be divided upon divorce. Most states say no. In such states, one way for the sacrificing ex-spouse to be compensated would be to give him or her reimbursement alimony.

OPPORTUNITY LOSS

Many women often postpone their own education and entry (or re-entry) into the workforce in order to stay at home to care for children and to run the household. As a result, they lose opportunities they would have had to build their own financial identity. In many states, an "opportunity loss" will lead to an increased share of the property division, or, if there is little property to divide, to a larger alimony award. Additionally, an opportunity loss may further demonstrate a stay-at-home mother's need for a generous award of rehabilitative alimony.

PAYOR'S ABILITY TO PAY

In addition to the payee's need for alimony, the ability of the payor to pay alimony must be determined. All of the payor's earnings and other financial resources are considered in determining ability to pay. The test for calculating earnings is not the payor's actual earnings; it is his or her realistic *earning potential* now and in the future. A spouse cannot plead poverty that could be substantially eliminated by using available or obtainable employment skills. Nor can a spouse create self-imposed poverty by giving away or squandering assets. (This admonition against dissipating assets also applies to property division, as we will see later when we study the case of *Gastineau v. Gastineau.*)

MARITAL FAULT

Note that the Uniform Marriage and Divorce Act states that alimony should be awarded "without regard to marital misconduct." Many courts follow this guideline, but some do not. There are courts that will decrease the amount of alimony to be paid to a spouse whose marital misconduct precipitated the divorce. More common are courts that will increase the amount of alimony to be paid by a spouse who has committed domestic violence or other marital fault if the wrongdoing has affected the victim's ability to be self-sufficient after the divorce. "In most cases, judges take fault into account only when the fault resulted in some tangible economic consequence—for example, if a husband's physical cruelty toward his wife rendered her unable to work, he might be required to pay greater alimony."[13]

Fault can also be relevant when one party seeks to *modify* an alimony award. We will consider modification of alimony shortly.

ALIMONY IN SAME-SEX DIVORCES

Divorcing couples in same-sex marriages are, of course, entitled to the same alimony rights as apply to divorcing couples in opposite-sex marriages. As indicated, one of the factors courts take into consideration in the alimony decision is the length of the marriage that is ending. In general, the shorter the marriage, the less likely a court will grant substantial alimony to a lower-earning or no-earning spouse. This criterion can place some same-sex partners at a disadvantage in their divorce.

Same-sex marriage did not become legal in some states until 2003 and in all states until 2015 (see Chapter 5). Yet, many recently divorced same-sex married couples were in long-term relationships well before same-sex marriage became legal. From a legal perspective, however, such couples were not in long-term *marriages*. Thus, today when one of the spouses asks the court for alimony, the marriage is viewed as a short-term marriage—one often slated for no alimony or modest alimony. To overcome this disadvantage, some states say that they will take into consideration the fact of a prior long-term relationship in making the alimony decision even if the marriage was short term. In such states, the needy spouse will not be viewed as someone looking for financial support after a short marriage. Rather, "the courts will agree to tack on prior years of cohabiting so it's viewed as a longer-term marriage than the legal date" would indicate.[14]

ASSIGNMENT 8.2

Answer the following questions after examining your state code. Also check state court opinions of your state if you cannot find an answer in the code. (See General Instructions for the State-Code and Court-Opinion Assignments in Appendix A.)

a. What standards will a court use in awarding alimony? For example, is marital fault relevant?

b. Are there any limitations or options on the form that alimony can take (e.g., periodic payments, lump sum, etc.)?

c. When alimony is awarded, is it always for an indefinite period? If not, under what circumstances can it be for a fixed period?

d. If the court denies the divorce to both parties, can alimony still be awarded?

ASSIGNMENT 8.3

a. Find an opinion decided within the last ten years by a court in your state that awarded alimony to a woman. List all the considerations that the court used in making its alimony decision. Try to find an opinion in which the court mentioned a specific dollar amount as alimony. To find cases, go to Google Scholar (scholar.google.com), click "Case law," then click, "Select courts," click the state courts of your state, click "Done," and enter the search "*aa alimony*," substituting the name of your state for *aa*.

b. Repeat the assignment, except this time find an opinion in which the court awarded alimony to a man.

c. Are the two opinions consistent with each other? Explain. (See also the General Instructions for the Court-Opinion Assignment in Appendix A.)

NEGOTIATING ALIMONY

During negotiations on a separation agreement, spouses often waive the right to receive spousal support (alimony) from each other after the divorce. They both know that the law does not favor long-term alimony for most marriages. They therefore are more likely to use property division as the main vehicle for settling their post-divorce financial lives.

Also, if the parties entered into a valid **premarital agreement**, its terms may specify whether alimony is waived in the event of a divorce, or if it is not waived, how much alimony will be paid and who will pay it. (See Chapter 4.)

Let's assume that the parties will include alimony in their separation agreement. As we examine the options for doing so, keep in mind that no individual clause in the agreement can be fully understood in isolation. The negotiation process involves a large variety of factors. A party may agree to a clause not so much because that clause gives the party what he or she wants, but rather because the party decided to concede that clause in order to gain another clause (e.g., a spouse may accept a lower alimony provision in exchange for the other spouse's agreement to give her or him sole physical and sole legal custody of their child). This is the nature of the bargaining process. Here are some of the main factors the parties must consider when negotiating alimony:

PERIODIC PAYMENTS OR LUMP SUM? In a few states, it is illegal for spouses to agree to fulfill the support obligation through *alimony in gross*, which is alimony in the form of a single lump-sum payment. In most states, however, alimony in gross is allowed. For example, instead of an alimony payment of $1,000 a month for ten years, the parties could agree that a single payment of $120,000 would satisfy the alimony obligation. Many variations of this arrangement are possible. For example, the $120,000 debt could be met by paying $50,000 when the divorce is granted and the remaining $70,000 in seven equal payments of $10,000 over the next seven months. From the perspective of the recipient, collectability is an important factor in deciding whether to seek a lump-sum alimony payment. A spouse may find it safer to take a lower lump-sum payment now rather than hassle with installment or periodic payments if there is any likelihood that the payor will fall behind in the payments. It can be expensive and psychologically draining to have to go after a delinquent payor.

FIXED OR FLUCTUATING PERIODIC PAYMENTS? If periodic payments are agreed to, the most common method is a fixed-dollar amount (e.g., $700 per month). A less common and more-difficult-to-enforce option is a fluctuating or flexible periodic payment. Under this method, the amount of the payment will fluctuate up or down depending upon the income of the ex-husband, ex-wife, or both. An alimony payment of 15 percent of the ex-husband's earnings (gross or net), for example, provides an automatic fluctuating standard. Another option is the gradual reduction of alimony payments over a designated period (e.g., alimony that decreases 10 percent every year). Gradually, decreasing alimony is known as "step-down support."

MEDICAL AND DENTAL INSURANCE As part of spousal support (alimony), do the parties want to include the payee's medical and dental insurance costs? We will cover medical care for children separately in Chapter 10 when we examine the qualified medical child support order (QMCSO).

LIFE INSURANCE Even though the duty of support usually ends at the death of the payor or of the payee, the parties might agree that the support payments will continue after the payor dies. If so, one way to do this is through a life insurance policy on the payor's life. The beneficiary would be the payee—the other spouse. If a life insurance policy already exists, the parties may decide to include a clause in the separation agreement that requires the payor to continue paying

---

premarital agreement
A contract by persons about to be married that can cover (a) financial and related matters once the marriage occurs and (b) spousal support, property division, and related matters in the event of separation, divorce, annulment, or death. Also called *prenuptial agreement*, *prenup*, and *antenuptial agreement*.

the premiums, to increase the amount of the policy, to name the payee as the **irrevocable** beneficiary (meaning that the payor cannot change the beneficiary), etc. The agreement could also specify whether an existing policy remains in force if either side remarries. If no life insurance policy exists, the parties need to decide whether to take one out. Unfortunately, if a payor violates a clause requiring him or her to take out a life insurance policy, a court might take the position that it is powerless to enforce the clause if the state has a law that alimony must end upon the death of the payor or payee.

irrevocable
Not capable of being altered, revoked, canceled, or recalled.

TERMINATION OF SUPPORT PAYMENTS The agreement should specify when alimony ends. After a designated number of months or years? After the payee becomes employed? After he or she remarries? Most payors want alimony to end if the payee remarries. Yet a clause to this effect might discourage the payee from remarrying. Hence, the payor might want to continue alimony after the payee's remarriage, but at a reduced amount and/or for a shorter period. (If the second marriage is later annulled, states differ on whether the original alimony obligation of the first husband is *revived*. See Chapter 6.)

In some states, cohabitation by the payee either terminates the alimony or is some evidence that alimony is no longer needed. Concerned about helping to support a live-in lover, some payors include a clause stating that alimony ends upon the payee's cohabitation with another adult. Cohabitation by the *payor* does not affect the payor's alimony obligation to the payee. (We will discuss cohabitation more fully when we cover modification of alimony.)

The termination of future alimony payments does not affect **arrears** (i.e., unpaid back payments). All delinquent payments must be paid.

arrears
Payments that are due but have not yet been made. Also called *arrearages*.

SECURITY When a payor fails to make a support payment, the payee can sue, but this is hardly a satisfactory remedy because of the delay and expense of litigation. The best way for a payee to avoid litigation is to be given *security* for the performance of the support obligation within the separation agreement itself. This security can be provided in a number of forms:

escrow
Property (e.g., money, a deed) delivered to a neutral person (e.g., bank, escrow agent) to be held until a specified condition occurs (e.g., nonpayment of a debt), at which time the property is to be delivered to a designated person.

- **Escrow.** The payor deposits a sum of money with an escrow agent (e.g., a bank), with instructions to pay the payee a designated amount of money in the event that the payor falls behind in a payment.

- **Surety bond.** The payor gives the payee a surety bond. The payor pays premiums to the surety company. The surety company guarantees that if the payor fails to fulfill the alimony obligation, the company will meet the obligation up to the amount of the bond.

surety bond
A bond given as insurance to guarantee that a contract will be completed within the agreed-upon time. An obligation by a guarantor to pay X if Y fails to perform a duty that Y owes to X. Also called *performance bond*.

Here are two additional forms of security that do not depend upon a breach by the payor of the alimony obligation. They are simply methods of transferring all of the support payments to the payee.

- **Annuity.** The payor purchases an annuity contract that provides a fixed income payable periodically to the payee (**annuitant**) in the amount of the alimony obligation.

- **Trust.** The payor transfers property (e.g., cash) to a **trustee** (e.g., a bank) with instructions to pay a fixed income to the payee (the beneficiary) in the amount of the alimony obligation. This is called an **alimony trust**.

annuity
A fixed sum payable periodically for life or for a specific period of time.

annuitant
Recipient of an annuity.

trust
A property arrangement by which its creator (the *settlor* or *trustor*) transfers property (the *corpus*) to a person (the *trustee*) who holds legal title for the benefit of another (the *beneficiary* or *cestui que trust*).

trustee
The person or company holding legal title to property for the benefit of another.

MODIFICATION OF ALIMONY

Generally, a court has no power to alter the terms of valid contracts. A separation agreement is a contract. Can its terms be modified? Clearly, the parties to any contract can mutually agree to modify its terms. But can the court *force* a modification on the parties when only one party wants it?

alimony trust
A trust to which a spouse or ex-spouse transfers funds that will be used to meet an alimony obligation.

The answer may depend on which terms of the separation agreement are in question. *Property-division* terms, as indicated earlier, are rarely modifiable (see Exhibit 8.5). *Child-custody* and *child-support* terms, however, are almost always modifiable according to the court's view of the best interests of the child (see Chapters 9 and 10 for special rules on modifying child-custody and child-support orders).

Can *alimony* (spousal support) terms be modified by a court? First, consider two extreme and relatively rare circumstances in which the court *can* modify alimony terms in most states:

- The separation agreement itself includes a provision allowing a court to modify its terms.

- The needy spouse becomes so destitute that he or she will become a public charge unless a modification is ordered.

If neither of these situations exists, can the court order a modification of the spousal-support terms of the separation agreement, particularly when the payor asserts a substantial change in his or her ability to pay? This raises two separate questions: Does the court have the power to modify? And if so, when will it exercise this power?

Power to Modify

First of all, a court cannot modify alimony if the court does not have **personal jurisdiction** over the ex-spouse payor who is being asked to pay more, or over the ex-spouse (payee) who is being asked to accept less than the original alimony award. In most states, if the court had personal jurisdiction over a party in the original proceeding that awarded the alimony, the court has **continuing jurisdiction** to revisit the award and modify it as needed.

A court does not need personal jurisdiction to dissolve a marriage (in rem jurisdiction is sufficient), but alimony orders (like child-support and property-division orders) require personal jurisdiction over the payor. (See Chapter 7 for a discussion of how a court obtains personal jurisdiction over a party.)

In a few states, a court has no power to modify a spousal-support term unless the parties have agreed in the separation agreement to allow the court to do so. Most states, however, will allow their courts to modify a separation agreement even if it has a *no-modification clause* that expressly states that neither side will request modification. A number of theories have been advanced to support this view. Some states hold that the separation agreement is merely advisory to the court, and that as a matter of public policy the court cannot allow the question of support to be determined solely by the parties. The state as a whole has an interest in seeing to it that this sensitive question is properly resolved. What the parties have agreed upon will be a factor in the court's determination, but it will not be the controlling factor.

Other states use the doctrine of merger. When a court accepts the terms of a separation agreement, the parties may ask the court to *incorporate* and *merge* the terms of the agreement into the divorce judgment. Incorporation occurs when the divorce judgment specifically refers to or mentions the alimony clauses in the separation agreement. Merger occurs when the separation agreement loses its separate identity once the divorce judgment is rendered. Upon **incorporation and merger**, the question is not whether the separation agreement can be modified, but whether the judgment can be modified. Courts are much less reluctant to modify their own judgments than they are to modify the private contracts of parties. Under the merger doctrine, the contract no longer exists.

personal jurisdiction
A court's power over a person to determine (adjudicate) his or her personal rights and duties. Also called *in personam jurisdiction.*

continuing jurisdiction
A court's power (by retaining jurisdiction) to modify its orders after entering a judgment.

incorporation and merger
The acceptance of the terms of one document (e.g., an agreement) and making the terms part of another document (e.g., a court decree) so that the former document ceases to exist as a separate entity.

Exercising the Power to Modify

Assuming the court has the power to modify alimony, when will the court use this power? As a general rule, a court will not consider a modification unless the following conditions are met:

- There has been a substantial change of circumstances of a continuing nature involving the payor's ability to pay and/or the payee's financial need.

- The ex-spouse is not using the change in circumstances as a pretext for avoiding the original alimony award.

Sometimes, a court may also consider whether the change in circumstances was foreseeable when the original alimony award was made. Suppose, for example, the parties knew that the payor was going to be out of work when his or her employer completed plans to relocate to Mexico. If such a change was foreseeable, a court might deny the modification on the ground that the parties factored in the change (or should have factored it in) when they negotiated the original clause on alimony.

Unfortunately, however, courts are not always consistent in how they resolve petitions for modification.

> Tom and Mary enter into a separation agreement that is incorporated and merged into a divorce judgment. Tom is required to pay $750 a month in alimony to Mary. A year later, Tom asks the court for a decrease, and/or Mary asks for an increase.

Consider the following variations on these facts on why the modification is being sought. Assume that the payor in these examples is the ex-husband and the payee is the ex-wife:

- *The ex-husband becomes sick and earns substantially less.* Most courts would modify the judgment to lessen the amount he must pay—at least during the period when his earning capacity is affected by the illness. If, however, the sickness was anticipated or foreseeable at the time the separation agreement was negotiated, a court may deny the modification on the ground that the parties factored the sickness into their calculations when they negotiated the agreement (or should have done so).

- *The ex-husband is bankrupt.* Bankruptcy does not eliminate (discharge) past-due *domestic-support obligations* (SDOs), such as alimony. If, however, the bankruptcy court grants the payor a bankruptcy, the payor may be able to go back to divorce court and request a modification downward of *future* support payments on the ground that he is genuinely unable to pay the original amount.

- *The ex-husband suddenly starts earning a great deal more.* The ex-wife usually will not be able to increase her alimony award simply because her ex-husband becomes more wealthy than he was at the time of the divorce judgment. The result might be different if she can show that the original alimony amount was inadequate due to his weaker earning capacity at that time.

- *The ex-wife violates the terms of the separation agreement relating to the visitation rights of the ex-husband/father.* Most courts will not modify alimony for the sole reason that the payee interferes with the visitation rights of the payor. There are a few courts, however, that disagree; they say that alimony payments and visitation rights *are* interdependent. If, for example, the ex-wife interferes with the father's visitation rights with the children, these courts might reduce her alimony, terminate her alimony, or cancel any unpaid past alimony obligations due her (*arrears*). For such a result, however, the interference must be substantial.

rebuttable presumption
An assumption or inference of fact that a party
will be allowed to try to disprove (rebut) but that
will be treated as true if it is not disproved.

- *The ex-wife cohabits.* In some states, cohabitation by the payee can lead to a termination or other modification of alimony, particularly if the cohabitation is ongoing and open. (The statute authorizing this result is sometimes called the "live-in-lover" statute.) Is this result due to a moral judgment of the court that the payee's conduct is immoral? If it is, the court is unlikely to say so explicitly. Instead, the court may say that the cohabitation creates a **rebuttable presumption** that the payee has a decreased need for alimony due to the new living arrangement. Of course, the main reason an ex-husband will petition the court for modification is his suspicion that his alimony payments are helping to support the new lover. Cohabitation means living together in an intimate (usually sexual) relationship in the manner of spouses. A single act of sexual intercourse is usually not enough to establish cohabitation. To cohabit, the parties must be acting in the way that spouses act such as by living together, having an ongoing sexual relationship, and sharing expenses.

- *The ex-husband cohabits.* Cohabitation by the payor does not affect the payor's alimony obligation to the payee.

- *The ex-husband wants to retire, change jobs, or go back to school.* When his income is reduced in this way, the courts will consider a downward modification of the alimony obligation if a number of conditions are met. First, the request for the reduction must be made in good faith (e.g., at an age when workers normally retire) and not be a mere strategy to avoid the original alimony award. A young, rich executive cannot "drop out" and become a poor farmer. Such an executive, however, may be able to take a lower-paying job if this is required for his health. Second, the reduction, if awarded, must not leave the payee in dire financial straits. The court will balance the genuineness of the request for a reduction against the impact that it would have on the payee.

- *The ex-wife wants to quit work.* Most courts will deny a request by a payee for increased alimony because the payee wants to quit a job.

- *The ex-wife remarries.* In most states, if the payee remarries, the alimony payments cease (the payor no longer owes them) *unless* the separation agreement or a court specifically provides that the payments continue after the payee's remarriage. Note, however, that if the ex-wife was allowed to receive lump-sum alimony (alimony in gross), her remarriage will not result in a court order to return any of the lump-sum amount.

- *The ex-husband remarries.* In most states, if the payor remarries, the alimony payments to the first spouse must continue *unless* the separation agreement or a court provides that the payments cease or are reduced. A court might be inclined to a reduction if it is clear that the payor cannot meet the burden of supporting two families, particularly when there are children from the second marriage.

- *The ex-wife dies.* Alimony ends upon the death of the payee.

- *The ex-husband dies.* Alimony ends upon the death of the payor *unless* the separation agreement or a court provides that the payments continue and must be paid by the payor's estate. If an ex-wife is concerned about the end of alimony because of the death of her ex-husband, she can try to negotiate a clause in the separation agreement that would make her the beneficiary of a life insurance policy on his life, or she can seek increased property division (payable in installments) in lieu of alimony.

- *The ex-wife undergoes a gender change.* In a Florida case, an ex-husband agreed in a separation agreement to pay his ex-wife $1,250 a month in alimony until she died or remarried. After the divorce judgment became final, the ex-wife physically changed her gender via surgeries (and her name from Julia to Julio). The payor then asked a court to cancel the alimony obligation because of this change. The court denied the request, reasoning that under Florida law, sex-change surgery cannot legally change a person's birth gender. Therefore, technically the alimony payments to the **transsexual** were not being made to a man.[15]

- *The ex-husband successfully challenges the basis of the alimony award.* In one divorce case involving a three-year marriage, the ex-wife was awarded $850 a month in alimony for life when she convinced the court that she was unable to work because of a car accident. When her ex-husband saw belly-dancing photos of her on an online blog, he went back to court and successfully argued that the alimony award should be canceled.[16]

transsexual
(1) A person who has undergone a sex-change operation. (2) A person who wants to be considered by society as having a gender of the opposite sex.

ASSIGNMENT 8.4

Find authority (e.g., a statute or a court opinion) in your state for the court's power to modify an alimony award. When will such a modification be made? (See also General Instructions for the State-Code Assignment and the Court-Opinion Assignment in Appendix A.)

ASSIGNMENT 8.5

Karen and Jim obtain a divorce decree that awards Karen $500 a month in alimony until she dies or remarries. A year after the divorce decree became final, Karen marries Paul. Jim stops the alimony payments. A year later, Karen's marriage to Paul is annulled. Karen now wants Jim to resume paying her $500 a month in alimony and to pay her $6,000 to cover the period when she was "married" to Paul ($500 x 12 months). What result? (See General Instructions for the Legal-Analysis Assignment in Appendix A.)

ENFORCING THE ALIMONY OBLIGATION

If the payor fails to fulfill his or her alimony obligation, the payee has a number of enforcement remedies that can be tried, such as the following:

- *Execution.* An **execution** is a command or writ to a court officer (e.g., sheriff) to seize and sell the property of the delinquent party in order to satisfy the judgment debt. Here, the judgment debt is the divorce judgment containing the order to pay alimony.

- *Garnishment.* **Garnishment** is a court proceeding by a creditor to force a third party in possession of the debtor's property to turn the property over to the creditor to satisfy a debt owed to the creditor. The alimony payee is a creditor of the payor who is a debtor owing the alimony debt. An example of the debtor's property that could be garnished is the salary of the debtor. The third party would be the debtor's employer who normally pays the salary to the debtor but instead turns it over to the creditor because of the garnishment.

- *Fine.* The court could impose a fine for failure to obey a court order (the order to pay alimony).

- *Civil contempt.* **Civil contempt** is the refusal of a party to comply with a court order (usually issued for the benefit of another), which can lead to punishment (including incarceration) until the party complies with the order. In general, civil contempt can be used to enforce an alimony obligation if the separation agreement containing the alimony clause has been incorporated and merged into the divorce judgment. (See the discussion earlier on incorporation and merger.) If the agreement has been incorporated and merged, then the failure to pay alimony is a violation of a court order for which civil contempt can result. If

execution
A command or writ to a court officer (e.g., sheriff) to seize and sell the property of the losing litigant (the judgment debtor) in order to satisfy the judgment debt to the winning litigant (the judgment creditor). Also called *general execution* and *writ of execution.* (See the glossary for an additional meaning.)

garnishment
A court proceeding by a creditor to force a third party in possession of the debtor's property (e.g., wages) to turn the property over to the creditor to satisfy the debt owed to the creditor.

civil contempt
The refusal of a party to comply with a court order (usually issued for the benefit of another), which can lead to punishment (including incarceration) until the party complies with the order.

incorporation and merger has not occurred, the alimony debt cannot be enforced by civil contempt. Sometimes, payors jailed for civil contempt protest that they are unable to pay and, therefore, the foundation for civil-contempt incarceration does not exist. You cannot use imprisonment to pressure someone to pay a debt that the debtor is unable to pay. In a Pennsylvania case, an ex-husband (a practicing attorney) was jailed for failing to produce $2.5 million that the court wanted to make available to pay the alimony award against him. After fourteen years, however, when investigators could not locate the money, the court was finally convinced that the money did not exist and released him.[17] Fourteen years is believed to be the longest time anyone has ever been jailed for civil contempt.

criminal contempt
The refusal of a party to comply with a court order, which can lead to punishment (including incarceration), because of the repeated or aggravated nature of the refusal.

- *Criminal contempt.* Civil contempt needs to be distinguished from **criminal contempt**. The purpose of criminal contempt is to punish a party for repeated violation of a court order; the purpose of civil contempt is to enforce compliance with a court order. If a payor flagrantly and repeatedly violates a court order to use available funds to pay alimony or to turn over available property pursuant to a property-division order, the payor can be held in criminal contempt.

IV-D agency
A state agency that helps custodial parents enforce child-support obligations.

Uniform Interstate Family Support Act (UIFSA)
A state law on establishing and enforcing alimony and child-support obligations against someone who does not live in the same state as the person to whom the alimony and child support is owed.

- *IV-D Agency.* In Chapter 10, we will learn how state child-support agencies, called **IV-D agencies**, can be used to collect child support. In most states, the IV-D agency can help in the collection of both spousal support and child support when the child lives with the custodial parent who is owed the alimony. When the delinquent spouse is in another state, the **Uniform Interstate Family Support Act (UIFSA)** allows the payee to use administrative and judicial tribunals to collect alimony. (We will discuss the UIFSA at length in Chapter 10 on child support.)

EFFECT OF BANKRUPTCY ON THE ALIMONY OBLIGATION

discharged
Extinguished; forgave a debt so that it is no longer owed.

nondischargeable
Not extinguished or forgiven by bankruptcy.

When debtors go into bankruptcy, some of their debts are **discharged** (they are forgiven) while others are **nondischargeable** (they survive and must be paid after bankruptcy). What is the effect of bankruptcy on divorce debts?

There are different categories of bankruptcy found in the chapters of the Bankruptcy Code. Our primary concerns are Chapter 7 bankruptcy and Chapter 13 bankruptcy. In a Chapter 7 bankruptcy, the debtor is asking the court to liquidate (discharge) debts; in a Chapter 13 bankruptcy, the debtor submits a plan on repaying his or her debts. Although some debts may be discharged in a Chapter 13 bankruptcy, the focus of Chapter 13 is on repayment.

Some debts, however, are nondischargeable under both Chapter 7 and Chapter 13:

- Domestic-support obligations (DSOs), such as alimony and child support, are nondischargeable under both Chapter 7 and under Chapter 13 bankruptcies.

- Property-division obligations are nondischargeable if the debtor obtains a bankruptcy under Chapter 7.

- Property-division obligations that are not DSOs are dischargeable if the debtor obtains a bankruptcy under Chapter 13 and certifies that he or she does not have any outstanding support obligations.

If a debtor/ex-spouse seeks to discharge a property-division debt by filing for bankruptcy under Chapter 13, the other ex-spouse can seek to challenge the discharge by arguing that the property division was, in fact, intended as support rather than as a division of marital assets and therefore is nondischargeable. (See the discussion above on the sometimes blurred distinction between alimony and property division.)

Although payors who have been granted bankruptcy may not be able to have their past alimony debts discharged by the bankruptcy court, as indicated earlier, they may be able to use the fact of bankruptcy as the basis of a request to the divorce court to modify the original alimony by reducing *future* payments because of a genuine inability to pay the original amount.

NECESSARIES AND SPOUSAL REFUSAL

Before leaving the topic of alimony, we need to cover two related topics that pertain to spousal support within an ongoing marriage: necessaries and spousal refusal.

NECESSARIES

The rule on **necessaries** is a seldom-used method for a spouse or child to obtain support by going to merchants, making purchases of necessaries, and charging them to the credit of the non-supporting spouse/parent. The latter must pay the bills whether or not he or she knows about them or authorizes them so long as:

necessaries
The basic items needed by family members to maintain a standard of living, particularly food, shelter, and clothing. Under the doctrine of necessaries, these items can be purchased and charged to the spouse or parent who has failed to provide them.

• They are in fact for necessaries, and

• The spouse/parent has not already provided them for the family.

Although the main necessaries are food, shelter, and clothing, other needs are also included as the court indicates in the following case:

The principle behind the suit for necessaries is that until the marriage relationship is severed, the husband is liable to his wife or his wife's creditors for her support and the support of his children. Although he cannot be charged with every expenditure that she may choose to make, the husband will be held responsible to the wife's creditors for all services and purchases found to have been necessary to support her in a style consistent with her habits and his means. The wife can maintain her action for necessaries even after the couple separates, as long as she did not cause the separation by her misconduct. Only termination of the marriage or a judicial or private financial settlement will relieve the husband of his liability for necessaries under most circumstances. Traditionally, the action for necessaries has included food, clothing, shelter, medical bills, and incidental living costs of various sorts. However, it has also been held to include necessary counsel fees that the wife may incur. Such fees have been allowed as "necessaries" for purposes ranging from the wife's defense against criminal charges to costs incurred in connection with the marital dispute itself.[18]

Some hospitals have used the rule on necessaries to provide expensive medical care for a wife or child and then sued the husband/father for the cost of the care. The hospital may be required to sue the patient first for the cost of the care and then, if still unpaid, to sue the other spouse on a necessaries theory.

Because merchants would have difficulty knowing whether a husband/father has already made provision for the necessaries of his family, few merchants are willing to extend credit without express authorization from the husband/father. Some states, however, have eliminated the requirement that there be evidence of a failure of the husband/father to provide necessaries before his credit can be charged.

Originally, the doctrine of necessaries applied against the husband only. At common law, a wife was not responsible for necessaries furnished to her child or husband. Today, states have either extended the doctrine so that it now applies equally to both spouses, or they have abolished the doctrine altogether.

SPOUSAL REFUSAL

As people grow older, the need for long-term care increases, particularly after strokes and debilitating ailments such as Alzheimer's disease. The cost of such care can be substantial. The poor can turn to Medicaid to pay most or all of this cost. To a large extent, others are on their own. Medicare covers hospitalization, doctor fees, and drug costs, but not the cost of nursing homes and similar long-term facilities. Private insurance can help, but its coverage is limited and expensive. Few purchase it.

One desperate strategy of some spouses is to declare that they will no longer support their spouses so that the ailing spouse can become poor and thereby qualify for Medicaid. The practice is called spousal refusal. Without the option of spousal refusal, say attorneys for the elderly, "American health care is like a ghoulish lottery. Those who need doctors' care for illnesses like cancer or heart disease are covered by Medicare, the insurance program for the elderly, while those who need more custodial care for Alzheimer's or stroke must pay for it themselves or dispose of their assets to qualify for Medicaid."[19]

The strategy has flaws. Eventually, the government can sue the healthy spouse for the Medicaid costs it covered. Yet some spouses still pursue the strategy: "Lawyers generally advise that even with the potential of being sued, spousal refusal makes sense because Medicaid pays less for nursing home care than private clients do."[20] Furthermore, the government is usually more amenable to lower negotiated settlements for the total amount owed than are nursing home providers.

Another desperate strategy is the so-called "Medicaid divorce." The parties end the marriage by divorce in the "hope" of sufficiently impoverishing the sick spouse so that the latter will qualify for Medicaid. The strategy assumes that the sick spouse will receive no alimony or assets in a property division. It is highly unlikely, however, that a court would permit a divorce on such terms if the other spouse has the means to pay for the sick spouse's healthcare expenses via alimony and property division.

spousal refusal
A person's formal declaration that he or she will no longer support his or her ailing spouse so that the latter will qualify for Medicaid or other means-based public benefits.

PROPERTY DIVISION

Next, we begin a more detailed look at property division, the distribution of community or marital property between spouses (or ex-spouses) after a legal separation or divorce. The five steps of property division are location, classification, valuation, tax-effecting, and distribution:

- Locating all of the property of the spouses,
- Classifying the property into what can and cannot be divided,
- Determining the worth (valuation) of the property,
- Tax-effecting the clauses to determine the tax implications of each clause, and
- Dividing the property according to the standard of division used in the state. In most states, the standard of division is equitable distribution.

(See Exhibit 8.7.)

EXHIBIT 8.7   The Process of Property Division

Locating all the property		Classifying property subject to division		Determining the value of the property		Tax-effecting each clause to determine its tax implications		Applying the governing principle in the state (usually equitable distribution) to divide the property

LOCATING PROPERTY TO DIVIDE AND FINANCIAL INFIDELITY

Before spouses can divide their property, they must know that the property exists. An early task of a family-law office is to help a client locate this property, which can be a difficult task. Studies have found that a large number of spouses are not truthful to each other about their finances—something that the media has called financial infidelity. "In a recent survey, one in three Americans (31%) admitted lying to their spouses about money, and another one-third of these adults said they'd been deceived." Although some of the deception involves minor purchases and petty cash, a significant number of spouses keep secret bank accounts and lie about their debt and earnings. According to the survey, "Financial infidelity may be the new normal."[21]

Elsewhere in the book, we discuss efforts to uncover assets that must be divided in a divorce and that may also be relevant to issues of alimony and child support. (See, for example, the extensive checklists in Chapter 3 and the interrogatories in Appendix C.) In this chapter, we cover the division of property that the parties have disclosed or that has been uncovered.

SEPARATION AGREEMENT

In their separation agreement, spouses are generally free to divide property as they wish. For example,

- A wife can give some or all of her separate property (defined below) to her husband.
- A husband can give some or all of his separate property to his wife.
- A wife can give some or all of her share of the marital property (defined below) to her husband.
- A husband can give some or all of his share of the marital property to his wife.
- Husband and wife can split all categories of property in any percentages they want.

A court must approve the division negotiated by the parties, and often it does so, subject to the guideline on unconscionability discussed earlier. If the parties entered into a valid *premarital agreement*, its terms may specify what property was brought into the marriage as separate property and how property acquired during the marriage should be divided in the event of a divorce (see Chapter 4).

When parties cannot agree on how to divide their property, the court will impose a division on them. Before we examine how a court will do so, we need to review some basic definitions and characteristics of different kinds of property. Paralegals are often asked to list and catalogue the property of spouses going through a divorce. The task requires an understanding of the major categories of property.

REAL AND PERSONAL PROPERTY; TANGIBLE AND INTANGIBLE PROPERTY

There are many ways to categorize property. We begin with the two broadest categories: real property and personal property:

- **Real property.** Land and anything attached or affixed to the land. Also called *real estate*. Examples of real property include: residence, vacation home, fences, trees, building used in a business, etc.
- **Personal property.** Anything tangible or intangible that can be owned other than land and things attached to land. Also called *chattels*. Examples of personal property include: cash, car, boat, stocks, bonds, furniture, jewelry, art objects, books, records, clothes, sports equipment, pets, business supplies (inventory), credits, accounts receivable, exclusive options to buy, insurance policies, etc.

real property
Land and anything attached or affixed to the land, such as buildings, fences, and trees. Also called *real estate*.

personal property
Anything tangible or intangible that can be owned other than land or things attached to land. Also called *chattel*.

account receivable
A business debt to a creditor that has not yet been collected.

tangible
Having a physical form; able to make contact through touch or other senses. Also called *corporeal*.

corporeal
Having a physical form.

intangible
Not having a physical form, though evidence of its existence may have a physical form. Also called *incorporeal*.

gift
The voluntary delivery of property with the present intent to transfer title and control, for which no payment or consideration is made. The person making the gift is the *donor*. The person receiving it is the *donee*.

bequest
A gift of personal property in a will. (In some states, a bequest can be a gift of personal property or real property in a will.)

devise
A gift of real property in a will. The person making the gift of property is the *devisor*. The person receiving it is the *devisee*. (In some states, a devise can be a gift of real property or personal property in a will.)

Personal property can be further broken down into two subcategories:

- **Tangible.** Having a physical form; you can make contact with it by touch or by the other senses. Examples: cash, car. Tangible property is also called *corporeal personal property*.
- **Intangible.** Not having a physical form though evidence of intangible property may consist of something physical such as a written contract. Examples: copyright, goodwill of a business, shares of stock. Intangible property consists primarily of a right to something. The right itself does not have a physical form. Also called *incorporeal* personal property.

Of course, all real property is tangible property.

GIFTS, BEQUESTS, DEVISES, AND INTESTATE SUCCESSION

Real and personal property can be acquired in a variety of ways:

- Property that was a **gift** to one spouse.
- Property that was a gift to both spouses.
- Property that was a **bequest** to one spouse.
- Property that was a bequest to both spouses.
- Property that was a **devise** to one spouse.
- Property that was a devise to both spouses.
- Property that one of the spouses receives by *intestate succession* (see the definition in Exhibit 8.2) from a person who died without a will.
- Property that both spouses receive by intestate succession.
- Property purchased with funds from the salary or investments of one spouse.
- Property purchased with funds from the salaries or investments of both spouses.

TIME OF ACQUISITION

There are different time periods in which property could be acquired:

- Before the marriage (either party brought the property into the marriage).
- During the marriage (either or both parties acquired it while married and still living together).
- After the DOS (date of separation) when the parties separated and at least one of them felt that the marital relationship was over.
- Before the DOF (date of filing) when the divorce petition was filed in court
- Before the DOJ (date of judgment) when the divorce judgment became final.

As we will see, when interviewing a client or conducting an investigation about assets, it can be important in many states to place each acquisition within these different time periods.

SOLE OWNERSHIP AND CONCURRENT OWNERSHIP

There are different ways in which parties can hold title to property. Titleholders should be identified (as well as the reason why title is held in a certain way), even though title is rarely controlling on the question of who receives property upon divorce. Here are the major title options:

1. *Sole ownership: title is in the name of one spouse only.* The title to the property can be in the name of only one of the parties. There could be a number of reasons why this is so:
   - The sole owner may be the person who brought the property into the marriage.

- The sole owner may have received the property during the marriage as a gift or as an inheritance (by intestate succession).
- The sole owner may have purchased the property during the marriage with his or her separate funds (see discussion of separate property below).
- One spouse may have purchased the property with his or her own separate funds but placed the title to the property in the sole name of the other spouse (perhaps in an attempt to insulate the property from the claims of the creditors of the spouse who purchased the property).
- The property may have been purchased with the funds of both spouses but they decided to place title in the name of only one of them.

2. *Concurrent ownership: title is in the names of more than one person.* A concurrent ownership occurs when property is owned by two or more persons at the same time. There are three kinds of concurrent ownership: joint tenancy, tenancy by the entirety, and tenancy in common. (The word *tenancy* here does not pertain to landlord-tenant law.)

concurrent
Acting, occurring, or operating at the same time. (See the glossary for an additional meaning.)

- *Joint tenancy.* In a **joint tenancy**, each joint tenant (there can be more than two) owns an equal share and has an equal right to possess the entire property. A single joint tenant does not own a piece of the property; each joint tenant owns it all. When one joint tenant dies, his or her interest passes to the surviving joint tenants by **right of survivorship**. The property automatically (i.e., by **operation of law**) goes to the surviving joint tenants. A joint tenancy is sometimes referred to as a joint tenancy with a right of survivorship—JTWROS.

joint tenancy
Ownership of property by two or more persons (called *joint tenants*) who have equal shares, equal rights to possess the whole property, and a right of survivorship. Also called *joint tenancy with right of survivorship (JTWROS)*.

- If a joint tenant dies with a valid will, can the will give the deceased's interest to someone other than a surviving joint tenant? No. The interest passes to the surviving joint tenants by operation of law.

right of survivorship
When one owner dies, his or her share automatically goes to the other owners; it does not go through the estate of the deceased owner.

- If a joint tenant dies without a valid will, can someone other than a surviving joint tenant receive the deceased's interest by intestate succession? No. The interest passes to the surviving joint tenants by operation of law.

Only surviving joint tenants can receive the interest of a deceased joint tenant.

operation of law
The means by which legal consequences are imposed by law, regardless of (or even despite) the intent of the parties involved.

- *Tenancy by the entirety.* A **tenancy by the entirety** is a joint tenancy held by a married couple. The characteristics described above for a joint tenancy apply to a tenancy by the entirety (e.g., both spouses own all of the property and upon the death of one spouse, the property goes to the other spouse by operation of law). In general, if the parties divorce, the tenancy by the entirety ends and, unless the separation agreement or the divorce judgment provides otherwise, the property becomes a tenancy in common (see below) with each spouse receiving an equal share of the property.

tenancy by the entirety
A joint tenancy held by a married couple.

- *Tenancy in common.* A **tenancy in common (TIC)** is ownership of property by two or more persons in shares that may or may not be equal, each person having an equal right to possess the whole property but without the right of survivorship. When one tenant in common dies, the property goes to whomever the deceased designates by will or it goes by intestate succession if the deceased tenant in common dies without a will. Hence, a major distinction between (1) a joint tenancy and a tenancy by the entirety and (2) a tenancy in common is that the property of a deceased tenant passes through the estate of that tenant (via will or intestacy) only in the case of a tenancy in common. In the other tenancies, the property passes immediately to the surviving tenants by operation of law.

tenancy in common (TIC)
Ownership of property by two or more persons (called *tenants in common*) in shares that may or may not be equal, each person having an equal right to possess the whole property but without a right of survivorship. Also called *estate in common*.

SEPARATE PROPERTY

Separate property is property that (1) is acquired by one spouse before marriage and brought into the marriage; (2) is acquired by one spouse by gift, will, or inheritance during the marriage; or (3) is any other property that is not marital or

separate property
Property that is (1) acquired by one spouse before marriage and brought into the marriage, or (2) is acquired by one spouse by gift, will, or inheritance during the marriage, or (3) is any other property that is not marital or community property.

community property. The parties can agree to divide separate property upon divorce, but they often do not do so. In most states, a court cannot force the parties to divide separate property, although there are some exceptions, as we will see.

There are at least ten types of separate property:

Categories of Separate Property

- *Property that one spouse acquired before the marriage.* This is property that one spouse brought into the marriage. Example: Ted had a bank account containing $5,000 when he married Fran. The $5,000 (which is still in Ted's same bank account) is the separate property of Ted.

- *Property one spouse acquired during the marriage by gift.* Example: A year after Sam married Mary, Sam's dad gives Sam a birthday gift of a gold watch. The watch is the separate property of Sam.

- *Property one spouse acquired during the marriage by will.* Example: A year after Rachel married Bill, Rachel's mother died; her will left a vacation home to Rachel. The vacation home is the separate property of Rachel.

- *Property one spouse acquired during the marriage by intestate succession.* Example: A year after Paul married George, Paul's aunt died. Paul is the only surviving relative of his aunt. The aunt did not leave a will. When she died, her only asset was 1,000 shares of IBM stock. Under the intestate law of the state, the IBM shares go to Paul as her closest relative. They are his separate property.

- *Property that one spouse acquired during the marriage in exchange for other separate property.* Example: Before Myles married Alice, he owned a diamond watch. A week after the marriage, he sold the watch and used the money to buy a boat. The watch was the separate property of Myles. Because he used money from the sale of separate property (the watch) to buy a boat, the boat is also his separate property.

passive income
Income that is earned from money or other property without direct involvement or active efforts by the earner.

- *Passive income earned from separate property during the marriage.* **Passive income** is income that is earned from money or other property without direct involvement or active efforts by the earner. Example: John has a bank account that contains $12,000 that he brought into his marriage with Diane. During the marriage, the account has earned $500 in interest. The original bank account is John's separate property. The $500 interest is also separate property because it is passive income earned from separate property. John did nothing active to earn the $500.

appreciation
An increase in the value of property after it is acquired.

passive appreciation
An increase in the value of property that is due to inflation or market forces rather than to the active efforts of the owner.

active appreciation
An increase in the value of property that is due to the active efforts of the owner rather than to inflation or market forces.

- *Passive appreciation of separate property during the marriage.* **Appreciation** is an increase in the value of property after it is acquired. **Passive appreciation** is an increase in the value of property that is due to inflation or market forces rather than to the active efforts of the owner. (**Active appreciation** would be an increase in value due to active efforts of the owner.) Example of passive appreciation: Georgia inherits a vacation home from her father during her marriage to Todd. The property is located in another county. Because Georgia and Todd never intend to use the home, she sells it five months after receiving it. When her father died, the value of the house was $100,000. She sold it for $110,000. The vacation home is Georgia's separate property. Its appreciation of $10,000 is also her separate property if the appreciation was due solely to the state of the real estate market rather than to anyone's active efforts such as making repairs or remodeling.

marital property
Any property acquired by either spouse during the marriage that is not separate property.

- *Marital property that both spouses have agreed to designate as the separate property of one of the spouses.* Example: After Pat and Fran married, they bought a house together. The house is **marital property**, which is any property acquired by either or both spouses during the marriage that is not separate property. In their separation agreement, they agree that the house will be the separate property of Fran. By mutual agreement, marital property has been transformed—transmuted—into separate property. (See *transmutation* below.)

- *The portion of an asset purchased with separate property if the asset was purchased with both separate property and marital property.* Example: During the marriage of Karen and Zeno, they decide to buy a vacation condo for $50,000. To raise the money for the purchase, Karen uses $10,000 from an inheritance she received from her mother. They also use $40,000 in a joint account containing their salary deposits during the marriage. One-fifth of the vacation home ($10,000) is Karen's separate property. Four-fifths ($40,000) is marital property. (This breakdown is sometimes due to the "source-of-funds" rule.)

- *Property acquired by either spouse after the date of separation (DOS) when at least one of the spouses considered the separation to be permanent.* Example: Ursula and Alex separate on April 1, 2018 and have no intention of resuming their relationship. The final divorce judgment is December 1, 2018. The salary that each spouse earned after April 1, 2018, is his or her separate property. (Note, however, that some states disagree and say that the cutoff date is not the DOS. Rather, they use the date of filing (DOF) for divorce or the date of the final judgment (DOJ). Anything acquired before these dates is still marital property. What is acquired after them is separate property.)

ASSIGNMENT 8.6

Before Mary married Charles, she owned 100 shares of stock valued at $20 a share. During the marriage, the company in which the shares were owned executed a stock split. (In a stock split, each individual share is split into a larger number of shares without changing the total number of shareholders.) Her 100 shares turned into 200 shares valued at $30 a share. Was the 100 shares @ $20 a share separate or marital property? What about the 200 shares @ $30 a share? (See the General Instructions for the Legal-Analysis Assignment in Appendix A.)

INTRODUCTION TO COMMON LAW PROPERTY AND COMMUNITY PROPERTY

States fall into two categories: common-law property states or community-property states. Although there are some differences between the two categories, there are substantial similarities in how they divide property when the divorcing parties are unable to agree on the division.

The community-property states are Arizona, California, Idaho, Louisiana, Nevada, New Mexico, Texas, and Washington (as well as Wisconsin, whose unique law is similar to these eight states). Every other state is a common-law property state.

- **Community property.** Property in which each spouse has a 50 percent interest because it was acquired during the marriage other than by gift, will, or intestate succession (inheritance) to only one of the spouses.

- **Common-law property.** Property acquired during the marriage in a state other than a community-property state. (Older definition: Property acquired during the marriage that is the separate property of the spouse who earned it or who has title to it.)

The law of community property is based on Spanish legal principles. Each spouse has a one-half interest in property acquired during the marriage. This half interest does not depend on who had title to the property or on whose income was used to purchase it. So long as the property was acquired during the marriage, it is community property and therefore subject to a one-half interest in each spouse. The exception is property that one spouse alone acquired by gift, will,

community property
Property in which each spouse has a 50 percent interest if the property was acquired during the marriage other than by gift, will, or intestate succession (inheritance) to only one of the spouses.

common-law property
Property acquired during the marriage in a state other than a community-property state. (Older definition: Property acquired during the marriage that is the separate property of the spouse who earned it or who has title to it.)

or intestate succession (inheritance) during the marriage; such property is solely owned by the spouse receiving it.

The underlying principle of community property is that the efforts of both spouses contributed to the acquisition of property during the marriage. One spouse, for example, could not have gone to the office each day to work if the other spouse had not stayed home to take care of the household, which could include child rearing, home economics, and social outreach.

When property is acquired during the marriage in a community-property state, there is a presumption that it is community property. This presumption can be rebutted by showing that it was acquired by one spouse alone through gift, will, or intestate succession (inheritance), or that the parties had agreed to treat community property as separate property (see *transmutation* below).

If the spouses acquire personal property (e.g., a car) in a common-law property state and then move to a community-property state, the property would be classified as **quasi-community property** and treated as community property if that property would have been community property if it had been acquired in a community-property state. Quasi-community property is personal property acquired during marriage by the spouses when they lived in a noncommunity-property state before moving to a community-property state and which would have been community property if they had acquired it in a community-property state.

At one time, there were major differences between community property and common law property in three areas:

- The management of the property during the marriage.
- The disposition of the property upon death while the parties were still married.
- The disposition of the property upon divorce.

Many of these differences still exist in the first two areas (management and death). Our main concern in this chapter is the third area (divorce), where the differences have all but disappeared in most states, as we will see.

Terminology

The meaning of *separate property* is clear in common-law states and in community property states. It is property that is (1) acquired by one spouse before marriage and brought into the marriage: (2) is acquired by one spouse by gift, will, or inheritance during the marriage; or (3) is any other property that is not marital or community property. Although the phrase *marital property* can refer to nonseparate property in both states, for purposes of discussion:

- We will use the phrase *marital property* to refer to nonseparate property in common-law property states.
- We will use the phrase *community property* to refer to nonseparate property in community-property states.
- We will use the phrase *marital/community property* when referring to nonseparate property in both states.

Finally, the phrase *marital estate* is sometimes used by courts to mean marital/community property. The court in the *Woodworth* case does so. (We will study *Woodworth v. Woodworth* later in this chapter.)

CUTOFF DATE

If a party acquires property after divorce, the property, of course, is not divided with the party's ex-spouse. What about property acquired before divorce, but after the parties separate or after the divorce action is filed?

quasi-community property
Personal property acquired during the marriage by the spouses when they lived in a non-community-property state before moving to a community-property state. If they had acquired it in a community-property state, it would have been community property.

Assume that Irene and Jack have decided to end their marriage. Consider the following pre-divorce dates:

- January 1, 2018: date of separation (DOS); Irene and Jack separate. The DOS is the date the parties separated at which time at least one of them felt that the marital relationship was over.

- February 20, 2018: date of filing (DOF); Irene files her divorce (dissolution) petition against Jack.

- March 20, 2018: date of judgment (DOJ). The divorce judgment of Irene and Jack becomes final.

Now assume that Irene wins $25,000 in the state's lottery on February 21, 2018. Is the $25,000 the separate property of Irene or is it marital/community property that she must divide with Jack? The answer depends on which cut-off date the state uses to determine separate property.

If the state uses the DOS:

- Property acquired prior to the DOS is marital/community property.
- Property acquired after the DOS is separate property.

If the state uses the DOF:

- Property acquired prior to the DOF is marital/community property.
- Property acquired after the DOF is separate property.

If the state uses the DOJ:

- Property acquired prior to the DOJ is marital/community property.
- Property acquired after the DOJ is separate property.

If Irene and Jack live in a DOS or a DOF state, the $25,000 won on February 21, 2018 is Irene's separate property. It was acquired after the DOS and after the DOF. If they live in a DOJ state, it is marital/community property because it was acquired before the DOJ.

TRANSMUTATION

The categorizations of property within common-law states and within community-property states are not static. The parties can voluntarily agree to reclassify their property. The change is called **transmutation**:

- In a common-law property state, the parties can agree that specific separate property of one spouse will become marital property.

- In a community-property state, the parties can agree that specific separate property of one spouse will become community property.

- In a common-law property state, the parties can agree that specific marital property will become the separate property of one of the spouses.

- In a community-law property state, the parties can agree that specific community property will become the separate property of one of the spouses.

The agreement is called a *transmutation agreement*. It is not always easy, however, to determine whether transmutation has occurred.

> *Jim and Diane own a vacation home as marital/community property. Both of their names are on the deed. They decide to change the deed so that only Diane has title. To accomplish this, Jim (the transferor)* **quitclaims** *the deed to Diane (the transferee) for $1. When the parties divorce five years later, the*

transmutation
The voluntary change of separate property into marital property or vice versa (in a common-law state); the voluntary change of separate property into community property or vice versa (in a community-property state).

quitclaim
A release or giving up of whatever claim or title you had in property. The party who quitclaims the property, turns over (transfers) whatever he or she has, without guaranteeing anything.

parties dispute whether the vacation home is marital/community property or is separate property.

States disagree on how they handle title-transfer cases such as this when the parties do not specifically indicate whether they intend a transmutation. In some states, transferring the title of marital/community property automatically transmutes it into the separate property of the spouse receiving title. In other states, the transfer of title is merely a *rebuttable presumption* that the parties intended transmutation. The party who transferred title (the transferor) can try to prove that the transfer was for reasons other than transmutation. For example, the spouses may have been trying to insulate the property from the transferor's creditors. This evidence may convince a court that the mere change in title did not create separate property out of marital/community property.

Some transmutation disputes can be bitter. For example, when Frank and Jamie McCourt bought the Los Angeles Dodgers, they were living in Massachusetts, a common-law property state. California is a community-property state. Would the Dodgers become community property when they moved to California? The parties signed six copies of a postnuptial agreement that attempted to clarify the transmutation intentions of the parties. The agreement declared the Dodgers to be the separate property of Frank and several homes around the world to be the separate property of Jamie. Unfortunately, several of the copies they signed contained a list stating that Frank's separate property did *not* include the Dodgers. Frank claimed that the list was an error that was later corrected on some of the copies. Jamie claimed that the corrections were made after the agreement was signed and notarized. She further asserted that she did not fully understand the agreement. Expensive litigation ensued on whether the Dodgers were community property. Ultimately, the parties sold the Dodgers and Frank agreed to give Jamie $135 million to settle the transmutation issue.

PROPERTY DIVISION IN COMMON-LAW STATES AND COMMUNITY-PROPERTY LAW STATES

We turn now to the question of how property is divided upon divorce in common-law states and in community-property states. Not all common-law property states have the same law of property division. The same is true of community-property states. Yet several major characteristics apply to both groupings of states. To understand the current law, we need to place it in the context of the *prior* law.

Property Division: Prior Law

At one time, the main definition of common-law property was property acquired during the marriage that is owned by the spouse who earned it or who has title to it. Under this definition, the spouse who owned particular property received it upon divorce in the property division. Ownership was determined by the name of the person on the title of the property or by the spouse who earned the money that was used to purchase it. Salaries, therefore, belonged to the spouse who earned it. These rules placed many stay-at-home spouses, usually the wife, at a disadvantage when it came time to divide property at divorce because the husband often controlled much of the family and business finances in his name alone. This inequity did not exist in community-property states where, in general, community property was divided equally upon divorce.

Property Division: Current Law

Now let's look at the current law of property division. As pointed out by the American Law Institute, the law has substantially changed in both common-law and community-property states:

> [The] sharp dichotomy between common law and community property traditions no longer prevails in the United States. All the common-law states now allow the divorce court to distribute the spouse's property between them on a basis other than common-law principles of ownership, under a doctrine known generally as "equitable distribution." Five of the eight community property states also instruct their divorce courts to divide the community property between the spouses "equitably" (rather than "equally"). Equitable distribution is therefore the dominant rule today, followed everywhere but in the three "equal division" community property states [of California, Louisiana, and New Mexico].[22]

Hence, in the majority of both common-law and community-property states, property division upon divorce is determined by **equitable distribution**, which is the just and fair, but not necessarily equal, division of property between spouses upon divorce. Although this is the general principle, not all equitable-distribution states define or apply equitable distribution in the same way.

Kitchen-Sink States

Under the general principle of equitable distribution, what property is divided? In most states, only marital/community property is divided. In a few states, however, a court has discretion to reach a party's separate property where it determines that the division of the marital/community property alone would not be equitable or fair. States that allow a court to divide all property are sometimes called *all-property states* or *kitchen-sink states*.

EQUITABLE DISTRIBUTION FACTORS

Equitable distribution requires a "just and fair" division. To accomplish this, many factors are considered. Before examining these factors, it should be pointed out that many courts take the position that the division should be roughly proportionate to the contribution that each spouse made to the acquisition of the property. In the *Gastineau* case we will be reading in this chapter, the New York court said:

> It is a guiding principle of equitable distribution that parties are entitled to receive equitable awards which are proportionate to their contributions, whether direct or indirect, to the marriage.

In some courts, however, there is a presumption that their contribution was equal and that therefore the division should be equal or approximately so.

Factors Considered in Equitable Distribution

- The length of the marriage.
- The contribution of each party in the acquisition, preservation, depreciation or appreciation of all assets, including the contribution of a stay-at-home party.
- The contribution by one party to the education, training, or increased earning power of the other party.
- Any interruption in the educational opportunities or personal career of either party, particularly the one who stayed home to take care of the children.
- The income and property of both at the time the marriage was entered.
- The sources of income of both parties, including, but not limited to, retirement, insurance, or other benefits.

equitable distribution
The just and fair, but not necessarily equal, division of property between spouses upon divorce.

- Whether either party has been granted alimony or maintenance.
- The opportunity of each party for future acquisitions of capital assets and income, including the vocational skills and employability of each party.
- Whether either party will be serving as the custodian of dependent minor children.
- The need of the party with physical custody of the children to use the marital home.
- The desirability of keeping any asset (e.g., a business) intact.
- The expense that would be involved in the sale, transfer, or liquidation of a particular asset.
- Intentional *dissipation* of marital assets (see the discussion of dissipation below).
- The federal, state, and local tax ramifications associated with each asset to be divided regardless of whether the ramifications are immediate or certain (see the discussion of *tax-effecting* under the section on "Taxes" below).
- The standard of living of the parties established during the marriage.
- The age and health of both parties.
- Any other factor that should be considered in order to achieve justice and fairness in the division.

Not all states use all of the above factors. Furthermore, a divorce judge has considerable discretion in applying the factors because states rarely mandate the weight or priority that judges must give them.

As indicated in the factors, contribution encompasses the full range of homemaking services that made the earnings possible and the financial opportunities that the stay-at-home spouse gave up so that the other spouse could devote greater attention to training, investment, and earning. Furthermore, at a time when the law disfavors long-term alimony, many courts are inclined to use property division as the main vehicle for achieving economic justice for a spouse who is about to leave a long-term marriage with no (or minimal) independent resources or marketable workforce skills.

MODIFICATION OF PROPERTY DIVISION

Earlier, we saw that *alimony* awards can be modified under certain circumstances. The situation is different with property division. Courts will rarely, if ever, modify the property-division clause of a separation agreement that a divorce court has approved. (See, however, the discussion below on the effect of mutual mistake.)

Death or remarriage of either ex-spouse does not affect property-division obligations. They continue no matter who dies or remarries. For example, as part of a property division (having nothing to do with support), John agrees to pay Mary $50,000. After John has paid Mary $1,000 of this amount, he dies. Mary can make a claim against John's estate for $49,000. If Mary dies after John has paid the $1,000, her estate can require John to pay the remaining $49,000 to the estate for distribution according to Mary's will or according to the laws of intestate succession if she died without leaving a valid will. The same is true if either party remarries. Whatever is still owed under the property-division clauses of a separation agreement remain due and owing no matter who remarries.

MARITAL FAULT AND ECONOMIC FAULT

Marital Fault

In most states, marital fault—who caused the marriage to break-up—is not a factor in the property division. Under the Uniform Marriage and Divorce Act (UMDA), property is to be divided "without regard to marital misconduct" in causing the break-up of the marriage. (The same is true in the award or alimony or maintenance as we saw earlier.) There are a few states, however, that take a different view. These states are inclined to increase the share of the marital property given to the "innocent" spouse.

Economic Fault: Dissipation

Marital fault is different from economic fault. Marital fault is the blameworthiness of a party in causing the demise of the marriage. Although most states do not consider marital fault in decisions on property division, they do consider economic fault as a factor. Economic fault is **dissipation**, which is the improper reduction or waste of marital/community assets that should have been available for property division upon divorce. For dissipation to exist, the marriage must be on the verge of a split or in serious relationship trouble at the time when a spouse improperly reduces or wastes a marital/community asset. To punish a spouse who has committed dissipation, a court might treat the dissipated funds as if they still existed when ordering the property division. This was the approach of the court in the *Gastineau* decision.

The most extreme example of dissipation is property destruction. In a highly contentious New York divorce, a spouse blew up a multi-million-dollar building to prevent his ex-wife from recovering her full share of its value in their property division. Reflecting on years of contentious cases, a veteran family-law attorney commented, "I've seen hundreds of thousands of dollars in property destroyed. People would rather break something than let the other party have it." In one of his cases in what he calls "soap-opera law," a spouse smashed an expensive collection of Dresden pottery.[23] Another attorney commented that "he has seen works of art and record collections slashed by angry spouses, a puppy put in the microwave and a cat in a washing machine. (The puppy died; the cat lived.)"[24]

Excessive spending can also constitute dissipation. In a recent case, a wife "spent a fortune on jewelry and clothes before filing for divorce—only to have the judge notice the timing of her spree and dock her property settlement."[25]

Finally, spouses cannot avoid support or property-division obligations by voluntarily becoming poor or drastically reducing their income. This was the major concern before the court in the *Gastineau* decision.

dissipation
The improper reduction or waste of marital/community assets that should have been available for property division or for support upon divorce.

CASE

Gastineau v. Gastineau
151 Misc. 2d 813, 573 N.Y.S.2d 819 (1991)
New York Supreme Court, Suffolk County

Background: *Marcus Gastineau was a professional football player for the New York Jets. His wife, Lisa, sued him for divorce and charged that he dissipated some of the marital assets. While the trial was in progress (i.e., pendente lite), the court ordered Marcus to make payments to Lisa to cover expenses. He fell $71,707 behind in these payments. The court then ordered the sequestration of his net severance pay of $83,000. (Sequestration is the removal or holding of assets until legal proceedings or legal claims are resolved.)*

Decision: *Marcus dissipated marital assets. In the equitable distribution of the marital assets, a court can treat dissipated assets as if they still exist. Marcus dissipated $484,437 in salary when he stopped playing football before his contract ended. When tax effected (i.e., when factoring in tax consequences of what he*

would have paid in taxes on this salary), the dissipated amount was $324,573.

OPINION OF THE COURT:

Justice LEIS delivered the opinion of the court.

This action for divorce, equitable distribution and other ancillary relief was tried on February 25, 28, March 5, and 6, 1991. The Plaintiff, Lisa Gastineau, is represented by counsel. The Defendant, Marcus Gastineau appeared pro se. . . . The parties were married in December of 1979. This action was commenced in September 1986. Consequently, this is a marriage of short duration. The Plaintiff is thirty-one years old and the Defendant is thirty-four. The parties have one child, Brittany, born on 11/6/82.

(continued)

Facts

The parties married just after Marc Gastineau had been drafted by the New York Jets to play professional football. The Plaintiff, at that time, was a sophomore at the University of Alabama. The Plaintiff never completed her college education, nor did she work during the course of the marriage.

In 1982, when Brittany was born, the parties purchased a house in Huntington, New York for $99,000. In addition to the purchase price, the Plaintiff and Defendant spent another $250,000 for landscaping and other renovations. This money came from the Defendant's earnings as a professional football player.

According to the uncontroverted testimony of the Plaintiff, in 1979 (the Defendant's first year in professional football) the Defendant earned a salary of $55,000. In his second year, 1980, the Defendant's salary was approximately $75,000. In 1981 it was approximately $95,000 and in 1982 he earned approximately $250,000. The Defendant's tax returns (which were not available for the years 1979 through 1982) indicate that the Defendant earned $423,291 in 1983, $488,994 in 1984, $858,035 in 1985, $595,127 in 1986, $953,531 in 1987 and in 1988, his last year with the New York Jets, his contract salary was $775,000 plus $50,000 in bonuses. It must be noted that in most years the Defendant earned monies in excess of his contract salary as a result of promotions, advertisements and bonuses.

In 1985 the parties purchased a home in Scottsdale, Arizona, for $550,000. During the course of the parties' marriage Plaintiff and Defendant acquired many luxury items including a power boat, a BMW, a Corvette, a Rolls Royce, a Porsche, a Mercedes and two motorcycles. They continually had a housekeeper who not only cleaned the house but prepared the parties' meals. In addition, the parties frequently dined out at expensive restaurants. The Plaintiff testified that as a result of this lifestyle she has become accustomed to buying only the most expensive clothes and going to the best of restaurants.

In 1988 the Defendant began an illicit relationship with Brigitte Nielsen. When Ms. Nielsen was diagnosed as having cancer the Defendant testified that he could no longer concentrate on playing football. At that time the Defendant was under contract with the New York Jets at a salary of $775,000. He left professional football in October 1988 (breaking his contract) after the sixth game of the 1988 season. The Defendant went to Arizona and remained with Ms. Nielsen while she underwent treatment for cancer.

Regardless of whether the Defendant wanted to be with his girlfriend while she underwent treatment for cancer, he had a responsibility to support his wife and child. The Court cannot condone Mr. Gastineau's walking away from a lucrative football contract when the result is that his wife and child are deprived of adequate support.

According to the testimony adduced at trial, there are sixteen games per season in the NFL. Players are paid one-sixteenth of their contract salary at the end of each game. Based on the

Defendant's salary for 1988 ($775,000), he received $48,437 per game. The Defendant played six games in the 1988 season and received approximately $290,622 plus $50,000 in bonuses. He was entitled to an additional $484,437 for the ten games remaining in the season. This Court finds that by walking away from his 1988–89 contract with the NFL the Defendant dissipated a marital asset in the amount of $484,437 [The Domestic Relations Law] § 236(B)(5)(d)(11) provides as follows: "In determining an equitable disposition of property..., the court shall consider: .... (11) the wasteful dissipation of assets by either spouse. . . ."]

Whether or not the Defendant would have been offered a contract by the New York Jets for the 1989/90 football season if he had not broken his 1988/89 contract is pure speculation. In professional football there are no guarantees. Variables such as age, how an athlete plays, the ability of other players seeking to fill his position, as well as possible injuries sustained during the season, make it impossible to determine with certainty whether or not the Defendant would have been re-signed by the New York Jets had he finished the 1988/89 season. It must also be noted that there has been no testimony offered by the Plaintiff to establish that the Defendant would have been re-signed by the New York Jets for the 1989/90 season had he not broken his contract.

The speculative nature of the Defendant's future in professional football is highlighted by the fact that in 1989 he tried out for the San Diego Chargers, the LA Raiders and the Minnesota Vikings, without success. The New York Jets also refused to offer him a contract. In 1990 the Defendant did acquire a position with the British Colombia Lions in the Canadian Football League at a salary of $75,000. He was cut, however, less than half way through the season. The Defendant played five of the 18 scheduled games and was paid approximately $20,000. The Defendant's performance in the Canadian Football League lends credence to his claim that he no longer has the capacity to earn the monies that he once made as a professional football player. Under these circumstances the court is limited to considering the dissipation of a marital asset valued at $484,437, to wit: the remaining amount of money that the Defendant was eligible to collect pursuant to his 1988/89 contract.

While Defendant admits that he has name recognition, he claims that his name has a negative rather than a positive connotation. The Defendant testified that because of his antics on the field (such as his victory dance after sacking a quarterback), the fact that he crossed picket lines during the NFL player's strike and because he walked away from his professional football career, his name has no value for promotions or endorsements. There has been no evidence presented to the contrary by the Plaintiff.

The Defendant testified that his chances of obtaining employment with a professional football team are almost nil. Although he is presently attempting to obtain a position at a Jack LaLanne Health Spa he could not provide details as to the potential salary. The Defendant has also attempted to enter professional boxing. No testimony has been elicited

(continued)

by the Plaintiff, however, as to the Defendant's financial potential as a professional boxer. Since the Defendant left professional football he has not worked or earned any money (except for the $20,000 that he earned when he played football in Canada). According to the Defendant, Ms. Nielsen paid for all of the Defendant's expenses during the period of time that they lived together.

After the Defendant failed to appear for a number of court dates and also failed to comply with this Court's pendente lite order, the Court directed that the Defendant's NFL severance pay be sequestered pursuant to Domestic Relations Law § 243 and the Plaintiff be appointed receiver and sequestrator of said funds (which amounted to approximately $83,000 after deducting taxes).

According to Plaintiff the entire $83,000 (reflecting the Defendant's total net severance pay from the NFL) was spent by her as follows: Thirty-two thousand dollars ($32,000) was used to pay mortgage arrears on the Huntington house (which still has approximately $15,000 outstanding in arrears), $22,000 went to the Plaintiff's attorneys, $15,000 went to repay loans taken out by the Plaintiff to pay necessary expenses and the rest, approximately $14,000, went for landscaping, medical insurance, electricity, fuel oil, telephone bills, dental and doctor bills.

Primary Marital Assets

With all of the money that the Defendant earned throughout the course of his professional football career he has retained only three significant marital assets.

(1) The Huntington house, which has been valued at approximately $429,000 and has an outstanding mortgage of $150,000.

(2) A house located in the state of Arizona which was purchased for approximately $550,000 and has a $420,000 mortgage (which in all probability will be sold at foreclosure);

(3) The Defendant's severance pay from the NFL of approximately $83,000.

It is clear that the Defendant has also dissipated a marital asset worth approximately $324,573 (to wit: $484,437 the Defendant was entitled to receive pursuant to his 1988/89 contract tax effected by 33%, reflecting approximate federal and state income tax). Although neither the Plaintiff nor the Defendant attempted to tax effect this dissipated marital asset, it is clear that the Defendant would not have actually received $484,437 had he finished the 1988/89 season. The Court therefore, on its own, has tax effected this amount by 33%, approximately what the defendant would have paid in federal and state taxes had he actually received the $484,437....

Equitable Distribution

It is a guiding principle of equitable distribution that parties are entitled to receive equitable awards which are proportionate to their contributions, whether direct or indirect, to the marriage, *Ullah v. Ullah*, 555 N.Y.S.2d 834 (2nd Dep't 1990).

In this case, the Plaintiff testified that during the course of the marriage she supervised the renovations made on the Huntington house, traveled with the Defendant wherever he trained and, with the assistance of a full-time nanny, raised and cared for their child.

This is not a long-term marriage, and there has been minimal testimony elicited concerning the Plaintiff's direct or indirect contributions to the Defendant's acquisition of marital assets. Although it was the defendant's own athletic abilities and disciplined training which made it possible for him to obtain and retain his position as a professional football player, equity dictates, under the facts of this case, that the Plaintiff receive one-third of the marital assets. The Defendant's decision to voluntarily terminate his contract with the New York Jets, depriving Plaintiff and the parties' child of the standard of living to which they had become accustomed, his failure to obtain meaningful employment thereafter and the indirect contributions made by the Plaintiff during the course of the marriage warrant an award to the Plaintiff of one third of the parties' marital assets. The Court is also mindful of the fact that during the years of the Defendant's greatest productivity, the Plaintiff enjoyed the fruits of Defendant's labors to the fullest...unlike the landmark *O'Brien* case (*O'Brien v. O'Brien*, 66 N.Y. 2d 576), where a newly licensed professional discarded his wife after she provided years of contributions to the attainment of his medical license.

There are only two marital assets to be considered in granting Plaintiff her one-third distributive award, (1) the Huntington house, and (2) the $324,573 dissipated marital asset. The Arizona house has no equity.

The Huntington house is valued at $429,000. It has a $150,000 mortgage with $15,000 owed in back mortgage payments. It thus has an equity of $264,000. One third of the equity would entitle the Plaintiff to $87,120. When one adds $107,109 (1/3 of the $324,573 tax effected marital asset which was dissipated), the Plaintiff would be entitled to $194,229. This would encompass Plaintiff's 1/3 distributive award of the parties' sole remaining marital asset (the Huntington house) and her 1/3 share of the marital asset dissipated by the Defendant. If one adds this $194,229 to the arrears owed by the Defendant on the pendente lite order ($71,707) Plaintiff could be awarded the total equity ($264,000) in the Huntington house in full satisfaction of her one-third distributive award of the parties' marital assets and still have approximately $1,936 remaining as a credit. The Court awards Plaintiff the Huntington house and grants her a Judgment for $1,936 for the remaining arrears owed to her.

Neither side has offered proof as to the present value of the Arizona house or the extent of arrears on mortgage payments (*Gluck v. Gluck*, 520 N.Y.S. 2d 581 (2nd Dep't 1987)). It would appear however, that there is no equity remaining in the Arizona house. The Court awards the Arizona house to the Defendant. The Court directs that each party take whatever steps are required to effect the transfer of the deed to the real property awarded to the other party so as to convey title to said property in said other's name alone.

APPRECIATION

Real or personal property can increase in value (appreciate) after it is acquired. In a property division, the treatment of the appreciation of marital/community property is relatively straightforward. Not so when *separate* property appreciates.

The appreciation of marital/community property is treated the same as the underlying property that appreciated regardless of why it appreciated. Suppose, for example, that a married couple used $100,000 of marital/community funds to buy stock during the marriage, which is worth $150,000 upon divorce. The stock has appreciated by $50,000. A court would decide how to divide the $50,000 the same way that it decides how to divide the $100,000. The entire value of the fund might be divided equally between the spouses or some other allocation to achieve an equitable distribution.

The appreciation of *separate* property can be more complicated. In many states, it is important to know why the appreciation occurred. Here are the main possibilities:

- The appreciation was due to inflation or market forces rather than to the active efforts by the parties. Such appreciation, as we saw earlier, is called *passive appreciation*.

- The appreciation was due to the labor or investment activity (active efforts) of one or both spouses. This is *active appreciation*.

> *After six months of marriage, Alex and Greg decide to divorce. They do not have children. Before the marriage, Alex bought a painting for $2,000. Due to the fame of the artist, the painting is now worth $10,000. Before the marriage, Greg bought an antique car for $4,000. Due to the refinishing work that Greg did himself, the car is now worth $5,000.*

Assume that Alex and Greg cannot decide how to divide the painting and the car. Hence, the court must decide the issue for them.

The painting is Alex's separate property. The car is Greg's separate property. Upon divorce, most states would grant the painting to Alex and the car to Greg because each brought the asset into the marriage. But both assets appreciated during the marriage, the painting by $8,000 and the car by $1,000. Is the appreciation marital/community property that can be divided? Does Alex get to keep the entire $8,000 (in addition to the original value of $2,000) or should Greg be given a share of the $8,000 as marital/community property? Does Greg get to keep the entire $1,000 (in addition to the original value of $4,000) or should Alex be given a share of the $1,000 as marital/community property? States answer these questions in different ways.

- In some states, the owner of separate property keeps the appreciation. The appreciated value of the separate property does not have to be divided. In such states, neither Alex nor Greg would have to share the appreciation.

- In some states, the appreciation of separate property must be divided only if the appreciation was due to the active efforts of one or both parties. *Passive appreciation* is not subject to property division. In the example, the appreciation of the painting was passive; it was due to market forces and inflation. Greg, therefore, does not share in the $8,000 appreciation. The appreciation of the car, however, was due to the active labor of Greg (e.g., he did the refinishing himself). It, therefore, is subject to property division with Alex.

- In some states, the appreciation of separate property must be divided regardless of whether the appreciation was active or passive.

COMMINGLING

Property division is further complicated when the parties mix or commingle assets in one account. For example:

> Before Mary married Ted, she had her own $10,000 checking account. After the marriage, she and Ted opened a joint checking account into which Mary deposited the $10,000 she brought into the marriage. They both started depositing their paychecks into the joint account.

There has been a **commingling** (mixing together) of funds. The pre-marriage $10,000 (clearly separate property) has been deposited into the same account as the post-marriage paychecks of both spouses (clearly marital/community property). A court may treat all commingled property as marital/community property unless the party claiming part of the account as separate property can trace the existence of the separate property by producing adequate records or other evidence—an increasingly difficult task as time passes. If **tracing** does not establish what is separate property, the court could treat all the commingled property as marital/community property. The court will presume that the spouse who commingled his or her separate property intended a gift of the property to the marriage so that the property became marital/community property.

Earlier, we discussed transmutation agreements in which spouses agree to convert separate property into marital/community property or vice versa. Commingling is evidence of transmutation. In and of itself, however, commingling does not prove that the parties intended a transmutation.

A related problem exists when one spouse brings separate property into a marriage (e.g., car, jewelry) and the other spouse uses it extensively. A claim is sometimes asserted that a gift of the separate property was made to the other spouse during the marriage because of this extensive use, a claim that is often successful.

PRACTICAL CONSIDERATIONS IN PROPERTY DIVISION

Once the decision is made on how to divide property, the next concern is to identify the most fair and *practical* way to accomplish the division. Cash, of course, is easy to split (e.g., a 50/50 or 60/40 percent division of a bank account). Not so for the division of homes, vehicles, and businesses. They cannot be conveniently chopped up. Sometimes, it is practical to sell an asset and divide the proceeds according to the allocation principle that applies. When this is not practical, other options are negotiated and/or ordered by the court:

- The wife will keep the house, and the husband will keep the car and his business.

- The wife will live in the house, but the husband will retain a designated amount of the equity in the house, which must be paid to him when the house is sold, which cannot occur until the children reach a designated age.

Commingling
(1) Any mixing of items of different categories.
(2) Mixing funds from different sources.
The verb is *commingle*. (See glossary for an additional meaning.)

tracing
Determining the ownership or characteristics of property from the time it came into existence.

- The wife receives $250,000 as a lump-sum payment, and the husband receives all of the other property.

Sometimes, such measures do not work because of the strained financial circumstances of the parties and a weak economy. Some ex-spouses have been forced to continue to live together after the divorce. In an article entitled *Alone Together in Tough Times*, the author said that "[w]ith the recession and the collapse of the housing market, more and more couples who have broken up are continuing to live under the same roof, according to judges and divorce lawyers. Some are waiting for housing prices to rebound; some are trying to get back on their feet financially."[26]

ASSIGNMENT   8.8

When parties in your state are are not able to agree on a division of marital/community property, what standards will a court use to divide it for them? Under what circumstances, if any, can a court divide *separate* property? (See General Instructions for the State-Code Assignment in Appendix A.)

PENSIONS, DEGREES/LICENSES, BUSINESSES, AND GOODWILL

Next, we examine four areas of possible contention involving property division:

- Pensions.
- Professional degrees (or occupational licenses).
- Businesses.
- Goodwill.

Until fairly recently, parties negotiating a separation agreement did *not* include these items in their bargaining. They were either considered too intangible or simply assumed to belong to one of the parties separately, usually the husband. Litigation and legislation, however, have forced drastic changes in this view. As a result, negotiations for a separation agreement now regularly take account of these items in one way or another. When the negotiations do not lead to agreement, the court will decide how these items will be handled in the divorce.

Pensions

PRIVATE PENSIONS Many workers are covered by one of the two main categories of private pension plans at their places of employment:

- **Defined-Benefit Plan (DBP).** A pension plan that provides a set or defined pension benefit upon retirement.
- **Defined-Contribution Plan (DCP).** A pension plan consisting of individual accounts for each worker (e.g., a 401(k) plan) whose retirement benefit depends on the amount in his or her account.

Accumulated benefits in these plans are **vested** or nonvested. They are vested when they have been earned and cannot be taken away. Under some plans, pension benefits can be vested before retirement. This is usually true of the amounts that the employee pays into the plan. An example of a nonvested benefit might be funds that are lost (particularly the amounts contributed by the employer to the plan) if the employee quits before working a minimum number of years.

---

defined-benefit plan (DBP)
A pension plan that provides a set or defined benefit upon retirement that is usually based on salary and years of employment.

defined-contribution plan (DCP)
A pension plan consisting of individual accounts for each worker whose retirement benefit depends on the amount in his or her account.

vested
Fixed so that it cannot be taken away by future events or conditions; accrued so that the right to present or future possession or enjoyment cannot be taken away.

Upon divorce, pension benefits can be divided between spouses even though only one spouse worked at a job with a pension plan. Some courts refuse to divide nonvested pensions, calling them mere **expectancies**. Many courts, however, take a different view and divide both vested and nonvested pensions.

If the worker began earning the pension before marriage, the amount of the pension earned during the marriage (called the **coverture fraction**) would have to be determined. In most states, only the pension benefits earned during the marriage is subject to property division.

In negotiations, the parties can agree on how to divide a pension. For example, the separation agreement might provide that each spouse will receive an agreed-upon percentage of every pension payout. Alternatively, one spouse might agree to relinquish all right to the other spouse's pension in exchange for a lump-sum cash payment or in exchange for some other benefit sought in the divorce. If they cannot agree, the court will decide what to do with the pension.

If the nonworking spouse is to receive a portion of a pension, the parties must obtain a court order to this effect and present it to the pension plan administrator where the worker has the pension. The order is called a **qualified domestic relations order (QDRO)**. It orders a company to divide the pension in a specified manner. Under a QDRO, a spouse, an ex-spouse, or a child can receive some or all of a worker's pension benefits. Any one of these individuals can become an **alternate payee** under the pension plan. In addition to being a way to divide a pension upon divorce, a QDRO can also be used to collect spousal support (alimony) or child support (see Chapter 10).

The use of QDROs to divide pensions represents a dramatic change in the law. Before 1984, when QDROs were created, individuals other than the worker or employee could not have pension benefits paid directly to them. (To see excerpts of QDROs, type "QDRO sample" in Google, Bing, or Yahoo.) In Chapter 10, we will consider a similar device called a *qualified medical child support order—QMCSO—*that covers health insurance for children.

Before an employee's pension plan can be divided, its value must be determined. Value will depend on factors such as:

- Type of pension plan.
- Amount contributed to the plan by the worker and by the employer (a plan is *contributory* if the employee pays part of his or her salary into the plan; it is noncontributory if the funds in the plan come from the employer only).
- How benefits are determined (e.g., when they accrue or are vested).
- Age of the worker.
- Worker's earliest retirement date.
- Worker's life expectancy.

The valuation process can be complex, often requiring the services of accounting specialists. Here, for example, is how a court described what steps would be needed to value the pension of a fifty-five-year-old plaintiff who was still employed at the time of the divorce:

> Since . . . plaintiff was 55 years old at the time of the divorce and was not eligible to receive any pension benefits until at least age 59, the [following steps would be needed to value his pension]:
>
>> First, the lower court would have to ascertain the likelihood of a 55-year-old man dying before he becomes 59. If, for instance, five 55-year-old males out of each 100 die by the age of 59, the value of the pension benefits would have to be reduced by 5%.

expectancy
The bare hope (but more than wishful thinking) of receiving a property interest.

coverture fraction
The portion of a pension earned during a marriage if part of the pension of a married worker was earned when the worker was not married.

qualified domestic relations order (QDRO)
A court order that allows a nonworker to reach all or part of the pension or other retirement benefits of a worker or former worker in order to satisfy the worker's support or other marital obligation.

alternate payee
A nonworker who is entitled to receive all or part of the pension or other retirement benefits of a current or former worker pursuant to a qualified domestic relations order (QDRO).

Second, the life expectancy of plaintiff at retirement age would have to be calculated. [Under statutory guidelines], a 59-year-old person has a life expectancy of 16.81 years.

Third, the life expectancy of plaintiff would have to be multiplied by the yearly pension benefits the plan provides.

Fourth, this figure must be reduced by the percentage of possibility that plaintiff would die before he is eligible for retirement. (In this example, we have used 5% for purposes of illustration only.)

Fifth, this figure must be reduced to **present value**. This sum will constitute a reasonably ascertainable present value for the pension.[27]

As you can see, the process can be complicated. Some law firms specialize in pension valuation and division. An attorney at one such firm claims that many attorneys are failing to provide competent representation in this area of practice. Flawed retirement-plan paperwork, he said, is a "ticking time bomb waiting to go off" in thousands of divorce cases across the country.[28]

SOCIAL SECURITY, MILITARY PENSIONS, AND OTHER PUBLIC PENSIONS Social Security is an insurance and social welfare program run by the federal government. Its benefits, unlike private pensions, are not divisible marital/community property. A recipient of Social Security cannot agree to (or be forced to) transfer (**assign**) future benefits to another person, such as an ex-spouse or a creditor. Divorced spouses, however, are entitled to collect Social Security benefits based upon the former spouse's earning record if the marriage lasted at least ten years immediately before the divorce became final and if the former spouse is entitled to or is receiving benefits. The divorced spouse seeking benefits through this route must be at least sixty-two years old.[29] This method of obtaining Social Security benefits is quite different from receiving a share of the other spouse's benefits. The latter is not allowed.

Although Social Security is not divisible marital/community property, a recipient's income from Social Security can be considered when calculating the amount of alimony and child support that he or she is required to pay. Also, some states take into account a party's receipt of Social Security benefits when making an over-all equitable distribution of marital property. (See the list of Factors Considered in Equitable Distribution earlier in the chapter.) Such states do not assume that these benefits do not exist. Critics complain that this approach results in an indirect division of Social Security benefits.

At one time, military pensions were also not divisible upon divorce. This was changed by the Uniformed Services Former Spouses' Protection Act (USFSPA).[30] Unlike Social Security benefits, military pensions can now be divided upon divorce.

At the state and local level, government employees are covered by more than 2,600 retirement systems. Although many of these systems have only limited benefits for spouses and no provisions for divorced spouses, aggressive attorneys, with court orders in hand, are sometimes able to break through the maze in order to obtain a share of benefits for ex-spouses.

Degrees and Licenses

Bill and Pat are married in 2013 immediately after both graduated from high school. While Bill goes through college, medical school, and an internship to become a doctor, Pat works full-time to support them. On the day he obtains his license to practice medicine, they decide to divorce. During the long years of Bill's education, they have accumulated no property. Pat earns $25,000 a year at her job. Because she is fully capable of supporting herself, the court decides that she should receive no alimony. They have no children.

present value
The amount of money an individual would have to be given now in order to generate a certain amount of money within a designated period of time through prudent investment, usually at compound interest. Also called *present cash value* and *present worth*.

assign
To transfer rights or property to someone. The person who makes the transfer is the *assignor*. The person who receives the transfer is the *assignee* or the *assign*. The noun is *assignment*.

Spouses such as Pat often make substantial contributions to the other spouse's *enhanced earning capacity* in the form of a degree, a license, or, in some instances, a potentially profitable celebrity status. Many would consider it an outrage if Pat walks away from the marriage with nothing. In our example, she is not eligible for alimony, and there is no property to divide. Bill walks away with a professional degree and a doctor's license ready to embark on a lucrative career.

What financial contributions and losses are relevant to the marriage and divorce of Pat and Bill? Consider these possibilities:

1. The amount Pat contributed to Bill's day-to-day living needs while he was in school, e.g., food, utilities, rent.
2. The amount Pat contributed to the payment of Bill's education expenses.
3. The amount Bill would have contributed to the marriage if he had worked during these years rather than going to school.
4. The increased earnings Pat might have had if she had taken a different job.
5. The increased earnings Pat would have had if she had continued her education rather than working to support Bill through his education.
6. The increased standard of living Pat would have enjoyed due to Bill's expected high earnings if they had stayed married.
7. The share of Bill's increased earnings to which Pat would have been entitled if they had stayed married.

Some courts have slowly come to the realization that supporting spouses such as Pat should be given a remedy. Yet the courts do not agree on what the remedy should be. Most courts will consider only the first two items listed above in providing Pat with a remedy. As a matter of equity, she is entitled only to **restitution**—a return of what she contributed while Bill was acquiring his degree and license. Such states do not consider a degree and license to be divisible property. They are personal to the holder. Under this view, it logically follows that she is not entitled to a share of his increased earnings as a result of the degree and license.

All of the above listed items (1–7) are taken into consideration in deciding the question of spousal support (alimony). Increased earnings as a result of the degree and license are taken into consideration because one of the factors in an alimony or maintenance judgment is the spouse's ability to pay. The problem, however, is that spouses such as Pat may not be eligible for alimony because of her own employability. Nor can equity be achieved by giving the wife a generous share of tangible property if little or no such property has been accumulated due to the fact that the husband had high educational expenses and little or no income of his own.

In such situations, a minimal remedy is a direct award for items (1) and (2) above, which amounts to little more than restitution. As we saw earlier in Exhibit 8.6, the award is sometimes awkwardly referred to as *reimbursement alimony* or *restitutional alimony*, even though its primary purpose is *not* to provide support. A few states will deny even this remedy, taking the position that the wife, in effect, was making a gift of her money and other resources to the husband during his education.

There is another remedy that the sacrificing ex-spouse might try to seek in this situation to prevent **unjust enrichment**. He or she may be able to sue the now-educated or now-licensed ex-spouse on a theory of **implied-in-law contract** (also called *quasi contract*), which would seek to recover the value of the contributions made by the sacrificing ex-spouse toward the other's achievement of the degree or license.

There is, however, a small minority of states that are more sympathetic to the plight of spouses in Pat's situation. These states have ruled that the degree and license *do* constitute divisible marital property and, as a result, more than restitution is needed. The following case of *Woodworth v. Woodworth* is an example of a case from such a state.

restitution
An equitable remedy that restores to the plaintiff the value of what he or she parted with. (See the glossary for another meaning.)

unjust enrichment
The receipt of a benefit in the form of goods or services that in fairness should be returned or paid for even though there was no express or implied promise to do so.

implied-in-law contract
An obligation created by the law to avoid unjust enrichment in the absence of an express or implied contract creating this obligation. Also called *quasi contract*.

 Woodworth v. Woodworth
126 Mich. App. 258, 337 N.W.2d 332 (1983)
Court of Appeals of Michigan

Background: *While Michael Woodworth went through law school in the 1970s, his wife, Ann, was a nursery school teacher. In their divorce action, she claimed that his law degree was a marital asset that should be divided. The trial court agreed. It valued the degree at $20,000 and ruled that he must pay her $2,000 per year for ten 10 years. The case is now on appeal before the Court of Appeals of Michigan. On appeal, Michael is the plaintiff and Ann is the defendant.*

Decision on Appeal: *A former husband's law degree, which was the end product of a concerted family effort, was marital property subject to distribution upon divorce. The case is remanded to the trial court to recalculate the value of the degree.*

OPINION OF THE COURT:

Judge BURNS delivered the opinion of the court.

On January 6, 1982, the parties' divorce was finalized. Both parties appeal as of right.

The parties were married on June 27, 1970, after plaintiff had graduated from Central Michigan University with a bachelor's degree in secondary education and defendant had graduated from Lansing Community College with an associate's degree. They then moved to Jonesville, where plaintiff worked as a teacher and coach

for the high school and defendant worked as a nursery school teacher in Hillsdale. In the Fall of 1973, they sold their house, quit their jobs [defendant had already quit her job the year before after the parties' first child was born], and moved to Detroit, where plaintiff attended Wayne State Law School. Three years later, they moved to Lansing where plaintiff took and passed the bar exam and accepted a job as a research attorney with the Court of Appeals. Plaintiff is now a partner in a Lansing law firm.

For all intents and purposes, the marriage ended on August 25, 1980, when the parties separated. The [Summary of Earnings chart] summarizes each party's earnings during the marriage.

The basic issue in this case is whether or not plaintiff's law degree is marital property subject to distribution. The trial court held that it was, valued it at $20,000, and awarded this amount to defendant in payments of $2,000 over ten years. Plaintiff contends that his law degree is not such a marital asset. We disagree.

The facts reveal that plaintiff's law degree was the end product of a concerted family effort. Both parties planned their family life around the effort to attain plaintiff's degree. Toward this end, the family divided the daily tasks encountered in living. While the law degree did not preempt all other facets of their lives, it did become the main focus and goal of their activities. Plaintiff left his job at Jonesville and the family relocated to Detroit so that plaintiff could

Summary of Earnings During the Marriage				
Year	**Plaintiff**		**Defendant**	
1970	$ 2,591	Jonesville HS teacher/coach	$ 1,422 $ 2,549	Nursery School Teacher Grant Company (clerk)
1971	$ 7,989 $ 410	Teacher St. Anthony Church (instructor)	$ 4,236 $ 280	Teacher St. Anthony Church (instructor)
1972	$ 9,691	Teacher	$ 2,525	Teacher
1973	$ 6,557	Teacher	$ 986	Bank Teller
1974	$ 2,483	Legal Aid (student lawyer)	$ 6,572	Bank Teller
1975	$ 2,588	Legal Aid (student lawyer)	$ 1,050 $ 8,191	Bank Teller Dept/Social Services (case worker)
1976	$ 6,342	Court of Appeals (attorney)	$10,276	Dept/Social Services (case worker)
1977	$12,493 $ 5,595	Court of Appeals (attorney) Asst. Pros. Atty.	$ 1,586	Dept/Social Services (case worker) (defendant quit this job in January after the parties' third child was born)
1978	$21,085	Asst. Pros. Atty.	$—0—	
1979	$27,247	Asst. Pros. Atty.	$—0—	
1980	$ 2,057 $30,000	Asst. Pros. Atty. Private Practice	$—0—	

(continued)

attend law school. In Detroit, defendant sought and obtained full time employment to support the family.

We conclude, therefore, that plaintiff's law degree was the result of mutual sacrifice and effort by both plaintiff and defendant. While plaintiff studied and attended classes, defendant carried her share of the burden as well as sharing vicariously in the stress of the [law school] experience known as the "paper chase."

We believe that fairness dictates that the spouse who did not earn an advanced degree be compensated whenever the advanced degree is the product of such concerted family investment. The degree holder has expended great effort to obtain the degree not only for him or herself, but also to benefit the family as a whole. The other spouse has shared in this effort and contributed in other ways as well, not merely as a gift to the student spouse nor merely to share individually in the benefits but to help the marital unit as a whole. . . .

We are aware that numerous other cases have held that an advanced degree is not a marital asset and may be considered only (if at all) in determining alimony. However, we reject the [following four main] reasons given in these cases to support their conclusions.

[I]

The cases first contend that an advanced degree is simply not "property":

An educational degree, such as an M.B.A., is simply not encompassed by the broad views of the concept of "property." It does not have an exchange value or any objective transferable value on an open market. It is personal to the holder. It terminates on death of the holder and is not inheritable. It cannot be assigned, sold, transferred, conveyed, or pledged. An advanced degree is a cumulative product of many years of previous education, combined with diligence and hard work. It may not be acquired by the mere expenditure of money. It is simply an intellectual achievement that may potentially assist in the future acquisition of property. In our view, it has none of the attributes of property in the usual sense of that term. Graham v. Graham, *194 Colo. 432, 374 P.2d 75 (1978).*

Yet whether or not an advanced degree can physically or metaphysically be defined as "property" is beside the point. Courts must instead focus on the most equitable solution to dissolving the marriage and dividing among the respective parties what they have.

[T]he student spouse will walk away with a degree and the supporting spouse will depart with little more than the knowledge that he or she has substantially contributed toward the attainment of that degree. Comment, The Interest of the Community in a Professional Education, *10 Cal. West. L. Rev. 590 (1974).*

In *DeLa Rosa v. DeLa Rosa*, 309 N.W.2d 758, (1981), the Minnesota Supreme Court added:

[O]ne spouse has forgone the immediate enjoyment of earned income to enable the other to pursue an advanced education on a full time basis. Typically, this sacrifice is made with the expectation that the parties will enjoy a higher standard of living in the future.

Where, as in this case, the family goal of obtaining the law degree was the purpose of the substantial contribution and sacrifice, both the degree holder and his or her spouse are entitled to share in the fruits of the degree. The trial judge recognized as much:

Here the plaintiff quit his job and entered law school. The defendant secured employment so plaintiff could become a professional with far greater earning capacity than he had, which would benefit him and their children. To permit this, upon divorce, to benefit only the party who secured the professional degree is unconscionable.

[II]

The next argument is that a marriage is not a commercial enterprise and that neither spouse's expectations are necessarily going to be met after the divorce:

I do not believe that a spouse who works and contributes to the education of the other spouse during marriage normally does so in the expectation of compensation. Sullivan v. Sullivan, *184 Cal. Rptr. 801 (1982) (Kaufman, P. J., concurring).*

Furthermore:

They do not nor do they expect to pay each other for their respective contributions in any commercial sense. Rather, they work together, in both income and nonincome-producing ways, in their joint, mutual and individual interests. The termination of the marriage represents, if nothing else, the disappointment of expectations, financial and nonfinancial, which were hoped to be achieved by and during the continuation of the relationship. It does not, however, in our view, represent a commercial investment loss. Recompense for the disappointed expectations resulting from the failure of the marital entity to survive cannot, therefore, be made to the spouses on a strictly commercial basis which, after the fact seeks to assign monetary values to the contributions consensually made by each of the spouses during the marriage. . . . If the plan fails by reason of the termination of the marriage, we do not regard the supporting spouse's consequent loss of expectation by itself as any more compensable or demanding of solicitude than the loss of expectations of any other spouse who, in the hope and anticipation of the endurance

(continued)

of the relationship in its commitments, has invested a portion of his or her life, youth, energy and labor in a failed marriage. Mahoney v. Mahoney, *182 N.J. Super. 612–614, 442 A.2d 1062 (1982).*

We agree that a marriage is not intrinsically a commercial enterprise. Instead, it is a relationship sanctioned by law governed at its essence by fidelity and troth. Neither partner usually expects to be compensated for his or her efforts. But that consideration does not end the discussion. We are not presently concerned with how best to characterize a marriage while it endures. Instead, we are concerned with how best to distribute between the parties what they have once the marriage has for all intents and purposes dissolved. In other words:

To allow a student spouse . . . to leave a marriage with all the benefits of additional education and a professional license without compensation to the spouse who bore much of the burdens incident to procuring these would be unfair. . . . O'Brien v. O'Brien, *452 N.Y.S.2d 801, 805 (1982).*

Furthermore, we also agree that divorce courts cannot recompense expectations. However, we are not talking about an expectation here. Defendant is not asking us to compensate for a failed expectation that her husband would become a wealthy lawyer and subsequently support her for the rest of her life. Instead, she is merely seeking her share of the fruits of a degree which she helped him earn. We fail to see the difference between compensating her for a degree which she helped him earn and compensating her for a house in his name which her earnings helped him buy.

[III]

The third argument against including an advanced degree as marital property is that its valuation is too speculative. In *Lesman v. Lesman,* 452 N.Y.S. 2d 938-939 (1982), the Court stated:

Gross inequities may result from predicating distribution awards [the term used in New York for property division] upon the speculative expectations of enhanced future earnings, since distributive awards, unlike maintenance, once fixed may not be modified to meet future realities. It is almost impossible to predict what amount of enhanced earnings, if any, will result from a professional education. The degree of financial success attained by those holding a professional degree varies greatly. Some, even, may earn less from their professional practices than they could have earned from nonprofessional work. Moreover, others, due to choice or factors beyond their control, may never practice their professions. . . .

Michigan has already recognized that:

Interests which are contingent upon the happening of an event which may or may not occur are not distributable. The party seeking to include the interest in the marital estate bears the burdens of proving a reasonably ascertainable value; if the

burden is not met, the interest should not be considered an asset subject to distribution. Miller v. Miller, *83 Mich. App. 672, 677, 269 N.W.2d 264 (1978).*

However, future earnings due to an advanced degree are not "too speculative." While a degree holder spouse might change professions, earn less than projected at trial, or even die, courts have proved adept at measuring future earnings in such contexts as personal injury, wrongful death, and workers' compensation actions. In fact, pain and suffering, professional goodwill and mental distress, within these general legal issues, have similar valuation "problems". . . . We, therefore, do not believe that the *Miller* contingency caveat applies to future earnings.

[IV]

The last argument is that these matters are best considered when awarding alimony rather than when distributing the property. . . .

A trial judge is given wide discretion in awarding alimony. . . . However, alimony is basically for the other spouse's support. The considerations for whether or not a spouse is entitled to support are different than for dividing the marital property. *McLain v. McLain,* 108 Mich. App. 166, 310 N.W.2d 316 (1981), listed eleven factors that the trial judge is to consider in determining whether or not to award alimony. Some of these deal with the parties' financial condition and their ability to support themselves. If the spouse has already supported the other spouse through graduate school, he or she is quite possibly already presently capable of supporting him or herself. Furthermore [trial courts in Michigan have] discretion to end alimony if the spouse receiving it remarries. We do not believe that the trial judge should be allowed to deprive the spouse who does not have an advanced degree of the fruits of the marriage and award it all to the other spouse merely because he or she has remarried. Such a situation would necessarily cause that spouse to think twice about remarrying.

Having determined that the defendant is entitled to compensation in this case, we must next determine how she is to be compensated. Two basic methods have been proposed—[1] a percentage share of the present value of the future earnings attributable to the degree or [2] restitution.

[Some courts limit] the recovery to restitution for any money given to the student spouse to earn the degree. While this solution may be equitable in some circumstances, we do not believe that restitution is an adequate remedy in this case. Limiting the recovery to restitution "would provide [the supporting spouse] no realization of [his or] her expectation of economic benefit from the career for which the education laid the foundation." Pinnel, *Divorce After Professional School: Education and Future Earning Capacity May Be Marital Property,* 44 Mo. L. Rev. 329, 335 (1979). Clearly, in this case, the degree was a family investment, rather than a gift or a benefit to the degree holder alone. Treating the degree as such a gift would unjustly enrich the degree holder to the extent that the

(continued)

degree's value exceeds its cost. . . . We note that this case does not involve the situation where both parties simultaneously earned substantially similar advanced degrees during the marriage. In such a situation, equity suggests that the parties have already amply compensated each other.

The trial court in this case valued plaintiff's law degree at $20,000 and ruled that plaintiff must pay defendant $2,000 per year for ten years. We are unable to determine how this value was reached and therefore, remand to the trial court to permit that court to revalue the degree in light of the following factors:

- the length of the marriage after the degree was obtained,
- the sources and extent of financial support given plaintiff during his years in law school, and
- the overall division of the parties' marital property.

In determining the degree's present value, the trial court should estimate what the person holding the degree is likely to make in that particular job market and subtract from that what he or she would probably have earned without the degree. . . . The ultimate objective in a property distribution is to be fair. . . . Both parties may present new evidence on these matters and the degree's valuation.

One of the tragedies of this divorce, as in so many others, is that what used to be financially adequate is no longer enough. As the trial court aptly stated: "The tablecloths . . . will not cover both tables." We, therefore, note that the trial court has discretion to order that the payments be made on an installment basis. . . . If the trial court should order such a payment schedule, the trial court should also consider the possibility of insuring these payments by a life insurance policy on plaintiff's life benefitting defendant. . . .

Pursuant to GCR [General Court Rules] 1963, 726.1, we order plaintiff to pay defendant reasonable attorney fees for this appeal. Costs to defendant.

Remanded with instructions to proceed in a manner consistent with this opinion. We do not retain jurisdiction.

ASSIGNMENT 8.9

a. Was the *Woodworth* case correctly decided? Why or why not?

b. Frank and Elaine are married in your state. Both work at low-paying jobs at a fast-food restaurant. Elaine wishes to become a paralegal, and Frank would like to become an electrician. A local Institute has a one-year paralegal training program and a nine-month-electrician-training program. Frank and Elaine decide that only one of them can go to school at a time. Frank volunteers to let Elaine go first, keeping his job at the restaurant to support them both while she is at the Institute. A month before Elaine is scheduled to graduate, Frank has a serious accident at the restaurant. He will not recover fully from his injury or be able to go to school for at least five years. When Elaine is graduated, she obtains a good job as a paralegal. The parties seek a divorce a month after graduation. There are no children from the marriage, and no tangible property to divide. In the divorce proceeding, Frank tells the court that the only asset that can be divided is Elaine's paralegal certificate. He asks the court to award him a percentage of the earnings that Elaine will have during the next five years as a paralegal.

   i. How would *Woodworth v. Woodworth* apply to this case?

   ii. How would your state resolve the case of Elaine and Frank? (See General Instructions for the Court-Opinion Assignment in Appendix A.)

Dividing a Business

When a divorce occurs, one of the assets to be divided may be a business that was acquired during the marriage or was acquired before the marriage but developed or expanded during the marriage. The business could be a large corporation, a small sole proprietorship, a partnership, a law practice, a medical practice, etc. (Our focus here is a functioning business rather than a degree or license.) In addition to commercial buildings and equipment, a number of intangible items must be valuated (e.g., patents, trademarks, employment agreements, copyrights, securities, and goodwill).

Many professional business appraisers are available for the task. Examples:

- Certified Public Accountant Accredited in Business Valuation
- Accredited Senior Appraiser
- Certified Valuation Analyst
- Certified Business Appraiser

Because property can fluctuate in value, particularly securities, the parties need to agree on the date that will be used for purposes of the valuation. The property to be divided will be valued as of the specific date (called the cutoff date) that they designate. Appraisers and other financial consultants will be asked to come up with valuations as of the cutoff date.

A great deal of documentation will be needed to perform the needed valuations. Here are some examples for corporate or partnership businesses:

- Federal, state, and local tax returns for the last five years.
- Annual and interim financial statements.
- Bank statements.
- Depreciation schedules.
- Articles of incorporation and bylaws or partnership agreements, including amendments.
- Minutes of meetings of shareholders and directors.
- Buy/sell agreements of shareholders or partners, including amendments.
- Loan applications.
- W-2 statements (or the equivalent) for the highest-paid employees.
- Leases.
- Production schedules.
- Inventory reports.
- Management reports.
- Billing records.[31]

There are three main approaches to valuing a business:

- *Asset-based approach.* In this approach, the focus is on the sum of the various business assets minus liabilities. An appraiser assigns a value to the business assets based on their replacement cost. Tangible assets, such as inventory, and intangibles, such as patents, trademarks, and accounts receivables, are included in the valuation.
- *Market approach.* Here, the focus is recent sales of similar businesses in the same market. The assessor looks at what ready, willing, and able buyers have paid to ready, willing, and able sellers in arm's length transactions involving comparable businesses.
- *Income-based approach.* This is the most commonly used method. The assessor determines the income of the company, normalizes costs such as salaries and expenses, and then applies a *capitalization rate* to the earnings in order to establish the value of the business. The **capitalization rate** is based on the income the business is likely to generate going forward in light of inherent risks.[32]

The fact that a business is a divisible part of the marital estate does not necessarily mean that the business must be sold so that the proceeds can be physically divided. The separation agreement will probably try to accommodate the need to keep the business in operation. The agreement, for example, might provide that the husband will give the wife $250,000 in exchange for the release of any

capitalization rate
The rate of interest investors would require as a return on their money before they would invest in income-producing property, taking into account all the risks involved in that particular enterprise. *City of Dallas v. Redbird Development Corp.* 143 S.W.3d 375 (Tex. App. 2004).

interest that the wife may have in his business, or vice versa if she is the one primarily responsible for the business. Similarly, a court may order such an exchange if the parties are not able to agree on dividing the business in their separation agreement.

Goodwill

One aspect of a business that is sometimes particularly difficult to evaluate is its goodwill, which is the reputation of a business or professional practice that causes it to generate additional customers. It is the value of a business or practice that exceeds the value of the combined assets used in the business or practice. Because of goodwill, the company is expected to have earnings beyond what is considered normal for the type of business involved. Individuals providing services, such as accountants and lawyers, can also have goodwill:

> If you are a lawyer facing divorce, it is open season on your practice. . . . Like it or not, law practices and lawyer's goodwill are assets. That you can't sell your practice doesn't mean it has no value. And there are almost no legal limits on the methods an appraiser may use in assigning a value to a law practice. . . . One approach is called the excess earnings method. An appraiser looks at published surveys to find the average income for a lawyer of your experience and type of practice, then compares your earnings with the average. If your earnings are higher than the average, the increment is said to be attributable to goodwill. If your ability to attract clients and collect substantial fees from them brings you more income than you would earn working for an average salary, you have built real goodwill.[33]

If goodwill was developed during the marriage, the spouse who stayed at home may be deemed to have contributed to it (as well as to the rest of the business).

A distinction should be made between enterprise goodwill and personal goodwill:

- **Enterprise goodwill** is an asset of a business or practice that exists by virtue of its business location, existing arrangements with suppliers and employees, and anticipated future customer base, but is not dependent on the continued presence of a particular individual in the business or practice.

- **Personal goodwill** is an asset of a business or practice that is dependent on the continued presence of a particular individual because the asset is attributed to that individual's personal skill, training, or reputation.

In many states only enterprise goodwill is divisible property upon divorce because this is an asset that is marketable—it is part of what could be sold when the business or practice is sold. By definition, personal goodwill is not marketable. It has no exchange value; it cannot be sold. Therefore, personal goodwill is not divisible in these states. Other states, however, take a different position and allow both enterprise and personal goodwill to be divided upon divorce.

goodwill
The reputation of a business or professional practice that causes it to generate additional customers. The value of a business or practice that exceeds the value of the combined assets used in the business or practice.

enterprise goodwill
An asset of a business or practice that exists by virtue of its business location, existing arrangements with suppliers and employees, and anticipated future customer base, but is not dependent on the continued presence of a particular individual in the business or practice.

personal goodwill
An asset of a business or practice that is dependent on the continued presence of a particular individual because the asset is attributed to that individual's personal skill, training, or reputation. Also called *professional goodwill*.

ASSIGNMENT 8.10

Does your state have any statutes on the division of (a) a pension, (b) a degree or license, (c) a business or profession, or (d) goodwill following a divorce? If so, summarize their major terms. (See General Instructions for the State-Code Assignment in Appendix A.)

MISCELLANEOUS PROPERTY-DIVISION PROBLEMS

The Two-List Method

When a marriage ends, most of the time and energy of the parties will be directed at the disposition of large items, such as the home, vehicles, pension, businesses, and the like. Yet there can also be a large number of household furnishings and miscellaneous personal property that must be divided. The list can be extensive for long-term marriages. The preferred method of dividing this property is, of course, a mutual agreement of the parties. Suppose, however, that the instinct of the parties is to fight over everything. One way that some courts have handled such a situation is to use the two-list method. Here is how it works:

- One spouse is asked to prepare two lists. The lists contain all the personal property to be divided. The two lists are mutually exclusive – anything placed on one list cannot also be on the other list.

- The two lists are then given to the other spouse who choses one of the lists to indicate what he or she will get. The items on the other list will be given to the spouse that made the two lists.

Initially, the spouse preparing the two lists does not know what list the other spouse will select. Hence, the list-making spouse has an incentive to make both lists equally appealing. "The idea" according to one court using this method, "is that, because the other spouse has the choice between the two lists, the list-preparing spouse will prepare balanced lists, and the division will be fair."[34]

Sports Tickets

In a recent case calling for the wisdom of Solomon, a judge had to decide how to divide season tickets to basketball games of the New York Knicks. Both spouses were passionate fans. The option of giving them each one ticket to every game was unacceptable, since this would mean they would have to sit together: "This court will not compel them to team up once again at courtside."[35] The judge decided to give the husband both tickets to every even-numbered game and the wife both tickets to every odd-numbered game. Each spouse could then take someone else to the game and avoid having to face the other in the already emotionally charged environment of professional basketball games.

Pets

Pets are personal property (chattels) that are subject to property division. If the parties cannot agree on who gets a beloved pet, the court must resolve the emotional battle. According to a veteran attorney, "Both parties will offer their version of why they are the best. They may have witnesses, neighbors who say, '[He] beat the dog,' or '[She] kissed the dog.' I have heard the story of a case where both parties were in the courtroom, with the dog in the middle, to see which way it would go. They both whistled and called. The dog ran to the husband. It was not the deciding factor, but it was one of the factors" in the outcome.[36]

A few states have enacted special laws on pets in divorce cases. The focus of such laws is pet *custody* rather than just pet *ownership*. In deciding which spouse gets a companion pet, the judge must take into consideration who is best able to provide proper care of the pet. In effect, the standard used by the court is "best interests of the pet," which is roughly equivalent to the standard used in child-custody cases – best interests of the child. If feasible, joint custody of a pet can be ordered.[37]

Tort Awards

What happens when one of the spouses receives damages from a tort case? For example, Harry wins $200,000 in a negligence case against a truck company for injuries he received in a collision with a driver of the company. A few months later, Harry and his wife, Alice, begin divorce proceedings. Is the $200,000 divisible property in the divorce? The answer may depend on what the $200,000 was for. Here are the main possibilities:

- Compensation for economic losses such as lost wages during the marriage, loss of earning capacity during the marriage, and medical bills that were paid during the marriage with marital funds. In most states, such compensation is marital/community property that is subject to property division upon divorce.

- Compensation for noneconomic losses such as pain and suffering. In most states, such compensation is the separate property of the spouse who won the tort case.

- Compensation for economic losses such as lost future wages and future medical expenses. In most states, such compensation is the separate property of the spouse who won the tort case.

States often assess the divisibility of workers-compensation awards in the same way. They will determine what is separate and what is divisible based on an analysis of what the award covers.

Note, however, that separate property such as compensation received for pain and suffering might be still relevant on the issues of alimony and child support. An ex-spouse may not be entitled to a share or a division of certain funds, but the ex-spouse will be allowed to point to the existence of such funds as evidence of the other's ability to pay alimony or child support.

ASSIGNMENT   8.11

Elaine has worked as an executive at ABC Company for twenty years. When she was laid off, she received a substantial severance package. Would the package be subject to property division if she divorced at the same time she was laid off? (See the General Instructions for the Legal-Analysis Assignment in Appendix A.)

Embryos

What happens to **embryos** that a married couple froze during the marriage for later implantation but never used as of the time of their divorce? How does a court resolve a disagreement between the divorcing spouses on what to do with the embryos? The dispute might center on whether they should be destroyed (often the ex-husband's wish) or kept in storage for later implantation by the ex-wife or by another woman to whom the embryos would be donated. Are the embryos "property" to be treated as part of a property division? Can one of the spouses allow another couple to "adopt" the embryos?

In most states, embryos are considered property that can be disposed of by contract between the spouses and/or between the spouses and the company they hired to freeze and store the embryos. If, however, a state seeks to give embryos the status of persons, their disposition in divorce cases becomes considerably more complex, as we will see in Chapter 16.

embryo
An egg that has been fertilized by a sperm and is in the early stage of development; it has undergone one or more divisions. The product of conception to about the eighth week of pregnancy.

OTHER MATTERS TO BE RESOLVED

Thus far in this chapter, we have covered two major components of separation agreements and divorces: alimony and property division. Before turning to child custody and child support (in Chapters 9 and 10), we need to look at some other matters that are often part of the dissolution process: debts, taxes, wills, insurance, and legal expenses.

DEBTS

Debts, like assets, must be divided upon divorce in order to determine who is responsible for paying them. A great variety of debts may be outstanding (unpaid) when the parties divorce:

- Personal debts a spouse incurred before the marriage.
- Family debts incurred by only one of the spouses.
- Business debts incurred by only one of the spouses.
- Business or family debts incurred by both spouses so that there is **joint and several liability** on the debts, meaning that a creditor could sue the spouses *together* on the debt, or could sue *either* spouse for payment of the whole debt.
- Debts between the spouses (e.g., a loan made by one spouse to the other during the marriage).

joint and several liability
Legally responsible together and individually. Each debtor is individually responsible for the entire debt; the plaintiff/creditor can choose to collect the full debt from one debtor or from all of them until the debt is satisfied.

The parties must decide who is going to pay what debts. This should be spelled out in the separation agreement. If they cannot agree, the court will decide the issue for them. States differ on how they make this decision. In some states, all debts can be divided, no matter who incurred them. Other states distinguish between separate debts of one spouse (e.g., a debt brought into the marriage) and marital/community debts. In these states, separate debts are the responsibility of the spouse who incurred them. Marital/community debts are allocated according to factors such as the parties' relative ability to pay, the party who incurred the debt, and the party who was the main financial manager of the debt. In short, just as most states seek an equitable distribution of property, so also do most courts seek to achieve an equitable allocation of marital/community (nonseparate) debts.

Future debts incurred after the divorce are the responsibility of the ex-spouse who incurred them. The normal expectation of the parties is that they will pay their own debts. A cautious party, however, will not only cancel all joint credit cards but also notify known large creditors that future debts will be the sole responsibility of the ex-spouse incurring the debts. Some separation agreements insert a clause in the agreement stating that each party promises not to attempt to use the credit of the other.

Finally, keep in mind that creditors are *not* bound by separation agreements or by court orders that allocate responsibility for paying debts between ex-spouses.

> *Paul and Karen are married. During the marriage, Paul buys a car on credit in his own name from Ford Motor Company. When they divorce, the balance owed on the car is $10,000. Because Karen was the primary user of the car throughout the marriage, the parties decide that the wife should pay the remaining $10,000 debt. This decision is stated in their separation agreement and approved by the court in the final divorce judgment.*

Ford can still sue Paul for the $10,000 debt if Karen fails to pay it. Parties do not have the right to switch debtors and force creditors to abide by the switch. The same is true if a court ordered Karen to pay the $10,000 as part of the divorce decree. Ford can still go after the party whose credit it relied on when extending credit—Paul. If Karen violates the separation agreement or divorce judgment by refusing to pay the debt, Paul can sue Karen. Such a suit, however, would not affect the contractual obligation that Paul has to Ford, which, of course, was not a party to the divorce judgment.

Another example:

> *The separation agreement of Jim and Alice gives their jointly owned Boston home to Alice. She must pay the remaining mortgage, which both she and Jim took out*

when they married. Jim quitclaims the Boston home to Alice so that his name is no longer on the title. A year after the divorce, Alice falls behind on her mortgage payments. Jim has remarried and has applied for a mortgage on a home in New York with his new wife. His application for the mortgage is denied because of the delinquent payments on the Boston home.

The separation agreement obligated Alice to pay the mortgage on their Boston home. The agreement did not (and could not) remove Jim's name from the Boston mortgage. When the court approved their separation agreement, the court order did not (and could not) remove Jim's name from the Boston mortgage. Only if the Boston mortgage company were a party to the divorce case would a divorce court have the power to alter the company's contractual relationship with Jim, a named mortgagor (borrower). The mortgage company can sue Alice and Jim for nonpayment.

TAXES

In Chapter 11, we will discuss the tax consequences of divorce. (They are summarized in Exhibit 8.5 above.) Our focus here is on the question of who pays the taxes and who will be able to take advantage of certain tax benefits. The following are the types of situations the parties need to anticipate:

- If the Internal Revenue Service (IRS) assesses a tax deficiency and penalty for a joint return filed in a year when the parties were still married, who pays the deficiency and penalty?

- If the parties file their last joint income tax return in the current tax year, and then, many months later, the IRS assesses a tax deficiency and penalty on that last tax return, who pays this deficiency and penalty?

During a marriage, a couple's tax returns are often prepared by one spouse with minimal involvement of the other. This situation, however, does not necessarily relieve the spouse who did not prepare the return from liability for underpayments, errors, or fraud committed by her or his spouse who prepared and submitted the returns. (Although, as we will see in Chapter 11, a spouse might be able to obtain relief as an "innocent spouse.")

In the negotiations for the separation agreement, one spouse might ask the other to insert a clause that he or she will **indemnify** him or her against any tax deficiencies and penalties that may arise out of the joint returns filed in any year during their marriage. Under such a *hold-harmless* clause, the tax-return-preparing spouse will have to pay the entire deficiency and penalty for which they both may be jointly and severally liable.

The parties must also agree on how tax refunds, if any, are to be divided. Such refunds are usually payable by government check to both of the parties. Two signatures may be required to cash such checks. Another concern is that the IRS might institute an audit years after a particular return is filed. It is a good idea to insert a clause in the separation agreement that both parties agree to cooperate with each other in responding to the issues raised during future audits.

Every clause in the separation agreement involving financial matters can have immediate or long-term tax consequences. The separation agreement will usually specify a dollar amount to be transferred pursuant to a support clause or a property-division clause. If, however, all the tax factors have not been considered, the parties may later be surprised by the discrepancy between such stated dollar figures and the *real* amounts that they receive and pay out. To **tax effect** a clause in a separation agreement means to determine the tax consequences of that clause. (Again, we will cover such consequences in Chapter 11.)

indemnify
To compensate another for any loss or expense incurred.

tax effect
(1) To determine the tax consequences of something. (2) The tax consequences of something.

WILLS

The parties must consider a number of questions involving wills and estates:

- Do the spouses already have wills naming each other as beneficiary? If so, are these wills to be changed? In most states, a divorce automatically revokes **testamentary** gifts to a surviving spouse unless the will specifically says otherwise. (Statutes requiring this result are called *revocation-on-divorce statutes*.) Nevertheless, the parties should make their wishes explicit in their separation agreement and also cover the contingency of death occurring after they sign the separation agreement but before the final divorce judgment.

- Have they named each other as **executor** of their estates? In most states, the divorce judgment will automatically revoke this appointment, but the revocation should be made explicit in the separation agreement.

- Does the will of a spouse name relatives of the other spouse as beneficiaries? (e.g., the sister of the spouse)? Changes in the will should be made to reflect current wishes. If the spouse dies before making such changes, some courts will presume that the deceased intended to revoke such gifts.

- Is either spouse mentioned as a beneficiary in the will of a relative of the other spouse? If so, the relative may want to change the will.

INSURANCE

Several different kinds of insurance policies could be in effect at the time the parties draft the separation agreement in anticipation of a divorce:

- Life insurance.
- Homeowner's insurance (covering fire and related damage to the home as well as liability claims by persons [e.g., mail carrier] injured on the premises).
- Hospitalization or other medical insurance.
- Liability insurance (for business).
- Comprehensive vehicle insurance.
- Disability insurance.
- Umbrella insurance (covering designated amounts that exceed the limits of standard liability policies).

Detailed information should be obtained about each policy. How much are the premiums? Who has paid them in the past? Who are the beneficiaries? Can the beneficiaries be changed? If so, by whom?

As we have seen, one ex-spouse usually has no obligation to support the other ex-spouse or the children after the payor dies. The latter, however, may want to assume this obligation voluntarily. One way of accomplishing this is to take out a life insurance policy on the payor's life, with the beneficiaries being the ex-spouse and/or the children. If such a life insurance policy already exists, then the payor may agree to keep it effective (e.g., pay the premiums) after the separation. The payee, however, will not gain much protection from such an agreement if the payor can change the beneficiaries. Hence, as part of the bargaining process, the payee might ask that the designation of the beneficiaries be made **irrevocable**.

What happens if the parties say nothing about an existing life insurance policy when they divorce and a death occurs? Assume that Joe has a life-insurance policy that names his wife, Sandra, as the sole beneficiary. After they divorce,

Joe marries George, but forgets to take Sandra's name off the policy. Sandra argues that the fact that Joe did not change the beneficiary means that his intent was to allow his ex-wife to remain as the beneficiary. Many states agree with her. If, however, the state has a revocation-on-divorce statute, the divorce automatically revokes the designation of his ex-spouse as a beneficiary. This would mean that the proceeds of the policy would go into Joe's estate to be distributed according to his will or, if he died without a will, to whomever is designated by the state's intestacy laws, usually his surviving spouse (George) and his children, if any.[38]

Qualified Medical Child Support Order (QMCSO)

Health insurance is often critically important in a separation agreement between two spouses. To protect the children, a **qualified medical child support order (QMCSO)** can be sought. A QMCSO is a court order that medical support or healthcare benefits for the child of a working parent must be included under a group healthcare insurance plan at work. (See Chapter 10 for more on QMCSOs.)

ELECTIVE SHARE, DOWER, AND CURTESY

In common-law property states, the death of a spouse gave the surviving spouse important rights in the estate of the deceased spouse, sometimes in spite of what the deceased spouse intended or provided for the surviving spouse in a will:

- **Elective share**. The percentage of a deceased spouse's estate that the surviving spouse can choose (elect) to receive despite what the will of the deceased spouse provided for the surviving spouse.
- **Dower**. The right of a widow to the lifetime use (called a *life estate*) of one-third of the land her deceased husband owned during the marriage.
- **Curtesy**. The right of a husband to the lifetime use (life estate) of all the land his deceased wife owned during the marriage (if **issue** were born of the marriage).

Rights such as dower and curtesy have been abolished or substantially changed in most common-law property states, often replaced by laws establishing the right to an elective share. The separation agreement should make clear what happens to these rights upon divorce. The parties frequently insert a clause that each side **releases** all such rights in the other's property.

Note, however, that the rights of dower, curtesy, and elective share are not applicable in community-property states. The death of a spouse in a community-property state automatically gives the surviving spouse a one-half interest in the community property. There is no need for the law to protect the survivor through devices such as dower and elective share.

LEGAL EXPENSES

One spouse can be ordered by the court to pay the attorney fees of the other spouse in a divorce action. The parties may want to specify this in the separation agreement itself. They should consider not only the legal costs (attorney fees, filing fees, etc.) of a potential divorce but also the legal costs incurred in connection with the preparation of the separation agreement itself. Of course, if both have adequate resources of their own, the parties may agree (and the court will probably order) that they pay their own legal bills.

qualified medical child support order (QMCSO)
A court order to an employer to extend its group health insurance benefits to the child of one of its workers, even if the child does not live with that worker.

elective share
The percentage of a deceased spouse's estate that the surviving spouse can choose (elect) to receive despite what the will of the deceased spouse provided for the surviving spouse. Also called *right of election, statutory share*, and *forced share*.

dower
The right of a widow to the lifetime use (called a *life estate*) of one-third of the land her deceased husband owned during the marriage. (Owned means *fee simple*, the most complete form of ownership possible.)

curtesy
The right of a husband to the lifetime use (called a *life estate*) of all the land his deceased wife owned during the marriage (if *issue* were born of the marriage).

issue
A child and anyone else who has descended from a common ancestor. (See the glossary for another meaning.)

release
To formally give up or relinquish (a claim or a right).

NONMOLESTATION

nonmolestation clause
A clause in an agreement that the parties will not disturb, annoy, or harass each other.

Most separation agreements contain a nonmolestation clause, in which both parties agree, in effect, to leave each other alone. Specifically, they will not try to live with the other person, interfere with each other's lifestyle, or bother each other in any way. This does not mean that they cannot have any future contact. If, for example, one spouse has physical custody of the children, communication may be necessary in order to make or reschedule visitation arrangements.

MUTUAL MISTAKE

rescind
To cancel something. The noun is *rescission*.

Mutual mistake is a commonly used theory when a party wants to rescind a contract. If, for example, a seller and buyer are both mistaken on whether the violin being sold is a Stradivarius, the contract can be invalidated on the ground of mutual mistake. The principle also applies to separation agreements. Many states will allow a party to force a reformation of the separation agreement if the spouses operated under a substantial mutual mistake about something in existence at the time the agreement was negotiated. Reformation is an equitable remedy to correct a writing so that it embodies the actual intent of the parties. The party seeking to reform the agreement is asking for what is called a *do-over*. Here is how one court expressed the test for reformation:

reformation
An equitable remedy to correct a writing so that it embodies the actual intent of the parties.

> *For a party to be entitled to reformation of a contract on the ground of mutual mistake, the mutual mistake must be material, i.e., it must involve a fundamental assumption of the contract. A party need not establish that the parties entered into the contract because of the mutual mistake, only that the "material mistake . . . vitally affects a fact or facts on the basis of which the parties contracted."*[39]

For example, assume that the divorcing spouses negotiate the division of a specific number of shares that both believe are currently available from the husband's employer. Later, however, they find out that the number of available shares was substantially less than they both assumed to exist. On these facts, a court would probably hold that the property division could be reformed to reflect the actual number.

One New York reformation case involved the divorce of two prominent attorneys (Steven Simkin and Laura Blank) and the notorious Madoff Ponzi scheme. "The Simkin-Blank dispute riveted the state's matrimonial bar."[40] After a marriage of thirty-three years, Steven Simkin (a real-estate attorney) and Laura Blank (a labor attorney) obtained a divorce in 2006. In their separation agreement, they agreed to an approximately equal division of their marital property. They also agreed that the property would be valued as of September 1, 2004. The largest asset to be divided was the account in Bernard Madoff Securities. It was valued at $5.4 million as of September 1, 2004. Blank received half of this amount in cash from Simkin to cover her share of the Madoff account, which Simkin would keep in his name.

Several years later, Simkin's account all but disappeared when Bernard Madoff was convicted of running a multi-billion dollar fraud, called "the world's largest Ponzi scheme" by the media. Simkin, therefore, had given Blank $2.7 million in cash to cover her share of an account that never existed in the amount stated in the records provided by Madoff. Simkin then sued Blank for a reformation of the property agreement based on mutual mistake. He argued that when they negotiated the property agreement, both he and Blank were under the mistaken impression that the Madoff account, in fact, existed. The widespread publicity to Simkin's suit dismayed some observers: "The decision could open the floodgates for people who want to challenge agreements after they go sour," said a divorce lawyer not involved in the case. "Deals are done every single day based on assumptions about what things are worth. If the court allows this lawsuit to go forward, how can we be certain that deals will hold up?"[41]

The New York Court of Appeals denied Simkin's request for a reformation. The court said that only in exceptional situations should separation agreements be set aside for mutual mistake. The Madoff account existed at the time the parties negotiated the separation agreement. Simkin, in fact, withdrew some money from it to pay Blank. The mistake was as to the value of the account. This mistake is not a sufficient basis to warrant reformation. According to the court:

> This situation, however sympathetic, is . . . akin to a marital asset that unexpectedly loses value after dissolution of a marriage; the asset had value at the time of the settlement but the purported value did not remain consistent. Viewed from a different perspective, had the Madoff account or other asset retained by husband substantially increased in worth after the divorce, should wife be able to claim entitlement to a portion of the enhanced value? The answer is obviously no.[42]

ARBITRATION AND MEDIATION

Separation agreements often contain an **arbitration** clause, which provides that disputes arising in the future about the agreement will be arbitrated. Arbitration is a method of **alternative dispute resolution (ADR)** that seeks to resolve disputes without litigation. In arbitration, the parties hire an arbitrator, who will examine all the evidence and render a decision on the dispute. Normally, an arbitrator will be chosen from a professional organization, such as the American Arbitration Association (www.adr.org). A professional arbitrator, however, is not required. The parties can select a mutually trusted friend as the arbitrator. The agreement should specify who the arbitrator will be or how the arbitrator will be selected and who will pay the arbitration expenses.

Another ADR method is **mediation**. Unlike an arbitrator, a mediator does not make a decision. The mediator tries to guide the parties to reach a decision on their own in much the same manner as a labor mediator tries to assist union and management to reach a settlement. If mediation does not work, the parties either agree to submit the dispute to an arbitrator (in which case the two-step process is called **med-arb**), or they are forced to litigate the dispute in court. (For more on mediation and how it can be used elsewhere in the divorce process, see Exhibit 7.6 in Chapter 7 on divorce procedure.)

RECONCILIATION

What happens if the parties become reconciled to each other *after* they **execute** the separation agreement but before the divorce becomes final? They certainly have the power to cancel or rescind their contract so long as both do so voluntarily. If it is clear that they want to cancel, no problem exists. Legally, the separation agreement goes out of existence. The problem arises when the parties say nothing about the separation agreement after they reconcile and resume

arbitration
A method of alternative dispute resolution (ADR) in which the parties avoid litigation by submitting their dispute to a neutral third person (the arbitrator) who renders a decision resolving the dispute.

alternative dispute resolution (ADR)
A method or procedure for resolving a legal dispute without litigating the dispute in a court or an administrative agency. ADR methods include *mediation*, *arbitration*, and *med-arb*.

mediation
A method of alternate dispute resolution (ADR) in which the parties avoid litigation by submitting their dispute to a neutral third person (the mediator) who helps the parties resolve their dispute but does not render a decision that resolves it for them.

med-arb
A method of alternative dispute resolution (ADR) in which the parties first try mediation, and if it does not work, they try arbitration.

execute
To take needed steps to create a legal document. (See the glossary for an additional meaning.)

cohabitation. Then, sometime thereafter, the parties separate again, and one of them tries to enforce the separation agreement, while the other argues that it no longer exists. Courts handle such cases in different ways:

- In some states, the reconciliation will cancel the alimony or spousal-support terms of the separation agreement but will not cancel the property-division terms.

executory
Unperformed as yet.

- In other states, the reconciliation will cancel the **executory** (unperformed) terms of the separation agreement but will not cancel the terms that have already been performed.

The case is substantially different if a divorce judgment exists that orders the parties to pay alimony or to divide the marital/community property. The parties cannot cancel a court judgment simply by reconciling. They must go back to court and petition for changes in the judgment that reflect the resumed relationship.

✔ INTERVIEWING AND INVESTIGATION CHECKLIST

Have the Parties Reconciled?

LEGAL INTERVIEWING QUESTIONS

1. On what date did you both sign the separation agreement?
2. When did you stop living together?
3. Where did you both live when you were separated?
4. Was the separation bitter? Describe the circumstances of the separation.
5. After you signed the separation agreement, when did the two of you have your first contact? Describe the circumstances.
6. Have the two of you had sexual relations with each other since the separation agreement was signed? When? How often?
7. Did you ever discuss getting back together again? If so, describe the circumstances (e.g., who initiated the discussion, was there any reluctance).
8. Did you move in together? If so, where? Did one of you give up a house or apartment in order to live together?
9. During this period, did the two of you abide by the terms of the separation agreement? If so, which parts or clauses? Which parts of the agreement did you ignore after you got together again?
10. Did you discuss what to do with the separation agreement?
11. Did the two of you assume that the separation agreement was no longer effective?
12. After you came together again, did either of you continue abiding by any of the terms of the separation agreement?

13. Did either of you give back whatever he or she received under the terms of the separation agreement?
14. When you resumed the relationship, did you feel that the reunion was going to be permanent? What do you think your spouse felt about it?
15. Did either of you attach any conditions to resuming the relationship?
16. What have the two of you done since you came together again to indicate that you both considered each other to be husband and wife (e.g., did you both sign joint tax returns, make joint purchases, spend considerable time together in public)?
17. Do you have a written reconciliation agreement? If so, what are its terms?
18. Have you separated again? If so, describe the circumstances of the most recent separation.

POSSIBLE INVESTIGATION TASKS

- Interview people who are well acquainted with the parties to find out what they know about the reconciliation.
- Obtain any documents executed after the separation agreement was signed that may indicate the extent to which the parties did things together during this time (e.g., rent receipts with both of their names on them, opening or continuing joint checking or savings accounts).

Reconciliation usually means the full and unconditional resumption of the marital relationship; occasional or casual contact will not suffice. The intent must be to abandon the separation agreement and to resume the marital relationship permanently.

The reconciliation can be relatively spontaneous or it can be negotiated. If the latter, the parties may want to formalize the terms of their revived relationship in a written agreement. If they do so, the agreement is an example of a postnuptial agreement. (See Exhibit 4.1 in Chapter 4.)

COMPUTER HELP

Computer companies have designed software to assist the law office in managing the large volume of data involved in the negotiation of a separation agreement. For example, Exhibit 8.8 presents a screen shot from software that enters data for the negotiation of property division. For more on the use of computers in a family-law practice, see Appendix B.

EXHIBIT 8.8   Software Used for Data Entry in a Property-Division Negotiation (Divorce of Lisa and Michael)

	Marital Equity Totals			Marital plus Separate Equity (Net Worth)		
Lisa's	Michael's			Lisa's	Michael's	
$86,263 (48.41%)	$91,928 (51.59%)			$86,263 (46.87%)	$97,782 (53.13%)	

	Who keeps? (for personal items)	Lisa % of Marital	Lisa Amount of Marital	Lisa Amount of Total	Michael % of Marital	Michael Amount of Marital	Michael Amount of Total
Securities and Real Estate:							
Joint Acct 23876		39	2,810	2,810	61	4,394	4,394
Stock fund 19-04		0	0	5,692	100	0	0
Personal Items:							
Lisa's Car	Lisa		7,200	7,200		0	0
Michael's car	Michael		0	0		11,300	11,300
Residences:							
Main home		50	75,785	75,785	50	75,786	75,786
IRAs and 401(k)s:							
Michael's IRA 72		0	0	0	100	6,140	6,302

DEBT:					
	Who will Pay This Debt?	Lisa Marital	Michael Marital	Lisa Separate	Michael Separate
Debt:					
BigBank VISA	Lisa	5,224	0	0	0

Reprinted with permission of Family Law Software, Inc. (www.familylawsoftware.com).

EXAMPLE OF A SEPARATION AGREEMENT

Exhibit 8.9 presents an example of a separation agreement with margin commentary on some of the clauses.

EXHIBIT 8.9   Example of a Separation Agreement

(For several of the clauses, alternatives are presented to demonstrate additional drafting options for different facts.)

SEPARATION AGREEMENT

1. **Introduction.** Agreement between John Smith (Husband) residing at
_____, and Mary Smith (Wife) residing at _____,
dated March 13, 2019, made in County of Essex, State of _____.

2. **Date of Marriage.** John Smith and Mary Smith were married in the City of
_____ on June 22, 2005.

3. **Children.** There are two children of the marriage:

Jessica Smith (born 7/31/2007)

Gabriel Smith (born 7/29/2010)

They are the only issue of the marriage.

4. **Reason for Separation Agreement.** The parties are now living apart because of
irreconcilable differences between them. They intend to continue living apart. It is the
parties' intention to enter into and abide by this Agreement, which determines the
financial, property, child custody, and visitation rights and obligations, and other rights and
obligations, which arise out of their relationship.

5. **Parties Represented by Attorneys.** Each of the parties has retained counsel. Husband
is represented by Ellen Foley, Esq. with offices at _____, and Wife is
represented by Trevor Youst, Esq. with offices at _____. The parties have
been advised of their legal rights and obligations as well as the terms and legal effect of this
Agreement by their own counsel. On the advice of independent counsel, both parties agree that
this Agreement is fair, equitable, just, and reasonable, and fully accept its terms and conditions.

   [Alternative clause 5]

   5. **Representation by Attorneys.** Wife was represented by Trevor Youst, Esq. whose
   address is _____. Husband acknowledges that he was advised
   by Wife's attorney that he should seek independent counsel and that he has refused
   to do so, it being his belief that he can represent himself properly. Wife has been
   advised by her attorney of her legal rights and obligations and the legal effect of
   this Agreement. Both parties agree that this Agreement is fair, equitable, just, and
   reasonable, and fully accept its terms and conditions.

6. **Parties May Live and Work As If They Were Single.** The parties will live separate
and apart. Each will be free from the other's interference and control as if he or she were
single and unmarried. Each may reside where he or she desires. Each may engage in any
business, profession, or employment that he or she chooses.

7. **Separate Property of Each Party.** Each party owns the real and personal property that is
now in his or her possession or is in his or her name alone, regardless of when acquired,
free of any claim of the other. Such property shall be the separate property of each spouse.
(A list of this separate property is attached to this agreement as Attachment #1.) However,
any personal belongings or clothing of either party that is in the other's possession will be
returned as quickly as possible.

- *The early clauses of the agreement state its purpose and identify all family members involved.*

- *Clause 4 makes clear that the parties have already separated and intend to remain so. This helps counter an argument that the separation agreement is conducive to divorce.*

- *Clause 5 says that each party has his or her own counsel. It may be, however, that one party is paying the legal fees of the other party.*

- *The alternative Clause (5) makes clear why the Husband does not have his own attorney. The clause will help rebut a later possible claim by the Husband that he was pressured into signing the agreement and that he did not understand it.*

- *Clause 6 on interference and control is a nonmolestation clause.*

- *Clause 7 identifies the real property and personal property that will not be divided because it is separate property. (The marital home is treated elsewhere in the agreement—in Clause 24). Clause 7 refers to an Attachment to this agreement (Attachment #1) containing a list of the separate property of each party. Other attachments are referred to elsewhere in the agreement.*

(continued)

Exhibit 8.9 *(continued)*

[Alternative clause 7]

7. **Separate Property of Each Party.** Each party owns the real and personal property that is now in his or her possession or in his or her name, regardless of when acquired, free of any claim of the other. However, any personal belongings or clothing of either party that is in the other's possession will be returned as quickly as possible. The parties jointly own the garage at _____. The garage is in both of their names and they are jointly and severally responsible for the property. (A copy of the deed to the garage is attached to this agreement as Attachment #2.) The garage shall become the separate property of the Husband. The Wife will execute documents needed to transfer the garage into the Husband's sole name. Once the transfer is final, Wife will have no financial or legal responsibility for said garage.

- *The garage is marital/community property, but Alternative Clause 7 transmutes the garage into the separate property of the Husband. In exchange for this transmutation, the Husband may have granted the Wife something else in the agreement that she desired as part of the bargaining process.*

8. **Payment of and Liability for Debts.** All of the parties' outstanding debts are listed in Attachment #3. Husband will pay these debts. Debts incurred by either of the parties after the date of this Agreement will not be the other party's responsibility.

- *The Husband and Wife have decided not to divide the debts. Under Clause 8, the Husband has agreed to pay all outstanding debts listed in Attachment #3*

9. **Mutual Release of Claims.** The parties mutually release and discharge each other and each other's heirs, executors, administrators and assigns from any and all causes of action and claims that either has against the other, by reason of their relationship as husband and wife or for any other reason, except for any cause of action or claim arising out of this Agreement or for an absolute divorce.

10. **Release of Rights in Each Other's Estates.** Neither party has any right to share in the estate of the other (including the right of election) or to be appointed Executor or Administrator of the other's estate. Nor shall either party have any right of dower or curtesy in each other's estate. All testamentary gifts, if any, to each other are revoked upon the signing of this separation agreement.

- *Clause 10 gives up (releases) the right of election (the elective share) against the each other's will. It also releases other estate rights that might exist.*

11. **Execution of Additional Documents.** Each party will sign and deliver to the other any additional writing or document that is necessary to enforce or carry out the purposes of this Agreement.

12. **Custody of the Children.** Wife will have sole physical custody and sole legal custody of the parties' children during their minority, except as provided elsewhere in this Agreement.

13. **Right to Visit Children.** Husband may visit the parties' children subject to the conditions that follow.

   a. **Place of Visitation.** Visitation by Husband will take place away from Wife's residence.

   b. **Pick Up and Return of Children: Regular Meals During Visitation.** Husband will pick up the children at Wife's residence and will provide the children with regular meals during the visitation. Husband will return the children to Wife's residence upon the completion of visitation.

   c. **Limitation of Visitation.** Visitation is limited to alternate weekends, commencing at 10 A.M. on Saturday and terminating at 6 P.M. on Sunday.

   d. **Each Child to Be Visited at the Same Time.** All rights of visitation, including vacation visitation rights, will be exercised with both children at the same time except in the event of unusual circumstances such as one child's illness.

   e. **Summer and Vacation Visitation Rights.** In addition to other visitation rights, Husband has the right to visit with the children for 6 consecutive weeks during the children's summer vacation, provided Husband is also on vacation and provides continuous personal supervision of the children. Husband is not to exercise this right unless he gives Wife reasonable notice and provided it does not substantially interfere with the children's other urgent activities during this period.

- *Clause 12 gives the Wife the right to make all major decisions on the raising of the children. Other clauses contain some restrictions on this right: Clause 13m (on moving out of state); Clauses 13g and 18 (on the right to notice and consultation on medical and dental treatment); and Clause 19 (higher education costs).*

- *For additional and more comprehensive visitation schedules, see Exhibits 9.4 and 9.5 in Chapter 9.*

(continued)

Exhibit 8.9 *(continued)*

f. **Non-Interference with Children's Education and Religious Activities.** No visitation is permitted if in Wife's judgment it will interfere with the children's education or religious activities or adversely affect the children's health or general welfare.

g. **Notification of Illness or Accident.** Each party will promptly notify the other of any serious illness, accident, or other incident affecting one or both of the children.

h. **Notice of Intent Not to Visit.** Husband will notify Wife if he does not intend to exercise visitation rights or will be late for a visitation. The purpose of advance notification is to prevent disappointing the children.

i. **Nothing to Estrange Children.** Neither party will do anything to estrange the children from the other party.

j. **Names of Children.** The children are to continue to be known by their present given and family names even if either parent remarries.

k. **Use of the Term Father or Mother.** The parties will not permit the children to call anyone "Father" or "Mother" other than the parties to this Agreement.

l. **Right to Visit Confined Child or Children.** If a child is confined because of serious illness or injury, the party with whom the child is confined will allow the other to visit the child at reasonable times during the confinement.

m. **Neither Child to be Removed from the State.** Neither child will be taken outside of the State of _____ by either party without the other party's prior written consent.

14. **Support and Maintenance of Spouse: Fixed Sum.** Husband will pay Wife for her support and maintenance the sum of $3,000 each month (totaling $36,000 a year), starting May 1, 2019 and continuing on the first day of each month, thereafter subject to the reduction in Clause 15.

    [Alternative A for clause 14]

    14. **Support and Maintenance of Spouse: Fixed Annual Amount Subject to Increase Based on Net Taxable Income.** Husband will pay Wife for her support and maintenance the sum of $24,000 per year in equal monthly installments starting on May 1, 2019. If Husband's net taxable income as shown on his federal income tax return exceeds $200,000 in any calendar year, then the payment to Wife for the next calendar year will be 15 percent of the net taxable income instead of $24,000. Husband will deliver to Wife a true and complete copy of his tax return for the prior calendar year on or before April 16th each year.

    [Alternative B for Clause 14]

    14. **Support and Maintenance of Spouse Amount Determined by Adjusted Gross Income: Establishment of Floors and Ceilings.** Husband will pay Wife for her support and maintenance the sum of $24,000 each year in equal monthly installments starting May 1, 2019. Husband will pay Wife for additional support and maintenance a sum equal to 2 percent of his adjusted gross income as shown on his federal income tax return for the previous calendar year, no later than April 16th of each year. In no event will the total yearly payment be less than $30,000 or more than $40,000.

    [Alternative C for clause 14]

    14. **Support and Maintenance of Spouse: Lump Sum Paid Over Fixed Number of Years.** In full and final settlement of Husband's obligation to provide support and maintenance to Wife, Husband will pay Wife the sum of $100,000 on May 1, 2019. Upon payment, Husband shall have no further obligation to support Wife.

- *Because the Wife has sole legal custody (see Clause 12), she will decide whether the interference mentioned in Clause 13f exists.*

- *Clause 13i is sometimes called the nonalienation-of-affections clause (see Chapter 9).*

- *Clause 14 provides for permanent alimony (with a reduction provided for in Clause 15 and termination provisions in Clause 16). Permanent alimony is relatively rare. See Alternatives A to E for Clause 14.*

- *Alternative A for Clause 14 also provides for permanent alimony but with fluctuating payments based on the Husband's net taxable income.*

- *Alternative C for Clause 14 is for a lump-sum, which is also called alimony in gross.*

(continued)

Exhibit 8.9 *(continued)*

[Alternative D for clause 14]

14. **Support and Maintenance of Spouse: Three Fixed Payments Over First Three Years.** Husband shall pay Wife the sum of $99,000 for her support and maintenance in three equal annual installments of $33,000 each on the 15th day of April in each year commencing with April 15, 2019. Upon the payment of the last of such installment, Husband shall have no further obligation to support Wife. Should Husband or Wife die before the last of the aforesaid installments has been made, payment thereof shall cease. Wife shall have no claim upon Husband's estate for any unpaid installments if Husband dies before Wife. If Wife dies before Husband, Wife's executors, administrators, or heirs shall have no claim upon Husband for any unpaid installments. Should Wife remarry before the last of the aforesaid installments has been made, payment thereof shall cease and Wife shall have no claim upon Husband for the unpaid installments.

> • *Alternative Clause D is typical of alimony payments in that they cease upon the death of the payor or the payee. The parties have also agreed to cease payments in the event that the Wife remarries before that last payment is made.*

[Alternative E for clause 14]

14. **Support and Maintenance of Spouse: Increasing Fixed Installments Over Five Years.** Husband shall pay Wife the following sums for her support and maintenance: (a) The sum of $30,000 in the first calendar year in which this agreement is in force; (b) the sum of $25,000 in the second calendar year; (c) the sum of $20,000 in the third calendar year; and (d) the sum of $15,000 annually in each of the fourth and fifth calendar years. Each payment shall be made on the 1st day of January in each year commencing with January 1, 2020. Upon the payment of the last of such installments, Husband shall have no further obligation to support Wife. Should Husband or Wife die before the last of the aforesaid installments has been made, payment thereof shall cease. Wife shall have no claim upon Husband's estate for any unpaid installments if Husband dies before Wife. If Wife dies before Husband, Wife's executors, administrators, or heirs shall have no claim upon Husband for any unpaid installments. Should Wife remarry before the last of the aforesaid installments has been made, payment thereof shall cease and Wife shall have no claim upon Husband for the unpaid installments.

15. **Reduction of Spouse's Support and Maintenance Payments.** The amount to be paid for Wife's support and maintenance has been set at $36,000 annually because Wife is not presently employed and has no income or assets other than those described in this Agreement. Should Wife become employed at an annual salary in excess of $36,000 or receive annual income from any other source in excess of $36,000, Husband's obligation to pay support and maintenance will be reduced by 50 percent of Wife's excess annual income for each year that such excess occurs.

16. **Termination of Support and Maintenance Payments.** Payments for Wife's support and maintenance will terminate upon the occurrence of any of the following events:

   a. **Death.** The death of either party.

   b. **Remarriage.** Wife's remarriage even if such marriage is annulled or otherwise terminated.

   c. **Meretricious Relationship.** The establishment by Wife of a relationship with a third party in which they hold themselves out to be married (even if they are not) or in which they maintain a single abode and openly and notoriously live together in the manner of a husband and wife (even if they are not married).

> *Clause 16b seeks to prevent a revival of alimony if the Wife's second marriage is annulled or otherwise terminated. For more on revival, see Chapter 6.*

(continued)

Exhibit 8.9 (continued)

17. **Child Support.** Husband will pay to Wife in addition to the payments provided for Wife's support and maintenance, the sum of $18,000 annually, per child, for the support and maintenance of each child of the marriage. The payments are to be made in equal monthly installments on the 1st day of each month, starting May 1, 2019. Wife agrees that so long as Husband makes the foregoing payments on a timely basis, he will be entitled to the income tax exemption for dependents for each of the children.

18. **Children's Medical and Dental Expenses.** The payments by Husband to Wife for the children's support and maintenance do not include the cost of the children's medical and dental care. These are Husband's obligations and Wife will cause all bills from physicians, dentists, and other health care professionals and facilities to be sent to Husband. Wife will notify and consult with Husband before either child enters into elective medical or dental treatment, such as plastic surgery or orthodontic treatment.

19. **Costs of Children's Education.** The payments by Husband to Wife for the children's support do not include tuition payments to private schools or to colleges, universities, professional schools, or trade schools. Tuition payments of this nature will be made by Husband, provided Wife and Husband agree that any such education should be undertaken.

20. **Termination of Child Support.** Payments for the support of any child of the marriage will terminate upon the occurrence of any of the following events:

    a. **Reaching Majority.** The child reaches the age of 18 years, provided the child is not in full-time attendance in a college, graduate school, or professional or trade school.

    b. **Completion of Education.** The child completes his or her college education, including graduate or professional school, or completes his or her trade school course.

    c. **Marriage.** The child marries, even though the marriage is later annulled or otherwise terminated.

    d. **Permanent Residence.** The child establishes a permanent residence away from Wife's residence, provided the residence was not established to attend school or because of active military service.

    e. **Death.** The child or Husband dies.

- *As we will see in Chapter 10, all states have mandatory guidelines on the minimum amount of child support that parents must provide. Parents can agree to provide support above the minimum, but not below the minimum.*

- *In addition to the annual child support payments listed here, Clause 18 provides that medical and dental costs are to be paid by the Husband.*

- *See Clause 12 above on sole legal custody, which includes the right to make final decisions on medical and dental treatment. The Wife makes these decisions pursuant to Clause 12, but the Husband pays for them pursuant to Clause 18. Clause 18 gives the Husband the right to notice and consultation, but the final decision on such matters is the Wife's to make.*

- *Clause 19 presents an exception to the sole legal custody of the Wife. Normally, such custody gives the final decision on education to the parent with such custody. In Clause 19, however, the parties have agreed that certain educational decisions must be made jointly — each parent has a veto. Clause 13m on moving out of state contains another restriction on the Wife's sole legal custody.*

- *See Chapter 14 on emancipation, which allows a child to live independently of his or her parent or guardian.*

(continued)

Exhibit 8.9 *(continued)*

f. **Full-Time Employment.** The child obtains full-time employment, provided such employment is not engaged in only during school vacations or summer recesses. If the full-time employment terminates before the child reaches the age of 18 years, child support payments will resume.

21. **Method of Payment of Support and Maintenance.** All payments of support and maintenance for the spouse and children of the marriage will be by cash, money order, bank check, or certified check. When payment is made by mail, the envelope containing the payment will be posted at least 3 days prior to the date on which the payment is due, addressed to Wife at the address given above or such other address as she may advise Husband of, in writing, from time to time.

22. **Adequacy of Support and Maintenance Payments.** Wife acknowledges that the support and maintenance payments provided for her and those provided for the children are adequate and in keeping with the living standards maintained by the parties immediately prior to the date of this Agreement.

- *Despite Clause 22, the court will have the final say on whether the child-support clauses are adequate for the needs of the children.*

23. **Arbitration.** If the parties have any dispute regarding any provision of this agreement, the controversy shall be determined by arbitration before the American Arbitration Association (AAA) in accordance with its rules. Husband will pay the full cost of such arbitration. The selection of the arbitrator shall be at the sole discretion of the AAA.

- *Arbitration is one of the methods of alternative dispute resolution (ADR).*

24. **Transfer of Marital Residence to Wife.** As their marital residence, the parties presently own as tenants by the entirety the real property at _____. Husband will convey his interest in the property to Wife by quitclaim deed once the final divorce judgment of the court is issued. In addition, Husband will transfer to Wife the fixtures, furnishings, and personal property listed in Attachment #4.

   [Alternative Clause 24]

   24. **Disposition of Marital Residence.** The parties presently own as tenants by the entirety the real property at _____. Husband will pay the mortgage, property taxes, insurance and repairs on said property. Wife will have the exclusive use and occupancy of said property until the occurrence of any of the following events:

      a. **Vacating Premises.** Wife leaves the premises and sets up a permanent abode elsewhere.

      b. **Remarriage.** Wife remarries even though the subsequent marriage is annulled or otherwise terminated.

      c. **Meretricious Relationship.** Wife establishes a relationship with a third party in which they hold themselves out to be married (even if they are not) or in which they maintain a single abode and openly and notoriously live together in the manner of a husband and wife (even if they are not married).

      d. **Emancipation of Children.** Both of the children of the marriage are emancipated.

   Husband will not institute any action for partition of the premises or any other litigation that would or could terminate Wife's occupancy. Upon termination of Wife's occupancy in accordance with the provisions of this Clause, the parties will sell the premises upon the best terms possible. The proceeds of the sale will be distributed in the following order:

      (1) Payment of the expenses and costs of the sale, including attorney fees and broker's commissions;

      (2) Repayment to Husband for payment of the mortgage, property taxes, insurance, and repairs during Wife's occupancy;

      (3) The balance divided equally between the parties.

(continued)

Exhibit 8.9 *(continued)*

25. **Life Insurance Policies.** Attachment #5 lists the life insurance policies Husband will maintain in full force and effect insuring his life. Husband will maintain Wife as beneficiary of these policies so long as he is obligated to make support and maintenance payment to Wife. The children of the marriage will be maintained as contingent beneficiaries, or prime beneficiaries if Wife is removed as prime beneficiary, of the policies with equal interest so long as Husband is obligated to make payments for any of the children's support. Husband will have possession of the policies and will deliver to Wife proof of timely payment of all premiums when made. Husband represents that he has not pledged, hypothecated, or encumbered any of the policies and will do nothing to impair their full value.

26. **Income Tax Returns.** The parties will sign and file joint federal, state, and local income tax returns for the year in which this agreement is executed. Any tax due will be paid by Husband and any refund will be Husband's sole property. Husband agrees to hold Wife harmless from any losses suffered as a result of additional assessments of tax, fines, or penalties arising out of audits of any income tax return signed jointly by both parties at any time.

  - *Clause 26 protects the Wife by a hold-harmless clause.*

27. **Right to Sue for Divorce: Incorporation of Separation Agreement in Divorce Decree.** Neither party will be precluded from obtaining a divorce. If a divorce action is brought by either party, this Agreement may be offered into evidence and may be incorporated in any decree or judgment, but this Agreement will survive and will not be merged into such decree or judgment.

  - *Under Clause 27, the parties wish the separation agreement to be incorporated but not merged into the divorce judgment. The parties want the agreement to survive as a separate contract.*

28. **Modification of Agreement: Effect of Waiver.** This Agreement or any part of it cannot be amended or modified except by an agreement in writing, executed with the same formality as this Agreement. Any oral waiver by either party of a breach of any provision of this Agreement will not prevent that party from enforcing the provision thereafter. The failure of either party to insist upon the strict performance by the other party will not be construed as a future waiver or relinquishment of any such term or provision.

29. **Illegality or Invalidity of Part of Agreement.** If any provision of this Agreement is held to be illegal or invalid, such holding will not affect the other provisions, all of which will continue in full force and effect.

  - *Clause 29 is a severability clause. It states that if one clause is illegal or invalid, the other valid clauses will not be affected.*

30. **Governing Law.** This Agreement will be governed and interpreted in accordance with the laws of the State of _____.

31. **Entire Understanding.** This Agreement constitutes the parties' entire understanding. They acknowledge that there have not been and are not now any representations, warranties, covenants, or understandings other than those expressly provided in this Agreement. This Agreement is binding upon the parties' heirs, assigns, executors, and administrators.

32. **Filing of Agreement with Public Official.** This Agreement or a Memorandum of this Agreement may be filed by either party with the Clerk of Court, County of _____, State of _____.

33. IN WITNESS WHEREOF, the parties have set their hands and seals this 13th day of March, 2019.

_____ Wife

_____ Husband

[Acknowledgment]

Attachments (not included here):

Attachment #1. List of real and personal property that is the separate property of each spouse (see Clause 7)

Attachment #2. Copy of the deed to the garage (see Alternative Clause 7)

Attachment #3. List of outstanding debts (see Clause 8)

Attachment #4. List of fixtures, furnishings, and personal property at the marital residence (see Clause 24)

Attachment #5. List of life insurance policies Husband will keep in force (see Clause 25)

Reprinted from Vincent DiLorenzo and Clifford Ennico, Basic Legal Transactions, § 43:32. Separation Agreement (West Group, November 2010) with permission of Thomson Reuters.

ASSIGNMENT   8.12

Two members of the class will role-play in front of the rest of the class a negotiation session between spouses who want to enter into a separation agreement. They have two children, ages two and three. The role-players can make up the facts as they go along, e.g., names of the parties, addresses, and assets involved. Use the checklist at the beginning of this chapter as an overview of the topics to be negotiated. In the negotiation session, the role-players should not act hostile toward each other. They should be courteous but anxious to protect their own rights. Finally, they should not leave any matters unresolved; everything should result in some form of agreement through the process of bargaining and negotiation. After the negotiators have concluded the negotiation, the rest of the class can ask questions of the negotiators. The questions should ask for clarification on what has been negotiated and should ask the negotiators to negotiate topics that they have not yet covered.

Each member of the class (including the two role-players) will draft a separation agreement that is based on the facts negotiated in the role-playing session. The agreement should conform to the standards for an effective separation agreement outlined in Exhibit 8.1. (See General Instructions for the Agreement-Drafting Assignment in Appendix A.)

PARALEGAL ROLES

- For an overview of paralegal roles in family-law cases, see Exhibits 1.5 and 1.6 in Chapter 1.
- For all financial issues covered in Chapter 8, a paralegal may be asked to help collect documents and facts outlined in:
  - The checklist in Exhibit 3.1 of Chapter 3.
  - The interrogatories in Appendix C.
- Paralegals often have important roles in the separation-agreement phase of a divorce case. According to one paralegal: "The identification and evaluation of a marital estate is often more complex than one might think. One of my favorite things to do is review documentation provided by our client and received through discovery. I do the following:
  - Prepare a detailed chart of the parties' assets and debts.
  - Note any challenges, such as claims that certain assets or debts are premarital or the non-marital property of one party.
  - Note any disagreement in the valuation of certain marital assets, such as real property, collections, and antiques.
  - Determine the marital portion of investment and retirement accounts that the parties owned prior to the marriage.
  - Identify any deficiencies in documentation needed to present evidence at trial."[43]
- Other Paralegal Duties
  - Compile factual data to support client's need for rehabilitative alimony.
  - Compile factual data to support client's petition for a modification of alimony.
  - Identify lists of appraisers for the valuation of marital/community property.
  - Collect documents and relevant data needed by the appraisers for their valuation.
  - Categorize property as separate property or marital/community property. Keep the lists of such property updated.
  - Categorize debts as separate or marital/community.
  - Organize documents and fact sheets to be used by the attorney in negotiating the separation agreement.

SUMMARY

A separation agreement is a contract by married persons who have separated (or who are about to separate) that can cover support, custody, property division, and other terms of their separation and likely divorce. A major goal of the law office is to prepare an effective separation agreement that will avoid litigation. The first step is the collection of extensive financial and family information pertaining to everyone involved. Detailed checklists can be helpful in this effort. Spouses must have the legal capacity to enter into a separation agreement. The agreement is enforceable if there was sufficient mutual disclosure of assets and liabilities; there was no fraud, duress, or overreaching; the agreement is not unconscionable; neither party is about to become a public charge; and both parties had the opportunity to seek independent advice before they signed.

Alimony is money or other property paid in fulfillment of a duty to support one's spouse (or ex-spouse) after a legal separation, a divorce, and, in some states, an annulment. Property division is the distribution of community or marital property between spouses (or ex-spouses) after a legal separation or divorce. The law office needs to be aware of the alimony and property-division rules concerning bankruptcy, remarriage and death, cohabitation, enforcement by contempt, and modification. Unfortunately, alimony and property division are not always easy to distinguish. The distinction is based on the intent of the parties as evidenced by the labels, contingencies, method of payment, and the type of property transferred.

In general, Alimony is not favored by the courts. The trend is to have short-term or no alimony and to rely on property division as the main vehicle of resolving financial issues after divorce. When alimony is awarded, the primary factors courts consider are the financial resources of the parties, the time needed by the payee to become self-sufficient, the length of the marriage, the age and physical condition of the parties, and the responsibility to care for others, particularly young children.

Rehabilitative alimony is support payments to an ex-spouse for a limited time to allow him or her to return to financial self-sufficiency through employment or job training. Reimbursement alimony repays a spouse who worked or made other financial contributions during the marriage so that the other spouse could obtain training or otherwise enhance his or her future earning capacity.

In most states, courts have the power to modify an alimony award. When they have this power, they will exercise it if there has been a substantial change in circumstances of a continuing nature affecting the payor's ability to pay or the likelihood that the needy spouse will become a public charge unless a modification is ordered. The payor must not be using the change in circumstances as a pretext for avoiding the original alimony award.

Methods for enforcing an alimony award include execution, garnishment, fines, civil contempt (if incorporation and merger has occurred), criminal contempt, and the enforcement tools of IV-D agencies (if the custodial parent who is owed alimony is living with a child who is owed child support). Support debts cannot be discharged (forgiven) in bankruptcy. It might be possible to discharge a property-division debt in a Chapter 13 bankruptcy. The law of necessaries provides a method for a spouse (and child) to obtain support by making purchases of necessaries and charging them to the credit of the other spouse/parent. In a "Medicaid divorce," the parties end the marriage by divorce in the hope of sufficiently impoverishing the sick spouse so that the latter will qualify for Medicaid healthcare benefits.

The five stages of property division are (1) locating assets, (2) classifying them, (3) determining their value, (4) tax-effecting them, and (5) distributing them between the spouses. There are many different ways to classify property: real property, personal property, tangible property, intangible property, property received as a gift (or as a bequest, as a devise, or by intestate succession), solely owned property, concurrently owned property, separate property, marital property, common-law property, community property, quasi-community property, transmuted property, appreciated property, commingled property, etc. In most states, the governing law of property division is equitable distribution based on factors such as the length of the marriage and the contribution each made to the acquisition of the property. In most states, marital fault (who caused the break-up of the marriage) is not relevant to property division but economic fault (dissipation) is relevant. Special problems can exist in the division of a pension, degree/license, business, and goodwill. In most states, only marital/community property is divided. In a few states (called kitchen-sink states), however, separate property can be divided as well.

Other matters often covered in separation agreements include clauses regarding debts, taxes, wills, insurance policies, legal expenses, nonmolestation, and alternative dispute resolution (arbitration, mediation, and med-arb). Parties sometimes try to rescind or modify the separation agreement because of mutual mistake. If the parties reconcile, states differ on the legal effect of the terms of the separation agreement. If the divorce judgment contained court orders, the reconciled parties may have to return to court to have the orders adjusted or canceled.

KEY TERMS

separation agreement
divorce
legal separation
postnuptial agreement
intestate succession
DOS
outstanding
instruments
financial statement
payor
obligor
payee
obligee
cohabits
emancipated
physical custody
legal custody
noncustodial parent (NCP)
custodial parent (CP)
hold harmless
reconciliation
conducive to divorce
public policy
bigamy
collusion
migratory divorce
foreign divorce
capacity
at common law
arm's length
fiduciary relationship
fraud
material
duress
aggrieved
overreaching
unconscionable
public charge
legal malpractice
consideration
cohabitation
alimony
property division
creditor
debtor
transferor
transferee
interest
liquid
contingent
lump-sum payment
periodic payments
alimony in gross

dowry
family expense act
separate maintenance
palimony
permanent alimony
temporary alimony
Uniform Marriage and Divorce Act (UMDA)
rehabilitative alimony
incapacity alimony
caregiver alimony
reimbursement alimony
premarital agreement
irrevocable
arrears
escrow
surety bond
annuity
annuitant
trust
trustee
alimony trust
personal jurisdiction
continuing jurisdiction
incorporation and merger
rebuttable presumption
transsexual
execution
garnishment
civil contempt
criminal contempt
IV-D agency
Uniform Interstate Family Support
    Act (UIFSA)
discharged
nondischargeable
necessaries
spousal refusal
real property
personal property
account receivable
tangible
corporeal
intangible
gift
bequest
devise
concurrent
joint tenancy
right of survivorship
operation of law
tenancy by the entirety
tenancy in common
separate property

passive income
appreciation
passive appreciation
active appreciation
marital property
community property
common-law property
quasi-community property
transmutation
quitclaim
equitable distribution
dissipation
commingling
tracing
defined-benefit plan (DBP)
defined-contribution plan (DCP)
vested
expectancy
coverture fraction
qualified domestic relations order
    (QDRO)
alternate payee
present value
assign
restitution
unjust enrichment
implied-in-law contract
capitalization rate
goodwill
enterprise goodwill
personal goodwill
embryo
joint and several liability
indemnify
tax effect
testamentary
executor
elective share
dower
curtesy
issue
release
qualified medical child support order
    (QMCSO)
nonmolestation clause
rescind
reformation
arbitration
alternative dispute resolution (ADR)
mediation
med-arb
execute
executory

CHECK THE CITE

Under the separation agreement of Joseph and Ida Richardson, Joseph was obligated to pay alimony (maintenance) to Ida. When Ida hired someone to murder Joseph, he filed a motion in court to terminate his alimony obligation. Why did the court deny his motion? See *Richardson v. Richardson*, 218 S.W.3d 426 (Mo. 2007). To read the opinion online: (1) Run this search in Google or Bing: "Richardson v. Richardson" "No. SC 87641". (2) Run a citation search ("218 S.W.3d 426") in the "Case law" database of Google Scholar (scholar.google.com).

PROJECT

Parties contemplating or undergoing divorce might hire a large variety of experts and professionals (in addition to the attorneys who represent them). In Google, Bing, or Yahoo, run the following search: *aa expert divorce* (substitute the name of your state for aa in the search, e.g., Georgia expert divorce). Identify as many *different* kinds of such experts and professionals (other than attorneys) as you can. Give an example of each category of professional or expert, his or her Internet address, the services offered in divorce cases, and, if available, the cost for his or her services.

ETHICS IN A FAMILY LAW PRACTICE

You are a paralegal working at the law office of James & James. The law firm represents the husband in a divorce action. One of the largest assets in the marriage is the husband's pension. The wife's attorney, however, fails to inquire into the pension because this attorney mistakenly believes that pensions are not divisible as marital property. Because the wife's attorney does not mention it, the James attorney is silent about the pension. Consequently, the final divorce decree does not divide the pension. Any ethical problems?

WRITING SAMPLE

Interrogatories are written questions that parties can send to each other before trial in order to uncover facts that will assist them in preparing for trial. You are a paralegal in an office that is representing a wife (Diane Richardson) who is divorcing her husband (David Richardson). draft interrogatories that will be sent to the husband. When doing this task, focus only on financial assets of the husband. During the marriage, he owned in his own name a printing company, a bakery-donut chain, a car dealership, and a horse ranch. The husband now claims that he lost all of these assets due to gambling in Reno, Nevada. Your questions should be detailed. They should seek the financial aspects of his acquisition of these assets, their profitability, their management, and their alleged loss. (See General Instructions for the Writing Sample in Appendix A. See also the General Instructions for the Interrogatories Assignment in Appendix A.)

REVIEW QUESTIONS

1. What is a separation agreement?
2. What are some of the reasons that separation agreements can come before a judge?
3. What are the characteristics of an effective separation agreement?
4. What financial checklists are needed to prepare for the drafting of a separation agreement?
5. When is a separation agreement conducive to divorce?
6. What financial disclosure obligation does each spouse have when divorcing?
7. What is fraud and duress, and how do they affect the separation agreement?
8. When is an agreement unconscionable?
9. What is the consideration for a separation agreement?
10. What is the effect of bankruptcy, remarriage, death, and cohabitation on alimony and property-division obligations?
11. When can civil contempt be used to enforce alimony and property-division obligations?
12. When will courts modify an alimony award or a property division?
13. What are the income tax consequences of alimony and property division?
14. How will a court distinguish between alimony and property-division obligations?

15. What is alimony in gross, permanent alimony, and temporary alimony?

16. What criteria will a court use when deciding if alimony should be awarded according to the Uniform Marriage and Divorce Act (UMDA)?

17. How does a court determine the amount of rehabilitative alimony to be awarded?

18. When will a court award reimbursement alimony?

19. What is the role of marital fault in the award of alimony?

20. What are some of the main options spouses should consider when including alimony in their separation agreement?

21. How can an alimony obligation be enforced?

22. What are necessaries?

23. What is spousal refusal and a Medicaid divorce?

24. What are the five steps in the process of property division?

25. What is financial infidelity?

26. What is the distinction between real and personal property?

27. What is the distinction between tangible and intangible property?

28. What are the different ways that real and personal property can be acquired?

29. What are the different time periods that should be identified for every property that is acquired?

30. What is the distinction between sole ownership and concurrent ownership?

31. What are the main concurrent estates?

32. What are the ten categories of separate property?

33. What is the distinction between community property and common-law property?

34. What are the main cutoff dates used by states to determine when separate property is acquired?

35. What is a transmutation agreement?

36. How is property divided today in most common-law property states and in most community-property states?

37. What factors are considered in equitable distribution?

38. How does economic fault (dissipation) affect property division?

39. How is appreciation divided?

40. What is commingling, and how does it affect property division?

41. How are private pensions divided?

42. How are Social Security, military pensions, and other public pensions treated upon divorce?

43. How have the courts handled degrees and licenses upon divorce?

44. How is a business divided upon divorce?

45. What categories of goodwill can and cannot be divided?

46. How are tort awards divided?

47. How are debts divided?

48. What are the ways in which tax law can affect a divorcing couple?

49. What happens to wills upon divorce?

50. What happens to dower, curtesy, and elective share upon divorce?

51. What insurance options should divorcing parties consider?

52. How are legal expenses paid?

53. What is a nonmolestation clause?

54. How does mutual mistake affect a separation agreement?

55. What role can alternative dispute resolution (ADR) play in disputes after a separation agreement is entered?

56. How does reconciliation affect a separation agreement?

HELPFUL WEBSITES

Your State

See Appendix D for links to the family law of your state on the topics covered in this chapter.

Fifty State Summaries of Divorce Law

- www.law.cornell.edu/wex/table_divorce
- www.americanbar.org/groups/family_law/resources/family_law_in_the_50_states.html

Alimony

- www.divorcenet.com/topics/alimony
- mensdivorce.com/men-alimony-child-support-rise

Property Division

- www.divorcenet.com/states/nationwide/property_division_by_state
- www.americanbar.org/groups/family_law/resources/family_law_in_the_50_states.html

Bankruptcy and Divorce

- www.womansdivorce.com/divorce-and-bankruptcy. html
- divorceinfo.com/bkrcybankruptcy.htm

Valuing a Business

- sunbusinessvaluations.com

Association of Divorce Financial Planners

- divorcefinancialplanner.org

Asset Search

- www.assetsearchblog.com
- www.wife.org/ss-hiddenassets.htm

Sample Separation Agreements or Forms

- family.findlaw.com/divorce/sample-separation-agreement.html
- www.flcourts.org/core/fileparse.php/293/urlt/902f3.pdf
- www.rosen.com/divorce/divorceforms/sample-separation-agreement
- www.sampleforms.com/separation-agreement-form. html

Google Scholar (scholar.google.com)

- Choose "Articles" and enter in the search box any of the key terms discussed in the chapter. Add the name of your state to the search term.

- Choose "Case law" and "Select courts". Select your state, click "Done," and enter in the search box any of the key terms discussed in the chapter. Add the name of your state to the search term.

Google, Bing, or Yahoo

(on these search engines, run the following searches, substituting your state for "aa")

- "separation agreement" aa
- UIFSA aa
- marital agreement aa
- QDRO aa
- alimony aa
- pension divorce aa
- alimony trust aa
- equitable distribution aa
- property division aa
- community property aa

YouTube

Run the same searches on YouTube listed above for Google, Bing, Yahoo searches. Even when the video clips are trying to entice you to retain an attorney, buy a book, or enroll in a course, they can provide useful overviews and references to primary authority.

Twitter, Reddit, and Facebook

On Twitter, Reddit, and Facebook, run the following search (substitute your state for *aa* in your searches; run the searches with and without the name of your state). Look for links to family-law developments in your state.

- alimony aa
- property division aa
- separation agreement aa

ENDNOTES

Note: All or most of the court opinions in these endnotes can be read online. To do so, go to Google Scholar (scholar.google.com), select "Case law," and in the search box, enter the cite (e.g., "646 A.2d 195") or name of the case (e.g., "Grayson v. Wofsey") that is given in the endnote.

[1] See, for example, Financial Advantage, *Dollars of Divorce* (www.dollarsofdivorce.com).

[2] John DeWitt Gregory et al., *Understanding Family Law* 97 (3d ed. 2005).

[3] Mississippi State Bar, Family Law Section, *Consumers Guide to Divorce* 4 (1990).

[4] Liesl Schillinger, *Playing Fair at Divorce, Cheating on the Other Stuff*, N.Y. Times, Dec. 23, 2007.

[5] Richard Shweder, *Reader, I Divorced Her*, N.Y. Times Book Review, Apr. 4, 1999 at 9 (a review of John Taylor, *The Story of One Marriage*).

[6] Lisa M. Schaffer, *Legal Tips to Handle Marital Separation During Divorce* (blogs.findlaw.com), (November 21, 2018).

[7] *Grayson v. Wofsey et al*, 646 A.2d 195 (Conn. 1994).

[8] *Orr v. Orr*, 440 U.S. 268 (1979).

[9] Robert Oliphant & Nancy Ver Steegh, *Family Law* 235 (3d ed. 2010); Harry D. Krause & David D. Meyer, *Family Law in a Nutshell* 296 (5th ed. 2007).

[10] Jim Tankersley, *'Hurry Up and Get a Divorce'? For the Rich, There's an Incentive*, N.Y. Times, July 2, 2018 at B1.

[11] Uniform Marriage and Divorce Act, § 308(b)(1974) (www.uniformlaws.org) (see also www.law.cornell.edu/uniform/vol9).

[12] Alexandra Harwin, *Ending the Alimony Guessing Game*, N.Y. Times, July 4, 2011, at A17.

[13] Joanna Grossman, *Punishing Adultery in Virginia*, FindLaw (Dec. 16, 2003).

[14] Sarah O'Brien, *Same-sex Divorce Poses Complications for Some Splitting Couples*, CNBC, Your Money, Your Future (www.cnbc.com) (November 10, 2017).

[15] *Sex Change Does Not Void Alimony Pact*, Los Angeles Times (Mar. 29, 2007) (articles.latimes.com/2007/mar/29/nation/na-alimony29).

[16] Tina Moore, *Staten Island Belly-Dancing Wife who Lost Alimony Claim*, NYDailyNews.com (Apr. 17, 2011).

[17] Mari Schaefer, *Judge frees Pa. Inmate who Served Record Term for Delinquent Alimony Amount*, Pittsburgh Post-Gazette (Jul. 11, 2009) (www.post-gazette.com/pg/09192/983301-454.stm).

[18] Phillips, Nizer et al. v. Rosenstiel, 490 F.2d 509, 517 (2d Cir. 1973) (internal cites omitted).

[19] Anemona Hartocollis, *Full Wallets, but Using Health Care for Poor*, N.Y. Times, Dec. 10, 2010 (www.nytimes.com/2010/12/12/nyregion/12medicaid.html).

[20] Ibid.

[21] Jenna Goudreau, Is Your Partner Cheating on You Financially? 31% Admit Money Deception, Forbes (Jan. 13, 2011). Jennifer Schultz, *Financial Infidelity*, N.Y. Times, Feb. 26, 2011, at B5.

[22] American Law Institute, *Principles of the Law of Family Dissolution*, 8 Duke Journal of Gender Law & Policy 1, 20 (2001).

[23] Mickey Rapkin, *Where There's Gay Marriage Comes . . . The Rise of Gay Divorce*, Details (Oct. 2001).

[24] Anemona Hartocollis, *Real Estate and Rubble: When Marriages Go Awry*, N.Y. Times, Jul. 12, 2006 at B6.

[25] Liesl Schillinger, *Playing Fair at Divorce, Cheating on the Other Stuff*, N.Y. Times, Dec. 23, 2007.

[26] Associated Press, *Alone Together in Tough Times*, Los Angeles Times (Dec. 4, 2008) (articles.latimes.com/2008/dec/04/business/fi-divorce4).

[27] *Boyd v. Boyd*, 323 N.W.2d 553, 555-56 (Mich. Ct. App. 1982).

[28] Lynn Asinof, *Divorcing? Attend to the Nest Egg*, Wall Street Journal, Nov. 13, 2000, at C1.

[29] Social Security Online (www.ssa.gov/gethelp1.htm) (www.benefits.gov/benefits/benefit-details/4388).

[30] 10 U.S.C § 1408 (www.dfas.mil/garnishment/usfspa/legal.html).

[31] List adapted from Business Valuation Research, Inc., (www.bvalu.com).

[32] McNees Wallace & Nurick LLC, *Valuing a Closely Held Business in Divorce: Pitfalls and Best Practices*, www.jdsupra.com/legalnews/valuing-a-closely-held-business-in-88519 (2018).

[33] Jan Gabrielson and Stuart Walzer, *Surviving Your Own Divorce*, California Lawyer 76 (Jun. 1987) (emphasis added).

[34] *Jundt v. Jundt*, 2006 WL 917592 (Minn. Ct. App. 2006).

[35] Salvatore Arena, *Couple Must Be Sports in Ducat Split*, Daily News (Feb. 6, 1998).

[36] Alexandra Zissu, *After the Breakup, Here Comes the Joint-Custody Pet*, N.Y. Times, Aug. 24, 1999, at B1, B4.

[37] See, for example, California Family Code § 2605 (2018).

[38] Revocation-on-divorce statues were recently declared constitutional by the U.S. Supreme Court, which held that the statutes did not constitute an unconstitutional impairment of contracts such as insurance policies. *Sveen v. Melin*, 138 S. Ct. 1815 (2018).

[39] *True v. True*, 882 N.Y.S.2d 261, 263 (N.Y. App. Div. 2009).

[40] Peter Lattman, *Madoff Victim Seeks Divorce Do-Over*, N.Y. Times, May 31, 2011, at B1.

[41] Ibid.

[42] *Simkin v. Blank*, 968 N.E.2d 459, 464 (N.Y. 2012).

[43] Lori Froistad, *My Specialty: Divorce Law*, 27 Paralegal Today 60 (Apr./Jun. 2010).

CHAPTER 9

Child Custody

CHAPTER OUTLINE

CHAPTER OBJECTIVES

After completing this chapter, you should be able to:

- Know how child-custody disputes were handled in our early history.
- Identify the major kinds of custody.
- List the major factors parents must consider when negotiating the custody terms of a separation agreement.
- Describe possible roles for a BIA, a GAL, a CASA, and a PC in child-custody cases.
- Know the main factors a court will consider when resolving a custody dispute between two biological parents.

- Know why legal preferences are disfavored.
- State the nexus test on lifestyle and morality in custody decisions.
- List the major components of an effective visitation schedule.
- Know how a court will resolve a dispute between a noncustodial parent and a custodial parent who wishes to relocate out of the area.
- List the major enforcement remedies for the violation of a custody order.

- Know how a court will resolve a custody dispute between a biological parent and a psychological parent.
- Understand when a court will modify its own custody order.
- Know how a court obtains jurisdiction to modify the custody order of another state.
- Identify when a court will refuse to use the custody jurisdiction that it has.
- Describe how international custody disputes are resolved.

INTRODUCTION

Facing two women who both claimed to be the mother of a baby, King Solomon said, "Bring me a sword." So they brought a sword for the king. He then gave an order: "Cut the living child in two and give half to one and half to the other." When the first woman exclaimed that the other woman could have the child, King Solomon said, "Give the living baby to the first woman. Do not kill him; she is his mother." 1 Kings 3:24–25, 27 (NIV)

Researchers estimate that 40 percent of children have experienced or will experience the divorce of their parents.[1] Unlike the drastic King Solomon example above, in most divorce cases there is little or no dispute over who should have custody of the children. The parties often negotiate a mutually acceptable arrangement. When the parents agree on custody and visitation, they ask a court to approve the arrangement they devise. In the vast majority of cases, the court does so.

When there is a dispute, however, the process can be intense. Between 10 and 20 percent of all divorces are called high-conflict divorces, defined as "a divorce process that lasts longer than two years, which is characterized by a high degree of anger, hostility and distrust, intensive custody litigation, ongoing difficulty in communicating about the care of [the] children, and higher than usual rates of nonpayment of child support."[2] Custody cases can be so draining that some family-law attorneys refuse to take cases involving custody disputes. "They will do everything else, but not custody."[3]

Forced into King Solomon's ruling role, judges say that child custody is one of the most painful issues they face. "We are asked to play God, a role we are neither trained nor prepared for," lamented a family-law judge. In a Michigan case, the child tragically died in the midst of his parents' marital difficulties. This did not stop the rancor. The divorcing parents could not agree on who should control the disposition of their thirteen-year-old son's body. In a decision "reminiscent of Solomon," the judge ruled that if they could not agree on who should bury their son, he would order the body cremated and each given "half the ashes."[4] While not all cases are this bitter, it does demonstrate the level of hostility that is possible in divorce proceedings. In this chapter, we will explore the spectrum of child-custody cases, from those in which the parties are in agreement to those in which their disagreement is little short of open warfare.

In our early history, child-custody disputes were rare because the wishes of the father were almost always followed. Children were considered to be his property. If he wanted custody upon divorce, the courts gave it to him. A radical change occurred in the early nineteenth century, when almost all courts began awarding custody based on a determination of the **best interests of the child**.[5] The new standard, however, was controversial. Applying the standard, courts often concluded—aided by presumptions about child rearing—that it would be in the best interests of a child that the mother be awarded custody. Critics argued that a father-dominated system was being replaced by a mother-dominated one. Yet the best-interests-of-the-child standard remains dominant today when the custody dispute is between biological parents. These are among the themes we will be exploring.

best interests of the child
A standard used by a court to decide what would best serve a child's welfare when the court must make custody, visitation, adoption, guardianship, and change-of-name decisions.

TYPES OF CUSTODY

The two main categories of child custody are legal custody and physical custody. The following custody definitions will refer to two parents, although, as we will see later in this chapter, guardians who are not parents can sometimes have custody rights.

legal custody
The right to make the major child-rearing decisions on healthcare, education, religion, discipline, and general welfare. Also called *decision-making responsibility*.

physical custody
(1) The right of an adult to have a child reside with the adult. Also called *residential custody* and *custodial responsibility*. (2) Where the child is actually living.

custodial parent (CP)
The parent with whom the child is living; the parent with physical custody of the child. Also called *residential parent*.

noncustodial parent (NCP)
The parent who is not living with the child; the parent who does not have physical custody of the child. Also called *nonresidential parent*.

visitation
The right to have access to a child who resides with another. Some states prefer the phrase *parenting time* when the person "visiting" the child is the noncustodial parent.

sole physical custody
Only one parent has the right to have the child reside with him or her.

sole legal custody
Only one parent has the right to make the major child-rearing decisions on healthcare, education, religion, discipline, and general welfare.

joint physical custody
The right of both parents to have the child reside with each of them for alternating (but not necessarily equal) periods of time. Also called *shared physical custody*.

joint legal custody
The right of both parents to make child-rearing decisions on healthcare, education, religion, discipline, and general welfare. Also called *shared legal custody*.

split custody
A custody arrangement in which siblings are in the physical custody of different parents.

bird nesting
A living arrangement in which parents take turns living with a child who stays in the same home as the parents alternate moving in and out. Also called *nesting*.

coparenting
(1) Shared responsibility by two adults to raise a child, regardless of the marital status or sexual orientation of the adults. (2) Communication and cooperation by separate parents on the raising of their children.

- **Legal custody** is the right to make the major child-rearing decisions on healthcare, education, religion, discipline, and general welfare.
- **Physical custody** is the right of an adult to have a child reside with the adult. When a court grants a parent physical custody, that parent is given the right to have the child live with him or her. The parent with physical custody is called the **custodial parent (CP)**. The other parent is the **noncustodial parent (NCP)**. Although the child lives with the CP, the NCP often has **visitation**, which is the right to have access to a child who resides with another.

If only one parent is granted both kinds of custody, he or she has **sole physical custody** and **sole legal custody**. Such phrases are more accurate than the phrase *sole custody*. If you are told that a parent has sole custody, you need to determine whether this includes physical *and* legal custody.

If *both* parents are granted physical and legal custody, they have *joint physical custody* and *joint legal custody*. These phrases are more accurate than the phrase *joint custody*. If you are told that parents have joint custody or that they share the task of parenting, you need to determine whether this includes both physical custody and legal custody. **Joint physical custody** means that the child spends alternating, but not necessarily equal, periods of time in the homes of the parents. **Joint legal custody** means that both parents must agree on the major child-rearing decisions such as where the child will go to school or whether a child will have a medical operation.

> *Grace and Peter Teller are divorced parents of ten-year-old Mary Teller. Under the terms of a separation agreement (that was approved by the divorce court), Mary lives year-round with Grace. Peter lives in a different state, one hundred miles away. He visits Mary several times a year when he is in town, and she spends two weeks a year during the summer at his home. Grace and Peter regularly talk on the phone about all the major decisions in Mary's life. No decision is made unless both agree.*

In this example, Grace and Peter have joint legal custody, and Grace has sole physical custody.

Let's examine some additional custody terms. When parents have more than one child, courts try to place all the children with the same parent in order to encourage sibling bonding. If this is not possible, the custody arrangement in which siblings are placed with different parents is called **split custody**. When parents have joint physical custody, the child usually alternates living with each parent. If the child stays in one home and the parents take turns living with the child in that home, the arrangement is called **bird nesting**.

Coparenting is shared responsibility by two adults to raise a child, regardless of the marital status or sexual orientation of the adults. (More generally, many courts use the term coparenting to mean communication and cooperation by separate parents on the raising of their children.)

States do not always use the same terminology for custody. In a few states, for example, the word *conservatorship* is used in place of *custody*, and the person with primary responsibility for raising the child is called the *managing conservator*. Some states prefer the phrase *parenting plan* or *coparenting plan* to the phrase *custody arrangement*. And some states prefer the phrase *parenting time* to the word *visitation* when the visiting parent is not the custodial parent.

Finally, it should be pointed out that these categories of custody could be somewhat fluid in spite of the living arrangement that the parents originally agreed upon or that a court imposed on them. For example, a mother and father may have joint physical and joint legal custody but the father's involvement with the children may gradually decrease. After a while, the mother may find herself making all the child-rearing decisions on her own and living with the child full-time. In another example, circumstances may force a father's visitation to become much more extensive than originally contemplated or authorized. He might take over the roles of sole physical and sole legal custodian when the mother becomes ill. Such rearranging often occurs without formal changes in the custody clauses of the original separation agreement. Unless child support becomes an issue, the courts may never become aware of these informal adjustments.

We turn now to the custody decision itself—both when the parties are able to reach agreement in their separation agreement, and when the custody decision is forced upon them because of their inability to agree.

SEPARATION AGREEMENT

In most cases, divorcing parents work out a mutually acceptable child-custody arrangement in the **separation agreement** that they will present to the court for approval.

separation agreement
A contract by married persons who have separated (or who are about to separate) that can cover support, custody, property division, and other terms of their separation and likely divorce. Also called *marital settlement agreement (MSA)*.

REACHING A MUTUALLY ACCEPTABLE CUSTODY DECISION

In attempting to negotiate the custody clauses of a separation agreement, the parties have many factors to consider:

- The kind of custody they want.
- The age and health of the child.
- The age and health of the parents. Which parent is physically and mentally more able to care for the child on a day-to-day basis?
- The parent with whom the child has spent the most time up to now. With whom are the emotional attachments the strongest?
- Which parent must work full-time?
- The availability of back-up assistance (e.g., from grandparents or close friends who can help in emergencies).
- The availability of daycare facilities.
- The visitation schedule of the noncustodial parent (NCP).
- Whether the custodial parent (CP) can move with the child out of the area.
- How decisions will be made on the child's medical care, schooling, religious upbringing, discipline, and other general welfare matters. Must one parent consult the other on such matters? Is consultation enough or is joint consent needed? Is obtaining such consent practical?
- Whether the child's surname will be changed if the mother remarries.
- Who will receive custody of a minor child if both parents die?
- If disputes arise between the parents concerning custody, how are they to be resolved? Informal discussions? Arbitration? Mediation?
- Do the parties agree to encourage the child to respect and love both parents?

Unfortunately, parents do not always give priority to the welfare of the child when negotiating the custody terms of the separation agreement. For example, a father's request for joint custody may be no more than a bargaining chip to pressure the mother to agree to a property settlement that favors him. If she agrees to the property settlement he wants, he may no longer challenge the sole custody she wants.

JOINT PHYSICAL CUSTODY AND JOINT LEGAL CUSTODY

The most common custody arrangement worked out by the parties is sole physical custody and sole legal custody with the mother and visitation for the father.

Parents do not often use joint physical custody. If the child is constantly changing households, the impact can be disruptive. Joint physical custody might work if the child is very young, the parents live close to each other, and the parents are relatively affluent. In most cases, however, such custody is not practical. Also, if either of the parties applies for public assistance, joint physical custody might raise questions about eligibility. For example, under the federal program **Temporary Assistance for Needy Families (TANF)**, benefits may depend in part on having an eligible child in the home. A parent may have difficulty meeting this requirement if the child spends long alternating periods with the other parent.

In contrast, joint legal custody is more common. In approximately 20 percent of separations and divorces, the parents have joint legal custody, with one parent having sole physical custody.[6] Some states use a **presumption** that joint legal custody is in the best interests of the child and should be ordered unless the facts of the case demonstrate that this arrangement would not work. Advocates of joint custody claim that it is psychologically the healthiest alternative for the child. It arguably produces the following:

- Less hostility between parents.
- Less hostility between child and individual parent.
- Less confusion in values for the child.
- Less sexual stereotyping of parental roles (one parent "works," the other raises the children).
- Less manipulation of the child by one or both parents.
- Less manipulation of one or both parents by the child.

Joint custody arrangements also dramatically increase the likelihood that child support will be consistently paid.

Critics, however, point out that joint custody will work only in exceptional circumstances. The parents have just separated. In this environment, it is often doubtful that they will be able to cooperate in the manner called for by a joint-legal-custody arrangement. A study of seven hundred divorce cases in one state concluded that couples with joint legal custody are more than twice as likely to reopen lawsuits over childcare arrangements than couples where only one parent had custody. In addition, it is by no means clear that a child is more likely to be better off when living under a joint-custody arrangement. Some studies have found no significant difference in a child's development under joint custody and under more traditional sole-custody arrangements.[7]

The following questions cover factors that are relevant to a decision on whether joint legal custody will work. Answers to any one of the following questions might tip the scale either way on whether joint legal custody is feasible:

- Is each parent fit and mentally stable?
- Do both parents agree to joint legal custody, or is one parent hesitant?
- Have the parents demonstrated that they are able to communicate at least to the extent necessary to reach shared decisions in the child's best interests?
- Is joint custody in accord with the child's wishes (if mature enough to state a preference), or does the child have strong opposition to such an arrangement?

Temporary Assistance for Needy Families (TANF)
The federal-state welfare program (42 U.S.C. § 601) that replaced Aid to Families with Dependent Children (AFDC). Unlike AFDC, benefits under TANF are limited to five years.

presumption
An assumption or inference that a certain fact is true once another fact is established. (Here, once it is clear that there are two capable parents, an assumption is raised that they both should have legal custody.)

COURT GUIDELINES FOR PARENTS

In contested custody cases, many courts require the parties to attend parenting classes. (Some states mandate such classes for all divorcing parties with children even if they have reached agreement on the custody issues.) For example, a county family-law court might require attendance at a four-hour seminar on how parents can help their children cope with separation and visitation. Using video and role-playing, the seminar emphasizes the emotional harm that fighting parents can continue to inflict on their children.

Most courts have guidelines they distribute to the parties on the effect of divorce on children, how to make coparenting work after divorce, and how to resolve disputes that arise under an approved custody arrangement. Sometimes, these guidelines are made part of the court's custody decree. For an example of parental guidelines, see Exhibit 9.1, which is written on the assumption that the mother is awarded custody.

contested
Challenged; opposed or disputed.

EXHIBIT 9.1   Court Guidelines for Parents

Relation toward Children

Although the court has the power to dissolve the bonds of matrimony, the court does not have the power to dissolve the bonds that exist between you, as parents, and your children. Both of you, therefore, are to continue your responsibility to emotionally support your children. You are to cooperate in the duty and right of each other to love those children. By love, the court means the training, the education, the disciplining, and motivation of those children. Cooperation means to present the other party to the children with an attitude of respect either for the mother or for the father. Neither of you should downplay, belittle, or criticize the other in the presence of those children because you may emotionally damage your children and foster a hatred for the demeaned parent. It is of utmost importance that you both recognize your children's right to love both parents without fear of being disloyal to either one of you.

In support of this admonition, the courts have drafted written guidelines on your future conduct relating to the best interests of your children. I sincerely urge that you preserve them, periodically read them, and always be guided by them.

Guidelines for Separated Parents

As you know, your children are usually the losers when their parents separate. They are deprived of full-time, proper guidance that two parents can give—guidance and direction essential to their moral and spiritual growth.

It is highly desirable that you abstain from making unkind remarks about each other. Recognize that such remarks are not about a former spouse but are about a parent of your children. Such comments reflect adversely upon the children.

It is urged that both parties cooperate to the end that mutual decisions concerning the interest of the children can be made objectively. Parents should remember that the mother, who has custody, should urge the children to find time to be with the father and encourage them to realize that their father has affection for them and contributes to their support. The father should recognize that his plans for visitation must be adjusted from time to time in order to accommodate the planned activities of the child. Visitation should be a pleasant experience rather than a duty. Cooperation in giving notice and promptness in maintaining hours of visitation are important to avoid ruffled feelings.

Although there is probably some bitterness between you, it should not be inflicted upon your children. In every child's mind there must and should be an image of two good parents. Your future conduct with your children will be helpful to them if you will follow these suggestions.

I. *Do Not's*

a. Do not poison your child's mind against either the mother or father by discussing their shortcomings.
b. Do not use your visitation as an excuse to continue the arguments with your spouse.
c. Do not visit your children if you have been drinking.

II. *Do's*

a. Be discreet when you expose your children to anyone with whom you may be emotionally involved.
b. Visit your children only at reasonable hours.

(continued)

Exhibit 9.1 *(continued)*

c. Notify your spouse as soon as possible if you are unable to keep your visitation. It's unfair to keep your children waiting—and worse to disappoint them by not coming at all.

d. Make your visitation as pleasant as possible for your children by not questioning them regarding the activities of your spouse and by not making extravagant promises that you know you cannot or will not keep.

e. Minimize the amount of time the children are in the care of strangers and relatives.

f. Always work for the spiritual well-being, health, happiness and safety of your children.

III. *General*

a. The parent with whom the children live must prepare them both physically and mentally for the visitation. The children should be available at the time mutually agreed upon.

b. If one parent has plans for the children that conflict with the visitation and these plans are in the best interests of the children, be adults and work out the problem together.

c. Arrangements should be made through visitation to provide the mother with some time "away" from the family. She needs the time for relaxation and recreation. Upon her return, she will be refreshed and better prepared to resume her role as mother and head of the household. Therefore, provide for extended periods of visitation such as weekends and vacations.

Bill of Rights for Children in a Divorce Action

1. The right to be treated as important human beings, with unique feelings, ideas, and desires and not as a source of argument between parents.

2. The right to a continuing relationship with both parents and the freedom to receive love from and express love for both.

3. The right to express love and affection for each parent without having to stifle that love because of fear of disapproval by the other parent.

4. The right to know that their parents' decision to divorce is not their responsibility and that they will live with one parent and will visit the other parent.

5. The right to continuing care and guidance from both parents.

6. The right to honest answers to questions about the changing family relationships.

7. The right to know and appreciate what is good in each parent without one parent degrading the other.

8. The right to have a relaxed, secure relationship with both parents without being placed in a position to manipulate one parent against the other.

9. The right to have the custodial parent not undermine visitation by suggesting tempting alternatives or by threatening to withhold visitation as a punishment for the children's wrongdoing.

10. The right to be able to experience regular and consistent visitation and the right to know the reason for a cancelled visit.

Source: Dane County Family Court, Madison, Wisconsin. See also familycourtservices.countyofdane.com/documents/PDFs/FC-ResourceBooklet.pdf.

---

mediation
A method of alternative dispute resolution (ADR) in which the parties avoid litigation by submitting their dispute to a neutral third person (the mediator) who helps the parties resolve their dispute but does not render a decision that resolves it for them.

mandatory
Required; commanded.

alternative dispute resolution [ADR]
A method or procedure for resolving a legal dispute without litigating the dispute in a court or administrative agency. ADR methods include *mediation*, *arbitration*, and *med-arb*.

CONTESTED CUSTODY

Parties who are able to agree on custody and visitation submit their plan to the court in writing, usually in the separation agreement. The court will approve the plan if it determines that the plan is in the best interests of the child. If, however, the parties cannot agree, or if the court determines that what they agreed to is not in the best interests of the child, a custody decision will be imposed on them by the court.

Often, the first step is for the court to require that the parents try **mediation**, where they will attempt to reach an agreement on a workable custody plan they both can support. Mediation is **mandatory** if it is ordered by the court. (Mediation is a form of **alternative dispute resolution [ADR]** that seeks the resolution of legal disputes without litigation.) In mandatory mediation, the mediator is a private citizen or a government employee, often in the family services division of the court, who meets with the parents to try to help them reach an agreement. The mediator does not force a decision on them. Although mediators may ultimately recommend a custody/visitation arrangement to the court, the primary objective of mediation is to pressure the parents to reach their own agreement, which they can take before the judge for approval. For an example of a mediation session, see Exhibit 7.6 in Chapter 7.

Throughout the divorce process, the parents are represented by their respective attorneys. In addition, most states have the power to appoint *separate* counsel for the child who will act independently of the attorneys for the parents. If the child is mature enough to express him- or herself, the child's attorney will perform traditional advocacy functions on behalf of and in consultation with the child. For children who do not have this level of maturity, the court may have the power to appoint what is called a **best interests attorney (BIA)**. A BIA is an attorney who provides legal representation for a child to protect the child's best interests without being bound by the child's directives or objectives.[8] The court may also have the power to appoint a **guardian ad litem (GAL)**. A GAL is an individual appointed to appear in court on behalf of a minor. An example of a function the court might assign to a GAL is to investigate the child's home environment. Often, the GAL is an attorney, although in some states, it can be a nonattorney, such as a social worker.

Finally, as we saw in Chapter 1, many courts can appoint a **court appointed special advocate (CASA)**. A CASA is a volunteer who undertakes special tasks, such as interviewing caregivers and relatives in order to recommend placement/treatment options for the child. A CASA does not have to be an attorney. Paralegals sometimes volunteer for this role.

In some custody cases, the parties use the services of a **parenting coordinator** to assist them in resolving custody disputes that arise under the parenting plan. (Parent coordinating is another method of alternative dispute resolution (ADR).) Here is how the Association of Family and Conciliation Courts describes the role:

> Parenting coordination is a child-focused alternative dispute resolution process in which a mental health or legal professional with mediation training and experience assists high conflict parents to implement their parenting plan by facilitating the resolution of their disputes in a timely manner, educating parents about children's needs, and with prior approval of the parties and/or the court, making decisions within the scope of the court order or appointment contract.[9]

As valuable as such individuals can be in child-custody cases, it is important to understand their limitations. For example, the **attorney-client privilege** does not apply to nonattorneys who are acting in coordinator or investigative roles unless special legislation exists that extends the privilege to them. An employee (e.g., paralegal) of an attorney representing a party *is* protected by the privilege, but usually these other individuals are not. Hence, they can be subpoenaed to give testimony on what they heard the child or one of the parents say.

PARENT VERSUS PARENT

The ultimate decider on custody is the court. The court must approve the custody agreement worked out by the parents, or the court must make the decision for them if they are not able to agree. How does the court make this decision?

best interests attorney (BIA)
An attorney who provides legal representation for a child to protect the child's best interests without being bound by the child's directives or objectives.

guardian ad litem (GAL)
A special guardian (often, but not always, an attorney) appointed by the court to appear in court proceedings on behalf of a person who is a minor, is insane, or is otherwise incapacitated.

court appointed special advocate (CASA)
A volunteer (who can be an attorney, a paralegal, or other nonattorney) appointed by the court to undertake special assignments pertaining to children in the court system.

parenting coordinator (PC)
A professional who assists parents in resolving custody disputes that arise under a parenting plan.

attorney-client privilege
A client or a client's attorney can refuse to disclose any confidential (private) communication between them if the purpose of the communication was to facilitate the provision of legal services to the client.

First, we consider the custody decision when the dispute is between the two *biological parents* who cannot agree on custody. The standard used by the court, as we have seen, is the best interests of the child. We will examine this standard through the following themes (which are not mutually exclusive):

- Court discretion
- Parenting plan
- Stability
- Attitude on visitation
- Availability
- Emotional ties
- Parental alienation syndrome
- Career choice

- Wealth
- Legal preferences
- Morality and lifestyle
- Domestic violence
- Religion
- Race
- Wishes of the child
- Expert witnesses

COURT DISCRETION

Trial judges are given considerable discretion in making the custody decision, so much so that critics claim that custody decisions are often unpredictable and sometimes arbitrary. Unlike determining child support (see Chapter 10), there are no formulas the court can use to reach the custody decision. There are guidelines but no formulas. The best-interests standard is very broad. Inevitably, the judge's personal views and philosophy of life help shape his or her concept of what is in the best interests of a child (e.g., views on the traditional family, alternate lifestyles, working women, child discipline). Of course, a judge would never admit that he or she is following his or her own personal views and philosophy; judges are supposed to be guided by "the law" and not by their individual biases. In reality, however, they are guided by both.

PARENTING PLAN

parenting plan
A child-custody plan for separated parents covering living arrangements, decision making, finances, and communication.

The starting point in the custody process is the submission to the court of the proposed **parenting plan** of each parent covering living arrangements, decision making, finances, and communication. See Exhibit 9.2 for the components of a parenting plan. Of course, if the two plans differ, each parent will have to litigate the differences by presenting evidence showing that his or her plan is in the best interests of the child.

EXHIBIT 9.2   Components of a Parenting Plan

(1) Where and with whom the child will live (physical custody);

(2) Who will make child-rearing decisions on schooling, discipline, religion, health, and general welfare (legal custody);

(3) If the child has special needs (e.g., illness, learning disability), how these needs will be met;

(4) What the visitation schedule of the noncustodial parent (NCP) will be;

(5) How the parties will communicate with each other on custody matters such as rescheduling visits;

(6) Who will pay what expenses related to the components of the parenting plan; and

(7) How the parents will resolve child-rearing disagreements between them.

STABILITY

By far, one of the most important considerations is stability. Courts are inclined to award custody to the parent who will cause the least amount of disruption to the life of the child, who is experiencing upheaval and stress due to the divorce. The loss of a household with two functioning parents can be a shattering experience for children. They will need as much stability as possible in their living arrangement, schooling, religious practice, access to relatives and friends, and participation in activities of their cultural heritage. The court will scrutinize each parenting plan to assess how the plan proposes to maintain maximum stability and continuity in these areas. As a guideline in achieving this goal, some courts apply an **approximation rule**: the proportion of custodial time the child spends with each parent should approximate the proportion of time each parent spent performing caretaking functions for the child prior to the parents' divorce.[10]

approximation rule
The caregiving of parents in the post-divorce world should be in rough proportion to that which predated the divorce.

ATTITUDE ON VISITATION

Attorneys often advise clients seeking sole physical or legal custody to tell the court that visitation by the noncustodial parent (NCP) is important and that they will fully cooperate with the NCP to make visitation work. Judges like to hear parents say that they want their children to stay in contact with the other parent and want to isolate the children from the precipitating (and perhaps ongoing) marital problems between the soon-to-be divorced parents. Of course, if there has been domestic violence in the home, a parent would be understandably reluctant to endorse significant visitation by a parent with a history of abuse. Nevertheless, the attorney is likely to tell the client that courts are inclined to grant visitation rights even to parents who have been abusive. Hence, the attorney will often advise the client to try to express at least some support for restricted visitation, such as supervised visitation (see discussion of domestic violence below). If, however, the domestic violence has been substantial, the client is unlikely to be able to express such a sentiment.

AVAILABILITY

Which parent will be available to spend the time required to respond to the day-to-day needs of the child? To gauge availability, the court will want to know which parent in the past:

- Took the child to doctor's appointments.
- Met with teachers.
- Took the child to church, synagogue, or mosque.
- Helped with homework.
- Attended school plays with the child.
- Involved the child in athletic activities.
- Arranged and attended birthday parties.
- Arranged for baby-sitters when needed.
- Changed diapers.
- Took care of the child's bathing, grooming, and dressing needs.
- Purchased, cleaned, and cared for the child's clothes.
- Administered discipline and taught manners.
- Stayed up with the sick child during the night.
- Taught elementary reading, writing, and arithmetic skills.

These activities are sometimes referred to as *indicia of parenthood*—indications that the adult is actively involved in the nurturing and care of a child.

deposition
A method of discovery by which one party questions another party (or questions the other party's witness) usually outside the courtroom. The person questioned is called the *deponent*.

An office representing a parent seeking custody should make sure that he or she is able to answer questions, such as the following, during a **deposition** or on the witness stand during a trial:

- What is the name of the child's pediatrician?
- When was the last time the child saw the pediatrician and for what reason?
- What is the name of the child's dentist?
- When was the last time the child saw the dentist and for what reason?
- Does the child have nightmares? If so, about what?
- What television programs do you watch with the child?
- What is the name of one of the child's teachers? What does this teacher think are the child's strengths and weaknesses as a student?
- In what subject has the child received the best grade and the worst grade?
- What are the names of some of the child's friends at school?
- What are the names of some of the child's friends at home?

A parent who is at work most of the day may not be able to answer all of these questions from direct knowledge, yet a responsible and engaged parent would be interested enough in the child to seek answers to such questions by talking with the other parent and with the child. There is no law that requires a parent to know the answers to the questions, but being able to answer as many as possible bolsters the parenting plan proposed by a parent.

Immediately after the separation, it is common for one of the parents to have temporary custody. Upon filing for divorce, the court will formally order a temporary-custody arrangement (including a decision on visitation) pending the final court proceeding, which may take place months later. During this interval, the court will inquire into the amount and kind of contact each parent had with the child. Again, the above list of questions becomes important, particularly with respect to the parent who moved out. How much time has this parent spent with the child? Have birthday cards, text messages, and gifts been sent? What about visits, telephone calls, Skype calls, and email messages? To what extent has this parent gone out of his or her way to be with the child?

EMOTIONAL TIES

Closely related to time availability is the emotional relationship that has already developed between a parent and child and the future prospects for this development. Which parent has been sensitive or insensitive to the psychological crisis that the child has experienced and will probably continue to experience because of the divorce? Of particular importance is the extent to which one parent has tried and succeeded in fostering the child's love for the *other* parent. Often, a qualification to become a custodial parent (CP) is the ability and inclination to cooperate in arranging visitations by the noncustodial parent (NCP). Hence, a major issue will be which parent can separate his or her own needs and lingering bitterness from the need of the child to maintain emotional ties with both parents.

A number of other factors are relevant to the emotional needs of the child:

- *Education.* The level of a parent's education may be some indication of the parent's ability to cope with difficult emotional needs of a child.
- *Psychological health.* Has the parent been in therapy for any reason? Has it been helpful? What is the parent's attitude about seeking such help? Positive? Realistic? Does the parent think that the *other* parent is the only one who needs help?
- *Work history.* How stable has the parent been in his or her work history?

- *Parenting norms.* What are the parent's views on discipline, TV watching, computer and video games, cell phones, texting, studying, religious activities, cleaning the child's room, etc.?

- *Siblings.* How do siblings get along in the home?

- *General home and neighborhood environment.* Are there cramped apartment conditions? What is the residential area like? Is there easy accessibility to school, friends, and recreational facilities?

Also, does the parent seeking sole custody plan to move from the area? If so, into what kind of environment? How will the proposed move affect the other parent's ability to visit the child? Depending upon the circumstances of the case, a court might award custody to a parent on condition that he or she *not* move out of a designated area without the consent of the other parent. We will return to the issue of parental relocations when we cover modification of custody orders.

PARENS PATRIAE

Parens patrae is the authority of the state to protect children and others in the state who suffer from a disability. The case of *Schultz v. Schultz* demonstrates how a court uses parens patriae to further the objectives we have been discussing on the issue of child custody.

parens patrae
"Parent of the country;" referring to the state's role in protecting children and others in the state who suffer from a disability.

CASE | Schutz v. Schutz
581 So. 2d 1290 (1991)
Supreme Court of Florida

Background: *Following a divorce, custody of the children was given to the mother, Laurel Schutz (the petitioner). When the trial court became concerned that the children had negative feelings about their father, Richard R. Schutz, (the respondent), it ordered Laurel to do everything in her power to create in the minds of the children a loving feeling toward their father. Laurel objected that this interfered with her First Amendment free speech rights and appealed. The case is now on appeal before the Supreme Court of Florida.*

Decision on Appeal: *Judgment affirmed. The state (as parens patriae) has an interest in protecting children and was properly pursuing this interest by encouraging meaningful contact between the children and their father.*

OPINION OF THE COURT:

Justice KOGAN delivered the opinion of the court. . . .

[T]he petitioner contends [that the order] requires her to affirmatively express feelings and beliefs which she does not have in violation of her first amendment right of free expression. . . . A final judgment dissolving the six-year marriage of petitioner, Laurel Schutz (mother) and respondent, Richard R. Schutz (father) was entered by the trial court on November 13, 1978. Although custody of the parties' minor children was originally granted to the father, the final judgment was later modified in 1979. Under the modified judgment, the mother was awarded sole custody of the children, and the father was both granted visitation rights and ordered to pay child support.

As noted by the trial court, the ongoing "acrimony and animosity between the adult parties" is clear from the record. The trial court found that in February 1981 the mother moved with the children from Miami to Georgia without notifying the father. After moving, the mother advised the father of their new address and phone number. Although the father and children corresponded after the move, he found an empty house on the three occasions when he traveled to Georgia to visit the children. The father was not notified that after only seven months in Georgia the mother and children had returned to Miami. Four years later in 1985, upon discovering the children's whereabouts, the father visited the children only to find that they "hated, despised, and feared" him due to his failure to support or visit them. After this visit, numerous motions concerning visitation, custody and support were filed by the parties.

After a final hearing on the motions, the trial court found that "the cause of the blind, brainwashed, bigoted belligerence of the children toward the father grew from the soil nurtured, watered and tilled by the mother." The court further found that "the mother breached every duty she owed as the custodial parent to the non-custodial parent of instilling love, respect and feeling in the children for their father." The trial court's findings are supported by substantial competent evidence.

Based on these findings, the trial court ordered the mother "to do everything in her power to create in the minds of [the children] a loving, caring feeling toward the father . . . [and] to convince the children that it is the mother's desire that they see their father

(continued)

and love their father." The court further ordered that breach of the obligation imposed "either in words, actions, demeanor, implication or otherwise" would result in the "severest penalties . . . , including contempt, imprisonment, loss of residential custody or any combination thereof.". . .

We begin our analysis by noting our agreement with the district courts of appeal that have found a custodial parent has an affirmative obligation to encourage and nurture the relationship between the child and the noncustodial parent. See *Gardner v. Gardner,* 494 So. 2d 500, 502 (Fla. 4th DCA 1986); *In re Adoption of Braithwaite,* 409 So. 2d 1178, 1180 (Fla. 5th DCA 1982). This duty is owed to both the noncustodial parent and the child. This obligation may be met by encouraging the child to interact with the noncustodial parent, taking good faith measures to ensure that the child visit and otherwise have frequent and continuing contact with the noncustodial parent and refraining from doing anything likely to undermine the relationship naturally fostered by such interaction.

Consistent with this obligation, we read the challenged portion of the order at issue to require nothing more of the mother than a good faith effort to take those measures necessary to restore and promote the frequent and continuing positive interaction (e.g., visitation, phone calls, letters) between the children and their father and to refrain from doing or saying anything likely to defeat that end. There is no requirement that petitioner express opinions that she does not hold, a practice disallowed by the first amendment. *Coca-Cola Co. v. Department of Citrus,* 406 So. 2d 1079, 1087 (Fla. 1981) ("the state may never force one to adopt or express a particular opinion"); *West Virginia State Board of Education v. Barnette,* 319 U.S. 624, 642 (1943) (state cannot "prescribe . . . matters of opinion or force citizens to confess by word or act their faith therein").

[The] order may be sustained against a first amendment challenge if "it furthers an important or substantial governmental interest . . . and if the incidental restriction on alleged First Amendment freedoms is no greater than is essential to the furtherance of that interest." *United States v. O'Brien,* 391 U.S. 367, 377 (1968). Accordingly, we must balance the mother's right of free expression against the state's parens patriae interest in assuring the wellbeing of the parties' minor children. However, as with all matters involving custody of minor children, the interests of the father and of the children, which here happen to parallel those of the state, must also factor into the equation.

In this case, the court, acting on behalf of the state as parens patriae, sought to resolve the dispute between the parties in accordance with the best interests of their children by attempting to restore a meaningful relationship between the children and their father by assuring them unhampered, frequent and continuing contact with him. . . . In resolving the matter, the court also properly considered the father's constitutionally protected "inherent right" to a meaningful relationship with his children. . . . [The United States Supreme Court has held that "the relationship between parents and child is constitutionally protected." The "custody, care, and nurture of the child reside first in the parents." *Quillion v. Walcott,* 434 U.S. 246, 255 (1978).]

There is no question that the state's interest in restoring a meaningful relationship between the parties' children and their father, thereby promoting the best interests of the children, is at the very least substantial. Likewise, any restriction placed on the mother's freedom of expression is essential to the furtherance of the state's interests because affirmative measures taken by the mother to encourage meaningful interaction between the children and their father would be for naught if she were allowed to contradict those measures by word or deed. . . .

Accordingly, construing the order as we do, we find no abuse of discretion by the trial court, nor impermissible burden on the petitioner's first amendment rights. . . . [T]he result reached is approved.

ASSIGNMENT   9.1

a. Would the court have reached the same result if the mother had been ordered to tell the children every day "Your father is a good man"?

b. Keeping in mind that the mother continued to be bitter about the father, give five examples of things she could say about the father to the children that would promote positive feelings about him without constituting opinions that she did not hold.

c. Would the mother violate the order if she refused to ever mention the father in the presence of the children?

d. What are the father's options if, a year after this case, he concludes that the children "still hate me"?

PARENTAL ALIENATION SYNDROME

In some custody disputes (such as the one involved in the case of *Schutz v. Schutz*), one of the parents (often the father) argues that he does not have a good relationship with his children because the mother has turned them against him. A controversial name for this charge is the parental alienation syndrome (PAS). PAS is said to be a disorder characterized by a child's obsessive and unjustified denigration of a parent that results both from the child's persistent attacks on the parent and from manipulation (brainwashing) by the other parent of the child's attitude toward the targeted parent.

Some women's groups have been highly critical of PAS, claiming that it is used mostly by men to discredit mothers unfairly. They say that PAS is junk science—a mere theory that has not been scientifically tested. Most courts agree. These courts will allow a parent to introduce specific evidence that the other parent has persistently portrayed him or her in a negative light in the eyes of the children, but the courts will not allow the alleged victimized parent to assert that the child is suffering from a disorder called PAS.

A more serious challenge against the use of PAS is that abusive parents have tried to use PAS as a defense against the domestic violence they have allegedly committed. The following caution about PAS has been issued by the National Council of Juvenile and Family Court Judges:

> The discredited "diagnosis" of PAS (or an allegation of "parental alienation"), quite apart from its scientific invalidity, inappropriately asks the court to assume that the child's behaviors and attitudes toward the parent who claims to be "alienated" have no grounding in reality. It also diverts attention away from the behaviors of the abusive parent, who may have directly influenced the child's responses by acting in violent, disrespectful, intimidating, humiliating, or discrediting ways toward the child or the other parent. The task for the court is to distinguish between situations in which the child is critical of one parent because they have been inappropriately manipulated by the other . . . , and situations in which the child has his or her own legitimate grounds for criticism or fear of a parent, which will likely be the case when that parent has perpetrated domestic violence.[11]

parental alienation syndrome (PAS)
A disorder characterized by a child's obsessive and unjustified denigration of a parent that results both from the child's persistent attacks on the parent and from manipulation (brainwashing) by the other parent of the child's attitude toward the targeted parent.

junk science
Unreliable and, therefore, potentially misleading scientific evidence.

CAREER CHOICE

Courts are sensitive to the need of many women to work outside the home after divorce. In a custody dispute, such women should not be penalized simply because their job commitments require them to use housekeepers, nannies, or daycare providers. A court will be impressed by a father who commits to being a stay-at-home dad, but this would not automatically lead to a custody ruling in his favor against a working mother. The parenting plans of both parents would have to be carefully scrutinized by the court to determine what custody arrangement would be in the best interests of the child. It may be that the balance could tip in favor of the working mother so long as her career choice does not adversely affect the child.

WEALTH

After a divorce, both parents have an equal obligation to provide child support based, in part, on their ability to pay. In a child-custody dispute, a wealthy parent is not preferred over a less well-to-do parent even if the wealthy parent is making most or all of the child-support payments. Although the relative wealth of the parents is a factor that the courts will consider in the custody decision, it is not a controlling factor.

LEGAL PREFERENCES

Up until recently, custody decisions of courts tended to favor one gender, the female, over the male. Today, however, courts use gender-neutral standards in the custody decision, although some critics argue that females/mothers are still preferred.

Tender-Years Presumption

tender-years presumption
A belief that mothers are better suited to raise their young children (usually under five years of age) and should be awarded custody of such children unless the mothers are unfit. Also called *maternal preference*.

The older custody rule was stated in the form of a presumption. A mother was presumed to be better suited to raising her young children (under five years of age) and should be awarded custody unless she is found to be unfit. This **tender-years presumption** was justified on the basis of biological dependence, socialization patterns, and tradition: "There is but a twilight zone between a mother's love and the atmosphere of heaven, and all things being equal, no child should be deprived of that maternal influence unless it be shown there are special or extraordinary reasons for so doing."[12] A strong case had to be made against the mother to overcome the tender-years presumption, primarily by proving that she was unfit.

Most states, however, have abolished the tender-years presumption. Fathers successfully argued that this gender-based presumption was an unconstitutional violation of the equal protection of the laws. Male anger and frustration over the presumption were main reasons for the growth of the men's rights movement. As a result, in the twenty-first century, more fathers are granted sole physical custody. "Single dads now account for 8 percent of American households with children, up from 6.3 percent in 2000 and 1.1 percent in 1950."[13] One in six custodial parents (CPs) today are fathers.[14] Not all of them became CPs because of decisions in disputed custody cases. Many "Mr. Moms" are widowers or assumed the CP role when mothers abandoned the child or voluntarily agreed with the father that he should be the CP. Yet a significant number of fathers are CPs because of custody decisions made after the tender-years presumption was abolished.

The cases in which fathers tend to be successful in custody cases are those in which they are seeking custody of an older male child. At one time, courts established a presumption that it was in the best interests of an older boy to be with his father. This gender-based presumption, however, is as constitutionally suspect as the tender-years presumption. No court today would openly acknowledge that it is using a pro-father presumption when the custody of an older male is in dispute.

Although the number of father CPs has increased, mothers are still granted custody in a large majority of cases. A number of factors account for this. Perhaps the primary reason is the fact that many fathers do not ask for custody. Becoming a full-time, at-home parent does not fit into the lifestyle of large numbers of men, particularly if it means significant interference with their occupations. Arguably, another major reason is that fathers are still handicapped by the tender-years presumption in spite of its formal abolition. Many older judges now sitting on the bench grew up with full-time mothers at home. Some experts feel it is difficult for these judges to accept the notion of giving sole custody to working fathers. But new judges are on the rise. It "will take a generation of judges who are brought up by, or married to career women" before there is more sympathy for granting custody to working parents—particularly fathers.[15]

The Primary-Caregiver Presumption

primary-caregiver presumption
A belief that custody should be granted to the parent who thus far has taken care of most of the daily needs of the child unless this parent is unfit.

In place of the tender-years presumption, a few courts have substituted a **primary-caregiver presumption**, by which the court presumes that custody should go to the parent who has thus far been the primary person who has taken care of the child's daily needs, unless this parent is unfit. The major caregiver tasks include making meals, bathing, grooming, dressing, cleaning, disciplining, tending to medical needs, and arranging the child's social, religious, educational, and cultural life. Fathers often claim that the primary-caregiver presumption means that the mother continues to receive sole custody in most cases, because she is often the parent who stays home to care for the child. Even when both the mother and the father work outside the home, the mother is more likely to be awarded custody as the primary caregiver. Hence, critics argue that this presumption is simply the tender-years presumption in disguise. In most states, therefore, primary caregiving is not a presumption; it is simply one of the factors a court will consider in determining what is in the best interests of the child.

Other Guidelines Used by Some Courts

Despite the controversy over presumptions, courts are anxious to provide as much stability as possible for children of divorcing parents. Toward this end, some courts apply the *approximation rule* discussed earlier. This rule states that the proportion of custodial time the child spends with each parent after divorce should approximate the proportion of time each parent spent performing caretaking functions for the child prior to the divorce. The rule is not a presumption; it is more of a guideline than a rigid rule to be followed in every case.

A less controversial presumption is that young brothers and sisters are best kept together with the same parent whenever possible. (In effect, this was a presumption that *split custody* should be avoided.) Older children are often treated differently. Most courts say that the preference of older, more mature children as to their own custody should be given great (though not necessarily controlling) weight.

The modern trend, however, is to avoid all presumptions and simply to apply the gender-neutral (degenderized) standard of best interests of the child with all of the factors being considered.

MORALITY AND LIFESTYLE: THE NEXUS TEST

Just as marital fault or misconduct should not control whether a court will grant a divorce (see Chapter 7), it should not determine who receives custody unless the fault affects the child. This is the *nexus test*. There must be a causal relationship—a nexus—between the parent's conduct or lifestyle and the child's well-being.

Smoking, for example, is considered a poor lifestyle choice. Yet a parent who smokes would not be automatically disqualified from obtaining custody. Suppose, however, that the parent's child has asthma. In such a case, a court would be concerned about the health effects of secondhand smoke on the child. This would be a nexus between lifestyle and child welfare that a court would consider. If, after all factors are considered, a court grants physical custody to a smoker, the court is likely to impose a condition that the parent not smoke in the presence of the child, especially in vehicles.

Similarly, a court would want to know if a parent's new romantic partner has had, or is likely to have, a negative effect on a child. According to one court:

> A judge should not base his decision upon his disapproval of the morals or other personal characteristics of a parent that do not harm the child. . . . We do not mean to suggest that a person's associational or even sexual conduct may not be relevant in deciding a custody dispute where there is compelling evidence that such conduct has a significant bearing upon the welfare of the children objectively defined.[16]

Assume that Bill and Mary are married with one child, Alice. After Mary and Bill separate, Mary and Alice move into an apartment where Mary begins living with her boyfriend. In the divorce proceeding, Bill argues that he should have sole physical custody because Mary is living in "illicit cohabitation" with her boyfriend. This argument will lose unless Bill can show that Mary's relationship with her boyfriend is having a detrimental effect on Alice. An example would be evidence that Alice is becoming emotionally upset because of the boyfriend's presence in the home and that this is negatively affecting her schoolwork. If, however, the relationship is not affecting Alice, the boyfriend's presence will not control the determination of custody despite Bill's plea that his daughter should not be exposed to the "sin and immorality" of Mary's conduct.

Some judges take a different position when the parent seeking custody has a homosexual partner in the home. For example, in a 2002 concurring opinion of the Alabama Supreme Court, the chief justice said that "[h]omosexual conduct by its very nature is immoral, and its consequences are inherently destructive to the natural order of society. Any person who engages in such conduct is presumptively unfit to have custody of minor children under the established laws of this State."[17] This is a minority view, however. Most judges apply the same nexus test in homosexual and heterosexual cases.

A court will want to know if the couple is discreet in the expression of their mutual affection. If sexuality is flaunted—whether heterosexual or homosexual—a court is likely to conclude that a child will be adversely affected. Courts have granted custody to a gay or lesbian parent when all of the factors point to a healthy home environment for the child, and there is no evidence that the homosexuality will have an adverse impact on the child. At one time, there was fear that a parent's homosexuality would cause the child to be homosexual. There are studies rejecting this conclusion, particularly because a child's sexual preference is developed during its infancy and very early years, which is often well before the homosexual parent seeks custody. It must be acknowledged, however, that a gay or lesbian parent has a substantial uphill battle in gaining or keeping custody. Homosexual parents have been most successful in winning or maintaining custody when their heterosexual spouse (the other parent) is either no longer available or is demonstrably unfit. In such cases, the homosexual parent wins by default unless his or her conduct is so offensive that the court will grant custody to neither biological parent.

The landmark cases of *Lawrence v. Texas* and *Obergefell v. Hodges* (discussed in Chapter 5) are not directly relevant to custody disputes involving gay or lesbian parents. The *Lawrence* case held that a state cannot criminalize private same-sex conduct between consenting adults,[18] and the *Obergefell* case held that a state cannot refuse to marry a same-sex couple.[19] Although there is language in these opinions about the positive home environments that many same-sex couples can provide, the opinions do not directly address the issue of custody disputes in which one of the disputants is homosexual.

DOMESTIC VIOLENCE

domestic violence (DV)
Actual or threatened injury or abuse of one member of a family or household by another member.

Domestic violence (DV) is actual or threatened injury or abuse of one member of a family or household by another member. Common examples are abuse between spouses (spousal abuse) and abuse against a child (child abuse).

Spousal Abuse

Most courts take the position that a parent who commits spousal abuse is not necessarily an unfit parent. The court will want to know what effect the abuse had on the child. Evidence of spousal abuse could be damaging if it was consistently committed in front of the child or if the anger and violence seriously disturbed the child's ability to function normally. It is possible, however, for the offending parent to show that the abuse was isolated and has not affected the home environment of the child. It may also help if this parent can show that he or she is seeking psychological counseling for anger control.

In some cases, both spouses charge each other with spousal abuse. One of the spouses, for example, may assert that he or she was acting in self-defense to the other's violent attack. The court may have to determine who was the primary aggressor and who was the primary victim. In general, a court will lean toward granting custody to the primary victim.

Child Abuse

If the domestic violence is directed at the child, the abuser will have great difficulty obtaining custody. **Child abuse** is serious physical, emotional, or sexual mistreatment of a child that is not the result of accident or circumstances beyond the control of the parent or guardian. A court is obviously unlikely to grant custody to a parent who has a history of child abuse. We will see this hesitancy when we study the *Allen* case in this chapter. Furthermore, the visitation rights of a violent parent are likely to be substantially restricted, such as by limiting the parent to supervised visitation, which we will examine shortly.

child abuse
Serious physical, emotional, or sexual mistreatment of a child that is not the result of an accident or circumstances beyond the control of the parent or guardian.

The "Terror Weapon"

"I had to face the fact that for one year [during unsupervised visitation], I sent my child off to her rapist."[20]

"For many parents engaged in seriously contested child-custody disputes, false allegations of child abuse have become an effective weapon for achieving an advantage in court."[21]

In alarming numbers, parents are being accused of sexually abusing their children, usually during visitation. The issue can also arise during an initial custody proceeding where one parent claims that the other committed sexual abuse during the marriage, and hence should not be granted custody, or should not be granted visitation rights in unsupervised settings.

The level of bitterness generated by this accusation is incredibly high. It is the equivalent of a declaration of total war between the parties. One attorney calls accusations of such abuse "the new terror weapon in child-custody cases."[22] The chances of reaching a settlement or of mediating the custody dispute—or anything else that is contested—often vanish the moment the accusation is made. Protracted and costly litigation is all but inevitable.

Nor does litigation always resolve the matter. Assume that a mother with sole physical and legal custody is turned down when she asks a court to terminate the father's right to visit the child because of an allegation of child abuse. The court finds the evidence of abuse to be insufficient and orders a continuation of visitation. Unable to accept this result, the mother goes underground out of desperation and a total loss of faith in the legal system. She flees with the child, or she turns the child over to sympathetic third parties who agree to keep the child hidden from the authorities. The child might be moved from one "safe house" to another to avoid detection. This underground network consists of a core of dedicated women, who at one time were in a similar predicament or who are former child-abuse victims themselves.

If the mother remains behind, she is hauled back into court. If she refuses to obey an order to produce the child, she faces an array of possible sanctions, including imprisonment for **civil contempt**, **criminal contempt**, or even prosecution for criminal kidnapping. Unfortunately, the media have an excessive interest in cases of this kind. Once reporters and cameras become involved, a circus atmosphere tends to develop.

Attorneys can find themselves in delicate situations. The first question they face is whether to take the case of an alleged child abuser, usually the father. Many attorneys need to believe in the father's innocence before agreeing to defend him. According to a prominent matrimonial attorney, "I have a higher duty to make sure

civil contempt
The refusal of a party to comply with a court order (usually issued for the benefit of another), which can lead to punishment (including incarceration) until the party complies with the order.

criminal contempt
The refusal of a party to comply with a court order, which can lead to punishment (including incarceration), because of the repeated or aggravated nature of the refusal.

Minnesota Multiphasic Personality Inventory Test (MMPI)
A psychological test designed to assess personality characteristics.

some wacko doesn't get custody of his child." Before proceeding, therefore, the attorney might ask the prospective client to:

- Take a lie detector test.

- Take the **Minnesota Multiphasic Personality Inventory Test (MMPI)**, which may help reveal whether someone has a propensity to lie and is statistically likely to be a child abuser.

- Be evaluated by a knowledgeable psychologist or psychiatrist.

Some attorneys have even insisted that the father undergo hypnosis as a further aid in trying to assess the truth of the allegation.

Attorneys representing the mother face similar concerns. Is she telling the truth? Is she exaggerating, knowingly or otherwise? Is she trying to seek some other strategic advantage from the father (e.g., more financial support, custody blackmail)? What advice should the attorney give her when she first reveals the charge of sexual abuse, particularly when the evidence of abuse is not overwhelming? Should she be advised to go public with the charge? As indicated, the consequences of doing so can be enormous. Bitter litigation is almost assured. What if the attorney talks her out of going public with the charge in order to settle the case through negotiation, and a month or two later, something terrible happens? Faced with a need to know if the accusation is true, the attorney may ask her to take a polygraph test or an MMPI, or to undergo an independent evaluation by a psychologist or psychiatrist.

Other attorneys disagree with this approach. They do not think that clients should be subject to such mistrust by their own attorney. They doubt the effectiveness of some of the devices used to assess the truth. Typical comments from such attorneys are that professionals "trained in sexual abuse are wrong very often"; "Frankly, I trust my horse sense more than I trust psychiatrists"; and "There is no research that says the polygraph or MMPI is of any use."[23]

Of course, attorneys for both sides will have to interview the child. This can be a delicate task. There is a danger of emotional damage every time the child is forced to focus on the events in question. Even though children are generally truthful, many are susceptible to suggestion and manipulation. Often, the charge is made that the child has been "brainwashed" into believing that abuse did or did not occur. Clearly, the child needs protection. A separate attorney can be appointed by the court to represent the child in the litigation. Guidelines may exist in the state on who can interview the child and whether the interview can be videotaped. Trained child counselors might be called in to conduct the interview. Using special anatomically correct dolls, the counselor will ask the child to describe what happened. When the time comes for a court hearing, the judge might interview the child outside the courtroom (e.g., in the judge's chambers) without either parent being present.

ASSIGNMENT 9.2

Diane and George are the parents of Mary. When the child is two years old, the parents divorce. The court awards Diane sole physical and sole legal custody with visitation rights to George on alternating weekends. Diane suspects that George is sexually abusing Mary during the visits. Answer the following questions for your state. (See General Instructions for the State-Code Assignment and General Instructions for the Court-Opinion Assignment in Appendix A.)

a. What options does Diane have?

b. Under what circumstances can the child be interviewed about the alleged sexual abuse? Are there any restrictions on such interviews?

c. Can Diane be jailed for contempt of court if she refuses to obey an order to disclose Mary's location following a court decision that there was no sexual abuse by George? If so, for how long? Indefinitely?

CASE

Allen v. Farrow
197 A.D.2d 327, 611 N.Y.S.2d 859 (1994)
Supreme Court, Appellate Division, New York

Background: *Woody Allen is an internationally famous director and actor. His custody case generated widespread publicity. When it was over, Allen commented, "I was on the cover of every magazine . . . all over the world. I couldn't believe the amount of interest." His opponent in the case was Mia Farrow, an actress who starred in thirteen of his movies. Allen had a romantic relationship with Farrow. She was formerly married to singer Frank Sinatra and conductor André Previn. (With Previn she had six children, three biological and three adopted. One of the adopted children was Soon-Yi Previn.) Farrow and Allen never married, but they had a child together, Satchel Farrow. Allen adopted two of Farrow's other children, Moses Amadeus Farrow and Dylan O'Sullivan Farrow. The relationship between Allen and Farrow fell apart when Allen began a romantic relationship with Soon-Yi when she was nineteen or twenty-one years old. (There is some doubt about her date of birth in Korea.) At the time the affair began, Allen was fifty-seven years old. Farrow discovered the relationship after finding sexually explicit pictures that Allen had taken of Soon-Yi. Farrow also accused Allen of sexually abusing Dylan. (He was never criminally prosecuted for this charge.) A drawn-out, well-financed, and highly publicized custody trial ensued. Allen (the petitioner) went to court asking for custody of Satchel, Moses, and Dylan or for better visitation than Farrow was allowing him. He objected to supervised visitation. The trial court denied his request. Farrow (the respondent) was granted custody and counsel fees. Allen's visitation with the three children was severely limited:*

1. He was granted supervised visitation with Satchel for two hours, three times a week.

2. Visitation with Dylan was to be "conducted in a therapeutic context" until the therapist recommended to the court that other visitation was appropriate.

3. Moses, who was fifteen years old at the time, refused to see Allen, and the court refused to force him to do so.

Allen appealed to the New York Supreme Court, Appellate Division.

Decision on Appeal: *The decision of the trial court in Farrow's favor on custody, visitation, and counsel fees was affirmed.*

Opinion of the Court

Justice ROSS delivered the opinion of the court. . . .

The petitioner and the respondent have brought themselves to this unhappy juncture primarily as a result of two recent events. These are, Mr. Allen's affair with Soon-Yi Previn and the alleged sexual abuse of Dylan O'Sullivan Farrow by Mr. Allen. While the parties had difficulties, which grew during Ms. Farrow's pregnancy with Satchel, it was the discovery of the relationship between Mr. Allen and Ms. Previn that intensified Ms. Farrow's concerns about Mr. Allen's behavior toward Dylan, and resulted in the retention of

counsel by both parties. While various aspects of this matter remain unclear, it is evident that each party assigns the blame for the current state of affairs to the other.

The parties' respective arguments are very clear. The petitioner maintains that he was forced to commence this proceeding in order to preserve his parental rights to the three infant children, because the respondent commenced and continues to engage in a campaign to alienate him from his children and to ultimately defeat his legal rights to them. The petitioner contends, inter alia, that the respondent seeks to accomplish her goals primarily through manipulation of the children's perceptions of him. He wishes to obtain custody, ostensibly to counteract the detrimental psychological effects the respondent's actions have had on his children, and to provide them with a more stable atmosphere in which to develop. Mr. Allen specifically denies the allegations that he sexually abused Dylan and characterizes them as part of Ms. Farrow's extreme overreaction to his admitted relationship with Ms. [Soon-Yi] Previn.

The respondent maintains that the petitioner has shown no genuine parental interest in, nor any regard for, the children's welfare and that any interest he has shown has been inappropriate and even harmful. Respondent cites the fact that the petitioner has commenced and maintained an intimate sexual relationship with her daughter Soon-Yi Previn, which he has refused to curtail, despite the obvious ill effects it has had on all of the children and the especially profound effect it has had on Moses. It is also contended that petitioner has, at best, an inappropriately intense interest in, and at worst, an abusive relationship with, the parties' daughter Dylan. Further, the respondent maintains that petitioner's contact with the parties' biological son, Satchel, is harmful to the child in that petitioner represents an emotional threat and has on at least one occasion threatened physical harm. Respondent contends that the petitioner's only motive in commencing this proceeding was to retaliate against the allegations of child sexual abuse made against him by Ms. Farrow.

Certain salient facts concerning both Mr. Allen's and Ms. Farrow's relationships to their children and to each other are not disputed. Review of these facts in an objective manner and the conclusions that flow from them, demonstrate that the determination of the [trial] court as to both custody and visitation is amply supported by the record before this Court.

From the inception of Mr. Allen's relationship with Ms. Farrow in 1980, until a few months after the adoption of Dylan O'Sullivan Farrow on June 11, 1985, Mr. Allen wanted nothing to do with Ms. Farrow's children. Although Mr. Allen and Ms. Farrow attempted for approximately six months to have a child of their own, Mr. Allen did so apparently only after Ms. Farrow promised to assume full responsibility for the child. Following the adoption, however, Mr. Allen became interested in developing a

(continued)

relationship with the newly adopted Dylan. While previously he rarely spent time in the respondent's apartment, after the adoption of Dylan he went to the respondent's Manhattan apartment more often, visited Ms. Farrow's Connecticut home and even accompanied the Farrow family on vacations to Europe. Allen also developed a relationship with Moses Farrow, who had been adopted by the respondent in 1980 and was seven years old at the time of Dylan's adoption. However, Allen remained distant from Farrow's other six children.

In 1986 Ms. Farrow expressed a desire to adopt another child. Mr. Allen, while not enthusiastic at the prospect of the adoption of Dylan in 1985, was much more amenable to the idea in 1986. Before the adoption could be completed Ms. Farrow became pregnant with the parties' son Satchel. While the petitioner testified that he was happy at the idea of becoming a father, the record supports the finding that Mr. Allen showed little or no interest in the pregnancy. It is not disputed that Ms. Farrow began to withdraw from Mr. Allen during the pregnancy and that afterwards she did not wish Satchel to become attached to Mr. Allen.

According to Mr. Allen, Ms. Farrow became inordinately attached to the newborn Satchel to the exclusion of the other children. He viewed this as especially harmful to Dylan and began spending more time with her, ostensibly to make up for the lack of attention shown her by Ms. Farrow after the birth of Satchel. Mr. Allen maintains that his interest in and affection for Dylan always has been paternal in nature and never sexual. The various psychiatric experts who testified or otherwise provided reports did not conclude that Allen's behavior toward Dylan prior to August of 1992 was explicitly sexual in nature. However, the clear consensus was that his interest in Dylan was abnormally intense in that he made inordinate demands on her time and focused on her to the exclusion of Satchel and Moses even when they were present.

The record demonstrates that Ms. Farrow expressed concern to Allen about his relationship with Dylan, and that Allen expressed his concern to Ms. Farrow about her relationship with Satchel. In 1990 both Dylan and Satchel were evaluated by clinical psychologists. Dr. Coates began treatment of Satchel in 1990. In April of 1991 Dylan was referred to Dr. Schultz, a clinical psychologist specializing in the treatment of young children with serious emotional problems.

In 1990 at about the same time that the parties were growing distant from each other and expressing their concerns about the other's relationship with their youngest children, Mr. Allen began acknowledging Farrow's daughter Soon-Yi Previn. Previously he treated Ms. Previn in the same way he treated Ms. Farrow's other children from her prior marriage, rarely even speaking to them. In September of 1991 Ms. Previn began to attend Drew College in New Jersey. In December 1991 two events coincided. Mr. Allen's adoptions of Dylan and Moses were finalized and Mr. Allen began his sexual relationship with their sister Soon-Yi Previn.

In January of 1992, Mr. Allen took the photographs of Ms. Previn, which were discovered on the mantelpiece in his apartment by Ms. Farrow and were introduced into evidence at the [trial court] proceeding. Mr. Allen in his trial testimony stated that he took the photos at Ms. Previn's suggestion and that he considered them erotic and not pornographic. We have viewed the photographs and do not share Mr. Allen's characterization of them. We find the fact that Mr. Allen took them at a time when he was formally assuming a legal responsibility for two of Ms. Previn's siblings to be totally unacceptable. The distinction Mr. Allen makes between Ms. Farrow's [older adopted children] and Dylan, Satchel and Moses is lost on this court. The children themselves do not draw the same distinction that Mr. Allen does. This is sadly demonstrated by the profound effect his relationship with Ms. Previn has had on the entire family.

Allen's testimony that the photographs of Ms. Previn ". . . were taken, as I said before, between two consenting adults wanting to do this . . ." demonstrates a chosen ignorance of his and Ms. Previn's relationships to Ms. Farrow, his three children and Ms. Previn's other siblings. His continuation of the relationship, viewed in the best possible light, shows a distinct absence of judgment. It demonstrates to this court Mr. Allen's tendency to place inappropriate emphasis on his own wants and needs and to minimize and even ignore those of his children. At the very minimum, it demonstrates an absence of any parenting skills.

We recognize Mr. Allen's acknowledgment of the pain his relationship with Ms. Previn has caused the family. We also note his testimony that he tried to insulate the rest of the family from the "dispute" that resulted, and tried to "de-escalate the situation" by attempting to "placate" Ms. Farrow. It is true that Ms. Farrow's failure to conceal her feelings from the rest of the family and the acting out of her feelings of betrayal and anger toward Mr. Allen enhanced the effect of the situation on the rest of her family. We note though that the reasons for her behavior, however prolonged and extreme, are clearly visible in the record. On the other hand, the record contains no acceptable explanation for Allen's commencement of the sexual relationship with Ms. Previn at the time he was adopting Moses . . ., or for the continuation of that relationship at the time he was supposedly experiencing the joys of fatherhood.

While the petitioner's testimony regarding his attempts to de-escalate the dispute and to insulate the family from it displays a measure of concern for his three children, it is clear that he should have realized the inevitable consequences of his actions well before his relationship with Ms. Previn became intimate. Allen's various inconsistent statements to Farrow of his intentions regarding Ms. Previn and his attempt to have Dr. Schultz explain the relationship to Dylan in such a manner as to exonerate himself from any wrong doing, make it difficult for this court to find that his expressed concern for the welfare of the family is genuine.

As we noted above, Mr. Allen maintains that Ms. Farrow's allegations concerning the sexual abuse of Dylan were fabricated by Ms. Farrow both as a result of her rage over his relationship with Ms. Previn and as part of her continued plan to alienate him from his children. However, our review of the record militates against

(continued)

a finding that Ms. Farrow fabricated the allegations without any basis. . . . [There is evidence to] suggest that the abuse did occur. While the evidence in support of the allegations remains inconclusive, it is clear that the investigation of the charges in and of itself could not have left Dylan unaffected.

Any determination of issues of child custody or visitation must serve the best interests of the child and that which will best promote the child's welfare (*Domestic Relations Law* § 70; *Eschbach v. Eschbach,* 56 N.Y.2d 167, 171). . . . It was noted by the [trial] court that the psychiatric experts agreed that Mr. Allen may be able to fulfill a positive role in Dylan's therapy. We note specifically the opinion of Dr. Brodzinsky, the impartial expert called by both parties, who concluded that contact with Mr. Allen is necessary to Dylan's future development, but that initially any such visitation should be conducted in a therapeutic context. The [trial] court structured that visitation accordingly and provided that a further review of Allen's visitation with Dylan would be considered after an evaluation of Dylan's progress.

Although the investigation of the abuse allegations have not resulted in a conclusive finding, all of the evidence received at trial supports the determination as to custody and visitation with respect to this child. There would be no beneficial purpose served in disturbing the custody arrangement. Moreover, even if the abuse did not occur, it is evident that there are issues concerning Mr. Allen's inappropriately intense relationship with this child that can be resolved only in a therapeutic setting. At the very least, the process of investigation itself has left the relationship between Mr. Allen and Dylan severely damaged. The consensus is that both Mr. Allen and Ms. Farrow need to be involved in the recovery process. The provision for further review of the visitation arrangement embodied in the trial court's decision adequately protects the petitioner's rights and interests at this time.

With respect to Satchel, the [trial] court denied the petitioner's request for unsupervised visitation. While the court stated that it was not concerned for Satchel's physical safety, it was concerned by Mr. Allen's "demonstrated inability to understand the impact that his words and deeds have upon the emotional well-being of the children." We agree. The record supports the conclusion that Mr. Allen may, if unsupervised, influence Satchel inappropriately, and disregard the impact exposure to Mr. Allen's relationship with Satchel's sister, Ms. Previn, would have on the child. His failure to understand the effect of such exposure upon Satchel as well as upon his other children is evidenced by his statement on direct examination in which he stated:

> If you ask me personally, I would say the children, the children adore Soon-Yi, they adore me, they would be delighted, if you asked me this personally, I would say they would be delighted and have fun with us, being taken places with us. But, I don't want to give you my amateur opinion on that. That's how I feel. And I know it counts for very little.

The record indicates that Ms. Previn when not at college spends most of her time with Mr. Allen. Contact between Ms. Previn and her siblings in the context of the relationship with Mr. Allen would be virtually unavoidable even if Mr. Allen chose to insulate his children from the relationship. Expert medical testimony indicated that it would be harmful for Ms. Previn not to be reintegrated into the family. However, the inquiry here concerns the best interests of Dylan, Moses and Satchel. Their best interests would clearly be served by contact with their sister Soon-Yi, personally and not in Mr. Allen's presence. Seeing both Ms. Previn and Mr. Allen together in the unsupervised context envisioned by Mr. Allen would, at this early stage, certainly be detrimental to the best interests of the children. It has been held that the desires of the child are to be considered, but that it must be kept in mind that those desires can be manipulated (*Friederwitzer v. Friederwitzer,* 55 N.Y.2d 89, 94).

In considering the custody and visitation decision concerning Moses, who is now a teenager, we cannot ignore his expressed desires. The record shows that he had a beneficial relationship with the petitioner prior to the events of December 1991. However, that relationship has been gravely damaged. While Moses' feelings were certainly affected by his mother's obvious pain and anger, we concluded that it would not be in Moses' best interests to be compelled to see Mr. Allen, if he does not wish to.

Therefore, we hold that in view of the totality of the circumstances, the best interests of these children would be served by remaining together in the custody of Ms. Farrow, with the parties abiding by the visitation schedule established by the trial court.

With respect to the award of counsel fees we note that the record demonstrates that Mr. Allen's resources far outpace those of Ms. Farrow. Additionally, we note the relative lack of merit of Mr. Allen's position in commencing this proceeding for custody. It became apparent, during oral argument, that there was serious doubt that Mr. Allen truly desired custody. It has been held that "in exercising its discretionary power to award counsel fees, a court should review the financial circumstances of both parties together with all the other circumstances of the case, which may include the relative merit of the parties' positions" (*DeCabrera v. Cabrera-Rosete,* 70 N.Y.2d 879, 881). We find no abuse of discretion in the court's award of counsel fees in this case.

Accordingly, the judgment [below] . . . , which, inter alia, denied the petitioner Woody Allen's request for custody of Moses Amadeus Farrow, Dylan O'Sullivan Farrow, and Satchel Farrow, set forth the terms of visitation between the petitioner and his children and awarded Ms. Farrow counsel fees, is affirmed in all respects, without costs.

CARRO, Justice (dissenting in part).

I agree with the majority's conclusions, except for the affirmance of the order of visitation with respect to Mr. Allen's son Satchel, which I find unduly restrictive.

There is strong evidence in the record from neutral observers that Mr. Allen and Satchel basically have a warm and loving

(continued)

father-son relationship, but that their relationship is in jeopardy, in large measure because Mr. Allen is being estranged and alienated from his son by the current custody and visitation arrangement. Frances Greenberg and Virginia Lehman, two independent social workers employed to oversee visitation with Satchel, testified how "Mr. Allen would welcome Satchel by hugging him, telling him how much he loved him, and how much he missed him." Also described by both supervisors "was a kind of sequence that Mr. Allen might say, I love you as much as the river, and Satchel would say something to the effect that I love you as much as New York City . . . then Mr. Allen might say, I love you as much as the stars, and Satchel would say, I love you as much as the universe."

Sadly, there was also testimony from those witnesses that Satchel had told Mr. Allen: "I like you, but I am not supposed to love you;" that when Mr. Allen asked Satchel if he would send him a postcard from a planned trip to California with Ms. Farrow, Satchel said "I can't [because] Mommy won't let me;" and on one occasion when Satchel indicated that he wanted to stay with Mr. Allen longer than the allotted two-hour visit, "Satchel did say he could not stay longer, that his mother had told him that two hours was sufficient." Perhaps most distressing, Satchel "indicated to Mr. Allen that he was seeing a doctor that was going to help him not to see Mr. Allen anymore, and he indicated that he was supposed to be seeing this doctor perhaps eight or ten times, at the end of which he would no longer have to see Mr. Allen."

In contrast to what apparently is being expressed by Ms. Farrow about Mr. Allen to Satchel, Mr. Allen has been reported to say only positive things to Satchel about Ms. Farrow, and conveys only loving regards to Moses and Dylan through Satchel. Thus I find little evidence in the record to support the majority's conclusion that "Mr. Allen may, if unsupervised, influence Satchel inappropriately, and disregard the impact exposure to Mr. Allen's relationship with Satchel's sister, Ms. Previn, would have on the child."

The majority's quotation of Mr. Allen's testimony with respect to Soon-Yi in support of its conclusion respecting visitation should be viewed in the context of Dr. David Brodzinsky's testimony. Dr. Brodzinsky is an expert in adoption with considerable experience in court-related evaluations of custody and visitation disputes. . . . . It was his clinical judgment that Mr. Allen had more awareness of the consequences of his actions than he was able to articulate in the adversarial process, and he was optimistic about Mr. Allen's ability to accept his share of responsibility for what had taken place in light of his love for his children, his capacity for perspective-taking and empathy, and his motivation and openness toward the ongoing therapeutic process. In addition, Dr. Susan Coates, Satchel's therapist until December 1992, and the only expert to testify about Satchel's mental health, stated that Mr. Allen's parental relationship with Satchel was essential to Satchel's healthy development. . . .

I do not believe that Mr. Allen's visitation with Satchel for a mere two hours, three times a week, under supervision, is reasonable and meaningful under the circumstances, or that exceptional circumstances are presented that warrant such significant restriction on visitation with Satchel. Mr. Allen and Satchel clearly need substantial quality time together to nurture and renew their bonds and to foster a warm and loving father-son relationship. Obviously this cannot occur overnight; but more significantly, it is almost inconceivable that it will occur even over an extended period of time if visitation is limited to three two-hour periods per week under the supervision of strangers, as ordered by the trial court and affirmed by the majority. Accordingly I would modify the judgment appealed from to provide that Mr. Allen shall have unsupervised visitation with Satchel for four hours, three times weekly, plus alternate Saturdays and Sundays for the entire day, plus alternate holidays to be agreed upon by the parties.

ASSIGNMENT 9.3

a. Was Allen denied custody because of his immoral behavior?

b. (i) For Allen, prepare a list of factual allegations that support his position that he should be given custody (not just visitation) rather than Farrow.
(ii) For Farrow, prepare a list of factual allegations that support her position that she should be given custody rather than Allen.
(iii) In class, be prepared to be called upon to debate who should have custody. Provide separate answers, as needed, for each child: Satchel, Dylan, and Moses.

c. Is it relevant that Allen married Soon-Yi soon after the case?

d. What responsibility, if any, did the court assign to the behavior of Mia Farrow? Did she help cause Allen's deterioration with the children? Does the parental alienation syndrome (PAS) apply?

e. If Allen were correct that Farrow has poisoned his relationship with the children, wouldn't keeping him away from them reward her efforts?

(continued)

f. The court said Allen agreed to have a biological child "apparently only after Ms. Farrow promised to assume full responsibility for the child." If Farrow did make this promise, what legal effect do you think it would have? For example, would it affect Allen's duty of child support? (See Chapter 10.)

g. The dissent says that in the "clinical judgment" of Dr. Brodzinsky, an adoption expert, "Allen had more awareness of the consequences of his actions than he was able to articulate in the adversarial process." What do you think Brodzinsky meant? Is a court-room the best place to resolve disputed custody cases? Is there an alternative?

RELIGION

Twenty-seven percent of married people live in religiously mixed marriages.[24] Most do so in harmony, but when a divorce occurs, the religion of minor children can become part of a custody dispute in the divorce. Under the U.S. Constitution, a court cannot resolve this dispute by favoring one religion over another or by preferring organized religion over less orthodox forms of religious beliefs. To do so could amount to an unconstitutional "establishment" of religion. The state must remain neutral.

The parenting plans of the parties will state how they propose to handle religion in the life of the child. In the court's response to these plans,

- the focus of the court must be to determine what effect, if any, the practice of religion in the parenting plan is likely to have on the child;

- courts are not as concerned about the religious *beliefs* that one parent will inculcate in the child as they are about the religious *conduct* that the parent will be asking the child to engage in;

- the focus of the court cannot be on whether one religion or religious practice is preferable or correct (1) according to the judge's personal standards, (2) according to the standards of the majority in the community, or (3) according to "respectable" minorities in the community.

The court will want to know what religion, if any, the child has practiced to date. Continuity is highly desirable. Also, will the practice of a particular religion tend to take the child away from other activities? For example, will the child be asked to spend long hours in door-to-door selling of religious literature and hence be unable to attend regular school? If so, the court will be reluctant to award custody to the parent who would require this of the child.

Courts sometimes have to walk a thin line between protecting a child and keeping out of religious disputes. In one case, for example, the mother was an observant orthodox Jew and the father was a fundamentalist Christian who believed that anyone who did not accept Jesus was destined for hell. During the marriage, the parents had agreed to raise the children in the Jewish tradition, including allowing their son, Ariel, to grow payes or payos (side curls). In the divorce, the mother was granted sole physical custody but both parents were given joint legal custody. The mother asked the court to limit the exposure of the children to their father's religion. The court appointed a guardian ad litem (GAL) to help the parents resolve future inter-religious conflicts and issued the following order:

RESTRICTIONS UPON RELIGIOUS EXPOSURE: Each parent shall be entitled to share his/her religious beliefs with the children with restrictions as follows: neither may indoctrinate the children in a manner which substantially promotes their . . . alienation from either parent or their rejection of either parent. The [father] shall not take the children to his church (whether to church services or Sunday School or church educational programs); nor engage them in prayer or bible study if it promotes rejection rather than acceptance, of their mother or their own Jewish self-identity. The [father] shall not share his religious beliefs with the children if those beliefs cause the children significant emotional distress or worry about their mother or about themselves. Thus, for example, [the father] may have pictures of Jesus Christ hanging on the walls of his residence, . . . [but he] may not take the children to religious services where they receive the message that adults or children who do not accept Jesus Christ as their lord and savior are destined to burn in hell. By way of further example, [he] may not shave off [their son's] payes. This provision shall not be construed so as to prevent [the father] from having the children with him at events involving family traditions at Christmas and Easter. In the event that there is a disagreement between the parents as to whether one or more of the children could be exposed to the religious belief(s) of [the father] without substantial negative impact upon their emotional health, the parents shall engage the services of Michael Goldberg, Ph.D., to act as G.A.L./investigator/evaluator on such issues and disputes. The fee of Dr. Goldberg shall be shared equally by the parties. In the event that Dr. Goldberg is unable to serve in this capacity, then the parties shall agree upon an alternate child psychologist, or an alternate shall be selected by the Court. . . .[25]

ASSIGNMENT 9.4

When Helen married John, she converted from Catholicism to his religion, Judaism. Neither Helen nor John, however, was a religious person. To a moderate extent, their two children were raised in the Jewish faith. The couple divorced when the children were aged four and five. Because of John's job, he could not spend much time with the children. Hence, he agreed that Helen receive sole physical and sole legal custody. But he asked the court to order Helen to continue raising the children in the Jewish faith.

a. Under what circumstances do you think a court can grant this request, so that, in effect, John will be granted *spiritual custody* of the children even though physical custody and legal custody (in all matters except religion) will be granted to Helen? (See General instructions for the Legal-Analysis Assignment in Appendix A.)

b. Suppose that Helen returns to her original religion and starts taking the children to Catholic services. What options does John have in your state? (See General Instructions for the State-Code Assignment and the Court-Opinion Assignment in Appendix A.)

RACE

A child's ethnic and cultural heritage is important. Suppose, for example, that a child has been raised in a Mexican-American community. If possible, a court will want to grant custody to the parent who will help the child maintain his or her contacts with this community. Race, however, cannot be the *sole* factor that determines custody. Assume that a divorced white parent asks a court for custody because the other parent (also white) has married a black person. A court's grant of custody for this reason would be an unconstitutional denial of the equal protection of the law.[26] Race cannot be the sole factor in a custody decision.

WISHES OF THE CHILD

Older children are almost always asked where they would prefer to live. Greater caution, however, is needed when the child-custody dispute centers on young children. If asking such children about their preferences became commonplace, there would be an incentive for both parents to pressure the child to choose one side or the other. If, however, the court is convinced that the child is mature enough to state a rational preference and that doing so would not harm the child, evidence of such a preference will be admissible. The judge might decide to speak to the child outside the formal courtroom (with the attorneys but not the parents present), or the judge might allow a professional (e.g., child psychologist, social worker) to interview the child at home.

EXPERT WITNESSES

Psychologists, psychiatrists, social workers, and other experts can be called as expert witnesses by either parent to testify on the home environment, the child's emotional development, the mental stability of the parents, and the suitability of various parenting plans. Experts can be asked to conduct investigations, make recommendations, give second opinions, and act as mediators.

Overreliance on experts, however, can be a problem. It would be an error, for example, for a court to rule that a parent should not have visitation rights until a psychiatrist or other professional concludes that such visitation would be beneficial. It is for the court to decide when custody and visitation is proper. Experts can give their opinions to the judge, who will make the decision on what is in the best interests of the child. The decision cannot be delegated to a professional.

Either parent or the guardian ad litem (GAL) for the child can make a motion that the court order a custody evaluation by an expert. Exhibit 9.3 gives an example of a custody-evaluation report by such an expert.

EXHIBIT 9.3   Example of a Custody Evaluation by an Expert

Psychiatric Custody Evaluation

Honorable James K. O'Brien
Supreme Court of New York
New York County
60 Centre Street
New York, New York 10007

Re: Johnson v. Johnson
Docket No. M-3784-16

Dear Judge O'Brien:

This report is submitted in compliance with your court order dated June 9, 2016, requesting that I conduct an evaluation of the Johnson family in order to provide the court with information that would be useful to it in deciding which of the Johnson parents should have custody of their children Tara, Elaine, and Charles.

My findings and recommendations are based on interviews conducted as itemized below:

July 6, 2016: Mrs. Carol Johnson and Mr. Frank Johnson, seen jointly	2 hours
July 7, 2016: Mr. Frank Johnson	1 hour
July 11, 2016: Mrs. Carol Johnson	1 hour
July 13, 2016: Tara Johnson	1½ hours
July 14, 2016: Mr. Frank Johnson	1 hour
July 20, 2016: Mrs. Carol Johnson	1 hour
July 21, 2016: Charles Johnson	¾ hour
July 21, 2016: Elaine Johnson	¾ hour

(continued)

Exhibit 9.3 *(continued)*

July 22, 2016: Tara Johnson	½ hour
July 22, 2016: Mrs. Carol Johnson and Tara Johnson, seen jointly	½ hour
July 24, 2016: Mrs. Carol Johnson	1 hour
July 27, 2016: Mrs. Carol Johnson and Mr. Frank Johnson, seen jointly	1 hour
Aug. 3, 2016: Elaine Johnson	¾ hour
Aug. 4, 2016: Tara Johnson	¼ hour
Aug. 4, 2016: Mr. Frank Johnson and Tara Johnson, seen jointly	½ hour
Aug. 10, 2016: Mr. Frank Johnson and Mrs. Carol Johnson, seen jointly	¾ hour
Aug. 11, 2016: Tara Johnson, Elaine Johnson, Charles Johnson, Mrs. Carol Johnson and Mr. Frank Johnson, seen jointly	¾ hour
Aug. 14, 2016: Tara Johnson, Elaine Johnson, Charles Johnson, Mrs. Carol Johnson and Mr. Frank Johnson seen jointly	1 hour
Total Time	16 hours

In addition, on August 16, 2016, Mr. and Mrs. Johnson were seen together for the purpose of my presenting these findings and recommendations to them. This interview lasted two hours, bringing to 18 the total number of hours spent with the Johnson family in association with this evaluation.

Mr. Frank Johnson, an airline pilot, is 43 years old. His first wife died soon after the delivery of Tara, who is now 16 years of age. He married Mrs. Carol Johnson when Tara was 2 years old. Mrs. Johnson, a housewife, who was formerly an elementary school teacher, is now 40. Her first marriage ended in divorce. A child of this relationship died soon after birth. There are two children of the Johnson marriage: Elaine, 11 and Charles, 7. Mrs. Johnson adopted her stepdaughter Tara in July 2005. In October 2015, Mr. Johnson initiated divorce proceedings because he felt that his wife no longer respected him and that she was a poor mother for the children, especially his daughter Tara. However, Mr. and Mrs. Johnson are still occupying the same domicile.

Both parents are requesting custody of all three children. It is this examiner's recommendation that Mr. Frank Johnson be granted custody of Tara and that Mrs. Carol Johnson be granted custody of Elaine and Charles. The observations that have led me to these conclusions will be divided into four categories:

1. Mr. Frank Johnson's assets as a parent,
2. Mr. Frank Johnson's liabilities as a parent,
3. Mrs. Carol Johnson's assets as a parent, and
4. Mrs. Carol Johnson's liabilities as a parent.

Following these four presentations I will comment further on the way in which my observations brought about the aforementioned recommendations. Although much information was obtained in the course of the evaluation, only those items specifically pertinent to the custody consideration will be included in this report.

(continued)

Exhibit 9.3 *(continued)*

1. MR. FRANK JOHNSON'S ASSETS AS A PARENT

Mr. Frank Johnson is Tara's biological father. The special psychological tie that this engenders is not enjoyed by Mrs. Carol Johnson and Tara. It is not the genetic bond per se that is crucial here; rather, it is the psychological attachment that such a bond elicits. Mr. Johnson had already started to develop a psychological tie with Tara while his first wife was pregnant with her. He was actually present at her birth and assumed an active role in her rearing - almost from birth because of the illness and early death of his first wife. This situation prevailed until the time of his marriage to Mrs. Johnson when Tara was 2 years of age. Although Mrs. Johnson has been Tara's primary caretaker since then, Mr. Johnson's early involvement with Tara during these crucial years of her development contributes to a very strong psychological tie between them that has continued up to the present time.

My observations have convinced me, and both parents agree, that at this time, Tara has a closer relationship with her father than her mother. Her relationship with Mrs. Johnson at this time is characteristically a difficult one in that there are frequent battles and power struggles. Although Tara is not completely free of such involvement with her father, such hostile interaction is far less common. In my interviews with Mr. Johnson and Tara, I found her to be far more friendly with him than I observed her to be with Mrs. Johnson in my joint interviews with them.

In every interview, both alone and in joint sessions with various members of the family, Tara openly and unswervingly stated that she wished to live with her father: "I want to live with my father. I am closer to him." "When I was younger, my mother did more things; but since I'm older, my father does more things." "My father listens to what I say; my mother doesn't."

Mr. Johnson and Tara both utilize a similar method of communication. Neither feels a strong need to give confirmation of examples to general statements that they make, and they are therefore comfortable with one another. Mrs. Johnson, on the other hand, is much more specific in her communications and this is a source of difficulty, not only in her relationship with Tara, but in her relationship with her husband as well.

All five family members agree that Mr. Johnson spends significant time with Charles, involved in typical father-son activities (sports, games, etc.). It is also apparent that Charles has a strong masculine identification and this arose, in part, from his modeling himself after his father.

2. MR. FRANK JOHNSON'S LIABILITIES AS A PARENT

Mr. Johnson states that he would not have involved himself in the custody evaluation conducted by this examiner if he had to contribute to its financing. Accordingly, Mrs. Johnson assumed the total financial obligation for this evaluation. I conclude from this that with regard to this particular criterion for comparing the parents, Mr. Johnson's position is less strong than Mrs. Johnson's.

On many occasions Mr. Johnson made general comments about his superiority over his wife with regard to parental capacity. For example, "She's a very poor mother," "She neglects the children," and "If you had all the information you would see that I'm a better parent." However, it was extremely difficult to elicit from Mr. Johnson specific examples of incidents that would substantiate these statements. I not only considered this to be a manifestation of Mr. Johnson's problem in accurately communicating, but also considered it to be a deficiency in his position. One cannot be convinced of the strength of such statements if no examples can be provided to substantiate them.

(continued)

Exhibit 9.3 *(continued)*

In the hope that I might get more specific information from Mr. Johnson I asked him, on at least three occasions, to write a list of specifics that might help corroborate some of his allegations. He came to three subsequent interviews without having written anything in response to my invitation. I consider such failure to reflect a compromise in his motivation for gaining custody of the three children. When he did finally submit such a list, it was far less comprehensive than that which was submitted by Mrs. Johnson and in addition, the issues raised had far less significance, e.g., "She's late once in a while," "She's sometimes forgetful," and "She doesn't like playing baseball with Charles."

Although I described Mr. Johnson's communication problem as a factor supporting his gaining custody of Tara, I would consider it a liability with regard to his gaining custody of Elaine and Charles. Tara (possibly on a genetic basis) communicates in a similar way and so, as mentioned, is comfortable with her father when they communicate. Elaine and Charles, however, appear to be identifying with their mother with regard to communication accuracy. Accordingly, intensive exposure to Mr. Johnson might compromise what I consider a healthier communicative pattern.

Mr. Johnson's profession as an airline pilot has not enabled him to have predictable hours. Not only is his schedule variable, but there are times when he is required to work on an emergency basis. All three children agree that Mrs. Johnson is more predictably present. Mr. Johnson's irregular schedule is not a significant problem for Tara who, at 16, is fairly independent and would not suffer significantly from her father's schedule. The younger children, however, are still in need of predictability of parental presence and Mr. Johnson has not demonstrated his capacity to provide such predictability. In my final interview with Mr. Johnson he stated that he would change his work pattern to be available to his children during non-school hours. Mrs. Johnson was very dubious that this could be arranged because his job does not allow such flexibility. Both parents agreed, however, that it had not occurred in the past and that such predictability was not taking place at the time of this evaluation.

Both Charles and Elaine stated that they wanted to live with their mother and not live with their father. Charles stated, "I want to be with my mother. I'd be alone when my father goes to work." Elaine stated, "I want to live with my mother. I'm closer to my mother. I'm not as close to my father."

In a session in which I was discussing his future plans with Mr. Johnson, he stated that he was considering moving to California because he could earn more money there by supplementing his income with certain business ventures that he had been invited to participate in. He stated also that he would still move even if he were only to be granted custody of Tara. Although I appreciate that a higher income could provide Mr. Johnson's children with greater financial flexibility, I believe that the disadvantages of such a move would far outweigh its advantages from their point of view. Specifically, the extra advantages they might enjoy from such a move would be more than offset by the even greater absence of their father who, his liabilities notwithstanding, is still an important figure for them.

In an interview in which I discussed with Mr. Johnson how he would react to the various custodial decisions, he was far more upset about the prospect of losing Tara than he was about the possibility of losing Charles and Elaine. In fact, he appeared to be accepting of the fact that Elaine would go to her mother. Although somewhat distressed about the possibility of Charles' living with his mother, he did not show the same degree of distress as his wife over the prospect of losing the younger two children.

(continued)

Exhibit 9.3 *(continued)*

3. MRS. CAROL JOHNSON'S ASSETS AS A PARENT

Mrs. Carol Johnson was far more committed to the custody evaluation than her husband. As mentioned, she was willing to make the financial sacrifices involved in the evaluation. I consider this to be a factor reflecting greater motivation than her husband for gaining custody of the children. Mrs. Johnson is more available to the children during non-school hours than her husband and this is one element in her favor regarding gaining custody, especially of the younger children. Mrs. Johnson is a more accurate and clearer communicator than her husband and this is an asset. As mentioned, the younger children do not seem to have been affected by their father's communication difficulty. Having them live with him might result in their acquiring this maladaptive trait.

During her pregnancy with Elaine, Mrs. Johnson suffered with toxemia and associated high blood pressure and convulsions. Most physicians generally discourage women with this disorder from becoming pregnant again because it is genuinely life endangering. However, Mrs. Johnson did wish to have a third child, primarily because her husband, she states, was so desirous of having a son. Her pregnancy with Charles was complicated by the exacerbation of a preexisting asthmatic condition from which she states that she almost died. A less maternal woman would not have become pregnant again.

Elaine stated on many occasions, and in every interview, both alone and with other family members, that she wished to live with her mother: "I'm closer to my mother," "She's home more than my father," "They call my father to do things at work all the time," and "My mother has more feelings for me than my father."

Charles also, both in individual session and in joint interviews, emphatically stated that he wished to live with his mother: "I want to stay with my mother because she doesn't work as much as my father." "If you get sick the father might not know what to do, but the mother does." "My mother knows how to take care of me." "She doesn't work that much." "She reads me books more than my father."

On one occasion Mr. Johnson stated: "Carol is closer to Elaine than I am. They are similar. They're both sore losers. Both get emotional if they don't have their way." Mrs. Carol Johnson agrees that she and her daughter Elaine have these traits, but not to the degree described by her husband. Although there are certainly negative elements regarding the reasons why Mr. Johnson sees Elaine to be closer to his wife, this statement is an admission of his recognition of this preference of Elaine for her mother. The situation is analogous to Mr. Johnson's involvement with Tara. They are closer to one another, yet maladaptive and undesirable factors are contributing to the closeness.

4. MRS. CAROL JOHNSON'S LIABILITIES AS A PARENT

Tara is not Mrs. Johnson's biological daughter. Although she has raised Tara from her infancy, as if she were her own biological child, and although she has adopted her, Mrs. Johnson is at a certain disadvantage regarding the development of a strong psychological parent-child tie. As mentioned, I believe that a biological relationship increases the strength of the psychological bond. Accordingly, Mrs. Johnson is at a disadvantage when compared to Mr. Johnson regarding this aspect of the custody consideration.

Mrs. Johnson and Tara have a poor relationship at this point. In my interviews with Mrs. Johnson and Tara I found the latter to view her mother scornfully and to be openly resentful of her authority. On one occasion Tara said: "She has a lot of nerve telling me what to do." Were this an isolated statement, it would probably not have much significance. However, all agreed that it epitomized her

(continued)

Exhibit 9.3 (*continued*)

general attitude toward her mother. Although some of the scornful attitude Tara exhibits toward her mother can be viewed as age-appropriate, I believe the extent goes beyond what is to be expected for teenagers.

Mrs. Johnson cannot provide Charles with the same kind of father model and father-type involvement that her husband can. Although she claims an interest in sports and a greater degree of facility than the average woman, it is still clear that her husband has been far more involved in this type of activity with his son than has Mrs. Johnson.

Mr. Johnson accuses Mrs. Johnson of being excessively punitive and too strong a disciplinarian. Mrs. Johnson claims that her husband is too lax with the children and does not implement proper disciplinary measures. I believe that it is most likely that Mrs. Johnson is a little too punitive and that Mr. Johnson is a little too lenient. However, neither parent exhibits these difficulties to a degree that would be significantly injurious to the children, nor would I consider this to be a factor compromising either of their capacities as parents. It is probable, however, that these differences are playing a role in Tara's antagonism to her mother and her gravitating toward her father.

In every interview, both individual and joint, Tara openly stated that she wished to live with her father. "I would be very unhappy if the judge made me go with my mother." "He can't make me live with my mother. I'd run away to my father if he did."

CONCLUSIONS AND RECOMMENDATIONS

Weighing the above factors as best I can, I believe that the evidence is strongly in favor of Mr. Johnson being given custody of Tara. I believe, also, that the above evidence strongly supports the conclusion that Elaine should be given to Mrs. Johnson. Although there are certain arguments supporting Mr. Johnson's gaining custody of Charles, I believe that these are greatly outweighed by arguments in favor of Mrs. Johnson's gaining custody. Were the court to conclude that Tara would be better off living with Mrs. Johnson, I believe that there would be a continuation of the present hostilities, and this could be disruptive to the healthy psychological development of the younger children if they were exposed to such hostile interactions over a long period. I believe that if Mr. Johnson were to be granted custody of Elaine and Charles it is most likely that they would suffer psychological damage. All things considered, I believe he is the less preferable parent for the young children and, if they had to live with him, they would suffer emotional deprivations that could contribute to the development of psychiatric disorders.

Reprinted with the permission of Richard A. Gardner. Family Evaluation in Child Custody Litigation, 318–25 (1982).

VISITATION (PARENTING TIME)

INTRODUCTION

parenting time
Visitation.

Courts want to preserve as much of the child's relationship with both parents as possible. Hence, visitation (or to use the preferred modern term, **parenting time**) is almost always granted to the noncustodial parent (NCP) even if it must be exercised in the presence of third-party strangers (see the discussion of *supervised visitation* below).

fit
Willing and able to provide what is needed to raise a child.

Whenever possible, the court will favor frequent and regular visitation by the NCP (e.g., every other weekend, alternating holidays, substantial summer vacation time). When two relatively **fit** parents seek sole physical custody, the court is even more inclined to grant greater visitation rights to the loser.

NEGOTIATING VISITATION

Negotiating a mutually acceptable visitation plan is not always easy: "For many family-law practitioners, the seemingly endless wrangling over days and even hours is one of the most time-consuming but least rewarding parts of custody practice."[27] In the negotiation, the parties need to work out a number of important details:

- When can the visitation occur by the NCP? Alternating weekends? School vacations? Holidays? Which ones? How much advance notice is needed if additional time is desired?

- At what time is the child to be picked up and returned?

- Can the NCP take the child on long trips? Is the consent of the custodial parent (CP) needed?

- Who pays the transportation costs, if any, when the child visits the NCP?

- When the NCP decides not to visit at a previously scheduled time, must he or she notify the CP in advance, or attempt to do so?

- Can the CP move out of the area even though this makes visitation more burdensome and costly? Should a clause be inserted in the separation agreement that the permission of the NCP is needed before the child can be moved more than a specified number of miles away?

- Do any third parties have visitation rights (e.g., grandparents)?

- If disputes arise between parents on visitation, how are they resolved? Arbitration? Mediation? Other method of Alternative dispute resolution (ADR)? Who pays for the ADR services?

- Will failure to visit as scheduled be a violation of the separation agreement or is visitation at the sole discretion of the NCP?

- What happens if one of the parties violates the agreement on visitation?

There are two major choices in selecting visitation times. First, the parties can simply state in their separation agreement that visitation will be at "reasonable" times to be mutually agreed upon by the parties in the future, with adequate advance notice to be given by the NCP when he or she wants visitation. Such flexibility, however, often turns out to be unworkable, particularly since many divorcing parents have ongoing difficulty communicating with each other. Second, the alternative is a visitation schedule that spells out precise times for the child and the NCP to interact. For an example, see Exhibit 9.4.

EXHIBIT 9.4   Sample Visitation Schedule

(This example assumes that the mother has sole physical and sole legal custody)

I. Father.

Father shall have the children with him at the following times:

A. Regular Visitation:

1. On alternate weekends from 7 p.m. Friday to 7 p.m. Sunday, commencing Friday, January 16, 2019.

2. The entire month of July, 2019, and the entire month of August, 2020, and alternating July and August in subsequent years.

B. Holidays and Special Days:

1. Lincoln's Birthday, 2019, from 7 p.m. the day before said holiday to 7 p.m. the day of said holiday, and thereafter on alternate years.

2. Washington's Birthday, 2019, from 7 p.m. the day before said holiday to 7 p.m. the day of said holiday, and thereafter on alternate years.

3. Memorial Day, 2019, from 7 p.m. the day before said holiday to 7 p.m. the day of said holiday, and thereafter on alternate years.

(continued)

Exhibit 9.4 *(continued)*

4. Independence Day, 2019, from 7 p.m. the day before said holiday to 7 p.m. the day of said holiday, and thereafter on alternate years.

5. Labor Day, 2019, from 7 p.m. the day before said holiday to 7 p.m. the day of said holiday, and thereafter on alternate years.

6. Columbus Day, 2019, from 7 p.m. the day before said holiday to 7 p.m. the day of said holiday, and thereafter on alternate years.

7. Veterans Day, 2019, from 7 p.m. the day before said holiday to 7 p.m. the day of said holiday, and thereafter on alternate years.

8. Thanksgiving Day, 2019, from 7 p.m. the day before said holiday to 7 p.m. the day of said holiday, and thereafter on alternate years.

9. Christmas, 2019, the first week of the Christmas school vacation, commencing 7 p.m. the last day of school before the vacation and ending at 11 a.m. Christmas Day and thereafter on alternate years.

10. Christmas Day, 2020, the second week of Christmas school vacation, commencing 11 a.m. Christmas Day to 5 p.m. New Year's Day, and thereafter on alternate years.

11. The entire Easter school vacation in the year 2019, including Easter Sunday, commencing 7 p.m. the last day of school before the vacation and ending at 7 p.m. the day before school resumes, and thereafter during the Easter vacation on alternate years.

12. On a child's birthday in the year 2019, from 7 p.m. the day before said birthday to 7 p.m. the day of said birthday, and thereafter on alternate years.

13. Every Father's Day, from 7 p.m. the day before said day to 7 p.m. on said day.

14. Every Father's birthday, from 7 p.m. the day before said day to 7 p.m. on said day.

15. Religious Holidays (where applicable):

    [*Note: Select option "a" or "b" below or insert comparable provision for other religions.*]

    a. Good Friday of 2019, from noon to 6 p.m. of said day, and thereafter on alternate years, or

    b. The first day of the Jewish Holidays of Yom Kippur, Rosh Hashanah, and Passover during 2019, commencing at 5 p.m. on the eve of each such day and terminating at 7 p.m. on such day, and thereafter on alternate years.

II. Mother.

1. Mother shall have the children with her on the holidays and special days listed in Clause I-B in the years alternate to the years in which Father has the children with him pursuant to Clause I-B.

2. Mother shall also have the children on every Mother's Day and on every Mother's birthday at comparable times listed for the Father in Clause I-B.

    [*Note: A common variation would be to split the holidays between Father and Mother and have them switch halves in alternate years. Another suggested addition if the children are young is Halloween in alternating years.*]

III. Priorities:

1. The rights of Mother under Clause II shall override the regular visitation rights of Father set forth in Clause I-A, in the event of conflict between Clause I-A and Clause II.

2. Father shall not be limited in his right to take the children out of the city during the period set forth in Clause I-A.2, even though Mother may thereby be deprived of the right she would otherwise have under Clause II to have the children with her during said period.

3. In the event of conflict between Clause I-B and Clause II, the rights of Father under Clause I-B shall override the rights of Mother under Clause II.

    [*Note: The significance of Clause III on priorities cannot be overemphasized. A key function of a drafter is to avoid disputes over meaning and intention. A provision establishing a hierarchy of clauses will help meet this goal.*]

Reprinted with permission of the Matrimonial Strategist (Law Journal Newsletters at www.lawjournalnewsletters.com).

VISITATION SOFTWARE

Computer programs exist to help parties plan and understand timesharing schedules. This can be particularly helpful in cases where the family has more than one child. Joint custody options in such cases are sometimes complex. Computer programs can generate color-coded calendar graphics to help the parties visualize their agreements. For an example of software that assists parents in devising a parenting plan, see Exhibit 9.5.

EXHIBIT 9.5   Example of Visitation Software for a Parenting Plan

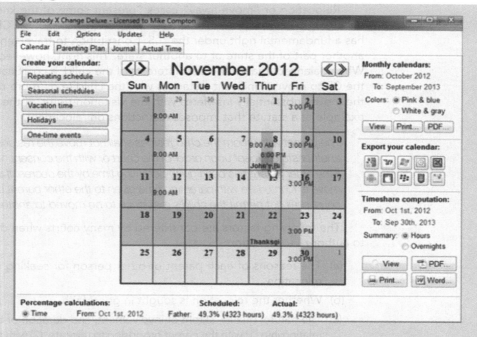

HOLIDAYS

Name	Parents' years	From time	From day	To time	To day
☐ New Year's Day					
☐ Martin Luther King's Birt					
☐ Lincoln's Birthday					
☐ President's Day (weeker					
☑ Easter	Mom odd / Dad even	9:00 AM	Day of holiday	6:00 PM	Day of holiday
☐ Spring Break 1st half					
☐ Spring Break 2nd half					
☑ Mother's Day	Mom all years	9:00 AM	Day of holiday	6:00 PM	Day of holiday
☐ Memorial Day (weekend					
☑ Father's Day	Dad all years	9:00 AM	Day of holiday	6:00 PM	Day of holiday
☑ Independence Day	Mom odd / Dad even	6:00 PM	Day of holiday	9:00 AM	1 day after
☐ Labor Day (weekend)					
☐ Columbus Day (weekenc					
☐ Halloween					
☐ Veteran's Day					
☑ Thanksgiving	Mom odd / Dad even	9:00 AM	Day of holiday	6:00 PM	Day of holiday
☐ Thanksgiving weekend					

☐ Include Jewish holidays   [Add new holiday...]   [View age-based ideas]

Source: Reprinted with permission of Custody X Change (www.custodyxchange.com).

ASSIGNMENT   9.5

Richard and Helen Dowd have been married for six years. They are both financial consultants who work out of their home. They have one child, four-year old Kevin. Recently, they decided to separate. Draft the clauses of their separation agreement that would provide joint physical custody and joint legal custody. Assume that both want to be active in raising Kevin. (See General Instructions for the Agreement-Drafting Assignment in Appendix A.)

RELOCATION: THE MOVE-AWAY CASE

Relocation or "move-away" cases "present some of the knottiest and most disturbing problems that courts are called upon to resolve."[28] A CP, like all citizens, has a fundamental right under the U.S. Constitution to travel (and to relocate) to another part of the state or to another state. This right, however, is not absolute. When balanced against the best interests of the child, a court can refuse to allow the CP to move significant distances with the child (e.g., more than fifty miles) if the move substantially interferes with the visitation rights of the NCP. Here is an example of a statute that imposes restrictions on relocation:

The parent with whom the child resides shall not move the residence of the child to another state except upon order of the court or with the consent of the other parent, if the other parent has been given parenting time by the decree. If the purpose of the move is to interfere with parenting time given to the other parent by the decree, the court shall not permit the child's residence to be moved to another state.[29]

The following factors are considered by many courts when deciding whether to authorize a relocation:

(a) The reasons of each parent or other person for seeking or opposing the relocation.

(b) Whether the relocation is sought in good faith.

(c) The nature, quality, extent of involvement, and duration of the child's current relationship (1) with the parent proposing to relocate, (2) with the nonrelocating parent, (3) with siblings, and (4) with other significant persons in the child's life.

(d) The age and developmental stage of the child, the needs of the child, and the likely impact the relocation will have on the child's physical, educational, and emotional development, taking into consideration any special needs of the child.

(e) The feasibility of preserving the relationship between the nonrelocating parent and the child through substitute arrangements that take into consideration the logistics of contact, access, visitation, and time sharing, as well as the financial circumstances of the parties; whether those factors are sufficient to foster a continuing meaningful relationship between the child and the nonrelocating parent; and the likelihood of compliance with the substitute arrangements by the relocating parent once he or she is out of the jurisdiction of the court.

(f) The child's preference, taking into consideration the age and maturity of the child.

(g) Whether the relocation will enhance the general quality of life for both the parent seeking the relocation and the child, including but not limited to financial or emotional benefits or educational opportunities.

(h) The current employment and economic circumstances of each parent and whether the proposed relocation is necessary to improve the economic circumstances of the parent seeking relocation of the child.

(i) The extent to which the objecting parent has fulfilled his or her financial obligations to the parent seeking relocation, including child support, spousal support, and marital property and marital debt obligations.

(j) The career and other opportunities available to the objecting parent if the relocation occurs.

(k) Any other factors affecting the best interests of the child.[30]

In extreme cases, the court might order the CP seeking to relocate to post a bond to secure compliance with the visitation rights of the NCP if relocation is allowed by the court.

VIRTUAL VISITATION

Courts are willing to accommodate the realities of modern living in order to preserve a child's contact with both parents. In one state, the court approved the CP's relocation out of state but gave the NCP the right to two virtual visits a week via Skype (an Internet calling service that uses video) so that the NCP could interact with his children by reading them bedtime stories. When a judge allows virtual visitation (also called *e-visitation*), limitations are usually imposed, such as when the visits can occur and how long they can last. Also, virtual visitation is not a replacement for traditional visits. When a NCP is allowed Skype or webcam visits, he or she is usually also allowed face-to-face visits.

THIRD-PARTY VISITATION AND THE *TROXEL* CASE

Another issue that is occasionally litigated is whether *third parties* can have visitation rights (e.g., grandparents, former stepparents) over the objection of the biological parents. The issue has profound implications for the relationship between the family and the state. If a state is allowed to force a parent to allow third parties to visit the parent's children, the question arises as to how far the state can go in overruling parental decisions. What is the boundary line between what parents think is good for their children and what the state thinks is good for them?

The U.S. Supreme Court was concerned about this boundary line when it faced the issue of third-party visitation in the case of *Troxel v. Granville*.[31] In this important case, the Court reinforced the "fundamental right of parents to make decisions concerning the care, custody, and control of their children." Specifically, the Court ruled that visitation by third parties must not substantially interfere with the primary right of fit parents to raise their children.

The *Troxel* case arose in the state of Washington, which had a statute that allowed "[a]ny person" "at any time" to petition the court for visitation, which could be granted if the court felt it would be in the best interests of child. The statute gave no special consideration or weight to the opinion of the parents on whether third-party visitation should be allowed. When a parent opposed such visitation, for example, the statute did not say that the third party had to overcome a presumption that the parent's opposition was valid. The statute gave no such presumption of validity to the parent's views.

This statute was called "breathtakingly broad" and declared unconstitutional in violation of the Due Process Clause. Here are the facts of the case:

- Tommie Granville and Brad Troxel were the unmarried parents of Isabelle and Natalie Troxel.

- After the parents separated, the girls lived with Tommie. Brad lived with his parents, Jenifer and Gary Troxel, the girls' paternal grandparents. Brad regularly brought his daughters to his parents' home for weekend visits.

- When Brad committed suicide, the grandparents continued to see the girls on a regular basis.

- Tommie informed the grandparents that she wished to limit their visitation with her daughters to one short visit per month.

- The grandparents used the Washington State statute to petition the court for two weekends of overnight visitation per month and two weeks each summer.

- Over Tommie's objection, the court granted them one weekend per month, one week during the summer, and four hours on both of the grandparents' birthdays.

Tommie's appeal eventually reached the U.S. Supreme Court.

The U.S. Supreme Court began its analysis by acknowledging the changing reality of family life in America:

> The demographic changes of the past century make it difficult to speak of an average American family. The composition of families varies greatly from household to household. While many children may have two married parents and grandparents who visit regularly, many other children are raised in single-parent households. In 1996, children living with only one parent accounted for 28 percent of all children under age 18 in the United States. U.S. Dept. of Commerce, Bureau of Census, Current Population Reports, 1997 Population Profile of the United States 27 (1998). [In 2018, it was more than 34 percent.] Understandably, in these single-parent households, persons outside the nuclear family are called upon with increasing frequency to assist in the everyday tasks of child rearing. In many cases, grandparents play an important role. For example, in 1998, approximately 4 million children—or 5.6 percent of all children under age 18—lived in the household of their grandparents. U.S. Dept. of Commerce, Bureau of Census, Current Population Reports, Marital Status and Living Arrangements: March 1998 (Update), p. i (1998).[32]

The Court specified, however, that if a fit parent is present in the home, his or her right to raise a child is entitled to constitutional protection. The Fourteenth Amendment to the U.S. Constitution provides that no state shall "deprive any person of life, liberty or property, without due process of law."[33] This clause gives parents the fundamental right to make decisions concerning the care, custody, and control of their children:

> The Fourteenth Amendment provides that no State shall "deprive any person of life, liberty, or property, without due process of law." We have long recognized that the Amendment's Due Process Clause . . . "guarantees more than fair process." Washington v. Glucksberg, 521 U.S. 702, 719 (1997). The Clause also includes a substantive component that "provides heightened protection against government interference with certain fundamental rights and liberty interests." Id., at 720. . . . The liberty interest at issue in this case—the interest of parents in the care, custody, and control of their children—is perhaps the oldest of the fundamental liberty interests recognized by this court. More than 75 years ago, in Meyer v. Nebraska, 262 U.S. 390, 399 (1923), we held that the "liberty" protected by the Due Process Clause includes the right of parents to "establish a home and bring up children" and "to control the education of their own." Two years later, in Pierce v. Society of Sisters, 268 U.S. 510, 534–535 (1925), we again held that the "liberty of parents and guardians" includes the right "to direct the upbringing and education of children under their control."[34]

There was no indication in this case that Tommie was an unfit parent. When fit parents make a decision in raising their child, they are entitled to a presumption that the decision is in the child's best interests. The presumption means that the parent's decision controls unless someone proves that the decision is not in the best interests of the child. It is not enough to show that someone else's decision is a good idea.

Tommie was not given the benefit of this presumption. Her opposition to the grandparents' request was given no "special weight." The judge simply disagreed with her on whether more extensive visitation with the paternal grandparents was in the best interests of the children. This troubled the U.S. Supreme Court:

> [S]o long as a parent adequately cares for his or her children (i.e., is fit), there will normally be no reason for the State to inject itself into the private realm of the family to further question the ability of that parent to make the best decisions concerning the rearing of that parent's children. . . . [T]he Due Process Clause does not permit a State to infringe on the fundamental right of parents to make childrearing decisions simply because a state judge believes a "better" decision could be made.[35]

Although the Court ruled that a fit parent must be given the presumption of correctness, the Court did not clarify what kind of evidence would overcome this presumption. The Court left this question for another day. Therefore, we do not know the precise scope of the constitutional right of parents to raise their children, but we do know that the Court will take a dim view of any effort by the state to interfere with the child-rearing decisions of a fit parent.

SUPERVISED VISITATION

Supervised visitation by the NCP occurs in the presence of a third party (someone other than the CP) who will monitor the visit. Occasionally, a CP will ask the court to deny all visitation rights to the NCP because of a fear that the child might be taken out of the state or country or might be physically or emotionally harmed by unrestricted visitation. As indicated, courts are reluctant to deny all visitation rights to a parent. If the court is convinced that unrestricted visitation would not be in the best interests of the child, supervised visitation is a possible alternative. When used, the CP usually takes the child to a facility that is equipped to monitor visitation in a safe environment. The facility might be a government agency or, more commonly, a private nonprofit group (e.g., a unit of the YWCA) that charges a fee for its services. After the CP drops off the child and leaves, the NCP has a visit of several hours (as designated by the court order) in rooms available in the facility. The CP then returns to pick up the child. Supervised visitation can also occur in less formal settings such as at the home of a relative that both parents trust. It is more common, however, for supervised visitation to occur at a facility that is professionally organized to offer such visitation.

supervised visitation
Visitation of a child while another adult (other than the custodial parent) is present to monitor the visit.

COHABITATION

In most cases, cohabitation by the NCP should not affect the NCP's visitation rights. If, however, the court determines that exposing a younger child to the NCP's romantic partner will (or has) unduly upset the child, the court might place restrictions on visitation, such as not allowing overnight visits with the NCP.

cohabitation
Living together in an intimate (usually sexual) relationship in the manner of spouses. A de facto husband and wife relationship. The verb is *cohabit*. Although a married couple cohabits, the word *cohabitation* is more often used in reference to unmarried couples.

ASSIGNMENT 9.6

Flora Smith and Harry Smith have one child, ten-year-old Mary. Flora and Harry are separated. Flora wants supervised visitation of Mary by Harry Smith because he often misses child-support payments and has a girlfriend who is an alcoholic. Flora is afraid that if Harry takes Mary to his home, she will be exposed to drinking. How should the court rule? (See General Instructions for the Legal-Analysis Assignment in Appendix A.)

SHARED CUSTODY AND COPARENTING

A parent can voluntarily enter into an agreement with a nonparent that allows the nonparent some measure of custody of the parent's child. Such agreements are called *shared-custody agreements*. In most states, the agreement can be between two opposite-sex adults or two same-sex adults. The arrangement is also referred to as *coparenting*, the shared responsibility by two adults to raise a child, regardless of the marital status or sexual orientation of the adults.

These arrangements do not violate the parent's *Troxel* rights because the parent voluntarily agrees to share custody with the nonparent. A court will enforce the agreement if the court concludes that the agreement is in the best interests of the child. In a recent case involving a suit for visitation rights by a former lesbian partner of a woman who gave birth to a child by in vitro fertilization while the unmarried women were living together, the court said that:

> [A] parent may voluntarily share with a nonparent the care, custody, and control of his or her child through a valid shared-custody agreement. The essence of such an agreement is the purposeful relinquishment of some portion of the parent's

right to exclusive custody of the child. A shared-custody agreement recognizes the general principle that a parent can grant custody rights to a nonparent and will be bound by the agreement. A valid shared-custody agreement is . . . an enforceable contract subject only to the court's determinations that the custodian is "a proper person to assume the care, training, and education of the child" and that the shared-legal-custody arrangement is in the best interests of the child.[36]

The court went further and said that a parent could enter into an enforceable agreement to relinquish his or her *full* custody to a third party.

In Chapter 10, we will consider the question of when a nonparent in a shared-custody arrangement can be ordered to pay child support.

ENFORCING THE RIGHT TO VISITATION

When a CP interferes with the visitation rights of a NCP, a number of remedies are possible:

- The court could issue a **ne exeat**, which is a writ that orders the CP not to remove the child from the area.
- The court could order an increase of the visitation rights of the NCP.
- The court could order that custody be given to the NCP.
- The CP could be held in civil contempt.
- The CP could be held in criminal contempt.
- The CP might be in violation of a criminal statute on custodial interference.[37]
- The CP could be ordered to place a designated amount of money in escrow or in a bond that can be reached by the NCP if the CP continues to interfere with visitation.
- The interference could be a step in the direction of terminating the parental rights of the CP (see Chapter 15).
- A few states allow a NCP to bring a tort action for interference with parental rights or tortious interference with custody (see Chapter 17).

Some of these remedies may also be available to the CP against the NCP if the latter seriously interferes with the parental/custodial rights of the CP. In a recent case, a mother refused to comply with court-ordered visitation between her children and their paternal grandparents. Due to willful disobedience, the mother was held in civil contempt, sentenced to 180 days in jail, and ordered to pay $14,000 in attorney fees.[38]

It is never permissible for a parent to stop making child-support payments in retaliation for the other parent's violation of visitation or other custody rights. In Chapter 10, we will discuss remedies against the NCP for failure to pay child support. Can a court terminate the visitation rights of the NCP for not paying child support? Yes, but this is seldom done.

BIOLOGICAL PARENT VERSUS PSYCHOLOGICAL PARENT

Thus far, most of our focus has been a custody dispute between two biological parents. Suppose, however, that the dispute over who receives custody is between a biological parent and a third party such as one of the following:

- Grandparent
- Other relative
- Former opposite-sex lover or stepparent (who never adopted the child)
- Former same-sex lover or stepparent (who never adopted the child)
- Foster parent (initially assigned to the child by a **foster care** agency)
- Neighbor
- Friend

ne exeat
A writ that forbids a person from leaving the state, country, or jurisdiction of the court; or from removing a child or property therefrom.

foster care
A government-funded child welfare service that provides shelter and substitute family care when a child's own family cannot provide this shelter and care.

Assume that the other biological parent is out of the picture because he or she has died, has disappeared, or does not care. The third party is usually someone with whom the child has established close emotional ties. Frequently, the child has lived with the third party for a substantial period of time. This may have occurred for a number of reasons:

- The parent was ill, out of state, out of work, in prison, etc.
- The parent was in school for substantial periods of time.
- The state asked the third party to care for the child temporarily as a foster parent (see Chapter 14).
- The parent once considered giving the child up for adoption.
- The child could not stay at home because of marital difficulties between the biological parents.

A third party who has formed such ties with a child is often referred to as a **psychological parent**. This is an adult who, in a substantial and continuing way, has provided for the physical and emotional needs of a child. The adult is usually someone other than a biological or adoptive parent. A court might refer to a psychological parent as being **in loco parentis**, which means standing in the place of a parent by assuming some or all of the parental responsibilities without being a biological or adoptive parent.

In a custody dispute between a biological parent and a psychological parent, the determining test in most states is whether the biological parent is **unfit**. In these states, the test is *not* the best interests of the child. Except in extraordinary circumstances, if the biological parent is fit, he or she is awarded custody.

Unfit means demonstrating abuse or neglect that is substantially detrimental to a child. As we will see in Chapter 14, **child neglect** is the failure of a parent or other caregiver to provide the basic needs of a child, including physical needs (e.g., food and shelter), emotional needs, medical needs, and educational needs; *child abuse* is serious physical, emotional, or sexual mistreatment of a child that is not the result of accident or circumstances beyond the control of the parent or guardian.

As we saw in the *Troxel* case, fit custodial parents have a constitutional (due process) right to raise their children and are entitled to a presumption that their child-rearing decisions are sound. When there is a custody dispute between a custodial biological parent and a psychological parent, the dispute is *not* resolved by asking who can provide the best home for the child—the biological parent or the psychological parent. The question is whether the biological parent is *fit*—that is, willing and able to provide what is needed to raise his or her child. If the biological parent is fit, he or she receives custody, not the psychological parent. Although a child may suffer some disruption if his or her relationship with the psychological parent is severed, this does not necessarily overcome the biological parent's overriding right to raise the child. The law is very reluctant to take children away from their natural parents because of a determination that someone else could do a better job raising them.

In practice, however, some courts tend to blur the distinction between the fitness of a biological parent and the comparative benefits that can be offered by a psychological parent. A court that emphasizes the rights of a biological parent might still undertake a comparison between the benefits to the child living with the biological parent and the benefits of living with the psychological parent. When the benefits to be derived from the latter are overwhelming, the court might be more inclined to find unfitness in the biological parent and to conclude that giving custody to the biological parent would be detrimental to the child. The interpretation of the evidence can be subjective. Often, there are enough data to support any conclusion the court wants to reach. A person's

psychological parent
An adult who, in a substantial and continuing way, has provided for the physical and emotional needs of a child.

in loco parentis
1. Standing in the place of a parent by assuming some or all parental responsibilities without being a biological or adoptive parent.
2. Acting as a temporary guardian or caretaker of a child.

unfit
Demonstrating abuse or neglect that is substantially detrimental to a child.

child neglect
The failure of a parent or other caregiver to provide the basic needs of a child, including physical needs (e.g., food and shelter), emotional needs, medical needs, and educational needs.

mistakes in raising children can be viewed either as an inability to be a competent parent or as an inevitable component of the nearly impossible job of parenting in today's society.

CHANGING THE CHILD'S SURNAME

Once the court decides who receives custody, the custodial parent (CP) might request that the surname of the child be changed. For example, a mother might ask that the child's surname be changed to her maiden name or to the surname of her new husband. This change-of-name request might also be made at a later time in a separate proceeding. Assume that the child has always had the surname of the noncustodial parent (NCP). The court must determine whether a surname change is in the best interests of the child. The following excerpt from a court opinion explains the factors that most courts consider in applying this standard:

> We first note that neither parent has a superior right to determine the initial surname their child shall bear. . . . However, once a surname has been selected for the child, be it the maternal, paternal, or some combination of the child's parents' surnames, a change in the child's surname should be granted only when the change promotes the child's best interests. In determining the child's best interests, the trial court may consider, but its consideration is not limited to, the following factors: the child's preference; . . . the effect of the change of the child's surname on the preservation and the development of the child's relationship with each parent; the length of time the child has borne a given name; the degree of community respect associated with the present and the proposed surname; and the difficulties, harassment or embarrassment that the child may experience from bearing the present or the proposed surname.[39]

The court stressed what when the NCP objects to the change, the evidence that the change is in the best interests of the child should be "clear and compelling."

A court's approval of a change in the surname of a child does not alter the parent-child relationship that the child has with both natural parents. Unless there has been an adoption or a termination of parental rights (see Chapter 15), a surname change has no effect on a parent's rights and responsibilities.

RAPE-CONCEIVED CHILDREN

Before discussing the modification of custody orders, we need to mention the unique custody and visitation issues that are raised in the case of rape-conceived children.

More than 25,000 rape-related pregnancies occur every year. Statistics vary on the number of these pregnancies that are ended by abortion. One study said 50 percent; another concluded 26 percent. What is clear is that a substantial number of women raise their children conceived by rape. Most do so alone because the rapists have no interest in the children they fathered. This is not so, however, in all cases. Some rapists seek the custody and visitation rights of a father. Remarkably, most states do not have laws that deny them this right. Only a few states allow the termination of a father's parental rights solely due to the fact that his child was the result of his act of rape. One woman exclaimed, "I was raped . . . and the rapist has been taking me to court for 5 years for the right to see his son."

> "Under most states' laws, a man who fathers a child through rape has the same legal rights to custody and visitation in regard to that child as does any other father of a child due to the absence of any laws restricting or terminating

such rights; as a result, many raped women face significant consequences following their decisions to raise the children they conceived through rape. They may be forced to share custody privileges of their children with their rapists, to ensure their rapists' access to their children, to foster their rapists' relationships with their children, and, in some cases, to make joint decisions about their children's welfare."[40]

To compound the problem, some women feel pressured into not cooperating with the state in the prosecution of the father for the crime of rape in the hope that the father will simply go away and never seek access to the child or that he will voluntarily relinquish his parental rights.

MODIFICATION BY THE STATE THAT ISSUED THE ORDER

Although child-custody decisions are often part of a divorce judgment, a custody decision is not considered a final judgment. Courts want to retain their jurisdiction over the child so that they can modify their decision if needed to protect the child.

In this section, we consider modification requests made to the same court that issued the initial custody decision. (Example: A parent petitions an Ohio court to modify the custody decision made earlier by the Ohio court.) In the next section, we will consider the more complex and controversial problem of interstate modifications, where the modification request is made to a court in another state. (Example: A parent petitions a Florida court to modify the custody decision made earlier by a California court.)

Two reasons justify a court in modifying its own custody order:

- There has been a substantial change in circumstances since the original order, or
- Relevant facts were not made available to the court at the time of its original order.

In either situation, the question is whether it is in the best interests of the child for the court to change its mind and award custody to the other parent or to adjust the custody/visitation arrangement. Given the disruption of such a change, the answer is *no* unless the new facts *substantially* alter the court's perception of the child's welfare. For example:

- The CP has been neglecting or abusing the child.
- The CP has moved from the area, contrary to the court's order, thus making visitation by the NCP extremely difficult or impossible.
- The CP has adopted an unorthodox lifestyle that has negatively affected the child's physical or mental health.

Given the potential for disruption in a child's life, the standard a parent must meet to obtain a change in custody is generally higher than the standard needed to obtain an initial custody order. To justify modification, it is not enough that the CP has experienced hard times such as sickness or loss of a part-time job since the initial order. Nor is it enough to show that mistakes have been made in raising the children. To justify a modification, the adverse circumstances or mistakes must be (1) ongoing, (2) relatively permanent, (3) serious, and (4) detrimental to the child. In some states, courts will not hear a request for modification within at least two years after the initial custody order unless the child has been abandoned or faces serious endangerment. (No such time limits apply, however, for requests to modify a visitation order.) For an argument by a NCP on why custody should be changed, see the affidavit in support of a motion to modify custody in Exhibit 9.6.

EXHIBIT 9.6   Affidavit in Support of a Motion to Modify a Custody Decree

AFFIDAVIT IN SUPPORT

STATE OF _____

COUNTY OF _____

John Davis v. Mary Davis

CV-2347-FC-2020

February 10, 2020

John Davis, being duly sworn, deposes and says:

1. This affidavit is submitted in support of an application for reconsideration of the decision of the court made in this action on March 13, 2017, insofar as custody of my children is concerned.

2. Custody of the children has been awarded to my ex-wife, Mary Davis. I did not contest her claim in the divorce. When I reported this to the children, they became extremely upset. My son told me that he did not want to live with his mother and that he felt it was unfair for a boy of his age to be forced to live with a parent contrary to his desires. My daughter had a similar reaction.

3. I love my children very much. A history of prior proceedings between my wife and myself indicates that she had been awarded custody of the children under a Family Court order on March 13, 2017. At that time, she lived with the children in our house in Peekskill. I paid support, as directed, for the children and my wife, and for the upkeep of the house. About two years ago, my wife ousted my son from the house and sent him to live with me. At that time, I occupied a small apartment in Peekskill so that I could be near the children. I would see them quite often and would take them to school on many mornings. When my son came to me, I made room for him and we lived together until my daughter came to live with us about a year ago. We made room for her. My wife made no objections to the children living with me and made no attempts to get them to come back to her. While we all lived in my small apartment, my wife continued to live in the Peekskill house by herself. I continued paying for the upkeep on the house, although my wife permitted it to fall into a state of deteriorating disrepair. I contributed to her support.

4. I took care of my children as best I could. They were grown and attended school most of the day. In the evening, we enjoyed a family life. We were together on the weekends. There were many weekends when their mother would not attempt to spend any time with them. My son stayed away from the Peekskill house. My daughter visited there with her mother on occasion. I know that on many occasions my wife stayed away from the Peekskill house for days at a time.

5. I have devoted my non-working hours to my children. I altered my schedule so that I would see them off to school each morning when I was not away from the City. If I was to be away, I would arrange adult supervision. I worked with my children on their homework and on anything else where they sought my participation. We shopped together and played together. My children were encouraged to maintain their friendships and to bring their friends to our home. Because of cramped quarters, my children would often visit with their friends and I encouraged them to maintain relationships with companions of their respective ages. I shared their problems and their joys. I tried to set responsible examples for them. My son had demonstrated to me that he is growing into a responsible young man who aspires to attend Massachusetts Institute of Technology. I am proud of his seriousness and of his healthy outlook in times like this. I have tried to maintain a closely knit family between my children and myself so that they should know the advantages of love, companionship, and security. I know that they did not find any such relationship at their mother's bosom.

6. My children have revealed to me that they were wrong in not having made a definite choice during the interview with the court back in 2017 on the matter of their preference of a home. I understand that they will still love their mother and I have not attempted to sway them from that plateau. They told me that they wanted the court to decide the problem for them and that they had hoped that they could be the force which could solve the rift between plaintiff and myself. They were unaware that at the time of the interview, my wife's prayer for divorce had already been granted. My son told me that he indicated to the court that he preferred to live with me although he did not state, unequivocally, that he did not desire to live with his mother.

7. I gather from my children's reaction and from what they have told me that they misunderstood what was required of them during their interview with the court. Had I not seen the effect of the custody decision on my children and had they not indicated their grief over it, I would sit back and abide by the will of the court.

8. I seriously question my wife's fitness as our children's custodian. She voluntarily relinquished their custody, as aforesaid. Under adverse living conditions (cramped quarters), my children have thrived and demonstrated a progression toward adulthood. I believe that my wife's having been competitive instead of being cooperative with the children operated to compromise their welfare. I believe that using the children as a pawn has lost our children's respect. I feel that my pleasures must be subservient to the

(continued)

Exhibit 9.6 *(continued)*

welfare of my children. They deserve as real a home as can be possible under the circumstances. They are entitled to eat a meal in peace and one that shows concern in its preparation. I believe that the children deserve some security in the knowledge that they have the genuine care and love of a parent. I believe that they cannot get this from their mother.

9. WHEREFORE, I respectfully pray that this application be granted and that upon reconsideration I be awarded custody of my children.

[Signature]

_____

Source: Reprinted from Joseph Marino, West's McKinney's Forms, Matrimonial and Family Law Form 20:152 (West 2011) with permission of Thomson Reuters.

ASSIGNMENT   9.7

How do you think the court will respond to the father's request for a change in custody in Exhibit 9.6? Do you think the court should grant it? What further facts, if any would you like to know about the case? (See the General Instructions for the Legal-Analysis and the investigation-Strategy Assignments in Appendix A.)

INTERSTATE MODIFICATION

INTRODUCTION

We have been discussing the modification of a child-custody order by the state that issued the order. The court's jurisdiction or power to modify its own order is rarely in doubt because all of the parties and the child are usually still in the state and, as indicated, in custody cases the court normally retains jurisdiction after it issues its initial order. Suppose, however, that a party tries to have the order modified by *another* state. Interstate modification of custody orders presents more serious problems.

> *Dan and Ellen are divorced in New York, where they live. The New York divorce court grants Ellen sole physical custody and sole legal custody of their child, with Dan receiving visitation rights. Dan moves to Delaware. During a visit of the child in Delaware, Dan petitions a Delaware court for a modification of the New York custody order. Ellen does not appear in the Delaware proceeding. Dan tells the Delaware court a horror story about the child's life with Ellen in New York. The Delaware court modifies the New York order on the basis of changed circumstances, awarding sole physical and sole legal custody to Dan.*

Or worse:

> *Dan and Ellen's child is playing in the yard of a New York school. Dan takes the child from the yard and goes to Delaware without telling Ellen. Dan petitions a Delaware court for a modification of the New York custody order. If he loses, he tries again in Florida. If he loses, he tries again in another state until he finds a court that will grant him custody.*

The latter situation involves what has been commonly called *child snatching.* A parent, without consulting the other parent, takes ("snatches") the child and then "shops" for a favorable **forum** (court) in which to re-litigate the custody issue. For years, the problem of such **forum shopping** reached epidemic proportions.

> *When a decree has been rendered awarding custody to one of the parties, this is by no means the end of the child's migrations. It is well known that those who lose a court battle over custody are often unwilling to accept the judgment of the court. They will remove the child in an unguarded moment or fail to return him*

forum
(1) A court. (2) The place where the parties are presently litigating their dispute. (3) A court or tribunal hearing a case.

forum shopping
When more than one court has jurisdiction over a claim, choosing the court that is most likely to issue a favorable ruling.

after a visit and will seek their luck in the court of a distant state where they hope to find - and often do find - a more sympathetic ear for their plea for custody. The party deprived of the child may then resort to similar tactics to recover the child and this "game" may continue for years, with the child thrown back and forth from state to state, never coming to rest in one single home and in one community. The harm done to children by these experiences can hardly be overestimated.[41]

Before Reforms Were Implemented

Before the law was reformed, courts were caught in a dilemma. They did not want to close their doors to children in need of custody changes; yet, their availability encouraged child snatching and forum shopping. Custody orders were always modifiable on the basis of changed circumstances that affected the welfare of the child. Under the traditional rule, if an order is not final, it is not entitled to **full faith and credit (FFC)** by another state (i.e., another state is not required to abide by it). Hence, other states were free to re-examine the case to determine whether new circumstances warranted a modification. To maintain flexibility, states required very little to trigger their jurisdiction to hear a modification case (e.g., the physical presence or domicile of the child in the state). The result was chaos: scandalous child snatching and unseemly forum shopping.

Reforms to End the Chaos

To solve the problem, uniformity in the law of custody jurisdiction among the states was required. To try to achieve this uniformity, three major legislative efforts occurred:

- In 1968, many states adopted the *Uniform Child Custody Jurisdiction Act* (UCCJA) proposed by the National Conference of Commissioners on Uniform State Laws (NCCUSL). Unfortunately, all states did not adopt the UCCJA. Furthermore, some states adopted their own version of the UCCJA, which meant that the "uniform" act was not uniform throughout the country.

- In 1980, Congress passed the *Parental Kidnapping Prevention Act* (PKPA) because of its concern that the UCCJA was not going to solve the problem of child snatching and the relitigation of custody disputes. The PKPA specified when the custody decrees of one state had to be accepted in (i.e., had to be given full faith and credit by) every other state.[42] Although the word "kidnapping" is used in the title of the PKPA, the act covers any custody decree that someone tries to modify in another state, not just cases involving child snatching.

- In 1997, the most important step toward uniformity occurred when the NCCUSL revised the UCCJA in order to conform it to the PKPA. The revision is called the *Uniform Child Custody Jurisdiction and Enforcement Act* (UCCJEA).[43]

We need to examine how the UCCJEA and the PKPA work together. These statutes do not decide which party should have custody. Rather, they decide which court should have the authority (jurisdiction) to make the custody determination.

UNIFORM CHILD CUSTODY JURISDICTION AND ENFORCEMENT ACT

The **Uniform Child Custody Jurisdiction and Enforcement Act (UCCJEA)** is designed to avoid jurisdictional competition and conflict among state courts that can arise when parents shift children from state to state in search of a favorable custody decision. Two important questions are covered in the UCCJEA:

- When does a court in the state have the power or jurisdiction to make the *initial* decision on child custody?

- When can a court modify a custody order of another state?

---

full faith and credit (FFC)
The obligation of one state to recognize and enforce the laws and court decisions of another state. This obligation is based on the U.S. Constitution, which provides that "Full Faith and Credit shall be given in each State to the public Acts, Records, and judicial Proceedings of every other State." Article IV, § 1.

Uniform Child Custody Jurisdiction and Enforcement Act (UCCJEA)
A model state statute on the enforcement of custody and visitation orders across state lines.

Jurisdiction to Make the Initial Child Custody Decision

Under the UCCJEA, mere physical presence of the child in the state is *not* sufficient to give the state jurisdiction to enter an initial custody order. Nor is the mere physical presence of one of the parents sufficient. There are four major foundations for custody jurisdiction under the UCCJEA:

- Home state custody jurisdiction.
- Significant connection/substantial evidence (sc/se) custody jurisdiction.
- Temporary emergency custody jurisdiction.
- Last resort custody jurisdiction.

Home state custody jurisdiction is the most important and has ultimate priority. It is based on where the child has lived for the last six months with a parent (or anyone acting as a parent) immediately before the commencement of a child-custody proceeding or since birth if the child is less than six months old. For a summary of the four categories of child-custody jurisdiction under the UCCJEA, see Exhibit 9.7.

home state
The state where the child has lived with a parent (or anyone acting as a parent) for at least six consecutive months immediately before the commencement of a child-custody proceeding or since birth if the child is less than six months old.

EXHIBIT 9.7   Jurisdiction to Make an Initial Custody Decision under the UCCJEA

General Rule: A state must have one of the following four kinds of custody jurisdiction to be able to make an initial custody order: [1] home state (this is the preferred basis of jurisdiction), [2] significant connection/substantial evidence (sc/se), [3] temporary emergency, or [4] last resort jurisdiction if no other state has or wants jurisdiction over the case.

Kind of Custody Jurisdiction	When Does a State Have This Type of Custody Jurisdiction?	Notes
Home State Custody Jurisdiction	A state has home state custody jurisdiction if one of two conditions exist: • This state is the home state of the child. A home state is the state in which the child has lived with a parent (or anyone acting as a parent) for at least six consecutive months immediately before the commencement of a child-custody proceeding or since birth if the child is less than six months old. (Temporary absences count as part of the six months or as part of the time since birth.) OR • This state *was* the home state of the child within six months before the court proceedings began and the child is now absent from the state, but a parent continues to live in this state.	• If the state that made the initial custody order had home state custody jurisdiction, that state will have *continuing jurisdiction* to make future custody determinations so long as at least one parent continues to live in the state. • A state with home state custody jurisdiction has priority over a state with sc/se custody jurisdiction.
SC/SE Custody Jurisdiction	A state has sc/se custody jurisdiction if three conditions exist: • No other state is the home state of the child (or if another state is the home state, it has declined to exercise the custody jurisdiction that it has). AND • The child and at least one parent have a significant connection (sc) with this state other than mere presence in this state. AND • There is substantial evidence (se) in this state concerning the child's care, protection, training, and personal relationships.	• A state with sc/se custody jurisdiction cannot enter a custody decision if another state has home-state jurisdiction unless the home state declines to act.

(continued)

Exhibit 9.7 (continued)

Kind of Custody Jurisdiction	When Does a State Have This Type of Custody Jurisdiction?	Notes
Temporary Emergency Custody Jurisdiction	A state has temporary emergency custody jurisdiction if two conditions exist: • The child is present in the state. AND • The child has been abandoned or there is an emergency requiring protection of the child because the child, a sibling, or a parent is being mistreated or abused or threatened with mistreatment or abuse (domestic violence).	• Temporary emergency custody jurisdiction can be exercised by a state that does not have home-state jurisdiction or sc/se jurisdiction. • The need to protect the child takes precedence because of the emergency. • But the custody order made by a court with temporary emergency jurisdiction can remain in effect only until a state with home state or sc/se jurisdiction intervenes. • Hence temporary emergency jurisdiction has a lower priority than home-state jurisdiction and sc/se jurisdiction.
Last Resort Custody Jurisdiction	A state has last resort jurisdiction if one of two conditions exist: • No other state has home-state jurisdiction or sc/se jurisdiction. OR • Every state that has jurisdiction has declined to exercise it.	

ASSIGNMENT 9.8

a. Fred and Jane were married in Iowa on 1/1/09. On 3/13/10 in Iowa, they had a child, Bob, in Iowa. From the first day of their marriage, however, they had been having marital difficulties. On 7/4/10, Fred moved to California. Bob continued to live with his mother in Iowa. By mutual agreement, Fred occasionally takes the child to California for visits. This occurs several times without incident.

After a scheduled one-day visit on 11/5/10, however, Fred decides not to return the child. He keeps Bob until 11/2/11, when Fred changes his mind and returns Bob to Jane in Iowa.

Fred joins the Army on 11/10/11.

When he is discharged from the Army on 10/1/13, he returns to California.

If an action for custody had been filed on the following dates, which state (Iowa or California) would have home-state jurisdiction under the UCCJEA to render a custody decision?

1. 4/4/10
2. 11/6/10
3. 1/1/11
4. 11/1/11
5. 10/6/13

(See General Instructions for the Legal-Analysis Assignment in Appendix A.)

b. Assume Fred is convinced that he is the better parent because of what he believes to be a pattern of neglect in Jane's care of Bob. What facts would you investigate in order to support or discredit Fred's position? Include questions that you would ask Fred. See General Instructions for the Investigation-Strategy Assignment in Appendix A.

Forum non Conveniens

You will note that Exhibit 9.7 refers to courts that decline to use the custody jurisdiction that they have. Assume that a court has jurisdiction to make the initial custody decision because it is the home state or because it is the state with sc/se. Nevertheless, this court may decline to exercise this jurisdiction because it determines that it is an *inconvenient forum*. This determination is based on **forum non conveniens**, which is the discretionary power of a court to decline the exercise of its jurisdiction when it would be more convenient and the ends of justice would be better served if the action were tried in another court.

How does a state decide whether it is an inconvenient forum? There is no rigid formula. It will consider a number of factors. Let's look at an example:

> Sid and Fran have lived in Tennessee since their marriage there in 2011. On 1/10/14, Fran gives birth to their child, Jim. On 2/10/15, Sid takes Jim to live with his mother in Oregon because of marital difficulties with Fran. On 12/10/15, Sid files for divorce in Oregon. In the divorce action, he asks the Oregon court to award him sole physical and sole legal custody of Jim. A month later (1/10/16), Fran files an action in Tennessee asking that she be granted sole physical and sole legal custody.

Oregon is Jim's home state. He has been with a parent (Sid) in Oregon for at least six consecutive months (from 2/10/15 to 12/10/15) immediately before the court action was filed in which Sid made the initial custody request. Under the UCCJEA, Oregon has jurisdiction to issue a custody order. Under the rule of forum non conveniens, however, Oregon can use its discretion to decline to exercise this jurisdiction if another state (e.g., Tennessee) would be a more convenient forum to litigate the custody dispute.

Here are some of the factors an Oregon court will consider in determining whether Tennessee is a more convenient forum for the parties to litigate the custody matter:

- *Domestic violence.* If domestic violence has been committed or threatened in Tennessee (e.g., Sid alleges that Fran was physically abusive to Jim in Tennessee), an Oregon court might decide that Tennessee is in the best position to resolve the allegation of child abuse and protect the parties. If so, Tennessee would be the most convenient state to make the custody decision.

- *Length of time the child has been outside the state.* Jim was in Tennessee from 1/10/14 to 2/10/15 (thirteen months). He was in Oregon from 2/10/15 to 12/10/15 (eight months). An Oregon court could conclude that this disparity of time bolsters the argument for letting Tennessee decide the custody issue.

- *Relative financial circumstances of the parties.* If litigating the custody case in Oregon would impose extreme financial burdens on the party in Tennessee (Fran) and if the party in Oregon (Sid) would have the financial resources to litigate in Tennessee, then an Oregon court might decide that Tennessee is the most convenient forum to make the custody decision.

- *Nature and location of the evidence.* If the important evidence needed to resolve the custody matter is in Tennessee, then an Oregon court might decide that Tennessee would be the most convenient forum to make the custody decision.

Again, the decision is discretionary with Oregon. In our example, we have assumed that Oregon has home state custody jurisdiction and has the right to exercise it. The UCCJEA encourages, but does not require, such a state to relinquish its jurisdiction if it decides that another state would be a more convenient state to render the custody decision.

forum non conveniens
The discretionary power of a court to decline the exercise of its jurisdiction when it would be more convenient, and the ends of justice would be better served, if the action were tried in another court.

Jurisdiction to Modify a Custody Order of Another State

Thus far, our primary focus has been the jurisdiction of a state to make an *initial* custody order under the UCCJEA. The examples we have used have involved more than one state, but our focus has been on identifying the state that has jurisdiction to make the first custody decision. (When does a court have jurisdiction to decide the custody question for the first time?) We now turn to the question of when a state has jurisdiction to *modify* a custody order of another state.

The underlying principle on jurisdiction in modification cases is as follows:

Once a court has made an initial custody order under the UCCJEA because it has home-state jurisdiction or sc/se jurisdiction, that court has **exclusive continuing jurisdiction (ECJ)** *over the case. Continuing means that the case is kept open;* exclusive *means that no other court has authority to act in the case unless the initial state declines to use its ECJ because another state is a more convenient forum.*

For example, if Florida was the home state and made the initial custody decision, then Florida has ECJ. North Carolina cannot modify Florida's custody order so long as Florida continues to have ECJ unless Florida declines to use its ECJ because it determines that North Carolina would be a more convenient forum.

If a state loses its ECJ, another state can become the home state and thereby modify the initial state's custody order. An initial state can lose its ECJ if both parents and the child no longer reside in the initial state or if substantial evidence about the child no longer exists in the state.

Suppose, for example, that Connecticut issues an initial custody order and has ECJ. The dissatisfied parent then takes the child to Maine. Can a Maine court modify the Connecticut order? Not if one of the parents remains in Connecticut. The dissatisfied parent would have to go back to Connecticut to ask the Connecticut court to modify its order or to rule that Maine is a more convenient forum.

An exception exists when there is an emergency, but only on a temporary basis. A state court with temporary emergency custody jurisdiction (see Exhibit 9.7) can modify the custody decision of any other court if the child is present in the state and has been abandoned, or if there is an emergency requiring protection of the child because the child, a sibling, or a parent is being mistreated or abused or threatened with mistreatment or abuse (domestic violence). In our Maine-Connecticut example, if the Maine court concluded that it had temporary emergency custody jurisdiction because of abandonment or violence in Maine, the Maine court could issue a custody order that would have the effect of modifying a Connecticut order. (A Maine court, for example, might issue a **protective order** or **restraining order** to keep a violent parent away from the child until a further hearing can be held.) As indicated in Exhibit 9.7, however, temporary emergency custody jurisdiction is *temporary*. A court with home-state jurisdiction—Connecticut in our example—can step in and change (modify) the temporary emergency custody order of a Maine court.

When a parent has **dirty hands**, a court might decline to exercise its jurisdiction. Dirty hands means wrongdoing or other inappropriate behavior that would make it unfair or inequitable to allow persons to assert a right or a defense they would normally have. Suppose, for example, that a parent engages in blatant forum shopping by moving a child from state to state for the sole purpose of trying to find a friendly court. In the unlikely event that this parent eventually finds a court that has jurisdiction under the UCCJEA, this court can decline to take the case because of the parent's dirty hands. But the court will make such a decision only if it determines that the refusal to take the case would not harm the child.

---

exclusive continuing jurisdiction (ECJ)
The authority of a court (obtained by compliance with the Uniform Child Custody Jurisdiction and Enforcement Act (UCCJEA)) to make all initial *and modifying* custody decisions in a case to the exclusion of courts in any other state.

protective order
A court order directing a person to refrain from inappropriate conduct such as harming or harassing another. Also called *order of protection.*

restraining order
A form of injunction, initially issued ex parte (with only one side present), to restrain the defendant from doing a threatened act or from contacting designated individuals. Also called *order of protection, personal protection order (PPO)*, and *protection from abuse.*

dirty hands
Wrongdoing or other inappropriate behavior that would make it unfair or inequitable to allow persons to assert a right or a defense they would normally have. Also called *unclean hands.* A person without dirty hands is said to have *clean hands.*

ASSIGNMENT 9.9

a. Ted and Ursula Jackson have one child, Sam. Sam was born on 4/13/15 in New York, where Ted, Ursula, and Sam have lived since the beginning of 2015. Upon discovering that Ted is having an affair with an office worker, Ursula takes Sam to Florida on 5/1/15, where her parents live. Ted continues to live in New York.

   1. On 5/1/15, could Ted go to a court in New York to obtain an initial custody order?

   2. Could Ursula obtain an initial custody order in Florida on 5/2/15?

b. Assume that Ted obtains a valid initial custody order in New York on 5/1/15. On 7/1/15 Ursula goes to a Florida court to seek a modification of the New York order. Under what circumstances, if any, will the Florida court modify the New York order? (See General Instructions for the Legal-Analysis Assignment in Appendix A.)

PARENTAL KIDNAPPING PREVENTION ACT

In addition to *state* laws on child-custody jurisdiction, there is also a *federal* statute designed to combat child snatching and forum shopping called the **Parental Kidnapping Prevention Act (PKPA)**. The PKPA covers all interstate child-custody disputes, not just those that involve child snatching or kidnapping. The PKPA requires states to give full faith and credit (FFC) to the custody decree of the state that issued the initial decree if this state had jurisdiction to do so (with priority given to the state with home-state jurisdiction). Another state "shall not modify" it. An exception exists if an emergency requires intervention because of abandonment, abuse, or neglect.

The PKPA also made available to the states the *Federal Parent Locator Service*, which can help locate an absent parent or child. As we will see in Chapter 10, this service was initially created as a tool for collecting child support. The PKPA makes the service available in child-custody cases where there is a need to locate a parent or child in order to enforce a child-custody order.

Parental Kidnapping Prevention Act (PKPA)
A federal statute that requires a state to enforce (give full faith and credit to) child-custody orders of other states when the orders comply with the PKPA (28 U.S.C. § 1738A).

CHILDREN ABROAD

As seen in this chapter, parental kidnapping within the United States can lead to complex jurisdictional problems. These problems multiply when the child is taken out of the country. The most difficult and frustrating reality for most parents whose children have been abducted abroad is that U.S. laws and U.S. court orders are not usually recognized in foreign countries and therefore are not directly enforceable abroad. A custody order in the United States can be meaningless abroad.[44]

When a child who is a U.S. citizen is abducted abroad, the U.S. State Department can work with U.S. embassies and consulates abroad to assist the child and the left-behind parent. The first step is to open an International Parental Child Abduction Case with the Department of State's Office of Children's Issues (OCI). The concerned parent should also contact local police, file a missing person report, and request that the child's name be entered into the National Crime Information Center (NCIC) computer database of the Federal Bureau of Investigation.[45]

The Hague Convention on the Civil Aspects of International Child Abduction (Hague Abduction Convention) is a treaty that seeks to deter international child abduction. It applies in countries that have ratified the treaty (referred to as Convention countries) when the following three conditions are met:

1. The child was "habitually resident" (it was the child's home for a significant amount of time) in one Convention country, and was wrongfully removed to or retained in another Convention country (taken or retained in violation of the aggrieved parent's custody rights).

2. The wrongful removal or retention occurred between two Convention countries that have a treaty relationship.

3. The child is under the age of sixteen.

Convention countries have agreed that a child who was living in one Convention country, and who has been removed to or retained in another Convention country in violation of the aggrieved parent's custodial rights, shall be promptly returned. Once the child has been returned, the custody dispute can then be resolved, if necessary, in the courts of that jurisdiction. The Hague Convention does not address who should have custody of the child; it addresses where the custody case should be heard.

Each Convention country has designated a central authority (a specific government office) to carry out specialized duties related to the Convention. Central authorities communicate with each other and assist parents in filing applications for return of (or access to) their children under the Convention. The central authority for the United States is the Department of State's Office of Children's Issues (OCI).

If the abducting parent does not voluntarily agree to return the child, the aggrieved parent may need to hire legal counsel in the foreign county to seek the return of the child pursuant to the Hague Convention. The U.S. Department of State's OCI does not provide representation, but it can provide information and coordination assistance. If the foreign country is not a Convention country, the process is similar except that the foreign country is not obligated to follow the procedures in the Convention.

EMBRYOS (EMBRYONIC CUSTODY DISPUTES)

embryo
An egg that has been fertilized by a sperm and is in the early stage of development; it has undergone one or more divisions. The product of conception to about the eighth week of pregnancy.

An **embryo** is an egg that has been fertilized by a sperm and is in the early stage of development; it has undergone one or more divisions. The embryo is the product of conception to about the eighth week of pregnancy. Child custody and adoption laws do not apply to embryos or sperm that are frozen for possible future use in attempting conception. Most states consider frozen embryos and sperm to be property that can be used or destroyed by contractual arrangements between the adults involved and the companies that do the freezing. As we will see in Chapter 16, however, the issue becomes more complex when a state attempts to define embryos as persons.

When a child is born using modern reproductive technologies such as in vitro fertilization, child-custody disputes can arise among the multiple parties involved in the child's conception and birth. We will also discuss such disputes in Chapter 16.

PARALEGAL ROLES

- For an overview of paralegal roles in family-law cases, see Exhibits 1.5 and 1.6 in Chapter 1.
- For financial issues related to child custody, a paralegal may be asked to help collect documents and facts outlined in:
  - The checklist in Exhibit 3.1 of Chapter 3.
  - The interrogatories in Appendix C.
- Interview the client and conduct an investigation into the facts that support parental involvement in the child's life to date in order to bolster the positions taken in the parent's parenting plan.
- "In cases where child-custody is an issue," comments an experienced paralegal, "be it the initial dissolution case or a modification of decree, the client provides me with names of potential witnesses to testify in their behalf. I contact each person and determine if they should be interviewed. As in a recent case, sometimes all witnesses live hours away, requiring me to travel and spend a few days interviewing. In these cases, it is a juggling [act] trying to schedule everyone."[46]

(continued)

- Miscellaneous duties:
  - Help prepare the client for deposition on custody issues.
  - Research potential expert witnesses for home evaluations.
  - Prepare a draft of the visitation schedule that has been negotiated by the parties.
  - Interview individuals concerning the home, school, and social environment of the child.
  - Draft affidavits for modification of custody orders.
  - Inform (and remind) the client of attendance at court-mandated mediation and parenting sessions for divorcing parents.
  - Conduct an investigation to collect evidence to demonstrate (or disprove) the nexus between a parent's lifestyle/morality and the welfare of the child.
  - Prepare a timeline of parent-child interactions since birth.
  - In interstate-custody cases, prepare a timeline of presence in both states of the child and the two parents in order to establish a state's jurisdiction to make the initial custody order and/or to modify an earlier order.
  - Act as liaison between the law office and the guardian ad litem (GAL), parenting coordinator (PC), and court appointed special advocate (CASA).
  - Research community resources to support the client's child-rearing responsibilities, particularly if the child has special needs.
  - Compile a health record of the client to demonstrate his or her suitability as a parent.
  - Compile a health record of the child.
  - Obtain police and other law-enforcement reports if domestic violence has occurred.
  - Obtain school records of the child.
  - Provide referrals to resources of the State Department in international custody cases.

SUMMARY

Legal custody is the right to make the major child-rearing decisions on healthcare, education, religion, discipline, and general welfare. Physical custody is the right of an adult (the custodial parent) to have a child reside with that adult. Both kinds of custody can be sole or joint. In negotiating custody and visitation clauses of a separation agreement, many factors need to be considered, such as the age and health of the parents and child, the emotional attachments of the child, the work schedules of the parents, etc. If negotiations fail and the parties cannot agree, litigation is necessary. This can be a stressful experience, not only for the parents but also for the person caught in the middle—the child. Courts often require divorcing parents to participate in short training programs to help relieve this stress.

When custody is contested, participants can include (in addition to parents, child, and judge) the attorneys for the parents, a best interests attorney (BIA), a guardian ad litem (GAL), a court appointed special advocate (CASA), and a parenting coordinator (PC). A custody dispute between the biological parents is resolved by a judge's considerable discretion in determining what is in the best interests of the child as reflected in competing parenting plans. The factors a judge will consider include stability in the child's life, availability to respond to the child's day-to-day needs, emotional ties that have already developed, amenability to visitation by the other parent, etc. At one time, courts applied guidelines such as the presumption that a child of tender years is better off with his or her mother. Today,

most courts reject gender-based presumptions, although fathers continue to complain that the mother is still given an undue preference. The moral values and lifestyles of the parent seeking custody are generally not considered by the court unless, under the nexus test, they negatively impact the child. Domestic violence that affects the child's welfare is also a factor. If the parents practice different religions, the court cannot prefer one religion over another, but it can consider any effect the practice of a particular religion will have on the child. To the extent possible, the court will try to maintain continuity in the child's cultural development. The custody decision cannot be based solely on race. If the child is old enough to express a preference, it will be considered. Often, the court will also consider the testimony of expert witnesses.

The court will generally favor liberal visitation rights for the noncustodial parent. Supervised visitation might be ordered if the court feels it is necessary because of violence or other serious concerns. Occasionally, such visitation rights will be granted to individuals other than biological parents (e.g., grandparents), if doing so does not interfere with the constitutional right of a fit custodial parent to make child-rearing decisions. When a custodial parent wants to move out of the area, the court will balance how the move will affect the noncustodial parent's visitation rights and the best interests of the child. Enforcement remedies can include ne exeat, civil and criminal contempt, and changes in the custody and visitation orders.

When the custody battle is between a biological parent and a nonparent (often called a psychological parent), the biological parent usually wins unless he or she can be shown to be unfit. If the parents disagree on whether the child's surname should be changed, the court will resolve the issue on the basis of whether the change is in the best interests of the child.

Occasionally, it is in the best interests of the child for a court to modify an earlier custody decision based primarily on changed circumstances. Frantic parents will sometimes engage in child snatching and forum shopping in order to find a court that will make a modification order. To cut down on this practice, two important laws have been enacted: the state Uniform Child Custody Jurisdiction and Enforcement Act and the federal Parental Kidnapping Prevention Act. The primary tool used by these statutes to cut down on forum shopping is to give priority to the child's home state among possible competing states that could be asked to issue or modify a custody decision. When the child has been taken to a foreign country, the aid of the Department of State and the Hague Convention on Child Abduction can be used.

KEY TERMS

best interests of the child	court appointed special advocate (CASA)	ne exeat
legal custody		foster care
physical custody	parenting coordinator	psychological parent
custodial parent (CP)	attorney-client privilege	in loco parentis
noncustodial parent (NCP)	parenting plan	unfit
visitation	approximation rule	child neglect
sole physical custody	deposition	forum
sole legal custody	parens patrae	forum shopping
joint physical custody	parental alienation syndrome (PAS)	full faith and credit (FFC)
split custody	junk science	Uniform Child Custody
bird nesting	tender-years presumption	Jurisdiction and Enforcement
coparenting	primary-caregiver presumption	Act (UCCJEA)
separation agreement	domestic violence (DV)	home state
Temporary Assistance for Needy Families (TANF)	child abuse	forum non conveniens
	civil contempt	exclusive continuing jurisdiction (ECJ)
presumption	criminal contempt	protective order
contested	Minnesota Multiphasic Personality Inventory Test (MMPI)	restraining order
mediation		dirty hands
mandatory	parenting time	Parental Kidnapping Prevention
alternative dispute resolution (ADR)	fit	Act (PKPA)
best interests attorney (BIA)	supervised visitation	embryo
guardian ad litem (GAL)	cohabitation	

CHECK THE CITE

A father has legal custody of his son. During the marriage, the boy was raised in the Russian Orthodox Church, which the mother still attends. At the time of the divorce, the father converted to Judaism and now wants to have his son circumcised. The mother has asked the court for an order preventing the circumcision or for an order granting her legal custody. How did the court resolve the conflict? Read *In re Marriage of Boldt*, 344 Or. 1, 176 P.3d 388 (Or. 2008). To read this opinion online: (1) Run a citation search ("176 P.3d 388") in the "Case law" database of Google Scholar (scholar.google.com). (2) Run this search in general search engines of Google or Bing: "Marriage of Boldt" circumcision.

PROJECT

In Google, Bing, or Yahoo, run the following search: aa "parenting coordinator" (substitute the name of your state for aa in the search). (a) Write a short essay in which you describe the benefits and potential difficulties of hiring a parenting coordinator. You must cite and quote from a minimum of three different sources that you find on the Internet. (b) Find three parenting coordinator services on the Internet (they can be the same three sites you selected in part (a)). How do the three services differ? In what ways are they the same? Compare what they offer, their experience, what they claim their strengths to be, their costs, etc.

ETHICS IN A FAMILY LAW PRACTICE

You are a paralegal working at the law office of Harris and Harris, which represents William Norton in a custody dispute with his wife, Irene Norton. Irene is represented by Davis & Davis. Your supervisor asks you to prepare interrogatories to be sent to Irene about her employment. You are not sure whether to include questions about her pension plan. Before you write any pension questions, you call Irene and ask her if she has a pension plan at her work. She is very cooperative, telling you that she does not have a pension. You then go back to drafting the interrogatories. Any ethical problems?

WRITING SAMPLE

George Smith and Alice O'Toole have one child, six-year-old Thomas. When George and Alice divorced, Alice was granted sole legal and sole physical custody of Thomas with visitation rights to George. The parties have always disagreed about how to raise their child. The disagreements continue after the divorce. Assume that George's attorney is going to draft a motion to modify the custody order so that George receives sole legal and sole physical custody. Alice's attorney will file an opposing motion. George's attorney asks George to write an affidavit that the attorney will file with the motion to modify. George's affidavit will state the facts that George believes justify the modification. Write the affidavit for George. (See Exhibit 9.6 for an example of a client affidavit.) You can make up the facts that are the basis of their custody dispute. The affidavit should have a strong factual basis to support its position. (See General Instructions for the Writing Sample in Appendix A.)

REVIEW QUESTIONS

1. What is meant by legal custody, physical custody, sole physical custody, sole legal custody, joint physical custody, joint legal custody, and split custody?

2. What are some of the factors the parents must consider when negotiating the child-custody clauses of their separation agreement?

3. When is joint legal custody likely to be effective?

4. What are some of the major guidelines that courts often present to divorcing parents to lessen the stress of divorce on children?

5. How is mediation often used in contested custody cases?

6. What are the roles of a best interests attorney (BIA), a guardian ad litem (GAL), a court appointed special advocate (CASA), and a parenting coordinator (PC)?

7. What factors do courts consider when determining the best interests of the child in a custody dispute between the two biological parents?

8. What are the components of a parenting plan?

9. How does a parent's attitude on visitation affect the court's decision on whether to allow that parent to become the custodial parent (CP)?

10. What are indicia of parenthood?

11. What is parental alienation syndrome (PAS), and why is it disfavored?

12. What is the tender-years presumption, and how is it used in custody decisions today?

13. What is the primary-caregiver presumption, and how is it used in custody decisions today?

14. What is the nexus test in regard to the morality and lifestyle of a parent seeking custody?

15. How does domestic violence affect a court's decision on custody?

16. What is the dilemma faced by attorneys asked to represent a parent who is accused of child sexual abuse?

17. What is the role of religion in the custody decision?

18. What is the role of race in the custody decision?

19. What roles do expert witnesses play in custody disputes?

20. What details should parents work out when negotiating the visitation clauses of the separation agreement?

21. What factors will a court consider in ruling on a request by the custodial parent to move away from the area?

22. What is virtual visitation?

23. What is the holding in the *Troxel* case?

24. When will a court require supervised visitation?

25. What is a shared-custody agreement?

26. What remedies are available to enforce a visitation order?

27. How does a court resolve a custody dispute between a biological parent and a psychological parent?

28. When can a divorced parent change the surname of a child?

29. What two reasons justify a court in modifying its own custody order?

30. What are child snatching and forum shopping?

31. What are the possible bases of jurisdiction under the Uniform Child Custody Jurisdiction and Enforcement Act?

32. When will a court use its discretion to refuse to exercise the custody jurisdiction that it has?

33. When does a court have jurisdiction to modify the custody order of another state?

34. What is the effect of the Parental Kidnapping Prevention Act (PKPA)?

35. What is the Hague Convention on the Civil Aspects of International Child Abduction?

36. Are embryos subject to the laws of child custody?

HELPFUL WEBSITES

Your State

See Appendix D for links to the family law of your state on the topics covered in this chapter.

Child Custody Jurisdiction

- www.ncjrs.gov/pdffiles1/ojjdp/189181.pdf
- en.wikipedia.org/wiki/Uniform_Child_Custody_Jurisdiction_and_Enforcement_Act

Shared Parenting: A Guide for Parents Living Apart

- www.mass.gov/files/documents/2016/08/tx/afcc-sharedparenting.pdf

A Judicial Guide to Child Safety in Child Custody Cases

- www.ncjfcj.org/images/stories/dept/fvd/pdf/judicial%20guide.pdf

Guidelines for Child Custody Evaluations

- www.apa.org/practice/guidelines/child-custody

Association of Family and Conciliation Courts

- www.afccnet.org

Principles of the Law of Family Dissolution

- papers.ssrn.com/sol3/papers.cfm?abstract_id=2014189

FBI Wanted List: Parental Kidnappings

- www.fbi.gov/wanted/parental-kidnappings

Grandparents Rights

- www.grandparentsrights.org
- family.findlaw.com/child-custody/grandparent-rights.html

Stepparents

- www.stepfamilies.info

Supervised Visitation Network

- www.svnworldwide.org

Court Appointed Special Advocates (CASA)

- www.casaforchildren.org

Child Custody and Visitation Software

- www.custodyxchange.com
- ParentingTime.net
- www.kidmate.com
- www.kidshare.com

Father's Rights

- www.dadsdivorce.com
- athomedad.org

Abuse-Excuse (unfounded claims of child abuse)

- www.abuse-excuse.com

Data on Children

- datacenter.kidscount.org

International Parental Kidnapping

- www.ncjrs.gov/pdffiles1/ojjdp/215476.pdf
- www.acf.hhs.gov/css/resource/hague-child-support-convention-judicial-guide

Google Scholar (scholar.google.com)

- Choose "Articles" and enter in the search box any of the key terms discussed in the chapter. Add the name of your state to the search term.

- Choose "Case law" and "Select courts". Select your state, click "Done," and enter in the search box any of the key terms discussed in the chapter. Add the name of your state to the search term.

Google, Bing, or Yahoo

(on these search engines, run the following searches, substituting your state for "aa")

- "child custody" aa
- joint custody divorce aa
- visitation divorce aa
- mediation "child custody" aa
- CASA child neglect aa
- "parenting plan" aa
- UCCJEA aa
- gay lesbian child custody aa
- PKPA custody aa
- international "child custody"
- "parenting coordinator" aa
- sole custody divorce aa

- coparenting aa
- "supervised visitation" aa
- guardian ad litem "child custody" aa
- "best interests of the child" aa
- "parental alienation syndrome" aa
- "primary caregiver" custody aa
- "tender years" "child custody" aa
- contempt "child custody" aa
- "child abuse" "child custody" aa

YouTube

Run the same searches on YouTube listed above for Google, Bing, Yahoo searches. Even when the video clips are trying to entice you to retain an attorney, buy a book, or enroll in a course, they can provide useful overviews and references to primary authority.

Twitter, Reddit, and Facebook

On Twitter, Reddit, and Facebook, run the following searches (substitute your state for aa in your searches. Look for links to family-law developments in your state.

- child custody aa
- parental kidnapping aa

ENDNOTES

Note: All or most of the court opinions in these endnotes can be read online. To do so, go to Google Scholar (scholar.google.com), select "Case law," and in the search box, enter the cite (e.g., "530 U.S. 57") or name of the case (e.g., "Troxel v. Granville") that is given in the endnote.

[1] Robert Oliphant and Nancy Ver Steegh, *Family Law* 103 (3d ed. 2010).

[2] Lisa Haddad et al, *High Conflict Divorce*, 29 American Journal of Family Law 243, 244 (2016).

[3] John Myers & Harry Krause, *Family Law in a Nutshell* 69, 72 (6th ed 2017).

[4] UPI, *A "Solomon Ruling—Half Son's Ashes"* Sydney Morning Herald (July 23, 1978); Chicago Daily Law Bulletin, July 21, 1978, at 1; Harry Krause et al., *Family Law* 628 (4th ed. 1998).

[5] Carl Schneider and Margaret Brinig, *An Invitation to Family Law* 62 (1996).

[6] Scott Coltrane and Randall Collins, *Sociology of Marriage and the Family* 530 (2001).

[7] Mary Ann Lamanna and Agnes Riedmann, *Marriages and Families* 481 (2000).

[8] National Conference of Commissioners on Uniform State Laws, *Uniform Representation of Children in Abuse, Neglect, and Custody Cases* (2006) (papers.ssrn.com/sol3/papers.cfm?abstract_id=938211).

[9] The AFCC Task Force on Parental Coordination, *Guidelines for Parental Coordination* 2 (May 2005) (www.afccnet.org).

[10] *In re Marriage of Hansen* 733 N.W.2d 683, 697 (Iowa 2007).

[11] National Council of Juvenile and Family Court Judges, *A Judicial Guide to Child Safety in Child Custody Cases* 13 (2008) (www.ncjfcj.org/images/stories/dept/fvd/pdf/judicial%20guide.pdf).

[12] *Tuter v. Tuter*, 120 S.W.2d 203, 205 (Mo. Ct. App. 1938).

[13] Joel Stonington and Frank Bass, *Single-Dad Courtroom Wins Show Greater Embrace of New Families*, Bloomberg News (July 25, 2011).

[14] Timothy Grall, *Custodial Mothers and Fathers and Their Child Support: 2009* (Current Population Reports, Dec. 2011) (www.census.gov/prod/2011pubs/p60-240.pdf).

[15] Jan Hoffman, *Divorced Fathers Make Gains in Battles to Increase Rights*, N.Y. Times, Apr. 26, 1995, at A11.

16 *In re Marriage of Wellman,* 164 Cal. Rptr. 148, 152 (Cal. Ct. App. 1980).

17 *Ex parte H.H.,* 830 So. 2d 21, 38 (Ala. 2002).

18 *Lawrence v. Texas,* 539 U.S. 558 (2003).

19 *Obergefell v. Hodges,* 135 S. Ct. 2584 (2015).

20 M. Szegedy-Maszak, *Who's to Judge,* N.Y. Times Magazine, May 21, 1989, at 28. (www.nytimes.com/1989/05/21/magazine/who-s-to-judge.html).

21 Cory Gordon, *False Allegations of Abuse in Child Custody Disputes,* 2 Minnesota Family Law Journal 225 (1985).

22 Catherine Paquette, *Handling Sexual Abuse Allegations in Child Custody Cases,* 25 New England Law Review 1415, 1419, n. 32 (1991) citing *Abuse: The New Weapon,* National Law Journal, July 17, 1989, at 20, col. 1.

23 Margaret Fisk, *Abuse: The New Weapon in Divorces,* National Law Journal, July 17, 1989, at 20.

24 Pew Forum on Religion & Public Life, *U.S. Religious Landscape Survey,* 34 (2007).

25 *Kendall v. Kendall,* 687 N.E.2d 1228, 1231 (Mass. 1997).

26 *Palmore v. Sidoti,* 466 U.S. 429 (1984).

27 James E. Manhood, *Kidmate Simplifies Custody Scheduling for Lawyers, Clients,* 16 Matrimonial Strategist 5 (Aug. 1998).

28 *Tropea v. Tropea,* 665 N.E.2d 145, 148 (N.Y. 1996).

29 Minnesota Statutes Annotated § 518.175(3).

30 Based on Florida Statutes, § 61.13001 (www.lrcvaw.org/laws/flrelocation.pdf).

31 *Troxel v. Granville,* 530 U.S. 57 (2000).

32 Id. at 63–64.

33 U.S. Const. amend. XIV, § 1.

34 *Troxel,* 530 U.S. at 65.

35 Id at 68, 72–73.

36 *In re Mullen,* 953 N.E.2d 302, 305-06 (Ohio 2011). Although the court affirmed the validity of shared-custody agreements, it denied the petitioner's request for visitation rights because of insufficient evidence that such an agreement had been entered into.

37 For example, see Revised Code of Washington, § 9A.40.060, Custodial Interference in the First Degree (apps.leg.wa.gov/rcw/default.aspx?cite=9A.40.060).

38 *D.G. v. W.M.,* 18A-MI-2115, Court of Appeals of Indiana (January 11, 2019) (www.in.gov/judiciary/opinions/pdf/01111902lmb.pdf).

39 *In re Saxton,* 309 N.W.2d 298, 301 (Minn. 1981).

40 Shauna R. Prewitt, *Giving Birth to a "Rapist's Child,"* 98 Georgetown Law Journal 827, 829, 831 (2010) (georgetown.lawreviewnetwork.com/files/pdf/98-3/Prewitt.PDF).

41 *Hafer v. Superior Court,* 126 Cal. App. 3d 856, 866 (Cal. Ct. App. 1981) quoting Commissioner's Comment to Uniform Child Custody Jurisdiction Act (UCCJA), 9 Uniform Laws Annotated 116–17 (1988).

42 28 U.S.C. § 1738A (www.law.cornell.edu/uscode/28/1738A.html).

43 Patricia Hoff, *Uniform Child Custody Jurisdiction and Enforcement Act,* Juvenile Justice Bulletin (2001) (www.ncjrs.gov/pdffiles1/ojjdp/189181.pdf).

44 U.S. Department of State, Office of Children's Issues, *International Parental Abduction* 3 (1997). See also travel.state.gov/content/travel.html.

45 Federal Bureau of Investigation, National Crime Information Center (www.fas.org/irp/agency/doj/fbi/is/ncic.htm).

46 Cathy Lenihan, *Role of the Family Law Paralegal,* 10 Oregon Legal Assistant Association Newsletter 7 (Aug. 1987).

CHAPTER 10

Child Support

CHAPTER OUTLINE

CHAPTER OBJECTIVES

After completing this chapter, you should be able to:

- State the role of state law and federal law on child support.
- Know who must pay child support, including persons other than biological parents.
- State when child support might continue after the age of majority.
- List the major issues divorcing parents should cover in the child-support clauses of their separation agreement.
- Explain how a state determines the amount of child support that is due.

- Know when income will be imputed for purposes of determining a child-support obligation.
- Identify the main kinds of assistance provided by an IV-D agency.
- List the methods of enforcing a child-support obligation.
- Explain when the government must pay for an attorney for an indigent obligor.

- Distinguish between obtaining jurisdiction over a resident and a nonresident parent in order to establish and enforce a child-support order.
- Explain how a support order can be enforced against a nonresident parent.
- Understand when a state will modify its child-support order.
- Know when one state can modify the support order of another state.

INTRODUCTION

Family law is primarily governed by state law. The law of child support, however, is a major exception. Although child support is still a function of state and local government, federal law has substantially influenced the field. In the 1970s, Congress began passing laws designed to increase the collection of child support and thereby decrease the cost of **public assistance** (welfare), which is funded in large measure by federal funds. When parents fail to pay child support, the last resort is often public assistance. Congress said to the states that their continued receipt of federal money was conditioned on their passing strong laws that establish and enforce the child-support obligations of parents. An example of such laws required employers to withhold child-support payments from the paychecks of delinquent parents, usually **noncustodial parents (NCP)** who do not have physical custody of their children. The result of such laws has been a dramatic increase in the collection of child support and a decline in the number of **custodial parents (CPs)** receiving public assistance on behalf of their children. Between 1995 and 2018, the national caseload of persons receiving **Temporary Assistance for Needy Families (TANF)**, the main public assistance program, declined by more than 50 percent.[1]

Unfortunately, however, collection of these support payments is still a huge problem. A large percentage of child-support obligations are not paid. Delinquent parents often disappear or devise elaborate methods of avoiding their support duty.

> [M]any "deadbeat dads" opt to work in the underground economy to shield their earnings from child support enforcement efforts. To avoid attempts to garnish their wages or otherwise enforce the support obligation, "deadbeats" quit their jobs, jump from job to job, become self-employed, work under the table, or engage in illegal activity.[2]

Often, delinquent parents move out of state in order to avoid payment. The total amount of **arrearages** (uncollected payments that are due) of all prior years is more than $110 billion (see Exhibit 10.1).

public assistance
Welfare and other forms of financial help from the government to the poor.

noncustodial parent (NCP)
The parent who is not living with the child and who does not have physical custody of the child. Also called *nonresidential parent*.

custodial parents (CP)
The parent with whom the child is living; the parent with physical custody of the child. Also called *residential parent*.

Temporary Assistance for Needy Families (TANF)
The federal-state welfare system (42 U.S.C. § 601) that replaced Aid to Families with Dependent Children (AFDC). Unlike AFDC, benefits under TANF are limited to five years.

arrearages
Payments that are due but have not been made. Also called *arrears*.

EXHIBIT 10.1 Child-Support Statistics

- The poverty rate of custodial parents (CPs) is 28.8%, which is twice as high as the poverty rate of the total population (14.5%).
- 14.7 million children receive child support with help from state child-support agencies (one in five children in the United States).
- The total annual amount of child support distributed to families with help from child-support agencies is $28.6 billion.
- 5.5 million noncustodial parents (NCPs) are delinquent (in arrears) in child-support payments of $114 billion.
- 5.7 million CPs have a court order or some type of agreement to receive financial support from the NCP.
- CPs are due an average of $480 a month from NCPs.
- Of this total:
  - 45.6% of the CPs received full payment.
  - 28.6% of the CPs received partial payment.
  - 25.9% of the CPs received no payments.

(continued)

Exhibit 10.1 *(continued)*

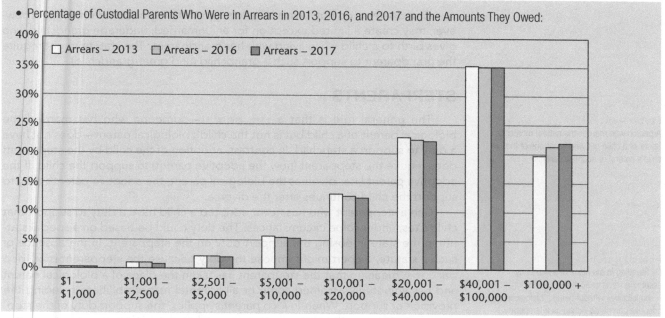

• Percentage of Custodial Parents Who Were in Arrears in 2013, 2016, and 2017 and the Amounts They Owed:

Source: Census Bureau, *Custodial Mothers and Fathers and Their Child Support* (Current Population Reports) (2016). (www.census.gov/content/dam/Census/library/publications/2016/demo/P60-255.pdf); (www.acf.hhs.gov/archive/css/css/resource/css/resource/fy-2015-preliminary-data-report); (www.acf.hhs.gov/css/ocsedatablog/2018/03/trends-in-child-support-debt-amounts); (www.acf.hhs.gov/sites/default/files/programs/css/fy_2018_preliminary_data_report.pdf).

WHO MUST PAY?

PARENTS

The traditional rule was that only the father had the legal duty to support his children. Today, however, each parent has an equal duty of support regardless of who has **physical custody** or who has **legal custody**. A parent who does not have physical or legal custody has the same duty of support as the parent with both physical and legal custody. The duty is not dependent on the existence of a marriage, on the sexual orientation of the parents, or on who caused the divorce. With limited exceptions, the duty is based on parentage.

The parent who must pay child support is the **obligor**; the child who is entitled to receive child support is the **obligee**. The obligor who pays (or who is obligated to pay) is also called the **payor**. The obligee to whom this payment is made (or to whom it must be paid) is also called the **payee**.

ADOPTIVE PARENTS

Once a child is adopted, the adoptive parent has the same child-support duty as any other parent. This reality became painfully clear to a woman in Tennessee who adopted a young boy from Russia. When she could no longer handle the boy's disruptive behavior and possible mental illness, she bought him a one-way ticket back to Russia and put him on a plane alone, with a note saying that she was returning him because of all the trouble he was causing. As will be discussed in Chapter 17, this is not the way to undo an adoption. The event became a world media story. The adoptive parent faced numerous legal problems as a result of what she did. One of those problems was child support. An American court ordered her to pay $150,000 in child support to the foster home in Russia where the boy has now been placed.[3]

physical custody
The right of an adult to have a child reside with the adult. Also called *residential custody* and *custodial responsibility*.

legal custody
The right to make the major child-rearing decisions on healthcare, education, religion, discipline, and general welfare. Also called *decision-making responsibility*.

obligor
One who has a legal obligation to do something, usually to make a payment.

obligee
One to whom a legal obligation is owed.

payor
One who makes a payment of money or who is obligated to do so.

payee
One to whom money is paid or is to be paid.

GRANDPARENTS

Grandparents do not have a duty to support their grandchildren. A state, however, may create a limited exception for an unmarried, underage grandchild who gives birth to a child while living with her grandparent. The statute might require the grandparent to support such a grandchild (and great-grandchild).

STEPPARENTS

stepparent
A person who marries the natural mother or father of a child but who is not one of the child's natural or adoptive parents.

The general rule is that a **stepparent**—someone who has married the biological parent of a child but is not the child's biological parent—does not have a duty to support a stepchild. In contrast, adoption of the child by the stepparent does require the stepparent (now the adoptive parent) to support the child. If the adoptive parent later divorces the biological parent, the adoptive parent's duty to support the child continues after the divorce.

Can a stepparent who has never adopted a child have a duty to support that child? Yes, under some circumstances. The duty could be based on a special statute in the state imposing the support duty on the stepparent. In the absence of such a statute, a court might impose the duty because the stepparent is **in loco parentis**, meaning that the stepparent has taken the place of a biological parent and has voluntarily assumed some or all parental responsibilities, including the provision of support. When *in loco parentis* applies, the support duty of the stepparent exists while the stepparent is married to the biological parent. In most states, when the relationship terminates, so does the support duty, unless **equitable estoppel** applies.

in loco parentis
(1) Standing in the place of a parent by assuming some or all of the parental responsibilities without being a biological or adoptive parent. (2) Acting as a temporary guardian or caretaker of a child.

equitable estoppel
The voluntary conduct of a person will preclude him or her from asserting rights against another who justifiably relied on the conduct and who would suffer damage or injury if the person is now allowed to repudiate the conduct. Also called *estoppel in pais*.

Under equitable estoppel, the voluntary conduct of a person will preclude him or her from asserting rights against another who justifiably relied on the conduct and who would suffer damage or injury if the person were now allowed to repudiate the conduct. For example, a stepparent would be **estopped** from denying a duty to support a child when the stepparent:

estopped
Prevented from asserting a right or a defense because it would be unfair or inequitable to allow the assertion. The noun is *estoppel*.

- Has been voluntarily supporting the child,
- Has allowed the child to be assimilated into the family,
- Has induced the child (and the biological parent) to rely on the stepparent's emotional and financial support, and
- May have encouraged the child to believe that the stepparent is a biological parent.

One possible hardship suffered by children as a result of their reliance on such a stepparent is the fact that they (and their biological parent) were discouraged from trying to locate the other biological parent for support.

Jane and Frank are the unmarried biological parents of baby Ann. When Frank withdraws from the family and moves to another state, Jane marries Kevin. Although Kevin does not adopt Ann, he supports her and encourages her to treat him as her father. Five years later, he and Jane divorce, at which time he stops providing support for Ann.

equitable parent
An adult on whom a court will impose the responsibilities of a legal or biological parent because of the close bond the adult has formed with a child and the reliance of the child on that bond even if the adult has no blood or adoptive relationship with the child. A *presumed parent* under the Uniform Parentage Act.

Because Kevin never adopted Ann, the divorce would normally end his provision of child support. On these facts, however, a court might apply equitable estoppel and order Kevin to continue supporting Ann. Kevin would become what some states call an **equitable parent** or what the Uniform Parentage Act calls a **presumed parent**. Over the past five years, he allowed Jane to rely on his support of Ann. Because of this reliance, Jane did not pursue Frank for support. Hence it would be unfair for Kevin to cease providing support. Under equitable estoppel, he is an equitable parent and would be estopped from denying an obligation to continue providing child support.

presumed parent
A person who, under the Uniform Parentage Act, is presumed to be the parent of a child if the person receives the child into his or her home and openly holds out the child as his or her child. The presumed parent does not have to be biologically related to the child.

COPARENTS

Coparenting is a general term that means shared responsibility by two adults to raise a child, regardless of the marital status or sexual orientation of the adults. The two adults can be married, single, of the opposite sex, of the same sex, transgender, etc. Assume, for example, that an unmarried lesbian couple wants to have a child that the two women will raise together. Using a sperm donor, one of the women becomes pregnant by **artificial insemination (AI)** or **in vitro fertilization (IVF)**. Upon birth, the women give the child a surname that is a hyphenated combination of their names. For two years, they care for the child and pay the expenses of upbringing. They let everyone know that the child is "theirs." When the women separate, the child stays with the woman who gave birth to the child. On these facts, some courts could rule that both women have an equal duty of child support even though one of the women (the one who left) is not biologically related to (and never adopted) the child.

Several theories could account for this result.

- *Statute.* The state may have a statute that gives rights and duties to adults who take a child into their home and hold the child out to the world as their natural child even though one or both adults are not biologically related to the child.
- *Breach of promise.* When one adult agrees to conceive a child upon the express or implied promise of the other adult to support that child, a court may enforce this contractual promise.
- *In loco parentis.* Both women assumed the full responsibilities of parents.
- *Equitable estoppel.* The birth mother relied on the departing partner in their joint plan to bring a child into the world and to raise it together. The reliance would cause hardship on the child if the departing partner is now able to walk away from the plan and leave the support burden on the birth mother alone. The departing adult has the responsibilities of an equitable parent.

As indicated, the Uniform Parentage Act (UPA) calls an equitable parent a presumed parent. Under the UPA, a presumed parent does not have to be biologically related to the child or married to the biological parent. The key criteria is receiving the child into the home and holding the child out as one's natural child. A "presumed parent is not just a casual friend of the other parent, or even a long-term boyfriend or girlfriend, but someone who has entered into a familial relationship with the child: someone who has demonstrated an abiding commitment to the child and the child's well-being, regardless of his or her relationship with the child's other parent."[4]

SPERM DONORS

A *sperm donor* is a male who provides his sperm to a woman so that she can have a child. The woman might be (1) the wife of another man, (2) a lesbian in a same-sex relationship, or a (3) a single person wishing to become a mother. Most women obtain donated sperm through a **sperm bank**, which is a facility that collects and stores human sperm from donors who will usually be anonymous to the women who use the sperm to become pregnant by AI or IVF. Many states require the AI or IVF process to be performed under the supervision of a licensed physician. If the woman is married and her spouse consents to AI or IVF under proper medical supervision, the sperm donor has no custody rights or support duties for the child, even if the donor and the mother agreed otherwise.

If the woman is unmarried, the same general rule applies—the donor has no rights or duties. Suppose, however, that the AI or IVF process is not supervised by a physician. In a recent Kansas case, two lesbians made a request on Craigslist for a man to donate his sperm to the couple. As a goodwill gesture, a stranger replied and

coparenting
Shared responsibility by two adults to raise a child, regardless of the marital status or sexual orientation of the adults. (See the glossary for an additional meaning.)

artificial insemination (AI)
Inserting sperm into the uterus by a method other than sexual intercourse in order to achieve conception.

in vitro fertilization (IVF)
The surgical removal of a woman's eggs from the ovaries, the fertilization of the eggs with sperm (in the laboratory), and the transfer of the resulting embryos (or pre-embryos) into the uterus through the cervix. A method of assisted reproductive technology (ART).

sperm bank
A facility that collects and stores human sperm from male donors who will usually be anonymous to any woman who uses the sperm to become pregnant by artificial insemination (AI) or by in vitro fertilization (IVF). Also called *cryobank.*

sent them his sperm with the written understanding that he would have no support obligations if a child resulted. He was not paid for this service. Via IVF, one of the women gave birth to a baby girl. Some years later, the state took the position that the donor was obligated to pay child support. Unknown to him, the mother did not use a licensed physician for the IVF procedure. This was a violation of state law. If IVF had been done properly, a sperm donor would not be liable for child support. The man is now contesting the state's ruling that he owes child support.[5]

Not all sperm donors wish to be anonymous. In fact, some donors want to become closely involved in the child's life. Such involvement, however, can trigger a duty to pay child support. The court will want to know if the donor formed a bonding relationship with the child, entered into an agreement with the unmarried mother to provide support, visited the child, regularly sent presents to the child, etc. Under such circumstances, the general rule on the liability of sperm donors for child support would not apply. The court would consider it to be unfair (inequitable) for such a donor to avoid paying child support. Such a donor would be classified as an equitable parent.

Suppose that a man has sexual intercourse with a woman solely to impregnate her, making no promise and having no expectation of assuming parental duties. Does he have a duty of child support? Yes. Only sperm donors via medically supervised AI or IVF processes can avoid the duty (with the exception just mentioned). A man who engages in sexual intercourse must support the resulting child, even if he and the woman agreed (prior to or after intercourse) that he would not be involved in raising the child and would not owe child support. (See the *Straub* case below.)

ASSIGNMENT 10.1

Under what circumstances, if any, will a sperm donor be required to pay child support in your state? (See the General Instructions for the State-Code Assignment and the Court Opinion Assignment in Appendix A.)

FOR HOW LONG?

With few exceptions, a parent's duty of child support ends when the child reaches the **age of majority** (usually age eighteen) or becomes **emancipated**. If an unemancipated child is still in school, the support duty may be extended (see the section below titled "College"). Similarly, a parent can be required to support a disabled child after the age of majority (see the section titled "Disability"). In most states, the death of the parent ends his or her duty of child support, although most states can require a parent to maintain a life insurance policy with the child as the beneficiary so that a measure of support continues after the parent's death.

EMANCIPATION

Emancipation means being legally independent of one's parent or legal guardian. Children can be emancipated before the age of majority if certain events take place that clearly indicate they are living independently with the consent of their parents or legal guardians. Such events include marriage and entering military service. We will have more to say on emancipation in Chapter 14.

COLLEGE

A good deal of litigation has centered on the issue of educational expenses, particularly higher education. Does a divorced parent have a duty to send his or her child to college? Arguments *against* imposing this duty are as follows:

age of majority
The age at which children reach legal adulthood (usually age eighteen) entitling them to many civil rights, such as the right to manage their own affairs.

emancipated
Legally independent of one's parent or legal guardian. The noun is *emancipation*.

- A parent's support duty is limited to providing a child with necessities (e.g., food, shelter, clothing). A large percentage of Americans do not attend college. College, therefore, is a luxury, not a necessity.

- A parent's support duty terminates when the child reaches the age of majority (e.g., eighteen). Children in college will be over the age of majority during some or most of their college years.

- Children of parents who are still married have no right to force their parents to send them to college. Why should children of divorced parents have the right to be sent to college?

Some states, however, have rejected these arguments and have required the divorced parent to pay for a college education if the parent has the ability to pay for college and the child has the capacity to go to college. Several arguments support this position, such as the following:

- In today's society, college is not a luxury. A college degree, at least the first one, is a necessity.

- A parent's duty to provide child support does not terminate in all cases when the child reaches majority. For example, a physically or mentally disabled child may have to be supported indefinitely. Some courts take the position that the support duty continues so long as the child's need for support continues (i.e., so long as the child remains dependent). This includes the period when the child is in college.

- It is true that married parents have no obligation to send their children to college. But there is a strong likelihood they will do so if they have the means and their children have the ability. When the court requires a divorced parent to send his or her children to college, the same tests are applied: ability to pay and capacity to learn. Thus, the court, in effect, is equalizing the position of children of divorced parents with that of children of married parents.

Whether or not a state says that college expenses are part of child support, divorcing parents often agree on their own to cover the expenses of college. Their separation agreement reflects this decision.

DISABILITY

In most states, as indicated, the duty of support extends beyond the age of majority if the child becomes physically or mentally disabled before that age. The duty continues during the disability. Suppose, however, that the disability arises during adulthood—after the child reaches the age of majority. An example is an adult child incapacitated in an automobile accident. Only a few states would impose the duty in such cases.

SUPPORT BEFORE BIRTH?

After a child is born, the father becomes jointly responsible with the mother for all pregnancy-related costs associated with the birth. When the parents are not married, the father's liability is determined by his acknowledgement of paternity or by the paternity tests that we will discuss in Chapter 13. Such tests are administered after the child is born. Suppose, however, that fatherhood could be established by safe paternity tests *during* the pregnancy. Should the unmarried father become liable for his share of pregnancy costs before the child is born? No state requires such payments, but the availability of safe prenatal paternity tests have encouraged some advocates to argue for a change in the law. One advocate would call the required payments *preglimony*.[6]

SEPARATION AGREEMENT

Approximately half of custodial parents (CPs) have an agreement or a court order requiring noncustodial parents (NCPs) to pay child support. The reasons CPs do not have formal agreements are outlined in Exhibit 10.2.

EXHIBIT 10.2 Reasons Custodial Parents Say They Do Not Have Formal Child-Support Agreements

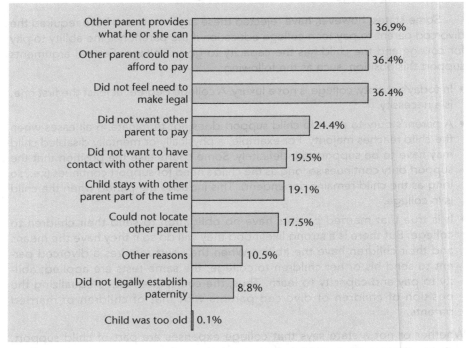

Source: Census Bureau, *Custodial Mothers and Fathers and Their Child Support: 2013* (Current Population Reports) (January 2016). (www.census.gov/content/dam/Census/library/publications/2016/demo/P60-255.pdf).

separation agreement
A contract by married persons who have separated (or who are about to separate) that can cover support, custody, property division, and other terms of their separation and likely divorce. Also called *marital settlement agreement (MSA)*.

child-support guidelines
State-mandated rules for calculating the amount of child support owed by adults obligated to pay such support (obligors).

lump-sum payment
A single payment of an amount of money rather than ongoing payments.

If parents have a **separation agreement**, here are the relevant factors they should keep in mind as they negotiate the child-support terms of the agreement:

- *State guidelines.* Each state has **child-support guidelines** on the amount of child support that must be paid. The guidelines set the minimum. The parents must decide whether they want to exceed the minimum. If they have the resources to meet the minimum, they cannot agree to a child-support amount that is *lower* than what the guidelines mandate. Parents cannot bargain away the basic need of their children for support as reflected in the guidelines.

- *Standard of living.* What standard of living was the child accustomed to during the marriage? Do the parents have the financial resources to maintain this standard of living?

- *Payment dates.* On what day is each child-support payment to be made?

- *Kinds of payments.* Although most child support is paid in cash on a periodic basis, the parties can decide to use other assets as child support, such as the marital home, stocks or other securities, and motor vehicles. (The custodial parent (CP) would then have to liquidate such assets to pay for the ongoing support needs of the child or use his or her own cash for such needs.) In many states, however, parties are not allowed to agree that child support will be paid as a one-time payment (a **lump-sum payment** is not allowed in such states).

- *Frequency of payments.* How many payments are to be made? Will they be monthly payments covering everyday expenses and separate payments covering large, emergency expenses (e.g., tuition, hospitalization)?

- *Insurance.* Will insurance be purchased (or maintained if already in existence)?
  - ◦ Medical insurance? Who will be covered? How will premiums be paid? (Later we will see that the obligor may be required to provide medical insurance for the child.)
  - ◦ Life insurance? Will the child be the beneficiary of a life insurance policy on the life of the obligor? If so, for how much, who pays the premiums, and can the beneficiaries be changed by the obligor?
  - ◦ Does the payment of premiums (and hence the insurance coverage) end when the child reaches the age of majority (usually 18)?

- *Escalation clause.* Will there be an **escalation clause**?
  - ◦ Will child-support payments be increased or decreased based on a factor over which the parties do not have complete control such as the Consumer Price Index?
  - ◦ Do the payments fluctuate with the income of either of the parents?
  - ◦ Do they fluctuate with the income of the child (e.g., summer jobs, inheritance)?

- *Termination of payments.* When do the child-support payments end? When the child reaches a certain age (e.g., the age of majority), marries, or moves out of the house? Although the separation agreement can specify the intention of the parents, the law may require continuation of support payments despite their intention.

- *Education expenses.* What education costs will be covered?
  - ◦ Private school? Tutors? College? Graduate school?
  - ◦ Will education-related expenses (e.g., transportation, books) be covered?
  - ◦ If tuition is to be paid, does the obligor send tuition money directly to the school or to the CP?

- *Reductions.* Will the amount of child support be reduced for every day the child spends overnight visiting the NCP (or a relative of the NCP)? Will there be a reduction if the child is away at boarding school?

- *Security for nonpayment.* Will there be security for the child-support payments that can be used in the event of nonpayment?
  - ◦ A **trust** account?
  - ◦ An **escrow** account?

- *Death of obligor.* When the obligor dies, is his or her estate obligated to continue child-support payments? If so, the separation agreement should state that the obligor's will must specify this continued obligation.

- *Disputes.* How will the parents resolve disputes concerning child support? Will they use arbitration or mediation?

- *Taxes.* The parties must keep in mind the tax effect of child-support payments:
  - ◦ The payor (obligor) of child support cannot deduct the payments on his or her tax return (the same is true of alimony payments).
  - ◦ The payee (obligee) who receives child support does not pay taxes on what is received (the same is true of alimony payments received).
  - ◦ Taxation will be discussed in Chapter 11.

Attempts in an agreement to remove a parent's continuing obligation of support are void. The case of *Straub v. B.M.T.* presents an even more extreme example of what parents cannot attempt to accomplish through agreement.

escalation clause
A provision in a contract or other document that provides for an increase or decrease in the amount to be paid based upon a factor over which the parties may or may not have complete control.

trust
A property arrangement by which its creator (the *settlor* or *trustor*) transfers property (the *corpus*) to a person (the *trustee*) who holds legal title for the benefit of another (the *beneficiary* or *cestui que trust*).

escrow
Property (e.g., money, a deed) delivered to a neutral person (e.g., bank, escrow agent) to be held until a specified condition occurs (e.g., nonpayment of a debt), at which time the property is to be delivered to a designated person.

CASE | Straub v. B.M.T., by Next Friend, Francine Todd
645 N.E.2d 597 (1994)
Supreme Court of Indiana

Background: *Edward Straub and Francine Todd had an affair. Straub impregnated Todd after she agreed not to hold him financially responsible for a child born from the union (a hold-harmless agreement). But three years after the birth of a child (referred to as B.M.T. by the court), Todd sued Straub for child support. The trial court ordered him to pay $130 per week. Straub appealed. The state court of appeals affirmed. The case is now on appeal before the Supreme Court of Indiana.*

Decision on Appeal: *Affirmed. The agreement to relieve a father of financial responsibility is void as a matter of public policy.*

OPINION OF THE COURT

Justice SHEPARD delivered the opinion of the court.

I. Summary of Facts . . .

[In] 1986, Francine Todd and Edward Straub engaged in a romantic relationship and sexual relations. In December of that year, Todd informed Straub of her desire to have a child. Straub was a divorcé with five children from a previous marriage, and he expressed resistance to fathering another child. Todd threatened to end the relationship, however, unless he agreed to impregnate her.

Straub handwrote the following statement and told Todd he would attempt to impregnate her if she signed it.

> *To whom it may concern. I Francine Todd in sound mind & fore thought have decided not to marry, but would like to have a baby of my own. To support financially & emotionally. I have approached several men who will not be held responsible financially or emotionally, who's [sic] names will be kept secret for life. Signed Francine E. Todd Dec. 15 1986*

Todd signed the statement, and the couple thereafter began having unprotected intercourse. Todd became pregnant in March 1987 and gave birth [to B.M.T.] that November. The birth certificate did not list anyone as the father. [Straub and Todd continued their relationship, but Straub did not establish a relationship with the child.]

On January 7, 1991, Todd filed a petition asking the trial court to declare Straub the father of the child and require him to pay child support and certain medical expenses. . . . The trial court found Straub to be the father of the child and ordered him to pay support in the sum of $130 per week, arrearages of $20 per week and certain medical expenses. . . .

Straub raises three issues, but the essence of all three may be stated as follows: whether a parent may contract away his or her rights and obligations to a child and/or the child's right to support through a preconception contract for fertilization. . . .

II. Some Agreements Concerning Children Are Void

Three rudimentary elements must be present before an agreement may be considered a contract: offer, acceptance of the offer and consideration. . . . If these components are present, a legal obligation results. . . . See, e.g., U.C.C. § 1-201(3).

There are instances, however, in which an agreement is not an enforceable contract despite proper formation. Where a properly formed agreement contravenes the public policy of Indiana, for instance, courts have traditionally said it is void and unenforceable. . . . Leading commentators frame the principle somewhat differently, saying that in such circumstances there is no contract, because such an agreement produces no legal obligation upon the part of the promisor. . . .

In any event, certain agreements are prohibited outright by statute [such as contingent fee agreements in criminal cases. This court demonstrated the public policy of protecting the welfare of children by adopting the Indiana Child Support Guidelines. The purpose of the Guidelines is threefold: establishing as state policy an adequate standard of support for children; making awards more equitable by ensuring a more consistent treatment of people in similar circumstances; and improving the efficiency of courts by promoting settlements.]

In keeping with this public policy, Indiana courts have from time to time voided agreements reached by parents. Agreements which yield up a support opportunity for a child have been especially suspect. We have treated custodial parents who receive child support as trustees of the payments for the use and the benefit of the child. *Stonehill v. Stonehill* (1896), 45 N.E. 600, 601 ("The person to whom money for support of a child is ordered paid by the court, receives it as a trustee, and can only expend the same for the benefit of the child."); . . . Neither parent has the right to contract away these support benefits. The right to the support lies exclusively with the child. Any agreement purporting to contract away these rights is directly contrary to this State's public policy of protecting the welfare of children, as it narrows the basis for support to one parent. . . .

[In addition,] consideration for this agreement, received by Straub, was sexual intercourse with Todd. Using sexual intercourse as consideration is itself against public policy. *Glasgo v. Glasgo*, (1980), Ind. App., 410 N.E.2d 1325, 1331. . . .

For these reasons, we hold the Todd agreement to be void and unenforceable. We affirm the trial court.

DeBRULER, Justice, dissenting.

I agree with the majority that one cannot contract away the right of a child to financial support from one of her parents. . . . [To make certain that B.M.T. receives adequate support, the contract should be treated as an assumption by Todd of Straub's obligation of support. Todd agreed to hold Straub harmless for his support obligation to B.M.T. Straub's support obligation to B.M.T. cannot be enforced against him unless Todd herself is without the means to pay that obligation.] If a person promises to pay the father's share of child support then, if that person is able, he or she should pay.

ASSIGNMENT   10.2

a. In the *Straub* case, is the majority opinion or the dissenting opinion correct? Is the majority opinion anti-female?

b. In the discussion of the *Marvin v. Marvin* case in Chapter 4 on cohabitation agreements, we learned that sexual intercourse cannot be a valid consideration for an enforceable contract. Was this rule also applied in the *Straub* case?

c. George and Helen are not married but are living together. George impregnates Helen. He asks her to have an abortion. She refuses. When the child is born, can she force George to support it? Would it make any difference if Helen became pregnant after lying to George about using contraceptives? (See General Instructions for the Legal-Analysis Agreement in Appendix A.)

HOW MUCH?

When a CP seeks help from a court, there are two main types of child support that can be asked for: temporary and permanent. If the parents are married and are in the process of seeking a divorce, the CP might ask a court for an award of temporary child support **pendente lite** while the case is being resolved in court. At the conclusion of the case, the court will decide on permanent child support.

When a court determines the amount of child support that must be paid, it will consider a number of factors, the most important of which are the child-support guidelines for determining child support.

pendente lite
Pending the [outcome of the] litigation.

CHILD SUPPORT GUIDELINES

At one time, the standard used by a court in determining the amount of child support was the best interests of the child. Today, states use a mathematical standard, at least initially. Every state has adopted child-support guidelines for the determination of child support. The guidelines use a formula to determine an amount of child support based on variables, such as a parent's income and the number of children to be supported. The guidelines also list circumstances that will allow a court to deviate from the amount set by the formula. The resulting amount establishes a **rebuttable presumption** on what should be awarded. The amount must be accepted as the minimum amount unless the court provides written findings on why this amount should not be used.

Courts may deviate from the guidelines only upon making a specific finding that application of the guidelines would be unjust or inappropriate. Factors that might cause a court to change the amount set by the guidelines include medical costs, private school costs, high parental income, the existence of other families that the parents must support, and the amount of time the child spends with each parent, particularly in cases of **joint physical custody**.

The federal law that establishes this rule provides as follows:

rebuttable presumption
An assumption or inference of fact that a party will be allowed to try to disprove (rebut) but that will be treated as true if it is not disproved.

joint physical custody
The right of both parents to have the child reside with both for alternating (but not necessarily equal) periods of time. Also called *shared physical custody*.

> *There shall be a rebuttable presumption . . . that the amount of the award which would result from the application of such guidelines is the correct amount of child support to be awarded. A written finding or specific finding on the record that the application of the guidelines would be unjust or inappropriate in a particular case, as determined under criteria established by the State, shall be sufficient to rebut the presumption in that case.*[7]

The starting point in using the guidelines is the identification of a parent's income. Income has a broad definition and includes any form of payment that a

net
The amount that remains after designated deductions and other allowances.

parent can receive, such as wages and salaries, self-employment income, commissions, bonuses, dividends, workers' compensation payments, disability payments, Social Security benefits, earned interest, pension payments, annuities, lottery winnings, and alimony income. From the total of such income, most states allow designated deductions, such as the income taxes the parent must pay. The result after the deductions is the parent's **net** income.

The guidelines are not the same in every state, although they are substantially similar. Most states base their calculations on either the *income-shares model* or the *percentage-of-income model*.

Income-Shares Model

The income-shares model is used in the majority of states. Child support under this model is calculated as a *share* of each parent's income that would have been spent on the children if the parents and children were living in the same household. In an intact household, the income of both parents is generally pooled and spent for the benefit of all household members, including any children.

The first step under this model is to calculate the net income (defined by the state) of each parent. For example, assume that the mother has net income of $2,000 a month and the father has net income of $6,000 a month. The combined income available for child support is $8,000. The mother's income is 25 percent of this total; the father's is 75 percent. These percentages will determine how much of the child's support needs each parent will pay.

The next step is to consult a state-mandated chart that identifies the amount of support that must be paid based on the number of children needing support. Assume, for example, that the chart says that parents with a combined net income of $8,000 must pay $1,600 a month for one child. The mother would be required to pay 25 percent of this amount ($400) and the father would be required to pay 75 percent ($1,200). If the chart says that they must pay $2,400 if they had two children, the mother's share would be 25 percent ($600) and the father's share would be 75 percent ($1,800).

Percentage-of-Income Model

Calculations under the percentage-of-income model are less complex. The noncustodial parent (NCP) pays a percentage of his or her income. The income of the custodial parent (CP) is not considered. Once the NCP's state-defined net income is calculated, a chart sets the percentage of that income that must be paid for child support. For example, child support for one child might be 24 percent if the net income is between $951 and $1,000 a month. The percentage increases if there are more children to be supported. There are two variations on the percentage: the flat percentage model (the percentage of income for child support stays constant for all income levels) and the varying percentage model (the percentage of income for child support varies according to level of income).

If a state does not use the income-shares model or the percentage-of-income model, it will use one of several alternatives, such as the *Melson-Delaware model*, which first identifies an amount needed for the parent's own basic needs and then designates a portion of the parent's remaining income for the child. There may also be variations among states using the same model. For a list of the states and the models they use, see Exhibit 10.3.[8]

Whatever model a state uses, adjustments can be made when the parties have joint physical custody of the child, when a child has special medical or childcare needs, or when there is extensive visitation with the NCP. There may also be separate guidelines when the combined incomes of the parents exceed a high amount, such as $100,000. (See the three-pony rule below.)

EXHIBIT 10.3 Child-Support Guidelines Used by the States

States Using Income-Shares Model		States Using the Percentage-of-Income Model	States Using Other Models
Alabama	Nebraska	Alaska	Delaware (Melson Model)
Arizona	New Hampshire	Arkansas	Hawaii (Melson Model)
California	New Jersey	Illinois	Montana (Melson Model)
Colorado	New Mexico	Mississippi	District of Columbia (Hybrid Model)
Connecticut	New York	Nevada	
Florida	North Carolina	North Dakota	
Georgia	Ohio	Texas	
Guam	Oklahoma	Wisconsin	
Idaho	Oregon		
Indiana	Pennsylvania		
Iowa	Rhode Island		
Kansas	South Carolina		
Kentucky	South Dakota		
Louisiana	Tennessee		
Maine	Utah		
Maryland	Vermont		
Massachusetts	Virginia		
Michigan	Washington		
Minnesota	West Virginia		
Missouri	Wyoming		

The calculation of child support under the guidelines is relatively mechanical. A number of commercial software companies sell computer programs that can be used to determine the amount of child support that is due under the guidelines used by a particular state. In addition, some child-support-enforcement agencies have calculation worksheets on their website. This allows a custodial parent, an NCP, and others to enter their own financial data to determine the amount of child support that would be required.

ASSIGNMENT 10.3

Answer the following questions by checking your state code and opinions of courts in your state. (See General Instructions for the State-Code Assignment and General Instructions for the Court-Opinion Assignment in Appendix A.)

a. How does a court determine the amount of child support in your state? Describe the main features of whatever guidelines exist and explain how they are used.

b. Make up a fact situation involving two parents (John Smith and Mary Smith) and one infant child (Billy Smith). Your facts should include the income and resources available to each parent. Now determine how much each parent would owe in child support in your state. Use any available online calculators or worksheets.

c. Under what circumstances, if any, does an NCP have an obligation to pay for his or her child's college education in your state?

d. Under what circumstances, if any, will your state make adjustments to what an NCP must pay if the NCP has additional children with a new spouse?

THREE-PONY RULE

For high-income parents, the strict application of the guidelines in some states can occasionally lead to large awards of child support. A state might take a share-the-wealth attitude and allow the child to share in the good fortune of the prosperous parent by ordering a high child-support award. Most states, however, do not want to order child support beyond the reasonable needs of the child. According to one court:

> While to some degree children have a right to share in each parent's standard of living, child support must be set in an amount which is reasonably and rationally related to the realistic needs of the children. This is sometimes referred to as the "Three Pony Rule." That is, no child, no matter how wealthy the parents, needs to be provided more than three ponies.[9]

The **three-pony rule** has come to mean that child support for children of parents with high incomes should be adjusted so that payments do not go beyond what is reasonably and rationally related to the realistic needs of the child. Once child-support payments exceed this level, the payments begin to look like alimony because the money is far beyond what can be spent to meet the needs of the child.

States have different methods of making this adjustment for high-income parents. For example, a state may use separate guidelines if the combined incomes of the parents exceed a certain amount, such as $100,000 a year or more than $4,000 a month. Alternatively, a state may provide that if the combined parents' monthly gross income exceeds the highest level specified in the schedule, the court has discretion to set the amount in accordance with the best interest of the child and the circumstances of each parent.

Of course, an NCP can always agree to provide a high level of child support, which, if not paid, can be the basis of a breach-of-contract suit to enforce the agreement. Our focus here has been on child-support payments that are ordered by a court when the parties cannot agree. The parties can always enter into enforceable agreements for higher amounts.

SECOND FAMILY

Many states will take into consideration the fact that the NCP has a second family to support. It could affect the amount of support the NCP owes to the first family. We will discuss second families later in this chapter when we cover modifications of child-support orders.

IMPUTED INCOME

When parents improperly reduce their income or their income capacity, a court can treat the reduction as if it is income that was actually earned. This **imputed income** will be used in the calculation of the income that is available to pay child support. The two major ways that NCPs improperly reduce their assets are fraudulent transfers and refusal to work at capacity. A **fraudulent transfer** is a transfer of an asset for little or no payment or consideration that is made to avoid an obligation to a creditor. An example is an NCP who places all of his salary in the bank account of his brother. An example of a refusal to work at capacity is a parent who is voluntarily unemployed or voluntarily underemployed. An example of the latter is a skilled NCP who voluntarily leaves a high-paying job to take a minimum-wage job. A court can *impute* to the NCP the salary transferred to the brother's account and can impute to the NCP the salary he or she is capable of earning. For an unskilled NCP who refuses to do any work, a court can impute the equivalent of the minimum wage.

three-pony rule
(No child needs more than three ponies.) Child support for children of parents with high incomes should be adjusted so that payments do not go beyond what is reasonably and rationally related to the realistic needs of the child.

imputed income
Income that will be assumed to be available, regardless of whether it is actually available.

fraudulent transfer
A transfer of an asset for little or no payment or consideration that is made to avoid an obligation to a creditor.

Assume that a parent stays home to care for a child even though the parent is capable of earning a decent wage in the workforce. Will the income this parent could have earned be imputed to him or her when the court calculates the support obligations of the parents? No. Under the **nurturing-parent doctrine**, a parent who stays home (or who works less) in order to care for a child will not have that income imputed to the parent.

nurturing-parent doctrine
For purposes of calculating child-support obligations, the income a parent could have earned will not be imputed to the parent if the failure to earn the income is due to the time needed by the parent to care for a child.

CASE | Goldberger v. Goldberger
96 Md. App. 313, 624 A.2d 1328 (1993)
Court of Special Appeals of Maryland

Background: *The Circuit Court awarded Esther Goldberger a divorce from Aron Goldberger and custody of their six children: Chana Frumit, Mamele, Meir, Chaim Tzvi, Eliezer, and Yaacov. The court also ordered Aron to pay $4,066 per month in child support for the six children. It found that he had impoverished himself voluntarily and that his potential income was $60,000 per year. The court based this figure on the amount of money others had contributed to his litigation expenses. The case is now on appeal before the Court of Special Appeals of Maryland. Aron is the appellant and Esther is the appellee.*

Decision on Appeal: *Affirmed in part; reversed in part. The trial court correctly concluded that Aron voluntarily impoverished himself but failed to properly calculate the amount he should pay for child support.*

OPINION OF THE COURT

Judge LEVITZ delivered the opinion of the court.

The odyssey of the young children of Aron and Esther Goldberger has led them from Lakewood, New Jersey, to Israel, to Belgium and England, and finally to Baltimore, Maryland. These children have been the subject of the attention of various courts including: The High Court of Justice, Family Division, London, England; the Ecclesiastical Court of the Chief Rabbi of London (Beth Din); and, finally, the Circuit Court for Baltimore City. [Eight judges of the Circuit Court (nearly 30% of the Bench) have been involved in the case to date.]

Prior to the trial of this matter before the Circuit Court, the parties and their children had been examined and evaluated by ten physicians or psychologists. When the trial began, Esther and Aron Goldberger were fighting only about the custody of their children and related matters of support and visitation. Allegations of sexual child abuse, kidnapping, insanity and unfitness were made by one or the other of the parents. Other extended family members were brought into the conflict and took an active part in it. Since both parties are devout Orthodox Jews, noted Rabbis in this country and in Europe and Israel were consulted by the parties for advice, guidance and support. . . .

[T]he evidence revealed that appellant was 32 years old and healthy, with many years of higher education. It was undisputed that appellant had earned no actual income, as he had never worked at any income-producing vocation. Appellant planned his life to be a permanent Torah/Talmudic student. He was a student before he was married and before any of his children were born. Appellant testified that he studies "for the sake of studying, which is a positive commandment to study the Torah for the sake of studying it." Further, appellant testified that it was his intention to continue his life of study forever: ". . . I should continue to study the rest of my life, to always be in studying. . . ." Throughout his life appellant has been supported by others, first, his parents, thereafter, his father-in-law, and most recently, friends in the Orthodox community. Nevertheless, appellant fathered six children whom he has refused to support, arguing that he has no means to support and never will have the means to provide support.

A life devoted to study is viewed by many in the Orthodox community as a true luxury that very few can enjoy. [Even Teveya, the fictional lead character of *Fiddler on the Roof,* recognizes that a life of study is a luxury when he sings, *"If I were a rich man. . . . Wouldn't have to work hard. . . . I'd discuss the Holy books with the learned men seven hours every day; that would be the sweetest thing of all."*] Unfortunately for the appellant's children, permanent Torah/Talmudic students must depend on the charity of others to provide the necessities of life. Those who support a Torah student have no legal obligation to continue such support in either duration or amount.

Nevertheless, through a network of family and Orthodox communities in Europe and the United States, approximately $180,000 had been contributed to appellant over a three-year period to enable him to pursue his custody claim. Approximately $3,000 of that sum was once used to purge appellant of contempt for failing to pay child support.

Based on these facts, the court determined (1) that appellant had voluntarily impoverished himself, and (2) that his potential income was equivalent to the money that had been contributed by others to his cause. It therefore regarded his income, for purposes of paying child support as

(continued)

$60,000 per year and ordered that he pay $4,066 per month for the support of his six children. Appellant challenges both the finding of voluntary impoverishment and the calculation of potential income.

The obligation of parents to support their minor children has been consistently upheld by the Court of Appeals of Maryland. In *Carroll County v. Edelman,* 577 A.2d 14, 23 (1990), the court stated,

> *Parenthood is both a biological and a legal status. By nature and by law, it confers rights and imposes duties. One of the most basic of these is the obligation of the parent to support the child until the law determines that he is able to care for himself. . . .*

The legislature of Maryland has made it a crime for parents to fail to support their minor children. Md. Code Ann., Fam. Law § 10–203 (1991). . . . [T]here can be no question that appellant has a legal obligation to financially support his children until they reach the age of legal majority. The more difficult question is how to calculate the proper amount of that support. Fortunately, that question has been answered by the Legislature of Maryland. Md. Code Ann., Fam. Law § 12-202(a)(1) (1991) states,

> *"[I]n any proceeding to establish or modify child support, whether pendente lite or permanent, the court shall use the child support guidelines set forth in this subtitle."*

In order to use the guidelines as required by § 12–202(a)(1), it is necessary to calculate the income of the parents. "Income" is defined in § 12–201(b) of the Family Law Article as: (1) actual income of a parent, if the parent is employed to full capacity; or (2) potential income of a parent, if the parent is voluntarily impoverished.

The legislature's purpose in including potential income was to implement state and federal policy of requiring adequate support by precluding parents from avoiding their obligation by deliberately not earning what they could earn. While the Code does not define the term "voluntarily impoverished," in *John O. v. Jane O.,* 90 Md. App. 406, 601 A.2d 149 (1992), we had occasion to address the meaning of that term. We noted that neither the Legislature nor the courts in existing case law had defined what "voluntarily impoverished" meant. We noted that no clear definition was found in any Maryland resource materials. Accordingly, we looked to the dictionary definitions of the words "voluntarily" and "impoverished." We noted that "voluntarily" means "done by design or intention; proceeding from the free and unrestrained will of the person; produced in or by act of choice. . . ." "Impoverished" means "to make poor, reduce to poverty or to deprive. . . of resources, etc.". . .

The issue of voluntary impoverishment most often arises in the context of a parent who reduces his or her level of income to avoid paying support by quitting, retiring or changing jobs.

The intent of the parent in those cases is often important in determining whether there has been voluntary impoverishment. Was the job changed for the purpose of avoiding the support obligation and, therefore, voluntary, or was it for reasons beyond the control of the parent, and thus involuntary?. . . A parent who chooses a life of poverty before having children and makes a deliberate choice not to alter that status after having children is . . ."voluntarily impoverished." Whether the voluntary impoverishment is for the purpose of avoiding child support or because the parent simply has chosen a frugal lifestyle for another reason, doesn't affect that parent's obligation to the child. Although the parent can choose to live in poverty, that parent cannot obligate the child to go without the necessities of life. A parent who brings a child into this world must support that child, if he has or reasonably could obtain, the means to do so. The law requires that parent to alter his or her previously chosen lifestyle if necessary to enable the parent to meet his or her support obligation.

Accordingly, we now hold that, for purposes of the child support guidelines, a parent shall be considered "voluntarily impoverished" whenever the parent has made the free and conscious choice, not compelled by factors beyond his or her control, to render himself or herself without adequate resources. To determine whether a parent has freely been made poor or deprived of resources the trial court should look to the factors enunciated in *John O. v. Jane O.,* 90 Md. App. 406, at 422:

1. his or her current physical condition;
2. his or her respective level of education;
3. the timing of any change in employment or financial circumstances relative to the divorce proceedings;
4. the relationship of the parties prior to the divorce proceedings;
5. his or her efforts to find and retain employment;
6. his or her efforts to secure retraining if that is needed;
7. whether he or she has ever withheld support;
8. his or her past work history;
9. the area in which the parties live and the status of the job market there; and
10. any other considerations presented by either party.

Based on a review of the evidence before the circuit court, there was no error in finding that appellant was "voluntarily impoverished."

Once a court determines that a parent is voluntarily impoverished, the court must then determine the amount of potential income to attribute to that parent in order to calculate the support dictated by the guidelines. Some of the factors the court should consider in determining the amount of potential income include:

1. age;
2. mental and physical condition;

(continued)

3. assets;

4. educational background, special training or skills;

5. prior earnings;

6. efforts to find and retain employment;

7. the status of the job market in the area where the parent lives;

8. actual income from any source;

9. any other factor bearing on the parent's ability to obtain funds for child support.

After the court determines the amount of potential income to attribute to the parent, the court should calculate the amount of support by using the standardized worksheet authorized in Family Law § 12–203(a) and the schedule listed in Family Law § 12–204(e) Once the guideline support figure is determined, the court must then determine whether the presumptive correctness of the guideline support figure has been overcome by evidence that application of the guidelines would be unjust or inappropriate. Md. Code Ann., Fam. Law § 12–202(a)(2) (1991).

Unfortunately, the court below erred in determining that appellant's potential income was $60,000 per year, based solely on his ability to raise funds to support and carry on this litigation. Although the court may consider the ability of appellant to persuade others to provide him with funds to pay child support in the future, the court cannot assume this will occur merely because appellant has been able to convince others to support this litigation up until now. The court needs to hear testimony and make findings regarding the factors relating to potential income previously enunciated. No such findings were made in this case. After calculating the guidelines using appellant's realistic potential income, the court must decide whether the presumptive correctness of the guidelines has been overcome. Accordingly, this matter must be remanded to the trial court for such determinations. . . .

We vacate the court's child support order and remand the matter to the trial court to recalculate the appellant's child support obligation in light of this opinion. Judgment affirmed in part.

ASSIGNMENT   10.4

a. Did the court violate Aron Goldberger's First Amendment right to freedom of religion by forcing him to pay child support?

b. Assume you work for the law firm that represents Esther Goldberger. To determine how much child support Aron should pay, what facts would you investigate as a result of the *Goldberger* opinion? (See General Instructions for the Investigation-Strategy Assignment in Appendix A.)

ENFORCEMENT OF CHILD SUPPORT ORDERS

When Congress concluded that the efforts of state governments to collect child support were inadequate, it enacted federal legislation that created national standards of enforcement. If states wanted federal dollars, they had to pass state enforcement laws that complied with these standards. The centerpiece of federal legislation was Title IV-D of the Social Security Act.[10]

IV-D AGENCY

Title IV-D of the Social Security Act created new enforcement tools that could be used in every state. Each state established a child-support enforcement agency, consisting of a central state office and units throughout the state, usually within each county. States use different names for the agency, such as Child Support Enforcement Division or Office of Recovery Services. They are collectively known as **IV-D agencies** because they were proposed in Title IV-D of the Social Security Act. To find the IV-D agencies in your state (and the rules governing the agency), see Appendix D. You can also run this search on Google, Bing, or Yahoo: "IV-D" aa "child support" (in place of aa, type the name of your state) (Example: "IV-D" Maine "child support").

IV-D agency
A state agency that helps custodial parents enforce child-support obligations.

There is a federal agency that coordinates, evaluates, and assists state IV-D agencies. It is the U.S. Office of Child Support Enforcement (OCSE) within the U.S. Department of Health and Human Services.[11]

The services provided by a state IV-D agency are substantial. The agency can

- Help locate absent parents.
- Help establish paternity.
- Help establish a child-support order.
- Help establish a medical-support order.
- Help modify a support order.
- Arrange for the withholding of the obligor's wages.
- Intercept federal and state tax refunds to make them available for support.
- Arrange for the withholding of the obligor's passive income.
- Help collect child support if the obligor is in another state (using the agency's Interstate Central Registry).

In addition to these enforcement remedies, the IV-D agencies can be quite persistent in going after the NCP through automatic billing, telephone reminders, delinquency notices, etc. When an IV-D agency collects child support from an obligor, the agency can deposit the funds directly into the bank account of the obligee through electronic funds transfer (EFT).

Any custodial parent (obligee) with a child under age eighteen is eligible for the services of an IV-D agency. For custodial parents receiving public assistance (e.g., Temporary Assistance for Needy Families (TANF)), IV-D services are free. Those not receiving public assistance may be charged a nominal fee ($25).

Obligees on public assistance must cooperate with the IV-D agency to establish paternity and collect child support. If, however, obligees can show "good cause," they are relieved of this requirement of cooperation. An example of good cause is a mother who faces a serious threat of physical violence from the father if she cooperates with the IV-D agency's efforts to collect child support from him.

Obligees who are on public assistance must **assign** (transfer) their support rights to the state IV-D agency or county welfare agency that collects support from obligors. The assignment means that the obligee gives the agency the right to keep any support money that it collects from the obligor up to the amount it has given the obligee in public assistance. This money is used to offset the TANF money the obligee has received. If an obligee fails to cooperate in assigning these rights, his or her share of the TANF benefits can be terminated, and the TANF benefits of the children can be sent to some other responsible adult who will agree to make them available for the children.

assign
To transfer rights or property to someone. The noun is *assignment*. The person who makes the transfer is the *assignor*. The person who receives the transfer is the *assignee* or the *assign*.

ASSIGNMENT   10.5

a. What is the name and website of the IV-D agency in your state?

b. Summarize the kinds of assistance the IV-D agency provides for custodial parents.

c. Is the IV-D agency's application for assistance online? If so, what is the website of the application? (See the General Instructions for the State-Code Assignment in Appendix A.)

LOCATING MISSING PARENTS

First things first: the NCP must be located. A very large number of NCPs disappear, or try to do so. It can sometimes be a challenge to find such NCPs in order to establish paternity, obtain a child-support order, and to enforce it. One of the services provided by an IV-D agency is its **State Parent Locator Service (SPLS)**, which helps locate parents through state sources such as:

- Records on birth, marriage, death, and other records containing **vital statistics**.
- Tax files.
- Real property records.
- Personal property records (e.g., vehicle ownership and registration records at the department of motor vehicles).
- Occupational and professional license records.
- Business filings.
- Employment security records.
- Public assistance (welfare) records.
- Law enforcement records (e.g., arrests).
- Records of public utilities and cable television companies.
- Credit bureau records.
- Information held by financial institutions, including asset and liability data.

The SPLS obtains assistance from the **Federal Parent Locator Service (FPLS)** within the U.S. Office of Child Support Enforcement. The FPLS has access to the vast databases of the federal government (e.g., Social Security numbers, data on veterans and current members of the military, IRS records, and FBI data), which it makes available to the state agencies. A unique part of the FPLS is the **National Directory of New Hires (NDNH)**, which, as we will see, collects data on newly hired employees throughout the country. One-third of all child-support cases involve parents living in different states. The NDNH is a major tool to locate such parents because of its extensive data on employment, unemployment insurance, and quarterly wages.

To begin the search for an NCP, the IV-D agency will ask the custodial parent to provide the following leads to the NCP:

- Social Security number (to be used to check old state and federal tax returns, hospital records, police records, bank accounts, insurance policies, credit cards, loan applications, pay slips, union records, etc.).
- Last known residential address.
- Current or recent employer's name and address.
- Prior employer names and addresses.
- Place of birth.
- Names and addresses of relatives and friends.
- Local clubs and organizations to which the NCP once belonged.
- Current and past local banks, public utilities, and other creditors of the NCP.
- Prior or present activity on social media.

SPLS will use the leads provided by the custodial parent to try to locate the NCP. If the NCP has moved to another state, the IV-D agency in that state can be asked to provide comparable search services. The success of the SPLS and the FPLS in finding NCPs has in large measure been due to the centralization and computerization of data on parents and children involved in child-support cases. The computer databases of state and federal child-support agencies are linked in order to facilitate matches between child-support orders and obligors.

These agencies, however, must be careful about the locator information they release, particularly in cases where domestic violence against a spouse or child is a reasonable possibility. Assume, for example, that the whereabouts of a husband is known but that he does not know where his wife and children are. They are in

State Parent Locator Service (SPLS)
A state government program that helps locate parents for purposes of child-support enforcement.

vital statistics
Data on major events, such as births, deaths, marriages, divorces, and abortions.

Federal Parent Locator Service (FPLS)
A program of the U.S. Office of Child Support Enforcement that uses data in federal databases to locate parents for purposes of child-support enforcement. Requests for information from the FPLS go through a State Parent Locator Service (SPLS).

National Directory of New Hires (NDNH)
A national database of wage and employment information used to assist state child-support agencies in locating noncustodial parents in order to establish paternity and enforce child-support obligations.

hiding because of a fear of violence from him. Without safeguards, he might attempt to locate them by using available IV-D locator services. In a system containing millions of records, this is a distinct possibility. To try to prevent it from happening, a "flag" called a **family violence indicator (FVI)** is placed on the name of a person who has been abused or threatened with abuse. The FVI goes on the victim's name in the state and federal case registries that are part of the vast network of databases in the enforcement system. The victim might have a **restraining order** (also called a *personal protection order* [*PPO*]) in effect against the abuser, or might have told the IV-D agency of the danger of family violence. This leads to the placement of a flag on her name and that of her children. States are prohibited from releasing information on the whereabouts of a "flagged" parent or child to someone who has committed or threatened domestic violence. Furthermore, the address of a victim is shielded or otherwise blocked out in the maze of online paperwork that will eventually be exchanged in the enforcement of a child-support order. Access to locator information such as addresses is highly restricted once a victim is flagged with an FVI.

family violence indicator (FVI)
A designation ("flag") placed on a participant in a child-support case indicating that he or she may be a victim of domestic violence so that access to information about the participant is restricted.

restraining order
A form of injunction, usually issued ex parte (with only one side present), to restrain the defendant from doing a threatened act or from contacting designated individuals. Also called *order of protection, personal protection order (PPO), protection from abuse (PFA).*

ASSIGNMENT	10.6

Run the following search in Google, Bing, or Yahoo: State Parent Locator Service aa (replace aa with the name of your state). How does the State Parent Locator Service of the IV-D agency in your state operate? Describe how the service functions. (See General Instructions for the State-Code Assignment in Appendix A.)

NEW HIRE REPORTING

Employers are required to report information about all newly hired employees to a *State Directory of New Hires (SDNH)* shortly after the hire date. (In many states, it is twenty days.) The "New Hire" report from the employer must provide the employee's name, address, and Social Security number as listed on his or her W-4 form. The SDNH will then match these data against its child-support records to locate delinquent parents so that income-withholding orders/notices can be issued. To help locate parents in other states, the SDNH submits its data to the National Directory of New Hires (NDNH), which is a national database that is part of the Federal Parent Locator Service (FPLS). To help locate parents who have moved across state lines, the NDNH compiles data on new hires from every state and federal agency and also unemployment-compensation data from every state. The NDNH is an important locator tool because of the large percentage of child-support cases (about 34 percent) that involve NCPs who do not live in the same state as their children.

The scope of the data collected in the NDNH is vast:

The National Directory of New Hires is a database that contains personal and financial data on nearly every working American, as well as those receiving unemployment compensation. Contrary to its name, the National Directory of New Hires includes more than just information on new employees. It is a database that includes information on (1) all newly hired employees, compiled from state reports (and reports from federal employers), (2) the quarterly wage reports of existing employees . . . , and (3) unemployment compensation claims. The National Directory of New Hires was originally established to help states locate noncustodial parents living in a different state so that child support payments could be withheld from that parent's paycheck. Since its enactment in 1996, the National Directory of New Hires has been extended to several additional programs and agencies to verify program eligibility, prevent or end fraud, collect overpayments, or assure that program benefits are correct.[12]

The new hire program has been quite successful. In the first two years of its operation, more than 2.8 million delinquent parents were uncovered. There have been side benefits as well. Citizens collecting unemployment compensation should not be working full-time. Yet the new hire program has found thousands who have been fraudulently collecting unemployment benefits while employed. In one year, for example, Pennsylvania identified 4,289 overpayments in unemployment with a dollar value of $2.3 million. Among the new hires, the government has also found numerous individuals who are in default on their student loans. Their names have been shared with the U.S. Department of Education, which has initiated successful loan-collection efforts. Clearly, the benefits of the new hire program have extended beyond improved child-support collection.

PATERNITY

Where needed, the IV-D agency will help a mother obtain a court order establishing paternity or an acknowledgement of paternity by the father. (We will cover paternity in depth in Chapter 13.) Every state has expedited paternity procedures, including standard forms in maternity wards on which unwed fathers are encouraged—voluntarily—to acknowledge paternity immediately after birth. (See Exhibit 13.6 in Chapter 13 for an example of such a form.)

ENFORCEMENT OPTIONS

The most dramatic modern development in the law of child support has been a substantial increase in the number of remedies that are available to enforce the duty of child support. For a summary of the remedies we will examine, see Exhibit 10.4.

EXHIBIT 10.4 Remedies to Enforce the Duty of Child Support

Name of Remedy	Description
Civil and Criminal Contempt	• Civil contempt is the refusal of a party to comply with a court order (e.g., to pay support), which can lead to punishment (including incarceration) until the party complies with the order. • Criminal contempt is the refusal of a party to comply with a court order (e.g., to pay support), which can lead to punishment (including incarceration) because of the repeated or aggravated nature of the refusal.
Criminal Nonsupport	The willful, repeated, or aggravated failure to pay support for a person that the defendant is obligated to support from available resources.
Execution	A command or writ to a court officer (e.g., sheriff) to seize and sell the property of the losing litigant in order to satisfy the judgment debt, such as delinquent child support.
Income Withholding	The process whereby an employer is required to deduct some of an employee's income, which will be used to meet the child-support obligations of the employee.
Garnishment	A court proceeding by a creditor to force a third party in possession of the debtor's property (e.g., wages) to turn the property over to the creditor to satisfy a debt, such as delinquent child support.
License and Registration Denial, Delay, or Revocation	Delinquent obligors can have their applications for an occupational license, driver's license, or vehicle registration denied or delayed (or have their current licenses or registrations revoked) for nonpayment of child support.
Passport Denial, Revocation, or Restriction	Delinquent obligors can have their application for a passport denied or have their current passport revoked or restricted for nonpayment of child support.
Tax Refund Offset	Delinquent obligors can have their federal and state tax refunds intercepted so that they can be used to pay child support.
IRS Full Collection	The Internal Revenue Service (IRS) can attempt to collect the full amount of delinquent child support in the same manner it collects a tax debt.

(continued)

Exhibit 10.4 *(continued)*

Name of Remedy	Description
Insurance Match Program	Delinquent obligors can have their insurance payment or award intercepted so that it can be used to pay child support.
Qualified Domestic Relations Order (QDRO)	A court order that allows a nonworker to reach all or part of the pension or other retirement benefits of a worker or former worker in order to satisfy the worker's child-support or other marital obligation.
Qualified Medical Child Support Order (QMCSO)	A court order to an employer to extend its group health insurance benefits to the child of one of its workers even if the child does not live with the worker.
Credit Bureau Referral (credit clouding)	Notification of a creditor or a credit bureau that an obligor/debtor is delinquent on certain debts, such as child support.
Financial Institution Data Match (FIDM) (freeze and seize)	Identification and seizure of funds that a delinquent obligor has in financial institutions so that they can be used for child support.
Lien	A security, encumbrance, or claim on property that remains until a debt such as child support is paid. The lien prevents the sale of an obligor's assets when the lien is imposed on cars, boats, and other property that must be registered.
Post Security	The delinquent obligor must post a bond or other guarantee to cover child support.
Wheel Boot	Placing a wheel boot on a delinquent obligor's car.
Wanted Posters	Placing the image of delinquent obligors on wanted posters.

Civil Contempt

contempt
Conduct that defies or disrespects the authority of a court or legislative body.

civil contempt
The refusal of a party to comply with a court order (usually issued for the benefit of another), which can lead to punishment (including incarceration) until the party complies with the order.

criminal contempt
The refusal of a party to comply with a court order, which can lead to punishment (including incarceration) because of the repeated or aggravated nature of the refusal.

Contempt is conduct that defies or disrespects the authority of a court or legislative body. The conduct is called *contempt of court* if a court is defied or disrespected. There are two types of contempt—civil and criminal—both of which can lead to the jailing of the offender. Civil contempt is the refusal of a party to comply with a court order (usually issued for the benefit of another), which can lead to punishment (including incarceration) until the party complies with the order. Criminal contempt is the refusal of a party to comply with a court order, which can lead to punishment (including incarceration) because of the repeated or aggravated nature of the refusal. The purpose of a civil contempt proceeding is to compel future compliance with the court order, whereas the purpose of a criminal contempt proceeding is to punish the offender because of the repeated or aggravated nature of the conduct.

When civil contempt occurs in child-support cases, the nonpaying obligor can be jailed until he or she agrees to comply with the court order. Suppose, however, that the offender has no resources and thus cannot comply. In effect, such a person would be imprisoned because of his or her poverty. This is unconstitutional.[13] Before ordering imprisonment for civil contempt, a court must conclude that the offender has the *present ability* to pay the child-support debt (from current or available resources) but refuses to do so. Such an individual is in control of how long the sentence will be. In effect, the keys to jail are in his or her pocket. As one court said,

> There is no constitutional impediment to imposition of contempt sanctions on a parent for violation of a judicial child support order when the parent's financial inability to comply with the order is the result of the parent's willful failure to seek and accept available employment that is commensurate with his or her skills and ability.[14]

house arrest
The confinement of an accused or convicted person to his or her home except for approved travel such as for employment. If an electronic devise (e.g., a bracelet) is attached to the body to monitor the arrest, it is called *Electronic House Arrest (EHA).*

In addition to jailing the obligor, most courts have the power to order the less drastic sanction of imposing a fine when the obligor is found to be in civil contempt. Also, an alternative to incarceration is house arrest, which confines the obligor to his or her home except for approved travel such as for employment.

Obligors faced with imprisonment for civil or criminal contempt can hire a private attorney to represent them. On whether they are entitled to a free attorney at government expense, see the section on Attorney Representation later in the chapter.

ASSIGNMENT 10.7

What steps must be taken in your state to use a civil contempt proceeding to enforce a child-support order? (See General Instruction for the Flowchart Assignment in Appendix A.)

Criminal Nonsupport

In most states, **criminal nonsupport** is the willful, repeated, or aggravated failure to pay support for a person the defendant is obligated to support from available resources. Criminal nonsupport is a *state* crime for which the obligor can be prosecuted. (This failure is separate from criminal contempt of court mentioned earlier, which is the failure to obey a specific court order.) The criminal-nonsupport statute might provide that the crime is committed if there is an intentional failure to pay spousal or child support for a designated number of consecutive days (e.g., 120). The punishment can consist of imprisonment or a fine.

Except for relatively wealthy offenders, locking someone up is seldom an effective method of enforcing child support. Most obligors are wage earners, and once they are jailed, their primary source of income obviously dries up. One way out of this dilemma is for the judge to agree to suspend the imposition of the jail sentence on condition that the obligor fulfill the support obligation, including the payment of arrearages. The obligor would be placed on **probation** under this condition.

criminal nonsupport
The willful, repeated, or aggravated failure to pay support for a person the defendant is obligated to support from available resources. Also called *nonsupport, criminal neglect of family, abandonment of children*.

probation
Living in the community (in lieu of institutionalization) so long as there is compliance with court-imposed conditions. (See the glossary for an additional meaning.)

ASSIGNMENT 10.8

a. Is it a crime in your state to fail to pay child support? If so, quote the elements of the crime. (See General Instructions for the State-Code Assignment in Appendix A.)

b. Prepare a list of questions that you would ask and facts that you would investigate in order to help determine whether this crime was committed. (See General Instructions for the Investigation-Strategy Assignment in Appendix A.)

c. What steps must be taken in your state to prosecute someone for committing this crime? (See General Instructions for the Flowchart Assignment in Appendix A.)

If a nonpayment case involves more than one state, a *federal* crime may have been committed under the **Deadbeat Parents Punishment Act (DPPA).** A sentence of between six months and two years can be imposed when the obligor repeatedly fails to pay child support for a child living in another state, or who crosses state lines in order to avoid paying child support.[15] To be prosecuted under the DPPA, the obligor must be financially able to pay the child support that is due. Federal prosecutors in the United States Attorney's Office, however, are reluctant to bring a case until civil and criminal remedies at the *state* level have been tried.

Furthermore, federal prosecutors will give priority to cases (1) where there is a pattern of moving from state to state to avoid payment, (2) where there is a pattern of deception such as the use of a false name or a false Social Security number,

Deadbeat Parents Punishment Act (DPPA)
A federal statute that makes it a crime for a parent to repeatedly fail to pay child support for a child living in another state or to cross state lines to avoid paying child support.

(3) where there is failure to make support payments after being held in contempt of court, and (4) where the failure to make support payments is connected to another federal offense, such as bankruptcy fraud.

The creation of federal crimes in this area by Congress has been criticized as inappropriately "federalizing" family law. For example, the former chief justice of the U.S. Supreme Court, William H. Rehnquist, complained that Congress was enacting too many federal laws to cover conduct that should be the exclusive domain of the state criminal justice system. One of the examples he cited was the DPPA.

Execution

Once an obligor fails to pay a judgment ordering child support, the sheriff can be ordered to seize the personal property or real property of the obligor in the state. This is called an **execution** or a *writ of execution*. The initial effect of execution is to create a **lien**, which is a claim on property that remains until a debt is paid. The property that is seized can be sold by the sheriff. The proceeds from this execution sale (also called a *forced sale*) are used to pay the judgment and the expenses of the execution. Not all property of the obligor, however, is subject to execution in every state. Certain property (e.g., clothes and cars) may be exempt from execution.

Income Withholding

One of the most successful enforcement programs is **income withholding**, which is a mandatory, automatic deduction by an employer from the paycheck (or other income) of an employee who falls behind in child-support payments. Nearly 75 percent of all child support is collected by employers through this method (more than $21 billion a year). An IWO (Income Withholding for Support Order) is sent to employers in any state where the obligor works. In addition to wages, employers can withhold commissions and retirement payments. Each pay period, the employer deducts a specified amount and sends it to the IV-D agency, to the court, or, in some cases, directly to the custodial parent. The process begins when the IV-D agency sends the employer an IWO to withhold income for child support. (See Exhibit 10.5.)

Employers must comply with all the requirements listed in the IWO. They can be fined or otherwise sanctioned for failure to withhold income. Most states allow employers to charge an employee an administrative fee for processing the withholding, but they cannot fire or discipline the employee because of the withholding.

If the employee quits or is terminated by the employer, the employer must send the IV-D agency or court a notice giving the date of termination, the employee's last known home address, and the new employer's address, if known.

Garnishment

Income withholding is similar to **garnishment**, which is a court proceeding by a creditor to force a third party (e.g., a bank or employer) in possession of the debtor's property (e.g., bank account, wages) to turn the property over to the creditor to satisfy a debt. Garnishment, however, is usually less effective than income withholding because of the more cumbersome procedures for instituting garnishment and the restrictions that may exist on how long it can be in effect.

License and Registration Denial, Delay, or Revocation

To engage in certain occupations, a person must obtain a license from the state. Examples of licensed occupations include plumber, hair stylist, real estate broker, accountant, electrician, teacher, doctor, and attorney. Many states will deny

---

execution
A command or writ to a court officer (e.g., sheriff) to seize and sell the property of the losing litigant in order to satisfy the judgment debt. Also called *general execution* and *writ of execution*. (See the glossary for an additional meaning.)

lien
A security, encumbrance, or claim on property that remains until a debt is paid.

income withholding
The process whereby an employer is required to deduct some of an employee's income, which will be used to meet the child-support obligations of the employee. (In some states, the deductions can also be used to meet spousal-support obligations.)

garnishment
A court proceeding by a creditor to force a third party in possession of the debtor's property (e.g., wages) to turn the property over to the creditor to satisfy the debt owed to the creditor.

EXHIBIT 10.5 IWO: Income Withholding for Support Order

INCOME WITHHOLDING FOR SUPPORT

- ☐ **INCOME WITHHOLDING ORDER/NOTICE FOR SUPPORT (IWO)**
- ☐ **AMENDED IWO**
- ☐ **ONE-TIME ORDER/NOTICE FOR LUMP SUM PAYMENT**
- ☐ **TERMINATION OF IWO**   **Date:** _____

☐ Child Support Enforcement (CSE) Agency ☐ Court ☐ Attorney ☐ Private Individual/Entity   (Check One)

NOTE: This IWO must be regular on its face. Under certain circumstances you must reject this IWO and return it to the sender (see IWO instructions www.acf.hhs.gov/css/resource/income-withholding-for-support-instructions). If you receive this document from someone other than a state or tribal CSE agency or a court, a copy of the underlying support order must be attached.

State/Tribe/Territory _____   Remittance ID (include w/payment) _____
City/County/Dist./Tribe _____   Order ID _____
Private Individual/Entity _____   Case ID _____

_____ RE: _____
Employer/Income Withholder's Name   Employee/Obligor's Name (Last, First, Middle)

Employer/Income Withholder's Address   Employee/Obligor's Social Security Number
_____
_____   Employee/Obligor's Date of Birth

_____   Custodial Party/Obligee's Name (Last, First, Middle)

Employer/Income Withholder's FEIN _____

Child(ren)'s Name(s) (Last, First, Middle)   Child(ren)'s Birth Date(s)

ORDER INFORMATION: This document is based on the support order from _____ (State/Tribe).
You are required by law to deduct these amounts from the employee/obligor's income until further notice.
$ _____ Per _____ current child support
$ _____ Per _____ past-due child support - **Arrears greater than 12 weeks?** ☐ Yes ☐ No
$ _____ Per _____ current cash medical support
$ _____ Per _____ past-due cash medical support
$ _____ Per _____ current spousal support
$ _____ Per _____ past-due spousal support
$ _____ Per _____ other (must specify) _____ .
for a **Total Amount to Withhold** of $ _____ per _____ .

AMOUNTS TO WITHHOLD: You do not have to vary your pay cycle to be in compliance with the *Order Information*. If your pay cycle does not match the ordered payment cycle, withhold one of the following amounts:
$ _____ per weekly pay period $ _____ per semimonthly pay period (twice a month)
$ _____ per biweekly pay period (every two weeks) $ _____ per monthly pay period
$ _____ **Lump Sum Payment:** Do not stop any existing IWO unless you receive a termination order.

Document Tracking ID _____

Income Withholding for Support (IWO)   OMB 0970-0154   Expiration Date: 08/31/2020   Page 1 of 4

Source: Office of Child Support Enforcement (www.acf.hhs.gov/sites/default/files/ocse/omb_0970_0154.pdf)

an initial application for a license, deny an application for a renewal of a license, or revoke the license of a parent who is delinquent in making child-support payments. For example, a state statute might specify that no persons shall be granted a license or renewal if they are more than thirty days delinquent in complying with a child support order.

Many states will also revoke or suspend the driver's license or vehicle registration of delinquent obligors. The state will send them an "intent to revoke" letter. If the child-support debt is not satisfied, an investigator might locate the vehicle, remove the license plate, and leave a bright orange decal on the driver's side window explaining the seizure and the steps to take through the IV-D agency to have the license plate restored.

Courts have rejected claims that these penalties violate the constitutional rights of obligors. Before the penalties are imposed, the obligor is notified of the penalty, given an opportunity for a hearing, and given the right to avoid the penalty by signing a payment agreement or otherwise satisfying the IV-D agency or the court that payment will be made. These procedures satisfy the due-process rights of the obligor.

Passport Denial, Revocation, or Restriction

Individuals who owe over $2,500 in child support can have their passport application denied. In addition, the U.S. Secretary of State, the federal official in charge of the Passport Office, can take action to revoke or restrict a passport previously issued to those who have this amount of child-support debt. Every year, the U.S. Department of State receives more than 4 million requests to block the passports of delinquent obligors.[16]

Federal Tax Refund Offset Program

Delinquent child support can be collected out of tax refunds that obligors would otherwise receive. This collection of funds occurs under the Federal Tax Refund Offset Program. Each year, IV-D agencies submit to the Internal Revenue Service (IRS) the names, Social Security numbers, and amounts of past-due child support owed by parents. The IRS then determines whether these individuals are scheduled to receive tax refunds on their returns. If so, the IRS sends them an offset notification that informs them of the proposed offset and gives them an opportunity to pay the past-due amount or to contest the amount with the IV-D agency. In addition, a program exists to intercept and offset tax refunds due on state returns. In a recent year, $2.3 billion was collected from federal tax intercepts and $204 million was collected from state tax intercepts.

IRS Full Collection

In addition to tax refund intercepts, the IRS can do an IRS Full Collection in which the power of the IRS is used to collect *all* of the obligor's delinquent child-support debt. In this collection effort, the IRS acts in the same manner as it would when collecting a tax debt. The amounts collected are then turned over to the obligee through the IV-D agency. IRS Full Collection can be used after the other major enforcement efforts have been tried without success.

Insurance Match Program

Assume that an obligor becomes entitled to receive an insurance payment or award. The insurance might be government insurance (e.g., unemployment compensation or workers' compensation) or private insurance (e.g., automobile or life insurance policy). The payment or award can be intercepted though the IV-D agency and made available to meet child-support delinquencies.

For example, computers at the unemployment-compensation agency and at the IV-D agency communicate with each other to identify delinquent parents who have applied for or who are eligible for unemployment compensation. (The identification is called a *match*.) An investigator from the IV-D agency will then contact surprised obligors to notify them of an intercept unless support payments are made. It may even be possible to intercept benefits across state lines pursuant to reciprocal agreements among cooperating states. In a recent year, more than $2 billion was collected from the unemployment-compensation intercept program.

Victim compensation funds are also subject to intercepts. For example, victims of disasters—such as 9/11 and the Deepwater Horizon oil spill—became eligible for billions of dollars in compensation for their losses. When IV-D agencies became involved, victims who were delinquent obligors were required to use their funds for child support.

Qualified Domestic Relations Order (QDRO)

Often, an obligor will have a pension or other retirement benefits through an employer. A special court order, called a **qualified domestic relations order (QDRO)**, allows a person other than the obligor to reach some or all of these benefits in order to meet a support obligation of the obligor, such as child support or alimony. Using a QDRO, the child or ex-spouse becomes an *alternate payee* under these benefit plans. This child or ex-spouse cannot receive benefits under the plan that the obligor would not have been able to receive. For example, if the obligor is not entitled to a lump-sum payment, the child as alternate payee is also subject to this limitation.

qualified domestic relations order (QDRO)
A court order that allows a nonworker to reach all or part of the pension or other retirement benefits of a worker or former worker in order to satisfy the worker's support or other marital obligation.

Qualified Medical Child Support Order (QMCSO)

Assume that a delinquent obligor parent works for a company that has a group health plan. But the parent either refuses to add the child to the plan, or the employer (and its insurance company) tells the parent that the child is ineligible because he or she does not live with the parent, does not live in the insurer's service area, is not claimed as a dependent on the parent's tax return, or was born to unmarried parents. In 1993, Congress passed a law that made it illegal for employers and their insurance companies to use such reasons to deny healthcare coverage to children. A court order can now be obtained to require such coverage. It is called the **qualified medical child support order (QMCSO)**. The child becomes an *alternate recipient* under the group health plan. The employer can deduct the cost of adding the child to the plan from the parent's pay.

qualified medical child support order (QMCSO)
A court order to an employer to extend its group health insurance benefits to the child of one of its workers, even if the child does not live with the worker.

Credit Bureau Referral (Credit Clouding)

An obligor can be warned that a credit bureau (e.g., Experian, TransUnion, Equifax) will be notified of a delinquency in making child-support payments unless satisfactory arrangements are made to pay the debt. Once the computers of a credit bureau have information on such payment problems, a "cloud" on the obligor's credit rating is created. **Credit clouding** notifies potential creditors that the obligor may be a bad credit risk. This method of pressuring compliance with child-support obligations is particularly effective with self-employed obligors, who often do not have regular wages that can be subjected to income withholding or garnishment.

credit clouding
Notifying a creditor or credit bureau that a debtor is delinquent on certain debts such as child support.

Financial Institution Data Match (FIDM) ("Freeze and Seize")

State IV-D agencies can attach and take ("freeze and seize") the accounts of delinquent obligors in financial institutions and use the funds for child support. The accounts can include savings, checking, time deposit, and money market

levy
The collection or seizure of property by a public official to satisfy a judgment. (See the glossary for an additional meaning.)

accounts at large banks, credit unions, and mutual funds. The IV-D agency issues a lien on the account. The debtor must satisfy the lien before the property may be sold or transferred. (The actual collection or seizure of the property is called a levy.) This IV-D method of collection is called Financial Institution Data Match (FIDM) or "Freeze and Seize."

Liens

Liens can be placed on any obligor property that must be registered, such as cars and boats. The effect of the lien is to inhibit the sale of the property by the obligor. No one would want to buy the property unless the liens were removed, and they can be removed only by paying the debt that caused the lien to be imposed. In some states, the obligee does not have to go to court to obtain the lien. An administrative agency can impose the lien. Such liens are called *administrative liens*.

Post Security

In some cases, the delinquent obligor can be required to post security in the form of a bond or other guarantee (including cash) that will cover future support obligations. This security will be held by the IV-D agency and used if the obligor falls behind in child-support payments.

Wheel Boot and Wanted Posters

prosecution
(1) Bringing and processing criminal proceedings against someone. The words *prosecution* and *prosecute* can also refer to bringing and processing *civil* proceedings against someone, although the words are more commonly used in criminal proceedings. (2) The attorney representing the government in a criminal case. Also called the *prosecutor*.

amnesty
Forgiveness; a pardon issued by the state.

A delinquent obligor's car can be immobilized by clamping a wheel boot on it until he or she pays past-due child support. Also, the threat of prosecution has encouraged some delinquent obligors to come forward. States can post "wanted lists" (e.g., the Ten Most Wanted Parents, the Deadbeat of the Month) containing the pictures of individuals who have been convicted of criminal nonsupport or for whom arrest warrants have been issued because of the amount of child support owed. (To find such lists, run the search "deadbeats wanted" on Google, Bing, or Yahoo.) Several states have launched highly publicized amnesty programs (see Exhibit 10.6).

EXHIBIT 10.6 Amnesty Ad Placed in Sports Section of Local Newspaper

DO YOU OWE CHILD SUPPORT?

—Has your luck run out?—

Beginning Monday morning, December 6, a substantial number of Kansas City area parents who have failed to make their court-ordered child support payments will be arrested, jailed, and prosecuted. Could you be one of those parents?

Rather than gamble, you can receive amnesty from criminal prosecution by coming in person to the child support enforcement office at 1805 Grand Avenue in Kansas City and making immediate payment arrangements. You only have until this Friday at 5 p.m. Next Monday, you may be in jail, and then it will be too late.

Come in—let's talk.

Missouri Division of Child Support Enforcement
www.dss.mo.gov/cse
1805 Grand Ave., Suite 300
Kansas City, MO 64108

Source: Missouri Division of Child Support Enforcement.

IMPROPER ENFORCEMENT

There are limits to what a state can do to enforce a child-support order. For example, as we have seen, a state cannot imprison parents for failure to pay child support when they do not have the financial resources or capability to make such payments. Furthermore, the failure of a parent to pay child support is not in and of itself grounds to terminate the parental rights of the parent. As we will see in Chapter 15, however, such failure can be an important factor in a court's decision to impose a termination.

A state's attempt to use its marriage statutes to enforce child support has been challenged as unconstitutional. One state refused to issue marriage licenses to individuals who had failed to support their children in the custody of someone else. As we saw in Chapter 5 on marriage formation, however, the U.S. Supreme Court has held that this method of child-support enforcement is invalid because it is an unconstitutional interference with the fundamental right to marry.[17]

Although the failure to pay child support cannot be used to interfere with the right to marry, can such failure be used to interfere with the right to procreate? Can the state say to a "deadbeat dad," stop having more children until you pay for the ones you already have? The U.S. Supreme Court has not yet answered this question. In 2001, however, the Supreme Court of Wisconsin answered it in the affirmative. The Wisconsin court held that a father who intentionally refused to pay child support can be required to avoid having another child until he makes sufficient efforts to support his existing children.[18]

In the Wisconsin case, David Oakley was convicted of intentionally failing to support the nine children he had fathered with four different women, even though nothing prevented him from obtaining gainful employment. He could have been sent to prison for eight years. Instead, the court released him on probation under the condition that he avoid fathering another child until he complied with his support obligation to the nine he had already fathered. He faced eight years in prison if he violated this condition. Oakley argued that the condition violated his fundamental right to procreate. The court acknowledged "the fundamental liberty interest of a citizen to choose whether or not to procreate."[19] Yet the court said that this interest had not been violated. Oakley was a convicted felon, and therefore, he was subject to more restrictions than ordinary citizens. Furthermore, the condition was reasonably related to his rehabilitation. To avoid eight years of prison (where he would face a total ban on his right to procreate), he merely had to make the efforts required by law to support his current children. The condition did no more than require him to avoid creating another victim of willful nonsupport.

The vote of the Wisconsin justices upholding the probation condition was four to three. The dissenters were concerned that the right to have children was based on a parent's financial resources. One dissenter said that the condition "is basically a compulsory, state-sponsored, court-enforced financial test for future parenthood."[20] Another dissenter commented that the condition creates a strong incentive for Oakley to demand an abortion from any woman he impregnates in the future. An attorney for the American Civil Liberties Union called the decision "a dangerous precedent" in the area of reproductive rights.[21] The case received widespread publicity. Some of the news accounts thought it relevant to point out that the four justices in the majority were male and that the three dissenters were female.

ATTORNEY REPRESENTATION

Because of the extensive assistance provided by the IV-D agency in collecting child support, most obligees do not need to hire private attorneys. Such attorneys are available for hire, but except in high-income cases, they are rarely used.

indigent
Poor; without means to afford something, such as a private attorney or filing fees.

The IV-D agency, of course, does not assist NCP obligors except to remind them of their duty to pay support and to work out payment options where appropriate. Obligors often need legal help when faced with severe sanctions, such as loss of an occupational license, a seizure of bank accounts, and imprisonment. The extensive amount of self-help information on the Internet for obligees and obligors may not be enough. When obligors cannot afford private counsel (i.e., when they are **indigent**), is the state required to provide free representation for them? The answer, in part, depends on what the obligor is being charged with—criminal contempt/criminal non-support or with civil contempt.

CRIMINAL CONTEMPT AND CRIMINAL NONSUPPORT CASES

If the obligor is charged with criminal contempt (or the crime of criminal non-support), the Sixth Amendment of the U.S. Constitution grants an indigent criminal defendant the right to counsel. In most serious criminal cases, the state will provide free counsel if the defendant is indigent and cannot afford his or her own attorney.

CIVIL CONTEMPT

As indicated earlier, the purpose of criminal contempt is to punish the obligor, whereas the purpose of civil contempt is to force the obligor to comply with an order. Imprisonment for criminal contempt can be ordered because of the affront that the defendant has shown the system. This affront can be punished regardless of whether the defendant is indigent.

Imprisonment for *civil* contempt is mainly an enforcement tool to pressure the obligor to pay support. Because of the punishment component that is part of criminal contempt, but not of civil contempt, obligors charged with civil contempt are entitled to fewer procedural rights than obligors charged with criminal contempt. For example, the Sixth Amendment of the U.S. Constitution requires the appointment of counsel in cases of criminal contempt. What about in civil contempt cases?

The Sixth Amendment does not apply to civil cases. Hence, the question is whether the due process of law clause of the Fourteenth Amendment requires the appointment of counsel in a civil contempt case. On this question, the U.S. Supreme Court has held that obligors charged with civil contempt are not entitled to free counsel (1) if the custodial parent (obligee) is not represented by counsel and (2) if the state has fair procedures that allow a noncustodial parent (obligor) to prove that he or she is unable to pay the child support. These procedures include an opportunity to contest the claim of child support; the use of a relatively straightforward method (e.g., a form) that allows the obligor to state his or her financial information; and adequate notice to the obligor that imprisonment for civil contempt will be not be imposed if the obligor is unable to pay the support alleged to be due. If, however, the obligee has counsel and the case is relatively complex, the state may have a duty to provide free counsel to an indigent obligor faced with civil contempt.[22]

DOMESTIC VIOLENCE

As indicated earlier, domestic violence against custodial parents is an ongoing concern. Some NCPs, particularly fathers, do not react kindly to requests that they meet their child-support obligations. Occasionally, they may physically assault the CP or threaten to do so. The police may be called. Usually, the threatened party can go to the local prosecutor or district attorney to obtain a restraining order, which warns the NCP that he or she will be arrested and jailed unless he or she stays away from the children and the CP. Initially, the order is usually issued by the court with only one party present in the court (**ex parte**)—the CP. At a later time, the target of the order is allowed to contest its validity in court. Some critics, however, have complained that the police and the legal system do not take so-called domestic disputes of this kind seriously. (For more on domestic violence, see Chapter 12.)

JURISDICTION

As we learned in Chapter 7, a divorce judgment can accomplish the following five objectives:

(1) Dissolve the marriage.

(2) Award spousal support.

(3) Divide marital property.

(4) Award child support.

(5) Award child custody.

For all five, a court needs **subject-matter jurisdiction**, which is the court's power to resolve a particular type of legal dispute and to grant a particular type of relief. In addition, a court order for each of the five objectives requires another kind of jurisdiction. (See Exhibit 7.5 in Chapter 7.) Our focus here is on the kind of jurisdiction needed (in addition to subject-matter jurisdiction) for an order of child support in the **forum** state where the CP is seeking child support from the NCP.

The additional jurisdiction needed to order an NCP to pay child support is **personal jurisdiction**. Such jurisdiction gives the court power to determine someone's personal rights and duties. If a court makes an order of child support against someone over whom it does not have personal jurisdiction, the court order is not enforceable in the court that issued the order and a court in another state does not have to enforce it—the support order is not entitled to **full faith and credit (FFC)** in other states.

How does a court acquire personal jurisdiction over a defendant NCP? To answer this question we will focus first on resident NCPs and then on nonresident NCPs.

JURISDICTION OVER A RESIDENT PARENT

The first step in acquiring personal jurisdiction over a resident parent is **service of process**, which is the formal delivery of notice to a defendant that a suit has been initiated (here, a suit for child support) to which he or she must respond. The defendant is also given a copy of the petition/complaint. If the defendant can be found, **personal service** consists of handing the service-of-process documents to the defendant in person. If the resident defendant cannot be found in the state, **substituted service** is often allowed, such as service by U.S. mail or by publication in a newspaper.

JURISDICTION OVER A NONRESIDENT PARENT

A more serious problem is collecting child support from a *nonresident* parent. A large number of child-support cases are brought by CPs against nonresident NCPs. The major concerns in collecting child support from nonresidents are jurisdiction and convenience. How does the forum state (where the CP and child live) obtain personal jurisdiction over a person who does not live in the forum state? How can a CP overcome the inconvenience (and often total impracticality) of traveling to the state where the NCP lives (assuming the NCP can be found) and bringing a support action in that state?

A related problem is the proliferation of child-support orders. Assume that after State #1 issues a child-support order, the NCP moves to State #2 and asks for a new or a modified order based on changed circumstances. Before the law was changed, State #2 did not have to give full faith and credit (FFC) to the

---

ex parte
With only one side present (usually the plaintiff or petitioner) when a court action is asked to do something.

subject-matter jurisdiction
The court's power to resolve a particular type of legal dispute and to grant a particular type of relief.

forum
(1) A court. (2) The place where the parties are presently litigating their dispute. (3) A court or tribunal hearing a case.

personal jurisdiction
A court's power over a person to determine (adjudicate) his or her personal rights and duties. Also called *in personam jurisdiction*.

full faith and credit (FFC)
The obligation of one state to recognize and enforce the laws and legal decisions of another state. The obligation is based on the U.S. Constitution, which provides that "Full Faith and Credit shall be given in each State to the public Acts, Records, and judicial Proceedings of every other State." Article IV, § 1.

service of process
A formal delivery of notice to a defendant that a suit has been initiated to which he or she must respond. *Process* is the means used by the court to acquire or exercise its power or jurisdiction over a person.

personal service
Handing the service-of-process documents to the person who is the target of the service.

substituted service
Service of process by mail, by publication in a newspaper, or by other approved methods that are alternatives to the personal service of hand delivering the process documents to the defendant (or to the defendant's authorized representative). Also called *constructive service*.

child-support order of State #1 because child-support orders were not final judgments and only final judgments were entitled to FFC.

- To help solve the problem of obtaining personal jurisdiction over nonresident NCPs, Congress pressured every state to enact the **Uniform Interstate Family Support Act (UIFSA)**. The UIFSA is a state law on establishing and enforcing alimony and child-support obligations against someone who does not live in the same state as the person to whom the alimony and child support is owed.

- To help solve the problem of proliferating child-support orders, Congress passed the *Full Faith and Credit for Child Support Orders Act (FFCCSOA)*.

We will examine the UIFSA next. We will examine the FFCCSOA later under the topic of modification. Under the UIFSA, there are seven ways a forum state can acquire personal jurisdiction over a nonresident defendant NCP. See Exhibit 10.7. States differ on whether they include all seven.

Presence and Consent

The first two UIFSA reasons in Exhibit 10.7 pose little difficulty. It is easy for a court to acquire personal jurisdiction over a nonresident defendant who is served with process while physically present in the forum state, who enters a **general appearance** and thereby litigates the merits of the case, or who shows up and files an answer or other **responsive pleading**.

A general appearance occurs when a person goes to court as a party without restrictions and thereby submits to the full jurisdiction of the court. A **pleading** is a formal litigation document (e.g., complaint, petition, answer) filed by a party that states or responds to claims or defenses of other parties. A *responsive pleading* is a pleading that replies to a prior pleading of an opponent.

Uniform Interstate Family Support Act (UIFSA)
A state law on establishing and enforcing alimony and child-support obligations against someone who does not live in the same state as the person to whom the alimony and child support is owed.

general appearance
Coming to court as a party without restrictions and thereby submitting to the full jurisdiction of the court.

responsive pleading
A pleading that replies to a prior pleading of an opponent.

pleadings
Formal litigation documents (e.g., a complaint or petition, an answer) filed by parties that state or respond to claims or defenses the parties have against each other.

EXHIBIT 10.7 Obtaining Personal Jurisdiction over a Nonresident under the Uniform Interstate Family Support Act (UIFSA)

Seven Possible Reasons a Forum State Can Assert Personal Jurisdiction over a Nonresident Under the UIFSA

1. *Presence.* The nonresident happens to be physically present in the forum state and is personally served while there.

2. *Consent.* The nonresident submits (i.e., consents) to the jurisdiction of the forum state in one of two ways: (a) by entering a general appearance, and thereby litigates the merits of the case, or (b) by filing a responsive pleading such as an answer to the complaint or petition. Filing such a pleading has the effect of waiving any objection to the assertion of personal jurisdiction over the nonresident.

3. *Former residence in the state with child.* The nonresident once resided with the child in the forum state.

4. *Former residence in the state, plus expenses or support.* The nonresident once resided in the forum state and paid prenatal expenses or support for the child.

5. *Possible conception in the state.* The nonresident engaged in sexual relations in the forum state, and the child may have been conceived from those relations.

6. *Asserting parentage in the state.* The nonresident asserted parentage in the forum state, such as through the putative father registry (discussed in Chapter 13).

7. *Catch-all alternative.* Any other basis consistent with the constitution of the forum state and the U.S. Constitution for the exercise of personal jurisdiction.

Source: 9 Uniform Laws Annotated pt. 1, § 201 (Supp. 1996).

Long-Arm Jurisdiction: Minimum Contacts

Reasons 3 to 6 in Exhibit 10.7 are based on the nonresident's **minimum contacts** with the state. The U.S. Supreme Court has said that it is not fair for a court to assert personal jurisdiction over a nonresident unless that nonresident has had (or currently has) enough activities in or connections with the state. Such contacts are called *minimum contacts.* They are activities in or connected with a state by a nonresident that are substantial and sufficiently purposeful so that it can be said that the nonresident has invoked the benefits and protections of the state, thereby making it fair for the state to assert personal jurisdiction over the nonresident.

The list of minimum contacts in 3 to 6 of Exhibit 10.7 includes residing in the forum state with the child at one time, residing in the forum state at one time and covering prenatal expenses or support for the child in the state (even if the nonresident never lived with the child in the state), engaging in sexual relations in the state that may have led to the conception of the child, and using the laws of the state to assert parentage of the child.

Because these contacts (3 to 6) with the state are considered sufficiently *purposeful*, it is fair and reasonable for a court in that state to resolve (i.e., to **adjudicate**) disputes arising out of those contacts. An example of such a dispute is whether the nonresident is the child's father and, therefore, should pay child support. The personal jurisdiction that a state acquires over a nonresident defendant because of his or her purposeful contact with that state is called **long-arm jurisdiction**. A statute authorizing it is called a **long-arm statute**. The state extends its "arm" of power across state lines to assert personal jurisdiction over someone who in fairness should answer to the authority of the court because of his or her sufficiently purposeful contacts with that state.

Not all contacts of a nonresident NCP with a forum state are sufficiently purposeful to meet the test of minimum contacts. For example, the U.S. Supreme Court has held that it is not enough for a nonresident NCP to do no more than allow his child to live in the forum state, even if he pays the airline ticket to fly the child to that state to live with the CP. The forum state cannot assert personal jurisdiction over the NCP if this is his only contact with the state.[23]

The long-arm jurisdiction provisions of the UIFSA can also be used in the enforcement of *spousal* support orders against obligors/spouses who live in another state. (See Chapter 8.)

Enforcing a Support Order against a Nonresident

Obtaining personal jurisdiction over a nonresident NCP is just the first step. Next, the CP must convince the court to order the NCP to pay child support. Fortunately, the IV-D agency can assist the CP. Within the IV-D agency in every state is an **interstate central registry** that handles the enforcement of child support across state lines. Let's examine two case examples:

CASE I. *Ted and Wilma live in New York, where they were married. While on a two-week vacation in Maine, they have sexual relations leading to the conception of their only child, Mary. Upon returning to New York, they decide to separate. Wilma and Mary then move to Maine. Except for the two-week vacation, Ted has never been to Maine. Before Wilma leaves, he tells her that if she moves to Maine, he will have nothing to do with her or Mary. She goes anyway, and Ted carries out his threat of having no contact with either. He never pays child support. After establishing domicile in Maine, Wilma obtains a divorce and a child-support order from a Maine court. Ted is given notice of the Maine action, but he was not served with process in Maine and he neither appears in Wilma's divorce action nor files any response in the action.*

minimum contacts
Activities in or connected with a state by a nonresident that are substantial and sufficiently purposeful so that it can be said that the nonresident has invoked the benefits and protections of the state, thereby making it fair for the state to assert personal jurisdiction over the nonresident.

adjudicate
To decide by judicial process; to judge.

long-arm jurisdiction
The personal jurisdiction that a state acquires over a nonresident defendant under a long-arm statute.

long-arm statute
A statute that allows a state to obtain personal jurisdiction over a nonresident defendant because of the latter's minimum contacts with the state.

interstate central registry
An office in each state that receives and responds to cases involving interstate child-support enforcement.

domicile
The place where a person has been physically present (a) with the intent to make that place a permanent home or (b) with no intent to make any other place a permanent home. The place to which one intends to return when away.

in rem jurisdiction
The court's power over a particular *res*, which is a thing (e.g., land) or a status (e.g., a marriage) that is located within the territory over which the court has authority.

Wilma's domicile in Maine gave the Maine court in rem jurisdiction to dissolve the marriage. With this jurisdiction, the court's judgment dissolving the marriage is entitled to full faith and credit (FFC) in every other state so long as Ted was given notice of the proceeding and an opportunity to appear if he so chose. Personal jurisdiction over the nonresident (Ted) is not needed to dissolve the marriage. (See Exhibit 7.5 in Chapter 7.)

Personal jurisdiction, however, *is* needed for a court to issue an order of child support. Did the Maine court have personal jurisdiction over Ted? Yes. Under one of the seven long-arm methods of the UIFSA, Maine had personal jurisdiction over Ted to make the child-support order—he engaged in sexual relations in Maine leading to conception. This was a sufficiently purposeful contact with the state of Maine to give it personal jurisdiction over him.

Once personal jurisdiction is acquired over a nonresident in this way, issues such as paternity and child support can be resolved. Hence, Wilma does not have to travel to New York to have these issues resolved. They can be resolved in a Maine court. Under the UIFSA, special rules exist for the proceeding against the nonresident. For example, the Maine court can accept testimony from witnesses in New York by telephone, video, or other electronic means. Also, assuming Ted continues to refuse to come to Maine, a Maine court can ask a New York court to force Ted to submit to discovery *in New York* on issues such as his financial resources.

Assume that the Maine court rules that Ted (the nonresident) is the father of Mary and issues an order that requires Ted to pay child support. How does Wilma enforce this order? What if Ted (still in New York) refuses to obey it? Wilma has two main choices:

- First, she can take the expensive and cumbersome step of traveling to New York and asking a New York court to enforce her Maine order. Such travel, however, is impractical for most CPs. The same is true of hiring a New York attorney.

- Second, the UIFSA allows her to use a special registration procedure to enforce the Maine order in New York. Without traveling to New York, she can ask the Maine IV-D agency to send the Maine order to the appropriate tribunal in New York for the purpose of registering the order. Once registered in New York, her order can be enforced in the same manner as a New York order could be enforced against a New York resident with the help of a New York IV-D agency. Thus, the UIFSA registration procedure allows a Maine resident (Wilma) to obtain and enforce a Maine support order against a New York resident (Ted), even if Wilma never travels to New York and Ted does not show up in Maine.

Here are the steps involved:

- Wilma asks a Maine IV-D agency to send her Maine order to a New York IV-D agency.

- The Maine order is registered in New York with the help of the New York IV-D agency.

- The New York IV-D agency then enforces the registered Maine order in New York.

initiating state
The state in which a support case is filed in order to forward it to another state (called the *responding state*) for enforcement proceedings under the Uniform Interstate Family Support Act (UIFSA).

responding state
The state to which a support case is forwarded for enforcement proceedings under the Uniform Interstate Family Support Act (UIFSA). The case was forwarded by the initiating state.

From Wilma's perspective, what would normally be a two-state lawsuit has become a one-state lawsuit. This efficiency was one of the main reasons the UIFSA was enacted.

In our example, Maine is the initiating state—the state in which a support case is filed in order to forward it to another state for enforcement. New York is the responding state—the state to which the case was forwarded for enforcement. A responding state can enforce, but cannot modify, an order registered from an initiating state.

Suppose, however, that Maine *cannot* obtain personal jurisdiction over Ted under the long-arm provisions of the UIFSA. Let's change some of the facts of our example:

> **CASE II.** *Ted and Wilma live in New York, where they were married and where their only child, Mary, was conceived and born. They decide to separate. Wilma and Mary move to Maine. Ted has never been to Maine. Before Wilma leaves, he tells her that if she moves to Maine, he will have nothing to do with her or Mary. She goes anyway, and Ted carries out his threat of having no contact with either. He never pays child support. After establishing domicile in Maine, Wilma obtains a divorce and a child-support order from a Maine court. Ted is given notice of the Maine action, but he was not served with process in Maine and he neither appears in Wilma's divorce action nor files any response in the action.*

Case II raises two questions under the UIFSA:

- Can Wilma obtain and enforce a *Maine* child-support order against a New York resident (who is a nonresident of Maine) without traveling to New York?

- Can Wilma obtain and enforce a *New York* child-support order against a New York resident (who is a nonresident of Maine) without traveling to New York?

On the facts of Case II, the answer to the first question is *no,* and the answer to the second question is *yes.*

MAINE CHILD SUPPORT ORDER The major fact difference between Case I and Case II is that Mary was not conceived in Maine. Reread the seven ways for a state to obtain personal jurisdiction over a nonresident under the UIFSA (Exhibit 10.7). *None* of them applies to Ted in Case II.

- He was not personally served in Maine.
- He never consented to Maine jurisdiction.
- He never lived in Maine with his child.
- He never lived in Maine and paid prenatal expenses or support for his child.
- He never had sexual relations in Maine leading to conception.
- He never asserted his parentage in Maine.

Therefore, in Case II, a Maine court could not obtain personal jurisdiction over Ted by the long-arm method, and Wilma could not use the efficient and inexpensive registration process in New York.

In Case II, the Maine court's dissolution of the marriage is valid and enforceable because Wilma's domicile in Maine gave the court in rem jurisdiction to dissolve the marriage. The Maine court also issued a child-support order against Ted. This order, however, is not enforceable in Maine and it is not entitled to FFC by New York or any other state because it was issued against a defendant over whom the court did not have personal jurisdiction. This is an example of **divisible divorce**, which we studied in Chapter 7, meaning only part of the divorce judgment is enforceable.

divisible divorce
(1) A divorce judgment that dissolves the marriage but does not resolve other divorce issues such as property division, support, and child custody. Also called a *bifurcated divorce.* (2) A divorce that is enforceable only in part. An example is a divorce judgment issued in one court that dissolves the marriage and makes an award of child support or alimony, but only the dissolution is enforceable in another court, not the child support or alimony order.

NEW YORK CHILD SUPPORT ORDER If Wilma wants child support from Ted in Case II, she will need a child-support order *from a New York court* where Ted is a resident. Obtaining a support order from a Maine court and registering it in New York for enforcement will not work because Maine cannot obtain personal jurisdiction over Ted. But a New York court can obtain personal jurisdiction over Ted with relative ease because he is a resident of New York. (See the discussion earlier about acquiring personal jurisdiction over a resident.)

To obtain a New York support order in Case II, does Wilma have to travel to New York and hire a New York attorney? Fortunately, under the UIFSA, she does not have to do either. Another efficient and inexpensive process is available to her. Here are the steps involved:

- Wilma files a petition for child support in Maine.
- A Maine IV-D agency helps her forward the petition to New York.
- New York obtains personal jurisdiction over Ted (e.g., by service of process in person or by substituted service).
- New York conducts an administrative or judicial proceeding on issues such as paternity and child support.
- The New York court orders Ted to pay child support.
- A New York IV-D agency uses its collection powers to force Ted to pay this support obligation.
- The New York IV-D sends what it collects to Wilma in Maine via the Maine IV-D agency.

In Case II, Maine again is the initiating state and New York is the responding state. Everything is handled on Wilma's behalf by the IV-D agency in Maine and the IV-D agency in New York. At no time is Wilma required to appear in New York. Her testimony can be received in New York by telephone, video, or other electronic means.

Note the procedural difference between Case I and Case II:

- Case I: A *Maine* support order is enforced against a New York resident in New York by the registration process.
- Case II: A *New York* support order is enforced against a New York resident in New York.

The difference is based on which state could obtain personal jurisdiction over Ted.

If Wilma does not want the IV-D agency to act on her behalf in Maine or New York, she can hire a private attorney to represent her. The role of the IV-D agency would then be to assist any attorney she decides to hire.

MODIFICATION OF CHILD SUPPORT ORDERS

After a court makes a child-support order, the parties can go back to court at a later time and argue that the amount of child support is too high (according to the obligor/NCP) or too low (according to the obligee/CP). In this section, we consider how courts resolve such requests for a modification of a child-support order.

CHANGED CIRCUMSTANCES

The standard rule is that a child-support order can be modified on the basis of a substantial change of circumstances that has arisen since the court granted the order. The changed circumstances must be serious enough to warrant the conclusion that the original award has become inequitable. For example:

- The child's welfare will be jeopardized if the child-support award is not increased due to an unexpected illness of the child, which requires costly medical care.
- The child has acquired independent resources or has moved out on his or her own, and therefore, child support should be ended or decreased.

Under federal law, parties can request a review of a child-support order every three years (or such shorter cycle as a state deems appropriate) to make sure that the order complies with the child-support guidelines and to add cost-of-living adjustments as needed.[24]

Frequently, the CP claims that child support should be increased because the NCP's ability to pay has increased since the time of the original order (e.g., by obtaining a better-paying job). This is a ground to increase child support only when it is clear that the original decree was inadequate to meet the child's needs. At the time of the original decree, a lesser amount may have been awarded because of an inability to pay more *at that time.* Hence, a later modification upward is a way for the court to correct an initially inadequate award.

What happens when the NCP seeks a modification downward because he or she can no longer afford the amount originally awarded? If the circumstances that caused this change are beyond the control of the parent (e.g., a long illness), a court will be sympathetic. Suppose, however, that the change is voluntary. For example:

> At the time of a 2018 child-support order, Dan was a fifty-year-old sales manager earning $120,000 a year. The order required him to pay his ex-wife $3,000 a month in child support. In 2018, Dan decides to go to evening law school. He quits his job as a sales manager and takes a part-time job as an investigator earning $10,000 a year. He then petitions the court to modify his child-support payments to $250 a month.

In many courts, Dan's petition would be denied because he has not lost the *capacity* to earn enough to pay the original support order. The test is earning capacity, not actual earnings. Self-imposed poverty is not a ground to reduce child support in such courts. Other courts, however, are not this dogmatic. They will grant the modification petition if:

- The child will not be seriously harmed, and
- The petitioner is acting in good faith.

The court will want to know whether the change of career or of lifestyle is legitimate. Is it the kind of change that the party would probably have made if the marriage had not ended? If so, the court will be inclined to grant a modification downward, so long as the child is not seriously harmed thereby. On the other hand, is the parent acting out of *bad faith* or malice (e.g., to avoid paying child support or to make life more miserable for the CP)? If so, the modification request will be denied.

ASSIGNMENT 10.9

Harry is fired from his job because of unsatisfactory performance. As a result, he is living on unemployment insurance. He no longer has enough money to pay child support. Will a court grant him a modification? (See the General Instructions for the Legal-Analysis Assignment in Appendix A.)

TWENTY-PERCENT RULE

Assume that a party is able to convince a court that the child-support order should be increased or decreased. The next question is: by how much? In some states, there is a 20 percent rule. After the child-support guidelines are applied to the new financial facts, a court in these states will apply a presumption that the current obligation should *not* be changed unless the result would be an increase or decrease of more than 20 percent of the amount originally ordered by the court. Special circumstances might overcome the presumption, but the court does not want to encourage the parties to keep coming back to court every time the financial facts of the parties change.

SECOND FAMILY

Another area of controversy concerns the NCP's responsibility of supporting others. Should the amount of child support be less because the NCP has taken on the responsibility of supporting a second family? Suppose there is a remarriage with someone who already has children and/or the NCP and new spouse have additional children of their own. The old view was that the parent's primary responsibility was to the first family. No adjustment would be made because the parent has voluntarily taken on additional support obligations.

Many courts, however, no longer take this hard line. Although they will not permit the parent to leave the first family destitute, they will take into consideration the fact that a second family has substantially affected the parent's ability to support the first. Given this reality, an appropriate adjustment might be made. It must be emphasized, however, that not all courts are this accommodating. Some continue to adhere to the old view.

FRAUD

Finally, suppose that a man asks a court to modify or cancel a child-support order when he finds out that he is not the child's biological father. The mother lied to him about his fatherhood. Because he believed her, he never challenged the court's initial finding of paternity and order of support. Years later, scientific tests prove that he is not the biological father. Hence he now wants to challenge the original paternity order and get out from under the order to pay child support.

States handle this situation in different ways.

- In some states, the man is relieved of his obligation to pay child support.
- In other states, he must continue paying child support because continuation is in the best interests of the child, which is the paramount consideration. As one court said, "Where a father challenges a paternity judgment, courts have pointed to the special needs of children that must be protected, noting that consideration of what is in a child's best interests will often weigh more heavily than the genetic link between parent and child."[25] A court might allow a finding of paternity to be challenged within a reasonable time after the finding is made, but not if years pass during which the man has held himself out to be the child's father, and a relationship has developed between him and the child. (See the earlier discussion about the duty that can be imposed on someone who has become an *equitable parent*.) Unless there is clear and convincing evidence that reopening a paternity judgment will serve the best interests of the child, a man will not be allowed to avoid paying child support by offering genetic proof that he is not the biological father.

ARREARAGES

Note that we have been discussing the modification of *future* child-support payments. What about arrearages? Can a court modify a delinquent obligation? There was a time when courts were sympathetic to requests by delinquent obligors to forgive past-due debts, particularly when the court was convinced that future obligations would be met. Congress changed this in 1986 when the Bradley Amendment banned retroactive modification of child-support arrearages in most cases.[26]

CHILD SUPPORT OR PROPERTY DIVISION?

We saw in Chapter 8 that separation agreements sometimes fail to distinguish between property division terms (which, in general, are not modifiable by a court) and support terms (which are). (See Exhibit 8.5 in Chapter 8.) For example, suppose that the parties agree to give to the "wife the exclusive use of the marital home until the youngest child reaches the age of eighteen." Is this a division of property or a child-support term? If it is the former, then the husband cannot modify it on the basis of changed circumstances. If it is a child-support term, then a modification is possible. Most courts would interpret the above clause to mean that the parties intended it as a child-support term because it is tied to a period of time when the child would most likely need support. Yet a court *could* rule the other way. Needless litigation often results from poor drafting of separation agreements.

ASSIGNMENT 10.10

a. What standards apply to a request to modify child-support payments in your state? (See General Instructions for the State-Code Assignment in Appendix A.)

b. Sara pays her ex-husband, Harry, $800 a month in child support under a 2015 court order that granted sole physical and sole legal custody of their child to Harry but gave liberal visitation rights to Sara. Due to continuing bitterness, Harry refuses to allow Sara to visit the child. Sara then petitions the court to reduce her child-support payments. How would her request for a modification be handled in your state? (See General Instructions for the Court-Opinion Assignment in Appendix A.)

c. Reread the facts involving Dan mentioned earlier in the chapter, the fifty-year-old sales manager, who wants to go to law school. How would this request for a modification be handled in your state? (See General Instructions for the Court-Opinion Assignment in Appendix A.)

MODIFYING OUT-OF-STATE ORDERS

Parents dissatisfied with a support order in one state might try to modify it (up or down) in another state. In such an environment, one judge commented that child-support orders can "proliferate like mushrooms."[27] The UIFSA tries to prevent this.

Once a court issues a valid support order under the UIFSA, that court has **continuing exclusive jurisdiction (CEJ)** over the case. (CEJ under the UIFSA is very similar to exclusive continuing jurisdiction—ECJ—which we examined in child-custody cases in Chapter 9.) CEJ under the UIFSA means that no other state can modify the order. A state retains its CEJ so long as the CP, or the NCP, or the child continues to reside in the state. If they all leave the state, the court loses its CEJ, and another state can acquire CEJ over the case. (A court can also lose its CEJ if all parties agree that another state can have CEJ to modify the order.)

Suppose, however, that the CP and the NCP seek simultaneous child-support orders in different states. Whenever there is a potential for competing child-support orders, the UIFSA gives preference to the order issued in the **home state**. This is the state in which a child has lived with a parent (or a person acting as a parent) for at least six consecutive months immediately before the support proceedings began. If the child is less than six months old, the home state is the state in which the child has lived since birth with the parent. Periods of temporary absence are counted as part of the six months or the time since birth. (As we saw in Chapter 9, the home state is also the basis of determining child-custody jurisdiction in interstate cases.) To further prevent proliferating child-support orders, Congress passed the **Full Faith and Credit for Child Support Orders Act (FFCCSOA)**, which requires states to enforce (i.e., give full faith and credit to) and not modify valid child-support orders of other states except in limited circumstances.[28]

NECESSARIES

A seldom-used method for a spouse and child to obtain support is to go to merchants, make purchases of **necessaries**, and charge them to the credit of the nonsupporting spouse or parent. For a discussion of this remedy, see Chapter 8.

---

continuing, exclusive jurisdiction (CEJ)
The authority of a court, obtained by compliance with the Uniform Interstate Family Support Act (UIFSA). to make all initial and modifying support decisions in a case to the exclusion of courts in any other state.

home state
The state where the child has lived with a parent (or anyone acting as a parent) for at least six consecutive months immediately before the support proceeding began or since birth if the child is less than six months old.

Full Faith and Credit for Child Support Orders Act (FFCCSOA)
A federal statute governing when a state must give full faith and credit to the child-support order of another state.

necessaries
The basic items needed by family members to maintain a standard of living, particularly food, shelter, and clothing. Under the doctrine of necessaries, these items can be purchased and charged to the spouse or parent who has failed to provide them.

BANKRUPTCY

As we saw in Chapter 8, child-support payments are not discharged (eliminated) in bankruptcy proceedings. Obligors who successfully obtain a Chapter 7 or a Chapter 13 bankruptcy must still pay past-due child support and future child support. Of course, obligors who are bankrupt have substantially less income and assets as a result of the financial plight that led them into bankruptcy. Although bankruptcy cannot discharge past-due child-support debts, the obligor's altered financial circumstances may be grounds for the obligor to go back to court and request a downward modification based on current ability to pay.

INTERNATIONAL CHILD SUPPORT CASES

As indicated in Exhibit 10.1, there are 14.7 million children who receive child support with help from state child-support agencies in the United States. More than 150,000 of them are international cases in which child support must be collected from an NCP in another country. In 2016, the United States joined the *Hague Convention on the International Recovery of Child Support and Other Forms of Family Maintenance*. It contains provisions to establish uniform and inexpensive procedures to process international child support cases.[29]

PARALEGAL ROLES

- For an overview of paralegal roles in family-law cases, see Exhibits 1.5 and 1.6 in Chapter 1.
- For all financial issues related to child support covered in Chapter 10, a paralegal may be asked to help collect documents and facts outlined in:
  - The checklist in Exhibit 3.1 of Chapter 3.
  - The interrogatories in Appendix C.
- Because of the availability of legal and administrative help from IV-D agencies, most custodial parent/obligees do not hire attorneys to obtain or enforce child-support orders. The exception is the high-income case in which the custodial parent/obligee is seeking an unusually large amount of child support. Noncustodial parent/obligors, however, are more likely to need legal help defending themselves against the large array of enforcement remedies that can be brought against them, including imprisonment. When attorneys represent a parent in child-support cases, duties of their paralegals can include the following:
  - Refer the custodial parent/obligee to the local IV-D agency for assistance.
  - Assist the custodial parent/obligee to collect documents (e.g., pay stubs) that will help locate the noncustodial parent/obligor.
  - Compile a detailed financial statement on both parents that will be relevant to the amount of child support that will be ordered.
  - Using worksheets and online calculators, apply the child-support guidelines to determine the amount of child support that a court is likely to order.
  - Compile documents for the attorney who will be negotiating the terms of a separation agreement between the parents (including the child-support terms).
  - Help the noncustodial parent/obligor compile documentation of child-support payments to date and current arrearages.
  - Collect evidence to help a nonparent (stepparent, coparent, or sperm donor) prove the extent of his or her involvement or noninvolvement in the rearing of the child.
- Many IV-D agencies employ paralegals in assisting custodial parents to establish paternity, obtain child-custody orders, and enforce such orders. The duties of a child-support paralegal in such an agency might include the following:
  - Assist an attorney or administrative supervisor in child-support enforcement.
  - Conduct extensive interviews of custodial parents on issues of paternity and child-support eligibility.
  - Compose correspondence in response to inquiries where considerable knowledge of child-support policy, procedures, and guidelines is required.
  - Contact attorneys and judicial personnel to collect needed data for agency files.
  - Provide clerical and administrative support.
  - See also *Duties of Child-Support Government Paralegal* in Chapter 1.

SUMMARY

Child support is heavily influenced by federal law, particularly in the rules on enforcing child-support obligations. Vast amounts of child-support debts are not paid. The primary criterion for paying child support is parentage; both parents (biological or adoptive) have an equal obligation to support their children. Others do not have this obligation unless a special statute says otherwise or equitable estoppel applies. With some exceptions, the duty of support ends upon the age of majority or emancipation. States differ on whether a parent has an obligation to pay for a child's college education. In most states, the duty to support a child extends beyond the age of majority if the child is physically or mentally disabled. When parents are negotiating the child-support terms of their separation agreement, they must consider a number of factors such as the child-support guidelines, standard of living, payment dates, kinds and frequency of payments, insurance, and tax considerations. Parents cannot make binding agreements that one of the parents will not owe child support or will owe an amount of child support that will fall below the minimum required in the state.

The amount of child support is determined primarily by the child-support guidelines of each state. The guidelines set the presumptively correct amount of support that is due. Factors that might cause a court to change the amount set by the guidelines include medical costs, private school costs, high parental income, the existence of other families that the parents must support, and the amount of time the child spends with each parent. Most states use calculations based on either the income-shares model or the percentage-of-income model. Under the three-pony rule, child support for children of parents with very high incomes should be adjusted so that payments do not go beyond what is reasonably and rationally related to the realistic needs of the child. When parents improperly reduce their income or their income capacity, a court can treat the amount of the reduction as if it is income that was actually earned—as imputed income.

All obligees in the state can use the services of an IV-D agency to establish child-support orders and to enforce child support. (The services are not limited to recipients of public assistance.) The assistance includes helping locate the noncustodial parent, establish paternity, and collect the support. Obligees on public assistance must assign their right of child support to the IV-D agency or county welfare agency. Major tools of the IV-D agency for use in locating missing noncustodial parents are the State Parent Locator Service (SPLS), the Federal Parent Locator Service (FPLS), and the National Directory of New Hires (NDNH). To protect abused custodial parents, a family violence indicator (FVI) can prevent the release of identifying information to unauthorized persons.

Enforcement remedies include civil and criminal contempt; criminal nonsupport (including the Deadbeat Parents Punishment Act); execution; income withholding; garnishment; license and registration denial, delay, or revocation; passport denial, delay, or revocation; tax refund offset; IRS Full Collection; insurance match; qualified domestic relations order (QDRO); qualified medical child support order (QMCSO); credit bureau referral (credit clouding); financial institution data match (FIDM); liens, posting security, wheel boots, and wanted posters. Indigent, delinquent obligors are not entitled to free attorney representation when charged with civil contempt if the obligee is unrepresented and the state provides procedural protections such as an opportunity to be heard and clear notice that imprisonment will not be ordered if the obligor cannot pay. A free attorney can be provided for serious cases of criminal contempt or criminal nonsupport. A state cannot refuse to give a marriage license to a person who has failed to pay child support for children in the custody of someone else. This interferes with the fundamental right to marry.

To issue a child-support order, a court needs personal jurisdiction over the obligor. Without such jurisdiction, the order is not entitled to full faith and credit (FFC). Personal jurisdiction over a resident obligor can be obtained by service of process. The long-arm statute can be used to obtain personal jurisdiction over nonresidents if they have sufficient minimum contacts with the forum state. A registration procedure can then be used to enforce the order in the state where the nonresident resides. If a custodial parent cannot use the long-arm statute to obtain personal jurisdiction over a nonresident defendant, the IV-D agency can assist the custodial parent in obtaining and enforcing a support order in the defendant's state.

A child-support order can be modified on the basis of a substantial change of circumstances that has arisen since the court granted the order, rendering the order inequitable. No downward modification will be ordered if a parent voluntarily reduces his or her income-earning capacity in order to avoid paying support. In some states, after the guidelines are applied to the new financial facts, a court will apply a presumption that the amount should not be changed unless the result would be an increase or decrease of more than 20 percent of the amount originally ordered by the court. If the obligor takes on a new family, some courts will take this into consideration when deciding whether to modify the child-support order downward so long as the first family is not left destitute thereby. Courts differ on whether a man can modify a child-support order that was issued against him by proving that he is not the biological father of the child.

In most cases, the Bradley Amendment forbids retroactive modification of arrearages. The Uniform Interstate

Family Support Act (UIFSA) and the Full Faith and Credit for Child Support Orders Act (FFCCSOA) seek to prevent a state from modifying an out-of-state child-support order by giving priority to the state that initially made the order. This state has continuing exclusive jurisdiction (CEJ), which all other states must respect, so long as the custodial parent, the noncustodial parent, or the child continues to reside in the state.

If the obligor obtains a bankruptcy, his or her child-support debts are not discharged.

KEY TERMS

public assistance
noncustodial parent (NCP)
custodial parent (CP)
Temporary Assistance for Needy Families (TANF)
arrearages
physical custody
legal custody
obligor
obligee
payor
payee
stepparent
in loco parentis
equitable estoppel
estopped
equitable parent
presumed parent
artificial insemination (AI)
in vitro fertilization (IVF)
sperm bank
coparenting
age of majority
emancipated
separation agreement
child-support guidelines
lump-sum payment
escalation clause
trust
escrow
pendente lite
rebuttable presumption

joint physical custody
net
three-pony rule
imputed income
fraudulent transfer
nurturing-parent doctrine
IV-D agency
assign
State Parent Locator Service (SPLS)
vital statistics
Federal Parent Locator Service (FPLS)
National Directory of New Hires (NDNH)
family violence indicator (FVI)
restraining order
contempt
civil contempt
criminal contempt
house arrest
criminal nonsupport
probation
Deadbeat Parents Punishment Act (DPPA)
execution
lien
income withholding
garnishment
qualified domestic relations order (QDRO)
qualified medical child support order (QMCSO)
credit clouding

levy
prosecution
amnesty
indigent
ex parte
subject-matter jurisdiction
forum
personal jurisdiction
full faith and credit (FFC)
service of process
personal service
substituted service
Uniform Interstate Family Support Act (UIFSA)
general appearance
responsive pleading
pleading
minimum contacts
adjudicate
long-arm jurisdiction
long-arm statute
interstate central registry
domicile
in rem jurisdiction
initiating state
responding state
divisible divorce
continuing exclusive jurisdiction (CEJ)
home state
Full Faith and Credit for Child Support Orders Act (FFCCSOA)
necessaries

CHECK THE CITE

Lois May Mills is the mother of a child born out of wedlock. She sued the alleged father to establish his paternity so that child support can be ordered. What statute-of-limitations argument did the alleged father raise in response to the suit against him? What constitutional arguments did Lois May Mills make to the alleged father's defense of the statute of limitations? How did the court rule? See *Mills v. Habluetzel*, 456 U.S. 91 (1982). To read this opinion online: (1) Run a citation search ("456 U.S. 91") in the "Case law" database of Google Scholar (scholar.google.com). (1) Run a citation search ("456 U.S. 91") in the general search engines of Google, Bing, or Yahoo.

PROJECT

In Google, Bing, or Yahoo, run the following search: aa military veteran "child support" (substitute the name of your state for aa in the search). Write an essay in which you explain how a custodial parent/obligee can collect child support from a current or former member of the military. You must cite and quote from a minimum of three different federal or state sources that you find on the Internet. At least two of these sources should be the actual language of statutes, court opinions, or other laws.

ETHICS IN A FAMILY LAW PRACTICE

You are a paralegal working at the law office of Helen Farrell, Esq. Claire Richardson asks Farrell to represent her in a child-support case. The court ordered the father of their child to pay $1,000 a month in child support. He is currently $25,000 in arrears. Farrell agrees to take the case. Her fee will be 40 percent of whatever amount of the arrears she collects. In addition, she will receive 10 percent of every future monthly child-support payment. Any ethical problems?

WRITING SAMPLE

Sam and Jill Adams were married and had two children in your state. Two years ago, Jill obtained a divorce from Sam in which the court gave Jill sole physical custody and sole legal custody of the two children. Sam was ordered to pay Jill $1,200 a month in child support. A month after this order, Sam moved to a neighboring state. He has paid no child support. Jill has come to the law firm where you work as a paralegal. Your supervisor has asked you to prepare a memo in which you outline what steps Jill can take to obtain and then enforce the child-support order against Sam. (See General Instructions for the Writing Sample in Appendix A.)

REVIEW QUESTIONS

1. Why did Congress write laws on child support, and how do they influence state child-support laws?
2. What are some of the ways in which noncustodial parents (NCPs) avoid paying child support?
3. What is an obligor/payor and an obligee/payee?
4. What is equitable estoppel?
5. What is a presumed parent?
6. When does the duty of support end?
7. When do some states require a parent to pay college expenses of a child over the age of majority?
8. What factors must parents take into consideration when negotiating the child-support terms of their separation agreement?
9. What is the role of child-support guidelines in determining the amount of child support?
10. What kinds of parental income does a court consider in determining child support?
11. When can a court deviate from the presumptively correct amount of support set by the guidelines?
12. What is the difference between the income-shares model and the percentage-of-income model?
13. What is the three-pony rule?
14. When will a court impute income to an obligor?
15. What is the role of an IV-D agency?
16. What is meant by assigning support rights to the government, and when does it occur?
17. How do the following entities function in locating noncustodial parents: State Parent Locator Service (SPLS), the Federal Parent Locator Service (FPLS), and the National Directory of New Hires (NDNH)?
18. What is a family violence indicator (FVI) and how is it used?
19. What is the scope of data contained in the National Directory of New Hires?
20. How do civil contempt and criminal contempt differ?
21. When is the crime of criminal nonsupport committed?
22. What is the Deadbeat Parents Punishment Act?
23. What is an execution of a court order or judgment?
24. How does income withholding work, and how does it differ from garnishment?
25. How can the license and registration process be used in the collection of child support?
26. How can the passport process be used in the collection of child support?
27. What is the tax offset program, and how does it differ from IRS Full Collection?

28. What is the Insurance Match program?

29. What are a QDRO and a QMCSO?

30. How do credit clouding and FIDM work?

31. What is a lien?

32. What is meant by posting security?

33. How does amnesty work?

34. When does the state have to provide a free attorney to indigent obligors who are in arrears?

35. Can a state refuse to give a marriage license to a person who has failed to pay child support for children in the custody of someone else?

36. What kinds of jurisdiction does a court need to issue a child-support order?

37. How does a state acquire personal jurisdiction over a resident obligor?

38. What is the Uniform Interstate Family Support Act (UIFSA)?

39. What is long-arm jurisdiction, and what are the ways in which it can be acquired?

40. What is an interstate central registry?

41. How does registration allow enforcement of a child-support order against a nonresident?

42. If the state of the obligor cannot obtain personal jurisdiction over the nonresident, how can the obligee obtain and enforce a child-support order against the obligor in the obligor's state without traveling to that state?

43. When will a court modify a child-support order?

44. What is the twenty-percent rule?

45. Will a court modify a child-support order because the obligor has remarried and must now support a new family?

46. How do courts respond to proof that a man is not the biological father of a child after a finding of paternity has been made?

47. What is the effect of the Bradley Amendment?

48. How do the UIFSA and the FFCCSOA seek to prevent a state from modifying an out-of-state child-support order?

49. What are necessaries?

50. What is the effect of bankruptcy on child-support debts?

HELPFUL WEBSITES

Your State

See Appendix D for links to the family law of your state on the topics covered in this chapter.

Handbook on Child Support Enforcement

- www.acf.hhs.gov/css/resource/handbook-on-child-support-enforcement
- www.acf.hhs.gov/sites/default/files/programs/css/2018_child_support_resource_guide_for_state_iv_d_directors_final.pdf

Child Support Guidelines: Fifty States

- www.supportguidelines.com
- www.supportguidelines.com/links.html

IV-D agencies and Child Support Enforcement

- www.acf.hhs.gov/css/resource/state-and-tribal-child-support-agency-contacts

Family Law Resources

- www.law.cornell.edu/wex/table_family

- guides.ll.georgetown.edu/familylaw
- www.hg.org/family.html
- www.ncsl.org/research/human-services/child-support-and-family-law.aspx

QDRO: Qualified Domestic Relations Orders

- www.dol.gov/general/siteindex (scroll down to the Q entries)

Establishment of Paternity

- www.ncsl.org/research/human-services/enforcement-establishing-paternity.aspx

International Child Support: Hague Child Support Convention

- www.acf.hhs.gov/sites/default/files/programs/css/ocse_judicial_guide.pdf

National Child Support Enforcement Association

- www.ncsea.org

National Council of Juvenile and Family Court Judges, *A Practice Guide: Making Child Support Orders Realistic and Enforceable*

- www.ncjfcj.org/resource-library/publications/practice-guide-making-child-support-orders-realistic-and-enforceable

National Center for Fathering

- www.fathers.com/programs/fathering-court

Interstate Child Support

- www.acf.hhs.gov/css/resource/interstate-child-support-hearings

Google Scholar (scholar.google.com)

- Choose "Articles" and enter in the search box any of the key terms discussed in the chapter. Add the name of your state to the search term.
- Choose "Case law" and "Select courts". Select your state, click "Done," and enter in the search box any of the key terms discussed in the chapter. Add the name of your state to the search term.

Google, Bing, or Yahoo

(on these search engines, run the following searches, substituting your state for "aa")

- "child support" aa
- "child support" guidelines aa
- UIFSA "child support" aa
- stepparent "child support" aa
- IV-D "child support"
- "child support" arrears aa

- jurisdiction "child support" aa
- "child support" enforcement aa
- "income withholding" "child support" aa
- "child support" coparenting aa
- estoppel "child support" aa
- paternity "child support" aa
- disability "child support" aa
- "initiating state" "child support" aa
- crime "child support" aa
- contempt "child support" aa
- emancipation "child support" aa
- interstate "child support" aa
- "long arm" "child support" aa
- FFCCSOA aa
- "father's rights" "child support" aa

YouTube

Run the same searches on YouTube listed above for Google, Bing, Yahoo searches. Even when the video clips are trying to entice you to retain an attorney, buy a book, or enroll in a course, they can provide useful overviews and references to primary authority.

Twitter, Reddit, and Facebook

On Twitter, Reddit, and Facebook, run the following search (substitute your state for *aa* in your searches, but also run the searches without the name of your state). Look for links to family-law developments in your state.

- child support aa
- fathers rights aa

ENDNOTES

Note: All or most of the court opinions in these endnotes can be read online. To do so, go to Google Scholar (scholar.google.com), select "Case law," and in the search box, enter the cite (e.g., "131 S. Ct. 2507") or name of the case (e.g., "Turner v. Rogers") that is given in the endnote.

[1] Pamela Loprest, *How Has the TANF Caseload Changed Over Time?* (www.acf.hhs.gov/opre/resource/how-has-the-tanf-caseload-changed-over-time) (2012); (1995 caseload) (www.acf.hhs.gov/ofa/resource/caseload-data-afdc-1995-total).

[2] *Turner v. Rogers*, 564 U.S. 431, 459-60 (2011) (Thomas dissent).

[3] Kirit Radia, *Adopted Boy Rejected by U.S. Mom Adjusts in Foster Care*, ABC News (Apr. 13, 2012).

[4] *E.C. v. J.V.*, 202 Cal. App. 4th 1076, 1085 (Cal. Ct. App. 2012).

[5] Joanna L. Grossman, *Why a Craigslist Sperm Donor Owes Child Support*, Verdict (January 27, 2014) (verdict.justia.com/2014/01/27/craigslist-sperm-donor-owes-child-support).

[6] Shari Motro, *Responsibility Begins at Conception*, N.Y. Times, July 7, 2012, at A15.

[7] 42 U.S.C. § 667(b)(2) (www.law.cornell.edu/uscode/text/42/667).

[8] See www.ncsl.org/research/human-services/guideline-models-by-state.aspx; web.archive.org/web/20110710144334/http://www.doover.com/Playground/Articles/ArticleType/ArticleView/ArticleID/307.aspx.

[9] *Downing v. Downing*, 45 S.W.3d 449, 456 (Ky. 2001).

[10] 42 U.S.C. §§ 651 et seq. (/www.law.cornell.edu/uscode/text/42/651).

[11] www.acf.hhs.gov/css.

[12]Carmen Solomon-Fears, *The National Directory of New Hires*, iii (Congressional Research Service 2011).

[13]*Moss v. Superior Court*, 950 P.2d 59 (Cal. 1998).

[14]*Moss*, 950 P.2d at 61.

[15]18 U.S.C. § 228 (codes.lp.findlaw.com/uscode/18/I/11A/228).

[16]Rebecca Hamil, *Western Hemisphere Travel Initiative*, 28 Child Support Report 6 (Office of Child Support Enforcement, Aug. 2006) (www.acf.hhs.gov/css/resource/overview-of-the-passport-denial-program).

[17]*Zablocki v. Redhail*, 434 U.S. 374 (1978).

[18]*State v. Oakley*, 629 N.W.2d 200 (Wis. 2001).

[19]629 N.W.2d at 207.

[20]629 N.W.2d at 221 (dissent).

[21]Tamar Lewin, *Father Owing Child Support Loses a Right to Procreate*, N.Y. Times, Jul. 12, 2001, at A14.

[22]*Turner v. Rogers*, 564 U.S. 431 (2011).

[23]*Kulko v. Superior Court*, 436 U.S. 84 (1978).

[24]42 U.S.C.. § 666(a)(10) (www.law.cornell.edu/uscode/text/42/666).

[25]*In re Paternity of Cheryl*, 746 N.E.2d 488, 495 (Mass. 2001).

[26]42 U.S.C.. § 666(a)(9)(c) (www.law.cornell.edu/uscode/text/42/666).

[27]Thomas J. Devine, *From the Bench*, 24 Vermont Bar Journal & Law Digest 10 (Mar. 1998).

[28]28 U.S.C. § 1738B (www.law.cornell.edu/uscode/text/28/1738B).

[29]Office of Child Support Enforcement, International (www.acf.hhs.gov/css/partners/international).

CHAPTER 11

Tax Consequences of Separation and Divorce

CHAPTER OUTLINE

CHAPTER OBJECTIVES

After completing this chapter, you should be able to:

- Know what is meant by the "tax effect" of a clause in a separation agreement.

- Explain the tax consequences of alimony and child support.

- Give an example of how a payor can obtain the equivalent of a deduction for nondeductible alimony after 2018.

- Explain the tax consequences of a property division.

- State the basis of property in the hands of the ex-spouse transferee as part of a property division.

- Know which fees paid obtaining a divorce are deductible.

- State the innocent-spouse rule.

- Explain the impact of the marital deduction.

- State some of the other tax considerations relevant to divorced parties.

tax effect
(1) To determine the tax consequences of something. (2) The tax consequences of something.

INTRODUCTION

Tax law can play an important role in the representation of divorce clients. The **tax effect** of every clause in a separation agreement must be determined. The phrase *tax effect* is also used as a verb. If, for example, you are asked to tax effect a clause in a proposed separation agreement, you are being asked to determine what, if anything, is deductible and what, if anything, is taxable if the clause is agreed to by the parties (or imposed on them by a court order). Tax effects often become part of (or should become part of) the bargaining process between the soon-to-be ex-spouses.

We will be examining the three major financial components of separation and divorce: alimony, child support, and property division. Exhibit 11.1 summarizes the tax law governing each.

In Chapter 8, we discussed how taxes are treated in the negotiation of a separation agreement. For example, who will pay the taxes on the last tax return filed by the parties, and who will pay any deficiencies or penalties the Internal Revenue Service (IRS) might impose on current and past returns. In Chapter 11, our main focus is the tax law itself.

alimony
Money or other property paid in fulfillment of a duty to support one's spouse (or ex-spouse) after a legal separation, a divorce, and in most states, an annulment. Also called *maintenance* and *spousal support*.

payor
One who makes a payment of money or who is obligated to do so.

payee
One to whom money is paid or is to be paid.

property division
The distribution of marital property between spouses after a legal separation or divorce. In a few states, separate property can be included in the property division. Also called *property settlement* and *property distribution*.

transferor
The person who transfers an interest in property.

transferee
The person to whom an interest in property is transferred.

ALIMONY

In 2019, a major change occurred in federal income taxation of **alimony**:

Before 2019:

- Alimony is deductible by the **payor** and is taxable to the **payee**.
- Child-support payments are not deductible by the payor and are not taxable to the payee.
- Property transferred as part of a **property division** is not deductible by the **transferor** and is not taxable to the **transferee**.

Starting in 2019:

- Alimony is *not* deductible by the payor and is *not* taxable to the payee.
- There was no change in child-support taxation. Child-support payments are not deductible by the payor and are not taxable to the payee.
- There was no change in property-division taxation. Property transferred as part of a property division is not deductible by the transferor and is not taxable to the transferee.

EXHIBIT 11.1 Tax Consequences of Separation and Divorce

Alimony	Child Support	Property Division
When alimony is paid: • The person who pays alimony (the payor) cannot deduct alimony payments. • The person who receives alimony (the recipient or payee) does not report it as income and does not pay taxes on it.	When child support is paid: • The person who pays child support (the payor) cannot deduct child-support payments. • The person who receives child-support payments (the recipient or payee) on behalf of a child does not report it as income and does not pay taxes on it.	When property is transferred as part of a property division: • The person who transfers cash or other property (the transferor) cannot deduct what is transferred. • The person who receives cash or other property (the transferee) does not report it as income and does not pay taxes on it. • The tax basis (discussed below) of the property in the hands of the transferee is the same as the transferor's tax basis.

Before 2019, when alimony was deductible, approximately 600,000 taxpayers claimed the alimony deduction each year. The deduction was so beneficial to payors that they often tried to disguise child support as alimony in order to increase the size of the deduction. For example, if the parties settled on $1,000 a month in alimony and $3,000 a month in child support, the clauses of the proposed separation agreement might say that the parties have agreed to $3,000 in alimony and $1,000 in child support. When this switch of figures was successful (by fooling the IRS), the payee ended up receiving additional alimony and hence owed more to the IRS on the taxable alimony received. To convince the payee to cooperate in the disguise, the payor (who got the benefit of the increased deduction) might offer the payee something else in the bargaining process that the payee wanted, such as better terms on child custody.

As a result, elaborate rules were enacted by the IRS to prevent payors from trying to disguise child support (or property division) as alimony. In 2019, however, new tax reforms made these IRS rules obsolete. Today, alimony is nondeductible by the payor and nontaxable to the payee. Note that the change was not **retroactive**. Thus, divorces entered into before 2019 still allow alimony to be deducted by the payors, and taxes still are paid on the alimony received by the payees.

In a recent survey of members of the American Academy of Matrimonial Lawyers, 95% of the lawyers said that the new alimony-taxation rules would result in significant changes in how divorces are settled. Sixty-four percent expect the tax change will make divorces more acrimonious.[1]

Did the change in the tax law mean the end of tax-planning maneuvers designed to restore some or all of the deductibility of spousal-support payments? No. Tax attorneys and accountants began looking for other ways to ease the pain of taxation now that traditional alimony is no longer deductible. One proposed strategy is to use pretax dollars from an IRA (individual retirement account), or another type of retirement account, to meet an alimony obligation. By *pretax*, we mean that the taxpayer did not pay taxes on the money when it was earned and placed in a retirement account. Taxes were to be paid when the money is withdrawn years later, usually when the taxpayer retires and is often in a lower tax bracket.

Suppose, for example, that during Tom's marriage to Sue (a full-time stay-at-home mother), he has been contributing to an IRA retirement account. The money in the account is pretax because no taxes have yet been paid on it. Taxes will be paid when he retires or reaches a designated age and starts to withdraw amounts from the account. Assume, however, that when Tom and Sue divorce in 2019, he meets his alimony obligation by transferring his IRA as lump-sum alimony to Sue. Sue will not pay taxes upon receipt of the IRA because 2019 alimony is nontaxable upon receipt. However, once she can access the IRA and starts withdrawing funds from it, she will be taxed on the income at what is likely to be her lower tax rate. The benefit to Tom is that he has met his alimony obligation with pretax money on which he has not had to pay taxes. He will not have to pay taxes when Sue starts withdrawing from the account; *she* will be responsible for the taxes at her lower rate. In effect, Tom is getting the equivalent of a deduction for his alimony. Of course, Sue may not be willing to cooperate in this alimony-tax strategy since she will be paying taxes as she withdraws money from what was once Tom's IRA. If in 2019 she had received traditional monthly alimony payments, she would not have had to pay taxes on the money. Now, however, she will be taxed on the money that comes out of the IRA.

In addition, another disadvantage for Sue in using Tom's retirement funds for alimony is that she may need the alimony funds right away—but the IRA funds may not be available to her until Tom reaches a certain age. Furthermore, there may be a penalty for early withdrawal of the funds from the IRA. To compensate for these disadvantages, Sue's attorney may bargain for something else in the separation agreement that she wants such as a custody or property-division that is more favorable to her. All of these factors must be carefully weighed in the negotiation process.

retroactive
Applying to facts that arise before a particular event or date.

Another example of a strategy that avoids taxes by the payor involves the transfer of an **annuity**. If a taxpayer owns a tax-deferred annuity (containing funds that have not yet been taxed), a transfer of this annuity as alimony (if allowed under the terms of the annuity) will result in the payee (not the taxpayer-payor) paying taxes when the funds are withdrawn.

Further complicating the tax picture is the fact that *state* income taxes may or may not conform to the new rules on federal deductibility of alimony. Most states impose state income taxes. In the past, states conformed their deductibility rules to the federal rules. If the federal government allowed a deduction for alimony on federal returns, the states allowed the deduction when calculating state income taxes. This may no longer be true. Some states have decided to continue to allow alimony to be deducted on state returns.

In short, the negotiation of separation agreements became considerably more involved in 2019.

PROPERTY DIVISION

In this section, our focus will be the division of marital property between spouses. Before discussing the tax consequences of a property division, we need to review some basic terminology.

> *Tom buys a house in 2007 for $260,000. He spends $30,000 to add a new storage room. In 2016, he sells the house to a stranger for $300,000.*

- Transferor. *The person who transfers an interest in property. Tom is the transferor. An* **interest** *is a legal share or right in something, which can often be sold or transferred. Here, the interest is the ownership of the house.*

- Transferee. *The person to whom an interest in property is transferred. The stranger in our example is the transferee.*

- Appreciation. **Appreciation** *is an increase in the value of property after it is acquired. Tom's house appreciated by $40,000 (from $260,000 to $300,000). He has made a profit, called a* gain. *The gain, however, is not $40,000. See the definition for* adjusted basis *below.*

- Depreciation. **Depreciation** *is a decrease in value of property after it is acquired. If the highest price Tom could obtain for his house had been $255,000, the house would have depreciated by $5,000.*

- Realize. *To* **realize** *is to receive an actual benefit or to suffer an actual loss from something as opposed to a mere potential (paper) benefit or loss. Income, gain, or loss is usually realized when it is received. Suppose that Tom has an offer to buy his house for $290,000, but he decides not to sell at the present time. He has not realized any income. During the time he was considering the offer, he had no more than a "paper" gain, a mere potential gain of $30,000 (the difference between his purchase price of $260,000 and $290,000). He does not have to pay taxes on a gain until he has realized a gain, such as by selling the house.*

- Fair Market Value. **Fair market value** *is the price that could be obtained in an open market between a willing buyer and a willing seller dealing at* **arm's length**, *neither being under any compulsion to buy or sell and both having reasonable knowledge of or access to the relevant facts. A transaction is at arm's length if the parties treat each other as strangers looking out for their own self-interests with no confidential or other relationship between them that would cause one to expect the other to provide a special advantage or to act with fairness. (Fairness here means impartiality. Strangers negotiating over a price are not impartial; they are*

---

annuity
A fixed sum payable periodically for life or for a specific period of time. The recipient of the annuity is called the *annuitant.*

interest
A legal share or right in something, which can often be sold or transferred.

appreciation
An increase in the value of property after it is acquired.

depreciation
A decrease in the value of property after it is acquired.

realize
To receive an actual benefit or to suffer an actual loss from something as opposed to a mere potential benefit or loss.

fair market value
The price that could be obtained in an open market between a willing buyer and a willing seller dealing at arm's length, neither being under any compulsion to buy or sell and both having reasonable knowledge of or access to the relevant facts.

arm's length
Pertaining to how parties would treat each other if they were strangers looking out for their own self-interests with no confidential or other special relationship between them that would cause one to expect the other to provide a special advantage or to act with fairness.

competitors looking out for their own interests.) A sale between a parent and a child will usually not be at fair market value; the fact that they are closely related will probably affect the price paid. It is possible for a happily married husband and wife to sell things to each other at fair market value, but the likelihood is that they will not. In our example, Tom sold his house for $300,000 to a stranger. There is no indication that the buyer or seller was pressured into the transaction or that either had any special relationship with each other that might have affected the price or the terms of the deal. The price paid, therefore, was the fair market value.

- Basis. **Basis** *is the initial* **capital investment**, *usually the cost of acquiring the property (also called* cost basis*). Tom's basis in his house is $260,000.*

- Adjusted Basis. *The* **adjusted basis** *is the basis of the property after adjustments and deductions are made. The basis is either adjusted upward (increased) by the amount of* **capital improvements** *(i.e., structural improvements on the property) or adjusted downward (e.g., for a casualty loss due to a natural disaster). Tom added a room to his house—a structural improvement. Assuming there are no deductions, his basis ($260,000) is increased by the amount of the capital expenditure ($30,000), giving him an adjusted basis of $290,000.*

When Tom sold his house for $300,000, he *realized* income. To determine whether he realized a gain or profit, we need to compare this figure with his adjusted basis. The amount of gain for tax purposes is determined as follows:

$$\text{SALE PRICE} - \text{ADJUSTED BASIS} = \text{TAXABLE GAIN}$$
$$\$300,000 \quad - \quad \$290,000 \quad = \quad \$10,000$$

Tom must declare this gain of $10,000 on his tax return. Of course, if the sale price had been *less* than the adjusted basis, he would have realized a loss. If, for example, he had sold the house for $265,000, his taxable loss would have been $25,000 ($290,000 − $265,000).

TAX CONSEQUENCES OF A PROPERTY DIVISION

The general rule on the tax treatment of property divisions is as follows:

Transfers of property because of a divorce (i.e., transfers that are incident to a divorce) are not deductible by the transferor, nor are they reportable as income by the transferee. The basis of the property in the hands of the transferee is the same as the transferor's basis, which is his or her adjusted basis.

A property division can be in cash or in noncash. To illustrate:

Cash Property Division: *An ex-wife receives a lump sum of $50,000 (or five yearly payments of $10,000) in exchange for the release of any rights she may have in property acquired during the marriage.*

Noncash Property Division: *An ex-wife receives the marital home, and an ex-husband receives stocks and the family business. They both release any rights they may have in property acquired during the marriage.*

A property division in cash is a nontaxable event; nothing is deducted and nothing is included in the income of either party. The IRS will assume that what was exchanged was of equal value.

Suppose, however, that property other than cash is transferred in a property division and that the noncash property so transferred has *appreciated* in value since the time it was acquired.

---

basis
One's initial capital investment in property, usually the cost of acquiring the property. Also called *cost basis*.

capital investment
The cost of acquiring property. Cost basis.

adjusted basis
The basis of property (its cost of acquisition) increased by the cost of capital improvements and decreased by allowable deductions.

capital improvements
Structural additions or improvements of property, as opposed to ordinary maintenance work.

In 1995, Tom and his wife, Tara, buy a cottage from their neighbor for $160,000. In 1996, they spend $30,000 to add a large porch to the cottage. Tom and Tara divorce in 2016. As part of their property division, Tom transfers the cottage to Tara. Assume that its fair market value in 2016 is $200,000.

The adjusted basis of the house in 2016 is $190,000 (the original purchase price of $160,000 plus the capital improvement of $30,000). If Tom had transferred the house to a stranger for 200,000, he would have realized a gain of $10,000 ($200,000 less his adjusted basis of $190,000). The picture is dramatically different, however, when property is transferred to a spouse because of (i.e., incident to) a divorce.

When *appreciated* property is transferred as part of a property division in a divorce, there is no gain or loss realized. In the example of Tara and Tom, the transferor (Tom) does not realize a gain, even though he transferred a $200,000 house with an adjusted basis of $190,000 to the transferee (Tara).

What is the transferee's basis in appreciated property that is transferred as part of a property division? The transferee's basis is the same as the adjusted basis of the transferor at the time of the transfer.[2] Hence, Tara's basis in the house when she receives it is $190,000, which was Tom's adjusted basis when he transferred it to her as part of the divorce settlement.

Assume that a week after Tara receives the cottage, she sells it to a stranger for $205,000. On these facts, she would realize a gain of $15,000 because her basis in the cottage is $190,000, which was its adjusted basis when she received it from Tom.

SALE PRICE − ADJUSTED BASIS = TAXABLE GAIN
$205,000　−　　$190,000　　=　　$15,000

Needless to say, it is essential that a spouse know the adjusted basis of the property in the hands of the other spouse before accepting that property as part of a property division. It can be meaningless, for example, to be told that property is "worth $150,000" on the market unless you are also told what the adjusted basis of that property is. Furthermore, the law office representing the transferee must insist that the transferor turn over records that will allow the transferee to determine the adjusted basis of the property. This could include a copy of the original purchase contract and all contractor bills or statements that will prove what capital improvements were made to the property. Without such records, the transferee will not be able to tell the IRS, perhaps years later, what the adjusted basis of the property is.

INCIDENT TO A DIVORCE

incident to divorce
(a) Occurring within one year after the date a marriage ends, or (b) relating to the ending of a marriage because it occurs within six years after a marriage ends pursuant to a divorce decree or separation agreement.

To take advantage of the basis rule we have been discussing, the property division must be **incident to divorce**. A property transfer is incident to a divorce when:

- The transfer occurs within one year after the marriage ends, or
- The transfer is related to the ending of the marriage.

A property transfer is presumed to relate to the ending of the marriage when:

- The transfer occurs within six years after the marriage ends, and
- The transfer is made under the divorce or separation agreement.

The presumption applies if the taxpayer can show that (1) the reason a transfer was made up to six years after the end of a marriage was a business or legal complication that prevented earlier transfer of the property, and that (2) the transfer was made promptly after those complications were resolved. For example, the transfer of the property may have taken six years because it took that long for the parties to settle a dispute over the purchase price and over payment terms.

LEGAL AND RELATED FEES IN OBTAINING A DIVORCE

Obtaining a divorce can be expensive. In addition to attorney fees, one or both parties may have to hire an accountant, actuary, and appraiser. Only two types of such fees are deductible:

- Fees paid for tax advice in connection with a divorce, and
- Fees paid to obtain alimony.

Other fees are not deductible. For example, you cannot deduct legal fees paid to negotiate the property division. Also, when legal fees are deductible, they must be your own legal fees. An ex-husband, for example, cannot deduct legal fees he is required to pay for his ex-wife's attorney even if the fees are for tax advice or alimony advice for her.

Bills from professionals received by a taxpayer should include a breakdown showing the amount charged for each service performed.

Examples:

For legal representation in divorce case	*$9,000*
For tax advice in connection with the divorce...	*$ 800*
Total bill..	*$9,800*

Only $800 is deductible.

For legal representation in divorce case..	*$6,500*
For legal representation in obtaining alimony...	*$1,200*
Total bill..	*$7,700*

Only $1,200 is deductible.

To deduct fees for these services, the taxpayer must itemize deductions in the year claimed. They go on Schedule A of IRS Form 1040 under Miscellaneous Deductions.

Fees paid to appraisers, actuaries, and accountants can also be deducted but only to the extent that their services are used to determine how much tax is owed or to assist in obtaining alimony.

INNOCENT SPOUSE RELIEF

What happens when the IRS determines that taxes, interest, and penalties are due on prior joint returns of spouses who have just divorced? Who pays? Frequently, one of the spouses simply signed the return prepared by the other spouse with little knowledge of the sources of income reported on the return or that should have been reported on the return. Although the less-involved spouse can be the husband or the wife, the following discussion will assume it is the homemaker/wife because this is the most common occurrence.

When the IRS audits the return, the ex-wife says, "I was not involved in his business; I just signed what he told me to sign; I never kept any of the records. I have no idea how to come up with records or anything involved with the return."

The general rule, however, is that the signers of a joint return are jointly *and individually* responsible for taxes, interest, and penalties due on the return. (It is called **joint and several liability**.) For all returns filed while the parties were married, the IRS has the right to collect taxes, interest, and penalties from either spouse even if:

- The spouses are now divorced.
- The separation agreement specifies that only the ex-husband must pay.
- The divorce decree orders only the ex-husband to pay.

The IRS could still demand payment from the wife. This, of course, could create a substantial hardship if the husband is unwilling or unable to pay due to obstinacy, disappearance, or financial setbacks.

joint and several liability
Legally responsible together and individually. Each debtor is individually responsible for the entire debt; the plaintiff/creditor can choose to collect the full debt from one debtor or from all of them until the debt is satisfied.

The IRS never signed the separation agreement and was not a party to the divorce litigation. Hence, the IRS is not bound by the separation agreement or divorce decree. The ex-husband is bound by them. If the ex-wife is forced to pay the IRS, she can sue the ex-husband for violating the separation agreement or court order, but she cannot escape the rule of joint and several liability with the IRS. There is, however, a possible way out for her if she qualifies for an exception to this rule.

The exception is called the **innocent-spouse doctrine**. The ex-spouse claiming this relief must prove that at the time she signed the return she did not know and had no reason to know that her husband had understated the taxes that were due. The IRS will decide whether, under all the facts and circumstances of the case, it would be unfair to hold her responsible for the understatement of tax due on the return.

Every year, the IRS receives more than 50,000 applications for innocent-spouse relief. Of this number, just over 15 percent are granted in full; just over 12 percent are partially granted.[3]

innocent-spouse doctrine
A former spouse will not be liable for taxes, interest, and penalties owed on prior joint returns if (a) he or she did not know or have reason to know that the other spouse understated the taxes due and (b) it would be unfair to hold the innocent spouse responsible for the understatement of tax on the return. An exception to the rule of joint and several liability of signers of a return.

MARITAL DEDUCTION

Most taxable events occur when property is transferred:

Tom gives $17,000 cash to Sally (his neighbor) as a gift or leaves the cash to her in his will. These transfers are taxable events. Tom may have to pay a gift tax (if the gift is an **inter vivos gift***) or his estate may have to pay an estate tax (if the gift is a* **testamentary gift***). Deductions may eliminate or reduce the tax, but the transfers are taxable transfers.*

inter vivos gift
A gift that takes effect while the donor is living.

testamentary gift
A gift made in a will.

marital deduction
A deduction on a federal tax return for lifetime and testamentary transfers between spouses.

Now suppose that Tom and Sally are married and that these same transfers occur. Are they still taxable transfers? Yes. There is, however, a **marital deduction** that the surviving spouse (Sally) enjoys. Sally does not have to pay a gift or estate gift tax on the transfers she received from Tom. She receives them tax-free. When she later transfers such assets, she will be responsible to pay the appropriate gift or estate taxes. Hence, the marital deduction delays the payment of taxes until the surviving spouse eventually transfers them during her life or at her death.

OTHER TAX CONSIDERATIONS

Here are some of the other family-tax considerations relevant to a divorce or separation (some of which have phase-out rules so that they are not available to high-income taxpayers):

adjusted gross income
The total income from all of a person's taxable sources less specifically allowed deductions.

- *Dependency Exemption.* A taxpayer can claim a dependency exemption for a qualifying child. (An exemption is an amount deducted from **adjusted gross income**.) If the child spends time with both parents, the exemption can be taken by the parent with whom the child lived for the longer period of time during the year. Divorcing parents cannot split the exemption, but the custodial parent (CP) can waive the exemption in favor of the noncustodial parent (NCP).
- *Head of Household.* A divorced parent living with a child can claim the status of Head of Household on his or her return, which has higher deductions and other tax benefits than filing as a single person.
- *Child Tax Credit.* A credit that can be taken for each dependent child under age seventeen who lives with the taxpayer for over half the year and who does not pay over half of his or her own expenses.
- *Child and Dependent Care Credit.* A credit that can be taken if the taxpayer paid someone to care for a child so that the taxpayer can work or look for work.
- *Earned Income Tax Credit.* A credit for taxpayers who earned less than a designated amount and who have a qualifying child or who meet other requirements.

- *Higher Education Credit.* An American Opportunity Credit (covering certain expenses for years one to four of higher education) or a Lifetime Learning Credit (covering certain expenses for non-degree courses that enable a student to acquire or improve job skills).

- *Adoption Credit.* A credit for certain expenses incurred in adopting a child.

ASSIGNMENT 11.1

The separation agreement of John and Carol requires John to pay Carol $500 a month as alimony for five years.

a. What is the tax consequence of the alimony clause if the parties were divorced in 2018?

b. What is its tax consequence if the parties were divorced in 2019?

(See General Instructions for the Legal-Analysis Assignment in Appendix A.)

ASSIGNMENT 11.2

Under a 2019 separation agreement and divorce decree, Helen transfers a building (which is her separate property) to her ex-husband, Ken, in exchange for his release of any rights he has in other property that Helen acquired during the marriage. The transfer is made on the day of the divorce. Helen bought the building in 1996 for $1 million. Over the years, she made $200,000 worth of capital improvements in the building (using her separate funds). Its fair market value on the date she transfers it to Ken is $1.5 million. A week later, however, the market crashes, and Ken is forced to sell the building for $800,000.

a. What was the basis of the building when Helen bought it?

b. What was the adjusted basis when she transferred it to Ken?

c. Was the transfer to Ken incident to a divorce?

d. Did Helen realize a gain when she transferred the building to Ken, which at that time had a fair market value of $1.5 million?

e. When Ken received the building from Helen, what was his basis in the building?

f. When Ken sold the building, what gain or loss did he realize?

PARALEGAL ROLES

- For an overview of paralegal roles in family-law cases, see Exhibits 1.5 and 1.6 in Chapter 1.
- For many of the financial issues related to taxation and divorce covered in Chapter 11, a paralegal may be asked to help collect documents and facts outlined in:
  - The checklist in Exhibit 3.1 of Chapter 3.
  - The interrogatories in Appendix C.
- Miscellaneous duties:
  - Enter due dates on tickler system for final income tax returns and estate tax returns.
  - Assist the attorney negotiating the separation agreement by collecting all documentation needed to argue the tax effect of proposed terms.
  - Use tax software to prepare reports on the tax effects of various negotiating positions the attorney will present.
  - Obtain needed tax return forms (state income, federal income, and estate).
  - Assist client in gathering needed data and support documentation for the tax returns.
  - Locate candidates for appraisers, accountants, and other professionals needed for the preparation of the returns.
  - Act as liaison with and monitor professionals hired by the firm.
  - Prepare a preliminary draft of the tax returns.
  - Secure client signature on the returns.

SUMMARY

Tax consequences should be a part of the negotiation process in a separation and divorce. The parties must know the tax effect of every financial component involved. Due to recent tax reforms, alimony is not deductible by the payor nor is it taxable for the payee. Child-support payments and property divisions are neither deductible nor taxable.

In a property division incident to a divorce, property is transferred from one ex-spouse to the other. The property can be cash (e.g., $50,000) or noncash (e.g., a house). When there is a transfer of cash, none of it is deducted by the transferor, and none of it is included in the income of the transferee. When there is a transfer of noncash property that has appreciated in value, (1) the transferor cannot deduct anything, (2) the transferee does not include anything in his or her income, (3) the transferor does not pay taxes on the amount of the appreciation, and (4) the basis of the property in the hands of the ex-spouse transferee is the adjusted basis that the property had in the hands of the transferor.

A fee paid to an attorney, accountant, or other professional is deductible if paid to obtain tax advice in connection with a divorce or if paid to help the client obtain alimony that is included in gross income. Under the innocent-spouse doctrine, a former spouse will not be liable for taxes, interest, and penalties owed on prior joint returns if he or she can prove that at the time he or she signed the return, he or she did not know, and had no reason to know, that the other spouse understated the tax due, and if the IRS concludes that it would be unfair to hold this spouse responsible for the understatement of tax on the return.

The marital deduction is a deduction on a federal tax return for lifetime and testamentary transfers between spouses. Other tax considerations relevant to a divorce or separation include the dependency exemption, head of household filing status, child tax credit, child and dependent care credit, earned income tax credit, higher education credits, and adoption credit.

KEY TERMS

tax effect	interest	capital improvement
alimony	appreciation	incident to divorce
payor	depreciation	joint and several liability
payee	realize	innocent-spouse doctrine
property division	fair market value	inter vivos gift
transferor	arm's length	testamentary gift
transferee	basis	marital deduction
retroactive	capital investment	adjusted gross income
annuity	adjusted basis	

CHECK THE CITE

James Guth formed a church (Universal Life Church) and named himself pastor for perceived tax advantages. He named his wife, Arlys Guth, treasurer of the church's bank account. They both signed the joint tax returns that were filed. The IRS later determined that deductions made on the returns for charitable purposes were improper. Why did the IRS assert that Arlys Guth was liable for the deficiencies that resulted from these deductions? Why was she successful in court in asserting the defense of innocent spouse? See *Guth v. C.I.R.*, 897 F.2d 441 (9th Cir. 1990). To read the opinion online, run a citation search ("897 F.2d 441") in the *Case law* database of Google Scholar (scholar.google.com), and in the general search engines of Google, Bing, or yahoo.

PROJECT

In Google, Bing, or Yahoo, run the following search: "dependency exemption" tax divorce. Write a short essay in which you explain how a divorced couple can determine who is entitled to the dependency exemption on the tax returns filed after the divorce. You must cite and quote from a minimum of three different sources that you find on the Internet. At least two of these sources should be the actual language of statutes, court opinions, regulations or other laws.

ETHICS IN A FAMILY LAW PRACTICE

You are a paralegal working at a law office that is representing David Harrison, a wealthy landowner whom everyone knows because of his exposure in the media. He is challenging the IRS's rejection of his claim of a deduction of more than $2 million. You work on this case because your supervising attorney is the main tax attorney at the firm. One day after a long day at work, your spouse asks you if you have had a bad day. You respond, "The Harrison case is driving me crazy; there is a good chance David Harrison may lose his $2 million deduction." Any ethical problems?

WRITING SAMPLE

Prepare a legal memo in which you discuss the federal law that applies to the facts of Assignment 11.2. You must cite and quote from a minimum of three different sources that you find on the Internet. All of the sources must be federal statutes, federal court opinions, federal regulations, or other federal laws. (See General Instructions for the Writing Sample in Appendix A.)

REVIEW QUESTIONS

1. What is meant by tax effecting a clause in a separation agreement?
2. After 2018, what are the tax consequences of alimony payments, child-support payments, and property division?
3. Give an example of an alimony payment after 2018 in which the payor avoids taxation.
4. When is gain or loss realized?
5. What is the fair market value of something?
6. How is the adjusted basis of property determined?
7. What are the tax consequences of a property division in cash?
8. What are the tax consequences of a property division of appreciated property?
9. When is a property transfer incident to a divorce?
10. What legal and related fees in obtaining a divorce are deductible?
11. When will an innocent spouse be given relief on past-due taxes, interest, and penalties on joint tax returns?
12. What is the effect of the marital deduction?
13. What other tax considerations are relevant to a divorce or separation?

HELPFUL WEBSITES

Divorce and Taxes

- divorceinfo.com/taxes.htm
- taxtopics.net/topic4.htm#div

Internal Revenue Service: Divorce and Separation

- www.irs.gov/pub/irs-pdf/p504.pdf

Internal Revenue Service: Innocent Spouse Relief

- www.irs.gov/forms-pubs/about-publication-971

Miscellaneous Tax Sites for Divorce and Separation

- search3.hrblock.com/?q=divorce
- www.divorcemag.com/?s=tax

Google Scholar

(scholar.google.com)

- Choose "Articles" and enter in the search box any of the key terms discussed in the chapter. Add the name of your state to the search term.
- Choose "Case law" and "Select courts". Select your state, click "Done," and enter in the search box any of the key terms discussed in the chapter. Add the name of your state to the search term.

Google, Bing, or Yahoo

(on these search engines, run the following searches, substituting your state for "aa")

- tax divorce aa
- alimony tax aa
- "incident to divorce" aa
- "child support" taxation aa

- "property division" tax aa
- "innocent spouse" divorce tax aa

YouTube

Run the same searches on YouTube listed above for Google, Bing, Yahoo searches. Even when the video clips are trying to entice you to retain an attorney, buy a book, or enroll in a course, they can provide useful overviews and references to primary authority.

Twitter, Reddit, and Facebook

On Twitter, Reddit, and Facebook, run the following search (substitute your state for aa in your searches; run the searches with and without the name of your state). Look for links to family-law developments in your state.

- divorce taxation aa

ENDNOTES

[1]Margaret Price, Investor's Business Daily, *Divorce Rules Change: Here's Your New Strategy For Alimony*, www. investors.com (6/14/2018).

[2]The rule was otherwise before 1984, when gain was recognized if appreciated property was transferred because of a divorce. This was the ruling of *United States v. Davis*, 370 U.S. 65 (1962). Transferors complained bitterly because they had to pay taxes on paper gains due to the appreciation. Congress changed the law in 1984 so that gains and losses were no longer recognized in property divisions due to a divorce. The change negated the ruling of *United States v. Davis*.

[3]Charles Delafuente, *Some Advice for Wary Spouses: Consider Filing a Separate Return*, N.Y. Times, Feb. 13, 2011, at BU11 (www.nytimes.com/2011/02/13/business/yourtaxes/13spouse.html).

CHAPTER 12

Legal Rights of Women

CHAPTER OBJECTIVES

After completing this chapter, you should be able to:

- Know the disabilities faced by married women at common law.
- Explain what disabilities no longer exist under current law.
- State the impact of the married women's property acts.
- Understand dower and curtesy and their substitute, elective share.
- Explain how a person can change a surname.
- List the prohibitions on discrimination against women in obtaining credit.
- Understand when a job requirement is a BFOQ.

- Explain when wage discrimination is illegal.
- Know what kinds of questions are illegal in a job interview.
- Explain the employment rights of a female employee with regard to pregnancy, breast milk expression, family leave, and medical leave.
- Distinguish between the two categories of sexual harassment.
- Explain why Paula Jones lost her claim of sexual harassment against Governor Bill Clinton.
- Describe how sex discrimination laws are enforced.

- State the right of individuals to contraceptives.
- Know when a person can be sterilized.
- State a woman's abortion rights.
- List the major categories of domestic violence and the available remedies to respond to it.
- Explain the battered woman syndrome.
- State whether marital rape is a crime.
- List ways in which sensitivity should be shown when assisting victims of domestic violence.

U.S. Supreme Court (1872):

Man is, or should be, woman's protector and defender. The natural and proper timidity and delicacy, which belongs to the female sex evidently unfits it for many of the occupations of civil life. The constitution of the family organization, which is founded in the divine ordinance, as well as in the nature of things, indicates the domestic sphere as that which properly belongs to the domain and function of womanhood. . . . The paramount destiny and mission of woman are to fulfill the noble and benign offices of wife and mother. This is the law of the Creator.

—Bradwell v. Illinois, *83 U.S. 130,141 (1872).*

_____

U.S. Supreme Court (1975):

No longer is the female destined solely for the home and the rearing of the family, and only the male for the marketplace, and the world of ideas.

—Stanton v. Stanton, *421 U.S. 7, 14-15 (1975).*

THE STATUS OF WOMEN AT COMMON LAW

Today, a married woman would consider it condescending to be told that she has the right to:

- Make her own will.
- Own her own property.
- Make a contract in her own name.
- Be a juror.
- Vote.
- Execute a deed.
- Keep her own earnings.
- Sue someone (and be sued) in her own name.

feme covert
"A covered woman." A married woman.

coverture
The legal status of a married woman whereby her civil existence for many purposes merged with (was covered up by) that of her husband.

There was a time in our history, however, when a married woman could engage in none of these activities, at least not without her husband's consent. When a woman married, "the common law took the view that she forfeited her legal existence and became the property of her husband, and her services and earnings belonged to him."[1] A married woman was a **feme covert**, or "a covered woman"— meaning, she was covered by the identity of her husband. The legal status of a married woman was called **coverture**, whereby her civil existence for many purposes merged with (and was covered up by) that of her husband. For example, she could not bring a suit against a third party unless her husband agreed to join in the suit as a party. There were substantial restrictions on her right to acquire and convey property in her own right. If she committed a crime in the presence of her husband, the law assumed that he forced her to commit it. If she worked outside the home, her husband was entitled to her earnings. If a woman had a will before marrying, her marriage automatically revoked the will.[2] To a large degree, a married woman was the property of her husband. In short, **at common law**, the husband and wife were considered one person, and the one person was the husband. This was the essence of the **unity of person** or the spousal-unity rule.

at common law
During a time in our early history when law was created by court opinions and legislatures, often before it was changed by later legislatures.

unity of person
The now-rejected view that the legal identity of a wife was subsumed into the legal identity of the husband.

An *unmarried* woman at common law was not as restricted; she could own property and enter into contracts in her own name. But she could not vote or serve on juries, and her inheritance rights were limited.[3]

Today, a married woman has her own legal identity: "In today's society, regardless of what individual couples believe and practice, the law does not recognize the husband as the 'one public voice' or as the automatic head of household with supreme authority over his nonresponsible feme covert. A married woman now has her own separate legal identity."[4] Hence, family law has gone through what is called degenderization, a gradual shifting away from a system that defines family roles and most property rights on the basis of gender.

CONTRACTS AND CONVEYANCES

Women now have the power to enter into all forms of contracts and conveyances in their own names, independent of their husbands. If, however, both spouses own property together, the wife normally must have the consent of her husband—and vice versa—to convey the property to someone else.

Contracts *between* the spouses in an ongoing marriage are also possible. Such agreements are often referred to as postnuptial agreements. (For examples of such agreements, see Exhibit 4.1 in Chapter 4.) There are, however, some restrictions on what spouses can do in a postnuptial agreement. For example, they cannot contract away their obligation to support each other (although this is possible in a separation agreement, as discussed in Chapter 8).

Courts tend to be suspicious of conveyances of property between husband and wife. Suppose, for example, that a husband transfers all of his property into his wife's name (for which she pays nothing), so that when he is sued by his creditors, he technically does not own any assets from which they can satisfy their claims. Because the transfer was made with little or no consideration and was made to avoid an obligation to a creditor, it is a fraudulent transfer and, if challenged, could be invalidated by a court.

Even nonfraudulent transactions between spouses can cause difficulty when a spouse uses his or her separate funds to buy property that he or she then places in the sole name of the other spouse:

- A husband buys a cottage with his separate funds and places the title to the cottage in his wife's name. (Assume that this is not a fraudulent transfer; he is not trying to defraud his creditors.)
- The wife buys stock with her separate funds and places the title to the stock in her husband's name. (Again, assume no intent to defraud her creditors.)

Many courts presume that when husbands or wives use their own money (their own separate property) to buy other property that they put into the names of their spouse, they are making a gift of the property to their spouse unless it is clear that they had a different intention. There are courts, however, that treat the two examples above differently. In the first, they presume the husband was making a gift to his wife, but in the second, they presume that the wife intended the husband to hold the property in trust for her. Yet some have argued that treating husbands and wives differently in this regard is unconstitutional as a violation of equal protection.

MARRIED WOMEN'S PROPERTY ACTS

Most states have enacted married women's property acts, which removes most of the disabilities that married women suffered at common law. Under the terms of such statutes, married women are now given the right to enter into contracts, own and dispose of their property, and be parties to litigation (suing and being sued) independent of their husbands. Without such laws, a married woman would not have a separate legal existence. The effect of the married women's

contract
A legally enforceable agreement. The elements of most contracts are offer, acceptance, and consideration. Some contracts must be in writing.

conveyance
The transfer of an interest in property. The verb is *convey*.

postnuptial agreement
A contract between married persons that covers specific matters, usually financial in nature. (Also called *postnup* and *midnup*.) The spouses may have no intention of separating. If they have this intention, the contract is commonly called a *separation agreement*.

consideration
Something of value that is exchanged between parties. It can be an act, a forbearance (not performing an act), a promise to perform an act, or a promise to refrain from performing an act.

fraudulent transfer
A transfer of an asset for little or no payment or consideration that is made to avoid an obligation to a creditor.

separate property
Property that (1) is acquired by one spouse before marriage and brought into the marriage, or (2) is acquired by one spouse by gift, will, or inheritance during the marriage, or (3) is any other property that is not marital or community property.

gift
The voluntary delivery of property with the present intent to transfer title and control, for which no payment or consideration is made. The person making the gift is the *donor*. The person receiving it is the *donee*.

trust
A property arrangement by which its creator (the *settlor* or *trustor*) transfers property (the *corpus*) to a person (the *trustee*) who holds legal title for the benefit of another (the *beneficiary* or *cestui que trust*).

trust
A device or arrangement by which its creator (the settlor or trustor) transfers property (the corpus) to a person (the trustee) who holds legal title for the benefit of another (the beneficiary or cestui que trust).

married women's property acts
Statutes removing all or most of a married woman's legal disabilities on matters such as entering into contracts, disposing of her property, and being a party to litigation independent of her husband.

property acts was to abolish most of the "unity of person" at common law. Why, you might ask, is it an advantage for a married woman to be able to be sued independent of her husband? The answer is that merchants are unlikely to do business with her if they know that they cannot sue if she breaches a business transaction with them.

EQUITABLE DISTRIBUTION

In Chapter 8, we examined the law of property division upon divorce in common-law states and in community-property states. We saw that changes in the law have resulted in a substantial leveling of the field in establishing the property rights of husbands and wives upon divorce. In most common-law states and in many community-property states, courts use varying versions of equitable distribution—the just and fair, but not necessarily equal, division of property between spouses upon divorce.

DOWER, CURTESY, AND ELECTIVE SHARE

At common law, when a husband died, the surviving wife was given the protection of dower, which was the right of a surviving wife to the lifetime use of one-third of all of the land her deceased husband owned during the marriage. (The right to use property during one's life is called a life estate.) The practical impact of dower was that the husband could not sell his property to others unless his wife waived her dower rights. Buyers were unlikely to want to buy property encumbered by the dower rights of the seller's wife. If the wife died first, the husband's comparable right at common law was called curtesy— his right to a life estate in all of the land his wife owned during the marriage.

Today, most states have abolished dower and curtesy. In its place, they give the surviving spouse an elective share in all of the property the deceased spouse owned at death. The elective share is also called a forced share because the surviving spouse can elect to take it in place of, and in spite of, what the will of the deceased spouse says the surviving spouse should receive.

- If the surviving spouse does not choose the elective share, he or she receives whatever is provided for him or her in the will of the deceased spouse.
- If the surviving spouse does choose the elective share, he or she usually receives the equivalent of an intestate share of the deceased spouse's assets. Intestacy means dying without a valid will. When someone dies intestate, certain relatives receive designated shares of the deceased's assets. When a surviving spouse chooses an elective share, the deceased's will is ignored. Indeed, the deceased is treated as if he or she had died intestate. Whatever share is given to the surviving spouse of a deceased intestate spouse is given to the surviving spouse who chooses the elective share. (In one state, for example, the elective share is $50,000 or one-third of the net estate of the deceased spouse, whichever is greater.)

Unfortunately, relics of the old law still exist on the books of many states. New Jersey, for example, did not repeal the following outrageous law until 2011:

> If a wife after being ravished, consent to the ravisher, she shall be disabled and forever barred from having her . . . dower, unless her husband is voluntarily reconciled to her and permits her to dwell with him, in which case she shall be restored to her . . . dower.[5]

---

property division
The distribution of community or marital property between spouses after a legal separation or divorce. In a few states, separate property can be included in the property division and some states allow property division in an annulment. Also called *property settlement* and *property distribution*.

equitable distribution
The just and fair, but not necessarily equal, division of property between spouses upon divorce.

dower
The right of a widow to the lifetime use (called a *life estate*) of one-third of the land her deceased husband owned during the marriage. (Owned means *fee simple*, the most complete form of ownership possible.)

life estate
An interest in property whose duration is limited to the life of an individual. An ownership of property that lasts as long as a designated person is alive. Also called *estate for life* or *life tenancy*.

curtesy
The right of a husband to the lifetime use (called a *life estate*) of all the land his deceased wife owned during the marriage (if issue were born of the marriage).

elective share
The percentage of a deceased spouse's estate that the surviving spouse can choose (elect) to receive despite what the will of the deceased spouse provided for the surviving spouse. Also called *right of election, statutory share,* and *forced share*.

intestate share
A designated portion of the estate of a person who dies intestate (i.e., without a valid will) to which certain relatives of the deceased are entitled according to state law.

ASSIGNMENT   12.1

If a surviving spouse in your state is not satisfied with the property left for him or her in the deceased spouse's will, what are the options of the surviving spouse? Can he or she elect against the will? If so, what can the election provide? (See General Instructions for the State-Code Assignment in Appendix A.)

Dower and curtesy were legal doctrines used in common-law states. In community-property states (see Chapter 8), there was no need for such doctrines because each spouse owned 50 percent of all marital (community) property by virtue of the marriage.

SURNAME CHANGE

In most states, there are two main ways that persons can legally change their surname: the *usage* method (called the common-law method) and the *statutory* method.

The Usage Method

The usage method simply involves using a new surname. The new name becomes one's legal name without going through court or agency procedures. The main requirement is that the use of the name must be:

- Exclusive (only one new name will be used),
- Consistent (the new name will be used for all purposes), and
- Nonfraudulent (the new name is not used to avoid creditors or to help commit some other illegal act).

The Statutory Method

The statutory method is a formal change-of-name procedure involving several steps (e.g., filing a petition to change one's name in the appropriate state court, stating the reasons for the change, paying a fee to the court, and publishing a notice of the court proceeding in a local newspaper). The procedure is usually not complicated so long as the court is convinced that the name change will not mislead anyone who may need to contact the individual (e.g., police officials, a former spouse, creditors). The main reason many persons use the statutory method is to have an official acknowledgement that the change has been made, an important step in the age of **identity theft**.

Once a new surname is changed, it is the responsibility of the individual to notify insurance companies, motor vehicle departments, banks, etc., of the change.

identity theft
Acquiring and using (or attempting to acquire and use) another person's private identifying information with the intent to commit an unlawful act.

Changing Surnames Upon Marriage

Many women change their surnames to those of their husbands at the time of marriage or use a hybrid (combination) name consisting of her maiden name and his surname. The change occurs by the usage method—they start using the new names immediately after the marriage. No formal procedures are necessary. Because name changes upon marriage are relatively common, newly married women rarely use the statutory method.

In some states, grooms are treated differently. If a man wishes to change his surname upon marriage, these states require him to use a version of the statutory method. Because brides do not have this requirement, the different treatment may be subject to constitutional challenge as a denial of the equal protection of law.

Brides who keep their maiden names are likely to be older, career women. About 23 percent of women kept their maiden names in the 1990s; the percentage fell to about 18 percent in the 2000s.[6] Women who take their husbands' names do so for one of two reasons:

- The law of the state gives them a choice of keeping their maiden names or taking their husbands' names, and they choose the latter.
- The law of the state gives them a choice that they do not know about; they use their husbands' names simply because that is the custom.

At one time, the law of some states *required* a woman to use her husband's name. Such laws either have been repealed or struck down as a violation of equal protection because husbands were not required to take the names of their wives.

Upon divorce, all courts will grant a woman's request that she be allowed to resume her maiden name or to use another name. Suppose, however, that she asks the divorce court to change the name of the children of the marriage. She may want them to have her new name or to take the name of the man she will marry when the divorce is final. Courts will not automatically grant such a request. They will want to be sure that the change would not harm the relationship between the child and the noncustodial father and that the change would be in the best interests of the child.

ASSIGNMENT 12.2

Prepare a flowchart of all the steps that an individual must go through to change his or her name in your state through the appropriate statutory procedure. (See General Instructions for the Flowchart Assignment in Appendix A.)

CREDIT

The federal Equal Credit Opportunity Act prohibits discrimination on the basis of sex or marital status in a credit application.[7] Creditors such as banks, finance companies, and department stores that violate the prohibition can be liable for damages, attorney fees, and court costs.

- When you apply for credit, a creditor:

    1. Must not discourage you from applying nor reject your application because of your marital status.
    2. Must not consider your gender.
    3. Must not impose different terms or conditions (e.g., higher interest rate or fees) based on your sex or marital status.
    4. Must not discount income because of your gender or marital status (e.g., a creditor cannot count a man's salary at 100 percent and a woman's at 75 percent; a creditor may not assume a woman of childbearing age will stop working to raise children).
    5. Must not ask if you are widowed or divorced.
    6. Must not ask about your marital status if you are applying for a separate, **unsecured** account. However, the creditor (a) may ask about your marital status if you live in a community-property state or (b) may ask about your marital status in every state if you are applying for a joint account or for an account **secured** by property.
    7. Must not request information about your spouse except (a) when your spouse is applying with you, (b) when your spouse will be allowed to use

unsecured
Not backed by collateral.

secured
Backed by collateral.

the account, (c) when you are relying on your spouse's income or on alimony or child-support income from a former spouse, or (d) when you live in a community-property state.

8. Must not ask about your plans for having or raising children (the creditor, however, can ask about expenses related to your dependents).

9. Must not ask if you receive alimony, child-support, or separate-maintenance payments unless you will be relying on these payments to obtain credit. If you are not relying on these payments to obtain credit, the creditor can ask if you receive these payments but must tell you that you do not have to provide this information. A creditor can ask if you are required to make alimony, child-support, or separate-maintenance payments.

10. Must not refuse your request that alimony, child-support, or separate-maintenance payments be considered. A creditor may ask you to prove you have received this income consistently.

- You also have a right to:

1. Have credit in your birth name (Mary Smith), your first name and your spouse's last name (Mary Jones), or your first name and a combined last name (Mary Smith-Jones).

2. Obtain credit without a **cosigner** if you meet the creditor's standards.

3. Have a cosigner other than your spouse if you need a cosigner.

4. Keep your own accounts with the creditor after you change your name, change your marital status, reach a certain age, or retire, unless the creditor has evidence that you are not willing or able to pay.

- If you suspect unlawful discrimination, you should:

1. Complain to the creditor; make it known that you are aware of your rights under the law.

2. Report violations to the appropriate government agency. If you are denied credit, the creditor must give you the name and address of the agency to contact.

3. Check with your state attorney general to see if the creditor violated state equal credit opportunity laws and, if so, whether the state will prosecute the creditor.

4. Bring a case in federal district court. If you win, you can recover your actual damages, plus **punitive damages** if the court finds that the creditor's conduct was willful. You also may recover reasonable attorney fees and court costs. Or, you might consider finding others with the same claim, and getting together to file a **class action** suit.[8]

The Federal Trade Commission adds this note of caution to women:

A good credit history—a record of your bill payments—often is necessary to get credit. This [requirement] can hurt many married, separated, divorced, and widowed women. Typically, there are two reasons women don't have credit histories in their own names: either they lost their credit histories when they married and changed their names, or creditors reported accounts shared by married couples in the husband's name only. If you're married, separated, divorced, or widowed, contact your local credit reporting companies to make sure all relevant bill payment information is in a file under your own name. Your credit report includes information on where you live, how you pay your bills, and whether you've been sued, arrested or filed for bankruptcy. National credit reporting companies sell the information in your report to creditors, insurers, employers, and other businesses that, in turn, use it to evaluate your applications for credit, insurance, employment, or renting a

cosigner
A person who signs a document along with the main signer, usually to agree to pay the debt created by the document in the event that the main signer fails to pay it.

punitive damages
Damages that are added to actual or compensatory damages in order to punish malicious, outrageous, or reckless conduct and to deter similar conduct in the future. Also called *exemplary damages*, *smart money*, and *vindictive damages*.

class action
A lawsuit in which one or more members of a group sue (or are sued) as representative parties on behalf of everyone in the group.

home. The Fair Credit Reporting Act (FCRA) requires each of the three nationwide credit reporting companies—Equifax, Experian, and TransUnion—to give you a free copy of your credit report, at your request, once every twelve months. To order your report, visit annualcreditreport.com or call 1-877-322-8228.[9]

EMPLOYMENT

BONA FIDE OCCUPATIONAL QUALIFICATION (BFOQ)

There are many laws that, in theory, have eliminated job discrimination against women. For example, the Equal Protection Clause in the Fourteenth Amendment of the U.S. Constitution provides that:

> *No State shall . . . deny to any person within its jurisdiction the equal protection of the laws.*

If a state passes a law that treats women differently from men, it will be invalidated unless the different treatment is substantially related to serve an important state interest. (See Exhibit 1.4 in Chapter 1, in which gender is listed as a **quasi-suspect class**. To determine whether discrimination against this class is legal, a court will apply the **intermediate-scrutiny test**.)

In addition, Title VII of the 1964 Civil Rights Act provides that:

> *It shall be an unlawful employment practice for an employer . . . to fail or refuse to hire or to discharge any individual, or otherwise to discriminate against any individual with respect to his compensation, terms, conditions, or privileges of employment, because of such individual's...sex....*[10]

This statute does not mean that all gender discrimination in employment is illegal. Job-related gender discrimination is permitted if gender is a **bona fide occupational qualification (BFOQ)**, meaning that the gender discrimination is reasonably necessary to the normal operation of a particular business or enterprise. When is discrimination (different treatment) of the sexes a BFOQ? Answer: when the essence of the business or enterprise would be undermined if the discrimination could not be used.

Examples of a BFOQ:

- It is a BFOQ for an advertising agency to hire only males to model for men's clothes.
- It is a BFOQ for a theater to hire only men to play fathers, sons, and uncles in a play.
- It is a BFOQ for a state prison to exclude women from being guards in an all-male prison where a significant number of the inmates are convicted sex offenders. It is reasonable to anticipate that some of the inmates would attack the female guards, creating a security problem. In this instance, discrimination based on sex (i.e., requiring that guards be male) in an all-male prison is a BFOQ because gender is related to the job of maintaining security.[11]

Examples of Non-BFOQs:

- It is not a BFOQ for a company to hire only women as bookkeepers because the male supervisor wants to work with women. Gender has no relationship to being a bookkeeper.
- It is not a BFOQ for an airline to hire only female flight attendants even though market research shows that most passengers prefer female flight attendants. Gender has no relationship to performing the job of a flight attendant.
- It is not a BFOQ for a battery manufacturer to discourage women (but not men) from working in jobs that expose them to lead. The exposure has the potential of harming the reproductive process of both women and men. The gender of the worker is not related to the worker's ability to perform the job of making batteries.[12]

quasi-suspect class
A class based on gender or on a child's legitimacy.

intermediate-scrutiny test
The classification must be substantially related to serve an important state interest. Also called *heightened scrutiny* or *elevated scrutiny*.

bona fide occupational qualification (BFOQ)
An employment qualification based on gender, religion, or other characteristic that is reasonably necessary for the normal operation of a particular business and hence is not an illegal requirement under federal employment discrimination laws.

Although employers are often angry when they are charged with wrongful job discrimination, it is illegal for them to retaliate against the employee making the charge even if an agency or court ultimately determines that the charge cannot be proven.

INTERVIEW QUESTIONS

In a job interview, there are some questions that should not be asked. For instance, questions about marital status or family life are often based on the assumption that female employees are not as work-oriented as male employees and will be less available and less productive than male employees. Such questions can violate federal or state employment discrimination laws.

Examples of Illegal Job Interview Questions:

* *Are you married? Are you Miss or Mrs.?* A woman is not required to disclose her marital status. After a person is hired, however, marital status will be relevant for insurance and tax matters.

* *What is your maiden name?* A woman is not required to disclose her marital status. It is not related to legitimate job requirements.

* *Do you have any children? Do you plan to have any children? What kinds of childcare arrangements do you have?* An employer cannot ask about children unless the applicant brings up the topic.

* *What is the name of your spouse? Does your spouse work? What does your spouse do for a living?* This is another indirect way of asking about marital status.

* *How tall are you? How much do you weigh?* Such questions cannot be asked unless height and weight are necessary job requirements.

Examples of Legitimate Job Interview Questions:

* *What are your career objectives?*
* *Can you make a long-term commitment (e.g., five years) to the employer?*
* *Would you be available to work overtime?*
* *Is there anything that you know of that could cause regular absences from work?*
* *Do you have any restrictions that would prevent you from traveling?*
* *Do you have any relatives who work for this company?* This information may be needed because of the company's nepotism policy.

nepotism
Favoritism shown to relatives. A rule against nepotism is called an *antinepotism rule*.

COMPENSATION

The pay gap between men and women has narrowed over the last fifty years according to the Industry and Occupation Statistics Branch at the U.S. Census Bureau. "However, the gender pay gap continues across the board in almost all occupations." In 2016, the median earnings for women was $40,675, compared with $50,741 for men.[13] See Exhibit 12.1.

Wage Discrimination

Wage discrimination on the basis of sex can be a violation of Title VII of the 1964 Civil Rights Act. One of the "unlawful employment practice[s]" under Title VII is to discriminate on a matter of compensation because of a person's sex. In addition, the Equal Pay Act of 1963 (EPA) prohibits discrimination on the basis of sex in the payment of wages or benefits, where men and women perform work of similar skill, effort, and responsibility for the same employer under similar working conditions.[14]

EXHIBIT 12.1 Women's Earnings by Occupation

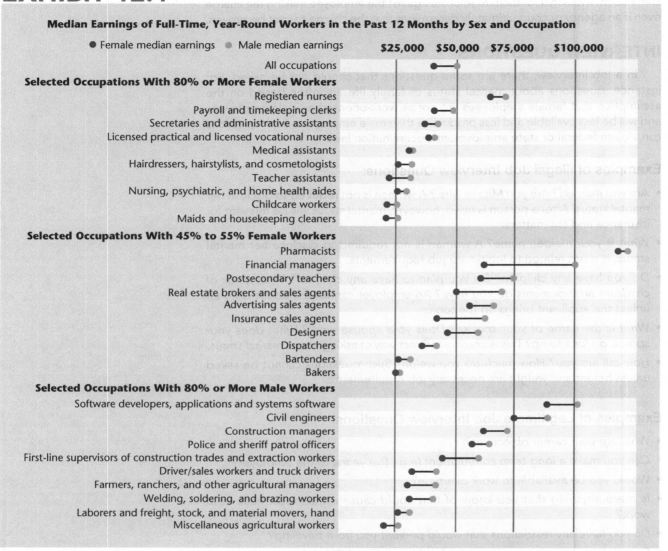

Median Earnings of Full-Time, Year-Round Workers in the Past 12 Months by Sex and Occupation

● Female median earnings   ● Male median earnings $25,000 $50,000 $75,000 $100,000

All occupations

Selected Occupations With 80% or More Female Workers

Registered nurses
Payroll and timekeeping clerks
Secretaries and administrative assistants
Licensed practical and licensed vocational nurses
Medical assistants
Hairdressers, hairstylists, and cosmetologists
Teacher assistants
Nursing, psychiatric, and home health aides
Childcare workers
Maids and housekeeping cleaners

Selected Occupations With 45% to 55% Female Workers

Pharmacists
Financial managers
Postsecondary teachers
Real estate brokers and sales agents
Advertising sales agents
Insurance sales agents
Designers
Dispatchers
Bartenders
Bakers

Selected Occupations With 80% or More Male Workers

Software developers, applications and systems software
Civil engineers
Construction managers
Police and sheriff patrol officers
First-line supervisors of construction trades and extraction workers
Driver/sales workers and truck drivers
Farmers, ranchers, and other agricultural managers
Welding, soldering, and brazing workers
Laborers and freight, stock, and material movers, hand
Miscellaneous agricultural workers

Source: U.S. Census Bureau (2016) (census.gov/library/stories/2018/05/gender-pay-gap-in-finance-sales.html).

Under the EPA:

- Employers may not reduce wages of either sex to equalize pay between men and women.

- Employers may not pay a different wage to a person who works in the same job before or after an employee of the opposite sex. (There can, however, be pay differences based on seniority or merit.)

Most of the pay-discrimination litigation centers on whether the compensation policy of a business or organization is gender neutral and whether wage disparities are due to legitimate business reasons such as the education, training, or experience requirements of a particular job.

PREGNANCY

An employer cannot:

- Refuse to hire a woman because of her pregnancy-related condition so long as she is able to perform the major functions necessary for the job.

- Terminate a female worker because of her pregnancy.
- Force a woman to go on leave at an arbitrary point during her pregnancy if she is still able to work.
- Penalize a woman in reinstatement rights, including credit for previous service, accrued retirement benefits, and accumulated seniority.

If a woman is temporarily unable to perform her job due to a medical condition related to pregnancy or childbirth, the employer must treat her the same as any other temporarily disabled employee (e.g., an employee recovering from heart surgery). For example, the employer may have to provide modified tasks, alternative assignments, disability leave, or unpaid leave. These rights are mandated by the Pregnancy Discrimination Act, which is part of Title VII of the Civil Rights Act.[15]

EXPRESSING BREAST MILK

The Fair Labor Standards Act (FLSA), a federal statute, requires employers to provide reasonable break time for an employee to express (remove) breast milk for her nursing child for one year after the child's birth. Once expressed, the mother would normally store the milk for later feeding of the child. Employers must provide a place, other than a bathroom, that is shielded from view and free from intrusion from coworkers and the public, which may be used by an employee to express breast milk. Some states have break-time laws that provide more extensive rights for the mother, such as requiring breastfeeding accommodation beyond one year of the baby's birth.[16]

FAMILY AND MEDICAL LEAVE

The Family and Medical Leave Act (FMLA), a federal statute, provides employees with up to twelve weeks of unpaid, job-protected leave per year. It also requires that their group health benefits be maintained during the leave. The FMLA applies to public agencies, public and private elementary and secondary schools, and companies with fifty or more employees. The employers must provide an eligible employee (male or female) with up to twelve weeks of unpaid leave each year for any of the following reasons:

- To attend to the birth and care of the newborn child of an employee;
- To attend to an adopted child or a child in foster care;
- To care for an immediate family member (spouse, child, or parent) with a serious health condition; or
- To take medical leave when the employee is unable to work because of a serious health condition.[17]

A few states offer *paid* family leave for these purposes. This, however, is not required under the FMLA.

SEXUAL HARASSMENT

Sexual harassment is unwanted and offensive sexual advances, contact, comments, or other interaction. On the job, two categories of sexual harassment constitute an unlawful employment practice under Title VII of the Civil Rights Act:

- **Quid pro quo sexual harassment** is the submission to or rejection of unwelcome sexual conduct used as a basis for employment decisions on promotion or other job-related benefits.
- **Hostile environment sexual harassment** is the pervasive unwelcome sexual conduct or sex-based ridicule that unreasonably interferes with an individual's job performance or that creates an intimidating, hostile, or offensive working environment, even if no tangible or economic consequences result.

sexual harassment
Unwanted and offensive sexual advances, contact, comments, or other interaction.

quid pro quo sexual harassment
Submission to or rejection of unwelcome sexual conduct used as a basis for employment decisions on promotion or other job-related benefits.

hostile environment sexual harassment
Pervasive unwelcome sexual conduct or sex-based ridicule that unreasonably interferes with an individual's job performance or that creates an intimidating, hostile, or offensive working environment, even if no tangible or economic consequences result.

An example of quid pro quo sexual harassment is a worker who is fired for refusing to become sexually intimate with a supervisor. An example of hostile environment sexual harassment is an office or other workplace that is pervaded by people telling dirty jokes, displaying obscene pictures, making graphic comments about the bodies of other persons, touching themselves sexually in the presence of others, persistently asking for dates, etc. This can be sexual harassment even if the person offended by such conduct is not being asked to engage in such behavior or is not being denied an employment benefit for refusing to do so.

Harassment does not have to be of a sexual nature; it can include offensive remarks about a person's sex. For example, it is illegal to harass a woman by making offensive comments about women in general. Both victim and the harasser can be either a woman or a man, and the victim and harasser can be the same sex. The harasser can be the victim's supervisor; a supervisor in another area; a coworker; or someone who is not an employee of the employer, such as a client or customer.[18]

An employer must actively combat sexual harassment by:

- Establishing a written policy against sexual harassment and distributing it throughout the office.
- Investigating all accusations of sexual harassment promptly.
- Establishing appropriate sanctions for employees who commit sexual harassment.
- Informing employees of their right to raise a charge of sexual harassment under Title VII.
- Telling employees how to assert a complaint of sexual harassment under Title VII.

It is not a defense for an employer to say that it did not know that one of its employees engaged in sexual harassment of another employee or that the harassment took place in spite of a company policy forbidding it. If the employer *should have known of the harassing conduct*, the employer must take immediate and appropriate corrective action, which usually entails more than merely telling all employees not to engage in sexual harassment.

SEXUAL HARASSMENT AND THE GOVERNOR

In 1991, Paula Corbin Jones was a low-level employee of the state of Arkansas. While attending a conference in a Little Rock hotel, then-governor Bill Clinton invited her to his hotel room after he thought she displayed "that come-hither look" because of the suggestive way she acted and dressed. The encounter in the suite led to an allegation that he committed sexual harassment. After he became President Clinton, she brought an action against him for sexual harassment and other wrongs. According to plaintiff Jones:

> [U]pon arriving at the suite and announcing herself, the Governor shook her hand, invited her in, and closed the door. She states that a few minutes of small talk ensued, which included the Governor asking her about her job and him mentioning that Dave Harrington, plaintiff's ultimate superior . . . and a Clinton appointee, was his "good friend." Plaintiff states that the Governor then "unexpectedly reached over to [her], took her hand, and pulled her toward him, so that their bodies were close to each other." She states she removed her hand from his and retreated several feet, but that the Governor approached her again and, while saying, "I love the way your hair flows down your back" and "I love your curves," put his hand on her leg, started sliding it toward her pelvic area, and bent down to attempt to kiss her on the neck, all without her consent. Plaintiff states that she exclaimed, "What are you doing?," told the Governor that she was "not that kind of girl," and "escaped" from the Governor's reach "by walking away from him." She states she was extremely upset and confused and, not knowing what to do, attempted to distract the Governor

by chatting about his wife. Plaintiff states that she sat down at the end of the sofa nearest the door, but that the Governor approached the sofa where she had taken a seat and, as he sat down, "lowered his trousers" [and requested oral sex]. She states that she was "horrified" by this and that she "jumped up from the couch" and told the Governor that she had to go, saying something to the effect that she had to get back to the registration desk. Plaintiff states that the Governor, [while fondling himself] said, "Well, I don't want to make you do anything you don't want to do," and then pulled up his pants and said, "If you get in trouble for leaving work, have Dave call me immediately and I'll take care of it." She states that as she left the room (the door of which was not locked), the Governor "detained" her momentarily, "looked sternly" at her, and said, "You are smart. Let's keep this between ourselves."

In her suit, Jones alleged both kinds of sexual harassment: quid pro quo and hostile environment, asserting that "[t]here are few more outrageous acts than a criminal sexual assault followed by unwanted exposure, coupled with a demand for oral sex by the most powerful man in the state against a very young, low-level employee."[19]

The trial judge, Susan Webber Wright, disagreed. She dismissed the action by granting the president's motion for a **summary judgment**. "While the Court will certainly agree that plaintiff's allegations describe offensive conduct, the . . . conduct as alleged by plaintiff describes a mere sexual proposition or encounter, albeit an odious one, that was relatively brief in duration, did not involve any coercion or threats of reprisal, and was abandoned as soon as plaintiff made clear that the advance was not welcome." There was no proof that Governor Clinton's conduct affected any tangible aspects of Jones's compensation, terms, conditions, or privileges of employment. Hence there was no quid pro quo harassment. "Moreover, notwithstanding the offensive nature of the Governor's alleged conduct, plaintiff admits that she never missed a day of work following the alleged incident . . . , she continued to go on a daily basis to the Governor's Office to deliver items and never asked to be relieved of that duty, she never filed a formal complaint or told her supervisors of the incident . . . , she never consulted a psychiatrist, psychologist, or incurred medical bills as a result of the alleged incident, and she acknowledges that her two subsequent contacts with the Governor involved comments made "in a light vein" and nonsexual contact that was done in a "friendly fashion." . . . Plaintiff certainly has not shown under the totality of the circumstances that the alleged incident in the hotel and her additional encounters with . . . the Governor were so severe or pervasive that it created an abusive working environment."[20]

While this court victory was welcomed by then-governor (and later, president) Clinton, his troubles were far from over. Before Judge Wright rendered her decision, the president had given a **deposition** in the case that gained worldwide notoriety and eventually was a major factor in his impeachment by the House of Representatives—only the second time in history up to that date that a President of the United States had been impeached. During the deposition, the president answered "none" when asked whether there were any female employees of the federal government with whom he had had sexual relations. In particular, he denied having such relations with Monica Lewinsky, a White House intern. A special prosecutor and almost all Republicans in Congress charged that his answers were intentionally false. They believed that lying in a deposition was one of the "high crimes and misdemeanors" that should lead to his removal from office. Ultimately, the U.S. Senate as a whole disagreed when it failed to convict the president (a Democrat) by the required two-thirds vote. (The vote on this count was 55 [not guilty] and 45 [guilty]. All the senators voting guilty were Republicans.) By acquitting the president, the Senate was saying either that it did not believe the president lied, or that even if he did, the lie and the other charges were not serious enough to remove him from office.

As indicated, the president also won the sexual harassment case when the trial court judge, Susan Wright, eventually ruled that his conduct did not constitute sexual harassment. In a stinging rebuke, however, Judge Wright ruled that he had

summary judgment
A court's judgment rendered without a full trial because of the absence of conflict on any of the material facts.

deposition
A method of discovery in which one party questions another party (or questions the other party's witness), usually outside the courtroom. The person questioned is called the *deponent*.

lied during his deposition and held him in contempt. One of the consequences of the lie was that the Jones legal team had to spend extra time preparing its case. Hence, the judge ordered the president to pay a fine of $90,000 for reasonable legal fees covering this time. The fee request included an hourly rate for the work of two paralegals on the Jones legal team.

In the meantime, Jones was set to appeal Judge Wright's ruling that the president did not commit sexual harassment. The President, however, did not relish the prospect of fighting the appeal, particularly since the appeal would have taken place before the impeachment proceeding in Congress was concluded. Hence, the President decided that the safest legal and political strategy was to settle the case in order to prevent the appeal from going forward. He agreed to pay Jones $850,000 in exchange for her decision to drop her appeal of Judge Wright's ruling against her on the sexual harassment and related claims.

ENFORCEMENT

Critics claim that the laws outlawing sex discrimination in employment have been inadequately enforced. The law of discrimination can be complex and confusing. Most often, bringing a discrimination case is time-consuming and expensive.

The **Equal Employment Opportunity Commission (EEOC)** is a federal agency with the primary responsibility of enforcing Title VII of the Civil Rights Act. A charge of employment discrimination (see Exhibit 12.2) can be made to the EEOC online and in its offices throughout the country. In 2017, for example, more than 84,000 workplace discrimination complaints were filed with the EEOC; 30.4 percent of them alleged sex discrimination.[21]

Equal Employment Opportunity Commission (EEOC)
The federal agency that enforces federal laws against employment discrimination.

EXHIBIT 12.2   Online EEOC Discrimination Complaint

TYPE OF EMPLOYER

The employer that I believe discriminated against me is a (choose one):

○ Business or non-profit organization that I applied to, work for, or worked for
○ State or Local Government that I applied to, work for, or worked for
○ Union that represents me
○ Temp agency or staffing firm that did not refer me to a job
○ Federal Government agency that I applied to, work for, or worked for
○ Other

TIMELINESS

On what day did the discriminatory action occur? For example, if you claim you were denied a promotion on April 19, 2017 because of your gender, then enter "4/19/2017".

If you allege more than one discriminatory action, please enter the most recent date. For example, if you claim you are being continually harassed at work because of your race, enter the date of the most recent act of harassment.

REASON

I believe I was discriminated against because of (check at least one, or as many as apply);

☐ Age - I am 40 years of age or older
☐ Color
☐ Disability
☐ Genetic information, my family medical history, or my participation in genetic services like counseling, education, or testing
☐ National origin and/or ethnicity

(continued)

Exhibit 12.2 *(continued)*

- ❑ Race
- ❑ Religion
- ❑ Sex (including pregnancy, sexual orientation, and gender identity)
- ❑ Retaliation - I filed a charge of job discrimination about any of the above
- ❑ Retaliation - I contacted a government agency to complain about job discrimination
- ❑ Retaliation - I complained to my employer about job discrimination
- ❑ Retaliation - I helped or was a witness in someone else's complaint about job discrimination
- ❑ Something Else

Do you believe you were **paid less** because of your sex/gender? (Pay includes salary, overtime pay, bonuses, stock options, profit sharing and bonus plans, life insurance, vacation and holiday pay, cleaning or gasoline allowances, hotel accommodations, reimbursement for travel expenses, and benefits.)

○ Yes   ○ No

LOCATION

Where did the discriminatory action occur?

The location you choose helps EEOC determine how much time you have to file a charge.

Source: Equal Employment Opportunity Commission (publicportal.eeoc.gov/portal/SignIn.aspx?ReturnUrl=OnlineInquiry.aspx).

Fair Employment Practices Agencies (FEPAs) and Dual Filing

Many states, counties, cities, and towns have their own laws prohibiting discrimination, as well as agencies responsible for enforcing those laws. These state and local agencies are called **fair employment practices agencies (FEPAs)**. The laws enforced by these agencies are often similar to those enforced by the EEOC. In some cases, however, the FEPAs enforce laws that offer greater protection to workers, such as protection from discrimination because of sexual orientation. There also may be different deadlines for filing a charge, different standards for determining whether someone is protected by these laws, and different types of relief available to victims of discrimination.

Victims can file discrimination charges with either the EEOC or with an FEPA.

- When an individual initially files with an FEPA that has a work-sharing agreement with the EEOC, and when the allegation is covered by a law enforced by the EEOC, the FEPA will dual file the charge with the EEOC. This means that the EEOC will receive a copy of the charge, but the FEPA will usually retain the charge for processing.

- When an individual initially files with the EEOC and the charge is also covered by state or local law, the EEOC will dual file the charge with the state or local FEPA. This means that the FEPA will receive a copy of the charge, but the EEOC will retain the charge for processing.

fair employment practices agency (FEPA)
A state or local government agency that enforces state or local employment discrimination laws, often in coordination with the Equal Employment Opportunity Commission (EEOC), which enforces federal employment discrimination laws.

SEXUALITY AND REPRODUCTIVE RIGHTS

Topics relevant to sexuality and reproductive rights include:

- Contraception
- Sterilization
- Abortion
- New routes to motherhood
- Same-sex relationships

The first three topics are discussed below. New routes to motherhood, such as surrogate motherhood, in vitro fertilization, and similar themes, are examined in Chapter 16. Legal problems involving same-sex relationships are covered in Chapter 5 on marriage and Chapter 15 on adoption.

CONTRACEPTION

Married and unmarried adult individuals cannot be denied access to contraceptives. The decision on whether to procreate is a **fundamental right**, part of the individual's constitutional **right to privacy**: "If the right of privacy means anything, it is the right of the individual, married or single, to be free from unwarranted governmental intrusion into matters so fundamentally affecting a person as the decision whether to bear or beget a child."[22] Restrictions on fundamental rights are valid only if they pass the **strict-scrutiny test**: The restriction must be narrowly tailored to serve a **compelling state interest**. (See Exhibits 1.3 and 1.4 in Chapter 1.) The U.S. Supreme Court has held that a law banning contraceptives to adults serves no compelling state interest, and therefore, is unconstitutional. (See also Chapter 5 on the Court's theory of personal dignity and autonomy to strike down government restrictions on same-sex intimacy.)

STERILIZATION

For much of the twentieth century, some states had laws that authorized the forced sterilization of persons who are legally considered intellectually disabled or insane. In fact, in 1927, the U.S. Supreme Court decided that a state could legally sterilize a person it termed "feeble-minded." The woman in question was an institutionalized eighteen-year-old who was the daughter of a feeble-minded woman in the same institution; the eighteen-year-old had already had a baby that was feeble-minded. In an infamous passage, Justice Oliver Wendell Holmes said, "Three generations of imbeciles are enough."[23]

Although today forced sterilization is no longer legal in most states, the states that continue to allow it have strict requirements for its use. California law, for example, allows the procedure when a guardian (called a **conservator**) petitions the court and the court finds beyond a reasonable doubt that the person named in the petition (1) is incapable of giving consent to sterilization; (2) is fertile and capable of procreation; (3) is likely to engage in sexual activity leading to pregnancy; and (4) is either permanently incapable of caring for a child (even with appropriate training and reasonable assistance) or would face a substantial medical risk if she became pregnant or gave birth to a child. Sterilization will be ordered only if all less-invasive contraceptive measures are unworkable.[24]

ABORTION

An **abortion** is an induced termination of a pregnancy in order to destroy an **embryo** or **fetus**. A **therapeutic abortion** is an abortion undertaken in order to safeguard the mother's life or health. An **elective abortion** is an abortion performed at the request of the woman for nonmedical reasons.

In the early 1970s, abortion was a crime in every state. It was permitted only when the health of the woman necessitated it (usually to preserve her life) or under special circumstances (e.g., when the pregnancy was caused by rape or incest).

Roe v. Wade

In 1973, the law was dramatically changed by the landmark case of *Roe v. Wade*,[25] in which the U.S. Supreme Court held that a pregnant woman's right to privacy included the fundamental right to terminate her pregnancy. A

fundamental right
A right that falls into one of the following three categories: The right (a) is specifically guaranteed in the U.S. Constitution, (b) is implicit in the concept of ordered liberty, or (c) is deeply rooted in the nation's history and tradition.

right to privacy
A constitutional right to make personal decisions without undue government interference on matters such as marriage, procreation, family relationships, child rearing and education, contraception, and abortion. The right is implied in specific provisions of the U.S. Constitution such as the Due Process Clause of the Fourteenth Amendment. Also called *right to personal autonomy*.

strict-scrutiny test
The government's action must be narrowly tailored to serve a compelling state interest. Also phrased as *necessary to serve a compelling state interest*.

compelling state interest
An interest that is of the highest order; an interest that has a clear justification in the necessities of national or community life.

conservator
A person appointed by the court to manage the affairs of persons who are not competent to do so on their own.

abortion
An induced termination of a pregnancy in order to destroy an embryo or fetus.

embryo
An egg that has been fertilized by a sperm in the early stage of development; it has undergone one or more divisions. The product of conception to about the eighth week of pregnancy.

fetus
A developing organism—unborn offspring—from the eighth week after conception until birth.

therapeutic abortion
An abortion undertaken in order to safeguard the mother's life or health. Also called *induced abortion*.

elective abortion
An abortion performed for nonmedical reasons; it is not undertaken to safeguard the mother's life or health.

woman's decision to terminate her pregnancy is a "liberty" protected against state interference by the Due Process Clause of the Fourteenth Amendment, which provides that no state shall "deprive any person of life, liberty, or property, without due process of law."[26] Under the of strict-scrutiny test, this fundamental right could not be restricted unless the restriction was narrowly tailored to serve a compelling state interest. The ruling in *Roe* was later modified by the 1992 case of *Planned Parenthood of Southeastern Pennsylvania v. Casey*. Before examining *Casey*, however, we need to look at the *Roe* decision.

In *Roe v. Wade*, the Court did not hold that a woman's right to have an abortion was absolute. The state can regulate the right. The extent of such regulation depended on the stage of a woman's pregnancy:

1. For the stage prior to approximately the end of the first **trimester** (the first three months), the abortion decision and its effectuation must be left to the medical judgment of the pregnant woman's attending physician.

2. For the stage subsequent to approximately the end of the first trimester, the state, in promoting its interests in the health of the mother, may, if it chooses, regulate the abortion procedure in ways that are reasonably related to maternal health.

3. For the stage subsequent to **viability**, the state in promoting its interest in the potentiality of human life may, if it chooses, regulate (and even **proscribe**) abortion except where it is necessary, in appropriate medical judgment, for the preservation of the life or health of the mother.

A major theme of *Roe* was that the state should not be regulating abortions until viability, unless the regulations were clearly necessary to protect the health of the mother. Here, the word *viable* means able to live indefinitely outside the womb by natural or artificial support systems. If the regulations are not necessary to protect the health of the mother, the state could not prohibit a woman from obtaining an abortion during the first trimester when an embryo or fetus is not viable.

Different considerations applied during the next twelve weeks, or the second trimester. Between the end of the first trimester and the beginning of the child's viability (a child is usually considered viable after about six months), the state could regulate medical procedures to make sure that abortions are performed safely but could not prohibit abortions altogether. Once the child is viable—during the third trimester—abortions could be prohibited unless they were necessary to preserve the life or health of the mother.

The court later reinforced *Roe* by holding that a wife's right to an abortion did not require the consent of her husband.

After *Roe* was decided, the Court approved some limits on abortion. Examples include the following:

• If a poor woman wanted an abortion for nonhealth reasons (i.e., a nontherapeutic abortion), the state was not required to pay for it, although a number of states decided to set aside funds to pay for such abortions.

• Abortions could be prohibited if not performed by licensed physicians.

• If a pregnant minor is living with and dependent on her parents, it is permissible for a state to require the parents to be notified of the child's desire to have an abortion. If the parents refuse to consent to the abortion, the minor can be denied the abortion so long as she has the opportunity to go to court to try to convince a judge (in what is called a "bypass proceeding" or a "judicial bypass") that she is a mature minor and that therefore parental notice and consent are not needed in her particular case.

trimester
Three months.

viability
Ability to live indefinitely outside the womb by natural or artificial support systems. The adjective is *viable*.

proscribe
To prohibit.

ASSIGNMENT   **12.3**

In Chapter 9 on child custody, we examined the U.S. Supreme Court case of *Troxel v. Granville* on the fundamental right of parents to make decisions concerning the care, custody, and control of their children. The *Troxel* Court held that court-ordered visitation by a nonparent (e.g., a grandparent) must not substantially interfere with the primary right of fit parents to raise their children. Is the authorization of a bypass proceeding for a pregnant minor consistent with the fundamental right of fit parents to raise their children, including the right to refuse to allow their minor daughter to have an abortion? (See the General Instructions for the Legal-Analysis Assignment in Appendix A.)

Planned Parenthood of Southeastern Pennsylvania v. Casey

Approximately 650,000 abortions are reported to the Center for Disease Control each year. It is one of the most common medical procedures performed in America. The U.S. Supreme Court has acknowledged that abortion continues to be "the most politically divisive domestic legal issue of our time."[27] Some activists argue for a constitutional amendment that would return the country to the pre-*Roe* days when states could outlaw abortion. Others hoped that the appointment of conservatives to the U.S. Supreme Court would lead to an overruling of *Roe* by the Court itself. This did not happen in 1992 when the Court reaffirmed the essential holding of *Roe* in the much-anticipated opinion of *Planned Parenthood of Southeastern Pennsylvania v. Casey*.[28]

The *Casey* case laid out three principles:

1. Before viability, a woman has a right to choose to terminate her pregnancy; this liberty right is guaranteed by the Due Process Clause of the Fourteenth Amendment.

2. A law that imposes an *undue burden* on a woman's decision before viability is unconstitutional. An **undue burden** exists when the purpose or effect of the state's regulation is to place a substantial obstacle in the path of a woman seeking an abortion of a nonviable fetus.

3. After viability, the state, in promoting its interest in the potentiality of human life, may, if it chooses, regulate, and even prohibit, abortions except where an abortion is medically necessary to preserve the life or health of the mother.

Under *Casey*, the key test continues to be viability. In *Roe*, the Court used a trimester analysis as a guide in the determination of viability. In *Casey*, the Court decided to reject this analysis as too rigid. In the future, the question of when a child is able to survive outside the womb will be determined by the facts of medicine and science as to when viability occurs rather than by rigid assumptions of what is possible during the trimesters of pregnancy.

Before viability, a state cannot place an "undue burden" on the right of a woman to seek an abortion. The state can pass laws designed to encourage women to choose childbirth over abortion and laws designed to further her health or safety so long as these laws do not place a "substantial obstacle" in the path of her decision to abort a nonviable fetus. "Regulations which do no more than create a structural mechanism by which the State, or the parent or guardian of a minor, may express profound respect for the life of the unborn are permitted, if they are not a substantial obstacle to the woman's exercise of the right to choose."

Using the undue-burden test, the Court in *Casey* reached the following conclusions about specific laws that were challenged in the case:

undue burden
A substantial and unwarranted obstacle to the enjoyment of a right.

- It is not an undue burden on the right to abortion for a state to require (except in a medical emergency) that a physician (at least twenty-four hours before performing an abortion) give a woman information about:

  - The nature of the procedure,
  - The health risks of abortion and of childbirth,
  - The probable gestational age of her unborn child,
  - Available medical assistance for childbirth,
  - Methods of obtaining child support from the father, and
  - A list of agencies that provide adoption and other services as alternatives to abortion.

Providing this information is not a substantial obstacle because the information allows women to give informed consent to whatever decision they make.

- It is an undue burden on the right to abortion for a state to require a signed statement from the woman that she has notified her spouse that she is about to undergo an abortion. This is a substantial obstacle because many women may not seek an abortion due to a fear of psychological and physical abuse from their husband if they tell him about their plan to have an abortion. Furthermore, a woman does not need her husband's consent to undergo an abortion. He does not have a veto. Therefore, notifying him about the planned abortion is not necessary.

The *Casey* case did not resolve the abortion controversy. Many states have enacted restrictions that the U.S. Supreme Court may one day have to decide are or are not "undue burdens" on a woman's right to abortion. The Court will have to rule on whether restrictions such as the following are constitutional:

- Mandatory waiting periods and counseling sessions (called needlessly onerous by critics);
- Requiring a woman to view an ultrasound of the fetus;
- Requiring abortion doctors to have admitting privileges at a local hospital;
- Prohibitions on abortion coverage in insurance policies;
- "Safety" rules on facilities that perform abortions, such as the width of hallways; and
- Prohibition of abortion after a fetal heartbeat is detected.

Other efforts to undermine the *Roe* and *Casey* decisions include proposed laws that grant legal rights to embryos and that define a fetus as a person. Mississippi almost passed a law that defined "person" to "include every human being from the moment of fertilization." Such laws would arguably make all abortions illegal.

Laws that regulate and restrict where and how abortions can be obtained are sometimes called TRAP laws—Targeted Regulation of Abortion Providers. The constitutionality of such laws are frequently challenged in the courts.

Partial-Birth Abortion

Partial-birth abortion is a late-term abortion in which the fetus is destroyed after it is partially extruded from the womb. Doctors use different terms for the procedure such as dilation and extraction (D & X) or intact dilation and evacuation (intact D & E).

In 2000, the U.S. Supreme Court held that a state's ban on partial-birth abortion was unconstitutional. One of the dissenting justices said that the opinion allowing partial-birth abortion would become as infamous as the Court's *Dred Scott* decision (protecting the rights of slave owners) and the *Korematsu* decision (allowing the internment of Japanese Americans during World War II).[29] Three years later, Congress passed the Partial-Birth Abortion Ban Act, which prohibited

gestational
Pertaining to the development of the embryo or fetus in the uterus until birth.

informed consent
Agreement to let something happen based on having a reasonable understanding of the benefits, risks, and available alternatives.

fertilization
The initial union of a sperm and an egg that becomes an embryo. Also called *conception*.

partial-birth abortion
An abortion in which the fetus is destroyed after it is partially extruded from the womb. Intact dilation and evacuation.

extrude
To force out.

abortions that involve partial delivery of a living fetus in late-term pregnancies. This time, the Court allowed the ban when it was challenged. The Partial-Birth Abortion Ban Act states that any physician who "knowingly performs a partial-birth abortion and thereby kills a human fetus shall be fined under this title or imprisoned not more than 2 years, or both. This subsection does not apply to a partial-birth abortion that is necessary to save the life of a mother whose life is endangered by a physical disorder, physical illness, or physical injury, including a life-endangering physical condition caused by or arising from the pregnancy itself."[30]

The act defines partial-birth abortion as "an abortion in which the person performing the abortion (A) deliberately and intentionally vaginally delivers a living fetus until, in the case of a head-first presentation, the entire fetal head is outside the body of the mother, or, in the case of breech presentation, any part of the fetal trunk past the navel is outside the body of the mother, for the purpose of performing an overt act that the person knows will kill the partially delivered living fetus; and (B) performs the overt act, other than completion of delivery, that kills the partially delivered living fetus."

The law was upheld by a divided U.S. Supreme Court.[31] The Court held that safe alternatives to the banned procedure are available to the woman, the act was not too vague, and most importantly, the act did not place a substantial obstacle in the path of a woman's decision to abort a nonviable fetus and hence did not violate the undue-burden test of *Casey*.

FETAL HOMICIDE

criminal homicide
Causing the death of a person without justification or excuse.

murder
Killing a person (1) with the intent to kill, (2) with the intent to cause grievous bodily harm, (3) with reckless disregard for human life, or (4) while committing a designated felony.

manslaughter
The unlawful killing of a person that does not constitute murder.

feticide
The unlawful killing of a fetus.

Criminal homicide is causing the death of a person without justification or excuse. The two major categories of criminal homicide are **murder** and **manslaughter**. When does a fetus become a person so that it can become the victim of a criminal homicide? In most states, the baby must be born alive for this to occur, usually meaning that the baby must have an independent circulation—it must be breathing. In a few states, however, the killing of a fetus can constitute murder. In New York, for example, homicide includes the death of an "unborn child" of a woman "pregnant for more than twenty-four weeks under circumstances constituting murder."[32]

It is also a crime to unlawfully terminate life before birth. The crime is called **feticide**, the unlawful killing of a fetus. In Georgia, for example, an unborn child is defined as "a member of the species homo sapiens at any stage of development who is carried in the womb." Feticide by vehicle in Georgia is committed if someone causes the death of an unborn child by any injury to the mother of such child that would be homicide by vehicle if it resulted in the death of the mother.[33] Similarly, an Indiana statute provides that a "person who knowingly or intentionally terminates a human pregnancy with an intention other than to produce a live birth or to remove a dead fetus commits feticide, a Level 3 felony." This section does not apply to an abortion performed in compliance with Indiana law.[34]

At the federal level, the Unborn Victims of Violence Act treats an unborn child as a victim by making it a federal crime to injure or kill a "child" "who is in utero" during the commission of one of over sixty specified federal crimes. The law defines "child in utero" as "a member of the species Homo sapiens, at any stage of development, who is carried in the womb."[35] Although the act contains an exception for abortion and does not say that a fetus is a child or a person, critics charge that it is step in the direction of granting that status to a fetus. An editorial in the New York Times, for example, said that the law is an attack on abortion rights masquerading as law enforcement: "This equivalence between a fetus in its earliest stages and a child sets a dangerous legal precedent."[36]

These laws on criminal liability are different from the *civil* liability of a defendant for killing a fetus. It is possible for a defendant to escape criminal liability for killing a fetus but still face civil liability. We will consider civil liability in Chapter 17 when we discuss prenatal torts.

VIOLENCE AGAINST WOMEN

INTRODUCTION

Domestic violence (DV) is actual or threatened injury or abuse of one member of a family or household by another member. DV can be committed against a spouse, a child, a same-sex partner, and in some states, against a dating partner. There are four major patterns of DV:

domestic violence (DV)
Actual or threatened injury or abuse of one member of a family or household by another member.

- *Coercive-control violence.* Classic battering. The abuser (often male) uses force as a tactic in a larger escalating pattern aimed at intimidating and controlling the victim. Physical violence and sexual abuse are often accompanied by threats, psychological and emotional abuse, isolation of the victim, manipulation of children, and exercise of economic control.

- *Violent resistance or self-defense.* The victim (usually female) uses violence to protect herself against a perpetrator who is using force as a part of a larger pattern of coercive control.

- *Conflict-instigated violence.* An unresolved disagreement spirals into a violent incident, but the violence is not part of a larger pattern of coercive control. It may be initiated by either the male or female partner, although female victims are more likely to suffer injury than are men. If the first violent incident occurs in response to the separation of the parties (and there is no history of coercive controlling behavior), the violence is sometimes called *separation-instigated violence.*

- *Violence caused by mental illness.* Violence resulting from abusers who suffer from severe mental illness such as psychosis and paranoia.[37]

Staggering Statistics

The statistics on intimate partner violence (IPV) in America are staggering:

- One in four women (and one in seven men) has been the victim of severe physical violence by an intimate partner.

- On average, more than three women (and one man) are murdered by their intimate partners every day.

- More than one million women per year are raped.

- One in five women has been raped in her lifetime (one in seventy-one men have been raped in their lifetime).

- One in six women has been the victim of **stalking** in her lifetime (one in nineteen men have been stalked in their lifetime).

stalking
A pattern of repeated and unwanted attention, harassment, contact, or any other course of conduct directed at a specific person that would cause a reasonable person to feel fear.

- Thirty percent of Americans say they know a woman who has been physically abused by her husband or boyfriend.

- About one in five female high school students reports being physically and/or sexually abused by a dating partner.

- About half of all female victims of intimate violence report an injury of some type, and about 20 percent of them seek medical assistance.

- Fifty percent of men who frequently assault their wives also frequently abuse their children.

- The health-related costs of intimate partner violence exceed $5.8 billion a year.[38]

As alarming as these statistics are, the numbers above are considered low estimates because the crimes involved are among the most unreported in the country. For example, the National Crime Victimization Survey reports that over a recent five-year period, police were not notified of half of all incidents of rape.[39] Only one out of every one hundred perpetrators of domestic violence is arrested.

There are, however, some positive trends. For example, although spouse-on-spouse violence continues to be alarmingly high, the rate of such violence has fallen by more than 30 percent over the last three decades "largely because individuals no longer feel forced to stay in a bad marriage."[40]

Historical Perspective on "Wife Beating"

As we saw earlier, wives were once considered the property of their husbands under the theory of the "unity of person" at common law. Unfortunately, this reality encouraged the use of violence against wives. Indeed, there was religious and legal approval for a husband's use of force against his wife. Around 1475, for example, Friar Cherubino of Siena compiled the following Rules of Marriage:

When you see your wife commit an offense, don't rush at her with insults and violent blows. . . . Scold her sharply, bully and terrify her. And if this still doesn't work . . . take up a stick and beat her soundly, for it is better to punish the body and correct the soul than to damage the soul and spare the body. . . . Then readily beat her, not in rage but out of charity and concern for her soul, so that the beating will redound to your merit and her good.[41]

Wife beating was acceptable and indeed was considered a duty of the husband. Society even condoned a particular weapon for the deed: a "rod not thicker than his thumb," a guideline that came to be called the rule of thumb.[42] Some authorities, however, say that the rule of thumb is more legend than fact.[43]

Eventually, of course, laws were passed outlawing wife beating. Yet the crime continues to be committed at an alarming rate today. As indicated, women frequently do not report such violence, particularly when they are still living with their abusers. Furthermore, when a woman does report the incident to the authorities, she often is not taken seriously. Many complain that the police handle violence in a "domestic quarrel" differently, that is, less seriously, than an assault on the street between strangers. Women's groups have campaigned for a change in the attitude and policies of courts, legislatures, and law enforcement agencies. (See the section on mandatory arrest and mandatory prosecution below.) In addition, they have fought for the creation of more shelters to which battered women can flee.

Remedies against Domestic Violence

Abuse is often defined as attempting to cause bodily injury; intentionally, knowingly, or recklessly causing bodily injury; or using threats of force that place another person in fear of imminent serious physical harm. If a woman is persistent and desperate enough, her main *civil* remedy is to go to court to ask for an **injunction**. This remedy seeks to stop the abuse against the plaintiff and/or her children. Depending on the state, the injunction is called a **restraining order**, an order of protection, personal protection order (PPO), a protection from abuse order (PFA), a stay-away order, or a no-contact order. The order often forbids the defendant from being in a designated area (e.g., within two hundred feet of the alleged domestic-violence victim), or from contacting the person except for approved reasons. Over twenty states authorize GPS tracking devices (usually in ankle braces), which can set off an alarm if the abuser goes to the victim's home or place of employment.

The first step in obtaining the restraining order is the filing of an application for a temporary injunction based on actual or threatened abuse. The petitioner usually files the application **ex parte**, meaning that only one party (the victim) is before the court. Once the judge (or sometimes a clerk) issues the order, the next step is to have it served on the defendant. As soon as it is served, the temporary injunction can be enforced by the police. A date is set for a hearing at which both sides can address the question of whether the injunction should be made permanent, which usually means being in effect for a year or more. The woman is urged to carry the temporary or permanent injunction with her at all times so that she can show it to the police in the event that the defendant violates its terms.

injunction
A court order that requires a person (or organization) to do or to refrain from doing a particular thing.

restraining order
A form of injunction, usually issued ex parte (with only one side present), to restrain the defendant from doing a threatened act or from contacting designated individuals. Also called *order of protection, personal protection order (PPO), protection from abuse order (PFA).*

ex parte
With only one side present (usually the plaintiff or petitioner) when a court is asked to do something.

In addition to the civil remedy of an injunction, a woman can ask the state to prosecute the defendant for a crime (e.g., assault, aggravated assault, battery, aggravated battery, reckless conduct, disorderly conduct, or harassment). Some states have special crimes that specifically cover violence committed by one family member against another, such as unlawful spouse-against-spouse violence.

The Violence against Women Act (VAWA)

An attempt to address the problem at the national level occurred when Congress passed the Violence Against Women Act (VAWA), which created an Office on Violence Against Women (OVW) in the U.S. Department of Justice.[44] The act (1) provided grants and support services to domestic-violence prevention programs throughout the country; (2) made it a federal crime to cross state lines with the intent to injure or harass a former or current spouse or intimate partner (opposite-sex or same-sex); (3) required states to give **full faith and credit** to the protection orders of other states; and (4) established a federal civil rights **cause of action** for victims of violence motivated by "animus" toward the victim's gender.

The U.S. Supreme Court, however, struck down the cause-of-action part of the VAWA as an unconstitutional exercise of the Commerce Clause of the U.S. Constitution.[45] The Court held that gender violence did not have a substantial enough effect on interstate commerce to justify the regulation of such violence through the VAWA. The Court also expressed its concern about imposing additional federal laws in this area of family relations, which should be the primary concern of state governments. The Court, however, left intact the other portions of the VAWA.

Another difficulty with VAWA is funding. There is some uncertainty as to whether Congress will continue to fund the programs supported by VAWA.

Freedom of Access to Clinic Entrances (FACE)

Another attempt by Congress to regulate gender-related violence was its passage of the Freedom of Access to Clinic Entrances Act (FACE), which gives a cause of action to anyone who is the victim of assault or other attack while seeking "reproductive health services," such as an abortion.[46] In view of the Court's rejection of the cause-of-action provision of VAWA, however, it is unclear whether FACE will eventually be held to be an unconstitutional intrusion by Congress on the right of the states to regulate family law.

Later, in Chapter 17, we will examine whether a spouse who is the victim of domestic violence can bring a traditional personal injury tort action (e.g., assault, battery, false imprisonment, and intentional infliction of emotional distress) against the other spouse in a state court.

MANDATORY ARREST; MANDATORY PROSECUTION

By some estimates, a large majority of domestic-violence cases are dismissed because of the refusal of the victims to cooperate with the prosecution.[47] Victims often fear further violence from their batterers if they cooperate. Some states have responded by passing mandatory-arrest laws that *require* the police to make an arrest if **probable cause** exists that a crime has been committed, regardless of the wishes of the victim. The law might prohibit the police from asking the victim whether an arrest should be made. Under such a law, victims are not asked if they wish to press charges. The policy of mandatory arrest is controversial.

> *Opponents of mandatory arrest argue that: (1) because domestic violence is a crime of passion, arrest is unlikely to deter crime; (2) arrest before all the facts are known leads to the arrest of innocent people; (3) mandatory arrest often punishes the alleged victim as well as the suspect since a bread-winner may lose his job after being arrested, or the arrest may cause the suspect to retaliate further against the victim upon release; and (4) fear of these adverse consequences may lead victims to refuse to call police for help out of fear that arrest will be the result.[48]*

full faith and credit (FFC)
The obligation of one state to recognize and enforce the laws and court decisions of another state. This obligation is based on the U.S. Constitution, which provides that "Full Faith and Credit shall be given in each State to the public Acts, Records, and judicial Proceedings of every other State." Article IV, § 1.

cause of action
(1) A legally acceptable reason for bringing a suit. A rule that constitutes a legal theory for bringing a suit. (2) The facts that give a person a right to judicial relief. When you *state a cause of action*, you list the facts that give you a right to judicial relief against the alleged wrongdoer.

probable cause
(1) A reasonable belief that a specific crime has been committed and that the accused committed the crime. (2) A reasonable belief that good grounds exist to bring civil proceedings against someone.

Furthermore, if a fight occurs, the police may have no way of sorting out who did what to whom, and end up arresting both parties. Dual arrests increased significantly in many mandatory-arrest states. Batterers have been known to sound convincing when they tell a police officer that they were just defending themselves.

Yet some states have gone even further and have instituted mandatory prosecution called a *no-drop policy*. The district attorney or prosecutor is not allowed to drop the charges. Government attorneys are required to bring criminal charges against batterers even if the victim refuses to cooperate.

RIGHT OF CONFRONTATION

When victims refuse to cooperate, they often refuse to answer further questions from the police and fail to show up for court proceedings against the alleged batterer. They may even say that it was all a mistake and that there was no violence. When this occurs, prosecutors have a serious problem of proof. How can they convict someone for what the victim now says did not happen?

Confrontation Clause
A clause in the U.S. Constitution stating that criminal defendants have a right to confront accusing witnesses face-to-face and to cross-examine them.

A further problem for prosecutors is the Confrontation Clause of the U.S. Constitution, which gives a criminal defendant the right to confront and cross-examine an accusing witness. A victim who refuses to show up cannot be confronted and cross-examined. Therefore, the defendant goes free. Suppose, however, that other evidence is available? Often, the police have a recording of a 911 phone call the victim made to the police in the middle of (or just after) the violent acts occurred. Can the statement on the recording be used against the defendant? Would the use of this statement violate the defendant's right of confrontation when the maker of the statement—the alleged victim—refuses to appear or say anything in court? The answer depends on how we characterize the statement.

- If it is a *testimonial* statement, the Confrontation Clause is violated by its use when the maker of the statement is not available for cross-examination.
- If it is a *nontestimonial* statement, the Confrontation Clause is not violated by its use when the maker of the statement is not available for cross-examination.

The distinction between testimonial and nontestimonial depends on the purpose and circumstances of the statement. Here is how the U.S. Supreme Court explained the difference:

> *Statements are nontestimonial when made in the course of police interrogation under circumstances objectively indicating that the primary purpose of the interrogation is to enable police assistance to meet an ongoing emergency. They are testimonial when the circumstances objectively indicate that there is no such ongoing emergency, and that the primary purpose of the interrogation is to establish or prove past events potentially relevant to later criminal prosecution.*[49]

Hence, if the statement is made as the police are trying to provide help, it is nontestimonial; if it is made while the police are trying to determine what happened, it is testimonial. Under these definitions, a panicked 911 call to the police would be considered nontestimonial if the caller is reaching out to the police for help in a crisis. The caller's statement can be introduced in court against the defendant even though the caller refuses to give testimony in court about what happened. On the other hand, if the police arrive after the emergency is over and take a written statement from the victim about what happened, the statement would be considered testimonial, and therefore, could not be used in court against the defendant unless the defendant had the right to cross-examine the maker of the statement.

PRIMARY AGGRESSOR LAW

Mandatory-arrest laws sometimes lead to the arrest of both parties. One way to avoid dual arrests when there are allegations of mutual violence is to require the police to determine who was the *primary* aggressor and to arrest only that person.

Some states have laws to this effect based on the *Model Code on Domestic and Family Violence* of the National Council of Juvenile and Family Court Judges. Under the model code:

> If a law enforcement officer receives complaints of domestic or family violence from two or more opposing persons, the officer shall evaluate each complaint separately to determine who was the primary aggressor. If the officer determines that one person was the primary physical aggressor, the officer need not arrest the other person believed to have committed domestic or family violence. In determining whether a person is the primary aggressor the officer shall consider:
> - *Prior complaints of domestic or family violence;*
> - *The relative severity of the injuries inflicted on each person;*
> - *The likelihood of future injury to each person; and*
> - *Whether one of the persons acted in self-defense.*[50]

BATTERED WOMAN SYNDROME

Some women have taken the extreme step of killing their husband (or other intimate partner) who has been abusing them. Does the killing constitute the crime of murder or manslaughter? In part, the answer depends on when the killing occurs. Compare the predicament of the women in the following two situations. Assume that both women had been physically abused by their husband or boyfriend for years:

- Carol is being physically attacked by her husband, who is coming at her with a knife. As he approaches, Carol shoots him.
- Hours after being beaten by her boyfriend, Helen takes a gun to his bedroom and shoots him in the head while he is asleep.

It is highly unlikely that Carol has committed a crime. She is protected by the traditional defense of **self-defense**. Citizens can use deadly force that they reasonably believe is necessary to protect themselves from **imminent** death or serious bodily injury.

What about Helen? Unless she can prove temporary insanity, she must establish the elements of self-defense to avoid conviction. But she apparently was not in *imminent* danger at the time she shot her boyfriend. Arguably, she could have left the home while he was sleeping if she felt that he might kill or maim her once he awoke. Women in Helen's situation have been prosecuted for crimes such as manslaughter and murder.

In these prosecutions, one argument that is often raised by the woman is the battered wife syndrome or, more broadly, the **battered woman syndrome**. She claims that she acted out of a psychological helplessness or paralysis. A variety of circumstances combined to block all apparent avenues of escape: financial dependence, loneliness, guilt, shame, and fear of reprisal from her husband or boyfriend.[51] From this state of "learned helplessness," she kills him. This argument is not an independent defense; it is an argument designed to bolster the self-defense argument. More accurately, it is an attempt to broaden the definition of *imminent danger* in self-defense. To a woman subjected to the psychological terror and paralysis of long-term abuse, the danger from her husband or boyfriend is real and close at hand. At any moment, his behavior might trigger a flashback in her mind to an earlier beating, causing her to honestly believe that she is in immediate danger.

Prosecutors are not sympathetic to the battered-woman-syndrome argument. They say it is too easy to exaggerate the extent of the abuse and the extent to which the abuse resulted in such a state of paralysis that the woman felt her only way to protect herself in the immediate short term was to kill her husband. Some courts, however, are at least willing to listen to testimony on the syndrome. This has been very helpful for the defendant because when jurors hear this testimony, they are often reluctant to return guilty verdicts despite the absence of clear facts that show

self-defense
The use of reasonable force to prevent harmful or offensive contact to one's person when there is an imminent danger of such contact.

imminent
Near at hand; coming soon; about to happen; immediate.

battered woman syndrome
A woman's psychological helplessness or paralysis because of conditions such as financial dependence, loneliness, guilt, shame, and fear of reprisal from her husband or boyfriend who has repeatedly subjected her to physical, sexual, and/or emotional abuse in the past.

voluntary manslaughter
The intentional, unlawful killing of someone but with extenuating circumstances such as provocation. Murder reduced to manslaughter because of the absence of malice or premeditation.

self-defense. Prosecutors are aware of this reluctance, and therefore many are more inclined to bring charges on lesser crimes such as **voluntary manslaughter** and, in some instances, not to bring any charges. Therefore, although prosecutors may deride the battered woman syndrome as an "abuse excuse," raising the syndrome can still be an important part of the strategy of the attorney representing the woman.

ASSIGNMENT 12.4

For the following questions, see General Instructions for the State-Code Assignment in Appendix A.

a. In your state, if a woman is threatened with violence, what remedies does she have?

b. When, if ever, can an injunction or protective order be issued when the defendant is not present in court (i.e., ex parte)?

c. Without justification, a husband stabs his wife but does not kill her. What are the possible crimes he can be charged with in your state?

ASSIGNMENT 12.5

a. Do you think that a court encourages killing when it allows evidence of the battered woman syndrome to be introduced in trials of women who kill their spouses or boyfriends? Explain why or why not.

b. Do you think it is possible for a battered *man* syndrome to exist? Explain why or why not.

MARITAL RAPE

The common-law rule was that a husband cannot rape his wife. The "husband cannot be guilty of a rape committed by himself upon his lawful wife, for by their mutual matrimonial consent and contract, the wife hath given up herself in this kind unto her husband which she cannot retract."[52] This view is still the law in a few states. Most states, however, allow prosecution if the couple is living apart and a petition has been filed for divorce or separate maintenance. The reluctance of courts and legislatures to allow the criminal law of rape to apply to married couples is, in part, based on a fear that a wife would lie about whether she consented to sexual intercourse. As we will see in the case of *Warren v. State*, however, this fear is largely unfounded.

CASE

Warren v. State
255 Ga. 151, 336 S.E.2d 221 (1985)
Supreme Court of Georgia

Background: *Daniel Steven Warren was indicted for rape and sodomy of his wife while they were still living together. He moved to dismiss the indictment on the ground that a husband cannot be convicted of committing these crimes against his wife. The motion was denied. He then appealed to the Supreme Court of Georgia, where he is the appellant.*

Decision on Appeal: *The denial of the motion to dismiss is affirmed. The rape statute in the state does not contain a marital exception.*

OPINION OF THE COURT:

Justice Smith delivered the opinion of the court.

"When a woman says I do, does she give up her right to say I won't?" This question does not pose the real question, because rape and aggravated sodomy are not sexual acts of an ardent husband performed upon an initially apathetic wife, they are acts of violence that are accompanied with physical and mental abuse and often leave the victim with physical and psychological damage that is almost always long lasting. Thus we find the more appropriate question:

When a woman says "I do" in Georgia does she give up her right to State protection from the violent acts of rape and aggravated sodomy performed by her husband[?]

The answer is no. We affirm. . . .

The appellant asserts that there exists within the rape statute an implicit marital exclusion that makes it legally impossible for a husband to be guilty of raping his wife. Until the late 1970s there was no real examination of this apparently widely held belief. Within the last few years several jurisdictions have been faced with similar issues and they have decided that under certain circumstances a husband can be held criminally liable for raping his wife.

What is behind the theory and belief that a husband could not be guilty of raping his wife? There are various explanations for the rule and all of them flow from the common law attitude toward women, the status of women and marriage.

Perhaps the most often used basis for the marital rape exemption is the view set out by Lord Hale in *1 Hale P.C. 629*. It is known as Lord Hale's contractual theory. The statement attributed to Lord Hale used to support the theory is: "but a husband cannot be guilty of a rape committed by himself upon his lawful wife, for by their mutual matrimonial consent and contract the wife hath given up herself in this kind unto her husband which she cannot retract."

There is some thought that the foundation of his theory might well have been the subsequent marriage doctrine of English law, wherein the perpetrator could, by marrying his victim, avoid rape charges. It was thus argued as a corollary, rape within the marital relationship would result in the same immunity. Another theory stemming from medieval times is that of a wife being the husband's chattel or property. Since a married woman was part of her husband's property, nothing more than a chattel, rape was nothing more than a man making use of his own property. A third theory is the unity in marriage or unity of person theory that held the very being or legal existence of a woman was suspended during marriage, or at least was incorporated and consolidated into that of her husband. In view of the fact that there was only one legal being, the husband, he could not be convicted of raping himself.

These three theories have been used to support the marital rape exemption. Others have tried to fill the chasm between these three theories with justifications for continuing the exemption in the face of changes in the recognition of women, their status, and the status of marriage. Some of the justifications include: Prevention of fabricated charges; Preventing wives from using rape charges for revenge; Preventing state intervention into marriage so that possible reconciliation will not be thwarted. A closer examination of the theories and justifications indicates that they are no longer valid, if they ever had any validity.

Hale's implied consent theory was created at a time when marriages were irrevocable and when all wives promised to "love, honor, and obey" and all husbands promised to "love, cherish, and protect until death do us part." Wives were subservient to their husbands, her identity was merged into his, her property became his property, and she took his name for her own.

There have been dramatic changes in women's rights and the status of women and marriage. Today our State Constitution provides that, "no person shall be deprived of life, *liberty*, or property except by due process," and "protection to person and property is the paramount duty of government and shall be impartial and complete. No person shall be denied the equal protection of the laws." Our state Constitution also provides that each spouse has a right to retain his or her own property. Our statutory laws provide that, "[t]he rights of citizens include, *without limitation*, the following: (1) The right of *personal security*, [and] (2) The right of personal liberty. . . ." (Emphasis supplied.) OCGA § 1–2–6.

Women in Georgia "are entitled to the privilege of the elective franchise and have the right to hold any civil office or perform any civil function as fully and completely as do male citizens." OCGA § 1–2–7. Couples who contemplate marriage today may choose either spouse's surname or a combination of both names for their married surname. No longer is a wife's domicile presumed to be that of her husband, and no longer is the husband head of the family with the wife subject to him. Marriages are revocable without fault by either party; either party, not just the husband, can be required to pay alimony upon divorce; and both parties have a joint and several duty to provide for the maintenance, protection, and education of their children. Couples may write antenuptial agreements in which they are able to decide, prior to marriage, future settlements; and our legislature has recognized that there can be violence in modern family life and it has enacted special laws to protect family members who live in the same household from one another's violent acts. . . .

One would be hard pressed to argue that a husband can rape his wife because she is his chattel. Even in the darkest days of slavery when slaves were also considered chattel, rape was defined as "the carnal knowledge of a female whether free or slave, forcibly and against her will." Georgia Code, § 4248 (1863). Both the chattel and unity of identity rationales have been cast aside. "Nowhere in the common law world—[or] in any modern society—is a woman regarded as chattel or demeaned—by denial of a separate legal identity and the dignity associated with recognition as a whole human being." *Trammel v. United States*, 445 U.S. 40, 52 (1980).

We find that none of the theories have any validity. The justifications likewise are without efficacy. There is no other crime we can think of in which all of the victims are denied protection simply because someone might fabricate a charge; there is no evidence that wives have flooded the district attorneys with revenge filled trumped-up charges, and once a marital relationship is at the point where a husband rapes his wife, state intervention is needed for the wife's protection. . . .

Judgment affirmed.

PRO BONO ASSISTANCE

A law office becomes involved in domestic-violence cases in a number of ways. In a divorce case, for example, there may have been violence or a threat of violence during the marriage. A criminal case could have begun when the police were called because of violence committed in the home.

Attorneys and paralegals may be involved in a **pro bono** project in which they give free legal services to victims of domestic violence. (For a poignant description of one paralegal's participation in such a pro bono program, see Exhibit 12.3.)

pro bono
Concerning or involving legal services that are provided for the public good (pro bono publico) without fee or compensation. Sometimes also applied to services given at a reduced rate.

EXHIBIT 12.3   A Paralegal's Experience with Domestic-Violence Cases

PROTECTION FROM ABUSE PROGRAM
by Laurie R. Mansell Reich, RP, Senior Paralegal
Equitable Resources, Inc.

I can still clearly remember my first day as a pro bono volunteer with the Protection From Abuse (PFA) Program in Allegheny County, Pennsylvania. I entered the PFA area of the City/County Building clutching a binder of sample forms, sweating profusely from nervousness and feeling very scared.

The PFA area of the building is an austere section just off the elevators on the eighth floor that has been partitioned off and "decorated" with old, well-worn government-issue tables and chairs. There is one desk. It is reserved for a volunteer. A sheriff's deputy sits on a plastic chair by the pay phone in case trouble breaks out between petitioners, which does happen. And did I mention that the building has no air conditioning and an overzealous heating system?

I had received my required one hour of training (from whence came the binder of forms) from the PFA coordinator of the Pittsburgh Paralegal Association. For some six years, the Association has participated in the PFA program, which is run by Allegheny County in conjunction with Neighborhood Legal Services and the women's shelters in the area.

I decided to volunteer one Monday a month. We were told at training that Monday is the worst day, especially following a three-day holiday weekend or a weekend sporting event. PFA assistance is available from 9:00 to 11:00 a.m. each day, Monday through Friday. If a PFA is needed over the weekend or in the evening, the petitioner must go to night court and obtain an emergency PFA until the program's office opens on Monday—thus the Monday crowd.

When I first arrived, I thought, how bad could this be? Well, on my first day, there were 50 petitioners. The PFA program had one paid counselor and three or four volunteer counselors. The volunteer counselors show up, unpaid, day in and day out. And then, there was me. I leave you to count the odds.

The stories the women tell are chilling. One woman's boyfriend held her by the neck from a third story apartment building. Another woman had gasoline poured down her throat and suffered permanent physical damage. One woman's fingernails were ripped off, and she could not even hold a pen. Sometimes these women are harassed at work or by telephone with as many as 30 or 40 calls during the night. Often their lives are threatened. Many are raising four or five children on $500 a month. I cannot tell you how humble I felt each time I left the PFA office.

In Pennsylvania, abuse is considered to have occurred if there is a family or sexual relationship between the parties and the abuse is imminent. So it is important first to establish that a family or sexual relationship exists. For example, a roommate cannot apply for a PFA against another roommate if there is no sexual relationship. If the defendant is a minor, the matter is referred to juvenile court. If the plaintiff is a juvenile, a parent or guardian must complete the paperwork on his or her behalf.

It is important to make sure that the abuse was very recent, usually within the last few days. Otherwise, the judge will dismiss the allegation as not meeting the imminence test, namely that the abuse is imminent, about to happen, close at hand, or immediate. If the abuse did not happen recently, the plaintiff would have to show a good reason for the delay in applying for the PFA, such as being hospitalized or perhaps having to flee the area.

I can remember bumbling my way through that first day, trying desperately to help and worrying that I would get something wrong and ruin someone's chances of getting the PFA. I think I spent more time frantically searching through my reference binder and asking questions of other staff than I did helping the clients.

Even now after two years of PFA volunteering, I have never stopped being nervous. It is a big responsibility to help someone to fill out a complaint that will be read by a judge. These people desperately need help. Most of the petitioners are women, but a few men

(continued)

Exhibit 12.3 *(continued)*

come in. Usually the men are there petitioning for a PFA at the same time their wives or girlfriends are petitioning for a PFA against them. It is important to note, however, that it is a *conflict of interest* for us to assist them both with their complaints, no matter how dispassionate we may feel.

It is also crucial to point out that at no time do we give legal advice even though we are asked for such advice. I explain to the people that I am not an attorney and refer them to Neighborhood Legal Services. . . . For this reason, when I became the PFA coordinator of the Pittsburgh Paralegal Association, I made nametags for paralegal volunteers with the Association's name on top and the first name of the paralegal below. This gave a clear message as to who we are. For safety's sake, we put only first names on the nametags so volunteers could not be contacted outside of the program.

The petitioners who come for help go through a full day of paperwork and hearings before they obtain a temporary PFA, assuming they get a sympathetic judge. The temporary PFA is good for ten days, at which time a hearing of both parties is held to determine whether a permanent PFA, good for one year, should be issued. The volunteer's role is to help an applicant obtain a temporary PFA.

Many of the women come in exhausted. They have been up all night and have their children with them. Recently, I brought in coloring books and crayons so the children could have something to do for the two hours that the parent is waiting and then filling out paperwork.

And the paperwork (five to six forms) is daunting, I can assure you. Some petitioners are illiterate. We are encouraged to have petitioners complete the paperwork themselves, mainly because there just are not enough volunteers to go around. If we do end up writing the actual description of the incident, we have to initial our description and have the petitioner read and initial it as well. This is to ensure that the petitioner will not tell the judge that he or she was unaware of what we wrote. The petitioner must initial the description to show he or she has read the description and agrees that it is accurate.

This volunteer experience has given me a whole new perspective on life and the use of my paralegal skills. Often when I would finish working with these women, they would have tears in their eyes as they thanked me for my help. They gratefully acknowledged that they could never have completed the forms without help. I listen to them carefully and try to help; they appreciate that.

Although the training session is essential, on-the-job experience is the best lesson. I encourage all paralegals to become involved in pro bono activity. You will never find a better or more rewarding way to use your skills. As few as two hours a month is not too much to ask—particularly considering the satisfaction you receive in return.

Reprinted with permission of Laurie R. Mansell Reich.

CLIENT SENSITIVITY

When working with a victim of domestic violence, special sensitivity is required. In the following guidelines, the victim is a woman and the perpetrator or batterer is a man, although similar guidelines apply if the roles are reversed or if the violence is being committed within a same-sex relationship. The guidelines assume that the paralegal works in a law office and that the victim is a client of the office. Although many of the guidelines also apply to volunteer settings, such as the one described in Exhibit 12.3, the guidelines assume that there will be an ongoing relationship between the client and the office, such as when the client is seeking the help of the office in obtaining a divorce.

- *Focus on immediate safety needs.* The client may be in immediate danger. The batterer, for example, may be following or stalking the client. Ask the client if she is safe at the present moment. Are the children safe? If danger exists, suggest to the client that she consider calling the police or the emergency 911 phone number from your office. Ask if the batterer knows where the client is. Does the client have any relatives where she can safely stay? Is the client interested in staying at a woman's shelter for the night? In short, before exploring the niceties of the law and legal procedures with the client, focus on any immediate safety concerns.

- *Take the client seriously.* If the client says there is danger, believe it. Too often, society does not take domestic violence seriously. The police, for example, may feel that nothing more than a "lover's quarrel" is taking place. Their attitude might be: "just go back and work things out." Many victims of domestic violence have been subjected to this attitude. They should not find it in a law office.

- *Know the community resources for battered women.* Run this search in Google, Bing, or Yahoo: domestic violence resources aa (with aa being the name of your city, county, or state). Someone in the city or county has probably already compiled a list of resources for domestic-violence victims, such as counseling, hotline numbers, overnight shelters, battered women's support groups, hospitals, emergency financial assistance from public welfare agencies, and information on obtaining a restraining order or a protective order. To find such a list, run the Internet search listed above. Also make inquiries about such a list at the police department, district attorney's office, the mayor's office, a local public library, religious charities, the Salvation Army, the YWCA, and any special offices or task forces on women's issues. You need to know where victims can turn for social, psychological, financial, and security assistance. In the unlikely event that this list does not exist where you live, start compiling your own.

- *Avoid being judgmental.* You may not approve of some of the client's decisions. You may think she has helped cause her own predicament. You may be shocked to learn that a client has regularly returned to the batterer after repeated incidents of violence over a long period of time. This is not the time to judge the morality or wisdom of the client's life choices. This is not the time for a lecture or sermon. Suggest alternatives to returning to the batterer but don't criticize the client's failure to find and use such alternatives in the past.

- *Understand the client's point of view.* The client may feel afraid, ashamed, confused, angry, or even guilty about the violence that has occurred. When you speak to her, she may be exhausted from being up all night on the run from her abuser, trying to protect herself and her children. She may be in physical pain. The crisis brought on by violence may be overwhelming. It is extremely important that you exhibit concern and understanding. The client may not be capable of grasping technical legal concepts. She needs information and a sympathetic ear.

- *Leave the critical decisions to the client.* It is the client's life that is on the line. Every decision she makes, including contacting the police, has the potential of escalating the violence when the batterer finds out what she has done. Let the client make the decisions. Provide options and information on the pros and cons of each option. Help the client think through the safety and other consequences of each step.

- *Alert the client to the danger of false security.* A restraining order or a protective order is a court document that orders the batterer to stay away from the victim and authorizes the police to arrest the batterer if he violates its terms. But these orders are not self-executing. Many batterers are not intimidated by them. In fact, such an order may provoke the batterer to further violence. Hence, clients should not feel 100 percent safe simply because they have the court order. They should carry it with them at all times but not have a false sense of security. Clients still need to take active steps to protect themselves, such as locating safe places to stay. In a crisis, a 911 call will probably be much more effective than showing the batterer another copy of the order.

- *Do not leave phone messages that will alert the batterer.* If the batterer does not know that the victim is seeking legal help, he may become enraged when he finds out. Thus, ask the client if it is safe to call her at home and leave a message. When you leave a message, it may not be wise to indicate that you are calling from a law office. It may also be unsafe to leave a phone number. If the batterer hears the message, he may call the number and find out you were calling from a law office. Arrange with the client ahead of time how to reach you so that you do not have to leave too much identifying information in a phone message. Alternatively, ask the client if she has a relative or close friend with whom messages can be left safely. This option may be critical if the batterer's phone lets him know the phone number of every call made to him.

- *Help the client develop a safety plan.* When the client leaves the office, she should have identified the locations and situations that are likely to lead to further violence. Help the client prepare a safety plan that will address these potential sources of further violence. The plan should outline how the client will try to avoid further violence (e.g., where to stay away from, what to avoid saying if/when she sees the batterer again) and what she will do if the violence recurs (e.g., what emergency phone numbers to call, where to take the children). Although every eventuality cannot be predicted, a safety plan should cover the major vulnerabilities in the client's life and give her some direction on how to respond to them.

PARALEGAL ROLES

- For an overview of paralegal roles in family-law cases, see Exhibits 1.5 and 1.6 in Chapter 1.
- For many of the financial issues related to women and the law covered in Chapter 12, a paralegal may be asked to help collect documents and facts outlined in:
  - The checklist in Exhibit 3.1 of Chapter 3.
  - The interrogatories in Appendix C.
- For paralegal tasks in pro bono domestic-violence cases, see Exhibit 12.3.
- Miscellaneous duties:
  - Investigate the facts of alleged employment discrimination.
  - Help the client answer questionnaire of the Equal Employment Opportunity Commission for purposes of filing a discrimination complaint.
  - Help draft a petition for filing a discrimination complaint before the local Fair Employment Practices Agency.
  - Help the client identify the assets of his or her deceased spouse in order to calculate the amount that would be received upon exercising the right to an elective share.
  - Help the client prepare needed documents for the statutory change-of-name procedures.
  - Help identify emergency resources (e.g., shelters) for battered women.
  - Help the client fill out a petition for a restraining order or an order of protection.

SUMMARY

Historically, under the common law, a married woman had few rights independent of her husband. Today, her situation is substantially different. For example, the married women's property acts gave women the right to dispose of their property and to enter into contracts in their own right. There are some restrictions on contracts and conveyances between spouses (e.g., they cannot enter into a contract to deny each other spousal support during the marriage, and they cannot transfer property to each other in order to defraud creditors). Such restrictions, however, apply equally to husbands and wives.

When a husband dies, his wife has a right of dower in his property. The corresponding right of the husband is called curtesy. Both of these rights have been replaced by the elective share in most common-law property states. A wife is not required to take her husband's surname upon marriage (though many do so by custom), nor, of course, is she required to keep it upon divorce if she used it when married.

An applicant for credit cannot be discriminated against on the basis of sex or marital status. Sex discrimination in employment is illegal unless sex is a bona fide occupational qualification (BFOQ). Wage discrimination on the basis of sex can be a violation of Title VII of the 1964 Civil Rights Act. Salaries cannot be determined on the basis of gender. The Equal Pay Act (EPA) prohibits discrimination on the basis of sex in the payment of wages or benefits, where men and women perform work of similar skill, effort, and responsibility for the same employer under similar working conditions. Pregnant women cannot be discriminated against on the job because of their pregnancy. Additional employment rights are provided by the Family and Medical Leave Act (FMLA).

The two categories of sexual harassment are quid pro quo harassment and hostile environment harassment. Employers must do more than forbid such harassment; they must actively combat it. Laws on sexual harassment are enforced by the federal Equal Employment

Opportunity Commission and by state fair employment practices agencies.

Adults cannot be denied access to contraceptives. Forced sterilization can be legal for someone who has severe intellectual disabilities or is insane. A state cannot place undue burdens on a woman's right to an abortion before viability. A state can encourage women to choose childbirth over abortion so long as these laws do not present a "substantial obstacle" in the path of her decision to abort a nonviable fetus. Feticide is a crime, but the crime does not apply to legal abortions. The Unborn Victims of Violence Act makes it a federal crime to injure or kill a "child" "who is in utero" during the commission of a specified federal crime.

Domestic violence (DV) is actual or threatened injury or abuse of one member of a family or household by another member. DV against women is a major national problem. Among the remedies women can use when they are victims of DV are restraining orders (initially obtained ex parte). The Violence Against Women Act (VAWA) has provisions that seek to strengthen laws against DV. The Free Access to Clinic Entrances Act (FACE) gives a cause of action to anyone who is the victim of assault or other attack while seeking "reproductive health services," such as an abortion. Mandatory arrest and mandatory prosecution require the arrest and prosecution of alleged batterers, even if the victim refuses to cooperate. The Confrontation Clause prohibits the use of testimonial statements made by an alleged victim, who now refuses to cooperate in the case against the alleged batterer. To avoid arresting both parties involved in DV, the law may require the arrest of the primary aggressor only. Some women have taken the drastic step of killing their abusers. In such cases, the defense of the battered woman syndrome is sometimes raised within the context of self-defense. Marital rape is not a crime in every state, although most states allow prosecution if the parties are separated and a petition has been filed for divorce or separate maintenance.

Important guidelines when assisting victims of DV include focusing on immediate safety needs, knowing the community resources for battered women, avoiding a judgmental attitude, understanding the client's point of view, taking the client seriously, leaving critical decisions to the client, alerting the client to the danger of false security, and helping the client develop a safety plan.

KEY TERMS

feme covert
coverture
at common law
unity of person
contract
conveyance
postnuptial agreement
consideration
fraudulent transfer
separate property
gift
trust
married women's property acts
property division
equitable distribution
dower
life estate
curtesy
elective share
intestate share
identity theft
unsecured
secured
cosigner
punitive damages
class action

quasi-suspect class
intermediate-scrutiny test
bona fide occupational qualification (BFOQ)
nepotism
sexual harassment
quid pro quo sexual harassment
hostile environment sexual harassment
summary judgment
deposition
Equal Employment Opportunity Commission (EEOC)
fair employment practices agency (FEPA)
fundamental right
right to privacy
strict-scrutiny test
compelling state interest
conservator
abortion
embryo
fetus
therapeutic abortion
elective abortion
trimester

viability
proscribe
undue burden
gestational
informed consent
fertilization
partial-birth abortion
extrude
criminal homicide
murder
manslaughter
feticide
domestic violence (DV)
stalking
injunction
restraining order
ex parte
full faith and credit (FFC)
cause of action
probable cause
Confrontation Clause
self-defense
imminent
battered woman syndrome
voluntary manslaughter
pro bono

CHECK THE CITE

A *class action* is a lawsuit in which one or more members of a class sue (or are sued) as representative parties on behalf of everyone in the class. More than 1.5 million current and former female employees of Wal-Mart sought a class action in which they asserted that the discretion exercised by Wal-Mart's local supervisors over pay and promotion matters violates Title VII by discriminating against women. Why did the U.S. Supreme Court refuse to allow the class action to be brought? See *Wal-Mart Stores, Inc. v. Dukes*, 564 U.S. 338 (2011). To read the opinion online: (1) Run a citation search ("564 U.S. 338") in the "Case law" database of Google Scholar (scholar.google.com). (2) Run a case name search ("Wal-Mart Stores, Inc. v. Dukes") or a citations search ("564 U.S. 338") in the search engines of Google, Bing, or Yahoo.

PROJECT

In Google, Bing, or Yahoo, run the following search: *aa discrimination complaint* (substitute the name of your state for aa in the search). Write a report in which you explain the options available to a woman in your state who alleges sex discrimination in the workplace. You must cite and quote from a minimum of five different sources that you find on the Internet. At least three of these sources should be the actual language of statutes, court opinions, or other laws.

ETHICS IN A FAMILY LAW PRACTICE

You are a paralegal who works in the office of Linda Williams, who is defending Richard Summer against a charge of raping his girlfriend. Linda asks you to do some paralegal work on the case. You have never told anyone that you were a victim of a sexual assault ten years ago. The assault was never reported. Any ethical problems?

WRITING SAMPLE

On the Internet, find a petition for a restraining order, an order of protection, or whatever the order is called in your state. Create a fact situation in which a woman alleges violence by her husband. Prepare the petition. (See General Instructions for the Writing Sample in Appendix A.)

REVIEW QUESTIONS

1. What rights were denied to married women at common law?
2. What is meant by coverture?
3. Describe the effect of the unity of person.
4. Today, what restrictions apply to contracts between spouses?
5. What is a fraudulent transfer?
6. What are the possible legal consequences of a spouse using his or her separate funds to buy property that is placed in the sole name of the other spouse?
7. What was accomplished by the married women's property acts?
8. What is equitable distribution?
9. What is the relationship among dower, curtesy, and elective share?
10. What are the two ways a surname can be changed?
11. What rights did the Equal Credit Opportunity Act give to women?
12. What is a BFOQ?
13. What are some examples of illegal job interview questions asked of women?
14. What does the Equal Pay Act provide?
15. What rights do pregnant women have on the job?
16. What right does a mother have to express breast milk on the job?
17. What rights is an employee given under the Family and Medical Leave Act (FMLA)?
18. How do the two kinds of sexual harassment differ?
19. What duties do employers have concerning sexual harassment?
20. On what basis did Governor Clinton win the claim of sexual harassment against him?

21. How are laws on sexual harassment enforced?

22. What contraceptive right does an adult have?

23. Can a person be forcibly sterilized?

24. What abortion rights were established by *Roe v. Wade*?

25. What abortion rights were established by *Planned Parenthood of Southeastern Pennsylvania v. Casey*?

26. What is the Partial-Birth Abortion Ban Act, and is it constitutional?

27. What is feticide?

28. What does the Unborn Victims of Violence Act provide?

29. What is domestic violence?

30. What remedies does a woman have when she is a victim of domestic violence?

31. How does a victim of domestic violence obtain a restraining order or an order of protection?

32. How does the Violence Against Women Act (VAWA) try to protect women who are victims of violence?

33. What does the Free Access to Clinic Entrances Act (FACE) provide?

34. What is mandatory arrest and mandatory prosecution?

35. When does the Confrontation Clause prevent the state from using the statement of an alleged victim who now refuses to cooperate in the case against the alleged batterer?

36. What is the primary aggressor law?

37. What is the battered woman syndrome, and how is it used in court?

38. What are some of the major guidelines for assisting victims of domestic violence?

HELPFUL WEBSITES

Your State

See Appendix D for links to the family law of your state on the topics covered in this chapter.

Women's Rights

- www.aclu.org (type *women's rights* in the search box)
- www.womensrights.org
- www.hrw.org/topic/womens-rights
- en.wikipedia.org/wiki/Women's_rights
- www.now.org

Women's Legal History

- wlh.law.stanford.edu

Employment Discrimination

- www.eeoc.gov/facts/qanda.html
- www.law.cornell.edu/wex/employment_discrimination
- www.hg.org/employment-discrimination-law.html

Equal Employment Opportunity Commission

- www.eeoc.gov

Abortion

- www.guttmacher.org/state-policy/explore /overview-abortion-laws
- llb2.com/2019/06/14/a-50-state-survey-of-abortion-laws
- en.wikipedia.org/wiki/Abortion_law

- www.ncsl.org (type *abortion* in the search box)
- www.law.duke.edu/voices/stenberg

Domestic Violence

- www.ncadv.org/statistics
- www.ncdbw.org

Institute for Women's Policy Research

- www.iwpr.org/press-room

Progress of the World's Women

- progress.unwomen.org

Google Scholar

(scholar.google.com)

- Choose "Articles" and enter in the search box any of the key terms discussed in the chapter. Add the name of your state to the search term.
- Choose "Case law" and "Select courts". Select your state, click "Done," and enter in the search box any of the key terms discussed in the chapter. Add the name of your state to the search term.

Google, Bing, or Yahoo

(on these search engines, run the following searches, substituting your state for "aa")

- coverture aa
- dower aa
- BFOQ aa
- pregnancy law aa

- "family leave" aa
- abortion law aa
- marital rape aa
- "married women's property" aa
- women "common law" aa

- "employment discrimination" aa
- EEOC discrimination aa
- "sexual harassment" aa
- "domestic violence" aa
- "battered woman syndrome" aa

Twitter, Reddit, and Facebook

On Twitter, Reddit, and Facebook, run the following searches (substitute your state for *aa* in your searches; run the searches with and without the name of your state). Look for links to family-law developments in your state.

- womens rights aa
- gender equality aa
- domestic violence aa

YouTube

Run the same searches on YouTube listed above for Google, Bing, Yahoo searches. Even when the video clips are trying to entice you to retain an attorney, buy a book, or enroll in a course, they can provide useful overviews and references to primary authority.

ENDNOTES

Note: All or most of the court opinions in these Endnotes can be read online. To do so, go to Google Scholar (scholar.google.com), select "Case law," and in the search box, enter the cite (e.g., "867 N.E.2d 903") or name of the case (e.g., "*State v. Donkers*") that is given in the endnote.

[1] Robert Oliphant and Nancy Ver Steegh, *Family Law* 239 (3d ed. 2010).

[2] At common law, marriage and the birth of a child automatically revoked a man's will. *Sveen v. Melin*, 138 S. Ct. 1815, 1819 (2018).

[3] Homer Clark, *The Law of Domestic Relations in the United States* § 8.1, p. 498 (Practitioner's ed. 2d ed. 1987).

[4] *State v. Donkers*, 867 N.E.2d 903, 939 (Ohio Ct. App., 2007).

[5] N.J.S.A. § 3A:37-3 (www.njleg.state.nj.us/2010/Bills /S3000/2665_I1.HTM).

[6] Sue Shellenbarger, *The Name Change Dilemma*, The Wall Street Journal (May 8, 2011) (blogs.wsj.com /juggle/2011/05/08/the-name-change-dilemma).

[7] Or on the basis of race, color, religion, national origin, or age. 15 U.S.C. § 1691 (www.law.cornell.edu/uscode /text/15/1691).

[8] Federal Trade Commission, *Your Equal Credit Opportunity Rights* (January 2013) (www.consumer.ftc.gov/ articles/0347-your-equal-credit-opportunity-rights)

[9] Ibid.

[10] 42 U.S.C. § 2000e-2(a)(1) (1974) (www.eeoc.gov/laws /statutes/titlevii.cfm).

[11] *Dothard v. Rawlinson*, 433 U.S. 321 (1977).

[12] *International Union, United Auto., Aerospace and Agr. Implement Workers of America, UAW v. Johnson Controls, Inc.*, 499 U.S. 187 (1991).

[13] Amy Newcomb, *Women's Earnings Lower in Most Occupations*, U.S. Census Bureau (May 22, 2018) (census.gov/library/stories/2018/05/gender-pay-gap-in-finance-sales.html)

[14] 29 U.S.C. § 206(d) (www.eeoc.gov/laws/statutes/epa.cfm).

[15] 42 U.S.C. § 2000e(k) (www.eeoc.gov/facts/fs-preg.html) (www.eeoc.gov/laws/statutes/pregnancy.cfm).

[16] United States Department of Labor, *Break Time for Nursing Mothers* (www.dol.gov/whd/nursingmothers).

[17] Family and Medical Leave Act (www.dol.gov/whd/fmla/#. UI3EDcU818E).

[18] U.S. Equal Employment Opportunity Commission, *Sexual Harassment* (www.eeoc.gov/laws/types/sexual_ harassment.cfm) (www.eeoc.gov/facts/fs-sex.html).

[19] *Jones v. Clinton*, 990 F. Supp. 657, 663–64, 677 (E.D. Ark 1998).

[20] Id. at 675, 677–78.

[21] U.S. Equal Employment Opportunity Commission, *Charge Statistics FY 1997 Through FY 2017* (www.eeoc. gov/eeoc/statistics/enforcement/charges.cfm).

[22] *Eisenstadt v. Baird*, 405 U.S. 438, 453 (1972).

[23] *Buck v. Bell*, 274 U.S. 200, 207 (1927).

[24] West's Annotated California Probate Code § 1958 (law. onecle.com/california/probate/1958.html).

[25] 410 U.S. 113 (1973).

[26] U.S. Const. amend. XIV (www.law.cornell.edu/ constitution/amendmentxiv).

[27] *Webster v. Reproductive Health Services*, 492 U.S. 490, 559 (1989) (Blackmun).

[28] 505 U.S. 833 (1992).

[29] *Stenberg v. Carhart*, 530 U.S. 914, 953 (2000) (Scalia dissenting).

[30] 18 U.S.C. § 1531(a) (www.law.cornell.edu/uscode/ text/18/1531).

[31] *Gonzales v. Carhart*, 550 U.S. 124 (2007).

[32] New York Penal Law § 125.00 (ypdcrime.com/penal.law/article125.htm).

[33] Georgia Code Annotated, § 40-6-393.1.

[34] Indiana Code, § 35-42-1-6.

[35] 18 U.S.C. § 1841 (www.law.cornell.edu/uscode/text/18/1841).

[36] Editorial, *A Misleading Fetal Violence Law*, N.Y. Times, Mar. 29, 2004 (www.nytimes.com/2004/03/29/opinion/a-misleading-fetal-violence-law.html).

[37] Nancy Ver Steegh and Clare Dalton, *Report from the Wingspread Conference on Domestic Violence and Family Courts*, 46 Family Court Review, 454, 458 (Jul. 2008).

[38] Domestic Violence Resource Center, *Domestic Violence Statistics* (www.dvrc-or.org). *The National Intimate Partner and Sexual Violence Survey* (www.cdc.gov/violenceprevention/NISVS/index.html).

[39] White House Council on Women and Girls, Women in America, 53 (Mar. 2011).

[40] Stephanie Coontz, *Marriage: Saying I Don't*, Los Angeles Times (Jan. 19, 2012).

[41] Quoted in T. Davidson, *Conjugal Crime* 99 (1978). See also The Language of Violence (cyber.law.harvard.edu/vaw00/History.html).

[42] United States Commission on Civil Rights, *Under the Rule of Thumb: Battered Women and the Administration of Justice* 2 (Jan. 1982).

[43] Ansgar Kelly, *Rule of Thumb and the Folklaw of the Husband's Stick*, 44 Journal of Legal Education 341 (Sept. 1994).

[44] www.justice.gov/ovw.

[45] *United States v. Morrison*, 529 U.S. 598 (2000).

[46] Freedom of Access to Clinic Entrances, 18 U.S.C. § 248 (www.law.cornell.edu/uscode/text/18/248)(www.justice.gov/crt-12).

[47] Michael Rips and Amy Lester, *When Words Bear Witness*, N.Y. Times, Mar. 20, 2006 (www.nytimes.com/2006/03/20/opinion/20rips.html).

[48] Paul Clark, *Mandatory Arrest for Misdemeanor Domestic Violence: Is Alaska's Arrest Statute Constitutional?*, 27 Alaska Law Review 151 (2010).

[49] *Davis v. Washington*, 547 U.S. 813, 822 (2006).

[50] National Council of Juvenile and Family Court Judges, *Family Violence: A Model State Code*, § 205(A)(1994) (www.ncjfcj.org/sites/default/files/modecode_fin_printable.pdf).

[51] Michael Buda and Theresa Butler, *The Battered Wife Syndrome*, 23 Journal of Family Law 359 (1984–85).

[52] M. Hale, *The History of the Pleas of the Crown* 629 (1736).

CHAPTER 13

Illegitimacy and Paternity

CHAPTER OUTLINE

CHAPTER OBJECTIVES

After completing this chapter, you should be able to:

- Describe the evolving terminology of illegitimacy and nonmarital children.
- Distinguish between marital and nonmarital children.
- Know the test used by the U.S. Supreme Court to determine whether a classification of nonmarital children violates equal protection of law.
- State the rights of nonmarital children in the areas of inheritance, wills, child support, wrongful death, workers' compensation, Social Security, annulment, and immigration.
- Explain the different types of artificial insemination and the paternity consequences of each.
- Describe medical and legal issues that arise in the operation of sperm banks.

- Identify the different ways that a child can be legitimated.
- Define the different categories of fathers.
- List the major reasons it is important to determine the paternity of a child.
- Know the federal requirements for paternity.
- State the standard of proof needed to determine paternity.
- Explain why it can be important to know whether a child had his or her own attorney in a paternity action.
- Know the type of jurisdiction a court needs to make a paternity determination and how it can obtain that jurisdiction.
- Explain Lord Mansfield's rule.

- Explain the presumption of legitimacy and how it can be overcome.
- Explain the presumption of paternity and how it can be overcome.
- Understand how some courts resolve conflicting presumptions of paternity.
- Explain how blood-group and DNA testing are used in determining paternity.
- List what mothers and fathers affirm when they sign a voluntary recognition of parentage (ROP).
- Know whether a person has standing to assert his paternity of a child born to a woman married to another man.
- Explain paternity by estoppel.

ILLEGITIMACY

INTRODUCTION

A child becomes a legitimate child is one of three ways:

1. Birth to parents who are married,
2. Birth to parents who marry after the child is born, or
3. Legitimation when the parents never marry.

An illegitimate child is one born to parents who were not married at the time of birth, who never married thereafter, and who never took the steps needed to legitimate the child. In 2016, there were 3,945,875 births in the United States; 39.8 percent of these births were to unmarried women.[1] This large number has contributed to the decline in the traditional negative stigma that society has attached to children of unmarried parents.

At one time, however, the stigma of being illegitimate was culturally and legally severe. The former legal term for a child born out of wedlock was bastard. His or her status was referred to as bastardy. We no longer use this terminology today. The predominant term is *nonmarital child*, although the term *illegitimate child* is still used. Other terms include *child of an informal relationship, child out of wedlock*, and *child with no presumed father*. The common term used to refer to a legitimate child is *marital child*.

At common law, the illegitimate child was filius nullius—the child of nobody and the kin of nobody. Many rights were denied to illegitimate children, such as the right to inherit from their parents and the right to be supported by their fathers. Fortunately, the pronounced discrimination that existed for centuries between the legitimate and the illegitimate child is eroding. States that have adopted the Uniform Parentage Act (UPA) have abolished the distinction between legitimate and illegitimate children. ("A parent-child relationship extends equally to every child and parent, regardless of the marital status of the parent."[2]) This change in the law has been due largely to decisions of the U.S. Supreme Court, which we will be examining in this chapter. In 1972, the Court summarized the change:

> The status of illegitimacy has expressed through the ages society's condemnation of irresponsible liaisons beyond the bonds of marriage. But visiting this condemnation on the head of an infant is illogical and unjust. Moreover, imposing disabilities on the illegitimate child is contrary to the basic concept of our system that legal burdens should bear some relationship to individual responsibility or wrongdoing. Obviously, no child is responsible for his birth and penalizing the illegitimate child is an ineffectual—as well as an unjust—way of deterring the parent. Courts are powerless to prevent the social opprobrium suffered by these hapless children, but the Equal Protection Clause does enable us to strike down discriminatory laws relating to status of birth where . . . the classification is justified by no legitimate state interest, compelling or otherwise.[3]

Not all discriminatory laws against nonmarital children, however, have been eliminated. As we will see, some of these laws have been upheld.

NONMARITAL CHILDREN AS A QUASI-SUSPECT CLASS

In Chapter 1, we saw that when the law treats one group differently from another group, it is setting up a class or a classification. We need to ask when such a classification is a violation of equal protection of law (EPL). There are different kinds of classifications. A class based on a child's legitimacy is an example

---

legitimate child
(1) A child born to parents who are married to each other. (2) A child born to parents who marry after the child is born. (3) A child legitimated through a process called *legitimation*.

illegitimate child
A child born to parents who are not married to each other at the time of birth, who never married thereafter, and who never took steps to legitimate the child. Also called *nonmarital child, child of an informal relationship, child out of wedlock, child with no presumed father*, and *bastard*.

bastard
An illegitimate child.

bastardy
The status of an illegitimate child.

filius nullius
"The son [or child] of no one." The status of an illegitimate child at common law.

kin
Relatives.

Uniform Parentage Act (UPA)
A model statute that has been adopted by most states on how paternity or parenthood is determined.

classification
(1) A group the government treats differently from another group in that the government discriminates for or against that group. (2) The government's different treatment of one group over another. (See the glossary for an additional meaning.)

equal protection of law (EPL)
The constitutional requirement that the government treats one group or class the same as it treats another group or class in like circumstances. Shortened to *equal protection*.

of what is called a **quasi-suspect class**. (See Exhibit 1.4 in Chapter 1.) Assume, for example, that a state passes a law that treats marital and nonmarital children differently by giving different inheritance rights to each. The test used by the courts to determine whether this different treatment of a quasi-suspect class violates EPL is the **intermediate-scrutiny** test. Under this test, the classification will be declared unconstitutional unless it can be shown that the classification is substantially related to the achievement of an important state interest.

In this chapter, we will examine some of the laws on nonmarital children that courts have held to be unconstitutional. The main test used by the courts in reaching this conclusion is the intermediate scrutiny test.

INHERITANCE

Assume that a parent dies **intestate** (without leaving a valid will). The estate of the deceased then passes by inheritance rather than by a will. The common-law rule was that nonmarital children could not inherit from their mothers or fathers. Today, however, they can inherit from their mothers and their fathers. For example, it would be a denial of equal protection to say that a *marital* child can inherit from an intestate mother or from an intestate father but that a *nonmarital* child can inherit only from an intestate mother, not from an intestate father.[4]

All inheritance discrimination, however, is not unconstitutional. Marital and nonmarital children can be treated differently when the alleged father dies before his paternity is determined.

Bill was born while Helen and Sam were living together. They never married. When Sam dies without a will (intestate), Bill seeks a share of Sam's estate under the laws of intestacy, which allows children of the deceased to claim rights in the estate of their deceased parents. Unfortunately, however, Sam's paternity of Bill was never established by a court before Sam died. A statute in the state requires a court order of paternity before a nonmarital child can claim an intestate share of an alleged father's estate. Such an order is not required of marital children.

Not all states discriminate against nonmarital children by insisting that such children obtain a court finding of paternity before the death of the alleged father. In some states, nonmarital children have intestate rights if, before death, the alleged father publicly acknowledged the nonmarital child as his, supported the child, or otherwise clearly indicated that he was the child's father.

Other states, however, are more restrictive on intestate rights. If a state requires a pre-death finding of paternity by a court, is the requirement constitutional? Yes, even though the requirement does not exist for marital children.[5] The pre-death requirement for nonmarital children is considered reasonable and is substantially related to the important public purpose of ensuring the orderly disposition of property at death and the prevention of false or fraudulent inheritance claims against the estate of an alleged father who is now deceased.

INTERPRETATION OF A WILL

If a clause in a will gives property "to my children" or "to my heirs," does the clause cover a nonmarital child of a father who dies **testate** (leaving a valid will)? This is not a constitutional question; it is simply a question of intent. Did the father intend to include nonmarital children in this clause? To resolve the question, the court must look at all of the circumstances (e.g., how much contact the nonmarital child had with the father at the time the father wrote the will and at the time he died). Although cases can go either way, in a significant number of cases, the court concluded that the nonmarital child was *not* intended to be included in the words "children" or "heirs."

quasi-suspect class
A class based on gender or on a child's legitimacy.

intermediate scrutiny
The classification must be substantially related to serve an important state interest. Also called *heightened scrutiny* and *elevated scrutiny*.

intestate
(1) Pertaining to someone who dies without a valid will. (2) A person who dies without a valid will.

paternity
The biological fatherhood of a child.

testate
(1) Pertaining to someone who dies with a valid will. (2) A person who dies with a valid will. (In older cases, if the testate was a man, he was also called *testator* and, if a woman, *testatrix*.)

SUPPORT

Today, both parents have an equal obligation to support their children, both marital and nonmarital. In most cases, a testate or an intestate father can decide to leave his marital or nonmarital children out of his will, but he cannot refuse to support them during his lifetime (see Chapter 10).

WRONGFUL DEATH

wrongful death
A death caused by a tort or other wrong.

When a parent dies due to the wrongful act of another, marital and nonmarital children have an equal right to bring wrongful death actions against defendants who have caused the death of the parent.

Suppose, however, that it is the child who dies. Mothers and fathers of marital children have an equal right to sue for the wrongful death of children born from their marriage. If the child is nonmarital, the mother can sue for its wrongful death. Can the father? Many courts are concerned about absent fathers who suddenly appear when there is the prospect of collecting tort damages due to the death of their nonmarital child. Hence, states may impose restrictions on a father's right to sue. The U.S. Supreme Court has upheld a state statute that denied the right of a father to sue for the wrongful death of his nonmarital child unless he had legitimated the child before its death.[6] (We will discuss legitimation steps later in this chapter.)

WORKERS' COMPENSATION

workers' compensation
A no-fault system of paying for medical care and providing limited wage benefits to a worker for an employment-related injury or illness regardless of who was at fault in causing the injury or illness.

When a parent dies from an injury on the job, the workers' compensation laws of the state permit the children of the deceased to recover benefits. If the state gives a preference to marital children over nonmarital children in claiming these benefits, the state is unconstitutionally denying equal protection of the law to the nonmarital children.[7]

SOCIAL SECURITY

survivors benefits
A form of life insurance from Social Security in which widows, children, and other designated survivors can receive monthly payments and other benefits upon the death of a worker. Also called *survivorship benefits*.

When a parent dies, it would be unconstitutional if survivors benefits (also called *survivorship benefits*)—provided by the Social Security Administration—were denied to a child solely because that child is nonmarital. Yet it is permissible to impose greater procedural burdens on nonmarital children than on marital children in applying for such benefits. Suppose, for example, that a child applies for survivorship benefits following the death of his or her parent. To be eligible under Social Security rules, the child must have been "dependent" on the deceased parent. Nonmarital children can be forced to *prove* that they were dependent on the parent, whereas no such requirement is imposed on marital children—the law will *presume* that a marital child was dependent on the parent without requiring specific proof of it. The difference in treatment is considered reasonable because nonmarital children are generally less likely to be dependent on their parent than marital children.[8]

in vitro fertilization (IVF)
The surgical removal of a woman's eggs from the ovaries, the fertilization of the eggs with sperm (in the laboratory), and the transfer of the resulting embryos (or pre-embryos) into the uterus through the cervix. A method of assisted reproductive technology (ART).

Other cases on survivors benefits have also come before the courts. For example, after the death of Karen Capato's husband in Florida, she gave birth to twins. They were conceived through in vitro fertilization (IVF) using her husband's sperm shortly after he died. (Children born after the death of a parent are called *posthumous children*. See Chapter 16.) When she applied for Social Security survivors benefits for the twins as survivors of a wage earner (their father), her application was denied. The U.S. Supreme Court upheld the denial. Under Social Security rules, children can qualify for survivors benefits if they are entitled to inherit from their parent under state law. In Florida, a child *born* after the death of the father can inherit from him, but a child *conceived* after his death cannot. Florida's inheritance law requires conception to occur before he died. The Caputo twins were conceived after their father's death through IVF and hence were not entitled to inherit from him. Under Social Security rules, this inability to inherit disqualified them from receiving survivors benefits.[9] Not all states have the same law as Florida. In other states, children conceived after the death of their father can inherit from his estate. In such states, they would be entitled to Social Security survivors benefits.

ANNULLED MARRIAGES

If a court grants an annulment to a married couple, the court has declared that a valid marriage never existed. If the couple had children while they were together, the children were born to unmarried parents. Consequently, the children are considered nonmarital children—and thus, illegitimate. At common law, they were called *retroactive bastards*. Today, however, all states have passed statutes declaring that children born during annulled marriages are legitimate. Furthermore, the rights of (and duties to) children are usually not dependent on whether they are legitimate.

annulment
A declaration by a court that a valid marriage never existed. Also called *declaration of invalidity of marriage* and *marital annulment*.

IMMIGRATION

Immigration law allows nonmarital children born abroad to become U.S. citizens when one of the parents is a U.S. citizen. The requirements for citizenship, however, differ depending on whether the citizen-parent is the mother or father. If the citizen-parent is the father, he must take affirmative steps in order for his child to acquire citizenship (i.e., initiate legitimation, declare paternity under oath, or obtain a court order of paternity). If, however, the citizen-parent is the mother, such steps are not required. Citizenship is automatic for nonmarital children born abroad if their mothers are U.S. citizens.

The U.S. Supreme Court has held that this discrimination does not violate equal protection of law. The government has an important interest (1) in ensuring that the child is biologically related to the U.S. citizen and (2) that there has been an opportunity for a meaningful relationship between the parent and child during the child's minority. It is significantly easier to verify the parentage of a mother (she is present at the birth!) and to verify her connecting relationship with the child than it is to verify a father's parentage and connecting relationship. In some cases, for example, the father may not be aware that conception or birth has occurred until many years later. Even if the father is present at the birth, his presence is not proof of his parentage nor does it prove that he developed a connecting relationship with the child. Therefore, the different citizenship requirements for mothers and fathers are justifiable.[10]

ASSIGNMENT 13.1

Explain whether you think the following feminist critique of the immigration decision on foreign-born children of fathers is correct: "Making parenthood a biological fact for women but legally optional for men promotes men's control over women and children, allowing men to take or leave fatherhood at their whim. It lets men decide whether their country has obligations to their progeny. And it defines women as mothers—alone, unless men choose to acknowledge the existence of children they jointly created." Catherine MacKinnon, *Can Fatherhood Be Optional?* N.Y. Times, June 17, 2001 at 15A.

ARTIFICIAL INSEMINATION (AI)

HUSBAND AND WIFE USING AI

artificial insemination (AI)
Inserting sperm into the uterus by a method other than sexual intercourse in order to achieve conception.

Assume that a woman is fertile but cannot conceive a child with her partner through sexual intercourse. His sperm may have poor motility, he may carry a genetically transmissible disease, or he may be sterile. In such cases, the couple might try **artificial insemination (AI)**. A physician uses a syringe to inject sperm into the woman's vagina during a time when she is ovulating.

There are three main types of AI that married couples can consider:

- AI with the semen of the husband (AIH).
- AI with the semen of a third-party donor (AID).
- AI in which the semen of the husband is mixed (confused) with that of a third-party donor (AIC).

The advantage in AIH is that the physician may be able to use "better" or concentrated sperm of the husband than would be achieved through sexual intercourse. One of the psychological advantages of AIC is the knowledge that the child *might* have been fathered by the husband.

AI was once controversial. "In 1954, a court ruled that donor insemination constituted adultery on the part of the woman, whether or not the husband had granted consent. The media referred to donor-conceived children as 'artificial bastards.'"[11] Today, no such characterizations are used as AI has become relatively common and, if proper procedures are followed, legal.

In cases where the donor is the mother's husband (AIH), the child is legitimate, and the husband has full parental rights and responsibilities. At one time, there was some doubt about the legitimacy of a child born through AID or AIC. Today, there is no longer any doubt in cases where the husband has consented to an AID or AIC procedure. Under § 5 of the Uniform Parentage Act:

> *If, under the supervision of a licensed physician and with the consent of her husband, a wife is inseminated artificially with semen donated by a man not her husband, the husband is treated in law as if he were the natural father of a child thereby conceived. The husband's consent must be in writing and signed by him and his wife. . . . The donor of semen . . . is treated in law as if he were not the natural father of a child thereby conceived.*[12]

Most states have adopted this statute or one similar to it. See Exhibit 13.1 for an example of a consent form used for AI.

OTHERS USING AI

sperm bank
A facility that collects and stores human sperm from male donors who will usually be anonymous to any woman who uses the sperm to become pregnant by artificial insemination (AI). Also called *cryobank*.

A single woman or a lesbian couple might also consider AI, using sperm that has been purchased anonymously from a commercial **sperm bank** or that has been donated by a known male. If both women want to conceive, they might decide to use the same sperm donor so that there is a biological link between each child. A same-sex male couple that wants a biological child would have to use the services of a surrogate mother. (We will study surrogacy arrangements in Chapter 16.)

SPERM DONORS

When a husband is involved in AI though AID or AIC, the sperm donor has no rights or duties with respect to the child born with his sperm. The sperm donor, for example, does not have to pay child support. The rights and duties of a sperm donor are not always as clear, however, when AI is used by a lesbian couple or a single heterosexual woman. Not many cases on such insemination have been

EXHIBIT 13.1   Consent for Artificial Insemination (AI)

SECTION I – TO BE COMPLETED BY BIRTH MOTHER AND BIRTH MOTHER'S SPOUSE/CIVIL UNION PARTNER

We, _____ and _____ ,
    (First)   (Middle)   (Last)   *(First)   (Middle)   (Last)*
         (Birth Mother)   **(Birth Mother's Spouse or Civil Union Partner)**

the undersigned, are each 18 years or older.

According to New Jersey law, if, under the supervision of a licensed physician, physician assistant, or advanced practice nurse, and with the consent of her spouse, a woman is inseminated artificially with semen donated by a man not her spouse or partner, the spouse or partner is treated in law as if he were the legal parent of a child thereby conceived. Pursuant to the Civil Union Act, N.J.S.A. 37:1-28, et seq., and New Jersey's recognition of same-sex marriage, female same-sex couples who are married or in a civil union may also avail themselves of the Artificial Insemination Statute.

Our signatures below indicate that we read and understand the above information and that we consent to the performance of artificial insemination with donor semen. We acknowledge that our relationship, rights and obligations to any child born as a result of artificial insemination herein consented to shall be the same for all legal intents and purposes as if the child had been naturally and legitimately conceived by us as a married couple or civil union couple.

We understand if a child is conceived as a result of the artificial insemination consented to herein, then the licensed physician, physician assistant, or advanced practice nurse, is required by law to file a copy of this consent with the Department of Health. Pursuant to N.J.S.A. 9:17-44(a), this document is a confidential record and is not available for public inspection. This document may be subject to inspection upon an order of the court.

Name of Birth Mother	Name of Birth Mother's Spouse or Civil Union Partner
(First) (Middle) (Last)	*(First) (Middle) (Last)*
Signature of Birth Mother	Signature of Birth Mother's Spouse or Civil Union Partner
Date	Date

SECTION II – TO BE COMPLETED BY PHYSICIAN	
Name of Physician, Physician Assistant, or Advanced Practice Nurse,	License Number
(First) (Middle) (Last)	
Practice Name	Telephone Number
Mailing Address (Street)	City State Zip Code

I certify that a child/children will be born to _____ on the anticipated date of delivery of _____ , that the individuals named above appeared before me and signed this form, and that the child /children were conceived as a result of artificial insemination that was performed on the following dates, in accordance with the above consent:

(List dates of insemination within one year prior to child/children's birth.)

Signature of Licensed Physician, Physician Assistant, or Advanced Practice Nurse, Named Above	Date

This consent is valid for one year or until the birth of a live child, whichever occurs first.

Source: New Jersey Department of Health (www.state.nj.us/health/forms/reg-64.pdf).

litigated. The few that do exist say that a donor of semen to someone other than his wife has no parental rights or duties to a child conceived through AI *unless* (1) the donor and the woman have entered into a written contract to the contrary, (2) the donor has established a bonding relationship with the child, or (3) the AI procedure did not comply with local law. (See Chapter 10 on child support for a discussion of the recent Kansas case in which a sperm donor found by a lesbian couple on Craigslist was held to be liable for child support because the couple failed to use a licensed physician for the AI procedure as required by local law.)

AI cases need to be distinguished from cases of one-night stands (or more extended affairs) involving traditional sexual intercourse. The father of a child conceived through the traditional method has the full duties of a father, including the duty to pay child support. It is not a defense for the man to say that he never intended to have or support a child or that his partner agreed with this intent.

As mentioned, sperm banks are facilities that collect and store human sperm. Sperm donors will usually be anonymous to the women who will later use the sperm to try to become pregnant by AI. (Anonymity, however, is not always easy to maintain as we will see.) Sperm banks have become a big business.

Ads for donors often appear in college newspapers and on the Internet. Because sperm is frequently sold to the banks, it is more accurate to say that the men are sperm vendors than sperm donors. Sellers can earn between $50 and $125 per acceptable sample. (Buyers of sperm pay sperm banks between $200 and $800 per vial.) Sperm banks often encourage repeat donations from males with specific characteristics (e.g., college educated, athletic, and no family history of serious disease). Popular donor males have said that the income they received from the sperm banks helped pay for their college education. Not surprisingly, some of these popular donors have fathered multiple children.

The system has worked well, but not without controversy. One sperm bank tried to recruit Nobel Prize winners as sperm donors. Not many came forward. Critics ridiculed the bank as elitist genetic engineering. It is no longer in existence. In 1992, a Virginia fertility doctor was arrested after it was discovered that he was using his own sperm to impregnate his patients through AI. Prosecutors said that he might have fathered up to seventy-five children. In 1991, in what the media called the "scrambled eggs" case, a white woman gave birth to a black child after the sperm bank accidentally injected her with the sperm of a black man. And in 2000, a trial court ordered a sperm bank to reveal the identity of "donor 276" when it became clear that the child born with his sperm had a genetic disease. There was no allegation in the case that the donor had lied about his medical condition when he agreed to donate. Nor was there an allegation that the donee (the mother) was not given sufficient information about the risks of AI. Doctors simply wanted more information about the father to help them in their diagnosis and treatment of the child. The court agreed and ordered the disclosure of the identity of the formerly anonymous donor 276.

ACCIDENTAL INCEST

Accurate statistics on the number of children born through sperm donation do not exist. Estimates vary from 30,000 to 60,000 babies a year. (For information on egg donation, see Chapter 16.) As the numbers of babies from anonymously donated semen increase, *accidental incest* becomes a concern. When the babies grow up, two of them who are unaware of their biological relationship might become sexually intimate. If they produce children, there is a risk of genetic diseases caused by inbreeding.

Even if the danger of incest is small, some health officials are worried about what is called *genetic bewilderment*—stress resulting from confusion about the identity of one's biological parents. Some European countries have passed laws banning the anonymous donation of genetic material, a controversial decision because of the steep decline in sperm donations that result from such laws. Less controversial are laws that limit the number of children that one donor can father.

consanguinity
Relationship by blood.

There is little or no official way for the vast majority of these children to find each other and learn of their potential consanguinity (relationship by blood). The voluntary DNA testing services have had some success in locating unknown relatives. A resource that has become popular is the Donor Sibling Registry, which helps persons conceived as a result of sperm, egg, or embryo donation to find others with whom they have genetic ties.[13] A sperm donor participates by voluntarily giving the registry his donor ID number. Users of sperm banks generally know the ID number of their donor and hence can use the number to search the registry for others who used a male with the same number. The registry claims to have helped connect more than 16,000 half-siblings and/or donors with each other. In one case, the mothers of twenty-one children of the same father established an ongoing network of contact: "These children are all 3 and under, and their families—four lesbian couples, three heterosexual couples and six single mothers—have formed their own Listserv, where photographs of the children (all blond, with a strong familial resemblance) are posted, and daily e-mail messages are exchanged about birthdays, toilet training and the like."[14]

THE END OF ANONYMITY?

Popular home DNA test kits allow anyone to submit a saliva sample to companies that will test it for its DNA (genetic) markers. Those submitting a sample can then construct a family tree, which can be compared to family trees constructed by others who also submitted their DNA samples. The DNA company sends users matches that reveal new family connections. "Results of home DNA tests can be compared among people to find relatives, who will have different amounts of matching DNA, measured in units called centimorgans, depending on their relationship.... Donors who were promised anonymity decades ago are now being contacted by offspring who have tracked them down with the help of consumer DNA tests from companies such as 23andMe and Ancestry, and Facebook groups such as DNA Detectives."[15]

LEGITIMATION

Legitimation confers the status of legitimacy on a nonmarital child. Legitimation is not the same as paternity. A paternity proceeding determines the identity of the biological father; legitimation confers the status of legitimacy on a child who is or who might be a nonmarital child.

States have different methods by which nonmarital children can be legitimated:

legitimation
(1) The declaration that a child is legitimate. The verb is *legitimate.* (2) The steps taken to declare that a child is legitimate.

- *Acknowledgment of paternity.* The father publicly recognizes or acknowledges the nonmarital child as his. States differ on how the acknowledgment takes place. In some states, it must be in writing and witnessed. (For a form acknowledging parentage that is used in many maternity wards, see Exhibit 13.6 at the end of this chapter.) In some states, a written acknowledgment of paternity is not required if the man's activities strongly indicate that he is the father of the child (e.g., the father treats the child the same as the children who were born legitimate).
- *Marriage.* If the mother and father of the nonmarital child marry, some states consider the child as automatically legitimated.
- *Combination of acknowledgment and marriage.* Some states require marriage of the parents, plus some form of acknowledgment by the father.
- *Legitimation proceeding.* A few states have special proceedings by which nonmarital children can be legitimated.
- *Paternity proceedings.* In a few states, a court finding of paternity also legitimates the child.
- *Legitimation by birth.* In some states, all children are legitimate whether or not their parents were married at the time of birth.

ASSIGNMENT   13.2

In what way(s) can an illegitimate child be legitimated in your state? (See General Instructions for the State-Code Assignment in Appendix A.)

PATERNITY

CATEGORIES OF FATHERS

There is no single standard definition of a father. Here are the major categories, some of which overlap:

- *Biological father.* A biological father is a man whose genes contributed to the birth of a child through conception. Also called the *genetic father.*
- *Acknowledged father.* An acknowledged father is a man who has formally declared that he is the father by signing an acknowledgement of paternity.
- *Adjudicated father.* An adjudicated father is a man who has been declared to be the father by a court.
- *Legal father.* A legal father is a man recognized by law as the father because he was married to the mother at the time of conception or birth of the child or because his paternity has been determined by a court.
- *Putative father.* A putative father is a man who is alleged to be the biological father, but who has not yet been medically or legally declared to be the father. Also called *alleged father* or *reputed father.*
- *Intended father.* An intended father is a man who takes affirmative steps to be recognized as the father.
- *Presumed father.* A presumed father is a man who is recognized as (presumed to be) the father until he is medically or legally declared not to be the father. Also called *presumptive father.*
- *Adoptive father.* An adoptive father is a man (often a stepparent) who has adopted a child.

CONSEQUENCES OF DETERMINING PATERNITY

Determining paternity of a nonmarital child can affect many different areas of a child's life as we have seen. Examples include:

- Child support.
- Inheritance from one's father.
- Social Security survivors benefits as the child of a deceased father.
- Insurance claims upon the death of the father.
- Citizenship status as a foreign-born child of a father who is a U.S. citizen.
- The right to share in damages for the wrongful death of a father.
- The child custody and visitation rights of the father.
- The identification of paternal grandparents and siblings.

For many young children, the most important of these consequences is child support from the noncustodial parent (NCP). A major method by which a father is forced to support his nonmarital child is through a paternity proceeding. Other names for this proceeding include a filiation action, a suit to determine parentage, or, in our early history, a *bastardy* proceeding. Once fatherhood is determined, the support obligation is imposed. Paternity proceedings are often instigated by the state to try to recover some of the welfare (public-assistance) money paid to custodial parents (CPs). These parents are required to cooperate in instituting paternity proceedings. The program has been very successful. In 2018, more than 1.4 million paternities were established or acknowledged with the help of state child-support agencies (IV-D agencies) that exist in every state. This is triple the number obtained in 1992.[16]

---

biological father
A man whose genes contributed to the birth of a child through conception. Also called the *genetic father.*

acknowledged father
A man who has formally declared that he is the father by signing an acknowledgement of paternity.

adjudicated father
A man who has been declared to be the father by a court.

legal father
A man recognized by law as the father because he was married to the mother at the time of conception or birth of the child, or because his paternity has been determined by a court.

putative father
A man who is alleged to be the biological father, but who has not yet been medically or legally declared to be the father. Also called *alleged father* and *reputed father.*

intended father
A man who takes affirmative steps to be recognized as the father.

presumed father
A man who is recognized as (presumed to be) the father until he is medically or legally declared not to be the father. Also called *presumptive father.*

adoptive father
A man (often a stepparent) who has adopted a child.

filiation
(1) A judicial determination of paternity. (2) The relation of child to a particular parent.

FEDERAL REQUIREMENTS

Congress has imposed the following federal requirements on paternity to which all states must adhere:

- Allow paternity to be establishment at any time before the child turns eighteen years old.
- Do not attempt to establish paternity in cases involving incest or forcible rape if it would not be in the best interests of the child to establish paternity.
- Do not attempt to establish paternity in cases where adoption proceedings are underway if the state's child support agency (the IV-D agency) believes that it would not be in the best interests of the child to establish paternity.
- Have procedures requiring paternity tests at the request of a child or parent alleging or denying paternity.
- Pay for state-ordered genetic tests (but require the challenging party to reimburse the state for the cost of the test if the test result is negative).
- Order a second paternity tests if the first results are contested (but require the party contesting the test to pay for the costs of the additional test).
- Have simplified procedures to allow males to voluntarily acknowledge paternity at hospitals and birth-records agencies.
- Include the father's name on the child's birth certificate only if both parents sign an acknowledgment of paternity, or if a court order requires both signatures.
- Provide written and oral notice of the consequences of paternity acknowledgement to both parents.
- Permit parties to contest acknowledgments and court orders within sixty days. Thereafter allow challenges only on the basis of fraud, duress, or mistake of fact.
- Admit genetic test results into evidence and create a rebuttable presumption of paternity if test results are positive to a certain probability (e.g., usually 95 percent or higher).
- Require Temporary Assistance to Needy Families (TANF) recipients to cooperate with paternity establishment proceedings in order to be eligible to receive TANF benefits.
- Permit a father to initiate a paternity action.
- Do not allow jury trials in paternity proceeding.[17]

PATERNITY QUESTIONNAIRE

The starting point in establishing paternity is to obtain detailed facts from the mother. The questionnaire in Exhibit 13.2 has this objective.

PATERNITY PROCEEDINGS

In most states, paternity must be established by a **preponderance of the evidence**—the evidence must show that it is more likely than not that the putative father is, in fact, the biological father. Some states, however, require a higher standard of proof: **clear and convincing evidence**. The **statute of limitations** is eighteen years so that the paternity action against the alleged father can be brought at any time before the child reaches the age of majority. In some states, however, there is no statute of limitations. In these states, the paternity action can be brought against the putative father at any time. (Exhibit 13.3 shows an example of a paternity petition.)

preponderance of the evidence
A standard of proof that is met when the evidence establishes that the existence of a disputed fact is more likely than its nonexistence. Also called *fair preponderance of evidence.*

clear and convincing evidence
A standard of proof that is met when the evidence demonstrates that the existence of a disputed fact is much more probable than its nonexistence. This standard is stronger than *preponderance of the evidence* but not as strong as *beyond a reasonable doubt.*

statute of limitations
A law stating that civil or criminal actions are barred if not brought within a specified period of time. The action is time-barred if not brought within that period.

EXHIBIT 13.2 Paternity Questionnaire

Please complete this form to the best of your ability.

CASE NAME

Privacy Statement

The Information Practices Act of 1977 (Civil Code Section 1798.17) and the Federal Privacy Act of 1974 (Public Law 93-579) requires that this notice be provided when collecting personal information from individuals. Information requested on this form, including your Social Security Number, is used by the Department of Child Support Services (DCSS) for purposes of identification and communication with you. The DCSS is required, under Section 466(a)(13) of the Social Security Act, to collect the Social Security Number of any individual who is subject to a divorce decree, support order, or paternity determination or acknowledgement. Social Security Number information is mandatory and will be kept on file at the local child support agency to locate and identify individuals and assets for the purpose of establishing, modifying, and enforcing child support obligations. Enrolling a child in health insurance may require the release of the child's Social Security Number and mailing address to the other parent's employer or the release of the other parent's Social Security Number to the other parent. The information in your case may be discussed with or given to the State, other public agencies that can legally receive such information, and to the other parent or his/her attorney to the extent required by law.

1. Please fill out the following personal information for the mother.

Name of Mother			Date of Mother's Birth
Address	Street	City	State	Zip Code
Social Security Number	Home Phone	Work Phone	Message Phone

2. Please fill out the following personal information for the child.

Name of Child		Date of Birth (or Expected Date)
Place of Birth	Social Security Number	

3. Please fill out the following personal information for the father.

Name of Father			Date of Birth
Last Known Address	Street	City	State	Zip Code
Last Known Phone	Home	Work	Message
Last Known Employment (Type, Business Name)			
Address of Last Known Employment			

Physical Description	Height	Weight	Hair Color	Eye Color	Complexion	Race

5. Were you married when you became pregnant? ☐ Yes ☐ No
If Yes, explain below:

Name of husband	Were you living with your husband at the time you became pregnant? ☐ Yes ☐ No
When did you separate?	Was your husband impotent or sterile at the time you became pregnant? ☐ Yes ☐ No

If you were living with your husband at the time you became pregnant and he was not impotent or sterile, then no further answers are required, sign below. If not, complete PART II after signing below.

If the father of your child(ren) is with you at your interview and will legally acknowledge paternity and cooperate in establishment of paternity, you do not need to complete Parts II and III at this time.

CASE NAME

1. Name of Mother

2. Date you became pregnant | Where?

   Why do you believe that this date is correct?

3. Name the father listed on the birth certificate

   If this is not the same person named in PART I, Question 3, please explain.

4. Did the father agree to the use of his name on your child's birth certificate?
   ☐ Yes ☐ No

5. Has the father ever seen the child? ☐ Yes ☐ No | If Yes, what did he say or do?

6. Did the father give you any money or articles for the child? ☐ Yes ☐ No | Explain:

7. Has the father ever lived with the child? ☐ Yes ☐ No | If Yes, when and where?

8. Did the father ever admit that the child was his? ☐ Yes ☐ No | Explain:

   Give the names and addresses of persons to whom the father has admitted paternity.

9. Is the father willing to sign a statement admitting that he is the father?
   ☐ Yes ☐ No

10. Have you ever received correspondence (cards and letters) from the father referring to your pregnancy, to you as mother, or to the child? ☐ Yes ☐ No | When?

    What did he say?

11. Did you and the father ever live together? ☐ Yes ☐ No | If Yes, give dates.

Exhibit 13.2 (continued)

12. Were you and the father ever married?
☐ Yes ☐ No   If Yes, date of marriage.

Date of separation

13. Did you have any sexual intercourse with anyone else during the month, the month before or the month after you became pregnant?
☐ Yes ☐ No   If Yes, give name(s) and address(es).

If the father of your child(ren) is with you at your interview and will legally acknowledge paternity and cooperate in establishment of paternity, you do not need to complete Parts II and III at this time.

CASE NAME

1. Name of Mother   Name of Father

2. Why do you believe this person is the father of your child?

3. When did you begin dating the father of your child?

4. When and in which city or town did you first have sexual intercourse with the father?

5. When and in which city or town did you last have sexual intercourse with the father?

6. Please give the name(s) and address(es) of people (friends, relatives, neighbors, landlord) who have seen you with the father and where they saw you:

7. Did you ever register at a motel or hotel with the father?   If Yes, where and when?
☐ Yes ☐ No
Please give the name(s) and address(es) of anyone who saw you there together.

8. Did the father use any birth control method?   If Yes, please list the method used.
☐ Yes ☐ No

9. What was the date of your last menstrual period before this pregnancy?

---

10. What was the weight of the child at birth?

11. What was the name of your doctor during pregnancy?

Doctor's Address:

12. Was the father informed of your pregnancy?   By whom?
☐ Yes ☐ No

What did the father say?

Who else was present when he was informed?

13. Did you ever discuss your pregnancy condition with the father?   What was said?
☐ Yes ☐ No

Who else heard the discussions?

14. Did the father ever pay or promise to pay any other money to you during your pregnancy?   Explain:
☐ Yes ☐ No

15. Did the father ever pay or promise to pay any doctor, hospital, or medical bills related to your pregnancy?   Explain:
☐ Yes ☐ No

16. Have you ever written to the father concerning the child?   When?
☐ Yes ☐ No

What did you say?

17. Does the child resemble the father?   In what way?
☐ Yes ☐ No

18. Has the father ever claimed the child on his income tax?   When?
☐ Yes ☐ No

19. Comments

I declare under penalty of perjury that the information on this form is true to the best of my knowledge and belief.

Signature   Day, Month, Year Signed

Executed at   City   County   State

Source: California Department of Child Support Services (2018) (www.childsup.ca.gov/portals/0/cp/docs/dcss0095_english.pdf).

EXHIBIT 13.3   Paternity Petition

FAMILY COURT OF
COUNTY OF
....

In the Matter of a Paternity Proceeding

——————————————————— Petitioner,

—against—

——————————————————— Respondent,
....

Docket No.

PATERNITY PETITION

(Parent)

TO THE FAMILY COURT:

The undersigned Petitioner respectfully shows that:

1. Petitioner resides at ————————————————————————————————.

2. Petitioner had sexual intercourse with the above named Respondent on several occasions covering a period of time beginning on or about the ————— day of ———————, 20 ——, and ending on or about the ————— day of ———————, 20 ——, and as a result thereof (Petitioner) became pregnant.

3. *(a) (Petitioner) gave birth to a (male) (female) child out of wedlock on the ————— day of ———————, 20 ——, at ————————————————————————————————

   *(b) (Petitioner) is now pregnant with a child who is likely to be born out of wedlock.

4. (Respondent) who resides at ————————————————————————————————— is the father of the child.

5. (Respondent) (has acknowledged) (acknowledges) paternity of the child (in writing) (and) (by furnishing support).

6. No previous application has been made to any court or judge for the relief sought herein (except ————————————————————————————————.)

WHEREFORE, Petitioner prays that this Court issue a summons or warrant requiring the Respondent to show cause why the Court should not enter a declaration of paternity, an order of support, and such other and further relief as may be appropriate under the circumstances.

——————————————————
Petitioner

Dated: ——————————, 20 ————,

*Alternative allegations.

REPRESENTATION

In paternity actions, the mother and alleged father can be represented by their own attorneys. In some paternity actions, the child may have his or her separate attorney, often appointed by the court. It can sometimes be important to determine whether the child had separate representation.

Mary, the mother of Sam, brings a paternity proceeding against Kevin, alleging that he is the father of Sam. The court finds that Kevin is not the father of Sam. Ten years later, Sam brings his own action against Kevin for support, alleging that he is the son of Kevin.

res judicata
"A thing adjudicated." A defense raised (a) to prevent the same parties from retrying (relitigating) a claim that has already been resolved on the merits in a prior case or (b) to prevent the litigation of a claim arising out of the same transaction involved in the first case that could have been raised in the first case but was not.

Is Sam's support action ten years later barred by the defense of **res judicata**? That is, was the fatherhood issue already resolved in the paternity proceeding so that it cannot be relitigated? States differ in their answer to this question. Some states will not allow the relitigation. Other states will allow it if Sam was not a formal party in the first case and if he did not have his own separate representation.

A related question is whether the mother can enter into a settlement with the alleged father under which she agrees to drop the paternity proceeding in exchange for the defendant's agreement to pay a certain amount for the support of the child and for the mother's expenses in giving birth to the child. In some states, it is illegal to enter into such an agreement. In states where this type of settlement is permitted, the child must have separate representation and/or the settlement must be approved by the court.

PERSONAL JURISDICTION OVER THE PUTATIVE FATHER

The paternity proceeding requires **personal jurisdiction** over the putative father (see Chapter 7). This generally means that service of process must be made on the defendant in person within the **forum** state (i.e., the state where the paternity proceeding is brought). If the defendant is not a resident of the forum state and is not in the forum state, **long-arm jurisdiction** over him may be obtainable on the ground that he engaged in sexual relations in the state, which may have led to the conception of the child. (Long-arm jurisdiction is the name for personal jurisdiction acquired under the state's long-arm statute.) For other ways to obtain long-arm jurisdiction, see Exhibit 10.7 on the Uniform Interstate Family Support Act (UIFSA) in Chapter 10.

LORD MANSFIELD'S RULE

In a paternity proceeding, it is understandable that a husband would want to raise the defense of **nonaccess**, which is the absence of opportunities for sexual intercourse with the mother around the time of conception. In most states, he is allowed to raise this defense. There was a time, however, when he was not allowed to do so. Under **Lord Mansfield's rule**, the testimony of either spouse was inadmissible on the question of whether the husband had access to the wife at the time of conception if such evidence would tend to "bastardize" the child (i.e., declare the child illegitimate). Hence, under this rule, if a defendant had not had sexual intercourse with his wife in years, he could not give testimony or introduce other evidence to this effect if it would lead to the conclusion that the child of the mother could not be legitimate. In most states today, Lord Mansfield's rule has been abolished so that the defense of nonaccess *can* be used.

PRESUMPTION OF LEGITIMACY

Another major evidentiary rule is the **presumption of legitimacy**—meaning that a child born to a married woman is presumed to be legitimate unless conclusively proven otherwise. This presumption has been called "one of the strongest and most persuasive known to the law."[18] If the defendant is the husband of the mother and denies paternity, he must introduce very strong evidence that he is not the father, e.g., blood or DNA test results or evidence that he is physically incapable of fathering a child because of impotence or sterility. (As indicated, however, when Lord Mansfield's rule applied, the husband or wife could not introduce evidence of nonaccess to rebut the presumption.)

PRESUMPTION OF PATERNITY

The focus of legitimacy is whether a child is a marital child (legitimate) or a nonmarital child (illegitimate). As indicated, most of the major discrimination against nonmarital children has been eliminated. Hence, the law governing *legitimacy* has become much less important than the law governing *paternity*. The focus of paternity is the biological fatherhood of a child.

---

personal jurisdiction
A court's power over a person to determine (adjudicate) his or her personal rights and duties. Also called *in personam jurisdiction*.

forum
(1) A court. (2) The place where the parties are presently litigating their dispute. (3) A court or tribunal hearing a case.

long-arm jurisdiction
The personal jurisdiction that a state acquires over a nonresident defendant under a long-arm statute.

nonaccess
Evidence of the absence of opportunities for sexual intercourse with the mother of a child around the time the child was conceived.

Lord Mansfield's rule
The testimony of either spouse is inadmissible on the question of whether the husband had access to the wife at the time of conception if such evidence would tend to "bastardize" (illegitimize) the child.

presumption of legitimacy
A child born to a married woman is presumed to be legitimate unless conclusively proven otherwise.

presumption of paternity
A man is presumed to be the father of a child if (a) he is married to the mother at the time of conception or birth, (b) the child is born within 300 days after the marriage ends, (c) he marries the mother after the child is born and agrees to support the child, or (d) he receives the child into his home and holds the child out as his own.

When paternity is in doubt, the most definitive way to prove the identity of the biological father is by using scientific tests, such as DNA testing. Before we examine these tests, we need to examine the starting point in many cases—the presumption of paternity. Very often, a statute will define when the presumption exits. For example, the statute may say that a man will be presumed to be the father of a child if (a) he is married to the mother at the time of conception or birth, (b) the child is born within 300 days after the marriage ends, (c) he marries the mother after the child is born and agrees to support the child, or (d) he receives the child into his home and holds the child out as his own. Other factors that the statute might list as triggering the presumption of paternity include signing a formal written acknowledgement of paternity and consenting to have his name placed on the child's birth certificate as the father.

In most cases, a presumption of paternity can be rebutted by acceptable evidence, such as by the results of paternity tests. There are some circumstances, however, in which a party will not be allowed to rebut the presumption, as we will see when we discuss *paternity by estoppel* later in this chapter.

CONFLICTING PRESUMPTIONS OF PATERNITY

Sometimes a conflict of presumptions can occur.

Carol is the daughter of Lena and Frank. When Carol was born, Lena and Frank were married, although they separated and divorced shortly thereafter. When Carol was six months old, Lena and Ted began living together. They never married. For six years, Ted has supported Carol in his home and told everyone that Carol is his child.

In many states, both Frank and Ted are presumed to be the father of Carol, Frank because he was married to the mother at the time of the birth, and Ted because he took Carol into his home and held her out as his child. States handle this conflict of presumptions differently. Some states will give priority to the presumption based on marriage and declare that Frank is presumed to be the father. Other states, however, use policy considerations to resolve the conflict. For example, a court may use the best-interests standard. The concern of the court will be the best interests of the child in deciding which man should be presumed to be the father.

Of course, blood-type or DNA tests can be used to try to resolve competing claims to paternity, as we will see shortly.

THREE PARENTS?

When there are conflicting claims of paternity, is another option to recognize both men as fathers? Can a child have more than two parents? The answer is *no* in most states. California, however, recently said otherwise when it passed a law that said, "In an appropriate action, a court may find that more than two persons with a claim to parentage... are parents if the court finds that recognizing only two parents would be detrimental to the child. In determining detriment to the child, the court shall consider all relevant factors, including, but not limited to, the harm of removing the child from a stable placement with a parent who has fulfilled the child's physical needs and the child's psychological needs for care and affection, and who has assumed that role for a substantial period of time. A finding of detriment to the child does not require a finding of unfitness of any of the parents or persons with a claim to parentage."[19]

In the multiple-parent arrangement envisioned by the California law, only two of the parents are genetically related to the child. In most cases, the third parent would be an adult who has formed a bonding relationship with the child without adopting the child or having a genetic link to him or her. In Chapter 16, however, we will consider the more dramatic question of whether it is possible for a child to have three parents (two women and a man), all of whom are genetically related to the child.

EVIDENCE OF PATERNITY

We turn now to an examination of the kind of evidence that can be considered by a court in paternity cases. In most of these cases, an unmarried man is trying to prove that he is not the father, or a married man (the presumed father) is trying to overcome the presumption that he is. In our early history, courts had few tools to help them decide whether a man had fathered a particular child: "Indeed, in former times, the most scientific method conceivable was to hold the child up before the jury for its consideration of whether it bore a physical resemblance to the putative father. Things have changed."[20]

Blood-Grouping Tests

The discovery of human blood groups and types has been of great assistance in paternity cases because they:

• Can be determined at birth or shortly thereafter,

• Remain constant throughout an individual's life, and

• Are inherited.

It is also possible for blood tests to determine paternity during pregnancy, although such tests are not often performed.

Here is what the U.S. Supreme Court has said about the operation and effectiveness of blood group tests:

> If the blood groups and types of the mother and child are known, the possible and impossible blood groups and types of the true father can be determined under the rules of inheritance. For example, a group AB child cannot have a group O parent, but can have a group A, B, or AB parent. Similarly, a child cannot be type M unless one or both parents are type M, and the factor rh' cannot appear in the blood of a child unless present in the blood of one or both parents. Since millions of men belong to the possible groups and types, a blood grouping test cannot conclusively establish paternity. However, it can demonstrate nonpaternity, such as where the alleged father belongs to group O and the child is group AB. It is a negative rather than an affirmative test with the potential to scientifically exclude the paternity of a falsely accused putative father. The ability of blood grouping tests to exonerate innocent putative fathers was confirmed by a 1976 report developed jointly by the American Bar Association and the American Medical Association. . . . The joint report recommended the use of seven blood test "systems" [ABO, Rh, MNSs, Kell, Duffy, Kidd, and HLA] when investigating questions of paternity. These systems were found to be reasonable in cost and to provide a 91% cumulative probability of negating paternity for erroneously accused Negro men and 93% for white men. The effectiveness of the seven systems attests the probative value of blood test evidence in paternity cases.[21]

DNA Testing

The effectiveness of paternity testing continues to increase significantly. Although traditional blood tests work on the principle of exclusion, **DNA testing** has the potential to go beyond exclusion to positive identification of the biological father.[22] Genes are the hereditary units that determine the particular characteristics

DNA testing
Genetic testing on deoxyribonucleic acid removed from cells.

of living organisms. The hereditary units consist of a DNA sequence. (DNA stands for deoxyribonucleic acid.) Hence, genetic testing for paternity is referred to as DNA testing.

The success of the test is due to the fact that the configuration of DNA is different in virtually all individuals except in identical twins. DNA, the "blueprint of life," determines each person's unique genetic individuality. The chances that two unrelated persons will have the same DNA fingerprint are as low as one in 30 billion. Although some authorities assert that this calculation of odds is exaggerated, there is almost universal agreement that DNA evidence is highly reliable.

To begin the test, the most common procedure is to remove DNA from cells obtained in a blood sample of a mother, child, and possible father. An alternative to drawing blood is to use a "buccal swab." To obtain cells by this method (most often used on small children), a cotton swab is rubbed on the inside of a person's cheeks.

Three separate tiers or determinations are made:

- Probability of exclusion.
- Paternity index.
- Probability of paternity.

The results will often state that:

- The tested man is not the biological father of the child, or
- The probability is greater than 99.9 percent that the tested man is the biological father of the child in comparison to the general population of men of the same race.

See Exhibit 13.4 for a sample DNA test result.

One consequence of the effectiveness of these tests is that most disputed paternity cases today are resolved on the basis of the tests rather than by a court trial. Testing, however, can be expensive. If the putative father is **indigent**, the state must pay for the tests. If he refuses to undergo the tests, many states will either force him to be tested or allow the trial court to take his refusal into consideration in making the paternity decision. The strong implication of such a refusal is that he has something to hide—his fatherhood.

Many states provide state-appointed counsel for an indigent putative father in these proceedings. As we saw in Chapter 10, if the state is charging a putative father with **civil contempt** for failure to pay child support (in which disputed paternity may have to be resolved), the state is not *required* to provide him with a free attorney if the mother is unrepresented and if the state provides procedural protections such as an opportunity to be heard and clear notice that he can avoid imprisonment if he is unable to pay child support.

indigent
Poor; without means to afford something such as a private attorney or filing fees.

civil contempt
The refusal of a party to comply with a court order (usually issued for the benefit of another), which can lead to punishment (including incarceration) until the party complies with the order.

ASSIGNMENT   13.3

Prepare a flowchart of all the procedural steps taken in your state to resolve contested paternity. (See General Instructions for the Flowchart Assignment Appendix A.)

Private DNA testing centers exist in every state. Testing has become big business. In some states, mobile testing is available. (See Exhibit 13.5 for an example of a mobile testing service.)

EXHIBIT 13.4 Sample DNA Test Result

the GENETICA DNA Test™

No. 79746 897	MOTHER	CHILD	ALLEGED FATHER
Patient Name	XXXX XXXXX	YYYY XXXXX	ZZZZ ZZZZZ
Date of Birth	January 1, 1979	January 1, 2011	January 1, 1975
Race	Caucasian		Caucasian
Date Collected	May 16, 2011	May 16, 2011	May 16, 2011
Test Number	79746-1	79746-2	79746-3

Genetic Systems Tested	Allele		Allele		Allele	
TPOX 2p23-2pter PI 1.25	7	9		9	8	9
D2S1338 2q35-37.1 PI 2.64	14	16	17	16	17	20
D3S1358 3p PI 4.21	15	16	15	18	17	18
FGA 4q28 PI 3.24	19	20		20		20
D5S818 5q21-31 PI 3.11	11	12	11	12	11	12
CSF1PO 5q33.3-34 PI 1.79	10	11	10	13	11	13
D7S820 7q PI 2.18	9	10	9	11	10	11
D8S1179 8 PI 5.69	12	14	12		12	
THO1 11p15.5 PI 1.45	9		9	6.3	8	6.3
vWA 12p12-pter PI 3.77	16	18	17	18	17	19
D13S317 13q22-31 PI 7.04	10	12	10		10	13
D16S539 16q24-qter PI 1.47	11		11		11	12
D18S51 18q21.3 PI 2.89	11	12	13	12	13	14
D19S433 19q12-13.1 PI 3.17	13.2	15		15	16	15
D21S11 21q11.2-q21 PI 5.21	29	31	28	31	28	30

Interpretation: Combined Parentage Index **8,393,003** Probability of Parentage **99.9999%**
The alleged father, ZZZZ ZZZZZ, cannot be excluded as the biological father of the child named YYYY XXXXX. Based on testing results obtained from analyses of 15 different DNA probes, the probability of paternity is 99.9999%. This probability of paternity is calculated by comparing to an untested, unrelated man of the North American Caucasian population (assumes prior probability equals .50). This DNA Parentage Test excluded greater than 99.99% of the male population from the possibility of being the biological father of the tested child.

COURT/ADMIN Case No.:   Report Date **May 17, 2011**

Source: Genetica, DNA Laboratories, Inc. 1737 Tennessee Ave, Cincinnati, OH, 45229, www.genetica.com.

will give him standing but may impose a time limit within which he must bring the suit to establish his paternity (e.g., within two years after the birth of the child). Other states would deny him standing. seek relief from a court.

A state that denied standing to the biological father came before the U.S. Supreme Court in 1989. The Court held that it is constitutional for a state to favor a husband (the presumed father) over a biological father and deny standing to the latter.[23] In this case, the plaintiff, Michael, sought to establish paternity of a child born to a woman who was married to (and still cohabitating with) another man, Gerald. Despite the fact that blood tests indicated a 98.07 percent probability that Michael was the father and the fact that Michael had established a relationship with the child, the court upheld the rights of the husband (Gerald) as the presumed father and denied Michael any rights. Under California's version of the presumption of legitimacy, only the husband and wife could rebut the presumption and neither wanted to do so in this case even though both knew that the husband was not the father. Hence it is constitutional for a state to deny the right of a biological father to prove that he is the father if the mother of the child was married to someone else when the child was born. A judge in another case commented that "interlopers" like Michael should not be allowed to "use their own adulterous behavior as a license to invade and disrupt the matrimonial circle."[24]

Not all states, however, go as far as California in their law on standing in paternity actions. There are states that will give standing to third parties (such as Michael) to prove their paternity if certain restrictions are met, such as the requirement that the suit be brought within two years after the child is born.

PATERNITY BY ESTOPPEL

equitable estoppel
The voluntary conduct of a person will preclude him or her from asserting rights against another who justifiably relied on the conduct and who would suffer damage or injury if the person were now allowed to repudiate the conduct. Also called *estoppel in pais*.

paternity by estoppel
Paternity that is established when a court does not allow the presumption of paternity to be rebutted even though there is no biological relationship between the presumed (putative) father and the child.

Suppose that a husband is the presumed (putative) father of a child under the presumption of paternity, but his wife denies that he is the father. In some cases, equitable estoppel will prevent her from asserting this denial despite paternity tests that prove she is right. In equitable estoppel, the voluntary conduct of a person will preclude him or her from asserting rights against another who justifiably relied on the conduct and who would suffer damage or injury if the person were now allowed to repudiate the conduct.

When equitable estoppel prevents a mother from denying paternity, the result is called paternity by estoppel. The court does not allow the presumption of paternity to be rebutted even though there is no biological relationship between the presumed (putative) father and the child. As we will see in the *Pettinato* case, the mother's conduct equitably estopped her from denying the paternity of her husband who, in fact, was not the biological father of her child.

CASE

Pettinato v. Pettinato
582 A.2d 909 (1990)
Supreme Court of Rhode Island

Background: *Gregory Pettinato sued Susanne Pettinato for divorce and custody of Gregory, Jr. During the litigation, she denied that he was the father. The Family Court granted the divorce and gave custody to the father. The case is now on appeal brought by Susanne before the Supreme Court of Rhode Island.*

Decision on Appeal: *Affirmed. Susanne is estopped from denying Gregory's paternity.*

OPINION OF THE COURT:

Justice Shea delivered the opinion of the court. . . .

Although many of the facts were disputed, it appears that a relationship developed between Gregory and Susanne

in the fall of 1984. The parties disagreed about the date when they began sexual relations. However, it is undisputed that the parties were engaging in sexual relations by February 1985. Susanne testified that she did not engage in sexual relations with Gregory between February 14, 1985, and April 7, 1985. During that period she traveled to Florida for two weeks. Moreover, Susanne testified, she did not speak with Gregory until after November 1985 when she returned to Rhode Island from her second trip to Florida.

Susanne gave birth to Gregory, Jr., on January 5, 1986. Despite the parties' discrepancies regarding events leading to the child's birth, Gregory was named as the child's father on the birth certificate filed on January 13, 1986.

Susanne testified that she told Gregory while in the hospital after giving birth that Gregory, Jr., was the child of the man she had stayed with while in Florida. Gregory disputed this testimony. He testified that Susanne telephoned him in April 1985, informed him of her pregnancy, and stated that he, Gregory, was the father. Gregory first became aware of Susanne's denial of his paternity at the time of this divorce action when she filed her answers to interrogatories.

The evidence established that the parties had a fairly nomadic existence after the birth of Gregory, Jr. For approximately one month after the child's birth, Susanne and the child lived at her parents' home. Gregory was forbidden by her parents to visit Susanne or Gregory, Jr., although the parties would arrange to meet at a friend's house without the knowledge of Susanne's parents. Thereafter, Susanne and the child shared a rented apartment with a friend for approximately three months before moving into an apartment with Gregory.

Gregory, Susanne, and Gregory, Jr., lived in an apartment from May 1986 until October 1986. All three then moved into Gregory's parents' home in October 1986. Gregory and Susanne married on December 21, 1986. Gregory testified that he married Susanne because he "thought it would be the proper thing to do to make a family and be on our own together and bring up our child." The parties remained at his parents' home until Susanne moved out on April 26, 1987. Susanne initially left Gregory, Jr., with Gregory and his parents. Susanne testified, however, that the Cranston police retrieved Gregory, Jr., the next day and brought the child to her at a friend's home. . . .

Over the objections of Gregory, the court heard testimony from Marjorie Kimball, a medical technologist at the Rhode Island Blood Center. Kimball testified that she performed genetic blood testing on Gregory, Susanne, and Gregory, Jr. As a result of this genetic blood testing, Kimball concluded that it was not possible for Gregory to be the biological father of Gregory, Jr.

The trial justice issued an interlocutory decision pending entry of final judgment on October 11, 1988. He granted the petition of Gregory for an absolute divorce and awarded Gregory permanent custody of Gregory, Jr., subject to all reasonable rights of visitation for Susanne. In his decision the trial justice based the award on the care given Gregory, Jr., by Gregory, the length of time Gregory, Jr., spent with Gregory, and the bonding that had occurred between Gregory, Jr., and Gregory. . . .

On appeal Susanne argues that the trial justice improperly overlooked and/or misconceived the expert testimony regarding the genetic blood testing that excluded Gregory as the biological father of Gregory, Jr. Susanne contends that as the natural parent of Gregory, Jr., she is entitled to custody of the child absent a showing of unfitness. . . .

In this case we consider for the first time the rights of parents whose legal presumption of paternity is later challenged during a divorce proceeding. It is undisputed that Gregory is the presumptive natural father of Gregory, Jr. . . .

[Rhode Island statutes provide as follows:]

§ 15–8–3 Presumption of paternity:

(a) A man is to be the natural father of a child if: . . . (3) After the child's birth, he and the child's natural mother have married, or attempted to marry, each other by a marriage solemnized in apparent compliance with law, although the attempted marriage could be declared invalid, and: (i) He has acknowledged his paternity of the child in writing filed with the clerk of the [F]amily [C]ourt; or (ii) With his consent, he is named as the child's father on the child's birth certificate; or, (iii) He is obligated to support the child under a written voluntary promise or by court order; (4) He acknowledges his paternity of the child in a writing filed with the clerk of the [F]amily [C]ourt, who shall promptly inform the mother of the filing of the acknowledgement, and she does not dispute the acknowledgement, within a reasonable time after being informed thereof, in a writing filed with the clerk of the [F]amily [C]ourt. If another man is presumed under this section to be the child's father, acknowledgement may be effected only with the written consent of the presumed father or after the presumption has been rebutted.

(b) A presumption under this section may be rebutted in an appropriate action only by clear and convincing evidence. If two (2) or more presumptions arise which conflict with each other, the presumption which on its facts is founded on the weightier considerations of policy and logic controls. The presumption is rebutted by a court decree establishing paternity of the child by another man.

Susanne admits that Gregory has met the requirements of § 15–8–3(a)(3)(ii). The parties married after Gregory, Jr.'s birth, and with his consent Gregory was named as the child's father on the birth certificate. Nevertheless, Susanne contends, the results of the genetic blood testing that excluded Gregory as the biological father provide the "clear and convincing" evidence required by § 15–8–3(b) to rebut the presumption of Gregory's paternity.

We are concerned about the situation before the court wherein a mother can tell a man that he is the father of her child, marry him and live together as a family, and then illegitimize the child during a divorce proceeding by attacking the legal presumption of paternity that she helped to bring about. The situation before us is a matter of first impression in this state. After reviewing the conclusions arrived at by other states that have considered this issue, we have reached the conclusion that Susanne may not defeat Gregory's legal presumption of paternity.

We are of the opinion that a mother should be equitably estopped from using the genetic blood testing permitted by § 15–8–11 to disestablish a child's paternity in connection with a routine divorce proceeding. The underlying rationale of the equitable estoppel doctrine is that "under certain circumstances, a person might be estopped from challenging paternity where that person has by his or her conduct accepted a given person as father of the child." *John M. v. Paula T.*, 524 Pa. 306, 318, 571 A.2d 1380, 1386 (1990). Where the equitable-estoppel doctrine is operative, evidence of genetic blood tests is considered irrelevant in a divorce proceeding wherein the basic issue is the termination of the marriage bond—not the paternity of a child. "[T]he law will not permit a person in these situations to challenge the status which he or she has previously accepted [or created]." Id.

(continued)

The circumstances of the case before us, in our opinion, compel the application of the equitable estoppel doctrine. Gregory has represented himself to be and has been accepted as Gregory, Jr.'s natural father. He married Susanne, believing her representation that the child was his child. He married her with the intention that the couple would raise their child in a family unit. Gregory consented to being named as the father on Gregory, Jr.'s birth certificate. The three lived together and represented themselves to the community as a family. Susanne never questioned Gregory's paternity until after he commenced divorce proceedings that followed her leaving him. At the time he filed for divorce, Susanne had become pregnant again but not by Gregory.

Taken together, this court's adherence to the statutory presumption of paternity in § 15–8–3(a)(3)(ii) and the court's application of the equitable-estoppel doctrine lead to the same point: the genetic blood test results offered into evidence were not relevant because legal paternity had been established and biological paternity was not at issue. *Scott v. Mershon*, 394 Pa. Super. 411, 417–418, 576 A.2d 67, 71 (1990). Therefore, the genetic blood test results disestablishing Gregory's paternity should not have been admitted. We reject Susanne's contention that the trial justice overlooked and/or misconceived the expert testimony regarding genetic blood testing. That testimony should have been excluded as irrelevant on Gregory's objection to its admission. . . .

For these reasons the defendant's appeal is denied and dismissed, the judgment appealed from is affirmed, and the papers of the case are remanded to the Family Court.

ASSIGNMENT 13.4

a. What is the difference between legal paternity and biological paternity? Why was the distinction important in the *Pettinato* case?

b. Assume that the paternity issue is not raised in the divorce case and that Susanne is granted custody of the son. Years later, Gregory refuses to pay child support. In a support action against him, he wants to introduce evidence of the genetic blood tests that prove he is not the father. Can he introduce this evidence?

c. In Chapter 9 on child custody, we discussed at length the U.S. Supreme Court case of *Troxel v. Granville*, which said that a fit parent has a fundamental constitutional right to raise his or her child against the wishes of a grandparent or other nonparent. Was Susanne Pettinato's fundamental constitutional right as a parent violated in the *Pettinato* case? Phrased another way, is *Pettinato v. Pettinato* consistent with *Troxel v. Granville*?

PARALEGAL ROLES

- For an overview of paralegal roles in family-law cases, see Exhibits 1.5 and 1.6 in Chapter 1.
- For many of the financial issues related to paternity covered in Chapter 13, a paralegal may be asked to help collect documents and facts outlined in:
  - The checklist in Exhibit 3.1 of Chapter 3.
  - The interrogatories in Appendix C.
- Miscellaneous duties:
  - Do fact research on the sperm bank used by or being considered for use by the client.
  - Assist the client in obtaining and filling out the paternity questionnaire for the child-support agency (the IV-D agency) and the court.
  - Explain the various paternity test options used in the state.
  - Investigate the chain of custody for the specimen used by the lab to assess paternity (e.g., who received it, when, and who handled it after the testing).
  - Prepare a preliminary draft of the paternity petition.
  - Draft documents needed for a legitimation proceeding.
  - Assist the client in filing for Social Security survivors benefits.
  - Investigate facts that tend to show whether the father took the child into his home, formed a bonding relationship with the child, and let the world know that the child was his.
  - Obtain birth certificates, hospital records, and other relevant documents.

SUMMARY

An illegitimate (nonmarital) child is one born to parents who are not married at the time of birth, who never married thereafter, and who never took the steps needed to legitimate the child. At one time, an illegitimate child had very few rights. This situation has changed, although discrimination between marital and nonmarital children has not been entirely eliminated. Nonmarital children are a quasi-suspect class; the constitutionality of discrimination against them is measured by the intermediate-scrutiny test. A nonmarital child can inherit from his or her father if the father dies intestate. Some states insist, however, that paternity be established before the intestate parent dies. Whether nonmarital children are included in the phrases "to my children" or "to my heirs" in the will of a testate father depends on the intent of the father.

Marital and nonmarital children have the same right to be supported, to bring wrongful death actions because of the death of a parent, and to receive workers' compensation benefits if the parent dies on the job. If the nonmarital child dies a wrongful death, a state can require the father to have legitimated the child before death in order to sue for his child's wrongful death. To obtain Social Security survivors benefits, a nonmarital child must prove that he or she was dependent on a deceased father, whereas the law presumes the dependence of a marital child. Children conceived (via artificial insemination—AI) after the death of their father can qualify for survivors benefits if they are entitled to inherit from their father under state law. Nonmarital children of annulled marriages are legitimate. The government can impose different requirements for citizenship of a nonmarital child born abroad to a citizen-mother as opposed to a citizen-father.

In most states, when a child is born through artificial insemination (AI) with the semen of a man other than the husband, the husband has a duty to support the child, and the child is considered legitimate if the husband consented to the AI and the AI was accomplished through a medically approved procedure. A donor of semen to someone other than his wife has no parental rights or duties to a child conceived through AI unless (1) the donor and the woman have entered into a written

contract to the contrary, (2) the donor has established a bonding relationship with the child, or (3) the AI procedure did not comply with local law.

Legitimation can occur in a number of ways: acknowledgment of paternity, marriage of the mother and father, legitimation proceeding, paternity proceeding, etc. In some states, all children are legitimate regardless of the marital status of their parents.

Categories of fathers include: biological father, acknowledged father, adjudicated father, legal father, putative (alleged) father, intended father, presumed father, and adoptive father. A major function of a paternity proceeding is to establish a father's duty of support. For this purpose, the court must have personal jurisdiction over the alleged father. The child should be joined as a party in the proceeding to ensure that the judgment will be binding on the child. In a paternity proceeding, if the defendant is married to the mother, he may face a number of evidentiary obstacles at the trial (e.g., the presumption of paternity). If more than one man is presumed to be the father of a child, the conflict might be resolved by giving preference to the married father or by assessing the best interests of the child.

Traditional blood-group testing can help establish the nonpaternity, though not the paternity, of a particular defendant. More modern scientific techniques such as DNA testing can establish a high probability of paternity. Another way that paternity can be established is by signing a voluntary recognition of parentage (ROP).

Some states deny standing to a man who wants to prove that he is the father of a child born to a woman married to another man. A state can subordinate his rights as a biological father to the rights of the husband as the presumed father even if the husband is not the biological father. Some states, however, will give the biological father standing to prove his paternity.

Equitable estoppel can prevent a person from denying the paternity of a particular person. Paternity by estoppel is paternity that is established when a court does not allow the presumption of paternity to be rebutted even though there is no biological relationship between the presumed (putative) father and the child.

KEY TERMS

legitimate child	classification	wrongful death
illegitimate child	equal protection of law	workers' compensation
bastard	quasi-suspect class	survivors benefits
bastardy	intermediate-scrutiny test	in vitro fertilization (IVF)
filius nullius	intestate	annulment
kin	paternity	artificial insemination (AI)
Uniform Parentage Act (UPA)	testate	sperm bank

consanguinity	filiation	presumption of legitimacy
legitimation	preponderance of the evidence	presumption of paternity
biological father	clear and convincing evidence	DNA testing
acknowledged father	statute of limitations	indigent
adjudicated father	res judicata	civil contempt
legal father	personal jurisdiction	putative father registry
putative father	forum	standing
intended father	long-arm jurisdiction	equitable estoppel
presumed father	nonaccess	paternity by estoppel
adoptive father	Lord Mansfield's rule	

CHECK THE CITE

Walter Little denies that he is the father of Kenyatta. He asked the court to order a blood test in order to prove his claim. At the time, Walter was incarcerated and could not afford the cost of the blood test. He therefore asked the state to pay for the test. How did the U.S. Supreme Court rule on his request and what reasons did the Court give for its decision? Read *Little v. Streater*, 452 U.S. 1 (1981). To read the opinion online: (1) Run a citation search ("452 US 1") in the *Case law* database of Google Scholar (scholar.google.com). (2) Run the citation search ("452 U.S. 1") in the general search engines of Google, Bing or Yahoo.

PROJECT

Using Google, Bing, or Yahoo, locate the sites for two different sperm banks. Select banks that have information on their sites that describe government laws and regulations that the bank must follow for the state where its primary office is located. Describe these laws and regulations as explained by the sites. Do not simply copy what the sites say. Prepare a report in which you compare what the two different sites say about the relevant laws and regulations. Indicate which site is more comprehensive in describing the laws and regulations. After you have completed the description, select any of the laws or regulations mentioned on one of the sites. Find that law or regulation on the Internet. Give the citation to the Internet address where you found it and quote any sentence in the law or regulation itself.

ETHICS IN A FAMILY LAW PRACTICE

You are a paralegal working at the law office of James Adams, Esq. On November 10, 2017, Adams is assigned by the court to represent John Edwinson against whom a paternity petition has been filed. There is a hearing scheduled for March 13, 2018. Edwinson is not a cooperative client. He frequently misses appointments at the law office. Frustrated, Adams sends Edwinson a short letter on March 10, 2018, that says, "Due to your noncooperation, I am withdrawing from the case as your representative effective immediately." Any ethical problems?

WRITING SAMPLE

The writing sample for this chapter will be a brief of a recent opinion of a state court in your state on paternity. The paternity opinion must involve a dispute over who is the father of a particular child. The brief should cover the name of the case, citation, facts, issues, holding, and reasoning. To find the opinion:

• In Google, Bing, or Yahoo, run the following search: aa paternity (substitute the name of your state for aa in the search).

Or:

• In Google Scholar (scholar.google.com), run the following search in the "Case law" database: aa paternity (substitute the name of your state for aa in the search).

Your instructor will let you know of any special instructions on preparing the brief. For additional guidance, run the search "how to brief a case" in Google, Bing, or Yahoo. (See General Instructions for the Writing Sample in Appendix A.)

REVIEW QUESTIONS

1. What is an illegitimate (nonmarital) child?
2. What was the status of nonmarital children at common law?
3. What does the Uniform Parentage Act say about the distinction between marital and nonmarital children?
4. What is the intermediate-scrutiny test for a classification based on legitimacy?
5. What distinctions, if any, exist between marital and nonmarital children on inheritance rights, suing for wrongful death, workers' compensation, Social Security survivors benefits, annulment, and immigration?
6. What will-interpretation problem might exist upon the death of the father of a nonmarital child?
7. Who has the duty of child support for a nonmarital child?
8. Can a child born or conceived after the death of his or her biological parent receive Social Security survivors benefits?
9. What is the status and duty of a husband who consents to the artificial insemination (AI) of his wife with the semen of another man, and what is the status of the child born from that AI?
10. What is the status of semen donors other than the husband?
11. What problems can result from the use of sperm banks?
12. In what ways can legitimation of a nonmarital child occur?
13. Define the different categories of father.
14. What are the consequences and benefits of establishing paternity?
15. What are the federal paternity requirements imposed by Congress?
16. What is the standard of proof in a paternity action?
17. What is the statute of limitations for bringing a paternity action against an alleged father?
18. What are the possible consequences of a child not having his or her own attorney in a paternity action?
19. What kind of jurisdiction is needed over a putative father?
20. What is Lord Mansfield's rule?
21. What is the presumption of legitimacy?
22. What is the presumption of paternity and when does it arise?
23. When could there be conflicting presumptions of paternity, and how will a court resolve the conflict?
24. How can blood-grouping and DNA tests be used in paternity cases?
25. Can a state prevent a man from proving that he is the biological father of a child given birth by a woman still married to another man?
26. What are equitable estoppel and paternity by estoppel?

HELPFUL WEBSITES

Your State

See Appendix D for links to the family law of your state on the topics covered in this chapter.

Paternity

- www.hg.org/paternity-law.html
- family.findlaw.com/paternity/paternity-law.html
- en.wikipedia.org/wiki/Paternity_(law)
- members.peak.org/~jedwards/paternity.html

Uniform Parentage Act

- apps.leg.wa.gov/rcw/default.aspx?cite=26.26

Paternity Establishment: State Use of Genetic Testing

- oig.hhs.gov/oei/reports/oei-06-98-00054.pdf

Voluntary Establishment of Paternity

- www.acf.hhs.gov/css/resource/voluntary-establishment-of-paternity

Donor Sibling Registry

- www.donorsiblingregistry.com

Father Knows Best, But Which Father

- digitalcommons.lmu.edu/cgi/viewcontent.cgi?article=1696&context=llr

Paternity Fraud

- www.paternityfraud.com

Paternity Forms

- www.uslegalforms.com/paternity

Gay and Lesbian Parents

- www.therainbowbabies.com

Google Scholar (scholar.google.com)

- Choose "Articles" and enter in the search box any of the key terms discussed in the chapter. Add the name of your state to the search term.
- Choose "Case law" and "Select courts". Select your state, click "Done," and enter in the search box any of the key terms discussed in the chapter. Add the name of your state to the search term.

Google, Bing, or Yahoo

(on these search engines, run the following searches, substituting your state for "aa")

- paternity aa
- bastardy aa
- paternity fraud aa
- sperm bank aa

- "Lord Mansfield's rule" aa
- genetic test paternity aa
- DNA paternity law aa
- "paternity by estoppel" aa
- "illegitimate child" aa
- "Uniform Parentage Act" aa
- paternity forms aa
- legitimation child aa
- "presumed father" aa
- "presumption of legitimacy" aa
- "presumption of paternity" aa
- gay lesbian paternity aa

YouTube

Run the same searches on YouTube listed above for Google, Bing, Yahoo searches. Even when the video clips are trying to entice you to retain an attorney, buy a book, or enroll in a course, they can provide useful overviews and references to primary authority.

Twitter, Reddit, and Facebook

On Twitter, Reddit, and Facebook, run the following searches (substitute your state for aa in your searches; run the searches with and without the name of your state). Look for links to family-law developments in your state.

- paternity aa
- legitimation aa
- DNA testing aa
- men's rights aa

ENDNOTES

Note: All or most of the court opinions in these endnotes can be read online. To do so, go to Google Scholar (scholar.google.com), select "Case law," and in the search box, enter the cite (e.g., "406 U.S. 164") or name of the case (e.g., "Weber v. Aetna Casualty & Surety Co") that is given in the endnote.

[1] National Center for Health Statistics, www.cdc.gov/nchs/fastats/unmarried-childbearing.htm (2017).

[2] Uniform Parentage Act, § 202 (2017) (www.uniformlaws.org).

[3] *Weber v. Aetna Casualty & Surety Co.,* 406 U.S. 164, 175 (1972).

[4] *Trimble v. Gordon,* 430 U.S. 762 (1977).

[5] *Lalli v. Lalli,* 439 U.S.259 (1978).

[6] *Parham v. Hughes,* 441 U.S. 347 (1979).

[7] *Weber v. Aetna Casualty & Surety Co.,* supra note 3.

[8] *Mathews v. Lucas,* 427 U.S. 495 (1976).

[9] *Astrue v. Capato,* 566 U.S. 541 (2012).

[10] *Nguyen v. Immigration and Naturalization Service,* 533 U.S. 53 (2001). See also *Flores-Villar,* 564 U.S. 210 (2011), affirming *U.S. v. Flores-Villar,* 536 F.3d 990 (9th Cir. 2008). Once it is clear, however, that a connecting relationship has been developed with the unwed father, other requirements (such as length of physical presence in the United States needed to convey automatic citizenship) cannot favor unwed mothers over unwed fathers. *Sessions v. Morales-Santana,* 137 S. Ct. 1678 (2017).

[11] Alice Park, *The Next Frontier in Fertility Treatments Time,* January 14, 2019, at 42.

[12] For a state that has adopted the Uniform Parentage Act, see Minnesota Statutes, § 257.56 (1987) (www.revisor. mn.gov/statutes/?id=257.56). States can always make changes in uniform laws. Minnesota, for example, uses the phrase "biological father" rather than "natural father" in the statute quoted in the text.

[13] www.donorsiblingregistry.com.

[14] Jennifer Egan, *Wanted: A Few Good Sperm,* N.Y. Times Magazine (Mar. 19, 2006).

[15] Emily Chung et. al, *Donor-Conceived People Are Tracking Down Their Biological Fathers, Even If They Want To Hide,* CBC NEWS (www.cbc.ca/news/technology/sperm-donor-dna-testing-1.4500517) (August 20, 2018).

[16] Office of Child Support Enforcement, *Preliminary Report FY 2018,* Table P-71, p. 77 (2019) (www.acf.hhs.gov/sites/default/files/programs/css/fy_2018_preliminary_data_report.pdf).,

[17] National Conference of State Legislators, *Establishing Paternity,* (March 19, 2014) (www.ncsl.org/research/human-services/enforcement-establishing-paternity.aspx).

[18] *In re Findlay,* 170 N.E. 471, 472 (N.Y. 1930).

[19] California Family Code § 7612(c) (codes.findlaw.com/ca/family-code/fam-sect-7612.html).

[20] *J.A.S. v. Bushelman,* 342 S.W.3d 850, 861 (Ky. 2011).

[21] *Little v. Streater,* 452 U.S. 1, 7-8 (1981)(emphasis added).

[22] Note, *Implications of DNA Testing on Posthumous Paternity Determination,* 35 Boston College Law Review 747, 798 (1994).

[23] *Michael H. v. Gerald D.,* 491 U.S. 110 (1989).

[24] *J.A.S.* supra note 20 at 866 (Ky. 2011)(dissent).

CHAPTER 14

The Legal Status of Children

CHAPTER OUTLINE

CHAPTER OBJECTIVES

After completing this chapter, you should be able to:

- Know in what sense minority is a disability.

- Explain emancipation and how a minor achieves it.

- List the contracts that a minor can and cannot disaffirm.

- State when, if ever, a parent has the right to keep a child's real and personal property (including earnings).

- State how a minor acquires a domicile.

- State when a child can write a will and what duties a guardian has when the parent of a minor dies and when a minor inherits property.

- Explain the requirement of compulsory education, when corporal punishment is allowed in school, and what constitutional rights students have.

- State the meaning of child maltreatment, child neglect, child abuse, dependency, and abandonment.

- Know when a parent's substance abuse can constitute child maltreatment.

- Explain the meaning of parens patriae.

- List the goals of the Child Abuse Prevention and Treatment Act (CAPTA).

- Explain mandatory reporting.

- Distinguish between the jurisdictional and dispositional stages of court proceedings on child maltreatment.

- Define juvenile delinquency and status offenses, and state how they are treated in the courts.

AGE OF MAJORITY AND EMANCIPATION

In most states and for most purposes, an adult is an individual who is eighteen years of age or older. When children reach the state's **age of majority**, they are entitled to many civil rights, such as the right to manage their own affairs. A **minor** (also called an *infant*) is anyone under the age of eighteen. **Minority** is the status of being under the age of legal adulthood—under the age of majority. Because minority prevents a person from being able to perform certain tasks legally, minority is an example of a **disability**.

Reaching the age of majority is one of the ways that a child is **emancipated**. Emancipation means being legally independent of parents or legal guardians. In most states, there are two ways that a child can be emancipated:

1. By **operation of law**, and
2. By a special court procedure.

OPERATION OF LAW

Emancipation can occur by operation of law. If a legal consequence results by operation of law, the consequence happens automatically once a designated event occurs. No special court procedure is required. The events that trigger this kind of emancipation include the following:

- Reaching the age of majority,
- Entering into a marriage,
- Joining the military,
- Abandonment of the child by the parent, and
- An explicit agreement between parent and child that the child can live independently.

COURT PROCEDURE

In the absence of one of the events that triggers emancipation by operation of law, a child can petition a court for an order or declaration of emancipation. The child must be a minimum age (sixteen, in many states) before making such a petition. In addition, most states require the applicant prove that he or she is financially self-sufficient. This requirement is particularly important in cases where a parent might be pressuring or forcing the child to seek emancipation.

Because one of the consequences of emancipation is that the parents are no longer obligated to support the child, some parents might be tempted to precipitate emancipation in order to avoid their support obligations. A court will not be interested in allowing an impoverished minor to be emancipated from relatively wealthy parents when there is a likelihood that the child will end up on **public assistance**.

CONSTRUCTIVE-EMANCIPATION DOCTRINE

Suppose, however, that a minor voluntarily, and without cause, abandons the parent's home, against the will of the parent for the purpose of avoiding parental control. In such cases, the minor may be barred from seeking support from the parent. Under the **constructive-emancipation doctrine**, the parental duty to provide child support ends if the minor was of employable age (capable of self-support) and in full possession of his or her faculties when the child avoided parental control. If, however, it is the parent who caused the breakdown in the

---

age of majority
The age at which children reach legal adulthood, usually age eighteen, entitling them to many civil rights such as the right to manage their own affairs.

minor
A person under age of legal adulthood, often eighteen. One who has not reached the age of majority. Also called *infant*.

minority
The status of being under the age of legal adulthood—under the age of majority.

disability
Not having the legal capacity to perform a certain task such as entering into a contract.

emancipated
Legally independent of one's parent or legal guardian. The noun is *emancipation*.

operation of law
The means by which legal consequences are imposed by law, regardless of (or even despite) the intent of the parties involved.

public assistance
Welfare or other forms of financial help from the government to those in need.

constructive-emancipation doctrine
When a minor of employable age and in full possession of his or her faculties, voluntarily and without cause, abandons the parent's home, against the will of the parent and for the purpose of avoiding parental control, he or she forfeits his or her right to demand support.

relationship with his or her child and the parent has made no serious effort to repair the relationship, the child will not be deemed to have forfeited his or her right to child support.

EMANCIPATION AND MINIMUM AGE REQUIREMENTS

As indicated, emancipation ends the parent's duty of child support. Also, emancipated children are no longer obligated to provide services to the parent (e.g., doing household chores), and are now able to do the following:

• Make their own health decisions.
• Live where they wish (see *domicile* below).
• Work without needing parental consent.
• Keep their own earnings.
• Sue and be sued in their own names.

Emancipation, however, does not necessarily mean that the child can do everything that an adult does. Specifically, the law imposes some age requirements that must be met whether or not emancipation has occurred. For example, a seventeen-year-old emancipated person must wait until he or she is eighteen to vote and twenty-one to purchase alcoholic beverages in most states.

ASSIGNMENT 14.1

a. Rich, age sixteen, becomes emancipated by operation of law when he marries Mary. Rich's parents stop supporting him on the date of his marriage. Six months after the marriage, Mary obtains a decree annulling the marriage on the ground of duress. Are Rich's parents now obligated to resume supporting him? If so, as of what date? (See the discussion of annulment in Chapter 6 and child support in Chapter 10; see also the General Instructions for the Legal-Analysis Assignment in Appendix A.)

b. Draft a flowchart of the procedural steps involved in petitioning a court for an order or declaration of emancipation in your state. (See General Instructions for the Flowchart Assignment in Appendix A.)

---

contract
A legally enforceable agreement. The elements of most contracts are offer, acceptance, and consideration. Some contracts must be in writing.

infancy
(1) The defense of being a minor, which allows the minor to disaffirm a voidable contract. (2) Minority.

disaffirm
(1) To repudiate or cancel. (2) To exercise a right to repudiate and refuse to perform one's own contract.

cosigner
A person who signs a document along with the main signer, usually to agree to pay the debt created by the document in the event that the main signer fails to pay it.

voidable
Of no legal effect but valid unless canceled or invalidated.

CONTRACTS AND MINORS

A **contract** is a legally enforceable agreement. When minors enter into contracts, however, they have an important defense called **infancy**, which they can raise if a merchant tries to sue them for breach of contract. In short, because of their infancy, minors have the right to **disaffirm** a contract and, in effect, to walk away from most of their contracts. Why are minors given this right? The objective of the law is to protect young people from their immaturity. Merchants or retailers, therefore, are on notice that if they do business with minors, they do so at their own risk. For this reason, many merchants refuse to enter into contracts with minors (particularly involving expensive goods or services), unless a parent or another financially responsible adult agrees to become a **cosigner** on the contract.

Contracts that a minor can disaffirm are **voidable**, meaning that they can be canceled or invalidated by choice—in this case, by the choice of the minor. A voidable contract, however, is valid and enforceable unless and until it is canceled.

Tom is fifteen years of age. He goes to ABC Micro Company and purchases an expensive new computer. The sales contract calls for a small down payment (which Tom pays) with the remainder to be paid in monthly installments— on credit. Six months later, Tom changes his mind about the computer and decides to take it back to ABC Micro Company. The computer is still in good working order.

If Tom were an adult, he would be bound by his contract, and he would have to continue paying for the computer. Once an adult and a merchant enter into a contract, they both are bound by it. Neither party can rescind or cancel a contract simply because of a change of mind. Store policy or a special consumer law might allow a change of mind by the customer within a certain number of days of purchase, but these are exceptions to the standard rule that a valid contract cannot be canceled at the whim of one of the parties.

In our example, however, Tom is a minor. Most states give minors the right to disaffirm such contracts if they do so while they are still minors or within a reasonable time (e.g., several months) after they reach the age of majority. In Tom's case, this would mean that he is *not* bound by the contract to buy the computer. He can return it and perhaps even force the company to refund whatever money he already paid on it. In some states, however, the merchant can keep all or part of the purchase price paid thus far to cover depreciation resulting from the minor's use of the item. When Tom disaffirms the contract, could he also refuse to return the computer? States differ in their answers to this question. Some states allow a minor to keep the goods after disaffirming, while other states require a return of what remains of the goods.

Not all contracts by minors can be disaffirmed. Here are examples of contracts that minors cannot disaffirm in many states:

- Contracts that minors entered into fraudulently by lying about their age (note, however, that some states *will* allow minors to disaffirm such contracts).
- Contracts by minors in the sports and entertainment industry (some states only).
- Contracts by minors with banks and other lending institutions (some states only).
- Contracts by minors for the purchase of *necessaries* (discussed below).
- Contracts for minors made by their guardians.
- Contracts made by guardians on behalf of minors under the Uniform Transfers to Minors Act (UTMA) (discussed below).

In some states, if minors commit fraud to induce the merchant to enter into a contract (e.g., lie about their age), the wrongdoing will prevent them from being able to disaffirm. They will be **estopped** from asserting the infancy defense. Other courts, however, argue that the policy of protecting minors from their own immaturity is so strong that even their own fraud will not destroy their right to disaffirm.

estopped
Prevented from asserting a right or a defense because it would be unfair or inequitable to allow the assertion. The noun is *estoppel*.

Special statutes have been passed in many states to limit the minor's right to disaffirm, particularly with respect to certain kinds of contracts. In several states, for example, some employment contracts—such as sports and show-business contracts—are binding on minors. Similarly, contracts with banks and other lending institutions cannot be disaffirmed in many states.

Necessaries

Finally, when a minor makes a contract with a merchant for **necessaries**, such as food or clothing, the contract can rarely be fully disaffirmed. (Necessaries are the basic items needed by family members to maintain a standard of living, particularly food, shelter, and clothing.) If minors are allowed to disaffirm a contract for necessaries, they may still be liable for the reasonable value of the goods or

necessaries
The basic items needed by family members to maintain a standard of living, particularly food, shelter, and clothing.

services provided but not necessarily for the full amount of the purchase price the minor initially agreed to pay. (As we saw in Chapter 10, however, the merchant can charge the minor's parent for the necessaries.)

Guardians

When a guardian has been appointed over a minor and the guardian enters into a contract on behalf of that minor, the contract generally cannot be disaffirmed by the minor. A **guardian** is someone who has legal authority to care for the person or property of another. A guardian who acts on behalf of the child in court is sometimes called a **guardian ad litem (GAL)**. If, for example, a GAL negotiates a settlement contract to end the court case on behalf of the minor, which the court finds is fair, the minor cannot later disaffirm the settlement.

Uniform Transfers to Minors Act (UTMA)

Most states have enacted the **Uniform Transfers to Minors Act (UTMA)**. Under this statute, gifts of certain kinds of property (e.g., securities) can be made to minors through guardians (called **custodians**) of the property. The custodian can sell the property on behalf of the minor. Contracts made by the custodian for this purpose cannot be disaffirmed by the minor.

Emancipated Minors and Disaffirmance

Suppose that a minor has become emancipated before reaching the age of majority (e.g., by marrying). Does this end the child's power to disaffirm? There is no absolute answer to this question. A minor so emancipated may be denied the power to disaffirm in some states, while in others, it will not affect the power.

Pregnant Minors and Adoption

Finally, an unemancipated pregnant minor has the capacity to consent to an adoption so long as her consent was not obtained with fraud or duress. In Chapter 15, we will consider when a woman can revoke (disaffirm) her consent to the adoption.

ASSIGNMENT   14.2

George is a wealthy sixteen-year-old who owns an expensive painting. He signs a contract to exchange the painting for a valuable horse owned by Helen, an equally wealthy sixteen-year-old. Both George and Helen are represented by their separate attorneys during the negotiations on the contract. Both George and Helen live independently in their separate homes. Once the contract is signed and the items are exchanged, what rights do George and Helen have? Can they disaffirm? Assume that there are no problems with the quality and condition of the painting and the horse. (See General Instructions for the Legal-Analysis Assignment in Appendix A.)

PROPERTY AND EARNINGS

Minors can own **real property** (e.g., land) and most **personal property** (e.g., clothes, cash) in their own names. The parents of a minor do not own and are not legally entitled to dispose of a minor's property; however, an exception exists for a minor's earnings (an example of personal property). A minor does *not* have a right to keep his or her own earnings. The parent with the duty to support the child has a right to keep the child's earnings. Because a mother and father are both obligated to support their child, they are equally entitled to the child's earnings. In most states, if a child is employed, the employer must pay wages directly to the child unless one of the parents instructs the employer to pay the parent. Once a child has been emancipated (e.g., by express agreement with the parents, by marriage, or by abandonment by the parents), the parents are no longer entitled to the child's earnings. A state may have special laws governing the pay of actors who are minors (e.g., a requirement that the parents deposit a designated percentage of the actor's earnings in a trust for the minor).

DOMICILE

The **domicile** of a minor is the domicile of the parents—even if the minor lives in a different state from the parents. (The child's domicile in such cases is called *domicile by operation of law.*) For example, if five-year-old Greg has lived for three years with his grandmother in Massachusetts while his parents are working at an extended job in New York, his domicile is New York. With parental consent, however, minors can acquire their own separate domicile (called *domicile by choice*). In most states, emancipated minors can acquire their own domicile even if they have not yet reached the age of majority.

domicile
The place where a person has been physically present (a) with the intent to make that place a permanent home or (b) with no intent to make any other place a permanent home. The place to which one intends to return when away. A *residence* is simply the place where you are living at a particular time. A person can have more than one residence but generally can have only one domicile.

ESTATES

Everyone, including a minor, has an estate. An **estate** consists of everything that one owns and owes (assets and liabilities), particularly at the time of death. The word *estate* also means the legal entity created upon a person's death consisting of all of the person's assets and liabilities. The estate, for example, must pay death (estate) taxes and can be sued.

One of the major estate **instruments** is a **will**, which specifies how the **decedent** wishes to dispose of his or her property upon death. States have specified a minimum age for a person to have the legal capacity to dispose of his or her property in a will. Some states have different minimum ages for the disposition of personal property and of real property. In many states, the emancipation of the minor by his or her marriage will enable the minor to make a valid will before reaching the minimum age.

If both parents die, the court will appoint a guardian over the minor and/or over the estate of the minor. This person appointed might be called a general guardian, a guardian of the estate, or a guardian ad litem (GAL). If the guardian is not an attorney and legal services are required, the guardian will hire an attorney on behalf of the minor. It is a guardian's duty to:

estate
(1) Everything that one owns and owes (assets and liabilities), particularly at the time of death. (2) The legal entity that exists upon a person's death, consisting of that person's assets and liabilities. (See the glossary for additional meanings.)

instruments
A formal written document that gives expression to or embodies a legal act or agreement (e.g., a contract or a will). (See the glossary for an additional meaning.)

will
An instrument (legal document) that specifies the disposition of one's property (and related instructions) upon death.

decedent
The person who has died; the deceased.

- Manage the minor's assets.
- Collect assets due to the minor.
- Sell, lease, or mortgage the minor's assets (with the approval of the court).
- Invest the minor's assets.
- Pay the minor's debts from the minor's assets.
- Support the minor from the minor's assets.
- Represent (or obtain representation for) the minor in court, when needed.

For such services, the minor must pay the guardian a fee, which might be a percentage of the minor's estate.

Even when parents are alive, most states give minors the right to inherit property in their own names (e.g., a gift of stock or of land from a deceased uncle). Again, a guardian would probably be appointed by the court to manage the

inter vivos gift
A gift that takes effect (becomes irrevocable) when the donor is living.

fundamental right
A right that falls into one of the following three categories: The right (a) is specifically guaranteed in the U.S. Constitution, (b) is implicit in the concept of ordered liberty, or (c) is deeply rooted in the nation's history and tradition.

truancy
The willful and unjustified failure to attend school by one who is required to attend.

corporal punishment
Punishment inflicted on the physical body.

in loco parentis
(1) Standing in the place of a parent by assuming some or all of the parental responsibilities without being a biological or adoptive parent. (2) Acting as a temporary guardian or caretaker of a child.

tort
A civil wrong (other than a breach of contract) that causes injury or other loss for which our legal system deems it just to provide a remedy, such as damages. Injury or harm can be to a person (a personal tort); to land and anything attached to the land (a real-property tort); to property other than land, called *personal property* and *movable property* (a personal-property tort); or to economic interests (an economic tort).

property. The most likely candidate to be such a guardian would be a parent of the minor. Title to the inherited property would remain in the name of the minor. Finally, minors can receive gifts in their own names that take effect during their lives (**inter vivos gifts**). For example, see the discussion earlier on the Uniform Transfers to Minors Act (UTMA) under the topic of contracts.

EDUCATION AND DISCIPLINE

COMPULSORY EDUCATION

All states have compulsory-education laws for children of designated ages, usually between five and seventeen. Education does not have to take place in a public school if an alternative private school (or home-schooling instruction) meets minimum educational standards. The liberty interest in the Due Process Clause of the U.S. Constitution includes the **fundamental right** of fit parents to raise their children, including the control of their education. (See Exhibit 1.3 in Chapter 1 on the Due Process Clause.) Violating compulsory-attendance laws can lead to criminal charges against the parents and juvenile-court proceedings against the child for **truancy**. The latter is the willful and unjustified failure to attend school by one who is required to attend. The state may have special categories of truants, such as a *habitual truant*—a student with four or more such absences.

CORPORAL PUNISHMENT

Children at home can be subjected to **corporal punishment** by their parents so long as the punishment does not constitute abuse (see discussion of child abuse below). Teachers are **in loco parentis**, which means that they stand in the place of parents and can assume some of the supervisory rights of the parents. As such, teachers can also impose corporal punishment on children if reasonably necessary for proper education and discipline. (In a recent year, the U.S. Department of Education estimated that more than 220,000 children were subjected to corporal punishment.[1])

Reasonable punishment at school is not cruel and unusual punishment under the U.S. Constitution, is not a crime, and is not a **tort**, such as battery, even if the punishment is carried out against the wishes of the parents. In some states, however, statutes exist that prohibit corporal punishment of students by teachers or school officials. The statute might prohibit teachers from hitting students except in self-defense or to protect others. New York State, for example, has specific regulations on when physical force can be used by teachers:

- To protect oneself from physical injury;
- To protect another pupil or teacher or any other person from physical injury;
- To protect the property of the school or of others; and
- To restrain or remove a pupil whose behavior is interfering with the orderly exercise and performance of school district functions, powers, or duties, if that pupil has refused to comply with a request to refrain from further disruptive acts, provided that alternative procedures and methods not involving the use of physical force cannot reasonably be employed.[2]

CONSTITUTIONAL RIGHTS

The U.S. Supreme Court has said that students have constitutional rights. For example, the Court ruled that a school violated the First Amendment right of free speech when it prohibited students from wearing black armbands in school to protest the Vietnam war if this activity did not substantially disrupt school activities:

> It can hardly be argued that either students or teachers shed their constitutional rights to freedom of speech or expression at the schoolhouse gate. . . . School officials do not possess absolute authority over their students. Students in school as well as out of school are "persons" under our Constitution. They are possessed of fundamental rights, which the State must respect, just as they themselves must respect their obligations to the State. In our system, students may not be regarded as closed-circuit recipients of only that which the State chooses to communicate. They may not be confined to the expression of those sentiments that are officially approved.[3]

Although wearing protest armbands in this case did not disrupt school activities in a substantial way, the U.S. Supreme Court took a different view when drugs were involved. It has held that a school could punish a student for refusing to take down a banner that read "Bong Hits 4 Jesus" once the school reasonably concluded that the banner promoted illegal drug use at a school-supervised event.[4]

The Fourth Amendment contains a right not to be subjected to an unreasonable search and seizure. The right, however, differs for adults and students:

- *Adults.* The search is allowed if there is **probable cause** to believe that an offense has been committed. For the search to be constitutional, there must be at least a fair probability or a substantial chance of discovering evidence of criminal activity by the adult.

- *Students.* The search is allowed if there is reasonable suspicion of illicit activity by the student. For the search to be constitutional, there must be at least a moderate chance of finding evidence of wrongdoing by the student.

probable cause
A reasonable belief that a specific crime has been committed and that the accused committed the crime. (See the glossary for an additional meaning.)

The standard is broader for students than it is for adults (thus allowing for more searches to be valid) because of the age of the students and the school environment of the search. It is still possible, however, to violate a student's Fourth Amendment right. In a recent case, the U.S. Supreme Court held that it was unconstitutional for school officials to strip search a thirteen-year-old girl to try to find prescription and over-the-counter drugs. There was an insufficient basis to suspect that the drugs presented a danger or that they were concealed in her underwear.[5] School officials can conduct a search of a student's locker, school bag, or body, but only if there is reasonable suspicion and at least a moderate chance of finding evidence of wrongdoing.

Schools also have the right to implement reasonable policies that deter illegal activities. For example, it is constitutional for a school to require all students who participate in competitive extracurricular activities to submit to random urinalysis drug testing. This is a reasonable means for deterring drug use.[6]

EXPULSION AND SUSPENSION

Students cannot be expelled or given a long-term suspension from school without being accorded certain procedural rights under the U.S. Constitution. For example:

- The right to receive written notice of the charges against them.

- The right to a hearing on the charges to determine whether they are valid.

- The right to an impartial hearing officer. (The latter cannot be directly involved in the matter. For example, the teacher who brought the charges against the student cannot be the hearing officer.)

- The right to be represented by counsel at the hearing.

- The right to present evidence and to confront the accuser at the hearing.

If the student is faced with a less severe punishment, such as a short-term suspension, all of these procedural rights are not required. The student has a right to know the basis of the charges and the right to respond to them, but not necessarily to a hearing with legal representation.

CHILD ABUSE AND NEGLECT

INTRODUCTION

Early in our history, children were considered the property of their parents. In colonial Massachusetts, a law based on the *Book of Deuteronomy* said that if a severely stubborn and rebellious son "disobeyed his father's voice, he could be put to death."[7] In nineteenth-century America, courts often refused to "interfere in the domestic government of families" by punishing a parent for correcting his child, however severe or unmerited the punishment, unless it produced permanent injury or was inflicted from malicious motives.[8]

Today, the situation is drastically different. A large network of law enforcement and social service agencies exist to respond to children at risk. Despite these efforts, however, child abuse and neglect continues to be a major problem in our society.

DEFINITIONS

Child Maltreatment

States use different terms to cover harm caused to children by parents or caregivers. All of the terms fall under the general category of **child maltreatment**, which is an act, or failure to act, by a parent or caretaker that intentionally or carelessly results in physical or emotional harm to a child or that presents an imminent risk of such harm to a child. Researchers prefer the term "child maltreatment," although all of the harms covered by this term may have different labels in the statutes of different states. The harms may be called:

- Abuse
- Child abuse
- Child abuse and neglect

Sometimes, the term **child abuse** is defined as serious physical, emotional, or sexual mistreatment of a child that is not the result of an accident or of circumstances beyond the control of the parent or guardian. In general, **child neglect** is the failure of a parent or other caregiver to provide the basic needs of a child, including physical needs (e.g., food and shelter), emotional needs, medical needs, or educational needs. Child neglect may be caused by poverty, unorthodox cultural or religious practices, or a lack of parenting skills.

Dependency is the condition of a child who has been placed in the custody of the state because the child has been abused, neglected, or abandoned. **Abandonment** is a major example of child maltreatment. It consists of relinquishing parental responsibilities by voluntarily leaving a child or ending communication with a child for a specific period or indefinitely without arranging for alternative care and supervision while away.

Exhibit 14.1 gives a further breakdown of the categories of maltreatment.

Statistics

For statistics on the scope of child maltreatment, see Exhibit 14.2. Note that these statistics are limited to cases that are reported and investigated. The numbers would be considerably higher if unreported cases were added.

---

child maltreatment
An act or failure to act by a parent or caretaker that intentionally or carelessly results in physical or emotional harm to a child or that presents an imminent risk of such harm to a child.

child abuse
Serious physical, emotional, or sexual mistreatment of a child that is not the result of an accident or circumstances beyond the control of the parent or guardian.

child neglect
The failure of a parent or other caregiver to provide the basic needs of a child, including physical needs (e.g., food and shelter), emotional needs, medical needs, or educational needs.

dependency
(1) The condition of a child who has been placed in the custody of the state because the child has been abused, neglected, or abandoned. (2) Pertaining to a child who lacks basic care through no fault of the parent or guardian.

abandonment
Relinquishing one's parental responsibility by voluntarily leaving a child or ending communication with a child for a specific period or indefinitely without arranging for alternative care and supervision while away. Conduct that constitutes a relinquishing of one's parental responsibilities.

EXHIBIT 14.1   Categories of Child Maltreatment

Sexual Abuse

- Intrusion sex without force
- Intrusion sex involving use of force
- Child's prostitution or involvement in pornography with intrusion
- Molestation with genital contact
- Exposure/voyeurism
- Providing sexually explicit materials
- Child's involvement in pornography without intrusion
- Failure to supervise child's voluntary sexual activity
- Attempted/threatened sexual abuse with physical contact
- Other sexual abuse

Physical Abuse

- Shake, throw, purposefully drop
- Hit with hand
- Hit with object
- Push, grab, drag, pull
- Punch, kick
- Other physical abuse

Emotional Abuse

- Close confinement: tying/binding
- Close confinement: other
- Verbal assaults and emotional abuse
- Threats of sexual abuse (without contact)
- Threats of other maltreatment
- Terrorizing the child
- Administering nonprescribed substances
- Other abuse

Other Maltreatment

- Lack of preventive healthcare
- General neglect (unspecified)
- Custody/child support problems
- Behavior control/family conflict issues
- Parent problem
- Other maltreatment

Physical Neglect

- Refusal to allow or provide needed care for diagnosed condition or impairment
- Unwarranted delay or failure to seek needed care
- Refusal of custody/abandonment
- Illegal transfers of custody
- Unstable custody arrangements
- Inadequate supervision
- Inadequate nutrition
- Inadequate personal hygiene
- Inadequate clothing
- Inadequate shelter
- Other disregard of child's physical needs and physical safety

Educational Neglect

- Chronic truancy
- Failure to register or enroll
- Other refusal to allow or provide needed attention to diagnosed educational need

Emotional Neglect

- Inadequate nurturance/affection
- Domestic violence
- Knowingly permitting drug/alcohol abuse
- Knowingly permitting other maladaptive behavior
- Refusal to allow or provide needed care for diagnosed emotional or behavioral impairment/problem
- Failure to seek needed care for emotional or behavioral impairment/problem
- Overprotectiveness
- Inadequate structure
- Inappropriately advanced expectations
- Exposure to maladaptive behaviors and environments
- Other inattention to development/emotional needs

Other

- Involuntary neglect
- Chemically dependent newborns

Source: Typology for Classifying Maltreatment, Table 6, Fourth National Incidence Study of Child Abuse and Neglect, *Design and Methods Study* (NIS-4), 19 (U.S. Department of Health and Human Services 2008) (www.nis4.org/DOCS/Nis4Design_Method_Summary.pdf).

A study of the perpetrators of child maltreatment concluded that:

- 81.2 percent are parents; 6.1 percent are other relatives of the victim.
- 45.2 percent are men, and 53.6 percent are women.
- 36.3 percent are between the ages of 20 and 29
- 84.2 percent are between the ages of 20 and 49.
- 84.2 percent of the parent perpetrators are the biological parent of the victim.[9]

EXHIBIT 14.2

Statistics on Child Maltreatment (Number of cases reported and investigated.)

Maltreatment Types of Victims, 2017

State	Victims	Medical Neglect	Neglect	Other	Physical Abuse	Psychological Maltreatment	Sexual Abuse	Unknown	Total Maltreatment Types
Alabama	10,847	92	4,669	-	5,720	41	1,590	-	12,112
Alaska	2,783	5	2,146	-	395	771	148	-	3,465
Arizona	9,909	-	9,152	-	806	2	319	-	10,279
Arkansas	9,334	1,461	5,043	3	2,051	153	1,783	-	10,494
California	65,342	103	57,027	353	5,321	6,857	3,497	-	73,158
Colorado	11,578	182	9,461	-	1,299	268	1,068	33	12,311
Connecticut	8,442	305	7,166	-	519	2,449	401	-	10,840
Delaware	1,542	22	447	269	294	592	109	-	1,733
District of Columbia	1,639	-	1,405	5	291	-	63	-	1,764
Florida	40,103	1,171	23,145	17,957	3,256	441	2,773	-	48,743
Georgia	10,487	257	8,115	-	1,055	1,603	624	-	11,654
Hawaii	1,280	15	167	1,146	111	18	60	-	1,517
Idaho	1,832	10	1,427	13	402	-	79	-	1,931
Illinois	28,751	637	20,740	-	5,660	50	4,140	-	31,227
Indiana	29,198	-	26,006	-	1,864	-	2,675	-	30,545
Iowa	10,643	103	8,626	591	1,278	72	786	-	11,456
Kansas	4,153	108	784	1,228	1,007	741	768	-	4,636
Kentucky	22,410	487	21,313	-	1,533	44	852	-	24,229
Louisiana	10,356	-	8,898	13	1,574	37	543	-	11,065
Maine	3,475	-	2,192	-	1,023	1,195	285	-	4,695
Maryland	7,578	-	4,597	-	1,688	10	1,772	-	8,067
Massachusetts	25,092	-	23,550	25	2,213	-	861	-	26,649
Michigan	38,064	724	30,256	-	9,479	132	1,412	-	42,003
Minnesota	8,709	20	5,666	-	2,648	135	1,525	-	9,994
Mississippi	10,429	397	7,891	31	1,547	1,557	1,164	-	12,587
Missouri	4,585	161	2,684	1	1,363	478	1,245	-	5,932
Montana	3,534	6	3,445	-	140	31	97	-	3,719
Nebraska	3,246	1	2,772	-	380	26	242	-	3,421
Nevada	4,859	82	4,018	-	1,065	10	252	-	5,427
New Hampshire	1,148	26	1,017	-	97	8	78	-	1,226
New Jersey	6,698	-	5,349	-	917	52	718	-	7,036
New Mexico	8,577	296	6,879	-	1,045	2,351	220	-	10,791
New York	71,226	4,606	67,669	20,190	6,884	561	2,158	-	102,068
North Carolina	7,392	57	3,848	96	1,814	118	1,439	85	7,457
North Dakota	1,981	43	1,522	-	157	788	48	-	2,558
Ohio	24,897	493	11,212	-	11,892	914	4,339	-	28,850
Oklahoma	14,457	179	11,369	-	2,032	3,841	692	-	18,113
Oregon	11,070	170	6,292	5,324	1,163	177	878	-	14,004
Pennsylvania	4,625	253	370	74	1,963	57	2,116	-	4,833
Puerto Rico	5,729	479	3,373	24	1,398	2,966	143	-	8,383
Rhode Island	3,095	48	1,786	65	454	1,092	101	-	3,546
South Carolina	17,071	361	9,673	63	9,219	130	838	-	20,284
South Dakota	1,339	-	1,202	-	155	18	59	-	1,434
Tennessee	8,983	137	2,234	-	5,424	199	2,517	-	10,511
Texas	61,506	1,168	50,785	2	8,772	378	6,097	1	67,203
Utah	9,947	46	2,925	148	4,478	2,808	1,713	-	12,118
Vermont	878	11	21	-	508	-	366	-	906
Virginia	6,277	137	4,102	4	1,910	84	694	-	6,931
Washington	4,386	-	3,466	-	914	-	467	-	4,847
West Virginia	6,496	290	2,629	-	5,083	4,050	229	-	12,281
Wisconsin	4,902	-	3,303	-	790	41	1,008	-	5,142
Wyoming	950	11	711	3	14	289	63	-	1,091
National	**673,830**	**15,160**	**504,545**	**47,628**	**123,065**	**38,635**	**58,114**	**119**	**787,266**
Reporting States	**52**	**41**	**52**	**24**	**52**	**46**	**52**	**3**	**52**

Source: Child Maltreatment 2017, U.S. Department of Health and Human Services, Children's Bureau (www.acf.hhs.gov/sites/default/files/cb/cm2017.pdf).

There are substantially more perpetrators in cohabiting families than in families where the parents are married:

- The rate of harm of children living with two married biological parents is 6.8 per 1,000 children.
- The rate of harm of children living with a parent who had an unmarried partner in the house was 57.2 per 1,000 children.[10]

Substance Abuse

Substance abuse can lead to child maltreatment. Here are some examples:

- Prenatal exposure of a child to harm due to the mother's use of an illegal drug or other substance.
- Manufacture of methamphetamine in the presence of a child.

- Selling, distributing, or giving illegal drugs or alcohol to a child.
- Using a controlled substance that impairs the caregiver's ability to adequately care for the child.[11]

Safe Haven Law

Some mothers are so overwhelmed by their personal problems (often involving drug addiction) that they cannot provide care for their babies. They are afraid, however, of seeking help for the child because of a concern that they might be prosecuted for criminal child neglect or some other crime. In extreme cases, infanticide has occurred as mothers throw babies into dumpsters. To encourage women in such straits to not abandon their infants in dumpsters or remote locations, some states have enacted safe haven laws that allow the mother to legally leave the child at designated locations such as a hospital, fire station, or doctor's office. Under these laws, a mother can do this anonymously or by disclosing information about herself and the child to the place where the child is brought. In return, she will not be prosecuted for abandonment so long as there is no evidence that the child has been abused. States have different requirements for these safe haven laws, such as the maximum age of the child that can be left.

infanticide
The unlawful killing of a newborn.

safe haven law
A law that protects a woman from prosecution if she abandons a baby at designated locations such as a hospital, fire station, or doctor's office where it can receive emergency medical assistance.

PARENS PATRIAE

Parens patriae is the state's role in protecting children and others under a disability. The state, as parent of the country, exerts its authority to enact laws that protect its vulnerable citizens. An example is the compulsory-education laws we examined earlier. Another major example of the parens-patriae power of the state is its law on child abuse. Parents have a fundamental constitutional right to raise their children, but the state can override that right when necessary to protect children.

Every state has an agency for child protective services designed to investigate child abuse and neglect, offer assistance to families of children at risk, and administer foster care or other placement programs. At the federal level, Congress enacted the Child Abuse Prevention and Treatment Act (CAPTA) to help fund state programs for the identification, prevention, and treatment of child abuse and neglect. CAPTA has also played an important role in defining and collecting data on child abuse and neglect.

As a condition for receiving federal funds under CAPTA, the states must agree that "in every case involving a victim of child abuse or neglect which results in a judicial proceeding, a guardian ad litem, who . . . may be an attorney or a court appointed special advocate [CASA] . . . (or both), shall be appointed to represent the child in such proceedings."[12] A paralegal can be a CASA. For more on CASAs, see Paralegal Roles at the end of the chapter.

parens patriae
Parent of the country, referring to the state's role in protecting children and others in the state who suffer from a disability.

child protective services
A state agency that investigates child neglect and abuse, offers assistance to families of children at risk, and administers foster care or other placement programs.

Child Abuse Prevention and Treatment Act (CAPTA)
A federal statute that helps fund state programs for the identification, prevention, and treatment of child abuse and neglect (42 U.S.C. § 5101).

court appointed special advocate (CASA)
A volunteer (who can be an attorney, a paralegal, or other nonattorney) appointed by the court to perform special assignments pertaining to children in the court system.

MANDATORY REPORTING

Every state has a mandatory reporting law. Under this law, designated individuals—such as teachers, doctors, nurses, social workers, day care workers, and counselors—are classified as "mandatory reporters" who are required to report suspected child abuse or neglect to the police, child protective services, or other child welfare authorities. For example, one state requires a mandated reporter to file a report when he or she "has knowledge of or observes a child whom the mandated reporter knows or reasonably suspects has been the victim of child abuse or neglect." For the purposes of this requirement, "reasonable suspicion" means that "it is objectively reasonable for a person to entertain a

mandatory reporting
Designated persons (e.g., teachers) must inform safety officials (e.g., police or child protective services) of suspected child abuse or neglect.

suspicion, based upon facts that could cause a reasonable person in a like position, drawing, when appropriate, on his or her training and experience, to suspect child abuse or neglect."[13]

In most states, if a report turns out to be false, the person making the report is granted **immunity** from civil liability so long as the report was made in **good faith**.

Some states have established a *central registry* that contains the names of persons involved in cases of suspected child abuse if there is credible evidence of the abuse. The registry is available to child-care employers so that they can do a background search of prospective employees.

JURISDICTIONAL STAGE AND DISPOSITIONAL STAGE

Child maltreatment can result in three major categories of court cases:

- *Criminal case.* The alleged perpetrator of child maltreatment is charged with a crime (e.g., child endangerment or sexual assault), and the case proceeds through the criminal courts.

- *Tort case.* The victim, or a representative of the victim, may be able to sue the perpetrator in a civil action for damages, such as a tort suit for battery. (See, however, Chapter 17 on when family members have immunity for torts committed against each other.)

- *Family or juvenile court case.* The most common judicial consequence of child maltreatment is intervention by the state to take steps to protect the child from further harm. This occurs primarily in family or juvenile court.

When the third option is taken by the state, a two-stage procedure usually occurs:

- *Jurisdictional stage.* The court determines if it has **subject-matter jurisdiction** by deciding whether the facts alleged in the case come within the definitions of abuse, neglect, or dependency as established by statutes and court opinions. A court does not have the power (jurisdiction) to hear the case unless the issues before the court fit within these definitions.

- *Dispositional stage.* If the court has jurisdiction, it must decide what to do—what disposition to make. The court's judgment is sometimes called a *dispositional* order. A number of options are possible. Examples:

  ○ Leave the child with the current parent or other caregiver under the supervision of child protective services or a child welfare agency and require counseling or other conditions designed to prevent future maltreatment.

  ○ Place the child in **foster care** or in an institution such as a state-operated orphanage.

  ○ Begin proceedings to terminate the parental rights of the parent so that the child can be adopted (see Chapter 15).

The normal procedure is for the parent or caregiver to be given notice of the alleged child maltreatment and an opportunity to be heard before the state takes any action. **Summary seizure**, however, is allowed if the child is in danger of serious **imminent** harm. In summary seizure, the state takes custody of the child without notice to the parent and without a prior hearing. Shortly after the child is removed, the parents are notified and given the right to contest the removal in court.

---

immunity
A defense that is granted because of a special relationship or status that operates to block litigation and liability whether or not wrongful conduct was committed. The defense prevents someone from being sued for what might be wrongful conduct.

good faith
A state of mind indicating honesty and lawfulness of purpose. The absence of wrongful intent or desire to take inappropriate advantage of someone. Also called *bona fides*.

subject-matter jurisdiction
The court's power to resolve a particular type of legal dispute and to grant a particular type of relief.

foster care
A government-funded child welfare service that provides shelter and substitute family care when a child's own family cannot provide this care.

summary seizure
Taking custody of a person or taking possession of property without notice or prior hearing.

imminent
Near at hand; coming soon; about to happen; immediate.

ASSIGNMENT 14.3

a. Prepare a checklist of questions you can use to help determine whether a child has been neglected or abused. (See General Instructions for the Checklist-Formulation Assignment in Appendix A.)

b. Draft a flowchart of the procedural steps that are necessary in your state to determine whether a child has been neglected or abused. (See General Instructions for the Flowchart Assignment in Appendix A.)

DELINQUENCY

At common law:

- A minor below the age of seven was incapable of committing a crime. This was a **conclusive presumption**, meaning that evidence that such a child was, in fact, capable of committing a crime (and intended to commit it) was inadmissible.

- A minor between the ages of seven and fourteen could be guilty of a crime if the prosecutor could show that the minor was mature enough to have formed the criminal intent necessary for the particular crime. For example, the crime of theft requires the intent to deprive someone permanently of his or her property. A **rebuttable presumption** existed that a minor between seven and fourteen could *not* possess the requisite criminal intent. This meant that the court would assume the absence of this intent unless the prosecutor affirmatively proved otherwise.

- A minor over age fourteen was treated and tried the same as adults.

In the early part of the twentieth century, a trend developed to remove the stigma of criminality from the misconduct of minors. Juvenile courts were created in which judges mandated counseling and social services for **juvenile delinquents**—young people under a designated age (e.g., sixteen) whose misconduct would constitute a crime if committed by an adult. Although a juvenile-court judgment could be severe (e.g., institutionalization), the goal was less to punish than to encourage responsible behavior and rehabilitation.

If, however, a minor commits a particularly heinous act, such as killing a parent, the state may have the authority to prosecute the minor in the regular criminal courts for adults.

Juvenile or family courts also handle what are called **status offenses**—disruptive behavior by a young person under a designated age (e.g., sixteen) that would not be considered illegal by an adult. Examples of such offenses include habitual truancy from school and incorrigibility at home.

Juvenile and family courts often go through the same two-stage process mentioned earlier for child neglect and abuse cases: (1) a *jurisdictional stage* to determine whether the court has jurisdiction and (2) a *dispositional stage* to design an appropriate judgment (disposition) that emphasized rehabilitation where appropriate. The court could order counseling, institutionalization in a juvenile facility, probation under the supervision of a youth counselor, foster home placement, etc.

conclusive presumption
A conclusion of law or fact that a party will not be allowed to try to disprove (rebut). Also called *irrebuttable presumption.*

rebuttable presumption
An assumption or inference of fact that a party will be allowed to try to disprove (rebut) but that will be treated as true if it is not disproved.

juvenile delinquent
A young person under a designated age (e.g., sixteen) whose misconduct would constitute a crime if committed by an adult. Sometimes called *PINS* (Person in Need of Supervision), *MINS* (Minor in Need of Supervision), or *CHIPS* (Child in Need of Protection and Services).

status offenses
Disruptive behavior by a young person under a designated age (e.g., sixteen) that would not be considered illegal by an adult. The status offender (or juvenile delinquent) is sometimes called a *PINS* (Person in Need of Supervision), *MINS* (Minor in Need of Supervision), or *CHIPS* (Child in Need of Protection and Services).

ASSIGNMENT   14.4

a. What is a juvenile delinquent in your state? (See General Instructions for the State-Code Assignment in Appendix A.)

b. Draft a flowchart of the procedural steps required in your state to process a juvenile delinquency case. (See General Instructions for the Flowchart Assignment in Appendix A.)

PARALEGAL ROLES

- For an overview of paralegal roles in family-law cases, see Exhibits 1.5 and 1.6 in Chapter 1.
- For many of the financial issues related to child neglect and dependency covered in Chapter 14, a paralegal may be asked to help collect documents and facts outlined in:
  - The checklist in Exhibit 3.1 of Chapter 3.
  - The interrogatories in Appendix C.
- *Court Appointed Special Advocate (CASA).* A CASA is a volunteer appointed by the court to undertake special assignments pertaining to children in the court system. Paralegals can become a volunteer CASA for children in abuse and neglect cases, particularly children in the foster care system. CASAs are not substitutes for attorneys, social workers, or other child welfare personnel. The CASA's role is to be an independent voice for the child, assisting the judge to obtain a better understanding of the child's needs. A CASA's tasks can include:
  - Conducting an independent investigation of the child's home environment.
  - Acting as a facilitator to achieve resolution of problems pertaining to a child's difficulties.
  - Appearing at all hearings to be available to offer views on the child's best interests, providing testimony when necessary.
  - Making recommendations for specific, appropriate services for the child and the child's family, and advocating for necessary services.
  - Monitoring implementation of case plans and court orders, checking to see that court-ordered services are provided in a timely manner.
- Administrative Agency Roles of Family Law Paralegals
  - Research administrative regulations of the agencies.
  - Obtain needed forms from child protective services and other child welfare agencies (often available online).
  - Research resources to be considered at the the dispositional hearing.
  - Determine status of the client's application for services from the agencies.
  - Monitor the service provided by the agencies.
  - Assist the client in a school suspension or revocation hearing.
  - Interview the client on the facts of the alleged child abuse, neglect, or abandonment.
  - Investigate the facts of the alleged child abuse, neglect, or abandonment.
  - Assist the client in designing alternative plans for the dispositional hearing on the child.

SUMMARY

The age of majority is eighteen in most states, but a state may impose different age requirements for performing different activities. Emancipation before the age of majority can make a minor eligible for some of these activities. Emancipation is legal independence from one's parents or legal guardians. It is obtained by operation of law (e.g., when the child reaches the age of majority or

marries) or by a special court procedure. The constructive-emancipation doctrine can apply to an unruly minor.

A number of special laws apply to minors. For example, they have the right to disaffirm certain contracts they have entered into. Some states will not allow disaffirmance of sports or entertainment contracts, or if the minors lied about their age. Minors can own real property and most personal property in their own names, but unless they have been emancipated, a parent has the right to keep their earnings. Also, minors cannot acquire their own domicile without parental consent. States have a minimum age for the making of a will by a minor. Many states allow emancipated minors to make a will even if they have not reached the minimum age. If the parents of a minor die, the court will appoint a guardian to oversee his or her affairs. Most states give minors the right to inherit property in their own names.

School is compulsory until a designated age. Teachers stand in the place of parents (in loco parentis) and, as such, can impose reasonable corporal punishment. Students have First Amendment free speech rights and Fourth Amendment search and seizure rights while in school. The exercise of these rights, however, must not be unduly disruptive of school discipline. Students are entitled to procedural rights (e.g., a hearing) if the school wants to impose expulsion or long-term suspension.

Child maltreatment is an act, or failure to act, by a parent or caretaker that intentionally or carelessly results in physical or emotional harm to a child or that presents an imminent risk of such harm to a child. Child abuse is serious physical, emotional, or sexual mistreatment that is not the result of an accident or circumstances beyond the control of the parent or guardian. Child neglect is the failure of a parent or other caregiver to provide the basic needs of a child, including physical needs, emotional needs, medical needs, or educational needs. Dependency is the condition of a child who has been placed in the custody of the state because the child has been abused, neglected, or abandoned. Abandonment is relinquishing one's parental responsibility by voluntarily leaving a child or ending communication with a child for a specific period or indefinitely without arranging for alternative care and supervision while away. Substance abuse can constitute child maltreatment, such as prenatal exposure of the child to the mother's use of illegal drugs. A safe haven law protects a woman from prosecution if she abandons a baby at designated locations where it can receive emergency medical assistance. The state's right to intervene in order to protect children is its parens patriae power. The Child Abuse Prevention and Treatment Act (CAPTA) funds state programs for the identification, prevention, and treatment of child abuse and neglect. CAPTA has helped define and collect data on child abuse and neglect. States have mandatory reporting laws that require certain individuals to report suspected child maltreatment to the police or child protective services.

Child maltreatment can result in a criminal case, a tort case, or a family/juvenile court case. If the latter, the jurisdictional stage determines whether the child fits within the state's definition of abuse, neglect, or other maltreatment. At the dispositional state, the court decides what order will best suit the rehabilitation needs of the child.

At common law, there was a conclusive presumption that a child below the age of seven could not commit a crime and a rebuttable presumption that a child between seven and fourteen cannot commit a crime. Minors over age fourteen were treated as adults. Today, misconduct by children is often handled as juvenile delinquency and status offenses in juvenile or family courts where the emphasis is on rehabilitation.

KEY TERMS

age of majority
minor
minority
disability
emancipated
operation of law
public assistance
constructive emancipation
contract
infancy
disaffirm
cosigner
voidable
estopped
necessaries
guardian
guardian ad litem (GAL)
Uniform Transfers to Minors Act (UTMA)
custodian

real property
personal property
domicile
estate
instrument
will
decedent
inter vivos gift
fundamental right
truancy
corporal punishment
in loco parentis
tort
probable cause
child maltreatment
child abuse
child neglect
dependency
abandonment

infanticide
safe haven law
parens patriae
child protective services
Child Abuse Prevention and Treatment Act (CAPTA)
court appointed special advocate (CASA)
mandatory reporting
immunity
good faith
subject-matter jurisdiction
foster care
summary seizure
imminent
conclusive presumption
rebuttable presumption
juvenile delinquent
status offense

CHECK THE CITE

Four-year-old Joshua DeShaney became comatose and then profoundly "retarded" after being beaten on the head by his father. Although the Winnebago County Department of Social Services responded to complaints of child abuse and took steps to protect Joshua, it did not remove him from the custody of his father. Joshua's mother then sued the social workers and local officials. What was her theory of recovery? What specific rights did she claim they violated by refusing to remove Joshua? How did the U.S. Supreme Court resolve the case and what were the reasons for its decision? Read *DeShaney v. Winnebago County Department of Social Services*, 489 U.S. 189 (1989). To read this opinion online, (1) go to Google Scholar (scholar.google.com) and enter the search "489 U.S. 189" in the *Case law* database; (2) in the general search engines of Google, Bing, or Yahoo, enter the search "489 U.S. 189".

PROJECT

In Google, Bing, or Yahoo, run the following search: aa children "mandatory reporting" (substitute the name of your state for aa in the search). Write a short essay in which you explain the mandatory reporting laws in your state. Cover the topics of who must report, when they must report, to whom they must report, the consequences of failing to report, and what happens if the report turns out to have been in error. You must cite and quote from a minimum of three different sources that you find on the Internet. At least two of these sources should be statutes, court opinions, or other laws. The citations from the laws must quote the relevant language of the laws. Do not simply copy long sections of the laws. Quote the essential language in the laws and summarize the rest.

ETHICS IN A FAMILY LAW PRACTICE

You are a paralegal working at the law office of Daniel Britton, Esq. At a Halloween party, you begin talking to a sixteen-year-old guest. The guest tells you he is having troubles at home. You tell him about applying for emancipation and explain how it is accomplished. You also give him your business card. Any ethical problems?

WRITING SAMPLE

In 2010, Torry Hansen, an unmarried nurse in Tennessee, became so frustrated over the behavior of the boy she had adopted in Russia that she put him on a plane back to Russia. Traveling alone, the boy carried a note from Hansen saying that she could no longer handle the boy's mental problems and violent behavior. Your supervisor has asked you to write a memo in which you explain what child maltreatment laws would apply to Torry Hansen if this case had arisen in your state. You can find out more facts on the case by running this search in Google, Bing, or Yahoo: *Russian adoption return child* *Tennessee Hansen*. The memo should cite specific laws of your state that would apply. Quote from these laws and explain how they might apply. Do not explain the law of adoption in your state. Your supervisor does not want to know what adoption law applied to the case. The supervisor wants coverage of child abuse, child neglect, or other child maltreatment laws. To find the laws, run this search: *child abuse neglect abandonment aa* (substitute the name of your state for aa in the search). (See the General Instructions for the Writing Sample in Appendix A.)

REVIEW QUESTIONS

1. What is the age of majority?
2. What is emancipation?
3. How is emancipation obtained by operation of law?
4. Describe the court procedure that can result in emancipation.
5. What is the constructive-emancipation doctrine?
6. When can minors disaffirm their contracts?
7. What is the Uniform Transfers to Minors Act (UTMA)?
8. What property can minors own in their own name?
9. What is the domicile of a minor?
10. What is an estate?
11. When can a minor make a will?
12. What happens if both parents of a minor die?

13. What are the duties of the guardian of a minor?

14. Can minors inherit property in their own names if their parents are still living?

15. Can minors receive inter vivos gifts in their own names?

16. What constitutional right do parents have over the education of their children?

17. What is meant by in loco parentis?

18. When can corporal punishment be used on a child?

19. Give an example of a First Amendment speech right that students have in school?

20. How does the Fourth Amendment right of an adult differ from that of a student?

21. What procedural rights do students have when the school wants to expel them or suspend them long term?

22. What is child maltreatment?

23. Distinguish between child abuse and child neglect.

24. What is dependency and abandonment?

25. When can substance abuse constitute child maltreatment?

26. What is a safe haven law?

27. What is parens patriae?

28. What is the Child Abuse Prevention and Treatment Act (CAPTA)?

29. How does mandatory reporting protect children?

30. What are the three major categories of court cases involving child maltreatment?

31. What is the distinction between the jurisdictional stage and the dispositional stage?

32. What are some of the options of a court at the dispositional stage if it finds that serious child maltreatment has occurred?

33. How did the common law treat crimes committed by children?

34. What is juvenile delinquency and what are status offenses?

HELPFUL WEBSITES

Your State

See Appendix D for links to the family law of your state on the topics covered in this chapter.

Emancipation

- www.law.cornell.edu/wex/table_emancipation
- en.wikipedia.org/wiki/Emancipation_of_minors

Contracts by Minors

- en.wikipedia.org/wiki/Capacity_(law)
- blogs.findlaw.com/law_and_life/2014/03/is-it-legal-to-sign-a-contract-with-a-minor.html

Corporal Punishment

- en.wikipedia.org/wiki/Corporal_punishment
- www.aclu.org/corporal-punishment-children

Child Welfare Information Gateway

- www.childwelfare.gov

Child Abuse Prevention Network

- child.cornell.edu

Child Abuse and Neglect Overview

- www.childwelfare.gov/topics/systemwide/statistics
- www.lawyers.com/legal-info/family-law/child-abuse-and-neglect

Reporting Child Abuse and Neglect

- www.childwelfare.gov/topics/responding/reporting
- www.childwelfare.gov/pubPDFs/manda.pdf

Abuse, Neglect, Adoption, and Foster Care Research

- www.acf.hhs.gov/programs/opre/abuse_neglect/natl_incid

Representation of Children at Child Abuse and Neglect Proceedings

- www.childwelfare.gov/topics/systemwide/laws-policies/statutes/represent

Online Resources for State Child Welfare Law and Policy

- www.childwelfare.gov/pubPDFs/resources.pdf

Statistics on Children in America

- datacenter.kidscount.org

Google Scholar (scholar.google.com)

- Choose "Articles" and enter in the search box any of the key terms discussed in the chapter. Add the name of your state to the search term.
- Choose "Case law" and "Select courts". Select your state, click "Done," and enter in the search box any of

the key terms discussed in the chapter. Add the name of your state to the search term.

Google, Bing, or Yahoo

(on these search engines, run the following searches, substituting your state for "aa")

- "age of majority" aa
- emancipation minor aa
- school discipline hearing aa
- "corporal punishment" aa
- "child abuse" aa
- safe haven law baby aa
- child abandonment aa
- "juvenile delinquency" aa
- child crimes prosecution aa
- minor disaffirm contract aa
- child earnings parent emancipated aa
- school expulsion hearing aa
- student constitution rights aa

- "child neglect" aa
- "parens patriae" aa
- "mandatory reporting" aa
- "status offense" aa

YouTube

Run the same searches on YouTube listed above for Google, Bing, Yahoo searches. Even when the video clips are trying to entice you to retain an attorney, buy a book, or enroll in a course, they can provide useful overviews and references to primary authority.

Twitter, Reddit, and Facebook

On Twitter, Reddit, and Facebook, run the following searches (substitute your state for *aa* in your searches; run the searches with and without the name of your state). Look for links to family-law developments in your state.

- child abuse aa
- child neglect aa

ENDNOTES

Note: All or most of the court opinions in these endnotes can be read online. To do so, go to Google Scholar (scholar.google.com), select "Case law," and in the search box, enter the cite (e.g., "393 U.S. 503") or name of the case (e.g., Tinker v. Des Moines Independent Community School District") that is given in the endnote.

[1] Dan Frosch, *A Trip to These Principals May Mean a Paddling*, N.Y. Times, Mar. 30, 2011 at A15).

[2] *New York Code, Rules and Regulations* (NYCRR) § 100.2(l)(3)(i) (government.westlaw.com/linkedslice /default.asp?SP=nycrr-1000)(title 8).

[3] *Tinker v. Des Moines Independent Community School District*, 393 U.S. 503, 506, 511 (1969).

[4] *Morse v. Frederick*, 551 U.S. 393 (2007).

[5] *Safford Unified School Dist. No. 1 v. Redding*, 557 U.S. 364 (2009).

[6] *Board of Ed. of Independent School District No. 92 of Pottawatomie City v. Earls*, 536 U.S. 822 (2002).

[7] Deuteronomy 21:18-21. Walter Weyrauch et al., *Family Law* 949 (1994).

[8] *State v. Jones*, 95 N.C. 588 (1886).

[9] U.S. Department of Health & Human Services, Children's Bureau, *Child Maltreatment 2010* x (2010).

[10] Sabrina Taverise, *More Unwed Parents Live Together, Report Finds*, N.Y. Times, Aug. 16, 2011.

[11] U.S. Department of Health and Human Services, *What Is Child Abuse and Neglect?* (2008).

[12] 42 U.S.C. § 5106a(b)(2)(B)(xiii)(emphasis added) (www.law .cornell.edu/uscode/text/42/5106a).

[13] California Penal Code § 11166.

CHAPTER 15

Adoption

CHAPTER OBJECTIVES

After completing this chapter, you should be able to:

- Know the definition and effect of adoption.
- Define second-parent adoption.
- Distinguish the four major categories of adoption.
- List the possible adoption facilitators.
- Know when an adoption becomes a black-market adoption.
- Explain when a court will approve the adoption of an adult.
- List the criteria that a court will use when deciding whether an adoption is in the best interests of the child.
- Explain the effect of the Multiethnic Placement Act (MEPA).

- Describe the difficulties faced by gays and lesbians when they want to adopt.
- List the procedures involved in an adoption.
- Explain the notice and consent rights of an unmarried father of a child whom others want to adopt.
- State when consent can be revoked.
- State the grounds for a termination of parental rights.
- Identify the major procedural issues in a proceeding to terminate parental rights.
- Explain the effect of the Adoption and Safe Families Act (ASFA).
- Explain why it is legally impossible for children to "divorce" their parents.

- Explain the challenges that can be brought against an adoption decree.
- Describe the function of a putative father registry.
- Explain how the Interstate Compact on the Placement of Children (ICPC) operates.
- List the consequences of an adoption.
- Distinguish between a confidential adoption and an open adoption.
- Know when an equitable adoption is created.
- Explain what is meant by an embryo adoption.

INTRODUCTION

TERMINOLOGY

adoption
The judicial process by which one person (the adoptive parent) becomes the legal parent of another person (the adoptee).

adoptive parent
A person who adopts another person.

adoptee
A person who is adopted.

intestate
(1) Pertaining to someone who dies without a valid will. (2) A person who dies without a valid will.

Adoption is the judicial process by which one person (the **adoptive parent**) becomes the legal parent of another person (the **adoptee**). Adoption establishes a permanent parent-child relationship between the child and a person who is not the biological parent of the child. In many states, an adoption leads to the reissuance of the child's birth certificate, listing the adoptive parent as the "mother" or "father" of the child. The relationship is permanent in that only a court can end the relationship by terminating the parental rights of the adoptive parent. The divorce or death of the adoptive parent does not end the relationship. Assume, for example, that Tom marries Linda and then adopts her son, Dave, by a previous marriage. If Tom subsequently divorces Linda (or if his marriage to her ends by annulment), he does not cease to be Dave's parent. His obligation to support Dave, for example, continues after the divorce or annulment. Similarly, if Tom dies **intestate** (without a valid will), Dave can inherit from Tom as if he were a biological child of Tom. In this sense, the parent-child relationship continues even after the death of the adoptive parent.

At the outset, we need to define and distinguish some important terms that relate to the law of adoption:

- **Custody** (1) The right to the care and control of something, either a person or a thing. (2) The actual care and control that someone has over a person or thing.

- **Legal custody** (in reference to children) The right to make the major child-rearing decisions on health, education, religion, discipline, and general welfare. Also called *decision-making responsibility*.

- **Ward** A person (e.g., minor) placed by the court under the care or protection of a guardian.

- **Guardian** A person who has legal authority to care for the person or property of another. Also called *custodian*.

- **Guardian ad litem (GAL)** A special guardian (often, but not always, an attorney) appointed by the court to appear in court proceedings on behalf of a person who is a minor, is insane, or is otherwise incapacitated or under a disability.

- **Paternity** The biological fatherhood of a child.

- **Foster care** A government-funded child welfare service that provides shelter and substitute family care when a child's own family cannot provide this shelter and care. Foster care is designed to last for a temporary period. The temporary home is called a *foster home*, which can be an individual family or a group home.

- **Stepparent** A person who marries the biological mother or father of a child, but who is not one of the child's biological parents. For example, assume that Ted and Mary marry each other. It is the second marriage for both. Ted has a son, Bill, from his first marriage. Mary has a daughter, Alice, from her first marriage. Ted is the biological father of Bill and the stepfather of Alice. Mary is the biological mother of Alice and the stepmother of Bill.

ASSIGNMENT 15.1

Run the following search in Google, Bing, or Yahoo (adoption aa), using the name of your state for aa (e.g., adoption Minnesota). Alternatively, go to the site that contains the statutes of your state (see Appendix D for leads). Use the search facility on the site (e.g., a search box) to find statutes on the adoption of children. (See General Instructions for the State-Code Assignment in Appendix A.)

a. Quote any sentence from any statute in your state on adoption.

b. Identify as many separate government agencies as you can that are involved with adoption. For each agency, state its name, Internet address, and its function (briefly stated).

SECOND-PARENT ADOPTION

The traditional rule is that an adoption terminates all prior parent-child relationships. If the child's biological parents are no longer living, there is nothing to terminate. Suppose, however, that one of the biological parents is alive and that this parent's romantic partner or new spouse wants to adopt the child. Examples:

- Georgia is a widow with one child. When Georgia remarries, her new husband, John, wishes to adopt her child.
- Ted is a single father in a romantic relationship with Ursula. Ursula wishes to adopt Ted's child.
- Helen becomes a single parent through artificial insemination from an anonymous donor. Helen's romantic partner, Paula, wishes to adopt Helen's child.

In each of these examples, the child has a biological parent who is the child's legal parent: Georgia, Ted, and Helen. This parent, of course, does not want to give up his or her parental rights in order to allow a romantic partner or new spouse to adopt the child. Yet how can this be avoided if an adoption terminates all prior parent-child relationships? States handle this predicament in one of three ways:

- The state makes an exception for stepparent adoptions. If a stepparent adopts the child, the parental rights of the biological parent are not terminated. Some states, however, apply this rule only if the stepparent marries the legal parent.

- The state allows all **second-parent adoptions**. This is an adoption of a child by an unmarried partner of a legal parent who does not give up (relinquish) his or her own parental rights when the adoption occurs.

- The state follows the traditional rule and will not allow the adoption without terminating the parental rights of the legal parent.

Where the third option applies, adoptions rarely occur unless the state imposes a termination of parental rights of the legal parent against the latter's wishes, usually because of child maltreatment, as we will see.

second-parent adoption
The adoption of a child by a partner of a legal parent when the latter does not give up (relinquish) his or her own parental rights when the adoption occurs.

STATISTICS

Exhibit 15.1 presents some of the major statistics that pertain to this area of family law.

CATEGORIES OF ADOPTION

There are four major categories of domestic adoption: public-agency adoption, licensed private-agency adoption, independent adoption, and facilitated/unlicensed agency adoption.[1] (See Exhibit 15.2.)

Ultimately, all adoptions require a court decision allowing the adoption. The four major categories differ primarily on how the adoptive parents and child are brought together:

- *Public-agency adoption.* An adoption that occurs directly through a public agency or through a private agency under contract with a public agency.

EXHIBIT 15.1   Adoption Statistics

- **Total Numbers**
  - Number of children in the United States who have been adopted: 1.5 million (some estimates, however, range from 2 million to 5 million)
  - Percentage of all children who have been adopted: over 2%
  - Number of children adopted per year: approximately 136,000
  - Number of families with children who have an adopted child: 1 in 15
  - Percentage of Americans who know someone who has been adopted: 58%
- **Adoptions by Source** (2008)
  - Adoptions that occurred through public child welfare agencies: 41% (55,303)
  - Intercountry adoptions: 13% (17,416) (since 2004 the number of intercountry adoptions had substantially declined)
  - Other types of adoption (private agency, tribal, facilitated, independent, and stepparent): 46% (63,094)
- **Categories of Adoptive Parents**
  - Married couples: 66%
  - Unmarried couples: 2%
  - Single females: 30%
  - Single males: 2%
  - Adoptive parents who knew the adoptee prior to the adoption: 33%
  - Adoptive parents who were relatives of the adoptee: 24%
- **Categories of Adoptees**
  - 37% were in foster care
  - 67% were White, non-Hispanic
  - 17% were Black, non-Hispanic
  - 5% were Hispanic
  - 8% were transracial (child and adoptive parents were of different races)
- **Ages of the Adoptees**
  - Under 1 year: 2%
  - 1–5 years: 46%
  - 6–10 years: 37%
  - 11–15 years: 13%
  - 16–18 years: 2%
- **Couples Seeking to Adopt**
  - For every actual adoption, there are approximately 5 to 6 couples seeking to adopt
  - More than one million couples compete for 30,000 healthy white infants each year (adoption agencies sometimes refer to such children born in this country as DWIs—domestic White infants)
- **Waiting Time to Adopt**
  - Healthy infant: 1 to 7 years
  - Intercountry: 6 to 18 months
- **Percentage of Unmarried Women who Place Their Babies for Adoption**
  - 1998: under 2%
  - Before 1973 (the year abortion was legalized): 9%
- **Women who Place their Babies for Adoption**
  - White women: 19% (from 1965 to 1972)
  - White women: 1.7% (from 1989 to 1995)
  - Black women: under 1% (a number that has remained constant)
  - Latina women: under 2% (a number that has remained constant)

- **Birth Parents and Adoptive Parents**
  - Traditional adoption. Percentage in which there is some contact between birth parent and adoptive parent before the adoption: 95%
  - Traditional adoption. Percentage in which they meet before the adoption: 69%
  - Open adoption. Percentage in which there is ongoing contact (including with the child) after the adoption: 55%
  - Mediated adoption. Percentage in which an adoption agency facilitates periodic exchanges of picture and letters, but not direct contact, after the adoption: 40%
- **Cost of Adoption to Adoptive Parent(s)**
  - Average cost of adoption through an agency in the United States (domestic adoption): $41,532
  - Average cost of adoption through an attorney in the United States (domestic adoption): $35,594
  - Cost range of adoption from foster care: $0 to $2,811
  - Average cost of an intercountry adoptions from South Korea: $36,412
  - Average cost of an intercountry adoption from Ethiopia: $38,667
  - Average cost of an intercountry adoption from China: $36,070
- **Some Specific Adoption Expenses**
  - Average attorney fee: $13,000
  - Average agency fee: $17,000
  - Average cost of home study: $2,345
  - Maternity home care during third trimester and postdelivery: $6,000
  - Prenatal and hospital care (normal delivery): $6,000
  - Prenatal and hospital care (caesarean section): $9,000
  - Prenatal and hospital care (major complications): $100,000
  - Home study and post-placement evaluation visits: $1,000 – $3,000
  - Other costs (travel, phone, insurance): $2,000 – $6,000
  - Additional costs of intercountry adoption: $7,000 – $10,000
- **Financial Assistance**
  - Federal tax credit for qualified adoption expenses: $14,300 per child (the amount of the credit, however, phases out for high-income taxpayers)
  - Some special needs children adopted from foster care are eligible to receive federal or state adoption assistance
- **Number of Adopted Adults who Search for Their Biological Parents:** 2% to 4%
- **Children in Foster Care**
  - 2012: 396,966
  - 2018: 510,000
  - Median age of children in foster care: 7.8
  - Percentage of foster children in homes of non-relatives: 45%
  - Percentage of foster children in homes of relatives (called *kinship care*): 32%
  - Percentage of foster children in institutions or group homes: 12%
  - Total number of children needing adoptive parent(s): 129,000 (photos may be available at adoptuskids.org)
  - Number of children older than 12 needing adoptive parent(s): 22,500+
  - Number of children in foster care adopted by a single adoptive parent: 28% (single female: 25%; single male: 3%)
  - Average time in foster care: 39.1 months
  - Total number of children adopted from foster care annually: 56,507

Sources: U.S. Department of Health and Human Services, Administration for Children and Families, *The Adoption and Foster Care Analysis and Reporting System (AFCARS)* (2018). Child Welfare Information Gateway, *Adoption Statistics (2019)*. Asher Fogle, *Surprising Facts. . . About Adoption* (December 8 2015) (www.goodhousekeeping.com). North American Council on Adoptable Children, *State Adoption Fact Sheets* (2019) (www.nacac.org).

EXHIBIT 15.2   Types of Adoption

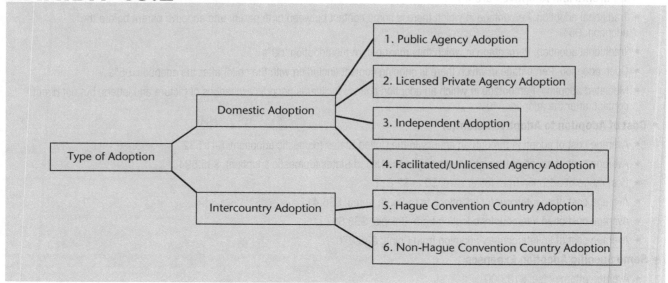

Source: U.S. Department of Health and Human Services, Child Welfare Information Gateway, Children's Bureau, *Adoption Options* (2015) (www.childwelfare.gov/pubPDFs/f_adoptoption.pdf#page=2&view=Step 1: Explore adoption options).

The public agency usually has legal and physical custody of the child in the foster-care system, often due to abuse or neglect. When efforts to reunite foster children with their birth parents fail, the agency searches for adoptive parents. Very few infants are available for adoption. Most of the children in the foster-care system are difficult to place because of special needs, such as being over eight years of age, having disabilities, and having siblings who need to be adopted together. Online adoption exchanges provide listings with pictures and brief descriptions of children in the foster-care system who need adoptive parents.

- *Licensed private-agency adoption.* An adoption that occurs through a private agency licensed by the state. It is often a nonprofit agency that has a religious focus. If the state allows the agency to be for-profit, it is more likely to be nonsectarian (and more expensive). Birth parents relinquish their parental rights to the agency. Adoptive parents usually seek healthy infants to adopt. The waiting time can be extensive (often several years). Many agencies encourage birth parents to choose a prospective adoptive family for their child based on profiles that prospective families create to share information about themselves.

independent adoption
An adoption that is arranged by the birth parents and the adoptive parents without the involvement of a public agency but often with the assistance of an attorney facilitator. Also called *private adoption, direct-placement adoption, private-placement adoption, facilitated adoption.*

- *Independent adoption.* In most **independent adoptions**, attorney-facilitators assist prospective adoptive parents and birth parents with the adoption process, which usually involves the adoption of an infant. Families adopting independently identify an expectant parent (e.g., a pregnant woman) without an agency's help. In some cases, the attorney may identify an expectant parent who is seeking an adoptive family. Infants usually are placed with the adoptive parents directly from the hospital after birth.

- *Facilitated/unlicensed agency adoption.* Some adoptions are arranged by facilitators and unlicensed agencies. A facilitator is any person who links prospective adoptive parents with expectant birth mothers for a fee. Facilitators may or may not be regulated in their state and may have varying degrees of expertise in adoption practice. Families who work with facilitators often have little recourse if the plan does not work out as they had hoped. Some states prohibit adoptions by paid facilitators.

Intercountry Adoptions

An *intercountry adoption* (also called an *international adoption*) is the adoption of a child who is a citizen of one country by persons who are citizens of a different country. Intercountry adoptions are finalized abroad or in the United States, depending on the laws of the country where the child resides. If the adoption is granted (finalized) abroad, it is often refinalized in the United States as a U.S. adoption in order (1) to assure compliance with the law of the state where the child will live and (2) to obtain a U.S. birth certificate. The United States is a member of the Hague Adoption Convention, which regulates adoptions between member nations.[2] A major concern of the Convention is to combat baby trafficking in which mothers in foreign countries are pressured into giving their children to orphanages, which then charge large fees to potential adoptive parents in the United States and other wealthy countries.

Native American Adoptions

One other unique category of adoption should be mentioned – the adoption of Native American children. Congress has declared in the Indian Child Welfare Act (ICWA) that in "any adoptive placement of an Indian child under State law, a preference shall be given, in the absence of good cause to the contrary, to a placement with (1) a member of the child's extended family; (2) other members of the Indian child's tribe; or (3) other Indian families."[3] Tribal courts can request exclusive jurisdiction to make the adoption decision, which, under tribal law, does not always require the termination of the parental rights of the birth parents.

FACILITATORS

A large network of service providers is available to facilitate adoptions. For many adoptions, the central service provider is the facilitator or intermediary who (for a fee) helps bring the biological parent (birth mother) and the adoptive parents together. The facilitator acts on behalf of a birth parent or on behalf of a prospective adoptive parent. The facilitator can be an attorney, a doctor, a member of the clergy, a relative, or an unregulated service agency with a large Internet presence. As indicated, however, some states limit the placement of children to licensed agencies and thereby prohibit the use of facilitators and intermediaries. Other states allow their use but impose restrictions, such as the amount of the fee they can charge.

Other facilitators include photographers and web designers who help childless couples design their own websites as part of their search for pregnant women thinking about adoption. Several insurance companies sell adoption cancellation policies to recover expenses if a birth mother changes her mind. Other available resources include numerous support groups, adoptive parent groups, and adoption exchanges that operate out of living rooms as well as office buildings. (An adoption exchange is often an organization that seeks adoptive parents for foster care or special needs children.) In states where ads are legal, you can find ads directed at young, unmarried pregnant women ("Loving couple wishes to adopt your child.") The ads are placed on websites, in newspapers and magazines, and on message boards, where young women are likely to see them.

The independent-adoption process can be arduous. Here is an example:

When Ralph and Nancy Smith discovered that they were infertile, they decided to adopt. Several visits to adoption agencies, however, were discouraging. One agency had a long waiting list of couples seeking to adopt healthy, white infants; the agency was not taking any new applications at the present time. Another agency accepted their application, but warned that the process might take up to five years, with no guarantee that an infant would eventually become available.

Nationally, hundreds of thousands of couples are waiting to adopt the few available healthy, white infants. The small number of adoptees is due to the widespread use of abortion and the declining social stigma attached to single-parent motherhood.

Acting on the advice of a friend, the Smiths placed personal ads on the Internet and in newspapers seeking to contact an unwed pregnant woman willing to relinquish her child for adoption. They created their own web page containing photographs and video clips of their home life in order to give a birth mother an idea of what life would be like for her child if she chose the Smiths as adoptive parents. They also sent their résumé and letters of inquiry to doctors, members of the clergy, and attorneys specializing in independent adoptions. Many attorneys with this specialty advertise online.

Their efforts were finally successful when an attorney led them to Diane Kline, a seventeen year-old pregnant girl. The Smiths prepared a scrapbook on their life, which Diane reviewed along with their web page. She then interviewed the Smiths and decided to allow them to adopt her child. The Smiths paid the attorney fees, Diane's medical bills, the cost of her psychological counseling, travel expenses, and living expenses related to the delivery of the baby. Eventually, Diane signed a consent form relinquishing her rights in the baby and agreeing to the adoption by the Smiths, who formally applied to the court for the adoption. A private agency investigated the case and made a home-study report to the court, which then issued an order authorizing the adoption.

In this example, the biological mother had personal contact with the adoptive parents. When, however, anonymity of the biological parents is desired, it can easily be accomplished.

ADOPTION ABUSE

black-market adoption
An adoption that is illegal because the payments to facilitate the adoption were in excess of reasonable expenses of facilitation. Also called *baby-buying.*

In the Smith example, the money paid by the adoptive parents covered medical, legal, and related expenses. In most states, a person may pay expenses that are naturally and reasonably connected with the adoption, so long as no cash or other consideration is given to induce someone to participate in the adoption. The law assumes that this is what occurs when there is a payment beyond reasonable expenses. Such payments turn the transaction into a **black-market adoption**, also called *baby buying*. Assume, for example, that Diane had hesitated about going through with the adoption, and the Smiths had offered her $20,000 above the usual pregnancy-related expenses. This would constitute baby-buying. You cannot pay someone (directly or indirectly) to give up a child. At the extreme end of this illegal practice are *baby brokers* who financially entice women to give up their children and then charge adoptive parents a large fee for arranging the adoption. Black-market adoptions can involve payments of up to $50,000. (The separate but related problem of payments for surrogate motherhood will be considered in the next chapter.)

It is difficult to know how many legitimate adoptions turn into black-market adoptions; the participants have an interest in keeping quiet about the illegal payment. To discourage illegal payments, most states require the adoptive parent to file with the court a list of all expenditures pertaining to the adoption. This, however, has not stopped black-market adoptions from occurring. Some argue that the only way to end the practice is to require that all adoptions be supervised by traditional public and licensed private agencies. Only a few states have taken this route.

Here are examples of other adoption abuses:

- A child was offered by an online adoption facilitator to two hopeful couples (one in the United States and one in England), neither of whom knew that the other was seeking to adopt the same child. After both couples paid the facilitator thousands of dollars in fees, the biological mother changed her mind about wanting to go through with the adoption.

- In Los Angeles, the police recently arrested a woman for promising her unborn child to seven couples seeking to adopt. She was charged with adoption fraud.

- A woman was charged with child abandonment when she tried to place her son for adoption with someone she met on eBay.

- A New York City attorney was convicted in the battery death of a six-year-old girl who had been placed in his care so that he might arrange an independent adoption. The attorney kept the child and then abused her when the prospective adoptive parents failed to pay his fee for the adoption.

Such stories always lead to calls for additional regulation. Proponents of independent adoptions, however, view these cases as aberrations and maintain that the vast majority of independent adoptions are legal and are adequately supervised.

ASSIGNMENT   15.2

Answer the following questions based on your state code. (See General Instructions for the State-Code Assignment in Appendix A.)

a. Are independent or private adoptions allowed in your state? If so, how do they differ from agency adoptions? In what ways does the state try to prevent black-market adoptions?

b. Is it a crime to "buy" a baby? If so, how is this crime committed?

WHO MAY BE ADOPTED?

In most cases, the person adopted (the adoptee) is a young child. Yet in many states it is possible for one adult to adopt another adult. The most common reason for this practice is that the adoptive parent wants the adopted adult (adoptee) to be able to inherit from the adoptive parent. In effect, the adoptive parent is naming an heir. In ancient Greece and Rome, perpetuating the family line by designating an heir was a main purpose of adoption. In addition to creating inheritance rights, a major reason that courts approve adult/adult adoptions is to provide long-term or perpetual care to a disabled adult adoptee.

Another use of adult/adult adoptions is to try to create a family so that a rent-controlled apartment can be transferred to a family member. If, for example, an adult tenant has a rent-controlled apartment (one that the landlord cannot rent at market rates), the tenant may not be able to transfer the apartment to another person unless that person is a member of the tenant's immediate family. To create such a member, the tenant might try to adopt another adult, e.g., an intimate companion. This strategy, however, is often challenged by landlords who are eager to convert rent-controlled apartments into market-rate units. Although the legality of this use of adoption is not clear, there are courts that have said that it is legal.[4] States that approve it are likely to say that adoption to confer the economic benefit of an apartment is similar to an adoption to confer the economic benefit of inheritance. Similarly, a recent case permitted a grandfather with disabilities to adopt his adult grandson in order to allow the grandson to qualify for financial aid available to children of disabled veterans.[5]

In 2012, a wealthy defendant adopted his girlfriend in an alleged strategy to shield some of his assets in the event that he was found liable in a wrongful-death case against him. The judge who granted the adoption did not know that the defendant was about to be sued for wrongful death at the time the adoption was approved. The adoption was then challenged on the ground that adoption cannot be used to shield assets from potential judgment creditors.[6]

When adult/adult adoptions are allowed, they differ from adoptions of minors in that adult/adult adoptions do not require a home study, and the consent of the biological parents of the adult adoptee is not required. The biological parents may have to be given notice of the adoption, but they cannot veto it.

WHO MAY ADOPT?

best interests of the child
A standard used by a court to decide what would best serve a child's welfare when the court must make custody, visitation, adoption, guardianship, and change-of-name decisions.

kinship adoptions
An adoption in which the adoptive parent is related to the adoptee.

In most cases, the petitioners (i.e., the persons seeking to become the adoptive parents) will be granted the adoption if it is in **best interests of the child**. Such a broad standard gives the judge considerable discretion. In many states, there is a presumption or a preference that the adoptive parent(s) should be a relative of the child. Although such **kinship adoptions** are desirable, other factors may lead a court to conclude that it would be in the best interests of the child to be placed with a nonrelated adoptive parent.

We turn now to an overview of the factors considered in most adoptions.

FACTORS CONSIDERED

To apply the best-interests standard, the judge will consider the following factors, no one of which is usually controlling:

1. Age
2. Marital status
3. Health
4. Race

5. Religion
6. Wishes of the child
7. Economic status
8. Home environment and morality

1. *Age of the petitioner.* Most states require the petitioner to be an adult. The preference is for someone who is not unusually older than the child. A court would be reluctant, for example, to allow a seventy-five-year-old to adopt an infant, unless special circumstances warranted it.

2. *Marital status of the petitioner.* Single persons are allowed to adopt, although the preference is for someone who is married. His or her spouse is usually required to join the petition as well.

3. *Health of the petitioner.* Adoptive parents are not expected to be physically and emotionally perfect. If a particular disability will not seriously interfere with the raising of the child, it will not by itself bar the adoption.

transracial adoptions
An adoption of a child whose race is different from the race of the adoptive parents. Also called *interracial adoption.*

Multiethnic Placement Act (MEPA)
A federal statute that forbids delay or denial of adoption on the basis of race, color, or national origin.

4. *Race.* Race can be a factor in the adoption decision of a court, but it cannot be the sole factor or the determining factor in the decision. Racial *matching* (placing children with adoptive parents of the same race as the child) cannot be required. **Transracial adoptions** have been controversial. In 1972, the National Association of Black Social Workers expressed strong opposition to such adoptions. The problem, however, is that there are not enough same-race adoptive parents available. The net effect of banning such adoptions would be to lengthen the time children must wait to be adopted, a reality referred to as *foster-care drift.* In an attempt to avoid this problem, Congress passed the **Multiethnic Placement Act (MEPA)**, which prohibits the delay or denial of adoptions on account of race:

A person or government that is involved in adoption or foster care placements may not (A) deny to any individual the opportunity to become an adoptive or a foster parent, on the basis of the race, color, or national origin of the individual, or of the child, involved; or (B) delay or deny the placement of a child for adoption or into foster care, on the basis of the race, color, or national origin of the adoptive or foster parent, or the child, involved.[7]

Native Americans in the United States, however, are treated differently. Congress has determined that "an alarmingly high percentage of Indian families are broken up by the removal, often unwarranted, of their children from them by nontribal public and private agencies and that an alarmingly high percentage of such children are placed in non-Indian foster and adoptive homes and institutions."[8] Consequently, the adoption of American Indian children by non-Indians today is relatively rare. As indicated earlier, tribal courts can request exclusive jurisdiction to make the adoption decisions involving Native American children.

5. *Religion.* When possible or practicable, the religion of the adoptive parents should be the same as the religion of the biological parents. Interfaith adoptions, though allowed, are generally not encouraged.

6. *Wishes of the child.* The court will consider the opinion of the prospective adoptee if he or she is old enough to communicate a preference.

7. *Economic status.* The adoptive parents must have the financial means (on their own or with available assistance from other sources) to care for the child. The court will examine their current financial status and prospects for the future in light of the child's support needs.

8. *Home environment and morality.* The goal is for the child to be brought up in a wholesome, loving home where values are important and where the child will be nurtured to his or her potential. Illegal or conspicuously unorthodox lifestyles are frowned upon and may lead to a denial of the adoption petition.

ASSIGNMENT   15.3

To answer the following questions, check your state code and court opinions. (See General Instructions for the State-Code Assignment and the Court-Opinion Assignment in Appendix A.)

a. In your state, who is eligible to adopt children? Who is not eligible?

b. What standards exist to guide a judge's decision in your state on whether to approve a particular adoption?

c. Mary Jones is a Baptist. She wants to place her one-year-old child for adoption. Mr. and Mrs. Johnson want to adopt the child and file the appropriate petition to do so in your state. The Johnsons are Jewish. Mary Jones consents to the adoption. What effect, if any, will the religious differences between Mary Jones and the Johnsons have on the adoption? Assume that Mary has no objection to the child's being raised in the Jewish faith.

d. Same facts as described in the (c) example above except that the Johnsons are professed atheists. Mary Jones does not care.

e. Under what circumstances can a single person—an adult who lives alone—adopt a minor in your state?

| ASSIGNMENT | 15.4 |

Both Paul and Helen Smith are deaf and mute. They wish to adopt the infant daughter of Helen's best friend, a widow who just died. Prepare an investigation strategy to collect evidence relevant to whether the adoption should be permitted. (See General Instructions for the Investigation-Strategy Assignment in Appendix A.)

GAYS AND LESBIANS

A gay or lesbian person who petitions for adoption could fall into one of several categories. He or she might:

- Live alone and hence seek to become the sole parent.
- Live with a same-sex partner who is a biological parent of the child. The same-sex partner would be seeking a second-parent adoption.
- Live with a same-sex partner who is not a biological parent of the child, so that both would petition the court for a **joint adoption**, which is an adoption by two adults who both seek to become adoptive parents of a child.

joint adoption
An adoption by two adults (usually married) who both seek to become adoptive parents of a child.

Exhibit 15.3 provides an overview of adoption by gays and lesbians.

Most states allow single adults of any sexual orientation to adopt children. The law in New York is typical of this position:

Applicants shall not be rejected solely on the basis of homosexuality. A decision to accept or reject when homosexuality is at issue shall be made on the basis of individual factors as explored and found in the adoption study process as it relates to the best interests of adoptive children.[9]

This policy decision on who should be allowed to adopt is supported by a 2004 resolution of the American Psychological Association that "[t]here is no scientific basis for concluding that lesbian mothers or gay fathers are unfit parents on the basis of their sexual orientation" and that "results of research suggest that lesbian and gay parents are as likely as heterosexual parents to provide supportive and healthy environments for their children."[10]

EXHIBIT 15.3   Adoption: Gays and Lesbians

- Of the 594,000 same-sex couple households in the United States, 115,000 have children. Approximately 65,000 of these children were adopted.
- Gay and lesbian couples are four times more likely than heterosexual couples to have an adopted child in their household.
- More than 50% of gay and lesbian parents adopt children from the foster care and child welfare system.
- More than 60% of gay and lesbian parents adopt children of a race different from their own (transracial adoptions).
- More than 10% of gay and lesbian parents adopt children who are six years of age or older (generally, a difficult age for a child to be adopted).
- More than 14,000 foster children live in homes headed by non-heterosexual individuals or couples.
- More than 2,000,000 gays, lesbians, or bisexuals are interested in adopting.

Sources: Evan B. Donalson Adoption Institute, *Expanding Resources for Children III* (2011). Gary Gates, et al, *Adoption and Foster Care by Gay and Lesbian Parents in the United States* (Williams Institute & Urban Institute, March 2007). Lifelong Adoptions (www.lifelongadoptions.com).

At one time, many states had explicit bans on adoptions by gays or lesbians. For example, a statute in Florida once provided that "No person eligible to adopt under this statute may adopt if that person is a homosexual." Such statutes no longer exist today primarily because of equal-protection challenges under federal and state constitutions. The Florida statute was held to violate the Equal Protection Clause of the Florida state constitution. Other bans have been subjected to similar state and federal constitutional challenges.

Although outright bans on such adoptions no longer exist, the agencies and judges applying adoption law can use their extensive discretion to disfavor prospective adoptive parents who are gay or lesbian. Critics charge that such discrimination exists to a very large extent.

Our earlier discussion of second-parent adoption affects the extent of adoptions by gays and lesbians:

- If a state allows second-parent adoptions (or stepparent adoptions) the gay or lesbian partner of a biological parent could adopt without terminating the existing partner's parental rights.[11]

- If, however, a state does not allow second-parent adoptions, the biological parent would have to give up his or her parental rights in order to let his or her partner adopt the child they are raising together. The state might make an exception when a stepparent wants to adopt the child, but only if the stepparent marries the biological parent.

A separate question is whether a gay or lesbian person has a duty to support the child he or she is seeking to adopt. If the rules on *equitable estoppel* and *in loco parentis* apply (see Chapter 10), the support duty may exist even if the application to adopt is denied.

ADOPTION PROCEDURE

It is not easy to adopt a child. Elaborate procedures have been created to protect the interests of the child, the biological parents, and the adoptive parents. When the most sought-after babies (i.e., healthy, DWIs—domestic white infants) are in short supply, the temptation to "buy" a baby on the black market is heightened. One way to try to control this is by increasing procedural safeguards in the process. Fewer safeguards, however, are usually needed in stepparent adoptions of children who will continue to live with a biological parent. In stepparent adoptions, courts may have discretion to use an **expedited procedure,** such as waiving (or doing a shortened version of) the home study. Some states, however, will not streamline the process in this way unless the biological parent has been married to the stepparent for at least a year.

expedited procedure
An accelerated procedure achieved by bypassing some of the procedural steps that are normally required.

JURISDICTION AND VENUE

Subject-matter jurisdiction is the power of a court to hear a particular kind of case and to grant a particular kind of relief. Not every court in a state has subject-matter jurisdiction to issue adoption decrees. The state constitution or a state statute will designate one or perhaps two courts that have authority to hear adoption cases (e.g., the state family court, probate court, surrogate court, or juvenile court). There are also rules on selecting the **venue** or place of the proceeding, which become important when more than one county or district has subject-matter jurisdiction over adoptions in the state. The selection is referred to as the *choice of venue.* It will often depend on the residence of one or more of the participants, usually the biological parents, the adoptive parents, or the child.

subject-matter jurisdiction
The court's power to resolve a particular type of legal dispute and to grant a particular type of relief.

venue
The place of the trial. The proper county or geographical area in which a court with subject-matter jurisdiction may hear a case.

PETITION

petition
A formal request that the court take some action. (See the glossary for an additional meaning.)

States differ on the form and content of the adoption **petition** filed by the adoptive parents to begin the adoption proceeding. In most states, the petition will contain such data as the names of the petitioners; the petitioners' ages; whether the petitioners are married and, if so, whether they are living together; the name and age of the child, etc. Not all states require that the biological parents be named in the petition itself. (See Exhibit 15.4 for the first page of an example of an adoption petition.)

EXHIBIT 15.4   Adoption Petition

PROBATE COURT OF HAMILTON COUNTY, OHIO
RALPH WINKLER, JUDGE

ADOPTION OF_____
                                    (Name after adoption)

CASE NO._____

PETITION FOR ADOPTION OF MINOR
[R.C. 3107.05]

The undersigned petitions to adopt_____,

a minor, and to change the name of the minor to_____.

PETITIONER

The petitioner states the following:

Full Name:_____ Age_____

Full Name:_____ Age_____

Place of Residence:_____
                                                    Street Address

_____

Post Office   State   Zip Code   Duration of residence

Marital Status:_____ Date and Place of Marriage:_____

Relationship of Minor to Petitioner:_____

The petitioner has facilities and resources suitable to provide for the nurture and care of the minor and it is the desire of the petitioner to establish the relationship of parent and child with the minor.

MINOR TO BE ADOPTED

Birth Name:_____ Date of Birth:_____

Place of Birth:_____

☐   The minor is living in the home of the petitioner, and was placed therein for adoption on the _____ day of
        _____, _____ by _____

☐   The minor is not living in the home of the petitioner, and resides at_____
        _____

A certified copy of the birth certificate of the minor is filed with this petition or is not available due to the following:
_____
_____

A Preliminary Estimate Accounting (Form 18.9), if required, is filed with this petition.

Source: Hamilton Probate Court, Ohio (www.probatect.org/forms/adoption).

In some states, once the adoption petition is filed, the child is placed with the prospective adoptive parents on a probation basis to assess how well the child adjusts to the new home. Of course, if the child is already living with the prospective parents (e.g., a foster parent or a stepparent who wants to adopt the child), the court will already have access to the data on adjustment.

ASSIGNMENT   15.5

a. What must a petition for adoption contain in your state? Must it name the biological parents? (See General Instructions for the State-Code Assignment in Appendix A.)

b. Draft an adoption petition. Assume that you are seeking to adopt the one-year-old baby of a friend, a woman who has recently been hospitalized. This friend has no other relatives. The biological father of the child is no longer alive. You can make up facts you need to draft the petition. (See General Instructions for the Complaint-Drafting Assignment in Appendix A.)

NOTICE

Procedural due process of law requires that both biological parents be given *notice* of the petition to adopt the child by the prospective adoptive parents. (Later, when we study the *Baby Richard* and *Baby Jessica* cases, we will see examples of the critical importance of this requirement.) The preferred method of providing notice is to personally serve the biological parents with process within the state where the adoption petition is brought. If this is not possible, the court may allow substituted service (e.g., by registered mail or publication in a newspaper).

There was a time when the father of a nonmarital (illegitimate) child was not entitled to notice of the adoption proceeding; only the mother of such a child was given notice. This has changed, however, as a result of decisions of the U.S. Supreme Court. Petitioners for the adoption are now required to use due diligence to locate and identify the father in order to give him notice. Although the full scope of the rights of the father of a nonmarital child has not yet been fully defined by the courts, it is clear that he can no longer be ignored in the adoption process. As we shall see, however, his right to receive notice of the adoption proceeding does not necessarily mean he can prevent the adoption by refusing to consent to it.

CONSENT

Consent of Biological Parents

Adoption occurs in two ways: with or without the consent of the biological parents. When consent is necessary, the state's statute will usually specify the requirements of consent:

- Whether the consent must be notarized and witnessed.
- Whether consent can be given before the birth of the child.
- Whether special steps must be taken if the birth mother is a minor (e.g., appointment of counsel or guardian ad litem for her).
- Whether the formalities for consent differ for agency adoptions as opposed to independent adoptions.
- Whether the consent form must mention the names of the parties seeking to adopt the child.

Along with consent, a formal relinquishment of parental rights (surrender) must be filed in court. A parent seeking the assistance of an adoption agency will usually be asked to sign a surrender of parental rights to the agency.

procedural due process
The constitutional requirement that the government provide fair procedures (such as adequate notice and an opportunity to be heard) whenever the government seeks to deprive someone of life, liberty, or property.

process
The means (e.g., a summons, writ, or other court order) used by the court to acquire its power or jurisdiction over a person.

substituted service
Service of process by mail, by publication in a newspaper, or by other approved methods that are alternatives to the personal service of hand delivering the process documents to the defendant (or his or her authorized representative). Also called *constructive service*.

due diligence
Reasonable efforts to find and verify factual information needed to carry out an obligation (e.g., to locate a parent) to avoid harming someone, or to make an important decision.

surrender
A voluntary relinquishment of rights.

opportunity interest
The right of a parent to develop a relationship with his or her child.

indicia of parenthood
Conduct that indicates or evidences a parental relationship with a child.

Women who change their minds about giving up their babies often claim that they were coerced or unduly pressured into consenting. In one case, the woman alleged that she was pressured to choose the adoptive parents while she was in labor and to sign the adoption papers while she was under the influence of the sedative Demerol. In light of such problems, most states say that the consent is not valid if it is obtained prior to the birth of the child. A state may not allow the consent to be sought until at least seventy-two hours after birth.

Both biological parents must consent to the adoption unless the parental rights of one or both of them have been formally terminated (see discussion of termination below) or unless one of the parents, mainly the father, has failed to take adequate steps to protect his *opportunity interest*, which is the constitutional right of a parent to develop a relationship with his or her child.

A father can prevent an adoption by withholding his consent, but only if he has shown sufficient *indicia of parenthood*. Indicia (indications or evidence) can include establishing his paternity, living with the child, supporting the child, or otherwise maintaining close contacts with the child. Such a father will be given the same rights as the mother. He *will* be allowed to veto a proposed adoption. A father who fails to demonstrate sufficient indicia of parenthood has, in effect, abandoned his opportunity interest and cannot prevent the adoption. The standard used by the courts is called "biology plus." The biological relationship between father and child is not sufficient to allow him to veto the adoption. To have this right, there must be biology *plus* indicia of parenthood.

Suppose, however, that a father fails to demonstrate sufficient indicia of parenthood (biology plus) because he never knew that he was a father (e.g., the birth mother lied about whether the baby was born alive). We will cover this issue later in this chapter when we discuss the *Baby Richard* case, the *Baby Jessica* case, and putative father registries.

Consent of Others

Who else may have to consent to an adoption?

- If the biological parents have already relinquished or surrendered their parental rights to an agency, then the consent of the adoption agency will be required.

- If the prospective adoptive parent is married, the consent of his or her spouse is often required, even if this spouse is not also adopting the child.

- In most states, the child to be adopted—the adoptee—must consent to the adoption if he or she has reached a specified age (e.g., twelve or fourteen), unless the court determines that it would not be in the child's best interests to ask the child.

- If the child is in foster care, the consent of foster parents is *not* required when the child is eventually adopted by someone else.

Foster parents cannot prevent the adoption from occurring. This does not mean that the foster parents can be ignored entirely. When an agency attempts to remove the child from the foster home, many states give the foster parents the right to object to the removal and to present their arguments against the removal. Although foster parents may be given a right to be heard on the removal, they cannot veto the adoption of the child.

ASSIGNMENT   15.6

In Assignment 15.5, part (b), you drafted an adoption petition based primarily on facts that you invented yourself. Using those facts, draft a consent form (to be signed by the mother) that complies with the statutory requirements for consent in your state. (Take a look at examples of consent forms by running a search (*adoption consent form*) in the Images option of Google or Bing.)

Revocation of Consent

A biological parent can change her mind and revoke her consent to the adoption. Most states allow the birth mother to revoke her consent at any time before the birth of the child. As indicated, however, a state may not allow consent to be sought until a designated time after birth (e.g., seventy-two hours) and may give her a designated time after birth (e.g., ten days) during which she can revoke her consent.

INVOLUNTARY TERMINATION OF PARENTAL RIGHTS

Parents, whose parental rights have been terminated, cannot prevent the adoption of their children. A **termination of parental rights (TPR)** is a judicial declaration that ends the legal relationship between parent and child when this is in the best interests of the child. The parent no longer has any right to participate in decisions affecting the welfare of the child and no longer has any duties toward the child.

termination of parental rights (TPR)
A judicial declaration that ends the legal relationship between parent and child when this is in the best interests of the child.

Grounds for Termination

TPR can be voluntary or involuntary.

- TPR is voluntary when the biological parent wants to end the parent-child relationship in order to allow someone to adopt the child. For an agency adoption, the biological parent executes a document called a *surrender* (a voluntary relinquishment of parental rights), which releases parental rights to the agency.

- TPR is involuntary when the termination is forced on the parent because of being ruled **unfit**.

unfit
Demonstrating abuse or neglect that is substantially detrimental to a child.

The grounds for involuntary termination of parental rights vary among the states, although a central theme of these grounds is the unfitness of the biological parent(s). These grounds are summarized in the following overview found in the statutes of many states:

> The relationship of parent and child may be terminated by a court order issued in connection with an adoption proceeding on the ground:
>
> - That the minor has been abandoned by the parent;
>
> - That by reason of the misconduct, faults, or habits of the parent or the repeated and continuous neglect or refusal of the parent, the minor is without proper parental care and control, or subsistence, education, or other care or control necessary for his physical, mental, or emotional health or morals, or, by reason of physical or mental incapacity the parent is unable to provide necessary parental care for the minor, and the court finds that the conditions and causes of the behavior, neglect, or incapacity are irremediable or will not be remedied by the parent, and that by reason thereof the minor is suffering or probably will suffer serious physical, mental, moral, or emotional harm; or
>
> - That in the case of a parent not having custody of a minor, his consent is being unreasonably withheld contrary to the best interests of the minor.[12]

abandonment
Relinquishing one's parental responsibility by voluntarily leaving a child or ending communication with a child for a specific period or indefinitely without arranging for alternative care and supervision while away. Conduct that constitutes a relinquishing of one's parental responsibilities.

A parent is unfit when he or she demonstrates abuse or neglect that is substantially detrimental to a child. Unfitness is demonstrated by conduct such as **abandonment**, extreme cruelty, chronic abuse and neglect, conviction of certain crimes, willful neglect, or substantial incapacity to provide care. Some states may list unfitness as one of several grounds for involuntary TPR rather than as a catchall to cover all the grounds. A statute might also refer to the children as being *dependent* or in a state of **dependency**, which can mean children who are abused, neglected, or abandoned, or children lacking basic care through no fault of their parent or guardian.

dependency
(1) The condition of a child who has been placed in the custody of the state because the child has been abused, neglected, or abandoned. (2) Pertaining to a child who lacks basic care through no fault of the parent or guardian.

Because parents have a fundamental right under the U.S. Constitution to raise their children, parental rights cannot be involuntarily terminated simply because someone else is more stable and has more resources than biological parents.

A showing of unfitness (or a comparable ground) is key to a forced severance of parental rights. The standard is *not* the best interests of the child. It may be in the best interests of the child to be placed with a wealthy family. However, only after a biological parent is found to be unfit because of abuse or neglect in failing to provide for a child's basic needs will a court determine if it is in the best interests of the child to be adopted by someone else. As one court put it:

> The inability of parents to provide the basic necessities of life for their children is certainly not in the child's best interest. However, even though it may be in a child's best interest to live with a family of comfortable means rather than a poorer family, this standard may not justify the state's intervention into a family relationship absent a finding of parental unfitness.[13]

As demonstrated in the following checklist, many factors are relevant to the question of whether a parent is unfit. A court will consider all of these factors in combination; no one factor is usually determinative.

☑ INTERVIEWING AND INVESTIGATION CHECKLIST

Factors Relevant to Determining Parental Unfitness

(Assume that the parent is not currently living with the child.)

QUESTIONS TO ASK A CLIENT CHARGED WITH UNFITNESS

- How old are you now?
- With whom is your child living?
- Is the person who is caring for the child your relative, a friend, or a stranger?
- How did the child get there?
- How long has the child been there?
- When was the last time you saw the child?
- How often do you see your child per month?
- How many times do you speak to your child on the phone per month?
- How often do you contact your child by letter, text, or email per month?
- Did you ever say to anyone that you did not want your child or that you wanted your child to find a home with someone else? If so, explain.
- Did you ever say to anyone that you wanted your child to live with someone else temporarily until you got back on your feet again? If so, explain.
- Have you ever placed your child with a public or private adoption agency? Have you ever discussed adoption with anyone? If so, explain.
- Have you ever been charged with neglecting, abandoning, or failing to support your child? If so, explain.
- Has your child ever been taken from you for any period of time? If so, explain.

- Have you ever been found by a court to be mentally ill?
- How much have you contributed to the support of your child while you were not living with the child?
- Did you give the child any presents? If so, what were they and when did you give them?
- While your child was not with you, did you ever speak to the child's teachers or doctors? If so, explain how often you did so and the circumstances involved.
- Were you on public assistance while the child was not living with you? If so, what did you tell the public assistance workers about the child?
- How well is the child being treated now?
- Could anyone claim that the child lived under immoral or unhealthy circumstances while away from you and that you knew of these circumstances?
- Has the child ever been charged with juvenile delinquency? Has the child ever been declared a Person in Need of Supervision (PINS), Minor in Need of Supervision (MINS), or Child in Need of Protection and Services (CHIPS)?

INVESTIGATION TASKS

- Find and interview relatives, friends, and strangers who may have information on whether the client visited or otherwise contacted the child.
- Find and interview anyone with whom the client may have discussed the reasons for leaving the child with someone else.
- Prepare an inventory of all the money and other assets given by the client for the support of the child while the child was living with someone else.

(continued)

☑ **INTERVIEWING AND INVESTIGATION CHECKLIST** (*continued*)

- Collect receipts (e.g., canceled check stubs) for all funds given by the client for such support.
- Locate all relevant court records, if any (e.g., custody order in divorce proceeding, neglect or juvenile delinquency petitions and orders).

- Interview employees of state agencies that have been involved with the child. Then assess how responsive the client has been to the efforts of the agency to help the child and the client.
- Prepare a parenting plan on how the client will be able to care for the basic needs of the child if parental rights are not terminated.

Procedural Issues in Terminating Parental Rights

To take the drastic step of ordering an involuntary termination of parental rights, there must be **clear and convincing evidence** that the parent is unfit. This is a higher standard of proof than **preponderance of the evidence**, which is commonly used in civil cases.

The parent can be represented by counsel at the termination proceeding. Some states provide state-appointed counsel if the parent cannot afford to pay one. The U.S. Supreme Court, however, has ruled that states are not required to provide free counsel to **indigent** defendants in every termination case. A court must decide on a case-by-case basis whether an indigent parent needs free counsel because of the complexity of the case.[14] In complex cases, the state must provide free representation.

Although an appointed attorney is not required in every indigent case, a guardian ad litem (GAL) must be appointed to represent the child's best interests whenever child abuse or neglect is alleged in a court case.[15] The GAL can be an attorney or a **court appointed special advocate (CASA)**, who can be a nonattorney. (For a list of the duties of a CASA, see Paralegal Roles at the end of Chapter 14.) If the CASA is a nonattorney and the child needs legal advice, an attorney must provide this advice.

A parent who loses in the trial court and wishes to appeal the termination of parental rights must be given a free transcript if he or she cannot afford the cost of the transcript, which can amount to several thousand dollars.[16]

If parental rights are terminated and there are adoptive parents available, a separate adoption procedure will take place, or the adoption will be finalized in the same proceedings that led to the termination of parental rights.

---

clear and convincing evidence
A standard of proof that is met when the evidence demonstrates that the existence of a disputed fact is much more probable than its nonexistence. This standard is stronger than *preponderance of the evidence* but not as strong as *beyond a reasonable doubt*.

preponderance of the evidence
A standard of proof that is met when the evidence establishes that the existence of a disputed fact is more likely than its nonexistence. Also called *fair preponderance of evidence*.

indigent
Poor; without means to afford something, such as a private attorney or filing fees.

court appointed special advocate (CASA)
A volunteer (who can be an attorney, a paralegal, or other nonattorney) appointed by the court to perform special assignments pertaining to children in the court system.

ASSIGNMENT 15.7

a. When will parental rights be terminated in your state? What are the grounds? What standard of proof must be met? Clear and convincing evidence? (See the General Instructions for the State-Code Assignment in Appendix A.)

b. Mary is the mother of two children. She is convicted of murdering her husband, their father. What facts need to be investigated in order to determine whether Mary's parental rights should be terminated? (See General Instructions for the Investigation-Strategy Assignment in Appendix A.)

c. Prepare a flowchart of all the procedural steps necessary to terminate parental rights in your state. (See General Instructions for the Flowchart Assignment in Appendix A.)

ADOPTION AND SAFE FAMILIES ACT (ASFA)

Adoption and Safe Families Act (ASFA)
A federal statute that requires states to take specific placement action on behalf of children in foster care, such as terminating parental rights in order to facilitate adoption after a designated period of time trying to reunite the child with its biological parents.

Many children spend substantial time in foster care (See Exhibit 15.1). While waiting to determine whether a reunion with biological parents is possible, some children can languish for years in multiple foster homes. In 1997, Congress passed the **Adoption and Safe Families Act (ASFA)**,[17] which had the effect of speeding up adoptions of children in foster care by forcing states to hold regularly scheduled hearings on whether a reunion with the biological parents is feasible and safe and, if not, whether termination of parental rights is warranted. States must seek termination of parental rights if a child has been in foster care for fifteen of the last twenty-two months unless special circumstances exist to warrant otherwise.

STANDING: CAN CHILDREN DIVORCE THEIR PARENTS?

unemancipated
Legally dependent on one's parent or legal guardian.

It is, of course, impossible to divorce someone to whom you are not married. The concept of *parental* divorce was created by the media in cases such as that of *Gregory K. v. Rachel K.* in which an eleven-year-old **unemancipated** child asked a Florida Court to terminate the rights of his biological mother so that his foster parents could adopt him. Because he was the party who initiated the action, the media described him as a child who wanted to "divorce" his parents. The trial court allowed him to bring the action, terminated the parental rights of his mother, and granted the adoption.

The decision sparked considerable controversy. Some hailed it as the beginning of a major child's rights movement, comparing Gregory to the black woman who began the civil rights movement by refusing to give up her seat on the bus. "Gregory is the Rosa Parks of the youth rights movement," according to the chairperson of the National Child Rights Alliance.[18] Others were deeply disturbed by the decision. They thought it would open a floodgate of litigation brought by disgruntled children against their parents. A presidential candidate lamented that "kids would be suing their parents for being told to do their homework or take out the trash."[19]

nonage
Below the required minimum age to enter into a relationship or to perform a task. Minority.

standing
The right to state a claim or to bring a case and seek relief from a court.

On appeal, however, the Florida Court of Appeals ruled it was an error for the trial court to allow Gregory to initiate the termination action. A minor suffers the disability of **nonage** and hence does not have **standing** to ask a court to terminate the rights of his or her biological parents. Yet the court agreed that the parental rights of Gregory's mother should be terminated. When Gregory filed his petition, his foster parent simultaneously brought his own petition to terminate the rights of Gregory's biological mother on the ground that she had abandoned him. Foster parents *do* have standing in Florida to bring such petitions, and in this case, the adult's termination petition had merit. Hence, although Gregory eventually obtained the result he wanted (termination of parental rights plus adoption), the court, in effect, shut the door to comparable actions initiated by children in the future: "Courts historically have recognized that unemancipated minors do not have the legal capacity to initiate legal proceedings in their own names."[20]

INTERLOCUTORY DECREE

interlocutory
Not final; interim.

In many states, an adoption decree does not become final immediately. An **interlocutory** (temporary) decree of adoption is first issued, which becomes final after a set period of time. If the child is not already living with the adoptive parents, he or she can be placed with them during the interlocutory period to assess the child's adjustment to the new home environment. After this period, the decree can be made final.

CHALLENGES TO THE ADOPTION DECREE

Because it would be disruptive for the child to be moved from place to place as legal battles continue to rage among any combination of adoptive parents, biological parents, and agencies, there is a time limit within which challenges to the adoption decree must be brought (e.g., two years). A major ground for a dissolution or abrogation of adoption (which annuls the adoption) is that the adoption decree was obtained by duress, fraud, or undue influence and undoing the adoption would be in the best interests of the child.

abrogation
A cancelation or nullification.

"JOURNALISTIC TERRORISM"

We turn now to one of the more dramatic cases in the history of family law, the Illinois case of *Baby Richard: In re Petition of John Doe and Jane Doe.* Before the glare of cameras and national media, a four-year-old boy was taken from his adoptive parents and turned over to his natural father, Otakar Kirchner, whom the boy had never met. One newspaper account said the biological father "took physical custody of the sobbing child as he frantically reached for his adoptive mother in front of the house where the boy had lived since he was four days old."[21] The public's reaction was intense. Newspapers, newscasts, and talk shows gave the story extensive coverage. The case was called "nightmarish," "monstrous," "absolutely horrible," and "state sanctioned child abuse." The governor of Illinois said that Baby Richard was being "brutally, tragically torn away from the only parents he has ever known." The opinion in the case (*In re Petition of John Doe and Jane Doe*) was written by Justice Heiple. When it was published, he was denounced. One columnist, Bob Greene, was particularly critical. Justice Heiple took the highly unusual step of responding to this criticism in the supplemental opinion he wrote denying a rehearing of the case. He referred to the criticism as "journalistic terrorism."

CASE | In re Petition of John Doe and Jane Doe . . . to Adopt Baby Boy Janikova
159 Ill. 2d 347, 638 N.E.2d 181 (1994)

Supreme Court of Illinois
Background: *Daniella Janikova and Otakar Kirchner were not married when their son, Baby Boy Janikova, was born. (The media called him Baby Richard.) Otakar was out of the country at the time. Four days after the birth, Daniella consented to have the baby adopted by John and Jane Doe. Daniella did not tell Otakar about the adoption by the Does. In fact, she told him the baby was born dead. Fifty-seven days after the boy's birth, Otakar learned the truth. Within two weeks, he challenged the legality of the adoption on the ground that he did not consent to it. Lengthy litigation and media attention followed. The trial court found that Otakar was unfit*

because he did not show sufficient interest in the child during the first thirty days of the child's life, and therefore his consent to the adoption was not required. On appeal before the appellate court, Justice Rizzi affirmed, ruling that the adoption was in the best interests of the child. The case is now on appeal before the Supreme Court of Illinois. (During the litigation, Daniella married Otakar and, therefore, joined him in seeking to revoke the adoption to which she initially had consented.)

Decision on Appeal: *Reversed. Justice Heiple of the Supreme Court of Illinois held that the adoption was invalid because it violated the rights of the natural father. The use of the* best-interests-of-the-child standard by Justice Rizzi in the appellate court "grossly misstated the law." When this decision was rendered, Baby Richard was four years old and had lived with John and Jane Doe for three years.

OPINION OF THE COURT:

Justice HEIPLE delivered the opinion of the court. . . .

Otakar and Daniella began living together in the fall of 1989, and Daniella became pregnant in June of 1990. For the first eight months of her pregnancy, Otakar provided for all of her expenses.

In late January 1991, Otakar went to his native Czechoslovakia to attend to his gravely ill grandmother for two weeks. During this time, Daniella received a phone call from Otakar's aunt saying that Otakar had resumed a former romantic relationship with another woman.

Because of this unsettling news, Daniella left their shared apartment, refused to talk with Otakar on his return, and gave birth to the child at a different hospital than where they had originally planned. She gave her consent to the adoption of the child by [John and Jane Doe], telling them and their attorney that she knew who the father was but would not furnish his name. Daniella and her uncle warded off Otakar's persistent inquiries about the child by telling him that the child had died shortly after birth.

Otakar found out that the child was alive and had been placed for adoption 57 days after the child was born. He then began the instant proceedings by filing an appearance contesting the Does' adoption of his son. . . . [T]he trial court ruled that Otakar was an unfit parent under section 1 of the Adoption Act (750 ILCS 50/1) because he had not shown a reasonable degree of interest in the child within the first 30 days of his life. Therefore, the father's consent was unnecessary under section 8 of the Act (750 ILCS 50/8).

The finding that the father had not shown a reasonable degree of interest in the child is not supported by the evidence. In fact, he made various attempts to locate the child, all of which were either frustrated or blocked by the actions of the mother. Further, the mother was aided by the attorney for the adoptive parents, who failed to make any effort to ascertain the name or address of the father despite the fact that the mother indicated she knew who he was. Under the circumstances, the father had no opportunity to discharge any familial duty.

In the opinion below, the appellate court, wholly missing the threshold issue in this case, dwelt on the best interests of the child. Since, however, the father's parental interest was improperly terminated, there was no occasion to reach the factor of the child's best interests. That point should never have been reached and need never have been discussed.

Unfortunately, over three years have elapsed since the birth of the baby who is the subject of these proceedings. To the extent that it is relevant to assign fault in this case, the fault here lies initially with the mother, who fraudulently tried to deprive the father of his rights, and secondly, with the adoptive parents and their attorney, who proceeded with the adoption when they knew that a real father was out there who had been denied knowledge of his baby's existence. When the father entered his appearance in the adoption proceedings 57 days after the baby's birth and demanded his rights as a father, the petitioners should have relinquished the baby at that time. It was their decision to prolong this litigation through a lengthy, and ultimately fruitless, appeal.

The adoption laws of Illinois are neither complex nor difficult of application. Those laws intentionally place the burden of proof on the adoptive parents in establishing both the relinquishment and/or unfitness of the natural parents and, coincidentally, the fitness and the right to adopt of the adoptive parents. In addition, Illinois law requires a good-faith effort to notify the natural parents of the adoption proceedings. These laws are designed to protect natural parents in their preemptive rights to their own children wholly apart from any consideration of the so-called best interests of the child. If it were otherwise, few parents would be secure in the custody of their own children. If best interests of the child were a sufficient qualification to determine child custody, anyone with superior income, intelligence, education, etc., might challenge and deprive the parents of their right to their own children. The law is otherwise and was not complied with in this case.

Accordingly, we reverse.

SUPPLEMENTAL OPINION UPON DENIAL OF REHEARING

Justice HEIPLE, writing in support of the denial of rehearing:

On Thursday, June 16, 1994, this court reversed a decision by a divided appellate court which had affirmed certain adoption proceedings in the circuit court of Cook County. Our reversal was the result of the failure of the courts below to correctly apply Illinois law in terminating the natural father's parental rights. This cause is now before the court on petitions for rehearing filed by the adoptive parents and the guardian ad litem for the child. The following is offered in support of today's order denying rehearing.

I have been a judge for over 23 years. In that time, I have seldom before worked on a case that involved the spread of so much misinformation, nor one which dealt with as straightforward an application of law to fact.

[A] . . . conspiracy was undertaken to deny the natural father any knowledge of his son's existence. It began when the biological mother, 8½ months pregnant, was misinformed that the father, her fiancé, had left her for another woman. She left their shared home and, at the encouragement of a social worker, agreed to give up her child. The social worker called her personal attorney, who contacted the adoptive mother (that attorney's friend and employee). At the behest of the adoptive parents and their attorney, the mother gave birth at a different hospital than she and the father had planned to avoid the father's intervention; the mother surrendered the baby to strangers four days after his birth; and then falsely told the father that the child had died. All of this occurred in the space of less than three weeks.

(continued)

The father did not believe the mother, and he immediately began an intensive and persistent search and inquiry to learn the truth and locate the child. On the 57th day following the child's birth, the father learned of his son's existence and of the pending adoption. On that day, he hired a lawyer and contested the adoption of his son by strangers. One may reasonably ask, What more could he have done? What more should he have done? The answer is that he did all that he could and should do.

The . . . adoptive parents should have relinquished the baby at that time. That is to say, on the 57th day. Instead of that, however, they were able to procure an entirely erroneous ruling from a trial judge that allowed the adoption to go forward. The father's only remedy at that stage was a legal appeal which he took. He is not the cause of the delay in this case. It was the adoptive parents' decision to prolong this litigation through a long and ultimately fruitless appeal. Now, the view has been expressed that the passage of time warrants their retention of the child; that it would not be fair to the child to return him to his natural parents, now married to each other, after the adoptive parents have delayed justice past the child's third birthday.

[In the lower court case, Justice Rizzi grossly misstated the law. If, as stated by Justice Rizzi, the best interests of the child is to be the determining factor in child custody cases, persons seeking babies to adopt might profitably frequent grocery stores and snatch babies from carts when the parent is looking the other way. Then, if custody proceedings can be delayed long enough, they can assert that they have a nicer home, a superior education, a better job or whatever, and that the best interests of the child are with the baby snatchers. Children of parents living in public housing or other conditions deemed less than affluent and children with single parents might be considered particularly fair game. The law, thankfully, is otherwise.

In 1972, the United States Supreme Court, in the case of *Stanley v. Illinois* (1972), 405 U.S. 645 ruled that unmarried fathers cannot be treated differently than unmarried mothers or married parents when determining their rights to the custody of their children. The courts of Illinois are bound by that decision. Subsequently, in 1990, a unanimous Illinois Supreme Court pointed out that when ruling on parental unfitness, a court is not to consider the child's best interests, since the child's welfare is not relevant in judging the fitness of the natural parent; that only after the parent is found by clear and convincing evidence to be unfit does the court proceed to consider the child's best interest and whether that interest would be served if the child were adopted by the petitioners. *In re Adoption of Syck* (1990), 138 Ill. 2d 255, 276–78, 562 N.E.2d 174.

Under Illinois law, a parent may be divested of his parental rights either voluntarily (e.g., consenting to an adoption (see Ill. Rev. Stat. 1991, ch. 40, par. 1513)) or involuntarily (e.g., finding of abuse, abandonment, neglect or lack of sufficient interest (see Ill. Rev. Stat. 1991, ch. 40, par. 1510)). . . . [T]he adoption laws of Illinois are neither complex nor difficult of application. These laws intentionally place the burden of proof on the adoptive parents. In addition, Illinois

law requires a good-faith effort to notify the natural father of the adoption proceedings. (Ill. Rev. Stat. 1991, ch. 40, par. 1509.) We call this due process of law. In the case at hand, both the adoptive parents and their attorney knew that a real father existed whose name was known to the mother but who refused to disclose it. Under these circumstances, the adoptive parents proceeded at their peril.

The best interest of the child standard is not to be denigrated. It is real. However, it is not triggered until it has been validly determined that the child is available for adoption. And, a child is not available for adoption until the rights of his natural parents have been properly terminated. Any judge, lawyer, or guardian ad litem who has even the most cursory familiarity with adoption laws knows that. Justice Rizzi, if he is to be taken at face value, does not know that.

Columnist Bob Greene apparently does not care. Rather, columnist Greene has used this unfortunate controversy to stimulate readership and generate a series of syndicated newspaper columns in the Chicago Tribune and other papers that are both false and misleading. In so doing, he has wrongfully cried "fire" in a crowded theatre, and has needlessly alarmed other adoptive parents into ill-founded concerns that their own adoption proceedings may be in jeopardy. In support of his position, Greene has stirred up contempt against the Supreme Court as an institution, concluding one of his columns by referring to all of the Justices with the curse, "Damn them all." Chicago Tribune, June 19, 1994, page 1.

Greene's implicit objective is to secure justice for a child. With that ethical and moral imperative, of course, no one could disagree. Greene, however, elevates himself above the facts, above the law, and above the Supreme Court of Illinois. He arrogates to himself the right to decide the case.

In support of his objective, Greene brings to bear the tools of the demagogue, namely, incomplete information, falsity, half-truths, character assassination and spurious argumentation. He has conducted a steady assault on my abilities as a judge, headlining one of his columns "The Sloppiness of Justice Heiple." Another was entitled "Supreme Injustice for a Little Boy." He has shown my picture in his columns with bylines reading, respectively, "Justice Heiple: Ruling takes boy from home," and "James D. Heiple: No justice for a child."

Make no mistake about it. These are acts of journalistic terrorism. These columns are designed to discredit me as a judge and the Supreme Court as a dispenser of justice by stirring up disrespect and hatred among the general population.

Lest we forget the place from which he comes, let us remind ourselves that Greene is a journalist with a product to sell. He writes columns for a living. His income is dependent on writing and selling his columns to newspapers. He cannot secure either sales or earnings by writing on subjects that lack impact or drama. So, he must seek out subjects that are capable of generating wide public interest. An adoption case involving two sets of parents contesting for the custody of a three-year-old boy is a ready-made subject for this type of journalist. So far, so good.

(continued)

The trouble with Greene's treatment of the subject, however, is that his columns have been biased, false and misleading. They have also been destructive to the cause of justice both in this case and in the wider perspective. Part of Greene's fury may be attributable to the fact that he staked out his views on this case in a published column that appeared on August 22, 1993. (Chicago Tribune, August 22, 1993, page 1.) Subsequently, on June 16, 1994, the Supreme Court had the audacity to base its decision on the law rather than on his newspaper column. So much for his self-possessed moralizing.

That Greene has succeeded to a limited degree cannot be denied. I have, indeed, received several pieces of hate mail with such epithets as idiot, jerk, etc. The Governor, in a crass political move, announced his attempt to intervene in the case. And the General Assembly, without meaningful debate of consideration, rushed into law a constitutionally infirm statute with the goal of changing the Supreme Court's decision.

Both the Governor and the members of the General Assembly who supported this bill might be well advised to return to the classroom and take up Civics 101. The Governor, for his part, has no understanding of this case and no interest either public or private in its outcome. The legislature is not given the authority to decide private disputes between litigants. Neither does it sit as a super court to review unpopular decisions of the Supreme Court. We have three branches of government in this land. They are designated as the legislative, the executive and the judicial. Legislative adjudication of private disputes went by the wayside generations ago. Moreover, this case cannot be decided by public clamor generated by an irresponsible journalist. Neither can it be decided by its popularity or lack thereof. This case can only be decided by a court of law. That is a judicial function pure and simple. For the Supreme Court to surrender to this assault would be to surrender its independence, its integrity and its reason for being. In so doing, neither justice to the litigants nor the public interest would be served. Under the circumstances, this case looms even larger than the child or the two sets of contesting parents.

Many law suits are painful matters. This case is no exception. Capital cases, for instance, demand the forfeiture of the life of the defendant. Damage suits take money away from some people and give it to others. No one ever claimed that both sides walk away from a law suit with smiles on their faces. No member of this court ever entertained any thought that the decision it rendered in this case would be easy to accept by the losing litigants. Such an event would be incredible.

As for the child, age three, it is to be expected that there would be an initial shock, even a longing for a time in the absence of the persons whom he had viewed as parents. This trauma will be overcome, however, as it is every day across this land by children who suddenly find their parents separated by divorce or loss to them through death. It will not be an insurmountable trauma for a three-year-old child to be returned, at last, to his natural parents who want to raise him as their own. It will work itself out in the fullness of time. As for the adoptive parents, they will have to live with their pain and the knowledge that they wrongfully deprived a father of his child past the child's third birthday. They and their lawyer brought it on themselves.

This much is clear. Adoptive parents who comply with the law may feel secure in their adoptions. Natural parents may feel secure in their right to raise their own children. If there is a tragedy in this case, as has been suggested, then that tragedy is the wrongful breakup of a natural family and the keeping of a child by strangers without right. We must remember that the purpose of an adoption is to provide a home for a child, not a child for a home.

ASSIGNMENT 15.9

a. Major blunders were obviously made in this case. From infancy, Baby Richard lived with one set of adults. Years later, he is forced to live with other adults. Who does Justice Heiple say is to blame? Why? Which of the following cast of characters do *you* think is to blame and why: the biological mother, her attorney, the relatives of the biological mother, her social worker, the biological father, his attorney, the adoptive parents, their attorney, Baby Richard's guardian ad litem, the trial court (which granted the adoption), the appellate court (which said it was in the best interests of the child that he go with the Does), or the Supreme Court of Illinois (which gave the child to his biological father)?

b. What do you think of the quality of the legal representation given to the Does by their attorney?

c. In Chapter 9, we learned that custody decisions are based on the best interests of the child. Did this case say that the best interests of the child are irrelevant?

(continued)

d. What do you think could have been done to avoid what occurred in this case?

e. Is it relevant that Daniella married Otakar and therefore agreed with him that the adoption should be set aside?

f. Explain whether it was wise for Justice Heiple to attack Bob Greene as a journalistic terrorist.

g. Justice Heiple said, "It will not be an insurmountable trauma for a three-year old child to be returned, at last, to his natural parents who want to raise him as their own." Do you agree? If Justice Heiple thought the trauma *would be* insurmountable, would he have ruled differently? Recall that he said the best interests of the child were irrelevant in this case.

h. Rich and Paula Davis are the biological parents of John. Following a divorce, Rich is granted custody of John. Rich illegally takes John to another state, where his girlfriend adopts him. During the adoption proceeding, Rich falsely tells the court that John's mother, Paula, is dead. Paula, therefore, never receives notice of the adoption proceeding. Years later, Paula learns about the adoption for the first time. Can she still challenge the adoption? How would this case be decided in Illinois in view of *In re Petition of John Doe and Jane Doe*?

BABY JESSICA

The *Baby Jessica* case is another highly publicized example of a biological father successfully challenging an adoption on the basis of the biological mother's lies. Cara Clausen gave birth to Baby Jessica in Iowa. Within days of the birth, she put her up for adoption to Jan and Roberta DeBoer, who took her to Michigan. In the adoption proceedings, Cara lied about who the biological father was. Three weeks later, she had a change of heart and told the biological father, Dan Schmidt, what had happened. He then sought to get Baby Jessica back from the adoptive parents. He argued that he had never consented to the adoption and had never been found to be unfit. After two and a half years of litigation, the Iowa and Michigan courts nullified the adoption and ordered Baby Jessica returned.[22] The federal courts refused to change this result. In *DeBoer v. Schmidt*, the U.S. Supreme Court said, "Neither Iowa law, Michigan law, nor federal law authorizes unrelated persons to retain custody of a child whose natural parents have not been found to be unfit simply because they may be better able to provide for her future and her education. . . . '[C]ourts are not free to take children from parents simply by deciding another home appears more advantageous.'"[23]

PUTATIVE FATHER REGISTRY

How do we protect the rights of an unmarried father who does not become aware of the adoption of his child until it is too late to intervene? How can we prevent heart-rending scenes of children being forced from their adoptive parents and returned to their biological father—sometimes years after their placement with the adoptive parents? The father needs notice of the proposed adoption so that he has time to intervene. Yet he cannot be given notice if the mother lies about who the father is or where he can be found.

At one time, Florida had a law providing that if a mother (seeking to allow her child to be adopted) said she did not know the identity or whereabouts of the father, she had to publish a notice in the newspaper that

> must contain a physical description, including, but not limited to, age, race, hair and eye color, and approximate height and weight of the minor's mother and of any person the mother reasonably believes may be the father; the minor's date of birth; and any date and city, including the county and state in which the city is located, in which conception may have occurred.[24]

This method of giving notice to fathers was widely criticized. To avoid the humiliation of publishing her sexual history, a young woman may be more likely to abort or abandon her baby than go through with an adoption procedure that has this publication requirement. In 2003, a Florida court ruled that the law was an unconstitutional invasion of privacy. Eventually, the Florida legislature repealed what the media called the "Scarlet Letter" adoption law.[25]

Today, the most common method used by states (including Florida) to try to protect the rights of an unmarried father is to establish a **putative father registry**. A **putative father** is the alleged biological father of a child. He will be given notice of the proposed adoption of his child (which would include the proposed termination of his parental rights) if he registers with the putative father registry within a specific time frame. By registering, he announces his intent to assert his rights and responsibilities as a parent. The failure to register may preclude his right to notice of the adoption proceedings. States have different names for the putative father registry. Among the names used are paternity registry, centralized paternity registry, parental claim registrar, fathers' adoption registry, and responsible father registry.

For an example of a putative father registry, see Exhibit 15.5.

putative father registry
A government office where the father of a child can register so that he can be notified of a proposed adoption of the child.

putative father
The man who is alleged to be the biological father, but who has not yet been medically or legally declared to be the father. Also called *alleged father, reputed father.*

EXHIBIT 15.5   Putative Father Registry

ALABAMA DEPARTMENT OF HUMAN RESOURCES
PUTATIVE FATHER INTENT TO CLAIM PATERNITY REGISTRATION

Information About the Father:

NAME
Last_____ First _____Middle _____

RACE_____ DOB_____SSN_____

Address_____

Information About the Child:

NAME

Last_____ First _____Middle _____

DOB_____ Place of Birth_____

Information About the Mother:
NAME
Last _____ First _____Middle _____

Other Names Mother May Have Used_____

RACE_____ DOB_____SSN_____

Address_____

_____

Possible Date(s) of Sexual Intercourse:_____

Alabama Department of Human Resources (dhr.alabama.gov/documents/Putative_Father_Form.pdf).

The registry is by no means a perfect solution. It can work well when the man knows about the registry and knows he has impregnated an unmarried woman. Difficulties arise when the woman with whom he is intimate does not tell him she is pregnant or falsely tells him that she had an abortion. Realistically, the only way he can protect his rights is to register every time he has sexual relations with an unmarried woman.

States are unsympathetic to the man who says, "I didn't know." A Utah statute, for example, provides that "[a]n unmarried biological father, by virtue of the fact that he has engaged in a sexual relationship with a woman . . . is considered to be on notice that a pregnancy and an adoption proceeding regarding that child may occur . . . and has a duty to protect his own rights and interests."[26] The burden, therefore, is on the unmarried man to find out whether he is about to become or has become a father and, if so, to take steps to protect his rights. If he knows about the child, he should help arrange prenatal and delivery care, pay child support, petition a court for an order of paternity, or make sure his name is on the birth certificate. If in doubt about whether a baby exists, register! Whether this approach violates the constitutional rights of the father is unclear. This is an area of the law in which we can expect continued litigation.

INTERSTATE COMPACT ON THE PLACEMENT OF CHILDREN

The **Interstate Compact on the Placement of Children (ICPC)** governs adoptions of a child born or living in one state (called the *sending state*), who will be adopted by someone in another state (called the *receiving state*). The ICPC does not cover all interstate adoptions. It applies mainly to so-called *stranger adoptions*, those undertaken by individuals other than relatives, guardians, or stepparents. (An adoption by a relative of a birth parent is a *kinship adoption*.)

Interstate Compact on the Placement of Children (ICPC)
A statute that governs adoption of a child born or living in one state, who will be adopted by someone in another state.

To coordinate the adoption, an ICPC office is established in each state. When a court approves the adoption, the ICPC office in the sending state gives written notice to the ICPC office in the receiving state of the proposed adoption. The notice provides identifying information about the child, the child's parents or guardians, and the person, agency, or institution with whom the child is to be placed. Also included are a statement of reasons for the proposed placement and "evidence of the authority pursuant to which the placement is proposed to be made." The ICPC office in the receiving state reviews this information. If approved, it submits to the ICPC office in the sending state a written notice that "the proposed placement does not appear to be contrary to the interests of the child."[27] The parties are then given permission to bring the child across state lines so that the placement can occur. A violation of these ICPC requirements can result in a voiding of the adoption.

CONSEQUENCES OF ADOPTION

Once the adoption becomes final, the adopted child and the adoptive parents have the rights and obligations toward each other that biological parents and children have. In most respects, an adopted child is treated the same as a biological child.

- *Surname.* Adoptees can be given the surname of their adoptive parents.
- *Birth certificate.* The birth certificate of the adoptee can be changed to reflect the surname of the adoptive parent.
- *Earnings and services.* An adoptive parent has a right to the services and earnings of an adoptee.

- *Support.* An adoptive parent must provide child support for the adoptee. This duty continues even if the adoptive parent divorces the biological parent or their marriage is annulled after the adoption.
- *Workers' compensation.* Adoptees are entitled to workers' compensation benefits in the event that an adoptive parent suffers an on-the-job injury.
- *Priority over biological grandparents.* An adoptive parent has priority over biological grandparents when the adoptive parent objects to their visitation. (See Chapter 9 on the rights of grandparents in custody and visitation cases.)

intestacy
The condition of dying without a valid will.

intestate
(1) Pertaining to someone who dies without a valid will. (2) A person who dies without a valid will.

intestate share
A designated portion of the estate of a person who dies intestate (i.e., without a valid will) to which specific relatives of the deceased are entitled according to state law.

Special rules sometimes exist in the area of intestacy—dying without a valid will. The standard rule is that if someone dies intestate (without a valid will), state law specifies which relatives of the deceased inherit an intestate share, which is a designated portion of the estate of the deceased. Can an adoptee receive an intestate share? The answer may depend on who died. If the deceased is the adoptive parent, the adoptee receives the same intestate share as a biological child of the deceased. Suppose, however, that a *relative* of the adoptive parent dies intestate.

> Mary is the biological mother of Kevin. After her parental rights are terminated, Paul adopts Kevin. Paul's brother, Bill, dies intestate. Can Kevin inherit from Bill?

States differ in their answer to this question. Some states will *not* allow an adoptee to inherit from a relative of his or her adoptive parent if the relative dies intestate. Other states, however, do not impose this restriction on adoptees.

Suppose that the biological parent of the adoptee dies intestate. In our example, Mary is Kevin's biological parent whose parental rights were terminated. What happens if Mary dies intestate? In most states adoptees cannot inherit from a biological parent whose parental rights have been terminated. The termination of parental rights also terminates intestate inheritance rights. There are, however, a few states that take a different view and allow adoptees like Kevin to inherit from a biological parent in Mary's situation. Of course, if Paul dies intestate, Kevin can inherit from Paul's estate in the same way that Paul's biological children could.

testate
(1) Pertaining to someone who dies with a valid will. (2) A person who dies with a valid will. (In older cases, if the testate was a man, he was also called *testator* and, if a woman, testatrix.)

testamentary
Pertaining to a will.

Thus far, we have limited our discussion to intestacy. The law is dramatically different when the deceased dies testate—leaving a valid will. There are no restrictions on persons to whom gifts can be made in a will. Testamentary gifts (i.e., gifts in a will) can be made to anyone. Hence, Kevin's uncle Bill and Kevin's biological mother (Mary) in our examples can leave Kevin a gift in their wills in the same manner as his adoptive parents can.

Occasionally, problems of interpretation arise over the language in wills. Suppose, for example, that an adoptive parent dies with a will leaving property to "my heirs" or to "my children" or to "my issue," without mentioning any individuals by name. Is an adoptee included within such language? Most (but not all) courts are inclined to conclude that the intention of the deceased adoptive parent was to include adopted children, as well as biological children within the designation of "heirs," "children," or "issue."

Can a biological parent be granted visitation rights even though this parent's parental rights were terminated in an adoption? In general, the answer is *no*. There are cases, however, in which a court has enforced an agreement between the biological parent and the adoptive parent to allow visitation by the biological parent. In these cases, the court concluded that the visits would be in the best interests of the child. Visits of this kind are relatively rare. A fit adoptive parent has the primary right to raise the child, including the decision on who should be allowed to visit the child. (For more on this right of fit parents, see Chapter 9.)

Finally, as we saw in Chapter 6 on annulment of marriages, states differ on whether a person can marry his or her adopted sibling. Most states say that they can. In these states, such a marriage is not a ground for an annulment.

CONFIDENTIALITY

In recent years, there has been great controversy over whether adopted children have a right to discover the identity of their biological parents. A traditional adoption was a **closed adoption** in which there is no disclosure of the identity of the birth parents, adoptive parent(s), or the adoptee. Once the adoption becomes final, the record is sealed. The data within it are confidential.

There were, however, some limited exceptions. If **good cause** can be shown, access to part of the adoption records may be allowed. For example, an adopted child may need medical or genetic information on his or her biological parents to help treat diseases that might be hereditary. Similarly, the adopted child may need some information about the identity of biological parents to avoid unknowingly marrying a biological brother or sister. Access to such information, however, is the exception. It is rare that *identifying* information is released. (Identifying facts are facts that would assist the recipient in determining who the biological parent is.) The norm is *nonidentifying* information consisting of social or medical facts that would not allow positive identification of any person who was a party to the adoption. The need for information must be great. Many courts have held that it is not enough for the adopted child to prove that he or she is experiencing emotional distress due to not knowing the identity of his or her biological parents.

Although many states continue to follow this narrow approach on confidentiality, the trend is going in the other direction. Some states have broadened the categories of nonidentifying information they will release without compromising anonymity. In one recent case, for example, an adult adoptee was allowed to discover information on the race of the birth parents, the general health of the adoptee at the time of the adoption, the reasons assigned for the adoption, and the length of time the adoptee was in the custody of her adoptive parents prior to the adoption. A few states (e.g., Kansas and Alaska) have created a system of complete openness. Adult adoptees, without restriction, can see their adoption records or original birth certificate. Reform in most other states has not been this radical.

Some states have created a **reunion registry**, which contains identifying information about adoptees and biological parents. There are two kinds of registries: passive and active.

- A *passive registry* (also called a *mutual consent registry*) requires both the adoptee and the biological parent to register their consent to release identifying information. When both have registered and a match is made, a registry employee lets them both know how to contact each other.

- An *active registry* does not require the adoptee and the biological parent to register their consent to release information. Once one of them registers, a registry employee will contact the other to determine his or her wishes for the release of information.

Contact vetoes are used in some states. A contact veto is a denial of consent to have contact between the adoptee and the biological parent, although permission for the release of identifying information might be given. In a few states, the release of information also requires the consent of the adoptive parents. Biological fathers can use the registry, but most states condition such use on the fathers' acknowledgment of paternity.

Some independent adoptions give the participants the option of maintaining limited contact between the biological parent and the child after the adoption. These are called **open adoptions**, involving an exchange of identifying information or face-to-face meetings with the child, usually after the biological parent has selected the adoptive parent(s). If there is no direct face-to-face contact but there is a periodic exchange of pictures and letters facilitated by an agency, the adoption is sometimes called a *mediated adoption*.

closed adoption
A traditional adoption in which there is no disclosure of the identity of the birth parents, adoptive parent(s), or the adoptee.

good cause
A legally sufficient ground or reason. Also called *just cause, sufficient cause*.

reunion registry
A central adoption file that could be used to release identifying information about, and allow contact between, adult adoptees and biological parents.

contact vetoes
A denial of consent to have contact between an adoptee and his or her biological parent, although permission for the release of identifying information might be given.

open adoption
An adoption in which the biological parent maintains certain kinds of initial and/or ongoing contact with the adoptee, whose adoptive parent(s) may have been selected by the biological parent. The contact might consist of letters or visits.

Some believe that open or mediated adoptions should be discouraged. Young women "are finding it harder to get on with their lives. . . . " "They start living for the photos that the adoptive parents send them every month." Adoptive parents sometimes "find themselves not only raising a new baby but providing counseling for the birth mother who often finds it difficult to break her bond with the child."[28] Not many adoptive parents, therefore, pursue open or mediated adoptions.

Many adoptees use the Internet to try to locate biological parents and other relatives regardless of whether their own adoption was traditional (confidential). One woman, for example, set up a Facebook page seeking help among her Facebook "friends" in her search for what she called her "first" family. In two days, she was in touch with her birth mother, and in six weeks, she was in contact with her biological father.[29]

In addition, online DNA testing companies, such as 23&Me or Ancestry.com, are available to try to provide links to blood relatives. For a fee, adoptees can send in a saliva sample or a swab of their cheek and receive back links of possible relatives. "Some DNA testing companies have been stepping up their efforts to reach out to this community over the past several years, posting advertisements on adoption message boards and testimonials on their websites."[30] The Internet "is changing nearly every chapter of adoption. It can now start with postings by couples looking for birth mothers who want to place children, and end years later with birth mothers looking to reunite with children they've placed. A process that once relied on gatekeepers and official procedures can now be largely circumvented with a computer, Wi-Fi and some luck."[31]

EQUITABLE ADOPTION

Assume that John Smith agrees with Mary Jones to adopt Mary's child, Bill, but fails to carry out the agreement. Such agreements are occasionally put in writing but more often are oral understandings between parties who know each other very well. Assume further that John takes custody of Bill, treats him as a member of his family, but never goes through formal adoption procedures as he had promised. John then dies intestate (i.e., without leaving a valid will). Technically, Bill cannot inherit from John because the adoption never took place. This argument might be used by John's biological children to prevent an unadopted child—in this case, Bill—from sharing in the intestate estate.

Many feel that it would be unfair to deny the child inheritance benefits simply because the deceased failed to carry out an agreement to adopt. To avoid the unfairness, some courts apply **equitable adoption**. Under this doctrine, a child will be considered the adopted child of a person who intended to adopt the child and acted as the child's parent but failed to go through the formal adoption procedures. The doctrine does not create a full parent-child relationship in the traditional sense. Its effect is limited to avoiding unfairness or injustice by allowing the child to claim specific benefits such as the intestate share of an adoptee. Other benefits are possible. For example, a court might allow the child to bring a **wrongful death** action as a surviving child of the deceased.

The doctrine is also called *adoption by estoppel*. Persons are **estopped** (i.e., prevented) from denying that such a child has been adopted. Suppose, for example, that the biological children do not want the unadopted child to share in the intestate estate of their deceased father. If the doctrine applies, the biological children would be estopped from taking this position.

Because it is relatively easy (and tempting) for someone to claim that a deceased person agreed to an adoption that was never formalized, a court may require that the agreement to adopt be proven by *clear and convincing evidence* rather than by the lower standard of preponderance of the evidence.

---

equitable adoption
A child will be considered the adopted child of a person who intended to adopt the child and acted as the child's parent but failed to go through the formal adoption procedures. Also called *adoption by estoppel, de facto adoption, virtual adoption.*

wrongful death
A death caused by a tort or other wrong.

estopped
Prevented from asserting a right or a defense because it would be unfair or inequitable to allow the assertion. The noun is *estoppel.*

A few courts will grant inheritance rights *even if there was no initial agreement to adopt*. If clear evidence exists that the deceased treated the child as his or her own in every way, a court might rule that a contract to adopt was *implied*. When the deceased dies intestate, equitable-adoption status will be accorded to the child so that he or she will have full inheritance rights from the deceased.

ASSIGNMENT   15.10

Contact a paralegal, an attorney, or a legal secretary in your state who has worked on adoption cases in the past. Obtain the answers to the following questions. (See General Instructions for the Systems Assignment in Appendix A.)

a. How many adoption cases have you worked on?

b. How many of them have been uncontested?

c. Approximately how long does it take to process an uncomplicated, uncontested adoption?

d. Is there a difference between working on an adoption case and working on another kind of case in the law office? If so, what is the difference?

e. What are the major steps for processing an adoption in this state? What documents must be filed? What court appearances must be made? Etc.

f. What formbook, manual, or other legal treatise do you use, if any, that is helpful? What software? What websites?

g. Does your office have its own internal manual that covers any aspect of adoption practice?

h. In an adoption case, what is the division of labor among the attorney, the paralegal, and the legal secretary?

EMBRYO "ADOPTION?"

An **embryo** is an egg that has been fertilized by a sperm in the early stage of development. Couples having difficulty conceiving will sometimes freeze their embryos for later implantation. In Chapter 16, we will cover the legal controversy that can exist when a couple divorces and cannot agree on what to do with unused frozen embryos.

Can these embryos be adopted? Probably not. Embryos can be *donated* as property to other couples (or to individual women), but no state requires persons to go through the adoption process described in this chapter before allowing others to use (implant) the embryos. This is true even in Louisiana where embryos are categorized as "juridical persons," as we will see in Chapter 16. Private agencies exist to help persons donate embryos in a process that has similarities to adoption, e.g., the agency will do a home study and provide the prospective donors with background information on the prospective recipients (donees) so that the donors would know what kind of home in which the baby from the embryo (if one is born) will live. (Children born from such agencies were invited to the White House by President George W. Bush. They wore t-shirts that read: "Former Embryos.") These embryo-adoption steps, however, are voluntary. There are no adoption laws that require them.

embryo
An egg that has been fertilized by a sperm and is in the early stage of development; it has undergone one or more divisions. The product of conception to about the eighth week of pregnancy.

WRONGFUL ADOPTION

For a discussion of the tort of **wrongful adoption**, covering the failure to disclose relevant information to the adoptive parents, see Chapter 17.

wrongful adoption
An action seeking damages for carelessly stating (or failing to disclose) to prospective adoptive parents available facts on the health or other condition of the adoptee that would be relevant to the decision on whether to adopt.

PARALEGAL ROLES

- For an overview of paralegal roles in family-law cases, see Exhibits 1.5 and 1.6 in Chapter 1.
- For many of the financial issues related to adoption covered in Chapter 15, a paralegal may be asked to help collect documents and facts outlined in:
  - The checklist in Exhibit 3.1 of Chapter 3.
  - The interrogatories in Appendix C.
- A veteran paralegal who has many years of experience working on adoption cases made the following comment about the challenges in this area of law:

  In adoption law, the most challenging aspect of working with families is the anxiety and other emotions involved with wondering whether the adoption will fall through. Another challenge is the deadlines that are the equivalent to a "race to the courthouse" since petitions often need to be filed the same day they are signed. Adoption laws change regularly, and keeping up with the changes can be a challenge. . . . My most memorable case was a maternal grandparent adoption. The birth mother was 100 percent sure she was going to place the child until she was asked to sign the consent for adoption. The birth mother was crying and shaking and saying she just wanted to try to parent her child. [Six months later, she signed.] It then took me about two years to secure the birth father's signature on the consent because he was always out of the country. [Perseverance paid off.] The greatest joy of my job is making families' dreams come true.[32]

- Miscellaneous duties:
  - Help prospective adoptive parents prepare a portfolio and website that will attract birth mothers seeking to place their children for adoption.
  - Help a birth mother locate prospective adoptive parents for her child.
  - Obtain certified copies of marriage records of the prospective adoptive parents and divorce decrees, if any.
  - Screen prospective adoptive parents for a mother seeking to place her child for adoption (e.g., do criminal-background checks).
  - Research federal and state adoption laws.
  - Conduct due diligence in locating an absent father.
  - Draft petitions and related pleadings needed for an adoption.
  - Arrange for a home study of the prospective adoptive parents.
  - Prepare consent or surrender documents in which the birth mother relinquishes her parental rights.
  - Investigate the extent to which a parent seeking to prevent an adoption has demonstrated indicia of parenthood.
  - Coordinate an out-of-state adoption under the Interstate Compact on the Placement of Children (ICPC).
  - Draft the agreement for an open adoption.
  - Document payments made for the medical and related expenses of the birth mother.
  - Document communication between the birth mother and the prospective adoptive parents.
  - Accompany client to court to provide needed support.
  - Assist adoptive parents in obtaining a new birth certificate or in verifying that one has been issued.
  - Assist an adult adoptee to obtain identifying or nonidentifying information about his or her natural parent(s).

SUMMARY

Adoption is the judicial process by which one person (the adoptive parent) becomes the legal parent of another person (the adoptee). For most adoptions, the parental rights of both biological parents are terminated. An exception exists for stepparent adoptions and for second-parent adoptions in some states. The four main categories of adoptions are (1) public-agency adoption, (2) licensed private-agency adoption, (3) independent adoption, and (4) facilitated/unlicensed agency adoption. Other categories include intercountry adoptions and Native American adoptions. A large network of service providers is available to facilitate adoptions: facilitators or intermediaries, doctors, clergy members, photographers, and web designers. A black-market adoption is an illegal adoption in which there is a payment to a biological parent beyond reasonable expenses in order to facilitate the adoption.

Most adoptees are infants. It is also possible to adopt an adult, which is usually done for inheritance purposes. In deciding whether an adoption of a minor is in the best interests of the child, judges have considerable discretion. Courts often presume that kinship adoptions are best for the child. The factors considered by a court include the petitioner's age, marital status, health, religion, economic status, home environment, and morality. Race can be considered, but it cannot be the sole or determining factor in the court's decision. Adoptions cannot be delayed or denied because of race. All states allow gays and lesbians to adopt minors, but discrimination against them still exists among agencies and judges who exercise discretion in adoption decisions.

An adoption must follow strict procedures. The court must have subject-matter jurisdiction and proper venue. The petition must contain the required information. The biological parents must be notified of the proceeding and must consent to the adoption unless their parental rights have been terminated or, in the case of the father of a nonmarital (illegitimate) child, there has been an insufficient indicia of parenthood. A parent without such indicia can lose his opportunity interest. Consent is also required of the agency if parental rights were initially surrendered to the agency. If the prospective adoptive parent is married, the consent of his or her spouse is often required, even if this spouse is not also adopting the child. If old enough, a court can ask for the consent of the adoptee. Foster parents must be notified of a proposed adoption, but they do not have the right to veto the adoption. Consent can be revoked in many states when given before birth and before a designated time after birth.

A termination of parental rights (TPR) is a judicial declaration that ends the legal relationship between the parent and the child when this is in the best interests of the child. The TPR can be voluntary because of the biological parent's consent, or involuntary if the parent is found to be unfit. The grounds for involuntary TPR must be proved by clear and convincing evidence. Some states provide free counsel for indigent defendants, but such counsel is not constitutionally required except in relatively complex cases. A guardian ad litem (GAL) must be appointed to represent the child in every court case that involves child abuse or neglect. The GAL can be an attorney or a nonattorney

court appointed special advocate (CASA). The Adoption and Safe Families Act (ASFA) requires states to take specific placement action on behalf of children in foster care, such as terminating parental rights in order to facilitate adoption after a designated period of time trying (without success) to reunite the child with its biological parents.

A child does not have standing to petition a court to terminate the parental rights of his or her parent. In many states, an adoption decree does not become final immediately. An interlocutory decree of adoption is first issued, and, while in effect, the child can be placed with the prospective adoptive parents.

A major ground for a dissolution (abrogation) of adoption (which annuls the adoption) is that the adoption decree was obtained by duress, fraud, or undue influence and dissolution would be in the best interests of the child. Unmarried fathers of nonmarital (illegitimate) children must register with a putative father registry if they want the right to be notified of a proposed adoption so that they can assert their objection. The Interstate Compact on the Placement of Children facilitates interstate adoptions.

Once the adoption becomes final, the adopted child is treated the same as a biological child with respect to support rights and most inheritance rights. A traditional adoption is a closed adoption in which the records are sealed. Matters such as the identity of the biological parents are kept confidential except in relatively rare circumstances. Some states have created active or passive reunion registries that can be the basis of the release of identifying information about adoptees and biological parents. In an open adoption, there may be varying degrees of contact between a biological parent and the child after the adoption becomes final.

An equitable adoption occurs when a person dies before carrying out an intention to adopt a child and when unfairness can be avoided only by treating the child as having been adopted for purposes of inheritance. Frozen embryos can be donated, but not legally adopted in the manner in which a child is adopted. The failure of an adoption agency to give available information about the health of the prospective adoptee might constitute the tort of wrongful adoption.

KEY TERMS

adoption	guardian ad litem (GAL)	kinship adoption
adoptive parent	paternity	transracial adoptions
adoptee	foster care	Multiethnic Placement Act (MEPA)
intestate	stepparent	joint adoption
custody	second-parent adoption	expedited procedure
legal custody	independent adoption	subject-matter jurisdiction
ward	black-market adoption	venue
guardian	best interests of the child	petition

procedural due process	court appointed special advocate (CASA)	intestate share
process		testate
substituted service	Adoption and Safe Families Act (ASFA)	testamentary
due diligence		closed adoption
surrender	unemancipated	good cause
opportunity interest	nonage	reunion registry
indicia of parenthood	standing	contact veto
termination of parental rights (TPR)	interlocutory	open adoption
unfit	abrogation	equitable adoption
abandonment	putative father registry	wrongful death
dependency	putative father	estopped
clear and convincing evidence	Interstate Compact on the Placement of Children (ICPC)	embryo
preponderance of the evidence		wrongful adoption
indigent	intestacy	

CHECK THE CITE

Terry Helms is a nonattorney GAL (guardian ad litem) appointed to represent two children in a termination-of-parental-rights proceeding against their father. Terry was later replaced by another nonattorney GAL, Karen Moorefield. The children were also represented by an attorney. When the father's parental rights were terminated, the GAL was not present in the courtroom. The attorney for the father objected, arguing that the GAL should have been present. How did the court rule on this objection, and what did the court say was the proper relationship between the nonattorney GAL and the children's attorney? Read *In the Matter of J.H.K. and J.D.K.*, 365 N.C. 171, 711 S.E.2d 118 (2011). To read the opinion online: (1) Run a citation search ("711 S.E.2d 118") in the *Case law* database of Google Scholar (scholar.google.com). (2) Run the same search in the general search engines of Google, Bing, or Yahoo.

PROJECT

In Google, Bing, or Yahoo, run the following search: aa "open adoption" (substitute the name of your state for *aa* in the search). Write an essay in which you describe the extent to which open adoption is allowed in your state. Cover the different circumstances that will allow contact among a birth parent, the adoptee, and the prospective adoptive parent(s) after the adoption. You must cite and quote from a minimum of four different sources that you find on the Internet. At least two of these sources should be statutes, court opinions, or other laws.

ETHICS IN A FAMILY LAW PRACTICE

a. You are a paralegal working at the law office of Daniel Johnson, Esq. The office takes adoption cases. While working on one of these cases, you learn that Mr. Johnson (your boss) told a birth mother that she can have a job as a receptionist at the law firm if she agrees to give up her baby for adoption to one of the firm's clients. You are asked to interview the birth mother for this job. During the interview, you learn that she is clearly not qualified for the job and that the only reason she is giving up her baby for adoption is that she needs the job. You do not say anything to anyone about her suitability for the job or her hesitancy about going through with the adoption. Any ethical problems?

b. You are a paralegal working at the law offices of Karen Smith, Esq. Smith represents Helen Owens, a birth mother who wants to place her child for adoption. Smith asks you to interview Rachael Davis, a prospective adoptive parent. You do so. When it becomes clear that Davis is a good candidate for the adoption, Smith explains the adoption process to Davis. Any ethical problems?

WRITING SAMPLE

Alice Thompson is fifteen years old and pregnant. A neighbor, Helen Foley, wishes to adopt Alice's child. Alice agrees. On January 10th of this year, Alice signs a consent form that relinquishes her parental rights to her baby. The baby is born the following March. Helen Foley is represented by the law firm where you work as a paralegal. Your supervisor asks you to write a memorandum of law in which you examine the issue of whether the prebirth consent is valid in your state. To locate the governing law, run this search in Google, Bing, or Yahoo: *aa consent adoption* (substitute the name of your state for *aa* in the search). Your memo must cite and quote from a minimum of four different sources that you find online. At least two of these sources should be statutes, court opinions, or other laws. (See General Instructions for the Writing Sample in Appendix A.)

REVIEW QUESTIONS

1. What is an adoption?
2. What is a second-parent adoption?
3. Approximately how many children are adopted every year?
4. What is a public agency adoption, a licensed private agency adoption, an independent adoption, a facilitated/unlicensed adoption, an intercountry adoption, and a Native American adoption?
5. What is an adoption facilitator?
6. How does a prospective adoptive parent go about finding a birth mother interested in placing her child for adoption?
7. When does an adoption become a black-market adoption?
8. For what reasons do persons sometimes adopt adults?
9. How do adult/adult adoptions differ from adoptions of minors?
10. What standard does a judge use in deciding whether to allow an adoption?
11. What is a kinship adoption?
12. What factors will a court consider in deciding whether an adoption is in the best interests of the child?
13. How does the Multiethnic Placement Act (MEPA) affect the adoption of children in foster care?
14. What obstacles do gays and lesbians face when adopting minors?
15. What court procedures govern adoption?
16. When does the father of a nonmarital (illegitimate) child lose his right to consent to an adoption?
17. What is a parent's opportunity interest and when is it lost?
18. What are the consent rights or duties, if any, of the agency, the spouse of a prospective adoptive parent, the adoptee, and the foster parents?
19. When can a biological parent revoke her consent to an adoption?
20. What are the grounds for an involuntary termination of parental rights (TPR)?
21. What is the standard of proof for an involuntary TPR?
22. When is an indigent defendant in an involuntary TPR case entitled to appointed (free) counsel?
23. What is the purpose of the Adoption and Safe Families Act (ASFA)?
24. Can a child divorce his or her parents through a TPR proceeding?
25. What is an interlocutory decree of adoption?
26. Under what grounds can an adoption decree be challenged?
27. What is the function of a putative father registry?
28. What is the Interstate Compact on the Placement of Children?
29. What are the intestate and testate consequences of an adoption?
30. What is the rule of confidentiality in a traditional adoption?
31. What is the distinction between an active and a passive reunion registry?
32. What is an open adoption?
33. When will an equitable adoption be ordered?
34. Can an embryo be adopted?
35. What is an action for wrongful adoption?

HELPFUL WEBSITES

Your State

See Appendix D for links to the family law of your state on the topics covered in this chapter.

Adoption Law

- www.childwelfare.gov/topics/adoption
- family.findlaw.com/adoption.html
- www.law.cornell.edu/wex/table_adoption
- www.adoption.org

National Adoption Statistics

- adoptionnetwork.com/adoption-statistics
- www.acf.hhs.gov/cb/research-data-technology/statistics-research

National Adoption Clearinghouse

- www.childwelfare.gov/topics/adoption/laws

State Child Welfare Resources

- www.childwelfare.gov/state-resources
- www.childwelfare.gov/topics/adoption/adopt-assistance

Child Welfare Policy Manual

- www.acf.hhs.gov/cb/laws-policies

Adoption Forms

- www.uslegalforms.com/adoption

State Adoption Photolisting Services

- www.adoptuskids.org

American Academy of Adoption & Assisted Reproduction Attorneys

- adoptionattorneys.org

Legal Center for Foster Care and Education

- www.fostercareandeducation.org

Search for Birth Parents

- www.adoption.com/reunion
- www.donorsiblingregistry.com
- www.omnitrace.com

Putative Father Registries

- adoptionart.org (enter *putative registry* in the search box)
- en.wikipedia.org/wiki/Putative_father_registry

Rights of Unmarried Fathers

- www.childwelfare.gov/pubPDFs/putative.pdf

Registries for Embryo Adoption

- www.embryodonation.org
- www.nrfa.org

Google Scholar (scholar.google.com)

- Choose "Articles" and enter in the search box any of the key terms discussed in the chapter. Add the name of your state to the search term.
- Choose "Case law" and "Select courts". Select your state, click "Done," and enter in the search box any of the key terms discussed in the chapter. Add the name of your state to the search term.

Google, Bing, Yahoo

(on these search engines, run the following searches, substituting your state for "aa")

- adoption aa
- paternity adoption aa
- black-market adoption aa
- independent adoption aa
- transracial adoption aa
- unfit adoption aa
- ASFA adoption aa
- open adoption aa
- mediated adoption aa
- ICPC adoption aa
- adoptive parent aa
- foster care" adoption aa
- second parent adoption aa
- kinship adoption aa
- opportunity interest child aa
- CASA adoption aa
- putative father registry aa
- gay lesbian adoption aa
- termination of parental rights aa

YouTube

Run the same searches on YouTube listed above for Google, Bing, Yahoo searches. Even when the video clips are trying to entice you to retain an attorney, buy a book, or enroll in a course, they can provide useful overviews and references to primary authority.

Twitter, Reddit, and Facebook

On Twitter, Reddit, and Facebook, run the following searches (substitute your state for *aa* in your searches; run the searches with and without the name of your state). Look for links to family-law developments in your state.

- adoption aa
- men's rights aa

ENDNOTES

Note: All or most of the court opinions in these end-notes can be read online. To do so, go to Google Scholar (scholar.google.com), select *Case law*, and in the search box, enter the cite (e.g., "503 N.Y.S.2d 752") or name of the case (e.g., "*333 East 53rd St. Assocs. v. Mann*") that is given in the endnote.

[1] Child Welfare Information Gateway, *Adoption Options* (*2015*) (www.childwelfare.gov/pubs/f-adoptoption).

[2] U.S. Department of State, *Intercountry Adoption* (travel.state.gov/content/travel/en/Intercountry-Adoption.html).

[3] 25 U.S.C. § 1915(a). See, however, *Brackeen v. Zinke*, 338 F. Supp. 3d 514 (N.D. Tex., 2018) holding that ICWA's mandatory placement preferences violated equal protection.

[4] *333 East 53rd St. Assocs. v. Mann*, 503 N.Y.S.2d 752 (N.Y. App. Div. 1986).

[5] *In re Adoption of Holland*, 965 So. 2d 1213 (Fla. Dist. Ct. App. 2007).

[6] *Keeping Assets in the Family: Millionaire Adopts Girlfriend*, www.wealthmanagement.com (February 1 2012).

[7] 42 U.S.C. § 1996b (www.law.cornell.edu/uscode/text/42/1996b).

[8] 25 U.S.C. § 1901 (www.law.cornell.edu/uscode/text/25/chapter-21).

[9] New York State Compilation of Codes, Rules & Regulations, 18 NYCRR 421.16(h)(2).

[10] American Psychological Association, *Sexual Orientation, Parents, and Children* (2004) (www.apa.org).

[11] Abby Bushlow, *Information Packet: Gay and Lesbian Second-Parent Adoptions* (National Resource Center for Foster Care and Permanency Planning, May 2002).

[12] See, for example, North Dakota Century Code Annotated, § 14-15-19 (2007) (www.legis.nd.gov/cencode/t14c15.pdf). See also Uniform Adoption Act (1971) (www.law.cornell.edu/uniform/vol9.html#adopt).

[13] *In re Kristina L.*, 520 A.2d 574, 581 (R.I. 1987).

[14] *Lassiter v. Department of Social Services of Durham County, North Carolina.*, 452 U.S. 18 (1981).

[15] Child Welfare Information Gateway, *Representation of Children in Child Abuse and Neglect Proceedings* (2011) (www.childwelfare.gov/systemwide/laws_policies/statutes/represent.pdf).

[16] *M.L.B. v. S.L.J.*, 519 U.S. 102 (1996).

[17] 42 U.S.C. § 671 (1997) (training.cfsrportal.acf.hhs.gov/section-2-understanding-child-welfare-system/2999).

[18] Mark Hansen, *Boy Wants "Divorce" from Parents*, 78 American Bar Association Journal 24 (July 1992).

[19] Mark Hansen, *Boy Wins "Divorce" from Mom*, 78 American Bar Association Journal 16 (Dec. 1992).

[20] *Kingsley v. Kingsley*, 623 So. 2d 780, 783 (Fla. Dist. Ct. App. 1993).

[21] *Unnecessary Cruelty*, San Diego Union-Tribune, May 4, 1995, at B12.

[22] *In re Baby Girl Clausen*, 502 N.W.2d 649 (Mich. 1993).

[23] *DeBoer v. Schmidt*, 509 U.S. 1301, 1302 (1993).

[24] 2001 Florida Session Law Service, Ch. 2001–3 (H.B. 141) (West Group).

[25] *G.P. v. State*, 842 So. 2d 1059 (Fla. Dist. Ct. App. 2003).

[26] Utah Statutes § 78B–6-110(1) (2018) (le.utah.gov/xcode/Title78B/Chapter6/78B-6-S110.html).

[27] icpcstatepages.org.

[28] Council of State Governments, *Adoption*, State Government News, Sept. 1989, at 31.

[29] Belinda Luscombe, *Adoption 2.0: Finding Mom on Facebook*, Time Magazine (Aug. 21, 2010) (www.time.com/time/magazine/article/0,9171,2008885,00.html).

[30] Rachel Swarns, *With DNA Testing, Suddenly They Are Family*, N.Y. Times, Jan. 23, 2012.

[31] Lisa Belkin, *I Found My Mom Through Facebook*, N.Y. Times, June 24, 2011.

[32] Danielle Stewart, *Adoption Law*, 25 Legal Assistant Today 88 (2007).

CHAPTER 16

The New Science of Motherhood

CHAPTER OUTLINE

CHAPTER OBJECTIVES

After completing this chapter, you should be able to:

- Define infertility and state its main causes.
- Define assisted reproductive technology (ART).
- Explain the process of in vitro fertilization (IVF).
- List the primary sources of eggs used in IVF.
- Explain how a court will resolve a dispute on the disposition of unused frozen embryos upon divorce.
- Distinguish between posthumous birth and posthumous conception or fertilization.

- Understand the ethical and legal controversy surrounding stem-cell research.
- Explain what is meant by a genetically altered embryo.
- What is the role of a surrogate mother?
- Define intended parent.
- Distinguish between traditional and gestational surrogacy.
- Explain the controversy involving Baby M.
- List the policy reasons for and against allowing surrogacy agreements.

- Explain the relationship between surrogacy and the following areas of law: adoption, paternity, child custody, and contracts.
- List the major restrictions different states place on surrogacy.
- List the factors a court will consider when deciding who is the legal mother when a surrogate refuses to give the child to the intended parent(s).

INTRODUCTION

Traditionally, courts have been a forum for establishing paternity, as we saw in Chapter 13. Only until recently have courts had to struggle with the issue of establishing *maternity* and of deciding whether it is possible for a child to have more than one mother. This is an area of family law in which legal principles have failed to keep pace with technological and scientific advances. As one court commented:

> In this area...there are few guideposts. Advances in medical technology have far outstripped the development of legal principles to resolve the inevitable disputes arising out of the new reproductive opportunities now available.[1]

And another court observed:

> [The] technological fragmentation of the procreative process . . . has engendered a bewildering variety of possibilities which are not easily reconciled with our traditional definitions of "mother," "father," and "parent."[2]

In this chapter, we will examine some of these "bewildering" possibilities of family creation in the twenty-first century.

INFERTILITY AND ITS TREATMENT

INFERTILITY

Infertility is the inability to conceive a child. Couples are infertile when they are sexually active, not using contraception, and unable to conceive in more than a year. Either or both partners can be the source of the infertility. The National Center for Health Statistics estimates that 10 to 15 percent of all married couples are infertile. The approximate causal percentages are as follows:

- Infertility cases due solely to the male: 33 percent
- Infertility cases due solely to the female: 33 percent
- Infertility cases due to both male and female (or no cause can be identified): 33 percent[3]

infertility
The inability to conceive a child. The failure of a couple to conceive in over a year in spite of having sexual relations without contraceptives.

Male infertility is due to low sperm count, poor semen motility, impaired delivery of sperm, overexposure to certain environmental factors, such as pesticides, and the effects of sexually transmitted diseases. Female infertility is due to blocked fallopian tubes, dysfunctional ovaries, hormonal imbalance, the effects of sexually transmitted diseases, and the postponement of childbearing.

One in eight couples in the United States today need some form of medical help to create their families:

- 12% of approximately 61 million women aged 15-44 have fertility problems
- 7% of married women aged 15-44 are infertile
- 12% of women aged 15-44 (7.3 million) have used infertility services

Every year, approximately $3 billion is spent on infertility services, such as medical tests to diagnose infertility, medical advice and treatments to help a woman become pregnant, and services other than routine prenatal care to prevent miscarriage.[4]

Fertility treatment for producing a child without sexual intercourse is called *assisted conception* or **assisted reproductive technology (ART)**—medical means to assist human reproduction. Here is a more complete definition:

> "Assisted conception" means a pregnancy resulting from any intervening medical technology, whether in vivo or in vitro, which completely or partially replaces sexual intercourse as the means of conception. Such intervening medical technology includes, but is not limited to, conventional medical and surgical treatment as

assisted reproductive technology (ART)
Medical means to assist human reproduction. All fertility treatments in which either eggs or embryos are handled. Also called *assisted conception.*

well as noncoital reproductive technology such as artificial insemination by donor, cryopreservation of gametes and embryos, in vitro fertilization, uterine embryo lavage, embryo transfer, gamete intrafallopian tube transfer, and low tubal ovum transfer.[5]

When assisted reproduction involves third parties, such as surrogates, the process is sometimes called "collaborative reproduction." See Exhibit 16.1 for biology terms involved in ART and related procedures.

EXHIBIT 16.1   Terminology: The Biology of Reproduction

Conception: Fertilization; the union of a sperm and an ovum; the formation of a viable zygote by the union of a sperm and an ovum. The union of male and female gametes to form a *zygote*.

Egg: An unfertilized female reproductive cell; also called an *ovum* or *oocyte*.

Embryo: An egg (ovum) that has been fertilized by a sperm and is in the early stage of development; it has undergone one or more divisions. The product of conception to about the eighth week of pregnancy. Called a *preembryo* before being implanted in the uterus.

Fallopian tube: The passageway for the eggs from the ovary to the uterus. Normal fertilization takes place in this tube. Also called *uterine tube* or *oviduct*.

Fertilization: Conception; the initial union of a sperm and an egg (ovum) that becomes an embryo. Penetration of an egg by a sperm.

Fetus: A developing organism—the unborn offspring—from the eighth week after conception until birth.

Fresh eggs, sperm, or embryos: Eggs, sperm, or embryos that have not been frozen.

Gamete: A reproductive cell, either a sperm or an egg (ovum). A reproductive cell with a specified number of chromosomes. A mature sperm or egg that is capable of fusing with the gamete of the opposite sex to produce a fertilized egg or *zygote*.

Gene: A hereditary unit (on a chromosome) that has a specific hereditary function determined by a DNA sequence.

Genetic: Pertaining to genes.

Genetic parent: A mother or father who is biologically related to a child. One who contributes a gamete that results in conception.

Gestation: Pregnancy; the period of development in the uterus from conception to birth.

Gestational carrier: (also called a *gestational surrogate*). A woman who gestates (carries), an embryo that was formed from the egg of another woman. The gestational carrier usually has a contractual obligation to give the infant to its intended parents.

Gonad: A gland that produces gametes. Gonads include an ovary or a testis.

In vitro: Any process that can be observed in an artificial environment such as a test tube.

In vitro fertilization (IVF): The surgical removal of a woman's eggs from the ovaries, the fertilization of the eggs with sperm (in the laboratory), and the transfer of the resulting embryos (or pre-embryos) into the uterus through the cervix. A method of assisted reproductive technology (ART).

In vivo: Any process occurring within the living body.

Oocyte: The female reproductive cell from which an *egg* develops.

Ovum: An egg; a female gamete or reproductive cell. Plural form is *ova*.

Ovary: One of the two female sex or reproductive glands that produce eggs; female sex cells.

Ovulation: The release of a mature egg from the ovary.

Ovum: A female gamete or reproductive cell prior to fertilization.

Pregnancy: The period of development of the fetus from conception to birth.

Preembryo: (pre-embryo) A fertilized egg up to 14 days old, before it becomes implanted in the uterus. (Also called a *prezygote*.) Note, however, that the terms *embryo* and *preembryo* are often used interchangeably.

Procreate: To reproduce, to bring forth offspring.

Semen: Sperm and other secretions expelled through the male reproductive tract.

Sperm: The male gamete or reproductive cell.

Uterus: A hollow, pear-shaped organ that holds a fertilized ovum during pregnancy.

Viable: Able to live indefinitely outside the womb by natural or artificial support systems.

Zygote: A fertilized ovum before it begins to divide.

In most ART procedures, a woman' eggs are surgically removed from her ovaries and combined with sperm in a laboratory. The result (a fertilized egg that becomes an embryo) is returned to that woman's body or to the body of another woman. These steps, occurring over a period of approximately two weeks, constitute an ART cycle. There are several categories of ART:

- *Nondonor eggs.* A woman uses her own eggs in the ART cycle.
- *Donor eggs.* A woman uses eggs from (donated by) another woman in the ART cycle.
- *Fresh embryos.* The embryos used in the ART cycle are newly fertilized eggs.
- *Frozen embryos.* The embryos used in the ART cycle are previously fertilized, frozen, and then thawed.

Worldwide, more than four million babies have been born through ART since 1978, when the first ART child, Louise Brown, was born in England. This is an area in which the science of motherhood (called "ovarian Olympics" on a "high-tech treadmill"[6]) is moving much faster than the law. Increasingly, courts are faced with legal issues for which there are no precedents.

A federal law called the Fertility Clinic Success Rate and Certification Act requires clinics performing ART to report their success rate to the Centers for Disease Control and Prevention.[7] (See Exhibit 16.2.)

EXHIBIT 16.2   ART Cycle Success Rate

- Number of ART procedures performed with the intent to transfer at least one embryo (as reported by 464 of the 499 clinics in the country): 182,111
- Number of ART pregnancies: 72,870
- Number of live-birth deliveries: 59,334
- Number of these live-birth deliveries that were single live-birth deliveries: 47,685
- Number of these live-birth deliveries that were multiple live-birth deliveries: 11,649
- Total percentage of all births in the country from ART procedures: 1.7%
- Total percentage of all multiple births in the country from ART procedures: 17%
- Average age of the women using ART procedures: 36
- Percentage of ART procedures that used fresh (not frozen) nondonor eggs or embryos: 70 percent
- Percentage of ART procedures that used eggs or embryos donated by another woman: 12 percent
- Percentage of ART procedures that used frozen nondonor embryos: 18 percent
- Number of pregnancies from ART procedures that ended in miscarriage, stillbirth, induced abortion, or maternal death: 6,837

Source: Centers for Disease Control and Prevention, *2009 Assisted Reproductive Technology Report* (November 2011). *2015 Assisted Reproductive Technology Surveillance* (2018). (www.cdc.gov/art/artdata/index.html).

IN VITRO FERTILIZATION (IVF)

At 70 percent, in vitro fertilization (IVF) is the most commonly performed ART. IVF is sometimes referred to as fertilization "in a glass," meaning in a petri dish (which the media often mischaracterizes as conception "in a test tube"). IVF consists of the surgical removal of a woman's eggs from her ovaries, their fertilization with a man's sperm in a petri dish in a laboratory, and the transfer of the resulting embryos (or preembryos) into the uterus through the cervix. The cost of each IVF cycle can be between $12,000 and $15,000. Because more than one IVF cycle is often needed, the estimated average cost per live birth is between $66,000 and $114,000.[8]

in vitro fertilization (IVF)
The surgical removal of a woman's eggs from the ovaries, the fertilization of the eggs with sperm (in the laboratory), and the transfer of the resulting embryos (or preembryos) into the uterus through the cervix. A method of assisted reproductive technology (ART).

Here is how a recent court opinion described the IVF procedure:

> *IVF involves injecting the woman with fertility drugs in order to stimulate production of eggs which can be surgically retrieved or harvested. After the eggs are removed, they are combined in a petri dish with sperm produced by the man, on the same day as the egg removal, in an effort to fertilize the eggs. If fertilization between any of the eggs and sperm occurs, preembryos are formed that are held in a petri dish for one or two days until a decision can be made as to which preembryos will be used immediately and which will be frozen and stored by the clinic for later use.*[9]

In most IVF procedures, the fertilized egg is implanted in the uterus of the woman from whom the egg was taken. If they are transferred to the uterus of *another* woman, a *surrogacy* arrangement (collaborative reproduction) is involved, as we will see later in this chapter.

Suppose that a woman's eggs are not usable. Assume that she is able to carry a child, but not an embryo created with her own egg. In this situation, one of her options is to be *implanted* with the egg of someone else—an *egg donor*—with whom the sperm of her husband (or of another male) is joined via IVF. Just as high-quality sperm donors are in demand (see Chapter 13 on paternity), there is also fierce competition for egg donors who meet certain criteria. To find such donors, advertisements are often placed in college media platforms—such as websites, newspapers, and posters—that urge female students to "donate eggs to pay for college."

The ad in Exhibit 16.3 was placed in several Ivy League college publications, such as those at Harvard and Yale. The ad was eventually given national publicity and generated hundreds of responses from women claiming to meet the requisite qualifications.

EXHIBIT 16.3   Egg Donor for Cash

EGG DONOR NEEDED

Large Financial Incentive: $50,000

Intelligent, Athletic Egg Donor Needed for a Loving Family

You must be at least 5'10" tall

Have a 1400 SAT score

Free Medical Screening

All Expenses Paid

Another ad sought a "Caucasian" with "proven college-level athletic ability." The price for the right woman was $100,000. A more typical fee for an egg donor would be in the range of $5,000 to $10,000. To obtain a sense of the "market" for this service, run this search in Google, Bing, or Yahoo, "egg donor wanted."

Egg donation typically requires daily hormone injections and minor surgery to remove the eggs; the entire process takes approximately sixty hours. It should be noted, however, that the risks of egg donation have not been adequately studied: "Although the consensus among most reproductive endocrinologists is that extraction is safe, five deaths have been reported in Britain." Moreover, "[e]thicists and some women's health advocates worry that lucrative payments are enticing young women with credit-card debt and steep tuition bills to sell eggs without seriously evaluating the risks."[10]

Although it is legal for a woman to donate her eggs to help another woman have a baby and to be paid a substantial fee for this service, the situation is different if the eggs are going to be used for research. Many states either ban paying women for eggs or place significant limitations on what they can be paid when the recipients of the eggs want to use them for research. As a matter of ethics and public policy, many in our society are uncomfortable about encouraging experimentation in this sensitive area of human existence.

OTHER ART METHODS

In addition to IVF, other major ART methods include:

- *Gamete intrafallopian transfer (GIFT)*. This method uses a fiber-optic instrument called a laparoscope to guide the transfer of unfertilized eggs and sperm (gametes) into the woman's fallopian tubes through small incisions in her abdomen.

- *Zygote intrafallopian transfer (ZIFT)*. This method fertilizes a woman's eggs in the laboratory and then uses a laparoscope to guide the transfer of the fertilized eggs (zygotes) into her fallopian tubes (combining IVF and GIFT).

- *Embryo transplant*. This method places a fertile woman's embryo into the uterus through the cervix. Also called *embryo transfer, ovum transfer,* or *ovum transplant*.

Artificial insemination (AI) is not an ART method. AI occurs by inserting sperm into the uterus by a method other than sexual intercourse. ART methods consist of fertility treatments in which both sperm and eggs are handled in the laboratory. In AI, only the sperm is handled (for more on AI, see Chapter 13).

The new science of motherhood has generated many legal issues of **first impression**—those that the courts have had to face for the first time. Among the areas of controversy that we will now examine are the following:

- The status of frozen embryos in a divorce,
- The ethical propriety of stem-cell research, and
- The legality of surrogacy contracts.

THE STATUS OF FROZEN EMBRYOS

Some embryos resulting from IVF are not immediately implanted into the uterus. Through **cryopreservation**, embryos can be frozen for transfer or implantation at a later time. More than 600,000 frozen embryos (or preembryos) are in storage throughout the country:

- Percentage stored for family building: 88 percent.
- Percentage stored for "adoption" by another woman: 2.3 percent.
- Percentage stored for research: less than 3 percent.
- Percentage stored for other reasons (e.g., storage facility lost contact with the person who hired the facility): 6.7 percent.

It is not known how long the embryos remain viable in storage.[11] Estimates range from ten to fifteen years. Annual storage costs can be $1,500 and higher.

DISPUTES OVER THE DISPOSITION OF EMBRYOS

Suppose that a husband and wife file for divorce *before* all of their frozen embryos are used. Who receives "custody" of these embryos? Who "owns" them? Are these frozen embryos no more than property subject to **property division** along with everything else the parties acquired during the marriage?

The problem of frozen embryos arises when the divorcing parties disagree about what should be done with the embryos. Suppose that the husband wants them destroyed because he does not want to become the father of a child with his

artificial insemination (AI)
Inserting sperm into the uterus by a method other than sexual intercourse in order to achieve conception.

first impression
Concerning an issue being addressed by a court for the first time.

cryopreservation
The storage of cells or whole tissues at sub-zero temperatures for later thawing and use. Example: freezing embryos from an ART cycle for potential transfer or implantation at a later time.

property division
The distribution of community or marital property between spouses after a legal separation or divorce, and in some states, after an annulment. Also called *property settlement* and *property distribution*.

soon-to-be ex-wife, but she wants them kept alive so that they can be implanted in her at a later time. Can he be forced to become a father against his will? In a different context, a man cannot force a woman whom he has impregnated to have an abortion in order to avoid being the father of a child he does not want. Is the situation different here? Can he force a laboratory to destroy a frozen embryo that the woman wants to preserve?

Davis v. Davis

The first major case to address this issue was the Tennessee case of *Davis v. Davis.*[12] Junior Lewis Davis sought a divorce from his wife, Mary Sue Davis. The parties were able to agree on all the terms of dissolution except for one: Who was to have custody of seven frozen preembryos stored in a Knoxville fertility clinic that the Davises hired in pursuit of a much-wanted pregnancy during a happier period of their relationship? Mary did not want to use the frozen embryos herself but wanted to donate them to a childless couple. Junior was adamantly opposed to such a donation; he wanted the preembryos destroyed. When the Davises enrolled in the IVF program at the Knoxville clinic, the agreement they signed did not specify what disposition should be made of any unused preembryos in the cryopreservation facility, nor was there any Tennessee statutes governing the facts of the case.

The Tennessee court resolved the dispute by writing guidelines on what to do when parties cannot agree on the fate of frozen preembryos:

- The party wishing to avoid procreation should ordinarily prevail, assuming the other party has a reasonable possibility of achieving parenthood by means other than the use of the frozen preembryos in question.

- If no other reasonable alternatives exist, the argument in favor of using the pre-embryos to achieve pregnancy should be considered.

- If, however, the party seeking control of the preembryos intends merely to donate them to another couple, the objecting party has the greater interest and should prevail.

Using these guidelines in the *Davis* case, Junior Lewis Davis prevailed because Mary Sue Davis did not want to use the preembryos herself. As a result, their preembryos were discarded.

Can an Embryo Sue Its Mother?

A much different result would have been reached if the *Davis* case had arisen in Louisiana. A statute in Louisiana specifies that a "human embryo" is a fertilized "human" ovum "with certain rights granted by law." The principles laid out in the Louisiana statute are as follows:

- A viable in vitro fertilized human ovum is a juridical person, which shall not be intentionally destroyed.

- If the IVF patients renounce their parental rights for in utero implantation, then the in vitro fertilized human ovum shall be available for adoptive implantation in accordance with written procedures of the facility where it is housed or stored.

- The in vitro fertilization patients may renounce their parental rights in favor of another married couple if the other couple is willing and able to receive the in vitro fertilized ovum.

- No compensation shall be paid or received by either couple to renounce parental rights.

- Disputes between parties should be resolved in the "best interest" of the in vitro fertilized ovum.[13]

If an embryo is a person, then it can be a party in litigation with someone appointed by the court to represent the embryo. Surprisingly, such a suit recently occurred when an embryo located in Louisiana sued its mother. The mother had created the embryo with her boyfriend. After the breakup of her relationship with the boyfriend (who did not want the embryos destroyed), the embryo sued the mother on the theory that destroying it was not in the embryo's "best interest."[14]

IVF Contracts Today

As a result of the difficulties that arose in the *Davis* Tennessee case, current IVF contracts that couples sign with fertility clinics almost always specify what should happen to unused frozen embryos or preembryos. (Florida, for example, *requires* couples to execute a written agreement on how "eggs, sperm, or pre-embryos" are to be disposed of in the event of death, divorce, or other unforeseen event.[15] Courts are generally inclined to enforce such an agreement, but there are exceptions. In Arizona, for example, a court must "award the in vitro human embryos to the spouse who intends to allow the in vitro human embryos to develop to birth."[16]

In a New York case several years after *Davis* case, the parties underwent several unsuccessful attempts to have a child through IVF at a cost in excess of $75,000. The agreement they signed said, "In the event that we no longer wish to initiate a pregnancy or are unable to make a decision" on the disposition of their frozen preembryos, they should be donated to the IVF clinic for research purposes and then disposed of by the clinic." After the parties divorced, the ex-wife wanted the preembryos implanted in her, claiming that it would be her only chance for genetic motherhood. The ex-husband, however, objected and asked the court to enforce the agreement so that the IVF clinic would dispose of them. The court ruled that the agreement was binding and should be enforced. The clinic kept the preembryos.[17]

Although most states (other than Louisiana) would follow this position, there are exceptions. In a Massachusetts case, for example, the court said that it would not enforce an agreement on the disposition of frozen preembryos if it has the effect of forcing one of the parties to become a parent against his or her will. The ex-wife in the case wanted to use the preembryos for implantation. The ex-husband objected, and the court ruled in his favor even though the agreement they signed appeared to favor the option the ex-wife now wanted.

> [The court] would not enforce an agreement that would compel one donor to become a parent against his or her will. As a matter of public policy, we conclude that forced procreation is not an area amenable to judicial enforcement. . . . We would not order either a husband or a wife to do what is necessary to conceive a child or to prevent conception, any more than we would order either party to do what is necessary to make the other happy."[18]

ASSIGNMENT   16.1

George's will leaves his girlfriend fifteen tubes of his frozen sperm, stating that he hopes his girlfriend will have his child. After George's death, an older child from one of George's previous marriages objects to this clause in the will and wants the court to order the sperm destroyed. For what reason would the older child make this request? How should the court rule? (See General Instructions for the Legal-Analysis Assignment in Appendix A.)

THE OCTOMOM AND THE SCRAMBLED EGGS CASE

Considerable disagreement exists over whether the science of motherhood is sufficiently regulated. Widespread media attention given to problems in the fertility industry suggests that more regulation is needed. Examples:

- A single mother of six children gave birth to eight *additional* children (octuplets) after undergoing IVF. Her doctor was disciplined for implanting an excessive number of embryos in his patient, referred to as "octomom" in the media after the eight babies were born. Ten years after the birth of the octuplets, media reports indicate that they (along with their six older siblings) are doing well.[19]

- In the famous "scrambled eggs" case, a white woman at a fertility clinic gave birth to unrelated twins, one white and one black. The clinic made a serious error. It was unclear whether a black couple's fertilized egg was mistakenly implanted in the white woman (along with her own fertilized egg), or whether the black man's sperm had been used to fertilize the white woman's egg. The twins were not genetically related. Fortunately, the couples amicably agreed that each twin would go home with its biological parents.

Publicity about fertility mix-ups has given rise to increased concern about IVF. One woman, worried about the procedures used by private clinics that store and handle eggs and embryos, asked, "What if they put them on the wrong shelf?"[20]

POSTHUMOUS REPRODUCTION

It is possible for a child to be born after the death of one or both of its parents—a posthumous birth. The most common example is a pregnant woman whose husband (or other male partner) dies before the birth of their child. It is also possible for a child to be *conceived* after the death of one or both of its parents—a posthumous conception. Here is how posthumous conception or fertilization can occur:

> Sperm is removed from a recently deceased man and either frozen for later IVF or immediately inserted into the uterus of a woman. Requests for such sperm have come from wives, girlfriends, and parents of the deceased. "In fact, retrieving sperm from the dead is now so common that the American Society of Reproductive Medicine has developed a protocol [Posthumous Reproduction] for dealing with it. And one bioethicist, Timothy Murphy, has coined a term for this new kind of father: the sperminator."[21]

Another example:

> Woman #1 freezes her own egg for later fertilization. Unfortunately, she dies soon thereafter. After her death, her egg is fertilized via IVF and the resulting embryo is implanted in Woman #2. This produces a baby who was conceived and born posthumously, after the death of its genetic (biological) mother, Woman #1. If the man who provided the sperm dies before fertilization and before implantation in Woman #2, the resulting baby would be conceived and born after the death of both genetic parents.

A major issue that can arise in situations such as these is whether the child born after the death of a genetic parent can inherit from that parent. The few cases that have addressed the issue have said that the child can inherit but only if there is sufficient proof that the deceased expressed a desire or intent to be a parent before death.

In Chapter 14 we discussed the related but separate question of whether a child conceived after the death of a parent is eligible for Social Security survivor benefits. We saw that they were eligible for such benefits if they were entitled to inherit from the deceased parent under local law.

STEM-CELL RESEARCH

The human embryo contains *stem cells* that can grow into (i.e., differentiate into) other cells that make up the heart, brain, kidney, and other organs. In a laboratory, stem cells can be removed from the embryo and grown into *cell lines* that multiply indefinitely. These laboratory-grown cells have the potential of being used to repair or replace damaged tissue or organs and to treat or cure various diseases. To remove stem cells for this purpose, however, the embryo must be destroyed. Opponents argue that the human embryo is the earliest stage of human life and, therefore, must be protected. Some church leaders and pro-life activists believe it is morally wrong to destroy embryos, because life begins at fertilization. In their view, the embryos should be donated to women who wish to use them in order to have children.

Scientists have two main sources of embryos from which they can extract stem cells:

- Embryos produced for in vitro fertilization (IVF) procedures but that are scheduled for destruction because the couples no longer need or want them.
- Embryos produced for the sole purpose of scientific research rather than for use in IVF procedures.

Conservatives oppose the destruction of both categories of embryos. They consider the latter particularly heinous because the embryos that are destroyed are not surplus embryos. Rather, they are created from donated eggs and sperm for the express purpose of medical experimentation. Others take the position that embryos not needed for IVF and already scheduled for destruction should be available for research.

There is widespread legal, ethical, and policy disagreement over what stem-cell research can be undertaken. Congress enacted the Dickey-Wicker Amendment, which prohibits federal funding for "research in which a human embryo or embryos are destroyed."[22] Different presidents have issued conflicting guidelines on the meaning of this prohibition and ongoing litigation has kept the issue unresolved. While the debate continues at the federal level, some states have spent *state*-government money and some private individuals have spent *private* money on embryo research, but advocates of expansive stem-cell research say that major breakthroughs will not occur until substantial federal funding is made available.

Stem cells are not limited to embryos. Adult stem cells can be found in blood, skeletal muscle, skin, and elsewhere. These cells can be extracted without destroying anything. Yet adult stem cells are more difficult than embryonic stem cells to grow in the laboratory. Also, embryonic stem cells are considered more versatile and promising for medical research.

ASSIGNMENT   16.2

Do you think that there should be restrictions on stem-cell research? Should there be limitations imposed on public or private funding of such research?

GENETICALLY ALTERED EMBRYOS

A more dramatic and controversial development in the science of reproduction is the *editing* of human genes in sperm, eggs, or embryos. For example, scientists can operate on strands of an embryo's DNA during an IVF procedure before inserting the embryo into the uterus. Although a number of scientists support gene editing for the treatment and prevention of disease, "experts have mostly agreed that gene editing shouldn't be used to make 'designer babies' whose physical looks or personality has been changed.... Currently, using a genetically engineered embryo to establish a pregnancy would be illegal in much of Europe and is prohibited in the United States."[23]

Nevertheless, experimentation will continue, particularly in countries where professional and governmental oversight is weak. "Where some see a new form of medicine that eliminates genetic disease, others see a slippery slope to enhancements, designer babies, and a new form of eugenics."[24] "In the future, will there be nations that allow fertility clinics to promise babies with genetically engineered perfect pitch of .400 batting averages? It's not Impossible." [25] To say that these possibilities have been alarming would be an understatement. Global institutions like the World Health Organization are anxious "to keep cowboy scientists from charging into the Wild West of embryo editing."[26]

A CHILD WITH THREE GENETIC PARENTS?

Most states do not allow a child to have more than two parents. (See Chapter 13 on paternity.) California is an exception. "In an appropriate action, a [California] court may find that more than two persons with a claim to parentage... are parents if the court finds that recognizing only two parents would be detrimental to the child.[27] A primary focus of this law is a person who has formed a bonding relationship with the child, but is not biologically related to the child and does not adopt him or her. In such cases, this third person could be recognized in California as a parent along with the two genetic parents: the father who provided the sperm and the mother who provided the egg. In this three-parent dynamic, only two are genetically related to the child.

Is it possible for a child to have three parents, all three of whom are genetically related to the child? Yes, if experiments underway in some countries come to fruition. Here is how this could happen:

- There is a structure within cells called mitochondria that contains genetic material needed for the body's energy.

- Assume that Woman #1 wants to have a child but has a defect in her mitochondria.

- Woman #2 donates some of her healthy mitochondria to Woman #1.

- Once the donated mitochondria is transplanted into the egg of Woman #1 and IVF is completed, the resulting embryo will have the DNA of the father and of both Woman #1 and Woman #2. If a child is born from the procedure, it will have three genetic parents.

The procedure is called mitochondrial replacement therapy (MRT), or mitochondrial donation. It is not legal in the United States, but it is being actively pursued in other countries.[28]

ARTIFICIAL EMBRYOS

"In a breakthrough that redefines how life can be created, embryologists working at the University of Cambridge in England have grown realistic-looking mouse embryos using only stem cells. No egg. No sperm. Just cells plucked from another embryo.... Synthetic human embryos would be a boon to scientists, letting them tease apart events early in development. And since such embryos start with easily manipulated stem cells, labs will be able to employ a full range of tools, such as gene editing, to investigate them as they grow."[29]

THE END OF SEX FOR REPRODUCTION?

Professor Hank Greely is the director of Stanford's Center for Law and the Biosciences and the university's Program on Neuroscience and Society. He "believes that within 20 to 40 years most people will procreate in a lab—not in bedroom. . . . Advances in DNA coding and research in cell creation have convinced Greely that soon people will be able to go to fertilization labs to produce embryos and test the DNA of as many as they choose. They will then pick the one that appears to promise the "best child" before implanting it in the mother's or surrogate's womb.... Greely predicted that the ability to use adult skin cells to create eggs and even sperm will make procreation in labs far more attractive."[30] Specifically, here is an example of Greely's future vision of sexual reproduction:

> *A man and woman walk into a fertility clinic. The man drops off some sperm. The woman leaves some skin cells, which are turned into eggs and fertilized with the man's sperm. Unlike in vitro fertilization today, which typically yields around eight eggs per try, the new method could result in 100 embryos. The embryos' complete library of DNA would be decoded and analyzed to reveal genetic predispositions, both for disease and personal traits. The man and woman would get dossiers on the embryos that pass minimum tests for suitability. Out of, say, 80 suitable embryos, the couple would then choose one or two to [artificially] implant."[31]*

SURROGACY

INTRODUCTION

Surrogacy is the status or act of being a substitute for another. For our purposes, surrogacy is the carrying and delivering of a child for another. The person performing this motherhood service is called the **surrogate mother**, or the surrogate. She becomes pregnant, usually by artificial insemination (AI) or in vitro fertilization (IVF) with the semen of a man who is not her husband, with the understanding that she will surrender her legal rights to the baby upon birth. The surrender leads to a **termination of parental rights (TPR)** of the surrogate mother. (In Florida, the surrogate mother is called a volunteer mother, and the surrogacy agreement is called a preplanned adoption agreement.)

It is also possible for a surrogate to become pregnant through sexual intercourse, called natural insemination (NI). An example is the biblical story in the book of Genesis in which Abram's then-barren wife, Sarai, told Abram to sleep with her slave, Hagar. ("The Lord has kept me from having children. Why don't you sleep with my slave girl? Perhaps I can build a family through her."[32]) In the vast majority of cases, however, pregnancy occurs through AI or IVF.

A person seeking to raise a child born with the services of a surrogate mother is called the **intended parent**. An intended parent is a person who wants to raise a child as its legal parent and who enters into an agreement with a surrogate mother to bear and deliver the child. The intended parent may or may not be genetically (biologically) related to the child depending on whose egg is used. If the intended parent's egg is used, she is the *genetic mother*. If the surrogate's egg is used, the surrogate is the genetic mother. Intended parents using the services of a surrogate mother can include:

- A wife who is infertile because she cannot produce her own healthy eggs. The semen of her husband fertilizes an egg provided by a surrogate mother who then carries and delivers the baby.

- A wife who is infertile because she does not have a functioning uterus, but she can produce healthy eggs. The semen of her husband fertilizes his wife's egg. A surrogate mother carries and delivers the baby.

- A single woman who is infertile because she does not have a functioning uterus, but she can produce healthy eggs. The semen of a donor (often anonymous) fertilizes her egg. A surrogate mother carries and delivers the baby.

- An unmarried man who wants to raise a child on his own. He fertilizes an egg provided by a surrogate mother who carries and delivers the baby.

surrogacy
(1) The status or act of being a substitute for another. (2) The carrying and delivering of a child for another.

surrogate mother
A woman who becomes pregnant (usually by artificial insemination or in vitro fertilization) with the sperm of a man who is not her husband, on the understanding that she will surrender her legal rights to the baby upon its birth.

termination of parental rights (TPR)
A judicial declaration that ends the legal relationship between parent and child when this is in the best interests of the child. The parent no longer has any right to participate in decisions affecting the welfare of the child and no longer has any duties toward the child.

intended parent
A person who wants to raise a child as its legal parent and who enters into an agreement with a surrogate mother to bear and deliver the child. The person hiring the surrogate mother may or may not be genetically (biologically) related to the child.

- Two gay men who want to raise a child together. One of them fertilizes an egg provided by a surrogate mother who carries and delivers the baby.

There are two main kinds of surrogacy: traditional and gestational.

traditional surrogacy
The carrying and delivering of a child for another in which the surrogate uses her own egg and is therefore genetically (biologically) related to the child.

- **Traditional surrogacy:** The carrying and delivering of a child for another in which the surrogate uses her own egg and is therefore genetically (biologically) related to the child. The surrogate agrees (1) to become impregnated (usually by artificial insemination) using her own egg and the sperm of the intended father or of another man, and (2) to relinquish her parental rights upon the birth of the child.

gestational surrogacy
The carrying and delivering of a child for another in which the surrogate does not use her own egg and is therefore not genetically (biologically) related to the child.

- **Gestational surrogacy:** The carrying and delivering of a child for another in which the surrogate does not use her own egg and is therefore not genetically (biologically) related to the child. The surrogate agrees (1) to have an embryo produced by the egg and sperm of the intended parents (or of other donors) implanted (by IVF) into her uterus and (2) to relinquish her parental rights upon the birth of the child.

Of course, under either method of surrogacy, the man who contributes the semen is genetically (biologically) related to the child.

We do not have accurate statistics on the number of births that occur through the use of a surrogate. During a recent four-year period, the estimate of the number of babies born through surrogacy arrangements is 5,238.[33] This number is incomplete, however, because it mainly covers gestational surrogacy; we do not have good data on traditional surrogacy.

SURROGACY CONTRACTS

In most cases surrogacy comes into existence by agreement. A nonpregnant woman enters into a contract to become pregnant, to give birth to a child, and to relinquish all parental rights to the couple (usually a husband and wife), who will then adopt the child. The couple agrees to pay her medical and related expenses. In addition, some states allow surrogates to be paid a fee. These are called commercial surrogacy contracts. The total cost to the intended parents who hire the surrogate can be between $90,000 and $130,000.[34] When a fee is to be paid, critics deride the arrangement as a "womb for hire" or "baby buying."

If no fee is involved and payment is limited to medical and related expenses, the arrangement is called noncommercial or compassionate surrogacy. In Kansas, for example, a woman became the surrogate for her daughter who was born without a uterus. The daughter's eggs were fertilized with the sperm of the daughter's husband in the laboratory before being implanted in the daughter's mother. She gave birth to twins—who were her own grandchildren.[35]

When the decision is made to use a commercial surrogate, the search can be frantic, giving rise to the phrase "Google baby," referring to donors and surrogates located online through search engines such as Google. A number of fertility agencies have recruited women in India to become surrogates because it is substantially less expensive than recruiting a surrogate in the United States: "Logistically, this involves freezing multiple donor embryos and shipping them to a surrogacy center [such as the one] in Anand, India, packaged in liquid nitrogen."[36] When surrogacy is performed abroad for Americans, the media calls it "reproductive outsourcing."

Unfortunately, surrogacy contracts do not always operate as planned. Suppose, for example, that the surrogate mother changes her mind and refuses to relinquish the child upon birth? In a recent case, a surrogate hired abroad gave birth to twins, but the couple who hired the surrogate returned home with only one of the children, leaving behind the twin that had Down Syndrome.[37] In the remainder of the chapter, we will examine how courts and legislatures have handled such problems. Exhibit 16.4 sets the stage by providing an overview of the policy and legal issues raised by surrogacy agreements.

EXHIBIT 16.4   Policy and Legal Issues in Surrogacy

I. THE *BABY M* CASE

In March 1987, the nation's attention focused on a breach-of-contract battle underway in New Jersey. The contract in question was between Elizabeth and William Stern and Mary Beth Whitehead. The Sterns contracted with Ms. Whitehead in 1985 to act as a surrogate mother. Under the terms of the contract, Ms. Whitehead was to be artificially inseminated with Mr. Stern's sperm, become pregnant, give birth to a baby, turn it over to the Sterns, and cooperate in the termination of her parental rights. Mrs. Stern would then adopt the baby. Upon the birth of the baby (known as Baby M), Ms. Whitehead reconsidered and refused to relinquish her parental rights. The Sterns then sued in an attempt to hold Ms. Whitehead to the terms of the contract.

A New Jersey trial court upheld the contract, granted permanent custody to the Sterns, permitted Mrs. Stern to adopt the child, and denied any rights to Ms. Whitehead. On appeal, the New Jersey Supreme Court approved only the custody portion of the lower court's decision, ruling that surrogate parenting contracts fell under the New Jersey "baby-selling" statutes and were therefore illegal.[38] In spite of the illegality of the contract, the court ruled that it would be in the best interests of Baby M to be in the custody of her biological father and his wife.

The publicity surrounding this case led to a flurry of activity in legislative bodies around the country as pro- and anti-surrogacy groups attempted to sway policymaking bodies to one side or the other.

II. DEFINITIONS

Although the term *surrogate parenting* has become widely used since the *Baby M* case, it can refer to more than one method of achieving parenthood. In addition, the parties involved in a surrogacy contract may not necessarily be limited to a married couple contracting with a single woman. The parties could involve a married surrogate mother, a single father, or same-sex couples. However, for ease of discussion, the terms "married couple," "husband," and "wife" will be used, keeping in mind that a broader definition may apply to these words.

A. METHODS

Four general methods of surrogate parenting are recognized. These methods are:

1. *Artificial Insemination by Husband (AIH)*. The AIH method is an arrangement in which the surrogate, a woman other than the wife of the sperm donor, is artificially inseminated with the sperm of the husband of a married couple.

2. *In Vitro Fertilization (IVF)*. In vitro fertilization is a process by which a sperm and an egg are joined in a laboratory and the fertilized egg is implanted in the surrogate.

3. *Artificial Insemination by Donor (AID)*. The AID method is a technique in which the surrogate is artificially inseminated with the sperm of a third-party donor—someone other than the male who has hired the surrogate. Such sperm is typically a specimen obtained from a sperm bank.

4. *Natural Insemination (NI)*. The NI consists of sexual intercourse between the surrogate and the husband of a married couple.

Of the four methods, AIH is the most common. It is often substantially less expensive than IVF. The remaining discussion will assume that AIH is the method chosen in the surrogate agreement.

B. AGREEMENTS

Here is an example of a typical surrogate agreement:

- Harry and Mary are married, and they hire the surrogacy services of Linda.

- Linda will be artificially inseminated with Harry's sperm, carry the child to term, and surrender her parental rights to Harry, the biological father, upon the birth of the child.

- Once Harry has full parental rights to the child, his wife, Mary (technically the child's stepmother) begins adoption proceedings.

- Harry and Mary agree to pay all of Linda's medical and other necessary expenses related to the pregnancy.

Brokers are often used in surrogacy contracts to bring the parties together and to coordinate the arrangement. The broker is usually an attorney or a private agency that receives a fee for this service. In some states, the surrogate mother is also paid a fee. Her fee cannot be paid in exchange for her agreement to give up her parental rights. This would be blatant baby selling. Fees beyond reasonable expenses also turn the transaction into illegal baby selling. Surrogacy arrangements also exist between family members or friends and do not involve the payment of a separate fee to the surrogate mother. If such a fee is paid, the arrangement is a *commercial surrogacy agreement*; if a fee is not paid, it is a *noncommercial surrogacy agreement*.

(continued)

Exhibit 16.4 *(continued)*

III. REASONS FOR CHOOSING SURROGATE PARENTING AGREEMENTS

According to a study of surrogacy in Wisconsin, the demand for surrogate mothers stems primarily from female infertility. The National Center for Health Statistics estimates that 10 to 15 percent of all married couples are infertile (defined as partners who are sexually active, not using contraception, and unable to conceive in over a year). These statistics do not include the surgically sterile. The Wisconsin study also cites evidence that the number of infertile women is on the rise due to the use of intrauterine birth control devices, greater incidence of sexually transmitted diseases, previous abortions, and the postponement of childbearing to establish careers. Studies indicate that women who delay having children have a greater risk of being infertile, bearing children with birth defects, and/or bearing children who are physically impaired. The most common treatments for female infertility are drugs and surgery. Until recently, when these treatments failed, adoption of an unrelated child was the only alternative available.

Couples who want children but cannot conceive usually consider adoption. Despite a marked increase in the number of live births to single women, fewer unrelated individuals are adopted. Adoption experts believe that the increasing willingness of single mothers to keep their children is a significant factor in limiting the number of infants available for adoption. The stigma once attached to single mothers has diminished. Peers and relatives often encourage single mothers to keep their babies. Medical personnel and social workers are less likely to encourage women to give babies up for adoption.

Not all couples who contract with a surrogate have failed at adoption. Some couples would rather be childless than adopt an unrelated child and, therefore, use traditional surrogacy. For such families, a genetic link to their child is of primary importance. For example, in the New Jersey *Baby M* case, William Stern had lost most of his family in Adolf Hitler's holocaust and wanted a child biologically linked to him. Newspaper interviews of intended fathers confirm the importance some of them place on a biological link when seeking surrogates. One father favored a surrogate birth because "that child will be biologically half-mine" while another father stated, "[W]e believe strongly in heredity."

IV. MAJOR ARGUMENTS FOR AND AGAINST SURROGATE PARENTING

A review of the literature on surrogate parenting reveals several common policy positions on each side of this issue: the side favoring surrogacy and the side that wants it banned.

A. SUPPORTING ARGUMENTS

Due to the decreasing number of babies available for adoption and the advancement of technology in the area of human reproduction, couples who desperately want children will continue to seek out surrogate mothers. Even though the vast majority of surrogacy agreements are completed without controversy, there is a need for additional protection for the intended parents, the surrogate mother, and the resulting child. Proposed regulations have included:

- Limitations on the fees charged by brokers, who should be better regulated to ensure competency, honesty, and legitimacy in the surrogacy process.
- Proper examination of both the intended parents and the surrogate mother to ensure:
  - i   That the couple is emotionally and financially ready to bear the responsibility of parenthood.
  - ii   That the couple is truly in need of this service, such as when the wife is unable to carry a child to term.
  - iii   That the woman who will bear the child is emotionally, physically, and psychologically able to carry the child and to give up her rights to the child at birth.

By and large, these safeguards do not exist and should be enacted into law rather than banning surrogacy altogether.

B. OPPOSING ARGUMENTS

People who advocate a ban on surrogacy contracts argue that:

- Children will be psychologically damaged when they discover that they were "bought."
- Surrogate parenting arrangements violate the Thirteenth Amendment of the U.S. Constitution; the Amendment applies to slavery and should be interpreted to forbid the buying and selling of people.
- Surrogate parenting is a form of economic exploitation by rich people over poor people. As exemplified by the *Baby M* case, the intended parents will almost always have an economic and educational advantage over the surrogate mother. Many surrogate mothers are unemployed or on some form of public assistance. Few have an education more than a high school diploma. Thus, surrogate parenting arrangements will serve to create a class of "womb-sellers."
- There are plenty of nonwhite babies, older children, and special needs children available for adoption. Surrogacy is not needed.

(continued)

Exhibit 16.4 *(continued)*

- Women will be forced (by the terms of the surrogacy agreement) to abort fetuses if the intended parents conclude that the child might be born with a defect. Also, the women might be contractually obligated to become pregnant again in the event of a miscarriage.

V. STATE LAW PROBLEMS

Traditional state laws governing parents and children do not always fit the facts of surrogacy arrangements. When disputes arise in a surrogacy case, courts may struggle to try to fit the traditional rules into the facts of the case. Four areas of state law that have raised concerns are (1) adoption, (2) paternity, (3) child custody, and (4) contract law. Here is an overview of these concerns and how proponents of surrogacy have responded to them:

A. ADOPTION LAWS

Two aspects of many state adoption laws (compensation and pre-birth consent) may restrict or prevent surrogate parenting agreements.

Adoption is part of the surrogacy process. The child that results from surrogacy is adopted by at least one of the intended parents. Some states prohibit the payment of compensation for an adoption. Other states limit the adoption expenses that can be paid in the adoption agreement. The major concern of these payment restrictions is the prevention of baby selling. Surrogacy jeopardizes the protections that adoption laws were designed to provide.

Proponents of surrogacy agreements disagree. A major goal of adoption restrictions is to protect unwed mothers. But in most surrogacy agreements, the intended father is the biological father. It cannot be said that he is buying his own child. Also, surrogates voluntarily agree to surrender the child. They are not doing so under pregnancy-related stress. Finally, the fees to the surrogate mother are paid primarily to replace lost work time or for pain and suffering she must endure.

Most states prohibit a mother from granting consent to the adoption of her child before a child's birth or for a designated period of time after birth. In one state, for example, a mother's consent to surrender a newborn for adoption is not valid until at least seventy-two hours after birth. These consent laws, however, have little bearing on surrogacy arrangements. Adoption consent laws, like those involving baby-selling laws, were designed to protect unwed mothers. The decisions facing an unwed mother are substantially different from those facing the surrogate mother who has voluntarily chosen to bear children for another couple.

As pointed out in the *Johnson v. Calvert* case [which we will read shortly], "The parties voluntarily agreed to participate in IVF and related medical procedures before the child was conceived; at the time when [the surrogate] entered into the contract, therefore, she was not vulnerable to financial inducements to part with her own expected offspring."

B. PATERNITY LAWS

Paternity laws may also affect surrogate arrangements. If the surrogate mother is married, her husband is presumed to be the father of the child in states that retain the common-law rule that the husband of a woman who gives birth to a child during the marriage is presumed to be the father. Courts in some of these states will not admit evidence to the contrary. A majority of states, however, allow a rebuttal to the presumption of paternity, even though they place a strict burden of proof on anyone challenging the presumption.

Surrogacy arrangements address this concern by having the husband of the surrogate sign the agreement between the surrogate and the intended parents. In the agreement, the husband acknowledges that he is not the biological father of the child and that he relinquishes any rights he may have in the child.

Supporters of surrogacy point out that paternity laws were designed to protect the child, particularly the rights to inheritance, and were not drafted in anticipation of surrogacy arrangements. Because the rights and duties outlined in a surrogacy agreement fall on the intended father, the child's inheritance and other rights are protected.

C. CHILD-CUSTODY ISSUES

The traditional basis for custody decisions is a determination of the *best interests of the child.* The standards for judging the suitability of prospective adoptive parents include marital and family status, mental and physical health, income and other assets, history of child abuse or neglect, and other relevant facts.

A spokesperson for the National Committee for Adoption objects to surrogate contracts because they are not required to take into account the best interests of the child. Unlike normal adoption proceedings, no one screens intended parents in surrogacy arrangements. Currently, surrogacy agreements require nothing more than the financial ability to hire a lawyer and pay the surrogate mother.

In response, supporters of surrogate agreements argue that the agreements are inherently in the best interests of the child because the intended parents have given much thought to their actions and have decided that they truly want a child. Adoption proceedings, on

(continued)

Exhibit 16.4 *(continued)*

the other hand, are devised to provide a permanent home for a child who otherwise would not have one. In a surrogacy agreement, the child's home is provided by contract.

Furthermore, many supporters would be in favor of new regulations that are designed to ensure that the intended parents are capable of responsible parenthood so that the child's best interests are protected.

D. CONTRACT LAW

Current law in most states does not address the issue of the surrogate's liability or of remedies if there is a breach of the surrogacy agreement. Nor does current law adequately address the responsibilities of the intended parents. A number of unanswered questions exist.

Surrogacy agreements impose a number of duties on one or both of the intended parents. The duties include the payment of expenses and fees and the assumption of responsibility for the child at birth. If the surrogate mother performs as agreed, does she have recourse if the other party refuses to pay all or part of the expenses and fees? What happens if the intended parents refuse to take the child? Can the surrogate mother sue the natural father for child support?

In Texas, a twenty-four-year-old surrogate mother died of heart failure in her eighth month of pregnancy; in Washington, D.C., a baby born through a surrogate agreement was diagnosed as having acquired immune deficiency syndrome (AIDS). Now, neither the surrogate mother nor the contracting parents want the baby with AIDS. These issues were not previously addressed in the contracts.

Enforcement of a surrogate mother's duties is even more difficult. She agrees to be inseminated, bear a child, and surrender all parental rights. She also must agree to refrain from sexual intercourse during the insemination period. (In a recent case, the surrogate's violation of the no-sex agreement resulted in a pregnancy of her own child so that she was already pregnant when she became pregnant with the fertilized egg of the intended parents. Hence, she gave birth to twins who had separate biological fathers!)

If medical clauses are included in the agreement, what recourse do the intended parents have if the surrogate refuses to follow them? If she refuses the insemination, are any expenses refunded to the intended parents? If the surrogate chooses to have an abortion in the first trimester, which is legally her right, can the intended parents sue for expenses? Can they sue for damages if the surrogate decides to keep the child?

These are some of the questions that have yet to receive clear answers from courts and legislatures.

VI. STATE REGULATION

As indicated, states differ on how they handle surrogacy contracts:

- Some states are silent on the subject. No statutes exist and no cases have yet been litigated in the courts.
- Some states have outright bans on all commercial and noncommercial surrogacy agreements.
- Some states prohibit commercial surrogacy contracts but allow noncommercial ones.
- Some states prohibit separate fees to the surrogate beyond the expenses involved.
- Some states prohibit fees to a broker or an intermediary.
- Some states allow surrogacy contracts, but closely regulate the process, including medical and psychological screening, home studies, the payment of fees, time periods within which the surrogate can change her mind, the identification of the legal parents, etc.

The National Conference of Commissioners on Uniform State Laws has drafted a Uniform Status of Children of Assisted Conception Act (later revised by the Uniform Parentage Act). The uniform act provides two alternatives ("A" and "B") for consideration by state legislatures:

Alternative A:

Under this alternative, the state would allow surrogate agreements and regulate them. A court hearing would be held at which both parties would be required to submit medical evidence to prove that the would-be mother cannot bear her own child and that the surrogate mother is mentally and physically fit to bear the child. The proposal also would allow the surrogate mother to withdraw from the agreement up to 180 days into her pregnancy.

Alternative B:

Under this alternative, all surrogate agreements are void, both commercial agreements (in which payments are involved) and noncommercial agreements.

Source: Adapted from Dina Bennett, *Surrogate Parenting* (Background Paper 88-2 prepared for the Legislative Counsel Bureau of Nevada (www.leg.state.nv.us/Division/Research /Publications/Bkground/BP88-02.pdf).

ASSIGNMENT   16.3

a. Should surrogacy contracts be banned? If not, what kind of regulation is needed? Do you favor the regulation in Alternative A of the Uniform Status of Children of Assisted Conception Act? Why or why not?

b. Do you approve of an advertisement such as the following, placed on Craigslist along with ads for accountants and truck drivers:

CASH AVAILABLE NOW. Married or single women needed as surrogate mothers for couples unable to have children. Conception to be by artificial insemination. We pay well! Contact the Infertility Clinic today.

WHO IS THE LEGAL MOTHER?

Next, we turn our attention again to the question of what happens if the surrogate mother changes her mind about turning over the baby to the person(s) who sought her services? The court must then decide who receives custody of the child based on a decision of who is the legal mother. There are three factors courts consider in making this decision:

- *Genetics.* Who is biologically related to the child?
- *Gestation.* Who carried the child to its date of birth?
- *Intent.* Who intended to be the permanent parent of the child?

We begin our examination of these factors with the case of *Johnson v. Calvert.*

CASE

Johnson v. Calvert
5 Cal. 4th 84, 851 P.2d 776 (1993)
Supreme Court of California

Background: *This is a case of gestational surrogacy in which the sperm and egg of a couple were combined in vitro (IVF) in a laboratory and the resulting embryo was then implanted in a surrogate mother who carried the child to term. The surrogate mother gave birth to a child with whom she had no genetic relationship.*

Anna Johnson, a licensed vocational nurse, agreed to become a gestational surrogate. (The opinion refers to her as a gestator.) An embryo created by the sperm and egg of Mark and Crispina Calvert was implanted in Johnson. The agreement, however, fell apart while Johnson was still pregnant. Crispina Calvert and Anna Johnson filed separate actions to be declared the mother of the child who was eventually born. (Anna named the child Matthew; the Calverts named him Christopher.) The cases were consolidated. The trial court ruled that Mark and Crispina were the child's "genetic, biological and natural" father and mother. It called Anna a "genetic stranger" to the child. The court of appeal affirmed. The case is now on appeal before the Supreme Court of California.

Decision on Appeal: *Judgment affirmed. In a gestational surrogacy contract, the natural mother of the child is the woman whose intent was to raise the child as her own. Only Crispina Calvert had this intent.*

OPINION OF THE COURT:

Justice PANELLI delivered the opinion of the court.

In this case we address several of the legal questions raised by recent advances in reproductive technology. When, pursuant to a surrogacy agreement, a zygote formed of the gametes of a husband and wife is implanted in the uterus of another woman, who carries the resulting fetus to term and gives birth to a child not genetically related to her, who is the child's "natural mother" under California law?. . . And is such an agreement barred by any public policy of this state? We conclude that the husband and wife are the child's natural parents, and that this result does not offend . . . public policy.

Mark and Crispina Calvert are a married couple who desired to have a child. Crispina was forced to undergo a hysterectomy in 1984. Her ovaries remained capable of producing eggs, however, and the couple eventually considered surrogacy. In 1989 Anna Johnson heard about Crispina's plight from a coworker and offered to serve as a surrogate for the Calverts.

On January 15, 1990, Mark, Crispina, and Anna signed a contract providing that an embryo created by the sperm of Mark and the egg of Crispina would be implanted in Anna and the child

(continued)

born would be taken into Mark and Crispina's home "as their child." Anna agreed she would relinquish "all parental rights" to the child in favor of Mark and Crispina. In return, Mark and Crispina would pay Anna $10,000 in a series of installments, the last to be paid six weeks after the child's birth. Mark and Crispina were also to pay for a $200,000 life insurance policy on Anna's life. The zygote was implanted on January 19, 1990. Less than a month later, an ultrasound test confirmed Anna was pregnant.

Unfortunately, relations deteriorated between the two sides. Mark learned that Anna had not disclosed she had suffered several stillbirths and miscarriages. Anna felt Mark and Crispina did not do enough to obtain the required insurance policy. She also felt abandoned during an onset of premature labor in June. In July 1990, Anna sent Mark and Crispina a letter demanding the balance of the payments due her or else she would refuse to give up the child. The following month, Mark and Crispina responded with a lawsuit, seeking a declaration they were the legal parents of the unborn child. Anna filed her own action to be declared the mother of the child, and the two cases were eventually consolidated....

The child was born on September 19, 1990, and blood samples were obtained from both Anna and the child for analysis. The blood test results excluded Anna as the genetic mother. The parties agreed to a court order providing that the child would remain with Mark and Crispina on a temporary basis with visits by Anna.

At trial in October 1990, the parties stipulated that Mark and Crispina were the child's genetic parents. After hearing evidence and arguments, the trial court ruled that Mark and Crispina were the child's "genetic, biological and natural" father and mother, that Anna had no "parental" rights to the child, and that the surrogacy contract was legal and enforceable against Anna's claims. The court also terminated the order allowing visitation. Anna appealed from the trial court's judgment. The Court of Appeal for the Fourth District, Division Three, affirmed. We granted review....

[In California, there are two kinds of evidence that can be used to establish the existence of a parent-child relationship: evidence on who gave birth to the child, and genetic evidence derived from blood testing. Our statutes do not say what a court must do when the two kinds of evidence lead to conflicting results. There is undisputed evidence that Anna, not Crispina, gave birth to the child and that Crispina, not Anna, is genetically related to him.] Both women thus have adduced evidence of a mother and child relationship.... Yet for any child California law recognizes only one natural mother, despite advances in reproductive technology rendering a different outcome biologically possible....

[We decline to accept the contention of the American Civil Liberties Union (ACLU) that we should find the child has two mothers. Even though rising divorce rates have made multiple parent arrangements common in our society, we see no compelling reason to recognize such a situation here. The Calverts are the genetic and intending parents of their son and have provided him, by all accounts, with a stable, intact, and nurturing home. To recognize parental rights in a third party—Anna—with whom the Calvert

family has had little contact since shortly after the child's birth would diminish Crispina's role as mother.]

Because two women each have presented acceptable proof of maternity, we do not believe this case can be decided without enquiring into the parties' intentions as manifested in the surrogacy agreement. Mark and Crispina are a couple who desired to have a child of their own genetic stock but are physically unable to do so without the help of reproductive technology. They affirmatively intended the birth of the child, and took the steps necessary to effect in vitro fertilization. But for their acted-on intention, the child would not exist. Anna agreed to facilitate the procreation of Mark's and Crispina's child. The parties' aim was to bring Mark's and Crispina's child into the world, not for Mark and Crispina to donate a zygote to Anna. Crispina from the outset intended to be the child's mother. Although the gestative function Anna performed was necessary to bring about the child's birth, it is safe to say that Anna would not have been given the opportunity to gestate or deliver the child had she, prior to implantation of the zygote, manifested her own intent to be the child's mother. No reason appears why Anna's later change of heart should vitiate the determination that Crispina is the child's natural mother.

We conclude that although [California law] recognizes both genetic consanguinity and giving birth as means of establishing a mother and child relationship, when the two means do not coincide in one woman, she who intended to procreate the child— that is, she who intended to bring about the birth of a child that she intended to raise as her own—is the natural mother under California law....

Anna urges that surrogacy contracts violate several social policies. Relying on her contention that she is the child's legal, natural mother, she cites the public policy embodied in Penal Code section 273, prohibiting the payment for consent to adoptions of a child. She argues further that the policies underlying the adoption laws of this state are violated by the surrogacy contract because it in effect constitutes a prebirth waiver of her parental rights.

We disagree. Gestational surrogacy differs in crucial respects from adoption and so is not subject to the adoption statutes. The parties voluntarily agreed to participate in in vitro fertilization and related medical procedures before the child was conceived; at the time when Anna entered into the contract, therefore, she was not vulnerable to financial inducements to part with her own expected offspring. As discussed above, Anna was not the genetic mother of the child. The payments to Anna under the contract were meant to compensate her for her services in gestating the fetus and undergoing labor, rather than for giving up "parental" rights to the child. Payments were due both during the pregnancy and after the child's birth. We are, accordingly, unpersuaded that the contract used in this case violates the public policies embodied in . . . the adoption statutes....

It has been suggested that gestational surrogacy may run afoul of prohibitions on involuntary servitude. (See U.S. Const., Amend. XIII.) Involuntary servitude has been recognized in cases of

(continued)

criminal punishment for refusal to work. (*Pollack v. Williams* (1944) 322 U.S. 4, 18; see, generally, 7 Witkin, *Summary of Cal. Law* (9th ed. 1988) Constitutional Law, §§ 411–414, pp. 591–596.) We see no potential for that evil in the contract at issue here, and extrinsic evidence of coercion or duress is utterly lacking. We note that although at one point the contract purports to give Mark and Crispina the sole right to determine whether to abort the pregnancy, at another point it acknowledges: "All parties understand that a pregnant woman has the absolute right to abort or not abort any fetus she is carrying. Any promise to the contrary is unenforceable." We therefore need not determine the validity of a surrogacy contract purporting to deprive the gestator of her freedom to terminate the pregnancy.

Finally, Anna and some commentators have expressed concern that surrogacy contracts tend to exploit or dehumanize women, especially women of lower economic status. Anna's objections center around the psychological harm she asserts may result from the gestator's relinquishing the child to whom she has given birth. Some have also cautioned that the practice of surrogacy may encourage society to view children as commodities, subject to trade at their parents' will.

We are all too aware that the proper forum for resolution of this issue is the Legislature, where empirical data, largely lacking from this record, can be studied and rules of general applicability developed. However, in light of our responsibility to decide this case, we have considered as best we can its possible consequences.

We are unpersuaded that gestational surrogacy arrangements are so likely to cause the untoward results Anna cites as to demand their invalidation on public policy grounds. Although common sense suggests that women of lesser means serve as surrogate mothers more often than do wealthy women, there has been no proof that surrogacy contracts exploit poor women to any greater degree than economic necessity in general exploits them by inducing them to accept lower-paid or otherwise undesirable employment. We are likewise unpersuaded by the claim that surrogacy will foster the attitude that children are mere commodities; no evidence is offered to support it. The limited data available seem to reflect an absence of significant adverse effects of surrogacy on all participants.

The argument that a woman cannot knowingly and intelligently agree to gestate and deliver a baby for intending parents carries overtones of the reasoning that for centuries prevented women from attaining equal economic rights and professional status under the law. To resurrect this view is both to foreclose a personal and economic choice on the part of the surrogate mother, and to deny intending parents what may be their only means of procreating a child of their own genetic stock. Certainly in the present case it cannot seriously be argued that Anna, a licensed vocational nurse who had done well in school and who had previously borne a child, lacked the intellectual wherewithal or life experience necessary to make an informed decision to enter into the surrogacy contract. . . .

The judgment of the Court of Appeal is affirmed.

ASSIGNMENT   16.4

a. Isn't it true that the child in the *Johnson* case has three parents, two of whom are mothers? Why couldn't there be a three-parent solution to this case?

b. Do you think a gestational mother can bond with her child prenatally? If so, would this be relevant to Anna Johnson's claim to be declared the natural or legal mother?

c. Do you think that a gestational mother makes a substantial or significant contribution to the birth of a child? If so, when a court must decide who is the legal/natural parent of a child, should the test be the best interests of the child? Would it be in the best interests of the child to be with the gestational mother or with the intended genetic mother? Since both women have serious claims, why shouldn't the test be: Who would make the better parent?

d. Assume that Anna Johnson was genetically related to the baby because she used her own egg but that all of the other facts in the case were the same. Who would the legal mother be?

Belsito v. Clark

Not all courts agree with the intent test used in the *Johnson* case. Similar facts arose in the Ohio case of *Belsito v. Clark*.[39] An embryo from the sperm and ovum of a husband and wife was transferred to a gestational mother (referred to in the opinion as the "surrogate host"). The wife asked the hospital to list her as the mother on the birth certificate. The hospital refused, telling her that the woman who gave birth to the child must be listed as the mother on the birth certificate. Furthermore, since the father was not married to the gestational (birth) mother, the child would be considered illegitimate. The husband and wife then asked a court to declare them the genetic and natural parents of the child so that they could both be listed on the birth certificate as the natural parents of a legitimate child. (The gestational mother was the wife's sister, who was not being compensated for carrying the child. Although the gestational mother was related to the child as an aunt, she was not a "genetic provider.")

The *Belsito* court was faced with the same question as the *Johnson* court: Who is the mother of the child? The woman who provided the genetic link via the egg or the woman who gave birth? Although the *Belsito* court and the *Johnson* court both concluded that the woman who provided the genetic link is the legal mother, the *Belsito* court refused to use the intent test to reach its conclusion. The following excerpt from *Belsito v. Clark* explains the court's reasoning:

> In Johnson v. Calvert (1993), 851 P.2d 776, the facts are very similar to this case, with a married couple supplying the egg and sperm and a surrogate agreeing to carry and deliver the child. . . . The court in Johnson looked for the intent to procreate and to raise the child, in order to identify the natural mother. Since the genetic mother in Johnson intended to procreate, she was the natural parent. The Johnson Court discarded both genetics and birth as the primary means of identifying the natural maternal parent, and replaced both with a test that involves intent of the parties. . . .
>
> [We do not find the Johnson case] to be persuasive. . . . Intent can be difficult to prove. Even when the parties have a written agreement, disagreements as to intent can arise. In addition, in certain fact patterns when intent is clear, the Johnson test of intent to procreate and raise the child may bring about unacceptable results. As an example, who is the natural parent if both a nongenetic-providing surrogate and the female genetic provider agree that they both intend to procreate and raise the child? It is apparent that the Johnson test presents problems when applied. . . .
>
> [In addition, it] has long been recognized that, as a matter of public policy, the state will not enforce or encourage private agreements or contracts to give up parental rights. . . . See Matter of Baby M. (1988), 109 N.J. 396, 537 A.2d 1227. . . . Through the intent to procreate, the Johnson case allows the nongenetic carrier/surrogate to be designated as the natural mother. The possibility of recognition as a parent means that a potential right is implicit in any agreement or contract to act as gestational surrogate. A surrogate who chooses not to be the natural parent forfeits her right to be considered the natural and legal parent. Because a fee is often involved in a surrogacy service, that assent amounts to selling a parental right, and is in contradiction to the public policy against private contracts to surrender parental rights.
>
> [The intent test also conflicts with] the underlying public policy of adoption law. Adoption laws of Ohio have long required that a relinquishing natural mother be given an unpressured opportunity before a disinterested magistrate to surrender her parental rights. R.C. 3107.08. Considering the substantial rights involved, the possible financial pressures, and the value our society places on procreation, the need for such procedures is evident.
>
> In addition to protecting the interest of the mother, adoption law has attempted to protect the interest of the child. By agreement or otherwise, the natural mother is not free to surrender her child to whomever she wishes. Through the use of its

parens patriae powers, the state closely supervises the process, and ultimately selects or approves of the new parents. . . . The underlying public policy is to provide for the best interest of the child: to ensure that the abandoned child is not given to persons who will abuse or neglect the child, but will be placed in a home with caring and competent parents. . . .

The Johnson *court's formulation of the intent-to-procreate test does not . . . provide a means to review and ensure the suitability of the gestational surrogate or her spouse as parents. In addition, because it is based on private agreement or intent that has not been sanctioned by a court proceeding, it raises the question of future legal challenges, and thus undermines the stability of the child-parent relationship. The* Johnson *intent formulation ignores those concerns and relies on the whims of private intent and agreement. It is, in effect, a private adoption process that is readily subject to all the defects and pressures of such a process. . . .*

[T]here is abundant precedent for using the genetics test for identifying a natural parent. For the best interest of the child and society, there are strong arguments to recognize the genetic parent as the natural parent. The genetic parent can guide the child from experience through the strengths and weaknesses of a common ancestry of genetic traits. Because that test has served so well, it should remain the primary test for determining the natural parent, or parents, in nongenetic-providing surrogacy cases. . . . When dealing with a nongenetic-providing surrogate, such a rule minimizes or avoids the question of the surrogate selling her right to be determined the natural parent. . . . In addition, given the relative certainty of DNA blood testing, such a foundation or test for parental identity would be simpler to apply and more certain in results than a Johnson-*type intent test. . . .*

In conclusion, under Ohio law, when a child is delivered by a gestational surrogate who has been impregnated through the process of in vitro fertilization, the natural parents of the child shall be identified by a determination as to which individuals have provided the genetic imprint for that child. If the individuals who have been identified as the genetic parents have not relinquished or waived their rights to assume the legal status of natural parents, they shall be considered the natural and legal parents of that child.[40]

parens patriae
Parent of the country, referring to the state's role in protecting children and others in the state who suffer from a disability.

ASSIGNMENT   16.5

a. Which court is correct: the *Johnson* court or the *Belsito* court? Explain your answer.

b. Mary and Beverly are a lesbian couple. Each wants to give birth to and raise a child together. Mary becomes pregnant from IVF and gives birth to a child whose genetic father is an anonymous sperm donor, and whose genetic mother is Beverly, who provided the egg that was implanted in Mary by IVF. Who should be declared the natural, legal mother? (See General Instructions for the Legal-Analysis Assignment in Appendix A.)

c. Same facts as in the (b) example above except that both Mary and Beverly have genetic links to the child. The embryo was formed from the egg of Beverly and the sperm of the anonymous male donor. Before the doctors implanted the embryo in Mary, they removed the nucleus from the egg of Beverly and inserted it into the egg of Mary. Who should be declared the natural, legal mother? (See General Instructions for the Legal-Analysis Assignment in Appendix A.)

PARALEGAL ROLES

- For an overview of paralegal roles in family-law cases, see Exhibits 1.5 and 1.6 in Chapter 1.
- For many of the financial issues related to surrogacy covered in Chapter 16, a paralegal may be asked to help collect documents and facts outlined in:
  - The checklist in Exhibit 3.1 of Chapter 3.
  - The interrogatories in Appendix C.
- Miscellaneous duties:
  - Help the client compile resources on assisted reproductive technology (ART), particularly in vitro fertilization (IVF).
  - Assist the attorney-intermediary in locating an egg donor or surrogate mother and in coordinating the transaction.
  - Help collect evidence of the parties' intentions when they froze the embryos that they did not use.
  - Obtain copies of agreements signed by the egg donor, the sperm donor, the surrogate, and others involved in the fertility procedure.
  - Prepare a draft of the agreements that the attorney-intermediary will ask his/her client(s) to sign.
  - Research statutory and case law on surrogacy in the state.
  - Prepare adoption pleadings for the nongenetic parent who will be adopting the child given birth by the surrogate mother.

SUMMARY

Infertility is the inability to conceive a child in over a year. Assisted reproductive technology (ART) consists of medical means to assist human reproduction. A major ART is in vitro fertilization (IVF), which involves surgically removing a woman's eggs from the ovaries, fertilizing the eggs with sperm (in the laboratory), and transferring the resulting embryos (or preembryos) into the uterus through the cervix. Fertility clinics performing ART must report their success rate to the Centers for Disease Control and Prevention. Some women undergoing IVF use an egg donor. Many states either ban egg donation for research or place significant limitations on such use. Other ART methods include gamete intrafallopian transfer (GIFT), zygote intrafallopian transfer (ZIFT), and embryo transplant.

Using cryopreservation, embryos from an ART cycle can be frozen for potential use at a later time. States do not agree on what to do with unused frozen embryos after a couple divorces or separates but are unable to agree on what to do with them. Louisiana will not allow the embryos to be destroyed. Other states will try to abide by the contract the couple signed regarding what to do with the unused frozen embryos. If there is no such contract, Tennessee gives preference to the party who wants to avoid procreation unless the other party does not have a reasonable chance of procreating without the frozen embryos. In Arizona, a court must award the in vitro human embryos to the spouse who intends to allow the in vitro human embryos to develop to birth. Massachusetts is reluctant to enforce an agreement that has the effect of compelling someone to be a parent against his or her will. Posthumous reproduction is the *conception* of a child after the death of one or both of its genetic parents. A child born after the death of its genetic parent can inherit from that parent if there is sufficient proof that the deceased expressed a desire or intent to be a parent before the death.

Stem cells in human embryos hold great promise for medical research. The country is divided, however, on the ethical and legal propriety of destroying embryos in order to extract such cells. The Dickey-Wicker Amendment prohibits federal funding for research in which a human embryo is destroyed. State and private funding may provide alternative resources for research prohibited by the amendment.

Even more controversial is the genetic alteration of embryos in which the DNA of an embryo is modified before being inserted into a woman. There is some support for such alteration when the goal is to treat or prevent disease in the child born from the ART procedure. There is little or no support for its use in producing babies with particular traits.

Under a surrogacy contract, a pregnant woman enters into a contract to become pregnant, to give birth to a child, and then to relinquish all parental rights to the couple who hired her services. Brokers are often used to bring the parties together and to coordinate the arrangement. If the surrogate supplies the egg, she is genetically related to the child; she is the genetic mother. This is called traditional surrogacy. If the surrogate carries an embryo that was formed from the egg of another woman, the surrogate is not genetically related to the child. This is called gestational surrogacy. States have different laws on surrogacy contracts. Some states ban them; other states permit them, but regulate how they are created and enforced.

Courts must sometimes determine who is the legal mother of a child when the surrogate mother refuses to give the child to the intended parents. Some courts say that the legal mother is the woman who had the intent to procreate and to raise the child even if she has no genetic link to the child. Other courts say that the legal mother is the woman who has the genetic link to the child.

KEY TERMS

infertility
assisted reproductive technology
    (ART)
in vitro fertilization (IVF)
artificial insemination (AI)

first impression
cryopreservation
property division
surrogacy
surrogate mother

termination of parental rights (TPR)
intended parent
traditional surrogacy
gestational surrogacy
parens patriae

CHECK THE CITE

Gina is a gestational surrogate who gives birth to a child pursuant to an agreement with Andrea and Peter, the biological parents. The court described the issue in the case as follows: "The novel issue presented in this surrogacy matter is whether or not a court may issue a pre-birth order directing a delivering physician to list the man and woman who provided the embryo carried by a third party as legal parents on a child's birth certificate." How did the court resolve the issue and what was its reasoning? Read *A.H.W. v. G.H.B.*, 339 N.J. Super. 495, 772 A.2d 948 (N.J. Super. Ct. Ch. Div., 2000). To read the opinion online, run a citation search ("772 A.2d 948") in the *Case law* database of Google Scholar (scholar.google.com).

PROJECT

In Google, Bing, or Yahoo, run the following search: aa surrogate mother (substitute the name of your state for aa in the search). Write an essay in which you describe the law governing surrogacy in your state. Cover what is legal and what is illegal. Explain the regulations governing this area of fertility. You must cite and quote from a minimum of three different sources that you find on the Internet. At least two of these sources should be statutes, court opinions, or other laws. (If your state bans all surrogacy agreements, do this project on the closest neighboring state that does not ban them.)

ETHICS IN A FAMILY LAW PRACTICE

You are a paralegal working at the law office of Franklin & Franklin. One of the clients at the office is a bio-technology company. When you learn that the company is about to announce the discovery of a new fertility drug, you buy 1,000 shares of its stock. Any ethical problems?

WRITING SAMPLE

You work for a law office where one of the clients is a married couple who have asked a woman to be the surrogate mother of their child. The surrogate will be a gestational mother, using an embryo from the egg and sperm of the married couple. The surrogate mother is the first cousin of the wife. Prepare a draft of the surrogacy agreement that the married couple and the surrogate will be asked to sign. (See General Instructions for the Agreement-Drafting Assignment and the Writing Sample in Appendix A.)

REVIEW QUESTIONS

1. What is infertility, and what are its major causes?
2. What is assisted reproductive technology (ART)?
3. What does the Fertility Clinic Success Rate and Certification Act require?
4. What is in vitro fertilization (IVF)?
5. What is an egg donor?
6. What risks does an egg donor face?
7. Can eggs be donated for purposes of research?
8. What is cryopreservation?
9. How do different states resolve a dispute between a divorcing couple on what to do with unused frozen embryos (or preembryos)?
10. What is posthumous reproduction?
11. What are the two main sources of embryos from which stem cells can be extracted?

12. What does the Dickey-Wicker Amendment provide?

13. What is a genetically altered embryo, and why is it controversial?

14. What is a surrogate mother?

15. What is the distinction between traditional surrogacy and gestational surrogacy?

16. What is an intended parent?

17. What was the controversy involving the *Baby M* case, and how was it resolved?

18. What are the policy reasons for and against surrogacy agreements?

19. How have different states regulated surrogacy agreements?

20. How do different states determine who is the legal mother when the surrogate mother refuses to give the child to the intended parents?

HELPFUL WEBSITES

Your State

See Appendix D for links to the family law of your state on the topics covered in this chapter.

Fertility Law and Ethics

- www.fertilitytoday.org/fertility_law_ethics.html
- www.ihr.com/infertility/articles/legal_rights.html
- www.ivf-infertility.com/ivf/standard/regulations.php

National Infertility Association

- resolve.org

Division of Frozen Embryos at Divorce

- repository.uchastings.edu/hwlj/vol25/iss2/4

Surrogacy

- www.creatingfamilies.com
- www.selectsurrogate.com/surrogacy-laws-by-state.html
- dl.tufts.edu/concern/rcrs/ht24wv75n

Gestational Surrogacy Agreement

- www.allaboutsurrogacy.com/sample_contracts /contracts.htm
- www.allaboutsurrogacy.com/sample_contracts /GScontract1.htm

National Embryo Adoption Center

- www.embryodonation.org

Google Scholar (scholar.google.com)

- Choose "Articles" and enter in the search box any of the key terms discussed in the chapter. Add the name of your state to the search term.
- Choose "Case law" and "Select courts." Select your state, click "Done," and enter in the search box any of the key terms discussed in the chapter. Add the name of your state to the search term.

Google, Bing, Yahoo

(on these search engines, run the following searches, substituting your state for "aa")

- infertility aa
- paternity adoption aa
- cryopreservation baby aa
- surrogate mother aa
- natural mother aa
- assisted reproductive technology aa
- in vitro fertilization aa
- genetic modification of embryos aa
- surrogacy aa
- legal mother aa
- intended parent aa

YouTube

Run the same searches on YouTube listed above for Google, Bing, Yahoo searches. Even when the video clips are trying to entice you to retain an attorney, buy a book, or enroll in a course, they can provide useful overviews and references to primary authority.

Twitter, Reddit, and Facebook

On Twitter, Reddit, and Facebook, run the following searches (substitute your state for *aa* in your searches; run the searches with and without the name of your state). Look for links to family-law developments in your state.

- surrogacy aa
- infertility aa
- genetically modified embryos aa

ENDNOTES

Note: All or most of the court opinions in these endnotes can be read online. To do so, go to Google Scholar (scholar.google.com), select "Case law" and in the search box, enter the cite (e.g., "783 A.2d 707") or name of the case (e.g., "J.B. v. M.B.") that is given in the endnote.

[1] *J.B. v. M.B.*, 783 A.2d 707, 175 (N.J. 2001).

[2] *In re C.K.G.*, 173 S.W.3d 714, 721 (Tenn. 2005).

[3] Mayo Clinic, *Infertility* (2018) (www.mayoclinic.com/health/infertility/DS00310/DSECTION=causes).

[4] Magdalina Gugucheva, *Surrogacy in America* 26 (Council for Responsible Genetics, 2010). National Center for Health Statistics, *Infertility* (2016) (www.cdc.gov/nchs/fastats/infertility.htm). National Center for Health Statistics, *National Survey of Family Growth* (2018) (www.cdc.gov/nchs/nsfg/index.htm).

[5] Virginia Code Annotated. § 20-156.

[6] Sheryl Gay Stolberg, *For the Infertile, a High-Tech Treadmill* N.Y. Times, Dec. 14, 1997 (www.nytimes.com/1997/12/14/us/for-the-infertile-a-high-tech-treadmill.html).

[7] 42 U.S.C. § 263a-1 (www.cdc.gov/art) (www.cdc.gov/art/nass/policy.html).

[8] Glen Cohen and Daniel Chen, *Trading-Off Reproductive Technology and Adoption*, 95 Minnesota Law Review 485, 486 (2010).

[9] *A.Z. v. B.Z.*, 725 N.E.2d 1051, 1053 (Mass. 2000).

[10] Roni Rabin, *As Demand for Donor Eggs Soars, High Prices Stir Ethical Concerns*, N.Y. Times, May 15, 2007.

[11] *How Many Frozen Human Embryos Are Available for Research?* (Society for Assisted Reproductive Technology and Rand (2003).

[12] 842 S.W.2d 588 (Tenn. 1992).

[13] Louisiana Statutes Annotated §§ 9-129 to 9-131 (2008) (law.justia.com/codes/louisiana/2011/rs/title9).

[14] Gina Vivinetto, *'Modern Family' Star Sofia Vergara Sued by Her Own Frozen Embryos*, Today (December 8, 2018) (www.today.com/health/sofia-vergara-sued-her-own-frozen-embryos-t105728).

[15] Florida Statutes Annotated § 742.17 (www.flsenate.gov/Laws/Statutes/2011/742.17).

[16] Ariz. Rev. Stat. Ann. § 25-318.03.

[17] *Kass v. Kass*, 696 N.E.2d 174 (N.Y. 1998).

[18] *A.Z. v. B.Z.*, 725 N.E.2d 1051, 1057-58 (Mass. 2000).

[19] Holly Scudero, Where Are They Now: Octomom Nadya Suleman, Mommyish (March 13 2019) (www.mommyish.com/where-are-they-now-octomom/1).

[20] Sarah Hall, *Whites Have Black Twins in In-Vitro Mix-Up*, N.Y. Times (July 9, 2002).

[21] Lori Andrews, *The Sperminator*, N.Y. Times, Mar. 28, 1999.

[22] Megan Kearl, *Dickey-Wicker Amendment*, 1996, The Embryo Project Encyclopedia (8/27/2010) (embryo.asu.edu/pages/dickey-wicker-amendment-1996).

[23] Antonio Regalado, *EXCLUSIVE: Chinese Scientists Are Creating CRISPR Babies*, MIT Technology Review (November 25, 2018) (www.technologyreview.com/s/612458/exclusive-chinese-scientists-are-creating-crispr-babies).

[24] Wesley Smith, *Eugenics Revisited: Scientists on the Verge of Genetically Engineering Babies*, Evolutionary News (November 26, 2018).

[25] Pam Belluck, *"Designer Babies" Still Seem Unlikely*, N.Y. Times, August 5, 2017, at A14.

[26] Pam Belluck, *Altered Genes, A U.S. Adviser and an Inquiry*, N.Y. Times, April 14, 2019, at A4.

[27] California Family Code § 7612(c) (codes.findlaw.com/ca/family-code/fam-sect-7612.html).

[28] Editorial, *This Is Not About Designer Babies*, N.Y. Times, April 13, 2019, at A18.

[29] Antonio Regalado, *Artificial Embryos*, MIT Technology Review (www.technologyreview.com/lists/technologies/2018).

[30] Nancy Gill, *Author Discusses Future of Human Reproduction at Morning Forum*, Los Altos Town Crier, June 22, 2016 at 16.

[31] Malcolm Ritter, *Parenting of the Future: Many Embryos, each with DNA Profile* (April 18, 2018) (www.apnews.com/daa979776f584c0da4bc8bb03fbd51af).

[32] *Genesis* 16:1–2 (NIV).

[33] Magdalina Gugucheva, *Surrogacy in America* 7 (Council for Responsible Genetics, 2010) (www.councilforresponsiblegenetics.org/pagedocuments/kaevej0a1m.pdf).

[34] Examples: www.westcoastsurrogacy.com; www.bankrate.com (enter *surrogacy* in the search box).

[35] Gina Kolata, *When Grandmother Is the Mother, Until Birth*, N.Y. Times, Aug. 5, 1991.

[36] Ginia Bellafante, *Google Baby: Surrogate Pregnancy Becomes Global*, N.Y. Times, Aug. 26, 2014.

[37] Thomas Fuller, *Thailand's Business in Paid Surrogates May Be Foundering in a Moral Quagmire*, N.Y. Times, Aug. 5, 1991.

[38] *In the Matter of Baby M*, 109 N.J. 396, 537 A.2d 1227 (N.J. 1988).

[39] 644 N.E.2d 760 (Ohio C.P. 1994).

[40] Id. at 764–67.

CHAPTER 17

Torts and Family Law

CHAPTER OUTLINE

INTRODUCTION

INTRAFAMILY TORTS AND IMMUNITY

SEXUAL TORTS

TORT CLAIMS BROUGHT WITHIN A DIVORCE ACTION

PRENATAL TORTS

WRONGFUL LIFE AND WRONGFUL BIRTH

WRONGFUL PREGNANCY

WRONGFUL ADOPTION

CONSORTIUM, SERVICES, AND EARNINGS
Loss of Consortium (Spousal Consortium)
Parental Consortium and Filial Consortium
Loss of Services and Earnings

HEART-BALM ACTIONS

Alienation of Affections
Criminal Conversation
Enticement of a Spouse
Tortious Interference with Custody
Seduction

VICARIOUS AND INDEPENDENT LIABILITY
Vicarious Liability
Independent Liability of a Parent

INTRAFAMILY CRIMES

CHAPTER OBJECTIVES

After completing this chapter, you should be able to:

- Explain why the legal system has historically disfavored intrafamily torts.
- List the different ways that states treat spouse-spouse torts and parent-child torts.
- State when spouses can sue each other for a sexual tort.

- Explain when prenatal torts can be brought.
- Explain when actions can be brought for wrongful life, wrongful birth, and wrongful pregnancy.
- Explain when an action for wrongful adoption can be brought.

- Describe the different kinds of consortium actions.
- Explain the action for loss of services and earnings.
- List the heart-balm actions.
- Explain the extent to which vicarious liability exists among family members.

INTRODUCTION

A **tort** is a civil wrong (other than a breach of contract) that causes injury or other harm for which our legal system deems it just to provide a remedy, such as monetary damages. Injury or harm can be to a person (a personal tort); to land and anything attached to the land (a real-property tort); to property other than land, called *personal property* and *movable property* (a personal-property tort); or to economic interests (an economic tort).

In this chapter, we consider torts committed by one family member against another, special categories of torts against family members, and the vicarious liability of one family member for a tort committed by another family member.

INTRAFAMILY TORTS AND IMMUNITY

An **intrafamily tort** is a tort committed by one family member against another. The two main categories of intrafamily torts are the martial tort and the parent-child tort. A **marital tort** is a tort that one spouse commits against another spouse, and a *parent-child tort* is a tort that a parent commits against a child or vice versa.

At one time, an immunity prevented most intrafamily torts from being litigated. An **immunity** is a defense that is granted because of a special relationship or status that operates to block litigation and liability. The immunity is a complete defense to a tort claim, whether or not the defendant committed the tort. The main types of family immunities are as follows:

- *Spousal immunity.* When spousal immunity applies, spouses cannot sue each other for designated torts. Also called *interspousal immunity.*
- *Parent-child immunity.* When parent-child immunity applies, children and parents cannot sue each other for designated torts.

Each of these immunities is referred to as an **intrafamily tort immunity**.

Historically, courts have been reluctant to allow family members to sue each other for torts. Three reasons accounted for this reluctance. First, a family's harmony might be threatened if members knew that they could sue each other in tort actions. Second, if the family carries **liability insurance**, there is a fear that family members will fraudulently try to collect under the policy by fabricating tort actions against each other. When the insurance company pays the tort claim, for instance, the payment might go into the same house where both the plaintiff and defendant continue to live, thereby allowing both to benefit from the payment. (Note, however, that insurance policies often have a *family exclusion clause* that denies liability coverage among family members living in the same household.) Third, **at common law**, husbands and wives could not sue each other because a husband and wife were considered to be one person, and that one person was the husband! Hence, to allow a suit between spouses would theoretically amount to one person suing himself, and any damages from the suit would be paid and received by the same person—the husband.

Today, the third reason under common law no longer applies because wives now have their separate legal identity, as we saw in Chapter 12. Consequently, husbands and wives have the same right to sue and be sued. This change has been due to the passage of **married women's property acts** and the enforcement of laws against sex discrimination.

Additionally, many, but not all, of the spousal and parent-child immunities have been abolished. To understand what still exists, we need to cover some preliminary definitions. There are two broad categories of harm that a tort can inflict:

1. Personal injury or harm.
2. Property interference.

tort
A civil wrong (other than a breach of contract) that causes injury or other harm for which our legal system deems it just to provide a remedy, such as damages.

intrafamily tort
A tort committed by one family member against another.

marital tort
A tort that one spouse commits against another. Also called *domestic tort*.

immunity
A defense that is granted because of a special relationship or status that operates to block litigation and liability whether or not wrongful conduct was committed. The defense prevents someone from being sued for what might be wrongful conduct.

intrafamily tort immunity
Designated family members cannot sue each other for designated categories of torts.

liability insurance
A contract that obligates an insurer to pay damages (within policy limits) that an insured must pay a third person because of a tort or other wrong for which the insured has become liable.

at common law
During a time in our early history when law was created by court opinions and legislatures, often before it was changed by later legislatures.

married women's property acts
Statutes removing all or most of a married woman's legal disabilities on matters, such as entering into contracts, disposing of her property, and being a party to litigation independent of her husband.

Both of these categories can be inflicted by intentional torts or by negligence.

- *Personal injury*. The tort causing a personal injury can be an intentional tort (e.g., intentionally knocking someone to the ground in an argument—a battery), or it can be the tort of negligence (e.g., carelessly colliding with someone).

- *Property interference*. This interference can be to a person's **real property** or **personal property**. The tort causing the interference can be an intentional tort (e.g., taking someone's money without permission—a conversion), or it can be the tort of negligence (e.g., carelessly damaging someone's trees).

There is considerable diversity among the states on when intrafamily tort immunities apply depending on:

- The kind of harm involved (personal injury or property interference?),
- The kind of tort that caused the harm (intentional tort or negligence?), and
- The identity of the victim of the tort (the spouse, an **emancipated** or **unemancipated** child, a parent, or another relative?).

Exhibit 17.1 uses these categories and definitions to identify what intrafamily torts are blocked by immunities and which can still be brought.

real property
Land and anything attached or affixed to the land, such as buildings, fences, and trees. Also called *real estate*.

personal property
Anything tangible or intangible that can be owned other than land or things attached or affixed to land. Also called *chattel*.

emancipated
Legally independent of one's parent or legal guardian. The noun is *emancipation*.

unemancipated
Legally dependent on one's parent or legal guardian.

EXHIBIT 17.1   Intrafamily Torts and Immunities

SPOUSE VERSUS SPOUSE

A. Property Interference

- In most states, spouses can sue each other for intentional torts and for negligence that wrongfully interferes with each other's personal property or real property. Spousal immunity has been abolished for all torts causing property interference in these states.

B. Personal Injury

- In some states, spouses can sue each other for personal injury caused by intentional torts or by negligence. Spousal immunity has been abolished for all torts causing personal injury in these states. (The most common torts for personal injury are those growing out of domestic violence, such as battery and intentional infliction of emotional distress.)

- In some states, spouses cannot sue each other for personal injury caused by intentional torts or by negligence. Spousal immunity exists for such torts in these states.

- In some states, spouses can sue each other for personal injury caused by intentional torts but not if the injury is caused by negligence. Spousal immunity exists for negligence but not for intentional torts in these states.

- In some states, if the tort is covered by liability insurance, spouses can sue each other for personal injury caused by intentional torts or by negligence. (See, however, the family exclusion clause below.)

CHILD-PARENT SUITS

A. Property Interference

- In most states, children and parents can sue each other for intentional torts and for negligence that wrongfully interferes with their personal property or real property. Parent-child immunity has been abolished for all such torts in these states. This is true regardless of whether the child is unemancipated or emancipated.

B. Personal Injury

- In some states, an unemancipated child can sue a parent for personal injury caused by intentional torts or by negligence, except if the tort arises out of the parent's exercise of discipline over the child. Parent-child immunity has been abolished for all such torts in these states. (Parents have a privilege to exercise discipline in raising their children, which can include physically hitting and confining the child as long as such force is reasonable.) Teachers and others who stand in the place of parents—*in loco parentis*—also have this privilege unless it has been restricted by statute or regulation.

- In many states, an unemancipated child cannot sue a parent for personal injury caused by intentional torts or by negligence. Parent-child immunity exists for such torts in these states.

Exhibit 17.1 *(continued)*

- In some states, an unemancipated child can sue a parent for personal injury caused by intentional torts but not if the injury was caused by negligence. Parent-child immunity exists for negligence but not for intentional torts in these states.

- In most states, an emancipated child can sue a parent for personal injury caused by intentional torts or by negligence. There is no parent-child immunity for such torts in these states.

- In most states, parents can sue their children for personal injury caused by intentional torts or by negligence. Parent-child immunity has been abolished for all such torts in these states.

OTHER RELATED PERSONS

Property Interference and Personal Harm

No intrafamily immunity exists for other related persons. Brothers and sisters, aunts and uncles, grandparents and grandchildren, and other relatives can sue each for intentional torts and for negligence that cause personal injury or that cause property interference. The restrictions imposed on spouse-spouse suits and on parent-child suits do not apply to tort actions involving other relatives.

FAMILY EXCLUSION CLAUSE

Liability insurance policies often have a *family exclusion clause* that denies liability coverage among family members living in the same household.

SEXUAL TORTS

In every state, unmarried persons can sue each other for negligence if they transmit a sexually transmitted disease (STD) to his or her partner by carelessly failing to disclose the disease or by committing fraud if false statements of fact were made (e.g., "I am clean") to induce a partner to engage in sexual relations. Can spouses sue each other for the same torts? Yes, if their state allows suits for personal injury between spouses. If spousal immunity does not exist for such torts (see Exhibit 17.1), one spouse can sue another for failing to disclose the presence of an STD that was passed on to the victimized spouse. According to the *Restatement of Torts*, "A husband or wife who fraudulently conceals from the other a physical condition that makes cohabitation dangerous to the health of the other spouse is subject to liability to the other spouse for the harm suffered as a result."[1] Similarly, in most states where marital rape is illegal, the victim can sue the spouse-rapist for the torts of battery or intentional infliction of emotional distress.

TORT CLAIMS BROUGHT WITHIN A DIVORCE ACTION

Spouses who commit serious torts against one another often divorce. When a state allows one soon-to-be ex-spouse to bring a tort action against another (see Exhibit 17.1), can the tort action be brought in the divorce action, or must the tort be brought in a separate action? Not all states answer this question in the same way. Some states are against allowing torts to be asserted in the divorce action because most marital torts are based on marital fault and introducing evidence of such fault is inconsistent with the reason **no-fault divorce** was created (see Chapter 7). Other states, however, take the view that it would be a waste of time and a needless expense to require two separate suits—one for the divorce and another for the tort even though this has the effect of reintroducing concepts of fault and blame, which are central to the resolution of most tort claims.

no-fault divorce
A divorce that is granted without having to prove marital wrongs that caused the break-up.

(See General Instructions for the Legal-Analysis Assignment in Appendix A.)

ASSIGNMENT   **17.1**

Dave knows that he has contagious genital herpes but does not tell Alice, who contracts the disease from Dave. Can Alice sue Dave for battery or intentional infliction of emotional distress? Does it make any difference whether the disease was communicated before or after Dave and Alice were married? Does it make any difference that they are now divorced? (See General Instructions for the Legal-Analysis Assignment in Appendix A.)

PRENATAL TORTS

fetus
A developing organism—the unborn offspring—from the eighth week after conception until birth.

prenatal tort
A tort committed against a fetus.

It is possible to commit a tort against a **fetus**, which is defined as a developing organism (unborn offspring) from approximately eight weeks after conception until birth. The tort would be called a **prenatal tort**.

> Mary is pregnant. While on the freeway, Tom negligently drives his car into Mary's car. The impact causes a head injury to the unborn child that Mary is carrying.

Mary, of course, can sue for her own injuries and for damage to her car caused by Tom's negligence. In addition, if Mary is married, her husband may be able to sue for *loss of consortium*, as we will see later in this chapter.

If the fetus is later born alive, an action can be brought on its behalf to cover the head injury. Suppose, however, that the prenatal injury results in the death of the fetus. A wrongful death statute might apply only to the death of "persons," which raises the widely debated issue of whether a fetus is a person. Many states will allow a wrongful death action, but only if the fetus was *viable* at the time of death. (**Viable** means able to live indefinitely outside the womb by natural or artificial support systems.) A few states, however, will allow a wrongful death action even if the fetus was not viable at the time of death.

viable
Able to live indefinitely outside the womb by natural or artificial support systems. The noun is *viability*.

embryos
An egg that has been fertilized by a sperm and is in the early stage of development; it has undergone one or more divisions. The product of conception to about the eighth week of pregnancy.

Suppose that a fertility clinic carelessly destroys **embryos** (which are eggs that have been fertilized by sperm in the early stage of development) that a couple had cryopreserved (frozen) for future implantation. Is this carelessness (negligence) considered a wrongful death? Most states would say no, because the embryo (in most states) is not a person or a viable fetus. The couple can recover damages for the loss of the embryo (e.g., medical expenses in creating the embryo) but not the more extensive damages that are usually associated with wrongful death actions.

WRONGFUL LIFE AND WRONGFUL BIRTH

Doctors and pharmaceutical companies have been sued for negligence that results in the birth of what is called an "unwanted" child. An unwanted child can occur because of the following:

1. The parents sought a procedure to prevent conception—such as a *vasectomy*, which is a minor medical sterilization procedure for men—and afterwards they still got pregnant; or
2. The child that is born is deformed or otherwise impaired—meaning the child is not in the condition that the parents had hoped for (i.e., not what they wanted).

Consequently, there are two categories of suits that have been attempted in these unwanted-child cases:

- **Wrongful life** is an action by or on behalf of an unwanted, impaired child for negligence that precluded an informed parental decision to avoid the child's conception or birth. The child seeks its own damages in this action.

- **Wrongful birth** is an action by parents of an unwanted, impaired child for negligence in failing to warn them of the risks that the child would be born with birth defects. The parents seek their own damages in this action.

Suppose, for example, that a woman contracts German measles early in her pregnancy. Her doctor negligently advises her that the disease will not affect the health of the child. In fact, the child is born with severe defects caused by the disease. If the woman had known the risks, she would have had an abortion. Can an action for wrongful life or wrongful birth be brought in such a case?

Most states do not allow suits for wrongful life to cover the child's damages. Courts are reluctant to recognize a right *not* to be born. Several reasons account for this result. First, there is the enormous difficulty of calculating damages. According to a New Jersey case we will examine shortly, it is literally impossible to measure the difference in value between life in an impaired condition and the "utter void of nonexistence." Second, some courts feel that allowing the suit might encourage unwanted children to sue for being born to a poverty-stricken family or to parents with criminal records. Finally, anti-abortion activists have argued that no one should be allowed to sue for missing the opportunity to have been aborted.

Recently, the highest court in France ruled for the first time that damages for wrongful life could be awarded to a severely handicapped child. The ruling created a public uproar and led to a national debate over the implication of the ruling. The head of gynecology at a Paris hospital said, "This is the first time that doctors have been condemned for not having killed." A leading legislator in the country told the press, "This sends a message to handicapped people that their life is worth less than their death."[2] Soon after the court's ruling, France's national legislature passed a statute that barred future suits asserting the right not to be born. The new law states that "nobody can claim to have been harmed simply by being born."[3]

In contrast, wrongful birth cases have been more successful. Here, the parents sue for their own damages to cover their emotional distress and the cost of prenatal care and delivery. Courts disagree on whether other categories of damages (e.g., extra caretaking expenses due to the impairment) can be obtained in a wrongful birth action.

WRONGFUL PREGNANCY

Next, we examine negligence that leads to the birth of an unwanted *healthy* child:

- **Wrongful pregnancy** is an action by parents of an unwanted healthy child for a wrong related to pregnancy, such as negligent performance of a sterilization procedure. Also called *wrongful conception*.

Actions for wrongful pregnancy are allowed in most states. Common examples for a wrongful pregnancy action would be a suit against a doctor for negligently performing a vasectomy or a suit against a pharmaceutical company for making defective birth-control pills. Damages are limited to the expenses of prenatal care and the child's delivery; they rarely extend to the costs of raising a healthy child. Furthermore, the unwanted healthy child usually is not allowed to bring the same type of wrongful pregnancy action in his or her own right.

wrongful life
An action by or on behalf of an unwanted, impaired child for negligence that precluded an informed parental decision to avoid the child's conception or birth. The child seeks its own damages.

wrongful birth
An action by parents of an unwanted, impaired child for negligence in failing to warn them of the risks that the child would be born with birth defects. The parents seek their own damages.

wrongful pregnancy
An action by parents of an unplanned, healthy child for a wrong related to pregnancy, such as negligent performance of a vasectomy. Also called *wrongful conception*.

CASE | Berman v. Allen
80 N.J. 421, 404 A.2d 8 (1979)
Supreme Court of New Jersey

Background: *Sharon Berman was born with Down's syndrome. Sharon's mother would have had an abortion if she had known this fact before Sharon's birth. Doctors Allen and Attardi had failed to tell Sharon's mother about the availability of amniocentesis as a technique to discover the presence of Down's syndrome in an embryo. In this medical malpractice action, the parents sued for wrongful life on behalf of Sharon and for wrongful birth on their own behalf. The trial court granted the doctors a summary judgment because the plaintiffs failed to state a cause of action. The case is now on appeal before the Supreme Court of New Jersey.*

Decision: *The Supreme Court of New Jersey ruled that the child could not sue for wrongful life, but the parents could sue for wrongful birth.*

OPINION OF THE COURT

Justice PASHMAN delivered the opinion of the court . . .

Plaintiffs allege that defendants deviated from accepted medical standards by failing to inform Mrs. Berman during her pregnancy of the existence of a procedure known as amniocentesis. This procedure involves the insertion of a long needle into a mother's uterus and the removal therefrom of a sample of amniotic fluid containing living fetal cells [that can indicate genetic abnormalities such as Down's syndrome].

Due to Mrs. Berman's age at the time of her conception [38], plaintiffs contend that the risk that her child, if born, would be afflicted with Down's syndrome was sufficiently great that sound medical practice at the time of pregnancy required defendants to inform her both of this risk and the availability of amniocentesis as a method of determining whether in her particular case that risk would come to fruition. Had defendants so informed Mrs. Berman, the complaint continues, she would have submitted to the amniocentesis procedure, discovered that the child, if born, would suffer from Down's syndrome, and had the fetus aborted.

As a result of defendants' alleged negligence, the infant Sharon, through her guardian *ad litem,* seeks compensation for the physical and emotional pain and suffering which she will endure throughout life because of her mongoloid condition. Mr. and Mrs. Berman, the child's parents, request damages in their own right both for the emotional anguish which they have experienced and will continue to experience on account of Sharon's birth defect, and the medical and other costs which they will incur in order to properly raise, educate and supervise the child. . . .

The claim for damages asserted on behalf of the infant Sharon has aptly been labeled a cause of action grounded upon "wrongful life." [The] gist of the infant's complaint is that had defendants informed her mother of the availability of amniocentesis, Sharon would never have come into existence. . . . In essence, Sharon claims that her very life is "wrongful. . . ."

The primary purpose of tort law is that of compensating plaintiffs for the injuries they have suffered wrongfully at the hands of others. As such, damages are ordinarily computed by "comparing the condition plaintiff would have been in, had the defendants not been negligent, with plaintiff's impaired condition as a result of the negligence." *Gleitman v. Cosgrove,* 49 N.J. 22, 28 (1967). In the case of a claim predicated upon wrongful life, such a computation would require the trier of fact to measure the difference in value between life in an impaired condition and the "utter void of nonexistence." *Gleitman,* supra. Such an endeavor, however, is literally impossible. As Chief Justice Weintraub noted, man, "who knows nothing of death or nothingness," simply cannot affix a price tag to non-life. *Gleitman* at 63. . . .

One of the most deeply held beliefs of our society is that life whether experienced with or without a major physical handicap is more precious than non-life. . . . We recognize that as a mongoloid child, Sharon's abilities will be more circumscribed than those of normal, healthy children and that she, unlike them, will experience a great deal of physical and emotional pain and anguish. We sympathize with her plight. We cannot, however, say that she would have been better off had she never been brought into the world . . . . Accordingly, we hold that Sharon has failed to state a valid cause of action founded upon "wrongful life."

The validity of the parents' [own] claim for relief calls into play considerations different from those involved in the infant's complaint. As in the case of the infant, Mr. and Mrs. Berman do not assert that defendants increased the risk that Sharon, if born, would be afflicted with Down's syndrome. Rather, at bottom, they allege that they were tortiously injured because Mrs. Berman was deprived of the option of making a meaningful decision as to whether to abort the fetus, a decision which, at least during the first trimester of pregnancy, is not subject to state interference. See *Roe v. Wade,* 410 U.S. 113 (1973). They thus claim that Sharon's "birth" as opposed to her "life" was wrongful.

Two items of damage are requested in order to redress this allegedly tortious injury: (1) the medical and other costs that will be incurred in order to properly raise, supervise and educate the child; and (2) compensation for the emotional anguish that has been and will continue to be experienced on account of Sharon's condition. . . .

The Supreme Court's ruling in *Roe v. Wade* clearly establishes that a woman possesses a constitutional right to decide whether her fetus should be aborted, at least during the first trimester of pregnancy. Public policy supports . . . the proposition that she not be impermissibly denied a meaningful opportunity to make that decision.

As in all other cases of tortious injury, a physician whose negligence has deprived a mother of this opportunity should be required to make amends for the damage which he has proximately caused. Any other ruling would in effect immunize from liability those in

(continued)

the medical field providing inadequate guidance to persons who would choose to exercise their constitutional right to abort fetuses which, if born, would suffer from genetic defects. Accordingly, we hold that a cause of action founded upon wrongful birth is a legally cognizable claim.

Troublesome, however, is the measure of damages. As noted earlier, the first item sought to be recompensed is the medical and other expenses that will be incurred in order to properly raise, educate and supervise the child. Although these costs were "caused" by defendants' negligence in the sense that but for the failure to inform, the child would not have come into existence, we conclude that this item of damage should not be recoverable. In essence, Mr. and Mrs. Berman desire to retain all the benefits inhering in the birth of the child, i.e., the love and joy they will experience as parents while saddling defendants with the enormous expenses attendant upon her rearing. Under the facts and circumstances here alleged, we find that such an award would be wholly disproportionate to the culpability involved, and that allowance of such a recovery would both constitute a windfall to the parents and place too unreasonable a financial burden upon physicians.

The parents' claim for emotional damages stands upon a different footing. In failing to inform Mrs. Berman of the availability of amniocentesis, defendants directly deprived her and, derivatively,

her husband of the option to accept or reject a parental relationship with the child and thus caused them to experience mental and emotional anguish upon their realization that they had given birth to a child afflicted with Down's syndrome. We feel that the monetary equivalent of this distress is an appropriate measure of the harm suffered by the parents deriving from Mrs. Berman's loss of her right to abort the fetus. . . .

[W]e do not feel that placing a monetary value upon the emotional suffering that Mr. and Mrs. Berman have and will continue to experience is an impossible task for the trier of fact. . . . [C]ourts have come to recognize that mental and emotional distress is just as "real" as physical pain, and that its valuation is no more difficult. Consequently, damages for such distress have been ruled allowable in an increasing number of contexts. Moreover . . . to deny Mr. and Mrs. Berman redress for their injuries merely because damages cannot be measured with precise exactitude would constitute a perversion of fundamental principles of justice.

Consequently, we hold that Mr. and Mrs. Berman have stated actionable claims for relief. Should their allegations be proven at trial, they are entitled to be recompensed for the mental and emotional anguish they have suffered and will continue to suffer on account of Sharon's condition. Accordingly,. . .this case remanded for a plenary trial.

WRONGFUL ADOPTION

Suppose that an adoption agency carelessly states the physical or mental health of a child or the medical history of the child's birth family.

Alice and Stan Patterson go to the Riverside Adoption Agency (RAA), where they adopt Irene, an infant. Before the adoption, RAA told the Pattersons that Irene did not have any genetic disorders. This statement turned out to be false. RAA knew that Irene had phenylketonuria (PKU) (a disorder that affects how the body processes protein), but it did not inform the Pattersons of her diagnosis. After Irene has been living with the Pattersons for a while, they discover that she has severe medical problems due to PKU.

What options do the Pattersons have? The period for challenging the adoption itself may have passed. Furthermore, they may have bonded with the child and do not want to "send the child back," even if it were possible to annul or abrogate the adoption. In such cases, some states have allowed the adoptive parents to sue the adoption agency, particularly when they made clear to the agency that they did not want to adopt a problem child.

The Pattersons' argument in court would be that information about the child's health was **material**—that is, the information was important enough to influence their decision. The Pattersons would not have adopted the child if they had been presented with all the facts. Of course, prospective adoptive parents cannot expect a guarantee that the child will be perfect. But they are entitled to available information that might indicate a significant likelihood of future medical problems. The careless failure to provide such information may constitute the tort of wrongful adoption.

- **Wrongful adoption** is an action seeking damages for carelessly stating (or failing to disclose) to prospective adoptive parents available facts on the health or other condition of the adoptee that would be relevant to the decision on whether to adopt.

material
(1) Serious and substantial. (2) Important enough to influence the decision that was made.

wrongful adoption
An action seeking damages for carelessly stating (or failing to disclose) to prospective adoptive parents available facts on the health or other condition of the adoptee that would be relevant to the decision on whether to adopt.

CONSORTIUM, SERVICES, AND EARNINGS

Consortium is a right to the benefits that are naturally expected in a particular family relationship. We will consider three categories of consortium: spousal, parental, and filial (relating to a son or a daughter).

LOSS OF CONSORTIUM (SPOUSAL CONSORTIUM)

Spousal consortium is the right of one spouse to the relational benefits that are naturally expected from the other spouse. The benefits include companionship, love, affection, sexual relations, and services (e.g., housekeeping or making repairs around the house). An interference with these benefits can lead to the recovery of damages. The interference is called loss of consortium, although a more accurate term would be *loss of spousal consortium*. At one time, only the husband could recover for loss of consortium. In every state, this view has been changed by statute or has been ruled unconstitutional as a denial of the equal protection of the laws. Either spouse can now recover for loss of consortium. Here is an example of how the loss is claimed:

- *Rich and Ann are married.*
- *Paul, a stranger, negligently injures Ann.*
- *Ann sues Paul for negligence. She receives damages to cover her medical bills, lost wages, pain and suffering, etc.*
- *Rich asserts a separate claim against Paul for loss of consortium. He receives damages to compensate him for whatever loss or impairment he can prove in the love, affection, sexual relations, and services that Ann gave him as his wife before the accident.*

To receive damages for loss of consortium, the loss or interference with the consortium must be wrongful. It is wrongful if the injury to the other spouse was wrongful. If Ann loses her negligence suit against Paul, Rich will not be able to win his consortium claim. To recover for loss of consortium, there must be an underlying successfully litigated tort brought by the other spouse.

Unmarried Couples Cannot Sue for Loss of Consortium

Most states deny recovery for loss of consortium to individuals who are not married.

> *Jim and Rachel are engaged to be married. The defendant negligently incapacitates Rachel the day before the wedding. Rachel sues the defendant to recover for her injuries.*

> *Mary and John have lived together for forty years. They have never married and do not live in a state that recognizes common-law marriage. The defendant negligently incapacitates John, who sues the defendant to recover for his injuries.*

In most states, Jim and Mary would not have a right to sue for loss of consortium because, as one court put it, "it would be inequitable to allow a cohabitant to reap the benefits of a legal marriage without being required to assume the burdens of marriage" and recognizing the right "would be the equivalent of recognizing common law marriage" in a state that does not allow such marriages. If the marriage-only rule were relaxed, how far would the right be extended? The "injured person has cousins, co-workers, drinking buddies and softball team members who may lose his society, companionship and guidance. For that matter, the dead or injured person may have been having an affair with his married neighbor, who also may suffer a loss of consortium."[4]

Restricting the right to only married couples may seem unfair, particularly to a couple who is hours away from being married. The law, however, must draw a line somewhere. A court would have a difficult time distinguishing between Jim and Rachel (a day away from their wedding) and an engaged couple whose wedding is six weeks, or six months away. The practical problem of drawing the line has led most (but not all) courts to limit the action for loss of consortium to married individuals.

An Exception for Domestic Partnerships

While the general rule is that only married couples can sue for loss of consortium, an exception is allowed for **domestic partnerships**. Before same-sex marriage was allowed, many states gave legal recognition to two same-sex (or opposite-sex) unmarried persons who are emotionally and financially interdependent. They are allowed some of the same benefits and duties as married couples, including the right of one partner to sue for loss of consortium when the other partner is injured.

domestic partnerships
A same-sex or opposite-sex legal relationship of unmarried individuals who are emotionally and financially interdependent and who have some of the same state benefits and responsibilities as individuals in a marriage.

PARENTAL CONSORTIUM AND FILIAL CONSORTIUM

In addition to spousal consortium, two other kinds of consortium exist: *parental consortium* and *filial consortium*. Not all states allow suits for loss of these categories of consortium.

Parental consortium is the right of a child to the normal companionship and affection of a parent. For example:

Bill is the father of Sam, a teenager. Bill's shoulder is negligently injured by Alice. The injury led to hospitalization for several months and a long recovery period at home. Bill sues Alice to recover for his injuries.

parental consortium
The right of a child to the normal companionship and affection of a parent.

Sam, as Bill's son, also suffered a loss—a loss of parental consortium—while his father was incapacitated due to the injury. States differ on whether they allow suits for interference with (loss of) parental consortium.

Filial consortium is the right of a parent to the normal companionship and affection of a child. For example:

Susan is the mother of ten-year-old Irene. Irene's leg is negligently injured by John. Irene's leg is in a cast for eight months. Irene sues John to recover for her injuries.

filial consortium
The right of a parent to the normal companionship and affection of a child.

Susan, as Irene's mother, also suffered a loss—a loss of filial consortium—while her daughter was incapacitated due to the injury. States differ on whether they allow suits for interference with (loss of) filial consortium.

What about other family relationships in which one member suffers the loss of the companionship and affection of another member due to a wrongful or tortious injury? Examples include brother and sister and grandparent and grandchild. Very few courts will allow actions for interference with (loss of) consortium in such relationships.

LOSS OF SERVICES AND EARNINGS

Parents have a right to the services of their unemancipated children. This would include tasks such as cutting the grass and running errands for the household. In the example of ten-year-old Irene's leg injury that was negligently caused by John, Irene's mother, Susan, can recover damages from John for causing a **loss of services** by Irene to her. A loss of services is an interference with the right of a parent to the services of his or her unemancipated child. The parents can recover for an interference with such services that is wrongfully caused.

loss of services
Interference with the right of a parent to the services of his or her unemancipated child, such as doing household chores.

A parent is also entitled to the *earnings* of unemancipated children, such as from part-time jobs. If the defendant's negligence interferes with the earning capacity of the unemancipated child, the parent can recover for this loss of earnings.

HEART-BALM ACTIONS

At common law, there were a number of tort causes of actions were designed to salve a broken heart:

- Alienation of affections.
- Criminal conversation.
- The enticement of a spouse.
- Tortious interference with custody.
- Seduction.

heart-balm actions
An action based on the loss of love and relationships—on a broken heart (e.g., breach of promise to marry, alienation of affections, and seduction).

heart-balm statute
A statute that abolishes heart-balm actions.

Such actions were called **heart-balm actions** because they were based on the loss of love and relationship.

Heart-balm actions also included *breach of promise to marry*. Today, however, many states have abolished most of these causes of action because of changing mores, difficulties of proof, and the danger of fabricating claims. A statute that abolishes a heart-balm action is called a **heart-balm statute**. Not all states, however, have such statutes, and some of the causes of action (particularly alienation of affections) are still available. A state that keeps the cause of action might restrict it such as by limiting (or not allowing) damages that can be collected by a successful plaintiff.

ALIENATION OF AFFECTIONS

alienation of affections
The tort of causing a diminishment of the marital relationship or an interference with consortium rights between the plaintiff and his or her spouse.

Alienation of affections consists of causing a diminishment of the marital relationship or an interference with consortium rights between the plaintiff and his or her spouse.

Elements

1. Intent to diminish the marital relationship of a married couple.
2. Affirmative conduct to carry out this intent.
3. Alienation between the spouses.
4. Causation of the alienation.

In North Carolina, for example, a local litigation attorney estimates that more than two hundred cases a year are filed for alienation of affections. The typical alienation case involves an ex-wife who sues "the other woman" for enticing her husband into having an affair, thereby destroying (alienating) his affections for the wife. In a recent case, the jury returned a verdict of $8.8 million against the husband's mistress.[5]

CRIMINAL CONVERSATION

criminal conversation
The tort that occurs when the defendant has sexual relations with the plaintiff's spouse.

Criminal conversation exists when the defendant has sexual relations with the plaintiff's spouse.

Element

- The defendant has sexual relations with the plaintiff's spouse (the latter thereby commits adultery).

ENTICEMENT OF A SPOUSE

Enticement of a spouse exists when the defendant encourages the plaintiff's spouse to leave or to stay away from the plaintiff.

enticement of a spouse
A tort in which the defendant encourages the plaintiff's spouse to leave or to stay away from the plaintiff.

Elements

1. Intent to diminish the marital relationship of a married couple.
2. Affirmative conduct that encourages a spouse to leave or stay away from his or her spouse.
3. The spouse leaves home or stays away.
4. Causation of the departure or staying away.

TORTIOUS INTERFERENCE WITH CUSTODY

Tortious interference with custody consists of serious interference with a parent's custody over his or her child.

tortious interference with custody
A tort in which the defendant seriously interferes with a parent's custody over his or her child.

Elements

1. Intent to interfere with a parent's custody of his or her child.
2. Affirmative conduct to carry out this intent.
3. Interference.
4. Causation of the interference.

The tort is sometimes called *tortious interference with parental relationships* and *abduction or enticement of a child*.

Under the *Restatement of Torts*, "One who, with knowledge that the parent does not consent, abducts or otherwise compels or induces a minor child to leave a parent legally entitled to its custody or not to return to the parent after it has . . . left him, is subject to liability to the parent." One parent, however, cannot sue another for this tort if both parents are entitled to custody of the child: "When the parents are by law jointly entitled to the custody and earnings of the child, no action can be brought against one of the parents who abducts or induces the child to leave the other. When by law only one parent is entitled to the custody and earnings of the child, only that parent can maintain [the action]. One parent may be liable to the other parent for the abduction of his own child if by judicial decree the sole custody of the child has been awarded to the other parent."[6]

Of course, third parties can also be liable for this tort. In a recent Virginia case, an unwed father of an infant sued an adoption attorney for tortious interference with parental rights. The attorney counseled the mother of the child to lie on adoption papers about whether she knew the address of the baby's father. The father was thereby kept in the dark about the adoption proceedings and was forced to initiate extensive custody proceedings to stop the adoption. The father then sued the attorney for tortious interference with parental rights. In allowing the suit, the court listed the following elements of the tort:

> (1) the complaining parent has a right to establish or maintain a parental or custodial relationship with his/her minor child; (2) a party outside of the relationship between the complaining parent and his/her child intentionally interfered with the complaining parent's parental or custodial relationship with his/her child by removing or detaining the child from returning to the complaining parent, without that parent's consent, or by otherwise preventing the complaining parent from exercising his/her parental or custodial rights; (3) the outside party's intentional interference caused harm to the complaining parent's parental or custodial relationship with his/her child; and (4) damages resulted from such interference.[7]

SEDUCTION

Seduction occurs when the defendant engages in sexual relations with the plaintiff's minor daughter by force or with the consent of the daughter.

Element

- Defendant has sex with the plaintiff's minor daughter by force or with the consent of the daughter.

VICARIOUS AND INDEPENDENT LIABILITY

With limited exceptions, one family member is not liable for the torts committed by another family member. Thus, a spouse is not liable for the torts committed by the other spouse. Parents are not liable for the torts committed by their children, and vice versa. The general rule (to which there are exceptions) is that *vicarious liability* does not exist among family members.

VICARIOUS LIABILITY

Vicarious liability is liability that is imposed on a person because of the conduct of another, based solely on the status of the relationship between the two. The person vicariously liable is not the person whose conduct led to the liability. For example, if a trucker negligently hits a pedestrian while making a delivery within the scope of employment, the trucker's *employer* is liable. The liability is vicarious because it is based on the status of the trucker as an employee. The employer is liable because of what someone else—the employee—has done.

The person injured could *also* sue the trucker-employee, who is directly responsible for the injury and, therefore, has independent liability. We are all personally liable for our own torts even if someone else is vicariously liable. Often, however, the one directly responsible has minimal resources out of which to satisfy a judgment. The person who is vicariously liable is usually the deep pocket, who has substantial resources. Being able to sue both the employee and the employer does not mean that the plaintiff can receive double recovery. The plaintiff can sue either or both but cannot obtain more than one recovery.

In general, one family member is not vicariously liable for the torts committed by another family member against someone outside the family.

> Mary is the ten-year-old daughter of Diane. Mary throws a brick through the window of Jim's hardware store.

Jim must sue *Mary* for the damage done to the store. Her parents are *not* vicariously liable for the tort of their daughter.

There are, however, two limited exceptions to the general rule of no vicarious liability among family members: parental-liability laws and the family-purpose doctrine.

Parental-Liability Laws

Many states have passed parental-liability laws (also called *parental responsibility laws*) that make parents vicariously liable for the torts of their children, but only up to a relatively modest amount (e.g., $1,000). If Diane lives in a state with such a law, Jim could sue Diane for the damage Mary did to his window, but he could not recover more than the maximum amount allowed by the parental-liability law.

Family-Purpose Doctrine

The second exception is the family-purpose doctrine. It makes a nondriver vicariously liable for an accident caused by a driver.

> *Jessica owns a car. She allows her teenage son Bob to drive the car. One day, Bob is driving to the supermarket alone and carelessly collides with Gary, the plaintiff.*

Under the family-purpose doctrine, Jessica is vicariously liable to Gary for the damage caused by her son, Bob. Not all states have adopted the family-purpose doctrine, however, and those that have do not all agree on its elements. In general, the elements are as follows:

- The defendant must be an owner of the car or be in control of the use of the car.
- The defendant must make the car available for family use rather than for the defendant's business. (In some states, the defendant must make it available for general family use rather than just for a particular occasion.)
- The driver must be a member of the defendant's immediate household.
- The driver must be using the car for a family purpose at the time of the accident.
- The driver must have had the defendant's express or implied consent to be using the car at the time of the accident.

The defendant does not have to be the traditional head of the household and does not have to be in the car at the time of the accident. Again, individual states, by case law or by statute, may use different elements of the doctrine or may reject it entirely.

Family-purpose doctrine
An owner of a car (or a person controlling the use of a car) is vicariously liable for the negligence committed by a family member using the car for a family purpose. Also called *family automobile rule.*

INDEPENDENT LIABILITY OF A PARENT

Sometimes, parents are independently liable for the torts of their children because of what the parents themselves have done or failed to do. Two major examples of such liability are negligent supervision and negligent entrustment:

- **Negligent supervision** is the careless monitoring or supervising of an incompetent person who thereby poses an unreasonable risk of harm to others.
- **Negligent entrustment** is carelessly allowing a vehicle, tool, weapon, or other dangerous object to be used by someone whose use poses an unreasonable risk of causing harm to others.

Assume that a father is aware that his young son plays with matches in the alley by their home. Hence, this conduct is a known **dangerous propensity**. If the father fails to use reasonable care to control this known habit of his son, the father could be liable for the fire damage the son causes to a neighbor's house in the alley. When parents act unreasonably in failing to use available opportunities to control their children, the parents are *independently* liable for negligence in a suit brought by the person injured by the child. The liability is called *negligent supervision*. Defendants, however, might have a difficult problem of proof when alleging negligent supervision. Parents often assert that they were unaware of the child's bad habit or that they did everything reasonably possible to control it. If either of these positions is accurate, there is no negligent supervision.

Another example of independent (not vicarious) parental liability is *negligent entrustment*. An example would be allowing a ten-year-old child to drive a tractor or a truck on a public highway, resulting in a collision with another vehicle.

negligent supervision
Carelessly monitoring or supervising an incompetent person who poses an unreasonable risk of harm to others.

negligent entrustment
Carelessly allowing the use of a vehicle, tool, or other object by someone who poses an unreasonable risk of harm to others.

dangerous propensity
A tendency to cause damage or harm.

INTRAFAMILY CRIMES

domestic violence
Actual or threatened injury or abuse of one member of a family or household by another member.

In addition to the tort actions we have been discussing, family members can be prosecuted for crimes committed against each other. Examples include incest and bigamy. The epidemic of **domestic violence** can lead to prosecutions for various crimes, including, in many states, marital rape.

Spouses can also be prosecuted for crimes against each other's separate property. For example, a husband is guilty of larceny if he uses his wife's password without her permission and withdraws money from her solely owned account containing only her separate property. Such criminal liability is different from the civil liability for intrafamily torts covered in Exhibit 17.1.

PARALEGAL ROLES

- For an overview of paralegal roles in family-law cases, see Exhibits 1.5 and 1.6 in Chapter 1. Many of the roles listed in these exhibits pertain to litigation, which are at the core of tort cases.
- For many of the financial issues related to the calculation and enforcement of damages for the torts covered in Chapter 17, a paralegal may be asked to help collect documents and facts outlined in:
  - The checklist in Exhibit 3.1 of Chapter 3.
  - The interrogatories in Appendix C.

SUMMARY

An intrafamily tort is a tort committed by one family member against another. An interspousal immunity bars certain torts between spouses; a parental immunity bars certain torts between parents and children. Courts traditionally have been reluctant to allow suits for intrafamily torts. In most states, spouses can sue each other for any tort that causes property interference. States differ on whether spousal immunity exists for torts that cause personal injury. Some states maintain some or all of the immunity for such torts. Children and parents can sue each other for torts that cause property interference. In general, there are more restrictions on parent-child suits for torts that cause personal injury, particularly if the parent was disciplining the child. There is no immunity for suits between other family members. If the interspousal immunity does not apply, one spouse can sue the other for carelessly transmitting sexually transmitted diseases. States differ on whether an action for a marital tort can be brought in a divorce action or must be brought in a separate action.

A prenatal tort is a tort against a fetus. The tort can be brought if the child is born alive. If the fetus dies from an injury, many states will allow a wrongful death action if the unborn child was viable. Wrongful life is an action by or on behalf of an unwanted, impaired child for negligence that precluded an informed parental decision to avoid the child's conception or birth. Wrongful birth is an action by parents of an unwanted, impaired child for negligence in failing to warn them of the risks that the child would be born with birth defects. Wrongful pregnancy is an action by

parents of an unwanted healthy child for a wrong related to pregnancy, such as the negligent performance of a sterilization procedure. Wrongful adoption is an action seeking damages for carelessly stating (or failing to disclose) to prospective adoptive parents available facts on the health or other condition of the adoptee (the child) that would be relevant to the decision of whether or not to adopt.

Loss of spousal consortium covers injury to the companionship, love, affection, sexual relationship, and services that one spouse provides another. States differ on whether parents and children can sue for tortious interference with parental or filial consortium. Parents can sue for loss of services of their unemancipated children and for interference with their right to receive the earnings of such children. Other family torts include the heart-balm actions, such as alienation of affections. Most states, however, have passed heart-balm statutes that abolish these actions.

Vicarious liability does not exist among family members, with two exceptions. First, some states have parental-liability laws that impose limited vicarious liability on parents for the torts committed by their children. (This is different from negligent supervision and negligent entrustment, both of which can make a parent independently liable for the torts of their children.) Second, under the family-purpose doctrine, the owner of a car can be vicariously liable for a tort committed by a family member driving the car for a family purpose. An intrafamily crime is a crime that one family member commits against another for which the former can be prosecuted.

KEY TERMS

tort	viable	heart-balm statute
intrafamily tort	embryos	alienation of affections
marital tort	wrongful life	criminal conversation
immunity	wrongful birth	enticement of a spouse
intrafamily tort immunity	wrongful pregnancy	tortious interference with custody
liability insurance	material	seduction
at common law	wrongful adoption	vicarious liability
married women's property acts	consortium	independent liability
real property	spousal consortium	deep pocket
personal property	loss of consortium	parental-liability law
emancipated	domestic partnerships	family-purpose doctrine
unemancipated	parental consortium	negligent supervision
no-fault divorce	filial consortium	negligent entrustment
fetus	loss of services	dangerous propensity
prenatal tort	heart-balm action	domestic violence

CHECK THE CITE

The following quote is from the opening paragraph of an opinion of the Supreme Court of California:

This case presents the question of whether a child born with an hereditary affliction may maintain a tort action against a medical care provider who—before the child's conception—negligently failed to advise the child's parents of the possibility of the hereditary condition, depriving them of the opportunity to choose not to conceive the child.

How did the court answer this question, and how does its answer differ from the answer given by the Supreme Court of New Jersey in the *Berman* case, which you read in this chapter? To find out, read *Turpin v. Sortini*, 31 Cal. 3d 220, 643 P.2d 954, 182 Cal. Rptr. 337 (Cal. 1982). To read the opinion online:

- In Google Scholar (scholar.google.com), select *Case law,* and enter "643 P.2d 954."
- In the general search engines of Google and Bing, enter "643 P.2d 954."

PROJECT

In Google, Bing, or Yahoo, run the following search: *aa* "loss of consortium" (substitute the name of your state for *aa* in the search, e.g., Georgia "loss of consortium"). Write a short essay in which you describe the circumstances under which someone can claim spousal consortium damages in your state. You can consult as many websites as you wish, but you must quote from at least three separate sites, two of which must allow you to quote the language of specific laws in the state.

ETHICS IN A FAMILY LAW PRACTICE

You are a paralegal working in the law office of Emerson & Emerson, which represents Barbara Kirkland in a wrongful pregnancy case. Barbara is very pleased with your performance in the case. On your birthday, she gives you her time-share apartment by the lake. She asks one of the attorneys at Emerson & Emerson to draft the needed documents to finalize this gift to you. What ethical problems, if any, might exist?

REVIEW QUESTIONS

1. What is a tort?
2. Name four categories of torts based on the category of injury or harm caused.
3. What is an intrafamily tort and a marital tort?
4. What is an immunity?
5. What are the two major intrafamily tort immunities?
6. Historically, why has the law been reluctant to allow suits for intrafamily torts?
7. What are the two main categories of harm that can be the subject of an intrafamily tort, and what are the two main categories of torts that can cause this harm?

8. What is the distinction between an emancipated and an unemancipated child?

9. Do states allow one spouse to bring a tort action against another for torts that cause property interference?

10. Do states allow one spouse to bring a tort action against another for torts that cause personal injury?

11. Do states allow a child to bring a tort action against a parent for torts that cause property interference?

12. Do states allow a child to bring a tort action against a parent for torts that cause personal injury?

13. What sexual torts can spouses bring against each other?

14. Why are some states against allowing marital torts to be brought in a divorce action?

15. What is a prenatal tort, and when can it be brought?

16. What is an action for wrongful life, and when can it be brought?

17. What is an action for wrongful birth, and when can it be brought?

18. What is an action for wrongful pregnancy, and when can it be brought?

19. What is an action for wrongful adoption and when can it be brought?

20. What is an action for loss of consortium (spousal consortium), and when can it be brought?

21. What is parental consortium and filial consortium and when can an action for their interference be brought?

22. What is loss of services, and when can a suit be brought for the loss?

23. What are the main heart-balm actions?

24. What is a heart-balm statute?

25. What is the distinction between vicarious liability and independent liability?

26. When are parents vicariously liable for the torts of their children?

27. When are parents independently liable for the torts of their children?

28. What intrafamily crimes can be prosecuted?

HELPFUL WEBSITES

Your State

See Appendix D for links to the family law of your state on the topics covered in this chapter.

- www.ncdsv.org/images/MaritalTortActionsFamily Law.pdf
- www.smartdivorce.com/articles/torts.shtml
- www.gourvitz.com/practice-areas/domestic-torts
- en.wikipedia.org/wiki/Loss_of_consortium
- scholar.valpo.edu/cgi/viewcontent.cgi?article=1645& context=vulr
- en.wikipedia.org/wiki/Wrongful_life
- en.wikipedia.org/wiki/Wrongful_birth

Google Scholar (scholar.google.com)

- Choose "Articles" and enter in the search box any of the key terms discussed in the chapter. Add the name of your state to the search term.
- Choose "Case law" and "Select courts". Select your state, click "Done," and enter in the search box any of the key terms discussed in the chapter. Add the name of your state to the search term.

Google, Bing, Yahoo

(on these search engines, run the following searches, substituting your state for "aa")

- family tort aa
- divorce tort aa
- tort immunity family aa
- domestic violence tort aa
- wrongful life aa
- wrongful birth aa
- wrongful adoption aa
- heart balm tort aa
- spousal consortium tort aa
- vicarious liability tort aa
- marital tort aa
- "no fault divorce" tort aa
- emancipation family tort aa
- intrafamily tort aa
- tortious interference parent aa
- wrongful pregnancy aa
- prenatal tort aa
- loss of consortium aa
- filial consortium aa
- loss of consortium aa

YouTube

Run the same searches on YouTube listed above for Google, Bing, Yahoo searches. Even when the video clips are trying to entice you to retain an attorney, buy a book, or enroll in a course, they can provide useful overviews and references to primary authority.

Twitter, Reddit, and Facebook

On Twitter, Reddit, and Facebook, run the following searches (substitute your state for *aa* in your searches; run the searches with and without the name of your state). Look for links to family-law developments in your state.

- marital tort aa
- loss of consortium aa

ENDNOTES

Note: All or most of the court opinions in these endnotes can be read online. To do so, go to Google Scholar (scholar.google.com), select "Case law," and in the search box, enter the cite (e.g., "66 P.3d 948") or name of the case (e.g., "Lozoya v. Sanchez") that is given in the endnote.

[1] *Restatement (Second) of Torts* § 554 (1977).

[2] Marlise Simmons, *French Uproar Over Right to Death for Unborn*, N.Y. Times, Oct. 19, 2001, at A3.

[3] *French Rejects Right Not to be Born*, BBC News (Jan. 10, 2002).

[4] *Lozoya v. Sanchez*, 66 P.3d 948, 954, 955 (N.M. 2003).

[5] Alics Gomstyn, *Wife's $9M Message to Mistresses: "Lay Off,"* ABC Good Morning America (Mar. 23, 2010). See also Virginia Bridges, *He Slept with a Married Woman. Now a Judge Says Pay the Jilted Husband $8.8 Million*, The Herald Sun (July 26, 2018) (www.heraldsun.com/news/local/crime/article215577310.html).

[6] *Restatement (Second) of Torts*, § 700, Comment c (1977).

[7] *Wyatt v. McDermott*, 725 S.E.2d 555, 562 (Va 2012).

APPENDIX A

General Instructions for the Assignments and Projects in the Book

INTRODUCTION

Throughout the chapters of this book, there are 13 major kinds of skill assignments and projects:

- State-Code Assignment
- Legal-Analysis Assignment
- Complaint-Drafting Assignment
- Agreement-Drafting Assignment
- Court-Opinion Assignment
- Checklist-Formulation Assignment
- Investigation-Strategy Assignment
- Interview Assignment
- Interrogatory Assignment
- Flowchart Assignment
- Systems Assignment
- Projects
- Writing Samples

On the pages where these assignments and projects are found, you will be given *specific instructions*. In addition, a set of *general instructions* is available for each of the 13 categories of assignments and projects. These general instructions are provided here in Appendix A. Throughout the chapters of the book, you are referred to Appendix A for *general instructions* for most of the assignments.

Caution: Some of the general instructions apply primarily to paralegals working in a law office so that they can be useful when you become employed. Most of the instructions, however, apply to assignments in the chapters of this book.

THE CARTWHEEL

Several of the assignments, particularly the state-code and court-opinion assignments, ask you to check basic law books, such as the statutory code (containing the full text of the statutes of the legislature) and to use search engines to locate family-law materials on the Internet. The CARTWHEEL will help you find items in these sources. The CARTWHEEL is a search technique. Its objective can be simply stated: to help you develop the habit of phrasing every word involved in the client's problem *in multiple ways!* When you go to the index of a law book, you naturally begin looking up the words and phrases that you think should lead you to the relevant material in the book. The same is true when you type key words into search engines, such as Google and Bing. If you do not find anything on point, two conclusions are possible:

- There is nothing on point in the law book or on the Internet.
- You checked the wrong words in the index or in the search boxes.

Too often, we make the mistake of thinking that the first conclusion is accurate. Nine times out of ten, the second conclusion is more accurate. The solution is to be able to phrase a word in as many different ways and in as many different contexts as possible—hence, the CARTWHEEL. See Exhibit A.1.

CARTWHEEL
A search technique designed to help you think of a large variety of words and phrases to check in indexes, tables of contents, and online search boxes.

EXHIBIT A.1   The CARTWHEEL: Generating Search Terms for Indexes and Search Engines

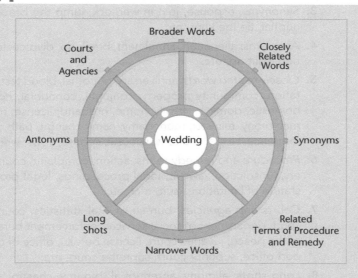

1. Identify all the *major words* from the facts of the client's problem or the assignment (e.g., wedding). One at a time, place each word or small set of related words in the center of the CARTWHEEL.
2. Look up all of these words in the index of law books or type them into a search engine.
3. Identify the *broader categories* of the major words.
4. Look up all of these broader words in the index of law books or type them into a search engine.
5. Identify the *narrower* categories of the major words.
6. Look up all of these narrower words in the index of law books or type them into a search engine.
7. Identify all *synonyms* of the major words.
8. Look up all of these synonyms in the index of law books or type them into a search engine.
9. Identify all of the *antonyms* (words that mean the opposite) of the major words.
10. Look up all of these antonyms in the index of law books or type them into a search engine.
11. Identify all words that are *closely related* to the major words.
12. Look up all of these closely related words in the index of law books or type them into a search engine.
13. Identify all terms of *procedure and remedy* related to the major words.
14. Look up all of these procedure and remedy terms in the index of law books or type them into a search engine.
15. Identify all *courts* and *agencies*, if any, that might have some connection to the major words.
16. Look up all of these courts and agencies in the index of law books or type them into a search engine.
17. Identify all *long shots*.
18. Look up all of these long shots in the index of law books or type them into a search engine.

Note: The above categories are not mutually exclusive.

Let's look at an example. A bride and a caterer have a dispute involving food that was ordered. Assume that one of the major words in the dispute is *wedding*. Place this word in the center of the CARTWHEEL. It will be the first word that will be CARTWHEEL-ed. Look up the word *wedding* in the index of every law book you are checking. Type the word in the search box of Google, Bing, or whatever search engine you are using. Also type the word in any search box on a relevant site you are checking—an example might be the search box in the main site of the legislature that would lead you to its statutes. If you are not successful with this word, it may be because (1) the word is not in the index, (2) the page or section references after the word in the index do not lead you to relevant material in the body of the book, or (3) the online material you are led to are equally unproductive.

The next step is to think of as many different phrasings and contexts of the word *wedding* as possible. This is where the 18 steps of the CARTWHEEL can be useful (see Exhibit A.1). If you applied the steps of the CARTWHEEL to the word *wedding*, here are some of the words and phrases that should come to mind:

1. *Broader words*: celebration, ceremony, custom, festivity, formality, matrimony, observance, rite, ritual, sacrament, service, etc.

2. *Narrower words*: church wedding, civil wedding, double wedding, formal wedding, golden wedding, group wedding, informal wedding, military wedding, proxy wedding, religious wedding, same-sex wedding, sham wedding, shotgun marriage, Vegas wedding, etc.

3. *Synonyms*: espouse, join in wedlock, jump the broom, marriage ceremony, nuptial, tie the knot, etc.

4. *Antonyms*: alienation, annulment, break-up, divorce, legal separation, separation, split-up, etc.

5. *Closely related words*: anniversary, betrothal, blood test, bride, children, cohabitation, community property, conjugal, connubial, consummation, contract, domestic, domicile, family, home, husband, license, marital, marital relations, matrimony, minister, monogamy, name change, path, premarital, relationship, residence, sexual relations, spousal, spouse, vows, wedlock, wife, etc.

6. *Procedure and remedy terms*: action, complaint, court case, defense, discovery, jurisdiction, lawsuit, legal proceedings, legal process, petition, process, statute of limitations, suit, trial, etc.

7. *Courts and agencies*: bureau of vital statistics, county clerk, county court, court, department of social services, enforcement bureau, family court, justice of the peace, juvenile court, license bureau, office of child support, child support office, superior court, supreme court, etc.

8. *Long shots*: alimony, antenuptial, bigamy, chastity, common law, consent, custody, dowry, fraud, gifts, illegitimate, impotence, incest, paternity, pregnancy, property division, religion, remarriage, separate maintenance, single, blood, support, virginity, etc.

If the CARTWHEEL can generate this many words and phrases from a starting point of just one word (wedding), potentially hundreds more can be generated when you subject all of the important words from the client's case or assignment to the CARTWHEEL.

Do you check them all in the index of every law book or type them all in search engines? No. You cannot spend your entire legal career working on one case or one assignment! Common sense will tell you when you are on the right track and when you are needlessly duplicating your efforts. You may get lucky and find what you are after in a few minutes. For important tasks in any line of work (or play), however, being comprehensive is usually time-consuming.

The categories in the CARTWHEEL will overlap; they are not mutually exclusive. Also, it is not significant whether you place a word in one category or another as long as the word comes to your mind. The CARTWHEEL is, in effect, a *word association game* that should become second nature to you with practice. Perhaps some of the word selections in the wedding example seem a bit far-fetched. You will not know for sure, however, whether a word will be fruitful until you try it. Be imaginative, and take some risks.

A legal thesaurus or a general thesaurus can often be helpful in generating word alternatives when using the CARTWHEEL technique. See, for example, West's *Legal Thesaurus/Dictionary* or *Roget's International Thesaurus*.

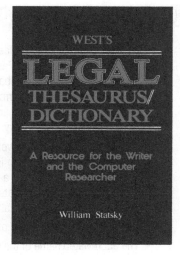

William Statsky, West's Legal Thesaurus (Delmar/Cengage Learning)

ASSIGNMENT   A.1

CHARTWHEEL the following words:

a. cruelty

b. support

c. paternity

STATE-CODE ASSIGNMENT

A great deal of family law consists of statutory law written by your state legislature. This law will be found within the state statutory code. (See Exhibit 1.7 on primary authority in Chapter 1.) It is important that you become acquainted with the family-law sections of your statutory code. (For links to such sections in the code of your state, see Appendix D.) Many of the assignments in this book ask you to examine this code on a particular family-law topic.

✔ GENERAL INSTRUCTIONS FOR THE STATE-CODE ASSIGNMENT

1. The first step is to make sure you know the name and location of the statutory code for your state. Some states have more than one code—usually from different publishers.

2. Be sure you are using the latest edition of the state code.

3. See Appendix D for leads to the online site to your state code that can be used without cost. The following sites will lead you to the online state codes of every state:

   • www.law.cornell.edu/statutes.html

   • statelaws.findlaw.com

   • law.justia.com

   In addition:

   • Go to the home page of your state government (www. aa.gov) (insert your state's abbreviation or its full name in place of *aa*). On this page, look for links to the legislature of your state. You will be told what statutes are available.

   • In Google, Bing, or Yahoo, do a legislature search (aa legislature) (insert your state's abbreviation or full name in place of *aa*). This search should lead you to your state legislature.

   Online statutory codes have search boxes. The CARTWHEEL will help you identify search terms to type in these boxes.

4. For statutory codes on the shelves of a law library, use the CARTWHEEL to help you use the various indexes in the code.

There is often a general index at the end of the code volumes, as well as smaller indexes after each volume or set of volumes covering the same topic area.

5. Statutes can change. There may be new sections added, revised language, or repeals. When you use the online version of the code (particularly at the site of the state legislature), these changes are usually already incorporated into the site. If you are using the *hard* copy of the code on the shelves of the library, you need to look for changes by:

   • Checking the pocket part, if any, of every volume you use.

   • Checking replacement volumes, if any.

   • Checking supplement volumes or pamphlets, if any.

   • Shepardizing the statute. To Shepardize something means to use the volumes of *Shepard's Citations* to obtain specific information about a document. When you Shepardize a statute, you go to the set of *Shepard's Citations* covering your state code and examine all of the references provided on your statute (e.g., amendments, repeals, opinions interpreting the statute). Find the citation of your statute in black bold print within each Shepard's pamphlet and bound volume. The references, if any, will be found in columns immediately beneath the citation of your statute.

(Continued)

☑ GENERAL INSTRUCTIONS FOR THE STATE-CODE ASSIGNMENT (*continued*)

6. You can also find statutes on fee-based online services, such as Westlaw, LexisNexis, and Fastcase. If you have access to these services, go to the database that contains the statutes of your state legislature and formulate a *query*, which is simply a question. The CARTWHEEL can help you decide what words or phrases to use in your query.

7. Give a complete citation for every statute that you think covers the assignment. (A citation is a reference to any material printed on paper or stored in a computer database. It is the "address" where you can locate and read the material.) The citation format for statues usually includes:

   - The title or chapter number of the statute.
   - The abbreviated name of the code.
   - The section number of the statute.
   - The date of the code edition you are using.

8. When you quote from a statute, use quotation marks around the language quoted.

9. If the assignment asks you to apply the statute to the facts of a problem in the assignment, follow the General Instructions for the Legal-Analysis Assignment below on applying elements.

10. When you need help in understanding a statute, use the following approaches:

   - See if there are definition statutes that define some of the words in the statute you are examining. (If such definition statutes exist, they will usually precede the statute you are examining at the beginning of the cluster of statutes on that topic.)

   - Examine opinions that have interpreted the statute. You can obtain leads to these opinions, if any exist, by checking the Notes of Decisions, which are summaries of opinions. They are found immediately after the text of the statute in annotated editions of the code. (Annotated means organized by subject matter with research references such as Notes of Decisions or other commentary.) You can also find opinions interpreting the statute by Shepardizing the statute.

   - If you cannot find what you are looking for in the statutory code, proceed as follows:

     ○ Repeat Step 4. Frequently, the difficulty lies in the failure to use indexes and search engines creatively. Do the CARTWHEEL again to try to come up with more words and phrases to check in the indexes and to type in the search boxes.

     ○ Check the court rules of your state courts to determine whether they treat the topic you are pursuing.

     ○ Check the constitution of your state to determine whether it treats the topic you are pursuing.

     ○ Find out if any court opinions have been written by your state courts on the topic you are pursuing. For techniques to find court opinions, see the General Instructions for the Court-Opinion Assignment below. See also the instruction on Notes of Decisions above.

ASSIGNMENT   A.2

a. What is the name of the statutory code of your state? (If more than one exists, list each one.)

b. Who publishes it?

c. How is it updated? By pocket parts? By supplemental pamphlets? Both?

d. Give the address of websites that give the full text of the statutes in your state.

e. In this question, you will locate the same statute (i) in the hard copy of the code volumes on the shelves in a law library and (ii) on the Internet. Go to your code in a law library and pick any statute on adoption. Quote the first line of the statute you select. Give the citation of the quote in the code. Now go on the Internet and find the same statute. Quote the first line. Give the citation of the quote on the Internet. If you cannot find the same code statute on the Internet, pick a different code statute.

---

legal analysis
The application of one or more rules to the facts of a client's case in order to answer a legal question that will help (a) avoid a legal dispute, (b) resolve a legal dispute that has arisen, or (c) prevent a legal dispute from becoming worse.

LEGAL-ANALYSIS ASSIGNMENT

Before we examine the general instructions for the legal-analysis assignment, here is a brief introductory refresher on legal reasoning, or legal analysis. The process of legal analysis can be diagrammed as follows:

$$\boxed{\text{Facts}} + \boxed{\text{Rule}} = \boxed{\begin{array}{c}\text{Application}\\ \text{of Rule to Facts}\\ \text{Leading to a Conclusion}\end{array}}$$

Let's look at a simple example.

Facts: George and Helen are married. One day, after a big argument, George walks out of the house and says, "Good-bye. Find someone else to take care of you." As he walks out, he resolves to stay away forever.

Rule (section 100): One spouse abandons another by leaving the family home without any intention of returning.

Application of rule to facts: When George walked out of the house resolving to stay away forever, he left the family home "without any intention of returning." This is abandonment under section 100.

Most legal analysis, however, is not this simple. This can be due to a number of factors, including the following:

- A word or phrase in the rule is ambiguous.
- You need more facts than you are given.

AMBIGUITY IN THE RULE

Facts: George and Helen are married. One day, after a big argument, George walks out of the apartment and says, "Good-bye. Find someone else to take care of you." As he walks out, he resolves to stay away forever. He moves downstairs to a vacant, never-used room in the same building that he and his wife jointly own. The room has its own exit to the street.

Rule (section 100): One spouse abandons another by leaving the family home without any intention of returning.

In this example, there is ambiguity in the rule. What does "leaving" mean? At least two interpretations are possible:

- Moving out of the entire family home.
- Moving out of whatever parts of the family home in which both spouses normally live together.

Which is the correct definition of "leaving"? The difference in the definitions is critical. Depending on which definition is adopted, a different result is reached:

- According to the first definition, George did not abandon Helen under section 100 because he did not move out of the entire family home.
- According to the second definition, George did abandon Helen under section 100, since he moved out of the rooms in the family home where they both normally lived. Under this definition, he can commit abandonment without moving out of the entire family home.

Your task in legal analysis is to be sensitive to such ambiguity in the rules that you are trying to apply to facts. Do not accept language at face value. Look at every word in the rule you are applying and ask yourself: What is the definition of this word? Is more than one definition possible?

When you are using legal analysis in an interoffice memorandum or in a school examination, one of the biggest mistakes you can make is to hit the reader over the head with one conclusion. Do not overlook ambiguity. When it exists, find it and write about it. Good legal analysis articulates both sides of the controversy.

If you personally favor one side over the other, you may state your opinion, but only after you have placed yourself in the shoes of both sides and presented the best argument for each.

Once you have identified ambiguity in the rule, how do you *resolve* the ambiguity? You do legal research. For example, you find out whether any courts have interpreted the ambiguous words/phrases. Are there court opinions that have defined the word *leaving* in section 100? If so, you need to find the opinions containing the definition. (For purposes of the legal-analysis assignments in this book, however, you will not do further legal research of this kind unless the instructions in the assignment, or your instructor, tell you otherwise.)

THE NEED FOR MORE FACTS

In the process of trying to connect rules to facts, you may sometimes feel that you need more facts to assess whether the rule applies. If so, state what additional facts you would like to have and *state why they may be helpful to your analysis.*

In the example involving George and Helen, suppose we are told that George said to Helen, "Good-bye. Find someone else to take care of you," but we are not told whether he walked out. In your analysis, you would have to indicate that the facts do not state what George did immediately after he made this statement to Helen. You need additional facts. You need to know whether he left the building or any part of the building after he made the statement. The rule refers to "leaving," and you do not know whether he left the home and if he did, where he went.

Also, if the facts do not clearly show that George left with the intent of never returning, you would need additional facts to help resolve the intent issue. For example:

- Did he take all of his clothes with him?
- Did he speak to anyone else (after he left) about what he was doing?
- How far away did he go when he left?
- Did he change his address officially (e.g., at the post office)?
- Did he open any new bank accounts or change old ones?
- Did he call Helen or otherwise contact her after he left? If so, how long after he left, how often, and about what?

State why you need these additional facts. For example, if George took all of his clothes with him when he left, this fact would be evidence that his departure was permanent (i.e., he had no intention of returning when he left). This should be stated as such in your legal analysis.

ANALYSIS OF ELEMENTS

One of the most important skills of legal analysis is the ability to break down any rule into its **elements**:

element
A portion of a rule that is a precondition to the applicability of the entire rule.

Element

1. A *portion* of a rule that can be conveniently discussed separately from the other elements, and is
2. A *precondition* to the applicability of the entire rule. If one of the elements of the rule does not apply, the entire rule does not apply).

To a very large extent, legal analysis proceeds by element analysis, as we shall see. In addition, we use element analysis as an aid in performing other tasks. For example:

- When drafting a petition or complaint, the drafter often tries to allege enough facts to establish each element of the **cause of action**.

cause of action
(1) A legally acceptable reason for bringing a suit. A rule that constitutes a legal theory for bringing a suit. (2) The facts that give a person a right to judicial relief. When you *state a cause of action*, you list the facts that give you a right to judicial relief against the alleged wrongdoer.

- When trial judges give instructions (the charge) to a jury, they must cover all of the elements of the cause of action and all of the elements of the defenses. When attorneys submit proposed instructions to the judge, the elements must likewise be covered.

- When attorneys conduct a **deposition**, they will frequently organize the questions around the elements of the causes of action and defenses in the case.

- The organization of a memorandum of law will often follow the list of elements of the rules being discussed.

> **deposition**
> A method of discovery by which one party questions another party (or questions the other party's witness), usually outside the courtroom. The person questioned is called the *deponent*.

A major characteristic of *sloppy* legal analysis is that it does not clearly take the reader through the elements of a rule. Good analysis discusses every element, with an emphasis on the element(s) in contention. No element is passed over.

Suppose you are analyzing the following rule found in a statute:

§ 25–403 A pharmacist must not sell prescription drugs to a minor.

Note that the rule is not broken down into elements. As with most rules, you must identify the elements on your own:

Elements of § 25–403

1. Pharmacist
2. Sells
3. Prescription drugs
4. To a minor

No violation exists unless all four elements of this statute are established. If a pharmacist sells simple aspirin (a nonprescription drug), he or she is not liable under the statute. The third element cannot be established; hence, there is no violation, because one of the elements (preconditions) cannot be met.

The consequence of all the elements applying is that there must be no sale, meaning that § 25–403 is violated if a sale is made.

For a number of reasons, rules such as statutes and regulations can be difficult to break down into elements. For example, the rule may be long or may contain:

- Lists
- Alternatives
- Exceptions or provisos

Nevertheless, the same process is used. You must take the time to dissect the rule into its component elements. Examine the following rule and its elements:

> **§ 5** While representing a client in connection with contemplated or pending litigation, a lawyer shall not advance or guarantee financial assistance to his client, except that a lawyer may advance or guarantee court costs, expenses of investigation, expenses of medical examination, and costs of obtaining and presenting evidence, provided the client remains ultimately liable for such costs or expenses.

Section 5 can be broken down into three elements:

Elements of § 5

1. A lawyer.
2. Representing a client in connection with contemplated litigation or in connection with pending litigation.
3. Advances financial assistance to his client or guarantees financial assistance to his client, except that the following is proper:

   a. lawyer advances or guarantees court costs, provided the client remains ultimately liable for these costs, or

    b. lawyer advances or guarantees expenses of investigation, provided the client remains ultimately liable for these expenses, or

    c. lawyer advances or guarantees expenses of medical examination, provided the client remains ultimately liable for these expenses, or

    d. lawyer advances or guarantees costs of obtaining and presenting evidence, provided the client remains ultimately liable for these costs.

The consequence of all the elements applying is that there must be no advancing or guaranteeing—§ 5 is violated if such advancing or guaranteeing occurs.

When an element is stated in the alternative, list all the alternatives within the same element. Alternatives related to one element should be kept within the phrasing of that element. The same is true of exception or proviso clauses. State them within the relevant element when they are intimately related to the applicability of that element.

In our § 5 example, the most complicated element is the third (3) one. It contains lists, alternatives, an exception, and a proviso. But they all relate to the same point—the advancing financial assistance. None of the subdivisions of the third element should be stated as a separate element.

Sometimes, you must do some unraveling of a rule in order to identify its elements. This certainly had to be done with the third element of § 5. Do not be afraid to pick the rule apart in order to cluster its thoughts around unified themes that should stand alone as elements. Place subjects and verbs together where this helps clarify meaning. Repeat subjects and verbs for the same reason so long as you are not adding anything to the rule. Diagram the rule for yourself as you examine it.

If more than one rule is involved in a statute, regulation, constitutional provision, charter, ordinance, etc., treat one rule at a time. (If there is more than one sentence in a rule, each sentence will often be its own rule and hence will need its own element breakdown.) Every rule should have its own elements, and, when appropriate, each element should be subdivided into its separate components, as in the third element of § 5.

ASSIGNMENT   A.3

Break the following rules into their elements:

a. **§ 800.** The parties can by mutual agreement elect to terminate their separation agreement.

b. **§ 52.** A court of this State shall not exercise its jurisdiction under this Act if at the time of filing the petition a proceeding concerning the custody of the child was pending in a court of another state exercising jurisdiction substantially in conformity with this Act, unless the proceeding is stayed by the court of the other state because this State is a more appropriate forum or for other reasons.

c. **§ 10.2.** With respect to a child who has no presumed father under Section 4, an action may be brought by the child, the mother or personal representative of the child, the appropriate state agency, the personal representative or a parent of the mother if the mother has died, a man alleged or alleging himself to be the father, or the personal representative or a parent of the alleged father if the alleged father has died or is a minor.

d. **§ 107(b).** When the mental or physical condition (including the blood group) of a party, or a person in the custody or under the legal control of a party, is in controversy, the court in which the action is pending may order the party to submit to a physical or mental examination by a physician or to produce for examination the person in his custody or legal control. The order may be made only on motion for good cause shown and upon notice to the person to be examined and to all parties and shall specify time, place, manner, conditions, and scope of the examination and the person or persons by whom it is to be made.

Once you have broken the rule into its elements, you have the structure of the analysis in front of you. Each element becomes a separate section of your analysis. You discuss one element at a time, concentrating on those that pose the greatest difficulties.

PHRASING ISSUES

To do legal analysis, you must identify the **legal issue**. To fail to identify the issue would be like trying to steer a ship without a rudder or to drive a car without the steering wheel: your legal analysis would drift aimlessly.

A legal issue has two components:

- A brief quote from the element of the rule in contention, and
- Several of the important facts relevant to that contention.

In formal legal analysis, both components should be present in your statement of the legal issue.

Every element of a rule is potentially the basis of a separate issue. A rule with five elements, for example, could lead to five separate issues, each structured around whether one of the elements applies. In practice, however, it is rare for every element to lead to a separate issue. This is because every element of a rule will probably not be an **element in contention**. To have such an element, the parties must disagree on whether the element applies. (In a course assignment, you may have to predict whether they will disagree.) If it is clear that both parties will agree on the applicability or nonapplicability of a particular element, it would be a waste of time to construct an issue around that element and to spend much time analyzing it.

At the time you write your memorandum, you may not know for certain what the other side will eventually say about the applicability of a rule. You must do your best to anticipate what your opponent *might* argue about the rule and any element within it.

There are three main kinds of disagreements that the parties can have about an element:

1. *Disagreement about definitions.* If you anticipate that the other side will disagree over the definition of an element, you should draft an issue around that element. We saw an example of this earlier when we asked whether "leaving" in the abandonment rule meant moving out of the entire family home or moving out of that part of the family home in which both spouses normally live together.

2. *Disagreement about whether the facts fit the element.* If you anticipate that the other side will disagree over whether the facts fit within an element, you should draft an issue around that element. In a child-custody case, for example, each parent may present numerous conflicting facts on whether it would be in the "best interests" of the child to be placed with one parent or the other. An issue clearly exists on the element of "best interests." Sometimes fact gaps will interfere with your ability to identify issues. (See the earlier discussion on the need for more facts.) If, for example, the marriage of a party can be annulled if that party was under age, but we are not told how old the person was, we have a fact gap. We will not know whether the annulment can be granted until we close this gap by finding out.

3. *A third possibility is that the parties may disagree over both the definition of an element and over whether the facts fit within that element.*

Let's return to the pharmacy example:

§ 25–403 A pharmacist must not sell prescription drugs to a minor.

legal issue
A question of law; a question of what the law is, or what the law means, or how the law applies to a set of facts. Also called *issue of law.* If the dispute is over the existence or nonexistence of the alleged facts, it is referred to as a *question of fact*, a *factual issue*, or an *issue of fact.*

element in contention
The portion or element of a rule about which the parties cannot agree. The disagreement may be over the definition of the element, whether the facts fit within the element, or both.

Suppose that Fred Jones owns a drugstore and is a licensed pharmacist. One day, he sells tetracycline to Phil, a seventeen-year-old male. Has Fred violated § 25–403? Step one in answering this question is to break § 25–403 into its elements:

Elements of § 25–403:

1. Pharmacist
2. Sells
3. Prescription drugs
4. To a minor

These elements become a checklist from which we begin to explore the presence of legal issues.

Elements 1 and 2 are not realistic candidates for legal issues. There is no reasonable doubt over whether Fred is a pharmacist and over whether he engaged in selling. The facts clearly tell us that he is a pharmacist who made a sale.

What about Element 3? Should it become the basis of a legal issue? Did Fred sell a "prescription drug"? Is tetracycline such a drug? The issue can be phrased as follows:

Is tetracycline a "prescription drug" within the meaning of § 25–403?

A fact gap exists on this issue. We were not told if tetracycline is sold over the counter in Fred's pharmacy. Our analysis should point out this gap.

Element 4 also poses some ambiguity that can become the basis of an issue. Who is a minor? Is a seventeen-year-old a minor? It is not clear. This ambiguity should prompt this issue:

Is a seventeen-year-old a "minor" within the meaning of § 25–403?

An alternate (more formal) phrasing of the issue would be as follows:

When a pharmacist sells tetracycline to a seventeen-year-old, has the pharmacist violated § 25–403, which prohibits sales of "prescription drugs" to "a minor"?

ASSIGNMENT   A.4

In each of the following situations, you are given a fact situation, plus a rule in the form of a statute. Phrase the legal issue involved in each situation.

a. *Facts:* Len's twenty-year-old son, Sam, has just graduated from Benton College, earning bachelor's degree. Len paid all of Sam's expenses at Benton. Sam has now been accepted by the Benton dental school. Len can afford to pay Sam's dental school expenses but refuses to do so. Sam says that his father is obligated to pay these expenses.

Statute: § 49(g). Child support shall include payment of college expenses if the child has the ability to attend and the parent has the ability to pay.

b. *Facts:* Jane and her two children by a former marriage receive public assistance. Jane's friend, Jack, who is a traveling salesman, stays at Jane's apartment during his monthly business trips. This allows him to stay in town five to ten days at a time. He does not give Jane any money while he is with her.

Statute: § 11351. Whenever unrelated adult males reside with a mother applying for or receiving public assistance, the male shall be required to make a financial contribution to the mother which shall not be less than it would cost him to provide himself with an independent living arrangement.

INTEROFFICE MEMORANDUM

One format in which you present your legal analysis to your supervisor is the interoffice memorandum. The component parts of the memo are as follows:

- *Heading*. Names of the author of the memo, whom it is addressed to, date it was written, and the identity of the case involved—its office file number, and if the case has been filed in court, its docket number.

- *RE*. This notation (meaning regarding or concerning) gives a brief statement of the subject matter of the memo, often in the form of a shorthand statement of the issue.

- *Statement of the Assignment*. It is a good idea at the outset to state what you have been asked to do in the memo.

- *Issue and Summary Conclusion*. State the legal issue(s) to be addressed in the memo. Also give a short answer to the issue(s), which will be elaborated on in the body of the memo.

- *Facts*. State the facts of the case.

- *Analysis*. In this section of the memo (also called Discussion), you identify the elements in contention and apply the facts to the elements, providing the perspective of both sides.

- *Conclusion*. Give your personal opinion of which side has the stronger position.

- *Next Steps*. State any recommendations about the case and next steps that should be considered.

Again, our focus here is an internal (interoffice) memorandum. No one outside the office will read it. Hence, it should present the strengths and weaknesses of the client's case. A very different kind of memo would be written when the audience is a court or an opposing attorney. Such a memo would emphasize the strengths of the client's case and would not suggest what further work needs to be done on the case.

Exhibit A.2 presents an example of an interoffice memorandum. It is written by George Wilson to his supervisor, Mary Adams.

interoffice memorandum
A written report addressed to someone in the office where you work, usually a supervisor. If the report explains how the law applies to a given set of facts, it is a *memorandum of law*.

EXHIBIT A.2 Interoffice Memorandum

INTEROFFICE MEMORANDUM

TO:	Mary Adams
FROM:	George Wilson
DATE:	March 26, 2019
NAME OF CASE:	Hagerty v. Hagerty
OFFICE FILE NO.:	19-49
COURT DOCKET NO.:	B-408-19

RE: "Serious marital discord" and the refusal to seek alcoholism treatment under § 402(b)

STATEMENT OF ASSIGNMENT

You have asked me to determine whether our client, Linda Hagerty, can prevent her husband from dissolving the marriage on the ground of "irretrievable breakdown" under § 402(b).

ISSUE AND SUMMARY CONCLUSION
ISSUE

Is there "serious marital discord" constituting an "irretrievable breakdown" of a marriage under § 402(b) when one party believes that the marriage can be saved if the other party seeks treatment for alcoholism, which the latter refuses to seek?

(continued)

Exhibit A.2 *(continued)*

SUMMARY CONCLUSION

Yes. Although our client has some reasonable arguments, her husband has the stronger position.

FACTS

Paul Hagerty has filed for dissolution of the marriage on the ground of "irretrievable breakdown of the marriage." Linda and Paul Hagerty have been married for four years. They have two children. Paul has a serious drinking problem according to our client. While intoxicated, he breaks furniture and is abusive to the children and his wife. Linda has repeatedly asked him to seek rehabilitation treatment through AA or a counseling service. Two months ago, she told him that he must leave unless he seeks treatment. He did leave but has refused treatment. She now insists that he return and undergo treatment. He has filed for a dissolution of the marriage on the ground of an "irretrievable breakdown of the marriage." He feels that their marriage is hopeless. Our client wants to defend the action and prevent the dissolution.

ANALYSIS

Section 402(b) provides as follows:

A court may make a finding that there has been an irretrievable breakdown of the marriage relationship if the finding is supported by evidence of serious marital discord adversely affecting the attitude of the parties toward the marriage.

Two elements of § 402(b) must be present before a court will declare the existence of an "irretrievable breakdown of the marriage":

(1) serious marital discord;

(2) adversely affecting the attitude of the parties toward the marriage.

Section 402(b) has been in existence for less than a year. No case law exists defining the terms of § 402(b), and no other statutes exist providing these definitions.

(1) SERIOUS MARITAL DISCORD

Two definitions of the phrase "serious marital discord" are possible. Mr. Hagerty will argue that such "discord" exists if either party to the marriage feels that there is no likelihood of reconciliation. Our client, on the other hand, should argue that both parties must agree that reconciliation is unlikely, or at least that evidence of marital collapse must exist in addition to the views of only one of the spouses. Under Mr. Hagerty's definition, there is "serious marital discord" because one party (himself in this case) feels that there is no likelihood of reconciliation. Our client feels that a reconciliation is likely if her husband will seek treatment for his alcoholism. Our client can argue that "marital discord" was meant to refer to the opinions of *two* people—the partners to the marriage. The agreement of both sides on the likelihood of reconciliation is critical to a determination of whether the marriage can survive. The lack of such a likelihood in the minds of *both* spouses amounts to an "irretrievable breakdown."

But our client is convinced that the marriage is retrievable. A court should not rule otherwise when one of the parties takes this position. In her view, Mr. Hagerty is sick and is in no position to judge whether a reconciliation is possible. His refusal to seek help for the treatable illness or sickness of alcoholism should disqualify him from making meaningful assessments as to whether the marriage can survive. The legislature could not have intended that a marriage would end simply at the whim of one of the parties, particularly when the party who wants out is too ill to make a considered judgment on the likelihood of reconciliation.

She can further argue that § 402(b) does not state that either party can obtain a dissolution of the marriage simply because one of the spouses says he or she wants it. The statute calls for "evidence" of "serious marital discord." There must be a showing of irretrievability. This must mean that a court is required to look at the underlying evidence of whether there is hope. A mere statement by one of the parties that the marriage is hopeless is not enough "evidence." More is required. The court should examine Mr. Hagerty's condition and listen to whatever expert witnesses she may be able to call. She will want an opportunity to prove through such witnesses that hope does exist because of treatment. This opportunity is destroyed if the court accepts Mr. Hagerty's statement at face value that the marriage cannot be saved. Section 402(b) calls for a more thorough probe by a court.

Mr. Hagerty, on the other hand, will argue that our client is using the wrong definition of "serious marital discord" for purposes of establishing an "irretrievable breakdown." If either side feels that there is no likelihood of reconciliation, a court should find evidence of "serious marital discord" for purposes of establishing an "irretrievable breakdown." Otherwise, one of the parties could force a dead marriage to continue out of stubbornness, unreasonableness, or malice. The legislature could not have intended such a result.

Mr. Hagerty will argue that our client told him to leave and to enter treatment. We can probably assume from the facts that Mr. Hagerty either does not want to enter treatment or that he thinks treatment will not be effective. In either event, Mrs. Hagerty has laid down a condition that Mr. Hagerty says cannot be met. He will argue that to force him into treatment would be as unproductive as to force him to continue his marriage.

(continued)

Exhibit A.2 *(continued)*

He will further try to argue that our client's actions demonstrate that even she feels that "serious marital discord" exists. She threw him out, and she insisted on an unacceptable condition. She may say that she thinks the marriage is salvageable, but her actions point to the opposite conclusion.

(2) ADVERSELY AFFECTING THE ATTITUDE OF THE PARTIES TOWARD THE MARRIAGE

It is unlikely that this element will be in contention. Both parties will probably agree that the difficulties have adversely affected their views of the marriage. The phrase "adversely affecting" is not defined in the statute or in any court opinions. An "attitude" that has been "adversely" affected means no more than negative feelings toward something—the marriage. Even Mrs. Hagerty cannot deny that she has negative feelings about the marriage as a result of the controversy surrounding alcoholism. She may not think the marriage is hopeless, but her feelings are certainly negative, as evidenced by the fact that she told him to leave the house.

It might be significant to note that the second element refers to "parties"—in the plural. The statute does not say "attitude of one of the parties." This point might bolster Mrs. Hagerty's argument on the first element that the legislature intended both parties to feel that reconciliation was not possible.

CONCLUSION

The only element in contention will be the first. I think that Mr. Hagerty has the stronger argument. If Mr. Hagerty feels that the treatment for his alcoholism will not help the marriage and if he refuses to undergo this treatment, it is difficult to avoid the conclusion that the parties to the marriage cannot be reconciled. The main argument favoring our client is that the legislature may not have intended a marriage to be terminated this easily.

NEXT STEPS

There are two things that I have not yet done on this case. Let me know if you want me to do either of them:

(1) I have not yet checked the legislative history of §402(b) to determine whether it will provide any guidance on the meaning of § 402(b).

(2) I have not yet checked the statutes of other states to see if they have the same language as our § 402(b). If such statutes exist, then I would check opinions interpreting these statutes as potential persuasive authority for our case.

ASSIGNMENT   A.5

Bill and Pat were married in State A on March 13, 1983, where they continue to live. They have one child, Brenda, age 15. Since 2000, Bill and Pat have been having marital difficulties. Bill is a traveling salesman who spends a good deal of time away from State A. From 2001 to 2004, he did not see his family at all. He returned on February 4, 2005. He and Pat attended marital-counseling sessions for about three months. By the summer of 2005, problems again arose. Bill left home. On the day he left, he said to Pat, "If you can straighten yourself out, I'll consider coming back." He packed all of his clothes and books but left behind the high school trophy he received for swimming. Although the departure was bitter, both sides agreed to maintain their joint checking account. Bill made deposits in the account. Pat wrote checks on the account to cover household expenses.

In September of 2005, Bill contacted a real estate broker in State B about renting an apartment for six months in that state. The broker suggested tax advantages of buying a condominium in State B as opposed to renting. Bill was persuaded. He had been in State B only once or twice for his job, but wanted to explore the possibility of more extensive business opportunities there. On October 1, 2005, the broker called to inform Bill of a good condominium prospect in State B. On October 5, 2005, Bill was killed in an automobile accident on a highway in State B while on the way to examine the condominium for the first time.

State B wants Bill's estate to pay a state inheritance tax on the theory that at the time of death, Bill was domiciled in State B. The representative of Bill's estate disagrees and claims

(continued)

that Bill was domiciled in State A at the time of death. In State B, the following statute exists, which is the basis of State B's claim:

> **§ 14.** Inheritance taxes are owed by persons who die domiciled in this state, which exists when the decedent had a physical presence in the state with the intent of making the state a permanent home.

Prepare an interoffice memorandum of law on the question of State B's right to inheritance taxes. Do not do any legal research on the problem. Do the memo solely on the basis of the information provided above.

The office file number is 05-421. There is no court docket number because no court action has yet been initiated. The Tax Department of State B has taken the position that inheritance taxes are due under § 14. The law office where you work has been retained by the representative of Bill's estate, which does not want to pay the inheritance tax to State B. Because the inheritance tax rate for State A is lower than for State B, it would be to the advantage of the estate to obtain a ruling that at the time of death, Bill was domiciled in State A.

For purposes of this assignment, you can assume the following definitions apply:

- *Physical presence:* actually being in a place

- *Intent of making the state a permanent home:* the desire to live in the state indefinitely; the place to which one intends to return when away (a person can have only one permanent home)

✔ GENERAL INSTRUCTIONS FOR THE LEGAL-ANALYSIS ASSIGNMENT

1. The starting point in the legal-analysis assignment is a set of facts in the assignment. It is to this set of facts that you must apply the rule or rules.

2. How do you find the rule or rules to apply to the facts?
   - By examining the text of the chapter immediately preceding the assignment, or
   - By examining the state code or court opinions of your state—if you are told to do so in the assignment.

3. Carefully examine each word/phrase in the rule being applied. Break the rule into its elements, and concentrate on those elements in contention.

4. Define each important word/phrase in each element in contention.

5. Determine whether more than one definition exists for each important word/phrase.

6. If more than one definition is possible, state each definition and show what effect the different definitions would have on the result of the analysis. How would each side use the definition that is favorable to itself?

7. State the legal issue(s).

8. Carefully examine each of the facts given to you in the assignment.

9. Note any differences between the fact situation given in the assignment and comparable fact situations discussed in the text of the chapter immediately preceding the assignment. Assess whether such fact differences are significant.

10. If you determine that you need more facts to provide the analysis, state what facts you need and why you would like to have the additional facts. Specifically, how will the additional facts assist in completing the analysis?

11. Analyze the facts from the perspective of both sides. Do not be dogmatic in your analysis. Whenever possible, show how the facts might be interpreted differently by both sides.

12. If requested by your instructor, give your answers in the format of an interoffice memorandum of law, as presented in Exhibit A.2.

13. Do not do any legal research on the assignment unless you are specifically instructed to do so. (See Instruction 2 above.)

COMPLAINT-DRAFTING ASSIGNMENT

Court litigation begins when one party files a petition or complaint against another party. This is the pleading that must state a cause of action such as negligence, breach of contract, or divorce on the ground of irretrievable breakdown. See Exhibit 7.7 in Chapter 7 for a sample divorce petition/complaint.

Before you begin drafting the complaint (or any document) from scratch, find out if someone has already prepared a standard form that you can use. These are available in a number of places. To locate forms on the Internet, run these searches on Google, Bing, or Yahoo:

- family law forms divorce aa
- family law forms agreement aa

In place of *aa*, type the name of your state. See also the links to forms for your state in Appendix D. In the law library, standard forms can be found in form-books, manuals, practice texts, some statutory codes, and some court rules. Many legal stationery stores print and sell them. Most are written by private attorneys. Occasionally, however, a standard form will be written by the legislature or by the court as the suggested or required format to be used.

Many law offices have a *forms file* (often on the computer) that contain forms used in prior cases that are usually adaptable for the case of a current client. The forms file may also contain commercial forms purchased by the office. As the forms file grows, it becomes a regular source of standard forms.

Considerable care must be exercised in the use of standard forms. They can be very deceptive in that they appear to require little more than a filling in of blanks. Intelligent use of the forms, however, usually requires much more. The guidelines in the following list should be kept in mind.

HOW TO AVOID ABUSING A STANDARD FORM

1. The cardinal rule is to *adapt* the form to the particulars of the client's case on which you are working.

2. Do not be afraid of changing the preprinted language of the form if you have a good reason for doing so. Whenever you make such a change, bring it to the attention of your supervisor for approval.

3. Never use a standard form unless and until you have satisfied yourself that you know the meaning of every word and phrase on it, especially **boilerplate**. The great temptation of most form users is to ignore what they do not understand because the form has been used so often in the past with no apparent difficulty. Do not give in to this temptation. Find out what everything means by:

   - Asking your supervisor.
   - Asking more experienced paralegals or other knowledgeable people.
   - Doing other legal research.
   - Using a legal dictionary.

boilerplate
Standard or often-used language that is commonly found in the same kind of document. Standard verbiage.

4. Once you have found a form that appears useful, look around for another form that covers the same topic. Analyze the different forms available. Which one is preferable? Why? Always be on the lookout for a better form.

5. Do not leave any blank spaces on the form. If a question does not apply to your case, write NA (not applicable) in the space for that question.

6. If the form was written for another state, be sure it can be adapted, and is adapted, to the law of your state. Often, out-of-state forms are unadaptable.

7. You may be told to go to an old case file to find a document in that file that might be used as a model for a similar document you need to draft for a current case. Many offices have collected older forms (and commercially bought forms) in a *forms file* stored on their computers. This file is a valuable source of standard forms. All of the above cautions apply equally to the adaptation of such forms.

✔ GENERAL INSTRUCTIONS FOR THE COMPLAINT-DRAFTING ASSIGNMENT

1. Your objective is to draft a complaint (called a petition in some states) that would be acceptable to a trial court in your state. For an example of the general structure of many divorce complaints, which you need to adapt to the law of your state, see Exhibit 7.7 in Chapter 7.

2. Go to your state statutory code and read everything you can about complaints in general and about complaints involving divorce and other family-law matters in particular. To help you find material in the statutory code, use the CARTWHEEL.

3. Go to the court rules of the courts of your state and read everything you can about complaints in general and about complaints involving divorce and other family-law matters in particular. To help you find material in the court rules, use the CARTWHEEL.

4. Find out if your state has any standard-form complaints written by the court or other official entity. Your state code or court rules will tell you if such forms exist and whether they are optional or required. Caution must be exercised in using standard forms. (See "How to Avoid Abusing a Standard Form" above.)

5. Many states have practice manuals, formbooks, or other practice materials written by attorneys. These materials often contain standard-form complaints that may be helpful. (See "How to Avoid Abusing a Standard Form" above.)

6. In the complaint-drafting assignments, you will often need additional facts in order to write the complaint (e.g., the names of the parties, the parties' addresses, the docket number of the case, some of the basic facts that prompted the plaintiff to file the complaint). You can make up the facts that you need so long as your facts are consistent with the limited facts that are provided in the assignment.

7. The major parts of a complaint are:
   - Caption
   - Jurisdiction and Venue
   - Body
   - Prayer for relief
   - Subscription
   - Verification

   For a description of these components, see the descriptions accompanying Exhibit 7.7 in Chapter 7.

8. Each paragraph is usually numbered separately. The content of each paragraph should be limited to a single allegation or to a small number of allegations that are closely related.

9. You cannot draft a complaint unless you know every component or element of the cause of action. For a divorce on the ground of living apart, for example, there must be a voluntary living apart for a designated period of time, and the time apart must be consecutive. In most states, there should be allegations of fact in the complaint that cover each of these elements of the ground.

10. With the exception of the citation to the statutes on jurisdiction and venue referred to in Instruction 7, you do not give citations to statutes, court rules, or opinions in the complaint. Limit yourself to the statement of facts—the essential facts.

11. If you are not sure of a fact, you can state it "on information and belief."

12. If the plaintiff has more than one cause of action or theory of recovery, you should state all of them. Each should be stated separately and numbered I, II, III, etc. Each separate theory or cause of action is called a *count*.

AGREEMENT-DRAFTING ASSIGNMENT

Some of the assignments in this book ask you to draft an agreement (e.g., prenuptial agreement, cohabitation agreement, separation agreement, custody agreement). For examples of agreements, see Exhibit 4.3 in Chapter 4 (premarital agreement, Exhibit 4.4 in Chapter 4 (cohabitation agreement) and Exhibit 8.9 in Chapter 8 (separation agreement).

✔ GENERAL INSTRUCTIONS FOR THE AGREEMENT-DRAFTING ASSIGNMENT

1. You will need additional facts in order to draft the agreement (e.g., you may need the names of the parties, their addresses, the property they own, how they own it, other economic facts). You can make up these facts unless the assignment tells you to obtain them otherwise (e.g., by interviewing a fellow student).

2. It is often useful to obtain copies of similar agreements that were written in the past for other clients and/or to

obtain copies of model agreements available online, in formbooks, manuals, practice books, etc. (The complaint-drafting instructions above give you suggestions on finding forms online.) Such material may provide effective starting points for your own drafting. Proceed with caution, however. (See "How to Avoid Abusing a Standard Form" above.)

(continued)

✔ GENERAL INSTRUCTIONS FOR THE AGREEMENT-DRAFTING ASSIGNMENT (*continued*)

3. It is critical that you know the law of the area covered by the agreement. What can and cannot be accomplished by the agreement? What legal pitfalls must be avoided? Research in the area of the law, therefore, is an essential precondition of drafting.

4. For purposes of the agreement-drafting assignments in this book, however, you do not have to do any legal research unless your instructor tells you otherwise. You will find all the law you need by reading the chapter text immediately preceding the drafting assignment you are doing.

5. When tax considerations are relevant, take them into account in drafting the agreement. For the basics of taxation, see Chapter 11.

6. Know what the client wants to accomplish by the agreement. Know the specific client objectives. (If you do not know what they are, see Instruction 1 above on obtaining facts for the agreement.) It is too general, for example, to say that the client wants to divide the property of the spouses in an equitable manner. A more *specific* and acceptable example of an objective would be to have the other spouse use the vacation home for ten years or until she remarries, whichever occurs earlier. Have all the specific objectives in mind when you draft. Each clause in the agreement should relate to one or more of the objectives. Your drafting guide is your statement of objectives.

7. At the beginning of the agreement, label the kind of agreement that it is (e.g., *Separation Agreement*). Also at the beginning,

state the names and addresses of the parties entering the agreement.

8. Number each paragraph consecutively (1, 2, 3, etc.). Limit the subject matter of each paragraph to a single topic or to closely related topics. Be as narrow as possible in selecting the topic of a paragraph. For example, in a separation agreement dealing with the disposition of the property that the spouses accumulated during the marriage, each paragraph should cover a separate category of property. Similarly, there should be separately numbered paragraphs covering custody of the children, visitation rights, alimony, etc.

9. A mistake made by many drafters is to assume that everyone will be using the same definition of words. *Major words* should always be defined. A major word is any important word that could have more than one meaning. The word *property*, for example, has several meanings (e.g., real property, personal property, property in one's possession now, property to be received in the future). What meaning did the parties intend for the word *property*? Such words should be carefully defined in the agreement.

10. One sign of an effective agreement is fairness. Avoid trying to take unfair advantage of the other side in drafting the agreement. The result may be an unworkable agreement leading to delay, animosity, and litigation expense. The cooperation of both sides is necessary to make the agreement work. An important incentive to such cooperation is a feeling by both parties that the agreement is fair.

COURT-OPINION ASSIGNMENT

You need to know how to locate court opinions on family-law topics for two reasons:

- To help you find opinions that have interpreted statutes on family-law topics.
- To help you find the **common law**. A considerable amount of family law is part of the common law, which is judge-made law in the absence of controlling statutory law or other higher law. If the legislature passes a statute that covers a controversy in litigation, the statute controls even if there is also common law that covers the controversy. Suppose, however, there are no statutes governing the dispute. In such a case, the court may be free to create new law to resolve the litigation. If it does so, the new law becomes part of the common law.

common law
Law created by courts in the absence of controlling statutory law or other higher law. (See the glossary for additional meanings.)

✔ GENERAL INSTRUCTIONS FOR THE COURT-OPINION ASSIGNMENT

1. To find court opinions (and other laws) written by your state online (without cost), see Appendix D and the following sites:
   - caselaw.findlaw.com
   - law.justia.com
   - www.plol.org
   - www.law.cornell.edu/states/listing.html

In addition:

- Go to the home page of your state government (www.aa.gov) (insert your state's abbreviation or full name in place of *aa*). On this page, look for links to the courts of your state. You will be told what opinions are available.

(continued)

✔ GENERAL INSTRUCTIONS FOR THE COURT-OPINION ASSIGNMENT (*continued*)

- In Google, Bing, or Yahoo, do a court search (aa courts) (insert your state's abbreviation or full name in place of *aa*). This search should lead you to your state courts.

2. Once you find a court site, look for links on the site to its opinions. Then use the CARTWHEEL technique to help you choose words or phrases to use in the search box for the opinions. The same is true if you are using any of the major fee-based search services, such as Westlaw, LexisNexis, and Fastcase.

3. Google Scholar
   - Go to scholar.google.com
   - Click "Case law"
   - Click "Select courts" and check the courts you want
   - Click "Done" and type the search term you want covered in opinions
   - If you already know the citation of an opinion that you want to read, enter it in the search box (e.g., "487 N.W.2d 484")

4. To find court opinions written by your state in a traditional law library, use these resources:
   - Notes to Decisions found within most annotated statutory codes.
   - The state digest or the regional digest covering opinions of your state, or the American Digest System.
   - *American Law Reports (A.L.R.).*
   - Footnote references in formbooks, hornbooks, manuals, legal encyclopedias, legal periodical literature, etc.
   - *Words and Phrases* (a multi-volume legal dictionary).

   We will briefly review each of these resources below.

5. You may not be familiar with all the legal resources mentioned above. If so, do not wait for a course in legal research before starting to learn how to use them. Start *now* by browsing through these resources on your own as often as you can. With practice and determination, you will soon be able to obtain materials from them.

6. *Notes to Decisions.* To know how to use Notes to Decisions, you must first know how to use an annotated statutory code. (Review the General Instructions for the State-Code Assignment.) The notes contain summaries of opinions that have interpreted statutes. Therefore, in order to find these notes, you must first find a statute that covers the topic under examination. If opinions exist interpreting this statute, they will be summarized in the Notes to Decisions following the statute. Be sure to check for more recent notes in the pocket parts and supplemental volumes of the code.

7. *Digests.* Digests are volumes containing thousands of small paragraph summaries of court opinions. They are organized by key topics and numbers. A digest is, in effect, a massive index to court opinions and consequently is often called a "case finder." There are three kinds of digests—all of which contain the same basic material and format:
   - State Digest. Most states have their own digest (i.e., volumes of small paragraph summaries of all the opinions written by courts in a particular state).
   - Regional Digest. There are a number of regional digests covering the opinions written by the state courts of several neighboring states.
   - American Digest System. This is the most comprehensive digest of all, covering the opinions of almost every court in the country.

   The main index in each of these digests is in separate volumes called the *Descriptive Word Index.* To use these indexes effectively, use the CARTWHEEL.

8. *American Law Reports (A.L.R.).* These volumes contain the full text of selected court opinions, plus extensive research material on issues in the opinions. The material in A.L.R. is called an *annotation.* The annotations often include a state-by-state breakdown of the legal issues treated in the annotation. Hence, when you find an annotation on a family-law topic, you can look for court opinions from your state on that topic. (The citations to these opinions are arranged alphabetically at the beginning of each annotation.) There are eight units of the *American Law Reports* volumes: A.L.R., A.L.R.2d, A.L.R.3d, A.L.R.4th, A.L.R.5th, A.L.R.6th, A.L.R. Fed., and A.L.R. Fed. 2d. The main index to these volumes is called the *Index to Annotations.* The CARTWHEEL will help you use this index.

9. *Footnote references in other books.* Sometimes, footnotes are the most valuable part of formbooks, hornbooks, manuals, legal encyclopedias, and legal periodical literature. These footnotes usually give citations to court opinions on the topics being discussed in the body of the text. In a set of books that has extensive footnotes, such as either of the major legal encyclopedias (*Corpus Juris Secundum* and *American Jurisprudence 2d*), the references to court opinions in the footnotes may be organized alphabetically by state, which will make it easier for you to determine if opinions of your state are provided.

10. *Words and Phrases.* This is a multivolume set of books containing thousands of definitions of legal terms. The definitions are quotations from court opinions. Try to find definitions of words from court opinions of your state on the family-law topic under examination.

ASSIGNMENT A.6

Answer the following questions by going to the nearest large law library to which you have access.

a. Give the name of every reporter in the library that will contain the full text of court opinions written by state courts of your state. Who publishes each reporter? What courts are covered in each?

b. Give the name of every digest that will provide small paragraph summaries of the court opinions of your state.

c. Go to one of the digests you mentioned in part (b) above. Use the index features of this digest to locate a key topic and number for *any* five family-law subjects. (Select five different family-law subject areas.) What are the key topics and numbers? Give the cite of the first opinion summarized under each key topic and number you selected.

CHECKLIST-FORMULATION ASSIGNMENT

It is important that you learn how to write checklists that could become part of a manual. Every rule that you are told about or that you read about can be "translated" into a checklist. Checklist formulation should eventually become second nature to you.

Suppose that you have before you the following statute of your state:

§ 1742 No marriage shall be solemnized without a license issued by the county clerk of any county of this state not more than thirty days prior to the date of the solemnization of the marriage.

One way to handle this statute is to create a checklist of questions that you would ask a client in order to determine whether the statute has been complied with or violated. Some of the questions would be:

1. Did you have a marriage license?

2. Where did you get the license? Did you obtain it from a county clerk in this state?

3. On what date did you obtain the license?

4. On what date did you go through the marriage ceremony ("solemnization")? (You want to determine if there were more than 30 days between the date the county issued the license and the date of the ceremony.)

These are some of the questions that must be asked as part of a large number of questions concerning the validity of a particular marriage. If you were creating a manual, the above four questions in your checklist for § 1742 could go under the manual topic of "Marriage Formation" or "Marriage License." Most laws can be translated into checklists in this way.

✔ GENERAL INSTRUCTIONS FOR THE CHECKLIST-FORMULATION ASSIGNMENT

1. The starting point in all the checklist-formulation assignments will be a rule. The rule usually will be found within a statute or a court opinion to which you will be referred.

2. Your objective is to make a list of questions that you would ask yourself, a client, or a witness for the purpose of determining whether the rule might apply.

3. Make sure you understand the rule. Closely analyze it. Make inquiries about what you do not understand in the rule. Consult a legal dictionary. Read closely related rules in order to see the rule you are examining in context. Read the rule again.

4. Break the rule down into elements, as discussed earlier.

5. For each element of the rule, design a question or a series of questions.

6. Every time the rule says that something must be done or that something must not be done, create a question or a series of questions designed to determine whether it was done.

7. Every time the rule imposes a precondition (i.e., *if* such and such occurs, *then* . . .), create a question or a series of questions designed to determine whether the precondition occurred.

8. Be alert to the word *and* in a rule. It usually refers to additional requirements. Create questions designed to determine whether all the additional requirements were met.

9. Be alert to the word *or* in a rule. It usually refers to alternative requirements. Create questions designed to determine if *both* alternatives were met.

10. If you have been diligent in creating checklists, you will be taking major steps toward the creation of your own manual. Even if you do not create manuals, checklist creation is still valuable as a practical way of thinking about any law. (For other components of such a manual, see the General Instructions for the Systems Assignment below.)

FACT-GATHERING ASSIGNMENTS

The next three categories of assignments cover various facets of fact-gathering in family law. A cardinal principle in this process is the necessity of obtaining relevant factual detail. One way to do so is through a technique called **fact particularization**. Once you identify the facts collected in the case thus far, you assume that these facts are woefully incomplete. For example, they fail to give more than one version of what happened. Then you identify a large number of basic *who*, *what*, *where*, *how*, *when*, and *why* questions that, if answered, will provide as complete a picture of what happened as is possible at this particular time.

fact particularization (FP)
A fact-gathering technique to generate a large list of factual questions (who, what, where, how, when, and why) that will help you obtain a specific and comprehensive picture of all available facts that are relevant to a legal issue.

Suppose you are working on a child-custody case. To particularize this case, you ask a series of questions centered on the following interrelated and overlapping clusters: participant details, place details, time details, incident details, and verification details.

1. *Participant details.* Who is involved in the case? Obtain the names of children, parents, grandparents, other relatives, neighbors, government agency workers connected with the case, friends of the children and of the parents, teachers and ministers who know the family, employers of the parents, medical personnel who have treated the children, witnesses to specific events, etc. What does each participant know about current and past family living conditions? How do you know? What have the participants said? What are the age and the educational background of each participant? Etc.

2. *Place details.* Where do the children live? Where else have they lived? Where do they go for school, religious services, recreational activities, medical care, cultural events, etc.? For each place, give the address, how far away from home it is, how the children get there, what costs are involved, who pays them, what happens there, what the feelings of the children are about the place, why they think so, what they have said about it, what other participants think about the place, etc.

3. *Time details.* In an average day, how much time do the children spend on their normal activities? When did any of the important events occur (e.g., abuse)? How long did it last? Has it occurred more than once in the past? When?

4. *Incident details.* What happened? What events are relevant to the well-being of the children and the fitness of the parents to be guardians? Explain ordinary and extraordinary occurrences in their day-to-day lives.

5. *Verification details.* Every fact you have obtained has a source (e.g., the client, a record). Assume that you wanted to obtain an additional source to verify the original source of every important fact. Where would you go? Whom would you ask? What additional records would you try to obtain? How would you try to obtain them? Assess the believability of each source, etc.

These categories of questions are interrelated. You will be simultaneously probing for details on people, incidents, dates, etc. There may be considerable overlap in your questions. This is not significant so long as you achieve comprehensiveness in factual detail (i.e., so long as you achieve factual particularity). Also, the above list of questions is just the tip of the iceberg. Scores and scores of additional questions of the same kind must be pursued. Given the complexity of human events and of human relationships, a great deal of factual detail is needed before you are able to achieve factual comprehensiveness. The objective of fact particularization is to get you into the habit of going beneath the surface in order to look at people and events from a variety of perspectives. Nothing is taken at face value.

INVESTIGATION-STRATEGY ASSIGNMENT

In many cases, an enormous number of facts must be gathered and verified. To keep from becoming overwhelmed, a plan of action must be developed. The investigation-strategy assignment is designed to help you construct such a plan in order to give the investigation some direction.

✔ GENERAL INSTRUCTIONS FOR THE INVESTIGATION-STRATEGY ASSIGNMENT

1. The starting point in this assignment is a set of facts you are given in the assignment. Assume you have entered the case after these facts have been collected by someone else.

2. Assume further that these facts are inadequate because *many* more facts are needed. Review the material on *fact particularization* discussed earlier.

3. Closely examine the facts you have. Are they arranged chronologically? If not, rearrange them chronologically so that the facts tell a story with a beginning, middle, and end. Of course, there will be many gaps in the story. Your task will be to identify these gaps and to raise the questions that the investigator would need to ask to try to fill or close the gaps. These questions will become the investigator's strategy or plan for further investigation.

4. Isolate the facts you have into small clusters of facts (e.g., the child is unhappy, the husband left the house in a rage). For each small set of facts that you identify or isolate in this way, make a *large* list of questions that fall into two interrelated categories:

   • Questions designed to obtain additional facts that will help you compile a much more detailed picture of what happened. To aid you in this list, ask the basic who, what, where, how, when, and why questions about every fact. (See also the material on fact particularization.)

   • Questions designed to obtain facts that will help substantiate (or prove) the facts that you already have.

There is no rigid formula to follow in making these lists of questions. The goal is a comprehensive list of questions that, if answered, would provide a comprehensive picture of what happened.

5. Consider structuring questions to elicit details on participants, places, times, and incidents.

6. Be particularly scrupulous about dates. Ask questions about the dates that you have and also about the dates that are missing.

7. In your questions on participants, try to identify a diversity of *versions.* Make a list of every person who is involved or who could be involved in the facts. Assume that each person potentially has a different version of a critical incident or series of incidents. Structure questions that will elicit these different versions.

8. Preceding most of the assignments will be a discussion of some legal principles or rules of law governing family-law topics. Include questions on the elements of any relevant rules of law. (On breaking rules into their elements, see the earlier discussion; see also General Instructions for the Checklist-Formulation Assignment.)

9. The list of questions in this assignment does not have to be written in any particular order. Select any format that is readable.

10. In some of the chapters, you will find checklists containing lists of interviewing questions and investigation tasks. If these lists are relevant to the area of the assignment, use the lists as points of departure for further fact particularization.

INTERVIEW ASSIGNMENT

The interview assignment relies on some of the skills covered earlier, especially fact particularization and checklist formulation.

✔ GENERAL INSTRUCTIONS FOR THE INTERVIEW ASSIGNMENT

1. In this assignment, you are asked to interview another person (e.g., a fellow student, someone at home).

2. Review the material on *fact particularization (FP)*. One of your objectives is to obtain substantial factual specificity. As the interviewer, you should strive for a comprehensive picture of the people and events involved in the assignment.

3. In some of the chapters, you will find lists of interviewing questions. If the lists are relevant to the area of the assignment, use the lists as points of departure for further fact particularization.

4. After you complete the interview, prepare a report from your notes. For the heading of your report, see Exhibit A.2, Interoffice Memorandum. (If you are interviewing a new client, label your report "Intake Memorandum.") Indicate who wrote the report or memo (you), who will receive it (your instructor or supervisor), the name of the person interviewed (the interviewee), the date of the interview, and the date you turned in the report or memo. The first paragraph should state the assignment (e.g., "You have asked me to interview [*name of the interviewee*] in order to [*state the purpose of the interview assignment*]).

5. In preparation for your interview, identify every rule of law that might be relevant to the fact situation (see the discussion in the text preceding the interview assignment). Break down each rule into its elements. Be sure to ask questions that are relevant to the applicability of every element. (See also the General Instructions for the Checklist Formulation Assignment.)

6. Try to arrange the facts in your intake memorandum in roughly chronological order so that the facts unfold as a story with a beginning, middle, and end.

7. *Instructions to Interviewee:* Tell the person you are interviewing (the interviewee) that he or she can make up the facts in the answer to your questions so long as the facts are reasonably consistent with the facts initially provided.

8. Your instructor may decide to role-play the interview in front of the class. If so, the class may be asked to comment on how the interview was conducted (e.g., did the interview follow the assignment, was there adequate fact particularization, did the interview ramble, was the interviewee placed at ease, how could the interview have been improved?).

INTERROGATORY ASSIGNMENT

interrogatories
A method of discovery by which one party sends written questions to another party.

The purpose of **interrogatories** is to obtain factual information about the other party's case in order to prepare for trial. See Appendix C for an example of comprehensive interrogatories.

✔ GENERAL INSTRUCTIONS FOR THE INTERROGATORY ASSIGNMENT

1. Your objective in writing the questions (i.e., the interrogatories) is to obtain as much information as possible from the other side in order to assist you in preparing a case. See the material on *fact particularization*. The material on preparing investigation strategies should also be helpful in drafting interrogatories.

2. The interrogatories you draft should be acceptable in your state, which means that you should know whatever restrictions exist in statutes and in court rules of your state on the scope and format of interrogatories in family-law cases. For example, is there a limit on the number of questions that can be sent? (The example of the interrogatories in Appendix C assumes that there is no limit on the number of questions that can be asked.)

3. The scope of questions you can ask is usually quite broad. The test is whether the question is reasonably calculated to lead to evidence that will be admissible in court. This is a much broader standard than whether the answer itself would constitute admissible evidence.

4. Avoid questions that improperly seek **privileged** information. For example:
   a. Questions that violate the privilege against self-incrimination (e.g., "Did you burn your house on purpose?").
   b. Questions that violate the attorney–client privilege (e.g., "What did you tell your attorney about the child?").
   c. Questions that violate the doctor–patient privilege (e.g., "What did you tell your doctor about the pain?").

(continued)

✔ GENERAL INSTRUCTIONS FOR THE INTERROGATORY ASSIGNMENT (*continued*)

d. Questions that violate the husband–wife privilege (e.g., "What did you tell your wife about the pain?"). This privilege does not apply when spouses are suing each other.

e. Questions that violate the attorney **work-product rule** (e.g., "Can I see the letter your attorney wrote you about the claim?").

5. In most states, it is permissible to ask a question that would involve the application of law to fact—sometimes called "contention interrogatories." Examples:

• "Do you contend that Mr. _____ had no intent to marry you at the time of the wedding ceremony?"

• "Is it your position that Ms. _____ took the child out of the state in order to avoid complying with the custody decree?"

If you ask such a question, be sure to follow it with a series of detailed questions that seek the factual reasons for the possible answers that could be given.

6. Be careful about the verb tense used in questions. Present tense (e.g., "is") is used to determine facts that are still current. Past tense (e.g., "was") is used to determine events that are over. If a question relates to past and present tense, break the question down into several questions.

7. It can be useful to try to find sample interrogatories online, in manuals, formbooks, and other practice materials. (See Appendix C.) Such interrogatories, of course, would have to be adapted to the particular needs of the client's case on which you are currently working. (See "How to Avoid Abusing a Standard Form" discussed earlier).

8. In a law office, it can be useful to go to the closed case file of another case that contains interrogatories in order to try to adapt them. Again, the use of such materials is only a point of departure. Great care is needed to determine what, if anything, can be borrowed from other interrogatories.

9. Before you draft your interrogatories, know the case (on which you are working) inside out. Read all pleadings filed to date (e.g., petition/complaint, answer, correspondences in the file, intake memorandum, etc.). Many ideas for questions will come from this knowledge. For purposes of the assignments in this book, however, you will not have access

to such data, since the assignments will be based on hypothetical cases.

10. Litigation involves causes of action and defenses. Each of these causes of action and defenses can be broken down into elements. Each of these elements should become the basis of a checklist. Ask interrogatory questions that seek facts that could potentially be used to support each of the elements. (See also the General Instructions for the Checklist-Formulation Assignment.)

11. Consider phrasing your questions in such a way that the "story" of the facts unfolds chronologically.

12. Be constantly concerned about dates, full names, addresses, exact amounts, etc.

13. Ask what documentation, physical things, or exhibits the other side will rely on to support its version of the facts. You may want to ask that such items be sent along with the answers to the interrogatories or that such items be brought to a later deposition. (When you ask that a witness appear at a deposition and bring specified items, you serve a **subpoena duces decum** on the witness.)

14. Avoid questions that call for simple "yes" or "no" answers unless you immediately follow up such questions with other questions that ask for details.

15. Include a definition section at the beginning of the interrogatories to avoid confusion and undue repetition in the later questions. This section will define words and phrases you intend to use in more than one question. For example: "A 'medical practitioner' as used in these interrogatories is meant to include any medical doctor, osteopathic physician, podiatrist, doctor of chiropractic, naturopathic physician, nurse, or other person who performs any form of healing art."

16. Ask follow-up questions on whether the person answering is talking from first-hand knowledge or second-hand knowledge (hearsay).

17. As to each fact, ask questions calculated to elicit the respondent's ability to comment on the fact (e.g., how far away was he or she, does he or she wear glasses, how long has he or she known the party and in what capacity?).

18. Avoid complicated and difficult-to-read questions. Be direct and concise.

---

privileged
Protected from disclosure; not discoverable.

work-product rule
Notes, working papers, memoranda, or similar things prepared by or for an attorney in anticipation of litigation are not discoverable by an opponent, absent a showing of substantial need. They are protected by privilege. Also called *attorney work product.*

subpoena duces decum
A command to appear at a certain time and place and bring specified things such as documents or jewelry for inspection.

FLOWCHART ASSIGNMENT

A flowchart is a step-by-step account of how something is done (e.g., a divorce or a particular kind of administrative proceeding such as an interstate enforcement of child support by IV-D agencies). A number of assignments in this book ask you to prepare a flowchart on the legal process under discussion.

☑ GENERAL INSTRUCTIONS FOR THE FLOWCHART ASSIGNMENT

1. Design the flowchart based upon the law of your state. The chart will give an overview of how something is done in your state (e.g., how to adopt a child, how to change your name).

2. The two primary sources of information for the flowchart are your state statutory code and the court rules for the courts in your state. (See General Instructions for the State-Code Assignment. See also the CARTWHEEL technique for using the index of statutory codes, court rules, or any reference materials on the shelf or online.)

3. You may be able to obtain information for the flowchart from manuals, formbooks, and other practice material online or in bound volumes on the shelf.

4. On Google or Bing, go to their "Images" option. Type the word flowchart and what you are working on, e.g., *adoption flowchart, divorce flowchart*. Also, try the search by adding the name of your state, *adoption flowchart Texas*.

5. The most important source of information for the flowchart is the current statutory code and the court rules for your state. The flowcharts in manuals or online may be out of date. Furthermore, to use secondary materials intelligently, you must know how to check the accuracy and timeliness of such materials by going to the primary sources, namely, the statutory code and the court rules (and occasionally the constitution).

6. The flowchart must be chronological, moving from the first step of the process to the last step.

7. The structure and graphics that present the steps in the flowchart can be varied:

   - Use a series of boxes (one step per box) with all the boxes connected by arrows to show the progression of the process.

   - Use a list of brief, numbered paragraphs with each paragraph stating one step.

   - Use an outline with the major headings being the key phrases of the process (e.g., agency contact, pretrial, conference etc.).

   Use your imagination in designing the sequence of events outlined in the flowchart. The examples of flowcharts in Google Images and Bing Images will give you format ideas.

8. The information in the chart should pertain primarily to procedural law rather than substantive law. **Procedural law** consists of the technical steps for bringing or defending actions in litigation before a court or an administrative agency. An example would be the number of days within which a party can request an extension of time to file an answer after

the complaint has been filed. Procedural law also consists of the formal steps required to obtain a benefit or other result. An example would be the steps needed to adopt a child. **Substantive law** consists of rights and obligations other than purely procedural matters. An example would be the right to a divorce on the ground of irreconcilable differences.

9. For each item of information in the flowchart, state your source (e.g., the citation to the statute or court rule that provided you with the procedural information you used in the flowchart).

10. Statutory codes and court rules may have sections that deal with litigation in general. Such sections are often listed in the index and table of contents of the codes and court rules under broad topics such as "Civil Procedure," "Actions," "Court Procedures," "Courts," etc. You should check these sections to see what, if anything, they say about the topic of your flowchart.

11. In addition, your state statutory code and court rules may have special sections that cover the procedural steps that are unique to the topic of your flowchart. Check these as well.

12. If you are flowcharting litigation of any kind, numerous steps are often involved at the pretrial, trial, appeal, and enforcement stages. These steps need to be incorporated into your flowchart. Here are some examples of questions you should ask yourself about most litigation. The answers to such questions must be outlined in your flowchart if they are relevant to whatever you are flowcharting.

    - What agency, if any, has jurisdiction over the case?
    - What is the application process at the agency?
    - What court(s) have jurisdiction?
    - How is service of process made?
    - How is venue determined?
    - Do you need to use any special format for the petition/complaint?
    - How is the petition/complaint served and filed?
    - Do you need to use any special format for the answer?
    - How is the answer served and filed?
    - Are there special rules for raising counterclaims?
    - What are the major motions that can be made (e.g., motion to dismiss)?
    - What rules govern pretrial discovery: depositions, interrogatories, requests for production (RFP) of documents and things, requests for admissions (RFA), and court-ordered examinations (physical and mental)?

(continued)

☑ GENERAL INSTRUCTIONS FOR THE FLOWCHART ASSIGNMENT (*continued*)

- What sanctions can be imposed for violation of the pretrial discovery rules?

- What preliminary orders can be requested, and how must the request be made?

- What rules govern the issuing of the final judgment?

- How many days does a party have to appeal?

- What court has jurisdiction to hear the appeal?

- How can a judgment be enforced?

The above list is not exhaustive. If there are other steps or more detailed steps that apply to the process you are flow-charting for your state, include them.

SYSTEMS ASSIGNMENT

A system is a method of organizing people and resources to accomplish a task. Skill is required in designing and implementing an effective system. A good way to start learning the necessary skills is to identify and describe a system currently used by others. The systems assignment is designed to help you make such a start.

procedural law
(1) The rules that govern the mechanics of resolving a dispute in court or in an administrative agency (e.g., a rule on the time by which a party must respond to a complaint). (2) The rules that govern the formal steps required to obtain a benefit or other result.

substantive law
Nonprocedural laws that define or govern rights and duties.

☑ GENERAL INSTRUCTIONS FOR THE SYSTEMS ASSIGNMENT

1. Your goal is to interview practicing attorneys, paralegals, law office administrators, and/or legal secretaries who handle family-law cases in order to identify their system for providing legal services on a certain kind of case.

2. You are seeking the following kinds of information about the system for handling the type of case involved in this assignment:

   - Who does what on the case? What does the attorney do? The paralegal? The secretary?

   - In what sequence is it all done?

   - How long does the process take from beginning to end? Does the time involved differ from case to case? If so, what are the main factors causing the differences?

   - What equipment is used (e.g., computers, calculators)?

   - What computer software, if any, is used (e.g., word processing, spreadsheet, specialty software)?

   - What websites, if any, are sometimes useful?

   - What standard forms are used?

   - Are any manuals particularly helpful? If so, were they written by the office or by someone else?

   - Has the office changed its system for handling this kind of case? If so, what were the changes, and why were they made?

   - Does anyone have any problems with how the present system now works? If so, what are they and what recommended improvements are contemplated?

3. If possible, try to interview someone from another firm that handles the same type of case so that you can compare the systems used.

4. For this assignment, how do you find practicing attorneys, paralegals, legal administrators, and secretaries in the field of family law?

   - Ask your instructor for guidance.

   - You may have fellow classmates who are secretaries or paralegals.

   - Check with your paralegal association.

   - Check with the local association of legal secretaries or legal administrators.

5. Another person who would have valuable information for this assignment is the law office manager or legal administrator of a law office.

6. Everyone is busy, and this is certainly true of people working in a law office. You must not give the impression that you are going to take up a lot of the time of the people you interview. Have a checklist of questions ready. Be prepared. Guard against giving the impression that you are not sure what you want.

7. People you interview should never reveal any information about any particular clients in their offices, including the identity of the clients. This information is confidential. You are seeking generic information on systems for handling categories of cases. If by mistake you learn information about particular clients, be sure that you keep it confidential and that you do not write it down.

CHAPTER PROJECTS

Most of the chapters in the book include a project that will expand on a major theme in the chapter.

✔ GENERAL INSTRUCTIONS FOR THE CHAPTER PROJECTS

1. The goal of the chapter project is to use the Internet to undertake research on a specific topic.

2. Be scrupulous about citing your sources. A major problem in research papers is that the writers use material on the Internet without citing the sources of the materials. This is plagiarism.

3. When you find comprehensive discussions on the Internet that are relevant to the chapter project, it is tempting to highlight the material, copy it, and drop it into your answer. Avoid this temptation. Lifting large segments of text is rarely adequate, even if you cite the material to avoid the charge of plagiarism. It is easy for an instructor to spot this cut-and-paste method of "writing." You need to organize your own answer. The outline of your presentation should be your own. Be selective in what you use.

4. The citation to an Internet page should contain:

   - The name of the person or organization authoring or sponsoring the site.
   - The name of the site (in italics).
   - The full Internet address.
   - The date you last visited the site (in parentheses).

Examples:

National Federation of Paralegal Associations, *What Is a Paralegal?,* www.paralegals.org (last visited January 22, 2021)

Peter W. Martin, *Introduction to Basic Legal Citation,* www.law.cornell.edu/citation (last visited March 13, 2020)

5. Many individual attorneys, law firms, and associations have summaries of the law on their web pages. These summaries are a major marketing tool to attract the public to their services. Be cautious about these summaries. They may contain errors and outdated material. You need to check multiple sources for everything that you use. The best sources to use are government sites containing primary authority such as statutes, court opinions, and agency regulations. Good attorney summaries will sometimes refer or link to such laws.

WRITING SAMPLES

For every course you take, you should have a file or portfolio of writing samples that can be used in a job search. A family-law course presents a number of opportunities to prepare such samples. Prospective employers are often impressed by well-drafted documents, particularly from job applicants who have not had prior legal experience.

✔ GENERAL INSTRUCTIONS FOR THE WRITING SAMPLE

1. The writing sample needs to be of the highest professional quality. It should be a document that you can present to a prospective employer.

2. Before a writing sample is ready for use in a job search, it needs to go through several drafts. It is rare for a sample to be ready after it is completed the first time. Hence, consider the writing sample you prepare for this course to be a first draft. It needs to be evaluated and rewritten based on the feedback you are given on how it can be improved. There probably will not be enough time in this course for you to do more than one draft. After the course is over, you need to seek further feedback from instructors, attorneys, and experienced paralegals.

3. Most of the writing samples will be on the law of your state. Follow the general guideline in the instructions on finding this law. See also Appendix D for additional leads to the law of your state.

4. Avoid plagiarism. Give a citation for any material that you use.

5. You need to know the citation system used in your state. See the following guide to citation formats in every state:

   - www.law.cornell.edu/citation (type the name of your state in the search box). If there are no special citation rules in your state, follow either of the following citation manuals:
   - *The Bluebook: A Uniform System of Citation* (www.legalbluebook.com)
   - *ALWD Guide to Legal Citation* (www.alwd.org/about-guide)

6. Avoid the cut-and-paste method of "writing." It is tempting to highlight large amounts of material on the Internet, copy it, and drop it into your paper. This is not writing. It is note-collecting dressed up as writing. An experienced reader (e.g., someone interviewing you for a job) can spot work that is pieced together from multiple sources rather than carefully thought through, outlined, and written.

7. Perfection in grammar and spelling is essential. One grammatical or spelling error is often enough to cause a prospective employer to reject a job candidate.

APPENDIX B

Computer-Generated Reports: The Divorce of Margaret and Nelson Paris

As we saw in Chapters 8 and 9, computer programs can be very helpful in the negotiation of custody and other issues in a divorce settlement. Here, we present a sample set of reports generated for such negotiation.

The reports in the following exhibits present the facts in the 2005 divorce of Margaret Paris and Nelson Paris. The couple has one child, Justine. Their major asset is a residence (242 Westerly Pl.).

Exhibit B.1   One-Page Summary of the Financial Data
Exhibit B.2   Projected After-Tax Cash Report for 20 Years
Exhibit B.3   Budget Report for Margaret
Exhibit B.4   Division of Marital Property
Exhibit B.5   Projected Net Worth for 20 Years
Exhibit B.6   Key Entries and Assumptions
Exhibit B.7   "What-If" Alimony and Child Support
Exhibit B.8   Alimony After Tax
Exhibit B.9   After-Tax Income on Sale of 242 Westerly Pl
Exhibit B.10   Pension Valuation Report
Exhibit B.11   Tax Calculation

EXHIBIT B.1   One-Page Summary of the Financial Data

One-Page Summary

Annual totals for Margaret Paris or Nelson Paris.

Total Income	Margaret	Nelson
Wages and Salary	$54,838	$24,000
Child Support Received	0	0
Alimony Received	12,000	0
All Other Income	28,000	28,000
TOTAL INCOME	94,838	52,000
Total Expenses		
Child Support Paid	0	0
Alimony Paid	0	12,000
All Other Expenses	89,623	16,205
TOTAL EXPENSES	89,623	28,205
Liquidations		
Liquidations	6,000	0
Taxes		
Federal Income Tax	13,390	8,077
State Income Tax	4,814	2,701
Other Taxes	4,195	1,836
TOTAL TAXES	22,399	12,614

(Continued)

Exhibit B.1 *(continued)*

After-Tax Cash	Margaret	Nelson
AFTER-TAX CASH	−17,184	11,181
Property		
Marital Property	168,858	220,196
Separate Property	16,110	−431
TOTAL PROPERTY	$184,968	$219,765
Miscellaneous		
Number of Dependents	1	0
Filing Status	Single	Single
Alimony Paid, % of Gross Income	0	23
Child Support Paid, % of Gross Income	0	0
Combined Pmts, % of Gross Income	0	23

Reprinted with permission of Family Law Software, Inc.

EXHIBIT B.2   Projected After-Tax Cash Report for 20 Years

Projected After-Tax Cash Report

Projected After-Tax Cash for Margaret Paris or Nelson Paris for 20 years.

	Margaret	Nelson		Margaret	Nelson
2005	($ 17,184)	$ 11,181	2015	($ 16,676)	$ 32,083
2006	$ 636	$ 11,655	2016	($ 18,712)	$ 33,215
2007	$ 3,202	$ 16,905	2017	($ 20,849)	$ 34,409
2008	$ 2,076	$ 17,551	2018	($ 23,104)	$ 35,618
2009	$ 885	$ 18,214	2019	($ 26,566)	$ 36,890
2010	($ 7,742)	$ 26,868	2020	($ 30,417)	$ 38,189
2011	($ 9,542)	$ 27,201	2021	($ 34,553)	$ 39,635
2012	($ 11,182)	$ 28,856	2022	($ 39,137)	$ 41,048
2013	($ 12,917)	$ 29,888	2023	($ 44,167)	$ 42,504
2014	($ 14,747)	$ 30,950	2024	($ 49,658)	$ 44,005

Reprinted with permission of Family Law Software, Inc.

EXHIBIT B.3 Budget Report for Margaret

Budget Report for 2005

Budget Report for Margaret for 2005

This report shows Margaret Paris's income, taxes, expenses, alimony, and child support.

	Weekly	Monthly	Annual
Income			
Wages	$1,054.58	$4,569.83	$54,838
Total Wage and Non-Wage Income	$1,054.58	$4,569.83	$54,838
Business Income			
Paris Plumbing Supply	$538.46	$2,333.33	$28,000
Total Business Income	$538.46	$2,333.33	$28,000
Support Received			
Alimony Received	$230.77	$1,000.00	$12,000
Total Support Received	$230.77	$1,000.00	$12,000
TOTAL INCOME	**$1,823.81**	**$7,903.17**	**$94,838**
Mortgage Payments			
242 Westerly Pl	$386.08	$1,673.00	$20,076
Total Mortgage Payments	$386.08	$1,673.00	$20,076
Living Expenses			
Union Dues	$19.23	$83.33	$1,000
Cable TV	13.15	57.00	684
Dry Cleaning	12.00	52.00	624
Furniture & Appliance repair/Replacement	3.92	17.00	204
Homeowners' Insurance	27.69	120.00	1,440
Household Maintenance/Repair	7.92	34.33	412
Household Supplies	1.15	5.00	60
Laundry	7.00	30.33	364
Lawn Service	4.62	20.00	240
Maid/cleaning Service	70.00	303.33	3,640
Snow Removal	5.77	25.00	300
Tax - Property Tax	145.00	628.33	7,540
Utilities - Electricity	145.38	630.00	7,560
Utilities - Gas/Propane Heat	17.31	75.00	900
Utilities - Oil Heat	25.00	108.33	1,300
Utilities - Phone	75.00	325.00	3,900
Utilities - Water/Sewer	28.85	125.00	1,500
Car Insurance	25.38	110.00	1,320
Car Gasoline/Oil	57.69	250.00	3,000
Car Maintenance and Repair	17.31	75.00	900
Car License/Stickers	0.96	4.17	50
Parking	2.31	10.00	120

(Continued)

Exhibit B.3 *(continued)*

Living Expenses (continued)	Weekly	Monthly	Annual
Public/alt. Transportation	15.00	65.00	780
Child Clothing/School Uniforms	4.81	20.83	250
Child Entertainment	70.00	303.33	3,640
Clothes	18.46	80.00	960
Church/Synagogue/Mosque etc.	9.62	41.67	500
Entertainment	29.23	126.67	1,520
Food/Groceries	69.23	300.00	3,600
Gifts	10.00	43.33	520
Hair	30.00	130.00	1,560
Internet Access	15.00	65.00	780
Misc Other	3.85	16.67	200
Pets	9.62	41.67	500
Restaurants	55.00	238.33	2,860
Therapist/Counselor	27.69	120.00	1,440
Toiletries/Grooming/Drug Store	5.77	25.00	300
Vacations	96.15	416.67	5,000
Health Insurance	110.00	476.67	5,720
Dental Exp	6.92	30.00	360
Optical Exp	4.62	20.00	240
Total Living Expenses	$1,303.62	$5,649.00	$67,788
Payments on Debt			
Sallie Mae Loan	$10.17	$44.08	$529
Citibank Visa	10.96	47.50	570
American Express Platinum	2.08	9.00	108
Student Loan	10.62	46.00	552
Total Payments on Debt	$33.83	$146.58	$1,759
TOTAL EXPENSES	$1,723.52	$7,468.58	$89,623
Taxes			
Federal Taxes	$257.50	$1,115.83	$13,390
FICA & Medicare	$80.67	$349.58	$4,195
State Taxes	$92.58	$401.17	$4,814
TOTAL TAXES	$430.75	$1,866.58	$22,399
Total Income	$1,823.81	$7,903.17	$94,838
Minus Total Expenses	(1,723.52)	(7,468.58)	(89,623)
Minus Total Taxes	(430.75)	(1,866.58)	(22,399)
AFTER-TAX CASH	$(330.46)	$(1,432.00)	$(17,184)

Reprinted with permission of Family Law Software, Inc.

EXHIBIT B.4 Division of Marital Property

Division of Marital Property

Property division report for Margaret Paris and Nelson Paris.

	Margaret Amount	Pct	Nelson Amount	Pct	Total Amount	
Residence Equity						
242 Westerly Pl	$135,250		$182,250		$317,500	1
Total Residence Equity	$135,250	43%	$182,250	57%	$317,500	
Investments						
Total Investments	$0	0%	$0	0%	$0	
Businesses						
Paris Plumbing Supply	$40,000		$40,000		$80,000	2
Total Businesses	$40,000	50%	$40,000	50%	$80,000	
Personal Items						
Car	$2,000		$0		$2,000	3
Sofa	$1,750		$0		$1,750	4
Oil Painting	$3,000		$0		$3,000	5
Sculpture	$0		$3,500		$3,500	6
Desk	$0		$1,750		$1,750	7
Total Personal Items	$6,750	56%	$5,250	44%	$12,000	
Subtotal Non-Retirement	**$182,000**	**44%**	**$227,500**	**56%**	**$409,500**	
Defined Benefit Pensions						
Federated Pension Plan	$14,515		$14,515		$29,030	8
Total Pensions	$14,515	50%	$14,515	50%	$29,030	
Subtotal Retirement	**$14,515**	**50%**	**$14,515**	**50%**	**$29,030**	
Total Assets	**$196,515**	**45%**	**$242,015**	**55%**	**$438,530**	
Debts						
Insurance Policies	$0		($1,593)		($1,593)	9
Bathroom Renovations	$0		($5,500)		($5,500)	10
Sallie Mae Loan	($8,696)		($8,696)		($17,392)	11
Citibank Visa	($4,717)		$4,717		$0	12
American Express Platinum	($1,749)		$1,749		$0	13
Student Loan	($12,495)		($12,495)		($24,990)	14
Total Debt	($27,657)	56%	($21,818)	44%	($49,475)	
Total Debts	**($27,657)**	**56%**	**($21,819)**	**44%**	**($49,476)**	
Total Property	**$168,858**	**43%**	**$220,196**	**57%**	**$389,054**	

Note: "Total Amount" column may not add due to rounding.

Reprinted with permission of Family Law Software, Inc.

EXHIBIT B.5   Projected Net Worth for 20 Years

Projected Net Worth Report

Projected Net Worth for Margaret Paris or Nelson Paris for 20 years.

	Margaret	Nelson
2005	$ 164,830	$ 226,639
2006	$ 154,224	$ 221,932
2007	$ 160,308	$ 241,244
2008	$ 165,189	$ 261,149
2009	$ 168,784	$ 281,645
2010	$ 163,638	$ 310,707
2011	$ 156,554	$ 339,775
2012	$ 147,665	$ 369,656
2013	$ 136,842	$ 400,371
2014	$ 123,950	$ 431,909
2015	$ 108,842	$ 464,292
2016	$ 91,352	$ 497,464
2017	$ 71,312	$ 531,415
2018	$ 48,522	$ 566,078
2019	$ 21,674	$ 601,421
2020	($ 9,736)	$ 637,350
2021	($ 46,223)	$ 673,784
2022	($ 88,336)	$ 710,587
2023	($ 136,704)	$ 747,624
2024	($ 192,028)	$ 784,697

Reprinted with permission of Family Law Software, Inc.

EXHIBIT B.6   Key Entries and Assumptions

Key Entries and Assumptions

This report presents the key assumptions behind the income and asset projections for Margaret Paris and Nelson Paris.

Key Rates

1. Inflation .... 3.1 %
2. After-tax rate of return on Accumulated Savings (reinvested income) .... 3.0 %
3. Cost of borrowing (%) for net deficits .... 8.0 %

Plan Start Date

1. The start year for plan is 2005.

Taxes

1. Federal taxes are calculated on a detailed basis using the tax laws for each year, including Earned Income Credit, Alternative Minimum tax, and phase-outs currently enacted.

2. Taxes for Margaret Paris

   Federal and state filing status for 2005 .... Single

   Filing status for subsequent years .... Single

   State taxes are estimated based on an abbreviated version of the New York State tax form.

Exhibit B.6 *(continued)*

3. Taxes for Nelson Paris

   Federal and state filing status for 2005 .... Single

   Filing status for subsequent years .... Single

   State taxes are estimated based on an abbreviated version of the New York State tax form.

Assumptions Relating to Children

		Custody	Tax Exemption
1.	Justine	Margaret	Margaret

Assumptions Relating to Child Support

1. No child support is entered.

Assumptions Relating to Alimony

1. Nelson paying alimony through 2009 .... $1,000 per month

Residence Assumptions - 242 Westerly Pl

1. Market Value $700,000

2. Rate of appreciation of residence .... With Inflation

3. This residence will be sold in 2006.

4. There is a first mortgage with a current mortgage balance of $335,000.

5. This mortgage will be paid by Margaret.

6. There is a second mortgage with a current mortgage balance of $47,500.

7. This mortgage will be paid by Margaret.

Assumptions Relating to Wages

		Margaret	Nelson
1.	Wage amount and period	$54,838/year	$2,000/month
2.	Rate of increase of wages	With Inflation	With Inflation
3.	Retirement age	65	65

Assumptions Relating to Cash & Investments

1. Chase [Checking]: The current market value is $4,000.

2. Chemical [Checking]: The current market value is $12,500.

3. Bank of America [Money market]: The current market value is $2,000.

4. Investment # 4: The current market value is $0.

Assumptions Relating to Defined Benefit Pensions

1. Federated Pension Plan.

   The plan is owned by Margaret Paris.

   The monthly benefit specified by the plan administrator is $1,231.

   This assumes the employee works until the cut-off date and begins receiving payments at age 65.

   The discount rate is 4.64%.

   We are using mortality table GAR-94.

Assumptions Relating to Debts

1. Insurance Policies. The current balance is $1,593. The current rate is 0.00%.

   No monthly payment has been entered.

2. Bathroom Renovations. The current balance is $5,500. The current rate is 3.00%.

   The monthly payment is $75.00.

(Continued)

Exhibit B.6 *(continued)*

3. Sallie Mae Loan. The current balance is $17,392. The current rate is 4.50%.
    The monthly payment is $88.00.

4. Citibank Visa. The current balance is $9,433. The current rate is 18.00%.
    The monthly payment is $95.00.

5. American Express Platinum. The current balance is $3,498. The current rate is 0.00%.
    The monthly payment is $18.00.

6. Student Loan. The current balance is $24,989. The current rate is 4.50%.
    The monthly payment is $92.00.

Reprinted with permission of Family Law Software, Inc.

EXHIBIT B.7   "What-If" Alimony and Child Support

"What-If" Alimony and Child Support

After-tax cash projections for Margaret Paris and Nelson Paris, for alimony paid by Nelson to Margaret.

What-If	Amount ($/mo.)	Through (year)
Alimony:	500	2009
Child Support:	1,000	2023

Results:

Year	Annual After-Tax Cash (*)		
	Margaret	Nelson	Combined
2005	−8,901	3,055	−5,846
2006	−10,468	3,317	−7,151
2007	−12,986	3,616	−9,370
2008	−15,346	3,911	−11,435
2009	−17,878	4,210	−13,668
2010	−24,202	8,392	−15,810
2011	−27,705	8,171	−19,534
2012	−31,276	9,255	−22,021
2013	−35,178	9,700	−25,478
2014	−39,434	10,156	−29,278
2015	−44,076	10,664	−33,412
2016	−49,137	11,154	−37,983
2017	−54,644	11,686	−42,958
2018	−60,645	12,214	−48,431
2019	−67,181	12,784	−54,397
2020	−74,282	13,360	−60,922
2021	−81,927	14,060	−67,867
2022	−90,300	14,706	−75,594
2023	−99,423	15,372	−84,051
2024	−121,335	28,059	−93,276

Reprinted with permission of Family Law Software, Inc.

(*) The After-Tax Cash calculation excludes down payments, refinancings, and income from sales of residences.

EXHIBIT B.8   Alimony After Tax

Alimony After-Tax

The total alimony payments are $60,000.

The total after-tax cost of the alimony to the payer is $45,428.

The total net benefit of the alimony to the recipient, after paying taxes, is $42,352.

There is a net tax *loss* of $3,076 due to the alimony payments.

(Note: The tax calculations cover the period when alimony was deductible by the payor and taxable to the payee. This was changed in 2019. See Chapter 11.)

Analysis:

The chart below shows the net tax savings to alimony.

Numbers in parentheses are negative – that is, net tax losses.

Net Tax Savings Due to alimony

Year	(a) Nelson's Tax Reduction Due to Alimony	(b) Margaret's Tax Increase Due to Alimony	(c) Net Tax Change Due to Alimony (a) - (b)
2005	$3,000	$3,488	($488)
2006	$2,968	$3,550	($582)
2007	$2,915	$3,620	($705)
2008	$2,867	$3,520	($653)
2009	$2,822	$3,470	($648)
Total tax svgs/pmts:	$14,572	$17,648	($3,076)
Total payments made:	$60,000	$60,000	
Cost/Inc after taxes:	$45,428	$42,352	

Explanation or Analysis:

When alimony is paid, the payer gets a tax deduction and the recipient pays tax on the alimony income.

The tax deduction is a benefit to the payer (Nelson). We calculate Nelson's tax with the alimony deduction. Then we calculate Nelson's tax as if there were no alimony payment. The difference is Nelson's tax benefit due to the alimony payment.

Note that we do not simply apply a marginal tax rate to the alimony amount. We do a complete tax calculation. This counts the impact of the alimony deduction on exemption phase-outs, itemized deduction phase-outs, the Alternative Minimum Tax, etc., and therefore it is the most accurate way to calculate the tax benefit.

We then do a similar set of calculations for Margaret, to find the extra tax that Margaret is paying due to the alimony income.

We then subtract Margaret's tax cost from Nelson's tax benefit, to get the net tax benefit.

Typically, the payer is in a higher tax bracket than the recipient. This means that the payer's tax savings is more than the recipient's tax cost. So there is a net tax benefit.

In this case, Margaret, after alimony payments, is in a higher tax bracket than Nelson, so there is actually a net tax loss due to alimony payments.

Reprinted with permission of Family Law Software, Inc.

EXHIBIT B.9 After-Tax Income on Sale of 242 Westerly Pl

After-Tax Income on Sale of 242 Westerly Pl

This report details the income, tax, and after-tax income on the sale of 242 Westerly Pl.

I. Calculating Income on Sale of 242 Westerly Pl:

1. Current Value of 242 Westerly Pl	$700,000
2. Times: Appreciation of 3.100% per year for 1 Year	1.031
3. Equals: Sale Price of 242 Westerly Pl	$700,000
4. Less: First Mortgage Balance on Sale Date	$338,484
5. Less: Second Mortgage Balance on Sale Date	$50,530
6. Less: Expense of Sale	$33,000
7. Equals: Equity After Mortgages and Expenses	$277,986
8. Percent of Equity to Margaret	43.00%
9. Percent of Equity to Nelson	57.00%
10. Income on Sale, for Margaret (line 7 * line 8)	$119,534
11. Income on Sale, for Nelson (line 7* line 9)	$158,452

II. Estimating Tax Payable on Sale of 242 Westerly Pl.

	Margaret	Nelson
1. Sale Price of 242 Westerly Pl	$301,000	$399,000
2. Less: Expense of Sale	$14,190	$18,810
3. Equals: Amount Realized	$286,810	$380,190
4. Less: Adjusted Basis	$0	$520,000
5. Equals: Potentially Taxable Gain	$0	$147,000
6. Less: Exclusion Amount	$250,000	$250,000
7. Equals: Taxable Gain	$0	$0
8. Federal Tax Payable (additional tax vs. home not sold) (Taxes may increase because of the loss of the mortgage deduction as well as gain on sale.)	$0	$0
9. Estimated State Tax Payable (addt'l vs. home not sold)	$0	$0

III. Estimating After-Tax Income on Sale of 242 Westerly Pl.

	Margaret	Nelson
1. Income on Sale (from Sections 1.10 and 1.11 above)	$119,534	$ 158,452
2. Less: Estimated Incremental Tax (from Sec II.8 & 9 above)	$0	$0
3. Equals: Estimated After-Tax Income on Sale	$119,534	$158,452

Reprinted with permission of Family Law Software, Inc.

EXHIBIT B.10   Pension Valuation Report

Pension Valuation Report

This valuation is for the plan: Federated Pension Plan.

This report values the plan as of the evaluation date, which is: 01/01/2004.

Based on the information entered (see below), the value of the pension as of the evaluation date is:

$37,589, using the RP-2000 mortality tables and a gender-specific approach.

As of 01/01/2004, 74.17% of this pension is so-called "marital property."

The "marital amount" is typically the amount the judge will divide. (The rest stays with the employee.)

Using a gender-specfic approach, the marital amount of the pension plan is $27,880 (that is, 74.17% of $37,589).

Using a gender-specific approach, if the judge divides the pension 50/50, for example, then $13,940.00 (half of $27,880) would be awarded to each spouse.

These comments about marital property apply in most states, even community property states.

Value of Pension at Retirement:

The value of the pension is $210,394 (gender-specific approach) as of regular retirement age.

This is typically more than the value as of the evaluation date because, like money in a bank account, a pension's value increases over time.

Knowing the value at earliest retirement age tends to be most useful if the worker is near retirement, or is likely to reach retirement with this company.

If the non-worker spouse is considering taking a share of the payout, as opposed to a cash buyout today, this number helps both spouses see what that payout might be.

This report is based on the following data entered:

Key Dates:

09/01/1975	Employee's birth date.
08/26/1990	Date the employee was married.
4,876	Number of days from marriage to separation.
1/1/1986	Date the employee started in the plan.
01/01/2004	Date the employment stopped being "marital." (This is usually the separation date).
01/01/2004	Date to evaluate the plan. (This should be the date on the pension benefits administrator's statement).
65	Employee's regular retirement age.
62	Employee's earliest retirement age.
NO	Is the employee already retired?

The Plan:

$1,231	Monthly benefit, provided by plan administrator, at "as if" retirement date.
1.0%	Cost of living adjustment (COLA) percent
4.64%	Interest rate (also known as the "discount rate").

Calculation Options Selected:

The pension benefit and marital portion are calculated "as if" the employee works until the cut-off date.

"Cut-off" means the date after which the plan is no longer marital. This is typically the separation date.

The pension's value is calculated assuming the employee retired or will retire on the regular retirement date.

The employee is a female.

Reprinted with permission of Family Law Software, Inc.

EXHIBIT B.11   Tax Calculation

Tax Calculation

Taxes for Margaret Paris in 2005 are $22,399, and taxes for Nelson Paris are $12,614.

Margaret	Nelson	
Single	Single	Filing Status in 2005
2	1	Number of exemptions
		Income:
54,838	24,000	Wages and salary.
0	0	Taxable interest income.
0	0	Taxable dividend income.
12,000	0	Alimony income.
28,000	28,000	Business and farm income.
0	0	Capital gain taxable.
0	0	Other gains and losses.
0	0	Taxable IRA and pension income.
0	0	Rent, royalty, partnership, S corporation.
0	0	Social Security taxable.
0	0	Other income.
94,838	52,000	Taxable Gross Income.
		Adjustments:
0	0	IRA deduction.
0	0	Moving expenses.
1,978	1,978	Deduction of 1/2 of self-employment tax.
0	0	Part of health insurance for self-employed people.
0	12,000	Alimony paid.
0	0	Interest on education loans.
0	0	Other deductions.
1,978	13,978	Total adjustments.
92,860	38,022	Adjusted Gross Income ("AGI") = gross income − total adjustments.
		Itemized Deductions:
795	0	Deductible medical expenditures.
6,093	2,701	State income taxes.
0	0	Local income taxes.
7,540	0	Property taxes.
20,076	0	Mortgage interest.
500	300	Charitable contributions.
1,000	324	Miscellaneous, subject to 2% AGI threshold.
0	0	Miscellaneous, after 2% AGI threshold.
0	0	Miscellaneous, not subject to 2% AGI threshold.
35,004	3,001	Itemized deductions before phase-out.
35,004	3,001	Itemized deductions after phase-out.
5,000	5,000	Compare: standard deduction.

(Continued)

Exhibit B.11 *(continued)*

Exemptions:

6,400	3,200	Deduction for exemptions before phase-out.
6,400	3,200	Deduction for exemptions after phase-out.

Tax Before Credits and Other Taxes:

51,456	29,822	Taxable Income
		= AG I − greater of itemized or standard deductions − exemptions.
9,534	4,121	Tax before credits and other taxes (from tax table or formula).

Non-refundable Credits:

0	0	Child care credit.
0	0	Hope education credit.
0	0	Lifetime learning credit.
0	0	Child credit, after phase-out, non-refundable portion.
0	0	Total Non-refundable Credits (reduce tax, but not below zero).

Refundable Credits:

100	0	Child credit, after phase-out, refundable portion.
0	0	Earned income credit.
100	0	Total Refundable Credits
		(can reduce tax below zero and generate a payment from the IRS).

Other Taxes on Form 1040:

0	0	Tax on retirement plan premature distribution.
0	0	Alternative minimum tax.
0	0	Lump-sum distribution 5- or 10-year averaging.
3,956	3,956	Self-employment tax.

Total Federal Income Tax:

		= tax before credits and other taxes
		− total nonrefundable credits (down to zero)
		− total refundable credits
		+ other taxes on Form 1040
13,390	8,077	Total Federal Income Tax.

Taxes Not on Form 1040:

3,400	1,488	FICA Taxes.
795	348	Medicare Taxes.
4,814	2,701	State Income Tax (NY: 10.5% of income).

Total Taxes:

22,399	**12,614**	**Total Taxes.**

APPENDIX C

Interrogatories on Financial Assets

INTRODUCTION

Gaining access to all the personal and financial information needed to negotiate a separation agreement or to prepare for trial is often a major task. In fact, one of the major reasons separation agreements are later challenged is that one of the parties was not given a complete and accurate inventory of the other spouse's financial assets before signing. In Chapter 7, we examined discovery devices that are designed to help an office obtain this kind of information.

One of these devices is interrogatories ("rogs"), which can be particularly effective when seeking financial assets. Interrogatories are a method of discovery in which one party sends written questions to another party in order to prepare for trial. Here, we will explore interrogatories directed at a spouse's finances. In some states, there are limits on the number of interrogatories one party can send another. For the interrogatories presented in this appendix, we will assume that there are no such limits.

Carefully examining these interrogatories will increase your understanding of the potential complexity of someone's financial affairs. As you read the questions, make note of the categories of financial data sought and the comprehensiveness of the questions in these categories. A paralegal must pursue the same kind of information with the same comprehensiveness when given interviewing and investigative tasks designed to help the office identify the financial assets of a client's spouse.

DOCUMENT HUNT

Uncovering financial assets is primarily a document hunt. Here is a list of the documents that our interrogatories will be seeking:

- Medical reports
- Physician letters
- Canceled rent checks
- Lease or rental agreements
- Real estate closing statements
- Deeds
- Real estate appraisals
- Real estate mortgages
- Real estate tax bills
- Contracts to buy real estate
- Contracts to sell real estate
- Pay stubs
- W-2 forms
- Employment contracts

- Car lease agreements
- Deferred compensation agreements
- Account statements for deferred compensation
- Federal income tax returns
- State tax returns
- Local tax returns
- Gift tax returns
- 1099 tax forms for miscellaneous income
- Partnership agreements
- Partnership tax returns
- Articles of incorporation

- Corporate tax returns
- Bank account statements
- Appraisals of livestock
- Appraisals of jewelry
- Appraisals of other collectibles
- Royalty statements
- Securities account statements
- Trust instruments
- Trustee accounting reports
- Pension account statements
- Credit card statements
- Financial statements
- Loan applications

Some of these documents only indirectly relate to someone's financial worth. Knowing a person's medical history, for example, is some evidence of whether health problems interfere with an ability to earn income.

INTERROGATORIES

These interrogatories must be answered by the defendant under oath. All answers should be supplemented after they are submitted if the defendant becomes aware of any new or changed facts that would alter any of the answers previously provided.

I. GENERAL MATTERS

1. State your full name, age, residence and post office address, home telephone number, Social Security number, business addresses, business phone numbers, personal and business e-mail addresses, and all personal and business Internet sites (including but not limited to blogs and social-network sites such as LinkedIn and Facebook).

2. Provide
    (a) The names, dates of birth, and current addresses of all children born or adopted during the marriage.
    (b) State whether any of the children have been emancipated.
    (c) Who has physical and legal custody of each minor child?
    (d) Does any minor child need medical or mental health care? If so, explain the details. What kind of treatment is needed? What are the names and addresses of medical care providers who have provided treatment or whose treatment will be needed? State the cost (past and projected) of such treatments and the anticipated length of the treatment needed. (Attach copies of reports or letters of medical care providers.)

3. (a) What is your own state of health at the present time?
    (b) What medical care needs do you currently have, if any?

4. (a) Describe your employment skills.
    (b) Do you have or have you ever had a license to practice any occupation? If so, describe each license, the dates received, and the name of the agency that granted the license.
    (c) What is your educational background? List the schools you attended and the years of attendance. List your degrees, certificates, or other indicia of completion.
    (d) For each school you attended, who paid the education expenses? If others provided gifts or loans for all or some of the expenses, state

the names and addresses of the persons who provided this aid, the amounts provided, and the circumstances of such assistance.

(e) While you attended schools or other training, did your spouse provide financial support for your education and living expenses? If so, describe the support provided in detail, including specific dollar amounts involved.

(f) Was your spouse working at any time you were obtaining your own education? If so, where did the spouse work, how much did your spouse earn, and how were the earnings used during your relationship?

5. Do you have any disabilities that have limited or that now limit your ability to perform your gainful work? If the answer is yes, attach medical reports on each disability and provide the following details:

(a) A description of each disability and how it affected your work.

(b) The medical care you received for each disability, including the names of doctors and other medical care providers, and the names of hospitals, clinics, and other facilities where you received treatment.

(c) The dates of the treatment.

(d) The expenses incurred for the treatment.

(e) The cost of the treatment.

(f) The resources used to pay for the treatment, including your own funds, insurance proceeds, employer contribution, and any other third-party assistance.

II. RESIDENCES

6. What is your primary residence? How long have you lived there?

7. For 10 years prior moving into your current primary residence, where did you reside and for what periods of time?

8. Do you currently live with your spouse? If not, do other persons live with you on a temporary or permanent basis? If so, what are their names and ages and their relationship to you?

9. Do you currently rent your primary residence? If so, what are the terms, including amount of rent, term of the rental or lease, and the name and address of the owner or other entity to whom payments are made? (Attach a copy of the lease and copies of canceled rent checks or other record of payment for the last twelve [12] months.)

10. What is the source of funds used to make rental payments? Give the name and address of anyone who assists you in making these payments. State the relationship between you and any such persons.

11. Do you own your present primary residence? If so, state:

(a) The percentage of the residence that you own.

(b) Does your spouse have an ownership interest in the residence? If so, what is the interest?

(c) Who else has an ownership interest and in what percentages?

(d) When did you acquire your interest?

(e) What was the tax basis of the residence on the date of purchase?

(f) What is the name of the seller(s)?

(g) How much did you pay for your ownership interest?

(h) Where did you obtain the funds for this payment?

(i) Where did your spouse obtain the funds to purchase his or her interest?

(j) What was the amount of the original mortgage on the residence?

(k) Who is the mortgagee?

    (l) What was the amount of the mortgage on the date you and your spouse separated?

    (m) How much is currently owed on the mortgage?

    (n) What was the market value of the residence on the date of separation?

    (o) For property tax purposes, what is the assessed value of the residence according to the county or other level of government? (Attach a copy of the government's notice on this value.)

    (p) What is the current market value of the residence?

    (q) What was the adjusted tax basis of the residence on the date of separation?

    (r) What is the current adjusted tax basis?

    (s) Are there any other mortgages, liens, or other encumbrances on the residence? If so, for how much? State the details of when they were acquired and from whom, as well as the source of funds used to make payments toward each.

    (t) List all annual, quarterly, monthly, and other recurring operating expenses for the residence, including taxes, mortgage payments, insurance, utilities, repairs, and maintenance.

    (u) What major expenses for capital improvements have been paid since the residence was purchased? For each improvement, state the nature of the improvement, the cost, the person or company performing the improvement, the source of the funds to pay the expense, and whether any balance remains for the expense.

    (v) What major capital improvements are now needed? For each need, state the estimated cost.

    (w) Attach copies of closing statements, deeds, appraisals, mortgages, contractor statements, and the most recent bills for property taxes.

12. Is your present primary residence your marital residence? If not, answer questions 11(a) to 11(w) for your marital residence.

13. Since the date of the separation, what has been the source of funds used to pay all mortgages and other costs for the residences referred to in the questions above? Indicate who made these payments.

14. Since the date of the separation, what has been the source of funds used to pay property taxes on all of the residences referred to in the questions above? Indicate who made these payments.

III. OTHER REAL PROPERTY

15. Do you have an ownership, possessory, or other interest in any real property other than indicated above? If so, for each such interest, provide the following information:

    (a) Address of the property.

    (b) The nature of your interest.

    (c) When you acquired your interest.

    (d) The date you acquired the interest.

    (e) The person or entity from whom you obtained the interest.

    (f) The names and addresses of other persons or entities who also have an interest in the property.

    (g) The manner in which you acquired the interest. If by purchase, state the price or other consideration paid.

    (h) The reason you acquired the interest.

    (i) The amount you owed on the interest on the date of separation from your spouse.

(j)   The amount currently owed.

(k)   The involvement, if any, of your spouse in acquiring the interest.

(l)   The market values of the property on the date you acquired it, on the date of separation, and currently.

(m) The assessed value of the property for property tax purposes.

(n)   The recurring operating expenses for the property, including property taxes, insurance, and utilities.

(o)   The source of funds used to pay these operating expenses.

(p)   The income generated by the property including but not limited to rental income.

(q)   Attach copies of the closing statements, deeds, and appraisals for each property covered in question 15.

16. Did you buy, sell, or otherwise transfer real property during the marriage and before the separation? If so, answer questions (a) to (q) of question 15 for each such property.

17. Did you buy, sell or otherwise transfer real property after the separation? If so, answer questions (a) to (q) of question 15 for each such property.

IV. INCOME AND EMPLOYMENT

18. For the last 10 years, state the names, street addresses, telephone numbers, e-mail addresses, and Internet addresses of your prior employers, with dates of each employment, positions held, salary, other compensation, and reasons for ending each employment.

19. What is the name, street address, e-mail address, and Internet address of your current employer?

(a)   How long have you been employed there?

(b)   Describe the kind of work you do.

(c)   How are your earnings determined? Include all forms of compensation, including salary, commissions, bonuses, and other remuneration.

(d)   Attach copies of pay stubs, W-2 forms, and other records you have received that demonstrate your answers to (c) for the past twelve (12) months.

20. Describe the employee benefits provided to you and/or to your family or dependents (indicating for each benefit the amount contributed by your employer and the amount contributed by you) in the following categories:

(a)   Health insurance for current employees

(b)   Health insurance for retirees

(c)   Life insurance

(d)   Disability insurance

(e)   Health and wellness programs

(f)   Child care subsidy

(g)   Pension, profit sharing, annuities, or retirement programs

(h)   Car or other vehicle allowance

(i)   Thrift savings plan

(j)   Stock options

(k)   Other benefits or perquisites

21. What deferred compensation in the form of cash, securities, or other assets are you currently entitled to (or might you be entitled to upon the happening of conditions) from any employment during the marriage?

(a)   State the details of such entitlement, including the person, company, or other entity that has or may have the duty of paying the deferred compensation and the amounts or value of the potential compensation involved.

(b)   Attach copies of contracts or other documents stating or indicating your entitlement to the deferred compensation.

22. For your current employment, list all the deductions from your gross earnings every pay period.

23. Do you have a written contract of employment or are you an at-will employee?
    (a) If the former, state the terms of the contract, including compensation, other benefits, and when the contract terminates.
    (b) If you currently have more than one written contract, answer this question for each.
    (c) Attach copies of all employment contracts.

24. In the last five years, have you had written contracts of employment other than those mentioned in question 23?
    (a) If so, for each state the terms of the contract, including compensation, other benefits, and when the contract terminates.
    (b) Attach copies of such contracts.

25. For any year during the marriage for which you earned income or other compensation, did you fail to file federal, state, or local income tax returns? If so, for what years and for what reason(s) were the returns not filed?

26. Attach copies of the federal, state, and local income tax returns that you filed in the last seven years.

27. Name each bank or other financial institution into which you deposit any salary or other compensation from your employment or other work endeavors. Include the account number(s) at each institution.

28. Do you expect to obtain a raise next year due to a promotion, union contract, regular incremental increase, performance review, or otherwise? Answer this question even if you do not know the exact amount of any such increase.

29. Have you ever received any government benefits such as unemployment compensation, workers' compensation, Social Security, etc.? If so, describe each including the dates received, amounts, etc.

30. Do you have any sources of income or economic benefits not covered in the above interrogatories? If so, describe each, including the nature of the income or benefit, amounts, sources, etc.

V. SELF-EMPLOYMENT

31. Are you self-employed? If so, describe the nature of your work.

32. State whether you are a sole proprietor, have an ownership interest in a partnership, work for or in a corporation in which you own any stock, or work for or in any other type of venture or entity in which you have an ownership interest.
    (a) Provide details on your ownership interest in said proprietorship, partnership, corporation, venture, or other entity, including the market value of your ownership interest and the source of funds you used to acquire the interest.
    (b) If others also have an ownership interest, state their names, the nature of their interest, and their relationship to you.

33. Have you ever sold any part of your ownership interests mentioned in 32(a)? If so, state what was sold, the names of the buyers, the dates of the sales, and the price or other consideration you received.

34. State the name and address of the following:
    (a) All accountants consulted during the last five years.
    (b) All attorneys consulted during the past five years.
    (c) Your stockbroker(s) during the past five years.
    (d) Your investment advisor(s) during the past five years.

VI. PERSONAL ASSETS

35. Give the name and address of every bank or other financial institution in which you wholly or partially own or once owned within the last five years any account offered by the bank or institution. Attach copies of the account statements for each account for the last six (6) months.

36. For each account listed in question 35, state the name and address of each co-owner.

37. For each account listed in question 35, state the current balance and, where applicable, the balance on the date of separation.

38. Within twelve (12) months prior to the date of separation, state the withdrawals you made from the accounts mentioned in your answer to question 35 and the purposes for such withdrawals.

39. Do you own or have access to the contents of a safe deposit box? If so, where is the box located? Itemize the contents of the box and itemize the withdrawals you have made from the box in the last three years.

40. Do you own or have a partial interest in cars, boats, or any other kind of vehicle? If so, describe each vehicle, when you obtained your interest, the purchase price, the amounts still owed, and the present location of said vehicles.

41. Do you own any jewelry that was purchased or that has a present value of $100 or more? If so, itemize each such piece of jewelry, indicating the circumstances of its purchase, its value, and its present location.

42. Itemize any personal property not mentioned in your answers to questions 35–41 (including but not limited to furnishings and collectibles) that has a value of over $300 that you own or in which you have an ownership interest.

43. Do you have a right to receive royalty income? If so, describe the source of your right and the amounts you have received from such royalties in the last three years.

44. Have you been a plaintiff in a lawsuit in any court in the last 10 years? If so, state the cause(s) of action asserted in the suit, the court(s) involved, the damages or other relief you sought, the outcome of the proceedings, and the names of the attorney(s) who represented you.

45. If any suit mentioned in question 44 is still pending, answer all parts of the question except for the outcome.

46. At any time during the marriage, did you receive any prize or gambling awards of over $100 in cash or value? If so, for each such prize or award, describe what you received, the date received, and the payor.

VII. SECURITIES, INHERITANCE, AND GIFTS

47. Do you currently own any securities not covered in previous interrogatories?
    (a) If so, for each security (as defined below), describe the security and your interest in it, the date of acquisition, the price paid, the source of the funds used to make the payment, the present value of the security, and the income currently derived from the security. Definition of security: A financial instrument that is evidence of a debt interest (e.g., a bond), an ownership/equity interest (e.g., a stock), or other specially defined rights (e.g., a futures contract).
    (b) Attach monthly statements on each security for the past five years.

48. In the last three years, have you sold, transferred, or exchanged any securities as defined in question 47? If so, for each sale, transfer, or exchange, state the nature of the transaction, the transaction date, and the price or other consideration received.

49. Does any person, institution, or organization owe you money or other assets, whether informally or as evidenced by instruments such as promissory notes, mortgages, accounts receivables, or other securities? If so, for each such debt, state its nature, amounts or values owed (whether principal, interest, or otherwise), and the terms of anticipated payment.

50. Did you receive any money or other asset by inheritance (will or intestate):
    (a) during the marriage?
    (b) before the marriage?
    (c) after the date of separation?
    (d) If so, for each inheritance listed in questions a through c, state what you received, the source, the date received, and what you did with what you received.

51. State (or estimate) the present market value of all noncash assets referred to in question 50.

52. For each gift you have made in the last five years in cash or other property in excess of $300, state the nature of the gift, the name and address of the recipient, the reason for the gift, and the date of the gift.

VIII. TRUSTS

53. Have you created a trust of any kind?
    (a) If so, for each trust, state the names of the beneficiaries, the names of the trustees, the amount in the trust (the corpus), and the major terms of the trust.
    (b) Attach a copy of each trust instrument.

54. Are any of the following the beneficiary of a trust: you, a member of your family, or any business or other entity in which you have an interest?
    (a) If so, for each trust, state the names of the beneficiaries, the names of the trustees, the amount in the trust (the corpus), and the major terms of the trust.
    (b) Attach a copy of each trust instrument and the most recent report or accounting statement received on the status of each trust.

IX. INSURANCE

55. What insurance policies do you have?
    (a) For each policy, state the kind of insurance, the name of the insurance company, the policy number, and, if applicable, the face amount of the policy, the premium, and the name of beneficiaries. Include life, disability, annuity, health, property, and any other kind of insurance.
    (b) On which of these policies do you have the right to change the beneficiaries?

56. Have you ever assigned any insurance policy? If so, provide the date, the name of the assignee(s), and the circumstances of each assignment.

57. Have you made a claim against an insurance policy in the last five years? If so, for each claim, state the date of the claim; the insurance company involved; and the action taken on your claim, including the monies you received on each claim.

X. LIABILITIES

58. List of all credit card balances on any card for which you have full or shared responsibility. For each card, state:
  (a) The name in which the card is listed and the names of all persons entitled to use the card.
  (b) The total amount currently due.
  (c) The total amount due on the date of the separation.
  (d) Attach copies of all credit card statements for the past twelve (12) months.

59. List any outstanding obligations, including mortgages, conditional sales contracts, contract obligations, promissory notes, or government agency loans not included in your answers to any previous interrogatory, stating for each:
  (a) The nature of the obligation.
  (b) The date(s) the obligation was incurred or renewed.
  (c) The names of each person responsible for payments in addition to yourself and the relationship of each person to you.
  (d) The name and address of each creditor and the creditor's relationship to you.
  (e) A description of any security or collateral given for the obligation.
  (f) The amount currently owed on the obligation.
  (g) The amount owed on the obligation on the date of separation.
  (h) The source(s) of the funds used to make payments on the obligation.

60. List all judgments outstanding against you or your spouse not included in your answer to a previous interrogatory, and for each state:
  (a) The names of the parties and their respective attorneys.
  (b) The courts in which the judgments were entered.
  (c) The amount of the judgment.
  (d) Attach a copy of the judgment.

61. List all pending suits against you or your spouse not included in your answer to a previous interrogatory, and for each, state:
  (a) The names of the parties and their respective attorneys.
  (b) The court in which the suit is pending.
  (c) The amount of the damages or other relief sought.
  (d) Attach a copy of the complaint.

62. List any lien or security interest not disclosed in a previous interrogatory to which any of your property or assets can be reached for payment. For each, state:
  (a) The name and address of the person or entity holding the lien or security interest.
  (b) The amount owed.

XI. ASSETS ACQUIRED BEFORE THE MARRIAGE

63. List the amount of cash not disclosed in prior interrogatories that you amassed before the marriage and that you brought into the marriage. For these amounts, state:
  (a) How it was obtained.
  (b) Where it was kept or deposited.
  (c) The extent to which your spouse had access to and could use it.
  (d) For what purposes all or part of it was spent.
  (e) The amount remaining on the date of separation.
  (f) The amount currently remaining.

64. List each asset valued over $300 not disclosed in prior interrogatories that you acquired before the marriage and that you brought into the marriage. For each asset, state:
    (a) The nature of the asset.
    (b) The source of the asset.
    (c) The funds used to acquire the asset.
    (d) The asset's market value on the date of the marriage.
    (e) The asset's market value on the date of the separation.
    (f) Your efforts that helped cause any appreciation.
    (g) Your spouse's efforts that helped cause any appreciation.

XII. ASSETS ACQUIRED DURING THE MARRIAGE

65. Explain the understanding of, and practice between, you and your spouse on the following matters:
    (a) Where monies earned by you would be deposited, whether your spouse had access to and could use the monies, and the extent to which your spouse did use any of them.
    (b) Where monies earned by your spouse would be deposited, whether you had access to and could use the monies, and the extent to which you did use any of them.

66. List each asset valued over $300 not disclosed in prior interrogatories that you, your spouse, or both acquired during the marriage. For each asset, state:
    (a) The nature of the asset.
    (b) The source of the asset.
    (c) The funds used to acquire the asset.
    (d) The asset's market value on the date of acquisition.
    (e) The asset's market value on the date of the separation.
    (f) The asset's current value.
    (g) Your efforts that helped cause any appreciation.
    (h) Your spouse's efforts that helped cause any appreciation.

67. List any gifts over the value of $300 received during the marriage by you, by your spouse, or by both of you not covered in prior interrogatories. For each gift, state:
    (a) The nature of the gift.
    (b) The amount or value of the gift on the date of receipt.
    (c) The source of the gift.
    (d) To whom the gift was given.
    (e) The gift's amount or market value on the date of the separation.
    (f) The current amount or market value of the gift.
    (g) Your efforts that helped cause any increase or appreciation.
    (h) Your spouse's efforts that helped cause any increase or appreciation.

68. List any inheritance over the value of $300 received during the marriage by you, by your spouse, or by both of you not covered in prior interrogatories. For each gift, state:
    (a) The nature of the inheritance.
    (b) The amount or value of the inheritance on the date of receipt.
    (c) The source of the inheritance.
    (d) To whom the inheritance was given.
    (e) Inheritance's amount or market value on the date of the separation.
    (f) Inheritance's current amount or market value.
    (g) Your efforts that helped cause any increase or appreciation.
    (h) Your spouse's efforts that helped cause any increase or appreciation.

XIII. ASSETS ACQUIRED AFTER THE SEPARATION

69. List the amount of cash not disclosed in prior interrogatories that you amassed after the date of separation. For this amount, state:
    (a) How it was obtained.
    (b) The extent to which your spouse had access to and could use it.
    (c) For what purposes all or part of it was spent.
    (d) The amount currently remaining.

70. List each asset valued over $300 not disclosed in prior interrogatories that you acquired after the date of separation. For each asset, state:
    (a) The nature of the asset.
    (b) The source of the asset.
    (c) The funds used to acquire the asset.
    (d) Asset's current market value.
    (e) Your efforts that helped cause any appreciation.
    (f) Your spouse's efforts that helped cause any appreciation.

XIV. MISCELLANEOUS

71. If you have prepared a financial statement of your assets and liabilities, either individually or for any business in which you have an interest within the past five years, state:
    (a) The dates of all such statements.
    (b) The name and address of the person, firm, company, partnership, corporation, or entity for whom they were prepared.
    (c) The name and address of all persons who worked on the preparation of such statements.
    (d) Attach copies of all such financial statements.

72. State whether you have made application for loan(s) with any individual, lending institutions, or other entity during the past five years. If so, state for each:
    (a) The name and address of the individual, lending institution, or other entity.
    (b) The date of the application.
    (c) The amount of the loan request.
    (d) Whether your application was approved or denied and in what amount.
    (e) Attach a copy of all such loan applications.

73. State what counsel fees you have paid or agreed to pay for services rendered in connection with the separation of the parties and the names of the attorney(s) to whom such fees have been paid or are owed.

APPENDIX D

Family Law in Your State

ALABAMA FAMILY LAW

Alabama Family Laws
- statelaws.findlaw.com/alabama-law/alabama-family-laws.html

Alabama Family Code/Domestic Relations Code
- law.onecle.com/alabama (click title 30)

Alabama Family Court
- www.alacourt.gov/FamilyCourtInfo.aspx
- montgomery.alacourt.gov/family-court

Alabama Marriage Law (formation)
- marriage.about.com/cs/marriagelicenses/p/alabama.htm
- www.law.cornell.edu/wex/table_marriage
- usmarriagelaws.com (enter your state or county)

Alabama Premarital Agreement Law
- Ala. Code § 321
- marriage.uslegal.com/permarital-agreements

Alabama Common Law Marriage
- See Exhibit 5-3 in Chapter 5.
- Ala. Code § 30-1-20
- www.buddybuddy.com/common.html
- www.unmarried.org/common-law-marriage-fact-sheet
- topics.law.cornell.edu/wex/table_marriage

Alabama Divorce Law
- Ala. Code § 30-2-1
- www.hg.org/divorce-law-alabama.html
- www.alabamalegalhelp.org/issues/families-and-children/divorce
- www.divorcelawinfo.com/states/AL/alabama.htm

Alabama Legal Separation Law
- Ala. Code § 30-2-40
- www.hg.org/divorce-law-alabama.html#7

Alabama Property Division Law
- www.divorcelawinfo.com/states/AL/alabama.htm

Alabama Child Custody Law
- Ala. Code § 30-3-160
- www.alabamalegalhelp.org/issues/families-and-children/custody

Alabama Relocation of Child
- Ala. Code § 30-3-163

Alabama Guardian Ad Litem and Attorney for Child
- Ala. Code §§ 26-14-11, 12-15-304
- www.childwelfare.gov/pubPDFs/represent.pdf

Alabama Child Support Law
- www.alacourt.gov/ChildSupportInfo.aspx
- www.alabamalegalhelp.org/issues/families-and-children/child-support

Alabama Paternity Law
- www.alabamalegalhelp.org/issues/families-and-children/paternity
- www.uslegalforms.com/paternity

Alabama Adoption Law
- Ala. Code, § 26-10A-1
- www.childwelfare.gov/pubPDFs/parties.pdf
- www.alabamalegalhelp.org/issues/families-and-children/adoption

Alabama Termination of Parental Rights
- Ala. Code § 12-15-319
- www.childwelfare.gov/pubPDFs/groundtermin.pdf

Alabama Putative Father Registry
- Ala. Code, § 26-10C-1
- www.ncsl.org/documents/cyf/putative_father_registries.pdf
- dhr.alabama.gov/services/Adoption/How_to_register.aspx
- adoption.about.com/od/adoptionrights/p/alabamafather.htm

Alabama Emancipation Law
- Ala. Code. § 26-13-1
- www.law.cornell.edu/wex/table_emancipation

Alabama Age of Majority
- Ala. Code § 26-1-1

Alabama Child Protection/Protective Services
- Ala. Code, § 26-14-3
- dhr.alabama.gov/services/Child_Protective_Services/Child_Protective_Services.aspx

Alabama Juvenile Law
- www.alacourt.gov/FamilyCourtInfo.aspx
- www.ncjj.org/pdf/1State_Juvenile_Justice_Profiles_2005.pdf
- www.alabamalegalhelp.org/issues/families-and-children/juveniles

Alabama Domestic Violence
- www.alabamalegalhelp.org/issues/families-and-children/domestic-violence
- www.domesticshelters.org/help/al

Alabama Surrogacy Law
- Ala. Code §§ 26-10A-34
- www.selectsurrogate.com/surrogacy-laws-by-state.html

Alabama Grandparent Rights
- Ala. Code §§ 30-3-4.1
- www.verywellfamily.com/grandparent-visitation-rights-state-by-state-1695938

Alabama Annulment Law
- www.hg.org/divorce-law-alabama.html

Alabama Family Law Forms
- eforms.alacourt.gov
- family.findlaw.com/divorce/divorce-forms-by-state.html
- www.uslegalforms.com/divorce/alabama-divorce-forms.htm?auslf=woman

Alabama Vital Records (Birth, Marriage, Divorce, Death)
- publicrecords.onlinesearches.com/Alabama.htm
- www.courtreference.com/Alabama-Courts.htm
- www.cdc.gov/nchs/w2w/alabama.htm
- www.cdc.gov/nchs/w2w.htm

Alabama Self-Help Services in Family Law Cases
- www.alabamalegalhelp.org
- www.courtreference.com/Alabama-Courts-Self-Help.htm

Alabama Legal Research on Family Law and Other Topics
- www.loc.gov/law/help/guide/states/us-al.php
- caselaw.findlaw.com/alabama.html

Alabama Court System
- judicial.alabama.gov

Alabama Legislature
- www.legislature.state.al.us/aliswww/default.aspx

Alabama Court Rules
- judicial.alabama.gov/Library/RulesOfCourt

Alabama Job Discrimination Based on Marital Status or Gender
- www.ncsl.org/documents/employ/DiscriminationChart-III.pdf

Google, Bing, or Yahoo Searches on Alabama Family Law
- "Alabama family law"
- "Alabama divorce"
- Alabama "property division"
- "Alabama adoption"
- Alabama paternity
- Alabama "child custody"
- Alabama "child support"
- Alabama abortion
- Alabama marriage
- Alabama "separation agreement"
- Alabama "premarital agreement"
- (also try these searches in the *Articles* and *Case law* databases of Scholar.google.com)

ALASKA FAMILY LAW

Alaska Family Laws
- statelaws.findlaw.com/alaska-law/alaska-family-laws.html

Alaska Family Code/Domestic Relations Code
- www.touchngo.com/lglcntr/akstats/Statutes/Title25/Chapter24.htm
- www.law.cornell.edu/wex/table_family

Alaska Marriage Law (formation)
- codes.findlaw.com/ak/title-25-marital-and-domestic-relations
- usmarriagelaws.com (enter your state or county)
- topics.law.cornell.edu/wex/table_marriage
- www.touchngo.com/lglcntr/akstats/Statutes/Title25/Chapter05.htm
- marriage.about.com/cs/marriagelicenses/p/alaska.htm

Alaska Premarital Agreement Law
- www.divorcenet.com/resources/prenuptial-agreements-alaska.html
- marriage.uslegal.com/permarital-agreements

Alaska Common Law Marriage
- www.law.cornell.edu/wex/table_marriage
- www.buddybuddy.com/common.html

Alaska Divorce Law
- www.courts.alaska.gov/shc/family/shcstart.htm
- www.hg.org/divorce-law-alaska.html
- www.divorcelawinfo.com/states/alaska/alaska.htm
- www.alaskalawhelp.org (under *Family*, click *Divorce*)

Alaska Discovery and Disclosure in Divorce
- courts.alaska.gov/shc/family/property.htm
- www.courts.alaska.gov/shc/family/docs/shc-185n.pdf

Alaska Legal Separation Law
- Alaska Stat. § 25.24.410
- www.hg.org/divorce-law-alaska.html#7

Alaska Alimony/Spousal Support/Maintenance Law
- Alaska Stat. § 25.24.160

Alaska Property Division Law
- Alaska Stat. § 25.24.160
- courts.alaska.gov/shc/family/property.htm
- www.hg.org/divorce-law-alaska.html

Alaska Child Custody Law
- Alaska Stat. § 25.20.090
- www.courts.alaska.gov/shc/family/shccustody.htm

- www.courts.alaska.gov/shc/family/jurisdictionfaq.htm
- www.divorcelawinfo.com/states/alaska/alaska.htm
- www.hg.org/divorce-law-alaska.html
- www.alaskalawhelp.org (click *Family* and *Divorce*)

Alaska Guardian Ad Litem and Attorney for Child
- Alaska Stat. § 47.10.050
- www.alaskalawhelp.org (click *Family* and *Divorce*)
- www.childwelfare.gov/pubPDFs/represent.pdf

Alaska Child Support Law
- childsupport.alaska.gov
- www.courts.alaska.gov/shc/family/shcins.htm

Alaska Paternity Law
- Alaska Stats. § 25.27.040; § 18.50.165
- www.courts.alaska.gov/shc/family/shcpaternity.htm
- www.divorcenet.com/resources/paternity-alaska.html
- www.uslegalforms.com/paternity

Alaska Adoption Law
- Alaska Stat. Ann. §§ 25.23.010 et seq.
- www.childwelfare.gov/pubPDFs/parties.pdf
- www.courts.alaska.gov/forms/index.htm#adopt
- www.alaskalawhelp.org (click *Family* and *More Issues*)

Alaska Termination of Parental Rights
- Alaska Stat. § 47.10.088
- www.law.cornell.edu/wex/table_emancipation
- www.childwelfare.gov/pubPDFs/groundtermin.pdf

Alaska Putative Fathers
- www.ncsl.org/documents/cyf/putative_father_registries.pdf

Alaska Emancipation Law
- Alaska Stat. Ann. § 09.55.590

Alaska Age of Majority
- Alaska Stat. Ann. § 25.20.010

Alaska Child in Need of Aid Rules
- touchngo.com/lglcntr/akstats/Statutes/Title47/Chapter10/Section011.htm

Alaska Juvenile Law
- alaskalawhelp.org/issues/family-and-life-planning/termination-of-parents-rights
- www.ncjj.org/pdf/1State_Juvenile_Justice_Profiles_2005.pdf

Alaska Domestic Violence Law
- courts.alaska.gov/shc/shcdv.htm
- www.andvsa.org
- alaskalawhelp.org

Alaska Surrogacy Law
- www.selectsurrogate.com/surrogacy-laws-by-state.html

Alaska Grandparent Rights
- www.courts.alaska.gov/shc/family/shcgrandparent.htm
- alaskalawhelp.org/search?q=grandparents
- www.verywellfamily.com/grandparent-visitation-rights-state-by-state-1695938

Alaska Annulment Law
- Alaska Stat. Ann. § 25.05.031
- www.touchngo.com/lglcntr/akstats/Statutes/Title25/Chapter05.htm
- www.hg.org/divorce-law-alaska.html

Alaska Family Law Forms
- www.courts.alaska.gov/shc/family/shcforms.htm
- family.findlaw.com/divorce/divorce-forms-by-state.html

Alaska Vital Records (Birth, Marriage, Divorce, Death)
- publicrecords.onlinesearches.com/Alaska.htm
- www.cdc.gov/nchs/w2w/alaska.htm
- www.cdc.gov/nchs/w2w.htm

Alaska Self-Help Services in Family Law Cases
- www.courts.alaska.gov/shc/family/shcabout.htm
- www.courts.alaska.gov/shc/family/selfhelp.htm
- alaskalawhelp.org

Alaska State Legal Research
- courts.alaska.gov/library/aklegal.htm
- www.loc.gov/law/help/guide/states/us-ak.php

Alaska Court Rules
- courts.alaska.gov/rules/index.htm
- www.llrx.com/courtrules-gen/state-Alaska.html

Alaska Job Discrimination Based on Marital Status or Gender
- www.ncsl.org/documents/employ/DiscriminationChart-III.pdf

Google, Bing, or Yahoo Searches on Alaska Family Law
- "Alaska family law"
- "Alaska divorce"
- Alaska "property division"
- "Alaska adoption"
- Alaska paternity
- Alaska "child custody"
- Alaska "child support"
- Alaska abortion
- Alaska marriage
- Alaska "separation agreement"
- Alaska "premarital agreement"
- (also try these searches in the *Articles* and *Case law* databases of Scholar.google.com)

ARIZONA FAMILY LAW

Arizona Family Laws
- statelaws.findlaw.com/arizona-law/arizona-family-laws.html

Arizona Family Code/Domestic Relations Code
- www.azleg.gov/arstitle (click *Title 25*)
- www.law.cornell.edu/wex/table_family
- www.azleg.gov

Arizona Courts: Family Department
- superiorcourt.maricopa.gov/family

Arizona Marriage Law (formation)
- marriage.about.com/cs/marriagelicenses/p/arizona.htm
- usmarriagelaws.com (enter your state or county)
- www.law.cornell.edu/wex/table_marriage

Arizona Premarital Agreement Law
- Ariz. Rev. Stat. § 25-201
- marriage.uslegal.com/permarital-agreements

Arizona Common Law Marriage
- topics.law.cornell.edu/wex/table_marriage
- www.buddybuddy.com/common.html

Arizona Covenant Marriage
- Ariz. Rev. Stat. § 25-901
- www.azlawhelp.org (enter *covenant marriage* in the search box)

Arizona Divorce Law
- www.divorcelawinfo.com/states/az/arizona.htm
- www.hg.org/divorce-law-arizona.html
- www.azlawhelp.org/documents/SelfServiceDivorceGuide.pdf
- www.azlawhelp.org/documents/azlawhelp_Divorce.pdf

Arizona Legal Separation
- Ariz. Rev. Stat. § 25-313
- www.hg.org/divorce-law-arizona.html#8

Arizona Property Division Law
- Ariz. Rev. Stat. § 25-318
- www.hg.org/divorce-law-arizona.html

Arizona Child Custody Law
- Ariz. Rev. Stat. § 25-403
- www.hg.org/divorce-law-arizona.html
- www.azlawhelp.org (enter *child custody* in the search box)

Arizona Guardian Ad Litem and Attorney for Child
- Ariz. Rev. Stat. §§ 8-523, 8-524
- Ariz. Rev. Stat. §§ 8-221; 25-321
- www.childwelfare.gov/pubPDFs/represent.pdf

Arizona Child Support Law
- www.azlawhelp.org (enter *child support* in the search box)
- www.supportguidelines.com/links.html

Arizona Paternity Law
- Ariz. Rev. Stat. § 25-812
- www.azlawhelp.org (Enter *paternity* in the search box.)
- www.uslegalforms.com/paternity/arizona-paternity-forms.htm

Arizona Adoption Law
- www.azleg.gov/ars/8/00103.htm
- www.azlawhelp.org (Enter *adoption* in the search box.)

Arizona Termination of Parental Rights
- Ariz. Rev. Stat. § 8-534
- www.childwelfare.gov/pubPDFs/groundtermin.pdf

Arizona Putative Father Registry
- Ariz. Rev. Stat. § 8-106.01
- www.courts.state.nh.us/probate/registrylist.pdf
- www.ncsl.org/documents/cyf/putative_father_registries.pdf

Arizona Emancipation Law
- Ariz. Rev. Stat. § 12-2451

Arizona Age of Majority
- Ariz. Rev. Stat. § 8-201(3)

Arizona Child Protection/Protective Services
- Ariz. Rev. Stat. § 8-800
- dcs.az.gov

Arizona Juvenile Law
- Ariz. Rev. Stat. §§ 8-201 et seq.
- azcourts.gov/PublicServices/JuvenileLaw.aspx
- www.ncjj.org/pdf/1State_Juvenile_Justice_Profiles_2005.pdf

Arizona Domestic Violence Law
- www.azcadv.org
- www.azcourts.gov/domesticviolencelaw/DomesticViolenceInformation.aspx

Arizona Premarital Agreement Law
- Ariz. Rev. Stat. § 25-201
- marriage.uslegal.com/permarital-agreements

Arizona Surrogacy Law
- Ariz. Rev. Stat. § 25-218
- www.selectsurrogate.com/surrogacy-laws-by-state.html

Arizona Grandparent Rights
- Ariz. Rev. Stat. § 25-409
- www.verywellfamily.com/grandparent-visitation-rights-state-by-state-1695938

Arizona Annulment Law
- Ariz. Rev. Stat. §§ 25-101, 25-302
- www.hg.org/divorce-law-arizona.html
- www.azlawhelp.org (enter *annulment* in the search box)

Arizona Family Law Forms
- www.azcourts.gov (type *divorce forms* in the search box)
- family.findlaw.com/divorce/divorce-forms-by-state.html

Arizona Vital Records (Birth, Marriage, Divorce, Death)
- www.cdc.gov/nchs/w2w.htm
- publicrecords.onlinesearches.com/Arizona.htm

Arizona Self-Help Services in Family Law Cases
- www.azcourts.gov (type *help* in the search box)
- www.azlawhelp.org

Arizona State Legal Research
- www.loc.gov/law/help/guide/states/us-az.php
- caselaw.findlaw.com/arizona.html

Arizona Court Rules
- government.westlaw.com/linkedslice/default.asp?SP=AZR-1000

Arizona Job Discrimination Based on Marital Status or Gender
- www.ncsl.org/documents/employ/DiscriminationChart-III.pdf

Google, Bing, or Yahoo Searches on Arizona Family Law
- "Arizona family law"
- "Arizona divorce"
- Arizona "property division"
- "Arizona adoption"
- Arizona paternity
- Arizona "child custody"
- Arizona "child support"
- Arizona abortion
- Arizona marriage
- Arizona "separation agreement"
- Alabama "premarital agreement"
- (also try these searches in the *Articles* and *Case law* databases of Scholar.google.com)

ARKANSAS FAMILY LAW

Arkansas Family Laws
- statelaws.findlaw.com/arkansas-law/arkansas-family-laws.html

Arkansas Family Code/Domestic Relations Code
- Ark. Code Ann. Title 9

Arkansas Marriage Law (formation)
- usmarriagelaws.com (enter your state or county)
- www.law.cornell.edu/wex/table_marriage

Arkansas Premarital Agreement Law
- Ark. Code Ann. § 9-11-402
- marriage.uslegal.com/permarital-agreements

Arkansas Common Law Marriage
- www.buddybuddy.com/common.html
- topics.law.cornell.edu/wex/table_marriage

Arkansas Covenant Marriage
- Ark. Code Ann. § 9-11-803
- www.arlegalservices.org/node/964/covenant-marriage

Arkansas Divorce Law
- Ark. Code Ann. § 9-12-301
- www.arlegalservices.org/node/1008/divorce

- www.divorcelawinfo.com/states/ark/arkansas.htm
- www.hg.org/divorce-law-arkansas.html

Arkansas Legal Separation Law
- Ark. Code Ann. § 9-11-808
- www.arlegalservices.org/node/931/legal-separation

Arkansas Alimony/Spousal Support Law
- Ark. Code Ann. § 9-12-312

Arkansas Property Division Law
- Ark. Code Ann. § 9-12-315
- www.hg.org/divorce-law-arkansas.html

Arkansas Child Custody Law
- Ark. Code Ann. § 9-13-101
- www.arlegalservices.org/node/912/child-custody-and-visitation

Arkansas Guardian Ad Litem and Attorney for Child
- Ark. Code Ann. § 9-27-316
- www.childwelfare.gov/pubPDFs/represent.pdf

Arkansas Child Support Law
- Ark. Code Ann. § 9-14-206
- www.arlegalservices.org/node/913/child-support-amounts-and-resources

Arkansas Paternity Law
- Ark. Code Ann. § 9-10-109
- www.dfa.arkansas.gov/child-support/custodial-party/paternity

Arkansas Legal Definition of Father
- Ark. Code Ann. § 20-18-701
- www.childwelfare.gov/systemwide/laws_policies/statutes/putative.pdf

Arkansas Adoption Law
- Ark. Code Ann. §§ 9-9-203 et seq.
- www.arlegalservices.org/node/906/adoption
- statelaws.findlaw.com/arkansas-law/arkansas-adoption-laws.html

Arkansas Termination of Parental Rights
- Ark. Code Ann. § 9-27-341
- www.childwelfare.gov/pubPDFs/groundtermin.pdf

Arkansas Putative Father Registry
- Ark. Code Ann. § 20-18-701
- www.arlegalservices.org/sites/default/files/putative-father-registry-pdf-form-by-arkansas-department-of-health-adh.pdf
- www.ncsl.org/documents/cyf/putative_father_registries.pdf

Arkansas Emancipation Law
- Ark. Code Ann. § 9-27-362
- www.arlegalservices.org/node/917/emancipation

Arkansas Age of Majority
- statelaws.findlaw.com/arkansas-law/arkansas-marriage-age-requirements-laws.html

Arkansas Child Protection/Protective Services
- humanservices.arkansas.gov/about-dhs/dcfs

Arkansas Child Welfare Agencies
- humanservices.arkansas.gov/about-dhs/dcfs

Arkansas Juvenile Law
- Ark. Code Ann. § 9-27-301
- www.ncjj.org/pdf/1State_Juvenile_Justice_Profiles_2005.pdf

Arkansas Domestic Violence Law
- Ark. Code Ann. § 9-15-103
- www.arlegalservices.org/node/965/domestic-violence

Arkansas Surrogacy Law
- Ark. Code Ann. § 9-10-201
- www.selectsurrogate.com/surrogacy-laws-by-state.html

Arkansas Grandparent Rights
- Ark. Code Ann. § 9-13-101
- www.verywellfamily.com/grandparent-visitation-rights-state-by-state-1695938

Arkansas Annulment Law
- Ark. Code Ann. § 9-11-105
- www.arlegalservices.org/node/907/annulment

Arkansas Family Law Forms
- www.arcourts.gov/forms-and-publications
- www.arlegalservices.org/node/1041/self-help-forms
- family.findlaw.com/divorce/divorce-forms-by-state.html

Arkansas Vital Records (Birth, Marriage, Divorce, Death)
- www.cdc.gov/nchs/w2w.htm
- publicrecords.onlinesearches.com/Arkansas.htm

Arkansas Self-Help Services in Family Law Cases
- www.arlegalservices.org/interactiveforms

Arkansas State Legal Research
- caselaw.findlaw.com/arkansas.html
- www.loc.gov/law/help/guide/states/us-ar.php

Arkansas Court Rules
- opinions.arcourts.gov/ark/cr/en/nav_date.do

Arkansas Job Discrimination Based on Marital Status or Gender
- www.ncsl.org/documents/employ/DiscriminationChart-III.pdf

Google, Bing, or Yahoo Searches on Arkansas Family Law
- "Arkansas family law"
- "Arkansas divorce"
- Arkansas "property division"
- "Arkansas adoption"
- Arkansas paternity
- Arkansas "child custody"
- Arkansas "child support"
- Arkansas abortion
- Arkansas marriage
- Arkansas "separation agreement"
- Arkansas "premarital agreement"
- (also try these searches in the *Articles* and *Case law* databases of Scholar.google.com)

CALIFORNIA FAMILY LAW

California Family Laws
- statelaws.findlaw.com/california-law/california-family-laws.html

California Family Code/Domestic Relations Code
- codes.findlaw.com/ca (Family Code)

California Family Court
- www.courts.ca.gov/ (enter "Family Court" in search box)

California Marriage Law (formation)
- Cal. Family Code §§ 300 et seq.
- usmarriagelaws.com (enter your state or county)

California Premarital Agreement Law
- Cal. Family Code § 1612
- marriage.uslegal.com/permarital-agreements

California Common Law Marriage
- topics.law.cornell.edu/wex/table_marriage
- www.buddybuddy.com/common.html

California Divorce Law
- Cal. Family Code § 2310
- www.courts.ca.gov/selfhelp-divorce.htm
- www.divorcelawinfo.com/states/ca/california.htm

California Legal Separation Law
- Cal. Family Code § 2310
- www.courts.ca.gov/selfhelp-divorce.htm

California Alimony/Spousal Support Law
- Cal. Family Code § 4330
- www.courts.ca.gov/1038.htm
- www.courts.ca.gov/9050.htm

California Community Property Division Law
- Cal. Family Code § 2550
- www.courts.ca.gov/1039.htm
- www.hg.org/divorce-law-california.html

California Child Custody Law
- Cal. Family Code § 3048
- www.courts.ca.gov/selfhelp-custody.htm

California Guardian Ad Litem and Attorney for Child
- www.childwelfare.gov/pubPDFs/represent.pdf

California Child Support Law
- Cal. Family Code §§ 4050 et seq.
- https://childsupport.ca.gov/

California Paternity Law
- Cal. Family Code § 7581
- www.courts.ca.gov/selfhelp-parentage.htm

California Legal Definition of Father
- Cal. Family Code §§ 7601, 7611
- www.childwelfare.gov/systemwide/laws_policies/statutes/putative.pdf

California Adoption Law
- Cal. Family Code § 8621
- www.courts.ca.gov/selfhelp-adoption.htm

California Termination of Parental Rights
- Cal. Welf. & Inst. Code § 366.26
- www.saccourt.ca.gov/family/parental-rights.aspx

California Putative Father Registry
- www.ncsl.org/documents/cyf/putative_father_registries.pdf

California Emancipation Law
- Cal. Family Code § 7820

California Age of Majority
- Cal. Family Code § 6500

California Child Protection/Protective Services
- www.cdss.ca.gov/Reporting/Report-Abuse/Child-Protective-Services

California Child Welfare Agencies
- www.childsworld.ca.gov
- https://cdss.ca.gov/inforesources/child-welfare-protection

California Juvenile Law
- www.courts.ca.gov/selfhelp-delinquency.htm
- www.cdcr.ca.gov/juvenile_justice/index.html
- www.ncjj.org/pdf/1State_Juvenile_Justice_Profiles_2005.pdf

California Domestic Violence Law
- Cal. Family Code §§ 6211 et seq.
- www.courts.ca.gov/selfhelp-domesticviolence.htm

California Assisted Reproduction/Surrogacy Law
- Cal. Family Code § 7606
- www.selectsurrogate.com/surrogacy-laws-by-state.html

California Grandparent Rights
- Cal. Family Code § 3047
- www.verywellfamily.com/grandparent-visitation-rights-state-by-state-1695938

California Annulment Law
- Cal. Family Code § 2210
- www.courts.ca.gov/1037.htm

California Family Law Forms
- www.courts.ca.gov/forms.htm
- family.findlaw.com/divorce/divorce-forms-by-state.html

California Vital Records (Birth, Marriage, Divorce, Death)
- publicrecords.onlinesearches.com/California.htm
- www.cdc.gov/nchs/w2w.htm

California Self-Help Services in Family Law Cases
- www.courts.ca.gov/selfhelp.htm
- www.courts.ca.gov/formsrules.htm

California State Legal Research
- www.loc.gov/law/help/guide/states/us-ca.php
- caselaw.findlaw.com/california.html

California Court Rules
- www.courts.ca.gov/rules.htm

California Job Discrimination Based on Marital Status or Gender
- www.ncsl.org/documents/employ/DiscriminationChart-III.pdf

Google, Bing, or Yahoo Searches on California Family Law
- "California family law"
- "California divorce"
- California "property division"
- "California adoption"
- California paternity
- California "child custody"
- California "child support"
- California abortion
- California marriage
- California "separation agreement"
- California "premarital agreement"
- (also try these searches in the *Articles* and *Case law* databases of Scholar.google.com)

COLORADO FAMILY LAW

Colorado Family Laws
- statelaws.findlaw.com/colorado-law/colorado-family-laws.html

Colorado Family Code/Domestic Relations Code
- Colo. Rev. Stat. Ann. Title 14

Colorado Marriage Law (formation)
- Colo. Rev. Stat. Ann. § 14-2-104
- usmarriagelaws.com (enter your state or county)

Colorado Premarital Agreement Law
- Colo. Rev. Stat. Ann. § 14-2-310
- marriage.uslegal.com/permarital-agreements

Colorado Common Law Marriage
- See Exhibit 5-3 in Chapter 5.
- Colo. Rev. Stat. Ann. § 14-2-109.5
- www.buddybuddy.com/common.html
- www.unmarried.org/common-law-marriage-fact-sheet

Colorado Divorce/Dissolution Law
- Colo. Rev. Stat. Ann. § 14-10-101
- www.courts.state.co.us/Forms/SubCategory.cfm?Category=Divorce
- www.divorcelawinfo.com/states/co/colorado.htm
- www.hg.org/divorce-law-colorado.html

Colorado Legal Separation Law
- Colo. Rev. Stat. Ann. § 14-10-106

Colorado Property Division Law
- Colo. Rev. Stat. § 14-10-113
- www.hg.org/divorce-law-colorado.html

Colorado Child Custody Law
- Colo. Rev. Stat. Ann. § 14-10-124
- www.courts.state.co.us/Forms/SubCategory.cfm?Category=Divorce

Colorado Guardian Ad Litem and Attorney for Child
- Colo. Rev. Stat. § 19-1-111
- www.childwelfare.gov/pubPDFs/represent.pdf

Colorado Child Support Law
- Colo. Rev. Stat. §§ 14-10-115
- www.courts.state.co.us/Forms/SubCategory.cfm?Category=Divorce

Colorado Paternity Law
- Colo. Rev. Stat. § 19-4-105
- www.courts.state.co.us/Forms/Forms_List.cfm?Form_Type_ID=81
- www.courts.state.co.us/Forms/SubCategory.cfm?Category=Divorce

Colorado Legal Definition of Father
- Colo. Rev. Stat. § 19-4-105
- www.ncsl.org/documents/cyf/putative_father_registries.pdf

Colorado Adoption Law
- Colo. Rev. Stat. § 19-4-201
- www.courts.state.co.us/Self_Help/adoption

Colorado Termination of Parental Rights
- Colo. Rev. Stat. § 9-5-105
- www.childwelfare.gov/pubPDFs/groundtermin.pdf

Colorado Emancipation Law
- Colo. Rev. Stat. § 13-21-107.5

Colorado Age of Majority
- statelaws.findlaw.com/colorado-law/colorado-legal-ages-laws.html

Colorado Child Protection/Protective Services
- https://www.colorado.gov/pacific/cdhs/child-welfare-0

Colorado Child Welfare Agencies
- www.colorado.gov/pacific/cdhs/child-welfare-0

Colorado Juvenile Law
- www.colorado.gov/pacific/cdhs/justice-services
- www.ncjj.org/pdf/1State_Juvenile_Justice_Profiles_2005.pdf

Colorado Domestic Violence Law
- Colo. Rev. Stat. § 18-6-800.3
- www.womenslaw.org/laws_state.php?state_code=CO

Colorado Grandparent Rights
- Colo. Rev. Stat. §§ 19-1-117
- www.verywellfamily.com/grandparent-visitation-rights-state-by-state-1695938

Colorado Annulment Law
- Colo. Rev. Stat. Ann. § 14-2-110
- https://www.courts.state.co.us/Forms/Forms_List.cfm?Form_Type_ID=84

Colorado Family Law Forms
- www.courts.state.co.us/Self_Help/Index.cfm
- www.courts.state.co.us/Forms/SubCategory.cfm?Category=Divorce
- family.findlaw.com/divorce/divorce-forms-by-state.html

Colorado Vital Records (Birth, Marriage, Divorce, Death)
- publicrecords.onlinesearches.com/Colorado.htm
- www.cdc.gov/nchs/w2w.htm

Colorado Self-Help Services in Family Law Cases
- www.courts.state.co.us/Self_Help/resources.cfm
- www.coloradolegalhelpcenter.us

Colorado State Legal Research
- www.loc.gov/law/help/guide/states/us-co.php
- caselaw.findlaw.com/colorado.html

Colorado Court Rules
- www.courts.state.co.us/Courts/Supreme_Court/Rule_Changes.cfm

Colorado Job Discrimination Based on Marital Status or Gender
- www.ncsl.org/documents/employ/DiscriminationChart-III.pdf

Google, Bing, or Yahoo Searches on Colorado Family Law
- "Colorado family law"
- "Colorado divorce"
- Colorado "property division"
- "Colorado adoption"
- Colorado paternity
- Colorado "child custody"
- Colorado "child support"
- Colorado abortion
- Colorado marriage
- Colorado "separation agreement"
- Colorado "premarital agreement"
- (also try these searches in the *Articles* and *Case law* databases of Scholar.google.com)

CONNECTICUT FAMILY LAW

Connecticut Family Laws
- statelaws.findlaw.com/connecticut-law/connecticut-family-laws.html

Connecticut Family Code/Domestic Relations Code
- Conn. Gen. Stats. Chapter 815
- www.jud.state.ct.us/lawlib/statutes.htm

Connecticut Premarital Agreement
- Conn. Gen. Stats. § 46b-36g
- www.jud.ct.gov/lawlib/Law/premarital.htm
- marriage.uslegal.com/permarital-agreements

Connecticut Marriage Law (formation)
- Conn. Gen. Stats. § 46b-20a
- www.jud.ct.gov/lawlib/law/marriage.htm
- usmarriagelaws.com (enter your state or county)
- www.law.cornell.edu/wex/table_marriage

Connecticut Cohabitation Law
- www.jud.ct.gov/lawlib/law/cohabitation.htm

Connecticut Divorce Law
- Conn. Gen. Stats. § 46b-40
- www.jud.ct.gov/forms/grouped/family/divorce.htm

- www.jud.ct.gov/lawlib/law/divorce.htm
- www.hg.org/divorce-law-connecticut.html

Connecticut Legal Separation Law
- Conn. Gen. Stats. § 46b-40
- www.jud.ct.gov/lawlib/law/separation.htm

Connecticut Alimony Law
- Conn. Gen. Stats. § 46b-82
- www.jud.ct.gov/lawlib/law/alimony.htm

Connecticut Property Division Law
- Conn. Gen. Stats. § 46b-81
- jud.ct.gov/LawLib/Notebooks/Pathfinders/EquitableDistribution.pdf

Connecticut Child Custody Law
- Conn. Gen. Stats. §§ 46b-56 et seq.
- www.jud.ct.gov/lawlib/law/custody.htm

Connecticut Parental Kidnapping Law
- www.jud.ct.gov/lawlib/law/parentalkidnapping.htm

Connecticut Relocation of Child
- Conn. Gen. Stats. § 46b-56d
- www.jud.ct.gov/lawlib/law/partrelocation.htm

Connecticut Guardian Ad Litem and Attorney for Child
- www.jud.ct.gov/lawlib/law/guardianship.htm
- www.childwelfare.gov/pubPDFs/represent.pdf

Connecticut Child Support Law
- Conn. Gen. Stats. § 36b-37
- www.jud.ct.gov/lawlib/law/childsupport.htm

Connecticut Paternity Law
- Conn. Gen. Stats. § 46b-160
- www.jud.ct.gov/lawlib/law/paternity.htm

Connecticut Legal Definition of Father
- Conn. Gen Stat. § 45a-604
- www.ncsl.org/documents/cyf/putative_father_registries.pdf

Connecticut Adoption Law
- Conn. Gen Stat. § 45a-707
- www.jud.ct.gov/lawlib/law/adoption.htm

Connecticut Termination of Parental Rights
- Conn. Gen Stat. § 45a-717
- www.jud.ct.gov/lawlib/law/tpr.htm
- www.childwelfare.gov/pubPDFs/groundtermin.pdf
- www.childwelfare.gov/pubPDFs/groundtermin.pdf

Connecticut Emancipation Law
- www.jud.ct.gov/lawlib/law/emancipation.htm
- www.jud.ct.gov/lawlib/law/minors.htm

Connecticut Child Protection/Protective Services
- www.ct.gov/ocpd/cwp/view.asp?a=4117&Q=481642&ocpdNav=|

Connecticut Child Welfare Agencies
- www.ct.gov/dcf/site/default.asp

Connecticut Juvenile Law
- www.jud.ct.gov/lawlib/law/minors.htm
- www.ct.gov/opm/cwp/view.asp?A=2974&Q=383628
- www.ncjj.org/pdf/1State_Juvenile_Justice_Profiles_2005.pdf

Connecticut Domestic Violence Law
- www.jud.ct.gov/lawlib/Law/domesticviolence.htm

Connecticut Surrogacy Law
- *Doe v. Doe*, 710 A.2d 1297 (Conn. 1998)
- www.selectsurrogate.com/surrogacy-laws-by-state.html

Connecticut Grandparent Rights
- Conn. Gen. Stats. § 46b-59
- www.jud.ct.gov/lawlib/law/grandparent.htm
- www.verywellfamily.com/grandparent-visitation-rights-state-by-state-1695938

Connecticut Annulment Law
- Conn. Gen. Stats. § 46b-40
- www.jud.ct.gov/lawlib/law/annulment.htm

Connecticut Domestic Tort Law
- www.jud.ct.gov/lawlib/law/domestic_torts.htm

Connecticut Parental Liability for Acts of Minors
- www.jud.ct.gov/lawlib/law/domestic_torts.htm

Connecticut Family Law Forms
- www.jud.ct.gov/webforms/#FAMILY2
- family.findlaw.com/divorce/divorce-forms-by-state.html

Connecticut Vital Records (Birth, Marriage, Divorce, Death)
- www.cdc.gov/nchs/w2w.htm
- publicrecords.onlinesearches.com/Connecticut.htm
- www.cdc.gov/nchs/w2w.htm

Connecticut Self-Help Services in Family Law Cases
- www.jud.ct.gov/faq/represent.html
- www.jud.ct.gov/selfhelp.htm
- www.slsct.org

Connecticut Family Law Legal Research
- www.jud.ct.gov/lawlib/law
- www.jud.ct.gov/lawlib/law/famdiscovery.htm

Connecticut State Legal Research (general)
- caselaw.findlaw.com/connecticut.html
- www.loc.gov/law/help/guide/states/us-ct.php

Connecticut Family Support Magistrate Decisions
- www.jud.state.ct.us/lawlib/fsm.htm

Connecticut Court Rules
- www.jud.ct.gov/PB.htm

Connecticut Job Discrimination Based on Marital Status or Gender
- www.ncsl.org/documents/employ/DiscriminationChart-III.pdf

Google, Bing, or Yahoo Searches on Connecticut Family Law
- "Connecticut family law"
- "Connecticut divorce"
- Connecticut "property division"
- "Connecticut adoption"
- Connecticut paternity
- Connecticut "child custody"
- Connecticut "child support"
- Connecticut abortion
- Connecticut marriage
- Connecticut "separation agreement"
- Connecticut "premarital agreement"
- (also try these searches in the *Articles* and *Case law* databases of Scholar.google.com)

DELAWARE FAMILY LAW

Delaware Family Laws
- statelaws.findlaw.com/delaware-law/delaware-family-laws.html

Delaware Family Code/Domestic Relations Code
- Del. Code Ann. Title 13
- delcode.delaware.gov/title13/c015/index.shtml
- www.law.cornell.edu/wex/table_family

Delaware Family Court
- courts.delaware.gov/family

Delaware Marriage Law (formation)
- 13 Del. Code Ann. 13, § 115
- usmarriagelaws.com (enter your state or county)
- delcode.delaware.gov/title13/c001/sc01/index.shtml
- www.law.cornell.edu/wex/table_marriage

Delaware Premarital Agreement Law
- 13 Del. Code Ann. § 321
- marriage.uslegal.com/permarital-agreements

Delaware Common Law Marriage
- topics.law.cornell.edu/wex/table_marriage
- www.buddybuddy.com/common.html

Delaware Divorce Law
- 13 Del. Code §§ 1501 et seq.
- courts.delaware.gov/forms/download.aspx?id=53648
- courts.delaware.gov/family/divorce
- www.divorcelawinfo.com/states/de/delaware.htm

Delaware Annulment Law
- 13 Del. Code § 1506
- courts.delaware.gov/forms/ownload.aspx?id=53648
- courts.delaware.gov/family/divorce
- delcode.delaware.gov/title13/c015/index.shtml

Delaware Alimony/Spousal Support Law
- 13 Del. Code § 1512
- www.maritallaws.com/states/delaware/alimony

Delaware Property Division Law
- 13 Del. Code § 1513
- www.maritallaws.com/states/delaware/property-division

Delaware Child Custody Law
- 13 Del. Code § 1920
- courts.delaware.gov/family/custody/answercustody.aspx
- courts.delaware.gov/family/custody
- courts.delaware.gov/family/legalcare.aspx

Delaware Guardian Ad Litem and Attorney for Child
- 29 Del. Code § 9007A
- www.childwelfare.gov/pubPDFs/represent.pdf

Delaware Child Support Law
- 13 Del. Code § 514
- courts.delaware.gov/family/support/index.aspx
- www.dhss.delaware.gov/dcse/index.html

Delaware Paternity Law
- 13 Del. Code § 8-3013
- www.childwelfare.gov/pubPDFs/putative.pdf
- www.dhss.delaware.gov/dcse/estpat.html

Delaware Legal Definition of Father
- 13 Del. Code § 8-102
- www.childwelfare.gov/pubPDFs/putative.pdf
- www.childwelfare.gov/systemwide/laws_policies/statutes/putative.pdf

Delaware Adoption Law
- 13 Del. Code § 903
- courts.delaware.gov/family/adoption

Delaware Termination of Parental Rights
- 13 Del. Code § 1103
- courts.delaware.gov/Family/tpr/index.aspx
- www.childwelfare.gov/pubPDFs/groundtermin.pdf

Delaware Putative Father Registry
- 13 Del. Code § 8-402
- www.ncsl.org/documents/cyf/putative_father_registries.pdf

Delaware Emancipation Law
- minors.uslegal.com/emancipation/delaware-emancipation-of-minor-law

Delaware Age of Majority
- 13 Del. Code § 701
- delcode.delaware.gov/title1/c007/index.shtml

Delaware Child Protection/Protective Services
- kids.delaware.gov/fs/fs_iseethesigns.shtml

Delaware Child Welfare Agencies
- kids.delaware.gov

Delaware Juvenile Law
- courts.delaware.gov/help/proceedings/fc_criminal.aspx#juvenile
- cjc.delaware.gov/juvenile-justice
- www.ncjj.org/pdf/1State_Juvenile_Justice_Profiles_2005.pdf

Delaware Domestic Violence Law
- 11 Del. Code § 3906
- courts.delaware.gov/family/pfa/index.aspx

Delaware Grandparent Rights
- 13 Del. Code § 2410
- www.verywellfamily.com/grandparent-visitation-rights-state-by-state-1695938

Delaware Family Law Forms
- courts.delaware.gov/family
- family.findlaw.com/divorce/divorce-forms-by-state.html

Delaware Vital Records (Birth, Marriage, Divorce, Death)
- www.cdc.gov/nchs/w2w.htm
- publicrecords.onlinesearches.com/Delaware.htm
- www.cdc.gov/nchs/w2w.htm

Delaware Self-Help Services in Family Law Cases
- courts.delaware.gov/Help
- courts.delaware.gov/family

Delaware State Legal Research
- www.loc.gov/law/help/guide/states/us-de.php
- caselaw.findlaw.com/delaware.html

Delaware Court Rules
- courts.delaware.gov/rules/index.aspx#family
- courts.delaware.gov/rules

Delaware Job Discrimination Based on Marital Status or Gender
- www.ncsl.org/documents/employ/DiscriminationChart-III.pdf

Google, Bing, or Yahoo Searches on Delaware Family Law
- "Delaware family law"
- "Delaware divorce"
- Delaware "property division"
- "Delaware adoption"

- Delaware paternity
- Delaware "child custody"
- Delaware "child support"
- Delaware abortion
- Delaware marriage
- Delaware "separation agreement"
- Delaware "premarital agreement"
- (also try these searches in the *Articles* and *Case law* databases of Scholar.google.com)

DISTRICT OF COLUMBIA FAMILY LAW

District of Columbia Family Laws
- statelaws.findlaw.com/dc-law/dc-family-laws.html

District of Columbia Family Code/Domestic Relations Code
- DC Code Title 46

District of Columbia Family Court
- www.dccourts.gov/services/family-matters

District of Columbia Marriage Law (formation)
- See Exhibit 5-3 in Chapter 5.
- usmarriagelaws.com (enter "Wash DC")
- www.unmarried.org/common-law-marriage-fact-sheet

District of Columbia Premarital Agreement Law
- DC Code § 46-501
- marriage.uslegal.com/permarital-agreements

District of Columbia Common Law Marriage
- *U.S. Fidelity v. Britton*, 269 F.2d 249 (C.A.D.C. 1959)
- www.buddybuddy.com/common.html

District of Columbia Divorce Law
- DC Code § 16-904
- www.dccourts.gov/services/divorce-matters
- www.lawhelp.org/dc (click Family Law)

District of Columbia Legal Separation Law
- DC Code § 16-904

District of Columbia Alimony/Spousal Support Law
- DC Code § 16-913
- www.lawhelp.org/dc (click Family Law)

District of Columbia Property Division Law
- DC Code § 16-910
- statelaws.findlaw.com/dc-law/district-of-columbia-marital-property-laws.html

District of Columbia Child Custody Law
- DC Code § 16-914
- www.lawhelp.org/dc (click Family Law)
- statelaws.findlaw.com/dc-law/district-of-columbia-child-custody-laws.html

District of Columbia Guardian Ad Litem and Attorney for Child
- DC Code § 16-2304
- www.childwelfare.gov/pubPDFs/represent.pdf

District of Columbia Child Support Law
- DC Code § 16-916.01
- www.lawhelp.org/dc (click Family Law)
- code.dccouncil.us/dc/council/code/sections/16-916.01.html

District of Columbia Paternity Law
- DC Code § 16-909
- paternity.uslegal.com/paternity-laws/district-of-columbia-paternity-law

District of Columbia Adoption Law
- DC Code § 16-304
- statelaws.findlaw.com/dc-law/district-of-columbia-adoption-laws.html
- www.dccourts.gov/services/family-matters/adoption

District of Columbia Termination of Parental Rights
- DC Code § 16-2353
- www.childwelfare.gov/pubPDFs/groundtermin.pdf

District of Columbia Putative Father Registry
- www.ncsl.org/documents/cyf/putative_father_registries.pdf

District of Columbia Age of Majority & Emancipation
- statelaws.findlaw.com/dc-law/district-of-columbia-legal-ages-laws.html

District of Columbia Child Protection/Protective Services
- cfsa.dc.gov/service/report-child-abuse-and-neglect

District of Columbia Child Welfare Agencies
- cfsa.dc.gov/DC/CFSA

District of Columbia Juvenile Law
- DC Code § 16-2301
- www.ncjj.org/pdf/1State_Juvenile_Justice_Profiles_2005.pdf

District of Columbia Domestic Violence Law
- DC Code §§ 16-1001 et seq.
- www.lawhelp.org/dc (click Family Law)

District of Columbia Surrogacy Law
- DC Code §16-401
- www.selectsurrogate.com/surrogacy-laws-by-state.html

District of Columbia Annulment Law
- DC Code § 16-904
- www.lawhelp.org/dc (click Family Law)

District of Columbia Family Law Forms
- www.dccourts.gov/services/forms
- family.findlaw.com/divorce/divorce-forms-by-state.html

District of Columbia Vital Records (Birth, Marriage, Divorce, Death)
- www.cdc.gov/nchs/w2w.htm
- publicrecords.onlinesearches.com/Districtofcolumbia.htm

District of Columbia Self-Help Services in Family Law Cases
- www.lawhelp.org/dc (click Family Law)

District of Columbia State Legal Research
- caselaw.findlaw.com/district-of-columbia.html
- www.loc.gov/law/help/guide/states/us-dc.php

District of Columbia Court Rules
- www.dccourts.gov/superior-court/rules

District of Columbia Job Discrimination Based on Marital Status or Gender
- www.ncsl.org/documents/employ/DiscriminationChart-III.pdf

Google, Bing, or Yahoo Searches on District of Columbia Family Law
- "District of Columbia family law"
- "District of Columbia divorce"

- District of Columbia "property division"
- "District of Columbia adoption"
- District of Columbia paternity
- District of Columbia "child custody"
- District of Columbia "child support"
- District of Columbia abortion
- District of Columbia marriage
- District of Columbia "separation agreement"
- District of Columbia "premarital agreement"
- (also try these searches in the *Articles* and *Case law* databases of Scholar.google.com)

FLORIDA FAMILY LAW

Florida Family Laws
- statelaws.findlaw.com/florida-law/florida-family-laws.html

Florida Family Code/Domestic Relations Code
- www.leg.state.fl.us/Statutes (scroll down to "Domestic Relations")

Florida Family Court
- www.flcourts.org/Resources-Services/Court-Improvement/Family-Courts/Family-Court-Basics2

Florida Marriage Law (formation)
- usmarriagelaws.com (enter your state or county)
- www.law.cornell.edu/wex/table_marriage

Florida Premarital Agreement Law
- Fla. Stat. § 61.079
- marriage.uslegal.com/permarital-agreements

Florida Common Law Marriage
- Fla. Stat. § 741.211
- www.buddybuddy.com/common.html

Florida Divorce Law
- Fla. Stat. § 61.052
- www.flcourts.org (click "Self-Help")
- www.hg.org/divorce-law-florida.html

Florida Alimony/Spousal Support Law
- Fla. Stat. § 61.08
- www.flcourts.org (click "Self-Help")
- www.hg.org/divorce-law-florida.html

Florida Legal Separation Law
- Fla. Stat. § 61.031

Florida Property Division Law
- Fla. Stat. § 61.075

Florida Child Custody Law
- Fla. Stat. §§ 61.13, 61.514
- www.flcourts.org (click "Self-Help")

Florida Relocation of Child
- Fla. Stat. § 61.13001

Florida Guardian Ad Litem and Attorney for Child
- Fla. Stat. § 39.822
- www.childwelfare.gov/pubPDFs/represent.pdf

Florida Child Support Law
- Fla. Stat. §§ 61.13, 61.29
- www.flcourts.org (click "Self-Help")

Florida Paternity Law
- Fla. Stat. § 742.10
- www.flcourts.org (click "Self-Help")

Florida Adoption Law
- Fla. Stat. § 63.012
- www.flcourts.org (click "Self-Help")

Florida Termination of Parental Rights
- Fla. Stat. § 39.806
- www.childwelfare.gov/pubPDFs/groundtermin.pdf

Florida Putative Father Registry
- Fla. Stat. § 63.054
- www.ncsl.org/documents/cyf/putative_father_registries.pdf

Florida Emancipation Law
- Fla. Stat. § 743.07

Florida Age of Majority
- Fla. Stat. § 743.07

Florida Child Protection/Protective Services
- www.myflfamilies.com

Florida Child Welfare Agencies
- www.myflfamilies.com

Florida Juvenile Law
- www.djj.state.fl.us
- www.ncjj.org/pdf/1State_Juvenile_Justice_Profiles_2005.pdf

Florida Domestic Violence Law
- Fla. Stat. § 741.28
- www.fcadv.org

Florida Grandparent Rights
- Fla. Stat. § 39.509
- www.verywellfamily.com/grandparent-visitation-rights-state-by-state-1695938

Florida Annulment Law
- Fla. Stat. § 741.21
- www.hg.org/divorce-law-Florida.html

Florida Family Law Forms
- www.flcourts.org (click "Family Law Forms")
- family.findlaw.com/divorce/divorce-forms-by-state.html

Florida Vital Records (Birth, Marriage, Divorce, Death)
- www.cdc.gov/nchs/w2w.htm
- publicrecords.onlinesearches.com/Florida.htm

Florida Self-Help Services in Family Law Cases
- www.flcourts.org (click "Self-Help")
- www.floridalawhelp.org

Florida State Legal Research
- caselaw.findlaw.com/florida.html
- www.loc.gov/law/help/guide/states/us-fl.php

Florida Court Rules
- www.flcourts.org/search/?query=court%20rules

Florida Job Discrimination Based on Marital Status or Gender
- www.ncsl.org/documents/employ/DiscriminationChart-III.pdf

Google, Bing, or Yahoo Searches on Florida Family Law
- "Florida family law"
- "Florida divorce"

- Florida "property division"
- "Florida adoption"
- Florida paternity
- Florida "child custody"
- Florida "child support"
- Florida abortion
- Florida marriage
- Florida "separation agreement"
- Florida "premarital agreement"
- (also try these searches in the *Articles* and *Case law* databases of Scholar.google.com)

GEORGIA FAMILY LAW

Florida Family Laws
- statelaws.findlaw.com/georgia-law/georgia-family-laws.html

Georgia Family Code/Domestic Relations Code
- Ga. Ann. Code Title 19

Georgia Marriage Law (formation)
- Ga. Code Ann., § 19-3-30
- usmarriagelaws.com (enter your state or county)

Georgia Premarital Agreement Law
- Ga. Ann. Code § 19-3-63
- marriage.uslegal.com/permarital-agreements

Georgia Common Law Marriage
- See Exhibit 5-3 in Chapter 5.
- Ga. Code Ann., § 19-3-1.1
- www.buddybuddy.com/common.html

Georgia Divorce Law
- Ga. Ann. Code § 19-5-3
- www.divorcelawinfo.com/states/ga/georgia.htm
- www.hg.org/divorce-law-Georgia.html

Georgia Separate Maintenance (Legal Separation) Law
- www.hg.org/divorce-law-Georgia.html

Georgia Alimony/Spousal Support Law
- Ga. Ann. Code § 19-6-1

Georgia Property Division Law
- Ga. Ann. Code § 19-3-9
- www.hg.org/divorce-law-Georgia.html
- www.divorcenet.com/states/georgia/ga_property

Georgia Child Custody Law
- Ga. Ann. Code § 19-9-1

Georgia Guardian Ad Litem and Attorney for Child
- Ga. Ann. Code §§ 15-11-15, 15-11-262
- www.childwelfare.gov/pubPDFs/represent.pdf

Georgia Child Support Law
- Ga. Ann. Code § 19-11-43
- childsupport.georgia.gov

Georgia Paternity Law
- Ga. Ann. Code § 19-7-43
- childsupport.georgia.gov/paternity-establishment

Georgia Legal Definition of Father
- Ga. Ann. Code § 19-8-1
- www.childwelfare.gov/systemwide/laws_policies/statutes/putative.pdf

Georgia Adoption Law
- Ga. Ann. Code §§ 19-8-3 et seq.

Georgia Termination of Parental Rights
- Ga. Ann. Code § 15-11-310
- www.childwelfare.gov/pubPDFs/groundtermin.pdf

Georgia Putative Father Registry
- dph.georgia.gov/putative-father-registry
- www.ncsl.org/documents/cyf/putative_father_registries.pdf

Georgia Emancipation Law
- Ga. Ann. Code § 15-11-725

Georgia Age of Majority
- statelaws.findlaw.com/georgia-law/georgia-legal-ages-laws.html

Georgia Child Protection/Protective Services
- dfcs.georgia.gov/services/child-abuse-neglect

Georgia Juvenile Law
- Ga. Ann. Code § 15-11-2
- www.djj.state.ga.us
- www.ncjj.org/pdf/1State_Juvenile_Justice_Profiles_2005.pdf

Georgia Interspousal Tort Immunity
- Ga. Ann. Code § 19-3-8

Georgia Domestic Violence Law
- Ga. Ann. Code § 19-13-1
- gcadv.org

Georgia Surrogacy Law
- www.surrogacy.com/legals/article/gaoverv.html

Georgia Grandparent Rights
- Ga. Ann. Code § 19-7-3
- www.verywellfamily.com/grandparent-visitation-rights-state-by-state-1695938

Georgia Annulment Law
- Ga. Ann. Code §§ 19-4-1 et seq.

Georgia Family Law Forms
- www.georgialegalaid.org/self-help-forms
- www.uslegalforms.com/familylaw/georgia
- family.findlaw.com/divorce/divorce-forms-by-state.html

Georgia Vital Records (Birth, Marriage, Divorce, Death)
- www.cdc.gov/nchs/w2w.htm
- publicrecords.onlinesearches.com/Georgia.htm

Georgia Self-Help Services in Family Law Cases
- www.georgialegalaid.org

Georgia State Legal Research
- caselaw.findlaw.com/georgia.html
- www.loc.gov/law/help/guide/states/us-ga.php

Georgia Court Rules
- www.gasupreme.us/rules

Georgia Job Discrimination Based on Marital Status or Gender
- www.ncsl.org/documents/employ/DiscriminationChart-III.pdf

Google, Bing, or Yahoo Searches on Georgia Family Law
- "Georgia family law"
- "Georgia divorce"

- Georgia "property division"
- "Georgia adoption"
- Georgia paternity
- Georgia "child custody"
- Georgia "child support"
- Georgia abortion
- Georgia marriage
- Georgia "separation agreement"
- Georgia "premarital agreement"
- (also try these searches in the *Articles* and *Case law* databases of Scholar.google.com)

HAWAII FAMILY LAW

Hawaii Family Laws
- statelaws.findlaw.com/hawaii-law/hawaii-family-laws.html

Hawaii Family Code/Domestic Relations Code
- Haw. Rev. Stat. Title 31
- www.law.cornell.edu/wex/table_family

Hawaii Family Court
- Haw. Rev. Stat. § 571-3
- www.courts.state.hi.us/courts/family/family_courts

Hawaii Marriage Law (formation)
- Haw. Rev. Stat. § 572-12
- usmarriagelaws.com (enter your state or county)
- www.law.cornell.edu/wex/table_marriage

Hawaii Premarital Agreement Law
- Haw. Rev. Stat. § 572D-11
- marriage.uslegal.com/permarital-agreements

Hawaii Common Law Marriage
- topics.law.cornell.edu/wex/table_marriage
- www.buddybuddy.com/common.html

Hawaii Divorce Law
- Haw. Rev. Stat. § 580-41
- www.lawhelp.org/hi (click Family)
- www.courts.state.hi.us/self-help/divorce/divorce
- www.courts.state.hi.us/self-help/help
- www.divorcelawinfo.com/states/hi/hawaii.htm

Hawaii Legal Separation Law
- Haw. Rev. Stat. § 580-71

Hawaii Alimony/Spousal Support Law
- Haw. Rev. Stat. § 580-47
- www.lawhelp.org/hi (click Family)

Hawaii Property Division Law
- Haw. Rev. Stat. §§ 510-9, 580-47
- www.lawhelp.org/hi (click Family)

Hawaii Child Custody Law
- Haw. Rev. Stat. § 571-46
- www.lawhelp.org/hi (click Family)

Hawaii Guardian Ad Litem and Attorney for Child
- Haw. Rev. Stat. § 587A-16
- www.childwelfare.gov/pubPDFs/represent.pdf

Hawaii Child Support Law
- Haw. Rev. Stat. § 576D-7
- hawaii.gov/ag/csea
- www.lawhelp.org/hi (click Family)

Hawaii Paternity Law
- Haw. Rev. Stat. § 584-4
- ag.hawaii.gov/csea/paternity

Hawaii Legal Definition of Father
- Haw. Rev. Stat. § 584-4
- www.childwelfare.gov/pubPDFs/putative.pdf

Hawaii Adoption Law
- Haw. Rev. Stat. § 578-8
- www.lawhelp.org/hi (click Family)

Hawaii Termination of Parental Rights
- Haw. Rev. Stat. § 571-61
- www.childwelfare.gov/pubPDFs/groundtermin.pdf

Hawaii Putative Father Registry
- None
- www.ncsl.org/documents/cyf/putative_father_registries.pdf

Hawaii Emancipation Law
- Haw. Rev. Stat. § 575-25

Hawaii Age of Majority
- Haw. Rev. Stat. § 577-1
- statelaws.findlaw.com/hawaii-law/hawaii-marriage-age-requirements-laws.html

Hawaii Child Protection/Protective Services
- humanservices.hawaii.gov/ssd

Hawaii Child Welfare Agencies
- humanservices.hawaii.gov/ssd/home/child-welfare-services

Hawaii Juvenile Law
- www.courts.state.hi.us/self-help/juvenile/juvenile_proceedings
- ag.hawaii.gov/cpja/jjis

Hawaii Domestic Violence Law
- Haw. Rev. Stat. § 321-471
- www.lawhelp.org/hi (click Family)
- www.hscadv.org

Hawaii Surrogacy Law
- Haw. Rev. Stat. § 327E-5
- www.selectsurrogate.com/surrogacy-laws-by-state.html

Hawaii Grandparent Rights
- Haw. Rev. Stat. § 571.46(a)(7)
- www.verywellfamily.com/grandparent-visitation-rights-state-by-state-1695938

Hawaii Annulment Law
- Haw. Rev. Stat. § 580-21

Hawaii Parental Liability for Acts of Minors
- Haw. Rev. Stat. § 577.3

Hawaii Family Law Forms
- www.courts.state.hi.us/self-help/help
- family.findlaw.com/divorce/divorce-forms-by-state.html

Hawaii Vital Records (Birth, Marriage, Divorce, Death)
- www.cdc.gov/nchs/w2w.htm
- publicrecords.onlinesearches.com/Hawaii.htm

Hawaii Self-Help Services in Family Law Cases
- www.courts.state.hi.us/self-help/help
- www.lawhelp.org/hi (click Family)

Hawaii State Legal Research
- www.loc.gov/law/help/guide/states/us-hi.php
- caselaw.findlaw.com/hawaii.html

Hawaii Court Rules
- www.courts.state.hi.us/legal_references/rules/rulesOfCourt

Hawaii Job Discrimination Based on Marital Status or Gender
- www.ncsl.org/documents/employ/DiscriminationChart-III.pdf

Google, Bing, or Yahoo Searches on Hawaii Family Law
- "Hawaii family law"
- "Hawaii divorce"
- Hawaii "property division"
- "Hawaii adoption"
- Hawaii paternity
- Hawaii "child custody"
- Hawaii "child support"
- Hawaii abortion
- Hawaii marriage
- Hawaii "separation agreement"
- Hawaii "premarital agreement"
- (also try these searches in the *Articles* and *Case law* databases of Scholar.google.com)

IDAHO FAMILY LAW

Idaho Family Laws
- statelaws.findlaw.com/idaho-law/idaho-family-laws.html

Idaho Family Code/Domestic Relations Code
- Idaho Code Ann. Title 32
- www.law.cornell.edu/wex/table_family

Idaho Family Court
- isc.idaho.gov/family-court/fc-home

Idaho Marriage Law (formation)
- See Exhibit 5-3 in Chapter 5
- Idaho Code Ann. § 32-202
- usmarriagelaws.com (enter your state or county)
- www.law.cornell.edu/wex/table_marriage

Idaho Premarital Agreement Law
- Idaho Code Ann. § 32-922
- marriage.uslegal.com/permarital-agreements

Idaho Common Law Marriage
- Idaho Code § 32-201
- topics.law.cornell.edu/wex/table_marriage
- www.buddybuddy.com/common.html
- www.unmarried.org/common-law-marriage-fact-sheet

Idaho Divorce Law
- Idaho Code Ann. § 26.09.030, § 32-601
- www.divorcelawinfo.com/states/id/idaho.htm
- www.hg.org/divorce-law-idaho.html

Idaho Legal Separation Law
- Idaho Code Ann. § 26.09.030
- www.hg.org/divorce-law-idaho.html

Idaho Alimony/Maintenance/Spousal Support Law
- Idaho Code Ann. § 32-705
- www.hg.org/divorce-law-idaho.html

Idaho Property Division Law
- Idaho Code Ann. § 32-712
- www.hg.org/divorce-law-idaho.html

Idaho Child Custody Law
- Idaho Code Ann. § 32-717

Idaho Guardian Ad Litem and Attorney for Child
- Idaho Code Ann. § 16-1614
- www.isc.idaho.gov/guardian/about-us
- www.childwelfare.gov/pubPDFs/represent.pdf

Idaho Child Support Law
- Idaho Code Ann. § 32-706
- www.healthandwelfare.idaho.gov

Idaho Paternity Law
- Idaho Code Ann. § 7-1116
- healthandwelfare.idaho.gov (enter "Paternity" in the search box)

Idaho Legal Definition of Father
- Idaho Code Ann. § 16-2002
- www.childwelfare.gov/systemwide/laws_policies/statutes/putative.pdf

Idaho Adoption Law
- Idaho Code Ann. § 16-1501
- statelaws.findlaw.com/idaho-law/idaho-adoption-laws.html

Idaho Termination of Parental Rights
- Idaho Code Ann. § 16-2005
- www.childwelfare.gov/pubPDFs/groundtermin.pdf

Idaho Putative Father Registry
- Idaho Code Ann. § 16-1513
- www.ncsl.org/documents/cyf/putative_father_registries.pdf

Idaho Emancipation Law
- Idaho Code Ann. § 32-101
- *Ireland v. Ireland*, 855 P.2d 40 (Id 1993)

Idaho Age of Majority
- Idaho Code Ann. § 32-101

Idaho Child Protection/Protective Services
- Idaho Code Ann. § 16-1605
- isc.idaho.gov/cp/manual/Idaho_CP_Manual-3rd_Edition.pdf
- healthandwelfare.idaho.gov/Children/AbuseNeglect/tabid/74/Default.aspx

Idaho Child Welfare Agencies
- healthandwelfare.idaho.gov/Children/tabid/57/Default.aspx

Idaho Juvenile Law
- isc.idaho.gov/ijr
- www.idjc.idaho.gov
- www.ncjj.org/pdf/1State_Juvenile_Justice_Profiles_2005.pdf

Idaho Domestic Violence Law
- Idaho Code Ann. § 18-918
- icdv.idaho.gov

Idaho Grandparent Rights
- Idaho Code Ann. § 32-719
- www.verywellfamily.com/grandparent-visitation-rights-state-by-state-1695938

Idaho Annulment Law
- Idaho Code Ann. § 32-501

Idaho Family Law Forms
- www.courtselfhelp.idaho.gov
- www.isc.idaho.gov/search/node/forms
- www.idaholegalaid.org/SelfHelp/family
- family.findlaw.com/divorce/divorce-forms-by-state.html
- www.idaholegalaid.org/node/2207/self-help-idaho-interactive-forms

Idaho Vital Records (Birth, Marriage, Divorce, Death)
- www.cdc.gov/nchs/w2w.htm
- publicrecords.onlinesearches.com/Idaho.htm

Idaho Self-Help Services in Family Law Cases
- www.courtselfhelp.idaho.gov
- www.idaholegalaid.org/node/2183/family-law-self-help-forms

Idaho State Legal Research
- www.isll.idaho.gov
- www.loc.gov/law/help/guide/states/us-id.php

Idaho Court Rules
- isc.idaho.gov/main/idaho-court-rules

Idaho Job Discrimination Based on Marital Status or Gender
- www.ncsl.org/documents/employ/DiscriminationChart-III.pdf

Google, Bing, or Yahoo Searches on Idaho Family Law
- "Idaho family law"
- "Idaho divorce"
- Idaho "property division"
- "Idaho adoption"
- Idaho paternity
- Idaho "child custody"
- Idaho "child support"
- Idaho abortion
- Idaho marriage
- Idaho "separation agreement"
- Idaho "premarital agreement"
- (also try these searches in the *Articles* and *Case law* databases of Scholar.google.com)

ILLINOIS FAMILY LAW

Illinois Family Laws
- statelaws.findlaw.com/illinois-law/illinois-family-laws.html

Illinois Family Code/Domestic Relations Code
- 750 Ill. Comp. Stat. Ann. § 5/101

Illinois Family Court
- www.19thcircuitcourt.state.il.us/1310/Family-Court

Illinois Marriage Law (formation)
- usmarriagelaws.com (enter your state or county)
- marriage.about.com/cs/marriagelicenses/p/illinois.htm
- www.law.cornell.edu/wex/table_marriage

Illinois Premarital Agreement Law
- 750 Ill. Comp. Stat. Ann. § 10/1
- marriage.uslegal.com/permarital-agreements

Illinois Common Law Marriage
- topics.law.cornell.edu/wex/table_marriage

Illinois Divorce Law
- 750 Ill. Comp. Stat. Ann. § 5/401
- www.divorcelawinfo.com/states/ill/illinois.htm
- www.hg.org/divorce-law-Illinois.html

Illinois Legal Separation Law
- 750 Ill. Comp. Stat. Ann. § 5/402
- www.hg.org/divorce-law-Illinois.html

Illinois Alimony/Spousal Support/Maintenance Law
- 750 Ill. Comp. Stat. Ann. § 5/504
- www.hg.org/divorce-law-Illinois.html

Illinois Property Division Law
- 750 Ill. Comp. Stat. Ann. § 5/503
- www.hg.org/divorce-law-Illinois.html

Illinois Child Custody Law
- 750 Ill. Comp. Stat. Ann. § 5/602.7
- www.hg.org/divorce-law-Illinois.html

Illinois Guardian Ad Litem and Attorney for Child
- 705 Ill. Comp. Stat. Ann. § 5/506
- www.childwelfare.gov/pubPDFs/represent.pdf

Illinois Child Support Law
- 705 Ill. Comp. Stat. Ann. § 46/801
- www.illinois.gov/hfs/ChildSupport/Pages/default.aspx

Illinois Paternity Law
- 750 Ill. Comp. Stat. Ann. § 46/201
- www.illinois.gov/hfs/ChildSupport/FormsBrochures/Pages/hfs3282.aspx

Illinois Legal Definition of Father
- 750 Ill. Comp. Stat. Ann. § 46/101
- www.ilga.gov/legislation/publicacts/99/099-0085.htm

Illinois Adoption Law
- 750 Ill. Comp. Stat. Ann. § 50/0.01
- statelaws.findlaw.com/illinois-law/illinois-adoption-laws.html

Illinois Termination of Parental Rights
- 750 Ill. Comp. Stat. Ann. § 50/17
- www.childwelfare.gov/pubPDFs/groundtermin.pdf

Illinois Putative Father Registry
- 750 Ill. Comp. Stat. Ann. 50/12.1
- www.ncsl.org/documents/cyf/putative_father_registries.pdf

Illinois Emancipation Law
- 750 Ill. Comp. Stat. Ann. § 30/1

Illinois Age of Majority
- minors.uslegal.com/age-of-majority/illinois-age-of-majority-law
- statelaws.findlaw.com/illinois-law/illinois-legal-ages-laws.html

Illinois Child Protection/Protective Services
- www.state.il.us/dcfs/child/index.shtml
- www.ilga.gov/legislation/ilcs/ilcs2.asp?ChapterID=32
- www2.illinois.gov/dcfs/Pages/default.aspx

Illinois Child Welfare Agencies
- www2.illinois.gov/dcfs/Pages/default.aspx

Illinois Juvenile Law
- 750 Ill. Comp. Stat. Ann. § 405/1-1
- www.ilga.gov/legislation/ilcs/ilcs3.asp?ActID=1863
- www.ncjj.org/pdf/1State_Juvenile_Justice_Profiles_2005.pdf

Illinois Domestic Violence Law
- 750 Ill. Comp. Stat. Ann. § 60/103
- www.ilcadv.org

Illinois Surrogacy Law
- 750 Ill. Comp. Stat. Ann. §§ 47/1 et seq.
- dph.illinois.gov/topics-services/birth-death-other-records /birth-records/surrogacy
- www.selectsurrogate.com/surrogacy-laws-by-state.html

Illinois Grandparent Rights
- 750 Ill. Comp. Stat. Ann. § 5/602.9
- www.verywellfamily.com/grandparent-visitation-rights-state-by-state-1695938

Illinois Annulment Law
- 750 Ill. Comp. Stat. Ann. § 5/301
- www.illinoislegalaid.org/search/site?keyword=annulment

Illinois Parental Liability for Acts of Minors
- 740 Ill. Comp. Stat. Ann. §115/1

Illinois Family Law Forms
- www.illinoislegalaid.org/index.cfm?fuseaction=home.formLibrary
- www.illinoiscourts.gov/Forms/approved/default.asp
- family.findlaw.com/divorce/divorce-forms-by-state.html

Illinois Vital Records (Birth, Marriage, Divorce, Death)
- www.cdc.gov/nchs/w2w.htm
- publicrecords.onlinesearches.com/Illinois.htm

Illinois Self-Help Services in Family Law Cases
- www.illinoislegalaid.org/index.cfm?fuseaction=home.formLibrary
- www.state.il.us/court/citizen.asp
- www.illinoislegalaid.org
- www.law.siu.edu/selfhelp

Illinois State Legal Research
- www.loc.gov/law/help/guide/states/us-il.php
- caselaw.findlaw.com/illinois.html

Illinois Court Rules
- www.state.il.us/court/supremecourt/rules

Illinois Job Discrimination Based on Marital Status or Gender
- www.ncsl.org/documents/employ/DiscriminationChart-III.pdf

Google, Bing, or Yahoo Searches on Illinois Family Law
- "Illinois family law"
- "Illinois divorce"
- Illinois "property division"
- "Illinois adoption"
- Illinois paternity
- Illinois "child custody"
- Illinois "child support"
- Illinois abortion
- Illinois marriage
- Illinois "separation agreement"
- Illinois "premarital agreement"
- (also try these searches in the *Articles* and *Case law* databases of Scholar.google.com)

INDIANA FAMILY LAW

Indiana Family Laws
- statelaws.findlaw.com/indiana-law/indiana-family-laws.html

Indiana Family Code/Domestic Relations Code
- Ind. Code Ann. Title 31

Indiana Marriage Law (formation)
- usmarriagelaws.com (enter your state or county)
- www.law.cornell.edu/wex/table_marriage

Indiana Premarital Agreement Law
- Ind. Code Ann. § 31-11-3-1
- marriage.uslegal.com/permarital-agreements

Indiana Common Law Marriage
- topics.law.cornell.edu/wex/table_marriage
- www.buddybuddy.com/common.html

Indiana Divorce Law
- Ind. Code Ann. § 31-15-2-3
- www.divorcelawinfo.com/states/ind/indiana.htm
- www.hg.org/divorce-law-Indiana.html

Indiana Legal Separation Law
- Ind. Code Ann. § 31-15-3-9
- www.hg.org/divorce-law-Indiana.html

Indiana Alimony/Spousal Support/Maintenance Law
- Ind. Code Ann. § 31-15-7-1
- divorce.laws.com/alimony/alimony-in-indiana

Indiana Property Division Law
- Ind. Code Ann. § 31-15-7-4
- www.hg.org/divorce-law-Indiana.html

Indiana Child Custody Law
- Ind. Code Ann. § 31-17-2-8
- www.in.gov/judiciary/rules/parenting

Indiana Relocation of Child
- Ind. Code Ann. § 31-17-2.2-2

Indiana Guardian Ad Litem and Attorney for Child
- Ind. Code Ann. § 31-32-3-1
- www.childwelfare.gov/pubPDFs/represent.pdf

Indiana Child Support Law
- www.in.gov/dcs/support.htm
- www.in.gov/judiciary/selfservice

Indiana Paternity Law
- Ind. Code Ann. § 31-14-5-6
- www.in.gov/dcs/2482.htm

Indiana Legal Definition of Father
- Ind. Code Ann. §§ 31-9-2-9
- www.childwelfare.gov/systemwide/laws_policies/statutes/putative.pdf

Indiana Adoption Law
- Ind. Code Ann. § 31-19-9-1
- statelaws.findlaw.com/indiana-law/indiana-adoption-laws.html

Indiana Termination of Parental Rights
- Ind. Code Ann. § 31-35-1-4.5
- www.childwelfare.gov/pubPDFs/groundtermin.pdf

Indiana Putative Father Registry
- Ind. Code Ann. § 31-19-5-2
- www.ncsl.org/documents/cyf/putative_father_registries.pdf

Indiana Emancipation Law
- Ind. Code Ann. § 31-16-6-6

Indiana Age of Majority
- statelaws.findlaw.com/indiana-law/indiana-legal-ages-laws.html

Indiana Child Protection/Protective Services
- Ind. Code Ann. § 31-33-5-1
- www.in.gov/dcs/2398.htm

Indiana Child Welfare Agencies
- www.in.gov/dcs/2354.htm

Indiana Juvenile Law
- www.doe.in.gov/student-services/attendance/juvenile-justice
- www.ncjj.org/pdf/1State_Juvenile_Justice_Profiles_2005.pdf

Indiana Domestic Violence Law
- Ind. Code Ann. § 34-6-2-34.5

Indiana Surrogacy Law
- Ind. Code Ann. § 31-20-1-1
- www.selectsurrogate.com/surrogacy-laws-by-state.html

Indiana Grandparent Rights
- Ind. Code Ann. § 31-17-5-1
- www.verywellfamily.com/grandparent-visitation-rights-state-by-state-1695938

Indiana Annulment Law
- Ind. Code Ann. § 31-11-9-1

Indiana Family Law Forms
- www.in.gov/judiciary/selfservice/2333.htm
- family.findlaw.com/divorce/divorce-forms-by-state.html

Indiana Vital Records (Birth, Marriage, Divorce, Death)
- www.cdc.gov/nchs/w2w.htm
- publicrecords.onlinesearches.com/Indiana.htm

Indiana Self-Help Services in Family Law Cases
- www.in.gov/judiciary/selfservice/2332.htm

Indiana Family Law Legal Research
- www.in.gov/judiciary/selfservice/2332.htm

Indiana State Legal Research (general)
- www.loc.gov/law/help/guide/states/us-in.php
- caselaw.findlaw.com/indiana.html

Indiana Court Rules
- www.in.gov/judiciary/2695.htm

Indiana Job Discrimination Based on Marital Status or Gender
- www.ncsl.org/documents/employ/DiscriminationChart-III.pdf

Google, Bing, or Yahoo Searches on Indiana Family Law
- "Indiana family law"
- "Indiana divorce"
- Indiana "property division"
- "Indiana adoption"
- Indiana paternity
- Indiana "child custody"
- Indiana "child support"
- Indiana abortion
- Indiana marriage
- Indiana "separation agreement"
- Indiana "premarital agreement"
- (also try these searches in the *Articles* and *Case law* databases of Scholar.google.com)

IOWA FAMILY LAW

Iowa Family Laws
- statelaws.findlaw.com/iowa-law/iowa-family-laws.html

Iowa Family Code/Domestic Relations Code
- Iowa Code Ann. Chapter 595

Iowa Marriage Law (formation)
- Iowa Code Ann. § 598.3
- usmarriagelaws.com (enter your state or county)

Iowa Premarital Agreement Law
- Iowa Code Ann. § 596.5
- marriage.uslegal.com/permarital-agreements

Iowa Common Law Marriage
- See Exhibit 5-3 in Chapter 5.
- *In re Dallman's Estate*, 228 N.W.2d 187 (Iowa 1975)
- www.buddybuddy.com/common.html

Iowa Divorce Law
- Iowa Code Ann. § 598.5
- www.iowalegalaid.org (under "Legal Topics" click "Family and Juvenile")

- www.divorcelawinfo.com/states/ia/iowa.htm
- www.hg.org/divorce-law-Iowa.html

Iowa Legal Separation Law
- www.iowalegalaid.org (enter "legal separation" in the search box)
- www.hg.org/divorce-law-Iowa.html

Iowa Alimony/Spousal Support Law
- Iowa Code Ann. § 598.21A
- www.hg.org/divorce-law-Iowa.html

Iowa Property Division Law
- Iowa Code Ann. § 598.21
- www.hg.org/divorce-law-Iowa.html

Iowa Child Custody Law
- Iowa Code Ann. § 597.15, 598.41
- www.iowalegalaid.org (under "Legal Topics" click "Family and Juvenile")
- www.hg.org/divorce-law-Iowa.html

Iowa Relocation of Child
- Iowa Code Ann. § 598.21D

Iowa Guardian Ad Litem and Attorney for Child
- Iowa Code §§ 232.71C, 232.89
- www.childwelfare.gov/pubPDFs/represent.pdf

Iowa Child Support Law
- Iowa Code Ann. § 598.21B
- www.iowalegalaid.org (under "Legal Topics" click "Family and Juvenile")

Iowa Paternity Law
- Iowa Code Ann. § 600B.7

Iowa Legal Definition of Father
- Iowa Code § 144.12A
- www.childwelfare.gov/systemwide/laws_policies/statutes/putative.pdf

Iowa Adoption Law
- Iowa Code § 600.4

Iowa Termination of Parental Rights
- Iowa Code Rule 600A.8
- www.childwelfare.gov/pubPDFs/groundtermin.pdf

Iowa Putative Father Registry
- Iowa Code Ann. § 144.12A
- www.ncsl.org/documents/cyf/putative_father_registries.pdf

Iowa Emancipation Law
- Iowa Code § 232C.1

Iowa Age of Majority
- Iowa Code § 599.1

Iowa Child Protection/Protective Services
- dhs.iowa.gov/child-services

Iowa Juvenile Law
- www.iowalegalaid.org (under "Legal Topics" click "Family and Juvenile")
- www.ncjj.org/pdf/1State_Juvenile_Justice_Profiles_2005.pdf

Iowa Domestic Violence Law
- www.iowalegalaid.org (under "Legal Topics" click "Family and Juvenile")

Iowa Surrogacy Law
- Iowa Code § 710.11
- www.selectsurrogate.com/surrogacy-laws-by-state.html

Iowa Grandparent Rights
- Iowa Code Ann. § 600C.1
- www.verywellfamily.com/grandparent-visitation-rights-state-by-state-1695938

Iowa Annulment Law
- Iowa Code Ann. § 595.29
- www.hg.org/divorce-law-Iowa.html

Iowa Parental Liability for Acts of Minors
- Iowa Code Ann. § 613.16

Iowa Family Law Forms
- www.iowacourts.gov/for-the-public/court-forms
- family.findlaw.com/divorce/divorce-forms-by-state.html

Iowa Vital Records (Birth, Marriage, Divorce, Death)
- www.cdc.gov/nchs/w2w.htm
- publicrecords.onlinesearches.com/Iowa.htm

Iowa Self-Help Services in Family Law Cases
- www.iowalegalaid.org

Iowa State Legal Research
- www.loc.gov/law/help/guide/states/us-ia.php
- caselaw.findlaw.com/iowa.html

Iowa Court Rules
- www.legis.iowa.gov/law/courtRules

Iowa Job Discrimination Based on Marital Status or Gender
- www.ncsl.org/documents/employ/DiscriminationChart-III.pdf

Google, Bing, or Yahoo Searches on Iowa Family Law
- "Iowa family law"
- "Iowa divorce"
- Iowa "property division"
- "Iowa adoption"
- Iowa paternity
- Iowa "child custody"
- Iowa "child support"
- Iowa abortion
- Iowa marriage
- Iowa "separation agreement"
- Iowa "premarital agreement"
- (also try these searches in the *Articles* and *Case law* databases of Scholar.google.com)

KANSAS FAMILY LAW

Kansas Family Laws
- statelaws.findlaw.com/kansas-law/kansas-family-laws.html

Kansas Family Code/Domestic Relations Code
- Kan. Stat. Ann. Chapter 23

Kansas Marriage Law (formation)
- usmarriagelaws.com (enter your state or county)

Kansas Premarital Agreement Law
- Kan. Stat. Ann. § 23-2407
- marriage.uslegal.com/permarital-agreements

Kansas Common Law Marriage
- See Exhibit 5-3 in Chapter 5.
- Kan. Stat. Ann. § 23-2502
- www.buddybuddy.com/common.html

Kansas Divorce Law
- Kan. Stat. Ann. § 23-2701
- www.kansaslegalservices.org/node/1882/divorce-no-minor-children-interactive-forms
- www.divorcelawinfo.com/states/ks/kansas.htm
- www.hg.org/divorce-law-Kansas.html

Kansas Separate Maintenance/Legal Separation Law
- Kan. Stat. Ann. § 23-2701
- www.hg.org/divorce-law-Kansas.html

Kansas Alimony/Spousal Support/Maintenance Law
- Kan. Stat. Ann. § 23-2902
- www.hg.org/divorce-law-Kansas.html

Kansas Property Division Law
- Kan. Stat. Ann. § 23-2802
- www.hg.org/divorce-law-Kansas.html

Kansas Child Custody Law
- Kan. Stat. Ann. § 23-3203
- www.hg.org/divorce-law-Kansas.html

Kansas Relocation of Child
- Kan. Stat. Ann. §§ 23-3222

Kansas Guardian Ad Litem and Attorney for Child
- Kan. Stat. Ann. § 38-2205
- www.childwelfare.gov/pubPDFs/represent.pdf

Kansas Child Support Law
- Kan. Stat. Ann. §§ 23-3002
- www.kansaslegalservices.org/node/235/child-custody-visitation-and-support
- www.kscourts.org/Rules-procedures-forms/Child-support-guidelines/default.asp

Kansas Paternity Law
- Kan. Stat. Ann. § 23-2208
- www.kansaslegalservices.org/node/1313/faq-paternity

Kansas Legal Definition of Father
- www.childwelfare.gov/systemwide/laws_policies/statutes/putative.pdf

Kansas Adoption Law
- Kan. Stat. Ann. § 59-2111
- statelaws.findlaw.com/kansas-law/kansas-adoption-laws.html

Kansas Termination of Parental Rights
- Kan. Stat. Ann. § 38-2269
- www.childwelfare.gov/pubPDFs/groundtermin.pdf

Kansas Putative Father Registry
- www.ncsl.org/documents/cyf/putative_father_registries.pdf

Kansas Emancipation Law
- www.kansaslegalservices.org/node/2050/emancipation

Kansas Age of Majority
- statelaws.findlaw.com/kansas-law/kansas-marriage-age-requirements-laws.html

Kansas Child Protection/Protective Services
- www.dcf.ks.gov/services/PPS/Pages/ChildProtectiveServices.aspx

Kansas Child Welfare Agencies
- www.dcf.ks.gov/Pages/Default.aspx

Kansas Juvenile Law
- www.ncjj.org/pdf/1State_Juvenile_Justice_Profiles_2005.pdf

Kansas Grandparent Rights
- Kan. Stat. Ann. § 23-3301
- www.verywellfamily.com/grandparent-visitation-rights-state-by-state-1695938

Kansas Annulment Law
- Kan. Stat. Ann. § 23-2702

Kansas Family Law Forms
- www.kansasjudicialcouncil.org
- www.kansaslegalservices.org/node/785/free-legal-forms
- family.findlaw.com/divorce/divorce-forms-by-state.html

Kansas Vital Records (Birth, Marriage, Divorce, Death)
- www.cdc.gov/nchs/w2w.htm
- publicrecords.onlinesearches.com/Kansas.htm

Kansas Self-Help Services in Family Law Cases
- www.kansaslegalservices.org
- www.kscourts.org/programs/self-help/default.asp

Kansas State Legal Research
- caselaw.findlaw.com/kansas.html
- www.loc.gov/law/help/guide/states/us-ks.php

Kansas Court Rules
- www.kscourts.org/rules/default.asp

Kansas Job Discrimination Based on Marital Status or Gender
- www.ncsl.org/documents/employ/DiscriminationChart-III.pdf

Google, Bing, or Yahoo Searches on Kansas Family Law
- "Kansas family law"
- "Kansas divorce"
- Kansas "property division"
- "Kansas adoption"
- Kansas paternity
- Kansas "child custody"
- Kansas "child support"
- Kansas abortion
- Kansas marriage
- Kansas "separation agreement"
- Kansas "premarital agreement"
- (also try these searches in the *Articles* and *Case law* databases of Scholar.google.com)

KENTUCKY FAMILY LAW

Kentucky Family Laws
- statelaws.findlaw.com/kentucky-law/kentucky-family-laws.html

Kentucky Family Code/Domestic Relations Code
- Ky. Rev. Stat. Title XXXV

Kentucky Family Court
- courts.ky.gov/courts/familycourt/Pages/default.aspx

Kentucky Marriage Law (formation)
- Ky. Rev. Stat. §§ 402.080
- usmarriagelaws.com (enter your state or county)

Kentucky Premarital Agreement Law
- www.divorcenet.com/resources/prenuptial-agreements-kentucky.html
- marriage.uslegal.com/permarital-agreements

Kentucky Common Law Marriage
- Ky. Rev. Stat. §§ 402.080

Kentucky Divorce Law
- Ky. Rev. Stat. §§ 403.140, 403.170
- kyjustice.org/home
- www.divorcelawinfo.com/states/ky/kentucky.htm
- www.hg.org/divorce-law-Kentucky.html

Kentucky Legal Separation Law
- Ky. Rev. Stat. §§ 403.050, 403.140
- www.hg.org/divorce-law-Kentucky.html

Kentucky Alimony/Spousal Support/Maintenance Law
- Ky. Rev. Stat. § 403.200
- www.hg.org/divorce-law-Kentucky.html

Kentucky Property Division Law
- Ky. Rev. Stat. § 403.190
- www.hg.org/divorce-law-Kentucky.html

Kentucky Child Custody Law
- Ky. Rev. Stat. § 403.270
- kyjustice.org/library/807
- www.hg.org/divorce-law-Kentucky.html

Kentucky Guardian Ad Litem and Attorney for Child
- Ky. Rev. Stat. § 620.100
- www.childwelfare.gov/pubPDFs/represent.pdf

Kentucky Child Support Law
- Ky. Rev. Stat. § 403.212
- kyjustice.org/topic_childsupport

Kentucky Paternity Law
- Ky. Rev. Stat. § 406.021
- paternity.uslegal.com/paternity-laws/kentucky-paternity-law

Kentucky Legal Definition of Father
- www.childwelfare.gov/systemwide/laws_policies/statutes/putative.pdf

Kentucky Adoption Law
- Ky. Rev. Stat. § 199-470

Kentucky Termination of Parental Rights
- Ky. Rev. Stat. § 625-090
- kyjustice.org/node/627
- www.childwelfare.gov/pubPDFs/groundtermin.pdf

Kentucky Putative Father Registry
- Ky. Rev. Stat. § 199-503
- www.ncsl.org/documents/cyf/putative_father_registries.pdf

Kentucky Emancipation Law
- minors.uslegal.com/emancipation/kentucky-emancipation-of-minor-law

Kentucky Age of Majority
- Ky. Rev. Stat. § 2.015

Kentucky Child Protection/Protective Services
- chfs.ky.gov/agencies/dcbs/dpp/cpb/Pages/default.aspx

Kentucky Child Welfare Agencies
- chfs.ky.gov/Pages/index.aspx

Kentucky Juvenile Law
- Ky. Rev. Stat. § 610.290
- djj.ky.gov
- www.ncjj.org/pdf/1State_Juvenile_Justice_Profiles_2005.pdf

Kentucky Domestic Violence Law
- Ky. Rev. Stat. § 403.720
- kyjustice.org/topic_domesticviolence

Kentucky Surrogacy Law
- *Surrogate Parenting v. Commonw.*, 704 S.W.2d 209 (Ky. 1986)
- www.selectsurrogate.com/surrogacy-laws-by-state.html

Kentucky Grandparent Rights
- Ky. Rev. Stat. § 405.021
- kyjustice.org/topic_visitation
- www.verywellfamily.com/grandparent-visitation-rights-state-by-state-1695938

Kentucky Annulment Law
- Ky. Rev. Stat. § 403.120
- www.hg.org/divorce-law-Kentucky.html

Kentucky Family Law Forms
- kyjustice.org/self-help-forms
- family.findlaw.com/divorce/divorce-forms-by-state.html

Kentucky Vital Records (Birth, Marriage, Divorce, Death)
- www.cdc.gov/nchs/w2w.htm
- publicrecords.onlinesearches.com/Kentucky.htm

Kentucky Self-Help Services in Family Law Cases
- kyjustice.org/home
- www.courtreference.com/Kentucky-Courts-Self-Help.htm

Kentucky State Legal Research
- www.loc.gov/law/help/guide/states/us-ky.php
- caselaw.findlaw.com/kentucky.html

Kentucky Court Rules
- government.westlaw.com/linkedslice/default.asp?SP=KYR-1000

Kentucky Job Discrimination Based on Marital Status or Gender
- www.ncsl.org/documents/employ/DiscriminationChart-III.pdf

Google, Bing, or Yahoo Searches on Kentucky Family Law
- "Kentucky family law"
- "Kentucky divorce"
- Kentucky "property division"
- "Kentucky adoption"
- Kentucky paternity
- Kentucky "child custody"
- Kentucky "child support"
- Kentucky abortion
- Kentucky marriage
- Kentucky "separation agreement"
- Kentucky "premarital agreement"
- (also try these searches in the *Articles* and *Case law* databases of Scholar.google.com)

LOUISIANA FAMILY LAW

Louisiana Family Laws
- www.familylawrights.net/louisiana

Louisiana Family Code/Domestic Relations Code
- legis.la.gov/Legis/LawSearchList.aspx

Louisiana Family Court
- familycourt.org/main/index.php?page=home

Louisiana Marriage Law (formation)
- usmarriagelaws.com (enter your state or county)
- www.law.cornell.edu/wex/table_marriage

Louisiana Premarital Agreement Law
- marriage.uslegal.com/permarital-agreements/louisiana-premarital-agreement-law
- marriage.uslegal.com/permarital-agreements

Louisiana Common Law Marriage
- topics.law.cornell.edu/wex/table_marriage

Louisiana Covenant Marriage
- La. Rev. Stats. § 9:272
- www.divorcereform.org/la01.html
- www.hg.org/divorce-law-Louisiana.html

Louisiana Divorce Law
- La. Stat. Ann. Civil Code Art. 103
- www.lawhelp.org/LA (click Family & Children)
- www.divorcelawinfo.com/states/la/louisiana.htm
- www.hg.org/divorce-law-Louisiana.html

Louisiana Alimony/Spousal Support Law
- La. Stat. Ann. Civil Code Art. 111
- www.lawhelp.org/LA (click Family & Children)
- www.hg.org/divorce-law-Louisiana.html

Louisiana Property Division Law
- La. Revised Statutes § 9:2801
- www.hg.org/divorce-law-Louisiana.html

Louisiana Child Custody Law
- La. Stat. Ann. 13:1813
- www.lawhelp.org/LA (click Family & Children)

Louisiana Relocation of Child
- La. Rev. Stats. § 9:355.14

Louisiana Guardian Ad Litem and Attorney for Child
- www.childwelfare.gov/pubPDFs/represent.pdf

Louisiana Child Support Law
- La. Stat. Ann. 9:312
- dss.louisiana.gov/index.cfm?md=pagebuilder&tmp=home&pid=137
- www.lawhelp.org/LA (click Family & Children)

Louisiana Paternity Law
- louisianalawhelp.org/issues/family-children/paternity
- ldh.la.gov/index.cfm/page/681/n/237

Louisiana Legal Definition of Father
- www.childwelfare.gov/pubPDFs/putative.pdf

Louisiana Adoption Law
- La. Stat. Ann. 9:461
- louisianalawhelp.org/issues/family-children/adoption
- statelaws.findlaw.com/louisiana-law/louisiana-adoption-laws.html

Louisiana Termination of Parental Rights
- La. Stat. Ann. Children's Code Art. 1015
- legis.la.gov/legis/Law.aspx?d=72540
- louisianalawhelp.org/issues/family-children/termination-of-parents-rights
- www.childwelfare.gov/pubPDFs/groundtermin.pdf

Louisiana Putative Father Registry
- La. Stat. Ann. 9:400
- www.ncsl.org/documents/cyf/putative_father_registries.pdf

Louisiana Emancipation Law
- La. Stat. Ann. Civil Code Title VIII, Art. 368
- codes.findlaw.com/la/civil-code/la-civ-code-tit-viii-art-368.html

Louisiana Age of Majority
- statelaws.findlaw.com/louisiana-law/louisiana-legal-ages-laws.html

Louisiana Child Protection/Protective Services
- www.dcfs.louisiana.gov/index.cfm?md=pagebuilder&tmp=home&pid=109

Louisiana Child Welfare Agencies
- www.dss.state.la.us

Louisiana Juvenile Law
- www.lawhelp.org/LA (click Family & Children)
- www.ncjj.org/pdf/1State_Juvenile_Justice_Profiles_2005.pdf

Louisiana Domestic Violence Law
- www.lawhelp.org/LA (click Family & Children)
- www.lcadv.org

Louisiana Employment Discrimination Law
- La. Rev. Stats. § 23:301

Louisiana Surrogacy Law
- La. Rev. Stat. Ann. § 9:2719
- www.selectsurrogate.com/surrogacy-laws-by-state.html

Louisiana Grandparent Rights
- La. Rev. Stats. § 9:344
- louisianalawhelp.org/issues/family-children/rights-of-grandparents-other-relatives
- www.verywellfamily.com/grandparent-visitation-rights-state-by-state-1695938

Louisiana Annulment Law
- La. Code Civil Proc Art. 2004
- www.hg.org/divorce-law-Louisiana.html

Louisiana Family Law Forms
- familycourt.org/main/index.php?page=home
- family.findlaw.com/divorce/divorce-forms-by-state.html

Louisiana Vital Records (Birth, Marriage, Divorce, Death)
- www.cdc.gov/nchs/w2w.htm
- publicrecords.onlinesearches.com/Louisiana.htm

Louisiana Self-Help Services in Family Law Cases
- www.lawhelp.org/LA (click Family & Children)
- www.courtreference.com/Louisiana-Courts-Self-Help.htm

Louisiana State Legal Research
- www.lasc.org/law_library/library_information.asp
- www.loc.gov/law/help/guide/states/us-la.php

Louisiana Court Rules
- www.lasc.org/rules

Louisiana Job Discrimination Based on Marital Status or Gender
- www.ncsl.org/documents/employ/DiscriminationChart-III.pdf

Google, Bing, or Yahoo Searches on Louisiana Family Law
- "Louisiana family law"
- "Louisiana divorce"
- Louisiana "property division"
- "Louisiana adoption"
- Louisiana paternity
- Louisiana "child custody"
- Louisiana "child support"
- Louisiana abortion
- Louisiana marriage
- Louisiana "separation agreement"
- Louisiana "premarital agreement"
- (also try these searches in the *Articles* and *Case law* databases of Scholar.google.com)

MAINE FAMILY LAW

Maine Family Laws
- statelaws.findlaw.com/maine-law/maine-family-laws.html

Maine Family Code/Domestic Relations Code
- Title 19-A, Me. Rev Stat. Ann.
- www.mainelegislature.org/legis/statutes/19-A/title19-Ach0sec0.html
- www.maine.gov/legis
- legislature.maine.gov/statutes/19-A/title19-Ach23sec0.html

Maine Courts (Family Division)
- courts.maine.gov/maine_courts/family/index.shtml

Maine Marriage Law (formation)
- 19-A Me. Rev Stat. Ann. Chapter 23
- usmarriagelaws.com (enter your state or county)
- statutes.laws.com/maine/title19a/title19-Ach23sec0
- www.law.cornell.edu/wex/table_marriage

Maine Premarital Agreement Law
- 19-A Me. Rev. Stat. Ann. § 608
- marriage.uslegal.com/permarital-agreements

Maine Common Law Marriage
- topics.law.cornell.edu/wex/table_marriage
- www.buddybuddy.com/common.html

Maine Divorce Law
- 19-A Me. Rev. Stat. Ann. § 902
- helpmelaw.org/library (click Family Law)
- www.divorcelawinfo.com/states/me/maine.htm
- www.hg.org/divorce-law-Maine.html

Maine Legal Separation Law
- 19-A Me. Rev. Stat. Ann. § 851
- www.hg.org/divorce-law-Maine.html

Maine Annulment Law
- 19-A Me. Rev. Stat. §§ 701, 752
- www.divorcenet.com/resources/annulment/annulment-basics/maine.htm

Maine Alimony/Spousal Support Law
- 19-A Me. Rev. Stat. Ann. § 951
- www.maritallaws.com/states/maine/alimony
- www.hg.org/divorce-law-Maine.html

Maine Property Division Law
- 19-A Me. Rev. Stat. Ann. § 953
- www.hg.org/divorce-law-Maine.html

Maine Child Custody Law
- 19-A Me. Rev. Stat. Ann. § 1501
- statelaws.findlaw.com/maine-law/maine-child-custody-laws.html
- www.hg.org/divorce-law-Maine.html

Maine Guardian Ad Litem and Attorney for Child
- 19-A Me. Rev. Stat. Ann. § 1507
- helpmelaw.org/library/3133
- www.childwelfare.gov/pubPDFs/represent.pdf

Maine Child Support Law
- 19-A Me. Rev. Stat. Ann. § 2011
- www.maine.gov/dhhs/ofi/dser
- helpmelaw.org/library (click Family Law)
- www.hg.org/divorce-law-Maine.html

Maine Paternity Law
- 19-A Me. Rev. Stat. Ann. § 1901
- www.maine.gov/dhhs/ofi/dser/paternity/aop.html

- helpmelaw.org/library (click Family Law)
- www.maine.gov/dhhs/ofi/dser/paternity

Maine Legal Definition of Father
- 18-A Me. Rev Stat. Ann. § 9-102
- 19-A Me. Rev. Stat. Ann. § 1601(1)
- www.childwelfare.gov/pubPDFs/putative.pdf

Maine Adoption Law
- 19-A Me. Rev. Stat. Ann. § 101
- helpmelaw.org/library (click Family Law)
- statelaws.findlaw.com/maine-law/maine-adoption-laws.html

Maine Termination of Parental Rights
- 18-A Me. Rev. Stat. Ann. § 9-204
- www.childwelfare.gov/pubPDFs/groundtermin.pdf

Maine Putative Father Registry
- www.ncsl.org/documents/cyf/putative_father_registries.pdf

Maine Emancipation Law
- 1 Me. Rev Stat. Ann. § 73
- minors.uslegal.com/emancipation/maine-emancipation-of-minor-law

Maine Age of Majority
- 1 Me. Rev Stat. Ann. § 73
- family.findlaw.com/emancipation-of-minors.html

Maine Child Protection/Protective Services
- www.maine.gov/dhhs/ocfs/cw/abuse.shtml
- helpmelaw.org/library (click Family Law)

Maine Child Welfare Agencies
- www.maine.gov/dhhs/ocfs/cw

Maine Juvenile Law
- www.maine.gov/corrections/juvenile/index.htm
- www.ncjj.org/pdf/1State_Juvenile_Justice_Profiles_2005.pdf

Maine Domestic Violence Law
- 17-A Me. Rev. Stat. Ann. § 207-A
- helpmelaw.org/library (click Family Law)

Maine Employment Discrimination Law
- 5 Me. Rev. Stat. Ann. § 4552

Maine Surrogacy Law
- surrogate.com/surrogacy-by-state/maine-surrogacy
- www.selectsurrogate.com/surrogacy-laws-by-state.html

Maine Grandparent Rights
- 19-A Me. Rev. Stat. Ann. 1801
- helpmelaw.org/library/3133
- www.verywellfamily.com/grandparent-visitation-rights-state-by-state-1695938

Maine Family Law Forms
- www.courts.state.me.us/fees_forms/forms/index.shtml#fm
- www.courts.state.me.us/fees_forms/forms/index.shtml
- family.findlaw.com/divorce/divorce-forms-by-state.html

Maine Vital Records (Birth, Marriage, Divorce, Death)
- www.cdc.gov/nchs/w2w.htm
- publicrecords.onlinesearches.com/Maine.htm

Maine Self-Help Services in Family Law Cases
- helpmelaw.org/library (click Family Law)

Maine State Legal Research
- www.loc.gov/law/help/guide/states/us-me.php
- caselaw.findlaw.com/maine.html

Maine Court Rules
- www.courts.state.me.us/rules_adminorders/rules/index.shtml

Maine Job Discrimination Based on Marital Status or Gender
- www.ncsl.org/documents/employ/DiscriminationChart-III.pdf

Google, Bing, or Yahoo Searches on Maine Family Law
- "Maine family law"
- "Maine divorce"
- Maine "property division"

- "Maine adoption"
- Maine paternity
- Maine "child custody"
- Maine "child support"
- Maine abortion
- Maine marriage
- Maine "separation agreement"
- Maine "premarital agreement"
- (also try these searches in the *Articles* and *Case law* databases of Scholar.google.com)

MARYLAND FAMILY LAW

Maryland Family Laws
- statelaws.findlaw.com/maryland-law/maryland-family-laws.html

Maryland Marriage Law (formation)
- usmarriagelaws.com (enter your state or county)
- www.law.cornell.edu/wex/table_marriage

Maryland Premarital Agreement Law
- www.divorcenet.com/resources/prenuptial-agreements-maryland.html
- marriage.uslegal.com/permarital-agreements

Maryland Common Law Marriage
- topics.law.cornell.edu/wex/table_marriage
- www.buddybuddy.com/common.html

Maryland Divorce Law
- Md. Code Ann. Family Law § 7-103
- www.divorcelawinfo.com/MD/flc.htm
- www.hg.org/divorce-law-Maryland.html

Maryland Legal Separation Law (Limited Divorce)
- Md. Code Ann. Family Law § 7-102
- www.hg.org/divorce-law-Maryland.html

Maryland Alimony/Spousal Support Law
- Md. Code Ann. Family Law § 11-101
- www.hg.org/divorce-law-Maryland.html

Maryland Property Division Law
- Md. Code Ann. Family Law §§ 8-203 et seq.
- www.hg.org/divorce-law-Maryland.html

Maryland Child Custody Law
- Md. Code Ann. Family Law § 5-203
- www.hg.org/divorce-law-Maryland.html

Maryland Relocation of Child
- Md. Code Ann. Family Law § 9-106

Maryland Guardian Ad Litem and Attorney for Child
- Md. Code Ann. Courts & Jud. Proc. § 3-813
- www.childwelfare.gov/pubPDFs/represent.pdf

Maryland Child Support Law
- Md. Code Ann. Family Law § 12-204
- dhs.maryland.gov/child-support-services/apply-for-support-services

Maryland Paternity Law
- Md. Code Ann. Family Law § 5-1001
- dhr.maryland.gov/csea/pat.php

Maryland Legal Definition of Father
- Md. Code Ann. Est. and Trusts § 1-208
- www.childwelfare.gov/systemwide/laws_policies/statutes/putative.pdf

Maryland Adoption Law
- Md. Code Ann. Family Law § 5-3B-25
- statelaws.findlaw.com/maryland-law/maryland-adoption-laws.html

Maryland Termination of Parental Rights
- Md. Code Ann. Family Law § 5-331
- www.childwelfare.gov/pubPDFs/groundtermin.pdf

Maryland Putative Father Registry
- www.ncsl.org/documents/cyf/putative_father_registries.pdf

Maryland Age of Majority & Emancipation
- Md. Code Ann. General Provisions § 1-103
- statelaws.findlaw.com/maryland-law/maryland-legal-ages-laws.html

Maryland Child Protection/Protective Services
- dhs.maryland.gov/child-protective-services

Maryland Child Welfare Agencies
- dhs.maryland.gov

Maryland Juvenile Law
- statelaws.findlaw.com/maryland-law/maryland-juvenile-crime-laws.html
- www.courts.state.md.us/family/forms
- www.ncjj.org/pdf/1State_Juvenile_Justice_Profiles_2005.pdf

Maryland Domestic Violence Law
- Md. Code Ann. Family Law § 4-513
- www.courts.state.md.us/legalhelp/domesticviolence

Maryland Surrogacy Law
- Md. Code Ann. Crim. Law § 3-603
- www.selectsurrogate.com/surrogacy-laws-by-state.html

Maryland Grandparent Rights
- Md. Code Ann. Family Law § 9-102
- www.verywellfamily.com/grandparent-visitation-rights-state-by-state-1695938

Maryland Annulment Law
- Md. Code Ann. Family Law § 2-202
- www.hg.org/divorce-law-Maryland.html

Maryland Family Law Forms
- www.courts.state.md.us/family/forms
- family.findlaw.com/divorce/divorce-forms-by-state.html

Maryland Vital Records (Birth, Marriage, Divorce, Death)
- www.cdc.gov/nchs/w2w.htm
- publicrecords.onlinesearches.com/Maryland.htm

Maryland Self-Help Services in Family Law Cases
- www.courts.state.md.us/family/familylawassistance
- www.peoples-law.org

Maryland State Legal Research
- www.loc.gov/law/help/guide/states/us-md.php
- caselaw.findlaw.com/maryland.html

Maryland Court Rules
- www.courts.state.md.us/rules
- caselaw.findlaw.com/maryland.html

Maryland Job Discrimination Based on Marital Status or Gender
- www.ncsl.org/documents/employ/DiscriminationChart-III.pdf

Google, Bing, or Yahoo Searches on Maryland Family Law
- "Maryland family law"
- "Maryland divorce"

- Maryland "property division"
- "Maryland adoption"
- Maryland paternity
- Maryland "child custody"
- Maryland "child support"
- Maryland abortion
- Maryland marriage
- Maryland "separation agreement"
- Maryland "premarital agreement"
- (also try these searches in the *Articles* and *Case law* databases of Scholar.google.com)

MASSACHUSETTS FAMILY LAW

Massachusetts Family Laws
- statelaws.findlaw.com/massachusetts-law/massachusetts-family-laws.html

Massachusetts Family Code/Domestic Relations Code
- Mass. Gen. Laws Ann. Title III

Massachusetts Family Court
- www.masslegalhelp.org/children-and-families/probate-and-family-court

Massachusetts Marriage Law (formation)
- usmarriagelaws.com (enter your state or county)

Massachusetts Antenuptial (Premarital) Agreement Law
- Mass. Gen. Laws Ann. Chap. 209, § 25
- marriage.uslegal.com/permarital-agreements

Massachusetts Common Law Marriage
- www.buddybuddy.com/common.html

Massachusetts Divorce Law
- Mass. Gen. Laws Ann. Chap. 208, § 1
- www.masslegalhelp.org (click "Children and Families")
- www.divorcelawinfo.com/states/ma/massachusetts.htm
- www.hg.org/divorce-law-Massachusetts.html

Massachusetts Legal Separation Law
- www.masslegalhelp.org (click "Children and Families")
- www.hg.org/divorce-law-Massachusetts.html

Massachusetts Alimony
- Mass. Gen. Laws Ann. Chap. 208, §§ 34, 48-55
- www.mass.gov/info-details/massachusetts-law-about-alimony
- www.hg.org/divorce-law-Massachusetts.html

Massachusetts Property Division Law
- Mass. Gen. Laws Ann. Chap. 208, §§ 34, 34A
- www.hg.org/divorce-law-Massachusetts.html

Massachusetts Child Custody Law
- Mass. Gen. Laws Ann. Chap. 208, §§ 31, 31A
- www.masslegalhelp.org (click Children and Families)
- www.hg.org/divorce-law-Massachusetts.html

Massachusetts Guardian Ad Litem and Attorney for Child
- Mass. Gen. Laws Ann. Chap. 119, § 39F6
- www.childwelfare.gov/pubPDFs/represent.pdf

Massachusetts Child Support Law
- Mass. Gen. Laws Ann. Chap. 208, § 28
- www.masslegalhelp.org (click "Children and Families")

Massachusetts Paternity Law
- Mass. Gen. Laws Ann. Chap. 209C, § 11
- www.masslegalhelp.org (click "Children and Families")

Massachusetts Legal Definition of Father
- Mass. Gen. Laws Ann. Chap. 209C, § 6

Massachusetts Adoption Law
- Mass. Gen. Laws Ann. Chap. 210, § 1
- statelaws.findlaw.com/massachusetts-law/massachusetts-adoption-laws.html

Massachusetts Termination of Parental Rights
- www.childwelfare.gov/pubPDFs/groundtermin.pdf

Massachusetts Putative Father Registry
- www.ncsl.org/documents/cyf/putative_father_registries.pdf

Massachusetts Emancipation Law
- www.masslegalhelp.org/children-and-families/emancipation

Massachusetts Age of Majority
- Mass. Gen. Laws Ann. Chap. 231, § 85P
- statelaws.findlaw.com/massachusetts-law/massachusetts-marriage-age-requirements-laws.html

Massachusetts Child Protection/Protective Services
- www.mass.gov/how-to/report-child-abuse-or-neglect

Massachusetts Juvenile Law
- www.mass.gov/info-details/massachusetts-law-about-the-juvenile-justice-system
- www.ncjj.org/pdf/1State_Juvenile_Justice_Profiles_2005.pdf

Massachusetts Domestic Violence Law
- www.masslegalhelp.org (click "Children and Families")

Massachusetts Employment Discrimination Law
- Mass. Gen. Laws Ann. Chap. 151B, § 3A

Massachusetts Artificial Insemination/Surrogacy Law
- Mass. Gen. Laws Ann. Chap. 46, § 4B
- *Culliton v. Beth Israel*, 756 N.E.2d 1133 (Mass. 2001)
- www.selectsurrogate.com/surrogacy-laws-by-state.html

Massachusetts Grandparent Rights
- Mass. Gen. Laws Ann. Chap. 119, § 26B
- www.verywellfamily.com/grandparent-visitation-rights-state-by-state-1695938

Massachusetts Annulment Law
- Mass. Gen. Laws Ann. Chap. 207, §§ 4 et seq.
- www.masslegalhelp.org (click "Children and Families")

Massachusetts Family Law Forms
- www.masslegalhelp.org/children-and-families/forms
- family.findlaw.com/divorce/divorce-forms-by-state.html

Massachusetts Vital Records (Birth, Marriage, Divorce, Death)
- www.cdc.gov/nchs/w2w.htm
- publicrecords.onlinesearches.com/Massachusetts.htm

Massachusetts Self-Help Services in Family Law Cases
- www.masslegalhelp.org (click Children and Families)

Massachusetts State Legal Research (general)
- caselaw.findlaw.com/massachusetts.html
- www.loc.gov/law/help/guide/states/us-ma.php

Massachusetts Court Rules
- www.mass.gov/guides/massachusetts-rules-of-court-and-standing-orders

Massachusetts Job Discrimination Based on Marital Status or Gender
- www.ncsl.org/documents/employ/DiscriminationChart-III.pdf

Google, Bing, or Yahoo Searches on Massachusetts Family Law
- "Massachusetts family law"
- "Massachusetts divorce"
- Massachusetts "property division"
- "Massachusetts adoption"
- Massachusetts paternity
- Massachusetts "child custody"
- Massachusetts "child support"
- Massachusetts abortion
- Massachusetts marriage
- Massachusetts "separation agreement"
- Massachusetts "premarital agreement"
- (also try these searches in the *Articles* and *Case law* databases of Scholar.google.com)

MICHIGAN FAMILY LAW

Michigan Family Laws
- statelaws.findlaw.com/Michigan-law/Michigan-family-laws.html

Michigan Family Code/Domestic Relations Code
- Mich. Comp. Laws Chapters 551, 552

Michigan Marriage Law (formation)
- usmarriagelaws.com (enter your state or county)
- www.law.cornell.edu/wex/table_marriage

Michigan Premarital Agreement Law
- marriage.uslegal.com/permarital-agreements/michigan-premarital-agreement-law
- marriage.uslegal.com/permarital-agreements

Michigan Common Law Marriage
- topics.law.cornell.edu/wex/table_marriage
- www.buddybuddy.com/common.html

Michigan Divorce Law
- Mich. Comp. Laws § 552.6
- michiganlegalhelp.org/self-help-tools/family
- www.divorcelawinfo.com/states/mi/michigan.htm
- www.hg.org/divorce-law-Michigan.html

Michigan Separate Maintenance Law
- Mich. Comp. Laws § 552.7
- www.hg.org/divorce-law-Michigan.html

Michigan Alimony/Spousal Support Law
- Mich. Comp. Laws § 552.151
- michiganlegalhelp.org (click "Family")
- www.hg.org/divorce-law-Michigan.html

Michigan Property Division Law
- Mich. Comp. Laws § 722.23
- www.hg.org/divorce-law-Michigan.html

Michigan Child Custody Law
- Mich. Comp. Laws § 557.27a
- michiganlegalhelp.org (click "Family")
- michiganlegalhelp.org (click Child Custody)
- www.michiganlegalaid.org/library_client (click Family Law)
- www.hg.org/divorce-law-Michigan.html

Michigan Guardian Ad Litem and Attorney for Child
- Mich. Comp. Laws §§ 722.630, 712A.17d
- www.childwelfare.gov/pubPDFs/represent.pdf

Michigan Child Support Law
- Mich. Comp. Laws § 400.232
- michiganlegalhelp.org (click "Family")
- michiganlegalhelp.org/self-help-tools/family

Michigan Child Support Specialty Court
- courts.michigan.gov (enter "support specialty court" in search box)

Michigan Paternity Law
- Mich. Comp. Laws § 722.714
- michiganlegalhelp.org (click "Family")
- michiganlegalhelp.org (click Paternity)

Michigan Legal Definition of Father
- Mich. Comp. Laws §§ 722.1002, 722-1003
- www.childwelfare.gov/systemwide/laws_policies/statutes/putative.pdf

Michigan Adoption Law
- Mich. Comp. Laws § 710.21

Michigan Termination of Parental Rights
- Mich. Comp. Laws § 712A.19b
- www.childwelfare.gov/pubPDFs/groundtermin.pdf

Michigan Putative Father Registry Alternative
- Mich. Comp. Laws § 710.33
- www.ncsl.org/documents/cyf/putative_father_registries.pdf

Michigan Emancipation Law
- michiganlegalhelp.org (click "Family")

Michigan Age of Majority
- statelaws.findlaw.com/michigan-law/michigan-legal-ages-laws.html

Michigan Child Protection/Protective Services
- www.michigan.gov (enter "protective services" in search box)

Michigan Juvenile Law
- www.michigan.gov (enter "juvenile justice" in search box)
- www.ncjj.org/pdf/1State_Juvenile_Justice_Profiles_2005.pdf

Michigan Teen Court
- courts.michigan.gov (enter "teen court" in search box)

Michigan Domestic Violence Law
- Mich. Comp. Laws § 400.1501
- courts.michigan.gov (enter "domestic violence" in search box)

Michigan Surrogacy Law
- Mich. Comp. Laws § 722.851
- www.selectsurrogate.com/surrogacy-laws-by-state.html

Michigan Grandparent Rights
- Mich. Comp. Laws § 722.27(1)(f)
- www.verywellfamily.com/grandparent-visitation-rights-state-by-state-1695938

Michigan Annulment Law
- Mich. Comp. Laws § 552.37
- www.hg.org/divorce-law-Michigan.html

Michigan Family Law Forms
- courts.michigan.gov/Search/Pages/Forms.aspx?k=court%20rules
- courts.michigan.gov/Administration/SCAO/Forms/Pages/Family-Division-Index.aspx
- family.findlaw.com/divorce/divorce-forms-by-state.html

Michigan Vital Records (Birth, Marriage, Divorce, Death)
- publicrecords.onlinesearches.com/Michigan.htm
- www.cdc.gov/nchs/w2w.htm

Michigan Self-Help Services in Family Law Cases
- courts.michigan.gov/self-help/center/pages/default.aspx
- michiganlegalhelp.org

Michigan State Legal Research
- caselaw.findlaw.com/michigan.html
- www.loc.gov/law/help/guide/states/us-mi.php

Michigan Court Rules
- courts.michigan.gov/search/pages/results.aspx?k=court%20rules

Michigan Job Discrimination Based on Marital Status or Gender
- www.ncsl.org/documents/employ/DiscriminationChart-III.pdf

Google, Bing, or Yahoo Searches on Michigan Family Law
- "Michigan family law"
- "Michigan divorce"
- Michigan "property division"
- "Michigan adoption"
- Michigan paternity
- Michigan "child custody"
- Michigan "child support"
- Michigan abortion
- Michigan marriage
- Michigan "separation agreement"
- Michigan "premarital agreement"
- (also try these searches in the *Articles* and *Case law* databases of Scholar.google.com)

MINNESOTA FAMILY LAW

Minnesota Family Laws
- statelaws.findlaw.com/minnesota-law/minnesota-family-laws.html

Minnesota Family Code/Domestic Relations Code
- www.revisor.mn.gov/statutes/?id=518

Minnesota Marriage Law (formation)
- www.revisor.mn.gov/statutes/?id=517
- usmarriagelaws.com (enter your state or county)
- www.law.cornell.edu/wex/table_marriage

Minnesota Premarital Agreement Law
- Minn. Stat. Ann. §§ 519.11
- marriage.uslegal.com/permarital-agreements

Minnesota Common Law Marriage
- Minn. Stat. Ann. §§ 517.01
- www.buddybuddy.com/common.html

Minnesota Divorce Law
- Minn. Stat. Ann. §§ 518.06, 518.10
- www.mncourts.gov/Help-Topics/Divorce.aspx
- www.mncourts.gov/Help-Topics.aspx
- www.hg.org/divorce-law-Minnesota.html

Minnesota Legal Separation Law
- Minn. Stat. Ann. §§ 518.06, 518.10
- www.mncourts.gov/Help-Topics.aspx
- www.mncourts.gov/Help-Topics/Annulment-and-Legal-Separation.aspx

Minnesota Alimony/Spousal Maintenance Law
- Minn. Stat. Ann. § 518.552
- www.oesw.leg.mn/cola/index.htm
- www.hg.org/divorce-law-Minnesota.html

Minnesota Property Division Law
- Minn. Stat. Ann. § 518.58
- www.hg.org/divorce-law-Minnesota.html

Minnesota Child Custody Law
- Minn. Stat. Ann. § 518.17
- www.mncourts.gov/Help-Topics/Child-Custody.aspx

Minnesota Guardian Ad Litem and Attorney for Child
- Minn. Stat. Ann. § 518.165
- Minn. Stat. Ann. § 260C.163(3)&(5)
- www.mncourts.gov/Help-Topics.aspx
- www.childwelfare.gov/pubPDFs/represent.pdf

Minnesota Child Support Law
- Minn. Stat. Ann. § 518A.27
- www.mncourts.gov/Help-Topics/Child-Support.aspx
- www.mncourts.gov/Help-Topics.aspx
- www.childsupport.dhs.state.mn.us/Action/Welcome

Minnesota Paternity Law
- Minn. Stat. Ann. § 257.57
- www.mncourts.gov/Help-Topics/Paternity.aspx
- www.mncourts.gov/Help-Topics.aspx

Minnesota Legal Definition of Father
- Minn. Stat. Ann. §§ 257.52, 257.55
- www.childwelfare.gov/systemwide/laws_policies/statutes/putative.pdf

Minnesota Adoption Law
- Minn. Stat. Ann. §§ 257.54, 257.74
- www.mncourts.gov/Help-Topics/Adoption.aspx

Minnesota Termination of Parental Rights
- Minn. Stat. Ann. § 260C.301
- www.mncourts.gov/Help-Topics.aspx
- www.childwelfare.gov/pubPDFs/groundtermin.pdf

Minnesota Putative Father Registry
- Minn. Stat. Ann. § 259.52
- www.ncsl.org/documents/cyf/putative_father_registries.pdf

Minnesota Emancipation Law
• www.mncourts.gov/Help-Topics.aspx

Minnesota Age of Majority
• statelaws.findlaw.com/minnesota-law/minnesota-marriage-age-requirements-laws.html

Minnesota Child Protection/Protective Services
• mn.gov/dhs (click "Report Abuse")
• www.lawhelpmn.org/issues/family-law/child-abuse-and-protection-chips

Minnesota Child Welfare Agencies
• mn.gov/dhs

Minnesota Juvenile Law
• www.mncourts.gov/Help-Topics.aspx
• www.ncjj.org/pdf/1State_Juvenile_Justice_Profiles_2005.pdf

Minnesota Domestic Violence Law
• Minn. Stat. Ann. § 518B.01
• www.domesticshelters.org/help/mn

Minnesota Surrogacy Law
• www.selectsurrogate.com/surrogacy-laws-by-state.html

Minnesota Grandparent Rights
• Minn. Stat. Ann. § 257C.08
• www.lawhelpmn.org/issues/family-law/relatives-caring-for-children
• www.verywellfamily.com/grandparent-visitation-rights-state-by-state-1695938

Minnesota Annulment Law
• Minn. Stat. Ann. § 518.05
• www.mncourts.gov/Help-Topics/Annulment-and-Legal-Separation.aspx
• www.mncourts.gov/Help-Topics.aspx

Minnesota Family Law Forms
• www.mncourts.gov/GetForms.aspx
• family.findlaw.com/divorce/divorce-forms-by-state.html

Minnesota Vital Records (Birth, Marriage, Divorce, Death)
• www.cdc.gov/nchs/w2w.htm
• publicrecords.onlinesearches.com/Minnesota.htm

Minnesota Self-Help Services in Family Law Cases
• www.mncourts.gov/Help-Topics.aspx
• www.lawhelpmn.org

Minnesota State Legal Research (general)
• caselaw.findlaw.com/minnesota.html
• www.loc.gov/law/help/guide/states/us-mn.php

Minnesota Court Rules
• www.mncourts.gov/SupremeCourt/Court-Rules.aspx

Minnesota Job Discrimination Based on Marital Status or Gender
• www.ncsl.org/documents/employ/DiscriminationChart-III.pdf

Google, Bing, or Yahoo Searches on Minnesota Family Law
• "Minnesota family law"
• "Minnesota divorce"
• Minnesota "property division"
• "Minnesota adoption"
• Minnesota paternity
• Minnesota "child custody"
• Minnesota "child support"
• Minnesota abortion
• Minnesota marriage
• Minnesota "separation agreement"
• Minnesota "premarital agreement"
• (also try these searches in the *Articles* and *Case law* databases of Scholar.google.com)

MISSISSIPPI FAMILY LAW

Mississippi Family Laws
• statelaws.findlaw.com/mississippi-law/mississippi-family-laws.html

Mississippi Family Code/Domestic Relations Code
• Miss. Code Ann. Title 93 (Domestic Relations)

Mississippi Marriage Law (formation)
• Miss. Code Ann. § 93-1-15
• statutes.laws.com/mississippi/title-93/1
• usmarriagelaws.com (enter your state or county)
• www.law.cornell.edu/wex/table_marriage

Mississippi Premarital Agreement Law
• www.divorcenet.com/resources/prenuptial-agreements-mississippi.html
• marriage.uslegal.com/permarital-agreements

Mississippi Common Law Marriage
• topics.law.cornell.edu/wex/table_marriage
• www.buddybuddy.com/common.html

Mississippi Divorce Law
• Miss. Code Ann. § 93-5-1
• www.msatjc.org/family-and-children-law
• www.mslegalservices.org (click *Family and Juvenile*)
• www.divorcelawinfo.com/states/miss/mississippi.htm
• www.hg.org/divorce-law-Mississippi.html

Mississippi Alimony/Spousal Support Law
• Miss. Code Ann. § 93-5-23
• www.hg.org/divorce-law-Mississippi.html

Mississippi Property Division Law
• www.maritallaws.com/states/mississippi/property-division
• www.hg.org/divorce-law-Mississippi.html

Mississippi Child Custody Law
• Miss. Code Ann. § 93-5-23
• www.msatjc.org/family-and-children-law
• www.mslegalservices.org (click *Family and Juvenile*)
• www.hg.org/divorce-law-Mississippi.html

Mississippi Guardian Ad Litem and Attorney for Child
• Miss. Code Ann. §§ 43-21-121
• www.childwelfare.gov/pubPDFs/represent.pdf

Mississippi Child Support Law
• Miss. Code Ann. §§ 93-5-23
• www.mdhs.ms.gov/child-support
• www.mslegalservices.org (click *Child Support*)

Mississippi Paternity Law
• Miss. Code Ann. §§ 93-9-1
• www.mslegalservices.org (click *Family and Juvenile*)
• www.mslegalservices.org (click Family and Juvenile)
• www.childwelfare.gov/systemwide/laws_policies/statutes/putative.pdf

Mississippi Legal Definition of Father
• www.childwelfare.gov/systemwide/laws_policies/statutes/putative.pdf

Mississippi Adoption Law
- Miss. Code Ann. § 93-17-3
- www.mslegalservices.org (click *Adoption*)
- www.msatjc.org/family-and-children-law
- statelaws.findlaw.com/mississippi-law/mississippi-adoption-laws.html

Mississippi Termination of Parental Rights
- Miss. Code Ann. § 93-15-101
- www.mslegalservices.org (click *Family and Juvenile*)
- www.msatjc.org/family-and-children-law
- www.childwelfare.gov/pubPDFs/groundtermin.pdf

Mississippi Emancipation Law
- Miss. Code Ann. § 93-19-3

Mississippi Age of Majority
- statelaws.findlaw.com/mississippi-law/mississippi-legal-ages-laws.html

Mississippi Child Protection/Protective Services
- www.mdcps.ms.gov

Mississippi Juvenile Law
- Miss. Code Ann. § 43-21-105
- www.mslegalservices.org (click *Abuse, Neglect...*)
- www.mdhs.ms.gov/youth-services
- www.ncjj.org/pdf/1State_Juvenile_Justice_Profiles_2005.pdf

Mississippi Domestic Violence Law
- Miss. Code Ann. § 93-21-3
- www.mslegalservices.org (click Family and Juvenile)

Mississippi Surrogacy Law
- www.selectsurrogate.com/surrogacy-laws-by-state.html

Mississippi Grandparent Rights
- www.mslegalservices.org (click *Family and Juvenile*)
- www.verywellfamily.com/
  grandparent-visitation-rights-state-by-state-1695938

Mississippi Annulment Law
- Miss. Code Ann. § 93-7-3
- www.hg.org/divorce-law-Mississippi.html

Mississippi Family Law Forms
- family.findlaw.com/divorce/divorce-forms-by-state.html

Mississippi Vital Records (Birth, Marriage, Divorce, Death)
- www.cdc.gov/nchs/w2w.htm
- publicrecords.onlinesearches.com/Mississippi.htm

Mississippi Self-Help Services in Family Law Cases
- www.msatjc.org
- www.mslegalservices.org (click Family and Juvenile)
- www.courtreference.com/Mississippi-Courts-Self-Help.htm
- www.familylawrights.net/mississippi

Mississippi State Legal Research
- www.loc.gov/law/help/guide/states/us-ms.php
- caselaw.findlaw.com/mississippi.html

Mississippi Court Rules
- courts.ms.gov/research/rules/rules.php

Mississippi Job Discrimination Based on Marital Status or Gender
- www.ncsl.org/documents/employ/DiscriminationChart-III.pdf

Google, Bing, or Yahoo Searches on Mississippi Family Law
- "Mississippi family law"
- "Mississippi divorce"
- Mississippi "property division"
- "Mississippi adoption"
- Mississippi paternity
- Mississippi "child custody"
- Mississippi "child support"
- Mississippi abortion
- Mississippi marriage
- Mississippi "separation agreement"
- Mississippi "premarital agreement"
- (also try these searches in the *Articles* and *Case law* databases of Scholar.google.com)

MISSOURI FAMILY LAW

Missouri Family Laws
- statelaws.findlaw.com/missouri-law/missouri-family-laws.html

Missouri Family Code/Domestic Relations Code
- revisor.mo.gov/main/OneChapter.aspx?chapter=451

Missouri Juvenile and Family Court Divisions
- www.courts.mo.gov/page.jsp?id=321

Missouri Marriage Law (formation)
- usmarriagelaws.com (enter your state or county)
- Ann. Mo. Stat. § 451.010

Missouri Premarital Agreement Law
- www.divorcenet.com/resources/prenuptial-agreements-missouri.html
- marriage.uslegal.com/permarital-agreements

Missouri Common Law Marriage
- topics.law.cornell.edu/wex/table_marriage
- www.buddybuddy.com/common.html

Missouri Divorce Law
- Ann. Mo. Stat. § 452.305
- www.divorcelawinfo.com/states/mo/missouri.htm
- www.hg.org/divorce-law-Missouri.html

Missouri Legal Separation Law
- Ann. Mo. Stat. § 452.305
- www.hg.org/divorce-law-Missouri.html

Missouri Alimony/Spousal Support/Maintenance Law
- Ann. Mo. Stat. § 452.335
- www.hg.org/divorce-law-Missouri.html

Missouri Property Division Law
- Ann. Mo. Stat. § 452.330
- www.hg.org/divorce-law-Missouri.html

Missouri Child Custody Law
- Ann. Mo. Stat. § 452.375
- www.lsmo.org/node/713/child-custody-and-visitation

Missouri Guardian Ad Litem and Attorney for Child
- Ann. Mo. Stat. § 210.160
- www.childwelfare.gov/pubPDFs/represent.pdf

Missouri Child Support Law
- Ann. Mo. Stat. § 452.340
- www.dss.mo.gov/cse

Missouri Paternity Law
- Ann. Mo. Stat. § 210.826
- paternity.uslegal.com/paternity-laws/missouri-paternity-law

Missouri Legal Definition of Father
- Ann. Mo. Stat. §§ 210.817(4), 210.822
- www.childwelfare.gov/systemwide/laws_policies/statutes/putative.pdf

Missouri Adoption Law
- www.lsmo.org/node/575/adoption
- statelaws.findlaw.com/missouri-law/missouri-adoption-laws.html

Missouri Termination of Parental Rights
- Ann. Mo. Stat. §211.447
- www.childwelfare.gov/pubPDFs/groundtermin.pdf

Missouri Putative Father Registry
- Ann. Mo. Stat. § 192.016
- www.ncsl.org/documents/cyf/putative_father_registries.pdf

Missouri Age of Majority & Emancipation
- statelaws.findlaw.com/missouri-law/missouri-legal-ages-laws.html
- www.lsmo.org/node/771/emancipation-minors-missouri

Missouri Child Protection/Protective Services
- dss.mo.gov/cd/keeping-kids-safe

Missouri Juvenile Law
- dss.mo.gov/dys
- www.ncjj.org/pdf/1State_Juvenile_Justice_Profiles_2005.pdf

Missouri Domestic Violence Law
- www.mocadsv.org

Missouri Surrogacy Law
- www.selectsurrogate.com/surrogacy-laws-by-state.html

Missouri Grandparent Rights
- Ann. Mo. Stat. § 452.402
- www.verywellfamily.com/grandparent-visitation-rights-state-by-state-1695938

Missouri Annulment Law (declaration of invalidity)
- Ann. Mo. Stat. § 451.020
- www.hg.org/divorce-law-Missouri.html

Missouri Family Law Forms
- www.courts.mo.gov/page.jsp?id=5240
- family.findlaw.com/divorce/divorce-forms-by-state.html

Missouri Vital Records (Birth, Marriage, Divorce, Death)
- www.cdc.gov/nchs/w2w.htm
- publicrecords.onlinesearches.com/Missouri.htm

Missouri Self-Help Services in Family Law Cases
- www.courts.mo.gov/page.jsp?id=5240

Missouri State Legal Research
- www.loc.gov/law/help/guide/states/us-mo.php
- caselaw.findlaw.com/missouri.html

Missouri Court Rules
- www.courts.mo.gov/page.jsp?id=46

Missouri Job Discrimination Based on Marital Status or Gender
- www.ncsl.org/documents/employ/DiscriminationChart-III.pdf

Google, Bing, or Yahoo Searches on Missouri Family Law
- "Missouri family law"
- "Missouri divorce"
- Missouri "property division"
- "Missouri adoption"
- Missouri paternity
- Missouri "child custody"
- Missouri "child support"
- Missouri abortion
- Missouri marriage
- Missouri "separation agreement"
- Missouri "premarital agreement"
- (also try these searches in the *Articles* and *Case law* databases of Scholar.google.com)

MONTANA FAMILY LAW

Montana Family Laws
- statelaws.findlaw.com/montana-law/montana-family-laws.html

Montana Family Code/Domestic Relations Code
- Mt. Code Ann. Title 40

Montana Marriage Law (formation)
- statutes.laws.com/montana/40
- www.montanalawhelp.org (click "Families and Kids")
- courts.mt.gov/Forms
- usmarriagelaws.com (enter your state or county)

Montana Common Law Marriage
- See Exhibit 5-3 in Chapter 5.
- Mt. Code Ann. § 40-1-403
- www.montanalawhelp.org (click "Families and Kids")
- *Snetsinger v. Montana Univ.*, 104 P.3d 445 (Mont., 2004)

Montana Premarital Agreement Law
- Mt. Code Ann. § 40-2-601
- marriage.uslegal.com/permarital-agreements

Montana Divorce Law
- Mt. Code Ann. § 40-4-107
- www.montanalawhelp.org (click "Families and Kids")

- courts.mt.gov/Forms
- www.divorcelawinfo.com/states/mont/montana.htm

Montana Legal Separation Law
- Mt. Code Ann. § 40-4-104

Montana Alimony/Spousal Support/Maintenance Law
- Mt. Code Ann. § 40-4-203

Montana Property Division Law
- Mt. Code Ann. § 40-4-202

Montana Child Custody Law
- Mt. Code Ann. § 40-4-212
- courts.mt.gov/Forms
- www.montanalawhelp.org (click "Families and Kids")

Montana Guardian Ad Litem and Attorney for Child
- Mt. Code Ann. §§ 41-3-112, 41-3-425, 40-4-205
- www.childwelfare.gov/pubPDFs/represent.pdf

Montana Child Support Law
- Mt. Code Ann. § 40-6-113
- courts.mt.gov/Forms
- www.dphhs.mt.gov/csed/index.shtml
- www.montanalawhelp.org (click "Families and Kids")

Montana Paternity Law
- Mt. Code Ann. § 40-4-204
- courts.mt.gov/Forms/paternity
- www.montanalawhelp.org (click "Families and Kids")

Montana Legal Definition of Father
- Mt. Code Ann. §§ 40-6-102(2), 42-1-103
- www.childwelfare.gov/systemwide/laws_policies/statutes/putative.pdf

Montana Adoption Law
- Mt. Code Ann. §§ 42-1-103 et seq.
- courts.mt.gov/Forms

Montana Termination of Parental Rights
- Mt. Code Ann. § 42-2-607
- www.childwelfare.gov/pubPDFs/groundtermin.pdf

Montana Putative Father Registry
- Mt. Code Ann. § 42-2-202
- www.ncsl.org/documents/cyf/putative_father_registries.pdf

Montana Emancipation Law
- courts.mt.gov/Forms/emancipation

Montana Age of Majority
- statelaws.findlaw.com/montana-law/montana-legal-ages-laws.html

Montana Child Protection/Protective Services
- www.dphhs.mt.gov/cfsd/index.shtml

Montana Juvenile Law
- mbcc.mt.gov/Juvenile-Justice
- courts.mt.gov/courts/ycourt
- www.ncjj.org/pdf/1State_Juvenile_Justice_Profiles_2005.pdf

Montana Domestic Violence Law
- Mt. Code Ann. § 45-5-206
- courts.mt.gov/Forms

Montana Grandparent Rights
- Mt. Code Ann. § 40-4-228
- www.verywellfamily.com/grandparent-visitation-rights-state-by-state-1695938

Montana Annulment Law
- Mt. Code Ann. § 40-1-402
- courts.mt.gov/Forms (click "Invalidity of Marriage")

Montana Family Law Forms
- courts.mt.gov/Forms
- courts.mt.gov/Forms
- family.findlaw.com/divorce/divorce-forms-by-state.html

Montana Vital Records (Birth, Marriage, Divorce, Death)
- www.cdc.gov/nchs/w2w.htm
- publicrecords.onlinesearches.com/Montana.htm

Montana Self-Help Services in Family Law Cases
- courts.mt.gov/selfhelp
- www.montanalawhelp.org

Montana State Legal Research
- caselaw.findlaw.com/montana.html
- www.loc.gov/law/help/guide/states/us-mt.php

Montana Court Rules
- courts.mt.gov/home/search-results?search=court%20rules

Montana Job Discrimination Based on Marital Status or Gender
- www.ncsl.org/documents/employ/DiscriminationChart-III.pdf

Google, Bing, or Yahoo Searches on Montana Family Law
- "Montana family law"
- "Montana divorce"
- Montana "property division"
- "Montana adoption"
- Montana paternity
- Montana "child custody"
- Montana "child support"
- Montana abortion
- Montana marriage
- Montana "separation agreement"
- Montana "premarital agreement"
- (also try these searches in the *Articles* and *Case law* databases of Scholar.google.com)

NEBRASKA FAMILY LAW

Nebraska Family Laws
- statelaws.findlaw.com/nebraska-law/nebraska-family-laws.html

Nebraska Family Code/Domestic Relations Code
- Neb. Rev. Stats. Chapter 42

Nebraska Marriage Law (formation)
- nebraskaccess.ne.gov/marriagelicense.asp
- usmarriagelaws.com (enter your state or county)
- www.law.cornell.edu/wex/table_marriage

Nebraska Premarital Agreement Law
- Neb. Rev. Stats. § 42-1011
- marriage.uslegal.com/permarital-agreements

Nebraska Common Law Marriage
- Neb. Rev. Stats. § 42-104
- www.buddybuddy.com/common.html

Nebraska Divorce Law
- Neb. Rev. Stats. § 42-361
- www.divorcelawinfo.com/states/ne/nebraska.htm
- www.hg.org/divorce-law-Nebraska.html

Nebraska Legal Separation Law
- Neb. Rev. Stats. § 42-372.03
- www.hg.org/divorce-law-Nebraska.html

Nebraska Alimony/Spousal Support Law
- Neb. Rev. Stats. § 42-365
- www.hg.org/divorce-law-Nebraska.html

Nebraska Property Division Law
- Neb. Rev. Stats. § 42-365
- www.hg.org/divorce-law-Nebraska.html

Nebraska Child Custody Law
- Neb. Rev. Stats. § 42-364
- www.hg.org/divorce-law-Nebraska.html

Nebraska Guardian Ad Litem and Attorney for Child
- Neb. Rev. Stats. §§ 42-358, 43-272, 43-3710
- www.childwelfare.gov/pubPDFs/represent.pdf

Nebraska Child Support Law
- Neb. Rev. Stats. § 42-364.16
- dhhs.ne.gov/Pages/Child-Support.aspx

Nebraska Paternity Law
- Neb. Rev. Stats. § 43-1412
- paternity.uslegal.com/paternity-laws/nebraska-paternity-law

Nebraska Legal Definition of Father
- www.childwelfare.gov/systemwide/laws_policies/statutes/putative.pdf

Nebraska Adoption Law
- Neb. Rev. Stats. § 43-103
- statelaws.findlaw.com/nebraska-law/nebraska-adoption-laws.html

Nebraska Termination of Parental Rights
- Neb. Rev. Stats. § 43-292
- www.childwelfare.gov/pubPDFs/groundtermin.pdf

Nebraska Putative Father Registry
- Neb. Rev. Stats. § 43-104.01
- www.ncsl.org/documents/cyf/putative_father_registries.pdf

Nebraska Emancipation Law
- Neb. Rev. Stats. §§ 43-4809, 43-4810
- nebraskaaccess.ne.gov/agemajority.asp

Nebraska Age of Majority
- nebraskaaccess.ne.gov/agemajority.asp

Nebraska Child Protection/Protective Services
- Neb. Rev. Stats. § 23-104.03

Nebraska Juvenile Law
- supremecourt.nebraska.gov/courts/separate-juvenile-courts
- www.ncjj.org/pdf/1State_Juvenile_Justice_Profiles_2005.pdf

Nebraska Domestic Violence Law
- statelaws.findlaw.com/nebraska-law/nebraska-domestic-violence-laws.html

Nebraska Surrogacy Law
- Neb. Rev. Stats. § 25-21,200
- www.selectsurrogate.com/surrogacy-laws-by-state.html

Nebraska Grandparent Rights
- Neb. Rev. Stats. § 43-1801
- www.verywellfamily.com/grandparent-visitation-rights-state-by-state-1695938

Nebraska Annulment Law
- Neb. Rev. Stats. § 42-373
- http://www.hg.org/divorce-law-Nebraska.html

Nebraska Family Law Forms
- www.uslegalforms.com/familylaw/nebraska
- family.findlaw.com/divorce/divorce-forms-by-state.html

Nebraska Vital Records (Birth, Marriage, Divorce, Death)
- www.cdc.gov/nchs/w2w.htm
- publicrecords.onlinesearches.com/Nebraska.htm

Nebraska Self-Help Services in Family Law Cases
- supremecourt.nebraska.gov/self-help
- supremecourt.nebraska.gov/programs-services/children-families/divorce-parenting-support

Nebraska State Legal Research
- www.loc.gov/law/help/guide/states/us-ne.php
- caselaw.findlaw.com/nebraska.html

Nebraska Court Rules
- supremecourt.nebraska.gov/rules

Nebraska Job Discrimination Based on Marital Status or Gender
- www.ncsl.org/documents/employ/DiscriminationChart-III.pdf

Google, Bing, or Yahoo Searches on Nebraska Family Law
- "Nebraska family law"
- "Nebraska divorce"
- Nebraska "property division"
- "Nebraska adoption"
- Nebraska paternity
- Nebraska "child custody"
- Nebraska "child support"
- Nebraska abortion
- Nebraska marriage
- Nebraska "separation agreement"
- Nebraska "premarital agreement"
- (also try these searches in the *Articles* and *Case law* databases of Scholar.google.com)

NEVADA FAMILY LAW

Nevada Family Laws
- statelaws.findlaw.com/nevada-law/nevada-family-laws.html

Nevada Family Code/Domestic Relations Code
- www.leg.state.nv.us/NRS/NRS-125.html

Nevada Marriage Law (formation)
- www.leg.state.nv.us/nrs/NRS-122.html
- usmarriagelaws.com (enter your state or county)
- www.law.cornell.edu/wex/table_marriage

Nevada Premarital Agreement Law
- Nev. Rev. Stat. § 123A.080
- marriage.uslegal.com/permarital-agreements

Nevada Common Law Marriage
- www.buddybuddy.com/common.html

Nevada Divorce Law
- Nev. Rev. Stat. § 125.010
- nevadalawhelp.org (click "Family and Juvenile")
- www.familylawselfhelpcenter.org

Nevada Legal Separation Law
- www.hg.org/divorce-law-Nevada.html

Nevada Alimony/Spousal Support/Maintenance Law
- Nev. Rev. Stat. § 125.150
- www.hg.org/divorce-law-Nevada.html

Nevada Property Division Law
- Nev. Rev. Stat. § 125.150
- www.hg.org/divorce-law-Nevada.html

Nevada Child Custody Law
- Nev. Rev. Stat. § 125C.0035
- nevadalawhelp.org (click "Family and Juvenile")
- www.familylawselfhelpcenter.org

Nevada Guardian Ad Litem and Attorney for Child
- Nev. Rev. Stat. §§ 432B.500, 432B.420
- www.childwelfare.gov/pubPDFs/represent.pdf

Nevada Child Support Law
- Nev. Rev. Stat. § 125B.020
- nevadalawhelp.org (click "Family and Juvenile")
- www.familylawselfhelpcenter.org

Nevada Paternity Law
- Nev. Rev. Stat. § 126.071
- www.familylawselfhelpcenter.org

Nevada Legal Definition of Father
- Nev. Rev. Stat. §§ 108.016, 126.051
- www.childwelfare.gov/systemwide/laws_policies/statutes/putative.pdf

Nevada Adoption Law
- Nev. Rev. Stat. §§ 127.020
- www.familylawselfhelpcenter.org

Nevada Termination of Parental Rights
- Nev. Rev. Stat. § 128.150
- www.familylawselfhelpcenter.org
- www.childwelfare.gov/pubPDFs/groundtermin.pdf

Nevada Putative Father Registry
- www.ncsl.org/documents/cyf/putative_father_registries.pdf

Nevada Emancipation Law
- www.familylawselfhelpcenter.org/self-help/other-topics/emancipation-of-a-minor

Nevada Age of Majority
- statelaws.findlaw.com/nevada-law/nevada-marriage-age-requirements-laws.html

Nevada Child Protection/Protective Services
- http://dcfs.nv.gov/Programs/CWS/CPS/CPS

Nevada Child Welfare Agencies
- dcfs.nv.gov

Nevada Juvenile Law
- dcfs.nv.gov/Programs/JJS
- www.ncjj.org/pdf/1State_Juvenile_Justice_Profiles_2005.pdf

Nevada Domestic Violence Law
- Nev. Rev. Stat. § 33.018
- ag.nv.gov/Hot_Topics/Victims/Domestic_Violence

Nevada Assisted Reproduction Law
- Nev. Rev. Stat. § 126.510
- www.selectsurrogate.com/surrogacy-laws-by-state.html

Nevada Grandparent Rights
- Nev. Rev. Stat. § 125C.050
- www.familylawselfhelpcenter.org/self-help/other-topics/visitation-for-non-parents
- www.verywellfamily.com/grandparent-visitation-rights-state-by-state-1695938

Nevada Annulment Law
- Nev. Rev. Stat. §§ 125.290 et seq.
- nevadalawhelp.org (click "Family and Juvenile")
- www.familylawselfhelpcenter.org

Nevada Family Law Forms
- www.familylawselfhelpcenter.org
- family.findlaw.com/divorce/divorce-forms-by-state.html

Nevada Vital Records (Birth, Marriage, Divorce, Death)
- www.cdc.gov/nchs/w2w.htm
- publicrecords.onlinesearches.com/Nevada.htm

Nevada Self-Help Services in Family Law Cases
- nevadalawhelp.org
- nvcourts.gov/ (Click "Self Help")
- www.familylawselfhelpcenter.org

Nevada State Legal Research
- www.loc.gov/law/help/guide/states/us-nv.php
- caselaw.findlaw.com/nevada.html

Nevada Court Rules
- www.leg.state.nv.us/courtrules

Nevada Job Discrimination Based on Marital Status or Gender
- www.ncsl.org/documents/employ/DiscriminationChart-III.pdf

Google, Bing, or Yahoo Searches on Nevada Family Law
- "Nevada family law"
- "Nevada divorce"
- Nevada "property division"
- "Nevada adoption"
- Nevada paternity
- Nevada "child custody"
- Nevada "child support"
- Nevada abortion
- Nevada marriage
- Nevada "separation agreement"
- Nevada "premarital agreement"
- (also try these searches in the *Articles* and *Case law* databases of Scholar.google.com)

NEW HAMPSHIRE FAMILY LAW

New Hampshire Family Laws
- statelaws.findlaw.com/new-hampshire-law/new-hampshire-family-laws.html

New Hampshire Family Code/Domestic Relations Code
- www.gencourt.state.nh.us/rsa/html/nhtoc.htm (click Title XLIII)

New Hampshire Courts Family Division
- www.courts.state.nh.us/fdpp/index.htm

New Hampshire Marriage Law (formation)
- usmarriagelaws.com (enter your state or county)
- www.law.cornell.edu/wex/table_marriage

New Hampshire Premarital Agreement Law
- N.H. Rev. Stat. § 460:2-a
- marriage.uslegal.com/permarital-agreements

New Hampshire Common Law Marriage
- See Exhibit 5-3 in Chapter 5.
- N.H. Rev. Stat. § 457:39
- www.buddybuddy.com/common.html
- www.unmarried.org/common-law-marriage-fact-sheet
- topics.law.cornell.edu/wex/table_marriage

New Hampshire Divorce Law
- NH Rev. Stats. § 458:7
- www.divorcelawinfo.com/states/nh/newhampshire.htm
- www.hg.org/divorce-law-NewHampshire.html

New Hampshire Legal Separation Law
- NH Rev. Stats. § 458:26

New Hampshire Alimony/Spousal Support Law
- NH Rev. Stats. § 458:19
- www.hg.org/divorce-law-NewHampshire.html

New Hampshire Property Division Law
- NH Rev. Stats. § 458:16-a
- www.hg.org/divorce-law-NewHampshire.html

New Hampshire Child Custody Law
- NH Rev. Stats. § 461-A:6
- www.courts.state.nh.us/fdpp/divorce_parenting.htm

New Hampshire Guardian Ad Litem and Attorney for Child
- NH Rev. Stats. § 169-C:10
- www.courts.state.nh.us/fdpp/guardianship_of_minors.htm
- www.childwelfare.gov/pubPDFs/represent.pdf

New Hampshire Child Support Law
- NH Rev. Stats. § 461-A:6
- www.dhhs.nh.gov/dcss/index.htm
- www.supportguidelines.com/links.html

New Hampshire Paternity Law
- NH Rev. Stats. § 168-A:2
- www.dhhs.nh.gov/dcss/index.htm

New Hampshire Legal Definition of Father
- NH Rev. Stat. Ann. § 170-B:2
- www.childwelfare.gov/pubPDFs/putative.pdf

New Hampshire Adoption Law
- NH Rev. Stat. Ann. § 170-B
- www.courts.state.nh.us/fdpp/adoption.htm

New Hampshire Termination of Parental Rights
- NH Rev. Stats. § 169-C:24-a
- www.courts.state.nh.us/fdpp/terminiation.htm
- www.childwelfare.gov/pubPDFs/groundtermin.pdf

New Hampshire Putative Father Registry
- www.dhhs.nh.gov/dcss/pfregistry.htm
- www.courts.state.nh.us/probate/registrylist.pdf
- www.ncsl.org/documents/cyf/putative_father_registries.pdf

New Hampshire Emancipation Law
- minors.uslegal.com/emancipation/new-hampshire-emancipation-of-minor-law

New Hampshire Age of Majority
- minors.uslegal.com/emancipation/new-hampshire-emancipation-of-minor-law
- icpcstatepages.org/newhampshire/ageofmajority

New Hampshire Child Protection/Protective Services
- www.dhhs.nh.gov/dcyf/index.htm
- www.dhhs.state.nh.us/dcyf/cps/index.htm

New Hampshire Child Welfare Agencies
- www.dhhs.nh.gov/dcyf/index.htm

New Hampshire Juvenile Law
- www.courts.state.nh.us/fdpp/juvenile_delinquency.htm
- www.dhhs.state.nh.us/djjs/index.htm
- www.ncjj.org/pdf/1State_Juvenile_Justice_Profiles_2005.pdf

New Hampshire Domestic Violence Law
- www.courts.state.nh.us/fdpp/dv_petitions.htm
- www.courts.state.nh.us/rules/family/fam-10.htm

New Hampshire Surrogacy Law
- NH Rev. Stat. Ann. § 168-B:1
- www.selectsurrogate.com/surrogacy-laws-by-state.html

New Hampshire Grandparent Rights
- NH Rev. Stats. § 461-A:13
- www.verywellfamily.com/grandparent-visitation-rights-state-by-state-1695938

New Hampshire Annulment Law
- NH Rev. Stats. § 5-C:59
- www.hg.org/divorce-law-NewHampshire.html

New Hampshire Family Law Forms
- www.courts.state.nh.us/superior/forms
- www.uslegalforms.com/familylaw/new-hampshire
- family.findlaw.com/divorce/divorce-forms-by-state.html

New Hampshire Vital Records (Birth, Marriage, Divorce, Death)
- www.cdc.gov/nchs/w2w.htm
- publicrecords.onlinesearches.com/Newhampshire.htm

New Hampshire Self-Help Services in Family Law Cases
- www.courts.state.nh.us/selfhelp/getting_started.htm
- www.courts.state.nh.us
- www.nhlegalaid.org

New Hampshire State Legal Research
- www.loc.gov/law/help/guide/states/us-nh.php
- caselaw.findlaw.com/new-hampshire.html

New Hampshire Court Rules
- www.courts.state.nh.us/rules/index.htm

New Hampshire Job Discrimination Based on Marital Status or Gender
- www.ncsl.org/documents/employ/DiscriminationChart-III.pdf

Google, Bing, or Yahoo Searches on New Hampshire Family Law
- "New Hampshire family law"
- "New Hampshire divorce"
- New Hampshire "property division"
- "New Hampshire adoption"
- New Hampshire paternity
- New Hampshire "child custody"
- New Hampshire "child support"
- New Hampshire abortion
- New Hampshire marriage
- New Hampshire "separation agreement"
- New Hampshire "premarital agreement"
- (also try these searches in the *Articles* and *Case law* databases of Scholar.google.com)

NEW JERSEY FAMILY LAW

New Jersey Family Laws
- statelaws.findlaw.com/new-jersey-law/new-jersey-family-laws.html

New Jersey Family Code/Domestic Relations Code
- NJ Stat. Ann. Title 37

New Jersey Courts Family Division
- www.njcourts.gov/courts/family/family.html

New Jersey Marriage Law (formation)
- www.lsnjlaw.org (click Family and Relationships)
- usmarriagelaws.com (enter your state or county)
- marriage.about.com/cs/marriagelicenses/p/newjersey.htm

New Jersey Premarital Agreement Law
- statelaws.findlaw.com/new-jersey-law/new-jersey-prenuptial-agreements.html
- marriage.uslegal.com/permarital-agreements

New Jersey Common Law Marriage
- https://marriage.laws.com/common-law-marriage-new-jersey
- www.buddybuddy.com/common.html

New Jersey Divorce Law
- NJ Stat. Ann. § 2A:34-2
- www.njcourts.gov/attorneys/rules.html
- www.lsnjlaw.org (click Family and Relationships)
- www.divorcelawinfo.com/NJ/flc.htm
- www.hg.org/divorce-law-NewJersey.html

New Jersey Legal Separation Law
- NJ Stat. Ann. § 2A:34-3
- www.hg.org/divorce-law-NewJersey.html

New Jersey Alimony/Spousal Support Law
- NJ Stat. Ann. § 2A:34-23
- www.lsnjlaw.org (click Family and Relationships)
- www.hg.org/divorce-law-NewJersey.html

New Jersey Property Division Law
- NJ Stat. Ann. § 2A:34-23.1
- www.hg.org/divorce-law-NewJersey.html

New Jersey Child Custody Law
- NJ Stat. Ann. § 2A:34-65
- www.njcourts.gov/attorneys/rules.html
- www.lsnjlaw.org (click Family and Relationships)
- statelaws.findlaw.com/new-jersey-law/new-jersey-child-custody-laws.html
- www.hg.org/divorce-law-NewJersey.html

New Jersey Guardian Ad Litem and Attorney for Child
- NJ Stat. Ann. § 9:6-8.23
- www.childwelfare.gov/pubPDFs/represent.pdf

New Jersey Child Support Law
- NJ Stat. Ann. § 2A:34-23a
- www.njchildsupport.org
- www.lsnjlaw.org (click Family and Relationships)

New Jersey Paternity Law
- www.njchildsupport.org/Search.aspx?searchtext=paternity

New Jersey Legal Definition of Father
- NJ Stat. Ann. § 9:17-43
- www.childwelfare.gov/systemwide/laws_policies/statutes/putative.pdf

New Jersey Adoption Law
- NJ Stat. Ann. §§ 9:3-38
- www.njcourts.gov/attorneys/rules.html
- www.lsnjlaw.org (click Family and Relationships)

New Jersey Termination of Parental Rights
- NJ Stat. Ann. § 30:4C-15.1
- www.childwelfare.gov/pubPDFs/groundtermin.pdf

New Jersey Putative Father Registry
- None
- www.ncsl.org/documents/cyf/putative_father_registries.pdf

New Jersey Emancipation Law
- statelaws.findlaw.com/new-jersey-law/new-jersey-legal-ages-laws.html

New Jersey Age of Majority
- NJ Stat. Ann. § 9:17B-3
- statelaws.findlaw.com/new-jersey-law/new-jersey-legal-ages-laws.html

New Jersey Child Protection/Protective Services
- www.visitmonmouth.com/page.aspx?ID=2695

New Jersey Child Welfare Agencies
- www.state.nj.us/humanservices/clients/welfare/

New Jersey Juvenile Law
- www.njcourts.gov/attorneys/rules.html
- www.ncjj.org/pdf/1State_Juvenile_Justice_Profiles_2005.pdf

New Jersey Domestic Violence Law
- NJ Stat. Ann. § 2C:25-19
- www.njcourts.gov/attorneys/rules.html
- www.lsnjlaw.org (click Family and Relationships)

New Jersey Surrogacy Law
- *AHW. v. GHB*, 772 A.2d 948 (NJ Super. 2000)
- www.selectsurrogate.com/surrogacy-laws-by-state.html

New Jersey Grandparent Rights
- NJ Stat. Ann. § 9:2-7.1
- www.verywellfamily.com/grandparent-visitation-rights-state-by-state-1695938

New Jersey Annulment Law
- NJ Stat. Ann. § 2A:34-1
- www.hg.org/divorce-law-NewJersey.html

New Jersey Family Law Forms
- www.judiciary.state.nj.us/prose/index.htm
- family.findlaw.com/divorce/divorce-forms-by-state.html

New Jersey Vital Records (Birth, Marriage, Divorce, Death)
- publicrecords.onlinesearches.com/NewJersey.htm
- www.cdc.gov/nchs/w2w.htm

New Jersey Self-Help Services in Family Law Cases
- www.njcourts.gov/selfhelp/index.html
- www.judiciary.state.nj.us/prose/index.htm
- www.lsnjlaw.org (click Family and Relationships)

New Jersey State Legal Research
- www.loc.gov/law/help/guide/states/us-nj.php
- caselaw.findlaw.com/new-jersey.html

New Jersey Court Rules
- www.njcourts.gov/attorneys/rules.html

New Jersey Job Discrimination Based on Marital Status or Gender
- www.ncsl.org/documents/employ/DiscriminationChart-III.pdf

- "New Jersey family law"
- "New Jersey divorce"
- New Jersey "property division"
- "New Jersey adoption"
- New Jersey paternity
- New Jersey "child custody"

- New Jersey "child support"
- New Jersey abortion
- New Jersey marriage
- New Jersey "separation agreement"
- New Jersey "premarital agreement"
- (also try these searches in the *Articles* and *Case law* databases of Scholar.google.com)

NEW MEXICO FAMILY LAW

New Mexico Family Laws
- statelaws.findlaw.com/new-mexico-law/new-mexico-family-laws.html

New Mexico Family Code/Domestic Relations Code
- NM Stats. Ann. Chapter 40

New Mexico Children's Court
- seconddistrictcourt.nmcourts.gov/family-court.aspx
- www.nmlea.dps.state.nm.us/legal/documents/Childrens_Code.pdf

New Mexico Marriage Law (formation)
- usmarriagelaws.com (enter your state or county)
- www.thespruce.com/get-married-in-new-mexico-2300779

New Mexico Premarital Agreement Law
- NM Stats. Ann. § 40-3A-1
- marriage.uslegal.com/permarital-agreements

New Mexico Common Law Marriage
- marriage.islaws.com/common-law-marriage-new-mexico

New Mexico Divorce Law
- NM Stats. Ann. § 40-4-1
- www.nmcourts.gov/Self-Help/self-help-guide.aspx
- www.lawhelpnewmexico.org/topics (click "Family Law")
- www.divorcelawinfo.com/states/nm/newmexico.htm
- www.hg.org/divorce-law-NewMexico.html

New Mexico Legal Separation Law
- www.hg.org/divorce-law-NewMexico.html
- www.divorcesource.com/ds/newmexico/new-mexico-legal-separation-5332.shtml

New Mexico Alimony/Spousal Support Law
- NM Stats. Ann. § 40-4-7
- www.nmcourts.gov/Self-Help/self-help-guide.aspx
- www.hg.org/divorce-law-NewMexico.html

New Mexico Property Division Law
- NM Stats. Ann. § 40-4-7
- www.hg.org/divorce-law-NewMexico.html

New Mexico Child Custody Law
- NM Stats. Ann. § 40-4-9
- www.lawhelpnewmexico.org/topics (click "Family Law")
- www.hg.org/divorce-law-NewMexico.html

New Mexico Guardian Ad Litem and Attorney for Child
- NM Stat. § 32A-4-10
- www.childwelfare.gov/pubPDFs/represent.pdf

New Mexico Child Support Law
- NM Stats. Ann. § 40-4-11.1
- www.nmcourts.gov/Self-Help/self-help-guide.aspx
- www.lawhelpnewmexico.org/topics (click "Family Law")

New Mexico Paternity Law
- NM Stats. Ann. §§ 40-11A-301 et seq.
- www.lawhelpnewmexico.org/topics (click "Family Law")

New Mexico Legal Definition of Father
- NM Stat. § 32A-5-3
- www.childwelfare.gov/systemwide/laws_policies/statutes/putative.pdf

New Mexico Adoption Law
- NM Stat. § 32A-5-1

New Mexico Termination of Parental Rights
- NM Stat. § 32A-4-28
- www.childwelfare.gov/pubPDFs/groundtermin.pdf

New Mexico Putative Father Registry
- NM Stat. § 32A-5-20
- www.ncsl.org/documents/cyf/putative_father_registries.pdf

New Mexico Emancipation Law
- NM Stat. §§ 32A-21-4, 32A-21-7

New Mexico Age of Majority
- statelaws.findlaw.com/new-mexico-law/new-mexico-legal-ages-laws.html

New Mexico Child Protection/Protective Services
- cyfd.org/child-abuse-neglect

New Mexico Child Welfare Agencies
- www.cyfd.org

New Mexico Juvenile Law
- www.nmlea.dps.state.nm.us/legal/documents/Childrens_Code.pdf
- www.ncjj.org/pdf/1State_Juvenile_Justice_Profiles_2005.pdf

New Mexico Domestic Violence Law
- NM Stat. § 31-12-12
- www.nmcourts.gov/Self-Help/self-help-guide.aspx

New Mexico Surrogacy Law
- NM Stat. § 32A-5-34
- www.selectsurrogate.com/surrogacy-laws-by-state.html

New Mexico Grandparent Rights
- NM Stats. Ann. § 40-9-2
- www.lawhelpnewmexico.org/topics (click "Family Law")
- www.verywellfamily.com/grandparent-visitation-rights-state-by-state-1695938

New Mexico Annulment Law
- NM Stats. Ann. § 40-1-9
- www.hg.org/divorce-law-NewMexico.html

New Mexico Family Law Forms
- www.nmcourts.gov/forms.aspx
- family.findlaw.com/divorce/divorce-forms-by-state.html

New Mexico Vital Records (Birth, Marriage, Divorce, Death)
- www.cdc.gov/nchs/w2w.htm
- publicrecords.onlinesearches.com/NewMexico.htm

New Mexico Self-Help Services in Family Law Cases
- www.nmcourts.gov/Self-Help/self-help-guide.aspx
- www.lawhelpnewmexico.org/topics (click "Family Law")

New Mexico State Legal Research
- www.loc.gov/law/help/guide/states/us-nm.php
- caselaw.findlaw.com/new-mexico.html

New Mexico Court Rules
- www.nmcompcomm.us/nmrules/NMRuleSets.aspx

New Mexico Job Discrimination Based on Marital Status or Gender
- www.ncsl.org/documents/employ/DiscriminationChart-III.pdf

Google, Bing, or Yahoo Searches on New Mexico Family Law
- "New Mexico family law"
- "New Mexico divorce"
- New Mexico "property division"
- "New Mexico adoption"
- New Mexico paternity
- New Mexico "child custody"
- New Mexico "child support"
- New Mexico abortion
- New Mexico marriage
- New Mexico "separation agreement"
- New Mexico "premarital agreement"
- (also try these searches in the *Articles* and *Case law* databases of Scholar.google.com)

NEW YORK FAMILY LAW

New York Family Laws
- statelaws.findlaw.com/new-york-law/new-york-family-laws.html

New York Family Court
- www.nycourts.gov/courts/nyc/family/infobycounty.shtml

New York Marriage Law (formation)
- usmarriagelaws.com (enter your state or county)
- www.law.cornell.edu/wex/table_marriage

New York Premarital Agreement Law
- www.nycprenup.com/pages/ny-law
- marriage.uslegal.com/permarital-agreements

New York Common Law Marriage
- www.divorcesource.com/ds/newyork/common-law-marriages-in-new-york-3719.shtml

New York Divorce Law
- NY Dom. Rel. Law § 170
- www.nycourts.gov/courthelp/Family/divorce.shtml
- www.lawhelp.org/NY (click "Family & Safety")
- www.divorcelawinfo.com/states/ny/newyork.htm
- www.hg.org/divorce-law-NewYork.html

New York Legal Separation Law
- NY Dom. Rel. Law § 200
- www.hg.org/divorce-law-NewYork.html

New York Alimony/Spousal Support Law
- NY Family Court Act § 411
- www.hg.org/divorce-law-NewYork.html

New York Property Division Law
- NY Dom. Rel. Law § 236
- statelaws.findlaw.com/new-york-law/new-york-marital-property-laws.html
- www.hg.org/divorce-law-NewYork.html

New York Child Custody Law
- NY Dom. Rel. Law § 240
- www.lawhelp.org/NY (click "Family & Safety")
- www.nycourts.gov/courthelp/Family/custody.shtml

New York Guardian Ad Litem and Attorney for Child
- NY Family Court Act § 1016
- www.childwelfare.gov/pubPDFs/represent.pdf

New York Child Support Law
- NY Dom. Rel. Law § 240
- www.nycourts.gov/courthelp/Family/support.shtml
- www.lawhelp.org/NY (click "Family & Safety")

New York Paternity Law
- NY Family Court Act § 563
- www.nycourts.gov/courthelp/Family/paternity.shtml
- www.lawhelp.org/NY (click "Family & Safety")

New York Legal Definition of Father
- www.childwelfare.gov/systemwide/laws_policies/statutes/putative.pdf

New York Putative Father Registry
- NY Soc. Serv. Law § 372-c

New York Adoption Law
- NY Dom. Rel. Law § 110
- www.lawhelp.org/NY (click "Family & Safety")
- www.nycourts.gov/courthelp/Family/adoption.shtml

New York Termination of Parental Rights
- NY Court Rule 205.49, Soc. Serv. Law § 384-b
- www.childwelfare.gov/pubPDFs/groundtermin.pdf

New York Putative Father Registry
- N.Y. Soc. Serv. Law § 372-c
- www.ncsl.org/documents/cyf/putative_father_registries.pdf

New York Age of Majority & Emancipation Law
- statelaws.findlaw.com/new-york-law/new-york-legal-ages-laws.html

New York Child Protection/Protective Services
- NY Family Court Act § 1012
- ocfs.ny.gov/main/cps

New York Juvenile Law
- www.nycourts.gov/courthelp/Criminal/crimesByChildren.shtml
- www.lawhelp.org/NY (click "Family & Safety")
- www.ncjj.org/pdf/1State_Juvenile_Justice_Profiles_2005.pdf

New York Domestic Violence Law
- NY Soc. Serv. Law § 459-a
- www.lawhelp.org/NY (click "Family & Safety")

New York Surrogacy Law
- NY Dom. Rel. Law § 122
- www.selectsurrogate.com/surrogacy-laws-by-state.html

New York Grandparent Rights
- www.lawhelpny.org/search?q=grandparent
- www.verywellfamily.com/grandparent-visitation-rights-state-by-state-1695938

New York Annulment Law
- NY Dom. Rel. Law § 140
- www.hg.org/divorce-law-NewYork.html

New York Family Law Forms
- www.lawhelpny.org/resource/interactive-forms
- www.nycourts.gov/divorce/forms.shtml
- family.findlaw.com/divorce/divorce-forms-by-state.html

New York Vital Records (Birth, Marriage, Divorce, Death)
- www.cdc.gov/nchs/w2w.htm
- publicrecords.onlinesearches.com/NewYork.htm

New York Self-Help Services in Family Law Cases
- www.lawhelpny.org
- www.nycourts.gov/courthelp

New York State Legal Research
- www.loc.gov/law/help/guide/states/us-ny.php
- caselaw.findlaw.com/new-york.html

New York Court Rules
- www.courts.state.ny.us/rules/trialcourts/index.shtml

New York Job Discrimination Based on Marital Status or Gender
- www.ncsl.org/documents/employ/DiscriminationChart-III.pdf

Google, Bing, or Yahoo Searches on New York Family Law
- "New York family law"
- "New York divorce"
- New York "property division"
- "New York adoption"
- New York paternity
- New York "child custody"
- New York "child support"
- New York abortion
- New York marriage
- New York "separation agreement"
- New York "premarital agreement"
- (also try these searches in the *Articles* and *Case law* databases of Scholar.google.com)

NORTH CAROLINA FAMILY LAW

North Carolina Family Laws
- statelaws.findlaw.com/north-carolina-law/north-carolina-family-laws.html

North Carolina Family Code/Domestic Relations Code
- NC Gen. Stat. Chapter 50

North Carolina Family Court
- www.nccourts.gov/courts/family-court

North Carolina Marriage Law (formation)
- statutes.laws.com/north-carolina/Chapter_51
- usmarriagelaws.com (enter your state or county)
- www.law.cornell.edu/wex/table_marriage

North Carolina Premarital Agreement Law
- NC Gen. Stat. §§ 52B-3
- marriage.uslegal.com/permarital-agreements

North Carolina Common Law Marriage
- topics.law.cornell.edu/wex/table_marriage
- www.buddybuddy.com/common.html

North Carolina Divorce Law
- NC Gen. Stat. § 50-11
- www.nccourts.gov/help-topics/divorce
- www.legalaidnc.org
- www.lawhelp.org/NC (click "Family and Juvenile")
- www.divorcelawinfo.com/states/nc/northcarolina.htm
- www.hg.org/divorce-law-NorthCarolina.html

North Carolina Legal Separation Law
- NC Gen. Stat. § 50-7
- www.hg.org/divorce-law-NorthCarolina.html

North Carolina Alimony/Spousal Support Law
- NC Gen. Stat. § 50-16.3A
- www.hg.org/divorce-law-NorthCarolina.html

North Carolina Property Division Law
- NC Gen. Stat. § 50-20
- www.hg.org/divorce-law-NorthCarolina.html

North Carolina Child Custody Law
- NC Gen. Stat. § 50-13.2
- www.legalaidnc.org
- www.lawhelp.org/NC (click "Family and Juvenile")
- www.hg.org/divorce-law-NorthCarolina.html

North Carolina Relocation of Child
- NC Gen. Stat. § 50-13.2

North Carolina Guardian Ad Litem and Attorney for Child
- NC Gen. Stat. § 7B-601
- www.childwelfare.gov/pubPDFs/represent.pdf

North Carolina Child Support Law
- NC Gen. Stat. § 8-57.2
- www.nccourts.gov/help-topics/family-and-children/child-support

North Carolina Paternity Law
- NC Gen. Stat. § 110-136.6
- www.lawhelp.org/NC (click "Family and Juvenile")

North Carolina Legal Definition of Father
- www.childwelfare.gov/systemwide/laws_policies/statutes/putative.pdf

North Carolina Adoption Law
- NC Gen. Stat. § 48-2-601
- www.lawhelp.org/NC (click "Family and Juvenile")
- www.nccourts.gov/documents/forms/adoption-forms-dhhs

North Carolina Termination of Parental Rights
- NC Gen. Stat. § 7B-1111
- www.lawhelp.org/NC (click "Family and Juvenile")
- www.childwelfare.gov/pubPDFs/groundtermin.pdf

North Carolina Putative Father Registry
- www.ncsl.org/documents/cyf/putative_father_registries.pdf

North Carolina Emancipation Law
- NC Gen. Stat. § 7B-3500

North Carolina Age of Majority
- statelaws.findlaw.com/north-carolina-law/north-carolina-legal-ages-laws.html

North Carolina Child Protection/Protective Services
- www.nc.gov/child-protection-services

North Carolina Juvenile Law
- www.lawhelp.org/NC (click "Family and Juvenile")
- www.ncjj.org/pdf/1State_Juvenile_Justice_Profiles_2005.pdf

North Carolina Domestic Violence Law
- NC Gen. Stat. § 50B-1
- www.lawhelp.org/NC (click "Family and Juvenile")

North Carolina Surrogacy Law
- NC Gen. Stat. § 48-10-102
- www.selectsurrogate.com/surrogacy-laws-by-state.html

North Carolina Grandparent Rights
- NC Gen. Stat. § 50-13.2
- www.verywellfamily.com/grandparent-visitation-rights-state-by-state-1695938

North Carolina Annulment Law
- NC Gen. Stat. § 50-4
- www.hg.org/divorce-law-NorthCarolina.html

North Carolina Family Law Forms
- www.nccourts.org/Forms/FormSearch.asp
- www.courtreference.com/North-Carolina-Court-Forms.htm
- family.findlaw.com/divorce/divorce-forms-by-state.html

North Carolina Vital Records (Birth, Marriage, Divorce, Death)
- www.cdc.gov/nchs/w2w.htm
- publicrecords.onlinesearches.com/NorthCarolina.htm

North Carolina Self-Help Services in Family Law Cases
- www.lawhelp.org/NC (click "Family and Juvenile")
- www.legalaidnc.org
- www.courtreference.com/North-Carolina-Courts-Self-Help.htm

North Carolina State Legal Research
- www.loc.gov/law/help/guide/states/us-nc.php
- caselaw.findlaw.com/north-carolina.html

North Carolina Court Rules
- www.nccourts.gov/courts/supreme-court/court-rules

North Carolina Job Discrimination Based on Marital Status or Gender
- www.ncsl.org/documents/employ/DiscriminationChart-III.pdf

Google, Bing, or Yahoo Searches on North Carolina Family Law
- "North Carolina family law"
- "North Carolina divorce"
- North Carolina "property division"
- "North Carolina adoption"
- North Carolina paternity
- North Carolina "child custody"
- North Carolina "child support"
- North Carolina abortion
- North Carolina marriage
- North Carolina "separation agreement"
- North Carolina "premarital agreement"
- (also try these searches in the *Articles* and *Case law* databases of Scholar.google.com)

NORTH DAKOTA FAMILY LAW

North Dakota Family Laws
- statelaws.findlaw.com/north-dakota-law/north-dakota-family-laws.html

North Dakota Family Law Manual
- www.legalassist.org/?id=128&page=ND+Family+Law+Manual

North Dakota Family Code/Domestic Relations Code
- www.legis.nd.gov/cencode/t14.html
- www.legis.nd.gov/information/statutes/cent-code.html
- www.legis.nd.gov/index.html
- www.law.cornell.edu/wex/table_family

North Dakota Marriage Law (formation)
- ND Cent. Code § 14-03-01
- usmarriagelaws.com (enter your state or county)

North Dakota Premarital Agreement Law
- ND Cent. Code § 14-03.2-01
- marriage.uslegal.com/permarital-agreements

North Dakota Common Law Marriage
- *Cermak v. Cermak* 569 N.W.2d 280, 284 (N.D. 1997)

North Dakota Divorce Law
- ND Cent. Code § 14-05-03
- www.ndcourts.gov/legal-self-help/divorce
- www.divorcelawinfo.com/states/nd/northdakota.htm

North Dakota Legal Separation Law
- ND Cent. Code § 14-05-03.1

North Dakota Alimony/Spousal Support Law
- ND Cent. Code § 14-05-24.1

North Dakota Property Division Law
- ND Cent. Code § 14-05-24

North Dakota Child Custody Law
- ND Cent. Code § 14-09-06.2

North Dakota Guardian Ad Litem and Attorney for Child
- ND Cent. Code § 50-25.1-08
- www.childwelfare.gov/pubPDFs/represent.pdf

North Dakota Child Support Law
- ND Cent. Code § 14-09-08.19
- www.nd.gov/dhs/services/childsupport

North Dakota Paternity Law
- ND Cent. Code § 14-20-14.(304)
- childsupport.dhs.nd.gov/services/establish-paternity

North Dakota Legal Definition of Father
- ND Cent. Code §§ 14-20-02, 14-20-10
- www.childwelfare.gov/systemwide/laws_policies/statutes/putative.pdf

North Dakota Adoption Law
- ND Cent. Code § 14-15-01
- statelaws.findlaw.com/north-dakota-law/north-dakota-adoption-laws.html

North Dakota Termination of Parental Rights
- ND Cent. Code § 27-20-44
- www.childwelfare.gov/pubPDFs/groundtermin.pdf

North Dakota Putative Father Registry
- www.ncsl.org/documents/cyf/putative_father_registries.pdf

North Dakota Age of Majority & Emancipation
- statelaws.findlaw.com/north-dakota-law/north-dakota-marriage-age-requirements-laws.html

North Dakota Child Protection/Protective Services
- www.nd.gov/dhs/services/childfamily/cps

North Dakota Child Welfare Agencies
- www.nd.gov/dhs/services/childfamily

North Dakota Juvenile Law
- www.ndcourts.gov/other-courts/juvenile-court
- www.ncjj.org/pdf/1State_Juvenile_Justice_Profiles_2005.pdf

North Dakota Domestic Violence Law
- ND Cent. Code § 14-07.1-01

North Dakota Surrogacy Law
- ND Cent. Code §14-18-05
- www.selectsurrogate.com/surrogacy-laws-by-state.html

North Dakota Grandparent Rights
- ND Cent. Code § 14-09-05.1
- www.verywellfamily.com/grandparent-visitation-rights-state-by-state-1695938

North Dakota Annulment Law
- ND Cent. Code § 14-04-01

North Dakota Parental Liability for Acts of Minors
- ND Cent. Code § 32-03-39

North Dakota Family Law Forms
- www.legalassist.org/?id=104
- www.ndcourts.gov/court/forms
- family.findlaw.com/divorce/divorce-forms-by-state.html

North Dakota Vital Records (Birth, Marriage, Divorce, Death)
- www.cdc.gov/nchs/w2w.htm
- publicrecords.onlinesearches.com/NorthDakota.htm

North Dakota Self-Help Services in Family Law Cases
- www.ndcourts.gov/legal-self-help
- www.ndcourts.gov/court/forms
- www.courtreference.com/North-Dakota-Courts-Self-Help.htm

North Dakota State Legal Research
- www.loc.gov/law/help/guide/states/us-nd.php
- caselaw.findlaw.com/north-dakota.html

North Dakota Court Rules
- www.ndcourts.gov/rules

North Dakota Job Discrimination Based on Marital Status or Gender
- www.ncsl.org/documents/employ/DiscriminationChart-III.pdf

Google, Bing, or Yahoo Searches on North Dakota Family Law
- "North Dakota family law"
- "North Dakota divorce"
- North Dakota "property division"
- "North Dakota adoption"
- North Dakota paternity
- North Dakota "child custody"
- North Dakota "child support"
- North Dakota abortion
- North Dakota marriage
- North Dakota "separation agreement"
- North Dakota "premarital agreement"
- (also try these searches in the *Articles* and *Case law* databases of Scholar.google.com)

OHIO FAMILY LAW

Ohio Family Laws
- statelaws.findlaw.com/ohio-law/ohio-family-laws.html

Ohio Family Code/Domestic Relations Code
- codes.ohio.gov/orc (click Title 31)

Ohio Domestic Relations Division of Courts of Common Pleas
- www.supremecourt.ohio.gov/JudSystem/default.asp
- www.supremecourt.ohio.gov/SCO/jurisdiction/structure.pdf
- www.sconet.state.oh.us/Boards/familyCourts/V109.pdf

Ohio Marriage Law (formation)
- codes.ohio.gov/orc/3101
- usmarriagelaws.com (enter your state or county)
- statelaws.findlaw.com/ohio-law/ohio-marriage-laws.html

Ohio Premarital Agreement Law
- statelaws.findlaw.com/ohio-law/ohio-prenuptial-agreements.html
- marriage.uslegal.com/permarital-agreements

Ohio Common Law Marriage
- See Exhibit 5-3 in Chapter 5.
- Ohio Revised Code § 3105.12
- topics.law.cornell.edu/wex/table_marriage
- www.buddybuddy.com/common.html
- www.unmarried.org/common-law-marriage-fact-sheet

Ohio Divorce Law
- Ohio Rev. Code Ann. § 3105.01
- www.divorcelawinfo.com/states/ohio/ohio.htm
- www.hg.org/divorce-law-Ohio.html

Ohio Legal Separation Law
- Ohio Rev. Code Ann. § 3105.17
- www.hg.org/divorce-law-Ohio.html

Ohio Alimony/Spousal Support Law
- Ohio Rev. Code Ann. §3105.18
- www.maritallaws.com/states/ohio/alimony
- www.hg.org/divorce-law-Ohio.html

Ohio Property Division Law
- Ohio Rev. Code Ann. § 3105.171
- www.divorcesource.com/ds/ohio/ohio-property-division-4753.shtml
- www.hg.org/divorce-law-Ohio.html

Ohio Child Custody Law
- Ohio Rev. Code Ann. § 3109.04
- statelaws.findlaw.com/ohio-law/ohio-child-custody-forms-and-process.html
- www.hg.org/divorce-law-Ohio.html

Ohio Guardian Ad Litem and Attorney for Child
- Ohio Rev. Code Ann. § 2151.281
- www.childwelfare.gov/pubPDFs/represent.pdf

Ohio Child Support Law
- Ohio Rev. Code Ann. § 3119.02
- jfs.ohio.gov/ocs

Ohio Paternity Law
- Ohio Rev. Code Ann. § 3111.04

Ohio Legal Definition of Father
- Ohio Rev. Code Ann. § 3111.03
- www.childwelfare.gov/systemwide/laws_policies/statutes/putative.pdf

Ohio Adoption Law
- Ohio Rev. Code Ann. § 3107.07
- statelaws.findlaw.com/ohio-law/ohio-adoption-laws.html
- fosterandadopt.jfs.ohio.gov/wps/portal/gov/ofc

Ohio Termination of Parental Rights
- Ohio Rev. Code Ann. § 2151.414
- www.childwelfare.gov/pubPDFs/groundtermin.pdf

Ohio Putative Father Registry
- Ohio Rev. Code Ann. § 3107.07
- jfs.ohio.gov/pfr
- www.ncsl.org/documents/cyf/putative_father_registries.pdf

Ohio Emancipation Law
- minors.uslegal.com/emancipation/ohio-emancipation-of-minor-law

Ohio Age of Majority
- Ohio Rev. Code Ann. § 3109.01
- statelaws.findlaw.com/ohio-law/ohio-legal-ages-laws.html

Ohio Child Protection/Protective Services
- jfs.ohio.gov/ocf/aps.stm

Ohio Child Welfare Agencies
- jfs.ohio.gov/ocf/index.stm

Ohio Juvenile Law
- www.dys.ohio.gov
- www.ncjj.org/pdf/1State_Juvenile_Justice_Profiles_2005.pdf

Ohio Domestic Violence Law
- Ohio Rev. Code Ann. § 2919.25
- www.odvn.org

Ohio Surrogacy Law
- Ohio Rev. Code Ann. § 3111.89
- www.selectsurrogate.com/surrogacy-laws-by-state.html

Ohio Grandparent Rights
- Ohio Rev. Code Ann. § 3109.11
- www.verywellfamily.com/grandparent-visitation-rights-state-by-state-1695938

Ohio Annulment Law
- Ohio Rev. Code Ann. § 3105.31
- statelaws.findlaw.com/ohio-law/ohio-annulment-and-prohibited-marriage-laws.html

Ohio Family Law Forms
- family.findlaw.com/divorce/divorce-forms-by-state.html

Ohio Vital Records (Birth, Marriage, Divorce, Death)
- publicrecords.onlinesearches.com/Ohio.htm
- www.cdc.gov/nchs/w2w.htm

Ohio Self-Help Services in Family Law Cases
- www.ohiolegalhelp.org

Ohio State Legal Research
- www.loc.gov/law/help/guide/states/us-oh.php
- caselaw.findlaw.com/ohio.html

Ohio Court Rules
- www.supremecourt.ohio.gov/LegalResources/Rules

Ohio Job Discrimination Based on Marital Status or Gender
- www.ncsl.org/documents/employ/DiscriminationChart-III.pdf

Google, Bing, or Yahoo Searches on Ohio Family Law
- "Ohio family law"
- "Ohio divorce"
- Ohio "property division"
- "Ohio adoption"
- Ohio paternity
- Ohio "child custody"
- Ohio "child support"
- Ohio abortion
- Ohio marriage
- Ohio "separation agreement"
- Ohio "premarital agreement"
- (also try these searches in the *Articles* and *Case law* Databases of Scholar.google.com)

OKLAHOMA FAMILY LAW

Oklahoma Family Laws
- statelaws.findlaw.com/oklahoma-law/oklahoma-family-laws.html

Oklahoma Family Code/Domestic Relations Code
- Okla. Stat. Title 43

Oklahoma Childrens's Court
- www.oscn.net/Sites/CourtImprovement/default.aspx

Oklahoma Marriage Law (formation)
- usmarriagelaws.com (enter your state or county)
- www.law.cornell.edu/wex/table_marriage

Oklahoma Premarital Agreement Law
- marriage.uslegal.com/permarital-agreements

Oklahoma Common Law Marriage
- See Exhibit 5-3 in Chapter 5.
- *Brooks v. Sanders*, 190 P.3d 357 (Okla. Civ. App. 2008)
- oklaw.org/issues/family/marriage
- www.buddybuddy.com/common.html
- www.unmarried.org/common-law-marriage-fact-sheet

Oklahoma Divorce Law
- 43 Okla. Stat. § 101
- oklaw.org/issues/family
- www.divorcelawinfo.com/states/ok/oklahoma.htm
- www.hg.org/divorce-law-Oklahoma.html

Oklahoma Legal Separation Law
- www.hg.org/divorce-law-Oklahoma.html

Oklahoma Alimony/Spousal Support Law
- 43 Okla. Stat. § 121
- www.hg.org/divorce-law-Oklahoma.html

Oklahoma Property Division Law
- 43 Okla. Stat. § 121
- www.hg.org/divorce-law-Oklahoma.html

Oklahoma Child Custody Law
- 43 Okla. Stat. § 112
- oklaw.org/issues/family
- www.hg.org/divorce-law-Oklahoma.html

Oklahoma Relocation of Child
- 43 Okla. Stat. § 112.3

Oklahoma Guardian Ad Litem and Attorney for Child
- 10A Okla. Stat. § 1-4-102, 1-4-306
- www.childwelfare.gov/pubPDFs/represent.pdf

Oklahoma Child Support Law
- 40 Okla. Stat. § 2-801
- www.okdhs.org/services/ocss/Pages/default.aspx
- oklaw.org/search?q=child+support

Oklahoma Paternity Law
- 43 Okla. Stat. § 109.2
- oklaw.org/issues/family

Oklahoma Legal Definition of Father
- 10 Okla. Stat. § 7700-102
- www.childwelfare.gov/systemwide/laws_policies/statutes/putative.pdf

Oklahoma Adoption Law
- 10 Okla. Stat. § 7501-1.2
- oklaw.org/issues/family

Oklahoma Termination of Parental Rights
- 10A Okla. Stat. § 1-4-904
- www.childwelfare.gov/pubPDFs/groundtermin.pdf

Oklahoma Putative Father Registry
- 10 Okla. Stat. Ann. § 7506-1.1
- www.ncsl.org/documents/cyf/putative_father_registries.pdf

Oklahoma Age of Majority & Emancipation Law
- statelaws.findlaw.com/oklahoma-law/oklahoma-legal-ages-laws.html

Oklahoma Child Protection/Protective Services
- www.okdhs.org/services/cps/Pages/default.aspx

Oklahoma Juvenile Law
- www.ok.gov/oja
- www.ncjj.org/pdf/1State_Juvenile_Justice_Profiles_2005.pdf

Oklahoma Domestic Violence Law
- oklaw.org (click "Relationship Abuse")

Oklahoma Surrogacy Law
- 21 Okla. Stat. § 866
- www.selectsurrogate.com/surrogacy-laws-by-state.html

Oklahoma Grandparent Rights
- 43 Okla. Stat. § 109.4
- www.verywellfamily.com/grandparent-visitation-rights-state-by-state-1695938

Oklahoma Annulment Law
- 43 Okla. Stat. § 2
- oklaw.org/issues/family/marriage

Oklahoma Family Law Forms
- www.oscn.net/oscn/scrules/scforms.html
- oklaw.org/self-help-forms
- family.findlaw.com/divorce/divorce-forms-by-state.html

Oklahoma Vital Records (Birth, Marriage, Divorce, Death)
- www.cdc.gov/nchs/w2w.htm
- publicrecords.onlinesearches.com/Oklahoma.htm

Oklahoma Self-Help Services in Family Law Cases
- oklaw.org
- oklaw.org/issues/family
- www.legalaidok.org

Oklahoma State Legal Research
- www.loc.gov/law/help/guide/states/us-ok.php
- caselaw.findlaw.com/oklahoma.html

Oklahoma Court Rules
- www.oscn.net/applications/oscn/index.asp?ftdb=STOK&level=1

Oklahoma Job Discrimination Based on Marital Status or Gender
- www.ncsl.org/documents/employ/DiscriminationChart-III.pdf

Google, Bing, or Yahoo Searches on Oklahoma Family Law
- "Oklahoma family law"
- "Oklahoma divorce"
- Oklahoma "property division"
- "Oklahoma adoption"
- Oklahoma paternity
- Oklahoma "child custody"
- Oklahoma "child support"
- Oklahoma abortion
- Oklahoma marriage
- Oklahoma "separation agreement"
- Oklahoma "premarital agreement"
- (also try these searches in the *Articles* and *Case law* databases of Scholar.google.com)

OREGON FAMILY LAW

Oregon Family Laws
- statelaws.findlaw.com/oregon-law/oregon-family-laws.html

Oregon Family Code/Domestic Relations Code
- Or. Rev. Stat. Ann. Title 11

Oregon Marriage Law (formation)
- usmarriagelaws.com (enter your state or county)
- www.osbar.org/public/legalinfo/1131_Marriage.htm
- www.law.cornell.edu/wex/table_marriage

Oregon Premarital Agreement Law
- marriage.uslegal.com/permarital-agreements

Oregon Divorce Law
- Or. Rev. Stat. Ann. § 107.025
- www.divorcelawinfo.com/states/or/oregon.htm
- www.hg.org/divorce-law-Oregon.html
- www.oregonlawhelp.org/OR (click "Family")
- www.courts.oregon.gov/help/Pages/default.aspx

Oregon Legal Separation Law
- www.oregonlawhelp.org/OR (click "Family")
- www.hg.org/divorce-law-Oregon.html

Oregon Alimony/Spousal Support Law
- Or. Rev. Stat. Ann. §§ 107.105
- www.oregonlawhelp.org/OR (click "Family")
- www.hg.org/divorce-law-Oregon.html

Oregon Property Division Law
- Or. Rev. Stat. Ann. § 107.105
- www.hg.org/divorce-law-Oregon.html

Oregon Child Custody Law
- Or. Rev. Stat. Ann. § 107.137
- www.oregonlawhelp.org/OR (click "Family")
- www.courts.oregon.gov/help/Pages/default.aspx

Oregon Guardian Ad Litem and Attorney for Child
- www.childwelfare.gov/pubPDFs/represent.pdf

Oregon Child Support Law
- www.oregonlawhelp.org/OR (click "Family")
- oregonchildsupport.gov
- www.courts.oregon.gov/help/Pages/default.aspx

Oregon Paternity Law
- Ore. Rev. Stat. § 109.070
- www.oregonlawhelp.org/OR (click "Family")

Oregon Legal Definition of Father
- Or. Rev. Stat. Ann. § 109.070
- www.childwelfare.gov/systemwide/laws_policies/statutes/putative.pdf

Oregon Adoption Law
- Or. Rev. Stat. Ann. § 109.315
- www.oregonlawhelp.org/OR (click "Family")

Oregon Termination of Parental Rights
- Or. Rev. Stat. Ann. § 419B.498
- www.childwelfare.gov/pubPDFs/groundtermin.pdf

Oregon Putative Father Registry
- www.ncsl.org/documents/cyf/putative_father_registries.pdf

Oregon Emancipation Law
- Or. Rev. Stat. Ann. § 419B.552

Oregon Age of Majority
- statelaws.findlaw.com/oregon-law/oregon-legal-ages-laws.html

Oregon Child Protection/Protective Services
- www.oregon.gov/dhs/children/child-abuse/Pages/CPS.aspx

Oregon Juvenile Law
- www.oregon.gov/oya/pages/juvrights.aspx
- www.ncjj.org/pdf/1State_Juvenile_Justice_Profiles_2005.pdf

Oregon Domestic Violence Law
- Or. Rev. Stat. Ann. § 132.586
- www.courts.oregon.gov/help/Pages/default.aspx

Oregon Sex Discrimination Law
- Or. Rev. Stat. Ann. § 659A.030

Oregon Surrogacy Law
- Or. Rev. Stat. Ann. § 163.537(2)(d)
- www.selectsurrogate.com/surrogacy-laws-by-state.html

Oregon Grandparent Rights
- Or. Rev. Stat. Ann. § 109.332
- www.verywellfamily.com/grandparent-visitation-rights-state-by-state-1695938

Oregon Annulment Law
- Or. Rev. Stat. Ann. § 106.020
- www.oregonlawhelp.org/OR (click "Family")

Oregon Parental Liability for Acts of Minors
- Or. Rev. Stat. Ann. § 30.765

Oregon Family Law Forms
- www.courts.oregon.gov/forms/Pages/default.aspx
- family.findlaw.com/divorce/divorce-forms-by-state.html

Oregon Vital Records (Birth, Marriage, Divorce, Death)
- www.cdc.gov/nchs/w2w.htm
- publicrecords.onlinesearches.com/Oregon.htm

Oregon Self-Help Services in Family Law Cases
- www.courts.oregon.gov/help/Pages/default.aspx
- www.oregonlawhelp.org/OR (click "Family")
- www.courtreference.com/Oregon-Courts-Self-Help.htm

Oregon State Legal Research
- www.loc.gov/law/help/guide/states/us-or.php
- caselaw.findlaw.com/oregon.html

Oregon Court Rules
- www.courts.oregon.gov/rules/Pages/default.aspx

Oregon Job Discrimination Based on Marital Status or Gender
- www.ncsl.org/documents/employ/DiscriminationChart-III.pdf

Google, Bing, or Yahoo Searches on Oregon Family Law
- "Oregon family law"
- "Oregon divorce"
- Oregon "property division"
- "Oregon adoption"
- Oregon paternity
- Oregon "child custody"
- Oregon "child support"
- Oregon abortion
- Oregon marriage
- Oregon "separation agreement"
- Oregon "premarital agreement"
- (also try these searches in the *Articles* and *Case law* databases of Scholar.google.com)

PENNSYLVANIA FAMILY LAW

Pennsylvania Family Laws
- statelaws.findlaw.com/pennsylvania-law/pennsylvania-family-laws.html

Pennsylvania Family Code/Domestic Relations Code
- Pa Consol. Stats. Ann. Title 23

Pennsylvania Family Court Division (Philadelphia)
- www.courts.phila.gov/common-pleas/family

Pennsylvania Marriage Law (formation)
- usmarriagelaws.com (enter your state or county)
- marriage.about.com/cs/marriagelicenses/p/pennsylvania.htm
- www.law.cornell.edu/wex/table_marriage

Pennsylvania Premarital Agreement Law
- 23 Pa.C.S.A. § 3106
- marriage.uslegal.com/permarital-agreements

Pennsylvania Common Law Marriage
- See Exhibit 5-3 in Chapter 5.
- 23 Pa.C.S.A. § 1103

- www.buddybuddy.com/common.html
- www.unmarried.org/common-law-marriage-fact-sheet

Pennsylvania Divorce Law
- 23 Pa Consol. Stats. Ann. § 3301
- www.palawhelp.org (click "Children and Families")

Pennsylvania Legal Separation Law
- www.hg.org/divorce-law-Pennsylvania.html
- www.palawhelp.org (click "Children and Families")

Pennsylvania Alimony/Spousal Support Law
- 23 Pa Consol. Stats. Ann. § 3701
- www.hg.org/divorce-law-Pennsylvania.html

Pennsylvania Property Division Law
- 23 Pa Consol. Stats. Ann. § 3502 (equitable division)
- www.divorcelawinfo.com/PA/papropdiv.htm
- www.hg.org/divorce-law-Pennsylvania.html

Pennsylvania Child Custody Law
- 23 Pa Consol. Stats. Ann. § 5328
- www.palawhelp.org (click "Children and Families")
- www.hg.org/divorce-law-Pennsylvania.html

Pennsylvania Guardian Ad Litem and Attorney for Child
- 42 Pa Consol. Stats. Ann. §§ 6311, 6342
- www.childwelfare.gov/pubPDFs/represent.pdf

Pennsylvania Child Support Law
- 23 Pa Consol. Stats. Ann. § 4322
- Pa. R. Civ. P. 1910.16-1
- statelaws.findlaw.com/pennsylvania-law/pennsylvania-child-support-guidelines.html

Pennsylvania Paternity Law
- 23 Pa Consol. Stats. Ann. § 4343
- www.palawhelp.org (click "Children and Families")

Pennsylvania Legal Definition of Father
- www.childwelfare.gov/systemwide/laws_policies/statutes/putative.pdf

Pennsylvania Adoption Law
- www.palawhelp.org (click "Children and Families")

Pennsylvania Termination of Parental Rights
- adoption.com/grounds-for-termination-of-parental-rights-pennsylvania
- www.childwelfare.gov/pubPDFs/groundtermin.pdf

Pennsylvania Putative Father Registry
- www.ncsl.org/documents/cyf/putative_father_registries.pdf

Pennsylvania Age of Majority & Emancipation Law
- statelaws.findlaw.com/pennsylvania-law/pennsylvania-legal-ages-laws.html
- www.palawhelp.org (click "Children and Families")
- www.nwls.org/emancipation_of_minors.htm

Pennsylvania Child Protection/Protective Services
- keepkidssafe.pa.gov/about/cpsl/index.htm

Pennsylvania Juvenile Law
- www.palawhelp.org (click "Children and Families")
- www.ncjj.org/pdf/1State_Juvenile_Justice_Profiles_2005.pdf

Pennsylvania Domestic Violence Law
- 23 Pa Consol. Stats. Ann. § 6102
- www.palawhelp.org (click "Children and Families")

Pennsylvania Surrogacy Law
- www.selectsurrogate.com/surrogacy-laws-by-state.html

Pennsylvania Annulment Law
- 23 Pa Consol. Stats. Ann. § 3303
- www.hg.org/divorce-law-Pennsylvania.html

Pennsylvania Family Law Forms
- www.palawhelp.org (click "Children and Families")
- family.findlaw.com/divorce/divorce-forms-by-state.html

Pennsylvania Vital Records (Birth, Marriage, Divorce, Death)
- www.cdc.gov/nchs/w2w.htm
- publicrecords.onlinesearches.com/Pennsylvania.htm

Pennsylvania Self-Help Services in Family Law Cases
- www.palawhelp.org (click "Children and Families")
- www.nwls.org/Resources.htm

Pennsylvania State Legal Research
- www.loc.gov/law/help/guide/states/us-pa.php
- caselaw.findlaw.com/pennsylvania.html

Pennsylvania Court Rules
- www.pacode.com/secure/data/231/231toc.html
- www.jenkinslaw.org/research/guides/pennsylvania-court-rules-state/pa-court-rules

Pennsylvania Job Discrimination Based on Marital Status or Gender
- www.ncsl.org/documents/employ/DiscriminationChart-III.pdf

Google, Bing, or Yahoo Searches on Pennsylvania Family Law
- "Pennsylvania family law"
- "Pennsylvania divorce"
- Pennsylvania "property division"
- "Pennsylvania adoption"
- Pennsylvania paternity
- Pennsylvania "child custody"
- Pennsylvania "child support"
- Pennsylvania abortion
- Pennsylvania marriage
- Pennsylvania "separation agreement"
- Pennsylvania "premarital agreement"
- (also try these searches in the *Articles* and *Case law* databases of Scholar.google.com)

RHODE ISLAND FAMILY LAW

Rhode Island Family Laws
- statelaws.findlaw.com/rhode-island-law/rhode-island-family-laws.html

Rhode Island Family Code/Domestic Relations Code
- RI Gen Laws Title 15
- www.rilin.state.ri.us/Statutes/TITLE15/15-5/INDEX.HTM

Rhode Island Family Court
- www.courts.ri.gov/Courts/FamilyCourt/Pages/default.aspx

Rhode Island Marriage Law (formation)
- usmarriagelaws.com (enter your state or county)
- www.law.cornell.edu/wex/table_marriage

Rhode Island Premarital Agreement Law
- www.divorcenet.com/resources/prenuptial-agreements-rhode-island.html
- marriage.uslegal.com/permarital-agreements

Rhode Island Common Law Marriage
- See Exhibit 5-3 in Chapter 5.
- *Fravala v. City of Cranston...*, 996 A.2d 696 (R.I., 2010)
- www.mcintyretate.com/blog/2016/november/how-is-a-common-law-marriage-established-in-rhod/
- www.buddybuddy.com/common.html
- www.unmarried.org/common-law-marriage-fact-sheet

Rhode Island Divorce Law
- RI Gen Laws §§ 15-5-2 et seq.
- www.divorcelawinfo.com/states/ri/rhodeisland.htm

Rhode Island Legal Separation Law
- RI Gen Laws § 15-5-9

Rhode Island Alimony/Spousal Support Law
- RI Gen Laws § 15-5-16
- www.hg.org/article.asp?id=18172

Rhode Island Property Division Law
- RI Gen Laws § 15-5-16.1

Rhode Island Child Custody Law
- RI Gen Laws § 15-5-16
- statelaws.findlaw.com/rhode-island-law/rhode-island-child-custody-laws.html

Rhode Island Guardian Ad Litem and Attorney for Child
- RI Gen Laws § 40-11-14
- www.childwelfare.gov/pubPDFs/represent.pdf

Rhode Island Child Support Law
- RI Gen Laws § 15-5-16.2
- www.cse.ri.gov

Rhode Island Paternity Law
- RI Gen Laws § 31-14-7-3
- www.cse.ri.gov/services/establishment_paternity.php

Rhode Island Legal Definition of Father
- RI Gen Laws § 15-8-3
- www.childwelfare.gov/systemwide/laws_policies/statutes/putative.pdf

Rhode Island Adoption Law
- RI Gen Laws § 15-7-2
- statelaws.findlaw.com/rhode-island-law/rhode-island-adoption-laws.html

Rhode Island Termination of Parental Rights
- RI Gen Laws § 15-7-7
- www.childwelfare.gov/pubPDFs/groundtermin.pdf

Rhode Island Emancipation Law
- RI Gen Laws § 14-1-59.1

Rhode Island Age of Majority
- statelaws.findlaw.com/rhode-island-law/rhode-island-legal-ages-laws.html

Rhode Island Child Protection/Protective Services
- www.dcyf.ri.gov/child-protective-services

Rhode Island Child Welfare Agencies
- www.adoptionservices.org/child_welfare_agencies/child_welfare_agencies_rhode_island.htm

Rhode Island Juvenile Law
- http://psga.ri.gov/documents/JJGUIDE2007.pdf
- www.ncjj.org/pdf/1State_Juvenile_Justice_Profiles_2005.pdf
- www.rikidscount.org/IssueAreas/JuvenileJustice.aspx

Rhode Island Domestic Violence Law
- RI Gen Laws § 12-29-2
- www.ricadv.org/en

Rhode Island Employment Discrimination Law
- RI Gen Laws § 28-51-2

Rhode Island Surrogacy Law
- RI Gen Laws §§ 23-16.4-1 et seq.
- www.selectsurrogate.com/surrogacy-laws-by-state.html

Rhode Island Grandparent Rights
- RI Gen Laws § 15-5-24.3
- www.verywellfamily.com/grandparent-visitation-rights-state-by-state-1695938

Rhode Island Annulment Law
- RI Gen Laws §§ 15-1-1 et seq.

Rhode Island Family Law Forms
- www.courts.ri.gov/PublicResources/forms/Pages/default.aspx
- family.findlaw.com/divorce/divorce-forms-by-state.html

Rhode Island Vital Records (Birth, Marriage, Divorce, Death)
- publicrecords.onlinesearches.com/RhodeIsland.htm
- www.cdc.gov/nchs/w2w.htm

Rhode Island Self-Help Services in Family Law Cases
- www.courts.ri.gov/Self%20Help%20Center/Pages/default.aspx
- www.helprilaw.org

Rhode Island State Legal Research
- caselaw.findlaw.com/rhode-island.html
- www.loc.gov/law/help/guide/states/us-ri.php

Rhode Island Court Rules
- www.courts.ri.gov/Courts/SupremeCourt/Pages/Supreme%20Court%20Rules.aspx

Rhode Island Job Discrimination Based on Marital Status or Gender
- www.ncsl.org/documents/employ/DiscriminationChart-III.pdf

Google, Bing, or Yahoo Searches on Rhode Island Family Law
- "Rhode Island family law"
- "Rhode Island divorce"
- Rhode Island "property division"
- "Rhode Island adoption"
- Rhode Island paternity
- Rhode Island "child custody"
- Rhode Island "child support"
- Rhode Island abortion
- Rhode Island marriage
- Rhode Island "separation agreement"
- Rhode Island "premarital agreement"
- (also try these searches in the *Articles* and *Case law* databases of Scholar.google.com)

SOUTH CAROLINA FAMILY LAW

South Carolina Family Laws
- statelaws.findlaw.com/south-carolina-law/south-carolina-family-laws.html

South Carolina Family Code/Domestic Relations Code
- Code of Laws of So. Car. Title 20

South Carolina Family Court
- www.sccourts.org/courtReg (click "Family")

South Carolina Marriage Law (formation)
- statutes.laws.com/south-carolina/title-20/chapter-1
- usmarriagelaws.com (enter your state or county)
- www.law.cornell.edu/wex/table_marriage

South Carolina Premarital Agreement Law
- *Holler v. Holler*, 612 S.E.2d 469 (S.C. Ct. App. 2005)
- marriage.uslegal.com/permarital-agreements

South Carolina Common Law Marriage
- See Exhibit 5-3 in Chapter 5.
- Code 1976 § 20-1-100
- www.buddybuddy.com/common.html
- www.unmarried.org/common-law-marriage-fact-sheet

South Carolina Divorce Law
- Code of Laws of So. Car. § 20-3-10
- www.lawhelp.org/sc (click Family and Juvenile)
- www.divorcelawinfo.com/states/sc/southcarolina.htm
- www.hg.org/divorce-law-SouthCarolina.html

South Carolina Legal Separation Law
- Code of Laws of So. Car. § 62-2-802
- www.hg.org/divorce-law-SouthCarolina.html

South Carolina Alimony/Separate Maintenance/Spousal Support Law
- Code of Laws of So. Car. § 20-3-130
- www.lawhelp.org/sc (click Family and Juvenile)

South Carolina Property Division Law
- Code of Laws of So. Car. § 20-3-620
- www.lawhelp.org/sc (click Family and Juvenile)
- www.hg.org/divorce-law-SouthCarolina.html

South Carolina Child Custody Law
- Code of Laws of So. Car. § 20-3-160
- www.lawhelp.org/sc (click Family and Juvenile)
- www.hg.org/divorce-law-SouthCarolina.html

South Carolina Guardian Ad Litem and Attorney for Child
- Code of Laws of So. Car. § 63-7-1620
- www.childwelfare.gov/pubPDFs/represent.pdf

South Carolina Child Support Law
- Code of Laws of So. Car. § 63-17-310
- www.lawhelp.org/sc (click Family and Juvenile)
- www.state.sc.us/dss/csed

South Carolina Paternity Law
- Code of Laws of So. Car. § 63-17-10
- www.lawhelp.org/sc (click Family and Juvenile)

South Carolina Legal Definition of Father
- Code of Laws of So. Car. § 63-9-310
- www.childwelfare.gov/systemwide/laws_policies/statutes/putative.pdf

South Carolina Putative Father Registry
- www.ncsl.org/documents/cyf/putative_father_registries.pdf

South Carolina Adoption Law
- Code of Laws of So. Car. §§ 63-9-10 et seq.
- www.lawhelp.org/sc (click "Family and Juvenile")

South Carolina Termination of Parental Rights
- Code of Laws of So. Car. § 63-7-2570
- www.lawhelp.org/sc (click Family and Juvenile)
- www.childwelfare.gov/pubPDFs/groundtermin.pdf

South Carolina Responsible Father Registry
- Code of Laws of So. Car. § 63-9-810

South Carolina Age of Majority & Emancipation Law
- statelaws.findlaw.com/south-carolina-law/south-carolina-legal-ages-laws.html

South Carolina Child Protection/Protective Services
- dss.sc.gov/abuseneglect/report-child-abuse-and-neglect

South Carolina Juvenile Law
- www.state.sc.us/djj
- www.ncjj.org/pdf/1State_Juvenile_Justice_Profiles_2005.pdf

South Carolina Domestic Violence Law
- Code of Laws of So. Car. § 16-25-20

South Carolina Surrogacy Law
- www.selectsurrogate.com/surrogacy-laws-by-state.html

South Carolina Grandparent Rights
- Code of Laws of So. Car. § 63-3-530(A)(33)
- www.verywellfamily.com/grandparent-visitation-rights-state-by-state-1695938

South Carolina Annulment Law
- Code of Laws of So. Car. §§ 20-1-80, 20-1-510
- www.lawhelp.org/sc (click Family and Juvenile)

South Carolina Family Law Forms
- family.findlaw.com/divorce/divorce-forms-by-state.html

South Carolina Vital Records (Birth, Marriage, Divorce, Death)
- www.cdc.gov/nchs/w2w.htm
- publicrecords.onlinesearches.com/SouthCarolina.htm

South Carolina Self-Help Services in Family Law Cases
- www.lawhelp.org/sc (click "Family and Juvenile")

South Carolina State Legal Research
- www.loc.gov/law/help/guide/states/us-sc.php
- caselaw.findlaw.com/south-carolina.html

South Carolina Court Rules
- www.sccourts.org/courtReg

South Carolina Job Discrimination Based on Marital Status or Gender
- www.ncsl.org/documents/employ/DiscriminationChart-III.pdf

Google, Bing, or Yahoo Searches on South Carolina Family Law
- "South Carolina family law"
- "South Carolina divorce"
- South Carolina "property division"
- "South Carolina adoption"
- South Carolina paternity
- South Carolina "child custody"
- South Carolina "child support"
- South Carolina abortion
- South Carolina marriage
- South Carolina "separation agreement"
- South Carolina "premarital agreement"
- (also try these searches in the *Articles* and *Case law* databases of Scholar.google.com)

SOUTH DAKOTA FAMILY LAW

South Dakoda Family Laws
- statelaws.findlaw.com/south-dakota-law/south-dakota-family-laws.html

South Dakota Family Code/Domestic Relations Code
- So. Dak. Codif. Laws Title 25

South Dakota Family Court
- judicial.sd.gov/Third_Circuit/Local_Procedures/familycourt.aspx

South Dakota Marriage Law (formation)
- usmarriagelaws.com (enter your state or county)

South Dakoda Premarital Agreement Law
- So. Dak. Codif. Laws § 25-2-16
- marriage.uslegal.com/permarital-agreements

South Dakota Common Law Marriage
- *Matter of Millers' Estate*, 243 N.W.2d 788 (SD 1976)
- www.buddybuddy.com/common.html

South Dakota Divorce Law
- So. Dak. Codif. Laws § 25-4-2
- www.divorcelawinfo.com/states/sd/southdakota.htm

South Dakota Legal Separation Law
- So. Dak. Codif. Laws § 25-4-17.2

South Dakota Alimony/Spousal Support/Maintenance Law
- So. Dak. Codif. Laws § 25-4-41

South Dakota Property Division Law
- So. Dak. Codif. Laws § 25-4-44

South Dakota Child Custody Law
- So. Dak. Codif. Laws § 25-4-45

South Dakota Guardian Ad Litem and Attorney for Child
- So. Dak. Codif. Laws §§ 26-8A-18, 15-6-17(c)
- www.childwelfare.gov/pubPDFs/represent.pdf

South Dakota Child Support Law
- So. Dak. Codif. Laws § 25-7A-1
- dss.sd.gov/childsupport

South Dakota Paternity Law
- So. Dak. Codif. Laws § 25-8-7.1

South Dakota Legal Definition of Father
- So. Dak. Codif. Laws § 25-5A-1
- www.childwelfare.gov/systemwide/laws_policies/statutes/putative.pdf

South Dakota Adoption Law
- So. Dak. Codif. Laws § 25-6-2

South Dakota Termination of Parental Rights
- So. Dak. Codif. Laws § 26-8A-26.1
- www.childwelfare.gov/pubPDFs/groundtermin.pdf

South Dakota Putative Father Registry
- www.ncsl.org/documents/cyf/putative_father_registries.pdf

South Dakota Emancipation Law
- So. Dak. Codif. Laws § 25-5-26

South Dakota Age of Majority
- statelaws.findlaw.com/south-dakota-law/south-dakota-legal-ages-laws.html

South Dakota Child Protection/Protective Services
- dss.sd.gov/childprotection

South Dakota Juvenile Law
- judicial.sd.gov/Fourth_Circuit/Procedures/juvenilecourt.aspx
- www.ncjj.org/pdf/1State_Juvenile_Justice_Profiles_2005.pdf

South Dakota Domestic Violence Law
- sdnafvsa.com/home

South Dakota Surrogacy Law
- www.selectsurrogate.com/surrogacy-laws-by-state.html

South Dakota Grandparent Rights
- So. Dak. Codif. Laws § 25-4-52
- www.verywellfamily.com/grandparent-visitation-rights-state-by-state-1695938

South Dakota Annulment Law
- So. Dak. Codif. Laws §§ 25-3-1 et seq.

South Dakota Family Law Forms
- www.uslegalforms.com/familylaw/south-dakota
- family.findlaw.com/divorce/divorce-forms-by-state.html

South Dakota Vital Records (Birth, Marriage, Divorce, Death)
- www.cdc.gov/nchs/w2w.htm
- publicrecords.onlinesearches.com/SouthDakota.htm

South Dakota Self-Help Services in Family Law Cases
- ujslawhelp.sd.gov
- www.courtreference.com/South-Dakota-Courts-Self-Help.htm

South Dakota State Legal Research
- www.loc.gov/law/help/guide/states/us-sd.php
- caselaw.findlaw.com/south-dakota.html

South Dakota Court Rules
- ujs.sd.gov/Supreme_Court/rules.aspx

South Dakota Job Discrimination Based on Marital Status or Gender
- www.ncsl.org/documents/employ/DiscriminationChart-III.pdf

Google, Bing, or Yahoo Searches on South Dakota Family Law
- "South Dakoda family law"
- "South Dakoda divorce"
- South Dakoda "property division"
- "South Dakoda adoption"
- South Dakoda paternity
- South Dakoda "child custody"
- South Dakoda "child support"
- South Dakoda abortion
- South Dakoda marriage
- South Dakoda "separation agreement"
- South Dakoda "premarital agreement"
- (also try these searches in the *Articles* and *Case law* databases of Scholar.google.com)

TENNESSEE FAMILY LAW

Tennessee Family Laws
- statelaws.findlaw.com/tennessee-law/tennessee-family-laws.html

Tennessee Family Code/Domestic Relations Code
- Tenn. Code Ann. Title 36

Tennessee Family Court
- www.tsc.state.tn.us/courts/juvenile-family-courts

Tennessee Marriage Law (formation)
- Tenn. Code Ann. § 36-3-103
- usmarriagelaws.com (enter your state or county)

Tennessee Common Law Marriage
- topics.law.cornell.edu/wex/table_marriage
- www.buddybuddy.com/common.html

Tennessee Premarital Agreement Law
- Tenn. Code Ann. § 36-4-501
- marriage.uslegal.com/permarital-agreements

Tennessee Divorce Law
- Tenn. Code Ann. § 36-4-101
- www.las.org/booklets/family_problems
- las.org/find-help/self-help-resource-center/legal-help-booklets /family-problems (click "divorce")
- www.divorcelawinfo.com/states/tn/tennesee.htm
- www.hg.org/divorce-law-Tennessee.html

Tennessee Legal Separation Law
- Tenn. Code Ann. § 36-4-102

Tennessee Alimony/Spousal Support Law
- Tenn. Code Ann. § 36-5-101
- www.hg.org/divorce-law-Tennessee.html

Tennessee Property Division Law
- Tenn. Code Ann. § 36-4-121
- www.hg.org/divorce-law-Tennessee.html

Tennessee Child Custody Law
- Tenn. Code Ann. § 36-6-106
- www.hg.org/divorce-law-Tennessee.html

Tennessee Relocation of Child
- Tenn. Code Ann. § 36-6-108

Tennessee Guardian Ad Litem and Attorney for Child
- Tenn. Code Ann. §§ 36-4-132, 37-1-149
- www.childwelfare.gov/pubPDFs/represent.pdf

Tennessee Child Support Law
- Tenn. Code Ann. § 36-5-101
- statelaws.findlaw.com/tennessee-law/tennessee-child-support-guidelines.html
- las.org/find-help/self-help-resource-center/legal-help-booklets /family-problems (click "child support")

Tennessee Paternity Law
- Tenn. Code Ann. §§ 24-7-112, 36-2-304

Tennessee Legal Definition of Father
- Tenn. Code Ann. §§ 36-2-302, 36-2-304(a)
- www.childwelfare.gov/systemwide/laws_policies/statutes /putative.pdf

Tennessee Adoption Law
- Tenn. Code Ann. § 36-1-102

Tennessee Termination of Parental Rights
- Tenn. Code Ann. § 36-1-113
- www.childwelfare.gov/pubPDFs/groundtermin.pdf

Tennessee Putative Father Registry
- Tenn. Code Ann. § 36-2-318
- www.ncsl.org/documents/cyf/putative_father_registries.pdf

Tennessee Emancipation Law
- Tenn. Code Ann. § 33-8-104

Tennessee Age of Majority
- Tenn. Code Ann. § 34-2-106

Tennessee Child Protection/Protective Services
- www.tn.gov/dcs.html

Tennessee Juvenile Law
- www.tsc.state.tn.us/courts/juvenile-family-courts/rules-juvenile-procedure
- www.ncjj.org/pdf/1State_Juvenile_Justice_Profiles_2005.pdf

Tennessee Domestic Violence Law
- Tenn. Code Ann. §40-14-109
- las.org/find-help/self-help-resource-center/legal-help-booklets (click "domestic violence")

Tennessee Surrogacy Law
- www.selectsurrogate.com/surrogacy-laws-by-state.html

Tennessee Grandparent Rights
- Tenn. Code Ann. § 36-6-302
- www.verywellfamily.com/grandparent-visitation-rights-state-by-state-1695938

Tennessee Annulment Law
- Tenn. Code Ann. § 36-4-119
- www.hg.org/divorce-law-Tennessee.html

Tennessee Family Law Forms
- www.tsc.state.tn.us/forms-publications
- family.findlaw.com/divorce/divorce-forms-by-state.html

Tennessee Vital Records (Birth, Marriage, Divorce, Death)
- www.cdc.gov/nchs/w2w.htm
- publicrecords.onlinesearches.com/Tennessee.htm

Tennessee Self-Help Services in Family Law Cases
- www.tncourts.gov/programs/self-help-center
- www.courtreference.com/Tennessee-Courts-Self-Help.htm

Tennessee State Legal Research
- www.loc.gov/law/help/guide/states/us-tn.php
- caselaw.findlaw.com/tennessee.html

Tennessee Court Rules
- www.tsc.state.tn.us/courts/rules

Tennessee Job Discrimination Based on Marital Status or Gender
- www.ncsl.org/documents/employ/DiscriminationChart-III.pdf

Google, Bing, or Yahoo Searches on Tennessee Family Law
- "Tennessee family law"
- "Tennessee divorce"
- Tennessee "property division"
- "Tennessee adoption"
- Tennessee paternity
- Tennessee "child custody"
- Tennessee "child support"
- Tennessee abortion
- Tennessee marriage
- Tennessee "separation agreement"
- Tennessee "premarital agreement"
- (also try these searches in the *Articles* and *Case law* databases of Scholar.google.com)

TEXAS FAMILY LAW

Texas Family Laws
- statelaws.findlaw.com/texas-law/texas-family-laws.html

Texas Family Code/Domestic Relations Code
- www.statutes.legis.state.tx.us (Click "Family Code")
- texaslawhelp.org/article/texas-family-law-handbook-houston-bar-association

Texas Marriage Law (formation)
- Texas Family Code §2.001
- usmarriagelaws.com (enter your state or county)
- www.law.cornell.edu/wex/table_marriage

Texas Premarital Agreement Law
- Texas Family Code § 4.006
- marriage.uslegal.com/permarital-agreements

Texas Common Law (Informal) Marriage
- See Exhibit 5-3 in Chapter 5.
- Texas Family Code § 2.401
- topics.law.cornell.edu/wex/table_marriage
- www.buddybuddy.com/common.html
- www.unmarried.org/common-law-marriage-fact-sheet

Texas Divorce Law
- Texas Family Code §§ 6.001 et seq.
- texaslawhelp.org/family-divorce-children
- www.divorcelawinfo.com/states/texas/texas.htm
- www.hg.org/divorce-law-Texas.html

Texas Legal Separation Law
- www.hg.org/divorce-law-Texas.html

Texas Alimony/Spousal/Maintenance Support Law
- Texas Family Code § 8.051
- cordellcordell.com/resources/texas/texas-maintenance/

Texas Property Division Law
- Texas Family Code § 7.001
- texaslawhelp.org/article/enforcing-property-division-divorce

Texas Child Custody Law
- Texas Family Code § 153.002
- texaslawhelp.org/family-divorce-children

Texas Guardian Ad Litem and Attorney for Child
- Texas Family Code §§ 107.001
- www.childwelfare.gov/pubPDFs/represent.pdf

Texas Child Support Law
- Texas Family Code § 154.001
- texaslawhelp.org/family-divorce-children

Texas Paternity Law
- Texas Family Code § 160.601
- texaslawhelp.org/family-divorce-children

Texas Legal Definition of Father
- Texas Family Code §§ 160.102, 160.204
- www.childwelfare.gov/systemwide/laws_policies/statutes/putative.pdf

Texas Adoption Law
- Texas Family Code § 162.001
- texaslawhelp.org/family-divorce-children

Texas Termination of Parental Rights
- Texas Family Code § 161.001
- www.childwelfare.gov/pubPDFs/groundtermin.pdf

Texas Registry of Paternity
- Texas Family Code § 160.401
- www.ncsl.org/documents/cyf/putative_father_registries.pdf

Texas Emancipation Law
- texaslawhelp.org/article/emancipation-minors

Texas Age of Majority
- statelaws.findlaw.com/texas-law/texas-legal-ages-laws.html

Texas Child Protection/Protective Services
- www.dfps.state.tx.us

Texas Child Welfare Agencies
- www.dfps.state.tx.us

Texas Juvenile Law
- Texas Family Code §§ 51.01 et seq.
- www.tjjd.texas.gov
- www.ncjj.org/pdf/1State_Juvenile_Justice_Profiles_2005.pdf

Texas Domestic Violence Law
- www.tcfv.org

Texas Surrogacy Law
- Texas Fam. Code Ann. § 160.762
- www.selectsurrogate.com/surrogacy-laws-by-state.html

Texas Grandparent Rights
- Texas Family Code § 153.434
- texaslawhelp.org/family-divorce-children
- www.verywellfamily.com/grandparent-visitation-rights-state-by-state-1695938

Texas Annulment Law
- Texas Family Code §§ 6.102 et seq.
- texaslawhelp.org/family-divorce-children

Texas Family Law Forms
- www.txcourts.gov/rules-forms/forms
- www.texaslawhelp.org (click "Forms Only")
- www.txaccess.org/forms
- www.uslegalforms.com/familylaw/texas
- family.findlaw.com/divorce/divorce-forms-by-state.html

Texas Vital Records (Birth, Marriage, Divorce, Death)
- publicrecords.onlinesearches.com/Texas.htm
- www.cdc.gov/nchs/w2w.htm

Texas Self-Help Services in Family Law Cases
- www.texaslawhelp.org
- tarlton.law.utexas.edu/c.php?g=457723&p=3128561#s-lg-box-9637674

Texas State Legal Research
- www.loc.gov/law/help/guide/states/us-tx.php
- caselaw.findlaw.com/texas.html

Texas Court Rules
- www.sll.texas.gov/the-courts/texas-court-rules

Texas Job Discrimination Based on Marital Status or Gender
- www.ncsl.org/documents/employ/DiscriminationChart-III.pdf

Google, Bing, or Yahoo Searches on Texas Family Law
- "Texas family law"
- "Texas divorce"
- Texas "property division"
- "Texas adoption"

- Texas paternity
- Texas "child custody"
- Texas "child support"
- Texas abortion
- Texas marriage

- Texas "separation agreement"
- Texas "premarital agreement"
- (also try these searches in the *Articles* and *Case law* databases of Scholar.google.com)

UTAH FAMILY LAW

Utah Family Laws
- statelaws.findlaw.com/utah-law/utah-family-laws.html

Utah Family Code/Domestic Relations Code
- Utah Code Ann. Title 30
- le.utah.gov/xcode/Title30/30.html?v=C30_1800010118000101

Utah Family Court
- Utah Code Ann. § 30-3-11.1

Utah Marriage Law (formation)
- www.utcourts.gov/howto/marriage/index.htm
- www.thespruce.com/how-to-get-married-in-utah-2300795
- usmarriagelaws.com (enter your state or county)
- www.law.cornell.edu/wex/table_marriage

Utah Premarital Agreement Law
- Utah Code Ann. § 30-8-6
- marriage.uslegal.com/permarital-agreements

Utah Common Law Marriage
- See Exhibit 5-3 in Chapter 5.
- Utah Code Ann. § 30-1-4.5
- topics.law.cornell.edu/wex/table_marriage
- www.buddybuddy.com/common.html
- www.unmarried.org/common-law-marriage-fact-sheet

Utah Divorce Law
- Utah Code Ann. § 30-3-1
- www.utcourts.gov/howto/divorce
- www.divorcelawinfo.com/states/utah/utah.htm
- www.hg.org/divorce-law-Utah.html

Utah Legal Separation Law
- www.hg.org/divorce-law-Utah.html

Utah Alimony/Spousal Support/Maintenance Law
- Utah Code Ann. § 30-3-5
- www.utcourts.gov/howto/divorce/alimony.html

Utah Property Division Law
- Utah Code Ann. § 30-3-5
- www.utcourts.gov/howto/divorce/property.html

Utah Child Custody Law
- Utah Code Ann. § 30-3-10
- www.utcourts.gov/howto/divorce/custody.html

Utah Guardian Ad Litem and Attorney for Child
- Utah Ann. Code §§ 78A-6-902
- www.childwelfare.gov/pubPDFs/represent.pdf
- www.utcourts.gov/howto/seniors/g_and_c.asp

Utah Child Support Law
- Utah Ann. Code § 78B-12-105
- www.ors.utah.gov
- www.supportguidelines.com/links.html

Utah Paternity Law
- Utah Ann. Code § 78B-15-622
- www.utcourts.gov/mediation/cpm/paternity.html
- www.utcourts.gov/resources/forms (click *Paternity*)

Utah Legal Definition of Father
- Utah Ann. Code § 78B-15-102
- www.childwelfare.gov/systemwide/laws_policies/statutes/putative.pdf

Utah Adoption Law
- Utah Ann. Code § 78B-6-137
- www.utcourts.gov/howto/family/adoption
- statelaws.findlaw.com/utah-law/utah-adoption-laws.html

Utah Termination of Parental Rights
- Utah Ann. Code § 62A-4a-203.5
- www.childwelfare.gov/pubPDFs/groundtermin.pdf

Utah Putative Father Registry
- Utah Ann. Code § 78B-6-110
- www.ncsl.org/documents/cyf/putative_father_registries.pdf

Utah Emancipation Law
- Utah Code Ann. § 78A-6-805
- www.utcourts.gov/courts/juv/juvyfaq.htm

Utah Age of Majority
- minors.uslegal.com/age-of-majority/utah-age-of-majority-law
- statelaws.findlaw.com/utah-law/utah-legal-ages-laws.html

Utah Child Protection/Protective Services
- dcfs.utah.gov/services/child-protective-services

Utah Child Welfare Agencies
- dcfs.utah.gov

Utah Juvenile Law
- www.utcourts.gov/courts/juv/juvyfaq.htm
- www.ncjj.org/pdf/1State_Juvenile_Justice_Profiles_2005.pdf

Utah Domestic Violence Law
- Utah Code Ann. § 77-36-1
- www.health.utah.gov/vipp/topics/domestic-violence

Utah Employment Discrimination Law
- Utah Code Ann. § 34A-5-107

Utah Surrogacy Law
- Utah Code Ann. §78B-15-801
- www.selectsurrogate.com/surrogacy-laws-by-state.html

Utah Grandparent Rights
- Utah Code Ann. § 30-5-2
- www.verywellfamily.com/grandparent-visitation-rights-state-by-state-1695938

Utah Annulment Law
- Utah Code Ann. §§ 30-1-1 et seq.
- www.utcourts.gov/howto/divorce/annulment.html

Utah Family Law Forms
- www.utcourts.gov/resources/forms
- family.findlaw.com/divorce/divorce-forms-by-state.html

Utah Vital Records (Birth, Marriage, Divorce, Death)
- www.cdc.gov/nchs/w2w.htm
- publicrecords.onlinesearches.com/Utah.htm

Utah Self-Help Services in Family Law Cases
- www.utcourts.gov/selfhelp
- www.utcourts.gov/resources/forms
- www.utahlegalservices.org
- www.utcourts.gov/selfhelp/#families

Utah State Legal Research
- www.loc.gov/law/help/guide/states/us-ut.php
- www.utcourts.gov/lawlibrary/research

Utah Court Rules
- www.utcourts.gov/resources/rules

Utah Job Discrimination Based on Marital Status or Gender
- www.ncsl.org/documents/employ/DiscriminationChart-III.pdf

Google, Bing, or Yahoo Searches on Utah Family Law
- "Utah family law"
- "Utah divorce"
- Utah "property division"
- "Utah adoption"
- Utah paternity
- Utah "child custody"
- Utah "child support"
- Utah abortion
- Utah marriage
- Utah "separation agreement"
- Utah "premarital agreement"
- (also try these searches in the *Articles* and *Case law* databases of Scholar.google.com)

VERMONT FAMILY LAW

Vermont Family Laws
- statelaws.findlaw.com/vermont-law/vermont-family-laws.html

Vermont Family Code/Domestic Relations Code
- Vt. Stats. Ann. Title 15

Vermont Family Court Division
- www.vermontjudiciary.org/family

Vermont Marriage Law (formation)
- 15 Vt. Stats. Ann. § 8
- usmarriagelaws.com (enter your state or county)
- www.law.cornell.edu/wex/table_marriage

Vermont Premarital Agreement Law
- marriage.uslegal.com/permarital-agreements

Vermont Divorce Law
- 15 Vt. Stats. Ann. § 551
- www.vermontjudiciary.org/GTC/Family/Pamphlets.aspx
- vtlawhelp.org (click "Family")
- www.divorcelawinfo.com/states/vermont/vermont.htm

Vermont Legal Separation Law
- 15 Vt. Stats. Ann. § 555

Vermont Alimony Law
- 15 Vt. Stats. Ann. § 634

Vermont Property Division Law
- 15 Vt. Stats. Ann. §§ 634, 751

Vermont Child Custody Law
- 15 Vt. Stats. Ann. §§ 665 et seq.
- vtlawhelp.org (click "Family")
- 15 Vt. Stats. Ann. § 634

Vermont Guardian Ad Litem and Attorney for Child
- 33 Vt. Stat. Ann. § 5112
- www.childwelfare.gov/pubPDFs/represent.pdf

Vermont Child Support Law
- 15 Vt. Stats. Ann. §et seq.654 et seq.
- dcf.vermont.gov/ocs
- www.vermontjudiciary.org/GTC/Family/Pamphlets.aspx
- vtlawhelp.org (click "Family")

Vermont Paternity Law
- 15C Vt. Stats. Ann. §204
- vtlawhelp.org/parentage

Vermont Legal Definition of Father
- 15A Vt. Stat. Ann. § 1-101
- www.childwelfare.gov/systemwide/laws_policies/statutes/putative.pdf

Vermont Adoption Law
- 15A Vt. Stat. Ann. § 1-101
- statelaws.findlaw.com/vermont-law/vermont-adoption-laws.html

Vermont Termination of Parental Rights
- 15A Vt. Stat. Ann. § 3-504
- www.childwelfare.gov/pubPDFs/groundtermin.pdf

Vermont Putative Father Registry
- www.ncsl.org/documents/cyf/putative_father_registries.pdf

Vermont Emancipation Law
- 12 Vt. Stats. Ann. § 7155

Vermont Age of Majority
- statelaws.findlaw.com/vermont-law/vermont-legal-ages-laws.html

Vermont Child Protection/Protective Services
- dcf.vermont.gov/protection/reporting

Vermont Juvenile Law
- www.vermontjudiciary.org/GTC/Family/Pamphlets.aspx
- www.ncjj.org/pdf/1State_Juvenile_Justice_Profiles_2005.pdf

Vermont Domestic Violence Law
- 15 Vt. Stats. Ann. § 1151
- www.vtnetwork.org
- vtlawhelp.org (click "Family")

Vermont Sexual Harassment Law
- 21 Vt. Stats. Ann. § 495h

Vermont Surrogacy Law
- 15C Vt. Stats. Ann. § 801
- www.selectsurrogate.com/surrogacy-laws-by-state.html

Vermont Grandparent Rights
- 15 Vt. Stats. Ann. § 1011
- www.verywellfamily.com/grandparent-visitation-rights-state-by-state-1695938

Vermont Annulment Law
- 15 Vt. Stats. Ann. §§ 511 et seq.

Vermont Family Law Forms
- www.vermontjudiciary.org/masterpages/Court-Formsindex.aspx
- family.findlaw.com/divorce/divorce-forms-by-state.html

Vermont Vital Records (Birth, Marriage, Divorce, Death)
- www.cdc.gov/nchs/w2w.htm
- publicrecords.onlinesearches.com/Vermont.htm

Vermont Self-Help Services in Family Law Cases
- vtlawhelp.org (click "Family")
- www.vermontjudiciary.org/GTC/Family/Pamphlets.aspx

Vermont State Legal Research
- www.loc.gov/law/help/guide/states/us-vt.php
- caselaw.findlaw.com/vermont.html

Vermont Court Rules
- www.lexisnexis.com/hottopics

Vermont Job Discrimination Based on Marital Status or Gender
- www.ncsl.org/documents/employ/DiscriminationChart-III.pdf

Google, Bing, or Yahoo Searches on Vermont Family Law
- "Vermont family law"
- "Vermont divorce"
- Vermont "property division"
- "Vermont adoption"
- Vermont paternity
- Vermont "child custody"
- Vermont "child support"
- Vermont abortion
- Vermont marriage
- Vermont "separation agreement"
- Vermont "premarital agreement"
- (also try these searches in the *Articles* and *Case law* databases of Scholar.google.com)

VIRGINIA FAMILY LAW

Virginia Family Laws
- statelaws.findlaw.com/virginia-law/virginia-family-laws.html

Virginia Family Code/Domestic Relations Code
- Va. Code Ann. Title 20

Virginia Family Court
- www.courts.state.va.us/courts/jdr/home.html
- www.courts.state.va.us/forms/district/jdr.html
- www.courts.state.va.us/courts/jdr/resources/manuals/jdrman/toc_jdr_manual.pdf

Virginia Marriage Law (formation)
- www.vsb.org/site/publications/marriage-in-virginia usmarriagelaws.com (enter your state or county)

Virginia Premarital Agreement Law
- Va. Code Ann. § 20-149
- marriage.uslegal.com/permarital-agreements

Virginia Common Law Marriage
- topics.law.cornell.edu/wex/table_marriage
- www.buddybuddy.com/common.html

Virginia Divorce Law
- Va. Code Ann. § 20-91
- www.vsb.org/site/publications/divorce-in-virginia
- www.valegalaid.org (click "Family and Domestic")
- www.hg.org/divorce-law-virginia.html

Virginia Legal Separation Law
- Va. Code Ann. § 20-95
- www.hg.org/divorce-law-virginia.html

Virginia Alimony/Spousal Support Law
- Va. Code Ann. §§ 20-107.1, 20-108.1
- www.hg.org/divorce-law-virginia.html

Virginia Property Division Law
- Va. Code Ann. § 20-107.3
- www.divorcelawinfo.com/VA/marprop/propdiv.htm
- www.hg.org/divorce-law-virginia.html

Virginia Child Custody Law
- Va. Code Ann. § 20-124.2
- www.valegalaid.org (click "Family and Domestic")
- www.hg.org/divorce-law-virginia.html

Virginia Guardian Ad Litem and Attorney for Child
- Va. Code Ann. §§ 16.1-266, 9.1-153
- www.courts.state.va.us/courtadmin/aoc/cip/programs/gal/home.html
- www.childwelfare.gov/pubPDFs/represent.pdf

Virginia Child Support Law
- Va. Code Ann. §§ 20-108.1 et seq.
- www.valegalaid.org (click "Family and Domestic")

Virginia Paternity Law
- Va. Code Ann. § 63.2-1913
- www.dss.virginia.gov/pub/pdf/dcse_paternity.pdf

Virginia Legal Definition of Father
- www.childwelfare.gov/systemwide/laws_policies/statutes/putative.pdf

Virginia Adoption Law
- Va. Code Ann. § 63.2-1200
- www.valegalaid.org (click "Family and Domestic")

Virginia Termination of Parental Rights
- Va. Code Ann. § 16.1-283
- www.childwelfare.gov/pubPDFs/groundtermin.pdf

Virginia Putative Father Registry
- Va. Code Ann. § 63.2-1250
- www.ncsl.org/documents/cyf/putative_father_registries.pdf

Virginia Emancipation Law
- Va. Code Ann. § 16.1-331

Virginia Age of Majority
- statelaws.findlaw.com/virginia-law/virginia-legal-ages-laws.html

Virginia Child Protection/Protective Services
- www.dss.virginia.gov/family/cps/index.cgi

Virginia Juvenile Law
- www.djj.virginia.gov
- www.courts.state.va.us/courts/jdr/resources/manuals/jdrman/toc_jdr_manual.pdf

Virginia Domestic Violence Law
- Va. Code Ann. § 9.1-1300
- www.valegalaid.org (click "Family and Domestic")

Virginia Surrogacy Law
- Va. Code Ann. §§ 20-156, 20-160
- www.selectsurrogate.com/surrogacy-laws-by-state.html

Virginia Grandparent Rights
- Va. Code Ann. § 20-124.1
- www.verywellfamily.com/grandparent-visitation-rights-state-by-state-1695938

Virginia Annulment Law
- Va. Code Ann. § 20-89.1
- www.hg.org/divorce-law-virginia.html

Virginia Family Law Forms
- www.valegalaid.org/self-help-forms
- www.courts.state.va.us/forms/district/jdr.html
- www.courts.state.va.us/forms/home.html
- family.findlaw.com/divorce/divorce-forms-by-state.html

Virginia Vital Records (Birth, Marriage, Divorce, Death)
- www.cdc.gov/nchs/w2w.htm
- publicrecords.onlinesearches.com/Virginia.htm

Virginia Self-Help Services in Family Law Cases
- www.valegalaid.org
- selfhelp.vacourts.gov

Virginia State Legal Research
- www.loc.gov/law/help/guide/states/us-va.php
- caselaw.findlaw.com/virginia.html

Virginia Court Rules
- www.courts.state.va.us/courts/scv/rules.html

Virginia Job Discrimination Based on Marital Status or Gender
- www.ncsl.org/documents/employ/DiscriminationChart-III.pdf

Google, Bing, or Yahoo Searches on Virginia Family Law
- "Virginia family law"
- "Virginia divorce"
- Virginia "property division"
- "Virginia adoption"
- Virginia paternity
- Virginia "child custody"
- Virginia "child support"
- Virginia abortion
- Virginia marriage
- Virginia "separation agreement"
- Virginia "premarital agreement"
- (also try these searches in the *Articles* and *Case law* databases of Scholar.google.com)

WASHINGTON FAMILY LAW

Washington Family Laws
- statelaws.findlaw.com/washington-law/washington-family-laws.html

Washington Family Law Handbook
- www.courts.wa.gov/newsinfo/content/pdf/FLHBMarriageEdition.pdf#search=family

Washington Family Code/Domestic Relations Code
- Wash. Rev. Code Title 26

Washington Marriage Law (formation)
- usmarriagelaws.com (enter your state or county)

Washington Premarital Agreement Law
- marriage.uslegal.com/permarital-agreements/washington-premarital-agreement-law
- marriage.uslegal.com/permarital-agreements

Washington Common Law Marriage
- topics.law.cornell.edu/wex/table_marriage
- www.buddybuddy.com/common.html

Washington Divorce Law
- Wash. Rev. Code § 26.09.030
- www.washingtonlawhelp.org/WA (click "Family & Safety")
- www.hg.org/divorce-law-washington.html

Washington Legal Separation Law
- Wash. Rev. Code § 26.09.030

Washington Alimony/Spousal Support Law
- Wash. Rev. Code § 26.09.090

Washington Community Property Division Law
- Wash. Rev. Code § 26.09.080

Washington Child Custody Law
- Wash. Rev. Code § 26.09.181
- www.washingtonlawhelp.org/WA (click "Family & Safety")

Washington Relocation of Child
- Wash. Rev. Code §§ 26.09.410 et seq.

Washington Guardian Ad Litem and Attorney for Child
- Wash. Rev. Code §§ 26.44.053, 13.34.100, 13.34.102
- www.childwelfare.gov/pubPDFs/represent.pdf

Washington Child Support Law
- Wash. Rev. Code § 26.18.020
- www.dshs.wa.gov/esa/division-child-support
- www.washingtonlawhelp.org/WA (click "Family & Safety")

Washington Paternity Law
- www.washingtonlawhelp.org/WA (click "Family & Safety")

Washington Legal Definition of Father
- Wash. Rev. Code §§ 26.26.011, 26.26.116
- www.childwelfare.gov/systemwide/laws_policies/statutes/putative.pdf

Washington Adoption Law
- Wash. Rev. Code §§ 26.33.010 et seq.
- www.washingtonlawhelp.org/WA (click "Family & Safety")

Washington Termination of Parental Rights
- Wash. Rev. Code § 13.34.145
- www.childwelfare.gov/pubPDFs/groundtermin.pdf

Washington Putative Father Registry
- www.ncsl.org/documents/cyf/putative_father_registries.pdf

Washington Emancipation Law
- Wash. Rev. Code § 13.64.010

Washington Age of Majority
- Wash. Rev. Code § 26.28.010

Washington Child Protection/Protective Services
- www.dcyf.wa.gov/services/child-welfare-system/cps

Washington Juvenile Law
- apps.leg.wa.gov/RCW/default.aspx?cite=13
- www.ncjj.org/pdf/1State_Juvenile_Justice_Profiles_2005.pdf

Washington Domestic Violence Law
- Wash. Rev. Code §§ 26.50.010 et seq.
- www.washingtonlawhelp.org/WA (click "Family & Safety")

Washington Surrogacy Law
- Wash. Rev. Code §§ 26.26A.700
- www.selectsurrogate.com/surrogacy-laws-by-state.html

Washington Grandparent Rights
- www.divorcenet.com/resources/do-grandparents-have-visitation-rights-washington.html
- www.verywellfamily.com/grandparent-visitation-rights-state-by-state-1695938

Washington Annulment Law
- Wash. Rev. Code §§ 26.04.010 et seq.

Washington Family Law Forms
- www.courts.wa.gov/forms
- family.findlaw.com/divorce/divorce-forms-by-state.html

Washington Vital Records (Birth, Marriage, Divorce, Death)
- www.cdc.gov/nchs/w2w.htm
- publicrecords.onlinesearches.com/Washington.htm

Washington Self-Help Services in Family Law Cases
- www.washingtonlawhelp.org/WA
- www.courts.wa.gov/newsinfo/index.cfm?fa=newsinfo.displayContent&theFile=content/selfhelp

Washington State Legal Research
- www.loc.gov/law/help/guide/states/us-wa.php
- caselaw.findlaw.com/washington.html

Washington Court Rules
- www.courts.wa.gov/court_rules

Washington Job Discrimination Based on Marital Status or Gender
- www.ncsl.org/documents/employ/DiscriminationChart-III.pdf

Google, Bing, or Yahoo Searches on Washington Family Law
- "Washington family law"
- "Washington divorce"
- Washington "property division"
- "Washington adoption"
- Washington paternity
- Washington "child custody"
- Washington "child support"
- Washington abortion
- Washington marriage
- Washington "separation agreement"
- Washington "premarital agreement"
- (also try these searches in the *Articles* and *Case law* databases of Scholar.google.com)

WEST VIRGINIA FAMILY LAW

West Virginia Family Laws
- statelaws.findlaw.com/west-virginia-law/west-virginia-family-laws.html

West Virginia Family Code/Domestic Relations Code
- www.legis.state.wv.us/WVCODE/Code.cfm (Chapter 38)

West Virginia Family Court
- www.courtswv.gov/lower-courts/family-courts.html

West Virginia Marriage Law (formation)
- usmarriagelaws.com (enter your state or county)

West Virginia Premarital Agreement Law
- W.Va. Code § 48-1-203
- marriage.uslegal.com/permarital-agreements

West Virginia Common Law Marriage
- topics.law.cornell.edu/wex/table_marriage
- www.buddybuddy.com/common.html

West Virginia Divorce Law
- W.Va. Code §§ 48-5-201 et seq.
- www.lawv.net/Resources/Self-Help-Library/Family
- www.divorcelawinfo.com/states/wva/westvirginia.htm

West Virginia Alimony/Spousal Support/Maintenance Law
- W.Va. Code §§ 48-1-242 et seq.
- www.hg.org/divorce-law-westvirginia.html

West Virginia Property Division Law
- W.Va. Code § 48-7-101
- www.hg.org/divorce-law-westvirginia.html

West Virginia Child Custody Law
- W.Va. Code §§ 48-9-101, 48-20-106
- www.lawv.net/Resources/Self-Help-Library/Family

West Virginia Guardian Ad Litem and Attorney for Child
- W.Va. Code § 49-4-601
- www.childwelfare.gov/pubPDFs/represent.pdf

West Virginia Child Support Law
- W.Va. Code § 48-5-603
- www.lawv.net/Resources/Self-Help-Library/Family

West Virginia Paternity Law
- W.Va. Code § 48-24-106
- www.lawv.net/Resources/Self-Help-Library/Family

West Virginia Legal Definition of Father
- W.Va. Code §§ 48-22-105, 48-23-209
- www.childwelfare.gov/systemwide/laws_policies/statutes/putative.pdf

West Virginia Adoption Law
- W.Va. Code §§ 48-22-103 et seq.
- www.lawv.net/Resources/Self-Help-Library/Family

West Virginia Termination of Parental Rights
- W.Va. Code § 49-4-607
- www.lawv.net/Resources/Self-Help-Library/Family
- www.childwelfare.gov/pubPDFs/groundtermin.pdf

West Virginia Putative Father Registry
- www.ncsl.org/documents/cyf/putative_father_registries.pdf

West Virginia Emancipation Law
- W.Va. Code § 49-4-115

West Virginia Age of Majority
- statelaws.findlaw.com/west-virginia-law/west-virginia-legal-ages-laws.html

West Virginia Child Protection/Protective Services
- www.wvdhhr.org/bcf/sams

West Virginia Child Welfare Agencies
- dhhr.wv.gov/bcf/Services/Pages/Child-Protective-Services.aspx

West Virginia Juvenile Law
- www.courtswv.gov/public-resources/CAN/juvenile-law-procedure/juvenile-law-procedure.html
- www.ncjj.org/pdf/1State_Juvenile_Justice_Profiles_2005.pdf

West Virginia Domestic Violence Law
- W.Va. Code §§ 48-27-202 et seq.
- www.courtswv.gov/public-resources/domestic/domestic-violence.html

West Virginia Surrogacy Law
- www.selectsurrogate.com/surrogacy-laws-by-state.html

West Virginia Grandparent Rights
- W.Va. Code §§ 48-10-401 et seq.
- www.lawv.net/Resources/Self-Help-Library/Family
- www.verywellfamily.com/grandparent-visitation-rights-state-by-state-1695938

West Virginia Annulment Law
- W.Va. Code §§ 48-3-104 et seq.
- www.lawv.net/Resources/Self-Help-Library/Family

West Virginia Family Law Forms
- www.courtswv.gov/lower-courts/family-forms/index-family-forms.html
- www.lawv.net/Resources/Guided-Self-Help-Forms
- www.courtswv.gov
- family.findlaw.com/divorce/divorce-forms-by-state.html

West Virginia Vital Records (Birth, Marriage, Divorce, Death)
- publicrecords.onlinesearches.com/WestVirginia.htm
- www.cdc.gov/nchs/w2w.htm

West Virginia Self-Help Services in Family Law Cases
- www.lawv.net
- www.lawv.net/Resources

West Virginia State Legal Research
- www.loc.gov/law/help/guide/states/us-wv.php
- caselaw.findlaw.com/west-virginia.html

West Virginia Court Rules
- www.courtswv.gov

West Virginia Job Discrimination Based on Marital Status or Gender
- www.ncsl.org/documents/employ/DiscriminationChart-III.pdf

Google, Bing, or Yahoo Searches on West Virginia Family Law
- "West Virginia family law"
- "West Virginia divorce"
- West Virginia "property division"
- "West Virginia adoption"
- West Virginia paternity
- West Virginia "child custody"
- West Virginia "child support"
- West Virginia abortion
- West Virginia marriage
- West Virginia "separation agreement"
- West Virginia "premarital agreement"
- (also try these searches in the *Articles* and *Case law* databases of Scholar.google.com)

WISCONSIN FAMILY LAW

Wisconsin Virginia Family Laws
- statelaws.findlaw.com/wisconsin-law/wisconsin-family-laws.html

Wisconsin Family Code/Domestic Relations Code
- docs.legis.wisconsin.gov/statutes/statutes/765

Wisconsin Family Court
- www.wicourts.gov/forms1/circuit/formcategory.jsp?Category=12

Wisconsin Marriage Law (formation)
- usmarriagelaws.com (enter your state or county)
- wilawlibrary.gov/topics/familylaw/marriage.php
- www.law.cornell.edu/wex/table_marriage

Wisconsin Premarital Agreement Law
- marriage.uslegal.com/permarital-agreements

Wisconsin Common Law Marriage
- topics.law.cornell.edu/wex/table_marriage

Wisconsin Divorce Law
- wilawlibrary.gov/topics/familylaw/divorce.php
- www.divorcelawinfo.com/states/wiscon/wisconsin.htm
- www.hg.org/divorce-law-wisconsin.html

Wisconsin Legal Separation Law
- Wisc. Stat. § 767-315
- www.hg.org/divorce-law-wisconsin.html

Wisconsin Property Division Law
- Wisc. Stat. § 767.61
- docs.legis.wisconsin.gov/statutes/statutes/766
- wilawlibrary.gov/topics/familylaw/maritalproperty.php

Wisconsin Child Custody Law
- wilawlibrary.gov/topics/familylaw/childcustody.php

Wisconsin Relocation of Child
- Wisc. Stat. § 767.481

Wisconsin Guardian Ad Litem and Attorney for Child
- Wisc. Stat. §§ 48.23, 48.235
- wilawlibrary.gov/topics/familylaw/gal.php
- www.childwelfare.gov/pubPDFs/represent.pdf

Wisconsin Child Support Law
- dcf.wisconsin.gov/bcs
- wilawlibrary.gov/topics/familylaw/childsupport.php

Wisconsin Paternity Law
- Wisc. Stat. § 767.84
- wilawlibrary.gov/topics/familylaw/paternity.php

Wisconsin Legal Definition of Father/Parent
- www.childwelfare.gov/systemwide/laws_policies/statutes/putative.pdf

Wisconsin Child Custody Law
- wilawlibrary.gov/topics/familylaw/childcustody.php

Wisconsin Adoption Law
- statelaws.findlaw.com/wisconsin-law/wisconsin-adoption-laws.html

Wisconsin Termination of Parental Rights
- wilawlibrary.gov/topics/familylaw/tpr.php
- www.childwelfare.gov/pubPDFs/groundtermin.pdf

Wisconsin Putative Father (Paternal Interest) Registry
- dcf.wisconsin.gov/paternalinterest/father
- www.ncsl.org/documents/cyf/putative_father_registries.pdf

Wisconsin Emancipation Law
- statelaws.findlaw.com/wisconsin-law/wisconsin-legal-ages-laws
  .html

Wisconsin Age of Majority
- statelaws.findlaw.com/wisconsin-law/wisconsin-legal-ages-laws
  .html

Wisconsin Child Protection/Protective Services
- dcf.wisconsin.gov

Wisconsin Child Welfare Agencies
- dcf.wisconsin.gov

Wisconsin Juvenile Law
- www.wicourts.gov/services/public/selfhelp/juvenile.htm
- www.ncjj.org/pdf/1State_Juvenile_Justice_Profiles_2005.pdf

Wisconsin Domestic Violence Law
- Wisc. Stat. § 905.045
- wilawlibrary.gov/topics/familylaw/domesticabuse.php

Wisconsin Employment Discrimination Law
- Wisc. Stat. § 111.321
- www.ncsl.org/documents/employ/DiscriminationChart-III.pdf

Wisconsin Surrogacy Law
- Wisc. Stat. § 69.14(h)
- www.selectsurrogate.com/surrogacy-laws-by-state.html
- www.surrogacyforall.com
- www.selectsurrogate.com/surrogacy-laws-by-state.html

Wisconsin Grandparent Rights
- wilawlibrary.gov/topics/familylaw/grandparents.php
- www.verywellfamily.com/grandparent-visitation-
  rights-state-by-state-1695938

Wisconsin Annulment Law
- Wisc. Stat. § 767.313
- wilawlibrary.gov/topics/familylaw/divorce.php#annul

Wisconsin Parental Liability for Acts of Minors
- Wisc. Stat. § 895.035

Wisconsin Family Law Forms
- www.wicourts.gov/forms1/circuit/index.htm
- wilawlibrary.gov/topics/countytopics.php?t=famm
- family.findlaw.com/divorce/divorce-forms-by-state.html

Wisconsin Vital Records (Birth, Marriage, Divorce, Death)
- www.cdc.gov/nchs/w2w.htm
- publicrecords.onlinesearches.com/Wisconsin.htm

Wisconsin Self-Help Services in Family Law Cases
- www.wicourts.gov/services/public/selfhelp/?
- wilawlibrary.gov/topics/shc.php

Wisconsin Family Law Legal Research
- wilawlibrary.gov/topics/familylaw/index.php

Wisconsin State Legal Research (general)
- www.loc.gov/law/help/guide/states/us-wi.php
- caselaw.findlaw.com/wisconsin.html

Wisconsin Court Rules
- wilawlibrary.gov/topics/wisconsinlaw.php#WCC

Wisconsin Job Discrimination Based on Marital Status or Gender
- www.ncsl.org/documents/employ/DiscriminationChart-III.pdf

Google, Bing, or Yahoo Searches on Wisconsin Family Law
- "Wisconsin family law"
- "Wisconsin divorce"
- Wisconsin "property division"
- "Wisconsin adoption"
- Wisconsin paternity
- Wisconsin "child custody"
- Wisconsin "child support"
- Wisconsin abortion
- Wisconsin marriage
- Wisconsin "separation agreement"
- Wisconsin "premarital agreement"
- (also try these searches in the *Articles* and *Case law* databases of
  Scholar.google.com)

WYOMING FAMILY LAW

Wyoming Family Laws
- statelaws.findlaw.com/wyoming-law/wyoming-family-laws.html

Wyoming Family Code/Domestic Relations Code
- statelaws.findlaw.com/wyoming-law/wyoming-legal-requirements-
  for-divorce.html

Wyoming Marriage Law (formation)
- marriage.about.com/cs/marriagelicenses/p/wyoming.htm
- usmarriagelaws.com (enter your state or county)

Wyoming Premarital Agreement Law
- www.divorcenet.com/resources/prenuptial-agreements-wyoming.html
- marriage.uslegal.com/permarital-agreements

Wyoming Common Law Marriage
- topics.law.cornell.edu/wex/table_marriage

Wyoming Divorce Law
- Wyo. Statutes Ann. Title 20, Chapter 2
- www.divorcelawinfo.com/states/wyo/wyoming.htm
- divorce.laws.com/divorce-in-wyoming
- www.womenslaw.org/laws/wy/divorce

Wyoming Judicial Separation Law
- Wyo. Statutes Ann. § 20-2-106

Wyoming Alimony Law
- Wyo. Statutes Ann. § 20-2-114

Wyoming Property Division Law
- Wyo. Statutes Ann. § 20-2-114
- www.maritallaws.com/states/wyoming/property-division

Wyoming Child Custody Law
- Wyo. Statutes Ann. § 20-5-301
- www.courts.state.wy.us/?s=child+custody&x=0&y=0
- www.familylawrights.net/wyoming/child-custody

Wyoming Guardian Ad Litem and Attorney for Child
- www.childwelfare.gov/pubPDFs/represent.pdf

Wyoming Child Support Law
- dfsweb.wyo.gov
- sites.google.com/a/wyo.gov/dfsweb
- childsupport.wyoming.gov

Wyoming Paternity Law
- Wyo. Statutes Ann. § 14-2-504
- paternity.uslegal.com/paternity-laws/wyoming-paternity-law

Wyoming Legal Definition of Father
- Wyo. Statutes Ann. § 1-22-101 ("parent" "putative father")
- www.childwelfare.gov/pubPDFs/putative.pdf

Wyoming Putative Father Registry
- Wyo. Statutes Ann. § 1-22-117
- www.ncsl.org/documents/cyf/putative_father_registries.pdf
- www.childwelfare.gov/pubPDFs/putative.pdf

Wyoming Adoption Law
- Wyo. Statutes Ann. §§ 1-22-102 et seq.
- statelaws.findlaw.com/wyoming-law/wyoming-adoption-laws.html

Wyoming Termination of Parental Rights Law
- Wyo. Statutes Ann. § 14-3-431
- www.childwelfare.gov/pubPDFs/groundtermin.pdf

Wyoming Emancipation Law
- Wyo. Statutes Ann. §§ 14-1-101 et seq.

Wyoming Age of Majority
- Wyo. Statutes Ann. § 14-1-101
- statelaws.findlaw.com/wyoming-law/wyoming-legal-ages-laws.html

Wyoming Child Protection/Protective Services
- Wyo. Statutes Ann. §§ 14-3-201 et seq.
- dfsweb.wyo.gov/social-services/child-protective-services

Wyoming Child Welfare Agencies
- dfsweb.wyo.gov

Wyoming Juvenile Law
- www.ncjj.org/pdf/1State_Juvenile_Justice_Profiles_2005.pdf
- www.ojp.usdoj.gov/saa/wy.htm

Wyoming Domestic Violence Law
- Wyo. Statutes Ann. §§ 35-21-101 et seq.
- www.domesticshelters.org/help/wy

Wyoming Employment Discrimination Law
- Wyo. Statutes Ann. § 27-9-105
- www.ncsl.org/documents/employ/DiscriminationChart-III.pdf

Wyoming Surrogacy Law
- www.selectsurrogate.com/surrogacy-laws-by-state.html

Wyoming Grandparent Rights
- Wyo. Statutes Ann. § 20-7-101
- grandparents.about.com/od/grandparentsrights/qt/Grandparent_Rights_in_Wyoming.htm
- www.verywellfamily.com/grandparent-visitation-rights-state-by-state-1695938

Wyoming Annulment Law
- Wyo. Statutes Ann. § 20-2-101
- statutes.laws.com/wyoming/Title20/chapter2

Wyoming Parental Liability for Acts of Minors
- Maximum liability $2,000
- Wyo. Statutes Ann. § 14-2-203

Wyoming Family Law Forms
- www.courts.state.wy.us/?s=forms&x=0&y=0
- www.courts.state.wy.us/legal-assistances-and-forms/court-self-help-forms
- family.findlaw.com/divorce/divorce-forms-by-state.html

Wyoming Vital Records (Birth, Marriage, Divorce, Death)
- publicrecords.onlinesearches.com/Wyoming.htm
- www.cdc.gov/nchs/w2w.htm

Wyoming Self-Help Services in Family Law Cases
- www.courts.state.wy.us/legal-assistances-and-forms/
- www.courts.state.wy.us/legal-assistances-and-forms/court-self-help-forms

Wyoming State Legal Research
- www.loc.gov/law/help/guide/states/us-wy.php
- caselaw.findlaw.com/wyoming.html

Wyoming Court Rules
- www.courts.state.wy.us/supreme-court/court-rules

Wyoming Job Discrimination Based on Marital Status or Gender
- www.ncsl.org/documents/employ/DiscriminationChart-III.pdf

Google, Bing, or Yahoo Searches on Wyoming Family Law
- "Wyoming family law"
- "Wyoming divorce"
- Wyoming "property division"
- "Wyoming adoption"
- Wyoming paternity
- Wyoming "child custody"
- Wyoming "child support"
- Wyoming abortion
- Wyoming marriage
- Wyoming "separation agreement"
- Wyoming "premarital agreement"
- (also try these searches in the *Articles* and *Case law* databases of Scholar.google.com)

A

abandonment Relinquishing one's parental responsibility by voluntarily leaving a child or ending communication with a child for a specific period or indefinitely without arranging for alternative care and supervision while away. Conduct that constitutes a relinquishing of one's parental responsibilities. See also *criminal nonsupport* and *desertion*.

abandonment of children See *criminal nonsupport*.

abrogation A cancelation or nullification.

abduction The unlawful taking away of another.

abduction or enticement of a child See *tortious interference with custody*.

abortion An induced termination of a pregnancy in order to destroy an embryo or fetus. See also *therapeutic abortion*.

absolute divorce A declaration by a court that the marriage is terminated so that the parties can remarry. Also called *complete divorce* and *divorce a vincula matrimonii* (divorce from the chains of marriage).

abuse See *child abuse* and *domestic violence*.

accounting See *financial statement*.

account receivable A business debt to a creditor that has not yet been collected.

acknowledged father A man who has formally declared that he is the father by signing an acknowledgment of paternity.

active appreciation An increase in the value of property that is due to the active efforts of the owner rather than to inflation or market forces.

adjudicate To decide by judicial process; to judge.

adjudicated father A man who has been declared to be the father by a court.

adjusted basis The basis of property (its cost of acquisition) increased by the cost of capital improvements and decreased by allowable deductions. See also *basis* and *tax effect*.

adjusted gross income (AGI) The total income from all of a person's taxable sources less specifically allowed deductions.

adoptee A person who is adopted.

adoption The judicial process by which one person (the adoptive parent) becomes the legal parent of another person (the adoptee).

Adoption and Safe Families Act (ASFA) A federal statute that requires states to take specific placement action on behalf of children in foster care, such as terminating parental rights in order to facilitate adoption after a designated period of time trying to reunite the child with its biological parents.

adoption by estoppel See *equitable adoption* and *estopped*.

adoptive father A man (often a stepparent) who has adopted a child.

adoptive parent A person who adopts another person.

ADR See *alternative dispute resolution*.

adultery (1) Voluntary sexual intercourse between a married person and someone other than his or her spouse. (2) Voluntary intimate sexual relations between a spouse and someone other than his or her spouse, irrespective of the specific sexual acts performed, the marital status of the nonspouse, or the gender of the nonspouse.

adversary (1) An opponent. (2) Involving a dispute between opposing sides who argue their case before a neutral official, such as a judge.

adversary proceeding A proceeding in which both sides appear and argue their positions when a court is asked to do something. See also *ex parte proceeding*.

adversary system A method of resolving a legal dispute whereby the parties (alone or through their advocates) argue their conflicting claims before a neutral (impartial) decision maker.

adverse (1) Opposed to. (2) Hostile. (3) Having an opposing position. (4) Harmful, unfavorable.

adverse interest A goal or claim of one person that is different from (or opposed to) the goal or claim of another person.

AFDC Aid to Families with Dependent Children, a public-assistance program. See also *Temporary Assistance for Needy Families*.

affiant A person who is making an affidavit.

affidavit A written or printed statement containing facts given under oath by a person (called the *affiant*) before someone with authority to administer the oath.

affinity Relationship by marriage rather than by blood.

affirmative defense A defense raising facts or arguments that will defeat the opponent's claim even if the opponent's allegations in the claim are true.

a fortiori With greater force; all the more so.

age of majority The age at which children reach legal adulthood, usually eighteen years, entitling them to many civil rights, such as the right to manage their own affairs.

aggrieved Injured or wronged and thereby entitled to a remedy.

AGI See *adjusted gross income*.

AI See *artificial insemination*.

alien A person who was born outside the United States, is still a subject of a foreign nation, and has not been naturalized in the United States.

alienage The condition of being an alien.

alienation of affections   The tort of causing a diminishment of the marital relationship or an interference with consortium rights between the plaintiff and his or her spouse.

alimony   Money or other property paid in fulfillment of a duty to support one's spouse (or ex-spouse) after a legal separation, a divorce, and, in most states, an annulment. Also called *maintenance, spousal support*. See also *rehabilitative alimony*.

alimony in gross   Alimony in the form of a single (lump-sum) payment. Also called *lump-sum alimony*.

alimony pendente lite   See *temporary alimony*.

alimony trust   A trust to which a spouse or ex-spouse transfers funds that will be used to meet an alimony obligation.

alleged father   See *putative father*.

alternate payee   A nonworker who is entitled to receive all or part of the pension or other retirement benefits of a current or former worker pursuant to a qualified domestic relations order (QDRO).

alternative dispute resolution (ADR)   A method or procedure for resolving a legal dispute without litigating it in a court or an administrative agency. ADR methods include *mediation, arbitration,* and *med-arb*.

ambulance chasing   Approaching accident victims (or others who might have a legal problem or claim of any kind) to encourage them to hire a particular attorney. If the attorney uses someone else to do the soliciting, the latter is called a *runner*. If this other person uses deception or fraud in the solicitation, he or she is sometimes called a *capper* or a *steerer*.

a mensa et thoro   See *divorce a mensa et thoro*.

American Bar Association   A voluntary, national organization of attorneys.

American Law Reports   A set of reporters that contain selected opinions from many different courts. In addition, the ALR volumes contain research papers—called *annotations*—that give surveys of the law on particular issues found in the opinions.

amnesty   Forgiveness; a pardon issued by the state.

annotated   Organized by subject matter with research references or other commentary.

annotation   (1) A note or commentary on something. (2) A research paper in one of the sets of American Law Reports.

annuitant   Recipient of an annuity.

annuity   A fixed sum payable periodically for life or for a specific period of time. The recipient of the annuity is called the *annuitant*.

annulment   A declaration by a court that a valid marriage never existed. Also called *declaration of invalidity of marriage, marital annulment*.

answer   (1) A party's pleading that responds to the pleading of an opposing party. (2) The first pleading of the defendant that responds to the plaintiff's claims.

antenuptial agreement   See *premarital agreement*.

anticontact rule   An advocate must not contact an opposing party without permission of the latter's attorney. Also called *no-contact rule*.

antimiscegenation law   A law that forbids marriage between persons of different races.

antinepotism   See *nepotism*.

appearance   Formally going before a court.

appellant   The party bringing an appeal because of disagreement with the decision of a lower tribunal.

appellate brief   A document that a party files with an appellate court (and serves on an opponent) in which the party presents arguments on why the appellate court should affirm (approve), reverse, vacate (cancel), or otherwise modify what a lower court has done.

appellee   The party against whom an appeal is brought.

appreciation   An increase in the value of property after it is acquired.

approximation rule   The caregiving of parents in the postdivorce world should be in rough proportion to that which predated the divorce.

arbitration   A method of alternate dispute resolution (ADR) in which the parties avoid litigation by submitting their dispute to a neutral third person (the arbitrator) who renders a decision resolving the dispute.

arm's length   Pertaining to how parties would treat each other if they were strangers looking out for their own self-interests with no confidential or other special relationship between them that would cause one to expect the other to provide a special advantage or to act with fairness.

arrearages   Payments that are due but have not yet been made. Also called *arrears*.

arrears   See *arrearages*.

ART   See *assisted reproductive technology*.

artificial insemination (AI)   Inserting sperm into the uterus by a method other than sexual intercourse in order to achieve conception.

ASFA   See *Adoption and Safe Families Act*.

assign   To transfer rights or property to someone. The noun is *assignment*. The person who makes the transfer is the *assignor*. The person who receives the transfer is the *assignee* or the *assign*.

assignee   The person to whom ownership or rights are transferred. See also *assign*.

assignment   See *assign*.

assignor   See *assign*.

assisted reproductive technology (ART)   Medical means to assist human reproduction. Any fertility treatment in which either eggs or embryos are handled in a laboratory. Also called *assisted conception*.

at arm's length   See *arm's length*.

at common law   During a time in early U.S. history when law was created by court opinions and legislatures, often before it was changed by later legislatures. See also *common law*.

attachment   (1) A court authorization of the seizure of a person's property so that it can be used to satisfy a judgment against him or her. (2) The seizure of property as security for such a judgment.

attestation clause   A formal statement that you saw (witnessed) someone sign a document or perform other tasks related to the validity of the document.

attorney-client privilege   A client or a client's attorney can refuse to disclose any confidential (private) communication between them if the purpose of the communication was to facilitate the provision of legal services to the client.

attorney in fact   See *power of attorney*.

attorney work product   See *work-product rule*.

autonomy, right to personal   See *right to privacy*.

a vinculo matrimonii   See *divorce a vinculo matrimonii*.

B

baby-buying   See *black-market adoption*.

basis   One's initial capital investment in property, usually the cost of acquiring the property. Also called *cost basis*. An *adjusted basis* is calculated after making allowed adjustments and deductions to the initial capital investment (e.g., an increase in the basis because of a capital improvement).

bastard   See *illegitimate child*.

bastardy   The status of an illegitimate child.

battered-woman syndrome   A woman's psychological helplessness or paralysis because of conditions such as financial dependence, loneliness, guilt, shame, and fear of reprisal from her husband or boyfriend who has repeatedly subjected her to physical, sexual, and/or emotional abuse in the past.

battery   An intentional infliction of a harmful or offensive bodily contact.

bench trial   A nonjury trial.

beneficial interest   A right to a benefit from something (e.g., property) whose legal ownership is in another.

beneficiary   The person named in a document, such as a will or insurance policy, to receive property or other benefit.

bequest   A gift of personal property in a will. (In some states, a bequest can be a gift of personal property or real property in a will.)

best interests attorney (BIA)   An attorney who provides legal representation for a child to protect the child's best interests without being bound by the child's directives or objectives.

best interests of the child   A standard used by a court to decide what would best serve a child's welfare when the court must make custody, visitation, adoption, guardianship, and change-of-name decisions.

BFOQ   See *bona fide occupational qualification*.

BIA   See *best interests attorney*.

bias   (1) An inclination, tendency, or predisposition to think or act in a certain way. (2) Prejudice for or against something or someone. (3) A danger of prejudgment.

bifurcated divorce   A divorce that resolves marital issues in separate proceedings, usually dissolving the marriage in one proceeding but requiring a separate proceeding to resolve property division and support issues.

bigamy   Marrying another while still in a valid, undissolved marriage with someone else.

bilateral divorce   A divorce granted by a court when both spouses are present before the court.

biological father   A man whose genes contributed to the birth of a child through conception. Also called the *genetic father*.

biological parent   One's parent by blood.

bird nesting   A living arrangement in which parents take turns living with a child who stays in the same home as the parents alternate moving in and out. Also called *nesting*.

black market adoption   An adoption that is illegal because the payments to facilitate the adoption were in excess of reasonable expenses of facilitation. Also called *baby-buying*.

boilerplate   Standard or often-used language that is commonly found in the same kind of document. Standard verbiage.

bona fide occupational qualification (BFOQ)   An employment qualification based on gender, religion, or other characteristic that is reasonably necessary for the normal operation of a particular business and hence is not an illegal requirement under federal employment discrimination laws.

bona fides   Good faith. The absence of wrongful intent or desire to take inappropriate advantage of someone.

bond   See *surety bond*.

book value   The value at which an asset is carried on the balance sheet.

bridge-the-gap alimony   See *rehabilitative alimony*.

bundled legal services   All tasks needed to represent a client on a legal matter; all-inclusive legal services. See also *unbundled legal services*.

burden of proof   The responsibility of proving a fact at trial.

C

canon   (1) A rule of behavior. (2) A maxim or guideline.

canon law   Church law; ecclesiastical law.

capacity   (1) The legal power to do something, such as enter into a contract or a relationship. Also called *legal capacity*. (2) The ability to understand the nature and effects of one's actions or inactions.

capital investment   The cost of acquiring property. Cost basis.

capital improvements   Structural additions or improvements of property, as opposed to ordinary maintenance work.

capitalization rate   The rate of interest investors would require as a return on their money before they would invest in income-producing property, taking into account all the risks involved in that particular enterprise. *City of Dallas v. Redbird Development Corp.* 143 S.W.3d 375 (Tex. App. 2004).

capper   See *ambulance chasing.*

CAPTA   See *Child Abuse Prevention and Treatment Act.*

caption   The heading or introductory part of a pleading or other document that identifies what it is, the names of the parties, the court involved, if any, etc.

caregiver alimony   Alimony for an ex-spouse who cannot be self-supporting because of his or her need to care for a disabled child.

CARTWHEEL   A search technique designed to help you think of a large variety of words and phrases to check in indexes, tables of contents, and online search boxes.

CASA   See *court appointed special advocate.*

case law   The body of law found in court opinions.

cause of action   (1) A legally acceptable reason for bringing a suit. A rule that constitutes a legal theory for bringing a suit. (2) The facts that give a person a right to judicial relief. When you *state a cause of action*, you list the facts that give you a right to judicial relief against the alleged wrongdoer.

ceremonial marriage   A marriage entered into in compliance with statutory formalities (e.g., obtaining a marriage license, having the marriage performed by an authorized person before witnesses). A marriage other than a common-law marriage. Also called *conventional marriage, traditional marriage, formal marriage,* and *statutory marriage.*

certificate of service   See *proof of service.*

chambers   A judge's private office.

chancellor   A judge in a court of equity.

chattel   See *personal property.*

child abuse   Serious physical, emotional, or sexual mistreatment of a child that is not the result of an accident or circumstances beyond the control of the parent or guardian.

Child Abuse Prevention and Treatment Act (CAPTA)   A federal statute that helps fund state programs for the identification, prevention, and treatment of child abuse and neglect (42 U.S.C. § 5101).

child in need of supervision and services (CHIPS)   See *status offense, juvenile delinquent.*

child maltreatment   An act or failure to act by a parent or caretaker that intentionally or carelessly results in physical or emotional harm to a child or that presents an imminent risk of such harm to a child.

child neglect   The failure of a parent or other caregiver to provide the basic needs of a child, including physical needs (e.g., food and shelter), emotional needs, medical needs, or educational needs.

child protective services   A state agency that investigates child neglect and abuse, offers assistance to families of children at risk, and administers foster care or other placement programs.

child-support guidelines   State-mandated rules for calculating the amount of child support owed by adults obligated to pay such support (obligors).

Chinese Wall   Screening that prevents a tainted worker (attorney, paralegal, secretary, or clerk) from having any contact with the case of a particular client in the office because the tainted worker has created a conflict of interest between that client and someone else. A tainted worker is also called a *contaminated worker.* Once the Chinese Wall is set up around the tainted worker, the latter is referred to as a *quarantined worker.* A Chinese Wall is also called *ethical wall, cone of silence.*

CHIPS   (child in need of protection and services) See *status offense, juvenile delinquent.*

choice of law   A selection of which law to apply when a court is being asked to apply the law of different legal systems, such as in two states or two countries.

choice of venue   See *venue.*

circumstantial evidence   Evidence of one fact from which another fact (not personally observed or known) can be inferred. Also called *indirect evidence.*

civil   Noncriminal.

civil contempt   The refusal of a party to comply with a court order (usually issued for the benefit of another), which can lead to punishment (including incarceration) until the party complies with the order.

civil union   A same-sex legal relationship of unmarried individuals who have some or all of the same state benefits and responsibilities as individuals in a marriage.

class action.   A lawsuit in which one or more members of a group sue (or are sued) as representative parties on behalf of everyone in the group.

classification   (1) A group or class that the government treats differently from another group or class in that the government discriminates for or against that group or class. (2) The government's different treatment of one group or class over another. (3) The identification of property as either separate property or marital property.

CLE   See *continuing legal education.*

clean hands   See *dirty hands.*

clear and convincing evidence   A standard of proof that is met when the evidence demonstrates that the existence of a disputed fact is much more probable than its nonexistence. This standard is stronger than *preponderance of the evidence* but not as strong as *beyond a reasonable doubt.*

closed adoption   A traditional adoption in which there is no disclosure of the identity of the birth parents, adoptive parent(s), or the adoptee.

code   A book or set of books that contain rules or laws organized by subject matter. The state code, also called the *state statutory code,* is a collection of statutes written by the state legislature, organized by subject matter.

cohabit   To live together in an intimate (usually sexual) relationship in the manner of spouses. The noun is *cohabitation.*

Although a married couple cohabits, the word is more often used in reference to an unmarried couple.

cohabitation Living together in an intimate (usually sexual) relationship in the manner of spouses. A de facto husband and wife relationship. The verb is *cohabit*. Although a married couple cohabits, the word cohabitation is more often used in reference to an unmarried couple.

cohabitation agreement A contract by persons in an intimate relationship who are not married to each other (and who intend to stay unmarried indefinitely) that covers financial and related matters while they are living together and upon the end of the cohabitation by separation or death.

cohabitants Two persons living together in an intimate (usually sexual) relationship.

collaborative law A method of practicing law in which the attorneys refuse to continue representing the parties if the parties cannot settle their dispute through mediation or other form of alternative dispute resolution (ADR).

collateral attack A challenge or attack against the validity of a judgment raised in a different proceeding from the one that rendered the judgment. A *direct attack* would be a challenge or an attack against the validity of a judgment raised in the *same* proceeding that rendered the judgment, such as during the trial or during a direct appeal of that judgment.

collusion (1) An agreement to commit fraud. (2) An agreement by spouses that one or both will lie to the court in order to help secure their divorce.

collusive divorce A divorce obtained in a proceeding in which the spouses agreed to lie to the court in order to facilitate the granting of the divorce.

comity The court's decision to give effect to the laws and court decisions of another state as a matter of deference and mutual respect even if no obligation exists to do so. (Most often applied to the laws and court decisions of another nation.)

commingling (1) Mixing what should be kept separate. (Example: depositing client funds in an account that also contains general operating funds of the office.) (2) Any mixing of items of different categories. (3) Mixing funds from different sources. The verb is *commingle*.

common law (1) Law created by courts in the absence of controlling statutory law or other higher law. (2) Court opinions, all of case law. (3) The legal system of England and of those countries such as the United States whose legal system is based on England's. (4) The case law and statutory law in England and in the American colonies before the American Revolution. See also *at common law*.

common-law marriage A marriage entered into without complying with statutory formalities (e.g., obtaining a marriage license, having the marriage performed by an authorized person before witnesses) by persons who (a) agree to marry, (b) live together as spouses , and (c) hold themselves out as married. A marriage by persons who have not gone through a ceremonial marriage. Called an *informal marriage* in Texas.

common-law property Property acquired during the marriage in a state other than a community-property state. (Older definition: Property acquired during the marriage that is the separate property of the spouse who earned it or who has title to it.)

common representation See *multiple representation*.

community estate The community property of a husband and wife.

community property Property in which each spouse has a 50 percent interest if the property was acquired during the marriage other than by gift, will, or intestate succession (inheritance) to only one of the spouses.

comparative rectitude A comparison of the wrongdoing of two spouses in causing the breakdown of the marriage so that the divorce can be given to the spouse least at fault.

compelling state interest An interest that is of the highest order; an interest that has a clear justification in the necessities of national or community life.

compensatory damages Money paid to restore an injured party to his or her position prior to the injury or other loss.

competent (1) Taking the time needed to prepare so that you are using the knowledge and skill that are reasonably necessary to represent a particular client. (2) Having the legal capacity to give testimony because the person understands the obligation to tell the truth, has the ability to communicate, and has knowledge of the topic of his or her testimony. (3) Allowed (having the legal capacity) to give testimony because the person understands the obligation to tell the truth, has the ability to communicate, and has knowledge of the topic of his or her testimony. The noun is *competency*.

complaint (1) A plaintiff's first pleading that states a claim against the defendant. Also called a *petition*. (2) A formal criminal charge.

conclusive presumption A conclusion of law or fact that a party will not be allowed to try to disprove (rebut). Also called *irrebuttable presumption*.

concurrent (1) Acting, occurring, or operating at the same time. (2) Having authority on the same matters.

concurrent jurisdiction Subject-matter jurisdiction that resides in more than one kind of court in the same judicial system.

condonation An express or implied forgiveness by the innocent spouse of the marital fault committed by the other spouse.

conducive to divorce Tending to encourage divorce.

confidential (1) Pertaining to information that others do not have a right to receive. (2) Pertaining to all information related to the representation of a client whatever its source, including the fact that someone is a client.

confidential marriage A ceremonial marriage entered into with fewer technical/procedural requirements and greater privacy than a traditional ceremonial marriage.

confidential relationship See *fiduciary relationship*.

conflict of interest   Divided loyalties that actually or potentially harm (or disadvantage) someone who is owed undivided loyalty.

conflict of laws   An inconsistency between the laws of different legal systems such as the laws of two states or the laws of two countries.

conflicts check   Finding out whether a conflict of interest exists that might disqualify a law office from representing a prospective client or from continuing the representation of a current client.

Confrontation Clause   A clause in the U.S. Constitution stating that criminal defendants have a right to confront accusing witnesses face-to-face and to cross-examine them. U.S. Const. amend. VI.

conjugal   Pertaining to marriage; appropriate for married persons.

connivance   A willingness or a consent by one spouse that a marital wrong be committed by the other spouse.

consanguinity   Relationship by blood.

consent   See *informed consent*.

conservator   A person appointed by the court to manage the affairs of persons who are not competent to do so on their own.

consideration   Something of value that is exchanged between parties. It can be an act, a forbearance (not performing an act), a promise to perform an act, or a promise to refrain from performing an act.

consortium   A right to the benefits that are naturally expected in a particular family relationship. See also *filial consortium, loss of consortium, parental consortium, spousal consortium*.

constitution   The basic legal document of a government that allocates power among the three branches of the government and that may also enumerate fundamental rights of individuals.

constitutionalization   (1) Changes in state law that result from interpretations of the U.S. Constitution by the U.S. Supreme Court and other federal courts. (2) The resolution of a matter through the enactment or interpretation of a constitutional provision rather than through a statute.

constructive desertion   (1) A spouse's conduct that justifies the other spouse's departure from the home. (2) A spouse's rejection of a sincere offer of reconciliation from the spouse who initially left the home without justification.

constructive-emancipation doctrine   When a minor of employable age and in full possession of his or her faculties, voluntarily and without cause, abandons the parent's home, against the will of the parent and for the purpose of avoiding parental control, he or she forfeits his or her right to demand support.

constructive service   See *substituted service*.

constructive trust   A trust created by operation of law to prevent unjust enrichment by someone who has improperly obtained property through fraud, duress, abuse of confidence, or other wrongful conduct.

consummation   (1) Sexual intercourse for the first time, particularly between spouses. (2) The completion of a marriage by the first act of sexual intercourse. (3) Bringing to completion; fulfillment.

contact veto   A denial of consent to have contact between an adoptee and his or her biological parent, although permission for the release of identifying information might be given.

contempt   Conduct that defies or disrespects the authority of a court or legislative body. When the court is defied or disrespected, it is called *contempt of court*. See also *civil contempt, criminal contempt*.

contempt of court   Obstructing or assailing the authority or dignity of the court such as by intentionally violating a court order. The purpose of a *civil* contempt proceeding is to compel future compliance with a court order. The purpose of a *criminal* contempt proceeding is to punish the offender.

contested   Challenged; opposed or disputed.

contested divorce   A divorce granted after both spouses appeared and disputed some or all of the claims made in the proceeding.

contingency   An event that may or may not occur.

contingent   Conditional; dependent on something that may or may not happen.

contingent fee   A fee that is paid only if the case is successfully resolved by litigation or settlement regardless of the number of hours spent on the case. (The fee is also referred to as a *contingency*.)

continuance   The postponement or adjournment of a proceeding to a later date.

continuing exclusive jurisdiction (CEJ)   The authority of a court, obtained by compliance with the Uniform Interstate Family Support Act (UIFSA) to make all initial and modifying support decisions in a case to the exclusion of courts in any other state. See also *exclusive continuing jurisdiction (ECJ)*.

continuing jurisdiction   A court's power (by retaining jurisdiction) to modify its orders after entering judgment.

continuing legal education (CLE)   Training in the law (usually short term) that a person receives after completing his or her formal legal training or after becoming employed.

contract   A legally enforceable agreement. The elements of most contracts are offer, acceptance, and consideration. Some contracts must be in writing. See also *cohabitation agreement, implied contract, premarital agreement*, and *separation agreement*.

contract cohabitation   See *cohabitation agreement*.

conversion   (1) Changing a legal separation into a divorce after the parties have lived apart for a designated period of time. (2) An intentional interference with another's personal property, consisting of an exercise of dominion over it.

conversion divorce, convertible divorce   See *conversion*.

conveyance   The transfer of an interest in property. The verb is *convey*.

coparenting   (1) Shared responsibility by two adults to raise a child, regardless of the marital status or sexual orientation of the adults. (2) Communication and cooperation by parents who are no longer married or in a relationship for the benefit of the child.

copulate   To engage in sexual intercourse.

corespondent   The person who had sexual relations with a defendant charged with adultery.

corporeal   Having a physical form or existence.

corporal punishment   Punishment inflicted on the physical body.

corporeal   See *tangible*.

corpus   The body of something; the aggregate of something.

corroborate   To introduce additional evidence of a fact in dispute.

corroboration   Additional evidence of a fact in dispute.

cosigner   A person who signs a document along with the main signer, usually to agree to pay the debt created by the document in the event that the main signer fails to pay it.

costs   See *court costs*.

count   A separate and independent claim or charge in a pleading, such as a petition or complaint.

counterclaim   A claim by one side in a case (usually the defendant) that is filed in response to a claim asserted by an opponent (usually the plaintiff).

court appointed special advocate (CASA)   A volunteer (who can be an attorney, a paralegal, or other nonattorney) appointed by the court to perform special assignments pertaining to children in the court system.

court costs   Charges or fees (imposed by and paid to the court) that are related to litigation in that court. An example is a court-filing fee.

court opinion   The written explanation by a court of why it reached a certain conclusion or holding.

court rules   Rules of procedure that govern the mechanics of litigation before a particular court.

covenant   A promise or agreement.

covenant marriage   A ceremonial marriage (a) that is entered upon proof of premarital counseling and a promise to seek marital counseling when needed during the marriage, and (b) that is dissolved upon separation for a designated period or upon proof of marital fault. Also called *high-test marriage*.

coverture   The legal status of a married woman whereby her civil existence for many purposes merged with (was covered up by) that of her husband. Also called *unity of person*, *doctrine of oneness*, *spousal-unity rule*, *unity of identity*.

coverture fraction   The portion of a pension earned during a marriage if part of the pension of a married worker was earned when the worker was not married.

CP   See *custodial parent*.

credit clouding   Notifying a creditor or credit bureau that a debtor is delinquent on certain debts such as child support.

creditor   Someone to whom a debt is owed.

criminal contempt   The refusal of a party to comply with a court order, which can lead to punishment (including incarceration) because of the repeated or aggravated nature of the refusal.

criminal conversation   The tort that occurs when the defendant has sexual relations with the plaintiff's spouse.

criminal homicide   Causing the death of a person without justification or excuse.

criminal law   The body of law covering acts declared to be crimes by the legislature for statutory crimes or by the courts for common-law crimes.

criminal neglect of family   See *criminal nonsupport*.

criminal nonsupport   The willful, repeated, or aggravated failure to pay support for a person the defendant is obligated to support from available resources. Also called *nonsupport*, *criminal neglect of family*, *abandonment of children*.

cruelty   The infliction of serious physical or mental suffering on another.

cryobank   See *sperm bank*.

cryopreservation   The storage of cells or whole tissues at sub-zero temperatures for later thawing and use. Example: freezing embryos from an ART cycle for potential use, transfer, or implantation at a later time.

curtesy   The right of a husband to the lifetime use (called a *life estate*) of all the land his deceased wife owned during the marriage (if issue were born of the marriage).

custodial parent (CP)   The parent with whom the child is living; the parent with physical custody of the child. Also called *residential parent*. The other parent is the *noncustodial parent (NCP)*.

custodial responsibility   See *physical custody*.

custodian   A person or an institution in charge of something. A caretaker. Also called *guardian*.

custody   (1) The right to the care and control of something, either a person or a thing. (2) The actual care and control that someone has over a person or thing.

D

damages   Money paid because of a wrongful injury or loss to person or property.

dangerous propensity   A tendency to cause damage or harm.

Deadbeat Parents Punishment Act (DPPA)   A federal statute that makes it a crime for a parent to repeatedly fail to pay child support for a child living in another state or who crosses state lines to avoid paying child support. 18 U.S.C. § 228.

debtor   One who owes a debt.

decedent   The person who has died; the deceased.

decision-making responsibility   See *legal custody*.

declaratory judgment   A court judgment that establishes (declares) rights or duties but does not order their enforcement.

deep pocket   (1) An individual, business, or other organization with resources to pay a potential judgment. (2) Sufficient assets for this purpose. The opposite of *shallow pocket*.

de facto adoption   See *equitable adoption*.

de facto marriage A marriage in fact. A relationship of a cohabiting couple that is recognized as a marriage for limited purposes when the couple has acted in a marriage-like manner even though the relationship does not meet the requirements of a ceremonial, common law, or putative marriage.

default divorce A divorce that is granted because of the failure of a spouse to appear, plead, or otherwise defend the divorce action of the other spouse.

default judgment A judgment against a party for failure to appear, plead, or otherwise respond to an opponent's claim.

defendant The party against whom a claim is brought at the commencement of litigation.

defense Allegations of fact or legal theories offered to offset or defeat claims or demands.

Defense of Marriage Act (DOMA) A federal statute that says (1) one state is not required to give full faith and credit to a same-sex marriage entered in another state (28 U.S.C. § 1738C), and (2) for federal purposes, only opposite-sex marriage is recognized (1 U.S.C. § 7).

defined-benefit plan (DBP) A pension plan that provides a set or defined pension benefit upon retirement, usually based on salary and years of employment.

defined-contribution plan (DCP) A pension plan consisting of individual accounts for each worker whose retirement benefit depends on the amount in his or her account.

dependency (1) The condition of a child who has been placed in the custody of the state because the child has been abused, neglected, or abandoned. (2) Pertaining to a child who lacks basic care through no fault of the parent or guardian.

deponent A person who is questioned in a deposition.

deposed To be asked questions in a deposition.

deposition A method of discovery by which one party questions another party (or questions the other party's witness), usually outside the courtroom. The person questioned is called the *deponent*.

depository The party or place where something is stored.

depreciation A decrease in the value of property after it is acquired.

descent Acquiring property by inheritance rather than by will; acquiring property from a decedent who died intestate.

desertion The voluntary and unjustified departure of one spouse from another. Also called *abandonment*. See also *constructive desertion*.

devise A gift of real property in a will. (In some states, a devise can be a gift of real property or personal property in a will.) The person making the gift of property is the *devisor*. The person receiving it is the *devisee*.

devisee/devisor See *devise*.

digest (1) Set of books containing brief summaries of court opinions arranged by topic and by court or jurisdiction. (2) A summary of a document or a series of documents.

dilatory Causing delay, often without merit or justification.

dirty hands Wrongdoing or other inappropriate behavior that would make it unfair or inequitable to allow persons to assert a right or a defense they would normally have. Also called *unclean hands*. A person without dirty hands is said to have *clean hands*.

disability Not having the legal capacity to perform a certain task, such as entering into a contract.

disaffirm (1) To repudiate or cancel. (2) To exercise a right to repudiate and refuse to perform one's own contract. (A right enjoyed by minors.)

disbursement Payment.

discharge Extinguish; forgive a debt so that it is no longer owed.

discipline Imposing correction or punishment.

discoverable Pertaining to information or materials an opponent can obtain through deposition, interrogatories, or other discovery methods.

discovery Methods used by parties to force information from each other before trial to aid in trial preparation. Examples of such methods include interrogatories and depositions. The methods can also be used to aid in the enforcement of a judgment.

discrimination Treating things or people differently depending on which group they are in. Differential treatment.

disinterested (1) Not working for one side or the other in a dispute. (2) Not deriving benefit if one side of a dispute wins or loses; objective.

dissipation The improper reduction or waste of marital/community assets that should have been available for property division or for support upon divorce.

dissolution (1) A divorce. A court's termination of a marriage for specified grounds. (2) In a few states, divorce and dissolution have different meanings. A divorce is the result of a court proceeding in which one spouse establishes grounds against the other, whereas a dissolution is the result of a joint petition in which both spouses ask the court for the same relief pursuant to a separation agreement they have negotiated.

distributable Subject to distribution to the parties; pertaining to property that can be divided and distributed to spouses upon divorce.

distributive share The portion of an estate that a person receives from a person who dies intestate (i.e., without leaving a valid will).

diversity of citizenship The disputing parties are citizens of different states and the amount in controversy exceeds $75,000. This diversity gives subject-matter jurisdiction to a federal trial court—a U.S. district court. It is called *diversity jurisdiction*.

divided custody See *split custody*.

divided loyalty Representing a client when a conflict of interest exists. See *conflict of interest*.

divisible Capable of being divided.

divisible divorce (1) A divorce judgment that dissolves the marriage but does not resolve other divorce issues such as property division, support, and child custody. Also called a *bifurcated divorce*. (2) A divorce that is enforceable only in part. An example is a divorce judgment issued in one court that dissolves the marriage and makes an award of alimony, but only the dissolution is enforceable in another court, not the alimony order.

divorce A declaration by a court that a validly entered marriage is terminated so that the parties are no longer married to each other. Also called *dissolution, marital dissolution, divorce a vinculo matrimonii* (divorce from the chains of marriage). See, however, *dissolution* for a distinction between divorce and dissolution in some states.

divorce a mensa et thoro [divorce from bed and hearth] A declaration by a court that parties can live apart although they are still married to each other. Also called *legal separation, judicial separation, limited divorce, separation from bed and board*.

divorce a vinculo matrimonii [divorce from the chains of marriage] A declaration by a court that a marriage is terminated so that the parties are no longer married to each other. Also called *divorce, absolute divorce*.

divorce kit A package of do-it-yourself materials containing standard forms and written instructions on how to obtain a divorce without an attorney.

DNA testing Genetic testing on deoxyribonucleic acid removed from cells.

doctor–patient privilege A patient or a patient's doctor can refuse to disclose any confidential (private) communications between them if the purpose of the communication was to facilitate the provision of medical services to the patient.

DOMA See *Defense of Marriage Act*.

domestic partners (1) Two same-sex or opposite-sex legal, unmarried individuals who are emotionally and financially interdependent and who have many of the same state benefits and responsibilities as individuals in a marriage. (2) "Two persons of the same sex or opposite-sex, not married to one another, who for a significant period of time share a primary residence and a life together as a couple." American Law Institute, *Principles of the Law of Family Dissolution*, § 6.03 (2000).

domestic partnership A same-sex or opposite-sex legal relationship of unmarried individuals who are emotionally and financially interdependent and who have many of the same state benefits and responsibilities as individuals in a marriage.

domestic-relations exception Federal courts do not have subject-matter jurisdiction over the granting of divorce, alimony, or child custody—even if there is diversity of citizenship among the parties.

domestic tort See *marital tort*.

domestic violence (DV) Actual or threatened injury or abuse of one member of a family or household by another member. Under § 102(1) of the *Model Code on Domestic and Family Violence*, "Domestic or family violence" means the occurrence of one or more of the following acts by a family or household member, but does not include acts of self-defense: (a) Attempting to cause or causing physical harm to another family or household member; (b) Placing a family or household member in fear of physical harm; or (c) Causing a family or household member to engage involuntarily in sexual activity by force, threat of force, or duress.

domicile The place where a person has been physically present (a) with the intent to make that place a permanent home or (b) with no intent to make any other place a permanent home. The place to which one intends to return when away. A *residence* is simply the place where you are living at a particular time. A person can have more than one residence, but generally can have only one domicile.

domicile by choice A domicile selected by a person with the legal capacity to choose.

domiciliary One who is domiciled in a particular place.

domiciliary state The state where one has a domicile.

donee The person who receives a gift.

donor The person who gives a gift.

DOS Date of separation; date the spouses stopped living together on a permanent basis.

dower The right of a widow to the lifetime use (called a *life estate*) of one-third of the land her deceased husband owned during the marriage. (Owned means *fee simple*, the most complete form of ownership possible.)

dowry The cash or other property given to the husband by the wife upon marriage.

DPL see *due process of law*.

draft (1) As a verb, draft means to write a document (e.g., a letter, contract, or memorandum). (2) As a noun, it means a version of a document that is not yet final or ready for distribution.

due diligence Reasonable efforts to find and verify factual information that is needed to carry out an obligation, to avoid harming someone, or to make an important decision.

due process of law (DPL) Both *procedural due process* and *substantive due process*. See these terms listed in this glossary.

durational alimony See *rehabilitative alimony*.

durational residency requirement The requirement that a party be a resident of the state for a specified period of time before being allowed to exercise a right, such as the right to petition a court for a divorce.

duress The unlawful use of force or threats to pressure or compel someone to do something he or she does not want to do. Illegal coercion.

E

ecclesiastical Pertaining to the church. See also *canon law*.

ecclesiastical court A court that resolves disputes on church matters; a church that applies canon law.

ECJ See *exclusive, continuing jurisdiction*.

EDD see *electronic data discovery*.

e-discovery Electronic data discovery (EDD). The discovery of data found in emails, spreadsheets, databases, videos, text messages, and other digital formats. Also called *electronic data discovery (EDD)*.

EEOC See *Equal Employment Opportunity Commission*.

elective abortion An abortion performed for nonmedical reasons; it is not undertaken to safeguard the mother's life or health.

elective share The percentage of a deceased spouse's estate that the surviving spouse can choose (elect) to receive despite what the will of the deceased spouse provided for the surviving spouse. Also called *right of election, statutory share, forced share*.

electronic data discovery (EDD) The discovery of data found in emails, spreadsheets, databases, texts, social-media posts, and other digital formats. Also called *e-discovery*.

electronic house arrest (EHA) See *house arrest*.

element A portion of a rule that is a precondition to the applicability of the entire rule.

element in contention The portion or element of a rule about which the parties cannot agree. The disagreement may be over the definition of the element, whether the facts fit within the element, or both.

elevated scrutiny See *intermediate scrutiny*.

emancipated Legally independent of one's parent or legal guardian. The noun is *emancipation*.

emancipation See *emancipated*.

embryo An egg that has been fertilized by a sperm and is in the early stage of development; it has undergone one or more divisions. The product of conception to about the eighth week of pregnancy.

encrypt Convert text into a code that renders it incomprehensible until it is reconverted to a readable format by an authorized recipient with the right software. The noun is *encryption*.

encumber To impose a burden, claim, lien, or charge on property.

encumbrance A claim, lien, or other charge against property.

enjoin To prohibit something through an injunction.

Enoch-Arden divorce A divorce granted on the ground that a spouse has disappeared for a designated number of years with no explanation.

Enoch-Arden presumption A spouse is presumed to be dead after being missing without explanation for a designated number of years despite due diligence in attempting to locate him or her.

enterprise goodwill An asset of a business or practice that exists by virtue of its business location, existing arrangements with suppliers and employees, and anticipated future customer base, but is not dependent on the continued presence of a particular individual in the business or practice.

enticement of a child See *abduction or enticement of a child*.

enticement of a spouse A tort in which the defendant encourages the plaintiff's spouse to leave or to stay away from the plaintiff.

EPL See *equal protection of law*.

Equal Employment Opportunity Commission (EEOC) The federal agency that enforces federal laws against employment discrimination (www.eeoc.gov).

equal protection of law (EPL) The constitutional requirement that the government treats one group or class the same as it treats another group or class in like circumstances. Also called *equal protection*.

equitable adoption A child will be considered the adopted child of a person who intended to adopt the child and acted as the child's parent but failed to go through the formal adoption procedures. Also called *adoption by estoppel, de facto adoption*, or *virtual adoption*.

equitable distribution The just and fair, but not necessarily equal, division of property between spouses upon divorce.

equitable estoppel The voluntary conduct of a person will preclude him or her from asserting rights against another who justifiably relied on the conduct and who would suffer damage or injury if the person were now allowed to repudiate the conduct. Also called *estoppel in pais*.

equitable parent An adult on whom a court will impose the responsibilities of a legal or biological parent because of the close bond the adult has formed with a child and the reliance of the child on that bond even if the adult has no blood or adoptive relationship with the child. A *presumed parent* under the Uniform Parentage Act.

equitable remedy A form of relief (e.g., injunction, specific performance, or constructive trust) that may be available when remedies at law (e.g., damages) are not adequate.

equity (1) Justice administered according to fairness in a particular case, as contrasted with the strictly formalized rules followed by common-law courts. (2) The system of justice administered in courts of equity. (3) Fairness.

escalation clause A provision in a contract or other document that provides for an increase or decrease in the amount to be paid based upon a factor over which the parties may or may not have complete control.

escrow Property (e.g., money, a deed) delivered to a neutral person (e.g., bank, escrow agent) to be held until a specified condition occurs (e.g., nonpayment of a debt), at which time the property is to be delivered to a designated person.

essentials test Did the matter go to the heart or essence of the marriage relationship?

estate (1) Everything that one owns and owes (assets and liabilities), particularly at the time of death. (2) The legal entity that exists upon a person's death, consisting of that person's assets and liabilities. (3) An interest in real or personal property. (4) The extent and nature of one's interest in real or personal property. (5) Land.

estate tax A tax on money or other property that is transferred by someone who dies leaving a valid will (testate) or without such a will (intestate). There is a federal estate tax and some states impose a state estate tax.

estopped Prevented from asserting a right or a defense because it would be unfair or inequitable to allow the assertion. The noun is *estoppel*.

estoppel See *estopped*.

ethics Rules or standards of behavior to which members of an occupation, profession, or other organization are expected to conform. Ethics governing attorneys are called *legal ethics, codes of professional responsibility*.

et ux And wife.

evidence Anything offered to establish the existence or non-existence of a fact in dispute.

exclusive, continuing jurisdiction (ECJ) The authority of a court (obtained by compliance with the Uniform Child Custody Jurisdiction and Enforcement Act (UCCJEA)) to make all initial and modifying custody decisions in a case to the exclusion of courts in any other state. See also *continuing exclusive jurisdiction*.

exclusive jurisdiction A court has exclusive jurisdiction when only that court has the power to hear a certain kind of case.

execute (1) To take needed steps to create a legal document. (2) To perform or carry out according to its terms.

executed Performed or carried out according to its terms.

execution (1) The process of carrying out or satisfying the judgment of a court. (2) A command or writ to a court officer (e.g., sheriff) to seize and sell the property of the losing litigant (now called the judgment debtor) in order to satisfy the judgment debt to the winning litigant (now called the judgment creditor). Execution is also called *general execution* and *writ of execution*.

executor A person designated in a will to carry out the terms of the will and to handle related matters. If a woman, this person is sometimes called an *executrix*. See also *personal representative*.

executory Unperformed as yet.

executory contract A contract in which the parties bind themselves to future activity. A contract that is not yet fully completed or performed.

executrix See *executor*.

exemplary damages See *punitive damages*.

ex parte With only one side present (usually the plaintiff or petitioner) when a court is asked to do something.

ex parte divorce A divorce granted by a court when only one of the spouses participates or appears in court. Also called *unilateral divorce*.

ex parte proceeding A proceeding in which only one side appears and argues its position when court action is requested. See also *adversary proceeding*.

expectancy The bare hope (but more than wishful thinking) of receiving a property interest.

expectation damages Money to compensate for the loss of what was reasonably anticipated from a contract that was not performed.

expedited procedure An accelerated procedure achieved by bypassing some of the procedural steps that are normally required.

express Explicitly stated, rather than merely implied or inferred.

express contract An agreement or contract whose terms are explicitly stated by the parties.

extrude To force out.

F

FACE See *Freedom of Access to Clinic Entrances Act*.

facilitation of divorce That which makes a divorce easier to obtain.

fact particularization (FP) A fact-gathering technique to generate a large list of factual questions—who, what, where, how, when, and why—that will help you obtain a specific and comprehensive picture of all available facts that are relevant to a legal issue.

fair employment practices agency (FEPA) A state or local government agency that enforces state or local employment discrimination laws, often in coordination with the Equal Employment Opportunity Commission (EEOC), which enforces federal employment discrimination laws.

fair market value The price that could be obtained in an open market between a willing buyer and a willing seller dealing at arm's length, neither being under any compulsion to buy or sell and both having reasonable knowledge of or access to the relevant facts. See also *arm's length*.

family-automobile rule See *family purpose doctrine*.

family expense act A state statute that makes spouses jointly liable for the basic support needs of the family.

family law The body of law that defines relationships, rights, and duties in the formation, ongoing existence, and dissolution of marriage and other family units.

family purpose doctrine An owner of a car (or a person controlling the use of a car) is vicariously liable for the negligence committed by a family member using the car for a family purpose. Also called *family automobile rule*.

family violence indicator (FVI) A designation ("flag") placed on a participant in a child-support case indicating that he or she may be a victim of domestic violence so that access to information about the participant is restricted.

fault grounds Marital wrongs that will justify the granting of a divorce (e.g., adultery).

federalism The division of powers between the federal government and the state governments.

federalization Changes in state law that result mainly from (a) laws written by the federal legislature (Congress) and (b) interpretations of the U.S. Constitution by federal courts.

Federal Parent Locator Service (FPLS) A program of the U.S. Office of Child Support Enforcement that uses data in federal databases to locate parents for purposes of child-support enforcement. Requests for information from the FPLS go through a State Parent Locator Service (SPLS).

fee-sharing   See *fee-splitting*.

fee-splitting   (1) The splitting (division) of a single client's fee between two or more attorneys who are not in the same law firm. (2) The splitting (division) of a single client's fee between an attorney and a nonattorney. Also called *fee-sharing, division of fees*.

felony   See *misdemeanor*.

feme covert   "A covered woman." A married woman.

FEPA   See *Fair Employment Practices Agency*.

fertilization   Conception. The initial union of a sperm and an egg that becomes an embryo.

feticide   The unlawful killing of a fetus.

fetus   A developing organism—the unborn offspring—from the eighth week after conception until birth.

FFC   See *full faith and credit*.

FFCCSOA   See *Full Faith and Credit for Child Support Orders Act*.

fiduciary   (1) Pertaining to the high standard of good faith and fair treatment that must be exercised on behalf of another (adjective). (2) A person who owes another good faith and fair treatment in protecting the other's interest (noun).

fiduciary relationship   The relationship that exists when one party (called the *fiduciary*) owes loyalty, candor, and fair treatment to another party. The fiduciary is required to act in the interest (and for the benefit) of the other party. Also called a *confidential relationship*.

filial consortium   The right of a parent to the normal companionship and affection of a child.

filiation   (1) A judicial determination of paternity. (2) The relation of a child to a particular parent.

filius nullius   ("The son [or child] of no one.") The status of an illegitimate child at common law.

financial statement   A report covering assets (e.g., income, investments) and debts of a person or business as of a particular date or over a designated period. A financial accounting or balance sheet.

first impression   Concerning an issue being addressed by a court for the first time.

fit   Willing and able to provide what is needed to raise a child.

flowchart   An overview of the step-by-step process by which something is done.

forced share   See *elective share*.

foreign divorce   A divorce obtained in another state or country. A divorce that was not obtained in the forum state where the parties are now in litigation. If, for example, you live in Florida and obtain a divorce in Ohio, you have a foreign divorce.

forensic   (1) Pertaining to the use of scientific techniques to discover and examine evidence. (2) Belonging to or suitable in courts of law. (3) Concerning argumentation. (4) Forensics (ballistics or firearms evidence).

formal marriage   See *ceremonial marriage*.

formbook   A practical treatise or manual containing standard forms along with checklists, summaries of the law, etc. See also *legal treatise*.

fornication   Voluntary sexual intercourse between unmarried persons.

forum   (1) A court. (2) The place where the parties are presently litigating their dispute. (3) A court or tribunal hearing a case.

forum non conveniens   The discretionary power of a court to decline the exercise of its jurisdiction when it would be more convenient, and the ends of justice would be better served, if the action were tried in another court.

forum shopping   When more than one court has jurisdiction over a claim, choosing the court that is most likely to issue a favorable ruling.

forum state   The state in which the case is now being litigated.

foster care   A government-funded child welfare service that provides shelter and substitute family care when a child's own family cannot provide this shelter and care.

foster home   A temporary home for children when their own families cannot provide care and when adoption either is not possible at the present time or is under consideration.

FPLS   See *Federal Parent Locator Service*.

fraud   An intentionally false statement of fact that (a) is material, (b) is made to induce reliance by the plaintiff, and (c) results in harm because of the reliance. Also called *deceit* and *intentional misrepresentation*.

fraudulent transfer   A transfer of an asset for little or no payment or consideration that is made to avoid an obligation to a creditor.

Freedom of Access to Clinic Entrances Act (FACE)   A federal statute that provides a remedy for victims of assault or other attack suffered while trying to obtain (or provide) reproductive health services (18 U.S.C. § 248(a)(1)).

friendly divorce   A divorce proceeding in which the husband and wife are not contesting the dissolution of the marriage or anything related thereto. An uncontested divorce.

full blood   Having the same mother and father. *Half blood* is having the same mother or father, but not both.

full faith and credit (FFC)   The obligation of one state to recognize and enforce the laws and court decisions of another state. This obligation is based on the U.S. Constitution, which provides that "Full Faith and Credit shall be given in each State to the public Acts, Records, and judicial Proceedings of every other State." Article IV, § 1.

Full Faith and Credit for Child Support Orders Act (FFCCSOA)   A federal statute governing when a state must give full faith and credit to the child-support order of another state.

fundamental right   A right that falls into one of the following three categories: The right (a) is specifically guaranteed in the U.S. Constitution, (b) is implicit in the concept of ordered liberty, or (c) is deeply rooted in the nation's history and tradition.

G

garnishment   A court proceeding by a creditor to force a third party in possession of the debtor's property (e.g., wages) to turn the property over to the creditor to satisfy the debt owed to the creditor.

general appearance   Coming to court as a party without restrictions and thereby submitting to the full jurisdiction of the court.

gestational   Pertaining to the development of the embryo or fetus in the uterus until birth.

gestational carrier   A woman who gestates (or carries) an embryo that was formed from the egg of another woman. The gestational carrier usually has a contractual obligation to give the infant to its intended parents. Also called a *gestational surrogate*.

gestational surrogacy   The carrying and delivering of a child for another in which the surrogate does not use her own egg and is therefore not genetically related to the child.

get   A document that grants a Jewish divorce.

gift   The voluntary delivery of property with the present intent to transfer title and control for which no payment or consideration is made. The person making the gift is the *donor*. The person receiving it is the *donee*.

good cause   A legally sufficient ground or reason. Also called *just cause* or *sufficient cause*.

good faith   A state of mind indicating honesty and lawfulness of purpose. The absence of wrongful intent or desire to take inappropriate advantage of someone. Also called *bona fides*.

goodwill   The reputation of a business or professional practice that causes it to generate additional customers. The value of a business or practice that exceeds the value of the combined assets used in the business or practice. See also *enterprise goodwill* and *personal goodwill*.

grantor   A transferor; a person who makes a grant.

gratuitous   Performed without expectation of payment.

green-card marriage   A marriage of a foreigner (alien) with an American citizen that entitles the foreigner to permanent resident status in the United States.

gross income   The total amount received or earned before deductions.

grounds   Reasons that are legally sufficient to obtain a particular remedy or result.

guarantee   A warranty or assurance that a particular result will be achieved.

guardian   A person who has legal authority to care for the person or property of another. Also called a *custodian*.

guardian ad litem (GAL)   A special guardian (often, but not always, an attorney) appointed by the court to appear in court proceedings on behalf of a person who is a minor, mentally incompetent, or otherwise incapacitated.

guardianship   The legal right to the custody of an individual.

H

half blood   Having the same mother or father, but not both. *Full blood* is having the same mother and father.

harassment   See *hostile environment harassment* and *quid pro quo harassment*.

harmless   Without injury or damage.

heart-balm action   An action based on the loss of love and relationships—on a broken heart (e.g., breach of promise to marry, alienation of affections, and seduction).

heart-balm statute   A statute that abolishes heart-balm actions.

heightened scrutiny   See *intermediate scrutiny*.

high-test marriage   See *covenant marriage*.

hold harmless   To assume any liability in a transaction thereby relieving another from responsibility or loss arising out of the transaction. Also called *save harmless*.

holding   A court's answer to one of the legal issues in a case.

holding out   Taking steps that will allow others to believe that something exists, such as a legal status. Making representations that something is true.

home state   The state where the child has lived with a parent (or anyone acting as a parent) for at least six consecutive months immediately before the commencement of a child-custody (or child-support) proceeding or since birth if the child is less than six months old.

homestead   One's dwelling house along with adjoining land and buildings.

hostile-environment sexual harassment   Pervasive unwelcome sexual conduct or sex-based ridicule that unreasonably interferes with an individual's job performance or that creates an intimidating, hostile, or offensive working environment, even if no tangible or economic consequences result.

house arrest   The confinement of an accused or convicted person to his or her home except for approved travel, such as for employment. If an electronic devise (e.g., a bracelet) is attached to the body to monitor the arrest, it is called *Electronic House Arrest (EHA)*.

husband-wife immunity   See *interspousal immunity*.

husband-wife privilege   See *marital communications privilege*.

hypothetical   Assumed to exist solely for purposes of discussion.

I

ICPC   See *Interstate Compact on the Placement of Children*.

identity theft   Acquiring and using (or attempting to acquire and use) another person's private identifying information with the intent to commit an unlawful act.

illegitimacy   Pertaining to a child born to unmarried parents who never legitimated the child. Also called *bastardy*.

illegitimate child A child born to parents who are not married to each other at the time of birth, who never married thereafter, and who never took steps to legitimate the child. Also called *nonmarital child, child of an informal relationship, child out of wedlock, child with no presumed father, bastard.*

illicit cohabitation Sexual intercourse between unmarried persons who are living together. See also *cohabitation.*

IME See *independent medical examination.*

imminent Near at hand; coming soon; about to happen; immediate.

immunity A defense that is granted because of a special relationship or status that operates to block litigation and liability whether or not wrongful conduct was committed. The defense prevents someone from being sued for what might be wrongful conduct.

impeach To challenge; to attack the credibility of.

impediment A legal obstacle that prevents the formation of a valid marriage or other contract.

implicate (1) May apply or be relevant to. (2) May involve or affect.

implied contract See *implied-in-fact contract* and *implied-in-law contract.*

implied-in-fact contract A contract that is not created by an express agreement between the parties but is inferred as a matter of reason and justice from their conduct and the surrounding circumstances. A contract that is manifested by conduct and circumstances rather than by words of agreement. A contract whose existence could be inferred by a reasonable person, even in the absence of an express agreement to create it. Also called a *contract implied-in-fact.*

implied-in-law contract An obligation created by the law to avoid unjust enrichment in the absence of an express or implied contract creating this obligation. Also called a *quasi contract.*

impotence The inability to engage in sexual intercourse. For males, it is often the inability to achieve or maintain an erection.

imputed disqualification The disqualification of every attorney in a law office from representing a client solely because of an actual conflict of interest caused by one of the attorneys in the office. Also called *vicarious disqualification.*

imputed income Income that will be assumed to be available regardless of whether it is actually available.

in camera In the judge's private chambers; not in open court.

incapacity alimony Alimony, usually long-term, for an ex-spouse unable to be self-supporting because of a physical or mental incapacity.

incest Sexual relations between two people who are too closely related to each other as defined by law.

inchoate Partial; not yet complete.

incident to Closely connected to something else.

incident to divorce (a) Occurring within one year after the date a marriage ends or (b) relating to the ending of a marriage because it occurs within six years after a marriage ends pursuant to a divorce decree or separation agreement.

income withholding The process whereby an employer is required to deduct some of an employee's income, which will be used to meet the child-support obligations of the employee. (In some states, the deductions can also be used to meet spousal-support obligations.)

incompatibility A no-fault ground for divorce that is established when there is such discord between spouses that it is impossible for them to live together in a normal marital relationship.

incorporation and merger The acceptance of the terms of one document (e.g., an agreement) and making the terms part of another document (e.g., a court decree) so that the former document ceases to exist as a separate entity.

incorporeal See *intangible.*

incorrigible Habitually disobedient and disruptive.

indemnify To compensate another for any loss or expense incurred.

indemnity The right to have another person pay you the amount you were forced to pay.

independent adoption An adoption that is arranged by the birth parents and the adoptive parents without the involvement of a public agency but often with the assistance of an attorney-facilitator. Also called *private adoption, direct-placement adoption, private-placement adoption* and *facilitated adoption.*

independent liability Liability of an individual based on what the individual did himself or herself. The opposite of vicarious liability, which is liability based on what someone else has done.

independent medical examination (IME) A method of discovery by which a party obtains a court order for a professional examination of a person whose physical or mental condition is in controversy.

independent professional judgment Advice given by an attorney who is not subject to a conflict of interest. See *conflict of interest.*

indicia of parenthood Conduct that indicates or evidences a parental relationship with a child.

indigent Poor or without means to afford something, such as a private attorney or filing fees.

induced abortion See *therapeutic abortion.*

infancy (1) The defense of being a minor, which allows the minor to disaffirm a voidable contract. (2) Minority.

infant See *minor.*

infanticide The unlawful killing of a newborn.

infertility The inability to conceive a child. The failure of a couple to conceive in spite of having sexual relations without contraceptives in more than a year.

informal marriage A common-law marriage in Texas.

in forma pauperis As a poor person who is allowed to proceed without paying certain filing fees and other court costs.

informed consent Agreement to let something happen based on having a reasonable understanding of the benefits, risks, and available alternatives.

informed consent Agreement to let something happen based on having a reasonable understanding of its benefits, risks, and available alternatives.

inheritance Property received from someone who dies without leaving a valid will—by intestate succession. The state determines which relatives receive such property.

initiating state The state in which a support case is filed in order to forward it to another state (called the *responding state*) for enforcement proceedings under the Uniform Interstate Family Support Act (UIFSA).

injunction A court order that requires a person or organization to perform, or to refrain from doing, a particular thing.

in loco parentis (1) Standing in the place of a parent by assuming some or all parental responsibilities without being a biological or adoptive parent. (2) Acting as a temporary guardian or caretaker of a child.

innocent spouse doctrine A former spouse will not be liable for taxes, interest, and penalties owed on prior joint returns if (a) he or she did not know or have reason to know that the other spouse understated the taxes due and (b) it would be unfair to hold the innocent spouse responsible for the understatement of tax on the return. An exception to the rule of joint and several liability of signers of a return.

in personam jurisdiction See *personal jurisdiction*.

in praesenti At present; now.

in propria persona See *pro se*.

in rem jurisdiction The court's power over a particular *res*, which is a thing (e.g., land) or a status (e.g., a marriage) that is located within the territory over which the court has authority.

insider trading Improperly using (or passing on to others) any nonpublic information that could provide a financial advantage when used to buy or sell shares in a company.

instrument (1) A formal written document that gives expression to or embodies a legal act or agreement (e.g., contract, will). (2) A means by which something is achieved.

insupportability The no-fault ground for divorce consisting of discord or conflict of personalities that destroys the legitimate ends of the marital relationship and prevents any reasonable expectation of reconciliation.

intake memorandum A written report that summarizes an interview with a new client of the office. It normally contains basic facts on the client and on his or her legal problems. See also *interoffice memorandum* and *memorandum of law*.

intangible Not having a physical form, though evidence of its existence may have a physical form. Also called *incorporeal*.

intended father A man who takes affirmative steps to be recognized as the father.

intended parent A person who wants to raise a child as its legal parent and who enters into an agreement with a surrogate mother to bear and deliver the child. The person hiring the surrogate mother may or may not be genetically (biologically) related to the child.

intentional infliction of emotional distress (IIED) Intentionally causing severe emotional distress by extreme or outrageous conduct.

inter alia Among other things.

intercept program A procedure by which the government seizes designated benefits owed to a parent in order to cover the latter's delinquent child-support payments.

interest A legal share or right in something, which can often be sold or transferred.

interference with contract relations Intentionally encouraging or provoking a breach of contract that exists between or among other persons. Also called *tortious interference with contractual relations*.

interlocutory Not final; interim.

intermediate-scrutiny test The classification must be substantially related to serve an important state interest. Also called *heightened scrutiny* and *elevated scrutiny*.

interoffice memorandum A written report addressed to someone in the office where you work, usually a supervisor. If the report explains how the law applies to a given set of facts, it is a *memorandum of law*.

interracial adoption An adoption of a child whose race is different from the race of the adoptive parents. Also called *transracial adoption*.

interrogatories ("rogs") A method of discovery by which one party sends written questions to another party.

interspousal Between or pertaining to a husband and wife.

interspousal immunity Spouses cannot sue each other for designated categories of torts. Also called *husband-wife immunity*.

interstate central registry An office in each state that receives and responds to cases involving interstate child-support enforcement.

Interstate Compact on the Placement of Children (ICPC) A statute that governs adoption of a child born or living in one state who will be adopted by someone in another state.

inter vivos gift A gift that takes effect (becomes irrevocable) while the donor is living.

intestacy The condition of dying without a valid will.

intestate (1) Pertaining to someone who dies without a valid will. (2) A person who dies without a valid will.

intestate share A designated portion of the estate of a person who dies intestate (i.e., without a valid will) to which certain relatives of the deceased are entitled according to state law.

intestate succession The transfer of a decedent's property to state-designated relatives of the decedent who dies without leaving a valid will. Also called *descent and distribution* and *hereditary succession*.

intrafamily tort A tort committed by one family member against another. See also *marital tort*.

intrafamily tort immunity Designated family members cannot sue each other for designated categories of torts.

in vitro fertilization (IVF)   The surgical removal of a woman's eggs from the ovaries, the fertilization of the eggs with sperm (in the laboratory), and the transfer of the resulting embryos (or pre-embryos) into the uterus through the cervix. A method of *assisted reproductive technology (ART)*.

irrebuttable presumption   A conclusion of law or fact that a party will not be allowed to try to disprove (rebut). Also called *conclusive presumption*.

irreconcilable differences   A no-fault ground for divorce that is established when there is such discord between the spouses that there has been an irremediable breakdown of the marriage.

irremediable breakdown   See *irreconcilable differences*.

irrevocable   Not capable of being altered, revoked, canceled, or recalled.

issue   (1) A child and anyone else who has descended from a common ancestor. (2) A legal question. See also *legal periodical*.

IV-D agency   A state agency that helps custodial parents enforce child support obligations.

IVF   See *in vitro fertilization*.

J

joint adoption   An adoption by two adults (usually married) who both seek to become adoptive parents of a child.

joint and several liability   Legally responsible together and individually. Each debtor is individually responsible for the entire debt; the plaintiff/creditor can choose to collect the full debt from one debtor or from all of them until the debt is satisfied.

joint custody   See *joint legal custody* and *joint physical custody*.

joint legal custody   The right of both parents to make the child-rearing decisions on healthcare, education, religion, discipline, and general welfare. Also called *shared legal custody*.

joint physical custody   The right of both parents to have the child reside with each of them for alternating (but not necessarily equal) periods of time. Also called *shared physical custody*.

joint representation   See *multiple representation*.

joint tenancy   Ownership of property by two or more persons (called joint tenants) who have equal shares, equal rights to possess the whole property, and a right of survivorship. Also called *joint tenancy with right of survivorship (JTWROS)*.

joint venture   A business or profit-seeking activity of two or more persons who each participate and control the activity (or who have the right of participation and control).

JTWROS   See *joint tenancy*.

judgment debtor   The person who loses and therefore must pay a money judgment to the judgment creditor.

judgment creditor   The person who wins and therefore has a right to collect a money judgment from the judgment debtor.

judicial review   (1) The power of a court to determine the constitutionality of a statute or other law, including the power to refuse to enforce it if the court concludes that it violates the constitution. (2) The power of a court to determine the correctness of what a lower tribunal has done.

judice   See *sub judice*.

judicial separation   See *legal separation*.

junk science   Unreliable and, therefore, potentially misleading scientific evidence.

jurisdiction   (1) The power of a court to act in a particular case to resolve a legal matter. There are three major types of power jurisdiction: subject-matter jurisdiction, in rem jurisdiction, and personal jurisdiction. (2) The geographic area over which a particular court has authority or power. See also *concurrent jurisdiction*, *exclusive jurisdiction*, *in rem jurisdiction*, *personal jurisdiction*, and *subject-matter jurisdiction*.

juvenile delinquent   A young person under a designated age (e.g., sixteen years) whose misconduct would constitute a crime if committed by an adult. Sometimes called *PINS* (Person in Need of Supervision), *MINS* (Minor in Need of Supervision), or *CHIPS* (Child in Need of Protection and Services).

K

kin   Relatives.

kinship adoption   An adoption in which the adoptive parent is related to the adoptee.

L

last-in-time-marriage presumption   If more than one marriage is alleged to exist, the most recent marriage is presumed to be valid.

legal advice   A statement or conclusion that applies the law or legal principles to the facts of a specific person's legal problem in an attempt to help resolve that problem.

legal aid office   An office of attorneys (and paralegals) that provides free legal services to persons who cannot afford standard legal fees.

legal analysis   The application of one or more rules to the facts of a client's case in order to answer a legal question that will help (a) avoid a legal dispute, (b) resolve a legal dispute that has arisen, or (c) prevent a legal dispute from becoming worse.

legal capacity   See *capacity*.

legal custody   The right to make the major child-rearing decisions on healthcare, education, religion, discipline, and general welfare. Also called *decision-making responsibility*.

legal father   A man recognized by law as the father because he was married to the mother at the time of conception or birth of the child or because his paternity has been determined by a court.

legal information   A general statement about the law or about a client's case that does not apply the law or legal principles and hence does not attempt to help resolve a legal problem in the specific facts of a specific person.

legal issue   A question of law; a question of what the law is, or what the law means, or how the law applies to a set of facts. Also called *issue of law*. If the dispute is over the existence or nonexistence of the alleged facts, it is referred to as a *question of fact*, a *factual issue*, or an *issue of fact*.

legal malpractice   The failure of an attorney to use the knowledge and skill commonly applied under similar circumstances by attorneys in good standing in the same area of practice.

legal separation   A declaration by a court that parties can live apart even though they are still married to each other. Also called *judicial separation, limited divorce, divorce a mensa et thoro*, and *separation from bed and board*.

legal treatise   A book written by a private individual (or by a public official writing as a private citizen) that provides an overview, summary, or commentary on a legal topic. Hornbooks, manuals, and formbooks are treatises.

legislative divorce   A divorce granted by an act of the legislature rather than by the decree of a court.

legitimacy   The status or condition of being born within a lawful marriage. See also *presumption of legitimacy*.

legitimate child   (1) A child born to parents who are married to each other. (2) A child born to parents who marry after the child is born. (3) A child legitimated through a process called legitimation. See *legitimation*.

legitimate state interest   Any government objective that the state has the authority to pursue, such as providing for public safety.

legitimation   (1) The declaration that a child is legitimate. The verb is *legitimize*. (2) The steps taken to declare that a child is legitimate.

legitimize   To formally declare that children born out of wedlock are legitimate.

letter of nonengagement   A letter sent to prospective clients that explicitly states that the law office will not be representing them.

levy   (1) The collection or seizure of property by a public official to satisfy a judgment. (2) An assessment or tax.

Lexis–Nexis   A legal database for computer research.

lex loci celebration   Law of the place where the marriage or other contract was entered.

lex loci contractus   Law of the place where the contract was executed.

liabilities   That which one owes; debts.

liability insurance   A contract that obligates an insurer to pay damages (within policy limits) that an insured must pay a third person because of a tort or other wrong for which the insured has become liable.

lien   A security, encumbrance, or claim on property that remains until a debt is paid.

life estate   An interest in property whose duration is limited to the life of an individual. An ownership of property that lasts as long as a designated person is alive. Also called *estate for life* and *life tenancy*.

limited divorce   A declaration by a court that parties can live apart although they are still married to each other. Also called *legal separation, judicial separation, separation from bed and board*, and *divorce a mensa et thoro* (divorce from board and hearth).

liquid   Pertaining to cash or property that can be readily converted into cash.

living apart   A no-fault ground for divorce that is established when spouses live separately for a designated period of consecutive time during which their intent was to end the marriage. Also called *living separate and apart*.

loco parentis   See *in loco parentis*.

long-arm jurisdiction   The personal jurisdiction that a state acquires over a nonresident defendant under a long-arm statute.

long-arm statute   A statute that allows a state to obtain personal jurisdiction over a nonresident defendant because of the latter's minimum contacts with the state.

Lord Mansfield's rule   The testimony of either spouse is inadmissible on the question of whether the husband had access to the wife at the time of conception if such evidence would tend to "bastardize" (illegitimize) the child.

loss of consortium   Interference with the companionship, love, affection, sexual relations, and services that a person naturally expects to receive from his or her spouse.

loss of services   Interference with the right of a parent to the services of his or her unemancipated child such as doing household chores.

lucid interval   A period of time during which a mentally ill or insane person had the mental capacity to understand what he or she is doing before the mental illness or insanity returned.

lump-sum alimony   See *alimony in gross*.

lump-sum payment   A single payment of an amount of money rather than ongoing payments.

M

maintenance   Food, clothing, shelter, and other necessaries of life. See also *alimony*.

majority   See *age of majority*.

malice   (1) The intent to inflict injury or other wrongful harm. (2) Reckless disregard of what is right. (3) Animosity or ill will.

malicious   (1) Pertaining to a wrongful act that is done intentionally and without just cause or excuse. (2) Pertaining to conduct that is certain or almost certain to cause harm.

malpractice   See *legal malpractice*.

mandatory   Required; commanded.

mandatory reporting   Designated persons (e.g., teachers) must inform safety officials (e.g., police or child protective services) of suspected child abuse or neglect.

manslaughter   The unlawful killing of a person that does not constitute murder.

manual   A practical treatise often containing standard forms along with checklists, summaries of the law, etc. Sometimes called a *practice manual*. See also *legal treatise*.

marital-communications privilege   A person can refuse to testify and can prevent his or her spouse or ex-spouse from testifying about any confidential (private) communications made between them during their marriage. Also called *marital privilege* or *husband-wife privilege*.

marital deduction   A deduction on a federal tax return for lifetime and testamentary transfers between spouses.

marital dissipation   See *dissipation*.

marital privilege   See *marital-communications privilege*.

marital property   Any property acquired by either or both spouses during the marriage that is not separate property. See also *separate property*.

marital separation agreement   See *separation agreement*.

marital tort   A tort that one spouse commits against another. Also called *domestic tort*. See also *intrafamily tort*.

market value   See *fair market value*.

marriage   The legal union of two persons as spouses with designated rights and obligations to each other. See also *ceremonial marriage* and *common-law marriage*.

marriage by estoppel   A relationship that is recognized as a marriage because a party is prevented from asserting the invalidity of the marriage even though grounds for its invalidity may exist.

married women's property acts   Statutes removing all or most of a married woman's legal disabilities on matters such as entering contracts, disposing of her property, and being a party to litigation independent of her husband.

material   (1) Serious and substantial. (2) Important enough to influence the decision that was made.

maternal preference   See *tender years presumption*.

matrimonii, a vinculo   See *divorce*.

med-arb   A method of alternative dispute resolution (ADR) in which the parties first try mediation, and if it does not work, they try arbitration.

mediation   A method of alternate dispute resolution (ADR) in which the parties avoid litigation by submitting their dispute to a neutral third person (the mediator) who helps the parties resolve their dispute but does not render a decision that resolves it for them.

medical examination   See *independent medical examination*.

memorandum of law   A written explanation of how the law applies to a given set of facts. See also *intake memorandum*.

mensa et thoro   See *divorce a mensa et thoro*.

MEPA   See *Multiethnic Placement Act*.

meretricious   (1) Pertaining to prostitution or unlawful sexual relations. (2) Vulgar or tawdry. (3) In Washington State, a meretricious relationship means a stable, marital-like relationship where both parties cohabit with knowledge that a lawful marriage between them does not exist.

merger   See *incorporation and merger*.

meritorious   Having merit; having a reasonable basis to believe that a person's claim or defense will succeed.

metadata   Data about data. Data about an electronic document that are hidden within the document itself, e.g., earlier versions of the document.

migratory divorce   A divorce obtained in a state to which one or both of the spouses traveled before returning to their state of domicile.

minimum contacts   Activities in or connected with a state by a nonresident that are substantial and sufficiently purposeful so that it can be said that the nonresident has invoked the benefits and protections of the state, thereby making it fair for the state to assert personal jurisdiction over the nonresident.

Minnesota Multiphasic Personality Inventory Test (MMPI)   A psychological test designed to assess personality characteristics.

minor   A person under age of legal adulthood, often eighteen years of age. One who has not reached the age of majority. Also called an *infant*.

minority   The status of being under the age of legal adulthood or under the age of majority.

MINS (minor in need of supervision)   See *status offense*, *juvenile delinquent*.

miscegenation   Marriage between persons of different races.

misdemeanor   Any crime that is not as serious as a felony. In many states, a misdemeanor is any crime punishable by fine or by detention (often for a year or less) in an institution other than a prison. A *felony* is any crime that is more serious than a misdemeanor. In many states, a felony is any crime punishable by death or imprisonment (often for more than a year).

MMPI   See *Minnesota Multiphasic Personality Inventory Test*.

Model Rules of Professional Responsibility   The canons of ethics of the American Bar Association and adopted in whole or part by most states.

moot   (1) Pertaining to a nonexistent controversy where the issues have ceased to exist from a practical point of view. (2) Subject to debate.

mortgage   An interest in land that provides security for the performance of a duty or the payment of a debt.

movant   A person making a motion.

Multiethnic Placement Act (MEPA)   A federal statute that forbids delay or denial of adoption on the basis of race, color, or national origin (42 U.S.C. § 1996B).

multiple representation   Representation by the same attorney of more than one side in a controversy or other legal matter. Also called *joint representation* or *common representation*.

murder   Killing a person (1) with the intent to kill, (2) with the intent to cause grievous bodily harm, (3) with reckless disregard for human life, or (4) while committing a designated felony.

N

narrowly tailored No more than needed to maintain the effectiveness of a goal; no broader than absolutely necessary.

National Directory of New Hires (NDNH) A national database of wage and employment information used to assist state child-support agencies in locating noncustodial parents in order to establish paternity and enforce child-support obligations.

NCP See *noncustodial parent*.

NDNH See *National Directory of New Hires*.

necessaries The basic items needed by family members to maintain a standard of living, particularly food, shelter, and clothing. Under the doctrine of necessaries, these items can be purchased and charged to the spouse or parent who has failed to provide them.

ne exeat A writ that forbids a person from leaving the state, country, or jurisdiction of the court; or from removing a child or property therefrom.

neglect See *child neglect*.

negligence The failure to use reasonable care that an ordinary prudent person would have used in a similar situation, resulting in injury or other loss.

negligent entrustment Carelessly allowing the use of a vehicle, tool, or other object by someone who poses an unreasonable risk of harm to others.

negligent supervision Carelessly monitoring or supervising an incompetent person who poses an unreasonable risk of harm to others.

nepotism Favoritism shown to relatives. A rule against nepotism is called an *antinepotism rule*.

net The amount that remains after designated deductions and other allowances.

net worth The total assets of a person or business less the total liabilities.

neutral evaluation A method of alternative dispute resolution (ADR) in which both sides hire an experienced attorney or an expert in the area involved in the dispute who will listen to an abbreviated version of the evidence and arguments of each side and offer an evaluation in the hope that this will stimulate more serious settlement discussions. Sometimes called *case evaluation*.

nisi Not final; interim.

no-contact order See *stay-away order*.

no-fault divorce A divorce that is granted without having to prove marital wrongs that caused the break-up.

nonaccess Evidence of the absence of opportunities for sexual intercourse with the mother of a child around the time the child was conceived.

nonage Below the required minimum age to enter a relationship or to perform a task. Minority.

noncustodial parent (NCP) The parent who is not living with the child; the parent who does not have physical custody of the child. Also called *nonresidential parent*.

nondischargeable Not extinguished or forgiven by bankruptcy.

nondomiciliary One who is not domiciled in a particular place.

nonengagement See *letter of nonengagement*.

nonmolestation clause A clause in an agreement that the parties will not disturb, annoy, or harass each other.

nonresident Someone who does not have a residence in a particular place.

nonresidential parent See *noncustodial parent*.

nonsupport See *criminal nonsupport*.

notarize To certify or attest to something, e.g., the authenticity of a signature.

nullity Legally void.

nurturing-parent doctrine For purposes of calculating child-support obligations, the income a parent could have earned will not be imputed to the parent if the failure to earn the income is due to the time needed by the parent to care for a child.

O

objective standard A standard that measures something by comparing (1) what a particular person actually knew, felt, or did with (2) what a reasonable person would have known, felt, or done under the same or similar circumstances. See also *subjective standard*.

objectivity The state of being dispassionate; the absence of a bias.

obligee One to whom a legal obligation is owed. See also *payee*.

obligor One who has a legal obligation to do something, usually to make a payment. See also *payor*.

offer To present something that can be accepted or rejected.

officiant One who leads or performs a ceremony, often a religious service.

open adoption An adoption in which the biological parent maintains certain kinds of initial and/or ongoing contact with the adoptee, whose adoptive parent(s) may have been selected by the biological parent. The contact might consist of letters or visits. See also *closed adoption*.

operation of law The means by which legal consequences are imposed by law, regardless of (or even despite) the intent or wishes of the parties involved.

opinion See *court opinion*.

opportunity interest The right of a parent to develop a relationship with his or her child.

order of protection See *protective order* and *restraining order*.

outstanding (1) Unpaid. (2) To be collected.

overreaching Taking unfair advantage of another's naiveté or other vulnerability, especially by deceptive means.

P

palimony   Support payments ordered after the end of a non-marital relationship (a) if the party seeking support was induced to enter or stay in the relationship by a promise of support or (b) if ordering support is otherwise equitable.

paralegal   A person with legal skills who works under the supervision of an attorney or who is otherwise authorized to use those skills.

paralegal fees   Fees that attorneys can collect for the nonclerical work of their paralegals on client cases.

parens patriae   "Parent of the country," referring to the state's role in protecting children and others in the state who suffer from a disability.

parental alienation syndrome (PAS)   A disorder characterized by a child's obsessive and unjustified denigration of a parent that results both from the child's persistent attacks on the parent and from manipulation (brainwashing) by the other parent of the child's attitude toward the targeted parent.

parental consortium   The right of a child to the normal companionship and affection of a parent.

Parental Kidnapping Prevention Act (PKPA)   A federal statute on when a state must enforce (give full faith and credit to) child custody orders of other states when the orders comply with the PKPA (28 U.S.C. § 1738A).

parental-liability law   A statute that imposes vicarious liability (up to a limited dollar amount) on parents for the torts committed by their children. Also called *parental responsibility law*.

parental-responsibility law   See *parental-liability law*.

parenting coordinator (PC)   A professional who assists parents in resolving custody disputes that arise under a parenting plan.

parenting plan   A child-custody plan for separated parents covering living arrangements, decision making, finances, and communication.

parenting time   Visitation.

Parent Locator Service   See *Federal Parent Locator Service*, *State Parent Locator Service*.

partial-birth abortion   An abortion in which the fetus is destroyed after it is partially extruded from the womb. Intact dilation and evacuation.

partition   The dividing of land held by joint tenants or by tenants in common. The division results in individual ownership.

partnership   A voluntary association of two or more persons to place their resources in a jointly owned business or enterprise, with a proportional sharing of profits and losses.

passim   Here and there, throughout.

passive appreciation   An increase in the value of property that is due to inflation or market forces rather than to the active efforts of the owner.

passive income   Income that is earned from money or other property without direct involvement or active efforts by the earner.

passive registry   A reunion registry that requires both the adoptee and the biological parent to register their consent to release identifying information. When both have registered and a match is made, an agency employee will contact both. Also called *mutual consent registry*.

paternity   The biological fatherhood of a child.

paternity by estoppel   Paternity that is established when a court does not allow the presumption of paternity to be rebutted even though there is no biological relationship between the presumed (putative) father and the child.

payee   One to whom money is paid or is to be paid.

payor   One who makes a payment of money or who is obligated to do so.

PC   See *parenting coordinator*.

PDP   See *procedural due process*.

pecuniary   Relating to money. (A pecuniary interest is a financial interest.)

pendente lite   Pending the [outcome of the] litigation. See also *temporary alimony*.

periodic payments   Payments to be made over a period of time as opposed to a single (lump-sum) payment.

perjury   Making a false statement under oath concerning a material matter with the intent to provide false testimony. Also called *false swearing*.

permanent alimony   Alimony that is awarded periodically (e.g., monthly) until a designated date or indefinitely without a termination date. Also called *traditional alimony*.

per se   In and of itself. Without additional facts or support.

personal autonomy, right to   See *right to privacy*.

personal goodwill   An asset of a business or practice that is dependent on the continued presence of a particular individual because the asset is attributed to that individual's personal skill, training, or reputation. Also called *professional goodwill*.

personal jurisdiction   A court's power over a person to determine (adjudicate) his or her personal rights and duties. Also called *in personam jurisdiction*.

personal property   Anything tangible or intangible that can be owned other than land or things attached or affixed to land. Also called *chattel*.

personal protection order (PPO)   See *restraining order*.

personal representative   An executor or administrator of the estate of the deceased; someone who formally acts on behalf of the estate of the deceased.

personal service   Handing the service-of-process documents to the person who is the target of the service (or to the defendant's authorized representative).

person in need of supervision (PINS)   See *status offense* and *juvenile delinquent*.

petition   (1) A complaint. (2) A formal request that the court take some action.

petitioner   (1) A party who files a petition or complaint; a plaintiff. (2) A party who files an appeal; an appellant.

physical custody (1) The right of an adult to have a child reside with the adult. Also called *residential custody* or *custodial responsibility*. (2) Where the child is actually living.

physical examination See *independent medical examination*.

PINS (person in need of supervision) See *status offense* and *juvenile delinquent*.

PKPA See *Parental Kidnapping Prevention Act (PKPA)*.

plaintiff The party bringing a claim against another.

plead (1) To file a pleading, a formal document that asserts or responds to court claims or defenses. (2) To make a formal assertion or response. (3) To argue a case in court.

pleadings Formal litigation documents (e.g., a complaint or petition, an answer) filed by parties that state or respond to the claims and defenses the parties have against each other.

police power The inherent power of a government to impose laws deemed necessary and proper for public security, health, morality, and general welfare.

polyandry The condition or practice of having more than one husband at the same time.

polygamy The condition or practice of having more than one spouse at the same time.

polygyny The condition or practice of having more than one wife at the same time.

posthumous Existing or occurring after death.

posthumous child A child born after the death of a parent.

postnuptial After marriage; after the parties have been married.

postnuptial agreement A contract between married persons that covers specific matters, usually financial in nature. (Also called *postnup* and *midnup*.) The spouses may have no intention of separating. If they have this intention, the contract is commonly called a *separation agreement*.

power of attorney (1) A document that authorizes another to act as one's agent or attorney in fact. (An attorney in fact is someone who is authorized to act in place of or for another, often in a business transaction. An attorney in fact may or may not be an attorney at law.) (2) The authority itself.

PPO personal protection order See *restraining order*.

practice manual See *manual*.

practice of law Using or attempting to use legal skills to help resolve a specific person's legal problem when the assistance requires a license to practice law or other authorization.

praesenti See *in praesenti*.

prayer A formal request.

precedent A decision made in a prior case that can be used as a standard or guide in a later case, which raises a similar issue.

premarital agreement A contract by persons about to be married that can cover (1) financial and related matters once the marriage occurs and (2) spousal support, property division, and related matters in the event of separation, divorce, annulment, or death. Also called *prenuptial agreement* ("prenup"), *antenuptial agreement*.

prenatal tort A tort committed against a fetus.

prenup A prenuptial agreement See *premarital agreement*.

prenuptial Before marriage.

prenuptial agreement See *premarital agreement* and *prenup*.

preponderance of the evidence A standard of proof that is met when the evidence establishes that the existence of a disputed fact is more likely than its nonexistence. Also called *fair preponderance of evidence*.

present value The amount of money an individual would have to be given now in order to generate a certain amount of money within a designated period of time through prudent investment, usually at compound interest. Also called *present cash value*, *present worth*.

presumed father A man who is recognized as (presumed to be) the father until he is medically or legally declared not to be the father. Also called *presumptive father*.

presumption An assumption or inference that a certain fact is true once another fact is established. The presumption is *irrebuttable* (conclusive) if a party is not allowed to introduce evidence to try to show that the assumption is false. The presumption is *rebuttable* if a party is allowed to introduce evidence to try to show that the assumption is false.

presumption of legitimacy A child born to a married woman is presumed to be legitimate unless conclusively proven otherwise.

presumption of paternity A man is presumed to be the father of a child (a) if he is married to the mother at the time of conception or birth, (b) if the child is born within 300 days after the marriage ends, (c) if he marries the mother after the child is born and agrees to support the child, or (d) if he receives the child into his home and holds the child out as his own.

presumptive Created or arising out of a presumption; based on inference.

pretrial conference A meeting of the attorneys and the judge (or magistrate) before the trial begins to attempt to narrow the issues, secure stipulations, make a final effort to settle the case without a trial, and cover other preliminary matters. Also called a *trial management conference*.

prima facie case A party's presentation of evidence that will prevail unless the other side offers more convincing counterevidence.

primary authority Any law written by one of the three branches of government (legislative, judicial, and executive).

primary-caregiver presumption A belief that custody should be granted to the parent who thus far has taken care of most of the daily needs of the child unless this parent is unfit.

privacy See *right to privacy*.

private judging A method of alternative dispute resolution (ADR) consisting of arbitration or mediation in which the arbitrator or mediator is a retired judge. Sometimes misleadingly called *rent-a-judge*.

privilege (1) A special legal benefit, right, exemption, or protection. (2) The right to act contrary to the right of another without being subject to tort or other liability. (3) A defense that authorizes conduct that would otherwise be wrongful.

privilege for marital communication See *marital-communications privilege*.

privileged Protected from disclosure; not discoverable.

probable cause (1) A reasonable belief that a specific crime has been committed and that the accused committed the crime. (2) A reasonable belief that good grounds exist to bring civil proceedings against someone.

probate A court proceeding at which a will is proved to be valid or invalid.

probation (1) Living in the community (in lieu of institutionalization) so long as there is compliance with court-imposed conditions. (2) A trial or test period.

pro bono Concerning or involving legal services that are provided for the public good (pro bono publico) without fee or compensation. Sometimes also applied to services given at a reduced rate.

procedural due process (PDP) The constitutional requirement that the government provide fair procedures (such as adequate notice and an opportunity to be heard) whenever the government seeks to deprive someone of life, liberty, or property.

procedural fairness Sufficient financial disclosure, sufficient opportunity to consult with others, voluntariness, and the absence of duress and fraud. Informed consent.

procedural law (1) The rules that govern the mechanics of resolving a dispute in court or in an administrative agency (e.g., a rule on the time by which a party must respond to a complaint). (2) The rules that govern the formal steps required to obtain a benefit or other result.

process The means (e.g., a summons, writ, or other court order) used by a court to acquire or exercise its power or jurisdiction over a person.

proctor A person appointed for a particular purpose (e.g., protect the interests of a child).

production See *request for production*.

professional goodwill See *personal goodwill*.

pro hac vice For this particular occasion.

proof of service A sworn statement (or other evidence) that the requirements of in-person or substituted (constructive) service of process have been followed. Also called *certificate of service*, *return of service*.

pro per See *pro se*.

property See *personal property*, *real property*, *property division*.

property division The distribution of community or marital property between spouses (or ex-spouses) after a legal separation or divorce. In a few states, separate property can be included in the property division and some states allow property division in an annulment. Also called *property settlement*, *property distribution*.

property tort A tort that damages or interferes with a person's real property or personal property.

proscribe To prohibit.

pro se (1) On one's own behalf. (2) Representing oneself; not represented by an attorney. Also called *in propria persona* (abbreviated *in pro per*).

prosecute To commence and proceed with a lawsuit.

prosecution (1) Bringing and processing criminal proceedings against someone. The words *prosecution* and *prosecute* can also refer to bringing and processing *civil* proceedings against someone, although the words are more commonly used in criminal proceedings. (2) The attorney representing the government in a criminal case. Also called the *prosecutor*.

pro se divorce A divorce obtained when a party represents himself or herself.

protective order A court order directing a person to refrain from inappropriate conduct such as harming or harassing another. Also called *order of protection*.

prove-up The presentation of sufficient evidence to support one's claims even if they are unopposed.

provocation Inciting the conduct that constitutes the marital wrong by the other spouse.

proxy marriage A ceremonial marriage in which agents ("stand-ins") take the place of (and can act on behalf of) one or both of the prospective spouses who are not present at the ceremony.

psychological parent An adult who, in a substantial and continuing way, has provided for the physical and emotional needs of a child. Most often the adult is someone other than a biological or adoptive parent.

public assistance Welfare and other forms of financial help from the government to those in need.

public charge An individual who is primarily dependent on the government for subsistence or support, as demonstrated by either the receipt of cash assistance for income maintenance or by institutionalization for short- or long-term care at government expense.

public policy The principles inherent in the customs, morals, and notions of justice that prevail in a state; the foundation of public laws; the principles that are naturally and inherently right and just.

punitive damages Damages that are added to actual or compensatory damages in order to punish malicious, outrageous, or reckless conduct and to deter similar conduct in the future. Also called *exemplary damages*, *smart money*, *vindictive damages*.

purported (1) Claimed, reputed. (2) Rumored, often falsely.

putative Alleged or reputed.

putative father A man who is alleged to be the biological father, but who has not yet been medically or legally declared to be the father. Also called *alleged father* or *reputed father*.

putative father registry A government office where the father of a child can register so that he can be notified of a proposed adoption of the child.

putative marriage See *putative spouse*.

putative spouse A person who believes in good faith that he or she entered into a valid marriage even though an impediment made the marriage invalid. The marriage with such a spouse is called a *putative marriage*.

Q

QDRO   See *qualified domestic relations order*.

QMCSO   See *qualified medical child support order*.

qualified domestic relations order (QDRO)   A court order that allows a nonworker to reach all or part of the pension or other retirement benefits of a worker or former worker in order to satisfy the worker's support or other marital obligation.

qualified medical child support order (QMCSO)   A court order to an employer to extend its group health insurance benefits to the child of one of its workers even if the child does not live with the worker.

quantum meruit   "As much as he deserves." An award of the reasonable value of services provided despite the absence of an express or implied agreement to pay for the services.

quasi-community property   Personal property acquired during the marriage by the spouses when they lived in a non–community property state before moving to a community property state. If they had acquired it in a community property state, it would have been community property.

quasi contract   A contract created by the law to avoid unjust enrichment. See *implied-in-law contract*.

quasi-suspect class   A group based on gender or on a child's legitimacy.

quid pro quo sexual harassment   Submission to or rejection of unwelcome sexual conduct used as a basis for employment decisions on promotion or other job-related benefits.

quitclaim   A release or giving up of whatever claim or title you had in property. The party who quitclaims the property, turns over (transfers) whatever he or she has, without guaranteeing anything.

R

rape   See *statutory rape*.

ratification   The approval of something after it has occurred. Approval retroactively by agreement, conduct, or any inaction that can reasonably be interpreted as an approval. The verb is *ratify*.

rational-basis test   The government's action must be reasonably related to a legitimate state interest or purpose. Also called *minimal-scrutiny test, rational-relation test*.

rational relation   The standard used to determine if a restriction or a classification complies with due process or equal protection (and is therefore constitutional); the restriction or the classification must be reasonably related to a legitimate state interest or purpose. Also called *rational basis*.

real estate   See *real property*.

realize   To receive an actual benefit or to suffer an actual loss from something as opposed to a mere potential benefit or loss.

real property   Land and anything attached or affixed to the land, such as buildings, fences, and trees. Also called *real estate*.

real time   Occurring now; happening as you are watching; able to respond immediately or within seconds.

reasonable   See *unreasonable*.

reasonably related   Logically connected (pertaining to any means used to achieve a goal that is reasonably likely to be successful).

rebut   To attack, dispute, or refute.

rebuttable presumption   An assumption or inference of fact that a party will be allowed to try to disprove (rebut) but that will be treated as true if it is not disproved.

receiver   A person appointed by the court to protect and manage property in litigation or property in the process of bankruptcy.

recital   A preliminary statement in a document covering its background or purpose.

reconciliation   The full resumption of the marital relationship.

record   To deposit a document with an official office or body, such as a county clerk's office.

recordation   Filing a document with a government body so that it becomes part of an official record.

recrimination   A serious marital wrong committed by the spouse seeking a divorce even though this spouse is charging the other spouse with committing a serious marital wrong.

reformation   An equitable remedy to correct a writing so that it embodies the actual intent of the parties.

regional reporter   The volumes that contain the full text of opinions from courts within a designated cluster of states.

regulation   A law enacted by an administrative agency.

rehabilitative alimony   Support payments to an ex-spouse for a limited time to allow him or her to return to financial self-sufficiency through employment or job training. Also called *durational alimony, transitional alimony, bridge-the-gap alimony*.

reimbursement alimony   Alimony that repays an ex-spouse who worked or made other financial contributions during the marriage so that the other spouse could obtain training or otherwise enhance his or her future earning capacity. Also called *restitutional alimony*.

relation-back rule   An act done (or a decision made) at a later time that is treated as if it had occurred at an earlier time. An example is a court's invalidation of a marriage after the parties have entered the marriage is treated as if the invalidity existed at the time the parties entered the marriage.

release   To formally give up or relinquish (a claim or a right).

rem   See *in rem jurisdiction*.

remand   To send back for further proceedings.

remedy   (1) The means by which a right is enforced or the violation of a right is prevented, compensated for, or otherwise redressed. (2) To correct. The plural is *remedies*.

remise   To give up or release.

rent-a-judge   See *private judging*.

request for admissions (RFA)   A method of discovery by which one party sends a request to another party that the latter agree that a certain fact or legal conclusion is true or valid so there will be no need to present proof or arguments about such matters during the trial.

request for production (RFP)   A method of discovery by which one party requests that another party provide access to electronically stored data, paper documents, or other tangible things for copying or inspection. The method can also include a request to enter the party's land for inspection.

res   (1) A thing (e.g., land) or a status (e.g., marriage). (2) The subject matter of a trust.

rescind   To cancel something. The noun is *rescission*.

rescission   The cancelation of something.

residence   The place where someone is living. See also *domicile*.

resident   Someone who lives at a particular place.

residential custody   See *physical custody*.

residential parent   See *custodial parent*.

res judicata   "A thing adjudicated." A defense raised (a) to prevent the same parties from retrying (relitigating) a claim that has already been resolved on the merits in a prior case or (b) to prevent the litigation of a claim arising out of the same transaction involved in the first case that could have been raised in the first case but was not.

respondeat superior   "Let the master [boss] answer." An employer is responsible (liable) for the wrongs committed by an employee within the scope of employment.

respondent   (1) The party responding to a position or claim of another party; the defendant. (2) The party against whom an appeal is filed. See also *appellee*.

responding state   The state to which a support case is forwarded for enforcement proceedings under the Uniform Interstate Family Support Act (UIFSA). The case was forwarded by the initiating state.

responsive pleading   A pleading that replies to a prior pleading of an opponent.

Restatement of Torts   A treatise written by the American Law Institute that articulates or restates the law of torts. The second edition is *Restatement (Second) of Torts*.

restitution   (1) An equitable remedy that restores to the plaintiff the value of what he or she parted with. (2) An equitable remedy in which a person is restored to his or her original position prior to the loss or injury.

restitutional alimony   See *reimbursement alimony*.

restraining order   A form of injunction, usually issued ex parte (with only one side present), to restrain the defendant from doing a threatened act or from contacting designated individuals. Also called *order of protection, personal protection order (PPO), protection from abuse (PFA)*. See also *ex parte*.

restraint of marriage   A condition in a contract or gift that a benefit will be lost upon marriage or remarriage.

retainer   (1) The act of hiring or engaging the services of someone, usually a professional. (The verb is *retain*.) (2) An amount of money (or other property) paid by a client as a deposit or advance against future fees, costs, and related expenses of providing services.

retroactive   Applying to facts that arose before a particular event or date.

return of service   See *proof of service*.

reunion registry   A central adoption file that could be used to release identifying information about, and allow contact between, adult adoptees and biological parents. See also *active registry, passive registry*.

revival   Restoration of what was once inoperative or terminated.

revocable   Capable of being altered, revoked, canceled, or recalled.

RFA   See *request for admission*.

right of election   See *elective share*.

right to privacy   A constitutional right to make personal decisions without undue government interference on matters such as marriage, procreation, family relationships, child rearing and education, contraception, and abortion. The right is implied in specific provisions of the U.S. Constitution such as the Due Process Clause of the Fourteenth Amendment. Also called *right to personal autonomy*.

right of survivorship   When one owner dies, his or her share automatically goes to the other owners; it does not go through the estate of the deceased owner.

rogs   See *interrogatories*.

RFP   See *request for production*.

runner   See *ambulance chasing*.

S

safe-haven law   A law that protects a woman from prosecution if she abandons a baby at designated locations such as a hospital, fire station, or doctor's office where it can receive emergency medical assistance.

sanction   (1) Penalty or other coercive measure that is imposed because of noncompliance. (2) Approval or authorization.

scienter   (1) Knowledge of the falsity of a statement, a lack of honest belief in its truth, or a reckless disregard of its truth or falsity. (2) Intent to deceive or mislead.

scope of employment   That which is foreseeably done by an employee for the employer's business under the employer's specific or general control.

SDNH   See *State Directory of New Hires*.

SDP   See *substantive due process*.

secondary authority   Any nonlaw that summarizes, describes, or explains the law but is not a law itself.

second-parent adoption   The adoption of a child by a partner of a legal parent when the latter does not give up (relinquish) his or her own parental rights when the adoption occurs.

secured   Backed by collateral.

security   (1) Collateral that guarantees a debt or other obligation. (2) A financial instrument that is evidence of a debt interest (e.g., a bond), an ownership/equity interest, (e.g., a stock) or other specially defined rights (e.g., a futures contract). (3) Surety. (4) The state of being secure.

seduction   (1) The tort of engaging in sexual relations with the plaintiff's minor daughter by force or with the consent of the daughter. (2) Inducing another, without the use of force, to engage in sexual relations.

self-defense   The use of reasonable force to prevent harmful or offensive contact to one's person when there is an imminent danger of such contact.

separate maintenance   Court-ordered spousal support while the parties are separated but still married. Also called *separate support, alimony without divorce.*

separate property   Property that is (a) acquired by one spouse before marriage and brought into the marriage, or (b) is acquired by one spouse by gift, will, or inheritance during the marriage, or (c) is any other property that is not marital or community property.

separate support   See *separate maintenance.*

separation   See *legal separation, separation agreement.*

separation agreement   A contract between married persons who have separated (or who are about to separate) that can cover support, custody, property division, and other terms of their separation and likely divorce. Also called *marital settlement agreement (MSA).*

sequester   (1) To remove or set apart. (2) To remove or hold until legal proceedings or legal claims are resolved. The noun is *sequestration.*

sequestration   The removal or holding of assets until legal proceedings or legal claims are resolved.

service of process   A formal delivery of notice to a defendant that a suit has been initiated to which he or she must respond. *Process* is the means used by the court to acquire or exercise its power or jurisdiction over a person.

settlor   See *trust.*

severability clause   A clause in an agreement stating that if any part of the agreement is declared invalid, the remaining valid portions of the agreement should be carried out (enforced).

severable   Removable without destroying what remains. Something is severable when what remains after it is taken away has legal force and can survive without it. The opposite of severable is *essential* or *indispensable.*

severally   Individually, separately.

sexual harassment   Unwanted and offensive sexual advances, contact, comments, or other interaction. See also *hostile-environment sexual harassment* and *quid pro quo sexual harassment.*

shallow pocket   See *deep pocket.*

sham   Pretended, counterfeit. Something false that purports to be genuine.

sham divorce   A divorce sought by parties who do not intend to stay divorced from each other once the divorce is granted. When they obtained the divorce, their intent was to remarry at the earliest opportune time.

sham marriage   A pretend or counterfeit marriage in which the parties never intended to live together as spouses.

shared legal custody   See *joint legal custody.*

shared physical custody   See *joint physical custody.*

Shariah   Islamic law.

shepardize   To use the set of law books called *Shepard's Citations* to obtain specific information about a document (e.g., whether an opinion has been overruled or whether a statute has been repealed). An online version of Shepard's is available on Lexis-Nexis.

sole custody   See *sole legal custody, sole physical custody.*

sole legal custody   Only one parent has the right to make the major child-rearing decisions on healthcare, education, religion, discipline, and general welfare.

solemnization   Formal steps taken in a public ceremony to enter into a status or contract. The verb is *solemnize.*

solemnize   To take formal steps in a public ceremony to enter into a status or contract. The verb is *solemnization.*

sole physical custody   Only one parent has the right to have the child reside with him or her.

sole proprietorship   A form of business in which one person owns all the assets.

solicitation   (1) An appeal or request for clients or business. (2) An attempt to obtain something by persuasion or application.

specialization   The development of experience and expertise in a particular area of practice.

specialty certification   A recognition of competency (often by a bar association) in a particular area of law.

specific performance   A remedy for breach of contract that forces the wrongdoing party to complete the contract as promised. It is an equitable remedy.

sperm bank   A facility that collects and stores human sperm from male donors who will usually be anonymous to any woman who uses the sperm to become pregnant by artificial insemination (AI) or by in vitro fertilization (IVF). Also called *cryobank.*

split custody   A custody arrangement in which siblings are in the physical custody of different parents.

spoliation   Intentionally destroying, altering, or concealing evidence.

SPLS   See *State Parent Locator Service.*

spousal consortium   The right of one spouse to the relational benefits naturally expected from the other spouse. The benefits include companionship, love, affection, sexual relations, and services (e.g., cooking, making repairs around the house).

spousal refusal   A person's formal declaration that he or she will no longer support his or her ailing spouse so that the latter will qualify for Medicaid or other means-based public benefits.

spousal support   See *alimony.*

spousal-unity rule   See *unity of person*.

stalking   A pattern of repeated and unwanted attention, harassment, contact, or any other course of conduct directed at a specific person that would cause a reasonable person to feel fear.

standard form   A frequently used format for a document such as contract, complaint, or tax return. The form is designed to be used by many individuals, often by filling in blanks that call for specific information commonly needed for such documents.

standing   The right to state a claim or to bring a case and seek relief from a court.

State Directory of New Hires (SDNH)   A child support database, maintained by each state, which contains information regarding newly hired employees for the respective state.

State Parent Locator Service (SPLS)   A state government program that helps locate parents for purposes of child-support enforcement. See also *federal parent locator service*.

status   A person's legal condition by which rights and obligations are imposed by law, often without regard to the consent or contract desires of the person involved.

status offense   Disruptive behavior by a young person under a designated age (e.g., sixteen years of age) that would not be considered illegal by an adult (e.g., leaving home without permission, habitual truancy). The state might refer to a status offender (or a juvenile delinquent) as a *PINS* (Person in Need of Supervision), *MINS* (Minor in Need of Supervision), or *CHIPS* (Child in Need of Protection and Services).

statute   An act of the state or federal legislature declaring, commanding, or prohibiting something.

statute of frauds   A law requiring some contracts (example: one that cannot be performed within a year of its making) to be in writing and signed by the parties to be bound by the contract.

statute of limitations   A law stating that civil or criminal actions are barred if not brought within a specified period of time. The action is time-barred if not brought within that period.

statutory code   See *code*.

statutory marriage   See *ceremonial marriage*.

statutory rape   Sexual intercourse with a person under a designated age (e.g., sixteen years of age) even if the latter consents.

statutory share   See *elective share*.

stay   The suspension or postponement of a judgment or proceeding.

stay-away order   A court order forbidding a person from being in a designated area (e.g., within 200 feet of a domestic-violence victim of the defendant) or for contacting the person except for approved purposes. Also called *no-contact order*.

steerer   See *ambulance chasing*.

stepparent   A person who marries the natural mother or father of a child, but who is not one of the child's biological parents.

sterility   Inability to have children; infertility.

stipulate   To enter into an agreement with an opposing party on a particular matter. The noun is *stipulation*.

stipulation   (1) An agreement between opposing parties about a particular matter. The verb is *stipulate*. (2) A condition or requirement.

strict-scrutiny test   The government's action must be narrowly tailored to serve a compelling state interest. Also phrased as *necessary to serve a compelling state interest*.

sua sponte   On its own motion.

subjective standard   A standard that measures something by what a particular person actually knew, felt, or did. See also *objective standard*.

subject-matter jurisdiction   The court's power to resolve a particular type of legal dispute and to grant a particular type of relief.

sub judice   Under judicial consideration; before the court.

subpoena   (1) A command to appear at a certain time and place. (2) To command that someone appear at a certain time and place.

subpoena duces tecum   A command to appear at a certain time and place and bring specified things such as documents or jewelry for inspection.

subscribe   To sign a document.

subscribed   Signed.

subscription   (1) A signature. (2) The act of signing one's name.

substantive due process (SDP)   The constitutional requirement that the government avoid arbitrary and capricious actions that deprive someone of life, liberty, or property regardless of how fair the government might be in the procedures that lead to the deprivation.

substantive fairness   Equitable in the sense that the terms are reasonable and mutually favorable.

substantive law   Nonprocedural laws that define or govern rights and duties.

substituted service   Service of process by mail, by publication in a newspaper, or by other approved methods that are alternatives to the personal service of hand delivering the process documents to the defendant (or to the defendant's authorized representative). Also called *constructive service*.

summary dissolution   A divorce obtained in an expedited manner because of the brevity of the marriage, the minimal amount of marital property, and the lack of controversy between the spouses.

summary judgment   A court's judgment rendered without a full trial because of the absence of conflict on any of the material facts.

summary seizure   Taking custody of a person or taking possession of property without notice or prior hearing.

summons   A court notice served on the defendant ordering him or her to appear and answer the allegations of the plaintiff or face a default judgment.

sunset Automatic termination or expiration upon a designated time or event.

supervised visitation Visitation of a child while another adult (other than the custodial parent) is present to monitor the visit.

Supremacy Clause The clause in the U.S. Constitution (art. VI, cl. 2) that has been interpreted to mean that when valid federal law conflicts with state law, federal law controls.

surety bond A bond given as insurance to guarantee that a contract will be completed within the agreed-upon time. An obligation by a guarantor to pay X if Y fails to perform a duty that Y owes to X. Also called a *performance bond*.

surrender A voluntary relinquishment of rights.

surrogacy (1) The status or act of being a substitute for another. (2) The carrying and delivering of a child for another.

surrogate mother A woman who becomes pregnant (usually by artificial insemination or in vitro fertilization) with the sperm of a man who is not her husband, with the understanding that she will surrender her legal rights to the baby upon its birth. (In Florida, the surrogate mother is called a volunteer mother, and the surrogacy agreement is called a preplanned adoption agreement.)

survivors benefits A form of life insurance from Social Security in which widows, children, and other designated survivors can receive monthly payments and other benefits upon the death of a worker. Also called *survivorship benefits*.

survivorship See *right of survivorship*.

suspect class A group based on race, national origin, or alienage. Alienage is the condition of being an alien. (An alien is a person who was born outside the United States, is still a subject of a foreign nation, and has not been naturalized in the United States.)

system An organized method of accomplishing a task that seeks to be more effective or efficient than alternative methods.

T

tacit Understood without being openly stated; implied by silence or conduct other than words.

tainted Having or causing a conflict of interest.

talak An Arab word meaning "I divorce you." For a Muslim divorce, the word is spoken three times by a husband to his wife.

TANF See *Temporary Assistance for Needy Families*.

tangible Having a physical form; able to make contact through touch or other senses. Also called *corporeal*.

task-based billing Charging a specific amount for each legal task performed. Also called *unit billing* or *project billing*.

tax basis See *basis*.

tax effect (1) To determine the tax consequences of something. (2) The tax consequences of something.

template (1) A file containing text and a format that can be used as the starting point for creating frequently used documents. (2) A set of formulas used to perform a designated task.

temporary alimony Alimony awarded on an interim basis before the court makes its final decision on alimony. Also called *alimony pendente lite*.

Temporary Assistance for Needy Families (TANF) The federal-state welfare program (42 U.S.C. § 601) that replaced Aid to Families with Dependent Children (AFDC). Unlike AFDC, benefits under TANF are limited to five years.

tenancy by the entirety A joint tenancy held by a married couple.

tenancy in common (TIC) Ownership of property by two or more persons (called tenants in common) in shares that may or may not be equal, each having an equal right to possess the whole property but without a right of survivorship. Also called *estate in common*.

tender-years presumption A belief that mothers are better suited to raise their young children (usually under five years of age) and should be awarded custody of such children unless the mothers are unfit. Also called *maternal preference*.

termination of parental rights (TPR) A judicial declaration that ends the legal relationship between parent and child when this is in the best interests of the child. The parent no longer has a right to participate in decisions affecting the welfare of the child and no longer has any duties toward the child.

testament A will.

testamentary Pertaining to a will.

testamentary gift A gift made in a will.

testate (1) Pertaining to someone who dies with a valid will. (2) A person who dies with a valid will. (In older cases, if the testate was a man, he was also called *testator* and, if a woman, testatrix.)

testator A man or woman who dies with a valid will. Sometimes called *testatrix* if a woman.

testatrix A woman who dies with a valid will. More commonly called *testator*.

therapeutic abortion An abortion undertaken in order to safeguard the mother's life or health. Also called *induced abortion*.

three-pony rule (No child needs more than three ponies.) Child support for children of parents with high incomes should be adjusted so that payments do not go beyond what is reasonably and rationally related to the realistic needs of the child.

tickler A paper or computer system designed to provide reminders of important dates.

time-barred Prevented (barred) from bringing a civil or criminal action because of the passage of a designated period of time without commencing the action. Being unable to sue because of the statute of limitations.

timeline   A chronological presentation of significant events, often using text and diagrams.

tort   A civil wrong (other than a breach of contract) that causes injury or other harm for which our legal system deems it just to provide a remedy such as damages. Injury or harm can be to a person (a personal tort); to land and anything attached to the land (a real-property tort); to property other than land, called personal property and movable property (a personal-property tort); or to economic interests (an economic tort).

tortious interference with parental relationships   See *tortious interference with custody*.

tortious interference with custody   A tort in which the defendant seriously interferes with a parent's custody over his or her child.

TPR   See *termination of parental rights*.

tracing   Determining the ownership or characteristics of property from the time it came into existence.

traditional alimony   See *permanent alimony*.

traditional surrogacy   The carrying and delivering of a child for another in which the surrogate uses her own egg and is therefore genetically (biologically) related to the child.

transcribed   Taken down in a word-for-word account. (The account is called a *transcript*.)

transcript   A word-for-word account. A written copy of oral testimony.

transferee   The person to whom an interest in property is transferred.

transferor   The person who transfers an interest in property.

transracial adoption   An adoption of a child whose race is different from the race of the adoptive parents. Also called *interracial adoption*.

transsexual   (1) A person who has undergone a sex-change operation. (2) A person who wants to be considered by society as having a gender of the opposite sex.

transitional alimony   See *rehabilitative alimony*.

transmutation   The voluntary change of separate property into marital property or vice versa (in a common-law state); the voluntary change of separate property into community property or vice versa (in a community-property state).

treatise   See *legal treatise*.

trespass   Wrongfully intruding on land in possession of another.

trial management conference   See *pretrial conference*.

trial notebook   A collection of documents, arguments, and strategies that an attorney plans to use during a trial.

triennial cohabitation   A rule by which a man was presumed to be impotent if his wife remained a virgin after three years of cohabitating together.

trimester   Three months.

truancy   The willful and unjustified failure to attend school by one who is required to attend.

trust   A property arrangement by which its creator (the *settlor* or *trustor*) transfers property (the *corpus*) to a person (the *trustee*) who holds legal title for the benefit of another (the *beneficiary* or *cestui que trust*).

trustee   The person or company holding legal title to property for the benefit of another.

U

UCCJEA   See *Uniform Child Custody Jurisdiction and Enforcement Act*.

UIFSA   See *Uniform Interstate Family Support Act*.

unauthorized practice of law (UPL)   (1) A nonattorney's performance of tasks in a law office without adequate attorney supervision when those tasks are part of the practice of law. (2) Delegating tasks to a nonattorney that only an attorney is authorized to perform. (3) Using or attempting to use legal skills to help resolve a specific person's legal problem when the assistance is provided by someone who does not have a license to practice law and when the kind of assistance provided requires such a license or other authorization.

unbundled legal services   Discrete task representation for which the client is charged per task. When performing such tasks, the attorney is providing limited-scope legal services rather than the full range (the full bundle) of legal services that may be needed on a legal matter.

unclean hands   See *dirty hands*.

unconscionable   (1) Shockingly unfair or unjust. (2) Shocking the conscience by heavily favoring one side together with an absence of meaningful choice and a highly unequal bargaining posture of the parties.

uncontested   Unchallenged; without opposition or dispute.

uncontested divorce   A divorce granted to a spouse when the other spouse does not appear or when the other spouse appears but does not dispute any of the other spouse's claims. See also *friendly divorce*.

undertaking   A promise, engagement, or enterprise.

undue burden   A substantial and unwarranted obstacle to the enjoyment of a right.

undue influence   Improper persuasion, coercion, force, or deception.

unemancipated   Legally dependent on one's parent or legal guardian.

unethical conduct   See *ethics*.

unfit   Demonstrating abuse or neglect that is substantially detrimental to a child.

Uniform Child Custody Jurisdiction and Enforcement Act (UCCJEA)   A model state statute on the enforcement of custody and visitation orders across state lines.

Uniform Interstate Family Support Act (UIFSA)   A state law on establishing and enforcing alimony and child-support obligations against someone who does not live in the same state as the person to whom the alimony and child support is owed.

uniform laws Laws proposed to state legislatures in areas where uniformity is deemed appropriate. Each state can adopt, modify, or reject the proposals. Sometimes called *model acts*.

Uniform Marriage and Divorce Act (UMDA) A model statute on marriage and divorce proposed to the states for adoption.

Uniform Parentage Act (UPA) A model statute that has been adopted by most states on how paternity or parenthood is determined.

Uniform Premarital Agreement Act (UPAA) A model statute adopted by many states that governs the legality of premarital agreements.

Uniform Probate Code A law adopted by some states that covers (1) the probating of wills and (2) the distribution of the estate of persons who die without wills (intestate succession).

Uniform Transfers to Minors Act (UTMA) A statute adopted by many states that allows transfers of property to minors and allows custodians to manage the property.

unilateral divorce (1) See *ex parte divorce*. (2) A divorce that can be granted when only one party wants to dissolve the marriage.

unity of identity See *unity of person*.

unity of person The now-rejected rule that the legal identity of a wife is subsumed into the legal identity of the husband. Also called *doctrine of oneness*, *spousal-unity rule*, or *unity of identity*.

unjust enrichment The receipt of a benefit in the form of goods or services that in fairness should be returned or paid for even though there was no express or implied promise to do so.

unreasonable That which is contrary to the behavior of an ordinary, prudent person under the same circumstances.

unsecured Not backed by collateral.

UPA See *Uniform Parentage Act*.

UPAA See *Uniform Premarital Agreement Act*.

UPL See *unauthorized practice of law*.

UTMA See *Uniform Transfers to Minors Act*.

ux (uxor) Wife. See also *et ux*.

V

venue (1) The place of the trial. (2) The proper county or geographical area in which a court with subject-matter jurisdiction may hear a case. When more than one court has subject-matter jurisdiction to hear a particular kind of case, the selection of the court is called *choice of venue*.

verification A formal declaration that a party has read a document (e.g., a pleading) and swears that it is true to the best of his or her knowledge.

vested Fixed so that it cannot be taken away by future events or conditions; accrued so that your right to present or future possession or enjoyment cannot be taken away.

viability Ability to live indefinitely outside the womb by natural or artificial support systems. The adjective is *viable*.

viable Able to live indefinitely outside the womb by natural or artificial support systems. The noun is *viability*.

vicarious liability Liability imposed on a person because of the conduct of another, based solely on the status of the relationship between the two. The person vicariously liable is not the person whose conduct led to the liability.

vinculo matrimonii See *divorce a vinculo matrimonii*.

virtual adoption See *equitable adoption*.

visitation The right to have access to a child who resides with another. Some states prefer the phrase "parenting time" when the person "visiting" the child is the noncustodial parent.

vital statistics Data on major events such as births, deaths, marriages, divorces, and abortions.

void Of no legal effect; invalid whether or not a court declares it so.

void ab initio Invalid from the beginning, from the time something started.

voidable Of no legal effect but valid unless canceled or invalidated.

voidable marriage A marriage that is invalid but that is treated as valid unless a court declares its invalidity.

void marriage A marriage that is invalid even if no court ever declares its invalidity.

voir dire Jury selection.

voluntary By choice; proceeding from a free and unrestrained will.

voluntary manslaughter The intentional, unlawful killing of someone but with extenuating circumstances such as provocation. Murder reduced to manslaughter because of the absence of malice or premeditation.

W

waive To relinquish or to give up a right or privilege because of an explicit rejection of it or because of a failure to take appropriate steps to claim it at the proper time.

ward A person (e.g., minor) placed by the court under the care or protection of a guardian.

welfare See *public assistance*.

will An instrument (legal document) that specifies the disposition of one's property (and related instructions) upon death.

workers' compensation A no-fault system of paying for medical care and providing limited wage benefits to a worker for an employment-related injury or illness regardless of who was at fault in causing the injury or illness.

work-product rule   Notes, working papers, memoranda, or similar things prepared by or for an attorney in anticipation of litigation are not discoverable by an opponent, absent a showing of substantial need. They are protected by privilege. Also called *attorney work product*.

writ   A court order to do or refrain from doing something.

writ of execution   See *execution*.

wrongful adoption   An action seeking damages for carelessly stating (or failing to disclose) to prospective adoptive parents available facts on the health or other condition of the adoptee that would be relevant to the decision on whether to adopt.

wrongful birth   An action by parents of an unwanted impaired child for negligence in failing to warn them of the risks that the child would be born with birth defects. The parents seek their own damages.

wrongful death   A death caused by a tort or other wrong.

wrongful life   An action by or on behalf of an unwanted impaired child for negligence that precluded an informed parental decision to avoid the child's conception or birth. The child seeks her or his own damages.

wrongful pregnancy   An action by parents of an unplanned healthy child for a wrong related to pregnancy such as negligent performance of a vasectomy. Also called *wrongful conception*.

Z

zygote   A fertilized ovum before it begins to divide.

INDEX

Cengage

ISBN-13: 978-1-337-91760-5
ISBN-10: 1-337-91760-5